THE

1997

A&E®

ENTERTAINMENT
ALMANAC

An Information Please® Almanac

D1118255

THE 1997

A&E® ENTERTAINMENT ALMANAC

AN INFORMATION PLEASE® ALMANAC

A WORKING MEDIA BOOK

Robert Moses, Alicia Potter and Beth Rowen, **EDITORS**

PRODUCTION EDITOR
Madeleine Newell

DESIGNER
Eleanor Ramsay

DESIGN AND PRODUCTION STAFF
Linda Bean-Pardee, Teresa Lopas, Elizabeth Murphy
and John T. Perry III

GENERAL MANAGER
Timothy Haley

HOUGHTON MIFFLIN COMPANY
BOSTON   NEW YORK

The A&E® Entertainment Almanac

ISBN: 0-395-82855-4

Printed in the United States of America
WP 10 9 8 7 6 5 4 3 2 1

Many organizations and individuals were generous with their time and expertise: Susan Chicoski, Ann-Marie Imbornoni and Beth Anderson for proofreading; Todd Kaplan, J. Drew Todd and Keith Hamel for editorial assistance; Jesse Haley for his patience and perseverance; Erich Rachlis and Michael Shulman at Archive Photos; Susan Kaplan at Billboard Publications; Gary Ink at *Publishers Weekly*; Dick Stone of Briggs and Briggs; The League of American Theatres and Producers; Pat McCrummen, M Street Radio Directory; and Ted Kozlowski, *Radio and Records*.

1997

A&E® ENTERTAINMENT ALMANAC

TABLE OF CONTENTS

HOME ENTERTAINMENT
1995–1996

HOME ENTERTAINMENT REFERENCE

PERFORMING ARTS
1995–1996

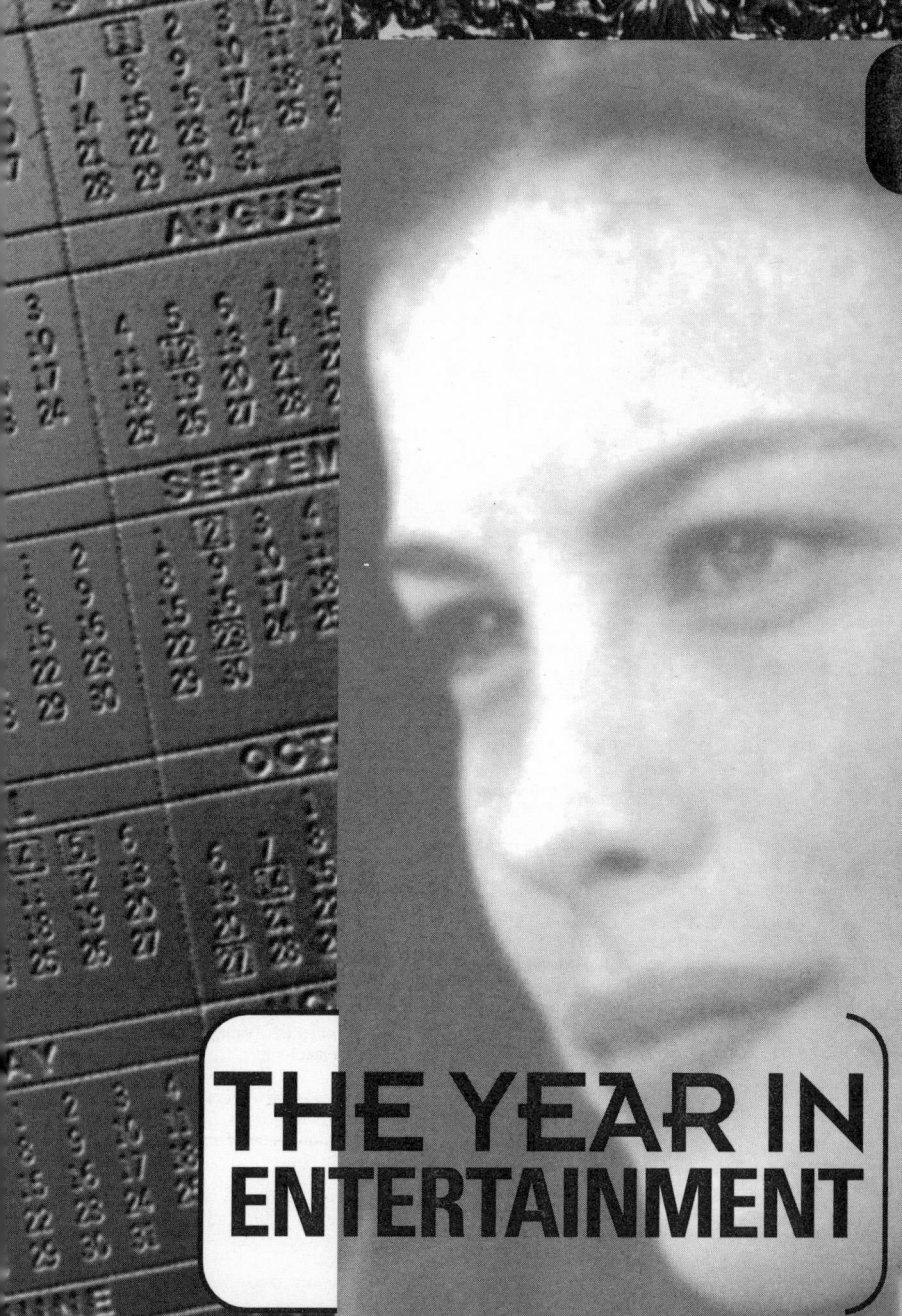

THE YEAR IN ENTERTAINMENT

SEPTEMBER 1995

TLC

◆ **Neil Young and Martin Davis,** former Paramount Communications chairman, team up to buy Lionel Trains Inc. Young, a train enthusiast, has in the past worked to make the trains easier for the handicapped to manipulate. He has two sons with cerebral palsy.

◆ **Trip Hawkins,** founder and chief executive of 3DO, bows to the PC market and announces he will produce a version of 3DO's M2 technology for PCs.

◆ **NBC charges nearly $1 million** per commercial minute for *Seinfeld,* the highest fee ever collected for a regularly scheduled series.

◆ **Sony Corp. and Philips Electronics** agree to combine technology with rivals Toshiba and Time Warner to develop digital videodiscs. Format wars — similar to the VHS-Beta scuffle of the early 1980s — loomed in January 1995 when Sony and Philips announced they would pursue technology incompatible with that of Toshiba and Time Warner. The DVD disc is the same size as audio CDs, but has the same capacity as a full length movie and multichannel sound.

◆ **The networks limp off to a slow start** with the launch of an unprecedented 42 new series. The big-three networks were disappointed early on, with a cumulative ratings drop of 9 percent. Unlike the fall 1994 season, there was no runaway hit the likes of *ER* and *Friends.*

◆ **Houghton Mifflin Company** buys publisher D.C. Heath for $455 million, making the Boston-based publisher the fourth largest educational publisher in the country.

◆ **Miramax Films and Twitching Image Inc.,** a stop-motion animation company, form an alliance to produce animated movies. Don't be surprised if you see the names Tarantino and Rodriguez attached to bloody, violent animated projects.

1 **The Rock and Roll Hall of Fame and Museum** opens in Cleveland, Ohio, with a weekend of festivities, including a seven-hour concert featuring Bob Dylan, Bruce Springsteen, Melissa Etheridge, Jerry Lee Lewis, Aretha Franklin and dozens of others.

Infinity Broadcasting agrees to pay $1.75 million in fines levied by the FCC against Howard Stern for indecent programming. The settlement with the FCC also calls for Infinity to release an indecency policy statement and begin an educational program for on-air employees. Industry insiders predict that shock jocks will have to clean up their acts else dish out big bucks.

2 **The Catholic Communication Campaign** debuts a toll-free hotline that rates movies according to their compliance (or lack of) with family values. The ratings, meant to supplement the MPAA's set of standards, range from A-I (general patronage) to A-IV and O (offensive).

7 *George* **hits the newsstands.** John F. Kennedy's long-awaited political slick features Cindy Crawford dressed as a bare-midriffed George Washington.

TLC dominates the 1995 MTV Video Music Awards, winning Best Video of the Year, Viewers' Choice Award, Best Group Award and Best R&B Video. Weezer's "Buddy Holly" also picks up four awards.

9 **The 32-bit Sony Playstation** debuts selling for $299, creating a battle for control of the $6 billion video-game industry with Sega's Saturn machine.

10 **The 1994–1995 Emmy Awards** are presented with *NYPD Blue* capturing best drama honors and *Frasier* getting the best comedy nod.

Congress votes to cut National Endowment for the Arts funding by 40 percent.

Software king Bill Gates announces his purchase of the Bettmann Archive, a photo collection with millions of photos in its inventory. Gates plans to digitize the photos so they can be packaged on computer discs or sold over computer networks.

15 **Savoy Pictures Entertainment** announces it is shifting focus from the motion picture business to television programming and station acquisitions. For its projects under contract, including an untitled Sylvester Stallone deal in which the actor will earn $20 million, Savoy will seek co-financing and, in some cases, will surrender distribution rights. Chairman Victor Kaufman said, "...the real triggering event is the change in the size and shape of the major companies in this business." His comment reflects the media business imperative to merge or die.

Colin Powell's *My American Journey* debuts and immediately hits the bestseller charts.

16 **James Webb, author and former Secretary of the Navy,** and Esparza-Katz Productions announce negotiations are almost complete for the first U.S.-produced feature film shot in Vietnam. The film, *Fields of Fire,* will be based on Webb's novel.

Christopher Reeve makes his first public appearance after the riding accident that left him paralyzed. He attended a New York fundraiser.

22 **A federal judge gives Spa'am (the puppet)** the go-ahead to appear in an upcoming Muppets film, ruling against Hormel Foods, which tried to block the pig's debut.

23 **Time Warner Inc. agrees to buy Turner** Broadcasting Systems Inc. for $7.5 billion in stock creating the world's largest entertainment corporation. As vice chairman of the new mega-corporation, Ted Turner will receive more than $100 million in compensation over five years. From the period January 1, 1996–December 31, 2000, his annual salary and bonus will be $5 million; long-term incentive will be $10 million a year; and stock options will total an estimated $36 million.

24 **PBS's 10-part** *Rock & Roll* **debuts** to strong reviews. The series, produced by the BBC with WGBH in Boston, chronicles the history of rock.

An ocean outing turns deadly when Gloria and Emilio Estefan's 30-foot powerboat collides with a jet ski driven by Howard Clark. Clark dies in the accident.

27 **Time Warner sells its 50 percent stake** in gangsta rap label Interscope Records back to the label's founders, Ted Field and Jimmy Iovine. Michael J. Fuchs, chairman of Time Warner's music division, denied that pressure from Sen. Bob Dole and William Bennett influenced the move.

28 **Bobby Brown** is involved in a gunfight in Boston, Massachusetts, that results in the death of his sister's fiancé.

Dennis Franz at the 1994–1995 Emmy Awards

OCTOBER 1995

O.J. Simpson

♦ **Between October 2 and 11,** Mariah Carey, Whitney Houston, Janet Jackson and Madonna release much-anticipated recordings, prompting many to speculate on which diva will win the race to the top of the charts.

♦ **Houghton Mifflin and the American Booksellers Association** settle a suit against Houghton and four other publishers. In the suit, the ABA challenged pricing and promotional allowances. Houghton agrees to pay the ABA $275,000 to help pay for the ABA's legal fees and to revamp its selling policies to retailers, making the process fair and profitable to all booksellers.

1 **Kenneth Branagh and Emma Thompson** announce their separation.

Tommy Tune, director and star of Broadway-bound *Busker Alley,* breaks his foot during a pre-Broadway, Tampa, Florida, performance of the musical. The show has been plagued by bad publicity, delayed arbitration and shaky reviews.

2 **The Metropolitan Opera** opened its season with *Othello* and introduced Met Titles. The $2.7-million system projects the words of operas to seatback monitors.

3 **The verdict in the O.J. Simpson double-murder trial** is announced on national television. An estimated 150 million people tune in to see and hear the shocking results. Media analysts say that 80 percent of the U.S. population watched at least some of the live courtroom coverage.

5 **Mo Ostin, former Time Warner music executive,** joins DreamWorks SKG Music as head of the record division. Ostin left Time Warner in 1994 during a period of heavy infighting. He will be joined at the mega-company by his son Michael Ostin and Lenny Waronker, both also former Time Warner executives.

9 **O.J. Simpson and NBC** announce that Tom Brokaw and Katie Couric will interview Simpson in a one-hour, commerical-free live *Dateline NBC.* Simpson said there would be no conditions to his interview, his first public appearance since the jury reached the not-guilty verdict.

11 **O.J. Simpson cancels his NBC interview,** saying his lawyers had advised against the no-conditions format. The cancellation wreaked havoc on NBC and the other networks, which shifted their programming anticipating low ratings.

12 **CBS announces the first casualty** of the 1995–1996 television season with the cancellation of *If Not for You* starring Elizabeth McGovern and Hank Azaria. Azaria lands on his feet with a recurring role on *Mad About You.* He plays the Buchman's dog walker. Azaria is the real-life boyfriend of *Mad*'s Helen Hunt.

With $1.4 million, Death Row Records bails Tupac Shakur out of jail (pending appeal). The bad-boy rapper served eight months of a 1½–4½-year sentence for sexual assault.

13 *Busker Alley* **producers Barry and Fran Weissler** officially cancel the show's Broadway run after they could not find a dancer with enough name recognition to draw audiences to the show. Tommy Tune dropped out after breaking his foot earlier in the month.

16 **The U.S. House of Representatives** passes legislation permitting copyright owners to collect royalties each time a recording is transmitted digitally.

The big-three networks form a coalition opposing mandatory children's programming quotas recommended by FCC Chairman Reed Hundt, who campaigned for a three-hour-a-week educational programming requirement.

17 **Rhino Home Video** releases on video 58 epidsodes of *The Monkees,* the largest boxed set ever released.

The 399-seat Laura Pels Theater at Broadway and West 45th Street (next to the Roundabout, in the Criterion Centre), Off-Broadway's newest addition, opens with Harold Pinter's *Moonlight,* starring Jason Robards and Blythe Danner.

22 **Some viewers are not happy** when a clip from the movie *S.O.B.,* in which Julie Andrews's breasts are exposed, is shown on *60 Minutes.*

23 **Intel Corp., television broadcasters and** 12 of the country's largest personal computer makers announce a new technology called Intercast that will turn PCs into television receivers and give broadcasters the ability to transmit computer data with programs. This means that in addition to television shows, the networks and advertisers will be able to send text, still pictures and graphics in the form of interactive World Wide Web pages four times faster than the fastest available computer modem.

Digicash, an Amsterdam company and Mark Twain Bankshares of St. Louis, offer Internet users E-Cash for electronic transactions. To use E-Cash, customers must set up an account with Mark Twain and use software provided by Digicash, which automatically deducts from the account when a transaction is completed. Only a few companies on the Internet initially accept E-Cash, but more are expected to join the fray.

At an industry screening of *Powder,* 20-year-old Nathan Winters confronts the movie's director, Victor Salva, and announces to the crowd that Salva had raped him eight years ago. Disney stands by the director, saying he had paid his debt when he served a three-year prison term.

Danny Goldberg, former Time Warner music executive, signs with PolyGram to head its Mercury Records label. Goldberg, an outspoken defender of rap music, made headlines in 1994 when he was forced to resign from Time Warner during a battle for control between Michael Fuchs and Doug Morris.

Yolanda Saldivar is found guilty of the March 31, 1995, murder of *tejano* singer Selena. On October 26 the jury sentenced Saldivar to life in prison.

24 **Bob Herman** announces that he has ended his one-man campaign to save New York's Fillmore East from becoming a modern apartment building. In August, Herman started his drive to raise $12 million to save the rock shrine that hosted the Doors, The Allman Brothers, the Who, Janis Joplin, Jerry Garcia and Jim Morrison. He planned to convert the building into a multimedia center that would occasionally stage concerts.

Jay Leno signs on with NBC to host *The Tonight Show With Jay Leno* until 2000.

25 **ABC and Jim Henson Productions** announce an alliance, which will result in the creation of several children's series. The deal puts into question ABC's relationship with DreamWorks, as children's programming was a major part of their original deal.

Posing as Canadian prime minister Jean Chrètien, a Canadian radio host talks to Queen Elizabeth via phone for 17 minutes about Quebec's attempt to secede from Canada.

Alec Baldwin is arrested for popping photographer Alan Zanger, who was attempting to videotape Baldwin's wife, Kim Basinger, and their newborn daughter, as they returned home from the hospital.

After a year of posturing, the League of American Theatres and Producers and the International Alliance of Theatrical Stage Employees reach an agreement, preventing a strike that would have crippled Broadway. The controversy involved the work rules for stagehands; the producers wanted to revamp what they called outdated work rules.

27 **William Bennett, moral crusader** and former education czar under President Reagan, announces a campaign against the daytime talk-show industry. One day later, U.S. Health and Human Services Secretary Donna Shalala expresses similar concern.

30 *The War of the Worlds,* **Orson Welles's** 1938 radio broadcast that caused a nationwide panic, debuts on the World Wide Web at http://www.realaudio.com and http://radioclassics.com.

31 **The Academy of Motion Picture Arts** and Sciences announces that Whoopi Goldberg, not David Letterman, will host the Oscars.

NOVEMBER 1995

The Beatles

♦ **Sylvester Stallone** joins the exodus from Creative Artists Agency and signs with ICM, which recently landed Steven Seagal, also from CAA.

1 **IBM unveils a new service,** InfoMarket, dedicated to protecting publishers' rights on the Internet. InfoMarket will charge Internet users for certain information that until now has been free. Companies such as the Associated Press, Simba Information Inc., Netscape, Yahoo! and other companies sign on early.

2 **Multi-bestselling author, John Grisham,** hires his editor, Doubleday's David Gernert, to also act as his agent, replacing his former agent and mentor, Jay Garon, who died in August 1995.

6 **Major League Baseball** announces that the league has signed a $1.7-billion contract to have Fox, NBC, ESPN and Fox's new Sports/Fox air games from 1996 through 2000. The four networks will have to work out an arrangement among themselves. Good luck.

Microsoft enlists Michael Kinsley, former editor of *The New Republic* and co-host of CNN's *Crossfire,* to edit *Slate,* an on-line magazine. *Slate* will be targeted at "people who are not Web fanatics," and will include politics, commentary and culture, modeled on *The New Yorker, The New Republic* and *The Economist.*

Michael Jackson's ATV Music Publishing and Sony Music Publishing form a joint venture worth an estimated $500 million ($100 million should fill Jackson's pockets). ATV owns the rights to 251 Beatles songs and songs popularized by Elvis Presley and Little Richard among others. The deal creates the world's third-largest music-publishing company.

8 **CBS's lawyers prohibit** *60 Minutes* executives from broadcasting an interview with a former cigarette company executive. In the interview, the former employee of Brown & Williamson Tobacco Corp. was critical of the industry. CBS said they were concerned about a potential lawsuit because the executive had signed a non-disclosure agreement.

MCI Communications unveils "1-800 MUSIC NOW," a call-in music service that allows customers to sample from more than 20,000 songs and order CDs either online or by touch-tone phone.

9 **Steven Spielberg** signs on to direct Michael Crichton's *The Lost World,* the sequel to *Jurassic Park.* The film, to be released in 1997, will be a co-production of Amblin Entertainment and Universal Pictures.

Marcia Clark, lead prosecutor in the O.J. Simpson trial, signs a $4.2-million book deal with Viking, one of the most lucrative in history for a nonfiction book. Clark's book will cover the trial and "how the trial has challenged and violated the very foundation of our justice system."

10 **Carolco Pictures** files for bankruptcy and plans to sell its assets to Twentieth Century-Fox for $50 million.

10-12 *Ace Ventura: When Nature Calls* grosses $40.3 million in its opening weekend, becoming the highest grossing November premiere and the fourth-highest in history

13 **The Associated Press** announces it will begin to distribute news and photos on the World Wide Web.

Sega announces it is creating a software company, Sega Soft, that will develop multi-player games for both PCs and its video-game machines. The games will be available over the Internet and will allow players at different locations to play simultaneously.

15 O.J. **Simpson defense attorney** Johnnie Cochran signs a book deal with the Ballantine Publishing Group to write an autobiography. Cochran won't get as much as Marcia Clark, though; he will only pocket roughly $2.5 million. Poor Johnnie. Robert Shapiro, another Simpson defense attorney, signs with Warner for $1.5 million.

Producer John Hart announces *Company* will close. The musical, which opened in early October at Broadway's Roundabout Theater, was supposed to move to the Brooks Atkinson Theatre on December 19. But because of a casting dispute over the lead actor, Boyd Gaines, Hart canceled the show. Gaines took a three-week leave from *Company* because of vocal-cord problems, and during that time Hart auditioned other actors. He picked Michael Rupert, another Broadway vet, to replace Gaines, but the *Company* company wanted to keep Gaines.

16 **K-III Communications Corp.** announces it will buy 13 magazines from Cahners Consumer Magazines. The magazines include *American Baby* and *Modern Bride*.

A big day for shakeups in the music industry. Michael Fuchs, the recently named head of the Warner Music Group and long-time chief of HBO, is forced out of the company. Some Time Warner insiders attribute the ouster to Fuchs's public opposition to Time Warner's acquisition of Turner Broadcasting. Elsewhere in the music biz, Al Teller, chairman of MCA's music division, quit because of philosophical differences with COO Ron Meyer and was replaced by Doug Morris, who was, until recently, in charge of Time Warner's music division.

17 **James Bond returns with a bang** and a $26.2-million opening weekend. Critics praise Pierce Brosnan's performance. Equally impressive is MGM's marketing department.

19 **Beatlemania (Part II) begins** with ABC's broadcast of *The Beatles Anthology*, a three-part miniseries chronicling The Beatles's story. During the first installation, ABC premieres the video of "Free as a Bird," the "new" Beatles song, in which Paul McCartney, Ringo Starr and George Harrison perform with a recording of John Lennon's voice.

20 **Capitol records releases** the much-marketed and anticipated *The Beatles Anthology I*. The two-CD set includes two hours of previously unreleased music including "Free as a Bird." The release of the CD coincided with Beatles week on ABC.

22 **Westinghouse** officially takes possession of CBS.

For the first time in four years, NBC wins the November sweeps.

23 **Director Louis Malle, 63,** dies of lymphoma.

24 **Barry Diller's Silver King** television network agrees to buy the controlling stake, 41 percent of the equity and 80 percent of the voting stock, in the Home Shopping Network from Tele-Communications, Inc. In a separate transaction, Diller announces that he will use $210 million of Silver King's stock to buy Savoy Pictures, which also owns four television stations. He hopes to build Silver King into a media empire as he did with the Fox network in the 1980s.

Penguin releases Bill Gates's *The Road Ahead,* in which the software king predicts the fate of the Internet and reveals his plan to dominate that industry. In an unusual marketing strategy, Penguin did not release any review copies of the book and guardedly protected its contents. The book, with a first run of 850,000 copies, was released in several countries on the same day, virtually guaranteeing it will immediately top the bestseller lists.

25 **Disney's** *Toy Story* **debuts** and takes in $39.1 million over Thanksgiving weekend, a record-breaker for the holiday weekend.

26 **In what Sen. Bob Dole calls a copycat** crime, burglars set fire to a Brooklyn toll booth, and the worker eventually dies. A similar crime appeared in *Money Train* starring Wesley Snipes and Woody Harrelson. Dole urges Americans to boycott the film.

30 **Howard Stern** brings with him to *The Tonight Show* two women dressed in bikinis and persuades them to kiss. Host Jay Leno is outraged and cuts the shot.

DECEMBER 1995

Frank Sinatra

1 **CBS announces a deal with Bill Cosby** for a sitcom for the fall 1996 season. Cosby will reunite with Marcy Carsey and Tom Werner, the team responsible for *The Cosby Show.* The show will be based on the British sitcom, *One Foot in the Grave,* about a cranky man fed up with life's irritations.

Eleven days before his 80th birthday, crooner Frank Sinatra auctions off some of his personal goodies, raking in more than $2 million.

West 42nd Street's oldest theater, the Victory, reopens as the New Victory Theater. The theater will cater to families, providing entertainment for children. The $11.4-million restoration is the first project to be completed in an urban renewal plan that was announced in 1981, which seeks to restore all the street's historic theaters.

4 **John Travolta** inks a $17-million deal to play identical characters in *The Double,* directed by Roman Polanski. Not a bad paycheck, considering he did *Pulp Fiction* for $500,000.

Emir Kusturica, the Bosnian director who won the Palme d'Or for *Underground* at the 1995 Cannes Film Festival, announces that he has quit filmmaking. He did not give specifics, but he faced intense criticism from Bosnian Muslims and French intellectuals who claimed that *Underground* was pro-Serb.

5 **Capital Cities/ABC** announces plans to launch in 1997 a 24-hour cable news channel that will rival CNN.

Michael P. Schulhof resigns under pressure as president and chief executive of Sony Corporation of America. Norio Ohga, Sony's chairman and chief executive, will run the American operations from Tokyo. Sources speculate that Sony's poor performance in American movies and music over the past year and his extravagant spending were major factors in Schulhof's departure.

7 **Michael Jackson** passes out during rehearsal for an HBO special at New York's Beacon Theater. An irregular heartbeat and dehydration caused the fainting spell, which left the King of Pop in intensive care for two days.

Bill Gates, Microsoft's chairman, announces that his company will begin concentrating on Internet technology. His plan includes licensing Java, software that is essential to World Wide Web navigation, and incorporating Internet links into each Microsoft product.

8 **The Grateful Dead** announces the long, strange trip is over and remaining band members will disband. The death of Jerry Garcia prompted the decision.

10 **A 22-year-old researcher** discovers a flaw in data security technology, public-key encryption, that threatens electronic transactions, including banking and shopping. Public-key encryption involves scrambling data so that it can only be read by people equipped with the mathematical keys to the code. Paul C. Kocher, the researcher, found that the code could be broken by repeatedly monitoring the unscrambling process.

12 **Donna L. Hoffman,** a business professor at Vanderbilt University, asserts that a Commercenet/Nielsen Internet Demographic Survey inflated the number of Internet users by millions. Nielsen found that 24 million adults in the United States and Canada use the Internet, while Hoffman puts the figure at fewer than 10 million users.

NBC inks a $2.3-billion deal with the International Olympic Committee to broadcast the 2004, 2006 and 2008 Olympics. It is the highest price ever paid for sports programming.

Frank Sinatra turns 80.

Michael Jackson

13 DreamWorks partners, Steven Spielberg, Jeffrey Katzenberg and David Geffen, announce plans to build a studio, backlot and a 3,246-home neighborhood in Los Angeles. They will call the 1,000-acre studio and backlot The DreamWorks Studio at Playa Vista, which will be built on what was Howard Hughes's hangar where he built his Spruce Goose. A groundbreaking has not yet been determined, but construction will take approximately 2½ years at an estimated cost of $770 million.

14 NBC and Microsoft announce a joint venture to create a 24-hour, all-news channel, MSNBC, and a companion interactive on-line news service. Both will compete with CNN and its home page on the World Wide Web. NBC will reformat *America's Talking*, its all-talk cable channel, over the next six months, reincarnating it as MSNBC. Microsoft paid NBC $220 million for a 50 percent share in the channel.

ABC and Walt Disney hire away Geraldine Laybourne from Nickelodeon in an attempt to become a big player in children's television. Laybourne, one of television's most powerful women, was president of Nickelodeon and vice president of MTV Networks and is credited with building Nick into one of cable's biggest success stories.

18 Encyclopedia Britannica Inc. announces the company will be sold to an investment group led by Swiss businessman Jacob E. Safra. The price paid for the 224-year-old publisher was not disclosed, but sources say the books could bring $400 million.

19 Janet Wilder, a 29-year-old stunt woman, is killed while filming Disney's film, *Gone Fishing*, which stars Danny Glover and Joe Pesci.

21 The Samuel Goldwyn Company, which had been for sale for months, receives an offer from Metromedia International Group. Metromedia's proposal for the independent film company totals $115.3 million, almost double what PolyGram N.V. agreed to pay only hours before Metromedia's offer.

25 Entertainer Dean Martin, 78, dies from acute respiratory failure.

28 CBS News president Eric W. Ober announces he is being replaced. Andrew Heyward, the producer of *CBS Evening News*, assumes the driver's seat.

Compuserve Inc. denies subscribers access to more than 200 indecent discussion groups and photo databases. The move follows a decision in Munich, Germany, that said such material violates Germany's pornography laws, and the company does not yet have the resources to filter material accessible to certain countries or users.

29 CNNfn, Ted Turner's new financial cable network, debuts with 5.5 million subscribers. The network broadcasts daily from 7 a.m. to 7 p.m. and includes 12 daily series. CNNfn competes with CNBC.

31 *Calvin and Hobbes*, a favorite comic strip among adults and children, appears for the last time as Calvin creator Bill Watterson calls it quits. We'll miss you Calvin and Hobbes.

Steven Spielberg, Jeffrey Katzenberg and David Geffen

JANUARY 1996

Michael Eisner and Thomas Murphy

◆ **PolyGram Filmed Entertainment** buys Universal's 50 percent share of Gramercy Pictures for an estimated $5–$10 million.

◆ **MCA Inc.** negotiates with Interscope Records owners, Jimmy Iovine and Ted Field, to buy 50 percent of the company for $200 million and the option to purchase the other 50 percent over the next five years. In an unusual move, MCA included in the deal an agreement that would allow the company to distribute some controversial titles but not others. MCA also plans to donate to charity proceeds from sales of gangsta rap titles.

◆ **Neil Young** launches a new record label, Vapor, with his manager, Elliott Roberts. The label's first release will be an album of guitar improvisations that Young recorded for the forthcoming Jim Jarmusch film *Dead Man*.

◆ **Putnam** wins the hardcover and paperback rights to publish an uncompleted autobiography by Lucille Ball. The publisher will pay $1 million for the book, which does not include rights to the audio and electronic products. Ball wrote the 312-page manuscript in the 1960s, but each typewritten page contains edits, which were probably made in the 1980s before she died in 1989. Ball's daughter, Lucie Arnez, will write an introduction and edit the memoir.

◆ *Showgirls* hits the video stores. Depending where you shop, you could find either the NC-17- or R-rated version. Because Blockbuster refuses to carry any videos with the NC-17 rating, director Paul Verhoeven cut the film to adhere to R-rating standards (he didn't cut very much, however).

2 **Chris Elliot** stars in a live commercial for Baked Tostitos, which ran during halftime at the Fiesta Bowl. It cost an estimated $500,000 to produce.

3 **DreamWorks Records** releases its first recording, "Jesus to a Child," a George Michael single.

Money **magazine** fires columnist Dan Dorfman, who also works as a commentator on CNBC, because he refused to reveal to his editors confidential sources that he frequently cited in his columns.

4 **Walt Disney and Capital Cities/ABC** shareholders approve the merger of the two companies, leaving only one hurdle to make the transaction official — a nod by the Federal Communications Commission.

Bryant Gumbel announces that 1996 will be his last year as anchor of NBC's *Today* show. He joined *Today* in 1982.

5 **Toshiba American Consumer Products** unveils two new compact-disc players that play the two-sided digital video disks. Each side of the DVD can store up to two hours of audio and video. The players should be available to the consumer in fall 1996 for $599 and $699.

8 **The Metropolitan Opera** cancels the premiere of Janacek's *Makropulos Case* because of a blizzard. It is the first time the Met has canceled a performance because of the weather since 1965. It was the second time the premiere of the opera was canceled; it was originally scheduled to open on January 5, but was called off after a singer died on stage. The weather also caused the cancellation of Broadway shows at the Winter Garden, the Minskoff, the Majestic and the Broadway Theater.

11 *Tonight Show* host Jay Leno signs a $4-million deal with HarperCollins to write a humorous autobiography about his experience on the comedy-club circuit.

Highly regarded Glimmerglass Opera director Paul Kellogg is announced as the new general and artistic director of the New York City Opera, assuming the post left vacant by the 1995 death of Christopher Keene. Kellogg will continue as artistic director of Glimmerglass and plans to transfer three or four Glimmerglass productions each year to City Opera.

12 Janet Jackson signs a record-setting $80-million deal with Virgin Records. The five-album deal includes a $35-million advance, $5 million for each album, a 24 percent royalty rate and a $25-million video budget. The deal makes Jackson the highest paid musician in history.

A backlash against O.J. Simpson grows as some TV stations refuse to air an ad for his $29.95 video, *O.J. Simpson: The Interview*, telling his side of the double-murder trial. Outraged radio listeners and Internet users urge a boycott of the video and encourage people to call the toll-free order number to tie it up.

15 Jerry Seinfeld announces his series *Seinfeld* will return for an eighth season. Prior to his announcement, there was speculation that the comedian would call it quits after the 1995–1996 season. *Murphy Brown* and *Roseanne* executives also announce this week that both sitcoms will return for another season, dispelling rumors that they would permanently sign off at the end of the 1995–1996 season.

16 CBS investigates allegedly racist remarks made by one of its senior executives, John Pike, at a programming meeting. He reportedly said that African-Americans are an important segment of the network's late-night audience because they don't have to get up in the morning for work. David Lipsky reported the incident in the February issue of *Details* magazine.

NBC announces that *Dateline NBC* will expand to a fourth night of programming in March and occupy the Sunday 7:00-8:00 P.M. timeslot — challenging CBS's *60 Minutes*.

Helen Gurley Brown announces she will step down as editor in chief of *Cosmopolitan*, the magazine she took over in 1965 and transformed into the voice of the newly liberated single career girl. Bonnie Fuller will assume Brown's responsibilities after an 18-month training period under Brown.

First Lady Hillary Clinton kicks off an 11-city book tour promoting *It Takes a Village: And Other Lessons Children Teach Us*.

17 In a surprise move, Sumner Redstone, chairman of Viacom, Inc., fires the company's president and CEO, Frank Biondi, Jr. Redstone said he would assume Biondi's duties, which include overseeing Paramount Pictures.

The Rock and Roll Hall of Fame Foundation inducts its newest members in a ceremony at New York City's Waldorf Astoria hotel. The ceremony is telecast live via satellite to Cleveland's new Rock and Roll Hall of Fame Museum. New inductees are Jefferson Airplane, The Velvet Underground, Gladys Knight and the Pips, The Shirelles, Little Willie John, Pete Seeger and Tom Donahue.

25 In a joint venture, Rupert Murdoch's News Corp. and MCI Communications agree to pay the government $682 million for the last available satellite slot. The companies plan to launch a $1-billion television and communications system within two years. The television portion of the system will compete with DirecTV and PrimeStar, satellite services that offer up to 150 channels.

Rent composer and librettist Jonathan Larson, 35, dies of an aortic aneurysm.

28 Super Bowl XXX fetches $1.2 million for a 30-second commercial.

29 MCI signs a pact with Microsoft to jointly develop and market an array of on-line and Internet services.

Turner Entertainment Group agrees to pay a record $105.6 million for syndication rights to 88 episodes of *ER*. The price translates into $1.2 million per episode. The reruns should start appearing on either TNT or TBS in fall 1998.

30 PolyGram withdraws its $62-million offer for Samuel Goldwyn, citing frustration with negotiations.

Rupert Murdoch, chairman of News Corp., announces that by the end of the year he will have launched a 24-hour news channel to rival CNN. He said Roger Ailes, former president of CNBC, will head the channel.

31 O.J. Simpson's video begins shipping.

FEBRUARY 1996

Seal

◆ **Signet announces plans to release Stephen King's** *The Green Mile,* a serial novel about death row published in six paperback installments.

◆ **In a joint venture with Sony Music,** pop wonder boys Boys II Men form their own label, Stonecreek Recordings. The crooners will fulfill their contract with Motown while developing new talent for Stonecreek.

◆ **Film director Spike Lee** seeks to squelch fears that his shoot of a new Michael Jackson video in a Rio de Janeiro shanty town would damage the city's image. Brazilian authorities had expressed concern that filming would hurt the city's efforts to woo back tourists.

1 *Rent* **moves from Off-Broadway** to Broadway to rave reviews, injecting new life in the modern musical.

5 **CBS's longest-running program,** *60 Minutes,* announces it will switch to a new format that adds coverage of breaking news stories and commentaries by prominent columnists. The network's most popular program also says it will abandon its practice of airing repeats in the summer and will broadcast new stories 52 weeks a year.

6 **In a Manhattan courtroom,** actress/author Joan Collins takes the stand as testimony opens for her breach-of-contract dispute with Random House. The publisher has asked that Collins return her $1.2-million advance after judging her submitted manuscript to be incomplete and unpublishable. In a countersuit, Collins asserts that the manuscript draft was within the terms of her contract and the publisher owes her another $4 million.

8 **President Clinton signs the sweeping** Telecommunications Bill of 1996 into law. The bill includes the controversial Computer Decency Act, which makes it a felony, punishable by prison terms and hefty fines, to distribute indecent or offensive materials on computer systems. Opponents of the bill rally for freedom of speech by "blacking out" their Web-page backgrounds.

The digital entry to the "Day in the Life" photojournalism series goes online with "24 Hours in Cyberspace" at http://www.cyber24.com.

13 **CompuServe restores worldwide access** to most of the 200 sex-related computer databases it had blocked under pressure from German prosecutors. The on-line service states its intent to leave Internet censorship to individual tastes.

Filmmaker Mike Nichols pays $1.5 million for the film rights to *Primary Colors,* the controversial roman á clef about the 1992 Clinton campaign by anonymous author Joe Klein.

A Manhattan jury decides that Random House must pay actress/author Joan Collins for the manuscript that its editors have already deemed unreadable. The ruling means Collins can keep her $1.2-million advance and potentially collect more.

The Oscar nominations are announced. The Best Picture nominees include *Apollo 13, Babe, Braveheart, The Postman (Il Postino)* and *Sense and Sensibility.*

15 **ABC, CBS, NBC and Fox** look into a ratings system, similar to the Motion Picture Association of America's code, to regulate the content of television programs. The move is seen by industry officials as a defensive strategy to preempt government intervention.

20 **The** *New York Times* **reports** that new National Endowment for the Arts grant guidelines have caused widespread anger and confusion in the arts community. Republican objections to arts funding led to an almost 40 percent decrease in endowment funding, and grants to individuals have been virtually eliminated. Applications have declined drastically, and staffers have been traveling across the country to help clarify the new regulations.

21 **MCA agrees to buy 50 percent** of Interscope Records, the label most famous for its "gangsta rap" releases.

The jury that acquitted rap artist Snoop Doggy Dogg and his former bodyguard of murder charges earlier this year remains deadlocked on lesser charges of voluntary manslaughter, despite the judge's orders to break the 9-to-3 split in favor of acquittal. The court declares a mistrial.

26 **Elizabeth Taylor appears in cameo roles** on all four of CBS's Monday night sitcoms as part of the network's February sweeps strategy.

After months of speculation, Consortium des Realisations, the French holding company that owns Metro-Goldwyn-Mayer Inc., decides to put the Hollywood studio up for sale.

A judge dismisses subpoenas issued by tobacco company Brown & Williamson seeking dirt from *60 Minutes* correspondents about its former research chief turned whistle-blower, Jeffrey Wigand. The executive had appeared on the CBS news magazine accusing the tobacco company of using carcinogenic additives and lying about nicotine's addictive effects.

Snoop Doggy Dogg

AT&T offers five hours of free Internet time each month for a year to its phone customers. The phone-titan's announcement brings computer network connection closer to becoming a standard utility like electricity or water.

28 **Seal, Alanis Morissette and Hootie & the** Blowfish dominate the 38th Annual Grammy Awards, which were presented at Los Angeles's Shrine Auditorium. Seal wins Record and Song of the Year honors for his "Kiss From a Rose;" Morissette took home four trophies, including Best Rock Album for her *Jagged Little Pill;* and Hootie was named Best New Artist.

29 **Japanese researchers succeed** in transmitting information at a rate of one trillion bits a second through an optical fiber — the equivalent of transmitting 300 years' worth of daily newspapers in one second.

A Detroit judge orders the owners and producers of *The Jenny Jones Show* to stand trial in a $25-million lawsuit related to the slaying of a man who had appeared on the show. Last year, guest Jonathan Schmitz allegedly killed a fellow guest who revealed his homosexuality and crush on Schmitz on air.

Inés Clouzot, the widow of Henri-Georges Clouzot, the director of the original 1955 classic thriller *Diabolique*, sues Morgan Creek, the American producers of a remake starring Sharon Stone and Isabelle Adjani. Clouzot, who read of the new version while at her hairdresser's, claims she is the soul beneficiary of the film's rights. Morgan Creek maintains it was within its rights and that Clouzot had agreed to an undisclosed payment in 1995.

Director Joel Schumacher, whose *Batman Forever* topped 1995 as the highest-grossing film, exits the Creative Artists Agency after 10 years, claiming the firm botched negotiations with Bat-star Val Kilmer. Kilmer had backed out of the next Batman installment to pursue a starring role in Paramount's *The Saint*. *ER* heartthrob George Clooney will don the cape and mask for the summer release of *Batman and Robin*.

MARCH 1996

Mel Gibson at the Oscars

◆ **Warner Bros.** announces that George Clooney will replace Val Kilmer (who replaced Michael Keaton) as the Caped Crusader in 1997's Batman and Robin.

1 **Viacom, the parent company of MTV,** gives the go-ahead for a new network, tentatively titled MTV2, to be launched in the summer. For viewers who want more of their MTV, the network will feature an "edgier," music-focused format, while the original MTV will continue on its more lifestyle-oriented programming track.

4 **DreamWorks SKG** joins the computer-animated film boom through a partnership with Pacific Data Images of Sunnydale, California. Under the terms of the agreement, DreamWorks will acquire a 40 percent stake in the company and begin immediate production on a feature-length project.

The three remaining Beatles decline a $225-million offer to perform on a world tour. A consortium of American and German business executives offered the whopping sum in exchange for 22 concerts in Japan, Europe and the United States.

News Corporation owner Rupert Murdoch recruits his British-born protégée Anthea Disney to be president and chief executive of the faltering HarperCollins publishing division. A former executive producer of Fox's *A Current Affair,* Disney triumphed as editor in chief of *TV Guide,* where she

brought in record profits. The book publishing newcomer hopes to strike a balance between a slick and serious product, while using her marketing savvy to raise the house's profile.

6 **The Telecommunications Act of 1996** hits home as the FCC orders cable operators carrying the Playboy Channel and other adult entertainment to either fully scramble their sex webs or broadcast the material only between 10 p.m. and 6 a.m.

7 **The Spice Network,** an adult entertainment provider, charges the Telecommunications Act provision violates its First Amendment rights and receives a temporary restraining order to prevent government-ordered scrambling.

9 **Dashing Microsoft's hopes** for Internet dominance, CompuServe announces a broad licensing agreement that will allow its users to choose Netscape's Internet browser over the software giant's browser, Internet Explorer.

8 **Senior Fox executives appeal to Nielsen** Media Research with a list of demands to improve its ratings service. Among its beefs, the network blasts the current Nielsen viewership measuring system for ignoring young adults and households with kids and teens.

11 **Playboy Enterprises** wins a temporary restraining order in its battle against the Telecommunications Act. The provision in question, Section 505, requires that blocking equipment be installed in every household with cable systems carrying adult programming, whether or not consumers request it.

The Clinton administration declares it will use World Trade Organization rules to challenge Canadian restrictions on American magazine publishing. Objections arose when Canada imposed an 80 percent excise tax on revenue from Canadian ads placed in *Sport's Illustrated*'s Canadian version. The case could have a wide impact on Canada's attempts to control American information and entertainment-industry imports.

12 **It's a big day for announcements** from America Online — not only will the on-line service leader discount some of its on-line features to customers of AT&T's Worldnet service, but it will also provide Netscape's Navigator browser software as part of its Internet offering.

13 **America Online has a change of heart** and taps Microsoft Explorer as its browser software partner over Netscape Navigator.

Jarvis Cocker of the British pop band Pulp is cleared of assaulting three children who appeared on stage with Michael Jackson at a London music awards ceremony.

Polish director Krzysztof Kieslowski, 54, dies of heart failure.

15 **Senate Budget Committee members** fail to support majority leader Bob Dole's plan to raise money by forcing broadcast companies to compete in an auction for digital television licenses valued at $10 billion to $70 billion. Broadcasters claim they need free licenses to continue free television transmissions, a stand attacked by Dole as "corporate welfare."

Sega Enterprises, MCA Inc. and Dreamworks SKG ally and plan to open more than 100 entertainment centers in the next four years.

Atari reports a nearly $28-million loss for the fourth quarter of 1995. The once-dominant gaming manufacturer points to sluggish sales of its 64-bit Jaguar entertainment system and inventory writedowns as factors in its downward spiral.

AT&T Worldnet's Internet service goes online with 212,000 subscribers.

The Federal Trade Commission charges nine companies that market on the Internet with making false or misleading advertising claims in its broadest crackdown ever on deceptive cyberspace marketing.

18 **MCI Communications Corp.** joins the telecommunications Internet fray by introducing a sweeping initiative that aims to triple its internetMCI network capacity and expand its consumer Internet package.

19 **A judge sentences actress Tori Spelling's** former assistant and her attorney to three years probation in an attempted blackmail case. The two women were charged with conspiracy and extortion after allegedly approaching Spelling to fork over $30,000 to keep private details of her life from becoming public.

The makers of 1993's *Philadelphia*, TriStar Pictures, admit the film was based in part on the life of a New York lawyer who was fired after his employer learned he had AIDS. The acknowledgment came after five days of testimony in a lawsuit filed by the family of the attorney, Geoffrey Bowers, who died in 1987. TriStar had maintained the film was a fictional work based on a variety of sources. The terms of the settlement are not disclosed.

MCA/Universal Home Video scrambles to keep up with the consumer demand for *Babe*.

20 **The National Academy of Recording Arts and Sciences** announces that the Grammy Awards will return to New York for the March 1997 ceremony after two years at Los Angeles's Shrine Auditorium. The event will move to Madison Square Garden, which can accommodate 20,000 people, to make the 1997 Awards the biggest Grammy event ever.

22 **Alec Baldwin is found not guilty** of misdemeanor battery charges resulting from a run-in with a photographer in October. Baldwin popped the paparazzo in the nose after he rushed the actor and his wife, Kim Basinger, as they were returning home from the hospital with their newborn baby.

25 *Braveheart* **and its director, Mel Gibson,** win Best Picture and Best Director at the 68th Academy Awards, broadcast live from the Dorothy Chandler Pavilion. Nicolas Cage picked up his first Oscar for his performance in *Leaving Las Vegas* and Susan Sarandon her first for portraying a crusading nun in *Dead Man Walking*.

"Gangsta" rap pioneer Dr. Dre leaves the controversial yet hugely successful company he cofounded, Death Row Records, to launch his own label, to be funded in part by Interscope Records.

31 *Getting Away With Murder*, Stephen Sondheim's first non-musical Broadway show, ends its run at San Diego's Old Globe Theater after 31 previews and only 17 performances. The comedy-thriller becomes the first flop of the spring theater season.

APRIL 1996

Picket Fences

◆ **Writer Andre Dubus** wins the $30,000 Rea Award for the Short Story. The Dungannon Foundation, which annually awards the prize to a living American writer, said Dubus was cited for "his conspicuous and enduring chronicles of the American soul . . . under his hand the form of the story thrives with basic life." *Dancing After Hours* is Dubus's most recent short-story collection.

◆ **In an effort headed by David Geffen,** DreamWorks SKG pays more than $1 million for the recording rights to Jonathan Larson's Pulitzer Prize- and Tony Award-winning rock opera, *Rent*.

◆ **After 12 seasons,** 11 Emmy nominations and four Golden Globes, Angela Lansbury calls it quits, announcing the 1995–1996 television season will be her last.

3 **Sylvester Stallone announces his plans** to build a center in Miami where young independent filmmakers can live while developing their projects.

Rapper Hammer files for bankruptcy in Oakland, California, claiming debts of $10 million.

9 **Within a month** of suspect Ted Kaczynski's arrest, Simon & Schuster's Pocket Books division announces the April 25 publication of a quick and dirty Unabomber wrap-up. Authors will be retired F.B.I. serial-killer expert John Douglas and writer Mark Olshaker, the team

that formerly produced *Mindhunter: Inside the F.B.I.'s Elite Serial Crime Unit.*

Two professors stumble upon Louisa May Alcott's first novel, *Inheritance*, written in 1849, while researching the author at Harvard University's Houghton Library.

The Smashing Pumpkins's double album *Mellon Collie and the Infinite Sadness* is certified at six million units, tying it with Michael Jackson's *HIStory* as the best-selling double CD in history.

The Pulitzer Prizes are announced at Columbia University. Richard Ford's *Independence Day* and Jonathan Larson's *Rent* win literature's most prestigious award.

DreamWorks principal and former Disney executive Jeffrey Katzenberg files a $250-million lawsuit against Disney, claiming the mouse denied him his "incentive bonus" of 2 percent of the profits generated from projects with which he was involved in his 10-year tenure with the company.

12 **The introduction of the digital video disc** is delayed once again as technical and marketing glitches push back the anticipated fourth-quarter roll-out.

16 **As if the return of The Beatles** wasn't enough, glam rockers Kiss announce a comeback tour complete with makeup, leather outfits and pyrotechnics. The four original members, Gene Simmons, Paul Stanley, Ace Frehley and Peter Criss, reunite for the band's first international tour in 15 years.

17 **ICM Artists, Ltd.** becomes worldwide representative of the New York City Ballet. To celebrate its 50th anniversary, the ballet company will launch a countrywide tour of three 30-member troups, with the goal of performing in every state. The gala tour, which is ICM's kickoff assignment, will also include educational and outreach activities.

18 **Conservative talk radio host Bob Grant** is fired from his long-running syndicated show on WABC after remarking that he feared Commerce Secretary Ron Brown might have survived a fatal plane crash in Croatia.

Rent

19 **Planet Hollywood goes public with an** initial price offering of $18 a share. The stock closes at $31. Not a bad day's work for Sly, Willis and Schwarzie.

22 **Bobby Brown** is busted for drunk driving in Atlanta.

Nationally syndicated columnist and best-selling author Erma Bombeck, 69, dies.

23 **MCA Inc. appoints former Viacom** executive Frank Biondi, recently fired from Viacom, as its new chairman and chief executive and puts him in charge of overhauling the company's management.

Business Week, Outside, Civilization and *The Sciences* win General Excellence citations in the National Magazine Awards. *The New Yorker* won two awards, for reporting and essays and criticism.

Virgin Retail Group opens a Virgin Megastore, billed as the world's largest home entertainment store, in New York City's Times Square. The 75,000-square-foot retailer carries music CDs, laserdiscs, videos, books and multimedia products.

24 *Picket Fences* **ends its four-year run** on CBS. The program won two Emmys for outstanding drama series.

The Stone Temple Pilots cancels upcoming concert dates, announcing singer Scott Weiland "has become unable to rehearse …due to his dependency on drugs."

25 **Macaulay Culkin calls 911,** claiming abuse by his father. Police didn't charge the elder, as the dispute erupted over the younger's dirty room.

26 **Three alleged Asian gang members** are charged with the murder of Haing Ngor, the Cambodian actor who won an Oscar for his portrayal of life under the Khmer Rouge in the 1984 movie *The Killing Fields*. Ngor was supposedly shot to death when he refused to hand over a gold chain and locket containing a picture of his late wife, who was killed by the Khmer Rouge.

27 **Sean Penn and Robin Wright** marry, making their stormy eight-year relationship official. The couple have two children, 5-year-old Dylan and 2-year-old Hopper.

30 **Microsoft shifts the MSN News** component of its million-member Microsoft News Network on-line service to the Web, where it will be available without charge.

MAY 1996

Friends

♦ Talk-show maven Kathie Lee Gifford's perma-grin quickly fades when the National Labor Committee announces that her Wal-Mart clothing line was manufactured by Honduran children. She didn't fare any better when she moved the operation to Manhattan. She later discovered the New York outfit was a sweatshop.

♦ Sony Computer Entertainment slashes the price of its PlayStation 32-bit game system to $199 from $299.

1 The three executive producers of NBC's megahit *Friends* sign what industry insiders call an "unprecedented" five-year deal that includes new series and feature-film development rights. Estimated at about $35 million, the deal comes in as one of the most lucrative programming agreements in TV history.

2 Hootie & the Blowfish's sophomore effort, *Fairweather Johnson*, debuts at No. 1 on the *Billboard* charts with first week sales of 411,000, more than double that of its closest rival.

Silver-haired talk pioneer Phil Donahue wraps up 29 years on the air with the taping of his 7,000th show. Declining ratings prompted the show's sign off.

4 Tina Turner struts her sequined stuff on a Paris stage to kick off her "Wildest Dreams World Tour '96." Bruce Willis and his band, the Accelerators, open for the 56-year-old rocker's two-hour show.

6 President Clinton tapes his cameo appearance for the television movie *A Child's Wish* about the hardships a family endures when their daughter is diagnosed with cancer. The film, to be aired on CBS following the November presidential election, highlights the significance of the Family Medical Leave Act, which Clinton signed into law.

The 50th annual Tony Award nominations are announced. The popular rock opera *Rent* sweeps up 10 nominations, the most of any show. *Bring in 'da Noise, Bring in 'da Funk* follows with nine nominations. The two musicals, which got their starts Off-Broadway, steal the spotlight from big-budget, commercial competitors, *Victor/Victoria* and *Big*, in one of the most surprising snubs in the awards' half-century history.

7 NBC and CNN announce they will offer presidential candidates free air time during prime-time hours leading up to the November elections. The two networks join CBS and Fox.

13 Michael Jackson cancels a concert tour of Germany because a change in German tax laws would cost him about $100,000 more for each of the eight planned shows.

14 John Tesh announces he's leaving his post as cohost of *Entertainment Tonight* to concentrate on his music career. Weekend host/correspondent Bob Goen will replace Tesh.

15 PepsiCo secures the promotion rights to the re-release of the *Star Wars* trilogy. The deal is considered the largest of its kind in history. Pepsi beat out McDonald's and values the promotion at $2 billion.

Melanie Griffith and Antonio Banderas marry in a private civil ceremony in London. The couple are expecting a baby in September.

Tri-Vision Electronics of Scarborough, Ontario, wins the rights to manufacture the first television attachment incorporating the V-chip, a technology that allows parents to block violent or explicit television programs.

The Fugees's *Score* pulls ahead of Hootie & the Blowfish's *Fairweather Johnson* on the *Billboard* charts.

17 **Retailers preview Nintendo 64** at Los Angeles's Electronic Entertainment Expo.

19 **Angela Lansbury solves her last mystery** as Jessica Fletcher as the 12-year run of *Murder, She Wrote* ends.

One of America's 10 most wanted criminals is arrested in Guatemala after an Internet surfer recognized his mug on the FBI's World Wide Web home page.

Apple Computer unveils the new "Pippin," a multimedia device that sits on top of a TV to bring the Internet, games and personal finance software to households not interested in owning a computer. Naysayers predict the $599 price tag will be too steep for most consumers.

20 **Internet News,** the first world-wide online broadcast highlighting hot Web sites and breaking Internet news, debuts at http://www.netnewstoday.com.

Julie Andrews, star of *Victor/Victoria* takes her name out of the running for Best Actress in a Musical to protest the Tony Awards's committee decision not to nominate her musical or other cast members in any other categories.

The 1996 Obie Awards are awarded to outstanding Off-Broadway and Off-Off Broadway productions and performers. Adrienne Kennedy's *June and Jean in Concert* and *Sleep Deprivation Chamber* receive Best Play honors, while Uta Hagen is recognized with a Special Achievement Award for her performance in *Mrs. Klein*.

21 **As if the Tony Awards** weren't already dramatic enough, 84-year-old *State Fair* producer David Merrick files a lawsuit seeking $2 million in damages and an injunction against the awarding of a Tony for Best Score of a Musical. Merrick contends that songs from the two Rodgers and Hammerstein film versions of *State Fair* were unfairly excluded from consideration. In other Tony news, the producers of *Victor/Victoria* decline to perform a number at the Tony telecast in support of star Julie Andrews's beef with the awards committee.

22 **Netscape, Oracle Corp., Sun Microsystems, IBM and Apple** agree on a set of standards to build a new, affordable breed of "network computers" for surfing the Internet, sending E-mail and word processing.

23 **NBC comes out on top** of the 1995–1996 Nielsen ratings, the first time the network has won since the 1990–1991 season. Following NBC were ABC, CBS, Fox, UPN and WB, respectively.

ABC announces it has scuttled plans for a 24-hour, all-news channel. ABC executives cited prohibitively high distribution fees the network would have to pay cable providers to carry the channel as the reason.

Walt Disney Co. and McDonald's form a $1-billion promotional alliance that will see McDonald's marketing Disney output and Snow White promoting Big Macs.

24 **Score one for *Victor/Victoria*.** Julie Andrews and cast win Outer Critics Circle awards for Outstanding Actress in a Musical and Outstanding Broadway Musical.

25 **A fire ravages Eric Clapton's house,** but the rocker manages to salvage his guitars.

27 *Mission: Impossible,* the action-adventure spectacle starring Tom Cruise, sets a new Memorial Day weekend gross, taking in $56.9 million. The take shattered former record holder, *The Flintstones*, which earned $37.2 in its debut weekend. The film also breaks the box-office record for a Wednesday opener, grossing $11.76 million on its opening day. *Terminator 2: Judgment Day* previously held the record with $11.66 million first-day receipts.

Jumping on the Internet-device bandwagon, TransPhone LLC announces plans for a $500 telephone-sized gadget that will surf the Web, place phone calls and carry out commercial banking transactions.

28 **David Gahan,** lead singer of Depeche Mode, is arrested after overdosing on a speed ball, a combination of heroin and cocaine.

A New York State Supreme Court judge denies David Merrick's request for an injunction to halt voting in the Tony Awards's original score category.

29 **NBC White House correspondent** Brian Williams is appointed anchor and managing editor of prime-time news for MSNBC, the cable network formed by Microsoft and NBC.

30 *Wired* magazine files for an initial public-stock offering valued at $450 million.

JUNE 1996

The Hunchback of Notre Dame

♦ **Keanu Reeves** announces he is backing out of *Speed II,* which was scheduled to begin shooting in September, to tour with his rock band, Dogstar.

♦ **Christopher Reeves** signs a deal with HBO to direct In the Gloaming, a one-hour AIDS drama. Filming of his helming debut will begin in October.

♦ **Fed up with annoying mourners,** Courtney Love announces she will tear down the greenhouse in which her husband, Kurt Cobain, committed suicide on April 5, 1994.

2 **Despite the swirl of controversy** leading up to the event, CBS broadcasts the Tony Awards ceremony to lackluster ratings. *Rent, Bring in 'da Noise, Bring in 'da Funk* and Terrence McNally's play, *Master Class,* emerge as the evening's big winners.

3 **Broadcasters, beware.** A study reveals that 58 percent of the computer users polled were cutting back on their TV viewing to go online.

5 **Anthony LaPaglia** lands a role on ABC's *Murder One,* replacing Daniel Benzali. Show producer Steven Bochco hopes LaPaglia, whose credits include the film *The Client* and the television special *Never Give Up: The Jim Valvano Story,* will carry the show in its second season.

Royal Opera House Chief Jeremy Isaccs defends his decision to spend more than $300 million rebuilding the London performance center. The project will provide modern facilities for the Royal Opera, Royal Ballet and Birmingham Royal Ballet.

6 **Jodie Foster files suit against PolyGram** Entertainment, claiming the company orally agreed that she would star in *The Game* and later dropped her from the cast.

8 **A pissed off Mel Gibson** makes a quick exit from an interview with Janeane Garofalo when the host of the MTV Movie Awards asked him questions about her career and her appearance. The interview never made it on the air, though, as the scene was cut from the broadcast.

9 **KRIS, a Corpus Christi television station,** airs a commercial for Seagram, ending a self-imposed industry-wide convention that prevented televised hard-liquor ads.

Courtney Love makes *Time* **magazine's list** of the 25 most influential people in America. Other entertainment types on the list include Jerry Seinfeld, Wynton Marsalis, Oprah Winfrey, Robert Redford, Toni Morrison and Martha Stewart.

10 **Another big-name star** goes the talk-show route. Rosie O'Donnell's self-titled show debuts with a champagne- and flower-bearing George Clooney. O'Donnell promises to go easy on the trash talk. Her show meets immediate critical and ratings success.

13 **A Federal panel in Philadelphia** unanimously declares unconstitutional key parts of a new law drafted to regulate indecent material on the Internet. Praising the Internet as a symbol of free speech, the three judges grant a temporary restraining order that prohibits the Justice Department from investigating or enforcing violations of the Communications Decency Act's ban on indecent and offensive subject matter on the Internet.

15 Ella Fitzgerald, 79, the "first lady of song," dies of complications from diabetes.

Marianna Tcherkassky, 43, one of the dance world's most admired stars, ends her 26-year career with American Ballet Theater. She dances the role of Juliet in Kenneth Macmillan's *Romeo and Juliet.*

15-16 **Rappers and alternative bands** rock fo Tibet at San Francisco's Golden Gate Park. Crowds of 50,000 saw the Beastie Boys, Smashing Pumpkins, Sonic Youth, the Fugees, A Tribe Called Quest, De La Sol, Beck, Richie Havens, Yoko Ono and John Lee Hooker perform in the bill organized by Beastie Adam Yauch and Erin Potts, who, with Yauch, founded Milarepa, a Tibetan charity.

Walt Disney Co. announces plans to reduce by 50 percent the number of films produced annually, citing increased marketing and production costs.

17 *The New Republic* announces Michael Kelly, a writer and editor at *The New Yorker,* will succeed Andrew Sullivan as editor of the magazine.

19 *The Hunchback of Notre Dame* premieres to 65,000 at New Orleans's Superdome. Not only did viewers get a first look at Disney's latest animated feature, they also saw a musical show featuring 100 dancers and a 500-member choir. A two-mile parade kicked off the day of Quasi.

ABC hires Jamie Tarses, formerly known as Jamie McDermott and NBC programming executive responsible for *Friends,* as president of its entertainment division. It also named Ted Harbert, whose tenure at ABC has been dubious, chairman of ABC Entertainment.

20 **Westinghouse Electric Corp.** announces it plans to buy Infinity Broadcasting for $3.9 billion. The transaction merges the country's two largest radio broadcasters and creates an empire with 83 radio stations and personalities that include Howard Stern and Don Imus. The new telecommunications bill made the deal possible.

21 **Michael Greene, CEO of the National** Academy of Recording Arts and Sciences, announces that NARAS has organized a substance abuse program, headed by label executives, that will try to stem the drug (read: heroin) problem that is ravaging the industry. The program includes an 800-number hotline, an intervention system, financial help for treatment programs and referrals. Drugs have recently claimed Kurt Cobain, Kristen Pfaff of Hole, Jerry Garcia, Dwayne Goettel of Skinny Puppy, Shannon Hoon of Blind Melon and Brad Nowell of Sublime.

22 **Actor Robert Downey, Jr.** is arrested in Malibu, California, on charges of drug possession and having a concealed weapon in his car. He had cocaine, heroin and an unloaded .357 magnum in his truck.

23 **The Sex Pistols return to the stage** after 19 years and play for a crowd of 30,000 in England as part of their "The Filthy Lucre Tour," for which each band member will earn an estimated one million pounds (approximately $1.5 million).

24 **Microsoft unveils** its much-anticipated entry in the Webzine category, *Slate,* edited by former *New Republic* chief Michael Kinsley. Its editorial content focuses on politics, pop culture and public policy.

Id Software, creators of the standard-setting *Doom,* make its much-anticipated new title, *Quake,* available over the Internet.

The governors of 10 Western states pledge to create a virtual university, aptly dubbed "Western Governors' University," where students would take courses by computer and earn degrees online.

The James Dean postage stamp debuts.

26 **Van Halen** announces it is working once again with former vocalist David Lee Roth, but it is not clear if his return is permanent. Sammy Haggar, who replaced Roth, has left the band.

'Netheads scoff at Microsoft for introducing a print edition of *Slate,* its on-line Webzine. Many interpret the paper companion as evidence Gates and Co. just don't understand the Internet.

Shaquille O'Neal, on-line sports celebrity, jumps from a deal with the Microsoft Network to Sportsline U.S.A., a World Wide Web sports service. The move brings attention to the fierce competition to affiliate a celebrity with on-line content.

27 **Lollapalooza opens in Kansas City,** Missouri. The touring festival is criticized for abandoning its mission of showcasing alternative talent. This year's fest features Metallica, Soundgarden, The Ramones, Screaming Trees and Rancid.

28 **Kiss kicks off its first tour since 1983,** and it is no small production. The group is in full makeup and costume and sold out their shows in record time.

Independence Day

♦ **David Letterman** inks a deal with CBS to host *The Late Show With David Letterman* through the 2001–2002 season.

♦ **Sarajevo-born filmmaker Emir Kusturica** announces he will start filming a comedy in April. In December 1995, he said he had quit directing films.

♦ **Hootie & the Blowfish** announce they will not honor more than 500 tickets that were sold by scalpers for August shows at New York's Jones Beach. Ticket holders will be reimbursed the tickets' $25 face value.

♦ **Vivid Video,** a porno movie production outlet, takes out a $1-million insurance policy on Steven St. Croix's genitalia after he bought a motorcycle. St. Croix is Vivid's biggest star.

♦ **The Recording Industry Association of America** announces that Alanis Morissette's *Jagged Little Pill* has sold 11-million copies, making her the second-best-selling female recording artist behind Whitney Houston.

♦ **Microsoft** privately demonstrates software designed to merge the Internet's multimedia technology with its Windows '95 operating system. The blending of desktop computing and global networking is hailed as the most significant change in the personal computer industry since the 1970s.

7 A 23-year-old student streaks across center court during the men's finals at Wimbledon.

9 *Independence Day* grosses $104.3 million in six days, becoming the fastest film in history to pass the $100-million mark.

11 **CBS and Sony** team up with management company 3 Arts Entertainment in an effort to produce prime-time television shows for the foundering network. It is the first deal of its kind to unite a network, studio and agency.

Leslie Nielsen, best known for his sight gags and puns in the spoofs *Airplane!* and the *Naked Gun* series, returns to his roots as a serious stage actor. He will make his comeback in a one-man play titled *Darrow.*

12 Former *NBC Nightly News* correspondent John Chancellor, 68, dies.

Jonathan Melvoin, 34, keyboardist touring with Smashing Pumpkins, dies of a heroin overdose at a Manhattan hotel. The band's drummer, Jimmy Chamberlain, was arrested on charges of possessing a controlled substance.

Conservative political commentator Rush Limbaugh announces he is quitting his syndicated television show. He said he will "concentrate on finding the best way to integrate TV work into the rest of my expansive media empire." Many in the television industry expect him to join Fox's 24-hour news network.

15 **MSNBC, the all-news cable channel** and Internet site, debuts, though not without a few glitches. Internet users could not sign on to the service for about an hour and the news anchors were touting on-line features that weren't available. MSNBC is a joint venture of Microsoft and NBC and reaches an estimated 22.5-million cable subscribers.

AT&T reveals its plans to introduce a $500 cellular phone through which users will be able to send and receive E-mail.

The six friends on *Friends* band together and ask for $100,000 each per episode — averaging a $60,000-per-episode raise for each actor.

16 **Cranberries singer Dolores O'Riordan** wins $15,500 in a libel case against British tabloid *The Daily Star.* The paper ran a story that said she was not wearing undies while performing in Hamburg, Germany.

17 **News Corp. agrees to buy New World** Communications for $2.48 billion in stock. The transaction makes News Corp. the country's largest owner of television stations.

CompuServe posts a loss in its first complete quarter as a public company. Shares for the second-largest on-line service are down 20 percent, adding to concerns that the major commercial on-line services may ultimately fold in the wake of the Internet's popularity.

Hot on the heels of *Slate*, Microsoft announces plans for an Internet travel magazine, *Mungo Park.* Named for an 18th century Scottish explorer who disappeared exloring the Nile River, the on-line publication will feature daily visual and text uploads from travel teams and destination features from well-known journalists.

After months of denying it, Joe Klein, *Newsweek* columnist and CBS commentator, fesses up to writing the one-million-selling *Primary Colors.*

The F.T.C. OKs the merger of Time Warner and Turner Broadcasting Systems, with the condition that the company's cable systems offer a cable news channel that will compete with CNN. The merger will create the world's largest media company.

Robert Downey, Jr. is arrested again on charges of being under the influence of drugs. He was found sleeping on a child's bed in a neighbor's house.

Smashing Pumpkins fires its drummer, Jimmy Chamberlain, who was arrested July 12 on charges of possessing heroin.

19 **Fox announces it will launch** its 24-hour cable news network on October 7, 1996. The Fox News Channel will reach an estimated 10-million cable subscribers.

The XXVIth Olympics open and are broadcast on NBC. The peacock network eclipses the ratings of the other big four, averaging a 22.5/42 share. An estimated 210-million viewers watched at least some of the event coverage.

20 **Robert Downey, Jr.** is arrested for the third time in a month, this time for leaving the drug rehab center he had been ordered to as a condition of his bail.

21 **Jim Carrey** finally pops the question to on-again, off-again girlfriend Lauren Holly.

23 **Fox hires its first anchor, Neil Cavuto,** for its Fox News Channel, which is scheduled to launch on October 7. Cavuto, a business reporter for CNBC, will preside over a daily financial program and continuous business updates.

24 **Pearl Jam** announces North American and European tour dates. The tour, promoting *No Code,* kicks off September 16 in their hometown, Seattle.

Tough times prompt Chicago's Organic and Touchstone theaters to join together to become the Organic-Touchstone Theater, the first known merger of two nonprofit theaters in the country.

Newsweek's **editor in chief,** Richard M. Smith, asks columnist Joe Klein to take a few weeks off to reflect on the controversy he stirred by lying about his authorship of *Primary Colors.* Smith also asked Klein to talk to the magazine's staff about the issue.

25 **Joe Klein** resigns from CBS, citing the need to simplify his life. He was a consultant and occasionally contributed opinion pieces to the network.

26 **Kirk Kerkorian** backs the $1.3-million purchase of MGM by the management of the studio.

AT&T and Microsoft agree to distribute each other's on-line software.

27 **While performing** at Atlanta's House of Blues, a block away from Atlanta's Olympic Centennial Park, James Brown's show is interrupted by the pipe bomb that rocked the city and shocked the world. Other music legends performing at the Olympics include Ray Charles, Little Richard, Jerry Lee Lewis, B.B. King and Al Green.

28 **Macromedia, Inc.** unveils software that makes voice and music clips received over the Internet sound as clear as traditional music CDs.

29 **The broadcast industry agrees to air** at least three hours of educational children's programming each week. The Federal Communications Commission will oversee the new programming regulation.

A New York panel of Federal judges unanimously rules that the Government's efforts to stop indecent material on the Internet were unconstitutionally unsound.

AUGUST 1996

◆ **Robert De Niro and Miramax** buy film rights to Jonathan Larson's rock opera *Rent*. Sources say the deal is in the ballpark of $2.5 million. Don't expect to see the film for at least three years, until the Broadway and touring productions have completed their runs.

1 **Playboy Enterprises,** which already runs one of the World Wide Web's most frequented sites, reveals it is developing a fee-based site that will provide access to five decades of features and Playmates. Insiders estimate the service will cost about five dollars a month to subscribe.

MTV debuts M2, an interactive spinoff of the groundbreaking cable channel. M2 offers a wider variety of videos and will appeal to an older audience.

2 **Aerosmith fires their manager,** Tim Collins, who helped the band make a huge comeback in the early 1980s and overcome drug problems that originally caused their undoing in the 1970s.

A flood of more than 50,000 visitors log on to the NBC Internet site to chat with heroic Olympic gymnast Kerri Strug, whose dramatic vault while injured won the United States a gold medal. The cyberevent nearly crashes the host computers.

Philips Electronic NV and Sony Corporation announce plans to license digital video disc (DVD) technology to bring the home entertainment industry closer to what experts predict will be a high-growth product.

7 **America Online blacks out for 19 hours as** a result of software bugs and human error.

Matsushita Electric Ltd. of Japan announces plans to base its $25 million digital video disc manufacturing operation, Panasonic Disc Services Corp., in the Los Angeles suburb of Torrance. The plant will be the first United States facility dedicated solely to manufacturing DVD players and DVD-ROM products.

13 **At the Edinburgh International Festival,** dancer and choreographer Mark Morris follows his opening program (for which he danced solo in pink satin pajamas) with an uncharacteristic 40-minute dance performed by his company to no music and scenery.

14 **The White House and Random House** announce that President Clinton has written a book, *Between Hope and History: Meeting America's Challenges for the 21st Century,* about his hopes and goals for the future. The book will ship to stores on August 21. Clinton did not receive an advance to write the book, nor will he see any royalties from sales.

15 **Smashing Pumpkins** replace drummer Jimmy Chamberlain with Matt Walker and keyboardist Jonathan Melvoin with Dennis Flemion. The two will finish the band's 1996–1997 world tour.

16 **Nintendo announces its new 64-bit** video-game console will be priced below $200 when it goes on sale in the United States in September. The machine was originally priced at $249.95

Tony Bennett and the Gin Blossoms christen *Billboard* Live, Hollywood's newest music club. The three-story, tony establishment, owned by *Billboard* magazine, will host up-and-coming artists.

Walt Disney announces five concert performances of the Alan Menken-Tim Rice oratoria *King David* will inaugurate its New Amsterdam Theater on Broadway in the fall.

20 **Microsoft threatens Netscape's** dominance of the Internet browser category with the latest version of its Internet Explorer. By giving away the software, the corporate behemoth is likely to boost its market share from less than 10 percent to as much as 40 percent by the end of 1997. Striking back, Netscape announces plans to release a new version of its Navigator Internet software that promises "home delivery" of Web pages featuring customized news and sports information to users' mailboxes.

ENTERTAINMENT
BUSINESS

The Smoke Clears

■ BY MARTY O'LOUGHLIN

Marty O'Loughlin is a freelance writer specializing in media and technology.

Fairy-tale logic tells us that every time people find a magic lamp, they end up running around fixing the fruits of their own misguided wishes. This year, via the Telecommunications Act, and even just the rising smoke that heralded its magical appearance, some mighty powerful people in the entertainment industry have watched their wishes come true after rubbing away for years. But somehow, watching the results has not been nearly as entertaining as watching an episode of *I Dream of Jeannie*.

After four years in the making, both the House and Senate passed the Telecommunications Act of 1996 on February 8, easing restrictions on the activities and ownership of media and communications giants. The Act lifts the FCC ban on one company owning more than 12 TV stations and boosts a broadcaster's allowable national TV audience reach from 25 percent to 35 percent. It also ends rate limits on cable service as of 1999, allows cable and phone companies to compete in each others' businesses, adds an anti-violence-and-sex feature to new televisions (the V-chip), bans pornography over computer networks and sets aside airwaves for digital television services. Whether phone companies will be providing digital television and video services, cable companies will be providing phone service or what either would mean to consumers and their pocketbooks remains to be seen. "This unleashes a digital free-for-all," said Rep. Ed Markey (D-Mass.). "Life will never be the same."

THE BUSINESS

Months before the Telecommunications Act was law, megadeals brewed in anticipation as the smoke swirled from the lamp. Disney began its purchase of Capital Cities/ABC in August 1995, creating one of the world's largest entertainment entities, followed the very next day by the Westinghouse Corporation purchase of CBS. The first megadeal after the genie appeared involved Westinghouse as well, when the company acquired radio powerhouse Infinity Broadcasting for $3.9 billion in June 1996. In addition to CBS network radio stations, Westinghouse now owns the voices of some of radio's top personalities, including Howard Stern, Don Imus and Charles Osgood. More importantly, the company would have had 32 percent of the total 1995 radio ad revenue ($814 million) in the top 10 markets and will now dwarf its rivals' audiences in local markets. One month later, Rupert Murdoch made news as his News Corp. acquired New World Communications Group in a $2.48 billion stock deal. News Corp. became the largest owner of TV stations in the country, and Murdoch's Fox network now has stations in 11 of the nation's 12 biggest TV markets and the power to reach 40 percent of American homes.

By far, the biggest wish granted by the genie went to Ted Turner, cable giant TCI's John Malone and Time Warner's Gerald Levin. In July, in what seemed to be almost a gentleman's agreement, the Federal Trade Commission ended months of hand-wringing by approving the $7.5 billion merger of Time Warner and Turner Broadcasting, creating the world's largest media conglomerate. In part, the merger teams film

President Clinton

Ted Turner and Gerald Levin

studios Warner Bros., New Line, Castle Rock and Turner Pictures; cable networks HBO, CNN, TBS, and percentages of Comedy Central, E!, Black Entertainment TV, as well as international entities; music companies Elektra, Atlantic Records and Warner Music; adds Turner Publishing to the Time Warner Publishing empire of *Time*, *Fortune*, *Sports Illustrated*, *People Weekly*, Little Brown & Co. and Warner Books; and Turner sports teams, interactive and entertainment venue interests. The deal overcame months of Justice Department and FTC scrutiny, and resistance from competitors as well as reluctant Time Warner Entertainment partner US West, with what seems to be pretty soft terms. The behemoth-to-be promised to limit TCI's role in the new company, act in a non-discriminatory way towards rival cable operators and programmers and carry a second news service in addition to Turner's CNN. The company that will reach nearly 50 percent of the U.S. cable households essentially promised to act nice. But there is still the Federal Communications Commission to appease.

Early cries of foul came from NBC president and CEO Bob Wright in the 24-hour news channel arena. Wright speculated on competitive conflict in July as NBC and partner Microsoft launched MSNBC (the formidable cable television and Internet project designed to compete with CNN). While ABC had postponed its plans for a 24-hour news service, Rupert Murdoch's Fox Broadcasting did not and aggressively pursued cable operators with lucrative offers to carry the channel. While MSNBC replaced NBC's America's Talking cable channel on some cable systems, Time Warner and TCI had not agreed to add the programming at press time. While Time Warner and TCI denied a deal or any wrongdoing, Wright saw them favoring the upcoming Fox project, bullying MSNBC out of half the U.S. cable homes.

Even months before the megadeal was done, Time Warner's Levin dealt with the first repercussion of his wishful thinking in a situation with Michael Fuchs. Fuchs was a longtime ally of Levin and the head of Warner Music Group and HBO, the pay cable pioneer he piloted from a start-up. Not deemed ready to take over Turner cable operations and Warner's music business, and coming up short against the Warner Bros. management team of Bob Daly and Terry Semel, suddenly the man who thought he'd be number two at the new entity was squeezed out at the end of 1995. And with the pressure of a $16-billion debt, Time Warner should undergo significant further restructuring as the Turner wish becomes a reality, including a rumored spin-off of Levin's beloved cable systems to US West, thereby removing some antitrust concerns and a quarrelsome partner.

The entertainment industry revenues listed below equaled $140.51 billion. Figures are based on 1995 statistics.

INDUSTRY	SALES
FILM	$5.51 billion in box-office receipts
TELEVISION	
NETWORK, NATIONAL SPOT AND LOCAL SPOT	$30.63 billion based on 1995 advertising revenue (network: $11.69 billion; national spot: $9 billion; local spot: $9.94 billion)

Toy Story

CABLE	$29 billion based on 1995's pay-per-view and premium subscription fees and advertising revenue (basic services: $18 billion; premium: $5.4 billion; advertising revenue: $5.3 billion)
RADIO	$11.32 billion based on network, national spot and local spot advertising revenue
RECORDED MUSIC	$12.3 billion based on manufacturers recommended retail price
PUBLISHING	
BOOK	$19.8 billion based on end-user spending
MAGAZINE	$10.11 billion based on advertising revenue

Also ousted as this year's smoke cleared was Frank Biondi, former chief executive of Viacom, Inc. In January, Viacom chair Sumner Redstone claimed sole dominion over the kingdom that includes MTV, Blockbuster, Paramount Pictures, Simon & Schuster, as well as multiple theme parks and TV and radio stations. Redstone pointed to Biondi's lack of aggression on the international front, à la Rupert Murdoch, and his failure to keep Paramount Pictures under control (after himself supporting a boost in production to 23 films). After fielding numerous offers, Biondi landed on his feet at MCA.

The sheer number of films, made even more expensive by the skyrocketing costs of marketing, star salaries and production, is an issue many studios grappled with this year, in part as a fallout from merger frenzy. Evidence of the increasing struggle to make money in the movie business is seen in Metro-Goldwyn-Mayer and Castle Rock Entertainment, both of which went on the sales block. MGM sold in July 1996 for $1.3 billion to a management group backed by Kirk Kerkorian, the third time MGM would be in Kerkorian's hands. Even with record-breaking films like *Mission: Impossible* and *Independence Day* scoring big at the box office, more frequent films in the $100 million budget range are making studio bosses nervous.

Ever watchful of bottom lines, Disney inaugurated the talk of cutbacks. The company not only dismantled its Hollywood Pictures production entity, but also is reportedly planning to reduce the number of films it produces from nearly 40 in 1996 to 25 in 1997. The studio even wrote off several projects in the first quarter developed under Jeffrey Katzenberg's regime due to escalating production costs. At the same time, Disney is unlikely to turn its back on turning films into franchises, as it created a $2 billion monster out of *The Lion King* and has signed an exclusive agreement with McDonald's for more toys and fun. Disney's new honchos, Michael Eisner and Michael Ovitz, have concurrently been trying to revive the ratings of the ABC network, help mold a fall schedule to restore the network's luster and integrate two very different corporate cultures. All eyes will be on Jamie Tarses, lured her post guiding such successful NBC programs as *Friends* and *Frazier*, who filled the post of president at ABC Entertainment in June 1996.

For his part, Seagram Co.'s Edgar Bronfman, Jr. who spearheaded the company's purchase of an 80 percent stake in MCA last year, simply stated, "There are in my view too many films being produced, driving the margins of everyone's films down. I believe if fewer films were produced, margins would improve." Fewer films, maybe, but not cheaper. MCA's Universal Pictures has a nearly $100-million film slated in volcano thriller *Dante's Peak*. The price tag is so daunting that the studio supposedly spoke to Fox, also producing a lava-flow film, about the possibility of joining efforts — but to no avail. While Bronfman has stated that he sees a two-to-three year period before MCA is producing

Edgar Bronfman, Jr.

profits up to his standards, he is certainly taking steps to move forward. Most notably, he paired MCA president and COO Ron Meyer with former Viacomer Biondi, who took over as MCA chairman and CEO, as well as cutting nearly 100 staff positions at the MCA Television group.

At Sony Corporation, where Nobuyuki Idei took the reigns as president in 1995, a little restructuring may be a very good thing. Idei ousted Michael P. Schulhof, president of Sony Corporation of America, to take direct control of the company's Hollywood operations. After disappointing results in its first film forays, Sony's film business did return to profitability in 1995 with hits like *Sense and Sensibility* and *Jumanji*. And Idei has tightened the buckle, bringing the average cost per film down below the industry average of $36 million. The results were marginal enough, however, to fuel continu-

Joan Marcus

A Funny Thing Happened on the Way to the Forum

PERFORMING ARTS

THEATER	$131.33 million in ticket sales based on a survey of 215 theaters nationwide, assuming ticket sales account for 46.7 percent of annual earned income
OPERA	No comprehensive data available
DANCE	No comprehensive data available

HOME ENTERTAINMENT
CD-ROM

Educational Software	$572 million based on end-user spending
Video Games	$3 billion based on end-user spending
ON-LINE	$2.79 billion in subscription fees of consumer-oriented services (Dialog, Lexis/Nexis, Dow Jones News Retrieval and CompuServe are not included)

VIDEO

Rentals	$9.88 billion based on 1995 consumer spending
Sales	$5.47 billion based on 1995 consumer spending

Sources: Association of American Publishers; Magazine Publishers of America; Opera America; Radio Business Report; Recording Industry Association of America; Theatre Communications Group; Variety; and Veronis, Suhler & Associates, Inc.

ing speculation about the leadership of Sony's film business. One name floated (and denied by Sony): Michael Fuchs. Idei's focus on Sony's electronics, somewhat surprisingly, will be in personal computers, aiming to deliver high-quality audio and video for the digital revolution.

Nearly two years later, the titans at DreamWorks SKG are still building what the genie dumped on their doorstep. Aside from their Playa Vista compound outside Los Angeles, Steven Spielberg, Jeffrey Katzenberg and David Geffen are building relationships. In the film arena, *The Peacemaker,* an action film set to star George Clooney and Nicole Kidman, may be the trio's first release in 1997. Though not scheduled for release until 1998, Katzenberg

Michael Eisner

is also hard at work on *Prince of Egypt,* an animated musical epic depicting Moses and the Ten Commandments. In television, DreamWorks has signed on such luminaries as Gary David Goldberg and the team of Linda Bloodworth-Thomason and Harry Thomason. Goldberg's first effort for DreamWorks, *Champs,* did not fare well with ABC, but his two new series, *Spin City,* with Michael J. Fox for ABC, and *Ink* with Ted Danson and Mary Steenburgen for CBS, have both received positive early reviews (though CBS shelved the first four episodes of *Ink* just as the season debuted, apparently deeming the episodes merely so-so). Dream-Works SKG Records has also made significant headway by enlisting former Warner Music executives and industry legends Mo Ostin and Lenny Waronker.

Warner refugee Doug Morris is in the ranks as well, heading up the music scene at MCA, distributor for the fledgling SKG label. Morris was savvy enough in February to pull in another Warner escapee in the form of Interscope Records. Grabbing such controversial, but money-making, acts as Nine Inch Nails and the crew at Death Row Records, MCA purchased half of Interscope for $200 million, an investment Morris and Bronfman are counting on to be a big winner. MCA has the option to buy out the rest of Interscope from owners Jimmy Iovine and Ted Field in five years.

But such significant deals take more than the consent of the folks for whom the genie has appeared. Interested and influential parties like Wall Street have the power to create smoke as well, as witnessed in US West Media Group's proposed purchase of Continental Cablevision and the take-over of Scripps Howard cable systems by Comcast. Wall Street this year began to cast a leery eye on the media industry's mega-mergers and the increasing debt many of the players were carrying. While US West planned to pay $10.8 billion to buy Continental and its $5 billion debt and Comcast was offering a $1.6 billion stock swap, Wall Street had other plans. The parties involved watched the markets nervously as both Comcast and US West Media Group's stocks hit the skids, triggering "collars" in the deals that protect buyer and seller from decreases in market value of either entity. But Wall Street is probably as fickle as the entertainment moguls themselves, and the entertainment stocks are likely to return to favor as their prices become more attractive.

And five years from now, it may be a very different picture. The government may decide it's time to break up Entertainment and Communication, Inc., the sole disseminator of information and entertainment on the face of the globe. Or competition may grow to a point at which we're paying $20 a month for wireless cable, telephone and Internet connections combined. But undoubtedly, whatever genie comes out of the bottle next, and no matter who's in charge or how much restructuring and belt-tightening goes on at media conglomerates, consumers will never stop paying to be entertained and industry moguls will never stop wishing for more. ■

Who Owns What?

A major media company can no longer content itself with a quaint concentration on making movies or publishing books. It must be a vertically integrated colossus able to market entertainment in any form. This is our guide to who controls what you watch, listen to and read. (Note that these media properties are extremely fluid. This is a snapshot of domestic businesses taken in August 1996.)

TIME WARNER INC./TURNER

The largest (pending final approvals) entertainment conglomerate in the world also encompasses various sports teams, theme parks and retail emporiums. Time Warner's cable and movie businesses are partially owned by US West (25.5%) with Japanese companies Hochu Corp. and Toshiba Corp. (11.2%).

MOVIES
Warner Bros., HBO Independent Productions, Castle Rock Entertainment, New Line Cinema Corporation (includes Fine Line Features), Turner Pictures Worldwide

MUSIC
WARNER BROS. RECORDS — Warner Bros., Reprise, Giant, Maverick, Qwest, Sire, Warner/Nashville, American Recordings, Slash, Tommy Boy, Luaka Bop, 4AD
ATLANTIC RECORDING GROUP — Atlantic, Interscope, Rhino, Select, Beggars Banquet, Big Beat, Mammoth, TAG Recordings, Celtic Heartbeat, Curb, Lava, Atlantic Nashville, Atlantic Theatre, Atlantic Classics/Nonesuch, 143, Lava, Big Beat
ELEKTRA ENTERTAINMENT — Elektra, East/West America, Asylum, Nonesuch

MUSIC PUBLISHING — Warner/Chappell;
OTHER — Columbia House music club; investment in Music Choice cable radio; investment in Accolade computer game company

PUBLISHING
MAGAZINES — *Time, Life, Fortune, Sports Illustrated, Money, People, Sports Illustrated for Kids, Entertainment Weekly, InStyle, Southern Living, Progressive Farmer, Southern Accents, Cooking Light, Parenting, Baby Talk, Martha Stewart Living, Sunset, Health, Hippocrates, Asiaweek, President, Dancyu, Elle Japon, Who, Vibe, Time for Kids*
BOOK PUBLISHING — Little, Brown, Warner Books, Turner Publishing, Oxmoor House, Sunset Books, Time Life Books, Book-of-the-Month Club, History Book Club, Children's Book of the Month Club, Crafter's Choice book club, Quality Paperback Club, Home Style book club, Time Warner Audio Books
MULTIMEDIA — Pathfinder Web site, Line Runner cable modem service, Turner New Media
OTHER — D.C. Comics, magazine/direct reponse catalogs *BBC Music, Jazziz, huH*

TELEVISION
CABLE PROGRAMMING — HBO, Cinemax, Warner Bros. Pay TV, CNN, CNN Headline News, TBS, TNT, Turner Classic Movies, Cartoon Network, The Airport Channel, SportSouth (44%), Full Service Network interactive TV test, Court TV (33%), Comedy Central (50%), E! Entertainment TV (58%), The Sega Channel (33%), Black Entertainment Television (15%), QVC (8%), Catalog 1 (50%), n-tv (33%), DreamShop, Time Warner cable systems, Advance/Newhouse joint venture

BROADCAST PROGRAMMING — New York 1 News, Warner Bros. Television, Witt-Thomas Productions, The WB Television Network, Time TelePictures Television, Warner Bros. Distribution

GAMES — 3DO (13%), Crystal Dynamics (10%), Atari (25%)

HOME VIDEO — Warner Home Video, Turner Domestic Home Video, Time Life Video

BERTELSMANN AG

MUSIC

BMG Music, Arista Records, Arista/Nashville, BMG/Ariola, Career Records, BMG Classics/RCA Victor, Private Music, RCA Records, Reunion Records, Imago Recording Company, Windham Hill, Zoo Entertainment

MUSIC PUBLISHING — BMG Songs, Killer Tracks, Reunion Music Group; BMG Direct music clubs

TELEVISION

VIDEO PRODUCTION — BMG Video, Nice Man (50%), Blanton/Harrell Management (50%)

PUBLISHING

MAGAZINES — *Parents, YM, Family Circle, McCall's, American Homestyle, Fitness, Child*

BOOK PUBLISHING — Bantam Doubleday Dell Publishing Group; Bantam Books, Doubleday, Broadway Books, Delacorte, Dell, BDD Young Readers, Bantam Classics, Golden Apple, Loveswept, New Age Books, New Fiction, New Sciences, Peacock Press, Perigord Press, Spectra, Sweet Dreams; Doubleday book clubs

MULTIMEDIA — America Online (5%), BMG Interactive Entertainment, Pixel Park, Telemedia

THE SEAGRAM COMPANY LTD.

In April 1995, The Seagram Company acquired 80 percent of MCA, Inc.

MOVIES

Universal Pictures, Cinema International (49%), United International Pictures (33%)

MUSIC

MCA Records, MCA Music Entertainment International, GRP Recording Company, Geffen Records, Uni Distribution, (510), Radioactive (joint venture), Fort Apache/MCA, MCA Publishing

CONCERT PROMOTION — Winterland Productions, MCA Concerts

PUBLISHING

BOOK PUBLISHING — The Putnam Berkley Group (Ace, Berkley Prime Crime, Coward-McCann, Diamond, Grosset & Dunlap, Grosset Books, HP Books, Jove, Perigee Books, Philomel, Platt & Munk, Price Stern Sloan, G.P. Putnam's Sons, Riverhead Books, Sandcastle, Serendipity, Jeremy P. Tarcher, Wee Sing, Wonder Books)

MULTIMEDIA — Universal Interactive, Interplay (minority holder)

TELEVISION

USA Network (50%), MCA TV, MCA Home Video, Universal Pay Television

VIACOM

Viacom's domain also includes video and music retailer Blockbuster and Paramount Parks theme parks.

MOVIES

Paramount Pictures, United International Pictures, Nickelodeon Films, Cinamerica Theatres (50%), Famous Players theaters in Canada

PUBLISHING

BOOK PUBLISHING — Simon & Schuster Trade, Pocket Books, Scribner, The Free Press, Simon & Schuster Children's, Macmillan Computer Publishing USA: Macmillan Reference, Macmillan Library, Prentice Hall, Simon & Schuster Education Group

MAGAZINES — *Nickelodeon Magazine, Nick-At-Nite Magazine*

MULTIMEDIA — Simon & Schuster Interactive, Viacom New Media, Viacom Interactive Services, Macmillan Digital, Macmillan Online USA, Computer Curriculum Corporation, StarSight (26%), Byron Preiss Multimedia (20%), Kaplan Interactive, NBC Digital

TELEVISION

CABLE PROGRAMMING — Showtime, The Movie Channel, FLIX, MTV, VH-1, Nickelodeon, Sundance Film Channel (33%), USA Network (50%), Comedy Central (50%), Sci-Fi Channel (50%), All News Channel (50%), Showtime Satellite Networks

BROADCAST OPERATIONS — United Paramount Network, Paramount Stations Group (12 TV stations), Viacom Radio (12 radio stations)

BROADCAST PROGRAMMING — Paramount Television, Viacom Productions, Laurel Entertainment, Paramount TV Syndication

HOME VIDEO — Paramount Home Video, Republic Home Video, MTV Home Video (partnership with Sony)

TELE-COMMUNICATIONS, INC.

TELEVISION

CABLE OPERATIONS — TCI Communications Inc., cable systems

CABLE PROGRAMMING — Liberty Media: Discovery Channel (49%), The Learning Channel, QVC networks (43%), Home Shopping Networks (41%), the Turner Television networks (23% - see **Time Warner/Turner** above), The Family Channel (20%), Starz! (48%), Encore and its multiplex channels (90%), f/x Network (50%), Court TV (33%), Black Entertainment Television (22%), E! Entertainment (10%), Prime Sports (various ownership in regional sports networks), SportsChannel (various ownership in regional sports networks), Fox Sports (50%), SportsSouth (44%), Sunshine Network (36%), Request TV (40%), Viewer's Choice (10%), The Box (5%), MacNeil/Lehrer Productions, The International Channel (45%), Odyssey Channel (49%), Digital Music Express cable radio (11%), FIT TV, Republic Pictures TV (50%), Southern Satellite Systems program distribution

NEW TECHNOLOGY — TCI Technology Ventures: Sega Channel (33%), Primestar satellite television (partnership with six cable operators), EPG (Viewer's Guide) (25%), @Home Network high-speed Internet service, AND Interactive (investment), Acclaim Entertainment (9%), Netscape provider of on-line access (2%), Western Telecommunications provider of long-distance voice and data (investment)

BROADCASTING — Netlink USA, Silver King (23%)

OTHER — TCI Telephony Services, Sprint Spectrum joint venture digital PCS service, Teleport local access provider

RADIO

Prime Sports Radio

SONY CORPORATION

MOVIES

Columbia Pictures, TriStar Pictures, Sony Pictures Classics, Triumph Films, Sony Pictures Releasing, Sony Theatres, Columbia TriStar International Distribution

MUSIC

Sony Music Entertainment: Columbia Records Group (Columbia, The WORK Group), Epic Records Group (Epic, Epic Associated, Epic Soundtrax, Sony 550 Music), TriStar Music Group (TriStar Music, Relativity), Sony Classical, Sony Music International, Sony Wonder

TELEVISION

PROGRAMMING — Columbia TriStar Television, Columbia TriStar Television Distribution
HOME VIDEO — Columbia TriStar Home Video

THE NEWS CORPORATION, LTD.

News Corp. boasts extensive international holdings, particularly in publishing and satellite television.

MOVIES

Twentieth Century-Fox Film, Fox 2000, Fox Searchlight, Fox Family Films, Fox Animation Studios

MUSIC

Twentieth Century-Fox Records

TELEVISION

BROADCAST PROGRAMMING: Twentieth Century Fox Television, Twentieth Television, Fox Broadcasting, ASkyB satellite TV (50%), Sky MCI satellite TV (50%)
CABLE PROGRAMMING: f/x Network (50%), f/xM Network, Fox Sports (50%), Fox News, The Golf Channel (33%)
HOME VIDEO: Fox Video
BROADCAST OPERATIONS: Fox Television stations (22 stations, including recent purchase of New World stations)

PUBLISHING

MAGAZINES — *TV Guide*
BOOK PUBLISHING — HarperCollins (Harper Collins, Harper Perennial, Harper Children's Books, Collins San Francisco, Harper San Francisco, Harper Reference, Harper Business, Basic Books), ReganBooks, Scott, Foresman, Zondervan;
NEWSPAPERS — The *New York Post*, the *Weekly Standard*, News American FSI
ONLINE — iGuide, Kesmai Corporation

THE WALT DISNEY COMPANY

The Magic Kingdom contains theme parks, of course, as well as theater productions and retail stores.

MOVIES

Walt Disney Pictures, Touchstone Pictures, Miramax Film Corp.

MUSIC

Walt Disney Records, Disney Music Publishing

TELEVISION

BROADCAST OPERATIONS — KCAL-TV, Los Angeles and 8 ABC television stations
BROADCAST PROGRAMMING — ABC television network, Buena Vista Television, Touchstone Television, Walt Disney Television
PRODUCTION — DreamWorks SKG (partnership), DIC Animation City
CABLE PROGRAMMING — The Disney Channel, Arts & Entertainment Network (37.5%), ESPN (80%), ESPN 2, Lifetime (50%), The History Channel (37.5%)
HOME VIDEO — Walt Disney Home Video

RADIO

ABC Radio Networks (11 AM, 10 FM radio stations)

PUBLISHING

MAGAZINES — *Discover, Disney Adventures, FamilyFun, Family PC* (joint venture with Ziff-Davis), shopping guides, diversified publishing group, agricultural publishing, Chilton Publications, Grupo Editorial Expansion (LA), NILS Publishing Co., *W, Women's Wear Daily, Institutional Investor*, International Medical News Group
BOOK PUBLISHING — Hyperion Press, Disney Press, Mouse Works, Miramax Books
NEWSPAPERS: *Fort Worth Star-Telegram,* The *Kansas City (MO) Star* newspapers and related publications in 13 states
MULTIMEDIA — Disney Software

MOVIES

Cinergy?

■ BY JOHN ANDERSON

John Anderson is a film critic for *Newsday*.

MOVIES. IS THERE ANOTHER POPULAR ENTERTAINMENT THAT generates so much anxiety? Over the last year, cinema and cinema-hype seemed to become as pervasive as politics, and it's not clear which had more influence over the mind of America. This year's election returns will probably get more attention than the opening weekend grosses of *Independence Day*, but more people probably saw *Independence Day* than can name their member of Congress.

At a time when the film industry is assumed to be on its way to a kinder, gentler and far more conservative sensibility — thanks in part to politicians who are willing to condemn movies they haven't seen — the best film of 1995 was judged to be a medieval splatter epic about a bunch of men in skirts (OK, kilts). This doesn't make much sense. But neither did the state of cinema as it entered its second century.

The most talked-about films of 1995 — *Apollo 13, Braveheart, Leaving Las Vegas* and *Babe* — illustrated what we have begun to see in film at large: a growing schism between what's considered art and what's considered profitable; a widening gap between what might be called the corporate movie and the strictly cinematic; a not-kinder but more shameless exploitation of media power to promote dubious screen product and the further marginalization of so-called independent film, which itself became harder to define.

MOVIES

The exaltation of *Braveheart* was half celebration, half symptom. A sincere, well-made adventure, it shared Best Picture Oscar nominations with those "foreign" films *The Postman (Il Postino), Babe* and *Sense and Sensibility*. But those-in-the-know always knew that *Braveheart*'s only real competition for the Academy Award was *Apollo 13*, another blockbuster in the classic Hollywood style, a film that boasted excitement, near-tragedy and inflated patriotism but never challenged any accepted tenet of industry filmmaking.

And when Mel Gibson also took home the Best Director prize, it followed a tradition of honoring actors-turned-directors — who have ranged from Laurence Olivier to Kevin Costner — and seemed quite logical, considering that the majority of Oscar voters are actors, and self-preservation is the first law of Hollywood.

It's a law that continues to apply, despite the ongoing consolidation of media entities and creation of mega-studios such as Disney. And it has brought about what might be perceived as a troubling development — one best illustrated by the hoopla surrounding *Twister*, which was one of 1996's blockbuster summer releases (and an example of Hollywood's growing preference for special effects over story or character).

The week the film opened, there was a sort of electronic coalescence around the event. PBS showed "killer weather" specials early in the week. CBS ran *The Wizard of Oz* (a film often quoted in *Twister*) on the night of the film's release. Local newscasts chimed in with special tornado reports (which, given that the film opened at the height of tornado season, wasn't hard to pull off). It seemed that the entirety of mass media had greeted the film with welcoming and decidedly self-interested arms.

The oft-heard concern about the concentration of media power among fewer and fewer companies failed to take into account this very "unofficial" (and presumably non-collusive)

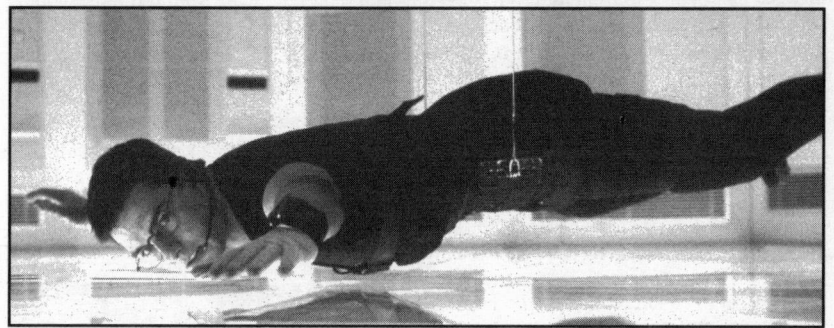

Twister, Independence Day, The Postman and *Mission: Impossible*

strain of symbiosis. On the Sundays leading up to the opening of *Mission: Impossible,* ABC aired two Tom Cruise movies. *MI* was not a Disney movie; there was no concrete corporate connection. In *The Hunchback of Notre Dame* — which, depending on your taste, marked either the continuation of the trend toward solid family fare or the arrival of Disney's animated musicals into a formulaic trench — Esmeralda, with both the voice and physique of Demi Moore, did an erotic spin around a pole that was an unmistakable plug for *Striptease.* There was no link between the films, except a desire to exploit whatever publicity each could provide the other.

Of course, entertainment companies occasionally plugged their own films. For *Independence Day,* Fox Television concocted "newscasts" that were obvious takeoffs on Orson Welles's "War of the Worlds" broadcast (while the film itself was essentially a rework-

Heat

ing of the original story by that other Wells, H.G.). During a scene in the Whoopi Goldberg comedy *Eddie,* shot outside the Plaza Hotel in New York, the actors were virtually haloed by a nearby theater marquee bearing the title *Belle de Jour* — the Catherine Deneuve film that had been re-released by Miramax, a Disney company. *Eddie* was a Disney movie.

Coincidence? Or synergy?

Basically, the movie business has resorted to a saturation-bombing of our psyches. Which is not to say that what came out of Hollywood always came out badly. Or that the quality of advertising has anything to do with the quality of the movies — even if the audience consensus seems to be one of dissatisfaction. There was certainly ambitious work out there: *12 Monkeys*, *Nixon*, the Jane Austen adaptations (*Persuasion, Sense and Sensibility, Emma*), *Heat*, *Seven*, *Clockers, Georgia, Devil in a Blue Dress, Get Shorty* and *Dead Man Walking*. Curiously, none of these were the beneficiaries of the massive campaigns that supported someone such as . . . Liv Tyler. Then again, she'll be around a lot longer than any of those movies.

But longevity isn't what it used to be. Jim Carrey became the biggest commodity in pictures, at least before *The Cable Guy* crossed his wires. John Travolta completed his round trip from idol to has-been to idol (and grabbed a seat in the big-money club). Eddie Murphy, another star coming off the ropes, made *Vampire in Brooklyn* and then *The Nutty Professor*, showing at least some forward motion. In terms of public image and staying power, Sharon Stone accomplished the miraculous transformation from movie babe to movie babe with a brain.

On the other hand, Quentin Tarantino, whose *Pulp Fiction* resurrected Travolta and made the director himself a demi-god of the New Nihilism, directed one of *Four Rooms* and acted in and wrote *From Dusk Till Dawn*. Not much to write home about. Neither was Demi Moore's $15-million performance in *Striptease* or her continued association with the assassination of literature (*The Scarlet Letter, The Hunchback of Notre Dame*).

The perceived reason for the perceived drop in movie quality was an all-too-real increase in output. There was a move — inaugurated by Disney — to cut back on the number of films produced and, in theory, maximize profits. At the same time, there was the sense of massive technological advancement throughout the filmmaking process, an ability, basically, to put on screen whatever a director could possibly want. Whether either of these developments will mean better movies is another question. We may simply be poised at a time when intellect and sensibility need to catch up with technique. It's happened before — the invention of talking pictures, for example.

Movies don't, of course, serve strictly as art, or strictly as entertainment, or anything in between. They serve as mirrors of the Zeitgeist, reflecting how we view ourselves and our culture. And how our culture views us.

When *Waiting to Exhale* opened to an unexpectedly popular response, it corresponded to the same phenom-

The Scarlet Letter

enon that has followed gay film, Hispanic film — any genre that embraces people marginalized first by society and then by its popular entertainment. Put characters on screen to whom these same people can relate, and they will come out in droves. Few critics gave *Waiting to Exhale* much credit as cinema, but the turnout by black women eager to see their story portrayed onscreen — by attractive, believable characters, set in reasonably authentic circumstances — proved that identification with self is an irresistible marquee attraction.

This is something accomplished more often on the fringes of film than in its mainstream, where throwing money onto the screen continued to be a popular pastime — Exhibit A might be Sylvester Stallone, rewarded for the barely releasable *Assassins* and *Judge Dredd* with a three-picture, $60 million deal. The fascination with remakes and continuing series continued — *Diabolique, Sabrina, The Birdcage, Goldeneye* — as did the bizarre practice of converting old TV shows to the big screen, something that indicated not just a lack of imagination but complete ignorance of taste outside the studio boardroom. In addition to *Mission: Impossible* there were *Sgt. Bilko, Flipper* and *A Very Brady Sequel*, and the planned appearance of a *McHale's Navy* feature, *The Saint, Beavis and Butt-Head* ... need I continue? Need they?

This is called playing it safe. What else would you call Robert Redford and Michelle Pfeiffer in *Up Close and Personal*? Or Jim Carrey in *Ace Ventura: When Nature Calls*? This may be the biggest failing of the studios, considering their resources. But it does make people, some people, hungry for something more real, something even a big-budget ad campaign can't satisfy. When *Fargo* was released early in 1996 — too early, it's commonly assumed, for the memories of end-of-year awards voters — it got a decent response, partly because the Coen brothers had made an imaginative film and partly because there was simply nothing else out there to prick the interest of intelligent moviegoers. When John Sayles's *Lone Star* opened in early summer, it was warmly received because it was human and dramatic and also because a steady diet of plastic explosives and

1995's HIGHEST GROSSING FILMS

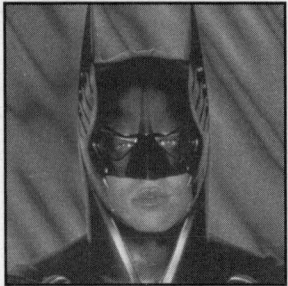

Batman Forever

Title	Gross through 1/2/96 (in millions)
1. *Batman Forever*	$184.0
2. *Apollo 13*	172.0
3. *Toy Story*	150.0
4. *Pocahontas*	141.5
5. *Ace Ventura: When Nature Calls*	104.4
6. *Casper*	100.3
7. *Die Hard With a Vengeance*	100.0
8. *Goldeneye*	93.2
9. *Crimson Tide*	91.3
10. *Waterworld*	88.2

Source: Exhibitor Relations

1995's TOP 10 MONEYMAKERS IN FOREIGN MARKETS

Title	1995 Gross (in millions)
1. *Die Hard With a Vengeance*	$254
2. *Casper*	180
3. *Pocahontas*	176
4. *Waterworld*	167
5. *Apollo 13*	160
6. *Batman Forever*	149
7. *Outbreak*	120
8. *Goldeneye*	107
9. *The Bridges of Madison County*	105
10. *While You Were Sleeping*	101

Figures from the Hollywood Reporter *and* Variety

hurtling bodies does not make for a healthy, or even happy, audience.

Sayles's film was politically correct (ooooohhh), but in the best sense: It showed various peoples separated, but separated by differences that can be overcome and the American people want to overcome. Sayles employed a cross-section of America for his story of murder and mythmaking in the Southwest and, by extension, exposed his audience to a broader-than-usual spectrum of humanity.

And this was precisely what began to go missing from American theaters, thanks to a reluctance on the part of distributors — with the notable exceptions of Miramax and the very independent October Films — to take a chance on subtitled movies. Emir Kusturica's *Underground,* winner of the Palme d'Or at Cannes in 1995, went unreleased in the United States. A lackluster response from the *New York Times,* which was virtually alone in its judgment but carries enormous clout, put film companies off Andre Techine's *Wild Reeds,* a film that eventually made money wherever it went and won several prestigious critics prizes. The major distributors passed, and Strand picked it up.

Lone Star

In 1996, Miramax, rightly, took great pride in the fact that it was opening a raft of foreign-language films — having made *The Postman,* the biggest foreign release in U.S. history — but otherwise, you had to look hard to find films you had to read.

And this, in light of the domination of world markets by U.S. film, made for lopsided international relations. Our films go everywhere; no one else's come here. This is due for the most part to the mechanics of film distribution and the rise of home video. Foreign films don't do well in rental, because people want to read subtitles even less at home than they do in the theater. And distribution deals hinge largely on a film's video potential. This is basic business. It isn't fair, and it isn't smart. And it also diminishes us as people. Shouldn't the death of Krzysztof Kieslowski, one of the giants of world cinema, the director of *Blue, White* and *Red*, have been given more attention than *Showgirls*? Krzysztof who?

We learn much of what we know, and think we know, from movies. If movies only offer us what we already know — and often, what we've already seen again and again — then they lose a great deal of their usefulness. One of the more notable developments in film during late 1995 was the number of films about women (cast other than as hookers or killers) and female relationships. But these films (*Now and Then, How to Make an American Quilt, Moonlight and Valentino*) weren't very good. Audiences didn't turn out. Hollywood could go back to business as usual.

Which was pretty good, all things considered. No one was losing money (although such indies as the Samuel Goldwyn Co. teetered financially). And there certainly was a wide range of choice in the theaters. During a year that saw the masterpiece of *Toy Story*, we also got *Trainspotting*, a film eager to offend but which, in its own perverse way, was as exciting as anything we saw last year. What that Scottish film ultimately proved, yet again, is that when it comes to movies, it's a big tent with something for everyone. Of course, sometimes you have to go find it. And other times, it's right there in your face. ■

How to Make an American Quilt

1995's TOP 10 DOMESTIC MONEYMAKERS

Title	Cost (in millions)	1995 Gross (in millions)
1. Toy Story	$30	$146.2
2. Apollo 13	62	172.0
3. Pocahontas	55	141.5
4. Batman Forever	100	184.0
5. Ace Ventura: When Nature Calls	30	104.2
6. While You Were Sleeping	17	81.1
7. Seven	30	87.0
8. Waiting to Exhale	15	75.0
9. Grumpier Old Men	25	80.0
10. The Bridges of Madison County	22	70.1

Figures from the Hollywood Reporter *and* Variety

1995's BOX-OFFICE BOMBS

Money Train

Title	Cost (in millions)	1995 Gross (in millions)
1. Cutthroat Island	$92	$ 6.5
2. Judge Dredd	90	34.7
3. Jade	50	9.8
4. The Scarlet Letter	50	10.4
5. Fair Game	50	11.2
6. First Knight	75	37.6
7. Nixon	50	6.9
8. Strange Days	42	7.9
9. Money Train	68	34.5
10. Steal Little, Steal Big	35	3.1

Figures from the Hollywood Reporter *and* Variety

Movies Released in U.S. Theaters in 1995–1996

The following films debuted domestically between September 1, 1995 and August 1, 1996.

ACE VENTURA: WHEN NATURE CALLS

Director/Writer: Steve Oedekerk; **Director of Photography:** Donald E. Thorin; **Editor:** Malcolm Campbell; **Music:** Robert Folk; **Production Designer:** Stephen J. Lineweaver; **Producer:** James G. Robinson
Warner Bros.; PG-13; 105 minutes
Release: 11/95
Cast: Jim Carrey, Ian McNeice, Simon Callow, Maynard Eziashi, Bob Gunton, Sophie Okonedo, Tommy Davidson, Andrew Steel and Bruce Spence
Pretty much the same movie as its predecessor, *Ace Ventura: Pet Detective*, but with a better title and a different milieu. Though many of the jokes have been recycled, Carrey scores big again, setting a box-office record with a $40-million opening weekend. After a raccoon falls to its untimely death in a scene out of *Cliffhanger*, Ace Ventura (Carrey) retreats to a Tibetan monastery to mourn. It's a short-lived refuge as British emissary Fulton Greenwell (McNeice) enlists Ventura to recover a white bat that is needed to ensure peace between two African tribes. The plot is secondary here to Carrey's shtick that has him twisting in mind-bending contortions, affecting hilarious expressions and overdoing everything. All this and animal rights, too.

THE ADDICTION

Director: Abel Ferrara; **Writer:** Nicholas St. John; **Director of Photography:** Ken Kelsch; **Editor:** Mayin Lo; **Music:** Joe Delia; **Production Designer:** Charles Lagola; **Producers:** Denis Hann and Fernando Sulichin
October Films; NR; 84 minutes
Release: 10/95
Cast: Lili Taylor, Christopher Walken, Annabella Sciorra, Kathryn Erbe and Father Robert Castle
Shot in New York in gritty black-and-white, this film provides the perfect look and feel for a dark vampire film. We expect nothing less from director Ferrara. Philosophy student Kathleen Conklin (Taylor) is the unsuspecting victim of Casanova (Sciorra), a vampire. Craving blood as an addict would drugs, the transformed Conklin begins biting other people. Adding a darkly comic tone to the tale, Peina (Walken), another vampire, encourages her to break the habit or at least drink in moderation.

The American President

THE ADVENTURES OF PINOCCHIO

Director: Steve Barron; **Writers:** Sherry Mills, Steve Barron, Tom Benedek and Barry Berman; **Director of Photography:** Juan Ruiz Anchia; **Editor:** Sean Barton; **Music:** Rachel Portman; **Production Designer:** Allan Cameron; **Producers:** Raju Patel and Jeffrey Sneller
New Line; G; 90 minutes
Release: 7/96
Cast: Martin Landau, Jonathan Taylor Thomas, Rob Schneider, Udo Kier, Bebe Neuwirth, David Doyle, Corey Carrier and Genevieve Bujold
Based on the novel by Carlo Collodi
The creators of this version of the beloved *Pinocchio* have to be given credit: Few would want to toy with the 1940 animated classic. It was a formidable task, and comparisons were certain. It's not that the update, which combines puppet animation and live action, is bad, it's just not as well done. The magic and charm are lacking. Landau's Geppetto is a sincere, heart-warming character, and Thomas is a convincing title character, but it's not the Pinocchio we so fondly remember from childhood.

AMAZING PANDA ADVENTURE

Director: Christopher Cain; **Writers:** Jeff Rothberg and Laurice Elehwany; **Director of Photography:** Jack N. Green; **Editor:** Jack Hofstra; **Music:** William Ross; **Producers:** Lee Rich, John Wilcox, Gary Foster and Dylan Sellers

Warner Bros.; PG; 93 minutes
Release: 9/95
Cast: Stephen Lang, Yi Ding, Ryan Slater and Huang Fei
Ryan (Slater) travels to China to visit his father
(Lang) who he hasn't seen since his parents'
divorce two years earlier. Ryan joins his father's
crusade to save a mother panda and her cub
from poachers. Ryan and his new friend (Ding)
lose their group and struggle to find their way
back to the panda reserve and evade the poachers to save the cub they have hidden in a back-
pack.

THE AMERICAN PRESIDENT
Director/Producer: Rob Reiner; **Writer:** Aaron Sorkin;
Director of Photography: John Seale; **Editor:** Bob
Leighton; **Production Designer:** Lilly Kilvert
Castle Rock Entertainment; PG-13; 115 minutes
Release: 11/95
Cast: Michael Douglas, Annette Bening, Martin
Sheen, Michael J. Fox, Anna Deveare Smith, David
Paymer, Shawna Waldron and Samantha Mathis
Liberal president — and widower — Andrew
Shepherd (Douglas) occupies the White House
with his teenage daughter (Waldron). Intelligent,
stunning environmental lobbyist Sydney Wade
(Bening) captures his heart. His Republican rival
(Dreyfuss) attempts to exploit the relationship
and bring down the president's remarkable 63
percent approval rating. This sleek effort captures some of the Capraesque feelings that
movies once gave audiences about their leaders.

ANGELA
Director/Writer: Rebecca Miller; **Director of
Photography:** Ellen Kuras; **Editor:** Melody London;
Music: Michael Rohatyn; **Production Designer:**
Daniel Talpers; **Producer:** Ron Kastner
Tree Farm Pictures; NR; 103 minutes
Release: 1/96
Cast: Miranda Stuart Rhyne, Charlotte Blythe, Anna
Thomson, John Ventimiglia, Ruth Maleczech and
Hynden Walch
As her mother's mental stability erodes, 10-year-
old Angela (Rhyne) leads her 6-year-old sister,
Ellie (Blythe), through a series of rituals meant
to ward off evil spirits. Angela realizes her moth-
er's condition is hopeless and decides that she
and her sister must leave home for "the big nothing," the place she says is "the same place as
dying." The movie turns into a disturbing, surreal journey and a commentary on how children
perceive and are affected by their surroundings.

ANGELS AND INSECTS
Director: Philip Haas; **Writers:** Philip Haas and
Belinda Haas; **Director of Photography:** Bernard
Zitzermann; **Editor:** Belinda Haas; **Music:** Alexander
Balanescu; **Production Designer:** Jennifer Kernke;
Producers: Belinda Haas and Joyce Herlihy
Samuel Goldwyn; NR; 116 minutes

Release: 1/96
Cast: Mark Rylance, Patsy Kensit and Kristin Scott
Thomas
Based on the novella *Morpho Eugenia* by A.S. Byatt
Bizarre and haunting, but a beautiful and mesmerizing depiction of human nature and its parallels with the insect world. Entomologist
William Adamson (Rylance) has just returned to
1850s England after a research stint in the
Amazon ended in disaster when his specimens
were lost at sea. The Alabaster family takes in
the impoverished Adamson, and he is enticed by
and marries Eugenia Alabaster (Kensit). She is
an enigma to Adamson: cold and distant during
the day, yet hot and passionate at night. He
begins a study of ants with Matty Crompton
(Thomas), a relative of the Alabasters, who is as
dark and cerebral as Eugenia is light and physical. Their working relationship deepens when
Adamson learns haunting secrets about his
wife's family.

ANGUS
Director: Patrick Read Johnson; **Writer:** Jill Gordon;
Director of Photography: Alexander Grusynski;
Editor: Janice Hampton; **Music:** David Russo;
Production Designer: Larry Miller; **Producers:** Dawn
Steel and Charles Roven
New Line Cinema; PG-13; 91 minutes
Release: 9/95
Cast: George C. Scott, Rita Moreno, Chris Owen,
Lawrence Pressman, Ariana Richards, Anna
Thompson, Charlie Talbert, Kathy Bates, James Van
Der Beek
Based on the short story by Chris Crutcher
A large high-school student (Talbert) faces indig-
nities and torment but remains a nice guy
throughout. The struggles with bullies and the
teenage need for popularity are fairly pre-
dictable, but the cast is strong and one could
imagine worse fare for teens.

ANNE FRANK REMEMBERED
Director/Writer/Producer: Jon Blair; **Director of
Photography:** Barry Ackroyd; **Editor:** Karen
Steininger; **Music:** Carl Davis
Sony Pictures Classics; PG; 122 minutes
Release: 2/96
With: Kenneth Branagh, Glenn Close, Miep Gies,
Hanneli Goslar and Peter Pfeffer
Anne Frank's heart-wrenching story, narrated by
Branagh with diary excerpts read by Close, is
perfectly told here without the hyper-emotional
Hollywood coloring. Frank's diary and inter-
views with Gies, who brought food and news to
the eight residents of the attic, chronicle the
time in hiding, their capture and their intern-
ment in concentration camps. A moving, true
portrait of courage.

ANTONIA'S LINE

Director/Writer: Marleen Gorris; **Director of Photography:** Willy Stassen; **Editors:** Michiel Reichwein and Wim Louwrier; **Music:** Ilona Sekacz; **Producer:** Hans de Weers
First Look Pictures; NR; 105 minutes
Release: 2/96
Cast: Willeke van Ammelrooy, Els Dottermans, Jan Decleir, Mil Seghers, Catherine ten Bruggencate and Jan Steen
In Dutch with English subtitles
A feminist yarn beautifully spun with magical realism and fantasy. Beginning and ending on the day of her death, Antonia (van Ammelrooy) looks back on her life and the maturation of her descendants.

THE ARRIVAL

Director/Writer: David Twohy; **Director of Photography:** Hiro Narita; **Editor:** Martin Hunter; **Music:** Arthur Kempel; **Production Designer:** Michael Novotny; **Producers:** Thomas G. Smith and Jim Steele
Live Entertainment; PG-13; 109 minutes
Release: 5/96
Cast: Charlie Sheen, Ron Silver, Lindsay Crouse, Tony T. Johnson and Teri Polo
Extraterrestrials bent on taking over Earth by overheating the planet disguise themselves as humans and set up camp in third world countries. NASA radio astronomer Zane Ziminski (Sheen) receives an intergalactic signal from one of their power stations and sets out to expel them from the planet. Getting nowhere with his superiors, Ziminski continues alone, and his quest leads him to Mexico where he teams up with climatologist Ilana Green (Crouse). Lots of inconsistencies and a plot that gets lost in gimmickry.

ASSASSINS

Director: Richard Donner; **Writers:** Andy Wachowski, Larry Wachowski and Brian Helgeland; **Director of Photography:** Vilmos Zsigmond; **Editor:** Richard Marks; **Music:** Mark Mancina; **Production Designer:** Tom Sanders; **Producers:** Richard Donner, Joel Silver, Bruce Evans, Raynold Gideon, Andrew Lazar and Jim Van Wyck
Warner Bros.; R; 105 minutes
Release: 10/95
Cast: Sylvester Stallone, Antonio Banderas and Julianne Moore
Assassins is a slight improvement over Stallone's two recent disasters, *Judge Dredd* and *The Specialist*, but not by much. Robert Rath (Stallone) is the number-one assassin in the world, closely trailed by Miguel Bain (Banderas), who is determined to assume the top position. Bain foils two of Rath's assignments, in the process wiping out dozens of innocent bystanders. His next target is Rath, who has fallen in love with the woman he is supposed to kill, technological surveillance expert Electra (Moore). In keeping with Hollywood's recent fascination with high-tech thrillers, there is as much action at the computer keyboard as there is at the trigger.

AUGUST

Director: Anthony Hopkins; **Writer:** Julian Mitchell; **Director of Photography:** Robin Vidgeon; **Editor:** Edward Mansell; **Music:** Anthony Hopkins; **Production Designer:** Eileen Diss; **Producers:** June Wyndham Davies and Pippa Cross
Samuel Goldwyn; NR; 90 minutes
Release: 4/96
Cast: Anthony Hopkins, Kate Burton, Gawn Granger and Rhian Morgan
Based on Anton Chekhov's *Uncle Vanya*
Hopkins, in his directorial debut, turns in another laudable performance in this adaptation of Chekhov's *Uncle Vanya*, the story of an embittered country farmer (Hopkins) who slowly goes mad as his extended family visits him at his estate. Unfortunately, there are times when the production is in a bit over its head, and one can't help but recall 1994's *Vanya on 42nd Street*. Even with Hopkins's eye for composition and musical ear, *August* falters.

THE BABYSITTER

Director/Writer: Guy Ferland; **Director of Photography:** Rick Bota; **Editor:** Jim Prior; **Music:** Loek Dikker; **Production Designer:** Phil Leonard; **Producers:** Kevin J. Messick and Steve Perry
Spelling Films International; R; 90 minutes
Release: 11/95
Cast: Alicia Silverstone, J.T. Walsh, Lee Garlington, Nicky Katt, Jeremy London, George Segal and Lois Chiles
Originally released on video, this Silverstone vehicle was made shortly before her star turn in *Clueless*. Here, she gives two performances: one as a young, shy babysitter and the other as a sexually charged Lolita, appearing in the male characters' dreams. Silverstone is playing the character she knows best: nymphet.

THE BABY-SITTERS CLUB

Director: Melanie Mayron; **Writer:** Dalene Young; **Director of Photography:** Willy Kurant; **Editor:** Christopher Greenbury; **Music:** David Michael Frank; **Production Designer:** Larry Fulton; **Producers:** Jane Startz and Peter O. Almond
Columbia; PG; 85 minutes
Release: 9/95
Cast: Schuyler Fisk, Rachel Leigh Cook, Bre Blair, Christian Oliver, Ellen Burstyn and Peter Horton
Based on the book series by Ann M. Martin
The seven members of the Stoneybrook, Connecticut, baby-sitters club cope with problems typical to 13 year olds: boys, school and broken homes. Kristy (Fisk) has more to contend

The Baby-Sitters Club

with, though, when her estranged father returns to town and asks Kristy to keep his presence a secret from her mother and stepfather.

BALTO

Director: Simon Wells; **Writers:** Cliff Ruby, Elana Lesser, David Steven Cohen and Roger S.H. Schulman; **Editors:** Nick Fletcher and Sim Evan-Jones; **Music:** James Horner; **Production Design:** Hans Bacher; **Animation Production Supervisor:** Colin J. Alexander; **Producer:** Steve Hickner
Universal; G; 77 minutes
Release: 12/95
Voices of: Kevin Bacon, Bob Hoskins, Bridget Fonda, Jim Cummings, Phil Collins, Miriam Margolyes and Lola Bates-Campbell

Unlike most of the kid flicks in theaters today, *Balto* offers little to parents and only little more to children, save for its social message. Balto (voice of Bacon) doesn't fit in with other animals because of his mixed lineage (half dog, half wolf). Humans avoid him for the same reason. Despite this, Balto helps deliver medicine by sled to sick children. Steele (voice of Cummings), a villainous dog, tries to undermine Balto's every move, including his efforts to win over Jenna (voice of Fonda). The animation pales in comparison to other recent animated offerings. Inoffensive at best.

BARB WIRE

Director: David Hogan; **Writers:** Chuck Pfarrer and Ilene Chaiken; **Director of Photography:** Rick Bota; **Editor:** Peter Schink; **Music:** Michel Colombier; **Production Designer:** Jean-Philippe Carp; **Producers:** Brad Wyman, Mike Richardson and Todd Moyer
Gramercy; R; 90 minutes
Release: 5/96
Cast: Pamela Anderson Lee, Temuera Morrison, Steve Railsback and Victoria Rowell

In her skin-tight, cleavage-revealing black rubber minidress, stiletto heels and caked-on makeup, female action hero/mercenary Barb Wire (Lee) says, "Don't call me babe." It's 2017 and the Nazis control an American police state. Barb

Wire, her old boyfriend and current colleague (Morrison) and his scientist wife (Rowell) are out to restore order. But to do so, they must get their hands on a pair of contact lenses that get them through retina scans at government outposts. Little more than a vehicle for Lee and her body parts.

BEAUTIFUL GIRLS

Director: Ted Demme; **Writer:** Scott Rosenberg; **Director of Photography:** Adam Kimmel; **Editor:** Jeffrey Wolf; **Music:** David A. Stewart; **Production Designer:** Dan Davis; **Producer:** Cary Woods
Miramax; R; 113 minutes
Release: 2/96
Cast: Matt Dillon, Michael Rapaport, Martha Plimpton, Mira Sorvino, Lauren Holly, Timothy Hutton, Annabeth Gish, Natalie Portman, Uma Thurman, Pruitt Taylor Vince, Rosie O'Donnell, Noah Emmerich and Max Perlich

An attractive cast does not guarantee an enjoyable product. Witness *Beautiful Girls*. It's not terrible, but do we need a big-screen version of *Friends?* Any other version of *Friends* for that matter? A group of small-town, going-nowhere men screw up their relationships with women, and the women, for the most part, prove that beauty is only skin deep.

BED OF ROSES

Director/Writer: Michael Goldenberg; **Director of Photography:** Adam Kimmel; **Editor:** Jane Kurson; **Music:** Michael Convertino; **Production Designer:** Stephen McCabe; **Producers:** Allan Mindel and Denise Shaw
New Line; PG; 87 minutes
Release: 1/96
Cast: Christian Slater, Mary Stuart Masterson and Pamela Segall

Lonely workaholic Lisa (Masterson) has a secret admirer who deluges her with beautiful lavender roses. It doesn't take her (or the audience) long to figure the mystery man is also the delivery man, Lewis (Slater). Lewis figures he can calm Lisa and cure her loneliness by introducing her to his world of flowers. It works, and for some reason, so does the movie.

BEFORE AND AFTER

Director: Barbet Schroeder; **Writer:** Ted Tally; **Director of Photography:** Luciano Tovoli; **Editor:** Lee Percy; **Music:** Howard Shore; **Production Designer:** Stuart Wurtzel; **Producers:** Barbet Schroeder and Susan Hoffman
Hollywood Pictures; PG-13; 108 minutes
Release: 2/96
Cast: Meryl Streep, Liam Neeson, Edward Furlong, Julia Weldon and Alfred Molina

Teenager Jacob Ryan (Furlong) is accused of killing his girlfriend. His sculptor father, Ben (Neeson), will do anything, including obstruct justice, to prove his son's innocence, while his pediatrician mother (Streep) has faith in the judicial system. Both parents find that there is a side to their son they never knew. The actors shine, though the script offers few surprises.

BIG BULLY

Director: Steve Miner; **Writer:** Mark Steven Johnson; **Director of Photography:** Daryn Okada; **Editor:** Marshall Harvey; **Music:** David Newman; **Production Designer:** Ian Thomas; **Producers:** Lee Rich and Gary Foster
Warner Bros.; PG; 93 minutes
Release: 1/96
Cast: Rick Moranis, Tom Arnold, Julianne Phillips, Carol Kane, Jeffrey Tambor, Curtis Armstrong, Faith Prince, Tony Pierce, Blake Bashoff, Michael Zwiener, Justin Jon Ross and Don Knotts
Big Bully marks the end of Arnold's hot streak. He stole the show in *Nine Months* and *True Lies,* but neither he nor Moranis can salvage this one. Thinking he'll never see his tormentor again, 10-year-old Davey (Ross) gets revenge on bully Roscoe (Zwiener) and finks on him just before his family moves out of town. Twenty-five years later, Davey (Moranis) moves back to his home turf, and his own son (Bashoff) gets in trouble for picking on a classmate — the son of Roscoe (Arnold). Bad feelings resurface and immature pranks turn unnecessarily malicious.

THE BIG GREEN

Director/Writer: Holly Goldberg Sloan; **Director of Photography:** Ralf Bode; **Editor:** John F. Link; **Music:** Randy Edelman; **Production Designer:** Evelyn Sakash; **Producer:** Roger Birnbaum
Buena Vista; PG; 100 minutes
Release: 9/95
Cast: Steve Guttenberg, Olivia d'Abo, Jay O. Sanders, Anthony Esquivel and Patrick Renna
Little League soccer helps a small, backwater Texas town gain some self-respect when the town's team, the Big Green, progresses from utter inexperience to a spot in the state championship. Reminiscent of 1994's *Angels in the Outfield.*

BIG NIGHT

Directors: Campbell Scott and Stanley Tucci; **Writers:** Joseph Tropiano and Stanley Tucci; **Director of Photography:** Ken Kelsch; **Editor:** Suzy Elmiger; **Music:** Gary DeMichele; **Production Designer:** Andrew Jackness; **Producer:** Jonathan Filley
MGM-United Artists; NR; 107 minutes
Release: 3/96
Cast: Tony Shalhoub, Stanley Tucci, Minnie Driver, Isabella Rossellini, Ian Holm and Campbell Scott
Two immigrant brothers, Primo (Shalhoub) and Secondo (Tucci), realize their dream when they open Paradise, an Italian restaurant in New Jersey. But their dream will be short-lived if they don't attract customers. Their neighbor, Pascal (Holm), who operates a successful restaurant (though his food doesn't come close to the culinary masterpieces offered at Paradise), tells them they can turn things around if they invite Louis Prima and his band to dinner. As they prepare for the big night, Primo and Secondo demonstrate their affection for each other and their passion for fine cuisine. Subtle and delightful.

BIO-DOME

Director: Jason Bloom; **Writers:** Kip Koenig and Scott Marcano; **Director of Photography:** Phedon Papamichael; **Editor:** Christopher Greenbury; **Music:** Andrew Gross; **Production Designer:** Michael Johnston; **Producers:** Brad Krevoy, Steve Stabler and Brad Jenkel
MGM; PG-13; 95 minutes
Release: 1/96
Cast: Pauly Shore, Stephen Baldwin, William Atherton, Joey Adams, Teresa Hill and Roger Clinton
Two airheads (Shore and Baldwin) mistake the bio-dome for a mall. They get hermetically sealed inside. Antics follow. Ugh.

THE BIRDCAGE

Director: Mike Nichols; **Writer:** Elaine May; **Director of Photography:** Emmanuel Lubezki; **Editor:** Arthur Schmidt; **Music:** Jonathan Tunick; **Production Designer:** Bo Welch; **Producer:** Mike Nichols
United Artists; R; 117 minutes
Release: 3/96
Cast: Robin Williams, Gene Hackman, Nathan Lane, Dianne Wiest, Christine Baranski, Dan Futterman and Calista Flockhart
Based on the French film *La Cage Aux Folles* by Jean Poiret
Armand (Williams) and Albert (Lane) are a gay couple — a cabaret owner and producer and a drag-show superstar — who raised Armand's son, Val (Futterman). When Val announces his engagement to the daughter of ultra-conservative Sen. Keeley (Hackman), Armand and Albert attempt to straighten up for the future in-laws. The three tone down their Miami apartment and Albert poses as Armand's wife. The reunion of May and Nichols and first-rate performances make *The Birdcage* strong, hilarious and sometimes even touching.

BLUE IN THE FACE

Directors: Wayne Wang and Paul Auster; **Situations created by** Wayne Wang and Paul Auster in collaboration with the actors; **Director of Photography:** Adam Holender; **Editor:** Christopher Tellefsen; **Music:** John Lurie, Calvin Weston and Billy Martin; **Production Designer:** Kalina Ivanov; **Producers:** Greg Johnson, Peter Newman and Diana Phillips
Miramax; R; 90 minutes
Release: 10/95

Cast: Harvey Keitel, Lily Tomlin, Jared Harris, Giancarlo Esposito, Sharif Rashed, Madonna, RuPaul, Roseanne, Lou Reed, Jim Jarmusch, John Lurie, Michael J. Fox, Malik Yoba, Mel Gorham, Ian Frazier, Keith David and Victor Argo

Wang and Auster had such a great time filming *Smoke*, they weren't ready to call it quits. So they continued to occupy the Brooklyn Cigar Company and invited actors to drop by Augie Wren's (Keitel) shop and improvise while the cameras ran. Drop by they did. Most actors maintained the laid-back, hip environment, spewing forth in streams of consciousness. RuPaul gave Madonna a dance lesson; Reed explains his glasses and tries to remember his first smoking experience, but adds, "It, along with most of my childhood memories, are not available to me." Tomlin, dressed like a man, describes her craving for a Belgian waffle. The only discordant note: Roseanne, stiff and annoying with her gum chewing.

THE BLUE VILLA
Directors: Alain Robbe-Grillet and Dimitri de Clercq; **Director of Photography:** Laurence Tremolet; **Writer:** Alain Robbe-Grillet; **Editor:** France Duez; **Music:** Nikos Kypourgos; **Producer:** Jacques de Clercq
Nomad Films; NR; 100 minutes
Release: 9/95
Cast: Fred Ward and Arielle Dombasle
In French with English subtitles

A baffling puzzle of a film in the manner of Robbe-Grillet's screenplay for *Last Year at Marienbad*. A supernatural sailor (Ward) visits an island where a ghastly crime has been transformed into myth by a screenwriter struggling to transform the loss of his stepdaughter into words. A dreamy woman (Dombasle) rules the island, the local brothel and, perhaps, a drug and white-slavery ring.

BOTTLE ROCKET
Director: Wes Anderson; **Writers:** Owen C. Wilson and Wes Anderson; **Director of Photography:** Robert Yeoman; **Editor:** David Moritz; **Music:** Mark Mothersbaugh; **Production Designer:** David Wasco; **Producers:** Polly Platt and Cynthia Hargrave
Columbia; R; 95 minutes
Release: 2/96
Cast: Luke Wilson, Owen C. Wilson, Ned Dowd, Robert Musgrave and Lumi Cavazos

Anderson and Owen C. Wilson, college pals from the University of Texas, wrote this Generation X comedy about three friends (Luke Wilson, Owen C. Wilson and Musgrave), who desperately want to become big-time gangsters. The low-budget, slacker attitude gives this film a lightweight but enjoyable quality that is consistently funny and entertaining.

A BOY CALLED HATE
Director/Writer: Mitch Marcus; **Director of Photography:** Michael Ruscio; **Editor:** Michael Ruscio; **Music:** Pray for Rain; **Production Designer:** Caryn Marcus; **Producer:** Steve Nicolaides
Dove Entertainment; R; 96 minutes
Release: 5/96
Cast: Scott Caan, Missy Crider, Adam Beach, James Caan and Elliott Gould

Steve "Hate" Bason (Scott Caan — son of James), is looking for a reason to leave his nowhere town. He finds one when he sees a young woman (Crider) about to be raped by an older man (Gould). Hate shoots the man, and the pair take off with police on their tail. Hate, not too smart but certainly impulsive, makes some bad moves along the way. The chase ends, ironically, at a country club called Camelot.

BOYS
Director/Writer: Stacy Cochran; **Director of Photography:** Robert Elswit; **Editor:** Camilla Toniolo; **Music:** Stewart Copeland; **Production Designer:** Dan Bishop; **Producers:** Peter Frankfurt, Paul Feldsher and Erica Huggins
Buena Vista; PG-13; 88 minutes
Release: 5/96
Cast: Winona Ryder, Lukas Haas, Wiley Wiggins, Skeet Ulrich and Chris Cooper
Based on the short story "Twenty Minutes" by James Salter

Ryder can't pull it off as a fast woman, she's just too innocent looking. But the casting isn't the only problem with *Boys* — the film doesn't go anywhere. Prep school student John Baker, Jr. (Haas) finds twentysomething townie Patty Vare (Ryder) unconscious after a riding accident and brings her to his dorm room. Evading police and afraid to return home, Vare hides out in his room — a big no-no at the boarding school. It's no big surprise that the two fall in love. What is a surprise is how badly the movie ends.

Bottle Rocket

Broken Arrow

Director: John Woo; **Writer:** Graham Yost; **Director of Photography:** Peter Levy; **Editors:** John Wright, Steve Mirkovich and Joe Hutshing; **Music:** Hans Zimmer; **Production Designer:** Holger Gross; **Producers:** Mark Gordon, Bill Badalato and Terence Chang
Twentieth Century-Fox; R; 110 minutes
Release: 2/96
Cast: John Travolta, Christian Slater, Samantha Mathis, Delroy Lindo and Howie Long
Director Woo has taken America by storm, perhaps saying good-bye forever to the low-budget chop sockeys that made him an international cult favorite. Military pilot Vic Deakins (Travolta) ejects his partner Riley Hale (Slater) from their B-Stealth bomber, downs the plane and makes off with two nuclear warheads, threatening to blow up the world. Hale survives, and he and his new-found friend/forest ranger Terry Carmichael (Mathis) dodge bullets and jump on and off anything that moves fast in pursuit of Deakins. The stunts, special effects and over-the-top action in *Broken Arrow* surely contributed to its success, but one has to admit, Travolta got people into theaters. Fast, cool and physical.

Broken Harvest

Director: Maurice O'Callaghan; **Writers:** Maurice O'Callaghan and Kate O'Callaghan; **Director of Photography:** Jack Conroy; **Editor:** J. Patrick Duffner; **Music:** Patrick Cassidy; **Production Designer:** Alan Gallett; **Producer:** Jerry O'Callaghan
Kit Parker Films; NR; 98 minutes
Release: 10/95
Cast: Colin Lane, Marian Quinn, Niall O'Brien and Darren McHugh
New Yorker Jimmy O'Leary (McHugh) looks back to his adolescent years as a poor boy living in an Irish village, which is still reeling 30 years after the civil war. Central in Jimmy's life are the ongoing political and emotional conflicts between his embittered father, Arthur (Lane), and his neighbor Josie (O'Brien).

A Business Affair

Director: Charlotte Brandstrom; **Writer:** William Stadiem; **Director of Photography:** Willy Kurant; **Music:** Didier Vasseur; **Producers:** Xavier Larère, Clive Parsons and Davina Belling
Castle Hill Productions; NR; 101 minutes
Release: 11/95
Cast: Carole Bouquet, Christopher Walken, Jonathan Pryce and Sheila Hancock
Based on the memoirs of Barbara Skelton
Kate Swallow (Bouquet) finds her own literary voice as her neglectful husband (Pryce), a successful author, and his publisher (Walken) fight for her affection. Realizing he has lost his wife, the aloof Alec lists his feelings in alphabetical order: "... eviscerated, flagellated, gutted ...."

Butterfly Kiss

Director: Michael Winterbottom; **Writer:** Frank Cottrell Boyce; **Director of Photography:** Seamus McGarvey; **Editor:** Trevor Waite; **Music:** John Harle; **Producer:** Julie Baines
CFP Distribution; NR; 88 minutes
Release: 5/96
Cast: Amanda Plummer, Saskia Reeves and Des McAleer
Looking to earn the punishment she craves, psychotic Eunice (Plummer) travels English highways, killing people she encounters at roadside gas stations and convenience stores. She meets Miriam (Reeves), a partially deaf woman leading a nowhere life, the two become lovers and Miriam takes to the road with Eunice. Miriam tries to reform Eunice but doesn't understand the extent of Eunice's problems.

The Cable Guy

Director: Ben Stiller; **Writer:** Lou Holtz, Jr.; **Director of Photography:** Robert Brinkmann; **Editor:** Steven Weisberg; **Music:** John Ottman; **Production Designer:** Sharon Seymour; **Producers:** Andrew Licht, Jeffrey A. Mueller and Judd Apatow
Columbia; PG-13; 91 minutes
Release: 6/96
Cast: Jim Carrey, Matthew Broderick, Leslie Mann, Ben Stiller, Janeane Garofalo and Eric Roberts
It may be tough for Carrey to recover from this one. He's not completely at fault, however. His performance is uneven, but the script has him bordering on sociopathic. The cable guy (Carrey) meets recently dumped Steven (Broderick) while installing cable in Steven's apartment. Cable guy, a victim of pop culture who has assumed the role of classic television characters, tries to mend Steven's severed relationship. But cable guy's matchmaking turns into stalking and a disturbing obsession.

The Cable Guy

CANADIAN BACON

Director/Writer: Michael Moore; **Director of Photography:** Haskell Wexler; **Editors:** Wendey Stanzler and Michael Berenbaum; **Music:** Elmer Bernstein and Peter Bernstein; **Production Designer:** Carol Spier; **Producers:** Michael Moore, David Brown and Ron Rotholz
Gramercy Pictures; PG; 110 minutes
Release: 9/95
Cast: Alan Alda, John Candy, Rhea Perlman, Kevin Pollak, Rip Torn and G.D. Spradlin

His popularity waning, the inept President of the United States (Alda) declares a cold war with Canada and dubs it Operation Canadian Bacon: A Line in the Snow. Sheriff of Niagara County Bud B. Boomer (Candy) leads the invasion of Canada to rescue his gun-happy partner Deputy Honey (Perlman), who has been propagandized as the war's first hostage. A premise with promise, but the laughs fizzle early on.

CAPTIVES

Director: Angela Pope; **Writer:** Frank Deasy; **Director of Photography:** Remi Adefarasin; **Editor:** Dave King; **Music:** Colin Towns; **Production Designer:** Stuart Walker; **Producer:** David M. Thompson
Miramax; R; 99 minutes
Release: 5/96
Cast: Julia Ormond and Tim Roth

Not the nice-girl Ormond we're accustomed to seeing. Rachael Clifford (Ormond), an upper-middle-class woman who is divorcing her unfaithful husband, works as a part-time dentist in a London prison. Risking her job, Clifford responds to inmate Philip Chaney's (Roth) advances, and a routine dental examination turns erotic. But Chaney is in prison for a reason, and Clifford has a lot to think about when she learns of his crime.

CARRIED AWAY

Director: Bruno Barreto; **Writers:** Ed Jones and Dale Herd; **Director of Photography:** Declan Quinn; **Editor:** Bruce Cannon; **Music:** Bruce Broughton; **Production Designer:** Peter Paul Raubertas; **Producers:** Lisa M. Hansen and Paul Hertzberg
Fine Line; R; 104 minutes
Release: 3/96
Cast: Dennis Hopper, Amy Irving, Amy Locane, Julie Harris, Gary Busey and Hal Holbrook

A precocious, unstable high-school student (Locane) seduces a single teacher nearing 50 (Hopper), who gives in to her persistent advances. However, this is an intelligent film that raises a number of other ethical issues, including the medical treatment of a terminally ill senior citizen and the fate of an outstanding teacher who faces termination because he doesn't meet the state's certification requirements. Irving gives perhaps *the* performance of her career as the lover of Joseph Svenden, the teacher involved with the young student.

CARRINGTON

Director/Writer: Christopher Hampton; **Director of Photography:** Denis Lenoir; **Editor:** George Akers; **Music:** Michael Nyman; **Production Designer:** Caroline Amies; **Producers:** Ronald Shedlo and John McGrath
Gramercy; NR; 123 minutes
Release: 11/95
Cast: Emma Thompson, Jonathan Pryce, Steven Waddington, Samuel West, Rufus Sewell, Penelope Wilton and Janet McTeer
Based on the book *Lytton Strachey* by Michael Holroyd

Merchant-Ivory checklist: English countryside? Check. Tea? Check. Platonic relationships that never really become anything more? Check. Emma Thompson? Check. Merchant and Ivory? No, but even the most loyal fans of British team could be convinced otherwise. *Carrington* focuses on the life of Lytton Strachey (Pryce), wit of the Bloomsbury group, and his soul-mate Carrington (Thompson) (she dropped her first name, Dora, deeming it "sentimental"). The film's screenplay is clever, witty and smart, and Thompson and Pryce both turn in remarkable performances.

Carrington

CASINO

Director: Martin Scorsese; **Writers:** Nicholas Pileggi and Martin Scorsese; **Director of Photography:** Robert Richardson; **Editor:** Thelma Schoonmaker; **Production Designer:** Dante Ferretti; **Producer:** Barbara De Fina
Universal; R; 170 minutes
Release: 11/95
Cast: Robert De Niro, Joe Pesci, Sharon Stone, James Woods, Don Rickles, Alan King, Kevin Pollak, L.Q. Jones and Dick Smothers
Based on the book by Nicholas Pileggi

Scorsese and Pileggi team up again for an operatic look at Las Vegas in the 1970s and 1980s, the good old days when the town was run by the mob. Sam "Ace" Rothstein (De Niro) and Nicky Santoro (Pesci), two Midwest hoods and childhood friends, move in the ranks of organized crime and become bosses in Vegas. Rothstein works above board (so to speak) as the man in charge of Tangiers, the city's biggest casino; the psychopathic Santoro, banned from all casinos, forms his own clique of thugs working the underworld. Ginger (Stone), a former hustler, is the centerpiece of the entire film: a lowlife who made it big only to fall even lower than she started. Rothstein can control just about everything in his life, even the number of blueberries in the casino's muffins, but he can't control his wife, Ginger. True to Scorsese form, violence is an ever-present threat: melodramatic, too vivid and essential.

CATWALK

Director: Robert Leacock; **Editor:** Milton Moses Ginsberg; **Music:** Malcolm McLaren; **Producer:** Sug Villa
Arrow Releasing; NR; 95 minutes
Release: 2/96
With: Christy Turlington, Naomi Campbell, Kate Moss, John Galliano, Jean-Paul Gaultier, Giorgio Armani, Gianni Versace, Valentino, Karl Lagerfeld, Elizabeth Tilberis, Carla Bruni, Sharon Stone and Isaac Mizrahi

A fashion magazine for the big screen, *Catwalk* leaves us with a shallow moral: It sure is great to be beautiful. That is, if you don't mind being gaped at and complimented incessantly, a fate that befalls the film's focal point, the stunning and ubiquitous Turlington. *Catwalk* can only recall last year's *Unzipped*, a more entertaining, and in many ways, more critical look at the fashion industry. The plot follows Turlington wherever she goes — backstage primping, strutting her stuff on the runway and kissy-kissying haute couture's reigning royalty. Candid quips from the models backstage make for some amusing moments, but it's never enough to keep *Catwalk* from being any more interesting than a new tube of lipstick.

CELESTIAL CLOCKWORK

Director/Producer: Fina Torres; **Writer:** Fina Torres, with Daniel Odier, Blanca Strepponi, Telsche Boorman, Yves Dalaubre and Chantal Pelletier; **Director of Photography:** Ricardo Aronovich; **Editors:** Christiane Lack and Catherine Troillet
October Films; NR; 85 minutes
Release: 7/96
Cast: Ariadna Gil, Arielle Dombasle, Evelyne Didi, Frederic Longbois and Lluis Homar

A multicultural Cinderella story with magic at every turn. Aspiring opera singer Ana (Gil), fleeing her wedding in Caracas, boards a plane headed for Paris. A friend of a friend takes her into her already crowded apartment, and one of her roommates, Celeste (Dombasle), quickly develops a dislike for Ana. Ana finds her fairy godmother in Alcanie (Didi), a psychotherapist who also dabbles in opera. She moves in with Alcanie, and with the help of a magic potion, the two sleep together. Prince Charming is Italo Medici (Homar), a filmmaker who casts Ana in his film upon hearing her voice on tape. When Ana's visa expires, she marries gay clairvoyant waiter Armand (Longbois).Too much going on here to make much sense.

CELTIC PRIDE

Director: Tom De Cerchio; **Writer:** Judd Apatow; **Director of Photography:** Oliver Wood; **Editor:** Hubert de la Bouillerie; **Music:** Basil Poledouris; **Production Designer:** Stephen Marsh; **Producer:** Roger Birnbaum
Hollywood Pictures; PG-13; 91 minutes
Release: 4/96
Cast: Damon Wayans, Daniel Stern and Dan Aykroyd
Two insanely obsessed Boston Celtic fans (Stern and Aykroyd) panic when their beloved team loses the sixth game of the NBA playoffs to the Utah Jazz, tying the series, and kidnap the Jazz's star, Lewis Scott (Wayans). Foul. Airball. Brick.

CEMETERY MAN

Director: Michele Soavi; **Writer:** Gianni Romoli; **Director of Photography:** Mauro Marchetti; **Editor:** Franco Fraticelli; **Music:** Manuel De Sica; **Producers:** Tilde Corsi, Gianni Romoli and Michele Soavi
October Films; R; 100 minutes
Release: 4/96
Cast: Rupert Everett, Francois Hadji-Lazaro and Anna Falchi
Francesco Dellamorte (Everett) and his obese assistant, Gnaghi (Hadji-Lazaro), watch over the Buffalora Cemetery, smashing the heads of corpses as they rise out of the ground ready to rampage. When the corpses become too much to handle, Dellamorte pulls out a gun. The zombies range from boy scouts to bikers to yuppies. Oh, and Dellamorte is a necrophiliac. A comic horror film that is neither funny nor scary.

CITY HALL

Director: Harold Becker; **Writers:** Ken Lipper, Paul Schrader, Nicholas Pileggi and Bo Goldman; **Director of Photography:** Michael Seresin; **Editors:** Robert C. Jones and David Bretherton; **Music:** Jerry Goldsmith; **Production Designer:** Jane Musky; **Producers:** Edward R. Pressman, Ken Lipper, Charles Mulvehill and Harold Becker
Castle Rock; R; 110 minutes
Release: 2/96
Cast: Al Pacino, John Cusack, Bridget Fonda, Danny Aiello, Martin Landau, David Paymer, Anthony Franciosa and Lauren Velez
Even with a top-flight performance from Pacino and strong supporting work from Cusack and Aiello, *City Hall* can't get past its screenplay problem: too many cooks in the kitchen. This investigative thriller looks at political corruption in New York City that branches out in all direc-

City Hall

tions, reaching the mayor's office, police department and judicial system. The events are based on real-life scandals that have rocked Gotham in recent years.

CLOCKERS

Director: Spike Lee; **Writers:** Richard Price and Spike Lee; **Director of Photography:** Malik Sayeed; **Editor:** Sam Pollard; **Production Designer:** Andrew McAlpine; **Producers:** Martin Scorsese, Spike Lee and Jon Kilik
Universal Pictures; R; 129 minutes
Release: 9/95
Cast: Harvey Keitel, John Turturro, Delroy Lindo, Mekhi Phifer and Isaiah Washington
Based on the novel by Richard Price
Lee and Price collaborated on what should have been the defining film about the breakdown of inner-city life. Strike (Phifer), a clocker (a drug dealer who will make a sale at any time of the day), works for Rodney (Lindo), who considers Strike his protégé. Rodney asks Strike to kill another dealer who is stealing from him. When the dealer is found dead, slightly racist cop Rocco Klein (Keitel) fingers Strike, but Strike's hardworking brother Victor (Washington) confesses. Klein is determined to get the story straight, but what follows is not a mission to find the who, but the why.

COLD COMFORT FARM

Director: John Schlesinger; **Writer:** Malcolm Bradbury; **Director of Photography:** Chris Seager; **Editor:** Mark Day; **Music:** Robert Lockhart; **Production Designer:** Malcolm Thornton; **Producers:** Richard Broke for BBC Films and Antony Root for Thames International
Gramercy; PG; 95 minutes
Release: 5/96
Cast: Kate Beckinsale, Joanna Lumley, Rufus Sewell, Ian McKellan, Stephen Fry, Eileen Atkins, Sheila Burrell, Freddie Jones and Maria Miles

The National Board of Review, which publishes *Films in Review*, includes teachers, actors, writers and movie-production workers.

Best Picture
Sense and Sensibility

Best Actor
Nicolas Cage, *Leaving Las Vegas*

Best Actress
Emma Thompson, *Sense and Sensibility* and *Carrington*

Best Supporting Actor
Kevin Spacey, *Seven* and *The Usual Suspects*

Best Supporting Actress
Mira Sorvino, *Mighty Aphrodite*

Best Director
Ang Lee, *Sense and Sensibility*

Best Foreign Film
Shanghai Triad

Best Documentary
Crumb

Best Television Movie
The Boys of St. Vincent

Billy Wilder Award for a Directing Career
Stanley Donen

Outstanding Newcomer
Alicia Silverstone

Zhang Yimou, director of *Shanghai Triad,* was given a special freedom of expression award for his battle against censorship in China.

James Earl Jones received a career achievement award.

The cast of ***The Usual Suspects*** received a special ensemble-acting award.

Betty Comden and **Adolph Green** were recognized for their songwriting careers.

Ang Lee

Based on the novel by Stella Gibbons
Though the dialect is sometimes incomprehensible, the satirical story is right on target, down to the stereotypes of English countryfolk. Flora Poste (Beckinsale), an urban sophisticate, turns to her relatives when she finds herself in financial straits. She ends up at Cold Comfort Farm, run by cousins, the Starkadders, whom Poste finds intolerably quaint.

COLD FEVER
Director/Director of Photography: Fridrik Thor Fridriksson; **Writers:** Jim Stark and Fridrik Thor Fridriksson; **Editor:** Steingrimur Karlson; **Production Designer:** Arni Poll Johansson; **Producer:** Jim Stark Artistic License Films; NR; 82 minutes
Release: 3/96
Cast: Masatoshi Nagase, Lili Taylor, Fisher Stevens, Gisli Halldorsson, Laura Hughes and Seijun Suzuki
A clever Icelandic road movie loaded with chills and thrills. A Japanese man (Nagase) travels across Iceland to reach the village where his parents died so he can perform a ritual that will ensure their eternal happiness. Along the way he encounters a cab driver who interrupts his fare to baptize a flock of sheep, a "funeral collector" who travels worldwide to chronicle funerals and a group of drunken Icelandic cowboys. Beyond the strange meetings, the beautifully photographed film takes a serious look at death, portraying it as something to accept, not fear.

THE CONVENT
Director/Writer: Manoel de Oliveira; **Director of Photography:** Mário Barroso; **Editors:** Manoel de Oliveira and Valerie Loiseleux; **Production Designers:** Zé Branco and Ana Vaz da Silva; **Producer:** Paulo Branco
Strand Releasing; NR; 90 minutes
Release: 12/95
Cast: Catherine Deneuve, John Malkovich, Luís Miguel Cintra, Leonor Silveira, Duarte D'Almeida, Heloísa Miranda and Gilberto Gonçalves
Convinced that William Shakespeare was of Sephardic origin, American professor Michael Padovic (Malkovich) and his wife, Hélène (Deneuve), travel to an ancient Spanish convent to find proof. Black-garbed, sinister Baltar (Cintra) and his beautiful archivist, Piedade (Silveria), inhabit the convent, and the four begin an exchange that evolves into a haunting morality play about faith, God, the devil and human nature. A complex, masterful study of good and evil, faith and secularism from Portuguese octogenarian de Oliveira.

COPYCAT
Director: Jon Amiel; **Writers:** Ann Biderman and Jay Presson Allen; **Director of Photography:** Laszlo Kovacs; **Editors:** Alan Heim and Jim Clark; **Music:** Christopher Young; **Production Designer:** Jim Clay; **Producers:** Arnon Milchan and Mark Tarlov

The Craft

Warner Bros.; R; 124 minutes
Release: 10/95
Cast: Sigourney Weaver, Holly Hunter, Dermot Mulroney, William McNamara, Harry Connick, Jr., Will Patton, John Rothman and J.E. Freeman
Based on a story by David Madsen
Left agoraphobic after a terrifying attack by a homicidal maniac (Connick), serial killer expert Dr. Helen Hudson (Weaver) helps cops M.J. Monahan (Hunter) and Ruben Geotz (Mulroney) track down a murderer who copies the modus operandi of famous killers. A nail-biting thriller.

COURAGE UNDER FIRE

Director: Edward Zwick; **Writer:** Patrick Sheane Duncan; **Director of Photography:** Roger Deakins; **Editor:** Steven Rosenblum; **Music:** James Horner; **Production Designer:** John Graysmark; **Producers:** John Davis, Joseph M. Singer and David T. Friendly
Twentieth Century-Fox; R; 120 minutes
Release: 7/96
Cast: Denzel Washington, Meg Ryan, Lou Diamond Phillips, Michael Moriarty, Matt Damon, Seth Gilliam, Bronson Pinchot, Scott Glenn and Regina Taylor
Warm, intelligent and even-handed. Washington and Ryan turn Oscar-caliber performances; let's hope they are not forgotten come February. Helicopter pilot Capt. Karen Walden (Ryan) is up for a posthumous Medal of Honor, and Capt. Nathaniel Serling (Washington) investigates Walden to ensure there won't be any trouble (or embarrassing questions) down the road. What he finds is perplexing, and no two witnesses tell the same story. The assignment contributes to Serling's own epiphany: A number of his own men were killed by friendly fire, and the official report was a cover-up. A *Rashomon*-like story of dignity in the face of hard truths.

THE CRAFT

Director: Andrew Fleming; **Writers:** Peter Filardi and Andrew Fleming; **Director of Photography:** Alexander Gruszynski; **Editor:** Jeff Freeman; **Music:** Graeme Revell; **Production Designer:** Marek Dobrowolski; **Producer:** Douglas Wick
Columbia; R; 100 minutes
Release: 5/96
Cast: Robin Tunney, Fairuza Balk, Neve Campbell, Rachel True, Skeet Ulrich and Christine Taylor
Four troubled teenage girls, outcasts in their Los Angeles high school, form a coven and use black magic to get revenge. But revenge, however sweet, has its price, and the girls learn their lesson the hard way. Lots of potential lost to the overdone moral cliché, "Be careful of what you wish for, because you might just get it."

THE CROSSING GUARD

Director/Writer: Sean Penn; **Director of Photography:** Vilmos Zsigmond; **Editor:** Jay Cassidy; **Music:** Jack Nitzche and Bruce Springsteen; **Production Designer:** Michael Haller; **Producers:** Sean Penn and David S. Hamburger
Miramax; R; 117 minutes
Release: 11/95
Cast: Jack Nicholson, David Morse, Anjelica Huston, Robin Wright, Piper Laurie, Priscilla Barnes, Robbie Robertson, Kellita Smith, Eileen Ryan and Dr. William Dignam
A film that evokes John Cassavetes in his prime. Freddy Gale (Nicholson) has lived for nothing but revenge since his daughter was killed by a hit-and-run driver, John Booth (Morse). Gale intends to kill Booth the day he is released from prison. As the film proceeds toward its climax, parallels between Gale and Booth begin to emerge, some in subtle ways and others subtle as a sledgehammer. Penn shows himself to be a more-than-competent director.

CRY, THE BELOVED COUNTRY

Director: Darrell James Roodt; **Writer:** Ronald Harwood; **Director of Photography:** Paul Gilpin; **Editor:** David Heitner; **Music:** John Barry; **Production Designer:** David Barkham; **Producer:** Anant Singh
Miramax; PG-13; 108 minutes
Release: 12/95
Cast: Richard Harris, James Earl Jones, Vusi Kunene, Dambisa Kente, Charles S. Dutton and Eric Miyeni
Adapted from the novel by Alan Paton
Rev. Stephen Kumalo (Jones), whose son, Absolom (Miyeni), murdered a white man who spent his entire life helping South African blacks, tries to piece together the shreds of his family (including his prostitute sister and activist brother) and make a connection with the dead man's white supremacist father, James Jarvis (Harris). Though the script sticks closely to the quiet tone of Paton's novel, the cinematography and music allow the film to take on a life of its own.

CUTTHROAT ISLAND

Director: Renny Harlin; **Writers:** Robert King and Marc Norman; **Director of Photography:** Peter Levy; **Editors:** Frank J. Urioste and Ralph E. Winters; **Music:** John Debney; **Production Designer:** Norman Garwood; **Producers:** Renny Harlin, Joel B. Michaels, Laurence Mark and James Gorman
MGM; PG-13; 123 minutes
Release: 12/95
Cast: Geena Davis, Matthew Modine, Frank Langella, Maury Chaykin, Patrick Malahide, Harris Yulin and Stan Shaw

Just when you thought *Waterworld* was a thing of the past, *Cutthroat Island* emerges, evoking unpleasant memories of one of Hollywood's all-time most expensive disappointments. There are many similarities between the two movies: Both were huge productions set on boats and both were terrible. After Morgan Adams's (Davis) father is murdered by her uncle Dawg Brown (Langella), she removes his tattooed scalp, which is also a treasure map. However, she can't read the map because it's written in Latin. Ever resourceful, Adams buys a Latin-literate slave, Shaw (Modine). The pair embark on a quest for treasure, developing a love-hate relationship. They are pursued by Uncle Dawg, and it's a fight to the bitter end.

DEAD BEAT

Director: Adam Dubov; **Writers:** Janice Shapiro and Adam Dubov; **Director of Photography:** Nancy Schreiber; **Editor:** Lorraine Salk; **Producers:** George Moffley and Christopher Lambert
Northern Arts Releasing; R; 92 minutes
Release: 10/95
Cast: Bruce Ramsey, Balthazar Getty, Natasha Gregson Wagner, Meredith Salender and Sara Gilbert

Teenage romances and obsession take a twisted turn in this comic spoof set in 1965 Albuquerque. Kit (Ramsey), an Elvis wannabe, thinks he has the appeal of Don Juan and will go to any length for a girl. His best friend, Rudy (Getty), doesn't have the same success and tends to go after Kit's leftovers. Things start getting strange when Kit lures his former girlfriend, Kirsten (Gilbert), to the desert and shows her the body of a woman he claims he killed.

DEAD MAN

Director/Writer: Jim Jarmusch; **Director of Photography:** Robby Muller; **Editor:** Jay Rabinowitz; **Music:** Neil Young; **Producer:** Demetra J. MacBride
Miramax; R; 121 minutes
Release: 5/96
Cast: Johnny Depp, Gary Farmer, Lance Henriksen, Mili Avital, Iggy Pop, Crispin Glover, Gabriel Byrne, John Hurt and Robert Mitchum

Typical Jarmusch — hip with a large helping of ennui. True fans will be satisfied, the uninitiated will be bored. Heading west for an accounting job, William Blake (Depp) is told by a fellow train passenger that he will meet his death there. Once at his destination, Machine, a dark hellhole, Blake finds that his job has been filled and things don't get any better. He meets a woman (Avital) in a bar, goes to bed with her and is interrupted by her former boyfriend (Byrne). Blake kills the jealous man and ends up with a bullet in his chest. He heads farther west, with police and bounty hunters after him, leaving a trail of bodies. He survives only because he is accompanied by Nobody (Farmer), an Indian guide who thinks Blake is the reincarnation of the poet William Blake and that it is his duty to lead Blake to the next world.

DEAD MAN WALKING

Director/Writer: Tim Robbins; **Director of Photography:** Roger A. Deakins; **Editor:** Lisa Zeno Churgin; **Music:** David Robbins; **Production Designer:** Richard Hoover; **Producers:** Jon Kilik, Tim Robbins and Rudd Simmons
Gramercy Pictures; R; 120 minutes
Release: 12/95
Cast: Sean Penn, Susan Sarandon, Robert Prosky, Raymond J. Barry and R. Lee Ermey

Based on the memoir by Sister Helen Prejean Robbins writing and directing a movie about the death penalty with Sarandon as the star? Surely it must be preachy and self-righteous. Not so. Robbins's position seems clear, but *Dead Man Walking* depends less on the message than on the characters and questions raised by the issue. Matthew Poncelet (Penn) has been accused of murdering two teenagers and is days away from death. Sister Helen Prejean (Sarandon) becomes his spiritual adviser and crusader for his life. Prejean also has to contend with the victims' parents and their outrage, which leads her to question her role as spiritual guide and her obligation to the families.

DEAD PRESIDENTS

Directors: Albert and Allen Hughes; **Writer:** Michael Henry Brown; **Director of Photography:** Lisa Rinzler; **Editor:** Dan Lebenthal; **Music:** Danny Elfman; **Production Designer:** David Brisbin; **Producers:** Albert and Allen Hughes and Michael Bennett
Hollywood Pictures; R; 120 minutes
Release: 10/95
Cast: Larenz Tate, Chris Tucker and Bokeem Woodbine

More a letdown than a sophomore slump, *Dead Presidents* isn't as effective at portraying street violence as *Menace II Society*. Anthony (Tate) is 18 years old when he joins the Marines in 1968, perfect timing for Vietnam. His Bronx sidekick Skip (Tucker) follows, they meet Cleon (Woodbine) and the trio learn to kill. Returning home four years later, Anthony, in need of money to support his wife and daughter and out to gain

Devil in a Blue Dress

respect, recruits his war buddies to rob an armored car.

DENISE CALLS UP

Director/Writer: Hal Salwen; **Director of Photography:** Michael Mayers; **Editor:** Gary Sharfin; **Music:** Lynn Geller; **Production Designer:** Susan Bolles; **Producer:** J. Todd Harris
Sony Pictures Classics; NR; 82 minutes
Release: 3/96
Cast: Alanna Ubach, Tim Daly, Caroleen Feeney, Dan Gunther, Dana Wheeler-Nicholson, Liev Schreiber, Aida Turturro and Sylvia Miles
In an age in which telephones, fax machines and modems are the preferred means of communication, why would anyone need human contact? *Denise Calls Up* proves that interaction isn't necessary, even to get pregnant. The characters live, die, have sex and, of course, telecommunicate over the wire.

DEVIL IN A BLUE DRESS

Director/Writer: Carl Franklin; **Director of Photography:** Tak Fujimoto; **Editor:** Carole Kravetz; **Music:** Elmer Bernstein; **Production Designer:** Gary Frutkoff; **Producers:** Jesse Beaton and Gary Goetzman
TriStar; R; 102 minutes
Release: 9/95
Cast: Denzel Washington, Tom Sizemore, Jennifer Beals, Don Cheadle, Maury Chaykin and Terry Kinney
Based on the book by Walter Mosley
Set in 1940s Chicago, Easy Rawlins (Washington) is out of a job and on the verge of losing his house. A friend introduces Rawlins to a sleazy private detective (Sizemore) who needs a black man to track down Daphne Monet (Beals). Washington excels in this film noir that evokes Roman Polanski's classic *Chinatown*.

DIABOLIQUE

Director: Jeremiah Chechik; **Writer:** Don Roos; **Director of Photography:** Peter James; **Editor:** Carol Littleton; **Music:** Randy Edelman; **Production Designer:** Leslie Dilley; **Producers:** Marvin Worth and James G. Robinson
Warner Bros.; R; 105 minutes
Release: 3/96
Cast: Sharon Stone, Isabelle Adjani, Chazz Palminteri and Kathy Bates
Based on the novel *Celle Qui N'Etait Plus* by Pierre Boileau and the 1956 French film
Chilling suspense that leaves you on the edge of your seat. Sexual tension that makes you squirm. The features that made the 1955 original a masterpiece are nowhere to be found in the 1996 remake. The casting is just about the only thing that works in the film. Demure Mia (Adjani) and coarse Nicole (Stone) team up to kill Mia's husband and Nicole's lover, Guy (Palminteri). The women think they have committed the perfect crime until a detective (Bates) begins to piece together their scheme.

DON'T BE A MENACE TO SOUTH CENTRAL WHILE DRINKING YOUR JUICE IN THE HOOD

Director: Paris Barclay; **Writers:** Shawn Wayans, Marlon Wayans and Phil Beauman; **Director of Photography:** Russ Brandt; **Editors:** William Young and Marshall Harvey; **Music:** John Barnes; **Production Designer:** Aaron Osborne; **Producer:** Keenen Ivory Wayans
Miramax; R; 88 minutes
Release: 1/96
Cast: Shawn Wayans, Marlon Wayans, Tracey Cherelle Jones, Chris Spencer, Suli McCullough, Darrell Heath, Helen Martin, Isaiah Barnes, Lahmard Tate, Keenen Ivory Wayans
The Wayans brothers send up 'hood movies. The jokes are predictable, and even those that are worth remembering get old the second and third time around.

THE DOOM GENERATION

Director/Writer/Editor: Gregg Araki; **Director of Photography:** Jim Fealy; **Music:** Jesus and Mary Chain, Nine Inch Nails, Showdive, Curve, Pizzicato Five and others; **Production Designer:** Therese Deprez; **Producers:** Andrea Sperling, Gregg Araki and Why Not Productions
Trimark Pictures; NR; 90 minutes
Release: 10/95
Cast: James Duval, Rose McGowan, Jonathan Schaech, Margaret Cho, Parker Posey and Heidi Fleiss
Gay filmmaker Araki billed *Doom* a "heterosexual movie," but that's not entirely true. "Nihilistic" and "hip" would have been better choices to describe this parody of teen-wasteland films that rivals the graphic, satirical violence in *Natural Born Killers*. Jordan (Duval) and his girlfriend

Amy (McGowan) pick up troubled Xavier (Schaech) in LA, the carnage begins and the sex has intricate permutations.

DOWN PERISCOPE

Director: Kelsey Grammer; **Writers:** Hugh Wilson, Andrew Kurtzman and Eliot Wald; **Director of Photography:** Victor Hammer; **Editor:** William Anderson; **Music:** Randy Edelman; **Production Designer:** Michael Corenblith; **Producer:** Robert Lawrence
Twentieth Century-Fox; PG-13; 100 minutes
Release: 3/96
Cast: Kelsey Grammer, Lauren Holly, Rob Schneider, Ken Hudson Campbell, Toby Huss, Harry Dean Stanton, Bruce Dern and Rip Torn
This spoof of submarine adventures could have been the underseas *Airplane!* but unfortunately never even becomes *Naked Gun II.* Grammer, in his big-screen debut as the Stingray's commander, heads a crew of misfits, including *Saturday Night Live* alumnus Schneider as his over-eager officer and Holly as a pretty experiment to see if women can integrate into the ranks. Dern takes a half-hearted stab as Grammer's nemesis in this war-games mission but seems oddly miscast. While the rich archive of submarine classics should provide plenty of fuel for razzing, *Down Periscope* repeatedly misses the mark.

DRACULA: DEAD AND LOVING IT

Director/Producer: Mel Brooks; **Writers:** Mel Brooks, Rudy De Luca and Steve Haberman; **Director of Photography:** Michael D. O'Shea; **Editor:** Adam Weiss; **Music:** Hummie Mann; **Production Designer:** Roy Forge Smith
Castle Rock; PG-13; 90 minutes
Release: 12/95
Cast: Leslie Nielsen, Peter MacNicol, Amy Yasbeck, Lysette Anthony, Harvey Korman, Anne Bancroft and Mel Brooks
Based on characters created by Bram Stoker
Not the best from Brooks, and certainly not the most daring, but *Dracula: Dead and Loving It* amuses and entertains. The enema and bat droppings jokes somehow remain fresh. The story sticks fairly close to Stoker's 1897 novel and recalls earlier takes on the Dracula tale. One of the best lines in the movie cites the first vampire film, the 1922 *Nosferatu:* "Yes, we have Nosferatu. We have Nosferatu today." Nielsen as Dracula was perfectly cast, providing the sense of being both inside and outside the movie at the same time. A good pick at the video store.

Eraser

DRAGONHEART

Director: Rob Cohen; **Writer:** Charles Edward Pogue; **Director of Photography:** David Eggby; **Editor:** Peter Amundson; **Music:** Randy Edelman; **Production Designer:** Benjamin Fernandez; **Producer:** Raffaella De Laurentiis
Universal; PG-13; 108 minutes
Release: 5/96
Cast: Dennis Quaid, David Thewlis, Pete Postlethwaite, Dina Meyer, Julie Christie and voice of Sean Connery
Cool dragon (what else would we expect from Industrial Light and Magic), and an interesting story, but somehow, the movie drags, especially when Draco the dragon (voice of Connery) is not in the picture. Bowen (Quaid), a knight, teaches young prince Einon royal ways at the request of the queen (Christie). But when Einon grows up (Thewlis), he becomes an evil ruler and Bowen joins the masses who want him slain. He enlists the help of Draco, and the two set out to overthrow the king. Their alliance is complicated as Draco has mixed feelings about the mission, because years earlier he donated half his heart to the ailing Einon, and as a result, they feel each other's pain.

DUNSTON CHECKS IN

Director: Ken Kwapis; **Writers:** John Hopkins and Bruce Graham; **Director of Photography:** Peter Collister; **Production Designer:** Rusty Smith; **Editor:** Jon Poll; **Music:** Miles Goodman; **Producers:** Todd Black and Joe Wizan
Twentieth Century-Fox; PG; 85 minutes
Release: 1/96
Cast: Jason Alexander, Faye Dunaway, Eric Lloyd, Rupert Everett, Graham Sack, Paul Reubens and Sam
Based on a story by John Hopkins
This silly movie had potential as a silly movie, but the talented actors, including the simian title character, were wasted. Animal-hating jewel thief Rutledge (Everett) checks into the high-brow Majestic Hotel posing as an aristocrat trav-

eling with monkey Dunston (Sam). Rutledge has instructed Dunston to scale ledges and enter guests' rooms through the windows to pilfer their pricey goods. Not enough attention is paid to Dunston's antics, and too much is given to the hotel manager (Alexander) and his two sons.

ED
Director: Bill Couturie; **Writer:** David Mickey Evans; **Director of Photography:** Alan Caso; **Editor:** Robert K. Lambert; **Music:** Stephen D. Endelman; **Production Designer:** Curtis A. Schnell; **Producer:** Rosalie Swedlin
Universal; PG; 94 minutes
Release: 3/96
Cast: Matt LeBlanc
OK, *Babe* was a commercial and critical success, but that doesn't mean every film with clever animatronics and cute animals will make it big, or even be watchable for that matter. Professional baseball mascot Ed, a chimp, makes the team when he reveals his fielding skills. He rooms with pitcher Jack Cooper (LeBlanc), and many stupid pet tricks, but no laughs, ensue.

EDDIE
Director: Steve Rash; **Writers:** Jon Connolly, David Loucka, Eric Champnella, Keith Mitchell, Steve Zacharias and Jeff Buhai; **Director of Photography:** Victor Kemper; **Editor:** Richard Halsey; **Music:** Stanley Clarke; **Production Designer:** Dan Davis; **Producers:** David Permut and Mark Burg
Hollywood Pictures; PG-13; 100 minutes
Release: 5/96
Cast: Whoopi Goldberg, Frank Langella, Dennis Farina, Richard Jenkins, Dwayne Schintzius, Eartha D. Robinson and Lisa Ann Walter
Manhattan limo driver Edwina "Eddie" (Goldberg), a die-hard New York Knicks fan, wins a contest that makes her honorary coach of the losing team for one game. The fans love the loud-mouthed, wisecracking "homegirl." Desperate to fill seats, team owner Wild Bill Burgess (Langella) hires her full-time. It takes a while for Eddie to get her groove, but when she does, with the help of some tough love, the team turns around. Forty-nine actual NBA players, including Dennis Rodman, Rick Fox and John (Spider) Salley, make appearances in the movie. Only Goldberg could pull off this one.

ERASER
Director: Charles Russell; **Writers:** Tony Puryear and Walon Green; **Director of Photography:** Adam Greenberg; **Editor:** Michael Tronick; **Music:** Alan Silvestri; **Production Designer:** Bill Kenney; **Producers:** Arnold Kopelson and Anne Kopelson
Warner Bros.; R; 105 minutes
Release: 6/96
Cast: Arnold Schwarzenegger, Vanessa Williams, James Coburn, James Caan, James Cromwell and Robert Pastorelli

Big guns, small plot. Federal marshal John Kruger (Schwarzenegger) helps people in the Witness Protection Program shed their old identities and live safely with new ones. When he protects Lee Cullen (Williams) from international terrorists who are involved in an arms deal with a major U.S. gun manufacturer, Kruger finds himself in the middle of the operation. Both characters look great, and Schwarzie, trimmed down a bit, hasn't forgotten any of his *Terminator* tricks. But this ain't no *Terminator*.

EXECUTIVE DECISION

Director: Stuart Baird; **Writers:** Jim Thomas and John Thomas; **Director of Photography:** Alex Thomson; **Editors:** Dallas Puett, Frank J. Urioste and Stuart Baird; **Music:** Jerry Goldsmith; **Production Designer:** Terence Marsh; **Producer:** Joel Silver
Warner Bros.; R; 105 minutes
Release: 3/96
Cast: Kurt Russell, Steven Seagal, Halle Berry, John Leguizamo, Oliver Platt, Joe Morton, David Suchet, B.D. Wong, J.T. Walsh, Marla Maples Trump and Whip Hubley
So you're thinking this is going to be another Seagal no-brainer. Wrong — *Executive Decision* proves to be a pleasant surprise. That Seagal's character meets an early demise probably contributes to the film's success. An Islamic terrorist group hijacks a plane destined for Washington D.C. and threatens to drop nerve gas over the city if its demands are not met. To save the city and face, the powers that be recruit an antiterrorist group led by Dr. David Grant (Russell) and Lt. Col. Austin Travis (Seagal). Their multiracial team includes Rat (Leguizamo), Louie (Wong), Cappy (Morton) and Cahill (Platt). Their biggest challenge is to board the plane mid-air, which provides stunning effects and action.

EYE FOR AN EYE

Director: John Schlesinger; **Writers:** Amanda Silver and Rick Jaffa; **Director of Photography:** Amir M. Mokri; **Editor:** Peter Honess; **Music:** James Newton Howard; **Production Designer:** Stephen Hendrickson; **Producer:** Michael I. Levy
Paramount; R; 101 minutes
Release: 1/96
Cast: Sally Field, Kiefer Sutherland, Ed Harris, Olivia Burnette, Alexandra Kyle, Joe Mantegna and Charlayne Woodard
Based on the novel by Erika Holzer
It's almost unnecessary to describe this movie — the trailer, which pretty much told the whole story, was ubiquitous on television for weeks. But in case anyone has forgotten: A teenager is raped and murdered as her mother listens from a cellular phone while stuck in LA traffic. Because of evidence mishandling too reminiscent of the O.J. trial, the killer (Sutherland) walks. The girl's mother, Karen McCann (Field), promises revenge. Bad. Bad. Bad.

FAIR GAME

Director: Andrew Sipes; **Writer:** Charlie Fletcher; **Director of Photography:** Richard Bowen; **Editors:** David Finfer, Christian Wagner and Steven Kemper; **Music:** Mark Mancina; **Production Designer:** James Spencer; **Producer:** Joel Silver
Warner Bros.; R; 110 minutes
Release: 11/95
Cast: William Baldwin, Cindy Crawford, Steven Berkoff and Christopher McDonald
Based on the novel by Paula Gosling
Crawford should stick to what she does best: slithering down the runway. Her movie debut finds her intimidated by her role as lawyer Kate McQuean running from the KGB. McQuean and her protector, Detective Max Kirkpatrick (Baldwin), narrowly escape explosion after explosion as the KGB employ heat sensors to track their quarry. There's plenty of heat between Kirkpatrick and McQuean.

FAITHFUL

Director: Paul Mazursky; **Writer:** Chazz Palminteri; **Director of Photography:** Fred Murphy; **Editor:** Nicholas C. Smith; **Music:** Phillip Johnston; **Production Designer:** Jeffrey Townsend; **Producers:** Jane Rosenthal and Robert De Niro
New Line; R; 91 minutes
Release: 3/96
Cast: Cher, Chazz Palminteri, Ryan O'Neal, Amber Smith and Paul Mazursky
Hitman Tony (Palminteri) enters the home of forlorn housewife Margaret (Cher), ties her to a chair and informs her that her husband, Jack (O'Neal), hired him to kill her. She won't die a fast death, however, because Jack needs an alibi and will let Tony know when he has one. So Tony and Margaret talk and talk. As it turns out, Tony ends up sympathizing with Margaret and wanting to kill Jack for the way he treats his wife. The film, based on Palminteri's play, is a bit claustrophobic for the big screen.

A FAMILY THING

Director: Richard Pearce; **Writers:** Billy Bob Thornton and Tom Epperson; **Director of Photography:** Fred Murphy; **Editor:** Mark Warner; **Music:** Charles Gross; **Production Designer:** Linda DeScenna; **Producers:** Robert Duvall, Todd Black and Randa Haines
United Artists; PG-13; 109 minutes
Release: 3/96
Cast: Robert Duvall, James Earl Jones, Michael Beach, Irma P. Hall and David Keith
White southern tractor salesman (and bigot) Earl (Duvall) travels to Chicago to find the black half-brother, Ray (Jones), he recently discovered. Earl and Ray are equally suspicious and uneasy with each other but eventually overcome their prejudices. Hall as Ray's Aunt T. steals the show with her amusing anecdotes and blunt advice. The cast saves this one from sentimentality.

Father of the Bride Part II

FARGO

Director: Joel Coen; **Writers:** Joel Coen and Ethan Coen; **Director of Photography:** Roger Deakins; **Editor:** Roderick Jaynes; **Music:** Carter Burwell; **Production Designer:** Rick Heinrichs; **Producers:** Eric Fellner, Tim Bevan, Ethan Coen and John Cameron
Gramercy; R; 95 minutes
Release: 3/96
Cast: Frances McDormand, Steve Buscemi, Peter Stormare, William H. Macy, Harve Presnell, Kristen Rudrüd, John Carroll Lynch and Steve Park
The Coen brothers' latest turns the *Twin Peaks*-esque weirdness up another notch or two. Jerry Lundegaard (Macy), a car salesman who's having trouble paying the bills, hires two thugs (Buscemi and Stormare) to kidnap his wife (but it's "strictly a no-rough-stuff" sort of deal, he says). The plan, of course, turns deadly. Marge Gunderson (McDormand), a very pregnant police chief, is the unflappable heroine who's equally at home snuggling with her husband as solving a triple homicide. Coenheads will be pleased: Their heroes are at their quirky best, and the Midwestern settings are sharply and affectionately observed.

FATHER OF THE BRIDE PART II

Director: Charles Shyer; **Writers:** Nancy Meyers and Charles Shyer; **Director of Photography:** William A. Fraker; **Editor:** Steven A. Rotter; **Music:** Alan Silvestri; **Production Designer:** Linda DeScenna; **Producer:** Nancy Meyers
Buena Vista; PG; 106 minutes
Release: 12/95
Cast: Steve Martin, Diane Keaton, Kimberly Williams, George Newbern, Martin Short, Eugene Levy, B.D. Wong and Jane Adams
Based on the screenplay *Father's Little Dividend* by Albert Hackett and Frances Goodrich
Safe. Happy. Suburban, middle-aged father (Martin) finds out he's going to be a grandfather and father *again* and panics. Nothing new in the seen-it-before mad dash to the hospital, labor and delivery scenes, which involve both mother (Keaton) and daughter (Williams) simultaneously. Short as decorator once again steals the show.

FEAR

Director: James Foley; **Writer:** Christopher Crowe; **Director of Photography:** Thomas Kloss; **Editor:** David Brenner; **Music:** Carter Burwell; **Production Designer:** Alex McDowell; **Producers:** Brian Grazer and Ric Kidney
Universal; R; 95 minutes
Release: 4/96
Cast: Mark Wahlberg, Reese Witherspoon, William Petersen and Amy Brenneman
Who would've thought that Marky Mark really had talent. Sure, he looks fine in his Calvin Klein undies, but can he act? *Fear* puts any doubts to rest. He's perfect as suave, sinister Seattle resident David McCall, who seduces the 16-year-old Alicia-Silverstone-wannabe Nicole Walker (Witherspoon), treats her like gold and turns into a crazed stalker. Nicole's protective father (Petersen) saw it coming all along but is helpless when it comes to McCall's grip on his daughter. Gets off to a good start but erodes into a formulaic bloodfest.

FEAST OF JULY

Director: Christopher Menaul; **Writer:** Christopher Neame; **Director of Photography:** Peter Sova; **Editor:** Chris Wimble; **Music:** Zbigniew Preisner; **Production Designer:** Christopher Robilliard; **Producers:** Henry Herbert and Christopher Neame
Touchstone Pictures; R; 118 minutes
Release: 10/95
Cast: Embeth Davidtz, Tom Bell, Gemma Jones, James Purefoy, Ben Chaplin, Kenneth Anderson and Greg Wise
Based on the novel by H.E. Bates
Bella Ford (Davidtz) travels by foot to a filthy industrial town looking for the man who impregnated her. After delivering a stillborn baby, she is taken in by the Wainwrights with the condition that she earn her keep. Similar to 1995's epic, *Legends of the Fall*, the three Wainwright sons fall for Bella and she chooses between them. Bella runs into trouble when she happens upon her former lover.

FLED

Director: Kevin Hooks; **Writer:** Preston A. Whitmore II; **Director of Photography:** Matthew F. Leonietti; **Editors:** Richard Nord and Joseph Gutowski; **Music:** Graeme Revell; **Production Designer:** Charles Bennett; **Producer:** Frank Mancuso, Jr.
MGM; R; 105 minutes
Release: 7/96
Cast: Laurence Fishburne, Stephen Baldwin, Salma Hayek, Will Patton, Robert John Burke, Robert Hooks and Victor Rivers
Fled tries, unsuccessfully, to be another *Lethal Weapon*. It also repeatedly alludes to other films, including *The Fugitive, Deliverance* and *What's Love Got to Do With It*. Having escaped a chain gang, Piper (Fishburne) and Dodge (Baldwin) find themselves trying to outrun and outwit mob-

Each year, Librarian of Congress James H. Billington adds 25 films to the National Film Registry. The Library of Congress ensures that each film selected will be preserved in its original form. The films, which must be at least 10 years old, are chosen based on "their historical, cultural and aesthetic significance."

The Adventures of Robin Hood
(Warner Bros./First National, 1938)

All That Heaven Allows (Universal, 1955)

American Graffiti (Universal, 1973)

The Band Wagon (MGM, 1953)

Blacksmith Scene (Edison, 1893)

Cabaret (Allied Artists, 1972)

Chan Is Missing (Wayne Wang, 1982)

The Conversation (Paramount, 1974)

The Day the Earth Stood Still (Fox, 1951)

El Norte (Independent Production/
Cinecom-Island Alive, 1983)

Fatty's Tintype Tangle
(Keystone Film Co./Mutual Film Corp., 1915)

The Four Horsemen of the Apocalypse
(MGM, 1921)

Fury (MGM, 1936)

Gerald McBoing Boing (United Productions of America/Columbia, 1951)

The Hospital (United Artists, 1971)

Jammin' the Blues
(Vitaphone/Warner Bros., 1944)

The Last of the Mohicans
(Tourneur Productions/Associated Prods., 1920)

Manhatta (Independent Production, 1921)

North by Northwest (MGM, 1959)

The Philadelphia Story (MGM, 1940)

Rip Van Winkle
(American Mutoscope and Biograph Co., 1896)

Seventh Heaven (Fox, 1927)

Stagecoach (Walter Wanger/United Artists, 1939)

To Fly (MacGillivray Freeman, 1976)

To Kill a Mockingbird (Universal, 1962)

sters and federal marshals. Neither character is as bad as he initially seems — Dodge, a computer hack, stole $25 million from a mob-fronted company and Piper is an undercover cop.

FLIPPER
Director/Writer: Alan Shapiro; **Director of Photography:** Bill Butler; **Editor:** Peck Prior; **Music:** Joel McNeely; **Production Designer:** Thomas A. Walsh; **Producers:** James J. McNamara and Perry Katz
Universal; PG; 96 minutes
Release: 5/96
Cast: Elijah Wood, Paul Hogan, Chelsea Field, Isaac Hayes, Jessica Wesson and Jonathan Banks
Straying little from the *Flipper* of the 1960s, the update looks much better and the dolphin has learned some new tricks, thanks to technological advances. Sandy (Wood), stinging from his parents' divorce, spends the summer with his aging hippie uncle, Porter (Hogan), in the Florida Keys. Sandy befriends the dolphin and saves him from fishermen looking for a feast and evil anti-environmentalists who want to dump toxic waste into the ocean.

Flirting With Disaster

FLIRTING WITH DISASTER
Director/Writer: David O. Russell; **Director of Photography:** Eric Edwards; **Editor:** Christopher Tellefsen; **Music:** Stephen Endelman; **Production Designer:** Kevin Thompson; **Producer:** Dean Silvers
Miramax; R; 86 minutes
Release: 3/96
Cast: Ben Stiller, Patricia Arquette, Téa Leone, Mary Tyler Moore, George Segal, Alan Alda, Lily Tomlin, Richard Jenkins and Josh Brolin
To describe *Flirting With Disaster* as a film about a twentysomething guy Mel Coplin (Stiller) tracking down his birth parents would do a disservice to a hilarious road movie packed with loony surprises at every turn. Mel, his wife (Arquette), and their new friend, adoption

researcher Tina Kalb (Leone), encounter a zany cast of characters as they endure a series of mistaken family identifications. The best lines are reserved for Mel's mother (Moore), who delivers her best performance in years.

FOR GOD AND COUNTRY
Director/Writer: Wolfgang Murnberger; **Director of Photography:** Fabian Eder; **Editor:** Maria Homolkova; **Music:** Robert Stiegler and Mischa Krausz; **Producers:** Danny Krausz and Milan Dor
Dor Film; NR; 115 minutes
Release: 12/95
Cast: Christoph Dostal, Andreas Lust, Andreas Simma, Marcus J. Carney and Leopold Altenburg
In German with English subtitles
This semi-autobiographical film depicts the Austrian army as a ridiculous institution that regularly and intentionally humiliates servicemen. Set in the 1980s, Private Berger (Dostal), an 18-year-old recruit, matures while serving on the Austro-Hungarian border. A fresh, day-by-day look at one man's moral education.

FOR THE MOMENT
Director/Writer: Aaron Kim Johnston; **Director of Photography:** Ian Elkin; **Editor:** Rita Roy; **Music:** Victor Davies; **Production Designer:** Andrew Deskin; **Producers:** Aaron Kim Johnston and Jack Clements
Twentieth Century-Fox Home Entertainment; PG-13; 120 minutes
Release: 4/96
Cast: Russell Crowe, Peter Outerbridge, Christianne Hirt, Wanda Cannon, Scott Kraft and Sara McMillan
It's 1942, and when they are not airborne, members of the volunteer British Commonwealth Air Training Plan, preparing for World War II, woo and seduce the local Canadian women. Not much more than a soap opera but one well acted and worth a look.

FOUR ROOMS
The Missing Ingredient
Director/Writer: Allison Anders; **Director of Photography:** Rodrigo Garcia; **Editor:** Margie Goodspeed; **Music:** Combustible Edison; **Production Designer:** Gary Frutkoff; **Producer:** Lawrence Bender
Cast: Tim Roth, Sammi Davis, Amanda de Cadenet, Valeria Golino, Madonna, Ione Skye, Lili Taylor and Alicia Witt

The Wrong Man
Director/Writer: Alexandre Rockwell; **Director of Photography:** Phil Parmet; **Editor:** Elena Maganini; **Music:** Combustible Edison; **Production Designer:** Gary Frutkoff; **Producer:** Lawrence Bender
Cast: Tim Roth, Jennifer Beals and David Proval

The Misbehavers
Director/Writer/Editor: Robert Rodriguez; **Director of Photography:** Guillermo Navarro; **Music:** Combustible Edison; **Production Designer:** Gary

Frutkoff; **Producer:** Lawrence Bender
Cast: Tim Roth, Antonio Banderas, Lana McKissack, Patricia Vonne Rodriguez, Tamlyn Tomita, Danny Verduzco and Salma Hayek

The Man From Hollywood
Director/Writer: Quentin Tarantino; **Director of Photography:** Andrzej Sekula; **Music:** Combustible Edison; **Production Designer:** Gary Frutkoff;
Producer: Lawrence Bender
Cast: Tim Roth, Quentin Tarantino, Jennifer Beals and Paul Calderon

Release: 12/95
Miramax; R; 96 minutes
The buzz about *Four Rooms* began in late 1994, a great idea from four of the hottest young directors. It's not exactly clear what or why it went wrong. But boy, did it go wrong. Each director, Anders, Rockwell, Rodriguez and Tarantino, had free rein (with the exception of including bellhop Ted (Roth) in the script) to depict a hotel room on New Year's Eve. *The Missing Ingredient* features a coven of witches led by Madonna dancing half-naked trying to summon the spirit of a witch who has long since disappeared. The missing ingredient is a semen specimen that they enlist Ted to supply. At this point, the movie can only get better. Or so we thought. In *Wrong Man*, armed Sigfried (Proval) ties up and gags Angela (Beals), and when she removes the gag, they engage in a battle of insults and accusations. Ted's role: to be the victim of both Sigfried's and Angela's outrageous behavior. Macho man Man (Banderas) hires Ted to babysit his two children while he romances his wife (Tomita) in *The Misbehavers*. Clearly the best segment. Tarantino's *The Man From Hollywood* has the director playing the lead: a filmmaker who has become affected by his overnight success.

FRANKIE STARLIGHT
Director: Michael Lindsay-Hogg; **Writers:** Chet Raymo and Ronan O'Leary; **Director of Photography:** Paul Laufer; **Editor:** Ruth Foster; **Music:** Elmer Bernstein; **Production Designer:** Frank Conway; **Producer:** Noel Pearson
Fine Line; R; 101 minutes
Release: 11/95
Cast: Anne Parillaud, Gabriel Byrne, Matt Dillon, Rudi Davies, Georgina Cates, Corban Walker, Alan Pentony and Niall Toibin
Based on Chet Raymo's novel
Psychic Frenchwoman Bernadette (Parillaud) has a vision that drives her from post-World War II France. She stows away on a U.S. troop ship and lands in Ireland, pregnant, and has an affair with Jack Kelly (Byrne). Despite Jack and Bernadette's relationship, Jack, his wife and their family take care of Bernadette and her dwarf son, Frankie (Pentony). Frankie tells this quirky tale as an adult in a novel that combines astronomy with his mother's life story.

THE FRIGHTENERS

Director: Peter Jackson; **Writers:** Fran Walsh and
Peter Jackson; **Directors of Photography:** Alun
Bollinger and John Blick; **Editor:** Jamie Selkirk;
Production Designer: Grant Major; **Producers:** Jamie
Selkirk and Peter Jackson
Universal Pictures; R; 106 minutes
Release: 7/96
Cast: Michael J. Fox, Trini Alvarado, Peter Dobson
and John Astin

After making his critically acclaimed feature,
Heavenly Creatures, Jackson follows up with this
lesser effort which features Fox as Frank
Bannister, a man who is able to see the spirit
world. Overflowing with special effects and hair-
raising moments, *The Frighteners* offers little else
to its viewers. In desperate need of more
thoughtful and economic editing, the film also
appears bulky and unfocused.

FRISK

Director/Editor: Todd Verow; **Writers:** Jim Dwyer,
George LaVoo and Todd Verow; **Director of
Photography:** Greg Watkins; **Music:** Mark Jan
Wlodarkiewicz; **Production Designer:** Jennifer
Graber; **Producers:** Marcus Hu and Jon Gerrans
Strand Releasing; NR; 87 minutes
Release: 3/96
Cast: Michael Gunther, Craig Chester, Parker Posey,
James Lyons, Mark Ewert, Alexis Arquette, Raoul
O'Connell and Michael Stock
Based on the novel by Dennis Cooper

Think you've pretty much seen it all on the big
screen? Guess again. *Frisk* will send even the
biggest fans of blood and guts running for the
exits. In letters to his former lover, Dennis
(Gunther) describes a fantasy that has him killing
his lovers. The grisly sex murders are played out
remarkably well, making them even more disturbing. The most graphic example of queercore,
a fringe form of gay cinema.

FROM DUSK TILL DAWN

Director/Editor: Robert Rodriguez; **Writer:** Quentin
Tarantino; **Director of Photography:** Guillermo
Navarro; **Music:** Graeme Revell; **Production
Designer:** Cecilia Montiel; **Producers:** Gianni Nunnari
and Meir Teper
Miramax Dimension Films; R; 100 minutes
Release: 1/96
Cast: Harvey Keitel, George Clooney, Quentin
Tarantino, Juliette Lewis, Cheech Marin, Fred
Williamson, Salma Hayek, Tom Savini and Ernest Liu

If Hipness were a *Fortune* 500 company, Tarantino
would be chairman of the board. His trademark
dialogue is the very reason he now runs with the
Hollywood big boys. However, one has to wonder

Get Shorty

how much longer Tarantino can carry a film,
especially if he continues to produce second-rate
plots and the same old hipspeak. Two bank-rob-
bing brothers, Seth (Clooney) and Richie
(Tarantino) Gecko, who have a propensity for
violence and witty talk (surprise!), kidnap an ex-
preacher (Keitel) and his children (Lewis and
Liu) and make their way to Mexico where they
meet up with a bar full of vampires. The last 40
minutes of the movie seem to have nothing to do
with the first hour, killing the movie. *From Dusk
Till Dawn* is not a Western; it's not horror; it's not
Tarantino-esque murder and mayhem — just a
mess, but an enjoyable mess, due to Rodriguez's
kinetic direction.

GEORGIA

Director: Ulu Grosbard; **Writer:** Barbara Turner;
Director of Photography: Jan Kiesser; **Editor:**
Elizabeth King; **Music:** Steven Soles; **Production
Designer:** Lester Cohen; **Producers:** Ulu Grosbard,
Barbara Turner and Jennifer Jason Leigh
Miramax; R; 117 minutes
Release: 10/95
Cast: Jennifer Jason Leigh, Mare Winningham, Ted
Levine, Max Perlich, John Doe, John C. Reilly, Jimmy
Witherspoon, Jason Carter, Tom Bower, Smokey
Hormel, Jimmy Z., Tony Marisco and Jamian Briar

Sadie (Leigh) doesn't get the title role in this tragic but nearly flawless film. Her sister does
(Winningham) and there's good reason: Georgia is
the source of Sadie's money and substance-abuse
problems. Sadie is a wannabe rocker, who has the
look but not the talent. Georgia has made it as a
country/pop star, wife and mother, and Sadie
does not do well in disguising her jealousy.
Despite growing resentment, Georgia comes to
the rescue. Leigh's mother, Turner, wrote the
screenplay.

Get Shorty

Director: Barry Sonnenfeld; **Writer:** Scott Frank; **Director of Photography:** Don Peterman; **Editor:** Jim Miller; **Music:** John Lurie; **Production Designer:** Peter Larkin; **Producers:** Danny DeVito, Michael Shamberg and Stacey Sher
MGM; R; 105 minutes
Release: 10/95
Cast: John Travolta, Gene Hackman, Rene Russo, Danny DeVito, Dennis Farina, Delroy Lindo, James Gandolfini, David Paymer and Bette Midler
Based on the novel by Elmore Leonard

Trailing a runaway dry cleaner from Miami to Los Angeles, debt collector Chili Palmer (Travolta) finds that being a Hollywood player isn't much different from loan sharking. He makes a move into the movie business when he meets debtor Harry Zimm (Hackman), a horror-movie producer in need of some creative help. The two maneuver their way past shady deals with even shadier characters to see Zimm's latest movie through production. A clever Hollywood satire with a superb performance from Travolta.

Getting Away With Murder

Director/Writer: Harvey Miller; **Director of Photography:** Frank Tidy; **Editor:** Richard Nord; **Music:** John Debney; **Production Designer:** Jay Moore; **Producers:** Frank Price and Penny Marshall
Savoy Pictures/Rank Distributors; R; 92 minutes
Release: 4/96
Cast: Dan Aykroyd, Jack Lemmon, Lily Tomlin and Bonnie Hunt

It's been a while since Aykroyd has done anything funny, and we're still waiting. Ethics professor Jack Lambert (Aykroyd) is convinced his neighbor, Max Mueller (Lemmon), is a Nazi war criminal, and takes justice into his own hands.

Girl 6

Director/Producer: Spike Lee; **Writer:** Suzan-Lori Parks; **Director of Photography:** Malik Sayeed; **Editor:** Sam Pollard; **Music:** The Artist Formerly Known as Prince; **Production Designer:** Ina Mayhew
Fox Searchlight Pictures; R; 105 minutes
Release: 3/96
Cast: Theresa Randle, Isaiah Washington, Spike Lee, Jenifer Lewis, Quentin Tarantino, Richard Belzer, Halle Berry, John Turturro, Madonna, Debi Mazur, Naomi Campbell and Ron Silver

Fed up with her continued failure to land an acting job, a young actress (Randle) takes a job as a dispenser of phone sex (her phone name is Girl 6). The phone sex sessions are tastefully and comically done with a subtly derisive tone. Tarantino plays a young, cocky director — not his most demanding role. A fun movie with a great soundtrack.

48th Annual Directors Guild of America Awards

The DGA Awards, which honor directorial excellence in film and television, were announced March 2, 1996. This is only the fourth time since 1949 that the DGA motion picture winner has not followed up with an Oscar. These are the film awards.

Crumb

Outstanding Directorial Achievement
Ron Howard, *Apollo 13*

Outstanding Directorial Achievement in a Documentary
Terry Zwigoff, *Crumb*

D. W. Griffith Award
Woody Allen

Overlooked Movies

These are the movies (with directors) released between September 1995 and July 1996 that we think deserved more attention or wider audiences than they received. If you missed them in the theater, give them a chance on video.

Carrington, Christopher Hampton

Clockers, Spike Lee

Crumb, Terry Zwigoff

Devil in a Blue Dress, Carl Franklin

Georgia, Ulu Grosbard

A Little Princess, Alfonso Cuarón

Persuasion, Roger Michell

Safe, Todd Haynes

Smoke, Wayne Wang

Theremin: An Electronic Odyssey, Steven M. Martin

GOLD DIGGERS: THE SECRET OF BEAR MOUNTAIN

Director: Kevin James Dobson; **Writer:** Barry Glasser; **Director of Photography:** Ross Berryman; **Editor:** Stephen W. Butler; **Music:** Joel McNeely; **Production Designer:** Michael Bolton; **Producers:** Martin Bregman, Rolf Deyhle and Michael S. Bregman
Universal; PG; 92 minutes
Release: 11/95
Cast: Christina Ricci, Anna Chlumsky, Polly Draper, Diana Scarwid and David Keith

What could be a refreshing story of two adolescent girls more interested in adventure than boys proves a lackluster disappointment, due to poor writing and acting. Beth Easton (Ricci) and her recently widowed mother (Draper) move from LA to the Pacific Northwest. Beth quickly finds a friend in tomboy Jody (Chlumsky), and they embark on a dangerous journey into the caves of Bear Mountain in search of a legendary stash of gold. The scenes that should be tense fall flat and the characters never seem believable.

GOLDENEYE

Director: Martin Campbell; **Writers:** Jeffrey Caine and Bruce Feirstein; **Director of Photography:** Phil Meheux; **Editor:** Terry Rawlings; **Music:** Eric Serra, Bono and the Edge; **Production Designer:** Peter Lamont; **Producers:** Michael G. Wilson and Barbara Broccoli
United Artists; PG-13; 130 minutes
Release: 11/95
Cast: Pierce Brosnan, Sean Bean, Izabella Scorupco, Famke Janssen, Joe Don Baker, Robbie Coltrane and Judi Dench

Based on the story by Michael France and characters created by Ian Fleming

Who cares if the action isn't as good as other Bond movies? So what if 33 years have tarnished this franchise? So what if the only relationship this movie has with Fleming is its title? So what if the Cold War isn't part of the plot? So what if there's more product placements than you can shake a stick at? So what if the theme music's gone? Pierce Brosnan looks *good*.

THE GREAT WHITE HYPE

Director: Reginald Hudlin; **Writers:** Tony Hendra and Ron Shelton; **Director of Photography:** Ron Garcia; **Editor:** Earl Watson; **Music:** Marcus Miller; **Production Designer:** Charles Rosen; **Producers:** Fred Berner and Joshua Donen
Twentieth Century-Fox; R; 90 minutes
Release: 5/96
Cast: Samuel L. Jackson, Damon Wayans, Michael Jace, Jeff Goldblum, Peter Berg, Jon Lovitz, Corbin Bernsen, Cheech Marin and Jamie Foxx

Can't get much closer to the Mike Tyson-Peter McNeely scenario than this. It's clever and comical on the big screen, and pathetic and sad in

Grumpier Old Men

real life. Frustrated that black vs. black matches no longer generate big bucks, fight promoter Rev. Fred Sultan (Jackson), looks far and wide for a white fighter who actually has a chance against the champ, James "The Grim Reaper" Roper (Wayans). Sultan finds Terry Conklin (Berg), a former boxer who once beat Roper and is now a politically correct punk rocker, and bills him as Irish Terry Conklin, though he's not Irish at all. Plenty of glitzy pre-fight buildup and scheming. Delightful sleaze and crafty satire.

GRUMPIER OLD MEN

Director: Howard Deutch; **Writer:** Mark Steven Johnson; **Director of Photography:** Tak Fujimoto; **Editors:** Billy Weber, Seth Flaum and Maryann Brandon; **Music:** Alan Silvestri; **Production Designer:** Gary Frutkoff; **Producers:** John Davis and Richard C. Berman
Warner Bros.; PG-13; 105 minutes
Release: 12/95
Cast: Walter Matthau, Jack Lemmon, Ann-Margret, Sophia Loren, Burgess Meredith, Daryl Hannah, Kevin Pollak and Ann Guilbert

They're back and despite the title, not quite so grumpy. Max (Matthau) and John (Lemmon) are both in love with beautiful women. John and Ariel (Ann-Margret) have married since the 1993 *Grumpy Old Men*, and Max has taken up with the sexy new woman in town, Maria (Loren), who opened a restaurant in what used to be his favorite bait shop. It wasn't love at first sight, though, as Max and John schemed to have her place closed. The title characters do have their moments, especially when their children (Hannah and Pollak) call off their wedding. John's father (Meredith) returns as a virile 95 year old. A pleasant surprise as far as sequels go.

HACKERS

Director: Iain Softley; **Writer:** Rafael Moreu; **Director of Photography:** Andrzej Sekula; **Editors:** Christopher Blunden and Martin Walsh; **Music:** Simon Boswell; **Production Designer:** John Beard; **Producers:** Michael Peyser and Ralph Winter
United Artists; PG-13; 105 minutes
Release: 9/95
Cast: Jonny Lee Miller, Angelina Jolie, Fisher Stevens, Matthew Lillard, Renoly Santiago, Alberta Watson and Lorraine Bracco

Though cyberspace films haven't seemed to make much of an impression on general audiences, this effort found appeal with kids. Dade Murphy (Miller), boy computer genius, now an adult hack, joins a group of other "elite" cyber pranksters, who try to outdo each other at the keyboard. Their video gaming and expert hacking turns serious when they find themselves in the middle of corporate skullduggery. Zippy, but more fun if you grew up with a keyboard in your lap.

HAPPY GILMORE

Director: Dennis Dugan; **Writers:** Tim Herlihy and Adam Sandler; **Director of Photography:** Arthur Albert; **Editor:** Jeff Gourson; **Music:** Mark Mothersbaugh; **Production Designer:** Perry Andelin Blake; **Producer:** Robert Simonds
Universal; PG-13; 92 minutes
Release: 2/96
Cast: Adam Sandler, Christopher McDonald, Frances Bay and Bob Barker

Sandler returns to the screen as an ice-hockey player who trades in his puck for a tee and becomes the boisterous bad boy of golf. His tantrums and swagger catapult him to overnight celebrity on the tournament circuit, and, sure enough, the sport's snobby stars can't wait to get him off the green. As the loudmouth of the links, Sandler never stretches the character far enough to elicit laughs and instead relies on wearisome sight gags. *Happy Gilmore* quickly falls into *Dumb and Dumber* territory, rather than mining the opportunities for satire the genteel sport presents.

HARRIET THE SPY

Director: Bronwen Hughes; **Writers:** Douglas Petrie and Theresa Rebeck; **Director of Photography:** Francis Kenny; **Editor:** Debra Chiate; **Music:** Jamshied Sharifi; **Production Designer:** Lester Cohen; **Producer:** Marykay Powell
Paramount; PG; 96 minutes
Release: 7/96
Cast: Michelle Trachtenberg, Rosie O'Donnell, Vanessa Lee Chester, Gregory Smith, J. Smith-Cameron, Robert Joy, Eartha Kitt, Don Francks, Eugene Lipinski and Charlotte Sullivan

The stuff that children's movies should be made of, but just the reason why *Harriet* may very well fail commercially. There are no adolescent crushes or fantasizing, no high-tech special effects and no video games to be seen. Harriet (Trachtenberg), a precocious sixth grader, imagines herself a spy, and records the comings and goings of her classmates and neighbors in a notebook. Her life comes apart when her nanny, Golly (O'Donnell), gives her notice and her snooty classmate Marion Hawthorne (Sullivan) finds the notebook and reads Harriet's observations aloud. Hawthorne cruelly turns Harriet's friends against her and organizes the Spy Catchers Club. Harriet gets revenge but is sent to a therapist as a result. Golly returns to guide Harriet through the mess.

HEAT

Director/Writer: Michael Mann; **Director of Photography:** Dante Spinotti; **Editors:** Dov Hoenig and Pasquale Buba; **Music:** Elliot Goldenthal; **Production Designer:** Neil Spisak; **Producers:** Michael Mann and Art Linson
Warner Bros.; R; 161 minutes
Release: 12/95
Cast: Al Pacino, Robert De Niro, Val Kilmer, Jon Voight, Tom Sizemore, Diane Venora, Amy Brenneman, Ashley Judd, Mykelti Williamson, Wes Studi, Ted Levine, Tom Noonan and Natalie Portman

Much was made of Pacino and De Niro working together again, but the hoopla led to disappointment. The megastars appeared in only two scenes together — once in a coffee shop in a meeting charged with superb dialogue and energy and in the last, overly dramatized scene. Individually, their performances are impressive, but neither had to stray far from earlier roles. Neil McCauley (De Niro) leads a group of high-tech thieves that will tackle almost any job as long as it pays big. McCauley insists that his men be willing to walk away from anyone or anything rather than risk getting caught, but each of the men is attached to his woman. Vincent Hanna (Pacino) is equally obsessed with his job as an LAPD detective, but he is willing to sacrifice his love life. Hanna and McCauley play a cat-and-mouse game that both know will end in death. Lots of shoot 'em up but too little character and relationship development.

HEAVEN'S PRISONERS

Director: Phil Joanou; **Writers:** Harley Peyton and Scott Frank; **Director of Photography:** Harris Savides; **Editor:** William Steinkamp; **Music:** George Fenton; **Production Designer:** John Stoddart; **Producers:** Albert S. Ruddy, Andre E. Morgan and Leslie Greif
New Line and Savoy Pictures; R; 104 minutes
Release: 5/96
Cast: Alec Baldwin, Kelly Lynch, Mary Stuart Masterson, Samantha Lagpacan, Eric Roberts and Teri Hatcher
Based on the novel by James Lee Burke

A moody portrayal of New Orleans and the surrounding bayous. Former cop Dave Robichaux

Home for the Holidays

(Baldwin) longs for the days on the beat. His wish comes true, though he will soon regret it. While he and his wife (Lynch) are on their boat, they witness a plane crash that leaves only one survivor, an 8-year-old Salvadoran girl (Lagpacan) whom the couple "adopt." Thugs start snooping around Robichaux's house and kill his wife. The plane crash turns out to be drug-related and Robichaux finds himself caught in the middle of a drug/Mafia turf war.

HEAVY

Director/Writer: James Mangold; **Director of Photography:** Michael Barrow; **Editor:** Meg Reticker; **Music:** Thurston Moore; **Production Designer:** Michael Shaw; **Producer:** Richard Miller
Cinepix Film Properties; NR; 105 minutes
Release: 6/96
Cast: Liv Tyler, Pruitt Taylor Vince, Shelley Winters, Deborah Harry, Joe Grifasi and Evan Dando
Touching and subtle with a first rate, albeit unusual, cast. Callie (Tyler) takes a waitressing job at Dolly's (Winters) roadside tavern, and changes the life of Dolly's son, a 250-pound pizza chef. Painfully shy, the mama's boy falls hard for Callie and fantasizes about her, knowing his fantasies will never materialize. Tyler proves she's not just another pretty face.

HEIDI FLEISS: HOLLYWOOD MADAM

Director/Producer: Nick Broomfield; **Director of Photography:** Paul Kloss; **Editor:** S.J. Bloom; **Music:** David Bergeaud
In Pictures; NR; 107 minutes
Release: 2/96
With: Heidi Fleiss, Ivan Nagy, Madam Alex and Victoria Sellers
OK, OK, you think you know what this documentary is all about: a nosy filmmaker looking to break the big story and reveal who was in that black book. Wrong. Instead, Broomfield tries to figure out the mind of the madam. He talks to pimps and haunts Fleiss's favorite hangouts in pursuit of the Real Heidi. He even got hold of some Fleiss home movies that reveal a happy, middle-class upbringing. The result: Some people talk, including Nagy and Madam Alex, both early builders of Fleiss's career, but they don't want to talk much about Heidi. Instead, they would rather focus on themselves. Typical.

HOMAGE

Director: Ross Kagan Marks; **Writer:** Mark Medoff; **Director of Photography:** Tom Richmond; **Editor:** Kevin Tent; **Music:** W. G. Snuffy Walden; **Production Designer:** Amy Ancona; **Producers:** Elan Sassoon and Mark Medoff
Arrow Releasing; R; 100 minutes
Release: 5/96
Cast: Blythe Danner, Frank Whaley, Sheryl Lee, Bruce Davison and Danny Nucci
Based on Mark Medoff's play *The Homage That Follows*
Told in flashbacks, *Homage* tries to determine what drove Archie (Whaley) to murder a television star who was the object of his obsession. Archie works for Katherine (Danner), caring for her estate. When her daughter, Lucy (Lee), a television sitcom star, comes home, psychological chaos ensues. Lucy plays mind games with her mother and sexually taunts the vulnerable Archie until he can take no more. Monologues and speechy dialogue overburden the otherwise sophisticated film.

HOME FOR THE HOLIDAYS

Director: Jodie Foster; **Writer:** W.D. Richter; **Director of Photography:** Lajos Koltai; **Editor:** Lynzee Klingman; **Music:** Mark Isham; **Production Designer:** Andrew McAlpine; **Producers:** Peggy Rajski and Jodie Foster
Paramount; PG-13; 103 minutes
Release: 11/95
Cast: Holly Hunter, Robert Downey, Jr., Anne Bancroft, Charles Durning, Dylan McDermott, Geraldine Chaplin, Steve Guttenberg, Cynthia Stevenson, Claire Danes and David Strathairn
Based on the short story by Chris Radant
Things aren't going well for single mother Claudia (Hunter): She just lost her job as a Chicago art restorer, and she has to go home to her dysfunctional family for Thanksgiving while her 15-year-old daughter (Danes) stays home and plans to lose her virginity. Claudia expects the worst from her visit and her expectations aren't far off. Her father (Durning) is rapidly falling into senility, her chain-smoking mother (Bancroft) is bitter, her aunt (Chaplin) still makes inopportune, off-the-cuff remarks and her yuppie sister and brother-in-law are as annoying as ever. Her gay brother, Tommy (Downey, Jr.), and his guest (McDermott) are the saving graces of her holiday.

HOMEWARD BOUND 2: LOST IN SAN FRANCISCO

Director: David R. Ellis; **Writers:** Chris Hauty and Julie Hickson; **Director of Photography:** Jack Conroy; **Editors:** Peter E. Berger and Michael A. Stevenson; **Music:** Bruce Broughton; **Production Designer:** Michael Bolton; **Producer:** Barry Jossen
Walt Disney; G; 89 minutes.
Release: 3/96
Voices of: Michael J. Fox, Sally Field, Ralph Waite and Carla Gugino
Based on characters from *The Incredible Journey* by Sheila Burnford
The endearing trio of pets — Chance (Fox), the headstrong bulldog, Sassy (Field), the high-strung Himalayan cat, and Shadow (Waite), the wizened golden retriever — escape from their cages in the airport as the Seaver family once again loses track of their menagerie. A wild week follows as the animals make their way home through unfamiliar urban turf. Along the way, they learn about the hardships of the city from a street-smart pack of strays, and, of course, some valuable lessons about understanding others' points of view. Solid family fare in an era when we just can't get enough of talking animals.

THE HORSEMAN ON THE ROOF

Director: Jean-Paul Rappeneau; **Writers:** Jean-Paul Rappeneau, Nina Companeez and Jean-Claude Carrière; **Director of Photography:** Thierry Arbogast; **Editor:** Noelle Boisson; **Music:** Jean-Claude Petit; **Producer:** René Cleitman
Miramax; R; 118 minutes
Release: 5/96
Cast: Juliette Binoche and Oliver Martínez
In French with English subtitles
In 1830s France, an outbreak of cholera threatens the population and creates a frenzy. And that's only the subplot. Freedom fighter Angelo Pardi (Martínez), escaping the Austrian Empire that threatens the revolutionary movement, lands in the home of Pauline de Théus (Binoche), a married woman who plans to return to her husband in Italy. The two make the journey together, fleeing both the plague and French soldiers pursuing them for ignoring the quarantine. They fall for each other, and the extent of their involvement and questions about their health keep viewers guessing to the end.

HOW TO MAKE AN AMERICAN QUILT

Director: Jocelyn Moorhouse; **Writer:** Jane Anderson; **Director of Photography:** Janusz Kaminski; **Editor:** Jill Bilock; **Music:** Thomas Newman; **Production Designer:** Leslie Dilley; **Producers:** Sarah Pillsbury and Midge Sanford
Universal; PG-13; 109 minutes
Release: 10/95

Cast: Winona Ryder, Maya Angelou, Anne Bancroft, Ellen Burstyn, Samantha Mathis, Kate Nelligan, Jean Simmons, Lois Smith, Alfre Woodard, Joanna Going, Derrick O'Connor, Kate Capshaw, Dermot Mulroney and Rip Torn
Based on the novel by Whitney Otto
Twenty-six-year-old confused graduate student Finn (Ryder) spends the summer with her grandmother, Hy (Burstyn), and great-aunt, Glady Jo (Bancroft), in Grasse, California, trying to write her thesis and decide if she should marry her carpenter-boyfriend Sam (Mulroney). Hy, Glady Jo and the members of their quilting bee reveal in flashbacks the turning points in their own marriages.

THE HUNCHBACK OF NOTRE DAME

Directors: Gary Trousdale and Kirk Wise; **Writers:** Tab Murphy, Irene Mecchi, Bob Tzudiker, Noni White and Jonathan Roberts; **Editor:** Ellen Keneshea; **Music:** Alan Menken and Stephen Schwartz; **Producer:** Don Hahn
Walt Disney; G; 95 minutes
Release: 6/96
Voices of: Tom Hulce, Demi Moore, Kevin Kline, Jason Alexander, Charles Kimbrough, Mary Wickes, Paul Kandel, Tony Jay, and Heidi Mollenhauer
Based on the book by Victor Hugo
A rehash of proven Disney gags, situations, themes and characters, *The Hunchback of Notre Dame* falls flat. Though based on Victor Hugo's grim classic, this revisionist animation ends all too happily, ultimately failing to capture the spirit of the tale. In spite of tuneful original music as well as fine voicing by Kline, Wickes and Moore, Disney could have found a project more in keeping with its uplifting mission.

IF LUCY FELL

Director/Writer: Eric Schaeffer; **Director of Photography:** Ron Fortunato; **Editor:** Susan Graef; **Music:** Charlton Pettus and Amanda Kravat; **Production Designer:** Ginger Tougas; **Producers:** Brad Krevoy, Steve Stabler and Brad Jenkel
TriStar; R; 93 minutes
Release: 3/96
Cast: Sarah Jessica Parker, Eric Schaeffer, Ben Stiller and Elle MacPherson
Lucy Ackerman (Parker) and Joe MacGonaughgill (Schaeffer) are roommates with a pact to jump off the Brooklyn Bridge if Ackerman doesn't find her true love by her 30th birthday. Sound crazy? Get this: She's a psychotherapist. That's about as sensible as this banter-fest gets. Stiller delivers some comic relief as Bwick, the loopy, eccentric painter. Try as it might, the looking-for-love-in-all-the-wrong-places plot doesn't offer any surprises, never mind whether Lucy takes a dive or not.

The 11th Independent Spirit Awards, honoring excellence in independent film, were presented on March 23, 1996, under a tent on Santa Monica beach and simulcast on the World Wide Web.

The Brothers McMullen

Feature
    Leaving Las Vegas
First Feature
    Edward Burns, *The Brothers McMullen*
Male Lead
    Sean Penn, *Dead Man Walking*
Female Lead
    Elisabeth Shue, *Leaving Las Vegas*
Supporting Male
    Benicio Del Toro, *The Usual Suspects*
Supporting Female
    Mare Winningham, *Georgia*
Debut Performance
    Justin Pierce, *Kids*
Director
    Mike Figgis, *Leaving Las Vegas*
Screenplay
    Christopher McQuarrie, *The Usual Suspects*
First Screenplay
    Paul Auster, *Smoke*
Cinematography
    Leaving Las Vegas
Foreign Film
    Before the Rain, Milcho Manchevski
    (Macedonia, Britain and France)

INDEPENDENCE DAY

Director: Roland Emmerich; **Writers:** Roland Emmerich and Dean Devlin; **Director of Photography:** Karl Walter Lindenlaub; **Editor:** David Brenner; **Music:** David Arnold; **Production Designers:** Patrick Tatopoulos and Oliver Scholl; **Producer:** Dean Devlin
Twentieth Century-Fox; PG-13; 135 minutes
Release: 7/96
Cast: Will Smith, Bill Pullman, Jeff Goldblum, Mary McDonnell, Judd Hirsch, Margaret Colin, Randy Quaid, Robert Loggia, James Rebhorn, Harvey Fierstein, Harry Connick, Jr., Vivica Fox, James Duval and Brent Spiner

It's finally here. We've been waiting for it since the 1996 Super Bowl teaser. Surprisingly, it was worth the wait. It's not often one can say that, especially about a summer blockbuster. *And,* the film is suitable for children. Yep, not much violence, blood, sex or profanity. The aliens that invade the planet over a July 4 weekend are so vile that you'll cheer out loud when the heroes (Goldblum and Smith) decimate them in an air war. It helps, too, that the characters are everyday people, even the president (Pullman). Good, clean fun.

INSTITUTE BENJAMENTA

Directors: The Brothers Quay; **Writers:** Allan Passes and the Brothers Quay; **Director of Photography:** Nic Knowland; **Editor:** Larry Sider; **Music:** Lech Jankowski; **Production Designer:** Jennifer Kernke; **Producers:** Keith Griffiths and Janine Marmot
Zeitgeist Films; NR; 105 minutes
Release: 3/96
Cast: Mark Rylance, Gottfried John, Daniel Smith and Alice Krige
Based on the novella *Jakob von Gunton* and other texts by Robert Walser

Aspiring butler Jakob von Gunten (Rylance) enrolls at the Institute Benjamenta, a school that teaches subservience and repetition. From here, the film becomes a strange, gothic fairy tale loaded with symbolism. The head of the school, Herr Benjamenta (John), and his sister, Lisa (Krige), compete for von Gunten's devotion and love, and it's not clear just how close the brother and sister really are.

I SHOT ANDY WARHOL

Director: Mary Harron; **Writers:** Mary Harron and Daniel Minahan; **Director of Photography:** Ellen Kuras; **Editor:** Keith Reamer; **Music:** John Cale; **Production Designer:** Therese Deprez; **Producers:** Tom Kalin and Christine Vachon
Samuel Goldwyn; NR; 100 minutes
Release: 3/96
Cast: Lili Taylor, Jared Harris, Stephen Dorff, Coco McPherson, Michael Imperioli, Reg Rogers and Craig Chester

Independence Day

A sympathetic take on the ultra-feminist who made her way into Andy Warhol's eccentric coterie and then shot the cult hero. The film traces Valerie Solanas's life from extremist college student and author of the *S.C.U.M. Manifesto* to Warhol wannabe at the pop artist's factory through the 1968 shooting. Harron accurately recreates the Factory's heady atmosphere. Surprisingly, you'll find sympathy with Solanas's extremism. Finally, Taylor has a role that will land her the praise and recognition she deserves.

IT'S MY PARTY
Director/Writer: Randal Kleiser; **Director of Photography:** Bernd Heinl; **Editor:** Ila Von Hasperg; **Music:** Basil Poledouris; **Production Designer:** Clark Hunter; **Producers:** Joel Thurm and Randal Kleiser
United Artists; R; 109 minutes
Release: 3/96
Cast: Eric Roberts, Gregory Harrison, Bruce Davison, Lee Grant, Devon Gummersall, Marlee Matlin, Roddy McDowall, Bronson Pinchot and George Segal
Upon discovering his condition will soon cause dementia, AIDS sufferer Nick Stark (Roberts) plans to commit suicide. The best way to say good-bye to friends and family? Throw a pre-suicide party. As can be expected, Stark's guests don't quite know how to react. His former lover, Brandon (Harrison), who bolted when he found out about Stark's infection, shows up for a final reunion, and the two reminisce about happier times. A little less treacly than it sounds.

IT TAKES TWO
Director: Andy Tennant; **Writer:** Deborah Dean Davis; **Director of Photography:** Kenneth D. Zunder; **Editor:** Roer Bondelli; **Music:** Sherman and Ray Foote; **Production Designer:** Edward Pisoni; **Producers:** James Orr and Jim Cruickshank
Warner Bros.; PG; 100 minutes
Release: 11/95

Cast: Kirstie Alley, Steve Guttenberg, Mary-Kate Olsen, Ashley Olsen, Jane Sibbett and Philip Bosco
The Prince and the Pauper meets *The Parent Trap.* Amanda Lemmon (Mary-Kate Olsen), from a Manhattan orphanage, and her look-alike, Alyssa Callaway (Ashley Olsen), the daughter of billionaire widower Roger (Guttenberg), meet at a summer camp and decide their guardians should be paired. Too many cute antics follow in the process to match Amanda's supervisor, Diane Barrows (Alley), and Roger. Roger's fiancée, Clarice (Sibbett), is the victim of the girl's pranks.

JACK AND SARAH
Director/Writer: Tim Sullivan; **Director of Photography:** Jean Yves-Escoffier; **Editor:** Lesley Walker; **Music:** Simon Boswell; **Production Designer:** Christopher J. Bradshaw; **Producers:** Pippa Cross, Simon Channing Williams and Janette Day
Gramercy; R; 100 minutes
Release: 3/96
Cast: Richard E. Grant, Bianca and Sophia Lee (baby Sarah), Sophia Sullivan (toddler Sarah), Samantha Mathis, Imogen Stubbs, Judi Dench, Ian McKellan, Cherie Lunghi and Eileen Atkins
Jack (Grant) is a turnoff even when he's supposed to be likable. He takes a less-than-active role in his wife's pregnancy, and his panic as she goes into labor causes an accident that leaves him unconscious. When he comes to, he learns his wife has died in childbirth and that he has a healthy daughter, Sarah. After a bout of depression, Jack finally takes responsibility for Sarah and hires a young, attractive nanny (Mathis) to care for her. It's not too hard to figure out what happens next. The movie may have been somewhat enjoyable had another actor played Jack. Hugh Grant comes to mind, but he's already done *Nine Months.*

JADE
Director: William Friedkin; **Writer:** Joe Eszterhas; **Director of Photography:** Andrzej Bartkowiak; **Editor:** Augie Hess; **Music:** James Horner; **Production Designer:** Alex Tavoularis; **Producers:** Robert Evans, Craig Baumgarten and Gary Adelson
Paramount; R; 90 minutes
Release: 10/95
Cast: David Caruso, Linda Fiorentino, Chazz Palminteri and Richard Crenna
Judging from *Jade* and his last film outing, *Kiss of Death,* Caruso made a big mistake leaving the small screen. His performances were OK, but the material wasn't. In *Jade,* Caruso is prosecutor David Corelli, who is investigating the murder of a millionaire. The case involves kinky sex and possibly the governor (Crenna). Katrina Gavin (Fiorentino) is a suspect; she's also Corelli's former lover and the wife of his best friend (Palminteri).

JAMES AND THE GIANT PEACH

Director: Henry Selick; **Writers:** Karey Kirkpatrick, Jonathan Roberts and Steve Bloom; **Directors of Photography:** Pete Kozachik and Hiro Narita; **Editor:** Stan Webb; **Music:** Randy Newman; **Conceptual Design:** Lane Smith; **Production Designer:** Harley Jessup; **Producers:** Denise Di Novi and Tim Burton
Walt Disney Pictures; PG; 80 minutes
Release: 4/96
Cast: Joanna Lumley, Miriam Margolyes, Pete Postlethwaite and Paul Terry
Voices of: Simon Callow, Richard Dreyfuss, Jane Leeves, Miriam Margolyes, Susan Sarandon and David Thewlis
Based on the story by Roald Dahl

Another top-notch technological effort from Disney. James (Terry), recently orphaned, is sent to live with two evil aunts (Lumley and Margoyles), who work him to the bone and serve him fish heads while they eat like queens. A strange old man (Postlethwaite) appears and gives James a bag of magic crocodile tongues. James spills the bag near a peach tree, the tree produces a giant peach and the film changes from live action to animation. James boards the peach and begins a magical adventure that brings him, and his new insect friends, across the ocean (with the help of sea gulls) to New York City. Dahl's dim view of adults may be a bit much for young children.

JANE EYRE

Director: Franco Zeffirelli; **Writers:** Hugh Whitemore and Franco Zeffirelli; **Director of Photography:** David Watkin; **Editor:** Richard Marden; **Music:** Alessio Vlad and Claudio Cappone; **Production Designer:** Roger Hall; **Producer:** Dyson Lovell
Miramax; PG; 112 minutes
Release: 4/96
Cast: William Hurt, Charlotte Gainsbourg, Geraldine Chaplin, Anna Paquin, Fiona Shaw, Elle MacPherson, John Wood, Leanne Rowe and Josephine Serre
Based on the novel by Charlotte Brontë

With the Jane Austen-mania hitting hard in Hollywood, it's no surprise that producers on the prowl for another literary lioness gave us one more version of this Brontë classic. Unfortunately, the resulting film is dark and brooding at one moment and romantic and flighty the next, without fully developing either aspect. Although Oscar-winner Paquin is marvelous once again and the film is bolstered by the fine direction of Zeffirelli, it disappoints compared to the high standard set by Robert Stevenson's 1944 version.

JOE'S APARTMENT

Director/Writer: John Payson; **Director of Photography:** Peter Deming; **Editor:** Peter Frank; **Music:** Carter Burwell and Kevin Weist; **Production Designer:** Carol Spier; **Producers:** Bonni Lee and Diana Phillips
Warner Bros.; PG-13; 80 minutes
Release: 7/96
Cast: Jerry O'Connell, Megan Ward, Robert Vaughn, Billy West, Jim Turner and Don Ho

MTV's first feature film falls short on story but not on awe-inspiring vermin. Thousands of cockroaches (the real thing, puppets and animated) sing, dance and take over Joe's (O'Connell) East Village apartment. Joe falls for Lily (Ward), the daughter of a U.S. senator (Vaughn), who wants to turn his decrepit building into a jail. Lily, on the other hand, wants to make the lot a community garden. *Joe's Apartment* could have worked if it focused on the bugs rather than the dull apartment dweller.

THE JOURNEY OF AUGUST KING

Director: John Duigan; **Writer:** John Ehle; **Director of Photography:** Slawomir Idziak; **Editor:** Humphrey Dixon; **Music:** Stephen Endelman; **Production Designer:** Patricia Norris; **Producers:** Nick Wechsler and Sam Waterston
Miramax Films; PG-13; 97 minutes
Release: 11/95
Cast: Jason Patric, Thandie Newton, Larry Drake and Sam Waterston
Based on the novel by John Ehle

August (Patric) is having a hard time coping with the recent death of his wife. Only his farm provides relief from a barren existence. He faces a moral dilemma when a runaway slave, Annalees (Newton), begs him to help her win freedom from her owner, Olaf (Drake). He resists at first, not wanting to break the law, but where he couldn't save his wife, he has the chance to save another woman from a miserable existence.

JUMANJI

Director: Joe Johnston; **Writers:** Jonathan Hensleigh, Greg Taylor and Jim Strain; **Director of Photography:** Thomas Ackerman; **Editor:** Robert Dalva; **Music:** James Horner; **Production Designer:** James Bissell; **Producers:** Scott Kroopf and William Teitler
TriStar Pictures; PG; 100 minutes
Release: 12/95
Cast: Robin Williams, Kirsten Dunst, Bradley Pierce, Adam Hann-Byrd, David Alan Grier and Bonnie Hunt
Based on the book by Chris Van Allsburg

The story takes a back seat to the visual effects, which prove too scary and realistic for most children. This leaves the movie in limbo, lacking enough substance for adults and too overwhelming for kids. Jumanji is a board game that

Jumanji

brings to life jungle animals with each roll of the dice. In 1969, a young boy Alan (Hann-Byrd) finds the game buried in a New Hampshire field and when he begins playing it, he is permanently swept into a mystical jungle. Twenty-six years later, two orphans (Dunst and Pierce) find the game, and when they begin playing, they free Alan, who emerges as a middle-aged man (Williams). Alan does not come alone, and the entire jungle overruns to the small town.

THE JUROR

Director: Brian Gibson; **Writer:** Ted Tally; **Director of Photography:** Jamie Anderson; **Editor:** Robert Reitano; **Music:** James Newton Howard; **Production Designer:** Jan Roelfs; **Producers:** Irwin Winkler and Rob Cowan
Columbia; R; 107 minutes
Release: 2/96
Cast: Alec Baldwin, Demi Moore, Joseph Gordon-Levitt, Anne Heche, James Gandolfini, Lindsay Crouse, Tony Le Bianco, Michael Constantine and Michael Rispoli
Based on the book by George Dawes
A John-Grisham-wannabe courtroom thriller (though light on the courtroom scenes) with a beautiful, tough woman as the hero. Taken that way, *The Juror* is surprisingly entertaining and chilling. Mob thug Teacher (Baldwin) has to terrorize one of the jurors to ensure the defendant, a high-ranking mobster, walks. Teacher picks Annie (Moore), a single mother and artist who puts up a hell of a fight.

KAZAAM

Director: Paul Michael Glaser; **Writers:** Christian Ford, Paul Michael Glaser and Roger Soffer; **Director of Photography:** Chuck Minsky; **Editor:** Michael E. Polakow; **Music:** Christopher Tyng; **Production Designer:** Don Burt; **Producers:** Bob Engelman, Paul Michael Glaser and Scott Kroopf
Buena Vista; PG; 93 minutes
Release: 7/96

Cast: Shaquille O'Neal, Francis Capra, Ally Walker, James Acheson and John Costlloe
Little more than a vehicle for Shaq to promote his rap career. A bratty kid (Capra), escaping another beating at the hands of bullies, runs into an abandoned building and finds a boom box he turns it on, accidentally freeing a rapping genie named Kazaam (O'Neal), who offers him the standard three wishes. Unlike the rest of us, he doesn't ask for a billion bucks. Instead, he asks to be reunited with his father (Acheson), a sleazy businessman involved in music piracy. Kazaam and Max bond, as they are stuck together until Max's wishes are granted. O'Neal deserves some praise, as he does add a dose of fun to the film.

KIDS IN THE HALL: BRAIN CANDY

Director: Kelly Makin; **Writers:** Norm Hiscock, Bruce McCulloch, Kevin McDonald, Mark McKinney and Scott Thompson; **Director of Photography:** David A. Makin; **Editor:** Christopher Cooper; **Music:** Craig Northey; **Production Designer:** Gregory P. Keen; **Producer:** Lorne Michaels
Paramount; R; 90 minutes
Release: 4/96
Cast: David Foley, Bruce McCulloch, Kevin McDonald, Mark McKinney and Scott Thompson
The Canadian television troupe takes its cross-dressing shtick to the big screen with unexpected success. Each actor plays several roles in skits based on a zany plot that mocks the Prozac generation. Dr. Chris Cooper (McDonald) has invented a pill, Gleemonex, that lifts people's moods from depression to elation. Cooper's boss, Don Roritor (McKinney), rushes the drug into the market without fully understanding the adverse effects. The skits show the patients' transformations and adverse effects of the drug. Another transvestite film that won't offend the mainstream.

KILLIAN'S CHRONICLE

Director/Writer: Pamela Berger; **Director of Photography:** John Hoover; **Editor:** Jon Neuberger; **Music:** R. Carlos Nakai and Bevan Manson; **Production Designer:** John Demeo; **Producers:** Pamela Berger and Mark Donadio
Lara Classics; NR; 112 minutes
Release: 10/95
Cast: Christopher Johnson, Robert McDonough, Eva Kim and Jonah Ming Lee
In English and Passamoquoddy with English subtitles
This epic about 10th-century Irish slave Killian (Johnson) who escapes to America tends to be preachy, sermonizing that people belong to the land, not vice versa. In America, Killian befriends some Native Americans and falls in love with Turtle (Kim), and the pair learns each other's languages in record time. War also plays a deadly role, with the Vikings provoking the Turtle's Native American tribe.

Last Dance

KINGPIN

Directors: Peter Farrelly and Bobby Farrelly; **Writers:** Barry Fanaro and Mort Nathan; **Director of Photography:** Mark Irwin; **Editor:** Christopher Greeenbury; **Music:** Freedy Johnston; **Production Designer:** Sidney Jackson Bartholomew, Jr.; **Producers:** Brad Krevoy, Steve Stabler and Bradley Thomas
MGM; PG-13; 113 minutes
Release: 7/96
Cast: Woody Harrelson, Randy Quaid, Bill Murray, Vanessa Angel and Chris Elliot
Another unfunny, tasteless road movie. Although it did have potential and the cast members give fine performances, the jokes cross the fine line between acceptably rude and offensively crude. Professional bowler Munson's (Harrelson) career grinds to a halt when he loses his bowling hand after being set up by sore loser Ernie McCracken (Murray). Nearly 20 years later, alcoholic-bowling-supplies salesman Munson stumbles upon Ishmael (Quaid), an Amish man, who, with the proper training, has the potential to win (and share equally with Munson) a $1-million bowling-tournament purse. So they head for Las Vegas and Munson introduces naive Ishmael to the guilty pleasures of the real world.

LAMERICA

Director: Gianni Amelio; **Writers:** Gianni Amelio, Andrea Porporati and Alessandro Sermoneta; **Director of Photography:** Luca Bigazzi; **Editor:** Simona Paggi; **Music:** Franco Piersanti; **Producers:** Mario and Vittorio Cecchi Gori
New Yorker Films; NR; 120 minutes
Release: 12/95
Cast: Enrico Lo Verso, Michele Placido, Carmelo De Mazzarelli and Piro Milkani
In Italian with English subtitles
Amelio's Italian neo-realist film is one of 1995's best and most moving films. Set in 1991 Albania, two slick Italian entrepreneurs, Fiore (Placido) and Gino (Lo Verso), travel to the newly open country looking to get rich from government subsidies by setting up a fake company. They need the help of their Albanian connection, a feeble old man, Spiro (Di Mazzarelli), whom they take from a labor camp. Gino, who separates from Fiore to watch Spiro, joins the unfortunate Albanians trying to emigrate to Italy, losing everything he has, including his identity. A compelling look at the new Europe.

LAST DANCE

Director: Bruce Beresford; **Writer:** Ron Koslow; **Director of Photography:** Peter James; **Editor:** John Bloom; **Music:** Mark Isham; **Production Designer:** John Stoddart; **Producer:** Steven Haft
Touchstone; R; 103 minutes
Release: 5/96
Cast: Sharon Stone, Rob Morrow, Randy Quaid, Peter Gallagher and Jack Thompson
Stone plays Cindy Liggett, a death row inmate who, with her boyfriend 12 years earlier, killed a young couple. High on drugs at the time of the murders, Liggett is rehabilitated and all too aware of her chances for clemency. Motivated by his attraction for Liggett and his belief in her case, zealous attorney Rick Hayes (Morrow) is willing to try anything to save his client. Stone proves once again that she can give a serious dramatic performance, but she's the only positive thing in the film. Part of the problem is *Last Dance* arrives on the heels of *Dead Man Walking*, which boasts wonderful performances, direction and writing, and it's only natural that comparisons are made.

LAST OF THE DOGMEN

Director/Writer: Tab Murphy; **Director of Photography:** Karl Walter Lindenlaub; **Editor:** Richard Halsey; **Music:** David Arnold; **Production Designer:** Trevor Williams; **Producer:** Joel B. Michaels
Savoy Pictures; PG; 120 minutes
Release: 9/95
Cast: Tom Berenger, Barbara Hershey, Kurtwood Smith, Steve Reevis, Andrew Miller and Wilfred Brimley
While following the trail of escaped prisoners, tracker Lewis Gates (Berenger) discovers a mysterious Indian arrow, which he suspects belongs to a Cheyenne Indian. A group of Cheyennes escaped into the woods in 1864 during the massacre of the tribe, and Gates thinks some of the Indians survived and their descendants still live in the woods. He enlists the help of anthropologist Lillian Sloan (Hershey), and together they venture into the woods in pursuit of the Indians.

LAST SUMMER IN THE HAMPTONS

Director: Henry Jaglom; **Writers:** Henry Jaglom and Victoria Foyt; **Director of Photography:** Hanania Baer; **Producer:** Judith Wolinsky
Rainbow Film Company; R; 105 minutes
Release: 12/95
Cast: Viveca Lindfors, Kristoffer Tabori, Victoria Foyt, Jon Robin Baitz, Savannah Bouchér, Roscoe Lee Browne, André Gregory, Nick Gregory, Melissa Leo, Roddy McDowall, Martha Plimpton, Ron Rifkin, Diane Salinger, Brooke Smith, Holland Taylor and Henry Jaglom

Like him or hate him, Jaglom is at least consistent. In this outing, Jaglom's guests assemble for the last days at his summer homestead. True to Jaglom's seemingly improvisational form, the actors are given more than enough room to explore their characters and most go overboard. With a Chekhovesque script that encourages wandering, Jaglom allows his actors to be so narcissistic that it often seems he cannot control them and wouldn't if he could. At times, the results are funny and insightful. Too often, however, the film pays the price for its excesses.

THE LAST SUPPER

Director: Stacy Title; **Writer:** Dan Rosen; **Director of Photography:** Paul Cameron; **Editor:** Luis Colina; **Music:** Mark Mothersbaugh; **Production Designer:** Linda Burton; **Producers:** Matt Cooper and Larry Weinberg
Columbia TriStar; R; 94 minutes
Release: 4/96
Cast: Cameron Diaz, Ron Eldard, Annabeth Gish, Jonathan Penner, Courtney B. Vance, Ron Perlman, Jason Alexander, Nora Dunn, Charles Durning and Bill Paxton

The Last Supper tries too hard to shock and instead comes off as a silly, low-budget outing. A group of five liberal graduate students invite a number of conservatives for dinner, poison them and bury them in the garden, one by one. Liberals don't need to resort to murder with Bob Dole leading the right.

LAWNMOWER MAN 2: BEYOND CYBERSPACE

Director/Writer: Farhad Mann; **Director of Photography:** Ward Russell; **Editors:** Joel Goodman and Peter Berger; **Music:** Robert Folk; **Production Designer:** Ernest H. Roth; **Producers:** Edward Simons and Keith Fox
New Line Cinema; PG-13; 93 minutes
Release: 1/96
Cast: Patrick Bergin, Matt Frewer, Ely Pouget, Austin O'Brien and Kevin Conway

Based on a story by Farhad Mann and Michael Miner
The surprise science-fiction/virtual reality hit from 1992 is back. Jobe (Frewer), the dim-witted gardener-turned-cybergenius, returns to create a computer chip for a sinister corporation that will link all of the world's computers in an inescapable network. What the corporation doesn't know is that the maniacal Jobe has plans of his own. Silly, but the effects are cool.

LEAVING LAS VEGAS

Director/Writer/Music: Mike Figgis; **Director of Photography:** Declan Quinn; **Editor:** John Smith; **Production Designer:** Waldemar Kalinowski; **Producers:** Lila Cazes and Annie Stewart
United Artists; R; 112 minutes
Release: 10/95
Cast: Nicolas Cage, Elisabeth Shue, Julian Sands and Valeria Golino

Based on the novel by John O'Brien
Alcoholic screenwriter Ben (Cage) knows he's run out of friends, family, work and time. Now, he just wants one last delirious binge in the city made for getting lost, Las Vegas. There he meets and falls in love with prostitute Sera (Shue), who has her own problems. Their bond is both mysterious and desperate. O'Brien, whose novel was semi-autobiographical, killed himself two weeks after he learned the book would be made into a movie.

LES MISÉRABLES

Director/Writer/Director of Photography/Editor/Producer: Claude Lelouch; **Music:** Francis Lai, Philippe Servain, Erik Berchot, Michel Legrand and Didier Barbelivien
Warner Bros.; R; 174 minutes
Release: 10/95
Cast: Jean-Paul Belmondo, Michel Boujenah, Alessandra Martines, Clémentine Célarié, Philippe Léotard, Annie Girardot and Paul Belmondo
In French with English subtitles
Based on the novel by Victor Hugo
In Lelouch's *Les Misérables*, an updated version of the Hugo classic, Jean Valjean has been transformed into boxer Fortin (Belmondo), who shows heroism not during the French Revolution, but during the period of occupied France during World War II. Fortin saves a family of Jews and is consistently compared to Valjean. In this ambitious but slow film, Lelouch repeats one main theme: There are only two or three stories in the history of the world, and they keep replaying themselves.

LITTLE INDIAN, BIG CITY

Director: Herve Palud; **Writers:** Herve Palud and Igor Aptekman; **Director of Photography:** Fabio Conversi; **Editor:** Roland Baubeau; **Music:** Manu Katche, Geoffrey Oryema and Tonton David; **Production Designer:** Ivan Maussion; **Producers:** Louis Becker and Thierry Lhermitte
Touchstone Pictures; PG; 90 minutes
Release: 3/96
Cast: Thierry Lhermitte, Patrick Timsit, Ludwig Briand, Miou Miou and Arielle Dombasle

One of the worst dubbing jobs in recent memory. The film was a blockbuster in France but doesn't stand a chance here. Mimi-Siku (Briand), a boy

1995 NEW YORK FILM CRITICS CIRCLE AWARDS

Jennifer Jason Leigh, *Georgia*

Best Picture
Leaving Las Vegas

Best Actor
Nicolas Cage, *Leaving Las Vegas*

Best Actress
Jennifer Jason Leigh, *Georgia*

Best Supporting Actor
Kevin Spacey, *Swimming With Sharks, The Usual Suspects* and *Seven*

Best Supporting Actress
Mira Sorvino, *Mighty Aphrodite*

Best Director
Ang Lee, *Sense and Sensibility*

Best Screenwriter
Emma Thompson, *Sense and Sensibility*

Best Cinematographer
Lu Yue, *Shanghai Triad*

Best Foreign Film
Wild Reeds

Best Documentary
Crumb

Best First Feature
Chris Noonan, *Babe*

Fabiano Canosa, former head of the now-defunct film program at the Joseph Papp Public Theatre, received a special citation for his work with the program.

raised in the Amazon by his mother, is transplanted to Paris by his father (Lhermitte). Predictable scenes follow: The loincloth-clad boy climbs the Eiffel Tower and strolls down the Champs Elysees.

LOADED
Director/Writer: Anna Campion; **Director of Photography:** Alan Almond; **Editor:** John Gilbert; **Music:** Simon Fisher; **Production Designer:** Alistair Kay; **Producer:** David Hazlett
Miramax; R; 105 minutes
Release: 4/96
Cast: Oliver Milburn, Nick Patrick, Catherine McCormick, Thandie Newton, Matthew Eggleton, Danny Cunningham and Biddy Hodson
In Jane Campion's younger sister's first feature film, seven characters visit a haunted house where they plan to shoot a horror movie. However, instead of focusing on comic elements built into the film-within-a-film, Campion turns her attention to the psychological problems of her characters. What might have been a funny and intriguing look into the artistic process becomes self-indulgent and aimless, especially due to its weak script.

LONE STAR
Director/Writer/Editor: John Sayles; **Director of Photography:** Stuart Dryburgh; **Production Designer:** Dan Bishop; **Producers:** R. Paul Miller and Maggie Renzi
Castle Rock; R; 138 minutes
Release: 6/96
Cast: Chris Cooper, Elizabeth Pena, Kris Kristofferson, Eddie Robinson and Joe Morton
Word is that this is the decade's brightest picture. It's the anti-summer blockbuster, replacing special effects and predictable plots with sincerity and acumen. Set in a small Texas border town, *Lone Star* is about a deputy (Kristofferson) searching for long-lost clues to his father's mysterious death. Resonant with borders crossed and the past unearthed, *Lone Star* succeeds with fluid editing (roaming between past and present effortlessly), expressive cinematography, fine acting and well-drawn characters.

LOTTO LAND
Director/Writer: John Rubino; **Director of Photography:** Rufus Standefer; **Editor:** Jack Haigis; **Music:** the Holmes Brothers; **Production Designer:** Paola Ridolfi; **Producers:** John Rubino and Michael J. Rubino
Cinepix Film Properties; NR; 87 minutes
Release: 4/96
Cast: Larry Gilliard, Jr., Wendell Holmes, Barbara Gonzalez, Suzanne Costallos and Jaime Tirelli
A low-budget tribute to the Park Slope section of Brooklyn that was shot in only 19 days (and it shows). Hank Stokes (Gilliard, Jr.), a young black

man, falls for his Hispanic neighbor Joy (Gonzalez); his father, Milt (Holmes), ignites a relationship with Joy's mother, Florence (Costallos). The two couples climb through windows, scale rooftops and maneuver fire escapes to secretly rendezvous while the neighborhood is consumed with finding the owner of a $27-million lottery ticket.

THE LOW LIFE

Director: George Hickenlooper; **Writers:** John Enbom and George Hickenlooper; **Director of Photography:** Richard Crudo; **Editor:** Yaffa Lerea; **Music:** Bill Boll; **Production Designer:** Deborah Smith; **Producers:** Donald Zuckerman and Tobin Heminway
Cabin Fever Entertainment; R; 98 minutes
Release: 7/96
Cast: Rory Cochrane, Sara Melson, Kyra Sedgwick, Sean Astin, Ron Livingston, Christian Meoli and James Le Gros
A group of recent Yale graduates have a hard time accepting their nowhere lives; their Ivy-League education should have placed them on top of the world, right? Many would think so. Instead, they do grunt work for a Hollywood accountant. When unsophisticated Andrew (Astin) moves in with John (Cochrane), he becomes a lightning rod for the group's frustrations. They wheedle him into buying expensive booze for them and then mock him behind his back. A smart lesson in getting over one's attitude and recognizing when something positive is staring you in the face.

MAGIC HUNTER

Director: Ildiko Enyedi; **Writers:** Ildiko Enyedi and Laszlo Revesz; **Director of Photography:** Tibor Mathe; **Editor:** Maria Rigo; **Production Designer:** Attila Ferenczfy-Kovacs; **Producers:** Andras Hamori and Wieland Schulz-Keil
Shadow Distribution; NR; 106 minutes
Release: 6/96
Cast: Gary Kemp, Sadie Frost, Alexander Kaidanovsky, Peter Vallai and Alexandra Wasscher
In Hungarian with English subtitles
Director Enyedi seems intent on being vague, esoteric and pretentious. Made in the vein of Krzysztof Kieslowski's films, *Magic Hunter* views fate and humanity as a connected entity. Unfortunately, Enyedi fails to weave the various themes, images and events as deftly as her predecessor. In the film's favor are wonderful composition and editing.

MAGIC IN THE WATER

Director: Rick Stevenson; **Writers:** Rick Stevenson and Icel Dobell Massey; **Director of Photography:** Thomas Burstyn; **Editor:** Allan Lee; **Music:** David Schwartz; **Producers:** Matthew O'Connor and Rick Stevenson
TriStar; PG; 98 minutes
Release: 9/95

Cast: Mark Harmon, Joshua Jackson, Harley Jane Kozak, Sarah Wayne, Frank Sotonoma Salsedo, Willi Nark-Orn, Morris Panych and Ben Cardinal
A divorced father (Harmon) takes his two children, to whom he rarely pays much attention, to a Canadian lake for vacation. He doesn't leave his work habits behind as he also brings two telephones and a computer and tells his children to have fun without him. Lurking in the lake is a good monster who preys on men just like dad and makes them more caring. Predictably, the monster catches dad and works family-bonding wonders.

Mallrats

MALLRATS

Director/Writer: Kevin Smith; **Director of Photography:** David Klein; **Editor:** Paul Dixon; **Music:** Ira Newborn; **Production Designer:** Dina Lipton; **Producers:** James Jacks, Sean Daniel and Scott Mosier
Gramercy; R; 97 minutes
Release: 10/95
Cast: Shannen Doherty, Jeremy London, Jason Lee, Claire Forlani, Jason Mewes, Kevin Smith, Brian O'Halloran and Stan Lee
Recently dumped by their girlfriends Rene (Doherty) and Brandi (Forlani), T.S. (London) and Brodie (Lee) head to the mall to forget their pain. They run into old friends Jay (Mewes) and Silent Bob (Smith), and the group schemes to sabotage a game show that is to be shot there that afternoon. Practical jokes, sex talk and pop culture references abound but never bore in Smith's low-budget (but not as low as Clerks), angst-filled film.

MANNY AND LO

Director/Writer: Lisa Krueger; **Director of Photography:** Tom Krueger; **Editor:** Colleen Sharp; **Music:** John Lurie; **Production Designer:** Sharon Lomofsky; **Producers:** Dean Silvers and Marlen Hecht
Sony Pictures Classics; R; 89 minutes
Release: 7/96
Cast: Mary Kay Place, Scarlett Johansson, Aleksa Palladino and Paul Guilfoyle
A story of second chances. Two sisters, 11-year-old Manny (Johansson) and 16-year-old Lo (Palladino), escape a foster home and try to make do on their own, stealing and taking refuge in empty houses. Their difficult lives become more challenging when Lo gets pregnant. Accustomed to taking what they need to survive, they kidnap a surrogate mother, Elaine (Place), whose craving for children of her own will never be realized. Elaine's initial anger softens, creating a happy ending that is subtle, not overly sentimental.

MAN OF THE YEAR

Director/Writer: Dirk Shaffer; **Director of Photography:** Stephen Timberlake; **Editors:** Barry Silver and Ken Solomon; **Music:** Peitor Angell; **Production Designer:** Michael Mueller; **Producer:** Matt Keener
Seventh Art Releasing; NR; 85 minutes
Release: 3/96
Cast: Dirk Shaffer, Vivian Paxton, Michael Ornstein, Mary Stein, Cal Bartlett, Claudette Sutherland, Thom Collins, Rhonda Dotson and Beth Broderick
A satirical documentary that takes a shot at the modeling industry. When Shaffer became *Playgirl's* 1992 Model of the Year, he became a recognizable star. His body was exposed, but one part of him was not: his homosexuality. In his film, Shaffer chronicles the charade he had to maintain as Man of the Year.

MARY REILLY

Director: Stephen Frears; **Writer:** Christopher Hampton; **Director of Photography:** Philippe Rousselot; **Editor:** Lesley Walker; **Music:** George Fenton; **Production Designer:** Stuart Craig; **Producers:** Ned Tanen, Nancy Graham Tanen and Norma Heyman.
TriStar; R; 118 minutes
Release: 2/96
Cast: Julia Roberts, John Malkovich, George Cole, Michael Gambon, Kathy Staff and Glenn Close
Based on the novel by Valerie Martin
Roberts takes a subdued turn in this retelling of the Jekyll and Hyde story from the timid maid Mary Reilly's perspective. Based on Martin's novel, not Robert Louis Stevenson's classic, the horror tale offers distracting anachronisms, starting with Reilly's curve-hugging maid's uniform. When the shy heroine finally puts the puzzle of her employer's creepy dual personality

Mary Reilly

together, we're already 10 steps ahead of her. The role never gives Roberts much leeway, though she does try hard to maintain a brogue throughout. Malkovich injects his trademark lasciviousness to give the film its only erotic edge, while Close falls victim to a case of bad casting in her role as an overly made-up tart.

MA SAISON PREFEREE

Director/Writer: Andre Techine; **Director of Photography:** Thierry Arbogast; **Editor:** Martine Giordano; **Music:** Philippe Sarde; **Production Designer:** Carlos Conti; **Producer:** Alain Sarde
Filmopolis Pictures; NR; 125 minutes
Release: 4/96
Cast: Catherine Deneuve, Daniel Auteuil, Marthe Villalonga, Jean-Pierre Bouvier, Chiara Mastroianni, Anthony Prada and Carmen Chaplin
In French with English subtitles
Honest and intelligent. A long-estranged brother (Auteuil) and sister (Deneuve) are reunited when their ailing mother, Berthe (Villalonga), can no longer live alone. When Berthe leaves her home to live with her daughter, Emilie, she quickly realizes the arrangement will not work. Emilie comes to the same conclusion and, against her husband's (Bouvier) wishes, finds her brother and asks for help. Techine doesn't pose easy solutions to a difficult emotional situation.

A MIDWINTER'S TALE

Director/Writer: Kenneth Branagh; **Director of Photography:** Roger Lanser; **Editor:** Neil Farrell; **Music:** Jimmy Yuill; **Production Designer:** Tim Harvey; **Producer:** David Barron
Castle Rock/Sony Pictures Classics; R; 98 minutes
Release: 2/96
Cast: Michael Maloney, Richard Briers, Julia Sawalha, Nicholas Farrell, John Sessions, Mark Hadfield, Gerard Horan, Celia Imrie and Joan Collins
A farcical, mocking look at the entertainment industry, *A Midwinter's Tale* follows an acting troupe of six players hired to play all 24 parts in

a local production of Hamlet. Though there is plenty of humor squeezed into the multiple characterizations, *A Midwinter's Tale* ends up being little more than a light-handed comedy.

MIGHTY APHRODITE

Director/Writer: Woody Allen; **Director of Photography:** Carlo DiPalma; **Editor:** Susan E. Morse; **Music:** Dick Hyman; **Production Designer:** Santo Loquasto; **Producer:** Robert Greenhut
Miramax; R; 93 minutes
Release: 10/95
Cast: Woody Allen, Helena Bonham Carter, F. Murray Abraham, Claire Bloom, Mira Sorvino, Michael Rapaport, Olympia Dukakis, David Ogden Stiers, Jack Warden and Peter Weller
Allen's work continues to enrich American cinema in the post-Mia Farrow days, and he has had no problem replacing his former leading lady. Lenny (Allen) and Amanda Winerib (Bonham Carter), an unhappily married New York couple, adopt a baby. But the addition doesn't solve their problems: He's still uninterested and she continues to flirt. Lenny becomes obsessed with finding the boy's birth mother and expects to find an intellectual like himself. He's shocked when he meets the mother, Linda (Sorvino), a prostitute/porno actress. Lenny desperately wants her to straighten out her life and sets her up with a boxer, Kevin (Rapaport). A Greek chorus, led by Stiers, regularly chimes in to provide commentary on fate and Lenny.

MISSION: IMPOSSIBLE

Director: Brian De Palma; **Writers:** David Koepp and Robert Towne; **Director of Photography:** Stephen H. Burum; **Editor:** Paul Hirsch; **Music:** Danny Elfman; **Production Designer:** Norman Reynolds; **Producers:** Tom Cruise and Paula Wagner
Paramount; PG-13; 110 minutes
Release: 5/96
Cast: Tom Cruise, Jon Voight, Emmanuelle Béart, Henry Czerny, Jean Reno, Ving Rhames, Kristin Scott-Thomas and Vanessa Redgrave
Based on the television series created by Bruce Geller
Your mission, if you choose to accept it, is to enjoy this film and take it as a big-budget vehicle for pretty-boy Cruise that is weak on story but strong on action (and confusion). Good-guy American spy Ethan Hunt (Cruise) blazingly trots the globe undertaking high-risk maneuvers to protect a disc that contains a list of secret agents. Some of his best and most suspenseful moves are straight out of the Hitchcock playbook. The Internet and lots of high-tech gadgetry play out well and are used for cat-and-mouse games between good and evil. A fun, wild ride.

MOLL FLANDERS

Director/Writer: Pen Densham; **Director of Photography:** David Tattersall; **Editors:** Neil Travis and James R. Symons; **Music:** Mark Mancina; **Production Designer:** Caroline Hanania; **Producers:** John Watson, Richard B. Lewis and Pen Densham
MGM; PG-13; 123 minutes
Release: 6/96
Cast: Robin Wright, Morgan Freeman, Aisling Corcoran, Stockard Channing, John Lynch and Brenda Fricker
Based on characters from Daniel Defoe's novel
The 1996 slate of summer films was overwhelmingly dominated by big action and lots of explosions — guy stuff. *Moll Flanders* was one of the few women's films. Moll Flanders (Wright) escapes an orphanage as a child and works as a servant for Mrs. Mazzawatti (Fricker), a good-hearted woman. When her jealous daughters have Flanders expelled from the house, she goes to work for Mrs. Allworthy (Channing), who isn't nearly as warm, and sells her into prostitution. Flanders falls in love with one of her clients, a gentle, charming artist (Lynch), who buys her services so she can model for him. Hibble (Freeman), Flanders's confidante, tells the story to Flander's daughter as they cross the Atlantic.

MONEY TRAIN

Director: Joseph Ruben; **Writers:** Doug Richardson and David Loughery; **Director of Photography:** John W. Lindley; **Editors:** George Bowers and Bill Pankow; **Music:** Mark Mancina; **Production Designer:** Bill Groom; **Producers:** Jon Peters and Neil Canton
Columbia; R; 103 minutes
Release: 10/95
Cast: Wesley Snipes, Woody Harrelson, Jennifer Lopez, Robert Blake and Chris Cooper
Based on a story by Doug Richardson
Foster brothers Charlie (Harrelson) and John (Snipes) are undercover New York subway cops stationed at a Wall Street stop. Both fantasize and joke about robbing the money train, the car that carries the day's fares, which often total in the millions. Charlie takes the dream one step further when he finds himself buried in gambling debt, and John, the responsible older brother, tries to prevent Charlie from screwing up his life. A high-speed action adventure that nicely showcases the chemistry between Harrelson and Snipes.

Money Train

A MONTH BY THE LAKE

Director: John Irvin; **Writer:** Trevor Bentham;
Director of Photography: Pasqualino De Santis;
Editor: Peter Tanner; **Music:** Nicola Piovani;
Production Designer: Giovanni Giovagnoni;
Producer: Robert Fox
Miramax; PG; 118 minutes
Release: 9/95
Cast: Vanessa Redgrave, Edward Fox, Uma Thurman,
Alessandro Gassman and Alida Valli

Set in 1930s Italy, *A Month by the Lake* is beautifully acted and equally enjoyable to watch. Miss Bentley (Redgrave), a middle-aged amateur photographer, returns to the lakeside resort she and her recently deceased father visited annually. She is immediately attracted to Major Wilshaw (Fox). Miss Beaumont (Thurman) and Vittorio (Gassman) interrupt Bentley's plan to win the vulnerable Wilshaw's affections.

MOONLIGHT AND VALENTINO

Director: David Anspaugh; **Writer:** Ellen Simon;
Director of Photography: Julio Macat; **Editor:** David
Rosenbloom; **Music:** Howard Shore; **Production
Designer:** Robb Wilson King; **Producers:** Alison
Owen, Eric Fellner and Tim Bevan
Gramercy Pictures; R; 107 minutes
Release: 9/95
Cast: Elizabeth Perkins, Whoopi Goldberg, Gwyneth
Paltrow, Kathleen Turner, Jon Bon Jovi and Peter
Coyote
Based on the play by Ellen Simon

Three women gather around their friend Rebecca (Perkins) to support her as she mourns the death of her husband. Rebecca is not the only woman with problems: Lucy's (Paltrow) negative body image prevents her from looking at her reflection; Sylvie (Goldberg) believes her husband (Coyote) is going to leave her; and Alberta (Turner) has "intimacy issues." Rocker Bon Jovi made his film debut here, looking pretty but doing little else.

MR. HOLLAND'S OPUS

Director: Stephen Herek; **Writer:** Patrick Sheane
Duncan; **Director of Photography:** Oliver Wood;
Editor: Trudy Ship; **Music:** Michael Kamen;
Production Designer: David Nichols; **Producers:** Ted
Field, Michael Nolin and Robert W. Cort
Hollywood Pictures; PG; 145 minutes
Release: 1/96
Cast: Richard Dreyfuss, Glenne Headly, Olympia
Dukakis, Jean Louisa Kelly, Nicholas John Renner,
Joseph Anderson, Anthony Natale, Jay Thomas, W.
H. Macy, Alicia Witt and Terrence Howard

The opus, of course, is a full and meaningful life, a la Capra's *It's a Wonderful Life*. Poor Mr. Holland can't support himself writing music, so he takes a short-term job as a high-school music teacher that lasts 30 years. The script may lack originali-

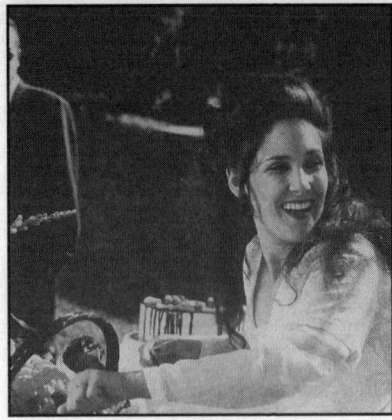

Mrs. Winterbourne

ty (the school principal, Dukakis, on Mr. Holland's supposed radical teaching style: "Mr. Holland, it has come to my attention that you are teaching the students rock and roll!") and brim with sentimentality, but you can't help liking it anyway. Even with all the moralizing, Dreyfuss and the film soar.

MR. WRONG

Director: Nick Castle; **Writers:** Chris Matheson,
Kerry Ehrin and Craig Munson; **Director of
Photography:** John Schwartzman; **Editor:** Patrick
Kennedy; **Music:** Craig Safan; **Production Designer:**
Doug Kraner; **Producer:** Marty Katz
Touchstone; PG-13; 92 minutes
Release: 2/96
Cast: Ellen DeGeneres, Bill Pullman, Joan Cusack,
Dean Stockwell, Joan Plowright, John Livingston,
Robert Goulet, Maddie Corman and Ellen Cleghorne

Maybe it's just us, but we don't think that a genuinely crazy guy stalking a woman is good comedy fodder. Martha Alston (DeGeneres) is a single woman pushed into romance with a total loser (Pullman). She dumps him and he starts to cling. More a premise for a DeGeneres sketch comedy than a feature film, *Mr. Wrong* is never really funny, despite valiant attempts from the leads.

MRS. WINTERBOURNE

Director: Richard Benjamin; **Writers:** Phoef Sutton
and Lisa-Marie Radano; **Director of Photography:**
Alex Nepomniaschy; **Editors:** Jacqueline Cambas
and William Fletcher; **Music:** Patrick Doyle;
Production Designer: Evelyn Sakash; **Producers:**
Dale Pollock, Ross Canter and Oren Koules
TriStar; PG-13; 104 minutes
Release: 4/96
Cast: Ricki Lake, Brendan Fraser, Shirley MacLaine,
Miguel Sandoval, Susan Haskell and Loren Dean

Based on Cornell Woolrich's novel *I Married a Dead Man*

Lake has come a long way since her John Waters days, but we're talking about her appearance, not her acting. The formerly rotund, current talk-show princess is a down-and-out pregnant woman, Connie Doyle, who meets a nice, rich married couple, Hugh (Fraser) and Patricia Winterbourne (Haskell), on a train. The train crashes, the couple dies, Doyle wakes up in the hospital having given birth and is mistaken for Patricia Winterbourne. She lives with her new in-laws and, after adjusting to the culture shock, falls for Hugh's twin, Bill (Fraser). No surprises here.

MULHOLLAND FALLS

Director: Lee Tamahori; **Writer:** Pete Dexter; **Director of Photography:** Haskell Wexler; **Editor:** Sally Menke; **Music:** Dave Grusin; **Production Designer:** Richard Sylbert; **Producers:** Richard D. Zanuck and Lili Fini Zanuck
MGM; R; 107 minutes
Release: 4/96
Cast: Nick Nolte, Melanie Griffith, Chazz Palminteri, Jennifer Connelly, Michael Madsen, Chris Penn, John Malkovich and Andrew McCarthy
Big names. Great visuals. Style. *Mulholland Falls* has each, but they weren't enough. Missing was a story to make the film a dark, LA-noir hit. The Hat Squad (a unit of the LAPD that was always seen in stylish fedoras and suits) had license to knock heads and ignore rules as long as they stemmed organized crime in the city. Investigating the murder of Allison Pond (Connelly), Heidi Fleiss-of-the-1950s and mistress of squad member Max Hoover (Nolte), the detectives' investigation leads them to the desert and the head of the Atomic Energy Commission (Malkovich). A disappointing Hollywood debut for Tamahori.

MULTIPLICITY

Director: Harold Ramis; **Writers:** Chris Miller, Mary Hale, Lowell Ganz, Babaloo Mandel and Harold Ramis; **Director of Photography:** Laszlo Kovacs; **Editors:** Pembroke Herring and Craig Herring; **Production Designer:** Jackson DeGovia; **Producer:** Trevor Albert
Columbia Pictures; PG-13; 110 minutes
Release: 7/96
Cast: Michael Keaton, Andie MacDowell, Harris Yulin, Richard Masur, Eugene Levy, Obba Babatunde, Ann Cusack, Zack Duhame and Katie Schlossberg
Though the film's premise is clever and ripe with cinematic possibility, *Multiplicity* falls short in its presentation. Suburban everyman Doug Kinney (Keaton) longs to be relieved of his cluttered schedule. When a local doctor (Yulin) offers to clone him, Kinney jumps at the chance to simplify his life: Not surprisingly, the presence of clones only makes it crazier.

1995 CHICAGO FILM CRITICS AWARDS

Best Picture
Apollo 13

Best Actor
Nicolas Cage, *Leaving Las Vegas*

Best Actress
Elisabeth Shue, *Leaving Las Vegas*

Best Supporting Actor
Kevin Spacey, *The Usual Suspects*

Best Supporting Actress
Joan Allen, *Nixon*

Best Director
Oliver Stone, *Nixon*

Best Screenplay
Christopher McQuarrie, *The Usual Suspects*

Best Cinematography
Darius Khondji, *Seven*

Best Foreign Film
The Postman (Il Postino), Italy

Best Original Score
Randy Newman, *Toy Story*

Most Promising Actor
Greg Kinnear, *Sabrina*

Most Promising Actress
Minnie Driver, *Circle of Friends*

Commitment to Chicago Award
Gary Sinise

Elisabeth Shue,
Leaving Las Vegas

Never Talk to Strangers

MUPPET TREASURE ISLAND

Director: Brian Henson; **Writers:** Jerry Juhl, Kirk R. Thatcher and James V. Hart; **Director of Photography:** John Fenner; **Editor:** Michael Jablow; **Music:** Hans Zimmer; **Production Designer:** Val Strazovec; **Producers:** Martin G. Baker and Brian Henson

Walt Disney Pictures; G; 99 minutes

Release: 2/96

Cast: Tim Curry, Kevin Bishop, Billy Connolly, Jennifer Saunders

Voices of: Steve Whitmire and Frank Oz

A completely off-beat retelling of the Robert Louis Stevenson classic ... and exactly what you would expect from the Muppets. Long John Silver (Curry) takes a young boy (Bishop) and his treasure map hostage, and it's up to the Muppets to rescue him. Guess which frog falls in love with which pig.

MUTE WITNESS

Director/Writer: Anthony Waller; **Director of Photography:** Egon Werdin; **Editor:** Peter Adam; **Music:** Wilbert Hirsch; **Production Designer:** Matthias Kammermeier; **Producers:** Alexander Buchman, Norbert Soentgen and Anthony Waller

Sony Pictures Classics; R; 98 minutes

Release: 9/95

Cast: Marina Sudina, Fay Ripley, Evan Richards, Oleg Jankowskif, Igor Volkow

Billy (Sudina) witnesses what she thinks is a gory murder on the set of a snuff film, but she can't tell anyone because she's mute. First-time director Waller has concocted a gritty, fast-moving tale that benefits from its gloomy Moscow setting, its cast of Russian actors and the intrinsic "is-it-real-or-is-it-special-effects" backdrop.

MYSTERY SCIENCE THEATER 3000: THE MOVIE

Director/Producer: Jim Mallon; **Writers:** Michael Nelson, Trace Beaulieu, Jim Mallon, Kevin Murphy, Mary Jo Pehl, Paul Chaplin and Bridget Jones; **Director of Photography:** Jeff Stonehouse; **Editor:** Bill Johnson; **Production Designer:** Jef Maynard; **Music:** Billy Barber

Gramercy; PG-13; 74 minutes

Release: 4/96

Cast: Trace Beaulieu and Michael Nelson

Voices of: Jim Mallon, Kevin Murphy and Trace Beaulieu

At the same time hilariously clever and innovative and yet insipid and stale, *Mystery Science Theater 3000: The Movie* is a sure-fire hit and miss. An exercise in post-modernist cinema, the film pokes fun at a 1950s B-sci-fi flick, *This Island Earth*, via its trio of orbiting film critics. Ripe with sexual innuendo and fast-paced humor, the film is crippled every time it shifts attention to its own silly B-movie subplot. All in all, the plentiful laughs make this watchable, especially if you're a fan of the cable-television series.

NEVER TALK TO STRANGERS

Director: Peter Hall; **Writers:** Lewis Green and Jordan Rush; **Director of Photography:** Elemer Ragalyi; **Editor:** Roberto Silvi; **Music:** Pino Donaggio; **Production Designer:** Linda Del Rosario; **Producers:** Andras Hamori, Jeffrey R. Neuman and Martin J. Wiley

TriStar; R; 86 minutes

Release: 10/95

Cast: Antonio Banderas, Rebecca De Mornay, Dennis Miller, Len Cariou, Harry Dean Stanton, Beau Starr, Tim Kelleher, Eugene Lipinski and Phillip Jarrett

Criminal psychologist Sarah Taylor (De Mornay), still spooked after an interview with serial killer Max Cheski (Stanton), doesn't really trust her gorgeous lover, Toni Ramirez (Banderas). Her distrust blooms into panic when her cat is delivered dead to her apartment, she catches Ramirez in a series of lies and she discovers she is being stalked. The surprise ending is a stretch.

NICK OF TIME

Director/Producer: John Badham; **Writer:** Patrick Sheane Duncan; **Director of Photography:** Roy H. Wagner; **Editors:** Frank Morriss and Kevin Stitt; **Music:** Arthur B. Rubinstein; **Production Designer:** Philip Harrison

Paramount; R; 89 minutes

Release: 11/95

Cast: Johnny Depp, Courtney Chase, Christopher Walken, Charles S. Dutton, Roma Maffia, Marsha Mason and Peter Strauss

Gene Watson (Depp) has one hour and one way to save his kidnapped daughter: He must kill the governor of California (Mason). Sounds like there should be a lot of nail-biting suspense, but there's not. Even Depp seems bored.

NICO ICON

Director/Writer: Susanne Ofteringer; **Directors of Photography:** Judith Kaufmann and Katarzyna Remin; **Editors:** Elfe Brandenburger and Guido Krajewski; **Producers:** Annette Pisacane and Thomas Mertens
Roxie Releasing; NR; 75 minutes
Release: 1/96
Interviews with: John Cale, Jackson Browne, Paul Morrissey, Viva, Billy Name, Tina Aumont, Ari Boulogne, Jonas Mekas and Sterling Morrison
In English, German and French with English subtitles
Christa Päffgen, who renamed herself Nico, seemingly had it all: looks to die for, a successful career as a singer, songwriter and model. But she hated being gorgeous and despised modeling even more. She did find pleasure in heroin and the destruction it wreaked on her body. It eventually killed her in 1988 at age 49. This documentary looks at Nico's life, from her German childhood to bohemian life in Paris to her association with Andy Warhol and the Velvet Underground and finally back to Europe where she had a child, Ari, whom she turned on to heroin. A spooky look at a product of the 1960s.

NIXON

Director: Oliver Stone; **Writers:** Stephen J. Rivele, Christopher Wilkinson and Oliver Stone; **Director of Photography:** Robert Richardson; **Editors:** Brian Berdan and Hank Corwin; **Music:** John Williams; **Production Designer:** Victor Kempster; **Producers:** Clayton Townsend, Oliver Stone and Andrew G. Vajna
Hollywood Pictures; R; 190 minutes
Release: 12/95
Cast: Anthony Hopkins, Joan Allen, Powers Boothe, Ed Harris, Bob Hoskins, E. G. Marshall, David Paymer, David Hyde Pierce, Paul Sorvino, Mary Steenburgen, J.T. Walsh, James Woods, Brian Bedford, Kevin Dunn, Fyvush Finkel, Annabeth Gish, Tony Goldwyn, Larry Hagman, Ed Herrmann, Madeline Kahn, Saul Rubinek and Tony Lo Bianco
Stone has the unfortunate role of being the only director in mainstream Hollywood with the courage to speak his mind and to put his opinion into film. With *Nixon*, Stone returns to the same ground he trod four years ago with *JFK* and is again lambasted for it. True, he has again rewritten history in many ways. True, Stone excuses Nixon's excesses because he wasn't loved as a child. However, anyone who takes the film as pure history deserves their myopia. This is the story of a man who could have been the most qualified and brilliant leader the country ever had, but, with his paranoia and lack of leadership, was responsible for his own undoing and his country's shame.

NOBODY LOVES ME

Director/Writer: Doris Dörrie; **Director of Photography:** Helge Weindler; **Editor:** Inez Regnier; **Music:** Niki Reiser; **Production Designer:** Tom Schlesinger; **Producers:** Gerd Huber and Renate Seefeldt
CFP Distribution; NR; 104 minutes
Release: 11/95
Cast: Maria Schrader, Pierre Sanoussi-Bliss and Michael Von Au
In German with English subtitles
This bizarre, morbidly comic film is not for everyone, but those who are fans of *Harold and Maude* will find *Nobody Loves Me* refreshing. Death-obsessed Fanny Fink (Schrader) can't get past her mania until she gets to know her neighbor, Orfeo (Sanoussi-Bliss), a psychic palm reader. Dörrie's theme of "don't sit back and mope, instead get up and enjoy the swing of life" at the surface seems like nothing but wackiness. But the film presents her daydream of a multicultural, free-spirited Germany.

NOW AND THEN

Director: Lesli Linka Glatter; **Writer:** I. Marlene King; **Director of Photography:** Ueli Steiger; **Editor:** Jacqueline Cambas; **Music:** Cliff Eidelman; **Production Designers:** Gershon Ginsburg and Anne Kuljian; **Producers:** Suzanne Todd and Demi Moore
New Line; PG-13; 96 minutes
Release: 10/95
Cast: Christina Ricci, Thora Birch, Gaby Hoffman, Ashleigh Aston Moore, Demi Moore, Rosie O'Donnell, Rita Wilson, Melanie Griffith and Bonnie Hunt
A girls' coming-of-age-story, *Now and Then* is a bland rip-off of the boys' coming-of-age-story, *Stand By Me*. The four girls (Ricci, Birch, Hoffman and Aston Moore) as 12 year olds have already developed their personalities, so there are few surprises when we see them as adults (briefly at the beginning and end of the movie). The girls share their summer vacation in an Indiana subdivision, flirting, sneaking out at night, holding seances in a cemetery and trying to solve the mystery of a 12-year-old's death.

THE NUTTY PROFESSOR

Director: Tom Shadyac; **Writers:** David Sheffield, Barry W. Blaustein, Tom Shadyac and Steve Oedekerk; **Director of Photography:** Julio Macat; **Editor:** Don Zimmerman; **Music:** David Newman; **Production Designer:** William Elliot; **Producers:** Brian Grazer and Russell Simmons
Universal; PG-13; 95 minutes
Release: 7/96
Cast: Eddie Murphy, Dave Chappelle, Jada Pinkett, James Coburn, Larry Miller and John Ales
Based on the 1963 movie by Jerry Lewis and Bill Richmond
A career-saving performance for Murphy. The morphing and makeup will blow any viewer away, but almost equally surprising is how nasty the

kind-hearted Sherman Klump (Murphy) becomes in his transformation to lady-killer Buddy Love (Murphy). The rotund chemistry professor desperately wants to be svelte and even tries acupuncture to shed pounds. He invents a magic potion that answers his dreams and morphs into his alter ego, the loud, obnoxious Love, who gives Klump's tormentors their just desserts. Murphy shines, especially in the dinner scenes, in which he plays five characters, including two women.

THE OLD LADY WHO WALKED IN THE SEA

Director: Laurent Heynemann; **Writer:** Dominique Roulet; **Producer:** Blue Dahlia Productions
CFP Distribution; NR; 95 minutes
Release: 9/95
Cast: Jeanne Moreau, Michel Serrault, Luc Thuillier, Geraldine Danon
Based on a novel by San Antonio
In French with English subtitles
Moreau and Serrault banter throughout this tale of cheerful swindles and sexual escapades of con artists in their golden years. Lady M (Moreau), who insists that she has had more than 2,000 lovers, takes an attractive young man (Thuillier) as a partner and heir — and, she hopes, a lover — while frustrating her old partner (Serrault).

ONCE UPON A TIME . . . WHEN WE WERE COLORED

Director: Tim Reid; **Writer:** Paul W. Cooper; **Director of Photography:** John Simmons; **Editor:** David Pincus; **Music:** Steve Tyrell; **Production Designer:** Michael Clausen; **Producers:** Tim Reid and Michael Bennett
Republic Pictures; PG; 145 minutes
Release: 1/96
Cast: Al Freeman, Jr., Phylicia Rashad, Richard Roundtree, Polly Bergen, Charles Earl Taylor, Jr., Willie Norwood, Jr. and Damon Hines
Based on the book by Clifton Taulbert
This series of vignettes set in the segregated south of the 1940s and 1950s provides an intimate portrait of a black family and its struggle with racial injustice. Rather than being preachy or political, the film relies on anecdotes, told by Taulbert at various stages of his life, to portray segregated life in the Mississippi Delta.

1-900

Director/Producer: Theo van Gogh; **Writers:** Johan Doesburg, Marcel Otten, Ad van Kempen and Ariane Schluter; **Director of Photography:** Tom Erisman; **Editor:** Ot Louw; **Music:** Ruud Bos
Zeitgeist Films; NR; 80 minutes
Release: 9/95
Cast: Ariane Schluter and Ad van Kempen
Based on the play *06* by Johan Doesburg
In Dutch with English subtitles

Sara (Schluter) and Thomas (van Kempen), two middle-aged Dutch adults, share soft-core sex talk, masturbating while they converse. Though the viewer eavesdrops on these intimate conversations and moments, little is learned about either character. An unexpected turn at the end provides a kick the film could have used earlier on.

OPEN SEASON

Director/Writer: Robert Wuhl; **Director of Photography:** Stephen Lighthill; **Editor:** Seth Flaum; **Music:** Marvin Hamlisch; **Production Designer:** Linda Burton; **Producer:** Daniel Raskov
Republic Entertainment; R; 97 minutes
Release: 5/96
Cast: Robert Wuhl, Rod Taylor, Gailard Sartain, Joe Piscopo, Maggie Han and Helen Shaver
A scathing satire of television that fails to deliver an effective punch. A glitch in the Fieldings (a fictionalization of the Nielsen ratings) has Public Broadcasting Television (PBT) rating ahead of the broadcast networks, forcing the mainstream outlets to produce cultural programming. The film portrays PBT as a liberal, cause-du-jour, network and the network executives as slimy go-getters who sacrifice quality for ratings.

ORIGINAL GANGSTAS

Director: Larry Cohen; **Writer:** Aubrey K. Rattan; **Director of Photography:** Carlos Gonzalez; **Music:** Vladimir Horunshy; **Producer:** Fred Williamson
Orion Pictures; R; 96 minutes
Release: 5/96
Cast: Fred Williamson, Jim Brown, Pam Grier, Paul Winfield, Isabel Sanford, Ron O'Neal and Richard Roundtree
The blaxploitation stars of the 1970s reunite in this gang-banger with a conscience. However, a moral message is the only thing *Original Gangstas* has to offer. Johnny Bowman (Williamson) returns to depressed Gary, Indiana, after his father was killed by members of the Rebels. Jake (Brown) is in town because his son was also shot down by the gang. Ironically, Jake and Johnny were founding members of the gang. They join other Rebels originals in an effort to win back the streets from the new, gone-bad toughies.

OTHELLO

Director: Oliver Parker; **Adapation:** Oliver Parker; **Director of Photography:** David Johnson; **Editor:** Tony Lawson; **Music:** Charlie Mole; **Production Designer:** Tim Harvey; **Producers:** Luc Roeg and David Barron
Castle Rock Entertainment; R; 125 minutes
Release: 12/95
Cast: Laurence Fishburne, Irène Jacob, Kenneth Branagh, Nathaniel Parker, Michael Maloney and Anna Patrick
Based on the play by William Shakespeare

Othello

Branagh has accomplished what a decade ago would have seemed impossible: redeemed Shakespearean acting from the old guard of mannered players to a new realism. He was the obvious choice to play Iago. Fishburne was a less obvious choice for Othello. This isn't the only renewal, though, as *Othello* is sexually and racially charged. Branagh gives the phenomenal performance we've come to expect from him. Fishburne captures the anger and on-edge quality of the title role, and Jacob as Desdemona also shines.

THE PALLBEARER

Director: Matt Reeves; **Writers:** Jason Katims and Matt Reeves; **Director of Photography:** Robert Elswit; **Editor:** Stan Salfas; **Music:** Stewart Copeland; **Production Designer:** Robin Standefer; **Producers:** Jeffrey Abrams and Paul Webster
Miramax; PG-13; 104 minutes
Release: 5/96
Cast: David Schwimmer, Gwyneth Paltrow, Michael Rapaport, Toni Collette, Carol Kane, Michael Vartan and Barbara Hershey
An attempt to make *The Graduate* of the 1990s, but chances are no one will remember *The Pallbearer* 30 years from now. Tom Thompson (Schwimmer), a 25-year-old who still lives at home, gets a call from Ruth Abernathy, a former classmate's mother (Hershey), who asks him to be a pallbearer at her son's funeral. Embarrassed he doesn't remember her son, he accepts. Abernathy seduces Thompson and the affair begins. At the funeral, he sees Julie (Paltrow), a woman he had a crush on in high school, and now the two share a mutual attraction. Bill Abernathy's suicide gets lost in the complications.

PERSUASION

Director: Roger Michell; **Writer:** Nick Dear; **Director of Photography:** John Daly; **Editor:** Kate Evans; **Music:** Jeremy Sams; **Production Designers:** William Dudley and Brian Sykes; **Producer:** Fiona Finlay
Sony Pictures Classics; PG; 103 minutes

Release: 9/95
Cast: Amanda Root, Ciaran Hinds, Susan Fleetwood, Corin Redgrave, Phoebe Nicholls, Fiona Shaw, John Woodvine, Samuel West, Sophie Thompson, Emma Roberts and Victoria Hamilton
Based on the novel by Jane Austen
Heeding the advice of a friend, Anne Elliot (Root) abandoned her love for Frederick Wentworth (Hinds) because he lacked the proper social status. Nine years later, as the 27-year-old Elliot faces spinsterhood, Wentworth, now a wealthy navy captain, and her cousin William (West) reenter her life and bring her hope of a late marriage.

THE PHANTOM

Director: Simon Wincer; **Writer:** Jeffrey Boam; **Director of Photography:** David Burr; **Editors:** O. Nicholas Brown and Bryan H. Carroll; **Music:** David Newman; **Production Designer:** Paul Peters; **Producers:** Robert Evans and Alan Ladd, Jr.
Paramount; PG; 96 minutes
Release: 6/96
Cast: Billy Zane, John Capodice, Kristy Swanson, Treat Williams, James Remar and Catherine Zeta Jones
Based on comic characters created by Lee Falk
Like many movies these days, *The Phantom* looks great but is lacking in every other respect. Depression-era American industrialist Xander Drax (Williams) needs the Skulls of Touganda — three skulls made of gold, silver and jade — to possess unlimited power. When he and his henchman travel to Bengalla to find the skulls, the Phantom (Zane) is the one thing that can foil the plan. The purple-clad Phantom is a superhero without any superpowers or superweapons (other than his wolf, pistol and horse). Plenty of action, but not much suspense.

PHENOMENON

Director: Jon Turteltaub; **Writer:** Gerald DiPego; **Director of Photography:** Phedon Papamichael; **Editor:** Bruce Green; **Music:** Thomas Newman; **Production Designer:** Garreth Stover; **Producers:** Barbara Boyle and Michael Taylor
Touchstone; PG; 117 minutes
Release: 7/96
Cast: John Travolta, Kyra Sedgwick, Forest Whitaker and Robert Duvall
A charming, Capraesque story that takes a paranoid, grim turn that nearly destroys the film. George Malley (Travolta) (no coincidence that the name rhymes with George Bailey) is a nice, simple blue-collar guy who everyone in town loves. When he is struck by lightning, he finds himself with supernatural powers that allow him to learn Portuguese in minutes, recite the names of wildflowers and become a chess expert. Malley struggles to reconcile his new mental abilities with the small-town life he leads. While an honest attempt to encourage thinking about the gifts that surround us every day, the main character becomes more symbol than human.

PIGALLE

Director/Writer: Karim Dridi; **Director of Photography:** John Mathieson; **Editor:** Lise Beaulieu; **Producers:** Romain Bremond and Patric Haddad
Seventh Art Releasing; NR; 93 minutes
Release: 12/95
Cast: Vera Briole, Francis Renaud, Raymond Gil, Philippe Ambrosini, Blanca Li, Younesse Boudache and Jean-Claude Grenier
In French with English subtitles

A steamy look at the underside of Paris, *Pigalle* examines the sex- and drug-filled life of the red light district. Assorted characters intermingle, from time to time inject nasty stuff into their bodies, occasionally have sex (at times for money) and often take off their clothes. We could see this by walking through any city's combat zone, but since this is *French* sex and drugs, it must be more glamorous.

THE POMPATUS OF LOVE

Director: Richard Schenkman; **Writers:** Jon Cryer, Adam Oliensis and Richard Schenkman; **Director of Photography:** Russell Lee Fine; **Editor:** Dan Rosen; **Music:** John Hill; **Production Designer:** Michael Krantz; **Producers:** D.J. Paul and Jon Resnik
In Pictures; NR; 99 minutes
Release: 7/96
Cast: Jon Cryer, Tim Guinee, Adam Oliensis, Adrian Pasdar, Kristen Wilson, Kristin Scott Thomas, Paige Turco and Dana Wheeler-Nicholson

Finally, a 1990s relationship film that doesn't focus on bratty, self-centered twentysomethings bellyaching about how terrible their lives are. Instead, we have four New York white guys in their 30s talking about their women problems. What sets *The Pompatus of Love* apart from other films and sitcoms is that these guys are intelligent and have literate conversations. Sure, they say silly things at times, but the script is smart. Oh, and what is the Pompatus of Love other than a line in an old Steve Miller song? See the film.

POWDER

Director/Writer: Victor Salva; **Director of Photography:** Jerzy Zielinski; **Editor:** Dennis M. Hill; **Music:** Jerry Goldsmith; **Production Designer:** Waldemar Kalinowski; **Producers:** Roger Birnbaum and Daniel Grodnik
Hollywood Pictures; PG-13; 111 minutes
Release: 10/95
Cast: Mary Steenburgen, Sean Patrick Flanery, Lance Henriksen and Jeff Goldblum

The hoopla surrounding Salva's prior child-molestation conviction added notoriety to the film, which would have otherwise gone ignored. Powder (Flanery) is an albino electromagnetic genius who was raised as a recluse until the sheriff (Henriksen) and a teacher (Steenburgen) discover and try to mainstream him. He experiences much of what most teens do, but with an extra dose of harassment.

Primal Fear

PRIMAL FEAR

Director: Gregory Hoblit; **Writers:** Steve Shagan and Ann Biderman; **Director of Photography:** Michael Chapman; **Editor:** David Rosenbloom; **Music:** James Newton Howard; **Production Designer:** Jeannine Oppewall; **Producer:** Gary Lucchesi
Paramount; R; 130 minutes
Release: 3/96
Cast: Richard Gere, Laura Linney, John Mahoney, Alfre Woodard, Frances McDormand and Edward Norton
Based on the novel by William Diehl
After a few bombs, Gere redeems himself. He's Martin Vail, a hotshot Chicago lawyer who looks great in Armani suits and loves the media. When he reads about the bludgeoning of an archbishop, he heads straight to prison and offers his services, pro bono, to the suspect, Aaron Stampler (Norton). Stampler, a victim of physical and emotional abuse, admits to being present at the murder but insists he didn't commit the crime. The case involves more than Vail anticipated, and possibly more than he can handle. Norton's performance steals the show.

PRINCE BRAT AND THE WHIPPING BOY

Director: Syd MacCartney; **Director of Photography:** Clive Tickner; **Editor:** Sean Barton; **Music:** Lee Holdridge; **Production Designers:** John Blezard and Norbert Scherer; **Producer:** Ellen Freyer
Jones Entertainment Group; G; 96 minutes
Release: 9/95
Cast: Truan Munro, Nic Knight, George C. Scott, Kevin Conway, Vincent Shiavelli, Karen Salt and Andrew Bicknell
Based on the novella by Sid Fleischman
Ill-behaved Prince Horace of Brattenburg (Knight) enjoys privileges only afforded to royalty — he even gets to pick another boy, Jemmy (Munro) to receive his spankings. Jemmy and his sister (Salt) move off the streets and into the palace, where Jemmy's intellect and manners put the prince to shame.

THE PROMISE

Director: Margarethe von Trotta; **Writers:** Peter Schneider and Margarethe von Trotta; **Director of Photography:** Franz Rath; **Editor:** Suzanne Baron; **Music:** Juergen Knieper; **Producer:** Eberhard Junkersdorf
Fine Line; R; 119 minutes
Release: 9/95
Cast: Corinna Harfouch, Meret Becker, August Zirner, Anian Zollner, Christian Herrschmann, Eva Mattes and Hans Kremer
In German with English subtitles
Two lovers who were separated by the Berlin Wall in 1960s Germany reunite three times (conceiving a child on their first tryst) over the course of 30 years. *The Promise* provides a historical look at the changes Germany endured during the period and a look at the sharply contrasting cultures of East and West Germany.

THE QUEST

Director: Jean-Claude Van Damme; **Writers:** Steven Klein and Paul Mones; **Director of Photography:** David Gribble; **Editors:** John F. Link and William J. Meshover; **Music:** Randy Edelman; **Production Designer:** Steve Spence; **Producer:** Moshe Diamant
Universal; PG-13; 95 minutes
Release: 4/96
Cast: Jean-Claude Van Damme, Roger Moore and James Remar
Van Damme has done what Steven Seagal did with *On Deadly Ground* — prove that he can neither act nor direct. Chris Dubois (Van Damme) starts out as a 1920s street performer and finds himself in outrageous circumstances, ranging from being a slave for gun runners to being captured by pirates. The far-fetched situations simply show off Asian and European fighting techniques. And to no one's surprise, Dubois always wins.

RACE THE SUN

Director: Charles T. Kanganis; **Writer:** Barry Morrow; **Director of Photography:** David Burr; **Editor:** Wendy Greene Bricmont; **Music:** Graeme Revell; **Production Designer:** Owen Paterson; **Producers:** Richard Heus and Barry Morrow
TriStar; PG; 105 minutes
Release: 3/96
Cast: Halle Berry, Casey Affleck, Eliza Dushku, Kevin Tighe, Anthony Ruivivar, J. Moki Cho, Sara Tanaka and James Belushi
Not a typical tale of underdog triumph. Led by their science teacher (Berry), a group of going-nowhere teenagers at a Hawaiian high school design and build a solar-powered car they dub Cockroach, which earns a bid in Australia's 2,000-mile race. The vehicle and the students endure obstacles during the race, as when their sleazy sponsor (Tighe) tries to have the team disqualified. You'll cheer for this unlikely group every mile of the way.

RECKLESS

Director: Norman René; **Writer:** Craig Lucas;
Director of Photography: Frederick Elmes; **Editor:**
Michael Berenbaum; **Music:** Stephen Endelman;
Production Designer: Andrew Jackness; **Producer:**
Amy J. Kaufman
Samuel Goldwyn; PG-13; 92 minutes
Release: 11/95
Cast: Mia Farrow, Scott Glenn, Mary-Louise Parker,
Tony Goldwyn, Eileen Brennan and Stephen Dorff
Based on the play by Craig Lucas

Had it with the gobs of sentimentality offered by
It's A Wonderful Life? Just don't think you can
take another cheery Bing Crosby Christmas? Try
Reckless. Rachel (Farrow), an obnoxiously
cheery housewife, has just about driven her husband (Goldwyn) crazy with her perkiness, and
he has put a contract on her life. If she is to live,
he says, she must leave at once. Out the window
she goes on Christmas Eve, clad in a nightgown
and slippers. A social worker (Glenn) and his
deaf, mute, paraplegic wife (Parker) take her in.
Their warm, fuzzy life is destroyed when secrets
begin to emerge. The surreal journeys that follow raise serious questions about the myths that
lull us into a sense of security.

RESTORATION

Director: Michael Hoffman; **Writer:** Rupert Walters;
Director of Photography: Oliver Stapleton; **Editor:**
Garth Craven; **Music:** James Newton Howard;
Production Designer: Eugenio Zanetti; **Producers:**
Cary Brokaw, Andy Paterson and Sarah Ryan Black
Miramax; R; 113 minutes
Release: 12/95
Cast: Robert Downey, Jr., Sam Neill, David Thewlis,
Polly Walker, Meg Ryan, Ian McKellen and Hugh
Grant
Based on the novel by Rose Tremain

Downey proves he can do just about anything in
front of the camera and do it well. In this
picaresque story set in 17th-century England, he
plays a roguish doctor, Merivel, who beds more
than his share of women. He cures King Charles
II's (Neill) dog and is then enlisted as the permanent vet to the royal canines. Charles himself is
a philanderer and finds he needs to do something about his mistress, Celia (Walker), who has
become an annoyance. Charles has Merivel
marry Celia but strictly prohibits conjugal contact or emotions. The doctor falls madly in love
with Celia and quickly falls out of royal favor.
Merivel seeks out his Quaker friend and colleague, Pearce (Thewlis), and finds him in an
asylum. Plenty of history thrown into the mix,
including the bubonic plague of 1665 and
London's Great Fire of 1666. An impressive work
on a lean $18.5-million budget.

The Rock

RHYTHM THIEF

Director/Editor: Matthew Harrison; **Writers:**
Christopher Grimm and Matthew Harrison; **Director
of Photography:** Howard Krupa; **Music:** Danny
Brenner and Hugh O'Donovan, John L. Horn and
Kevin Okerlund; **Producer:** Jonathan Starch
Strand Releasing; NR; 88 minutes
Release: 11/95
Cast: Jason Andrews, Eddie Daniels, Kevin Corrigan,
Kimberly Flynn, Sean Hagerty, Mark Alfred,
Christopher Cooke and Bob McGrath

Simon (Andrews) is a music pirate who smuggles
tape recorders into clubs, records concerts and
sells the tapes on the street. At times, he seems
to be only going through the motions of survival
— feeding his cat, eating spoonfuls of peanut
butter, getting drunk — until Marty (Daniels), an
unstable girl from his Long Island hometown,
arrives to tell him his mother has died.

RICHARD III

Director: Richard Loncraine; **Writers:** Ian McKellen
and Richard Loncraine; **Director of Photography:**
Peter Biziou; **Editor:** Paul Green; **Music:** Trevor
Jones; **Production Designer:** Tony Burrough;
Producers: Lisa Katselas Parè and Stephen Bayly
United Artists; R; 105 minutes
Release: 12/95
Cast: Ian McKellen, Annette Bening, Jim Broadbent,
Robert Downey, Jr., Nigel Hawthorne, Kristin Scott
Thomas, Maggie Smith and John Woods
Based on a stage production by Richard Eyre, which
was based on the play by William Shakespeare

McKellen has brilliantly adapted the stage production of *Richard III* for the big screen, cutting the
length of the play by more than one half. Richard
III (McKellen) reigns not in the Middle Ages as in
Shakespeare's work, but in a dark vision of the
1930s, which not coincidentally parallels the rise
of fascism. A brisk, violent tale of power and jealousy with a brilliant turn by McKellen.

THE ROCK

Director: Michael Bay; **Writers:** David Weisberg, Douglas S. Cook and Mark Rosner; **Director of Photography:** John Schwartzman; **Editor:** Richard Francis-Bruce; **Music:** Nick Glennie-Smith and Hans Zimmer; **Production Designer:** Michael White; **Producers:** Don Simpson and Jerry Bruckheimer

Buena Vista; R; 131 minutes

Release: 6/96

Cast: Sean Connery, Nicolas Cage, Ed Harris, David Morse, John C. McGinley and Bokeem Woodbine

This is the stuff that defines summer blockbusters: big, blow-ups, bravado. In a word, escapism. Marine general Francis X. Hummel (Harris) believes the government has ignored the men who died under his command in a covert operation, so he takes hostages at Alcatraz and threatens to launch chemical weapons unless the government promises to make reparations to the victim's families. The government enlists dorky chemical weapons expert Stanley Goodspeed (Cage), the Navy SEALS and Patrick Mason (Connery), the only person to ever break out of the rock. Goodspeed and Mason are the only two survivors, and it's up to them to save the day.

RUDE

Director/Writer: Clement Virgo; **Director of Photography:** Barry Stone; **Editor:** Susan Maggi; **Music:** Aaron Davis; **Production Designer:** Bill Fleming; **Producers:** Damon D'Oliveira and Karen A. King

Alliance International and KJM3 Entertainment Group; NR; 90 minutes

Release: 4/96

Cast: Maurice Dean Wint, Rachael Crawford, Clark Johnson, Richard Chevolleau, Sharon M. Lewis, Melanie Nicholls-King, Stephen Shellen and Ashley Brown

Rude (Lewis), a foul-mouthed DJ on a pirate radio station that broadcasts to a housing project, connects the three vignettes that develop over Easter weekend. In the first, Luke (Wint), just released from prison, returns home to his wife (Nicholls-King) (now a cop) and son. Luke is determined to stay clean but finds the pressure in the project unbearable. The second features a young, homosexual boxer (Chevolleau) whose friends are passionate homophobes. The other story watches as a recently dumped window dresser (Crawford) loses her composure after having an abortion.

RUMBLE IN THE BRONX

Director: Stanley Tong; **Writers:** Edward Tang and Fibe Ma; **Director of Photography:** Henry Chan; **Producer:** Barbie Tung

New Line; R; 87 minutes

Release: 2/96

Cast: Jackie Chan, Anita Mui and Françoise Yip

Hyperkinetic nonsense, but boy, is Chan fun to watch. *Rumble* might make him a superstar on these shores, but it will certainly reinforce his support among those who already love him. The title pretty much sums up the whole film.

THE RUN OF THE COUNTRY

Director: Peter Yates; **Writer:** Shane Connaughton; **Director of Photography:** Mike Southon; **Music:** Cynthia Millar; **Producers:** Peter Yates and Ruth Boswell

Castle Rock Entertainment; R; 100 minutes

Release: 9/95

Cast: Albert Finney, Matt Keeslar, Victoria Smurfit, Anthony Brophy, David Kelly and Dearbhla Molloy

Based on the novel by Shane Connaughton

Eighteen-year-old Danny (Keelsar) grows up quickly in his Irish village after his mother dies. He rebels against his volatile father (Finney) and gets his girlfriend, Annagh (Smurfit), pregnant. Danny suffers brutal humiliation when Annagh's family tars and feathers him as punishment.

SABRINA

Director: Sydney Pollack; **Writers:** Barbara Benedek and David Rayfiel; **Director of Photography:** Giuseppe Rotunno; **Editor:** Frederic Steinkamp; **Music:** John Williams, with original lyrics by Alan and Marilyn Bergman; **Production Designer:** Brian Morris; **Producers:** Scott Rudin and Sydney Pollack

Paramount; PG; 127 minutes

Release: 12/95

Cast: Harrison Ford, Julia Ormond, Greg Kinnear and Nancy Marchand

Based on the 1954 film by Billy Wilder, Samuel Taylor and Ernest Lehman

If it ain't broke, don't fix it. Someone should tell Hollywood that before any more classics are skewered by shoddy remakes. This updating of the 1954 gem looks lovely, the cast included, but it's a bore. And the cast, save for a charming Kinnear, exudes an another-day-another-dollar attitude. Ormond in the title role deserves some credit, though — few would dare take the part that was played to perfection by Audrey Hepburn.

THE SCARLET LETTER

Director: Roland Joffe; **Writer:** Douglas Day Stewart; **Director of Photography:** Alex Thomson; **Editor:** Thom Noble; **Music:** John Barry; **Production Designer:** Roy Walker; **Producers:** Andrew G. Vajna and Roland Joffe

Hollywood Pictures; R; 135 minutes

Release: 10/95

Cast: Demi Moore, Gary Oldman, Robert Duvall and Lisa Jolliff-Andoh

Based on the novel by Nathaniel Hawthorne

The Scarlet Letter received negative publicity before the movie was released because Joffe changed the ending. He made it a *happy* ending, a good indication that the movie should be taken as seriously as Joffe took the novel. Hawthorne's Hester Prynne was a woman with a conscience and a strong will; Joffe's Hester (Moore) hungers only for a man. The kind and guilty Rev. Dimmesdale (Oldman) described by Hawthorne is quick-tempered here. The many sex scenes are far from Puritanical, but are nonetheless predictable.

SCREAMERS
Director: Christian Duguay; **Writers:** Dan O'Bannon and Miguel Tejada-Flores; **Director of Photography:** Rodney Gibbons; **Editor:** Yves Langlois; **Music:** Normand Corbeil; **Production Designer:** Perri Gorrara; **Producers:** Tom Berry and Franco Battista
Triumph Films; R; 107 minutes
Release: 1/96
Cast: Peter Weller, Roy Dupuis, Jennifer Rubin, Andy Lauer, Charles Powell and Michael Caloz
Based on Philip K. Dick's short story "Second Variety"
Set on a distant planet in 2078, "screamers," sword-like machines designed to protect a mining outpost, have taken on a life of their own — and the ability to disguise themselves as humans. The screamers are out to destroy anything that lives on Sirius 6B, which is led by Col. Joseph Hendricksson (Weller). Another sci-fi thriller in which technology runs amok.

THE SEARCH FOR ONE-EYE JIMMY
Director/Writer: Sam Henry Kass; **Director of Photography:** Charles Levey; **Editor:** Mark Jurgens; **Music:** William Bloom; **Production Designer:** Ray Recht; **Producers:** Lisa Bruce and Robert Nickson
Northern Arts Entertainment; R; 82 minutes
Release: 6/96
Cast: Nick Turturro, Steve Buscemi, Michael Badalucco, Ray "Boom Boom" Mancini, Holt McCallany, Anne Meara, John Turturro, Samuel L. Jackson, Tony Sirico and Sam Rockwell
Kass, former head writer for *Seinfeld*, relies less on plot than on charisma to drive his stories. There is a plot here, but it's secondary to the cast of characters and their singular personalities. When Jimmy Hoyt (Rockwell) suddenly disappears, his brother Ed (Buscemi), his mother (Meara) and members of Ed's posse hit the streets of Brooklyn in search of One-Eye Jimmy. Members of the clique include car thief Junior (Turturro), the neighborhood's oldest virgin Joe Head (Badalucco), and Les (McCallany), a filmmaker who hopes the search will result in a box-office bonanza.

SENSE AND SENSIBILITY
Director: Ang Lee; **Writer:** Emma Thompson; **Director of Photography:** Michael Coulter; **Editor:** Tim Squyres; **Music:** Patrick Doyle; **Production Designer:** Luciana Arrighi; **Producer:** Lindsay Doran
Columbia; PG; 135 minutes
Release: 12/95
Cast: Emma Thompson, Kate Winslet, Hugh Grant, Alan Rickman, Greg Wise and Gemma Jones
Based on the novel by Jane Austen

Sgt. Bilko

This was the year of Austen, with *Persuasion*, *Clueless* (a loose interpretation of *Emma*) and *Sense and Sensibility* making their way to the big screen. *Sense* is the biggest production and arguably the best. The Dashwood women must vacate their home as it passes from the patriarch to his son. Taking up residence in a country cottage with a relative, the women begin a search for husbands for the two oldest sisters, Elinor (Thompson) and Marianne (Winslet). John Willoughby (Wise) and Colonel Brandon (Rickman) compete for Marianne's hand, and Edward Ferrars (Grant) seems to have clinched Elinor's heart. Beautifully lit, charmingly acted and with enough modern sensibility in the script to be thought provoking.

SERGEANT KABUKIMAN N.Y.P.D.
Directors: Lloyd Kaufman and Michael Herz; **Writers:** Lloyd Kaufman, Andrew Osborne and Jeffrey W. Sass; **Director of Photography:** Bob Williams; **Editors:** Ian Slater and Peter Novak; **Music:** Bob Mithoff; **Producers:** Michael Herz and Lloyd Kaufman
Troma Pictures; NR; 104 minutes
Release: 5/96
Cast: Rick Gianasi, Susan Byun, Bill Weeden, Thomas Crnkovich, Larry Robinson, Noble Lee Lester, Brick Bronsky, Pamela Alster, Shaler McClure and Daniel Boone
A jolly, fun spoof. Investigating the murder of a Japanese kabuki actor, New York cop Harry Griswold (Gianasi) finds himself in the middle of a shootout during a theater performance. The spirit of a dying kabuki actor with magical powers enters Griswold, and he becomes a samurai warrior. He alternates between personalities and learns from Lotus (Byun), the dead actor's granddaughter, that he has to battle "the evil one" as part of an ancient prophecy.

SEVEN

Director: David Fincher; **Writer:** Andrew Kevin Walker; **Director of Photography:** Darius Khondji; **Editor:** Richard Francis-Bruce; **Music:** Howard Shore; **Production Designer:** Arthur Max; **Producers:** Arnold Kopelson and Phyllis Carlyle
New Line; R; 107 minutes
Release: 9/95
Cast: Brad Pitt, Morgan Freeman, Gwyneth Paltrow, Richard Roundtree, R. Lee Ermey, Kevin Spacey and John C. McGinley

Two police detectives (Pitt and Freeman) search for a serial killer (Spacey) with a literary mind who commits a murder for each of the seven deadly sins: a gluttonous man is force fed to death, a model is bludgeoned for her vanity and a wealthy lawyer pays for his greed. We've seen this team dozens of times: The veteran cop has the brains and instinct *and* is a week away from retirement, and the green guy is impetuous and barely literate. The mood is bleak and the graphic images dark.

SGT. BILKO

Director: Jonathan Lynn; **Writer:** Andy Breckman; **Director of Photography:** Peter Sova; **Editor:** Tony Lombardo; **Music:** Alan Silvestri; **Production Designer:** Lawrence G. Paull; **Producer:** Brian Grazer
Universal; PG; 92 minutes
Release: 3/96
Cast: Steve Martin, Dan Aykroyd, Phil Hartman, Glenne Headly, Daryl Mitchell, Eric Edwards, Travis Tritt, Austin Pendleton and Chris Rock

For those non-baby boomers who weren't around to enjoy Phil Silvers as Sgt. Bilko in the 1950s, here's the lowdown: Sgt. Bilko heads a motor pool but knows little, if anything, about matters military. His expertise lies in gambling, and he corrupts his cadets as soon as they don their fatigues. It's obvious that Silvers was a big influence on Martin, who is a natural at turning each shifty gag. Aykroyd also does a great Paul Ford, who was Bilko's confused officer and dupe. New to the movie is Major Thorn (Hartman), who is out to even the score with Bilko. The real question is why.

SHANGHAI TRIAD

Director: Zhang Yimou; **Writer:** Bi Feiyu; **Director of Photography:** Lu Yue; **Editor:** Du Yuan; **Music:** Zhang Guangtian; **Production Designer:** Cao Jiu Ping; **Producers:** Jean-Louis Piel, Yves Marmion and Wu Yigong
Sony Pictures Classics; NR; 109 minutes
Release: 12/95
Cast: Gong Li, Li Baotian, Li Xuejian, Shun Chun, Wang Xiao and Jiang Baoying
Based on a novel by Li Xiao
In Mandarin with English subtitles

Shanghai Triad opened the 1995 New York Film Festival, but director Zhang was "asked" by the Chinese government not to attend the festival because NYFF officials refused to pull from the lineup *The Gate of Heavenly Peace,* a documentary about the Tiananmen Square uprising. Set in 1930s China, Xiao Jingbao "Jewel" (Gong) seems to live a life of privilege as the mistress of mobster Mr. Tang (Li Baotian), but the nightclub singer doesn't even control her own repertoire. Jewel's lifestyle, past and present, has left her embittered and cruel, and she exercises the only authority she has on her young servant Tang Shuisheng (Wang Xiao Xiao). Both Zhang and Gong seem more comfortable in the second half of the film when a gang war forces Jewel, Mr. Tang and his cronies away from the city to a beautiful island setting.

A SHORT FILM ABOUT LOVE

Director: Krzysztof Kieslowski; **Writers:** Krzysztof Kieslowski and Krzysztof Piesiewicz; **Director of Photography:** Witold Adamek; **Editor:** Ewa Smal; **Music:** Zbigniew Preisner; **Producer:** Ryszard Chutkowski
Film Polski; NR; 85 minutes
Release: 12/95
Cast: Olaf Lubaszenko and Grazyna Szapolowska
In Polish with English subtitles

Kieslowski often mused on voyeurism in his films, and in this 1988 psychological drama it is the central concern. Tomik (Lubaszenko), a shy postal worker, has fallen in love with his neighbor Magda (Szapolowska), an older woman who has many lovers and no window shades. This is not an innocent crush. He watches her trysts and devises schemes to lure her to the post office. Tomik reveals his passion to Magda, and she offers herself to him, which causes him to self-destruct and attempt suicide. Roles are reversed when Magda watches Tomik's apartment, waiting for him to return home. Not Kieslowski's best.

SHOPPING

Director/Writer: Paul Anderson; **Director of Photography:** Tomy Imi; **Production Designer:** Max Gottlieb; **Editor:** David Stiven; **Music:** Barrington Pheloung; **Producer:** Jeremy Bolt
Concorde-New Horizons; NR; 87 minutes
Release: 2/96
Cast: Sadie Frost, Jude Law, Sean Pertwee, Fraser James, Sean Bean, Marianne Faithfull and Jonathan Pryce

Fresh out of jail, Billy (Law), with his girlfriend Jo (Frost), resumes his life of crime by "shopping" — stealing cars, driving them through department store windows, looting and participating in car chases with police. Billy shops for thrills while his rival Tommy (Pertwee) does it to build inventory for his stolen-goods business. Not a pretty picture of a London in which hoodlums reign.

SHOWGIRLS

Director: Paul Verhoeven; **Writer:** Joe Eszterhas; **Director of Photography:** Jost Vacano; **Editors:** Mark Goldblatt and Mark Helfrich; **Music:** David A. Stewart; **Production Designer:** Allan Cameron; **Producers:** Alan Marshall and Charles Evans
United Artists; NC-17; 97 minutes
Release: 9/95
Cast: Elizabeth Berkley, Kyle MacLachlan, Gina Gershon, Glenn Plummer, Robert Davi, Alan Rachins and Gina Ravera
The director/writer team responsible for *Basic Instinct* set out to expose the Las Vegas lap-dancing scene, but they succeed only in creating an over-the-edge, voyeuristic debacle. Escaping her past, Nomi (Berkley) arrives in Vegas penniless and takes a job lap dancing (though she repeatedly insists she's not a whore) at a sleazy nightclub, aspiring to progress to a more upscale club. She makes it to the Stardust, where her rivalry with Cristal (Gershon) also includes some lesbian flirting. *Showgirls* gave new meaning to box-office "bust."

SOMEONE ELSE'S AMERICA

Director: Goran Paskaljevic; **Writer:** Gordan Mihic; **Director of Photography:** Yorgos Arbanitis; **Editor:** William Diver; **Music:** Andrew Dickson; **Production Designer:** Miljen Kljakovic; **Producers:** Antoine de Clermont-Tonnerre, David Rose and Helga Bahr
October Films; R; 96 minutes
Release: 5/96
Cast: Tom Conti, Miki Manojlovic, Maria Casares, Zorka Manojlovie and Sergej Trifunovic
A bittersweet story of immigrants pursuing the American dream in Brooklyn. Alonso (Conti), a Spaniard, owns a seedy bar and Bayo (Manojlovic), an illegal immigrant from Yugoslavia, runs the place in exchange for shelter. The two are constantly on each other's cases, but they remain steadfastly loyal. Bayo's mother (Manojlovie) and his three sons attempt to escape from Montenegro to join Bayo in New York. His youngest son dies en route, and this destroys Bayo. Unwilling to accept his child's death, he and Alonso travel to Texas to search for the boy. Meanwhile, Bayo's oldest son, Luka (Trifunovic), turns his father's bar into a successful restaurant.

SPY HARD

Director: Rick Friedberg; **Writers:** Rick Friedberg, Dick Chudnow, Jason Friedberg and Aaron Seltzer; **Director of Photography:** John R. Leonetti; **Editor:** Eric Sears; **Music:** Bill Conti; **Production Designer:** William Creber; **Producers:** Rick Friedberg, Doug Draizin and Jeffrey Konvitz
Hollywood Pictures; PG-13; 81 minutes
Release: 5/96
Cast: Leslie Nielsen, Nicollette Sheridan, Charles Durning, Andy Griffith, Stephanie Romanov, Ray Charles and Mr. T.
Nielsen, the king of low comedy, returns, spoofing espionage and action-adventure films, and he may prove more successful than the movies he mocks. Nielsen this time goes after *Mission: Impossible, True Lies* and *Butch Cassidy and the Sundance Kid*, to name a few. Perhaps the most humorous aspect of the film is the casting — Griffith as the evil nemesis, General Rancor, to Nielsen's WD-40. WD-40 teams up with fellow spy Veronique Ukrinsky (Sheridan) to save the daughter (Romanov) of an old girlfriend.

THE STAR MAKER

Director: Giuseppe Tornatore; **Writers:** Giuseppe Tornatore and Fabio Rinaudo; **Director of Photography:** Dante Spinotti; **Editor:** Massimo Quaglia; **Music:** Ennio Morricone; **Production Designer:** Francesco Bronzi; **Producers:** Vittorio and Rita Cecchi Gori
Miramax; R; 113 minutes
Release: 3/96
Cast: Sergio Castellitto and Tiziana Lodato
In the days of Italian Neo-Realism, anyone — and everyone — could be a star if they were "discovered." Castellitto is a scammer with a motion picture camera, claiming to be willing and able to discover the anonymous — for a small fee. He fools everyone until Beata (Lodato) breaks his heart. Sweet with some poignant stories and scenes, but a disappointing turn from the director of Cinema Paradiso.

THE STARS FELL ON HENRIETTA

Director: James Keach; **Writer:** Philip Railsback; **Director of Photography:** Bruce Surtees; **Editor:** Joel Cox; **Music:** David Benoit; **Production Designer:** Henry Bumstead; **Producers:** Clint Eastwood and David Valdes
Warner Bros.; PG; 110 minutes
Release: 9/95
Cast: Robert Duvall, Aidan Quinn, Frances Fisher, Brian Dennehy, Lexi Randall and Billy Bob Thornton
Duvall gives another fine performance as an eccentric who believes in the human spirit and the big payoff just around the corner. Would-be oil man in 1930s Texas, Mr. Cox (Duvall) imagines he hears oil below the ground of a farm owned by Don Day (Quinn). He convinces Day and his struggling family that they could soon be rich — despite having previously drilled 37 dry holes.

STEALING BEAUTY

Director: Bernardo Bertolucci; **Writer:** Susan Minot; **Director of Photography:** Darius Khondji; **Editor:** Pietro Scalia; **Music:** Richard Hartley; **Production Designer:** Gianni Silvestri; **Producer:** Jeremy Thomas
News Corp.; R; 110 minutes
Release: 6/96
Cast: Liv Tyler, Jeremy Irons, Sinead Cusack, Jean Marais, Donal McCann, Richard Reed, Stefania Sandrelli and Rachel Weisz

This film is all about breathtaking beauty, showcasing the exquisitely filmed Italian countryside and Cannes glamour-girl Tyler. Shortly after her mother's death, Lucy (Tyler) travels to an Italian idyll attended by bored expatriate dilettantes. She is searching for two men: her father, whom she never met, and another to deflower her. Of course, the stunning ingenue has no problem finding men willing to do the latter. Though visually pleasing, the dialogue is stiff and unbelievable.

STONEWALL

Director: Nigel Finch; **Writer:** Rikki Beadle Blair; **Director of Photography:** Chris Seager; **Music:** Michael Kamen; **Production Designer:** Therese DePrez; **Producer:** Christine Vachon
Strand Releasing; NR; 93 minutes
Release: 7/96
Cast: Guillermo Diaz, Frederick Weller, Brendan Corbalis, Duane Boutte and Bruce MacVittie
Based on the book by Martin Duberman
A fictionalized retelling of the 1969 uprising that signaled the era of gay liberation told through the comings and goings of drag queens LaMiranda (Diaz) and Bostonia (Boutte). Unfortunately, a history lesson and the personal dramas don't mix well, resulting in an all-too-obvious gap in continuity.

STRANGE DAYS

Director: Kathryn Bigelow; **Writers:** James Cameron and Jay Cocks; **Director of Photography:** Matthew F. Leonetti; **Editor:** Howard Smith; **Music:** Graeme Revell; **Production Designer:** Lilly Kilvert; **Producers:** James Cameron and Steven-Charles Jaffe
Twentieth Century-Fox; R; 145 minutes
Release: 10/95
Cast: Ralph Fiennes, Angela Bassett, Juliette Lewis, Tom Sizemore, Michael Wincott, Vincent D'Onofrio and Glenn Plummer
Based on a story by James Cameron
If virtual reality does become a commonplace form of entertainment for the masses, chances are the obsession will be with sleaze and violence. Director Bigelow underlines this with a fast-paced sci-fi thriller that has characters downloading into their heads other people's memories of sex, violence and murder. Lenny (Fiennes) is a VR junkie who deals the stuff as if it is a drug. Someone has provided him discs that contain brutal images of real crimes, including rape and murder. He is implicated in the crimes and must avoid arrest and find the real killer. Another in a string of millennium-countdown films.

STRIPTEASE

Director/Writer: Andrew Bergman; **Director of Photography:** Stephen Goldblatt; **Editor:** Anne V. Coates; **Music:** Howard Shore; **Production Designer:** Mel Bourne; **Producer:** Mike Lobell
Castle Rock; R; 115 minutes
Release: 7/96
Cast: Demi Moore, Burt Reynolds, Armand Assante, Ving Rhames, Robert Patrick and Rumer Willis
Based on the novel by Carl Hiaasen
After all the hype and talk, it's finally here. It's hard to say *Striptease* is a disappointment because it's doubtful anyone expected much from it. But we did hope to see more than two minutes of Moore's bare flesh. She takes herself too seriously in this comedy about a single mother who needs money to win a bitter custody battle with her scumbag ex-husband (Patrick). Reynolds goes over-the-top with his sex-crazed drunken congressman who rubs Moore the wrong way and gets her involved with sleazy sugar barons. Wait for the video.

THE SUBSTITUTE

Director: Robert Mandel; **Writers:** Roy Frumkes and Rocco Simonelli; **Director of Photography:** Bruce Surtees; **Producers:** Morrie Eisenman and Jim Steele
Live Entertainment; R; 114 minutes
Release: 4/96
Cast: Tom Berenger, Diane Venora and Ernie Hudson
Shale (Berenger), a former mercenary, takes over his girlfriend's teaching position after a high-school gang member clubs her knees. Out to get to the bottom of the incident, he finds much bigger problems at the school: The principal is involved in a drug smuggling operation with one of the school's gangs, KOD (Kings of Destruction). Shale also wants to teach, and after knocking a few kids around, he does. The film ends with a violent battle between Shales and his mercenary students and KOD. Awful.

Stealing Beauty

Sunset Park

SUDDEN DEATH
Director/Director of Photography: Peter Hyams; **Writer:** Gene Quintano; **Editor:** Steven Kemper; **Music:** John Debney; **Production Designer:** Philip Harrison; **Producers:** Moshe Diamant and Howard Baldwin
Universal; R; 110 minutes
Release: 12/95
Cast: Jean-Claude Van Damme, Powers Boothe, Raymond J. Barry, Whittni Wright, Ross Malinger and Dorian Harewood
One good thing can be said about *Sudden Death:* Van Damme doesn't do much talking. During a Stanley Cup hockey game at Pittsburgh's Civic Center, terrorist Foss (Boothe) demands that the vice president of the United States (who is in attendance) arrange to have $1 billion transferred to his bank accounts or else he'll blow up the place and the 17,000 fans watching the game. Not exactly a nail biter.

SUNSET PARK
Director: Steve Gomer; **Writers:** Seth Zvi Rosenfeld and Kathleen McGhee-Anderson; **Director of Photography:** Robbie Greenberg; **Editor:** Arthur Coburn; **Music:** Miles Goodman and Kay Gee; **Production Designer:** Victoria Paul; **Producers:** Danny DeVito, Michael Shamberg and Dan Paulson
TriStar; R; 100 minutes
Release: 4/96
Cast: Rhea Perlman, Fredro Starr, Antwon Tanner, Terrence DaShon Howard, Camille Saviola, De'Aundre Bonds, James Harris and Anthony Hall
Phyllis Saroka (Perlman), a teacher at Sunset Park High School, volunteers to coach the school's basketball team, though she knows nothing about the game. Facing resistance from team members, she perseveres, studies the game and seeks the players' help. Saroka wins over the inner-city kids and even develops a bond with them. *Sunset Park* resists falling into the typical underdog-on-the-rise mold by being warm and good-hearted rather than relying on cuteness.

SUPERCOP
Director: Stanley Tong; **Writers:** Edward Tang, Fibe Ma and Lee Wai Yee; **Director of Photography:** Ardy Lam; **Editor:** Cheung Yiu Chung; **Music:** Joel McNeely; **Production Designer:** Wong Yue Man; **Producers:** Willie Chan and Edward Tang
Miramax Dimension Films; R; 93 minutes
Release: 7/96
Cast: Jackie Chan, Michelle Khan, Maggie Cheung, Ken Tsang, Yuen Wah and Josephine Koo
The plot in any Chan movie is secondary to the sensational stunts (and everyone knows by now that Chan does them all himself). Chan had better watch out, though, because costar Khan may just overtake him as reigning action superstar. The partners in daredevilry travel to Southeast Asia to break up a major heroin ring. It's an old story of good guys vs. bad guys, but who cares when it's Chan doing battle against the forces of evil?

SWEET NOTHING
Director: Gary Winick; **Writer:** Lee Drysdale; **Director of Photography:** Makoto Watanabe; **Editor:** Niels Mueller; **Music:** Steven M. Stern; **Production Designer:** Amy Tapper; **Producers:** Rick Bowman and Gary Winick
Concrete Films; NR; 90 minutes
Release: 3/96
Cast: Michael Imperioli, Mira Sorvino, Paul Calderon, Patrick Breen and Richard Bright
Upon the arrival of his newborn child and at the urging of his best friend (Calderon), Angel (Imperioli), tries something new: crack. His casual drug use escalates to addiction and then dealing. He promises his wife, Monika (Sorvino), that he will quit dealing when they are out of debt. But it's not easy, and as Angel gets more involved in the drug culture, Monika becomes increasingly angry and finally kicks him out of the house. Unlike most films depicting the drug culture, *Sweet Nothing* is raw, true to life and void of clichés.

SWITCHBLADE SISTERS
Director: Jack Hill; **Writers:** Jack Hill, John Prizer and F.X. Maier; **Director of Photography:** Stephen Katz; **Editor:** Mort Tubor; **Production Designers:** Robinson Royce and B.B. Neel; **Producer:** John Prizer
Miramax Rolling Thunder; R; 90 minutes
Release: 6/96
Cast: Robbie Lee, Joanne Nail, Asher Brauner, Monica Gayle and Marlene Clark
Reportedly one of Quentin Tarantino's favorite films (in fact, the trendy director initiated this re-release), 1975's *Switchblade Sisters* is a perfect example of the exploitation films of the '60s and '70s. It centers around a gang of knife-wielding, bra-busting teenage toughies who call themselves the Jezebels, swearing and swaggering their youth away. Their male counterparts, the Silver Blades, run a prostitution/drug ring in the local high school. Marked by good editing and

unlikely power-to-the-people undertones, this retro kitsch classic at the very least provides ironic laughs.

TALK

Director: Susan Lambert; **Writer:** Jan Cornall; **Director of Photography:** Ron Hagen; **Editor:** Henry Dangar; **Music:** John Clifford White; **Production Designer:** Lissa Coote; **Producer:** Megan McMurchy
Filmopolis Pictures; NR; 90 minutes
Release: 10/95
Cast: Victoria Longley, Angie Milliken, Richard Roxburgh and John Jarratt

Two women who collaborate on graphic novels spend a day walking around Sydney, Australia, when they should be working. While meandering they discuss their lives, which they think they would like to swap. Julia (Longley) has a child with her lover and they live together in the country. Stephanie (Milliken) desperately wants a child. Their desires are played out in live-action fantasy sequences resembling comic-book adventures.

THEREMIN: AN ELECTRONIC ODYSSEY

Director/Producer: Steven M. Martin; **Directors of Photography:** Robert Stone, Cris Lombardi and Ed Lachman; **Editor:** David Greenwald; **Music:** Hall Willner
Orion Classics; NR; 84 minutes
Release: 9/95
With: Leon Theremin, Clara Rockmore, Robert Moog, Brian Wilson, Todd Rundgren and Nicolas Slonimsky

The theremin, the first electronic musical instrument, creates sounds not by playing keys on strings but by waving one's hands in the air. The instrument moved from concert halls in the 1920s to movie soundtracks and influenced musicians such as Brian Wilson and Todd Rundgren. Its Russian inventor, Leon Theremin, moved to New York in the 1920s and became part of the city's avant-garde music culture. He mysteriously disappeared in 1938, and it was later discovered that he was kidnapped by Soviet agents and brought back to the Soviet Union to work on electronic bugging. The story of the instrument and Theremin himself is skillfully told in this documentary that won Best Documentary honors at the 1994 Sundance Film Festival.

THINGS TO DO IN DENVER WHEN YOU'RE DEAD

Director: Gary Fleder; **Writer:** Scott Rosenberg; **Director of Photography:** Elliot Davis; **Editor:** Richard Marks; **Production Designer:** Nelson Coates; **Producer:** Cary Woods
Miramax; R; 104 minutes
Release: 12/95
Cast: Andy Garcia, Christopher Walken, Gabrielle Anwar, William Forsythe, Treat Williams, Christopher Lloyd, Bill Nunn, Jack Warden, Steve Buscemi and Fairuza Balk

The script is instantly cooler-than-thou, leaving the audience to feel like nerds for not getting the joke. Jimmy the Saint (Garcia) is a gangster who's left the life, but The Man With the Plan (Walken) wants him back to scare his daughter's new boyfriend out of marriage. Jimmy puts together a team. Needless to say, things go wrong. It's buckwheats (death in the most painful way) for everyone. It's cool to introduce new catch phrases into movies, but those catch phrases shouldn't have to be explained. Here the lingo is too inaccessible, and the film pays the price.

A THIN LINE BETWEEN LOVE AND HATE

Director: Martin Lawrence; **Writers:** Martin Lawrence, Bentley Kyle Evans, Kenny Buford and Kim Bass; **Director of Photography:** Francis Kenny; **Editor:** John Carter; **Music:** Roger Troutman; **Production Designer:** Simon Dobbin; **Producers:** Douglas McHenry and George Jackson
New Line; R; 107 minutes
Release: 3/96
Cast: Martin Lawrence, Lynn Whitfield, Regina King, Bobby Brown, Daryl M. Mitchell, Roger E. Mosley and Della Reese

Darnell (Lawrence) seduces hordes of women but has never had to say "I love you" to any of them. Things change when he meets Brandi Web (Whitfield), who turns out to be the black version of Glenn Close's character in *Fatal Attraction*. The film gets stuck somewhere between parody and thriller.

THREE WISHES

Director: Martha Coolidge; **Writer:** Elizabeth Anderson; **Director of Photography:** Johnny E. Jensen; **Editor:** Stephen Cohen; **Music:** Cynthia Millar; **Production Designer:** John Vallone; **Producers:** Gary Lucchesi, Clifford Green and Ellen Green
Savoy Pictures; PG; 105 minutes
Release: 10/95
Cast: Patrick Swayze, Mary Elizabeth Mastrantonio, Joseph Mazzello and Seth Mumy

Savoy and the crew of *Three Wishes* took out expensive full-page ads in several national newspapers promising that if Bob Dole and Bill Clinton watched the film together, Savoy would donate $150,000 to the Make-A-Wish Foundation. The deal was never done (but the donation was). Set in the 1950s, this fantasy tale tells the story of a single mother, Jeanne (Mastrantonio) and her two sons, Tom (Mazzello) and Gunny (Mumy). Jack (Swayze) is an eccentric who moves in with the family after Jeanne breaks his leg when she accidentally hits him with her car. With Jack's arrival into their lives comes fantasy sequences that make it hard to tell what is real and what is make believe.

TIE-DIED: ROCK 'N' ROLL'S MOST DEADICATED FANS

Director: Andrew Behar; **Director of Photography:** Hamid Shams; **Editors:** Andrew Behar and Sara Sackner; **Music:** Peter Fish with songs by Heads on the Lot; **Producers:** Marsha Oglesby and James Deutch
ISA Releasing; R; 88 minutes
Release: 9/95
With: Jahree Sullivan, Dianna Evans Sullivan, Ryan Massey, Al Dickens, Dan Adkins, Zane Kesey and Thin Man
Filming die-hard Grateful Dead fans as they camp out in parking lots, commune and dance in drug- and Dead-induced trances, director Behar tries to capture the Deadhead culture and mentality. He succeeds in chronicling the 1960s-like peace and happy scene, but the absence of Grateful Dead music (the band was not involved with the project) makes it hard to appreciate the fans' devotion.

A TIME TO KILL

Director: Joel Schumacher; **Writer:** Akiva Goldsman; **Director of Photography:** Peter Menzies, Jr.; **Editor:** William Steinkamp; **Music:** Elliot Goldenthal; **Production Designer:** Larry Fulton; **Producers:** Arnon Milchan, Michael Nathanson, Hunt Lowry and John Grisham
Warner Bros.; R; 128 minutes
Release: 7/96
Cast: Sandra Bullock, Samuel L. Jackson, Matthew McConaughey, Kevin Spacey, Brenda Fricker, Oliver Platt, Charles S. Dutton, Ashley Judd, Patrick McGoohan, Tonea Stewart, Chris Cooper, Donald Sutherland and Kiefer Sutherland
Based on the novel by John Grisham
Clearly the best film adaptation of a Grisham novel and often lauded as the best film of 1996. The cast, save for the overrated Bullock, shines in this thrilling, racially charged dramatic story of black vs. white, new South vs. old South. Young, gorgeous Mississippi lawyer Jake Brigance (McConaughey) defends Carl Lee Hailey (Jackson), who murdered the two white men who raped and nearly beat to death his 10-year-old daughter. The case stirs debate and bad feelings throughout the small, rural town, while the Ku Klux Klan is revived at the hands of Freddie Cobb (Kiefer Sutherland). And yes, McConaughey does live up to all the hype.

TO DIE FOR

Director: Gus Van Sant; **Writer:** Buck Henry; **Director of Photography:** Eric Alan Edwards; **Editor:** Curtiss Clayton; **Music:** Danny Elfman; **Production Designer:** Missy Stewart; **Producer:** Laura Ziskin
Columbia; R; 103 minutes
Release: 9/95

Cast: Nicole Kidman, Matt Dillon, Joaquin Phoenix, Casey Affleck, Illeana Douglas and Alison Folland
Based on the book by Joyce Maynard
Van Sant redeems himself in a big way after his disastrous *Even Cowgirls Get the Blues* with this dark satire on fame and tabloid culture. Suzanne Stone (Kidman) is a small-town, junior-college graduate who lives for the camera. As the local weather girl, she aspires to bigger things and revels in the media attention that surrounds the murder of her lughead husband (Dillon), which she convinced a local teen to commit. Kidman plays the hungry, vacuous Barbie to perfection.

TOM AND HUCK

Director: Peter Hewitt; **Writers:** Stephen Sommers and David Loughery; **Director of Photography:** Bobby Bukowski; **Editor:** David Freeman; **Music:** Stephen Endelman; **Production Designer:** Gemma Jackson; **Producers:** Laurence Mark and John Baldecchi
Buena Vista; PG; 93 minutes
Release: 12/95
Cast: Jonathan Taylor Thomas, Brad Renfro, Eric Schweig, Amy Wright and Rachael Leigh Cook
Based on *The Adventures of Tom Sawyer* by Mark Twain
Thomas sure knows how to charm. He knows exactly when to smile, flirt and roll his eyes for the camera. But the movie needed something more than charisma and cuteness. The script leaves Huck (Renfro) underdeveloped and almost ignored. A big mistake considering Renfro's talent. Tom (Thomas) and Huck see a murder and vow to keep their knowledge under wraps. When the wrong man is accused, Tom talks, fingering Injun Joe (Schweig) as the guilty party. Joe escapes from the courtroom and seeks revenge. A chase follows as does a predictable conclusion. Curiously, there's not one black character in the film.

TOTAL ECLIPSE

Director: Agnieszka Holland; **Writer:** Christopher Hampton; **Director of Photography:** Yourgos Arvanitis; **Editor:** Isabelle Lorente; **Production Designer:** Dan Weil; **Producer:** Jean-Pierre Ramsay
Fine Line; R; 110 minutes
Release: 11/95
Cast: Leonardo DiCaprio, David Thewlis, Romane Bohringer and Dominique Blanc
Based on Christopher Hampton's play
Holland tries to capture the brilliance and madness of French poet Arthur Rimbaud, and she nearly succeeds before losing continuity in the fights and love scenes. Both the loving and fighting involve Rimbaud (DiCaprio) and fellow poet Verlaine (Thewlis) as they try (successfully) to harm each other and Verlaine's wife, Mathilde (Bohringer).

To Wong Foo, Thanks for Everything, Julie Newmar

Director: Beeban Kidron; **Writer:** Douglas Carter Beane; **Director of Photography:** Steve Mason; **Editor:** Andrew Mondshein; **Music:** Rachel Portman; **Production Designer:** Wynn Thomas; **Producer:** G. Mac Brown
Universal Pictures; PG-13; 108 minutes
Release: 9/95
Cast: Wesley Snipes, Patrick Swayze, John Leguizamo, Stockard Channing, Chris Penn, Julie Newmar and Robin Williams
Transvestism must be big in Hollywood these days, if these three manly men had no problem doing the drag thing. In an obvious (and very bad) rip-off of *Priscilla, Queen of the Desert*, Noxeema (Snipes), Vida (Swayze) and Chi Chi (Leguizamo) road trip from New York to California for a fashion show. Their car breaks down in a small, unsophisticated town and the queens befriend and make over the residents.

Toy Story

Director: John Lasseter; **Writers:** Joss Whedon, Andrew Stanton, Joel Cohen and Alec Sokolow; **Supervising Technical Director:** William Reeves; **Supervising Animator:** Peter Docter; **Editors:** Robert Gordon and Lee Unkrich; **Music:** Randy Newman; **Producers:** Ralph Guggenheim and Bonnie Arnold
Walt Disney; G; 81 minutes
Release: 11/95
Voices of: Tom Hanks, Tim Allen, Don Rickles, Jim Varney, Wallace Shawn, John Ratzenberger, Annie Potts, John Morris, Erik Von Detten, Laurie Metcalf, R. Lee Ermey, Sarah Freeman and Penn Jillette
Based on the story by John Lasseter, Andrew Stanton, Pete Docter and Joe Ranft
Undeniably *the* technical and marketing success story of 1995. Sometimes kids' movies can seem more marketing tie-in than entertainment. *Toy Story* defies this expectation, and parents will probably take more pleasure in this clever film than their children. After all, Mr. Potato Head, Etch-a-Sketch and the Slinky are of *our* generation. Woody (voice of Hanks), a talking cowboy who is the head honcho in Andy's toy collection, senses he is about to be displaced on Andy's birthday. Sure enough, Andy's favorite gift is Buzz Lightyear (Allen), an astronaut, who assumes Woody's place on Andy's pillow. The technology (*Toy Story* is the first film to be entirely produced with computer animation) is so seamless that it is easy to forget that the characters are cartoons.

Trainspotting

Director: Danny Boyle; **Writer:** John Hodge; **Director of Photography:** Brian Tufano; **Editor:** Masahiro Hirakubo; **Production Designer:** Kave Quinn; **Producer:** Andrew MacDonald
Miramax Films; R; 94 minutes
Release: 7/96
Cast: Ewan McGregor, Ewen Bremner, Kevin McKidd, Robert Carlyle, Kelly Macdonald, Shirley Henderson and Johnny Lee Miller
Based on a novel by Irvine Welsh
With nearly as much shock value as *Kids* and as much sardonic, deadpan humor as *Delicatessen*, this new British hit is making noise across the globe. Following the hectic lives of young heroin addicts, *Trainspotting* has a rambunctious, anti-narrative quality. A disturbingly funny glimpse at a nihilistic subculture.

The Truth About Cats and Dogs

Director: Michael Lehmann; **Writer:** Audrey Wells; **Director of Photography:** Robert Brinkmann; **Editor:** Stephen Semel; **Music:** Howard Shore; **Production Designer:** Sharon Seymour; **Producer:** Cari-Esta Albert
Twentieth Century-Fox; PG-13; 96 minutes
Release: 4/96
Cast: Janeane Garofalo, Uma Thurman and Ben Chaplin
Brian (Chaplin) falls for pet advisor Abby (Garofalo) after calling in to her radio show. Abby, not comfortable with her physical appearance, describes her model neighbor Noelle (Thurman) instead of herself. Noelle, though beautiful, is not comfortable with her intelligence. Abby and Brian make a date, but Abby sends Noelle instead. Both fall for Brian, who doesn't really understand the charade. A charming modern Cyrano.

12 Monkeys

Director: Terry Gilliam; **Writers:** David Peoples and Janet Peoples; **Director of Photography:** Roger Pratt; **Editor:** Mick Audsley; **Music:** Paul Buckmaster; **Production Designer:** Jeffrey Beecroft; **Producer:** Charles Roven
Universal; R; 130 minutes
Release: 12/95
Cast: Bruce Willis, Brad Pitt, Madeleine Stowe and Christopher Plummer
Based on the 1962 film *La Jetee*
Gilliam, known for compelling, imaginative films such as Brazil and The Fisher King, has created

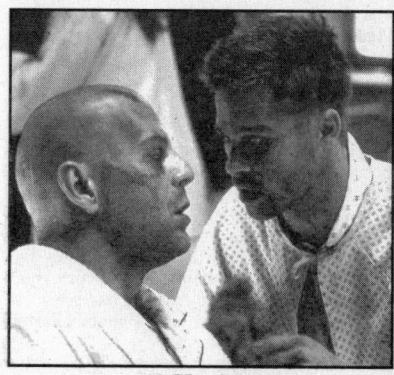

12 Monkeys

Twister

a post-apocalyptic sci-fi drama that is heavy on plot but leaner than his earlier offerings. Set in 2035 in a netherworld below Philadelphia, a group of crooked scientists want to know what caused a 1997 plague that wiped out 99 percent of the population. They send James Cole (Willis) back to 1997 to find out. The time travel apparatus is not perfect and Cole lands in a mental hospital in 1990, where he meets fellow patient Jeffrey Goines (Pitt) and psychiatrist Dr. Kathryn Railly (Stowe). Railly treats Cole and finds his warnings of doom at first normal behavior of a delusional man, but begins to believe him as his evidence becomes more conclusive. When Cole fails in his first mission, the scientists send him back again, this time successfully, and Cole is reunited with Railly and Goines, now the leader of the 12 Monkeys, an underground animal-rights group. A richly layered plot that manages to avoid being overwhelming.

TWISTER

Director: Jan de Bont; **Writers:** Michael Crichton and Anne-Marie Martin; **Director of Photography:** Jack N. Green; **Editor:** Michael Kahn; **Music:** Mark Mancina; **Production Designer:** Joseph Nemec III; **Producers:** Kathleen Kennedy, Ian Bryce and Michael Crichton
Warner Bros.; PG-13; 105 minutes
Release: 5/96
Cast: Helen Hunt, Bill Paxton, Jami Gertz, Lois Smith, Cary Elwes, Alan Ruck, Jeremy Davies, Joey Soltnick and Philip Seymour Hoffman
This is not a film, it's an amusement-park ride — lots of fun and excitement, though lacking in substance. While the effects and the sound blow you right out of your seat, the dialogue is silly. But who cares when a cow flies and a tanker truck falls from the sky. There are even bad scientists racing to beat tornado chasers Hunt and Paxton to the punch (or better, the eye of the storm). How can you tell they're bad guys? They drive sleek black vans while the good guys drive a red rig. A great kick-off to the summer movie season.

TWO BITS

Director: James Foley; **Writer:** Joseph Stefano; **Director of Photography:** Juan Ruiz-Anchia; **Editor:** Howard Smith; **Music:** Carter Burwell; **Production Designer:** Jane Musky; **Producer:** Arthur Cohn
Miramax; PG-13; 93 minutes
Release: 11/95
Cast: Al Pacino, Mary Elizabeth Mastrantonio and Jerry Barone
Narration: Alec Baldwin
On his deathbed, Grandpa (Pacino) promises to will his grandson Gennaro (Barone) a quarter to see a film in South Philadelphia's new air-conditioned movie palace. Gennaro can't wait for his inheritance, so he hits the streets and tries to earn the admission himself, experiencing some of life's lessons. An adult Gennaro (voice of Baldwin) recalls this Depression-era coming-of-age story and his grandfather's words of wisdom.

TWO DEATHS

Director: Nicolas Roeg; **Writer:** Allan Scott; **Director of Photography:** Witold Stok; **Editor:** Tony Lawson; **Music:** Hans Zimmer; **Production Designer:** Don Taylor; **Producers:** Carolyn Montagu and Luc Roeg
Castle Hill Productions; R; 102 minutes
Release: 5/96
Cast: Michael Gambon, Sonia Braga, Nickolas Grace, Patrick Malahide and John Shrapnel
A disturbing allegory of political oppression and sexual obsession. Set in an Eastern European country in the early days of perestroika, surgeon Daniel Pavenic (Gambon) hosts an elaborate dinner for friends while a bloody battle heats up on the streets outside his window. Cutting between the two scenes, Pavenic and his guests discuss their sexual obsessions, with Pavenic detailing his lust for his housekeeper (Braga) as she serves the meal.

TWO FRIENDS

Director: Jane Campion; **Writer:** Helen Garner; **Director of Photography:** Julian Penney; **Editor:** Bill Russo; **Music:** Martin Armiger; **Producer:** Jan Chapman
Milestone Films; NR; 76 minutes
Release: 4/96
Cast: Emma Coles, Kris Bidenko, Kris McQuade, Stephen Leeder and Debra May
Made in 1986, *Two Friends* is a melancholic, bleak look at friendship in a dreary, middle-class town on the outskirts of Sydney, Australia. The film accurately portrays the discomfort, confusion and unbridled anxiety of adolescence. Though not as technically solid as Campion's more recent films, *Two Friends* has its moments of cinematic genius; toward the end it boldly plunges into surrealism, mixing sped-up action and jumbled subtitles into a cinematic collage.

TWO IF BY SEA

Director: Bill Bennett; **Writers:** Denis Leary, Ann Lembeck and Mike Armstrong; **Director of Photography:** Andrew Lesnie; **Editor:** Bruce Green; **Music:** Nick Glennie-Smith and Paddy Moloney; **Production Designer:** David Chapman II; **Producers:** James G. Robinson and Michael MacDonald
Warner Bros.; R; 95 minutes
Release: 1/96
Cast: Sandra Bullock, Denis Leary, Stephen Dillane, Yaphet Kotto, Mike Starr, Jonathan Tucker, Wayne Robson, Michael Badalucco and Lenny Clarke
Softening his persona from his *No Cure for Cancer* stand-up act and his roles in *Demolition Man* and *The Ref*, Leary reemerges as a dimwitted thief who's really a marshmallow at heart. However, in writing the screenplay, Leary created a character too soft for his own good, and he struggles with his tough-guy persona. Bullock shines as his smart-cookie girlfriend, who keeps getting him out of jams and saving him from jail. The rest is fairly predictable romantic comedy, but the leads — Leary included — keep it from sinking.

TWO MUCH

Director: Fernando Trueba; **Writers:** Fernando and David Trueba; **Director of Photography:** Jose Luis Alcaine; **Editor:** Nena Bernard; **Music:** Michel Camilo; **Production Designer:** Juan Botella; **Producer:** Cristina Huete
Buena Vista; PG-13; 118 minutes
Release: 3/96
Cast: Antonio Banderas, Melanie Griffith, Daryl Hannah, Danny Aiello, Joan Cusack, Eli Wallach and Austin Pendleton
Based on the novel by Donald E. Westlake
The title could be referring to the exposure of Banderas and his new wife, Griffith. Maybe this movie will help push them out of the limelight for a while. Art (Banderas) poses as two different men to juggle relationships with two sisters, dim bombshell Betty (Griffith) and the less dim Liz (Hannah).

UNSTRUNG HEROES

Director: Diane Keaton; **Writer:** Richard LaGravenese; **Director of Photography:** Phedon Papamichael; **Editor:** Lisa Churgin; **Music:** Thomas Newman; **Production Designer:** Garreth Stover; **Producers:** Susan Arnold, Donna Roth and Bill Badalato
Hollywood Pictures; PG; 93 minutes
Release: 9/95
Cast: Andie MacDowell, John Turturro, Michael Richards, Maury Chaykin, Nathan Watt
Based on the book by Franz Lidz
A touching story of perseverance and strength from unlikely sources. Illness intrudes on a family blessed with a whimsical love of life. When his adored mother (MacDowell) is diagnosed with cancer and his inventor father (Turturro) succumbs to grief, young Steven (Watt) seeks solace with his two eccentric uncles. Not as grim as the storyline might indicate, *Unstrung Heroes* shines with warmth and genuine human feeling, a credit to Keaton and the adaptation of LaGravenese.

UP CLOSE AND PERSONAL

Director: Jon Avnet; **Writer:** Joan Didion and John Gregory Dunne; **Director of Photography:** Karl Walter Lindenlaub; **Editor:** Debra Neil-Fisher; **Music:** Thomas Newman; **Production Designer:** Jeremy Conway; **Producers:** Jon Avnet, David Nicksay and Jordan Kerner
Touchstone; PG-13; 124 minutes
Release: 3/96
Cast: Robert Redford, Michelle Pfeiffer, Stockard Channing, Joe Mantegna, Kate Nelligan and Glenn Plummer
The playful chemistry between Redford and Pfeiffer goes a long way to make this schmaltzy newsroom romance work. Warren Justice (Redford) turns his Svengali charms on fledgling talent Tally Atwater (Pfeiffer) and fashions her into an on-air sensation. While real-life news veterans scoff at how far Tally actually gets with a sound bite and a smile, the sparks between the muse and her maker lift the film above its more tedious moments. Solid supporting performances from Channing and Nelligan round out the film's guilty-pleasure quotient. Remotely inspired by Jessica Savitch's rise to TV-news stardom.

VAMPIRE IN BROOKLYN

Director: Wes Craven; **Writers:** Charles Murphy, Michael Lucker and Christopher Parker; **Director of Photography:** Mark Irwin; **Editor:** Patrick Lussier; **Music:** J. Peter Robinson; **Producers:** Eddie Murphy and Mark Lipsky
Paramount; R; 103 minutes
Release: 10/95
Cast: Eddie Murphy, Angela Bassett, Allen Payne, Kadeem Hardison, John Witherspoon and Zakes Mokae
Based on a story by Eddie Murphy, Charles Murphy and Vernon Lynch, Jr.
Before *The Nutty Professor*, Murphy just couldn't seem to find a script that did his talent justice. *Vampire* had potential, especially with Craven helming. Vampire Maximillian (Murphy) leaves Africa for Brooklyn, where he searches for a woman who is half vampire. He finds her in cop Rita (Bassett). Maximillian faces the challenge of luring her away from her partner and love interest, Justice (Payne). The laughs are few and far between.

VUKOVAR

Director: Boro Draskovic; **Writers:** Maja Draskovic and Boro Draskovic; **Director of Photography:** Aleksandar Petkovic; **Editor:** Snezana Ivanovic; **Producer:** Danka Muzdeka Mandzuka
Tara Releasing; NR; 94 minutes

Release: 2/96
Cast: Mirjana Jokovic, Boris Isakovic, Monica Romic, Nebojsa Glogovac and Svetlana Bojkovic
In Serbo-Croatian with English subtitles
This depressing antiwar film set in Yugoslavia tries hard to be objective, but in doing so it fails to develop a point of view and so seems cold and uncaring. Croat Anna (Jokovic) and Serb Toma (Isakovic) have only days to enjoy their wedded bliss before Toma is drafted into the Serbian army and sent to fight in the civil war. Anna, pregnant, barely scrapes by in hiding. Though a nonpartisan film, the Croat government banned a United Nations screening of the film, calling it "pro-Serbian propaganda."

WAITING TO EXHALE

Director: Forest Whitaker; **Writers:** Terry McMillan and Ronald Bass; **Director of Photography:** Toyomichi Kurita; **Editor:** Richard Chew; **Music:** Babyface; **Production Designer:** David Gropman; **Producers:** Ezra Swerdlow and Deborah Schindler
Twentieth Century-Fox; R; 120 minutes
Release: 12/95
Cast: Whitney Houston, Angela Bassett, Loretta Devine, Lela Rochon, Gregory Hines, Dennis Haysbert, Mykelti Williamson and Michael Beach
Based on the novel by Terry McMillan
The soundtrack to *Waiting to Exhale* received more pre-release publicity than the film itself and the attention was well deserved. The recording features Houston, Aretha Franklin, Toni Braxton and others, all of whom give peak performances. The music in the film provides more than a pleasant background; it serves as a Greek chorus to the four women dealing with their men and the problems they pose. Each of the women is successful in her career but in a state of flux when it comes to love. Savannah (Houston) can't decide if she should continue an affair with a married man; Bernadine (Bassett) has been dumped by her husband for his bookkeeper; Robin (Rochon) keeps picking the wrong man; and Gloria (Devine), recently separated from her bisexual husband, has hope for her developing relationship with Marvin (Hines). A fine directing debut for Whitaker that became a cultural phenomenon and surprise hit.

WALKING AND TALKING

Director/Writer: Nicole Holofcener; **Director of Photography:** Michael Spiller; **Editor:** Alisa Lepselter; **Music:** Billy Bragg; **Production Designer:** Anne Stuhler; **Producers:** Ted Hope and James Schamus
Miramax; NR; 90 minutes
Release: 3/96
Cast: Catherine Keener, Anne Heche, Liev Schreiber, Todd Field, Joseph Siravo, Kevin Corrigan and Randall Batinkoff
Not too much to this light date movie, but enjoyably neurotic all the same. Laura (Heche), upon accepting Frank's (Field) marriage proposal, worries about what her best friend, Amelia (Keener), will say. As the wedding approaches, Laura, training to be a therapist, grows increasingly anxious about the big day, while Amelia tries to get her own screwball love life together.

WELCOME TO THE DOLLHOUSE

Director/Writer: Todd Solondz; **Director of Photography:** Randy Drummond; **Editor:** Alan Oxman; **Music:** Jill Wisoff; **Production Designer:** Susan Block; **Producers:** Ted Skillman and Todd Solondz
Sony Pictures Classics; NR; 87 minutes
Release: 3/96
Cast: Heather Matarazzo, Eric Mabius, Brendan Sexton, Jr., Daria Kalinina, Angela Pietropinto and Matthew Faber
Everyone remembers those middle-school years. You were either always picked on by *everyone*, or you were one of the tormentors. Many of us can sympathize with 11-year-old Dawn Weiner (Matarazzo), the awkward, poorly dressed, bespectacled seventh grader who is the butt of her classmates' cruelty. Weiner falls for high-school hunk Steve Rodgers (Mabius), with heartbreakingly predictable results. Matarazzo provides an uncanny performance, but Solondz seems to change the point of view toward the characters, sending Weiner on a surreal wild goose chase. The film earned him the Grand Jury Prize at the 1996 Sundance Film Festival.

WHEN NIGHT IS FALLING

Director/Writer: Patricia Rozema; **Director of Photography:** Douglas Koch; **Editors:** Susan Shipton and Paul Bettis; **Music:** Lesley Barber; **Production Designer:** John Dondertman; **Producer:** Barbara Tranter
October Films; NR; 96 minutes
Release: 11/95
Cast: Pascale Bussières, Rachael Crawford, Henry Czerny and David Fox
Joining the circus was never like this. Camille (Bussières) and Martin (Czerny) are lovers and philosophy professors at a Calvinist college in Toronto. They've been asked by the school chaplain (Fox) to replace him as he retires, but they'll have to be married and approved by the board. It's not as easy as it sounds. Petra (Crawford), a lesbian circus performer, pursues Camille and eventually wins her affections. The MPAA rated *When Night Is Falling* NC-17, and October Films opted to distribute it without a rating.

THE WHITE BALLOON

Director/Editor/Producer: Jafar Panahi; **Writer:** Abbas Kiarostami; **Director of Photography:** Farzad Judat
October Films; NR; 85 minutes
Release: 2/96
Cast: Aida Mohammadkhani, Mohsen Kalifi, Fereshteh Sadr Orfani, Anna Bourkowska,

Mohammad Shahani and Mohammad Bahktiari
In Farsi with English subtitles
A big film with a thin plot. An hour-and-a-half before the new year, a young Iranian girl Razieh (Mohammadkhani) decides she wants a new goldfish for the event. She cajoles the money from her mother but loses it on her way to the store. The film progresses in real time, following Razieh as she urges strangers to help her retrieve the lost currency. A dramatic look at human nature as the film examines an entire community through a series of brief encounters.

WHITE MAN'S BURDEN

Director/Writer: Desmond Nakano; **Director of Photography:** Willy Kurant; **Production Designer:** Naomi Shohan; **Music:** Howard Shore; **Producer:** Lawrence Bender
Savoy Pictures; R; 96 minutes
Release: 12/95
Cast: John Travolta, Harry Belafonte, Kelly Lynch, Margaret Avery and Tom Bower
This didactic political film seems afraid to offend and, as a result, it does not develop its main premise: race relations viewed in reverse. White factory worker Louis Pinnock (Travolta) loses his job and his home after a misunderstanding at work. Pinnock becomes unraveled and kidnaps Thaddeus Thomas (Belafonte), the wealthy black man who caused his firing. In their travels, Pinnock and Thomas encounter white armed skinheads and black racist cops. Travolta agreed to star in this film before *Pulp Fiction* redefined his career.

WHITE SQUALL

Director: Ridley Scott; **Writer:** Todd Robinson; **Director of Photography:** Hugh Johnson; **Editor:** Gerry Hambling; **Music:** Jeff Rona; **Production Designers:** Peter J. Hampton and Leslie Tomkins; **Producers:** Mimi Polk Gitlin and Rocky Lang
Hollywood Pictures; PG-13; 128 minutes
Release: 2/96
Cast: Jeff Bridges, Caroline Goodall, John Savage, Scott Wolf, Jeremy Sisto, Julio Mechoso, Balthazar Getty and Ethan Embry
Skip the first hour and a half, and the film is worth a watch. A group of schoolboys grow up quickly while aboard the *Albatross* under the command of Christopher Sheldon (Bridges), their teacher and a skipper who believes in tough love. Nothing much of interest happens until the boys and their teachers battle the white squall, a hurricane that provides some of the best action seen in an oceangoing film.

WILD BILL

Director/Writer: Walter Hill; **Director of Photography:** Lloyd Ahern; **Editor:** Freeman Davies; **Music:** Van Dyke Parks; **Production Designer:** Joseph Nemec III; **Producers:** Richard D. Zanuck and Lili Fini Zanuck
United Artists; R; 97 minutes
Release: 12/95
Cast: Jeff Bridges, Ellen Barkin, Diane Lane, David Arquette, John Hurt, Marjoe Gortner, James Remar, Bruce Dern, Keith Carradine and Christina Applegate
Based on the novel *Deadwood* by Pete Dexter and the play *Father and Sons* by Thomas Babe
Hill turns in another fantastic revisionist Western, this time focusing on Wild Bill Hickok (Bridges). He's wild, he's crazy, and on his deathbed he's wondering how it all went wrong. There's no myth to the West; it's about one man, a loser, who rose to the top with a deadly talent, and morals that eventually broke him.

WORLD AND TIME ENOUGH

Director/Writer: Eric Mueller; **Director of Photography:** Kyle Bergersen; **Editor:** Laura Stokes; **Music:** Eugene Huddleston; **Production Designer:** Heather McElhatton; **Producers:** Julie Hartley and Andrew Peterson
Strand Releasing; NR; 90 minutes
Release: 9/95
Cast: Matt Guidry, Gregory G. Giles, Kraig Swartz, Peter Macon and Bernadette Sullivan
Garbage collector Joey (Giles) comes out to his parents by telling them he is bringing his girl-friend home for Thanksgiving dinner and arrives at the door with HIV-positive Mark (Guidry). That scene is the only entertaining one in a movie overloaded with maudlin emotion that mainly involves Mark and his dead parents.

THE YOUNG POISONER'S HANDBOOK

Director: Benjamin Ross; **Writers:** Jeff Rawle and Benjamin Ross; **Director of Photography:** Hubert Taczanowski; **Editor:** Anne Sopel; **Production Designer:** Maria Djurkovic; **Producer:** Sam Taylor
Touchstone; PG-13; 92 minutes
Release: 2/96
Cast: Hugh O'Conor, Antony Sher, Ruth Sheen, Charlotte Coleman, Roger Lloyd Pack and Paul Stacey
Based on the real-life exploits of Graham Young, the wee lad (O'Conor) dominated British tabloids in the 1970s by poisoning friends and loved ones with the teacup and the crumpet. Yet instead of morbidity, the film ends up being sweet, á la *Harold and Maude*.

1995 Academy Awards®

The 68th Annual Academy Awards were presented on March 25, 1996, at Los Angeles's Dorothy Chandler Pavilion.

Braveheart

BEST PICTURE
Apollo 13, Brian Grazer, producer (Universal)

Babe, George Miller, Doug Mitchell and Bill Miller, producers (Universal)

***Braveheart,* Mel Gibson, Alan Ladd, Jr. and Bruce Davey, producers (Paramount)**

The Postman (Il Postino), Mario and Vittorio Cecchi Gori and Gaetano Daniele, producers (Miramax)

Sense and Sensibility, Lindsay Doran, producer (Columbia)

ACTOR IN A LEADING ROLE
Nicolas Cage, *Leaving Las Vegas*

Richard Dreyfuss, *Mr. Holland's Opus*

Anthony Hopkins, *Nixon*

Sean Penn, *Dead Man Walking*

Massimo Troisi, *The Postman (Il Postino)*

ACTRESS IN A LEADING ROLE
Susan Sarandon, *Dead Man Walking*

Elisabeth Shue, *Leaving Las Vegas*

Sharon Stone, *Casino*

Meryl Streep, *The Bridges of Madison County*

Emma Thompson, *Sense and Sensibility*

ACTOR IN A SUPPORTING ROLE
James Cromwell, *Babe*

Ed Harris, *Apollo 13*

Brad Pitt, *12 Monkeys*

Tim Roth, *Rob Roy*

Kevin Spacey, *The Usual Suspects*

ACTRESS IN A SUPPORTING ROLE
Joan Allen, *Nixon*

Kathleen Quinlan, *Apollo 13*

Mira Sorvino, *Mighty Aphrodite*

Mare Winningham, *Georgia*

Kate Winslet, *Sense and Sensibility*

DIRECTING
Mike Figgis, *Leaving Las Vegas*

Mel Gibson, *Braveheart*

Chris Noonan, *Babe*

Michael Radford, *The Postman (Il Postino)*

Tim Robbins, *Dead Man Walking*

WRITING
SCREENPLAY WRITTEN DIRECTLY FOR THE SCREEN
Woody Allen, *Mighty Aphrodite*

Christopher McQuarrie, *The Usual Suspects*

Stephen J. Rivele, Christopher Wilkinson and Oliver Stone, *Nixon*

Randall Wallace, *Braveheart*

Joss Whedon, Andrew Stanton, Joel Cohen and Alec Sokolow, *Toy Story*

SCREENPLAY BASED ON MATERIAL PREVIOUSLY PRODUCED OR PUBLISHED

William Broyles, Jr. and Al Reinert, *Apollo 13*

Mike Figgis, *Leaving Las Vegas*

George Miller and Chris Noonan, *Babe*

Anna Pavignano, Michael Radford, Furio Scarpelli, Giacomo Scarpelli and Massimo Troisi, *The Postman (Il Postino)*

Emma Thompson, *Sense and Sensibility*

CINEMATOGRAPHY

Michael Coulter, *Sense and Sensibility*

Stephen Goldblatt, *Batman Forever*

Emmanuel Lubezki, *A Little Princess*

John Toll, *Braveheart*

Lu Yue, *Shanghai Triad*

ART DIRECTION

Tony Burrough, art direction, *Richard III*

Michael Corenblith, art direction; Merideth Boswell, set decoration, *Apollo 13*

Roger Ford, art direction; Kerrie Brown, set decoration, *Babe*

Bo Welch, art direction; Cheryl Carasik, set decoration, *A Little Princess*

Eugenio Zanetti, art direction, *Restoration*

SOUND

Rick Dior, Steve Pederson, Scott Millan and David MacMillan, *Apollo 13*

Donald O. Mitchell, Frank A. Montaño, Michael Herbick and Petur Hliddal, *Batman Forever*

Steve Maslow, Gregg Landaker and Keith A. Wester, *Waterworld*

Andy Nelson, Scott Millan, Anna Behlmer and Brian Simmons, *Braveheart*

Kevin O'Connell, Rick Kline, Gregory H. Watkins and William B. Kaplan, *Crimson Tide*

MUSIC

SONG

"Colors of the Wind," *Pocahontas,* Alan Menken, music; Stephen Schwartz, lyrics

"Dead Man Walkin'," *Dead Man Walking,* Bruce Springsteen, music and lyrics

"Have You Ever Really Loved a Woman," *Don Juan DeMarco,* Michael Kamen, Bryan Adams and Robert John Lange, music and lyrics

"Moonlight," *Sabrina,* John Williams, music; Alan and Marilyn Bergman, lyrics

"You've Got a Friend in Me," *Toy Story,* Randy Newman, music and lyrics

ORIGINAL SCORE

James Horner, *Apollo 13*

James Horner, *Braveheart*

John Williams, *Nixon*

Luis Bacalov, *The Postman (Il Postino)*

Patrick Doyle, *Sense and Sensibility*

ORIGINAL MUSICAL OR COMEDY SCORE

Marc Shaiman, *The American President*

Alan Menken, music; Stephen Schwartz, lyrics, *Pocahontas*

John Williams, *Sabrina*

Randy Newman, *Toy Story*

Thomas Newman, *Unstrung Heroes*

FILM EDITING

Marcus D'Arcy and Jay Friedkin, *Babe*

Richard Francis-Bruce, *Seven*

Mike Hill and Dan Hanley, *Apollo 13*

Chris Lebenzon, *Crimson Tide*

Steven Rosenblum, *Braveheart*

COSTUME DESIGN

James Acheson, *Restoration*

Jenny Beavan and John Bright, *Sense and Sensibility*

Shuna Harwood, *Richard III*

Charles Knode, *Braveheart*

Julie Weiss, *12 Monkeys*

MAKEUP

Ken Diaz and Mark Sanchez, *My Family: Mi Familia*

Greg Cannom, Bob Laden and Colleen Callaghan, *Roommates*

Peter Frampton, Paul Pattison and Lois Burwell, *Braveheart*

Nicolas Cage, *Leaving Las Vegas*

VISUAL EFFECTS

Scott E. Anderson, Charles Gibson, Neal Scanlan and John Cox, *Babe*

Robert Legato, Michael Kanfer, Leslie Ekker and Matt Sweeney, *Apollo 13*

SOUND EFFECTS EDITING

Lon Bender and Per Hallberg, *Braveheart*

John Leveque and Bruce Stambler, *Batman Forever*

George Watters II, *Crimson Tide*

SHORT FILMS

ANIMATION

The Chicken From Outerspace (John R. Dilworth, producer; Cartoons, Inc./Cartoon Network Production)

***A Close Shave* (Nick Park, producer; Aardman Animations Production)**

the end (Chris Landreth and Robin Bargar, producers; Alias/Wavefront Production)

Gagarin (Alexij Kharitidi, producer; Second Frog Animation Group Production)

Runaway Brain (Chris Bailey, producer; Walt Disney Pictures Production)

LIVE ACTION

Brooms (Luke Cresswell and Steve McNicholas, producers; Yes/No Production)

Duke of Groove (Griffin Dunne and Thom Colwell, producers; Chanticleer Films Production)

***Lieberman in Love* (Christine Lahti and Jana Sue Memel, producers; Chanticleer Films Production)**

Little Surprises (Jeff Goldblum and Tikki Boldberg, producers; Chanticleer Films Production)

Tuesday Morning Ride (Dianne Houston and Joy Ryan, producers; Chanticleer Films Production)

DOCUMENTARY

SHORT SUBJECT

Jim Dine: A Self-Portrait on the Walls (Nancy Dine and Richard Stilwell, producers; Outside in July, Inc. Production)

The Living Sea (Greg MacGillivray and Alec Lorimore, producers; MacGillivray Freeman Films Production)

Never Give Up: The 20th-Century Odyssey of Herbert Zipper (Terry Sanders and Freida Lee Mock, producers; American Film Foundation Production)

***One Survivor Remembers* (Kary Antholis, producer; Home Box Office and The United States Holocaust Memorial Museum Production)**

The Shadow of Hate (Charles Guggenheim, producer; Guggenheim Productions, Inc. Production)

FEATURE

***Anne Frank Remembered* (Jon Blair, producer; Jon Blair Film Company Limited Production)**

The Battle Over Citizen Kane (Thomas Lennon and Michael Epstein, producers; Lennon Documentary Group Production)

Fiddlefest: Roberta Tzavaras and Her East Harlem Violin Program (Allan Miller and Walter Scheuer, producers; Four Oaks Foundation Production)

Hank Aaron: Chasing the Dream (Mike Tollin and Fredric Golding, producers; Turner Original Production)

Troublesome Creek: A Midwestern (Jeanne Jordan and Steven Ascher, producers; West City Films, Inc. Production)

FOREIGN LANGUAGE FILM

All Things Fair, Sweden

***Antonia's Line*, The Netherlands**

Dust of Life, Algeria

O Quatrilho, Brazil

The Star Maker, Italy

GORDON E. SAWYER AWARD

Donald C. Rogers for "exceptional long-term accomplishments by an individual who has made substantial contributions toward the advancement of the science and technology of the motion picture"

SPECIAL ACHIEVEMENT AWARD

John Lasseter for the development and application of techniques that made possible the first feature-length computer-animated film

HONORARY AWARDS

Kirk Douglas for "50 years as a creative and moral force in the motion-picture community"

Chuck Jones for "the creation of classic cartoons and cartoon characters whose animated lives have brought joy to our real ones for more than half a century"

Kirk Douglas

Oscar's Big Night

■ BY BETH ROWEN

TASTEFUL. OVER-THE-TOP. SUBTLE. CHEESY. An odd selection of words to group together. Even stranger is that they describe the 68th annual Oscarcast. Tasteful works for the big picture. Over-the-top captures the emotional tributes. Subtle fits the stars' attire (this has to be a first). And cheesy belongs with the fashion show.

Overall, it was an uneventful evening — save for a few moving moments when emotions ran high. Christopher Reeve brought the audience to its feet with his introduction to a montage of socially compelling films. As did Miep Gies, who discovered Anne Frank's diary and was honored when *Anne Frank Remembered* won the Feature Documentary Oscar. Perhaps Paul Sorvino set the tone early on when he wept uncontrollably when his daughter, Mira, got the nod for Actress in a Supporting Role for *Mighty Aphrodite*. We saw that coming — he cried when she won the Golden Globe.

Whoopi Goldberg

There weren't many surprises or eyebrow raisers. Oh sure, we hoped, but did anyone think *Babe* really had a chance? Even Jesse Jackson toned down his outrage and, at the advice of producer Quincy Jones and Oprah Winfrey, abandoned plans to protest outside the venue, the Dorothy Chandler Pavilion. Instead, he and about 80 others picketed KABC, the local affiliate covering the ceremony. Jackson's outrage stemmed from the fact that only one African American, Dianne Houston, was nominated for an Academy Award. Houston received a nomination for her work in the short film *Tuesday Morning Ride*.

Jones compensated for the lack of African American representation by bookending the ceremony with Winfrey greeting guests as they arrived and Sidney Poitier presenting the Oscar for Best Picture, the last award of the evening. Host Whoopi Goldberg certainly helped the Academy defend itself against Jackson's charges. Still, there were several deserving African Americans who were overlooked on February 13 when the nominees were announced: Delroy Lindo, Laurence Fishburne, Spike Lee, Angela Bassett and Whitney Houston (for her soundtrack, not performance, in *Waiting to Exhale*).

Goldberg was a marked improvement over last year's host, David Letterman, and did not provide the equivalent of his "Umaaa, Opraaah" fiasco for critics to feast on the next day. She started with a bang, railing on outspoken Hollywood critic Bob Dole (who had to have been pleased with this year's Best Picture nominees), Pat Buchanan, whom she referred to as "the original boy in the hood" and the disastrous *Showgirls*, about which she deadpanned, "I haven't seen that many poles mistreated since World War II."

She even lashed out at Jackson. After she recognized the social causes represented by a panoply of symbolic ribbons she could have worn, she said, "I have something I want to say to Jesse right here, but he's not watching, so why bother?"

But Goldberg seemed to lose steam as the night progressed and her jokes, few and far between, fell flat. The stars didn't give her much fodder: For the most part, they behaved. Even Sharon Stone, who one-upped the who's-wearing-what-by-whom fashion police by mixing from

Part of the enjoyment of Hollywood's annual celebration of itself is imagining the outcome of the voting if the only vote that mattered was yours. The editors of *The Entertainment Almanac,* with the assistance of several contributing film writers and filmmakers, got together and argued, cajoled and orated in order to craft the list below.

Best Picture
Babe

Best Actor
Sean Penn, *Dead Man Walking*

Best Actress
Nicole Kidman, *To Die For*

Best Supporting Actor
Morgan Freeman, *Seven*

Morgan Freeman, *Seven*

Best Supporting Actress
Joan Allen, *Nixon*

Best Director
Bryan Singer, *The Usual Suspects*

Best Foreign Language Film
Shanghai Triad, China

Best Documentary
Crumb

her own closet and the Gap, was composed when the envelope with the winner for Best Dramatic Score was not at the podium. In a clever ad-lib, she united the audience for a "psychic moment" and turned what could have been a few agonizingly long seconds into one of the evening's unexpected high points.

That's not to say the night was free of fools. Jim Carrey left many wondering if he truly deserves to be the $20-million man. Does anyone know what Steven Seagal was rambling about? And, yes, while we realize she is only a puppet, Miss Piggy was pretty annoying with her *Babe* jokes.

On the fashion watch, shimmery pastel slip dresses were by far the most conspicuous trend. Armani dressed Sorvino in hers and Vera Wang

Sharon Stone

provided Mare Winningham's. Only a handful went for the ballgown look. Susan Sarandon was one of them, but pulled it off elegantly, even when her earrings broke en route. (By the way, which came first, the hair color or the dress? A new fad?) Our pick for best attired? Rita Wilson's blackwith-silver beads number from Armani.

But this year, the star parade down the pavilion's red carpet was unfortunately not enough of a fashion show for Oscar. In a creative yet ridiculous twist, the nominees for Best Costume Design — even the bulky space suits from *12 Monkeys* — were presented runway style by first-name-only models. If ever there was a moment when we collectively wished for the Supermodel fascination to die, this was it.

Aside from this example of errant bad taste, Oscar once again played it safe — a smidgeon of controversy, a handful of tacky gowns, a few high-falutin acceptance speeches and only two production numbers — giving us barely enough spectacle and surprise to gossip about the next day. ∎

Variety's 1995 Domestic Box Office

Variety magazine tracked the box-office gross of more than 450 films released domestically in 1995. Here are the films that earned more than $150,000.

Toy Story

Batman Forever (Warner Bros.)................$184,031,112

Apollo 13 (Universal) 172, 071,312

Toy Story (Buena Vista) 146,198,683

Pocahontas (Buena Vista)...........................141,523,195

Ace Ventura: When Nature Calls................104,194,467
  (Warner Bros.)

Casper (Universal) 100,328,194

Die Hard With a Vengeance 100,012,499
  (Twentieth Century-Fox)

Goldeneye (MGM/UA)...................................92,436,092

Crimson Tide (Buena Vista) 91,387,195

Waterworld (Universal) 88,246,220

Seven (New Line) 87,034,954

Dangerous Minds (Buena Vista) 84,211,543

While You Were Sleeping (Buena Vista) 81,057,016

Congo (Paramount)..81,022,333

Mortal Kombat (New Line)............................70,360,285

The Bridges of Madison County 70,112,709
  (Warner Bros.)

Nine Months (Twentieth Century-Fox).........69,690,778

Get Shorty (MGM/UA)...................................68,645,723

Outbreak (Warner Bros.) 67,823,573

Braveheart (Paramount)................................67,018,197

Bad Boys (Sony) 65,807,024

Species (MGM/UA) 60,054,449

Babe (Universal) 56,737,040

Clueless (Paramount)....................................$56,436,496

Jumanji (Sony)...53,745,261

Something to Talk About (Warner Bros.).....50,892,160

The Net (Sony) 50,727,965

The American President (Sony) 50,305,552

Under Siege 2: Dark Territory.......................50,024,083
  (Warner Bros.)

A Walk in the Clouds.....................................50,012,507
  (Twentieth Century-Fox)

Father of the Bride Part II (Buena Vista) 49,881,012

The Brady Bunch Movie (Paramount) 46,576,136

Man of the House (Buena Vista)...................40,070,995

French Kiss (Twentieth Century-Fox) 38,896,854

Higher Learning (Sony) 38,290,723

Mighty Morphin Power Rangers...................37,804,616
  (Twentieth Century-Fox)

First Knight (Sony) 37,600,435

Casino (Universal)..37,127,510

Just Cause (Warner Bros.) 36,853,222

To Wong Foo, Thanks for Everything,..........36,475,691
  Julie Newmar (Universal)

The Indian in the Cupboard (Paramount) 35,617,599

A Goofy Movie (Buena Vista) 35,348,597

Judge Dredd (Buena Vista)...........................34,693,581

Heat (Warner Bros.) 34,493,095

Get Shorty

Money Train (Sony) $34,461,327

Waiting to Exhale 33,356,203
  (Twentieth Century-Fox)

Forget Paris (Sony) 33,194,512

Tommy Boy (Paramount) 32,680,208

Rob Roy (MGM/UA) 31,596,468

Copycat (Warner Bros.) 31,203,644

Free Willy 2 (Warner Bros.) 30,077,111

Powder (Buena Vista) 29,768,475

Major Payne (Universal)..............................29,412,050

Assassins (Warner Bros.) 29,339,122

Sabrina (Paramount) 28,841,220

Grumpier Old Men (Warner Bros.) 28,004,723

Friday (New Line)..27,467,564

Now and Then (New Line) 26,342,995

Houseguest (Buena Vista)...........................26,325,256

Desperado (Sony) 25,625,110

Billy Madison (Universal) 25,588,734

Operation Dumbo Drop (Buena Vista)..........24,667,779

Dolores Claiborne (Sony) 24,361,867

Virtuosity (Paramount) 24,047,246

Dead Presidents (Buena Vista) 24,021,125

How to Make an American Quilt 23,574,130
  (Universal)

Boys on the Side (Warner Bros.)..................23,440,188

Circle of Friends (Savoy) 23,397,365

The Usual Suspects (Gramercy) 22,878,463

Don Juan DeMarco (New Line) 22,080,619

Tales From the Crypt: Demon Knight............21,088,568
  (Universal)

To Die For (Sony)..20,905,881

Showgirls (MGM/UA) 20,302,961

Johnny Mnemonic (Sony/Alliance) 19,075,720

Vampire in Brooklyn (Paramount).................19,031,346

The Quick and the Dead (Sony) 18,636,537

The Big Green (Buena Vista) 17,725,519

Heavyweights (Buena Vista).........................17,689,177

It Takes Two (Warner Bros.) 17,447,907

Murder in the First (Warner Bros.)...............17,381,942

Home for the Holidays (Paramount).............17,237,852

Jury Duty (Sony) 17,014,653

The Prophecy (Miramax)...............................16,115,878

Devil in a Blue Dress (Sony) 16,030,096

Mad Love (Buena Vista) 15,453,274

Muriel's Wedding (Miramax) 15,185,594

The Madness of King George (Goldwyn) 15,180,852

Unstrung Heroes

Halloween: The Curse of Michael Myers $15,126,948
  (Miramax)

Kiss of Death (Twentieth Century-Fox) 14,942,422

Candyman: Farewell to Flesh (Gramercy) ...13,940,383

Highlander III (Miramax/Malo)......................13,829,734

A Kid in King Arthur's Court (Buena Vista)..13,406,717

Lord of Illusions (MGM/UA) 13,293,081

Tom and Huck (Buena Vista) 13,233,053

Clockers (Universal) 13,040,603

Sudden Death (Universal) 12,260,935

Hideaway (Sony)...12,201,255

Roommates (Buena Vista).............................12,096,881

Bye Bye Love (Twentieth Century-Fox)........12,096,673

Tales From the Hood (Savoy)........................11,797,927

Far From Home: The Adventures of 11,642,946
  Yellow Dog (Twentieth Century-Fox)

Fair Game (Warner Bros.) 11,190,582

My Family: Mi Familia (New Line)................11,079,373

The Englishman Who Went Up a Hill 10,904,930
  but Came Down a Mountain (Miramax)

The Scarlet Letter (Buena Vista)...................10,378,982

The Brothers McMullen (Searchlight)........10,246,592

A Little Princess (Warner Bros.) 10,019,307

Jade (Paramount) 9,795,017

The Baby-Sitters Club (Sony) 9,685,976

Village of the Damned (Universal) 9,417,567

The Postman (Miramax/Alliance) 9,170,365

In the Mouth of Madness (New Line)	$8,946,580
Smoke (Miramax)	8,349,430
Tall Tale (Buena Vista)	8,247,627
Unstrung Heroes (Buena Vista)	7,929,241
Strange Days (Twentieth Century-Fox)	7,918,562
Nick of Time (Paramount)	7,877,270
Losing Isaiah (Paramount)	7,603,766
Dracula: Dead and Loving It (Sony)	7,564,936
The Jerky Boys (Buena Vista)	7,557,877
Hackers (MGM/UA)	7,555,834
The Amazing Panda Adventure (Warner Bros.)	7,506,759
Bushwhacked (Twentieth Century-Fox)	7,450,990
Kids (Shining Excalibur/Alliance)	7,417,210
Last of the Dogmen (Savoy)	7,026,165
Three Wishes (Savoy)	7,025,496
Nixon (Buena Vista)	6,973,187
Never Talk to Strangers (Sony/Alliance)	6,849,998
Panther (Gramercy)	6,834,525
The Hunted (Universal)	6,607,652
Cutthroat Island (MGM/UA)	6,554,449
The Secret of Roan Inish (First Look/CFP)	6,101,524
The Walking Dead (Savoy)	6,014,341
Balto (Universal)	5,953,535
The Tie That Binds (Buena Vista)	5,772,529
Beyond Rangoon (Sony)	5,750,110
Gold Diggers: The Secret of Bear Mountain (Universal)	5,721,671
Before Sunrise (Sony)	5,535,405
Miami Rhapsody (Buena Vista)	5,221,281
Top Dog (MGM/UA)	5,093,707
Mighty Aphrodite (Miramax)	5,026,135
Angus (New Line)	4,821,759
National Lampoon's Senior Trip (New Line/Alliance)	4,686,937
Wings of Courage (Sony Classics)	4,537,162
Exotica (Alliance/Miramax)	4,428,978
Priest (Miramax)	4,176,932
Belle de Jour (reissue; Miramax)	4,081,417
Tank Girl (MGM)	4,064,333
Sense and Sensibility (Sony)	4,032,165
Gordy (Miramax)	3,992,809
Fluke (MGM/UA)	3,987,649
The Pebble and the Penguin (MGM)	3,983,912
White Man's Burden (Savoy/CFP)	3,760,515
Born to Be Wild (Warner Bros.)	3,730,409
Bad Company (Buena Vista)	3,674,841
Persuasion (Sony Classics)	3,607,611

New Jersey Drive (Gramercy)	$3,587,823
Jeffrey (Orion/CFP)	3,487,767
The Glass Shield (Miramax)	3,313,633
Crumb (Sony Classics)	3,174,695
Steal Big, Steal Little (Savoy)	3,150,170
Shallow Grave (Gramercy)	2,881,508
Unzipped (Miramax)	2,875,086
The Perez Family (Goldwyn)	2,832,826
Dr. Jekyll and Ms. Hyde (Savoy)	2,763,020
The Show (Savoy)	2,702,578
Carrington (Gramercy)	2,697,902
Magic in the Water (Sony/Norstar)	2,643,346
Leaving Las Vegas (MGM/UA)	2,588,173
The Cure (Universal)	2,568,429
Moonlight and Valentino (Gramercy)	2,488,858
Jefferson in Paris (Buena Vista)	2,473,678
The Basketball Diaries (New Line/CFP)	2,424,439
Once Were Warriors (Fine Line)	2,201,126
Wild Bill (MGM/UA)	2,167,808
Four Rooms (Miramax)	2,155,523
Mallrats (Gramercy)	2,122,561
Farinelli (Alliance/Sony Classics)	2,122,948
A Month by the Lake (Miramax)	2,106,534
Strawberry and Chocolate (Miramax)	2,080,805
The Incredibly True Adventures of Two Girls in Love (Fine Line)	1,977,544
Endless Winter (Warren Miller)	1,966,454
The Mangler (New Line)	1,781,383
Blue in the Face (Miramax)	1,275,999
Mute Witness (Sony Classics)	1,204,430
Across the Sea of Time (Sony Classics)	1,184,317

Beyond Rangoon

Destiny Turns on the Radio (Savoy) $1,176,982

Living in Oblivion (Sony Classics) 1,148,752

Erotique (Group One) 1,109,822

Little Odessa (Fine Line) 1,095,885

Separate Lives (Trimark).....................................961,147

Picture Bride (Miramax) 940,446

When Night Is Falling (Alliance/October) 912,645

Stuart Saves His Family (Paramount) 911,310

Liste Noire (Astral) 886,018

Les Miserables (WB/CFP) 881,630

The Amateur (Sony Classics/Malo)....................856,422

The Crossing Guard (Miramax) 832,910

The Sum of Us (Goldwyn)....................................766,464

Before the Rain (Gramercy)................................763,847

Double Happiness (Malo/Fine Line) 759,393

Wigstock: The Movie (Goldwyn).........................688,512

The Run of the Country

Arabian Knight (Miramax) 669,276

The Wild Bunch (reissue; Warner Bros.) 650,235

Bar Girls (Orion Classics) 573,953

Le Confessionnal (Alliance) 562,069

Shanghai Triad (Sony Classics).........................561,032

The Innocent (Miramax) 553,454

The Underneath (Gramercy) 536,023

Funny Bones (Buena Vista)................................532,268

A Great Day in Harlem (Castle Hill) 527,924

Safe (Sony Classics) 512,245

Kicking and Screaming (Trimark)........................510,903

Horseman on the Roof (Alliance)........................487,784

Party Girl (First Look)..472,370

The Run of the Country (Sony) $470,768

A Pyromaniac's Love Story (Buena Vista)........468,240

Nadja (October/Astral)..446,934

Othello (Sony) 431,795

3 Ninjas Knuckle Up (Sony) 407,618

Bandit Queen (Alliance/Arrow)...........................399,748

Jason's Lyric (Gramercy).....................................399,360

Search and Destroy (October) 389,731

Eldorado (Alliance) 383,191

Gospa (Penland)...381,804

Bulletproof Heart (Keystone) 377,108

City of Lost Children 373,620
   (Alliance/Sony Classics)

Swimming With Sharks (Trimark) 370,928

Country Life (Miramax) 350,354

Un Indien Dans la Ville (CFP) 347,703

Total Eclipse (Fine Line) 339,889

Faster, Pussycat! Kill! Kill! 338,263
   (reissue; RM/CFP)

Gazon Maudit (CFP)..310,862

The Mystery of Rampo (Goldwyn) 305,434

Dance Me Outside (Cineplex)............................304,852

Empire Records (Warner Bros.) 303,841

The Addiction (October) 302,393

Feast of July (Buena Vista) 293,274

L'Enfant d'eau (Tonic) 292,226

Doctor Zhivago (reissue; MGM)..........................288,585

Red Firecracker, Green Firecracker 272,232
   (October)

Pather Panchali (reissue; Sony Classics) 270,712

The Doom Generation (Trimark).........................259,319

An Awfully Big Adventure (Fine Line) 258,195

Window to Paris (Sony Classics)........................255,088

Lie Down With Dogs (Miramax) 240,280

Mamma Roma (Milestone)..................................232,590

Cry, the Beloved Country (Miramax) 230,489

12 Monkeys (Universal) 224,624

Le Sphinx (CFP) 218,233

Sister, My Sister (7th Art) 217,881

My Fair Lady (reissue; Kit Parker) 208,992

Georgia (Miramax)...203,636

A Pure Formality (Sony Classics)........................202,458

Nina Takes a Lover (Sony) 189,509

Theremin: An Electronic Odyssey (Orion) 187,923

La Haine (France Film) 182,746

Movieline's 100 Best Movies

***Movieline*'s executive editors, Virginia Campbell and Edward Margulies, compiled a list of what they consider to be the best 100 English-language films ever made. Their comments are as entertaining to read as the list itself. The piece appeared in the December 1995 issue of the magazine.**

Blue Velvet

THE ADVENTURES OF ROBIN HOOD (1938)

Before that movie staple, Adventure Films for Boys of All Ages, degenerated into cinematic roller-coaster rides, the genre boasted articulated plots, real wit, stylish villainy and great players. This, the best of the lot, has all that and a great star, Errol Flynn, at his apex.

THE AFRICAN QUEEN (1951)

A floating paean to cranky, middle-aged single people. The best of the Hepburn/Tracy pictures, because Tracy isn't in it.

ALL ABOUT EVE (1950)

Power-crazed media figure comes to regret helping an ungrateful unknown to become a star. A film so close to our own experience at *Movieline,* we have to go lie down now.

ANNIE HALL (1977)

Unlikely Galahad's unlikely love poem to the most unlikely of screen queens.

BADLANDS (1973)

This nasty, bleak little take on Hollywood's favorite tale — psycho lovers on the lam from the law — gets better with every passing year. Two otherwise inexplicable stars can justly point with pride to their work here.

BAMBI (1942)

The only film masterpiece ever created for three-year-olds.

BEING THERE (1979)

In this film, when the idiot savant, who knows the world only through the garden he tends and the television he watches, makes gentle pronouncements that launch him to the heights of American power, the pseudo-aphorisms are a lot more clever than "Life is like a box of chocolates." Intelligent is as intelligent does.

THE BEST YEARS OF OUR LIVES (1946)

Director William Wyler's tale of soldiers returning home to small-town America after World War II may not ever have been the paragon of sensitive realism it was once taken for, but it's still an accurate, meaningful fantasy of the way we never were.

BLADE RUNNER (1982, DIRECTOR'S CUT)

An expensive, stylish, despairing vision of 21st-century L.A. in which Daryl Hannah and Sean Young, both perfectly cast, play androids. The most borrowed/stolen-from film of the last 20 years.

BLOW-UP (1966)

Those who think Antonioni's English-language film about a '60s London fashion photographer is dated should watch it again and try to name even one important item missing from this defining encyclopedia of what happened to us when we started looking at ourselves as cool objects.

BLUE VELVET (1986)

David Lynch's fabulously, authentically neo-Freudian fairy tale about the seriously dark and weird things going on in a small American town and/or in the mind of an over-curious young man who lives there. A masterpiece that slipped miraculously through the screens Hollywood keeps in place to prevent such original eruptions.

Breakfast at Tiffany's (1961)

A precariously thin veneer of charm helps put over this frankly amoral tale of venal users who deserve — and, surprise, wind up with — each other. Hit theme tune goes a long way to disguise the bitterness of this pill.

Cabaret (1972)

A precariously thin veneer of charm helps put over this frankly amoral tale of venal users who deserve — and, surprise, don't wind up with — each other. Flashy musical numbers go a long way to disguise the bitterness of this pill.

Casablanca (1942)

A time capsule of World War-II era glamour, nobility and romance. The only movie that could rival the average Shakespeare play for number of lasting phrases contributed to everyday speech.

Chinatown (1974)

The best thing Jack Nicholson will ever do. The best thing Faye Dunaway will ever do. The best thing Roman Polanski will ever do. The best thing Robert Towne will ever do. Etc.

Citizen Kane (1941)

A boy and his sled are separated. Problems ensue.

City Lights (1931)

Even if — like us — you can generally do without Charlie Chaplin, this one's a keeper.

The Conversation (1974)

Are we just being paranoid, or has everything this movie predicted about the invasion of personal privacy come to pass? In any case, the thinking man's *Sliver*.

Dodsworth (1936)

This tale of a self-made American millionaire industrialist who sells his factory and sails off to Europe with his flighty, pretentious wife is even more remarkable than it seemed upon first release, because Hollywood would never write as much virtue and benevolence into the character of a businessman now.

Don't Look Now (1973)

There's a lot more going on in this film than the question of whether Donald Sutherland and Julie Christie were or were not actually doing it during the filming of the sex scene. Basically a kinky and intellectual ghost story, outré director Nicolas Roeg's tale of things unseen becomes, thanks to his lucid, subversive eye, an Investigation of the Unseen.

Double Indemnity (1944)

So oft-imitated it should be old hat by now, but no — mix together the ruthlessness of the script, the director and the film's femme fatale star, and what you get is a poisonous cocktail that still has real kick to it.

Dr. Strangelove or: How I Learned to Stop Worrying and Love the Bomb (1964)

A classic black comedy about the Cold War. Stanley Kubrick's icy gallows humor is hyperbolic but dead-on accurate about the various species of crazed extremists who handled the Bomb back when it looked like we might be lobbing it momentarily.

The Elephant Man (1980)

Quite an odd film to come from Hollywood, where physical beauty is the town religion. David Lynch's true story of John Merrick, a legendarily ugly man with an exquisitely gentle soul despite all the misfortune and cruelty visited on him, makes you cry all the tears Merrick's kind doctor doesn't.

The Empire Strikes Back (1980)

The best of the *Star Wars* trilogy. All the fun-filled archetypes are in top form, and a perfect balance is achieved between special effects and story, humor and emotion and giddy action and dim-bulb philosophy.

E.T. the Extra-Terrestrial (1982)

By now, backlash has set in, claiming this movie's no *The Wizard of Oz*. They're wrong.

E.T. the Extra-Terrestrial

A Face in the Crowd (1957)

Power-crazed media figure comes to regret helping an ungrateful unknown to become a star. A film so close to our own experience at *Movieline,* we have to go lie down now.

Five Easy Pieces (1970)

Bob Rafelson tops our list of filmmakers with only one movie in 'em, but that one movie is a corker. Some people cannot buy Jack Nicholson as a piano virtuoso, but we have trouble getting past the early scenes depicting Jack as an oil rigger. From then on, smooth sailing.

Funny Face (1957)

Power-crazed media figure comes to regret helping an ungrateful unknown to become a star. A film so close to our own experience at *Movieline,* we have to go lie down now.

Gallipoli (1981)

One of the two best anti-war films ever made, starring a young Mel Gibson, whose outrageous good looks seduce you right into the heart of the battle.

Gigi (1958)

A gloriously gilded Easter egg of a movie. Despite the sugary trimmings, it's bracingly tart to the taste.

The Godfather Parts I and II (1972, 1974)

The very best of the gangster-glamorizing genre, if you give a damn about such things, and you really shouldn't.

Gone With the Wind (1939)

Long, Southern soaper closer to Jackie Collins than Shakespeare. Two big stars at their best. Still works, always will.

Gun Crazy (1949)

This nasty, bleak little take on Hollywood's favorite tale — psycho lovers on the lam from the law — has something that's missing from *Bonnie and Clyde, Thieves Like Us, True Romance* and all the others: irrepressible, irresistible Peggy Cummins, the gal we'd most like to be gunned down by.

A Hard Day's Night (1964)

Very funny, winning young guys run, hop, jump, flirt, wisecrack and make music. Our favorite Marx Brothers movie.

The Haunting (1963)

Two towering talents the movies completely misused — Claire Bloom and Julie Harris — provide the warm heart beating at the center of this cold-blooded haunted house thriller, which lets your imagination do all the work.

His Girl Friday (1940)

A classic of pre-shrill feminism. The one-liner chemistry between newspaper people Cary Grant and Rosalind Russell would probably result in mutual sexual harassment charges in real life today.

In a Lonely Place (1950)

A refreshingly off-putting Humphrey Bogart plays the self-involved, tormented writer with rage to spare, and the winningly sexy/creepy Gloria Grahame plays the woman who loves him to little avail. A remarkably grim and true portrait of a writer, a category of humans Hollywood so loathes and fears and needs that movies seldom present them realistically.

The Informer (1935)

John Ford's pointed political mood piece is a demanding partner, but still retains the power to haunt you afterwards.

The Innocents (1961)

Henry James's *The Turn of the Screw* makes for an alluring yet distant film, easily the movies' most ghostly ghost story. Great script, acting and direction, but one lone teardrop steals the show.

Intolerance (1916)

Difficult, daunting, dated and — OK, yes — challenging to sit through, yet D.W. Griffith's complex, four-part film lives up to its reputation as the first great epic produced in Hollywood.

It's a Wonderful Life (1946)

The only Frank Capra flick to make our list, and, sure, we'll admit we're sick of it by now, too. So try doing what we did — just knock off watching it for a few years. When you come back to it, it's even better than you first thought.

King Kong (1933)

A magical-looking movie that accomplishes the astounding feat of making a horny male (i.e. Kong) who lusts after a blond bimbo half his age seem sympathetic, tragic and downright endearing. Added plus: peerless native headgear.

The Lady Eve (1941)

The only film that could possibly make you want to become a cardsharp — anything, actually, that would put you in the fast company of smart, sexy, utterly corrupt Barbara Stanwyck, who is at her glorious, comic best.

BEST POLITICAL FILMS

Critic Roger Ebert listed chronologically what he considered to be the 20 best political films of the past two decades for *Mother Jones*. The piece appeared in the May/June 1996 issue.

Roger & Me

The War at Home, Barry Brown and
    Glenn Silber (1979)

Mephisto, Istvan Szabo (1981)

El Norte, Gregory Nava and Anna Thomas (1983)

Testament, Lynne Littman (1983)

Secret Honor, Robert Altman (1984)

Shoah, Claude Lanzmann (1985)

Dear America: Letters Home From Vietnam,
    Bill Couturie (1987)

Running on Empty, Sidney Lumet (1988)

Born on the Fourth of July, Oliver Stone (1989)

Do the Right Thing, Spike Lee (1989)

Roger & Me, Michael Moore (1989)

American Dream, Barbara Kopple (1990)

Hidden Agenda, Ken Loach (1990)

Boyz N the Hood, John Singleton (1991)

City of Hope, John Sayles (1991)

Grand Canyon, Lawrence Kasdan (1991)

The Blue Kite, Tian Zhuang-zhuang (1993)

Schindler's List, Steven Spielberg (1993)

Hoop Dreams, Steve James (1994)

Dead Man Walking, Tim Robbins (1995)

THE LAST PICTURE SHOW (1971)

Almost didn't make our cut, since, after all this is the movie that unleashed on an unsuspecting world everyone from Randy Quaid and Cloris Leachman to Timothy Bottoms and Cybill Shepherd to Peter Bogdanovich and Larry McMurtry. Truth is, this film could have survived Penelope Ann Miller, too, and still been great.

LETTER FROM AN UNKNOWN WOMAN (1948)

The incomparable director Max Ophuls brings the art of film as close as it can get to the art of music in this story of a woman who is destroyed by her obsessive love for a glamorous pianist who trifles with her and later doesn't even remember her. What would seem pathetic and alien if envisioned by another director is tragic and personal here.

THE LOST WEEKEND (1945)

A movie that still has the power to send you running into the arms of Bill W. The script, direction, acting, score, cinematography and that freaky bat, are all aces.

LOVE AFFAIR (1939)

Wit, charm and ideal performances keep this soaper afloat — and make it superior to its two remakes. The movies' greatest unheralded female star, Irene Dunne, thought it was her best movie, and she was right.

THE MANCHURIAN CANDIDATE (1962)

A cool, precise primer in the political, familial, romantic and personal paranoia that has plagued the American psyche since this film was released. Angela Lansbury is not really a good-hearted mystery-writing sleuth, she's an evil bitch who feeds her own son to the wolves. Laurence Harvey isn't really an English dish with great cheekbones, he's a tortured wimp. Asians aren't our valued trading partners in the great new global economy, they're . . . Well, you get the point.

MANHATTAN (1979)

Contemporary urban saga of mixed doubles and missed opportunities still strikes a nerve. The smooth, elegant production can't hope to gloss over all the heartache in the writing, playing and direction.

McCABE & MRS. MILLER (1971)

Sad spellbinder about how the West was settled by the losers who'd failed to score East. Winners here are Warren Beatty and Julie Christie, cast as star-crossed losers — neither one has ever been better.

Meet Me in St. Louis (1944)

Cornball costume period piece saved by director's neurotic interest in exposing the dark glints within a gaga American clan: imagine *Blue Velvet* made as a '40s MGM musical.

Miller's Crossing (1990)

A brainy gangster's simultaneous pursuit of integrity and self-destruction makes for verbal and visual combustion in Joel and Ethan Coen's most serious, lyrical and artistically successful comedy.

My Man Godfrey (1936)

More than slightly unhinged direction and distinctly unhinged scriptwriting set up Carole Lombard and William Powell for a screwball feast.

The Night of the Hunter (1955)

Charles Laughton's only directorial effort — which was remarkable enough for putting Robert Mitchum and Lillian Gish together in the same universe, not to mention movie — was a huge box-office failure, but is a masterpiece about two kids in peril. If the Grimm brothers had made movies, they would have been like this.

North by Northwest (1959)

Ernest Lehman's great screenplay fully exposes the hazards of going out for a drink in Manhattan and has a word-for-the-wise about traveling by bus, too.

Notorious (1946)

Cary Grant and Ingrid Bergman give us a ravishing look at their darker sides in one of Hitchcock's finest handbooks of cinematic eroticism and misogyny.

The Manchurian Candidate

CONTINUED ON NEXT PAGE ▶

◄ CONTINUED FROM PREVIOUS PAGE

Best Pictures Commemorating Tradition and Community
How Green Was My Valley (1941)
Fort Apache (1947)
She Wore a Yellow Ribbon (1948)
Rio Grande (1950)
The Quiet Man (1952)
The Life and Death of Colonel Blimp (1943)
A Canterbury Tale (1944)
I Know Where I'm Going (1945)

Special Lifetime Achievement
Frank Capra (1897–1991)

Best Picture Celebrating the American Dream
An American Romance (1944)

Best Picture Commemorating the Settling of America
My Darling Clementine (1946)

Best Scene of the American Idea
Since You Went Away (1944)

Best Picture About Defending America
Sergeant York (1941)

Best Fourth of July Movie
Yankee Doodle Dandy (1942)

Pictures to Make the Patriotic Blood Boil
The Hanoi Hilton (1987)
Heartbreak Ridge (1986)
Rambo: First Blood Part II (1985)
The Deer Hunter (1979)
Red Dawn (1984)
Thirty Seconds Over Tokyo (1944)
Wake Island (1942)

Winston Churchill's Favorite Movie
That Hamilton Woman (1941)

Ronald Reagan's Greatest Movies
King's Row (1942)
Knute Rockne — All American (1940)

Best Pictures Depicting the Evils of Communism
Repentance (1987)
The Inner Circle (1992)

Best Picture Predicting the Collapse of Communism
Ninotchka (1939)

Best Pictures Depicting the Inhumanity of Mass Revolution
Marie Antoinette (1938)
A Tale of Two Cities (1935)
Viva Villa! (1934)
Knight Without Armor (1937)

Best Pictures on the Limits of Good Intentions
There Was a Crooked Man (1971)
Heavens Above (1963)
Forbidden Planet (1956)

Best Movie Critique of Journalism
The Big Carnival (1951)

THE OX-BOW INCIDENT (1943)
This potent and plainspoken lesson about mob mentality is perhaps what you ought to have been watching instead of Court TV.

THE PALM BEACH STORY (1942)
Divorce, Preston Sturges-style. This writer-director reached his purely farcical peak with a dream script and a cast to match.

PATHS OF GLORY (1957)
The insanity of war — straight up, no chaser. May well be Stanley Kubrick's best film.

PEEPING TOM (1960)
Still shocking 35 years on, and a creepy reminder of where moviemakers' voyeurism runs if unchecked.

PETULIA (1968)
A precariously thin veneer of charm helps put over this frankly amoral tale of venal users who deserve — and, surprise, almost wind up with — each other. With no hit tunes, this is a bitter pill to swallow.

THE PHILADELPHIA STORY (1940)
A recent biography revealed that Philip Barry moved into the Hepburn family home, penned what he saw and heard and the result was the hit play that formed the basis of this movie. Interesting, sure, but not so surprising — when was Kate Hepburn ever playing anyone but herself?

PSYCHO (1960)
Genius married with such inspiration to cheese/horror that it rises above its own self-created campiness into a lasting tour de force of taxidermied screen terror.

THE PURPLE ROSE OF CAIRO (1985)
Before there was Prozac, people tolerated the Depression by going to the movies. If there were more movies like this, would fewer people need Prozac now?

QUEEN CHRISTINA (1933)
An eye-opener for anyone who believes censors caught even half of what Hollywood was up to in its heyday, this star vehicle reveals more about its star than its subject.

RAGING BULL (1980)

The cinematic record of the destruction of Robert De Niro's looks, and as moving and beautiful a film as anyone could make about an intolerably nasty, screwed-up man. Scorsese's best.

REAR WINDOW (1954)

Hitchcock's suitably subversive tribute to the voyeur in every filmgoer provides plenty to ogle at, like a peak-gorgeous Grace Kelly and a sexy, curmudgeonly Jimmy Stewart stuck in a wheelchair with nothing to do but spy on his neighbors while we stare at him. That the pathetic view of the human community Hitchcock presents from Stewart's window does not squelch his or our desire to snoop says everything.

REBECCA (1940)

Hitchcock's brilliant argument that there's nothing spookier than marriage.

THE ROAD WARRIOR (1981)

This fun, economical, smirk-free epic of heroic post-Apocalyptic individualism wasn't made in Hollywood because it couldn't have been. Director George Miller's renovation of the loner genre was so good it won't need a new coat of paint for a long time. Especially not from Kevin Costner.

SCHINDLER'S LIST (1993)

Who the hell would've thought that immature, moneybags director Steven Spielberg would make a movie that is (a) a serious, grown-up film, and (b) the best movie made by Hollywood in years?

THE SEARCHERS (1956)

This Western soaper cannot be dismissed (even by us). That door at the finale has reverberating echoes Ibsen only dreamt of.

SHADOW OF A DOUBT (1943)

It may be Hitchcock, it may be black-and-white, it may be realistic in style, but it's still the original *Blue Velvet*.

Schindler's List

SHAMPOO (1975)

A Beverly Hills black comedy/soaper closer to Judith Krantz than Molière. Admirably lacerating self-portraits by the entire cast. An entertaining warning against taking Hollywood's political opinions seriously.

SHERLOCK, JR. (1924)

You'd have selected Buster Keaton's other silent marvel, *The General?* We prefer this sweet romantic comedy, which provides stunning proof that just about every movie special effect — save morphing — was invented by Keaton back in '24.

SINGIN' IN THE RAIN (1952)

In an extraordinarily happy accident, Gene Kelly's de rigueur forced sunniness fails to disguise his steely, "I'd-kill-to-get-ahead" megalomania, which adds a needed touch of truth, and ballast, to what otherwise might have merely been the most entertaining of all show-biz musicals.

SNOW WHITE AND THE SEVEN DWARFS (1937)

The first of Disney's animated features remains unequaled in its charm, heart and pure terror — to this day, we've never taken an apple from a stranger.

SOME LIKE IT HOT (1959)

The "girls" in *Tootsie*, *Priscilla*, *Wong Foo* et al., cannot hope to match, let alone diminish, the stature of Billy Wilder's expertly constructed farce — nor do the latecomers have anything like this film's trio of generally uneven stars, each here at career-peak best.

A STAR IS BORN (1954)

Long, Tinseltown soaper closer to Sidney Sheldon than Euripides. Nevertheless, Moss Hart's screenplay makes you understand why Hollywood marriages don't ever work out. Judy Garland, James Mason and director George Cukor are all at the top of their game.

STRANGERS ON A TRAIN (1951)

A searing cautionary tale about the advisability of chatting with people to whom one has not been properly introduced — it turns out our mother was right about that.

SULLIVAN'S TRAVELS (1941)

This film about a too-successful comedy director who decides to disguise himself as a bum to get the experience he needs for the big "important" movie he feels he must make indulges in its own seriousness and overly-good intentions, but it ends up coming down solidly on the side of laughs (thanks to writer/director Preston Sturges), beauty (thanks to Veronica Lake) and self-effacing modesty (thanks to Joel McCrea).

Sunday, Bloody Sunday (1971)

An incisive screenplay and excellent direction chillingly demonstrate why most gay relationships fail to last — straight and bi ones, too, for that matter.

Sunrise (1927)

Murnau's silent has just got to be more interesting than whatever you saw last weekend at the 'plex. The poetic cinematography by Oscar-winners Karl Struss and Charles Rosher makes Janet Gaynor's feat in ascending above a thankless role all the more amazing, and puts a definite thrill into George O'Brien's transformation from homicidal lout to reborn romantic.

Sunset Blvd. (1950)

This valentine to the vagaries of who's up and who's down in the crapshoot that is Hollywood was dipped in acid, giving the black comedy an acrid air of hard-won home truths.

Sweet Smell of Success (1957)

Power-crazed media figure comes to regret helping assorted ungrateful unknowns to become stars. A film so close to our own experience at *Movieline*, we have to go lie down now.

Swing Time (1936)

Fred Astaire, Ginger Rogers and Jerome Kern — all this, plus the art deco dream of the Big Apple. Sublime nonsense, but oh, that fancy footwork!

The Third Man (1949)

Carol Reed's vertiginous direction and Robert Krasker's eerie photography take the dark, post-WWII story of a supposed good guy turned murderous war profiteer on the lam in Vienna and make it so brilliantly black it's like a one-film negation of the Victory in Europe.

The 39 Steps (1935)

The deceptive speed with which this charming thriller races along remains a tribute to Alfred Hitchcock, yes, but also to two of the most charismatic players he ever worked with: Robert Donat and Madeleine Carroll.

To Kill a Mockingbird (1962)

This story about how children look at and learn from the world around them, told through the lens of racial injustice in a Southern town, is proof that the best way for well-intentioned filmmakers to move audiences toward generosity is to curb Hollywood's natural inclinations — overspending, oversimplification and over-reliance on cheap emotion.

Touch of Evil (1958)

Well, more than a touch, actually. The whole subject is evil. Orson Welles, who plays a big, fat, corrupt cop, also directed. The result is a giant, baroque bad-mood piece in which everything is shot creepier-than-life. Certainly no other director would have dared to shoot Welles as unattractively as he appears here.

The Treasure of the Sierra Madre (1948)

Greedy, seedy, badly dressed men behaving unforgivably in a desolate landscape. In other words, virtually our Bible on what to expect here in Hollywood. John Huston's finest hour, not least because he brooked no star nonsense from the cast.

Trouble in Paradise (1932)

Ernst Lubitsch's glittering gem about jewel thieves is perfection — the most sophisticated and the most comic of all sophisticated comedies.

True Lies (1994)

Go ahead, laugh, but 10 years ago *Blade Runner* seemed like no one's idea of a classic, either. Given our divorce-torn times, this movie's downright radical message — that your dream mate is right there next to you in the partner you're taking for granted — is a daring and provocative theme which James Cameron has decorated with many of the greatest action set-pieces ever filmed. In years to come, *True Lies* will be studied not merely for its technical thrill-ride achievements, but to see how they were so deftly interwoven into a timely, pro-marriage update on Nick and Nora Charles.

Two for the Road (1967)

The reason most movies end at "and they lived happily ever after" is because marriage is so less upbeat a subject than romance. Here's the exception, however, the result of extraordinary contributions from writer Frederic Raphael, producer-director Stanley Donen, cinematographer Christopher Challis, composer Henry Mancini and stars Audrey Hepburn and Albert Finney.

2001: A Space Odyssey (1968)

Why is this cold, oddly optimistic, overreaching sci-fi poem so interesting? Because HAL, the computer on-board the spacecraft flying to Jupiter, has personal problems that make him a more engaging character than any of the humans in this or most other movies of the last few decades.

The Unbearable Lightness of Being

THE UNBEARABLE LIGHTNESS OF BEING (1988)
The personal problems of three little people do amount to a considerable hill of beans back in the halcyon days of the Soviet domination of Eastern Europe.

VERTIGO (1958)
Hitchcock's autobiographical film about show business investigates the inherent psychological troubles of earthy brunettes who become ethereal blond screen goddesses — and the attendant problems suffered by men who love the latter but not the former.

WEST SIDE STORY (1961)
Compared with today's drive-by thugs, the '50s homeboys who dance through this musical *Romeo and Juliet* are suitable for taking home to Mom and Dad. But they still cause enough problems to jerk major tears and support hyperemotional musical numbers. Think Natalie Wood is miscast as the Puerto Rican Maria? Today you'd get Marisa Tomei, so shut up and enjoy it.

THE WIND (1928)
One of the great silents, and the grandmother of all women's pictures. Lillian Gish delivers in this film alone a case-closed argument for her legendary status.

THE WIZARD OF OZ (1939)
Hopes, dreams and hallucinations in the original land of dysfunctionality. Flawless, even if you can't stand Judy Garland.

THE YEAR OF LIVING DANGEROUSLY (1983)
Director Peter Weir's sophisticated, uncynical view of love, romantic and otherwise, finds exotic expression in this story of an ambitious journalist in strife-torn Indonesia. The movie was taken to be a political thriller when it was released. It isn't.

1996 BRITISH ACADEMY OF FILM AND TELEVISION AWARDS

The BAFTA Awards, the British equivalent of our Oscar and Emmy awards (combined into one ceremony), were presented on Sunday, April 23, 1995, at the London Palladium. This year's awards celebrate 100 years of British cinema. Here are the winners in the film categories.

Film
Sense and Sensibility

British Film of the Year
The Madness of King George

Actor
Nigel Hawthorne, *The Madness of King George*

Actress
Emma Thompson, *Sense and Sensibility*

Supporting Actor
Tim Roth, *Rob Roy*

Supporting Actress
Kate Winslet, *Sense and Sensibility*

Direction
Michael Radford, *The Postman (Il Postino)*

Original Screenplay
Christopher McQuarrie, *The Usual Suspects*

Adapted Screenplay
John Hodge, *Trainspotting*

Foreign Film
The Postman (Il Postino), Italy

Director **John Schlesinger** was honored with a lifetime achievement trophy.

The Madness of King George

Film Comment's Guilty Pleasures

Guilty Pleasures began when Richard Corliss, then-editor of *Film Comment,* needed a *New Times* filler column during a slow movie season in May 1978. It was an annotated list of 10 films — among them *The Bobo, School Girl, Tenth Avenue Angel, Unknown World* — "films you hear universally reviled, if they're ever discussed at all, until your small, cracking voice can be heard saying, 'Well, I liked it.' " Corliss transferred the idea to *Film Comment* that summer; the first contributors were Roger Ebert, Martin Scorsese and David Newman, and the feature has continued irregularly since then. Some contributors fessed up; others picked fights. Here's a selection.

JOE BOB BRIGGS

Hundra (1983)
White Star (1985)
How to Make a Doll (1968)
The Hills Have Eyes (1977)
Billy Jack (1971)
Caged Heat (1974)
The Wild Angels (1966)
The Trip (1967)
Naughty Dallas (1964)
Funny Girl (1968)

VINCENT CANBY

Tarzan, the Ape Man (1932)
The Last Days of Pompeii (1935)
The Sign of the Cross (1932)
*The Adventures of Robin
    Hood* (1938)
Death Takes a Holiday (1934)
Topper (1937)
Mom and Dad (1944)
Rain (1932)
Captain From Castile (1947)
Ecstasy (1933)

JOE DANTE

Attack of the 50 Ft. Woman
    (1958)
Blood and Black Lace (1964)
*Confessions of an Opium
    Eater* (1962)
Exorcist II: The Heretic (1977)
The Sadist (1962)
*Frankenstein Meets the Wolf
    Man* (1943)
Invaders From Mars (1952)
The Gamma People (1955)
Truck Turner (1974)
Long John Silver (1954)

It's a Gift (1934)
Tomb of Ligeia (1965)

TERENCE DAVIES

The Clouded Yellow (1951)
The Blue Parrot (1953)
Dance Hall (1950)
Spare the Rod (1961)
It Always Rains on Sunday (1947)
Carry On Sergeant (1959)
Carry On Nurse (1959)
Carry On Constable (1960)
Carry On Regardless (1961)
Victim (1961)
Quartet (1949)
Singin' in the Rain (1952)
Young at Heart (1954)
Night of the Hunter (1955)
Mother Wore Tights (1947)
Shane (1953)
The Searchers (1956)
Psycho (1960)

BRIAN DE PALMA

El Topo (1971)
The Naked Kiss (1964)
White Dog (1982)

Homicidal (1961)
The Tenant (1976)
David Holzman's Diary (1968)
Night Dreams (1981)
Nightmare Alley (1947)
Two Rode Together (1961)
Get Carter (1971)
Savage Grace (1985)
The Damned (1969)
Ludwig (1973)

CHRISTOPHER DURANG

Going My Way (1944)
The Song of Bernadette (1943)
The Bells of St. Mary's (1945)
The Nun's Story (1959)
*There's No Business Like Show
    Business* (1954)
Woman's World (1954)
Pope Joan (1972)
Teorema (1968)
Until They Sail (1957)
Since You Went Away (1943)
Waterloo Bridge (1940)
Strangers When We Meet (1960)

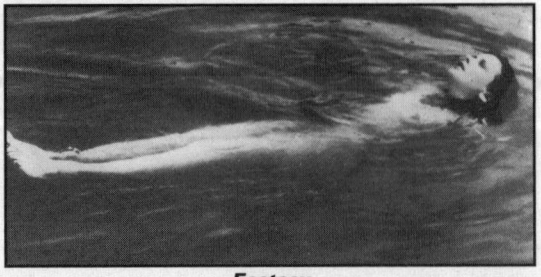

Ecstasy

STEPHEN KING

Bring Me the Head of Alfredo Garcia (1974)
Bloody Mama (1970)
Killers Three (1968)
Sorcerer (1977)
The Horror of Party Beach (1964)
The Amityville Horror (1979)
The Wild Angels (1966)
Suspiria (1977)
Night of the Juggler (1980)

JOHN MILIUS

The Wild One (1953)
The Losers (1970)
The Texas Chainsaw Massacre (1974)
Return to Paradise (1953)

ANDREW SARRIS

Sweet Adeline (1935)
South Riding (1937)
Mr. Lucky (1943)
The Adventuress (1947)
Love Letters (1945)
The Clouded Yellow (1951)
My Foolish Heart (1949)
Music for Millions (1944)
Her Highness and the Bellboy (1945)
Two Sisters From Boston (1946)
Miss Tatlock's Millions (1948)
I Know Where I'm Going (1947)
Vacation From Marriage (1945)
I Married an Angel (1942)

PAUL SCHRADER

Scorpio Rising (1963)
Wavelength (1983)
Two Thousand Maniacs (1964)
The Heart Is a Rebel (1958)
True Heart Suzie (1919)
Decision at Sundown (1957)
The Brain That Wouldn't Die (1963)
Peeping Tom (1969)
I, the Jury (1953)
Last Year at Marienbad (1961)
Reflections in a Golden Eye (1967)
Abbott and Costello Go to Mars (1953)

MARTIN SCORSESE

Land of the Pharaohs (1955)
Khartoum (1966)
The Ten Commandments (1956)
The Silver Chalice (1954)
Hell's Angels (1930)
The Counterfeit Traitor (1962)
Play Dirty (1969)
Twelve O'Clock High (1949)
In Harm's Way (1965)
Lady in the Dark (1944)
My Dream Is Yours (1949)
The Man I Love (1946)
Always Leave Them Laughing (1949)
The Road to Zanzibar (1941)
Blue Skies (1946)
Lost in a Harem (1944)
Abbott and Costello Go to Mars (1953)
House of Wax (1953)
The Uninvited (1944)
Frankenstein Created Woman (1967)
Exorcist II: The Heretic (1977)
One-Eyed Jacks (1961)
I Walk Alone (1947)
Night and the City (1950)
Station Six — Sahara (1963)
Dark of the Sun (1968)
Guns Don't Argue (1957)
Murder by Contract (1958)
The Magic Box (1951)

JULIA SWEENEY

Mahogany (1975)
The Parent Trap (1961)
The Trouble With Angels (1966)
Yours, Mine and Ours (1968)
The Singing Nun (1966)
Bless the Beasts and the Children (1971)
Brother Sun, Sister Moon (1973)
Divorce American Style (1967)
How to Save a Marriage and Ruin Your Life (1968)
The Last Married Couple in America (1980)
A Touch of Class (1973)

The Harrad Experiment (1973)
For Singles Only (1968)
Cactus Flower (1969)
Bob & Carol & Ted & Alice (1969)
How to Commit Marriage (1969)
The Love Bug (1969)
Herbie Rides Again (1974)

JOHN WATERS

Interiors (1978)
The films of Marguerite Duras
Brink of Life (1958)
Night Games (1966)
Teorema (1968)
Salo (1977)
A Cold Wind in August (1961)
Mademoiselle (1966)
Lancelot du Lac (1974)
Anything by Fassbinder

JAMES WOODS

Zontar, the Thing From Venus (1966)
R.P.M. (1970)
Believe in Me (1971)
Death Race 2000 (1975)
Gidget movies
Prime Cut (1972)
Earthquake (1973)
Dreamer (1978)
PT 109 (1963)
Fantastic Voyage (1966)

ROBERT ZEMECKIS

Macabre (1958)
House on Haunted Hill (1958)
The Tingler (1959)
13 Ghosts (1960)
I Saw What You Did (1965)
Two on a Guillotine (1965)
You'll Like My Mother (1972)
The Texas Chainsaw Massacre (1974)
The Beginning of the End (1957)
Nevada Smith (1960)
Hell Is for Heroes (1962)
The Great Escape (1963)
Where Eagles Dare (1969)

Major International Film Festivals

Our around-the-globe round-up of cinematic scenes

12TH ANNUAL SUNDANCE FILM FESTIVAL

The buzz starts here. Every January, Park City, Utah, sounds the call across America, and independents come running. Formerly synonymous with low-budget, fuzzy films about do-gooder subjects and the meaning of life, Sundance is now a full-blown, viable market for commercial hits. As founder Robert Redford explained, "There seems to be a maturing of the independent feature film. They're a little more mature, more sophisticated, more in tune with the times."

"See you in Park City," uttered unctuous studio exec Tim Robbins in *The Player*, immortalizing Sundance onscreen as a meet-and-greet must stop for Hollywood brass. Distributors such as Fine Line Features, Sony Pictures Classics and Miramax came to the 12th Sundance Film Festival prepared to do business and buy, buy, buy at the premier shopping mall for America's up-and-coming picture-makers.

Screening 175 features between January 18–28, the 1996 festival attracted some 9,000 Hollywood insiders and movie buffs. With more than 500 dramatic films and 200 documentaries submitted this year, organizers reported a 34 percent increase over last year.

The big news in 1996 was the escalation in money exchanging hands. The William Morris Agency alone reportedly had 18 agents working the festival. Bidding wars for unproven indies skyrocketed, most notoriously when Miramax film co-chairman Harvey Weinstein engaged in an all-too-public shouting match at a local restaurant over the rights to Scott Hicks's *Shine*. This Australian-made feature about pianist David Helfgot was ultimately scooped up by New Line Cinema for $2 million. As he was negotiating the deal, New Line exec Mark Ordesky reported, "the phone was ringing off the hook" with counteroffers

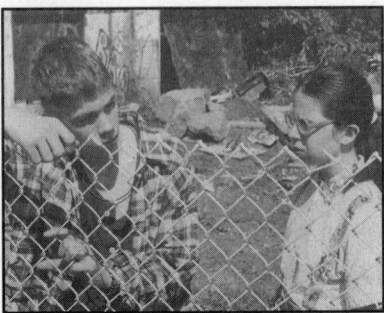

Welcome to the Dollhouse

from other parties, including Miramax. Sorry, Harv, New Line got there first.

The Spitfire Grill incensed some with its price tag. Castle Rock Entertainment paid $10 million for worldwide rights to the film. Sundance watchers felt that the Turner-owned company paid too much and falsely upped the stakes. Starring former fashion model Alison Eliott as an ex-con who befriends Ellen Burstyn and Marcia Gay Harden in a small Maine town, the drama won the Audience Award.

"I'm just stunned," writer and director Lee David Zlotoff, who also created the popular TV series *MacGyver*, told the *New York Times*. "My impression of Sundance was always the enthusiasms were for younger, hipper, more urban kinds of things. This movie is about as far away from hip as you can get. It's meant to be an emotional movie, without being sentimental or banal. And it's really striking a chord."

Another film that struck a chord — and won the coveted Grand Jury Prize for dramatic film — was Todd Solondz's adolescence-is-hell opus, *Welcome to the Dollhouse*, in which the under-recognized Solondz crafts a blistering portrait of suburban adolescence, riveting in its bleakness, bite and beauty. In searing, white-hot detail, the film reveals the torture suffered by a preteen loser, Dawn "Weiner Dog" Weiner, played by

Heather Matazzaro, at the hands of her family and classmates.

The documentary top honor went to husband-and-wife filmmakers Jeanne Jordan and Steve Ascher for their *Troublesome Creek: A Midwestern.* In a rare coup, this cinéma-vérité portrait of co-director Jordan's family's struggles to maintain their small farm also emerged as a viewer favorite, coming away with the Audience Award. Jordan's father stole the show when he took the stage after the screening, admitting that he hadn't thought anyone would be interested in their story. Hollywood was certainly interested, nominating *Troublesome Creek* for a Best Documentary Academy Award.

Another Sundance entry that would go on to define the 1996 cinematic landscape is Mary Harron's *I Shot Andy Warhol.* The first-time director's stylized portrait of lesbian playwright and part-time prostitute Valerie Solanas, who shot the pop icon, is produced by indie star Christine Vachon, a Sundance institution. *I Shot Andy Warhol* won lead actress Lili Taylor — a Sundance institution herself — a Special Jury Award.

Lili Taylor

This year saw the introduction of a new Sundance category, American Spectrum, showcasing emerging, home-grown filmmakers. Twenty works, both dramatic and documentary, played in this debut series. Notable screenings included Lisa Krueger's quirky and moving sisters-on-the-road film, *Manny and Lo,* and Stacy Title's dinner-party-from-hell satire, *The Last Supper.* "I'm on cloud nine," confessed writer and director Krueger after Sony Pictures Classics paid a reported $750,000 to distribute her film. Another standout was Russ Hexter's *Dadetown,* a powerful, toungue-in-cheek documentary about the David-and-Goliath relationship between a small town and its corporate uber-tenant. Hexter, 27, a recent NYU grad, seemed to have the world in his hands when, at the festival, he secured a William Morris agent. But, tragically, on April 29, 1996 just before a screening at the Philadelphia International Film Festival, he was rushed to the hospital, where he died of an aortic aneurysm.

In other Sundance news:

• Cinematography awards went to Rob Sweeney for the dramatic feature, *Color of a Brisk and Leaping Day,* and to Andrew Young for the documentary *Cutting Loose.*

• The Freedom of Expression Award went to *The Celluloid Closet,* producer/director Rob Epstein and Jeffrey Friedman's survey of gay images in Hollywood.

• The Waldo Salt Screenwriting Award went to Stanley Tucci and Joseph Tropiano for *Big Night,* a comedy about two brothers who open an Italian restaurant.

• Special Jury awards went to producer David Sonenberg's *When We Were Kings* and producer Lauren Zalaznick's *Girls Town.*

• Filmmaker trophies went to Jim McKay's drama, *Girls Town,* and Andrew Young and Susan Todd's documentary, *Cutting Loose.*

• The Latin American Cinema Award went to Cuban director Fernando Pérez's *Madagascar.*

• The Short Filmmaking Award went to *A Special Domain* by director Britta Sjogren.

— KIM CAVINESS

46TH INTERNATIONAL BERLIN FILM FESTIVAL

"The last time I was here was right after the war, when the amount of wreckage was truly frightening," commented guest American director Elia Kazan, 87, who witnessed the ravaged city before there was a Berlin Film Festival. "Today, Berlin is beautiful, and Berliners have tremendous energy, which I feel throughout the festival. I'm surprised how much I like it!"

The Berlin Film Festival, held annually in February, is the first major international festival out of the gate. It's the place where the world film community discovers what important movies have been produced in the months since Cannes, which is held in May. Traditionally, Berlin is a politically attuned festival and, in the late 1980s and early '90s, all the changes in Eastern Europe, from Glasnost to perestroika, were reflected in the movies playing there. When the East Germans decided to tear down the Wall, they did so at the most opportune moment, during the fest. That way, the festival guests could witness the Berlin Wall's destruction and then race back to the festival for movies.

The latter was easily accomplished: Berlin is among the busiest of festivals. Films unspool from 9 a.m. to way past midnight.

Highly commercial works stay clear. Berlin is, everyone agrees, a very serious-minded, artistic festival. The festival's Forum specializes in well-made documentaries and intelligent independent features. The Panorama features more formally experimental — and sometimes rawer — kinds of works done by young filmmakers. In the last decade, no major festival in the world has shown, by design, so many gay and lesbian films as Berlin, and the Forum is the place for them. In the last three years, Berlin has even offered a juried prize in this category: the Teddy, for best gay and/or lesbian film.

Finally, there's the Official Competition, in which a world-class jury of critics, actors and directors select the winner of the prestigious Golden Bear prize. In 1996, the unsurprising winner was Britain's *Sense and Sensibilty*. It was chosen over an unusually large number of Hollywood releases — *12 Monkeys, Toy Story, Dead Man Walking, Get Shorty, Nixon* — competing for the Golden Bear. "America is still the strongest film producer in the world, so

Elia Kazan

nobody should be surprised," explained Berlin Fest director Moritz de Hadelin.

Regrettably, the 46th fest made clear that faltering world economics, aside from Hollywood, has depleted film production. There wasn't a single film in the Official Competition category from India, Russia, Canada or Latin America. "I'm afraid of too much America on Polish screens," said Polish filmmaker Andrzej Wajda (*Ashes and Diamonds, Man of Iron*), who received this year's Lifetime Achievement Award. He complained that, after Communism, 90 percent of Polish theaters show only Hollywood movies.

Two non-Hollywood American pictures unveiled at Berlin were of special note. Greta Schiller's documentary *Paris Was a Woman,* an impressively researched homage to female literati in France during the 1920s, examines Gertrude Stein, Sylvia Beach, Janet Flanner and Djuna Barnes. Murray Lerner's *Message to Love: Isle of Wight Musical Festival*, is a stirring recreation, 25 years later, of the last pre-Altamont rockfest, with great music from Jimi Hendrix, Joni Mitchell and the Who.

Kazan was honored with a complete retrospective of his films — vintage prints of *On the Waterfront, A Streetcar Named Desire* and other, less famous, titles. At a press conference, the controversial Kazan was as pugnacious as ever, yelling at photographers, "If you flash those bulbs, I quit talking!" But he was a perfect gentleman when he took the stage for a sold-out screening of *Baby Doll*. As a result, Berliners at the Zoo Palast Theatre gave the American director a standing ovation. He could have been JFK.

— GERALD PEARY

Sense and Sensibility

1995 New York Film Festival

The 1995 New York Film Festival opened to controversy, when the Chinese government "asked" director Zhang Yimou, no stranger to political pressure, to cancel plans to attend the festival. Zhang's film, *Shanghai Triad,* kicked off the 17-day event, holding a coveted position on the festival circuit. The director was expected to speak following the screening of the film, and his absence left organizers scrambling to fill the void.

When Richard Peña, chairman of the festival, refused to bow to the Chinese government's request to pull the documentary *The Gate of Heavenly Peace* from the festival roster, Chinese officials issued their request to Yimou, though he had nothing to do with the film or its production.

"I was told the film was insulting to China and that it was made by Americans," Peña said. "There was no convincing reason, really, it was just 'You must not show this film.'"

The documentary focuses on the 1989 uprising in Tiananmen Square and was directed and produced by husband-and-wife filmmakers Richard Gordon and Carma Hinton. "They have not even seen our film, so it's like

Gong Li

a preemptive strike," Hinton said. "Instead of dealing with our film, they punish a filmmaker who has nothing to do with it and probably doesn't even know it is being made."

This was not the first roadblock Zhang faced with *Shanghai Triad.* The Chinese government halted production of the film because existing political problems with 1994's *To Live* had not been resolved. These problems kept him from 1994's Cannes Film Festival and prohibited him from working on foreign co-productions.

Gong Li, a regular in Zhang films and the director's former companion, stars in this

Strange Days

lavish mobster tale set in 1930s Shanghai. Ironically, the film is Zhang's most conventional, least political to date.

Aside from Zhang's difficulties, the 33rd annual festival went off smoothly, drawing a record number of viewers with 51,064 attending 44 screenings. Kathryn Bigelow's apocalyptic thriller *Strange Days* was the Festival Centerpiece, and the post-screening party reportedly rocked. In addition to the film's stars, Ralph Fiennes, Angela Bassett, Brigitte Bako, Tom Sizemore and Glenn Plummer, other notables, Robert De Niro, Liam Neeson, Natasha Richardson, Buck Henry and Rita Moreno, attended the night's events. Other hot tickets included Pedro Almodovar's *The Flower of My Secret,* about a romance novelist whose work turns dark when her marriage collapses; Rob Epstein's and Jeffrey Friedman's documentary *The Celluloid Closet,* a smart, entertaining history of gay stereotypes, sly subtexts and subversive messages in film; and Ulu Grosbard's perfectly cast *Georgia,* which earned Un Certain Regard at the 1995 Cannes Film Festival, about a troubled bar singer resentful of her sister's successful music career.

Premieres included Hal Hartley's *Flirt,* which moves between New York, Berlin and Tokyo, each city telling a similar story of a flirt wary of commitment; the Hughes brothers' sophomore outing *Dead Presidents,* about an 18 year old who returns from Vietnam and finds a different New York; and Gordon and Hinton's insightful, thoroughly researched *The Gate of Heavenly Peace.*

— Beth Rowen

Cannes Spotting

An hour outside of Cannes, the high-speed TGV that was taking me to the 49th Festival International du Film struck a despondent Frenchman, apparently not an uncommon occurrence. A case of literal train-spotting, and not the most upbeat portent for what proved to be a hard-to-top festival experience.

Ridicule, director Patrice Leconte's tale of dueling wits in Louis XVI's court, opened the festival to mouthfuls of praise. Festival director Gilles Jacob

Cast of *Trainspotting*

noted, "A fest director who opens his event with a movie called *Ridicule* and ends it with one called *Flirting With Disaster* cannot be said to lack a sense of humor." What's more, Jacob can be said to have excellent taste.

By coincidence or design, many films in the festival portrayed quests for identity. Looking for one's parents, be they biological or spiritual, occupied many of the 22 films in competition and the 45 films in the parallel sections Un Certain Regard and the Directors' Fortnight. Director Mike Leigh, whose gifted ensemble casts about for trustworthy roots in *Secrets and Lies*, said upon accepting the Golden Palm award: "This is incredibly encouraging for those of us who are trying to make films about real people and love and passion and relationships and caring and all the things that matter."

The 1996 festival also proved encouraging for leaps of faith (*Breaking the Waves*), micro-cinematography (*Microcosmos*) and lead performances from unconventional actors (Pascal Duquenne, an actor with Down's Syndrome). The jazz performances in Robert Altman's otherwise uneven period piece *Kansas City* drew raves and lanky Liv Tyler turned heads in Bernardo Bertolucci's *Stealing Beauty* (as did the billboard promoting her).

Combat gear would not have been out of place in the crush to get into *Crash*. Not since the lone press screening of *Pulp Fiction* in 1994 have so many journalists risked life and limb in the scramble for one of the 1,000 seats in the Debussy Auditorium. Opinions were evenly split as David Cronenberg's sleek, chilly adaptation of J.G. Ballard's 1973 cult novel had viewers squirming from either boredom or arousal. When *Crash* received a special jury prize for its "originality, audacity and innovation," jury president Francis Coppola was obliged to announce that some of the jurors had firmly abstained.

The Grand Fete award unofficially went to the half-million dollar *Trainspotting* party. Free samples of heroin weren't passed around in honor of the movie's addicted characters, but, before the night was over, a few would-be heroines passed out near the door. Mick Jagger and U2's Bono were trainspotted on the premises along with the entire cast and crew of the film. The mysterious never-ending party award went to the yacht stationed strategically in the harbor with giant letters spelling PRIVATE on one side. You had to speculate what message the other side carried: PARTS? EYE? Depending on whom you asked, the boat was either a floating brothel or simply a cocktail vessel.

In addition to every variety of glamour and debauchery, Cannes is famous for its blend of art and commerce. It was business as usual at the Majestic and Carlton hotels. Miramax paid nearly $1 million for U.S. distribution rights for *Ridicule*. They also paid handsomely for the festival sleeper, *Microcosmos*, a remarkable French documentary about insects.

Flirting With Disaster closed the festival and aptly described the evening's prize-giving ritual. The French excel at many things. Live award broadcasts are not among them. To some this lack of polish is refreshing. To others, its infuriating. Chinese actress Gong Li presented an award in Mandarin and no one bothered to translate her presentation into either English or French. Names flashed on the screen, seemingly at random. It has yet to occur to the organizers that photos may be taken backstage. Instead, the proceedings ground to a halt so Woody Harrelson or the Arquette sisters could brave a barrage of flashbulbs while viewers twiddled their thumbs.

Unprecedented hoopla will mark the 50th Cannes Film Festival in May 1997. Every creative type who has ever won a prize at Cannes will be invited back and, per Jacob, the festival will try to make up for films and filmmakers that have been overlooked for screenings or awards in the past. Although the festival staff will be hard-pressed to outdo this year's lineup on screen, there is room for more stars on the waterfront. As film heads into its second century, the seventh art is in first-rate hands on the French Riviera.

— GLENN MYRENT

Flirting With Disaster

1996 CANNES FILM FESTIVAL WINNERS

Fargo

Palme d'Or
Secrets and Lies, Mike Leigh (United Kingdom)

Grand Prize
Breaking the Waves, Lars von Trier (Denmark)

Best Actors
Pascal Duquenne and Daniel Auteuil,
Eighth Day (France)

Best Actress
Brenda Blethyn, *Secrets and Lies*
(United Kingdom)

Direction
Fargo, Joel Coen (United States)

Screenplay
A Self-Made Hero, Alain le Henry (France)

Special Jury Prize
Crash, David Cronenberg (Canada)

Camera d'Or for Film Debut
Love Serenade, Shirley Barrett (Australia)

Technique
Microcosmos (France)

Palme d'Or for Short Film
The Wind (Hungary)

Special Jury Prize for Short Film
Small Deaths, Lynne Ramsay (United Kingdom)

The Academy Awards

The Oscars®, awarded annually by the Academy of Motion Picture Arts and Sciences, showcase the best in movies and couture and always stir controversy. Critics and movie fans alike take great pleasure in second-guessing the Academy's picks. The 5,000-plus members of AMPAS select nominees and then vote for the winner in a secret ballot. Listed here is Oscar's 67-year history.

1927–1928

OUTSTANDING PICTURE
The Racket (Caddo; Paramount Famous Lasky)

7th Heaven (Fox)

***Wings* (Paramount Famous Lasky)**

ARTISTIC QUALITY OF PRODUCTION
Chang (Paramount)

The Crowd (MGM)

***Sunrise* (Fox)**

BEST ACTOR
Richard Barthelmess, *The Noose* and *The Patent Leather Kid*

Charles Chaplin, *The Circus* (Though nominated for best actor, the academy decided to remove Chaplin's name from the competitive classes and instead award him a Special Award for writing, acting, directing and producing *The Circus*.)

Emil Jannings, *The Last Command* and *The Way of All Flesh*

BEST ACTRESS
Louise Dresser, *A Ship Comes In*

Janet Gaynor, *7th Heaven*, *Street Angel* and *Sunrise*

Gloria Swanson, *Sadie Thompson*

DIRECTING
DRAMATIC PICTURE
Frank Borzage, *7th Heaven*

Herbert Brenon, *Sorrell and Son*

King Vidor, *The Crowd*

COMEDY PICTURE
Charles Chaplin, *The Circus* (Though nominated for best director of a comedy picture, the academy decided to remove Chaplin's name from the competitive classes and instead award him a Special Award for writing, acting, directing and producing *The Circus*.)

Lewis Milestone, *Two Arabian Knights*

Ted Wilde, *Speedy*

WRITING
ADAPTATION
Alfred Cohn, *The Jazz Singer*

Anthony Coldeway, *Glorious Betsy*

Benjamin Glazer, *7th Heaven*

ORIGINAL STORY
Lajos Biro, *The Last Command*

Ben Hecht, *Underworld*

TITLE WRITING
Gerald Duffy, *The Private Life of Helen of Troy*

Joseph Farnham

George Marion, Jr.

CINEMATOGRAPHY
George Barnes, *The Devil Dancer*, *The Magic Flame* and *Sadie Thompson*

Charles Rosher, *Sunrise*

Karl Struss, *Sunrise*

ART DIRECTION
Rochus Gliese, *Sunrise*

William Cameron Menzies, *The Dove* and *Tempest*

Harry Oliver, *7th Heaven*

ENGINEERING EFFECTS
Ralph Hammeras

Roy Pomeroy, *Wings*

Nugent Slaughter, *The Jazz Singer*

SPECIAL AWARDS
(Not necessarily given each year)

To **Warner Bros.** for producing *The Jazz Singer*, the outstanding pioneer talking picture, which has revolutionized the industry

To **Charles Chaplin** for versatility and genius in writing, acting, directing and producing *The Circus*

1928–1929

OUTSTANDING PICTURE
Alibi (Art Cinema; United Artists)

***The Broadway Melody* (MGM)**

Hollywood Revue (MGM)

In Old Arizona (Fox)

The Patriot (Paramount Famous Lasky)

BEST ACTOR
George Bancroft, *Thunderbolt*

Warner Baxter, *In Old Arizona*

Chester Morris, *Alibi*

Paul Muni, *The Valiant*

Lewis Stone, *The Patriot*

Mary Pickford, *Coquette*

BEST ACTRESS

Ruth Chatterton, *Madame X*

Betty Compson, *The Barker*

Jeanne Eagels, *The Letter*

Corinne Griffith, *The Divine Lady*

Bessie Love, *The Broadway Melody*

Mary Pickford, *Coquette*

DIRECTING

Lionel Barrymore, *Madame X*

Harry Beaumont, *The Broadway Melody*

Irving Cummings, *In Old Arizona*

Frank Lloyd, *The Divine Lady*

Frank Lloyd, *Weary River* and *Drag*

Ernst Lubitsch, *The Patriot*

WRITING

Tom Barry, *In Old Arizona* and *The Valiant*

Elliott Clawson, *The Leatherneck, The Cop, Sal of Singapore* and *Skyscraper*

Josephine Lovett, *Our Dancing Daughters*

Hans Kraly, *The Last of Mrs. Cheyney*

Hans Kraly, *The Patriot*

Bess Meredyth, *Wonder of Women* and *A Woman of Affairs*

CINEMATOGRAPHY

George Barnes, *Our Dancing Daughters*

Clyde De Vinna, *White Shadows in the South Seas*

Arthur Edeson, *In Old Arizona*

Ernest Palmer, *Four Devils* and *Street Angel*

John Seitz, *The Divine Lady*

ART DIRECTION

Hans Dreier, *The Patriot*

Cedric Gibbons, *The Bridge of San Luis Rey* and other pictures

Mitchell Leisen, *Dynamite*

William Cameron Menzies, *Alibi* and *The Awakening*

Harry Oliver, *Street Angel*

1929–1930

OUTSTANDING PRODUCTION

All Quiet on the Western Front (Universal)

The Big House (Cosmopolitan; MGM)

Disraeli (Warner Bros.)

The Divorcée (MGM)

The Love Parade (Paramount Famous Lasky)

BEST ACTOR

George Arliss, *Disraeli*

George Arliss, *The Green Goddess*

Wallace Beery, *The Big House*

Maurice Chevalier, *The Big Pond* and *The Love Parade*

Ronald Colman, *Bulldog Drummond* and *Condemned*

Lawrence Tibbett, *The Rogue Song*

BEST ACTRESS

Nancy Carroll, *The Devil's Holiday*

Ruth Chatterton, *Sarah and Son*

Greta Garbo, *Anna Christie* and *Romance*

Norma Shearer, *The Divorcée*

Norma Shearer, *Their Own Desire*

Gloria Swanson, *The Trespasser*

DIRECTING

Clarence Brown, *Anna Christie* and *Romance*

Robert Z. Leonard, *The Divorcée*

Ernst Lubitsch, *The Love Parade*

Lewis Milestone, *All Quiet on the Western Front*

King Vidor, *Hallelujah*

WRITING

George Abbott, Maxwell Anderson and Del Andrews, *All Quiet on the Western Front*

Howard Estabrook, *Street of Chance*

Julian Josephson, *Disraeli*

Frances Marion, *The Big House*

John Meehan, *The Divorcée*

CINEMATOGRAPHY

William Daniels, *Anna Christie*

Arthur Edeson, *All Quiet on the Western Front*

Gaetano Gaudio and Harry Perry, *Hell's Angels*

Victor Milner, *The Love Parade*

Joseph T. Rucker and Willard Van Der Veer, *With Byrd at the South Pole*

ART DIRECTION

Hans Dreier, *The Love Parade*

Hans Dreier, *The Vagabond King*

William Cameron Menzies, *Bulldog Drummond*

Jack Okey, *Sally*

Herman Rosse, *King of Jazz*

SOUND RECORDING

First National Studio Sound Dept., *Song of the Flame*
MGM Studio Sound Dept., *The Big House*
Paramount Famous Lasky Studio Sound Dept.,
    The Love Parade
RKO Radio Studio Sound Dept., *The Case of Sergeant Grischa*
United Artists Studio Sound Dept., *Raffles*

1930–1931

OUTSTANDING PRODUCTION

***Cimarron* (RKO Radio)**
East Lynne (Fox)
The Front Page (Caddo, United Artists)
Skippy (Paramount Publix)
Trader Horn (MGM)

BEST ACTOR

Lionel Barrymore, *A Free Soul*
Jackie Cooper, *Skippy*
Richard Dix, *Cimarron*
Fredric March, *The Royal Family of Broadway*
Adolphe Menjou, *The Front Page*

BEST ACTRESS

Marlene Dietrich, *Morocco*
Marie Dressler, *Min and Bill*
Irene Dunne, *Cimarron*
Ann Harding, *Holiday*
Norma Shearer, *A Free Soul*

DIRECTING

Clarence Brown, *A Free Soul*
Lewis Milestone, *The Front Page*
Wesley Ruggles, *Cimarron*
Norman Taurog, *Skippy*
Josef Von Sternberg, *Morocco*

WRITING

ADAPTATION
Howard Estabrook, *Cimarron*
Francis Faragoh and Robert N. Lee, *Little Caesar*
Horace Jackson, *Holiday*
Joseph L. Mankiewicz and Sam Mintz, *Skippy*
Seton Miller and Fred Niblo, Jr., *The Criminal Code*

ORIGINAL STORY
John Bright and Kubec Glasmon, *The Public Enemy*
Rowland Brown, *The Doorway to Hell*
Harry d'Abbadie d'Arrast, Douglas Doty and Donald Ogden
    Stewart, *Laughter*
Lucien Hubbard and Joseph Jackson, *Smart Money*
John Monk Saunders, *The Dawn Patrol*

CINEMATOGRAPHY

Edward Cronjager, *Cimarron*
Floyd Crosby, *Tabu*
Lee Garmes, *Morocco*
Charles Lang, *The Right to Love*
Barney "Chick" McGill, *Svengali*

ART DIRECTION

Richard Day, *Whoopee!*
Hans Dreier, *Morocco*
Stephen Goosson and Ralph Hammeras, *Just Imagine*
Anton Grot, *Svengali*
Max Ree, *Cimmaron*

SOUND RECORDING

MGM Studio Sound Department
Paramount Publix Studio Sound Department
RKO Radio Studio Sound Department
Samuel Goldwyn-United Artists Studio Sound Department

1931–1932

OUTSTANDING PRODUCTION

Arrowsmith (Goldwyn; United Artists)
Bad Girl (Fox)
The Champ (MGM)
Five Star Final (First National)
***Grand Hotel* (MGM)**
One Hour With You (Paramount Publix)
Shanghai Express (Paramount Publix)
The Smiling Lieutenant (Paramount Publix)

BEST ACTOR (TIE)

Wallace Beery, *The Champ*
Alfred Lunt, *The Guardsman*
Fredric March, *Dr. Jekyll and Mr. Hyde*

BEST ACTRESS

Marie Dressler, *Emma*
Lynn Fontanne, *The Guardsman*
Helen Hayes, *The Sin of Madelon Claudet*

DIRECTING

Frank Borzage, *Bad Girl*
King Vidor, *The Champ*
Josef Von Sternberg, *Shanghai Express*

WRITING

ADAPTATION
Edwin Burke, *Bad Girl*
Percy Heath and Samuel Hoffenstein, *Dr. Jekyll and Mr. Hyde*
Sidney Howard, *Arrowsmith*

ORIGINAL STORY
Lucien Hubbard, *The Star Witness*
Grover Jones and William Slavens McNutt, *Lady and Gent*
Frances Marion, *The Champ*
Adela Rogers St. Johns, *What Price Hollywood?*

CINEMATOGRAPHY
Lee Garmes, *Shanghai Express*
Ray June, *Arrowsmith*
Karl Struss, *Dr. Jekyll and Mr. Hyde*

ART DIRECTION
Richard Day, *Arrowsmith*
Lazare Meerson, *A Nous la Liberté*
Gordon Wiles, *Transatlantic*

SOUND RECORDING
MGM Studio Sound Dept.
Paramount Publix Studio Sound Department
RKO Radio Studio Sound Dept.
Warner Bros.-First National Studio Sound Dept.

SHORT SUBJECTS
CARTOON
***Flowers and Trees* (*Silly Symphony Series*) (Walt Disney Productions; United Artists)**
It's Got Me Again (Leon Schlesinger, producer; Warner Bros.)
Mickey's Orphans (*Mickey Mouse Series*) (Walt Disney Productions; Columbia)

COMEDY
The Loud Mouth (Mack Sennett, producer; Paramount Publix)
***The Music Box* (*Laurel and Hardy Series*) (Hal Roach, producer; MGM)**
Scratch-As-Catch-Can (*Headliner Series*) (RKO Radio)
Stout Hearts and Willing Hands (*Masquers Comedies Series*) (RKO Radio) (This film was originally announced as a nominee, but before the final voting, it was disqualified and replaced by *Scratch-As-Catch-Can*.)

NOVELTY
Screen Souvenirs (Paramount Publix)
Swing High (*Sports Champion Series*) (MGM)
***Wrestling Swordfish* (*Cannibals of the Deep Series*) (Mack Sennett, producer; Educational)**

SPECIAL AWARD
To **Walt Disney** for the creation of Mickey Mouse

1932–1933

OUTSTANDING PRODUCTION
***Cavalcade* (Fox)**
A Farewell to Arms (Paramount)
42nd Street (Warner Bros.)
I Am a Fugitive From a Chain Gang (Warner Bros.)
Lady for a Day (Columbia)
Little Women (RKO Radio)
The Private Life of Henry VIII (London Films; United Artists)
She Done Him Wrong (Paramount)
Smilin' Through (MGM)
State Fair (Fox)

Katharine Hepburn, *Morning Glory*

BEST ACTOR
Leslie Howard, *Berkeley Square*
Charles Laughton, *The Private Life of Henry VIII*
Paul Muni, *I Am a Fugitive From a Chain Gang*

BEST ACTRESS
Katharine Hepburn, *Morning Glory*
May Robson, *Lady for a Day*
Diana Wynyard, *Cavalcade*

DIRECTING
Frank Capra, *Lady for a Day*
George Cukor, *Little Women*
Frank Lloyd, *Cavalcade*

WRITING
ADAPTATION
Paul Green and Sonya Levien, *State Fair*
Victor Heerman and Sarah Y. Mason, *Little Women*
Robert Riskin, *Lady for a Day*

ORIGINAL STORY
Robert Lord, *One Way Passage*
Charles MacArthur, *Rasputin and the Empress*
Frances Marion, *The Prizefighter and the Lady*

CINEMATOGRAPHY
George J. Folsey, *Reunion in Vienna*
Charles Bryant Lang, Jr., *A Farewell to Arms*
Karl Struss, *The Sign of the Cross*

ART DIRECTION
William S. Darling, *Cavalcade*
Hans Dreier and Roland Anderson, *A Farewell to Arms*
Cedric Gibbons, *When Ladies Meet*

SOUND RECORDING
Paramount Studio Sound Dept., *A Farewell to Arms*
Warner Bros. Studio Sound Dept., *42nd Street*
Warner Bros. Studio Sound Dept., *Gold Diggers of 1933*
Warner Bros. Studio Sound Dept., *I Am a Fugitive From a Chain Gang*

ASSISTANT DIRECTOR (TIE)

Al Alborn, Warner Bros.

Charles Barton, Paramount

Scott Beal, Universal

Sidney S. Brod, Paramount

Charles Dorian, MGM

Benny Dull, MGM

Fred Fox, United Artists

Gordon Hollingshead, Warner Bros.

Percy Ikerd, Fox

Arthur Jacobson, Paramount

Eddie Killey, RKO Radio

Joe McDonough, Universal

W. J. Reiter, Universal

Frank X. Shaw, Warner Bros.

Benjamin Silvey, United Artists

Dewey Starkey, RKO Radio

William Tummel, Fox

John S. Waters, MGM

SHORT SUBJECTS

CARTOON

Building a Building (*Mickey Mouse Series*) (Walt Disney Productions; United Artists)

The Merry Old Soul (*Oswald the Rabbit Series*) (Walter Lantz Productions; Universal)

The Three Little Pigs (*Silly Symphony Series*) (Walt Disney Productions; United Artists)

COMEDY

Mister Mugg (*Comedies Series*) (Warren Doane, producer; Universal)

A Preferred List (*Headliner Series #5*) (Louis Brock, producer; RKO Radio)

So This Is Harris (Louis Brock, producer; RKO Radio)

NOVELTY

Krakatoa (Joe Rock, producer; Educational)

Menu (*Oddities Series*) (Pete Smith, producer; MGM)

The Sea (*Battle for Life Series*) (Educational)

1934

OUTSTANDING PRODUCTON

The Barretts of Wimpole Street (MGM)

Cleopatra (Paramount)

Flirtation Walk (First National)

The Gay Divorcée (RKO Radio)

Here Comes the Navy (Warner Bros.)

The House of Rothschild (Twentieth Century; United Artists)

Imitation of Life (Universal)

***It Happened One Night* (Columbia)**

One Night of Love (Columbia)

The Thin Man (MGM)

Viva Villa! (MGM)

The White Parade (Jesse L. Lasky; Fox)

**Clark Gable and Claudette Colbert,
*It Happened One Night***

BEST ACTOR

Clark Gable, *It Happened One Night*

Frank Morgan, *The Affairs of Cellini*

William Powell, *The Thin Man*

BEST ACTRESS

Claudette Colbert, *It Happened One Night*

Bette Davis, *Of Human Bondage* (Write-in candidate, not an official nomination)

Grace Moore, *One Night of Love*

Norma Shearer, *The Barretts of Wimpole Street*

DIRECTING

Frank Capra, *It Happened One Night*

Victor Schertzinger, *One Night of Love*

W. S. Van Dyke, *The Thin Man*

WRITING

ADAPTATION

Frances Goodrich and Albert Hackett, *The Thin Man*

Ben Hecht, *Viva Villa!*

Robert Riskin, *It Happened One Night*

ORIGINAL STORY

Arthur Caesar, *Manhattan Melodrama*

Mauri Grashin, *Hide-Out*

Norman Krasna, *The Richest Girl in the World*

CINEMATOGRAPHY

George Folsey, *Operator 13*

Victor Milner, *Cleopatra*

Charles Rosher, *The Affairs of Cellini*

ART DIRECTION

Richard Day, *The Affairs of Cellini*

Cedric Gibbons and Frederic Hope, *The Merry Widow*

Van Nest Polglase and Carroll Clark, *The Gay Divorcée*

SOUND RECORDING

Columbia Studio Sound Dept., *One Night of Love*

Fox Studio Sound Dept., *The White Parade*

MGM Studio Sound Dept., *Naughty Marietta*

Paramount Studio Sound Dept., *Cleopatra*

RKO Radio Studio Sound Dept., *The Gay Divorcée*

United Artists Studio Sound Dept., *The Affairs of Cellini*

Universal Studio Sound Dept., *Imitation of Life*

Warner Bros.-First National Studio Sound Dept.,
Flirtation Walk

ASSISTANT DIRECTOR

Scott Beal, *Imitation of Life*

Cullen Tate, *Cleopatra*

John Waters, *Viva Villa!*

MUSIC

SONG

"Carioca," *Flying Down to Rio,* Vincent Youmans, music;
Edward Eliscu and Gus Kahn, lyrics

**"The Continental," *The Gay Divorcée,* Con Conrad, music;
Herb Magidson, lyrics**

"Love in Bloom," *She Loves Me Not,* Ralph Rainger, music;
Leo Robin, lyrics

SCORE

Columbia Studio Music Dept., *One Night of Love*

RKO Radio Studio Music Dept., *The Gay Divorcée*

RKO Radio Studio Music Dept., *The Lost Patrol*

FILM EDITING

Anne Bauchens, *Cleopatra*

Gene Milford, *One Night of Love*

Conrad Nervig, *Eskimo*

SHORT SUBJECTS

CARTOON

Holiday Land (*Color Rhapsody Series*) (Screen Gems;
Columbia)

Jolly Little Elves (*Cartune Classic Series*) (Walter Lantz
Productions; Universal)

**The Tortoise and the Hare (*Silly Symphony Series*) (Walt
Disney Productions; United Artists)**

COMEDY

***La Cucaracha* (Pioneer Pictures; RKO Radio)**

Men in Black (*The Three Stooges Series*) (Jules White,
producer; Columbia)

What, No Men! (*Broadway Brevities Series*) (Warner Bros.)

NOVELTY

Bosom Friends (*Treasure Chest Series*) (Skibo Productions;
Educational-Fox)

***City of Wax* (*Battle for Life Series*) (Skibo Productions;
Educational-Fox)**

Strikes and Spares (*Oddities Series*) (Pete Smith, producer;
MGM)

SPECIAL AWARD

To **Shirley Temple** in grateful recognition of her outstanding
contribution to screen entertainment during the year 1934

1935

OUTSTANDING PRODUCTION

Alice Adams (RKO Radio)

Broadway Melody of 1936 (MGM)

Captain Blood (Cosmopolitan; First National)

David Copperfield (MGM)

The Informer (RKO Radio)

Les Misérables (Twentieth Century; United Artists)

The Lives of a Bengal Lancer (Paramount)

A Midsummer Night's Dream (Warner Bros.)

***Mutiny on the Bounty* (MGM)**

Naughty Marietta (MGM)

Ruggles of Red Gap (Paramount)

Top Hat (RKO Radio)

BEST ACTOR

Clark Gable, *Mutiny on the Bounty*

Charles Laughton, *Mutiny on the Bounty*

Victor McLaglen, *The Informer*

Paul Muni, *Black Fury* (Write-in candidate, not an official
nomination)

Franchot Tone, *Mutiny on the Bounty*

BEST ACTRESS

Elisabeth Bergner, *Escape Me Never*

Claudette Colbert, *Private Worlds*

Bette Davis, *Dangerous*

Katharine Hepburn, *Alice Adams*

Miriam Hopkins, *Becky Sharp*

Merle Oberon, *The Dark Angel*

DIRECTING

Michael Curtiz, *Captain Blood* (Write-in candidate, not an
official nomination)

John Ford, *The Informer*

Henry Hathaway, *The Lives of a Bengal Lancer*

Frank Lloyd, *Mutiny on the Bounty*

WRITING

ORIGINAL STORY

Moss Hart, *Broadway Melody of 1936*

Don Hartman and Stephen Avery, *The Gay Deception*

Ben Hecht and Charles MacArthur, *The Scoundrel*

Gregory Rogers, *G-Men* (Write-in candidate, not an
official nomination)

SCREENPLAY

Achmed Abdullah, John L. Balderston and Waldemar Young,
screenplay; Jules Furthman, Talbot Jennings and Carey
Wilson, *Mutiny on the Bounty*

Grover Jones and William Slavens McNutt, adaptation, *The
Lives of a Bengal Lancer*

Dudley Nichols, *The Informer*

Casey Robinson, *Captain Blood* (Write-in candidate, not an
official nomination)

CINEMATOGRAPHY

Ray June, *Barbary Coast*

Victor Milner, *The Crusades*

Hal Mohr, *A Midsummer Night's Dream* (Write-in candidate, not an official nomination)

Gregg Toland, *Les Misérables*

ART DIRECTION

Carroll Clark and Van Nest Polglase, *Top Hat*

Richard Day, *The Dark Angel*

Hans Dreier and Roland Anderson, *The Lives of a Bengal Lancer*

SOUND RECORDING

Columbia Studio Sound Dept., *Love Me Forever*

MGM Studio Sound Dept., *Naughty Marietta*

Paramount Studio Sound Dept., *The Lives of a Bengal Lancer*

Republic Studio Sound Department, *$1,000 a Minute*

RKO Radio Studio Sound Dept., *I Dream Too Much*

Twentieth Century-Fox Studio Sound Dept., *Thanks a Million*

United Artists Studio Sound Dept., *The Dark Angel*

Universal Studio Sound Dept., *The Bride of Frankenstein*

Warner Bros.-First National Studio Sound Dept., *Captain Blood*

ASSISTANT DIRECTOR

Clem Beauchamp and Paul Wing, *The Lives of a Bengal Lancer*

Joseph Newman, *David Copperfield*

Sherry Shourds, *A Midsummer Night's Dream* (Write-in candidate, not an official nomination)

Eric Stacey, *Les Misérables*

MUSIC

SONG

"Cheek to Cheek," *Top Hat,* Irving Berlin, music and lyrics

"Lovely to Look At," *Roberta,* Jerome Kern, music; Dorothy Fields and Jimmy McHugh, lyrics

"Lullaby of Broadway," *Gold Diggers of 1935*, Harry Warren, music; Al Dubin, lyrics

SCORE

MGM Studio Music Dept., *Mutiny on the Bounty*

Paramount Studio Music Dept., *Peter Ibbetson*

RKO Radio Studio Music Dept., *The Informer*

Warner Bros.-First National Studio Music Dept., *Captain Blood*

FILM EDITING

Margaret Booth, *Mutiny on the Bounty*

Ralph Dawson, *A Midsummer Night's Dream*

George Hively, *The Informer*

Ellsworth Hoagland, *The Lives of a Bengal Lancer*

Robert J. Kern, *David Copperfield*

Barbara McLean, *Les Misérables*

DANCE DIRECTION

Busby Berkeley, "Lullaby of Broadway" and "The Words Are in My Heart," *Gold Diggers of 1935*

Bobby Connolly, "Latin From Manhattan," *Go Into Your Dance* and "Playboy From Paree," *Broadway Hostess*

Dave Gould, "I've Got a Feeling You're Fooling," *Broadway Melody of 1936* and "Straw Hat," *Folies Bergere*

Sammy Lee, "Lovely Lady" and "Too Good to Be True," *King of Burlesque*

Hermes Pan, "Piccolino" and "Top Hat, White Tie and Tails," *Top Hat*

LeRoy Prinz, "It's the Animal in Me," *Big Broadcast of 1936* and "Viennese Waltz," *All the King's Horses*

Benjamin Zemach, "Hall of Kings," *She*

SHORT SUBJECTS

CARTOON

The Calico Dragon (*Happy Harmonies Series*) (Harman-Ising; MGM)

***Three Orphan Kittens* (*Silly Symphony Series*) (Walt Disney Productions; United Artists)**

Who Killed Cock Robin? (*Silly Symphony Series*) (Walt Disney Productions; United Artists)

COMEDY

***How to Sleep* (*Miniature Series*) (Jack Chertok, producer; MGM)**

Oh, My Nerves (*Broadway Comedies Series*) (Jules White, producer; Columbia)

Tit for Tat (*Laurel and Hardy Series*) (Hal Roach, producer; MGM)

NOVELTY

Audioscopiks (Pete Smith, producer; MGM)

Camera Thrills (Universal)

***Wings Over Mt. Everest* (Gaumont British and Skibo Productions; Educational)**

SPECIAL AWARD

To **David Wark Griffith** for his distinguished creative achievements as director and producer and his invaluable initiative and lasting contributions to the progress of the motion picture arts

1936

OUTSTANDING PRODUCTION

Anthony Adverse (Warner Bros.)

Dodsworth (Goldwyn; United Artists)

***The Great Ziegfeld* (MGM)**

Libeled Lady (MGM)

Mr. Deeds Goes to Town (Columbia)

Romeo and Juliet (MGM)

San Francisco (MGM)

The Story of Louis Pasteur (Cosmopolitan; Warner Bros.-First National)

A Tale of Two Cities (MGM)

Three Smart Girls (Universal)

BEST ACTOR

Gary Cooper, *Mr. Deeds Goes to Town*

Walter Huston, *Dodsworth*

Paul Muni, *The Story of Louis Pasteur*

William Powell, *My Man Godfrey*

Spencer Tracy, *San Francisco*

BEST ACTRESS

Irene Dunne, *Theodora Goes Wild*

Gladys George, *Valiant Is the Word for Carrie*

Carole Lombard, *My Man Godfrey*

Luise Rainer, *The Great Ziegfeld*

Norma Shearer, *Romeo and Juliet*

ACTOR IN A SUPPORTING ROLE

Mischa Auer, *My Man Godfrey*

Walter Brennan, *Come and Get It*

Stuart Erwin, *Pigskin Parade*

Basil Rathbone, *Romeo and Juliet*

Akim Tamiroff, *The General Died at Dawn*

ACTRESS IN A SUPPORTING ROLE

Beulah Bondi, *The Gorgeous Hussy*

Alice Brady, *My Man Godfrey*

Bonita Granville, *These Three*

Maria Ouspenskaya, *Dodsworth*

Gale Sondergaard, *Anthony Adverse*

Frank Capra

DIRECTING

Frank Capra, *Mr. Deeds Goes to Town*

Gregory La Cava, *My Man Godfrey*

Robert Z. Leonard, *The Great Ziegfeld*

W. S. Van Dyke, *San Francisco*

William Wyler, *Dodsworth*

WRITING

ORIGINAL STORY

**Pierre Collings and Sheridan Gibney,
*The Story of Louis Pasteur***

Adele Comandini, *Three Smart Girls*

Robert Hopkins, *San Francisco*

Norman Krasna, *Fury*

William Anthony McGuire, *The Great Ziegfeld*

SCREENPLAY

**Pierre Collings and Sheridan Gibney,
*The Story of Louis Pasteur***

Frances Goodrich and Albert Hackett, *After the Thin Man*

Eric Hatch and Morris Ryskind, *My Man Godfrey*

Sidney Howard, *Dodsworth*

Robert Riskin, *Mr. Deeds Goes to Town*

CINEMATOGRAPHY

George Folsey, *The Gorgeous Hussy*

Gaetano Gaudio, *Anthony Adverse*

Victor Milner, *The General Died at Dawn*

ART DIRECTION

Albert S. D'Agostino and Jack Otterson, *The Magnificent Brute*

William S. Darling, *Lloyds of London*

Richard Day, *Dodsworth*

Perry Ferguson, *Winterset*

Cedric Gibbons, Frederic Hope and Edwin B. Willis, *Romeo and Juliet*

Cedric Gibbons, Eddie Imazu and Edwin B. Willis, *The Great Ziegfeld*

Anton Grot, *Anthony Adverse*

SOUND RECORDING

Columbia Studio Sound Dept., *Mr. Deeds Goes to Town*

Hal Roach Studio Sound Dept., *General Spanky*

MGM Studio Sound Dept., *San Francisco*

Paramount Studio Sound Dept., *The Texas Rangers*

RKO Radio Studio Sound Dept., *That Girl From Paris*

Twentieth Century-Fox Studio Sound Dept., *Banjo on My Knee*

United Artists Studio Sound Dept., *Dodsworth*

Universal Studio Sound Dept., *Three Smart Girls*

Warner Bros. Studio Sound Dept., *The Charge of the Light Brigade*

ASSISTANT DIRECTOR

Clem Beauchamp, *The Last of the Mohicans*

William Cannon, *Anthony Adverse*

Joseph Newman, *San Francisco*

Eric G. Stacey, *Garden of Allah*

Jack Sullivan, *The Charge of the Light Brigade*

MUSIC

SONG

"Did I Remember," *Suzy*, Walter Donaldson, music; Harold Adamson, lyrics

"I've Got You Under My Skin," *Born to Dance*, Cole Porter, music and lyrics

"A Melody From the Sky," *Trail of the Lonesome Pine*, Louis Alter, music; Sidney Mitchell, lyrics

"Pennies From Heaven," *Pennies From Heaven*, Arthur Johnston, music; Johnny Burke, lyrics

"The Way You Look Tonight," *Swing Time*, Jerome Kern, music; Dorothy Fields, lyrics

"When Did You Leave Heaven," *Sing, Baby Sing*, Richard A. Whiting, music; Walter Bullock, lyrics

SCORE

Paramount Studio Music Dept., *The General Died at Dawn*

RKO Radio Studio Music Dept., *Winterset*

Selznick International Pictures Music Dept.,
The Garden of Allah

Warner Bros. Studio Music Dept., *Anthony Adverse*

Warner Bros. Studio Music Dept., *The Charge
of the Light Brigade*

FILM EDITING

Edward Curtiss, *Come and Get It*

Ralph Dawson, *Anthony Adverse*

William S. Gray, *The Great Ziegfeld*

Barbara McLean, *Lloyds of London*

Otto Meyer, *Theodora Goes Wild*

Conrad A. Nervig, *A Tale of Two Cities*

DANCE DIRECTION

Busby Berkeley, "Love and War," *Gold Diggers of 1937*

Bobby Connolly, "1,000 Love Songs," *Cain and Mabel*

**Seymour Felix, "A Pretty Girl Is like a Melody,"
*The Great Ziegfeld***

Dave Gould, "Swingin' the Jinx," *Born to Dance*

Jack Haskell, "Skating Ensemble," *One in a Million*

Russell Lewis, "The Finale," *Dancing Pirate*

Hermes Pan, "Bojangles of Harlem," *Swing Time*

SHORT SUBJECTS

CARTOON

**The Country Cousin (*Silly Symphony Series*) (Walt Disney
Productions; United Artists)**

Old Mill Pond (*Happy Harmonies Series*) (Harman-Ising; MGM)

Sinbad the Sailor (*Popeye Series*) (Paramount)

ONE-REEL

**Bored of Education (*Our Gang Series*) (Hal Roach,
producer; MGM)**

Moscow Moods (*Headliners Series*) (Paramount)

Wanted, A Master (*Pete Smith Specialties Series*)
(Pete Smith, producer; MGM)

TWO-REEL

Double or Nothing (*Melody Masters Series*) (Warner Bros.)

Dummy Ache (*Edgar Kennedy Comedies Series*) (RKO Radio)

The Public Pays (*Crime Doesn't Pay Series*) (MGM)

COLOR

Give Me Liberty (*Broadway Brevities Series*) (Warner Bros.)

La Fiesta de Santa Barbara (*Musical Revues Series*)
(Lewis Lewyn, producer; MGM)

Popular Science J-6-2 (*Popular Science Series*) (Paramount)

SPECIAL AWARDS

To the **March of Time** for its significance to motion pictures
and for having revolutionized one of the most important
branches of the industry — the newsreel

To **W. Howard Greene** and **Harold Rosson** for the color
cinematography of the Selznick International Production,
The Garden of Allah

1937

OUTSTANDING PRODUCTION

The Awful Truth (Columbia)

Captains Courageous (MGM)

Dead End (Goldwyn; United Artists)

The Good Earth (MGM)

In Old Chicago (Twentieth Century-Fox)

The Life of Emile Zola (Warner Bros.)

Lost Horizon (Columbia)

One Hundred Men and a Girl (Universal)

Stage Door (RKO Radio)

A Star Is Born (Selznick International Pictures; United Artists)

BEST ACTOR

Charles Boyer, *Conquest*

Fredric March, *A Star Is Born*

Robert Montgomery, *Night Must Fall*

Paul Muni, *The Life of Emile Zola*

Spencer Tracy, *Captains Courageous*

BEST ACTRESS

Irene Dunne, *The Awful Truth*

Greta Garbo, *Camille*

Janet Gaynor, *A Star Is Born*

Luise Rainer, *The Good Earth*

Barbara Stanwyck, *Stella Dallas*

ACTOR IN A SUPPORTING ROLE

Ralph Bellamy, *The Awful Truth*

Thomas Mitchell, *The Hurricane*

Joseph Schildkraut, *The Life of Emile Zola*

H. B. Warner, *Lost Horizon*

Roland Young, *Topper*

ACTRESS IN A SUPPORTING ROLE

Alice Brady, *In Old Chicago*

Andrea Leeds, *Stage Door*

Anne Shirley, *Stella Dallas*

Claire Trevor, *Dead End*

Dame May Whitty, *Night Must Fall*

DIRECTING

William Dieterle, *The Life of Emile Zola*

Sidney Franklin, *The Good Earth*

Gregory La Cava, *Stage Door*

Leo McCarey, *The Awful Truth*

William Wellman, *A Star Is Born*

WRITING

ORIGINAL STORY

Niven Busch, *In Old Chicago*

Heinz Herald and Geza Herczeg, *The Life of Emile Zola*

Hans Kraly, *One Hundred Men and a Girl*

Robert Lord, *Black Legion*

William A. Wellman and Robert Carson, *A Star Is Born*

Spencer Tracy, *Captains Courageous*

SCREENPLAY
Alan Campbell, Robert Carson and Dorothy Parker, *A Star Is Born*

Vina Delmar, *The Awful Truth*

John Lee Mahin, Marc Connolly and Dale Van Every, *Captains Courageous*

Morris Ryskind and Anthony Veiller, *Stage Door*

CINEMATOGRAPHY
Karl Freund, *The Good Earth*

Gregg Toland, *Dead End*

Joseph Valentine, *Wings Over Honolulu*

ART DIRECTION
Carroll Clark, *A Damsel in Distress*

William S. Darling and David Hall, *Wee Willie Winkie*

Richard Day, *Dead End*

Hans Dreier and Roland Anderson, *Souls at Sea*

Cedric Gibbons and William Horning, *Conquest*

Stephen Goosson, *Lost Horizon*

Anton Grot, *The Life of Emile Zola*

Wiard Ihnen, *Every Day's a Holiday*

John Victor Mackay, *Manhattan Merry-Go-Round*

Jack Otterson, *You're a Sweetheart*

Alexander Toluboff, *Walter Wanger's Vogues of 1938*

Lyle Wheeler, *The Prisoner of Zenda*

SOUND RECORDING
Columbia Studio Sound Dept., *Lost Horizon*

Grand National Studio Sound Dept., *The Girl Said No*

Hal Roach Studio Sound Dept., *Topper*

MGM Studio Sound Dept., *Maytime*

Paramount Studio Sound Dept., *Wells Fargo*

RKO Radio Studio Sound Dept., *Hitting a New High*

Twentieth Century-Fox Studio Sound Dept., *In Old Chicago*

United Artists Studio Sound Dept., *The Hurricane*

Universal Studio Sound Dept., *One Hundred Men and a Girl*

Warner Bros. Studio Sound Dept., *The Life of Emile Zola*

ASSISTANT DIRECTOR
C. C. Coleman, Jr., *Lost Horizon*

Russ Saunders, *The Life of Emile Zola*

Eric Stacey, *A Star Is Born*

Hal Walker, *Souls at Sea*

Robert Webb, *In Old Chicago*

MUSIC
SONG
"Remember Me," *Mr. Dodd Takes the Air*, Harry Warren, music; Al Dubin, lyrics

"Sweet Leilani," *Waikiki Wedding*, Harry Owens, music and lyrics

"That Old Feeling," *Walter Wanger's Vogues of 1938*, Sammy Fain, music; Lew Brown, lyrics

"They Can't Take That Away From Me," *Shall We Dance*, George Gershwin, music; Ira Gershwin, lyrics

"Whispers in the Dark," *Artists and Models*, Frederick Hollander, music; Leo Robin, lyrics

SCORE
Columbia Studio Music Dept., *Lost Horizon*

Goldwyn Studio Music Dept., *The Hurricane*

Grand National Studio Music Dept., *Something to Sing About*

Hal Roach Studio Music Dept., *Way Out West*

MGM Studio Music Dept., *Maytime*

Paramount Studio Music Dept., *Souls at Sea*

Principal Productions, *Make a Wish*

Republic Studio Music Dept., *Portia on Trial*

RKO Radio Studio Music Dept., *Quality Street*

Selznick International Pictures Music Dept., *The Prisoner of Zenda*

Twentieth Century-Fox Studio Music Dept., *In Old Chicago*

Universal Studio Music Dept., *One Hundred Men and a Girl*

Walt Disney Studio Music Dept., *Snow White and the Seven Dwarfs*

Warner Bros. Studio Music Dept., *The Life of Emile Zola*

FILM EDITING
Bernard W. Burton, *One Hundred Men and a Girl*

Al Clark, *The Awful Truth*

Gene Havlick and Gene Milford, *Lost Horizon*

Elmo Vernon, *Captains Courageous*

Basil Wrangell, *The Good Earth*

DANCE DIRECTION
Busby Berkeley, "The Finale," *Varsity Show*

Bobby Connolly, "Too Marvelous for Words," *Ready, Willing and Able*

Dave Gould, "All God's Children Got Rhythm," *A Day at the Races*

Sammy Lee, "Swing Is Here to Stay," *Ali Baba Goes to Town*

Hermes Pan, "Fun House," *A Damsel in Distress*

LeRoy Prinz, "Luau," *Waikiki Wedding*

SHORT SUBJECTS
CARTOON
Educated Fish (*Color Classics Series*) (Paramount)

The Little Match Girl (Charles Mintz, producer; Columbia)

***The Old Mill* (Walt Disney Productions; RKO Radio)**

ONE-REEL
A Night at the Movies (*Robert Benchley Series*) (MGM)
The Private Life of the Gannetts (Skibo Productions; Educational)
Romance of Radium (*Pete Smith Specialties Series*) (Pete Smith, producer; MGM)

TWO-REEL
Deep South (*Radio Musical Comedies Series*) (RKO Radio)
Should Wives Work? (*Leon Errol Comedies Series*) (RKO Radio)
Torture Money (*Crime Doesn't Pay Series*) (MGM)

COLOR
The Man Without a Country (*Broadway Brevities Series*) (Warner Bros.)
Penny Wisdom (*Pete Smith Specialties Series*) (Pete Smith, producer; MGM)
Popular Science J-7-1 (*Popular Science Series*) (Paramount)

IRVING G. THALBERG MEMORIAL AWARD
(Not necessarily given each year)
Darryl F. Zanuck

SPECIAL AWARDS
To **Mack Sennett** for his lasting contribution to the comedy technique of the screen

To **Edgar Bergen** for his outstanding comedy creation, Charlie McCarthy

To the **Museum of Modern Art Film Library** for its significant work in collecting films dating from 1895 to the present, and for the first time making available to the public the means of studying the historical and aesthetic development of the motion picture as one of the major arts

To **W. Howard Greene** for the color photography of *A Star Is Born*

1938

OUTSTANDING PRODUCTION
The Adventures of Robin Hood (Warner Bros.-First National)
Alexander's Ragtime Band (Twentieth Century-Fox)
Boys Town (MGM)
The Citadel (MGM)
Four Daughters (Warner Bros.-First National)
Grand Illusion (Realization D'Art Cinematographique; World Pictures)
Jezebel (Warner Bros.)
Pygmalion (MGM)
Test Pilot (MGM)
You Can't Take It With You (Columbia)

BEST ACTOR
Charles Boyer, *Algiers*
James Cagney, *Angels With Dirty Faces*
Robert Donat, *The Citadel*
Leslie Howard, *Pygmalion*
Spencer Tracy, *Boys Town*

BEST ACTRESS
Fay Bainter, *White Banners*
Bette Davis, *Jezebel*
Wendy Hiller, *Pygmalion*
Norma Shearer, *Marie Antoinette*
Margaret Sullavan, *Three Comrades*

ACTOR IN A SUPPORTING ROLE
Walter Brennan, *Kentucky*
John Garfield, *Four Daughters*
Gene Lockhart, *Algiers*
Robert Morley, *Marie Antoinette*
Basil Rathbone, *If I Were King*

ACTRESS IN A SUPPORTING ROLE
Fay Bainter, *Jezebel*
Beulah Bondi, *Of Human Hearts*
Billie Burke, *Merrily We Live*
Spring Byington, *You Can't Take It With You*
Miliza Korjus, *The Great Waltz*

DIRECTING
Frank Capra, *You Can't Take It With You*
Michael Curtiz, *Angels With Dirty Faces*
Michael Curtiz, *Four Daughters*
Norman Taurog, *Boys Town*
King Vidor, *The Citadel*

WRITING
ORIGINAL STORY
Irving Berlin, *Alexander's Ragtime Band*
Rowland Brown, *Angels With Dirty Faces*
Marcella Burke and Frederick Kohner, *Mad About Music*
Eleanore Griffin and Dore Schary, *Boys Town*
John Howard Lawson, *Blockade*
Frank Wead, *Test Pilot*

SCREENPLAY
Lenore Coffee and Julius J. Epstein, *Four Daughters*
Ian Dalrymple, Elizabeth Hill and Frank Wead, *The Citadel*

Bette Davis, *Jezebel*

John Meehan and Dore Schary, *Boys Town*

Robert Riskin, *You Can't Take It With You*

George Bernard Shaw, writer; Ian Dalrymple, Cecil Lewis and W. P. Lipscomb, adaptation, *Pygmalion*

CINEMATOGRAPHY

Norbert Brodine, *Merrily We Live*

Robert de Grasse, *Vivacious Lady*

Ernest Haller, *Jezebel*

James Wong Howe, *Algiers*

Peverell Marley, *Suez*

Ernest Miller and Harry Wild, *Army Girl*

Victor Milner, *The Buccaneer*

Joseph Ruttenberg, *The Great Waltz*

Leon Shamroy, *The Young in Heart*

Joseph Valentine, *Mad About Music*

Joseph Walker, *You Can't Take It With You*

ART DIRECTION

Richard Day, *The Goldwyn Follies*

Hans Dreier and John Goodman, *If I Were King*

Cedric Gibbons, *Marie Antoinette*

Stephen Goosson and Lionel Banks, *Holiday*

Charles D. Hall, *Merrily We Live*

Bernard Herzbrun and Boris Leven, *Alexander's Ragtime Band*

Jack Otterson, *Mad About Music*

Van Nest Polglase, *Carefree*

Alexander Toluboff, *Algiers*

Carl J. Weyl, *The Adventures of Robin Hood*

Lyle Wheeler, *The Adventures of Tom Sawyer*

SOUND RECORDING

Columbia Studio Sound Dept., *You Can't Take It With You*

Hal Roach Studio Sound Dept., *Merrily We Live*

MGM Studio Sound Dept., *Sweethearts*

Paramount Studio Sound Dept., *If I Were King*

Republic Studio Sound Dept., *Army Girl*

RKO Radio Studio Sound Dept., *Vivacious Lady*

Twentieth Century-Fox Studio Sound Dept., *Suez*

United Artists Studio Sound Dept., *The Cowboy and the Lady*

Universal Studio Sound Dept., *That Certain Age*

Warner Bros. Studio Sound Dept., *Four Daughters*

MUSIC

SONG

"Always and Always," *Mannequin*, Edward Ward, music; Chet Forrest and Bob Wright, lyrics

"Change Partners," *Carefree*, Irving Berlin, music and lyrics

"The Cowboy and the Lady," *The Cowboy and the Lady*, Lionel Newman, music; Arthur Quenzer, lyrics

"Dust," *Under Western Stars*, Johnny Marvin, music and lyrics

"Jeepers Creepers," *Going Places*, Harry Warren, music; Johnny Mercer, lyrics

"Merrily We Live," *Merrily We Live*, Phil Charig, music; Arthur Quenzer, lyrics

"A Mist Over the Moon," *The Lady Objects*, Ben Oakland, music; Oscar Hammerstein II, lyrics

"My Own," *That Certain Age*, Jimmy McHugh, music; Harold Adamson, lyrics

"Now It Can Be Told," *Alexander's Ragtime Band*, Irving Berlin, music and lyrics

"Thanks for the Memory," *The Big Broadcast of 1938*, Ralph Rainger, music; Leo Robin, lyrics

SCORE

Victor Baravalle, *Carefree*

Cy Feuer, *Storm Over Bengal*

Marvin Hatley, *There Goes My Heart*

Boris Morros, *Tropic Holiday*

Alfred Newman, *Alexander's Ragtime Band*

Alfred Newman, *The Goldwyn Follies*

Charles Previn and Frank Skinner, *Mad About Music*

Max Steiner, *Jezebel*

Morris Stoloff and Gregory Stone, *Girls' School*

Herbert Stothart, *Sweethearts*

Franz Waxman, *The Young in Heart*

ORIGINAL SCORE

Russell Bennett, *Pacific Liner*

Richard Hageman, *If I Were King*

Marvin Hatley, *Block-Heads*

Werner Janssen, *Blockade*

Erich Wolfgang Korngold, *The Adventures of Robin Hood*

Alfred Newman, *The Cowboy and the Lady*

Louis Silvers, *Suez*

Herbert Stothart, *Marie Antoinette*

Franz Waxman, *The Young in Heart*

Victor Young, *Army Girl*

Victor Young, *Breaking the Ice*

FILM EDITING

Ralph Dawson, *The Adventures of Robin Hood*

Tom Held, *The Great Waltz*

Tom Held, *Test Pilot*

Gene Havlick, *You Can't Take It With You*

Barbara McLean, *Alexander's Ragtime Band*

SHORT SUBJECTS

CARTOON

Brave Little Tailor (*Mickey Mouse Series*) (Walt Disney Productions; RKO Radio)

Ferdinand the Bull (Walt Disney Productions; RKO Radio)

Good Scouts (*Donald Duck Series*) (Walt Disney Productions; RKO Radio)

Hunky and Spunky (Paramount)

Mother Goose Goes Hollywood (*Silly Symphony Series*) (Walt Disney Productions; RKO Radio)

ONE-REEL

The Great Heart (*Miniature Series*) (MGM)

That Mothers Might Live (*Miniature Series*) (MGM)

Timber Toppers (*Ed Thorgensen-Sports Series*) (Twentieth Century-Fox)

TWO-REEL

Declaration of Independence (*Historical Featurette Series*) (Warner Bros.)

Swingtime in the Movies (*Broadway Brevities Series*) (Warner Bros.)

They're Always Caught (*Crime Doesn't Pay Series*) (MGM)

IRVING G. THALBERG MEMORIAL AWARD
Hal B. Wallis

SPECIAL AWARDS

To **Deanna Durbin** and **Mickey Rooney** for their significant contribution in bringing to the screen the spirit and personification of youth, and as juvenile players setting a high standard of ability and achievement

To **Harry M. Warner** in recognition of patriotic service in the production of historical short subjects presenting significant episodes in the early struggle of the American people for liberty

To **Walt Disney** for *Snow White and the Seven Dwarfs*, recognized as a significant screen innovation which has charmed millions and pioneered a great new entertainment field for the motion picture cartoon

To **Oliver Marsh** and **Allen Davey** for the color cinematography of the MGM production *Sweethearts*

For outstanding achievement in creating special photographic and sound effects in the Paramount production, *Spawn of the North;* special effects by **Gordon Jenning**; assisted by **Jan Domela, Dev Jennings, Irmin Roberts** and **Art Smith**; transparencies by **Farciot Edouart**; assisted by **Loyal Griggs**; sound effects by **Loren Ryder**; assisted by **Harry Mills, Louis H. Mesenkop** and **Walter Oberst**

To **J. Arthur Ball** for his outstanding contributions to the advancement of color in motion picture photography

1939

OUTSTANDING PRODUCTION
Dark Victory (Warner Bros.-First National)
***Gone With the Wind* (Selznick International Pictures; MGM)**
Goodbye, Mr. Chips (MGM)
Love Affair (RKO Radio)
Mr. Smith Goes to Washington (Columbia)
Ninotchka (MGM)
Of Mice and Men (Hal Roach; United Artists)
Stagecoach (Walter Wanger; United Artists)
The Wizard of Oz (MGM)
Wuthering Heights (Goldwyn; United Artists)

BEST ACTOR
Robert Donat, *Goodbye, Mr. Chips*
Clark Gable, *Gone With the Wind*
Laurence Olivier, *Wuthering Heights*
Mickey Rooney, *Babes in Arms*
James Stewart, *Mr. Smith Goes to Washington*

BEST ACTRESS
Bette Davis, *Dark Victory*
Irene Dunne, *Love Affair*
Greta Garbo, *Ninotchka*
Greer Garson, *Goodbye, Mr. Chips*
Vivien Leigh, *Gone With the Wind*

ACTOR IN A SUPPORTING ROLE
Brian Aherne, *Juarez*
Harry Carey, *Mr. Smith Goes to Washington*

Brian Donlevy, *Beau Geste*
Thomas Mitchell, *Stagecoach*
Claude Rains, *Mr. Smith Goes to Washington*

ACTRESS IN A SUPPORTING ROLE
Olivia de Havilland, *Gone With the Wind*
Geraldine Fitzgerald, *Wuthering Heights*
Hattie McDaniel, *Gone With the Wind*
Edna May Oliver, *Drums Along the Mohawk*
Maria Ouspenskaya, *Love Affair*

DIRECTING
Frank Capra, *Mr. Smith Goes to Washington*
Victor Fleming, *Gone With the Wind*
John Ford, *Stagecoach*
Sam Wood, *Goodbye, Mr. Chips*
William Wyler, *Wuthering Heights*

WRITING

ORIGINAL STORY
Mildred Cram and Leo McCarey, *Love Affair*
Lewis R. Foster, *Mr. Smith Goes to Washington*
Felix Jackson, *Bachelor Mother*
Melchior Lengyel, *Ninotchka*
Lamar Trotti, *Young Mr. Lincoln*

SCREENPLAY
Charles Brackett, Walter Reisch and Billy Wilder, *Ninotchka*
Sidney Buchman, *Mr. Smith Goes to Washington*
Ben Hecht and Charles MacArthur, *Wuthering Heights*
Sidney Howard, *Gone With the Wind*
Eric Maschwitz, R. C. Sherriff and Claudine West, *Goodbye, Mr. Chips*

CINEMATOGRAPHY

BLACK-AND-WHITE
Joseph H. August, *Gunga Din*
Norbert Brodine, *Of Mice and Men*
George Folsey, *Lady of the Tropics*
Tony Gaudio, *Juarez*
Bert Glennon, *Stagecoach*
Arthur Miller, *The Rains Came*
Victor Milner, *The Great Victor Herbert*
Gregg Toland, *Intermezzo*
Gregg Toland, *Wuthering Heights*
Joseph Valentine, *First Love*
Joseph Walker, *Only Angels Have Wings*

COLOR
Ernest Haller and Ray Rennahan, *Gone With the Wind*
Georges Perinal and Osmond Borradaile, *Four Feathers*
Sol Polito and W. Howard Greene, *The Private Lives of Elizabeth and Essex*
Ray Rennahan and Bert Glennon, *Drums Along the Mohawk*
Hal Rosson, *The Wizard of Oz*
William V. Skall and Bernard Knowles, *The Mikado*

ART DIRECTION
Lionel Banks, *Mr. Smith Goes to Washington*
James Basevi, *Wuthering Heights*

Stagecoach

William Darling and George Dudley, *The Rains Came*

Hans Dreier and Robert Odell, *Beau Geste*

Cedric Gibbons and William A. Horning, *The Wizard of Oz*

Anton Grot, *The Private Lives of Elizabeth and Essex*

Charles D. Hall, *Captain Fury*

John Victor Mackay, *Man of Conquest*

Jack Otterson and Martin Obzina, *First Love*

Van Nest Polglase and Al Herman, *Love Affair*

Alexander Toluboff, *Stagecoach*

Lyle Wheeler, *Gone With the Wind*

SOUND RECORDING

Columbia Studio Sound Dept., *Mr. Smith Goes to Washington*

Denham Studio Sound Dept., *Goodbye, Mr. Chips*

Hal Roach Studio Sound Dept., *Of Mice and Men*

MGM Studio Sound Dept., *Balalaika*

Paramount Studio Sound Dept., *The Great Victor Herbert*

Republic Studio Sound Dept., *Man of Conquest*

RKO Radio Studio Sound Dept., *The Hunchback of Notre Dame*

Samuel Goldwyn Studio Sound Dept., *Gone With the Wind*

Twentieth Century-Fox Studio Sound Dept., *The Rains Came*

Universal Studio Sound Dept., *When Tomorrow Comes*

Warner Bros. Studio Sound Dept., *The Private Lives of Elizabeth and Essex*

MUSIC

SONG

"Faithful Forever," *Gulliver's Travels*, Ralph Rainger, music; Leo Robin, lyrics

"I Poured My Heart Into a Song," *Second Fiddle*, Irving Berlin, music and lyrics

"Over the Rainbow," *The Wizard of Oz*, Harold Arlen, music; E. Y. Harburg, lyrics

"Wishing," *Love Affair*, Buddy de Sylva, music and lyrics

SCORE

Phil Boutelje and Arthur Lange, *The Great Victor Herbert*

Aaron Copland, *Of Mice and Men*

Roger Edens and George E. Stoll, *Babes in Arms*

Cy Feuer, *She Married a Cop*

Lou Forbes, *Intermezzo*

Richard Hageman, Frank Harling, John Leipold and Leo Shuken, *Stagecoach*

Erich Wolfgang Korngold, *The Private Lives of Elizabeth and Essex*

Alfred Newman, *The Hunchback of Notre Dame*

Alfred Newman, *They Shall Have Music*

Charles Previn, *First Love*

Louis Silvers, *Swanee River*

Dimitri Tiomkin, *Mr. Smith Goes to Washington*

Victor Young, *Way Down South*

ORIGINAL SCORE

Anthony Collins, *Nurse Edith Cavell*

Aaron Copland, *Of Mice and Men*

Lud Gluskin and Lucien Moraweck, *The Man in the Iron Mask*

Werner Janssen, *Eternally Yours*

Alfred Newman, *The Rains Came*

Alfred Newman, *Wuthering Heights*

Max Steiner, *Dark Victory*

Max Steiner, *Gone With the Wind*

Herbert Stothart, *The Wizard of Oz*

Victor Young, *Golden Boy*

Victor Young, *Gulliver's Travels*

Victor Young, *Man of Conquest*

FILM EDITING

Charles Frend, *Goodbye, Mr. Chips*

Gene Havlick and Al Clark, *Mr. Smith Goes to Washington*

Hal C. Kern and James E. Newcom, *Gone With the Wind*

Otho Lovering and Dorothy Spencer, *Stagecoach*

Barbara McLean, *The Rains Came*

SPECIAL EFFECTS

John R. Cosgrove, Fred Albin and Arthur Johns, *Gone With the Wind*

Roy Davidson and Edwin C. Hahn, *Only Angels Have Wings*

Farciot Edouart, Gordon Jennings and Loren Ryder, *Union Pacific*

A. Arnold Gillespie and Douglas Shearer, *The Wizard of Oz*

E. H. Hansen and Fred Sersen, *The Rains Came*

Byron Haskin and Nathan Levinson, *The Private Lives of Elizabeth and Essex*

Roy Seawright, *Topper Takes a Trip*

SHORT SUBJECTS

CARTOON

Detouring America (*Merrie Melodies Series*) (Warner Bros.)

Peace on Earth (Hugh Harmon, producer; MGM)

The Pointer (*Mickey Mouse Series*) (Walt Disney Productions; RKO Radio)

The Ugly Duckling (***Silly Symphony Series***) **(Walt Disney Productions; RKO Radio)**

ONE-REEL

Busy Little Bears (***Paragraphics Series***) **(Paramount)**

Information Please (RKO Radio)

Prophet Without Honor (*Miniature Series*) (MGM)

Sword Fishing (*Vitaphone Variety Series*) (Warner Bros.)

TWO-REEL

Drunk Driving (*Crime Doesn't Pay Series*) (MGM)

Five Times Five (Pathé; RKO Radio)

Sons of Liberty (***Historical Featurette Series***) **(Warner Bros.)**

IRVING G. THALBERG MEMORIAL AWARD
David O. Selznick

SPECIAL AWARDS

To **Douglas Fairbanks** (Commemorative Award) recognizing his unique and outstanding contribution of Douglas Fairbanks, first president of the Academy, to the international development of the motion picture

To the **Motion Picture Relief Fund** acknowledging its outstanding services to the industry during the past year and its progressive leadership; presented to **Jean Hersholt**, president; **Ralph Morgan,** chairman of the executive committee; **Ralph Block,** first vice president; and **Conrad Nagel**

To **Judy Garland** for her outstanding performance as a screen juvenile during the past year

To **William Cameron Menzies** for outstanding achievement in the use of color for the enhancement of dramatic mood in the production of *Gone With the Wind*

To the **Technicolor Company** for its contributions in successfully bringing three-color feature production to the screen

1940

OUTSTANDING PRODUCTION

All This, and Heaven Too (Warner Bros.)
Foreign Correspondent (Walter Wanger; United Artists)
The Grapes of Wrath (Twentieth Century-Fox)
The Great Dictator (Charles Chaplin Productions; United Artists)
Kitty Foyle (RKO Radio)
The Letter (Warner Bros.)
The Long Voyage Home (Argosy-Wanger; United Artists)
Our Town (Sol Lesser; United Artists)
The Philadelphia Story (MGM)
Rebecca (Selznick International Pictures, United Artists)

Preston Sturges

BEST ACTOR

Charles Chaplin, *The Great Dictator*
Henry Fonda, *The Grapes of Wrath*
Raymond Massey, *Abe Lincoln in Illinois*
Laurence Olivier, *Rebecca*
James Stewart, *The Philadelphia Story*

BEST ACTRESS

Bette Davis, *The Letter*
Joan Fontaine, *Rebecca*
Katharine Hepburn, *The Philadelphia Story*
Ginger Rogers, *Kitty Foyle*
Martha Scott, *Our Town*

ACTOR IN A SUPPORTING ROLE

Albert Basserman, *Foreign Correspondent*
Walter Brennan, *The Westerner*
William Gargan, *They Knew What They Wanted*
Jack Oakie, *The Great Dictator*
James Stephenson, *The Letter*

ACTRESS IN A SUPPORTING ROLE

Judith Anderson, *Rebecca*
Jane Darwell, *The Grapes of Wrath*
Ruth Hussey, *The Philadelphia Story*
Barbara O'Neil, *All This, and Heaven Too*
Marjorie Rambeau, *Primrose Path*

DIRECTING

George Cukor, *The Philadelphia Story*
John Ford, *The Grapes of Wrath*
Alfred Hitchcock, *Rebecca*
Sam Wood, *Kitty Foyle*
William Wyler, *The Letter*

WRITING

ORIGINAL STORY
Hugo Butler and Dore Schary, *Edison, the Man*
Benjamin Glazer and John S. Toldy, *Arise, My Love*
Stuart N. Lake, *The Westerner*
Leo McCarey, Bella Spewack and Samuel Spewack, *My Favorite Wife*
Walter Reisch, *Comrade X*

ORIGINAL SCREENPLAY
Charles Bennett and Joan Harrison, *Foreign Correspondent*
Norman Burnside, Heinz Herald and John Huston, *Dr. Ehrlich's Magic Bullet*
Charles Chaplin, *The Great Dictator*
Ben Hecht, *Angels Over Broadway*
Preston Sturges, *The Great McGinty*

SCREENPLAY
Nunnally Johnson, *The Grapes of Wrath*
Dudley Nichols, *The Long Voyage Home*
Robert E. Sherwood and Joan Harrison, *Rebecca*
Donald Ogden Stewart, *The Philadelphia Story*
Dalton Trumbo, *Kitty Foyle*

CINEMATOGRAPHY
BLACK-AND-WHITE
George Barnes, *Rebecca*

Gaetano Gaudio, *The Letter*

Ernest Haller, *All This, and Heaven Too*

James Wong Howe, *Abe Lincoln in Illinois*

Charles B. Lang, Jr., *Arise, My Love*

Rudolph Maté, *Foreign Correspondent*

Harold Rosson, *Boom Town*

Joseph Ruttenberg, *Waterloo Bridge*

Gregg Toland, *The Long Voyage Home*

Joseph Valentine, *Spring Parade*

COLOR
Oliver T. Marsh and Allen Davey, *Bitter Sweet*

Arthur Miller and Ray Rennahan, *The Blue Bird*

Victor Milner and W. Howard Greene, *Northwest Mounted Police*

Georges Perinal, *The Thief of Bagdad*

Leon Shamroy and Ray Rennahan, *Down Argentine Way*

Sidney Wagner and William V. Skall, *Northwest Passage*

ART DIRECTION
BLACK-AND-WHITE
Lionel Banks and Robert Peterson, *Arizona*

James Basevi, *The Westerner*

Richard Day and Joseph C. Wright, *Lillian Russell*

Hans Dreier and Robert Usher, *Arise, My Love*

John DuCasse Schulze, *My Son, My Son!*

Cedric Gibbons and Paul Groesse, *Pride and Prejudice*

Alexander Golitzen, *Foreign Correspondent*

Anton Grot, *The Sea Hawk*

John Victor Mackay, *The Dark Command*

John Otterson, *The Boys From Syracuse*

Van Nest Polglase and Mark-Lee Kirk, *My Favorite Wife*

Lewis J. Rachmil, *Our Town*

Lyle Wheeler, *Rebecca*

COLOR
Richard Day and Joseph C. Wright, *Down Argentine Way*

Hans Dreier and Roland Anderson, *Northwest Mounted Police*

Cedric Gibbons and John S. Detlie, *Bitter Sweet*

Vincent Korda, *The Thief of Bagdad*

SOUND RECORDING
Columbia Studio Sound Dept., *Too Many Husbands*

General Service Sound Dept., *The Howards of Virginia*

Hal Roach Studio Sound Dept., *Captain Caution*

MGM Studio Sound Dept., *Strike Up the Band*

Paramount Studio Sound Dept., *Northwest Mounted Police*

Republic Studio Sound Dept., *Behind the News*

RKO Radio Studio Sound Dept., *Kitty Foyle*

Samuel Goldwyn Studio Sound Dept., *Our Town*

Twentieth Century-Fox Studio Sound Dept., *The Grapes of Wrath*

Universal Studio Sound Dept., *Spring Parade*

Warner Bros. Studio Sound Dept., *The Sea Hawk*

MUSIC
SONG
"Down Argentine Way," *Down Argentine Way,* Harry Warren, music; Mack Gordon, lyrics

"I'd Know You Anywhere," *You'll Find Out,* Jimmy McHugh, music; Johnny Mercer, lyrics

"It's a Blue World," *Music in My Heart,* Chet Forrest and Bob Wright, music and lyrics

"Love of My Life," *Second Chorus,* Artie Shaw, music; Johnny Mercer, lyrics

"Only Forever," *Rhythm on the River,* James Monaco, music; John Burke, lyrics

"Our Love Affair," *Strike Up the Band,* Roger Edens and Arthur Freed, music and lyrics

"Waltzing in the Clouds," *Spring Parade,* Robert Stolz, music; Gus Kahn, lyrics

"When You Wish Upon a Star," *Pinocchio,* Leigh Harline, music; Ned Washington, lyrics

"Who Am I?," *Hit Parade of 1941,* Jule Styne, music; Walter Bullock, lyrics

SCORE
Anthony Collins, *Irene*

Aaron Copland, *Our Town*

Cy Feuer, *Hit Parade of 1941*

Erich Wolfgang Korngold, *The Sea Hawk*

Alfred Newman, *Tin Pan Alley*

Charles Previn, *Spring Parade*

Artie Shaw, *Second Chorus*

Georgie Stoll and Roger Edens, *Strike Up the Band*

Victor Young, *Arise, My Love*

ORIGINAL SCORE
Aaron Copland, *Our Town*

Louis Gruenberg, *The Fight for Life*

Richard Hageman, *The Howards of Virginia*

Richard Hageman, *The Long Voyage Home*

Leigh Harline, Paul J. Smith and Ned Washington, *Pinocchio*

Werner Heymann, *One Million B.C.*

Alfred Newman, *The Mark of Zorro*

Miklos Rozsa, *The Thief of Bagdad*

Frank Skinner, *The House of Seven Gables*

Max Steiner, *The Letter*

Herbert Stothart, *Waterloo Bridge*

Franz Waxman, *Rebecca*

Roy Webb, *My Favorite Wife*

Meredith Willson, *The Great Dictator*

Victor Young, *Arizona*

Victor Young, *The Dark Command*

Victor Young, *Northwest Mounted Police*

FILM EDITING
Anne Bauchens, *Northwest Mounted Police*

Hal C. Kern, *Rebecca*

Warren Low, *The Letter*

Robert E. Simpson, *The Grapes of Wrath*

Sherman Todd, *The Long Voyage Home*

SPECIAL EFFECTS

Lawrence Butler, photography; Jack Whitney, sound,
The Thief of Bagdad

Jack Cosgrove, photography; Arthur Johns, sound, *Rebecca*

Paul Eagler, photography; Thomas T. Moulton, sound,
Foreign Correspondent

Farciot Edouart and Gordon Jennings, photography,
Dr. Cyclops

Farciot Edouart and Gordon Jennings, photography;
Loren Ryder, sound, *Typhoon*

John P. Fulton, photography; Bernard B. Brown and Joseph
Lapis, sound, *The Boys From Syracuse*

John P. Fulton, photography; Bernard B. Brown and William
Hedgecock, sound, *The Invisible Man Returns*

A. Arnold Gillespie, photography; Douglas Shearer, sound,
Boom Town

Byron Haskin, photography; Nathan Levinson, sound,
The Sea Hawk

R. T. Layton and R. O. Binger, photography; Thomas T. Moulton,
sound, *The Long Voyage Home*

Howard J. Lydecker, William Bradford and Ellis J. Thackery,
photography; Herbert Norsch, sound, *Women in War*

Roy Seawright, photography; Elmer Raguse, sound,
One Million B.C.

Fred Sersen, photography; E.H. Hansen, sound, *The Blue Bird*

Vernon L. Walker, photography; John O. Aalberg, sound,
Swiss Family Robinson

SHORT SUBJECTS

CARTOON
The Milky Way (*Rudolph Ising Series*) (MGM)

Puss Gets the Boot (*Cat and Mouse Series*) (MGM)

A Wild Hare (*Bugs Bunny Series*) (Leon Schlesinger, producer;
Warner Bros.)

ONE-REEL
London Can Take It (*Vitaphone Varieties Series*) (Warner Bros.)

More About Nostradamus (*Miniature Series*) (MGM)

**Quicker 'n a Wink (*Pete Smith Specialties Series*)
(Pete Smith, producer; MGM)**

Siege (*Reelism Series*) (RKO Radio)

TWO-REEL
Eyes of the Navy (*Crime Doesn't Pay Series*) (MGM)

Service With the Colors (*National Defense Series*)
(Warner Bros.)

**Teddy, the Rough Rider (*Historical Featurette Series*)
(Warner Bros.)**

SPECIAL AWARDS

To **Bob Hope** in recognition of his unselfish services to the
motion picture industry

To **Colonel Nathan Levinson** for his outstanding service to the
industry and the Army during the past nine years, which has
made possible the present efficient mobilization of the motion
picture industry facilities for the production of Army training films

1941

OUTSTANDING MOTION PICTURE

Blossoms in the Dust (MGM)

Citizen Kane (Mercury; RKO Radio)

Here Comes Mr. Jordan (Columbia)

Hold Back the Dawn (Paramount)

How Green Was My Valley (Twentieth Century-Fox)

The Little Foxes (Goldwyn; RKO Radio)

The Maltese Falcon (Warner Bros.)

One Foot in Heaven (Warner Bros.)

Sergeant York (Warner Bros.)

Suspicion (RKO Radio)

BEST ACTOR

Gary Cooper, *Sergeant York*

Cary Grant, *Penny Serenade*

Walter Huston, *All That Money Can Buy*

Robert Montgomery, *Here Comes Mr. Jordan*

Orson Welles, *Citizen Kane*

BEST ACTRESS

Bette Davis, *The Little Foxes*

Olivia de Havilland, *Hold Back the Dawn*

Joan Fontaine, *Suspicion*

Greer Garson, *Blossoms in the Dust*

Barbara Stanwyck, *Ball of Fire*

ACTOR IN A SUPPORTING ROLE

Walter Brennan, *Sergeant York*

Charles Coburn, *The Devil and Miss Jones*

Donald Crisp, *How Green Was My Valley*

James Gleason, *Here Comes Mr. Jordan*

Sydney Greenstreet, *The Maltese Falcon*

ACTRESS IN A SUPPORTING ROLE

Sarah Allgood, *How Green Was My Valley*

Mary Astor, *The Great Lie*

Patricia Collinge, *The Little Foxes*

Teresa Wright, *The Little Foxes*

Margaret Wycherly, *Sergeant York*

DIRECTING

John Ford, *How Green Was My Valley*

Alexander Hall, *Here Comes Mr. Jordan*

Howard Hawks, *Sergeant York*

Orson Welles, *Citizen Kane*

John Ford

William Wyler, *The Little Foxes*

WRITING

ORIGINAL STORY

Richard Connell and Robert Presnell, *Meet John Doe*

Monckton Hoffe, *The Lady Eve*

Thomas Monroe and Billy Wilder, *Ball of Fire*

Harry Segall, *Here Comes Mr. Jordan*

Gordon Wellesley, *Night Train*

ORIGINAL SCREENPLAY

Harry Chandlee, Abem Finkel, John Huston and Howard Koch, *Sergeant York*

Paul Jarrico, *Tom, Dick and Harry*

Norman Krasna, *The Devil and Miss Jones*

Herman J. Mankiewicz and Orson Welles, *Citizen Kane*

Karl Tunberg and Darrell Ware, *Tall, Dark and Handsome*

SCREENPLAY

Charles Brackett and Billy Wilder, *Hold Back the Dawn*

Sidney Buchman and Seton I. Miller, *Here Comes Mr. Jordan*

Philip Dunne, *How Green Was My Valley*

Lillian Hellman, *The Little Foxes*

John Huston, *The Maltese Falcon*

CINEMATOGRAPHY

BLACK-AND-WHITE

Edward Cronjager, *Sun Valley Serenade*

Karl Freund, *The Chocolate Soldier*

Charles Lang, *Sundown*

Rudolph Maté, *That Hamilton Woman*

Arthur Miller, *How Green Was My Valley*

Sol Polito, *Sergeant York*

Joseph Ruttenberg, *Dr. Jekyll and Mr. Hyde*

Gregg Toland, *Citizen Kane*

Leo Tover, *Hold Back the Dawn*

Joseph Walker, *Here Comes Mr. Jordan*

COLOR

Wilfred M. Cline, Karl Struss and William Snyder, *Aloma of the South Seas*

Karl Freund and W. Howard Greene, *Blossoms in the Dust*

Bert Glennon, *Dive Bomber*

Harry Hallenberger and Ray Rennahan, *Louisiana Purchase*

Ernest Palmer and Ray Rennahan, *Blood and Sand*

William V. Skall and Leonard Smith, *Billy the Kid*

ART DIRECTION

BLACK-AND-WHITE

Lionel Banks, art direction; George Montgomery, interior decoration, *Ladies in Retirement*

Richard Day and Nathan Juran, art direction; Thomas Little, interior decoration, *How Green Was My Valley*

Hans Dreier and Robert Usher, art direction; Sam Comer, interior decoration, *Hold Back the Dawn*

John DuCasse Schulze, art direction; Edward G. Boyle, interior decoration, *The Son of Monte Cristo*

Perry Ferguson and Van Nest Polglase, art direction; Al Fields and Darrell Silvera, interior decoration, *Citizen Kane*

Cedric Gibbons and Randall Duell, art direction; Edwin B. Willis, interior decoration, *When Ladies Meet*

Alexander Golitzen, art direction; Richard Irvine, interior decoration, *Sundown*

Stephen Goosson, art direction; Howard Bristol, interior decoration, *The Little Foxes*

John Hughes, art direction; Fred MacLean, interior decoration, *Sergeant York*

Vincent Korda, art direction; Julia Heron, interior decoration, *That Hamilton Woman*

Martin Obzina and Jack Otterson, art direction; Russell A. Gausman, interior decoration, *The Flame of New Orleans*

COLOR

Richard Day and Joseph C. Wright, art direction; Thomas Little, interior decoration, *Blood and Sand*

Raoul Pene du Bois, art direction; Stephen A. Seymour, interior decoration, *Louisiana Purchase*

Cedric Gibbons and Urie McCleary, art direction; Edwin B. Willis, interior decoration, *Blossoms in the Dust*

SOUND RECORDING

Columbia Studio Sound Dept., *The Men in Her Life*

General Service Sound Dept., *That Hamilton Woman*

Hal Roach Studio Sound Dept., *Topper Returns*

MGM Studio Sound Dept., *The Chocolate Soldier*

Paramount Studio Sound Dept., *Skylark*

Republic Studio Sound Dept., *The Devil Pays Off*

RKO Radio Studio Sound Dept., *Citizen Kane*

Samuel Goldwyn Studio Sound Dept., *Ball of Fire*

Twentieth Century-Fox Studio Sound Dept., *How Green Was My Valley*

Universal Studio Sound Dept., *Appointment for Love*

Warner Bros. Studio Sound Dept., *Sergeant York*

MUSIC

SONG

"Baby Mine," *Dumbo*, Frank Churchill, music; Ned Washington, lyrics

"Be Honest With Me," *Ridin' on a Rainbow*, Gene Autry and Fred Rose, music and lyrics

"Blues in the Night," *Blues in the Night*, Harold Arlen, music; Johnny Mercer, lyrics

"Boogie Woogie Bugle Boy of Company B," *Buck Privates*, Hugh Prince, music; Don Raye, lyrics

"Chattanooga Choo Choo," *Sun Valley Serenade*, Harry Warren, music; Mack Gordon, lyrics

"Dolores," *Las Vegas Nights*, Lou Alter, music; Frank Loesser, lyrics

"The Last Time I Saw Paris," *Lady Be Good*, Jerome Kern, music; Oscar Hammerstein II, lyrics

"Out of the Silence," *All-American Co-Ed*, Lloyd B. Norlind, music and lyrics

"Since I Kissed My Baby Goodbye," *You'll Never Get Rich*, Cole Porter, music and lyrics

SCORING OF A DRAMATIC PICTURE

Cy Feuer and Walter Scharf, *Mercy Island*

Louis Gruenberg, *So Ends Our Night*

Richard Hageman, *That Woman Is Mine*

Bernard Herrmann, *All That Money Can Buy*

Bernard Herrmann, *Citizen Kane*

Werner Heymann, *That Uncertain Feeling*

Edward Kay, *King of the Zombies*

Alfred Newman, *Ball of Fire*

Alfred Newman, *How Green Was My Valley*

Miklos Rozsa, *Lydia*

Miklos Rozsa, *Sundown*

Frank Skinner, *Back Street*

Max Steiner, *Sergeant York*

Morris Stoloff and Ernst Toch, *Ladies in Retirement*

Edward Ward, *Cheers for Miss Bishop*

Edward Ward, *Tanks a Million*

Franz Waxman, *Dr. Jekyll and Mr. Hyde*

Franz Waxman, *Suspicion*

Meredith Willson, *The Little Foxes*

Victor Young, *Hold Back the Dawn*

SCORING OF A MUSICAL PICTURE
Frank Churchill and Oliver Wallace, *Dumbo*

Anthony Collins, *Sunny*

Robert Emmett Dolan, *Birth of the Blues*

Cy Feuer, *Ice-Capades*

Emil Newman, *Sun Valley Serenade*

Charles Previn, *Buck Privates*

Heinz Roemheld, *The Strawberry Blonde*

Morris Stoloff, *You'll Never Get Rich*

Herbert Stothart and Bronislau Kaper, *The Chocolate Soldier*

Edward Ward, *All-American Co-Ed*

FILM EDITING

James B. Clark, *How Green Was My Valley*

William Holmes, *Sergeant York*

Harold F. Kress, *Dr. Jekyll and Mr. Hyde*

Daniel Mandell, *The Little Foxes*

Robert Wise, *Citizen Kane*

SPECIAL EFFECTS

Lawrence Butler, photography; William H. Wilmarth, sound, *That Hamilton Woman*

Farciot Edouart and Gordon Jennings, photography; Louis Mesenkop, sound, *Aloma of the South Seas*

Farciot Edouart and Gordon Jennings, photography; Louis Mesenkop, sound, *I Wanted Wings*

John Fulton, photography; John Hall, sound, *The Invisible Woman*

A. Arnold Gillespie, photography; Douglas Shearer, sound, *Flight Command*

Byron Haskin, photography; Nathan Levinson, sound, *The Sea Wolf* (This was not one of the original nominees; it replaced *Dive Bomber,* another Warner Bros. production.)

Roy Seawright, photography; Elmer Raguse, sound, *Topper Returns*

Fred Sersen, photography; E.H. Hansen, sound, *A Yank in the R.A.F.*

SHORT SUBJECTS

CARTOON

Boogie Woogie Bugle Boy of Company B (Walter Lantz Productions; Universal)

Hiawatha's Rabbit Hunt (*Merrie Melodies Series*) (Leon Schlesinger, producer; Warner Bros.)

How War Came (*Raymond Gram Swing Series*) (Columbia)

***Lend a Paw* (*Mickey Mouse Series*) (Walt Disney Productions; RKO Radio)**

The Night Before Christmas (*Tom and Jerry Series*) (MGM)

Rhapsody in Rivets (*Merrie Melodies Series*) (Leon Schlesinger, producer; Warner Bros.)

Rhythm in the Ranks (*George Pal Puppetoon Series*) (George Pal Productions; Paramount)

The Rookie Bear (*Bear Series*) (MGM)

Superman (*Superman Series #1*) (Max Fleischer, producer; Paramount)

Truant Officer Donald (*Donald Duck Series*) (Walt Disney Productions; RKO Radio)

ONE-REEL

Army Champions (*Pete Smith Specialties Series*) (Pete Smith, producer; MGM)

Beauty and the Beach (*Headliner Series*) (Paramount)

Down on the Farm (*Speaking of Animals Series*) (Paramount)

Forty Boys and a Song (*Melody Master Series*) (Warner Bros.)

Kings of the Turf (*Color Parade Series*) (Warner Bros.)

***Of Pups and Puzzles* (*Passing Parade Series*) (MGM)**

Sagebrush and Silver (*Magic Carpet Series*) (Twentieth Century-Fox)

TWO-REEL

Alive in the Deep (Woodard Productions, Inc.)

Forbidden Passage (*Crime Doesn't Pay Series*) (MGM)

The Gay Parisian (*Minature Featurette Series*) (Warner Bros.)

***Main Street on the March!* (MGM)**

The Tanks Are Coming (*National Defense Series*) (U.S. Army; Warner Bros.)

DOCUMENTARY

SHORT SUBJECT

Adventures in the Bronx (Film Associates)

Bomber (U.S. Office for Emergency Management Film Unit; Motion Picture Committee Cooperating for National Defense)

Christmas Under Fire (British Ministry of Information; Warner Bros.)

***Churchill's Island* (National Film Board of Canada; United Artists)**

Letter From Home (British Ministry of Information; United Artists)

Life of a Thoroughbred (Truman Talley; Twentieth Century-Fox)

Norway in Revolt (March of Time; RKO Radio)

A Place to Live (Philadelphia Housing Authority; Philadelphia Housing Association)

Russian Soil (Amkino)

Soldiers of the Sky (Truman Talley; Twentieth Century-Fox)

War Clouds in the Pacific (National Film Board of Canada; MGM)

IRVING G. THALBERG MEMORIAL AWARD

Walt Disney

SPECIAL AWARDS

To **Rey Scott** for his extraordinary achievement in producing *Kukan,* the film record of China's struggle, including its photography with a 16mm camera under the most difficult and dangerous conditions

To the **British Ministry of Information** for its vivid and dramatic presentation of the heroism of the R.A.F. in the documentary film *Target for Tonight*

To **Leopold Stokowski** and his associates for their unique achievement in the creation of a new form of visualized music in Walt Disney's production, *Fantasia*, thereby widening the scope of the motion picture as entertainment and as an art form

To **Walt Disney, William Garity, John N. A. Hawkins** and the **RCA Manufacturing Company** for their outstanding contribution to the advancement of the use of sound in motion pictures through the production of *Fantasia*

1942

OUTSTANDING MOTION PICTURE

The Invaders (Ortus; Columbia)

Kings Row (Warner Bros.)

The Magnificent Ambersons (Mercury; RKO Radio)

***Mrs. Miniver* (MGM)**

The Pied Piper (Twentieth Century-Fox)

The Pride of the Yankees (Goldwyn; RKO Radio)

Random Harvest (MGM)

The Talk of the Town (Columbia)

Wake Island (Paramount)

Yankee Doodle Dandy (Warner Bros.)

BEST ACTOR

James Cagney, *Yankee Doodle Dandy*

Ronald Colman, *Random Harvest*

Gary Cooper, *The Pride of the Yankees*

Walter Pidgeon, *Mrs. Miniver*

Monty Woolley, *The Pied Piper*

BEST ACTRESS

Bette Davis, *Now, Voyager*

Greer Garson, *Mrs. Miniver*

Katharine Hepburn, *Woman of the Year*

Rosalind Russell, *My Sister Eileen*

Teresa Wright, *The Pride of the Yankees*

ACTOR IN A SUPPORTING ROLE

William Bendix, *Wake Island*

Van Heflin, *Johnny Eager*

Walter Huston, *Yankee Doodle Dandy*

Frank Morgan, *Tortilla Flat*

Henry Travers, *Mrs. Miniver*

ACTRESS IN A SUPPORTING ROLE

Gladys Cooper, *Now, Voyager*

Agnes Moorehead, *The Magnificent Ambersons*

Susan Peters, *Random Harvest*

Dame May Whitty, *Mrs. Miniver*

Teresa Wright, *Mrs. Miniver*

DIRECTING

Michael Curtiz, *Yankee Doodle Dandy*

John Farrow, *Wake Island*

Mervyn LeRoy, *Random Harvest*

Sam Wood, *Kings Row*

William Wyler, *Mrs. Miniver*

James Cagney, *Yankee Doodle Dandy*

WRITING

ORIGINAL MOTION PICTURE STORY

Irving Berlin, *Holiday Inn*

Robert Buckner, *Yankee Doodle Dandy*

Paul Gallico, *The Pride of the Yankees*

Sidney Harmon, *The Talk of the Town*

Emeric Pressburger, *The Invaders*

ORIGINAL SCREENPLAY

W. R. Burnett and Frank Butler, *Wake Island*

Frank Butler and Don Hartman, *Road to Morocco*

Michael Kanin and Ring Lardner, Jr., *Woman of the Year*

George Oppenheimer, *The War Against Mrs. Hadley*

Michael Powell and Emeric Pressburger, *One of Our Aircraft Is Missing*

SCREENPLAY

Rodney Ackland and Emeric Pressburger, *The Invaders*

Sidney Buchman and Irwin Shaw, *The Talk of the Town*

George Froeschel, James Hilton, Claudine West and Arthur Wimperis, *Mrs. Miniver*

George Froeschel, Claudine West and Arthur Wimperis, *Random Harvest*

Herman J. Mankiewicz and Jo Swerling, *The Pride of the Yankees*

CINEMATOGRAPHY

BLACK-AND-WHITE

Charles Clarke, *Moontide*

Stanley Cortez, *The Magnificent Ambersons*

Edward Cronjager, *The Pied Piper*

James Wong Howe, *Kings Row*

Rudolph Maté, *The Pride of the Yankees*

John Mescall, *Take a Letter, Darling*

Arthur Miller, *This Above All*

Joseph Ruttenberg, *Mrs. Miniver*

Leon Shamroy, *Ten Gentlemen From West Point*

Ted Tetzlaff, *The Talk of the Town*

COLOR

Edward Cronjager and William V. Skall, *To the Shores of Tripoli*

W. Howard Greene, *Jungle Book*

Milton Krasner, William V. Skall and W. Howard Greene, *Arabian Knights*

Victor Milner and William V. Skall, *Reap the Wild Wind*

Sol Polito, *Captains of the Clouds*

Leon Shamroy, *The Black Swan*

ART DIRECTION

BLACK-AND-WHITE

Lionel Banks and Rudolph Sternad, art direction; Fay Babcock, interior decoration, *The Talk of the Town*

Ralph Berger, art direction; Emile Kuri, interior decoration, *Silver Queen*

Albert S. D'Agostino, art direction; Al Fields and Darrell Silvera, interior decoration, *The Magnificent Ambersons*

Richard Day and Joseph Wright, art direction; Thomas Little, interior decoration, *This Above All*

Hans Dreier and Roland Anderson, art direction; Sam Comer, interior decoration, *Take a Letter, Darling*

Perry Ferguson, art direction; Howard Bristol, interior decoration, *The Pride of the Yankees*

Cedric Gibbons and Randall Duell, art direction; Edwin B. Willis and Jack Moore, interior decoration, *Random Harvest*

John B. Goodman and Jack Otterson, art direction; Russell A. Gausman and Boris Leven, art direction and interior decoration, *The Shanghai Gesture*

Max Parker and Mark-Lee Kirk, art direction; Casey Roberts, interior decoration, *George Washington Slept Here*

Edward R. Robinson, interior decoration, *The Spoilers*

COLOR

Richard Day and Joseph Wright, art direction; Thomas Little, interior decoration, *My Gal Sal*

Hans Dreier and Roland Anderson, art direction; George Sawley, interior decoration, *Reap the Wild Wind*

Alexander Golitzen and Jack Otterson, art direction; Russell A. Gausman and Ira S. Webb, interior decoration, *Arabian Nights*

Vincent Korda, art direction; Julia Heron, interior decoration, *Jungle Book*

Ted Smith, art direction; Casey Roberts, interior decoration, *Captains of the Clouds*

SOUND RECORDING

Columbia Studio Sound Dept., *You Were Never Lovelier*

MGM Studio Sound Dept., *Mrs. Miniver*

Paramount Studio Sound Dept., *Road to Morocco*

RCA Sound, *The Gold Rush*

Republic Studio Sound Dept., *Flying Tigers*

RKO Radio Studio Sound Dept., *Once Upon a Honeymoon*

Samuel Goldwyn Studio Sound Dept., *The Pride of the Yankees*

Sound Service, Inc., *Friendly Enemies*

Twentieth Century-Fox Studio Sound Dept., *This Above All*

Universal Studio Sound Dept., *Arabian Nights*

Walt Disney Studio Sound Dept., *Bambi*

Warner Bros. Studio Sound Dept., *Yankee Doodle Dandy*

MUSIC

SONG

"Always in My Heart," *Always in My Heart*, Ernesto Lecuona, music; Kim Gannon, lyrics

"Dearly Beloved," *You Were Never Lovelier*, Jerome Kern, music; Johnny Mercer, lyrics

"How About You?," *Babes on Broadway*, Burton Lane, music; Ralph Freed, lyrics

"It Seems I Heard That Song Before," *Youth on Parade*, Jule Styne, music; Sammy Cahn, lyrics

"I've Got a Gal in Kalamazoo," *Orchestra Wives*, Harry Warren, music; Mack Gordon, lyrics

"Love Is a Song," *Bambi*, Frank Churchill, music; Larry Morey, lyrics

"Pennies for Peppino," *Flying With Music*, Edward Ward, music; Chet Forrest and Bob Wright, lyrics

"Pig Foot Pete," *Hellzapoppin'*, Gene de Paul, music; Don Raye, lyrics (This song was declared ineligible because it does not appear in *Hellzapoppin'*. The song did appear in the 1941 film *Keep 'Em Flying*.)

"There's a Breeze on Lake Louise," *The Mayor of 44th Street*, Harry Revel, music; Mort Greene, lyrics

"White Christmas," *Holiday Inn*, Irving Berlin, music and lyrics

SCORING OF A DRAMATIC OR COMEDY PICTURE

Frank Churchill and Edward Plumb, *Bambi*

Richard Hageman, *The Shanghai Gesture*

Leigh Harline, *The Pride of the Yankees*

Werner Heymann, *To Be or Not to Be*

Frederick Hollander and Morris Stoloff, *The Talk of the Town*

Edward Kay, *Klondike Fury*

Alfred Newman, *The Black Swan*

Miklos Rozsa, *Jungle Book*

Frank Skinner, *Arabian Nights*

Max Steiner, *Now, Voyager*

Herbert Stothart, *Random Harvest*

Max Terr, *The Gold Rush*

Dimitri Tiomkin, *The Corsican Brothers*

Roy Webb, *I Married a Witch*

Roy Webb, *Joan of Paris*

Victor Young, *Flying Tigers*

Victor Young, *Silver Queen*

Victor Young, *Take a Letter, Darling*

SCORING OF A MUSICAL PICTURE

Roger Edens and Georgie Stoll, *For Me and My Gal*

Robert Emmett Dolan, *Holiday Inn*

Leigh Harline, *You Were Never Lovelier*

Ray Heindorf and Heinz Roemheld, *Yankee Doodle Dandy*

Alfred Newman, *My Gal Sal*

Charles Previn and Hans Salter, *It Started With Eve*

Walter Scharf, *Johnny Doughboy*

Edward Ward, *Flying With Music*

FILM EDITING

George Amy, *Yankee Doodle Dandy*

Harold F. Kress, *Mrs. Miniver*

Daniel Mandell, *The Pride of the Yankees*

Otto Meyer, *The Talk of the Town*

Walter Thompson, *This Above All*

SPECIAL EFFECTS

Lawrence Butler, photography; William H. Wilmarth, sound, *Jungle Book*

Jack Cosgrove and Ray Binger, photography; Thomas T. Moulton, sound, *The Pride of the Yankees*

Farciot Edouart, Gordon Jennings and William L. Pereira, photography; Louis Mesenkop, sound, *Reap the Wild Wind*

John Fulton, photography; Bernard B. Brown, sound, *Invisible Agent*

A. Arnold Gillespie and Warren Newcombe, photography; Douglas Shearer, sound, *Mrs. Miniver*

Byron Haskin, photography; Nathan Levinson, sound, *Desperate Journey*

Howard Lydecker, photography; Daniel J. Bloomberg, sound, *Flying Tigers*

Ronald Neame, photography; C. C. Stevens, sound, *One of Our Aircraft Is Missing*

Fred Sersen, photography; Roger Heman and George Leverett, sound, *The Black Swan*

Vernon L. Walker, photography; James G. Stewart, sound, *The Navy Comes Through*

SHORT SUBJECTS

CARTOON

All Out for "V" (*Terrytoons Series*) (Twentieth Century-Fox)

Blitz Wolf (MGM)

Der Fuehrer's Face (Walt Disney Productions; RKO Radio)

Juke Box Jamboree (*Swing Symphony Series*) (Walter Lantz Productions; Universal)

Pigs in a Polka (*Blue Ribbon Series*) (Leon Schlesinger, producer; Warner Bros.)

Tulips Shall Grow (*George Pal Puppetoon Series*) (George Pal Productions, Paramount)

ONE-REEL

Desert Wonderland (*Magic Carpet Series*) (Twentieth Century-Fox)

Marines in the Making (*Pete Smith Specialties Series*) (Pete Smith, producer; MGM)

Speaking of Animals and Their Families (*Speaking of Animals Series*) (Paramount)

United States Marine Band (*Melody Master Bands Series*) (Warner Bros.)

TWO-REEL

Beyond the Line of Duty (*Broadway Brevities Series*) (U.S. War Department; Warner Bros.)

Don't Talk (*Crime Doesn't Pay Series*) (MGM)

Private Smith of the U.S.A. (*This Is America Series*) (RKO Radio)

DOCUMENTARY

Africa, Prelude to Victory (March of Time; Twentieth Century-Fox)

The Battle of Midway (U.S. Navy; Twentieth Century-Fox)

Combat Report (U.S. Army Signal Corps)

Conquer by the Clock (*America Speaks Series*) (U.S. War Information Office; RKO Pathé)

The Grain That Built a Hemisphere (Walt Disney, producer; Office of the Coordinator of Inter-American Affairs)

Henry Browne, Farmer (U.S. Department of Agriculture;

The Battle of Midway

Republic)

High Over the Borders (National Film Board of Canada)

High Stakes in the East (Netherlands Information Bureau; Netherlands Information Bureau/Service)

Inside Fighting China (*World in Action Series*) (National Film Board of Canada; United Artists)

It's Everybody's War (U.S. War Information Office; Twentieth Century-Fox)

Kokoda Front Line! (Australian News and Information Bureau)

Listen to Britain (British Ministry of Information)

Little Belgium (Belgian Ministry of Information)

Little Isles of Freedom (*Broadway Brevities Series*) (Victor Stoloff and Edgar Loew, producers; Warner Bros.)

Moscow Strikes Back (Artkino; Republic)

Mr. Blabbermouth! (U.S. War Information Office; MGM)

Mr. Gardenia Jones (U.S. War Information Office; MGM)

The New Spirit (Walt Disney, producer; U.S. Treasury Department)

Prelude to War (U.S. Army Special Services)

The Price of Victory (U.S. War Information Office; Paramount)

A Ship Is Born (U.S. Merchant Marine; Warner Bros.)

Twenty-One Miles (British Ministry of Information)

We Refuse to Die (U.S. War Information Office; Paramount)

White Eagle (Concanen Films)

Winning Your Wings (U.S. Army Air Force; Warner Bros.)

IRVING G. THALBERG MEMORIAL AWARD

Sidney Franklin

SPECIAL AWARDS

To **Charles Boyer** for his progressive cultural achievement in establishing the French Research Foundation in Los Angeles as a source of reference for the Hollywood motion picture industry

To **Noel Coward** for his outstanding production achievement in *In Which We Serve*

To **MGM** for its achievement in representing the American way of life in the production of the *Andy Hardy* series of films

1943

OUTSTANDING MOTION PICTURE

Casablanca (Warner Bros.)
For Whom the Bell Tolls (Paramount)
Heaven Can Wait (Twentieth Century-Fox)
The Human Comedy (MGM)
In Which We Serve (Two Cities; United Artists)
Madame Curie (MGM)
The More the Merrier (Columbia)
The Ox-Bow Incident (Twentieth Century-Fox)
The Song of Bernadette (Twentieth Century-Fox)
Watch on the Rhine (Warner Bros.)

BEST ACTOR

Humphrey Bogart, *Casablanca*
Gary Cooper, *For Whom the Bell Tolls*
Paul Lukas, *Watch on the Rhine*
Walter Pidgeon, *Madame Curie*
Mickey Rooney, *The Human Comedy*

BEST ACTRESS

Jean Arthur, *The More the Merrier*
Ingrid Bergman, *For Whom the Bell Tolls*
Joan Fontaine, *The Constant Nymph*
Greer Garson, *Madame Curie*
Jennifer Jones, *The Song of Bernadette*

ACTOR IN A SUPPORTING ROLE

Charles Bickford, *The Song of Bernadette*
Charles Coburn, *The More the Merrier*
J. Carrol Naish, *Sahara*
Claude Rains, *Casablanca*
Akim Tamiroff, *For Whom the Bell Tolls*

ACTRESS IN A SUPPORTING ROLE

Gladys Cooper, *The Song of Bernadette*
Paulette Goddard, *So Proudly We Hail!*
Katina Paxinou, *For Whom the Bell Tolls*

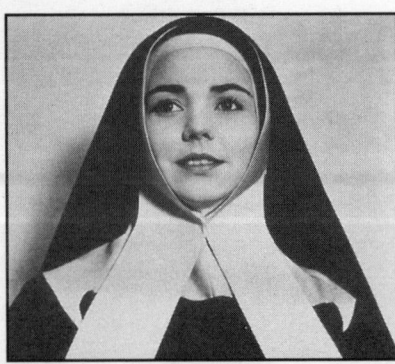

Jennifer Jones,
The Song of Bernadette

Anne Revere, *The Song of Bernadette*
Lucile Watson, *Watch on the Rhine*

DIRECTING

Clarence Brown, *The Human Comedy*
Michael Curtiz, *Casablanca*
Henry King, *The Song of Bernadette*
Ernst Lubitsch, *Heaven Can Wait*
George Stevens, *The More the Merrier*

WRITING

ORIGINAL MOTION PICTURE STORY
Steve Fisher, *Destination Tokyo*
Guy Gilpatric, *Action in the North Atlantic*
Gordon McDonell, *Shadow of a Doubt*
Frank Ross and Robert Russell, *The More the Merrier*
William Saroyan, *The Human Comedy*

ORIGINAL SCREENPLAY
Noel Coward, *In Which We Serve*
Lillian Hellman, *The North Star*
Norman Krasna, *Princess O'Rourke*
Dudley Nichols, *Air Force*
Allan Scott, *So Proudly We Hail!*

SCREENPLAY
Julius J. Epstein, Philip G. Epstein and Howard Koch,
**   *Casablanca***
Richard Flournoy, Lewis R. Foster, Frank Ross and Robert
    Russell, *The More the Merrier*
Dashiell Hammett, *Watch on the Rhine*
Nunnally Johnson, *Holy Matrimony*
George Seaton, *The Song of Bernadette*

CINEMATOGRAPHY

BLACK-AND-WHITE
Arthur Edeson, *Casablanca*
Tony Gaudio, *Corvette K-225*
James Wong Howe, *The North Star*
James Wong Howe, Elmer Dyer and Charles Marshall,
    Air Force
Charles Lang, *So Proudly We Hail!*
Rudolph Maté, *Sahara*
Arthur Miller, *The Song of Bernadette*
Joseph Ruttenberg, *Madame Curie*
John Seitz, *Five Graves to Cairo*
Harry Stradling, *The Human Comedy*

COLOR
Charles G. Clarke and Allen Davey, *Hello, Frisco, Hello*
Edward Cronjager, *Heaven Can Wait*
George Folsey, *Thousands Cheer*
Hal Mohr and W. Howard Greene, *Phantom of the Opera*
Ray Rennahan, *For Whom the Bell Tolls*
Leonard Smith, *Lassie Come Home*

ART DIRECTION

BLACK-AND-WHITE
James Basevi and William Darling, art direction; Thomas
**   Little, interior decoration, *The Song of Bernadette***
Albert S. D'Agostino and Carroll Clark, art direction; Darrell
    Silvera and Harley Miller, interior decoration, *Flight for
    Freedom*

Hans Dreier and Ernst Fegte, art direction; Bertram Granger, interior decoration, *Five Graves to Cairo*

Perry Ferguson, art direction; Howard Bristol, interior decoration, *The North Star*

Cedric Gibbons and Paul Groesse, art direction; Edwin B. Willis and Hugh Hunt, interior decoration, *Madame Curie*

Carl Weyl, art direction; George J. Hopkins interior decoration, *Mission to Moscow*

COLOR
James Basevi and Joseph C. Wright, art direction; Thomas Little, interior decoration, *The Gang's All Here*

Hans Dreier and Haldane Douglas, art direction; Bertram Granger, interior decoration, *For Whom the Bell Tolls*

Cedric Gibbons and Daniel Cathcart, art direction; Edwin B. Willis and Jacques Mersereau, interior decoration, *Thousands Cheer*

Alexander Golitzen and John B. Goodman, art direction; Russell A. Gausman and Ira S. Webb, interior decoration, *Phantom of the Opera*

John Hughes and Lt. John Koenig, art direction; George J. Hopkins, interior decoration, *This Is the Army*

SOUND RECORDING
Columbia Studio Sound Dept., *Sahara*

MGM Studio Sound Dept., *Madame Curie*

Paramount Studio Sound Dept., *Riding High*

RCA Sound, *So This Is Washington*

Republic Studio Sound Dept., *In Old Oklahoma*

RKO Radio Studio Sound Dept., *This Land Is Mine*

Samuel Goldwyn Studio Sound Dept., *The North Star*

Sound Service, Inc., *Hangmen Also Die*

Twentieth Century-Fox Studio Sound Dept., *The Song of Bernadette*

Universal Studio Sound Dept., *Phantom of the Opera*

Walt Disney Studio Sound Dept., *Saludos Amigos*

Warner Bros. Studio Sound Dept., *This Is the Army*

MUSIC
SONG
"Black Magic," *Star Spangled Rhythm*, Harold Arlen, music; Johnny Mercer, lyrics

"A Change of Heart," *Hit Parade of 1943*, Jule Styne, music; Harold Adamson, lyrics

"Happiness Is a Thing Called Joe," *Cabin in the Sky*, Harold Arlen, music; E. Y. Harburg, lyrics

"My Shining Hour," *The Sky's the Limit*, Harold Arlen, music; Johnny Mercer, music

"Saludos Amigos," *Saludos Amigos*, Charles Wolcott, music; Ned Washington, lyrics

"Say a Pray'r for the Boys Over There," *Hers to Hold*, Jimmy McHugh, music; Herb Magidson, lyrics

"They're Either Too Young or Too Old," *Thank Your Lucky Stars*, Arthur Schwartz, music; Frank Loesser, lyrics

"We Mustn't Say Goodbye," *Stage Door Canteen*, James Monaco, music; Al Dubin, lyrics

"You'd Be So Nice to Come Home To," *Something to Shout About*, Cole Porter, music and lyrics

"You'll Never Know," *Hello, Frisco, Hello*, Harry Warren, music; Mack Gordon, lyrics

SCORING OF A DRAMATIC OR
COMEDY PICTURE
C. Bakaleinikoff and Roy Webb, *The Fallen Sparrow*

Philip Boutelje, *Hi Diddle Diddle*

Gerard Carbonara, *The Kansan*

Aaron Copland, *The North Star*

Hanns Eisler, *Hangmen Also Die*

Louis Gruenberg and Morris Stoloff, *Commandos Strike at Dawn*

Leigh Harline, *Johnny Come Lately*

Arthur Lange, *Lady of Burlesque*

Alfred Newman, *The Song of Bernadette*

Edward H. Plumb, Paul J. Smith and Oliver G. Wallace, *Victory Through Air Power*

Hans J. Salter and Frank Skinner, *The Amazing Mrs. Holliday*

Walter Scharf, *In Old Oklahoma*

Max Steiner, *Casablanca*

Herbert Stothart, *Madame Curie*

Dimitri Tiomkin, *The Moon and Sixpence*

Victor Young, *For Whom the Bell Tolls*

SCORING OF A MUSICAL PICTURE
Robert Emmett Dolan, *Star Spangled Rhythm*

Leigh Harline, *The Sky's the Limit*

Ray Heindorf, *This Is the Army*

Alfred Newman, *Coney Island*

Edward H. Plumb, Paul J. Smith and Charles Wolcott, *Saludos Amigos*

Frederic E. Rich, *Stage Door Canteen*

Walter Scharf, *Hit Parade of 1943*

Morris Stoloff, *Something to Shout About*

Herbert Stothart, *Thousands Cheer*

Edward Ward, *Phantom of the Opera*

FILM EDITING
George Amy, *Air Force*

Doane Harrison, *Five Graves to Cairo*

Owen Marks, *Casablanca*

Barbara McLean, *The Song of Bernadette*

Sherman Todd and John Link, *For Whom the Bell Tolls*

SPECIAL EFFECTS
Farciot Edouart and Gordon Jennings, photography; George Dutton, sound, *So Proudly We Hail!*

A. Arnold Gillespie and Donald Jahraus, photography; Michael Steinore, sound, *Stand By for Action*

Hans Koenekamp and Rex Wimpy, photography; Nathan Levinson, sound, *Air Force*

Fred Sersen, photography; Roger Heman, sound, *Crash Dive*

Clarence Slifer and R. O. Binger, photography; Thomas T. Moulton, sound, *The North Star*

Vernon L. Walker, photography; James G. Stewart and Roy Granville, sound, *Bombardier*

SHORT SUBJECTS
CARTOON
The Dizzy Acrobat (*Woody Woodpecker Series*) (Walter Lantz Productions; Universal)

The 500 Hats of Bartholomew Cubbins (*George Pal Puppetoon Series*) (George Pal Productions; Paramount)

Greetings, Bait! (Merrie Melodies Series) (Leon Schlesinger, producer; Warner Bros.)

Imagination (Color Rhapsodies Series) (Dave Fleischer, producer; Columbia)

Reason and Emotion (Walt Disney Productions; RKO Radio)

Yankee Doodle Mouse (Tom and Jerry Series) (Frederick Quimby, producer; MGM)

ONE-REEL
Amphibious Fighters (Grantland Rice Spotlight Series) (Grantland Rice, producer; Paramount)

Cavalcade of Dance With Veloz and Yolanda (Melody Master Bands Series) (Gordon Hollingshead, producer; Warner Bros.)

Champions Carry On (Ed Thorgerson's Sports Reviews Series) (Edmund Reek, producer; Twentieth Century-Fox)

Hollywood in Uniform (Screen Snapshots Series) (Ralph Staub, producer; Columbia)

Seeing Hands (Pete Smith Specialties Series) (Pete Smith, producer; MGM)

TWO-REEL
Heavenly Music (Jerry Bresler and Sam Coslow, producers; MGM)

Letter to a Hero (This Is America Series) (Frederic Ullman, Jr., producer; RKO Radio)

Mardi Gras (Musical Parade Series) (Walter MacEwen, producer; Paramount)

Women at War (Technicolor Special Series) (Gordon Hollingshead, producer; Warner Bros.)

DOCUMENTARY

SHORT SUBJECT
Children of Mars (This Is America Series) (RKO Radio)

December 7th (U.S. Office of Strategic Services Field Photographic Bureau; U.S. Navy)

Plan for Destruction (MGM)

Swedes in America (U.S. War Information Office Overseas Motion Picture Bureau)

To the People of the United States (Walter Wanger; U.S. Public Health Service)

Tomorrow We Fly (U.S. Navy Bureau of Aeronautics)

Youth in Crisis (March of Time Series) (Twentieth Century-Fox)

FEATURE
Baptism of Fire (Fighting Men's Series) (U.S. Army)

The Battle of Russia (Special Service Division of the U.S. War Department; Twentieth Century-Fox)

Desert Victory (British Ministry of Information; Twentieth Century-Fox)

Report From the Aleutians (Combat Film Series) (U.S. Army Pictorial Service)

War Department Report (Office of Strategic Services Field Photographic Bureau)

The following titles were originally announced as Feature nominees, but they did not appear on the final ballot.

For God and Country (U.S. Army Pictorial Service)

Silent Village (British Ministry of Information; Czechoslovak Ministry of Foreign Affairs)

We've Come a Long Way (Negro Marches On, Inc.)

IRVING G. THALBERG MEMORIAL AWARD
Hal B. Wallis

SPECIAL AWARD
To **George Pal** for the development of novel methods and techniques in the production of short subjects known as Puppetoons

1944

BEST MOTION PICTURE
Double Indemnity (Paramount)

Gaslight (MGM)

Going My Way (Paramount)

Since You Went Away (Selznick International Pictures; United Artists)

Wilson (Twentieth Century-Fox)

Ingrid Bergman, *Gaslight*

BEST ACTOR
Charles Boyer, *Gaslight*

Bing Crosby, *Going My Way*

Barry Fitzgerald, *Going My Way*

Cary Grant, *None but the Lonely Heart*

Alexander Knox, *Wilson*

BEST ACTRESS
Ingrid Bergman, *Gaslight*

Claudette Colbert, *Since You Went Away*

Bette Davis, *Mr. Skeffington*

Greer Garson, *Mrs. Parkington*

Barbara Stanwyck, *Double Indemnity*

ACTOR IN A SUPPORTING ROLE
Hume Cronyn, *The Seventh Cross*

Barry Fitzgerald, *Going My Way*

Claude Rains, *Mr. Skeffington*

Clifton Webb, *Laura*

Monty Woolley, *Since You Went Away*

ACTRESS IN A SUPPORTING ROLE
Ethel Barrymore, *None but the Lonely Heart*
Jennifer Jones, *Since You Went Away*
Angela Lansbury, *Gaslight*
Aline MacMahon, *Dragon Seed*
Agnes Moorehead, *Mrs. Parkington*

DIRECTING
Alfred Hitchcock, *Lifeboat*
Henry King, *Wilson*
Leo McCarey, *Going My Way*
Otto Preminger, *Laura*
Billy Wilder, *Double Indemnity*

WRITING
ORIGINAL MOTION PICTURE STORY
David Boehm and Chandler Sprague, *A Guy Named Joe*
Edward Doherty and Jules Schermer, *The Sullivans*
Leo McCarey, *Going My Way*
Alfred Neumann and Joseph Than, *None Shall Escape*
John Steinbeck, *Lifeboat*

ORIGINAL SCREENPLAY
Jerome Cady, *Wing and a Prayer*
Richard Connell and Gladys Lehman, *Two Girls and a Sailor*
Preston Sturges, *Hail the Conquering Hero*
Preston Sturges, *The Miracle of Morgan's Creek*
Lamar Trotti, *Wilson*

SCREENPLAY
John L. Balderston, Walter Reisch and John Van Druten, *Gaslight*
Irving Brecher and Fred F. Finkelhoffe, *Meet Me in St. Louis*
Frank Butler and Frank Cavett, *Going My Way*
Raymond Chandler and Billy Wilder, *Double Indemnity*
Jay Dratler, Samuel Hoffenstein and Betty Reinhardt, *Laura*

CINEMATOGRAPHY
BLACK-AND-WHITE
Stanley Cortez and Lee Garmes, *Since You Went Away*
George Folsey, *The White Cliffs of Dover*
Charles Lang, *The Uninvited*
Joseph LaShelle, *Laura*
Lionel Lindon, *Going My Way*
Glen MacWilliams, *Lifeboat*
Joseph Ruttenberg, *Gaslight*
John Seitz, *Double Indemnity*
Robert Surtees and Harold Rosson, *Thirty Seconds Over Tokyo*
Sidney Wagner, *Dragon Seed*

COLOR
Edward Cronjager, *Home in Indiana*
George Folsey, *Meet Me in St. Louis*
Rudolph Maté and Allen M. Davey, *Cover Girl*
Ray Rennahan, *Lady in the Dark*
Charles Rosher, *Kismet*
Leon Shamroy, *Wilson*

ART DIRECTION
BLACK-AND-WHITE
Lionel Banks and Walter Holscher, art direction; Joseph Kish, interior decoration, *Address Unknown*
Albert S. D'Agostino and Carroll Clark, art direction; Darrell Silvera and Claude Carpenter, interior decoration, *Step Lively*
Hans Dreier and Robert Usher, art direction; Sam Comer, interior decoration, *No Time for Love*
Perry Ferguson, art direction; Julia Heron, interior decoration, *Casanova Brown*
Cedric Gibbons and William Ferrari, art direction; Edwin B. Willis and Paul Huldschinsky, interior decoration, *Gaslight*
John J. Hughes, art direction; Fred MacLean, interior decoration, *The Adventures of Mark Twain*
Mark-Lee Kirk, art direction; Victor A. Gangelin, interior decoration, *Since You Went Away*
Lyle Wheeler and Leland Fuller, art direction; Thomas Little, interior decoration, *Laura*

COLOR
Lionel Banks and Cary Odell, art direction; Fay Babcock, interior decoration, *Cover Girl*
Hans Dreier and Raoul Pene du Bois, art direction; Ray Moyer, interior decoration, *Lady in the Dark*
Ernst Fegte, art direction; Howard Bristol, interior decoration, *The Princess and the Pirate*
Cedric Gibbons and Daniel B. Cathcart, art direction; Edwin B. Willis and Richard Pefferle, interior decoration, *Kismet*
John B. Goodman and Alexander Golitzen, art direction; Russell A. Gausman and Ira S. Webb, interior decoration, *The Climax*
Wiard Ihnen, art direction; Thomas Little, interior decoration, *Wilson*
Charles Novi, art direction; Jack McConaghy, interior decoration, *The Desert Song*

SOUND RECORDING
Columbia Studio Sound Dept., *Cover Girl*
MGM Studio Sound Dept., *Kismet*
Paramount Studio Sound Dept., *Double Indemnity*
RCA Sound, *Voice in the Wind*
Republic Studio Sound Dept., *Brazil*
RKO Radio Studio Sound Dept., *Music in Manhattan*
Samuel Goldwyn Studio Sound Department, *Casanova Brown*
Sound Service Inc., *It Happened Tomorrow*
Twentieth Century-Fox Studio Sound Dept., *Wilson*
Universal Studio Sound Dept., *His Butler's Sister*
Warner Bros. Studio Sound Dept., *Hollywood Canteen*

MUSIC
SONG
"I Couldn't Sleep a Wink Last Night," *Higher and Higher*, Jimmy McHugh, music; Harold Adamson, lyrics
"I'll Walk Alone," *Follow the Boys*, Jule Styne, music; Sammy Cahn, lyrics
"I'm Making Believe," *Sweet and Lowdown*, James V. Monaco, music; Mack Gordon, lyrics
"Long Ago and Far Away," *Cover Girl*, Jerome Kern, music; Ira Gershwin, lyrics

"Now I Know," *Up in Arms*, Harold Arlen, music; Ted Koehler, lyrics

"Remember Me to Carolina," *Minstrel Man*, Harry Revel, music; Paul Webster, lyrics

"Rio de Janeiro," *Brazil*, Ary Barroso, music; Ned Washington, lyrics

"Silver Shadows and Golden Dreams," *Lady, Let's Dance*, Lew Pollack, music; Charles Newman, lyrics

"Sweet Dreams Sweetheart," *Hollywood Canteen*, M. K. Jerome, music; Ted Koehler, lyrics

"Swinging on a Star," *Going My Way*, James Van Heusen, music; Johnny Burke, lyrics

"Too Much in Love," *Song of the Open Road*, Walter Kent, music; Kim Gannon, lyrics

"The Trolley Song," *Meet Me in St. Louis*, Ralph Blane and Hugh Martin, music and lyrics

SCORING OF A DRAMATIC OR COMEDY PICTURE

C. Bakaleinikoff and Hanns Eisler, *None but the Lonely Heart*

Karl Hajos, *Summer Storm*

Franke Harling, *Three Russian Girls*

Arthur Lange, *Casanova Brown*

Michel Michelet and Edward Paul, *The Hairy Ape*

Michel Michelet, *Voice in the Wind*

Alfred Newman, *Wilson*

Edward Paul, *Up in Mabel's Room*

Frederic E. Rich, *Jack London*

David Rose, *The Princess and the Pirate*

Miklos Rozsa, *Double Indemnity*

Miklos Rozsa, *Woman of the Town*

H. J. Salter, *Christmas Holiday*

Walter Scharf and Roy Webb, *The Fighting Seabees*

Max Steiner, *The Adventures of Mark Twain*

Max Steiner, *Since You Went Away*

Morris Stoloff and Ernst Toch, *Address Unknown*

Robert Stolz, *It Happened Tomorrow*

Herbert Stothart, *Kismet*

Dimitri Tiomkin, *The Bridge of San Luis Rey*

SCORING OF A MUSICAL PICTURE

C. Bakaleinikoff, *Higher and Higher*

Robert Emmett Dolan, *Lady in the Dark*

Carmen Dragon and Morris Stoloff, *Cover Girl*

Leo Erdody and Ferde Grofé, *Minstrel Man*

Louis Forbes and Ray Heindorf, *Up in Arms*

Ray Heindorf, *Hollywood Canteen*

Werner R. Heymann and Kurt Weill, *Knickerbocker Holiday*

Edward Kay, *Lady, Let's Dance*

Mahlon Merrick, *Sensations of 1945*

Alfred Newman, *Irish Eyes Are Smiling*

Charles Previn, *Song of the Open Road*

H. J. Salter, *The Merry Monahans*

Walter Scharf, *Brazil*

Georgie Stoll, *Meet Me in St. Louis*

FILM EDITING

Roland Gross, *None but the Lonely Heart*

Hal C. Kern and James E. Newcom, *Since You Went Away*

Owen Marks, *Janie*

Barbara McLean, *Wilson*

Leroy Stone, *Going My Way*

SPECIAL EFFECTS

David Allen, Ray Cory and Robert Wright, photography; Russell Malmgren and Harry Kusnick, sound, *Secret Command*

John R. Cosgrove, photography; Arthur Johns, sound, *Since You Went Away*

Paul Detlefsen and John Crouse, photography; Nathan Levinson, sound, *The Adventures of Mark Twain*

Farciot Edouart and Gordon Jennings, photography; George Dutton, sound, *The Story of Dr. Wassell*

A. Arnold Gillespie, Donald Jahraus and Warren Newcombe, photography; Douglas Shearer, sound, *Thirty Seconds Over Tokyo*

Fred Sersen, photography; Roger Heman, sound, *Wilson*

Vernon L. Walker, photography; James G. Steward and Roy Granville, sound, *Days of Glory*

SHORT SUBJECTS

CARTOON

And to Think I Saw It on Mulberry Street (*George Pal Puppetoon Series*) (George Pal Productions; Paramount)

Dog, Cat and Canary (*Color Rhapsody Series*) (Screen Gems; Columbia)

Fish Fry (*Cartunes*) (Walter Lantz Productions; Universal)

How to Play Football (*Goofy Series*) (Walt Disney Productions; RKO Radio)

Mouse Trouble (*Tom and Jerry Series*) (Frederick Quimby, producer; MGM)

My Boy Johnny (*Terrytoons Series*) (Paul Terry, producer; Twentieth Century-Fox)

Swooner Crooner (*Looney Tunes Series*) (Warner Bros.)

ONE-REEL

Blue Grass Gentlemen (*Ed Thorgerson's Sports Review Series*) (Edmund Reek, producer; Twentieth Century-Fox)

Jammin' the Blues (*Melody Master Bands Series*) (Gordon Hollingshead, producer; Warner Bros.)

Movie Pests (*Pete Smith's Specialties Series*) (Pete Smith, producer; MGM)

Screen Snapshots' 50th Anniversary of Motion Pictures (*Screen Snapshots Series*) (Ralph Staub, producer; Columbia)

Who's Who in Animal Land (*Speaking of Animals Series*) (Jerry Fairbanks, producer; Paramount)

TWO-REEL

Bombalera (*Musical Parade Series*) (Louis Harris, producer; Paramount)

I Won't Play (*Featurette Series*) (Gordon Hollingshead, producer; Warner Bros.)

Main Street Today (Jerry Bresler, producer; MGM)

DOCUMENTARY

SHORT SUBJECT

Arturo Toscanini (U.S. War Information Office Overseas Motion Picture Bureau)

New Americans (*This Is America Series*) (RKO Radio)

With the Marines at Tarawa (U.S. Marine Corps)

FEATURE
The Fighting Lady (U.S. Navy; Twentieth Century-Fox)

Resisting Enemy Interrogation (U.S. Army Air Force)

IRVING G. THALBERG MEMORIAL AWARD
Darryl F. Zanuck

SPECIAL AWARDS
To **Margaret O'Brien**, outstanding child actress of 1944

To **Bob Hope** for his many services to the Academy (a life membership in the Academy of Motion Picture Arts and Sciences)

1945

BEST MOTION PICTURE
Anchors Aweigh (MGM)

The Bells of St. Mary's (Rainbow Productions; RKO Radio)

The Lost Weekend (Paramount)

Mildred Pierce (Warner Bros.)

Spellbound (Selznick International Pictures; United Artists)

BEST ACTOR
Bing Crosby, *The Bells of St. Mary's*

Gene Kelly, *Anchors Aweigh*

Ray Milland, The Lost Weekend

Gregory Peck, *The Keys of the Kingdom*

Cornel Wilde, *A Song to Remember*

BEST ACTRESS
Ingrid Bergman, *The Bells of St. Mary's*

Joan Crawford, Mildred Pierce

Greer Garson, *The Valley of Decision*

Jennifer Jones, *Love Letters*

Gene Tierney, *Leave Her to Heaven*

ACTOR IN A SUPPORTING ROLE
Michael Chekhov, *Spellbound*

John Dall, *The Corn Is Green*

James Dunn, A Tree Grows in Brooklyn

Robert Mitchum, *G. I. Joe*

J. Carrol Naish, *A Medal for Benny*

ACTRESS IN A SUPPORTING ROLE
Eve Arden, *Mildred Pierce*

Ann Blyth, *Mildred Pierce*

Angela Lansbury, *The Picture of Dorian Gray*

Joan Loring, *The Corn Is Green*

Anne Revere, National Velvet

DIRECTING
Clarence Brown, *National Velvet*

Alfred Hitchcock, *Spellbound*

Leo McCarey, *The Bells of St. Mary's*

Jean Renoir, *The Southerner*

Billy Wilder, The Lost Weekend

Joan Crawford, *Mildred Pierce*

WRITING
ORIGINAL MOTION PICTURE STORY
Alvah Bessie, *Objective, Burma!*

Charles G. Booth, The House on 92nd Street

Laszlo Gorog and Thomas Monroe, *The Affairs of Susan*

Ernst Marischka, *A Song to Remember*

John Steinbeck and Jack Wagner, *A Medal for Benny*

ORIGINAL SCREENPLAY
Myles Connolly, *Music for Millions*

Milton Holmes, *Salty O'Rourke*

Harry Kurnitz, *What Next, Corporal Hargrove?*

Richard Schweizer, Marie-Louise

Philip Yordan, *Dillinger*

SCREENPLAY
Leopold Atlas, Guy Endore and Philip Stevenson, *G. I. Joe*

Charles Brackett and Billy Wilder, The Lost Weekend

Frank Davis and Tess Slesinger, *A Tree Grows in Brooklyn*

Ranald MacDougall, *Mildred Pierce*

Albert Maltz, *Pride of the Marines*

CINEMATOGRAPHY
BLACK-AND-WHITE
George Barnes, *Spellbound*

Ernest Haller, *Mildred Pierce*

Arthur Miller, *The Keys of the Kingdom*

John F. Seitz, *The Lost Weekend*

Harry Stradling, The Picture of Dorian Gray

COLOR
George Barnes, *The Spanish Main*

Tony Gaudio and Allen M. Davey, *A Song to Remember*

Robert Planck and Charles Boyle, *Anchors Aweigh*

Leon Shamroy, Leave Her to Heaven

Leonard Smith, *National Velvet*

ART DIRECTION
BLACK-AND-WHITE
James Basevi and William Darling, art direction; Thomas Little and Frank E. Hughes, interior decoration, *The Keys of the Kingdom*

Albert S. D'Agostino and Jack Okey, art direction; Darrell Silvera and Claude Carpenter, interior decoration, *Experiment Perilous*

Hans Dreier and Roland Anderson, art direction; Sam Comer and Ray Moyer, interior decoration, *Love Letters*

Cedric Gibbons and Hans Peters, art direction; Edwin B. Willis, John Bonar and Hugh Hunt, interior decoration, *The Picture of Dorian Gray*

Wiard Ihnen, art direction; A. Roland Fields, interior decoration, *Blood on the Sun*

COLOR
Hans Dreier and Ernst Fegte, art direction; Sam Comer, interior decoration, *Frenchman's Creek*

Cedric Gibbons and Urie McCleary, art direction; Edwin B. Willis and Mildred Griffiths, interior decoration, *National Velvet*

Stephen Goosson and Rudolph Sternad, art direction; Frank Tuttle, interior decoration, *A Thousand and One Nights*

Ted Smith, art direction; Jack McConaghy, interior decoration, *San Antonio*

Lyle Wheeler and Maurice Ransford, art direction; Thomas Little, interior decoration, *Leave Her to Heaven*

SOUND RECORDING
Columbia Studio Sound Dept., *A Song to Remember*

General Service, *The Southerner*

MGM Studio Sound Dept., *They Were Expendable*

Paramount Studio Sound Dept., *The Unseen*

RCA Sound, *Three Is a Family*

Republic Studio Sound Dept., *Flame of Barbary Coast*

RKO Radio Studio Sound Dept., *The Bells of St. Mary's*

Samuel Goldwyn Studio Sound Dept., *Wonder Man*

Twentieth Century-Fox Studio Sound Dept., *Leave Her to Heaven*

Universal Studio Sound Dept., *Lady on a Train*

Walt Disney Studio Sound Dept., *The Three Caballeros*

Warner Bros. Studio Sound Dept., *Rhapsody in Blue*

MUSIC
SONG
"Accentuate the Positive," *Here Come the Waves*, Harold Arlen, music; Johnny Mercer, lyrics

"Anywhere," *Tonight and Every Night*, Jule Styne, music; Sammy Cahn, lyrics

"Aren't You Glad You're You," *The Bells of St. Mary's*, James Van Heusen, music; Johnny Burke, lyrics

"The Cat and the Canary," *Why Girls Leave Home*, Jay Livingston, music; Ray Evans, lyrics

"Endlessly," *Earl Carroll Vanities*, Walter Kent, music; Kim Gannon, lyrics

"I Fall in Love Too Easily," *Anchors Aweigh*, Jule Styne, music; Sammy Cahn, lyrics

"I'll Buy That Dream," *Sing Your Way Home*, Allie Wrubel, music; Herb Magidson, lyrics

"It Might as Well Be Spring," *State Fair*, Richard Rodgers, music; Oscar Hammerstein II, lyrics

"Linda," *G. I. Joe*, Ann Ronell, music and lyrics

"Love Letters," *Love Letters*, Victor Young, music; Eddie Heyman, lyrics

"More and More," *Can't Help Singing*, Jerome Kern, music; E. Y. Harburg, lyrics

"Sleighride in July," *Belle of the Yukon*, James Van Heusen, music; Johnny Burke, lyrics

"So in Love," *Wonder Man*, David Rose, music; Leo Robin, lyrics

"Some Sunday Morning," *San Antonio*, Ray Heindorf and M. K. Jerome, music; Ted Koehler, lyrics

SCORING OF A DRAMATIC OR COMEDY PICTURE
Daniele Amfitheatrof, *Guest Wife*

Louis Applebaum and Ann Ronell, *G. I. Joe*

Dale Butts and Morton Scott, *Flame of the Barbary Coast*

Robert Emmett Dolan, *The Bells of St. Mary's*

Lou Forbes, *Brewster's Millions*

Hugo Friedhofer and Arthur Lange, *The Woman in the Window*

Karl Hajos, *The Man Who Walked Alone*

Werner Janssen, *Captain Kidd*

Werner Janssen, *Guest in the House*

Werner Janssen, *The Southerner*

Edward J. Kay, *G. I. Honeymoon*

Alfred Newman, *The Keys of the Kingdom*

Miklos Rozsa, *The Lost Weekend*

Miklos Rozsa and Morris Stoloff, *A Song to Remember*

Miklos Rozsa, *Spellbound*

H. J. Salter, *This Love of Ours*

Herbert Stothart, *The Valley of Decision*

Alexander Tansman, *Paris, Underground*

Franz Waxman, *Objective, Burma*

Roy Webb, *The Enchanted Cottage*

Victor Young, *Love Letters*

SCORING OF A MUSICAL PICTURE
Robert Emmett Dolan, *Incendiary Blonde*

Lou Forbes and Ray Heindorf, *Wonder Man*

Walter Greene, *Why Girls Leave Home*

Ray Heindorf and Max Steiner, *Rhapsody in Blue*

Charles Henderson and Alfred Newman, *State Fair*

Edward J. Kay, *Sunbonnet Sue*

Jerome Kern and H. J. Salter, *Can't Help Singing*

Arthur Lange, *Belle of the Yukon*

Edward Plumb, Paul J. Smith and Charles Wolcott, *The Three Caballeros*

Morton Scott, *Hitchhike to Happiness*

Marlin Skiles and Morris Stoloff, *Tonight and Every Night*

Georgie Stoll, *Anchors Aweigh*

FILM EDITING
George Amy, *Objective, Burma!*

Doane Harrison, *The Lost Weekend*

Robert J. Kern, *National Velvet*

Harry Marker, *The Bells of St. Mary's*

Charles Nelson, *A Song to Remember*

SPECIAL EFFECTS
Lawrence W. Butler, photography; Ray Bomba, sound, *A Thousand and One Nights*

Jack Cosgrove, photography, *Spellbound*

John Fulton, photography; Arthur W. Johns, sound, *Wonder Man*

A. Arnold Gillespie, Donald Jahraus and Robert A. MacDonald, photography; Michael Steinore, sound, *They Were Expendable*

Fred Sersen and Sol Halprin, photography; Roger Heman and Harry Leonard, sound, *Captain Eddie*

SHORT SUBJECTS

CARTOON
Donald's Crime (*Donald Duck Series*) (Walt Disney Productions; RKO Radio)

Jasper and the Beanstalk (*George Pal Puppetoon-Jasper Series*) (George Pal Productions; Paramount)

Life With Feathers (*Merrie Melodies Series*) (Eddie Selzer, producer; Warner Bros.)

Mighty Mouse in Gypsy Life (*Terrytoon Series*) (Paul Terry, producer; Twentieth Century-Fox)

The Poet and Peasant (*Lantz Technicolor Cartune Series*) (Walter Lantz Productions; Universal)

Quiet Please! (***Tom and Jerry Series***) (**Frederick Quimby, producer; MGM**)

Rippling Romance (*Color Rhapsodies Series*) (Screen Gems; Columbia)

ONE-REEL
Along the Rainbow Trail (*Movietone Adventure Series*) (Edmund Reek, producer; Twentieth Century-Fox)

Screen Snapshots' 25th Anniversary (*Screen Snapshots Series*) (Ralph Staub, producer; Columbia)

Stairway to Light (***John Nesbitt Passing Parade Series***) (**Herbert Moulton, producer; MGM**)

Story of a Dog (*Vitaphone Varieties Series*) (Gordon Hollingshead, producer; Warner Bros.)

White Rhapsody (*Grantland Rice Spotlights Series*) (Grantland Rice, producer; Paramount)

Your National Gallery (*Variety Views Series*) (Joseph O'Brien and Thomas Mead, producers; Universal)

TWO-REEL
A Gun in His Hand (*Crime Doesn't Pay Series*) (Chester Franklin, producer; MGM)

The Jury Goes Round 'N' Round (*All Star Comedies Series*) (Jules White, producer; Columbia)

The Little Witch (*Musical Parade Series*) (George Templeton, producer; Paramount)

Star in the Night (***Broadway Brevities Series***) (**Gordon Hollingshead, producer; Warner Bros.**)

DOCUMENTARY

SHORT SUBJECT
Hitler Lives? (***Featurette Series***) (**Gordon Hollingshead, producer; Warner Bros.**)

Library of Congress (U.S. War Information Office Overseas Motion Picture Bureau)

To the Shores of Iwo Jima (U.S. Marine Corps.)

FEATURE
The Last Bomb (U.S. Army Air Force)

The True Glory (**Governments of Great Britain and the United States; Columbia**)

SPECIAL AWARDS

To **Walter Wanger** for his six years service as President of the Academy of Motion Picture Arts and Sciences

To **Peggy Ann Garner**, outstanding child actress of 1945

To **The House I Live In**, tolerance short subject; produced by Frank Ross and Mervyn LeRoy; directed by Mervyn LeRoy; screenplay by Albert Maltz; song "The House I Live In," music by Earl Robinson, lyrics by Lewis Allen; starring Frank Sinatra; released by RKO Radio

To **Republic Studio, Daniel J. Bloomberg** and the **Republic Sound Department** for the building of an outstanding musical scoring auditorium which provides optimum recording conditions and combines all elements of acoustic and engineering design

1946

BEST MOTION PICTURE
The Best Years of Our Lives (**Goldwyn; RKO Radio**)

Henry V (J. Arthur Rank-Two Cities Films; United Artists)

It's a Wonderful Life (Liberty Films; RKO Radio)

The Razor's Edge (Twentieth Century-Fox)

The Yearling (MGM)

BEST ACTOR
Fredric March, *The Best Years of Our Lives*

Laurence Olivier, *Henry V*

Larry Parks, *The Jolson Story*

Gregory Peck, *The Yearling*

James Stewart, *It's a Wonderful Life*

BEST ACTRESS
Olivia de Havilland, ***To Each His Own***

Celia Johnson, *Brief Encounter*

Jennifer Jones, *Duel in the Sun*

Rosalind Russell, *Sister Kenny*

Jane Wyman, *The Yearling*

ACTOR IN A SUPPORTING ROLE
Charles Coburn, *The Green Years*

William Demarest, *The Jolson Story*

Claude Rains, *Notorious*

Harold Russell, ***The Best Years of Our Lives***

Clifton Webb, *The Razor's Edge*

Fredric March, *The Best Years of Our Lives*

ACTRESS IN A SUPPORTING ROLE

Ethel Barrymore, *The Spiral Staircase*
Anne Baxter, *The Razor's Edge*
Lilian Gish, *Duel in the Sun*
Flora Robson, *Saratoga Trunk*
Gale Sondergaard, *Anna and the King of Siam*

DIRECTING

Clarence Brown, *The Yearling*
Frank Capra, *It's a Wonderful Life*
David Lean, *Brief Encounter*
Robert Siodmak, *The Killers*
William Wyler, *The Best Years of Our Lives*

WRITING

ORIGINAL MOTION PICTURE STORY
Charles Brackett, *To Each His Own*
Clemence Dane, *Vacation From Marriage*
Jack Patrick, *The Strange Love of Martha Ivers*
Vladimir Pozner, *The Dark Mirror*
Victor Trivas, *The Stranger*

ORIGINAL SCREENPLAY
Muriel Box and Sydney Box, *The Seventh Veil*
Raymond Chandler, *The Blue Dahlia*
Ben Hecht, *Notorious*
Norman Panama and Melvin Frank, *Road to Utopia*
Jacques Prévert, *Children of Paradise*

SCREENPLAY
Sergio Amidei and Federico Fellini, *Open City*
Sally Benson and Talbot Jennings, *Anna and the King of Siam*
Anthony Havelock-Allan, David Lean and Ronald Neame, *Brief Encounter*
Robert E. Sherwood, *The Best Years of Our Lives*
Anthony Veiller, *The Killers*

CINEMATOGRAPHY

BLACK-AND-WHITE
George Folsey, *The Green Years*
Arthur Miller, *Anna and the King of Siam*

COLOR
Charles Rosher, Leonard Smith and Arthur Arling, *The Yearling*
Joseph Walker, *The Jolson Story*

ART DIRECTION

BLACK-AND-WHITE
Richard Day and Nathan Juran, art direction; Thomas Little and Paul S. Fox, interior decoration, *The Razor's Edge*
Hans Dreier and Walter Tyler, art direction; Sam Comer and Ray Moyer, interior decoration, *Kitty*
Lyle Wheeler and William Darling, art direction; Thomas Little and Frank E. Hughes, interior decoration, *Anna and the King of Siam*

COLOR
John Bryan, art direction, *Caesar and Cleopatra*
Cedric Gibbons and Paul Groesse, art direction; Edwin B. Willis, interior decoration, *The Yearling*
Paul Sheriff and Carmen Dillon, art direction, *Henry V*

SOUND RECORDING

Columbia Studio Sound Dept., *The Jolson Story*
RKO Radio Studio Sound Dept., *It's a Wonderful Life*
Samuel Goldwyn Studio Sound Dept., *The Best Years of Our Lives*

MUSIC

SONG
"All Through the Day," *Centennial Summer*, Jerome Kern, music; Oscar Hammerstein II, lyrics
"I Can't Begin to Tell You," *The Dolly Sisters*, James Monaco, music; Mack Gordon, lyrics
"Ole Buttermilk Sky," *Canyon Passage*, Hoagy Carmichael, music; Jack Brooks, lyrics
"On the Atchison, Topeka and the Santa Fe," *The Harvey Girls*, Harry Warren, music; Johnny Mercer, lyrics
"You Keep Coming Back Like a Song," *Blue Skies*, Irving Berlin, music and lyrics

SCORING OF A DRAMATIC OR COMEDY PICTURE
Hugo Friedhofer, *The Best Years of Our Lives*
Bernard Herrmann, *Anna and the King of Siam*
Miklos Rozsa, *The Killers*
William Walton, *Henry V*
Franz Waxman, *Humoresque*

SCORING OF A MUSICAL PICTURE
Robert Emmett Dolan, *Blue Skies*
Lennie Hayton, *The Harvey Girls*
Ray Heindorf and Max Steiner, *Night and Day*
Alfred Newman, *Centennial Summer*
Morris Stoloff, *The Jolson Story*

FILM EDITING
Arthur Hilton, *The Killers*
William Hornbeck, *It's a Wonderful Life*
Harold Kress, *The Yearling*
William Lyon, *The Jolson Story*
Daniel Mandell, *The Best Years of Our Lives*

SPECIAL EFFECTS
Thomas Howard, visual, *Blithe Spirit*
William McGann, visual; Nathan Levinson, audible, *A Stolen Life*

SHORT SUBJECTS

CARTOON
***The Cat Concerto* (*Tom and Jerry Series*) (Frederick Quimby, producer; MGM)**
Chopin's Musical Moments (*Musical Miniatures Series*) (Walter Lantz, producer; Universal)
John Henry and the Inky Poo (*George Pal Puppetoon Series*) (George Pal, producer; Paramount)
Squatter's Rights (*Mickey Mouse Series*) (Walt Disney Productions; RKO Radio)
Walky Talky Hawky (*Merrie Melodies Series*) (Edward Selzer, producer; Warner Bros.)

ONE-REEL
Dive-Hi Champs (*Grantland Rice Spotlights Series*) (Jack Eaton, producer; Paramount)

Facing Your Danger (*Sports Parade Series*) (Gordon Hollingshead, producer; Warner Bros.)

Golden Horses (*Ed Thorgerson's Sports Review Series*) (Edmund Reek, producer; Twentieth Century-Fox)

Smart as a Fox (*Vitaphone Varieties Series*) (Gordon Hollingshead, producer; Warner Bros.)

Sure Cures (*Pete Smith Specialty Series*) (Pete Smith, producer; MGM)

TWO-REEL
A Boy and His Dog (*Featurettes Series*) (Gordon Hollingshead, producer; Warner Bros.)

College Queen (*Musical Parade Series*) (George B. Templeton, producer; Paramount)

Hiss and Yell (*All Star Comedies Series*) (Jules White, producer; Columbia)

The Luckiest Guy in the World (*Crime Doesn't Pay Series*) (Jerry Bresler, producer; MGM)

DOCUMENTARY
SHORT SUBJECT
Atomic Power (*March of Time Series*) (Twentieth Century-Fox)

Life at the Zoo (Artkino; Artkino Pictures)

Paramount News Issue #37 (*Twentieth Anniversary Issue! 1927–1947*) (Paramount)

Seeds of Destiny (U.S. War Department)

Traffic With the Devil (*Theatre of Life Series*) (Herbert Morgan, producer; MGM)

IRVING G. THALBERG MEMORIAL AWARD
Samuel Goldwyn

SPECIAL AWARDS
To **Laurence Olivier** for his outstanding achievement as actor, producer and director in bringing *Henry V* to the screen

To **Harold Russell** for bringing hope and courage to his fellow veterans through his appearance in *The Best Years of Our Lives*

To **Ernst Lubitsch** for his distinguished contributions to the art of the motion picture

To **Claude Jarman, Jr.**, outstanding child actor of 1946

1947

BEST MOTION PICTURE
The Bishop's Wife (Goldwyn; RKO Radio)

Crossfire (RKO Radio)

Gentleman's Agreement **(Twentieth Century-Fox)**

Great Expectations (J. Arthur Rank-Cineguild; Universal-International)

Miracle on 34th Street (Twentieth Century-Fox)

BEST ACTOR
Ronald Colman, *A Double Life*

John Garfield, *Body and Soul*

Gregory Peck, *Gentleman's Agreement*

William Powell, *Life With Father*

Michael Redgrave, *Mourning Becomes Electra*

BEST ACTRESS
Joan Crawford, *Possessed*

Susan Hayward, *Smash Up — The Story of a Woman*

Dorothy McGuire, *Gentleman's Agreement*

Rosalind Russell, *Mourning Becomes Electra*

Loretta Young, *The Farmer's Daughter*

ACTOR IN A SUPPORTING ROLE
Charles Bickford, *The Farmer's Daughter*

Thomas Gomez, *Ride the Pink Horse*

Edmund Gwenn, *Miracle on 34th Street*

Robert Ryan, *Crossfire*

Richard Widmark, *Kiss of Death*

ACTRESS IN A SUPPORTING ROLE
Ethel Barrymore, *The Paradine Case*

Gloria Grahame, *Crossfire*

Celeste Holm, *Gentleman's Agreement*

Marjorie Main, *The Egg and I*

Anne Revere, *Gentleman's Agreement*

Loretta Young, *The Farmer's Daughter*

DIRECTING
George Cukor, *A Double Life*

Edward Dmytryk, *Crossfire*

Elia Kazan, *Gentleman's Agreement*

Henry Koster, *The Bishop's Wife*

David Lean, *Great Expectations*

WRITING
ORIGINAL MOTION PICTURE STORY
Georges Chaperot and Rene Wheeler, *A Cage of Nightingales*

Herbert Clyde Lewis and Frederick Stephani, *It Happened on Fifth Avenue*

Valentine Davies, *Miracle on 34th Street*

Eleazar Lipsky, *Kiss of Death*

Dorothy Parker and Frank Cavett, *Smash Up — The Story of a Woman*

ORIGINAL SCREENPLAY
Sergio Amidei, Adolfo Franci, C. G. Viola and Cesare Zavattini, *Shoeshine*

Charles Chaplin, *Monsieur Verdoux*

Ruth Gordon and Garson Kanin, *A Double Life*

Abraham Polonsky, *Body and Soul*

Sidney Sheldon, *The Bachelor and the Bobby-Soxer*

SCREENPLAY
Moss Hart, *Gentleman's Agreement*

David Lean, Ronald Neame and Anthony Havelock-Allan, *Great Expectations*

Richard Murphy, *Boomerang!*

John Paxton, *Crossfire*

George Seaton, *Miracle on 34th Street*

CINEMATOGRAPHY
BLACK-AND-WHITE
George Folsey, *Green Dolphin Street*

Guy Green, *Great Expectations*

Charles Lang, Jr., *The Ghost and Mrs. Muir*

COLOR
Jack Cardiff, *Black Narcissus*

Harry Jackson, *Mother Wore Tights*

Peverell Marley and William V. Skall, *Life With Father*

ART DIRECTION
BLACK-AND-WHITE
John Bryan, art direction; Wilfred Shingleton, set decoration, *Great Expectations*

Lyle Wheeler and Maurice Ransford, art direction; Thomas Little and Paul S. Fox, set decoration, *The Foxes of Harrow*

COLOR
Robert M. Haas, art direction; George James Hopkins, set decoration, *Life With Father*

Alfred Junge, art direction and set decoration, *Black Narcissus*

SOUND RECORDING
Samuel Goldwyn Studio Sound Department, *The Bishop's Wife*

MGM Studio Sound Department, *Green Dolphin Street*

Sound Service, Inc., *T-Men*

MUSIC
SONG
"A Gal in Calico," *The Time, the Place and the Girl*, Arthur Schwartz, music; Leo Robin, lyrics

"I Wish I Didn't Love You So," *The Perils of Pauline*, Frank Loesser, music and lyrics

"Pass That Peace Pipe," *Good News*, Ralph Blane, Hugh Martin and Roger Edens, music and lyrics

"You Do," *Mother Wore Tights*, Josef Myrow, music; Mack Gordon, lyrics

"Zip-a-Dee-Doo-Dah," *Song of the South*, Allie Wrubel, music; Ray Gilbert, lyrics

SCORING OF A DRAMATIC OR COMEDY PICTURE
Hugo Friedhofer, *The Bishop's Wife*

Alfred Newman, *Captain From Castile*

David Raksin, *Forever Amber*

Miklos Rozsa, *A Double Life*

Max Steiner, *Life With Father*

SCORING OF A MUSICAL PICTURE
Daniele Amfitheatrof, Paul J. Smith and Charles Wolcott, *Song of the South*

Robert Emmett Dolan, *Road to Rio*

Johnny Green, *Fiesta*

Ray Heindorf and Max Steiner, *My Wild Irish Rose*

Alfred Newman, *Mother Wore Tights*

FILM EDITING
Monica Collingwood, *The Bishop's Wife*

Harmon Jones, *Gentleman's Agreement*

Francis Lyon and Robert Parrish, *Body and Soul*

Fergus McDonnell, *Odd Man Out*

George White, *Green Dolphin Street*

SPECIAL EFFECTS
Farciot Edouart, Devereux Jennings, Gordon Jennings, Wallace Kelley and Paul Lerpae, visual; George Dutton, audible, *Unconquered*

A. Arnold Gillespie and Warren Newcombe, visual; Douglas Shearer and Michael Steinore, audible, *Green Dolphin Street*

SHORT SUBJECTS
CARTOON
Chip an' Dale (*Donald Duck Series*) (Walt Disney Productions; RKO Radio)

Dr. Jekyll and Mr. Mouse (*Tom and Jerry Series*) (Frederick Quimby, producer; MGM)

Pluto's Blue Note (*Pluto Series*) (Walt Disney Productions; RKO Radio)

Tubby the Tuba (*George Pal Puppetoon Series*) (George Pal, producer; Paramount)

***Tweetie Pie* (*Merrie Melodies Series*) (Edward Selzer, producer; Warner Bros.)**

ONE-REEL
Brooklyn, U.S.A. (*Variety View Series*) (Thomas Mead, producer; Universal-International)

***Goodbye Miss Turlock* (*John Nesbitt Passing Parade Series*) (Herbert Moulton, producer; MGM)**

Moon Rockets (*Popular Science Series*) (Jerry Fairbanks, producer; Paramount)

Now You See It (*Pete Smith Specialty Series*) (Pete Smith, producer; MGM)

So You Want to Be in Pictures (*Joe McDoakes Series*) (Gordon Hollingshead, producer; Warner Bros.)

TWO-REEL
Champagne for Two (*Musical Parade Featurette Series*) (Harry Grey, producer; Paramount)

***Climbing the Matterhorn* (*Color Series*) (Irving Allen, producer; Monogram)**

Fight of the Wild Stallions (*Featurette Series*) (Thomas Mead, producer; Universal-International)

Give Us the Earth (Herbert Morgan, producer; MGM)

A Voice Is Born: The Story of Niklos Gafni (*Musical Featurette Series*) (Ben Blake, producer; Columbia)

DOCUMENTARY

SHORT SUBJECT
First Steps (United Nations Division of Films and Visual Education)

Passport to Nowhere (*This Is America Series*) (Frederic Ullman, Jr., producer; RKO Pathé)

School in the Mailbox (Australian News and Information Bureau)

FEATURE
Design for Death (Theron Warth and Richard O. Fleischer, producers; RKO Radio)

Journey Into Medicine (U.S. State Department Office of Information and Educational Exchange)

The World Is Rich (Paul Rotha, producer; British Information Services)

SPECIAL AWARDS

To **James Baskett** for his able and heartwarming characterization of Uncle Remus, friend and storyteller to the children of the world in Walt Disney's *Song of the South*

To *Bill and Coo*, in which artistry and patience blended in a novel and entertaining use of the medium of motion pictures

To *Shoeshine* — The high quality of this motion picture, brought to eloquent life in a country scarred by war, is proof to the world that the creative spirit can triumph over adversity.

To **Colonel William N. Selig, Albert E. Smith, Thomas Armat** and **George K. Spoor**, the small group of pioneers whose belief in a new medium and whose contributions to its development blazed the trail along which the motion picture has progressed, in their lifetime, from obscurity to worldwide acclaim

1948

BEST MOTION PICTURE
Hamlet (British) (J. Arthur Rank-Two Cities; Universal-International)

Johnny Belinda (Warner Bros.)

The Red Shoes (J. Arthur Rank-Archers; Eagle-Lion)

The Snake Pit (Twentieth Century-Fox)

The Treasure of the Sierra Madre (Warner Bros.)

BEST ACTOR
Lew Ayres, *Johnny Belinda*

Montgomery Clift, *The Search*

Dan Dailey, *When My Baby Smiles at Me*

Laurence Olivier, *Hamlet*

Clifton Webb, *Sitting Pretty*

BEST ACTRESS
Ingrid Bergman, *Joan of Arc*

Olivia de Havilland, *The Snake Pit*

Irene Dunne, *I Remember Mama*

Barbara Stanwyck, *Sorry, Wrong Number*

Jane Wyman, *Johnny Belinda*

ACTOR IN A SUPPORTING ROLE
Charles Bickford, *Johnny Belinda*

José Ferrer, *Joan of Arc*

Laurence Olivier, *Hamlet*

Oscar Homolka, *I Remember Mama*

Walter Huston, *The Treasure of the Sierra Madre*

Cecil Kellaway, *The Luck of the Irish*

ACTRESS IN A SUPPORTING ROLE
Barbara Bel Geddes, *I Remember Mama*

Ellen Corby, *I Remember Mama*

Agnes Moorehead, *Johnny Belinda*

Jean Simmons, *Hamlet*

Claire Trevor, *Key Largo*

DIRECTING
John Huston, *The Treasure of the Sierra Madre*

Anatole Litvak, *The Snake Pit*

Jean Negulesco, *Johnny Belinda*

Laurence Olivier, *Hamlet*

Fred Zinnemann, *The Search*

WRITING

MOTION PICTURE STORY
Borden Chase, *Red River*

Frances Flaherty and Robert Flaherty, *Louisiana Story*

Emeric Pressburger, *The Red Shoes*

Richard Schweizer and David Wechsler, *The Search*

Malvin Wald, *The Naked City*

SCREENPLAY
Charles Brackett, Billy Wilder and Richard L. Breen, *A Foreign Affair*

John Huston, *The Treasure of the Sierra Madre*

Frank Partos and Millen Brand, *The Snake Pit*

Richard Schweizer and David Wechsler, *The Search*

Irmgard Von Cube and Allen Vincent, *Johnny Belinda*

CINEMATOGRAPHY

BLACK-AND-WHITE
Joseph August, *Portrait of Jennie*

William Daniels, *The Naked City*

Charles B. Lang, Jr., *A Foreign Affair*

Ted McCord, *Johnny Belinda*

Nicholas Musuraca, *I Remember Mama*

COLOR

Charles G. Clarke, *Green Grass of Wyoming*

Robert Planck, *The Three Musketeers*

William Snyder, *The Loves of Carmen*

**Joseph Valentine, William V. Skall and Winton Hoch,
*Joan of Arc***

ART DIRECTION

BLACK-AND-WHITE

**Roger K. Furse, art direction; Carmen Dillon, set decoration,
*Hamlet***

Robert Haas, art direction; William Wallace, set decoration,
Johnny Belinda

COLOR

Richard Day, art direction; Edwin Casey Roberts and Joseph
Kish, set decoration, *Joan of Arc*

**Hein Heckroth, art direction; Arthur Lawson, set decoration,
*The Red Shoes***

SOUND RECORDING

Republic Studio Sound Dept., *Moonrise*

Twentieth Century-Fox Studio Sound Dept., *The Snake Pit*

Warner Bros. Studio Sound Dept., *Johnny Belinda*

MUSIC

SONG

**"Buttons and Bows," *The Paleface*, Jay Livingston and Ray
Evans, music and lyrics**

"For Every Man There's a Woman," *Casbah*, Harold Arlen,
music; Leo Robin, lyrics

"It's Magic," *Romance on the High Seas*, Jule Styne, music;
Sammy Cahn, lyrics

"This Is the Moment," *That Lady in Ermine*, Frederick
Hollander, music; Leo Robin, lyrics

"The Woody Woodpecker Song," *Wet Blanket Policy*, Ramey
Idriss and George Tibbles, music and lyrics

SCORING OF A DRAMATIC OR COMEDY PICTURE

Brian Easdale, *The Red Shoes*

Hugo Friedhofer, *Joan of Arc*

Alfred Newman, *The Snake Pit*

Max Steiner, *Johnny Belinda*

William Walton, *Hamlet*

SCORING OF A MUSICAL PICTURE

Johnny Green and Roger Edens, *Easter Parade*

Lennie Hayton, *The Pirate*

Ray Heindorf, *Romance on the High Seas*

Alfred Newman, *When My Baby Smiles at Me*

Victor Young, *The Emperor Waltz*

FILM EDITING

Reginald Mills, *The Red Shoes*

Christian Nyby, *Red River*

Frank Sullivan, *Joan of Arc*

Paul Weatherwax, *The Naked City*

David Weisbart, *Johnny Belinda*

COSTUME DESIGN

BLACK-AND-WHITE

Roger K. Furse, *Hamlet*

Irene, *B.F.'s Daughter*

COLOR

Edith Head and Gile Steele, *The Emperor Waltz*

Dorothy Jeakins and Karinska, *Joan of Arc*

SPECIAL EFFECTS

**Paul Eagler, J. McMillan Johnson, Russell Shearman and
Clarence Slifer, visual; Charles Freeman and James G.
Stewart, audible, *Portrait of Jennie***

Ralph Hammeras, Fred Sersen and Edward Snyder, visual;
Roger Heman, audible, *Deep Waters*

SHORT SUBJECTS

CARTOON

***The Little Orphan* (*Tom and Jerry Series*) (Frederick Quimby,
producer; MGM)**

Mickey and the Seal (*Mickey Mouse Series*) (Walt Disney
Productions; RKO Radio)

Mouse Wreckers (*Merrie Melodies Series*) (Edward Selzer,
producer; Warner Bros.)

Robin Hoodlum (*Fox and Crow Series*) (United Productions of
America; Columbia)

Tea for Two Hundred (*Donald Duck Series*) (Walt Disney
Productions; RKO Radio)

ONE-REEL

Annie Was a Wonder (*John Nesbitt Passing Parade Series*)
(Herbert Moulton, producer; MGM)

Cinderella Horse (*Sports Parade Series*) (Gordon Hollingshead,
producer; Warner Bros.)

So You Want to Be on the Radio (*Joe McDoakes Series*)
(Gordon Hollingshead, producer; Warner Bros.)

***Symphony of a City* (*Movietone Specialty Series*) (Edmund H.
Reek, producer; Twentieth Century-Fox)**

You Can't Win (*Pete Smith Specialty Series*) (Pete Smith, producer; MGM)

TWO-REEL

Calgary Stampede (*Technicolor Special Series*) (Gordon
Hollingshead, producer; Warner Bros.)

Going to Blazes (Herbert Morgan, producer; MGM)

Samba-Mania (*Musical Parade Featurette Series*) (Harry Grey,
producer; Paramount)

***Seal Island* (*True Life Adventure Series*) (Walt Disney
Productions; RKO Radio)**

Snow Capers (Thomas Mead, producer; Universal-
International)

DOCUMENTARY

SHORT SUBJECT

Heart to Heart (Herbert Morgan, producer; Fact Film
Organization)

Operation Vittles (U.S. Army Air Force)

***Toward Independence* (U.S. Army)**

FEATURE

The Quiet One (Film Documents; Mayer-Burstyn)

***The Secret Land* (U.S. Navy; MGM)**

IRVING G. THALBERG MEMORIAL AWARD

Jerry Wald

SPECIAL AWARDS

To **Monsieur Vincent** (France), voted by the Academy Board of Governors as the most outstanding foreign language film released in the United States during 1948

To **Ivan Jandl** for the outstanding juvenile performance of 1948 in *The Search*

To **Sid Grauman,** master showman, who raised the standard of exhibition of motion pictures

To **Adolph Zukor,** a man who has been called the father of the feature film in America, for his services to the industry over a period of 40 years

To **Walter Wanger** for distinguished service to the industry in adding to its moral stature in the world community by his production of the picture *Joan of Arc*

1949

BEST MOTION PICTURE

All the King's Men **(Robert Rossen Productions; Columbia)**
Battleground (MGM)
The Heiress (Paramount)
A Letter to Three Wives (Twentieth Century-Fox)
Twelve O'Clock High (Twentieth Century-Fox)

BEST ACTOR

Broderick Crawford, *All the King's Men*
Kirk Douglas, *Champion*
Gregory Peck, *Twelve O'Clock High*
Richard Todd, *The Hasty Heart*
John Wayne, *Sands of Iwo Jima*

BEST ACTRESS

Jeanne Crain, *Pinky*
Olivia de Havilland, *The Heiress*
Susan Hayward, *My Foolish Heart*
Deborah Kerr, *Edward, My Son*
Loretta Young, *Come to the Stable*

Broderick Crawford, *All the King's Men*

ACTOR IN A SUPPORTING ROLE

John Ireland, *All the King's Men*
Dean Jagger, *Twelve O'Clock High*
Arthur Kennedy, *Champion*
Ralph Richardson, *The Heiress*
James Whitmore, *Battleground*

ACTRESS IN A SUPPORTING ROLE

Ethel Barrymore, *Pinky*
Celeste Holm, *Come to the Stable*
Elsa Lanchester, *Come to the Stable*
Mercedes McCambridge, *All the King's Men*
Ethel Waters, *Pinky*

DIRECTING

Joseph L. Mankiewicz, *A Letter to Three Wives*
Carol Reed, *The Fallen Idol*
Robert Rossen, *All the King's Men*
William A. Wellman, *Battleground*
William Wyler, *The Heiress*

WRITING

MOTION PICTURE STORY

Harry Brown, *Sands of Iwo Jima*
Virginia Kellogg, *White Heat*
Clare Boothe Luce, *Come to the Stable*
Douglas Morrow, *The Stratton Story*
Shirley W. Smith and Valentine Davies, *It Happens Every Spring*

SCREENPLAY

Carl Foreman, *Champion*
Graham Greene, *The Fallen Idol*
Joseph L. Mankiewicz, *A Letter to Three Wives*
Robert Rossen, *All the King's Men*
Cesare Zavattini, *The Bicycle Thief*

STORY AND SCREENPLAY

Sidney Buchman, *Jolson Sings Again*
T. E. B. Clarke, *Passport to Pimlico*
Alfred Hayes, Federico Fellini, Sergio Amidei, Marcello Pagliero and Roberto Rossellini, *Paisan*
Helen Levitt, Janice Loeb and Sidney Meyers, *The Quiet One*
Robert Pirosh, *Battleground*

CINEMATOGRAPHY

BLACK-AND-WHITE

Joseph LaShelle, *Come to the Stable*
Frank Planer, *Champion*
Leon Shamroy, *Prince of Foxes*
Leo Tover, *The Heiress*
Paul C. Vogel, *Battleground*

COLOR

Charles G. Clarke, *Sand*
Winton Hoch, *She Wore a Yellow Ribbon*
Robert Planck and Charles Schoenbaum, *Little Women*
William Snyder, *Jolson Sings Again*
Harry Stradling, *The Barkleys of Broadway*

ART DIRECTION

BLACK-AND-WHITE
Cedric Gibbons and Jack Martin Smith, art direction; Edwin B. Willis and Richard A. Pefferle, set decoration, *Madame Bovary*

John Meehan and Harry Horner, art direction; Emile Kuri, set decoration, *The Heiress*

Lyle Wheeler and Joseph C. Wright, art direction; Thomas Little and Paul S. Fox, set decoration, *Come to the Stable*

COLOR
Edward Carrere, art direction; Lyle Reifsnider, set decoration, *The Adventures of Don Juan*

Cedric Gibbons and Paul Groesse; Edwin B. Willis and Jack D. Moore, *Little Women*

Jim Morahan, William Kellner and Michael Relph, art direction, *Saraband*

SOUND RECORDING
Republic Studio Sound Department, *Sands of Iwo Jima*

Twentieth Century-Fox Studio Sound Department, *Twelve O'Clock High*

Universal-International Studio Sound Department, *Once More, My Darling*

MUSIC

SONG
"Baby, It's Cold Outside," *Neptune's Daughter*, Frank Loesser, music and lyrics

"It's a Great Feeling," *It's a Great Feeling*, Jule Styne, music; Sammy Cahn, lyrics

"Lavender Blue," *So Dear to My Heart*, Eliot Daniel, music; Larry Morey, lyrics

"My Foolish Heart," *My Foolish Heart*, Victor Young, music; Ned Washington, lyrics

"Through a Long and Sleepless Night," *Come to the Stable*, Alfred Newman, music; Mack Gordon, lyrics

SCORING OF A COMEDY OR DRAMATIC PICTURE
Aaron Copland, *The Heiress*

Max Steiner, *Beyond the Forest*

Dimitri Tiomkin, *Champion*

SCORING OF A MUSICAL PICTURE
Roger Edens and Lennie Hayton, *On the Town*

Ray Heindorf, *Look for the Silver Lining*

Morris Stoloff and George Duning, *Jolson Sings Again*

FILM EDITING
John Dunning, *Battleground*

Harry Gerstad, *Champion*

Frederic Knudtson, *The Window*

Robert Parrish and Al Clark, *All the King's Men*

Richard L. Van Enger, *Sands of Iwo Jima*

COSTUME DESIGN

BLACK-AND-WHITE
Edith Head and Gile Steele, *The Heiress*

Vittorio Nino Novarese, *Prince of Foxes*

COLOR
Kay Nelson, *Mother Is a Freshman*

Leah Rhodes, Travilla and Marjorie Best, *The Adventures of Don Juan*

SPECIAL EFFECTS
***Mighty Joe Young* (Arko Production; RKO Radio)**

Tulsa (Walter Wanger; Eagle Lion)

SHORT SUBJECTS

CARTOON
Canary Row (*Merrie Melodies Series*) (Warner Bros. Cartoons, Inc.; Warner Bros.) (Nomination withdrawn by producer.)

***For Scent-imental Reasons* (*Merrie Melodies Series*) (Warner Bros. Cartoons, Inc.; Warner Bros.)**

Hatch Up Your Troubles (*Tom and Jerry Series*) (Frederick Quimby, producer; MGM)

The Magic Fluke (*Fox and Crow Series*) (United Productions of America; Columbia)

Toy Tinkers (*Donald Duck Series*) (Walt Disney Productions; RKO Radio)

ONE-REEL
***Aquatic House-Party* (*Grantland Rice Spotlights Series*) (Jack Eaton, producer; Paramount)**

Roller Derby Girl (*Pacemaker Series*) (Justin Herman, producer; Paramount)

So You Think You're Not Guilty (*John McDoakes Series*) (Gordon Hollingshead, producer; Warner Bros.)

Spills and Chills (*Sports News Review Series*) (Walton C. Ament, producer; Warner Bros.)

Water Trix (*Pete Smith Specialties Series*) (Pete Smith, producer; MGM)

TWO-REEL
The Boy and the Eagle (William Lasky, producer; RKO Radio)

Chase of Death (Irving Allen Productions)

The Grass Is Always Greener (Gordon Hollingshead, producer; Warner Bros.)

Snow Carnival (*Two-reel Technicolor Series*) (Gordon Hollingshead, producer; Warner Bros.)

***Van Gogh* (Gaston Diehl and Robert Haeessens, producers; Canton-Weiner Films)**

DOCUMENTARY

SHORT SUBJECT (TIE)
***A Chance to Live* (*March of Time Series*) (Richard de Rochemont, producer; Twentieth Century-Fox)**

1848 (A. F. Films; French Cinema General Cooperative)

The Rising Tide (National Film Board of Canada; St. Francis-Xavier University)

***So Much for So Little* (Warner Bros. Cartoons, Inc.; Warner Bros.)**

FEATURE
***Daybreak in Udi* (British Information Services; Crown Film Unit)**

Kenji Comes Home (Paul F. Heard, producer; Protestant Film Commission)

SPECIAL AWARDS
To ***The Bicycle Thief*** (Italy), voted by the Academy Board of Governors as the most outstanding foreign language film released in the United States during 1949

To **Bobby Driscoll**, oustanding juvenile actor of 1949

To **Fred Astaire** for his unique artistry and his contributions to the technique of musical pictures

To **Cecil B. DeMille,** distinguished motion picture pioneer, for 37 years of brilliant showmanship

To **Jean Hersholt** for distinguished service to the motion-picture industry

1950

BEST MOTION PICTURE
All About Eve **(Twentieth Century-Fox)**
Born Yesterday (Columbia)
Father of the Bride (MGM)
King Solomon's Mines (MGM)
Sunset Boulevard (Paramount)

BEST ACTOR
Louis Calhern, *The Magnificent Yankee*
José Ferrer, *Cyrano de Bergerac*
William Holden, *Sunset Boulevard*
James Stewart, *Harvey*
Spencer Tracy, *Father of the Bride*

BEST ACTRESS
Anne Baxter, *All About Eve*
Bette Davis, *All About Eve*
Judy Holliday, *Born Yesterday*
Eleanor Parker, *Caged*
Gloria Swanson, *Sunset Boulevard*

ACTOR IN A SUPPORTING ROLE
Jeff Chandler, *Broken Arrow*
Edmund Gwenn, *Mister 880*
Sam Jaffe, *The Asphalt Jungle*
George Sanders, All About Eve
Erich von Stroheim, *Sunset Boulevard*

ACTRESS IN A SUPPORTING ROLE
Hope Emerson, *Caged*
Celeste Holm, *All About Eve*
Josephine Hull, *Harvey*
Nancy Olson, *Sunset Boulevard*
Thelma Ritter, *All About Eve*

DIRECTING
George Cukor, *Born Yesterday*
John Huston, *The Asphalt Jungle*
Joseph L. Mankiewicz, All About Eve
Carol Reed, *The Third Man*
Billy Wilder, *Sunset Boulevard*

WRITING
MOTION PICTURE STORY
Edna Anhalt and Edward Anhalt, *Panic in the Streets*
William Bowers and Andre de Toth, *The Gunfighter*
Giuseppe De Santis and Carlo Lizzani, *Bitter Rice*
Sy Gomberg, *When Willie Comes Marching Home*
Leonard Spigelgass, *Mystery Street*

All About Eve

SCREENPLAY
Michael Blankfort, *Broken Arrow*
Frances Goodrich and Albert Hackett, *Father of the Bride*
Ben Maddow and John Huston, *The Asphalt Jungle*
Joseph L. Mankiewicz, All About Eve
Albert Mannheimer, *Born Yesterday*

STORY AND SCREENPLAY
Charles Brackett, Billy Wilder and D. M. Marshman, Jr.,
Sunset Boulevard
Carl Foreman, *The Men*
Ruth Gordon and Garson Kanin, *Adam's Rib*
Virginia Kellogg and Bernard C. Schoenfeld, *Caged*
Joseph L. Mankiewicz and Lesser Samuels, *No Way Out*

CINEMATOGRAPHY
BLACK-AND-WHITE
Robert Krasker, The Third Man
Milton Krasner, *All About Eve*
Victor Milner, *The Furies*
Harold Rosson, *The Asphalt Jungle*
John F. Seitz, *Sunset Boulevard*

COLOR
George Barnes, *Samson and Delilah*
Ernest Haller, *The Flame and the Arrow*
Ernest Palmer, *Broken Arrow*
Charles Rosher, *Annie Get Your Gun*
Robert Surtees, King Solomon's Mines

ART DIRECTION
BLACK-AND-WHITE
Hans Dreier and John Meehan, art direction; Sam Comer and
Ray Moyer, set decoration, Sunset Boulevard
Cedric Gibbons and Hans Peters, art direction; Edwin B. Willis
and Hugh Hunt, set decoration, *The Red Danube*
Lyle Wheeler and George Davis, art direction; Thomas Little
and Walter M. Scott, set decoration, *All About Eve*

COLOR

Hans Dreier and Walter Tyler, art direction; Sam Comer and Ray Moyer, set decoration, *Samson and Delilah*

Ernst Fegte, art direction; George Sawley, set decoration, *Destination Moon*

Cedric Gibbons and Paul Groesse, art direction; Edwin B. Willis and Richard A. Pefferle, set decoration, *Annie Get Your Gun*

SOUND RECORDING

Pinewood Studio Sound Dept., *Trio*

Samuel Goldwyn Studio Sound Dept., *Our Very Own*

Twentieth Century-Fox Studio Sound Department, *All About Eve*

Universal-International Studio Sound Dept., *Louisa*

Walt Disney Studio Sound Dept., *Cinderella*

MUSIC

SONG

"Be My Love," *The Toast of New Orleans*, Nicholas Brodszky, music; Sammy Cahn, lyrics

"Bibbidi-Bobbidi-Boo," *Cinderella*, Mack David, Al Hoffman and Jerry Livingston, music and lyrics

"Mona Lisa," *Captain Carey*, Ray Evans and Jay Livingston, music and lyrics

"Mule Train," *Singing Guns*, Fred Glickman, Hy Heath and Johnny Lange, music and lyrics

"Wilhelmina," *Wabash Avenue*, Josef Myrow, music; Mack Gordon, lyrics

SCORING OF A DRAMATIC OR COMEDY PICTURE

George Duning, *No Sad Songs for Me*

Alfred Newman, *All About Eve*

Max Steiner, *The Flame and the Arrow*

Franz Waxman, *Sunset Boulevard*

Victor Young, *Samson and Delilah*

SCORING OF A MUSICAL PICTURE

Adolph Deutsch and Roger Edens, *Annie Get Your Gun*

Ray Heindorf, *The West Point Story*

Lionel Newman, *I'll Get By*

André Previn, *Three Little Words*

Oliver Wallace and Paul J. Smith, *Cinderella*

FILM EDITING

Oswald Hafenrichter, *The Third Man*

Barbara McLean, *All About Eve*

James E. Newcom, *Annie Get Your Gun*

Arthur Schmidt and Doane Harrison, *Sunset Boulevard*

Ralph E. Winters and Conrad A. Nervig, *King Solomon's Mines*

COSTUME DESIGN

BLACK-AND-WHITE

Edith Head and Charles LeMaire, *All About Eve*

Jean Louis, *Born Yesterday*

Walter Plunkett, *The Magnificent Yankee*

COLOR

Edith Head, Dorothy Jeakins, Elois Jenssen, Gile Steele and Gwen Wakeling, *Samson and Delilah*

Walter Plunkett and Valles, *That Forsyte Woman*

Michael Whittaker, *The Black Rose*

SPECIAL EFFECTS

***Destination Moon* (George Pal Productions; Eagle Lion Classics)**

Samson and Delilah (Cecil B. DeMille Productions; Paramount)

SHORT SUBJECTS

CARTOON

***Gerald McBoing-Boing* (*Jolly Frolics Series*) (United Productions of America; Columbia)**

Jerry's Cousin (*Tom and Jerry Series*) (Frederick Quimby, producer; MGM)

Trouble Indemnity (*Mr. Magoo Series*) (United Productions of America; Columbia)

ONE-REEL

Blaze Busters (*Vitaphone Novelties Series*) (Robert Youngson, producer; Warner Bros.)

Grandad of Races (*Sports Parade Series*) (Gordon Hollingshead, producer; Warner Bros.)

Wrong Way Butch (*Pete Smith Specialty Series*) (Pete Smith, producer; MGM)

TWO-REEL

Grandma Moses (Falcon Films, Inc.; A.F. Films)

In Beaver Valley (*True-Life Adventure Series*) (Walt Disney Productions; RKO Radio)

My Country 'Tis of Thee (*Featurette Series*) (Gordon Hollingshead, producer; Warner Bros.)

DOCUMENTARY

SHORT SUBJECT

The Fight: Science Against Cancer (Medical Film Institute of the Association of American Medical Colleges; National Film Board of Canada)

The Stairs (Film Documents, Inc.)

Why Korea? (Twentieth Century-Fox Movietone; Twentieth Century-Fox)

FEATURE

The Titan: Story of Michelangelo (Michelangelo Co.; Classics Pictures, Inc.)

With These Hands (Jack Arnold and Lee Goodman, producers; Promotional Films Co., Inc.)

IRVING G. THALBERG MEMORIAL AWARD

Darryl F. Zanuck

HONORARY AWARDS

To **George Murphy** for his services in interpreting the film industry to the country at large

To **Louis B. Mayer** for distinguished service to the motion picture industry

To ***The Walls of Malapaga*** (France/Italy) voted by the Board of Governors as the most outstanding foreign language film released in the United States in 1950

1951

BEST MOTION PICTURE

An American in Paris, Arthur Freed, producer (MGM)

Decision Before Dawn, Anatole Litvak and Frank McCarthy,
producers (Twentieth Century-Fox)

A Place in the Sun, George Stevens, producer (Paramount)

Quo Vadis, Sam Zimbalist, producer (MGM)

A Streetcar Named Desire, Charles K. Feldman, producer
(Warner Bros.)

BEST ACTOR

Humphrey Bogart, The African Queen

Marlon Brando, A Streetcar Named Desire

Montgomery Clift, A Place in the Sun

Arthur Kennedy, Bright Victory

Fredric March, Death of a Salesman

BEST ACTRESS

Katharine Hepburn, The African Queen

Vivien Leigh, A Streetcar Named Desire

Eleanor Parker, Detective Story

Shelley Winters, A Place in the Sun

Jane Wyman, The Blue Veil

ACTOR IN A SUPPORTING ROLE

Leo Genn, Quo Vadis

Karl Malden, A Streetcar Named Desire

Kevin McCarthy, Death of a Salesman

Peter Ustinov, Quo Vadis

Gig Young, Come Fill the Cup

ACTRESS IN A SUPPORTING ROLE

Joan Blondell, The Blue Veil

Mildred Dunnock, Death of a Salesman

Lee Grant, Detective Story

Kim Hunter, A Streetcar Named Desire

Thelma Ritter, The Mating Season

Humphrey Bogart, The African Queen

DIRECTING

John Huston, The African Queen

Elia Kazan, A Streetcar Named Desire

Vincente Minnelli, An American in Paris

George Stevens, A Place in the Sun

William Wyler, Detective Story

WRITING

MOTION PICTURE STORY

Budd Boetticher and Ray Nazarro, Bullfighter and the Lady

Paul Dehn and James Bernard, Seven Days to Noon

Alfred Hayes and Stewart Stern, Teresa

Oscar Millard, The Frogmen

Robert Riskin and Liam O'Brian, Here Comes the Groom

SCREENPLAY

James Agee and John Huston, The African Queen

Jacques Natanson and Max Ophuls, La Ronde

Tennessee Williams, A Streetcar Named Desire

Michael Wilson and Harry Brown, A Place in the Sun

Philip Yordan and Robert Wyler, Detective Story

STORY AND SCREENPLAY

Philip Dunne, David and Bathsheba

Clarence Greene and Russell Rouse, The Well

Alan Jay Lerner, An American in Paris

Robert Pirosh, Go for Broke!

Billy Wilder, Lesser Samuels and Walter Newman,
The Big Carnival

CINEMATOGRAPHY

BLACK-AND-WHITE

Norbert Brodine, The Frogmen

Robert Burks, Strangers on a Train

William C. Mellor, A Place in the Sun

Frank Planer, Death of a Salesman

Harry Stradling, A Streetcar Named Desire

COLOR

Alfred Gilks and John Alton, An American in Paris

Charles Rosher, Show Boat

John F. Seitz and W. Howard Greene, When Worlds Collide

Leon Shamroy, David and Bathsheba

Robert Surtees and William V. Skall, Quo Vadis

ART DIRECTION

BLACK-AND-WHITE

**Richard Day, art direction; George James Hopkins, set
decoration, A Streetcar Named Desire**

D'Eaubonne, art direction and set decoration, La Ronde

Cedric Gibbons and Paul Groesse, art direction; Edwin B.
Willis and Jack D. Moore, set decoration, Too Young
to Kiss

Lyle Wheeler and John DeCuir, art direction; Thomas Little and
Paul S. Fox, set decoration, House on Telegraph Hill

Lyle Wheeler and Leland Fuller, art direction; Thomas Little
and Fred J. Rode, set decoration, Fourteen Hours

COLOR

Cedric Gibbons and Preston Ames, art direction; Edwin B. Willis and Keogh Gleason, set decoration, *An American in Paris*

Hein Heckroth, art direction and set decoration, *Tales of Hoffmann*

William A. Horning, Cedric Gibbons and Edward Carfagno, art direction; Hugh Hunt, set decoration, *Quo Vadis*

Lyle Wheeler and George Davis, art direction; Thomas Little and Paul S. Fox, set decoration, *David and Bathsheba*

Lyle Wheeler and Leland Fuller, art direction; Joseph C. Wright, musical settings; Thomas Little and Walter M. Scott, set decoration, *On the Riviera*

SOUND RECORDING

MGM Studio Sound Dept., *The Great Caruso*

RKO Radio Studio Sound Dept., *Two Tickets to Broadway*

Samuel Goldwyn Studio Sound Dept., *I Want You*

Universal-International Studio Sound Dept., *Bright Victory*

Warner Bros. Studio Sound Dept., *A Streetcar Named Desire*

MUSIC

SONG

"In the Cool, Cool, Cool of the Evening," *Here Comes the Groom,* Hoagy Carmichael, music; Johnny Mercer, lyrics

"A Kiss to Build a Dream On," *The Strip,* Bert Kalmar, Harry Ruby and Oscar Hammerstein II, music and lyrics

"Never," *Golden Girl,* Lionel Newman, music; Eliot Daniel, lyrics

"Too Late Now," *Royal Wedding,* Burton Lane, music; Alan Jay Lerner, lyrics

"Wonder Why," *Rich, Young and Pretty,* Nicholas Brodszky, music; Sammy Cahn, lyrics

SCORING OF A DRAMATIC OR COMEDY PICTURE

Alfred Newman, *David and Bathsheba*

Alex North, *Death of a Salesman*

Alex North, *A Streetcar Named Desire*

Miklos Rozsa, *Quo Vadis*

Franz Waxman, *A Place in the Sun*

SCORING OF A MUSICAL PICTURE

Peter Herman Adler and Johnny Green, *The Great Caruso*

Adolph Deutsch and Conrad Salinger, *Show Boat*

Johnny Green and Saul Chaplin, *An American in Paris*

Alfred Newman, *On the Riviera*

Oliver Wallace, *Alice in Wonderland*

FILM EDITING

Adrienne Fazan, *An American in Paris*

William Hornbeck, *A Place in the Sun*

Chester Schaeffer, *The Well*

Dorothy Spencer, *Decision Before Dawn*

Ralph E. Winters, *Quo Vadis*

COSTUME DESIGN

BLACK-AND-WHITE

Lucinda Ballard, *A Streetcar Named Desire*

Edith Head, *A Place in the Sun*

Charles LeMaire and Renie, *The Model and the Marriage Broker*

Walter Plunkett and Gile Steele, *Kind Lady*

Edward Stevenson and Margaret Furse, *The Mudlark*

COLOR

Hein Heckroth, *Tales of Hoffmann*

Charles LeMaire and Edward Stevenson, *David and Bathsheba*

Herschel McCoy, *Quo Vadis*

Orry-Kelly, Walter Plunkett and Irene Sharaff, *An American in Paris*

Helen Rose and Gile Steele, *The Great Caruso*

SPECIAL EFFECTS

***When Worlds Collide* (Paramount)**

SHORT SUBJECTS

CARTOON

Lambert, the Sheepish Lion (Walt Disney Productions; RKO Radio)

Rooty Toot Toot (*Jolly Frolics Series*) (United Productions of America; Columbia)

Two Mouseketeers (***Tom and Jerry Series***) **(Frederick Quimby, producer; MGM)**

ONE-REEL

Ridin' the Rails (*Grantland Rice Spotlight Series*) (Jack Eaton, producer; Paramount)

The Story of Time (Signal Films Production; Cornell Film Company)

World of Kids (***Vitaphone Novelties Series***) **(Robert Youngson, producer; Warner Bros.)**

TWO-REEL

Balzac (Les Films du Compass; A.F. Films, Inc.)

Danger Under the Sea (Tom Mead, producer; Universal-International)

Nature's Half Acre (***True-Life Adventure Series***) **(Walt Disney Productions; RKO Radio)**

DOCUMENTARY

SHORT SUBJECT

Benjy **(Fred Zinnemann, producer; Paramount)**

One Who Came Back (U.S. Department of Defense; Association of Motion Picture Producers)

The Seeing Eye (Gordon Hollingshead, producer; Warner Bros.)

FEATURE

I Was a Communist for the F.B.I. (Bryan Foy, producer; Warner Bros.)

Kon-Tiki **(Artfilm Production; RKO Radio)**

IRVING G. THALBERG MEMORIAL AWARD

Arthur Freed

HONORARY AWARDS

To **Gene Kelly** in appreciation of his versatility as an actor, singer, director and dancer, and specifically for his brilliant achievements in the art of choreography on film

To ***Rashomon*** (Japan) voted by the Board of Governors as the most outstanding foreign language film released in the United States during 1951

The Greatest Show on Earth

1952

BEST MOTION PICTURE
The Greatest Show on Earth, Cecil B. DeMille, producer (Paramount)

High Noon, Stanley Kramer, producer (United Artists)

Ivanhoe, Pandro S. Berman, producer (MGM)

Moulin Rouge, John Huston, producer (United Artists)

The Quiet Man, John Ford and Merian C. Cooper, producers (Republic)

BEST ACTOR
Marlon Brando, *Viva Zapata!*

Gary Cooper, *High Noon*

Kirk Douglas, *The Bad and the Beautiful*

José Ferrer, *Moulin Rouge*

Alec Guinness, *The Lavender Hill Mob*

BEST ACTRESS
Shirley Booth, *Come Back, Little Sheba*

Joan Crawford, *Sudden Fear*

Bette Davis, *The Star*

Julie Harris, *The Member of the Wedding*

Susan Hayward, *With a Song in My Heart*

ACTOR IN A SUPPORTING ROLE
Richard Burton, *My Cousin Rachel*

Arthur Hunnicutt, *The Big Sky*

Victor McLaglen, *The Quiet Man*

Jack Palance, *Sudden Fear*

Anthony Quinn, *Viva Zapata!*

ACTRESS IN A SUPPORTING ROLE
Gloria Grahame, *The Bad and the Beautiful*

Jean Hagen, *Singin' in the Rain*

Colette Marchand, *Moulin Rouge*

Terry Moore, *Come Back, Little Sheba*

Thelma Ritter, *With a Song in My Heart*

DIRECTING
Cecil B. DeMille, *The Greatest Show on Earth*

John Ford, *The Quiet Man*

John Huston, *Moulin Rouge*

Joseph L. Mankiewicz, *Five Fingers*

Fred Zinnemann, *High Noon*

WRITING
MOTION PICTURE STORY
Edna Anhalt and Edward Anhalt, *The Sniper*

Frederic M. Frank, Theodore St. John and Frank Cavett, *The Greatest Show on Earth*

Martin Goldsmith and Jack Leonard, *The Narrow Margin*

Leo McCarey, *My Son John*

Guy Trosper, *The Pride of St. Louis*

SCREENPLAY
Carl Foreman, *High Noon*

Roger MacDougall, John Dighton and Alexander Mackendrick, *The Man in the White Suit*

Frank S. Nugent, *The Quiet Man*

Charles Schnee, *The Bad and the Beautiful*

Michael Wilson, *Five Fingers*

STORY AND SCREENPLAY
Sydney Boehm, *The Atomic City*

T. E. B. Clarke, *The Lavender Hill Mob*

Ruth Gordon and Garson Kanin, *Pat and Mike*

Terence Rattigan, *Breaking the Sound Barrier*

John Steinbeck, *Viva Zapata!*

CINEMATOGRAPHY
BLACK-AND-WHITE
Russell Harlan, *The Big Sky*

Charles B. Lang, Jr., *Sudden Fear*

Joseph LaShelle, *My Cousin Rachel*

Virgil E. Miller, *Navajo*

Robert Surtees, *The Bad and the Beautiful*

COLOR
George J. Folsey, *Million Dollar Mermaid*

Winton C. Hoch and Archie Stout, *The Quiet Man*

Leon Shamroy, *The Snows of Kilimanjaro*

Harry Stradling, *Hans Christian Andersen*

F. A. Young, *Ivanhoe*

ART DIRECTION
BLACK-AND-WHITE
Cedric Gibbons and Edward Carfagno, art direction; Edwin B. Willis and Keogh Gleason, set decoration, *The Bad and the Beautiful*

Matsuyama, art direction; H. Motsumoto, set decoration, *Rashomon*

Hal Pereira and Roland Anderson, art direction; Emile Kuri, set decoration, *Carrie*

Lyle Wheeler and John DeCuir, art direction; Walter M. Scott, set decoration, *My Cousin Rachel*

Lyle Wheeler and Leland Fuller, art direction; Thomas Little and Claude Carpenter, set decoration, *Viva Zapata!*

COLOR

Richard Day and Clave, art direction; Howard Bristol, set decoration, *Hans Christian Andersen*

Cedric Gibbons and Paul Groesse, art direction; Edwin B. Willis and Arthur Krams, set decoration, *The Merry Widow*

Frank Hotaling, art direction; John McCarthy, Jr. and Charles Thompson, set decoration, *The Quiet Man*

Paul Sheriff, art direction; Marcel Vertes, set decoration, *Moulin Rouge*

Lyle Wheeler and John DeCuir, art direction; Thomas Little and Paul S. Fox, set decoration, *The Snows of Kilimanjaro*

SOUND RECORDING

London Film Sound Dept., *Breaking the Sound Barrier*

Pinewood Studios Sound Dept., *The Promoter*

Republic Studio Sound Dept.; Daniel J. Bloomberg, *The Quiet Man*

Samuel Goldwyn Studio Sound Dept., *Hans Christian Andersen*

Twentieth Century-Fox Studio Sound Dept., Thomas T. Moulton, *With a Song in My Heart*

MUSIC

SONG

"Am I in Love," *Son of Paleface*, Jack Brooks, music

"Because You're Mine," *Because You're Mine*, Nicholas Brodszky, music; Sammy Cahn, lyrics

"High Noon" (Do Not Forsake Me, Oh My Darlin'), *High Noon*, Dimitri Tiomkin, music; Ned Washington, lyrics

"Thumbelina," *Hans Christian Andersen*, Frank Loesser, music and lyrics

"Zing a Little Zong," *Just for You*, Harry Warren, music; Leo Robin, lyrics

SCORING OF A DRAMATIC OR COMEDY PICTURE

Herschel Burke Gilbert, *The Thief*

Alex North, *Viva Zapata!*

Miklos Rozsa, *Ivanhoe*

Max Steiner, *The Miracle of Our Lady of Fatima*

Dimitri Tiomkin, *High Noon*

SCORING OF A MUSICAL PICTURE

Lennie Hayton, *Singin' in the Rain*

Ray Heindorf and Max Steiner, *The Jazz Singer*

Gian-Carlo Menotti, *The Medium*

Alfred Newman, *With a Song in My Heart*

Walter Scharf, *Hans Christian Andersen*

FILM EDITING

William Austin, *Flat Top*

Anne Bauchens, *The Greatest Show on Earth*

Ralph Kemplen, *Moulin Rouge*

Warren Low, *Come Back, Little Sheba*

Elmo Williams and Harry Gerstad, *High Noon*

COSTUME DESIGN

BLACK-AND-WHITE

Edith Head, *Carrie*

Charles LeMaire and Dorothy Jeakins, *My Cousin Rachel*

Jean Louis, *Affair in Trinidad*

Sheila O'Brien, *Sudden Fear*

Helen Rose, *The Bad and the Beautiful*

COLOR

Clave, Mary Wills and Madame Karinska, *Hans Christian Andersen*

Edith Head, Dorothy Jeakins and Miles White, *The Greatest Show on Earth*

Charles LeMaire, *With a Song in My Heart*

Helen Rose and Gile Steele, *The Merry Widow*

Marcel Vertes, *Moulin Rouge*

SPECIAL EFFECTS

Plymouth Adventure (MGM)

SHORT SUBJECTS

CARTOON

Johann Mouse (*Tom and Jerry Series*) (Frederick Quimby, producer; MGM)

Little Johnny Jet (*MGM Series*) (Frederick Quimby, producer; MGM)

Madeline (*Jolly Frolics Series*) (United Productions of America; Columbia)

Pink and Blue Blues (*Mister Magoo Series*) (United Productions of America; Columbia)

Romance of Transportation (Tom Daly, producer; National Film Board of Canada)

ONE-REEL

Athletes of the Saddle (*Grantland Rice Sportlights Series*) (Jack Eaton, producer; Paramount)

Desert Killer (*Sports Parade Series*) (Gordon Hollingshead, producer; Warner Bros.)

Light in the Window (*Art Film Series*) (Art Film Productions; Twentieth Century-Fox)

Neighbours (National Film Board of Canada; Arthur Mayer-Edward Kingsley, Inc.)

Royal Scotland (Crown Film Unit; British Information Services)

TWO-REEL

Bridge of Time (London Films; British Information Services)

Devil Take Us (*Theatre of Life Series*) (Herbert Morgan, producer; Theatre of Life Production)

Thar She Blows! (*Technicolor Special Series*) (Gordon Hollingshead, producer; Warner Bros.)

Water Birds (*True-Life Adventure Series*) (Walt Disney Productions; RKO Radio)

DOCUMENTARY

SHORT SUBJECT

Devil Take Us (Herbert Morgan, producer; Theatre of Life Production)

The Garden Spider (Epeira Diadema) (Cristallo Films; I.F.E. Releasing Corp.)

Man Alive! (United Productions of America; American Cancer Society)

Neighbours (National Film Board of Canada; Arthur Mayer-Edward Kingsley, Inc.)

FEATURE

The Hoaxters (Dore Schary, producer; MGM)

Navajo (Bartlett-Foster Productions; Lippert Pictures, Inc.)

The Sea Around Us (Irwin Allen, producer; RKO Radio)

IRVING G. THALBERG MEMORIAL AWARD

Cecil B. DeMille

HONORARY AWARDS

To **George Alfred Mitchell** for the design and development of the camera which bears his name and for his continued and dominant presence in the field of cinematography

To **Joseph M. Schenck** for long and distinguished service to the motion picture industry

To **Merian C. Cooper** for his many innovations and contributions to the art of motion pictures

To **Harold Lloyd,** master comedian and good citizen

To **Bob Hope** for his contribution to the laughter of the world, his service to the motion picture industry and his devotion to the American premise

To *Forbidden Games* (France), best foreign language film first released in the United States during 1952

1953

BEST MOTION PICTURE

From Here to Eternity, Buddy Adler, producer (Columbia)
Julius Caesar, John Houseman, producer (MGM)
The Robe, Frank Ross, producer (Twentieth Century-Fox)
Roman Holiday, William Wyler, producer (Paramount)
Shane, George Stevens, producer (Paramount)

BEST ACTOR

Marlon Brando, *Julius Caesar*
Richard Burton, *The Robe*
Montgomery Clift, *From Here to Eternity*
William Holden, *Stalag 17*
Burt Lancaster, *From Here to Eternity*

BEST ACTRESS

Leslie Caron, *Lili*
Ava Gardner, *Mogambo*
Audrey Hepburn, *Roman Holiday*
Deborah Kerr, *From Here to Eternity*
Maggie McNamara, *The Moon Is Blue*

From Here to Eternity

ACTOR IN A SUPPORTING ROLE

Eddie Albert, *Roman Holiday*
Brandon de Wilde, *Shane*
Jack Palance, *Shane*
Frank Sinatra, *From Here to Eternity*
Robert Strauss, *Stalag 17*

ACTRESS IN A SUPPORTING ROLE

Grace Kelly, *Mogambo*
Geraldine Page, *Hondo*
Marjorie Rambeau, *Torch Song*
Donna Reed, *From Here to Eternity*
Thelma Ritter, *Pickup on South Street*

DIRECTING

George Stevens, *Shane*
Charles Walters, *Lili*
Billy Wilder, *Stalag 17*
William Wyler, *Roman Holiday*
Fred Zinnemann, *From Here to Eternity*

WRITING

MOTION PICTURE STORY

Ray Ashley, Morris Engel and Ruth Orkin, *Little Fugitive*
Alec Coppel, *The Captain's Paradise*
Beirne Lay, Jr., *Above and Beyond*
Dalton Trumbo, *Roman Holiday*

SCREENPLAY

Eric Ambler, *The Cruel Sea*
Helen Deutsch, *Lili*
A. B. Guthrie, Jr., *Shane*
Ian McLellan Hunter and John Dighton, *Roman Holiday*
Daniel Taradash, *From Here to Eternity*

STORY AND SCREENPLAY

Charles Brackett, Walter Reisch and Richard Breen, *Titanic*
Betty Comden and Adolph Green, *The Band Wagon*
Millard Kaufman, *Take the High Ground*
Richard Murphy, *The Desert Rats*
Sam Rolfe and Harold Jack Bloom, *The Naked Spur*

CINEMATOGRAPHY

BLACK-AND-WHITE

Joseph C. Brun, *Martin Luther*
Burnett Guffey, *From Here to Eternity*
Hal Mohr, *The Four Poster*
Frank Planer and Henry Alekan, *Roman Holiday*
Joseph Ruttenberg, *Julius Caesar*

COLOR

Edward Cronjager, *Beneath the 12-Mile Reef*
George Folsey, *All the Brothers Were Valiant*
Loyal Griggs, *Shane*
Robert Planck, *Lili*
Leon Shamroy, *The Robe*

ART DIRECTION

BLACK-AND-WHITE

Cedric Gibbons and Edward Carfagno, art direction; Edwin B. Willis and Hugh Hunt, set decoration, *Julius Caesar*

Fritz Maurischat and Paul Markwitz, art direction and set decoration, *Martin Luther*

Hal Pereira and Walter Tyler, art direction and set decoration, *Roman Holiday*

Lyle Wheeler and Leland Fuller, art direction; Paul S. Fox, set decoration, *The President's Lady*

Lyle Wheeler and Maurice Ransford, art direction; Stuart Reiss, set decoration, *Titanic*

COLOR

Cedric Gibbons, Preston Ames, Edward Carfagno and Gabriel Scognamillo, art direction; Edwin B. Willis, Keogh Gleason, Arthur Krams and Jack D. Moore, set decoration, *The Story of Three Loves*

Cedric Gibbons and Paul Groesse, art direction; Edwin B. Willis and Arthur Krams, set decoration, *Lili*

Cedric Gibbons and Urie McCleary, art direction; Edwin B. Willis and Jack D. Moore, set decoration, *Young Bess*

Alfred Junge and Hans Peters, art direction; John Jarvis, set decoration, *Knights of the Round Table*

Lyle Wheeler and George W. Davis, art direction; Walter M. Scott and Paul S. Fox, set decoration, *The Robe*

SOUND RECORDING

Columbia Studio Sound Dept., John P. Livadary, *From Here to Eternity*

MGM Studio Sound Dept., *Knights of the Round Table*

Paramount Studio Sound Dept., *The War of the Worlds*

Universal-International Studio Sound Dept., *The Mississippi Gambler*

Warner Bros. Studio Sound Dept., William A. Mueller, *Calamity Jane*

MUSIC

SONG

"The Moon Is Blue," *The Moon Is Blue*, Herschel Burke Gilbert, music; Sylvia Fine, lyrics

"My Flaming Heart," *Small Town Girl*, Nicholas Brodszky, music; Leo Robin, lyrics

"Sadie Thompson's Song" (Blue Pacific Blues), *Miss Sadie Thompson*, Lester Lee, music; Ned Washington, lyrics

"Secret Love," *Calamity Jane*, Sammy Fain, music; Paul Francis Webster, lyrics

"That's Amore," *The Caddy*, Harry Warren, music; Jack Brooks, lyrics

SCORING OF A DRAMATIC OR COMEDY PICTURE

Louis Forbes, *This Is Cinerama*

Hugo Friedhofer, *Above and Beyond*

Bronislau Kaper, *Lili*

Miklos Rozsa, *Julius Caesar*

Morris Stoloff and George Duning, *From Here to Eternity*

SCORING OF A MUSICAL PICTURE

Adolph Deutsch, *The Band Wagon*

Ray Heindorf, *Calamity Jane*

Frederick Hollander and Morris Stoloff, *The 5,000 Fingers of Dr. T.*

Alfred Newman, *Call Me Madam*

André Previn and Saul Chaplin, *Kiss Me Kate*

FILM EDITING

Everett Douglas, *The War of the Worlds*

Otto Ludwig, *The Moon Is Blue*

William Lyon, *From Here to Eternity*

Robert Swink, *Roman Holiday*

Irvine (Cotton) Warburton, *Crazylegs*

COSTUME DESIGN

BLACK-AND-WHITE

Edith Head, *Roman Holiday*

Charles LeMaire and Renie, *The President's Lady*

Jean Louis, *From Here to Eternity*

Walter Plunkett, *The Actress*

Helen Rose and Herschel McCoy, *Dream Wife*

COLOR

Charles LeMaire and Emile Santiago, *The Robe*

Charles LeMaire and Travilla, *How to Marry a Millionaire*

Mary Ann Nyberg, *The Band Wagon*

Walter Plunkett, *Young Bess*

Irene Sharaff, *Call Me Madam*

SPECIAL EFFECTS

The War of the Worlds (Paramount)

SHORT SUBJECTS

CARTOON

Christopher Crumpet (*Jolly Frolics Series*) (United Productions of America; Columbia)

From A to Z-Z-Z-Z (*Loony Tunes Series*) (Warner Bros. Cartoons, Inc.; Warner Bros.)

Rugged Bear (*Donald Duck Series*) (Walt Disney Productions; RKO Radio)

The Tell Tale Heart (*UPA Cartoon Special Series*) (United Productions of America; Columbia)

Toot, Whistle, Plunk and Boom (*Adventures in Music Series*) (Walt Disney Productions; Buena Vista)

ONE-REEL

Christ Among the Primitives (Vincenzo Lucci-Chiarissi Production; I.F.E. Releasing Corp.)

Herring Hunt (*Canada Carries on Series*) (National Film Board of Canada; RKO Pathé, Inc.)

Joy of Living (*Art Film Series*) (Art Film Productions; Twentieth Century-Fox)

The Merry Wives of Windsor Overture (*Overture Series*) (Johnny Green, producer; MGM)

Wee Water Wonders (*Grantland Rice Spotlight Series*) (Jack Eaton, producer; Paramount)

TWO-REEL

Bear Country (*True Life Adventure Series*) (Walt Disney Productions; RKO Radio)

Ben and Me (Walt Disney Productions; Buena Vista)

Return to Glennascaul (Dublin Gate Theatre Production; Arthur Mayer-Edward Kingsley, Inc.)

Vesuvius Express (*CinemaScope Shorts Series*) (Otto Lang, producer; Twentieth Century-Fox)

Winter Paradise (*Technicolor Special Series*) (Cedric Francis, producer; Warner Bros.)

DOCUMENTARY

SHORT SUBJECT
The Alaskan Eskimo (Walt Disney Productions; RKO Radio)

The Living City (John Barnes, producer; Encyclopaedia Britannica Films, Inc.)

Operation Blue Jay (U.S. Army Signal Corps.)

They Planted a Stone (World Wide Pictures; British Information Services)

The Word (John Healy and John Adams, producers; Twentieth Century-Fox)

FEATURE
The Conquest of Everest (Countryman Films, Ltd. and Group 3 Ltd.; United Artists)

The Living Desert (*True Life Adventure Series*) (Walt Disney Productions; Buena Vista)

A Queen Is Crowned (J. Arthur Rank Organization Ltd.; Universal-International)

IRVING G. THALBERG MEMORIAL AWARD
George Stevens

HONORARY AWARDS
To **Pete Smith** for his witty and pungent observations on the American scene in his series of *Pete Smith Specialities*

To **Twentieth Century-Fox Film Corporation** in recognition of their imagination, showmanship and foresight in introducing the revolutionary process known as CinemaScope

To **Joseph I. Breen** for his conscientious, open-minded and dignified management of the Motion Picture Production Code

To **Bell and Howell Company** for their pioneering and basic achievements in the advancement of the motion picture industry

1954

BEST MOTION PICTURE
The Caine Mutiny, Stanley Kramer, producer (Columbia)

The Country Girl, William Perlberg, producer (Paramount)

On the Waterfront, Sam Spiegel, producer (Columbia)

On the Waterfront

Seven Brides for Seven Brothers, Jack Cummings, producer (MGM)

Three Coins in the Fountain, Sol C. Siegel, producer (Twentieth Century-Fox)

BEST ACTOR
Humphrey Bogart, *The Caine Mutiny*

Marlon Brando, *On the Waterfront*

Bing Crosby, *The Country Girl*

James Mason, *A Star Is Born*

Dan O'Herlihy, *Adventures of Robinson Crusoe*

BEST ACTRESS
Dorothy Dandridge, *Carmen Jones*

Judy Garland, *A Star Is Born*

Audrey Hepburn, *Sabrina*

Grace Kelly, *The Country Girl*

Jane Wyman, *Magnificent Obsession*

ACTOR IN A SUPPORTING ROLE
Lee J. Cobb, *On the Waterfront*

Karl Malden, *On the Waterfront*

Edmond O'Brien, *The Barefoot Contessa*

Rod Steiger, *On the Waterfront*

Tom Tully, *The Caine Mutiny*

ACTRESS IN A SUPPORTING ROLE
Nina Foch, *Executive Suite*

Katy Jurado, *Broken Lance*

Eva Maria Saint, *On the Waterfront*

Jan Sterling, *The High and the Mighty*

Claire Trevor, *The High and the Mighty*

DIRECTING
Alfred Hitchcock, *Rear Window*

Elia Kazan, *On the Waterfront*

George Seaton, *The Country Girl*

William Wellman, *The High and the Mighty*

Billy Wilder, *Sabrina*

WRITING

MOTION PICTURE STORY
François Boyer, *Forbidden Games*

Jed Harris and Tom Reed, *Night People*

Ettore Margadonna, *Bread, Love and Dreams*

Lamar Trotti, *There's No Business Like Show Business*

Philip Yordan, *Broken Lance*

SCREENPLAY
Albert Hackett, Frances Goodrich and Dorothy Kingsley, *Seven Brides for Seven Brothers*

John Michael Hayes, *Rear Window*

Stanley Roberts, *The Caine Mutiny*

George Seaton, *The Country Girl*

Billy Wilder, Samuel Taylor and Ernest Lehman, *Sabrina*

STORY AND SCREENPLAY
Valentine Davies and Oscar Brodney, *The Glenn Miller Story*

Joseph L. Mankiewicz, *The Barefoot Contessa*

Norman Panama and Melvin Frank, *Knock on Wood*

William Rose, *Genevieve*

Budd Schulberg, *On the Waterfront*

CINEMATOGRAPHY

BLACK-AND-WHITE

George Folsey, *Executive Suite*

Boris Kaufman, *On the Waterfront*

Charles Lang, Jr., *Sabrina*

John Seitz, *Rogue Cop*

John F. Warren, *The Country Girl*

COLOR

Robert Burks, *Rear Window*

George Folsey, *Seven Brides for Seven Brothers*

Milton Krasner, *Three Coins in the Fountain*

Leon Shamroy, *The Egyptian*

William V. Skall, *The Silver Chalice*

ART DIRECTION

BLACK-AND-WHITE

Richard Day, art direction and set decoration, *On the Waterfront*

Cedric Gibbons and Edward Carfagno, art direction; Edwin B. Willis and Emile Kuri, set decoration, *Executive Suite*

Max Ophuls, art direction and set decoration, *Le Plaisir*

Hal Pereira and Roland Anderson, art direction; Sam Comer and Grace Gregory, set decoration, *The Country Girl*

Hal Pereira and Walter Tyler, art direction; Sam Comer and Ray Moyer, set decoration, *Sabrina*

COLOR

Malcolm Bert, Gene Allen and Irene Sharaff, art direction; George James Hopkins, set decoration, *A Star Is Born*

Cedric Gibbons and Preston Ames, art direction; Edwin B. Willis and Keogh Gleason, set decoration, *Brigadoon*

John Meehan, art direction; Emile Kuri, set decoration, *20,000 Leagues Under the Sea*

Hal Pereira and Roland Anderson, art direction; Sam Comer and Ray Moyer, set decoration, *Red Garters*

Lyle Wheeler and Leland Fuller, art direction; Walter M. Scott and Paul S. Fox, set decoration, *Desirée*

SOUND RECORDING

Columbia Studio Sound Dept., *The Caine Mutiny*

MGM Studio Sound Dept., *Brigadoon*

Paramount Studio Sound Dept., *Rear Window*

RKO Radio Studio Sound Dept., *Susan Slept Here*

Universal-International Studio Sound Dept., *The Glenn Miller Story*

MUSIC

SONG

"Count Your Blessings Instead of Sheep," *White Christmas*, Irving Berlin, music and lyrics

"The High and the Mighty," *The High and the Mighty*, Dimitri Tiomkin, music; Ned Washington, lyrics

"Hold My Hand," *Susan Slept Here*, Jack Lawrence and Richard Myers, music and lyrics

"The Man That Got Away," *A Star Is Born*, Harold Arlen, music; Ira Gershwin, lyrics

"Three Coins in the Fountain," *Three Coins in the Fountain*, Jule Styne, music; Sammy Cahn, lyrics

SCORING OF A DRAMATIC OR COMEDY PICTURE

Larry Adler, *Genevieve*

Leonard Bernstein, *On the Waterfront*

Max Steiner, *The Caine Mutiny*

Dimitri Tiomkin, *The High and the Mighty*

Franz Waxman, *The Silver Chalice*

SCORING OF A MUSICAL PICTURE

Adolph Deutsch and Saul Chaplin, *Seven Brides for Seven Brothers*

Joseph Gershenson and Henry Mancini, *The Glenn Miller Story*

Herschel Burke Gilbert, *Carmen Jones*

Ray Heindorf, *A Star Is Born*

Alfred Newman and Lionel Newman, *There's No Business Like Show Business*

FILM EDITING

Ralph Dawson, *The High and the Mighty*

William A. Lyon and Henry Batista, *The Caine Mutiny*

Gene Milford, *On the Waterfront*

Elmo Williams, *20,000 Leagues Under the Sea*

Ralph E. Winters, *Seven Brides for Seven Brothers*

COSTUME DESIGN

BLACK-AND-WHITE

Georges Annenkov and Rosine Delamare, *The Earrings of Madame De…*

Christian Dior, *Indiscretion of an American Wife*

Edith Head, *Sabrina*

Jean Louis, *It Should Happen to You*

Helen Rose, *Executive Suite*

COLOR

Charles LeMaire and Rene Hubert, *Desirée*

Charles LeMaire, Travilla and Miles White, *There's No Business Like Show Business*

Jean Louis, Mary Ann Nyberg and Irene Sharaff, *A Star Is Born*

Irene Sharaff, *Brigadoon*

Sanzo Wada, *Gate of Hell*

SPECIAL EFFECTS

Hell and High Water (Twentieth Century-Fox)

Them! (Warner Bros.)

***20,000 Leagues Under the Sea* (Walt Disney Productions; Buena Vista)**

SHORT SUBJECTS

CARTOON

Crazy Mixed Up Pup (Walter Lantz Productions; Universal-International)

Pigs Is Pigs (Walt Disney Productions; RKO Radio)

Sandy Claws (*Looney Tunes Series*) (Warner Bros. Cartoons, Inc.; Warner Bros.)

Touché, Pussy Cat (*Tom and Jerry Series*) (Frederick Quimby, producer; MGM)

***When Magoo Flew* (*Mr. Magoo Series*) (United Productions of America; Columbia)**

ONE-REEL

The First Piano Quartette (*Music Series*) (Otto Lang, producer; Twentieth Century-Fox)

The Strauss Fantasy (*Musical Gems Series*) (Johnny Green, producer; MGM)

This Mechanical Age (Warner Variety Series) (Robert Youngson, producer; Warner Bros.)

TWO-REEL

Beauty and the Bull (*Technicolor Specials Series*) (Cedric Francis, producer; Warner Bros.)

Jet Carrier (Otto Lang, producer; Twentieth Century-Fox)

Siam (*People and Places Series*) (Walt Disney Productions; Buena Vista)

A Time Out of War (Denis Sanders and Terry Sanders, producers; Carnival Productions)

DOCUMENTARY

SHORT SUBJECT

Jet Carrier (Otto Lang, producer; Twentieth Century-Fox)

Rembrandt: A Self-Portrait (Morrie Roizman Production; Distributors Corporation of America)

Thursday's Children (World Wide Pictures and Morse Films; British Information Services)

FEATURE

The Stratford Adventure (National Film Board of Canada; Continental Distributing, Inc.)

The Vanishing Prairie (True-Life Adventure Series) (Walt Disney Productions; Buena Vista)

HONORARY AWARDS

To **Bausch and Lomb Optical Company** for their contributions to the advancement of the motion picture industry

To **Kemp R. Niver** for the development of the Renovare Process, which has made possible the restoration of the Library of Congress Paper Film Collection

To **Greta Garbo** for her unforgettable screen performances

To **Danny Kaye** for his unique talents and his service to the Academy, the motion picture industry and the American people

To **Jon Whiteley** for his outstanding juvenile performance in *The Little Kidnappers*

To **Vincent Winter** for his outstanding performance in *The Little Kidnappers*

To *Gate of Hell* (Japan) best foreign language film first released in the United States during 1954

1955

BEST MOTION PICTURE

Love Is a Many Splendored Thing, Buddy Adler, producer (Twentieth Century-Fox)

Marty, Harold Hecht, producer (United Artists)

Mister Roberts, Leland Hayward, producer (Warner Bros.)

Picnic, Fred Kohlmar, producer (Columbia)

The Rose Tattoo, Hal Wallis, producer (Paramount)

Anna Magnani, *The Rose Tattoo*

BEST ACTOR

Ernest Borgnine, *Marty*

James Cagney, *Love Me or Leave Me*

James Dean, *East of Eden*

Frank Sinatra, *The Man With the Golden Arm*

Spencer Tracy, *Bad Day at Black Rock*

BEST ACTRESS

Susan Hayward, *I'll Cry Tomorrow*

Katharine Hepburn, *Summertime*

Jennifer Jones, *Love Is a Many Splendored Thing*

Anna Magnani, *The Rose Tattoo*

Eleanor Parker, *Interrupted Melody*

ACTOR IN A SUPPORTING ROLE

Arthur Kennedy, *Trial*

Jack Lemmon, *Mister Roberts*

Joe Mantell, *Marty*

Sal Mineo, *Rebel Without a Cause*

Arthur O'Connell, *Picnic*

ACTRESS IN A SUPPORTING ROLE

Betsy Blair, *Marty*

Jo Van Fleet, *East of Eden*

Peggy Lee, *Pete Kelly's Blues*

Marisa Pavan, *The Rose Tattoo*

Natalie Wood, *Rebel Without a Cause*

DIRECTING

Elia Kazan, *East of Eden*

David Lean, *Summertime*

Joshua Logan, *Picnic*

Delbert Mann, *Marty*

John Sturges, *Bad Day at Black Rock*

WRITING

MOTION PICTURE STORY

Joe Connelly and Bob Mosher, *The Private War of Major Benson*

Daniel Fuchs, *Love Me or Leave Me*

Beirne Lay, Jr., *Strategic Air Command*

Jean Marsan, Henry Troyat, Jacques Perret, Henri Verneuil and Raoul Ploquin, *The Sheep Has Five Legs*

Nicholas Ray, *Rebel Without a Cause*

SCREENPLAY
Richard Brooks, *Blackboard Jungle*

Paddy Chayefsky, *Marty*

Daniel Fuchs and Isobel Lennart, *Love Me or Leave Me*

Millard Kaufman, *Bad Day at Black Rock*

Paul Osborn, *East of Eden*

STORY AND SCREENPLAY
Betty Comden and Adolph Green, *It's Always Fair Weather*

William Ludwig and Sonya Levien, *Interrupted Melody*

Melville Shavelson and Jack Rose, *The Seven Little Foys*

Milton Sperling and Emmet Lavery, *The Court-Martial of Billy Mitchell*

Jacques Tati and Henri Marquet, *Mr. Hulot's Holiday*

CINEMATOGRAPHY
BLACK-AND-WHITE
Arthur E. Arling, *I'll Cry Tomorrow*

Russell Harlan, *Blackboard Jungle*

James Wong Howe, *The Rose Tattoo*

Charles Lang, *Queen Bee*

Joseph LaShelle, *Marty*

COLOR
Robert Burks, *To Catch a Thief*

Harold Lipstein, *A Man Called Peter*

Leon Shamroy, *Love Is a Many Splendored Thing*

Harry Stradling, *Guys and Dolls*

Robert Surtees, *Oklahoma!*

ART DIRECTION
BLACK-AND-WHITE
Cedric Gibbons and Malcolm Brown, art direction; Edwin B. Willis and Hugh B. Hunt, set decoration, *I'll Cry Tomorrow*

Cedric Gibbons and Randall Duell, art direction; Edwin B. Willis and Henry Grace, set decoration, *Blackboard Jungle*

Edward S. Haworth and Walter Simonds, art direction; Robert Priestley, set decoration, *Marty*

Hal Pereira and Tambi Larsen, art direction; Sam Comer and Arthur Krams, set decoration, *The Rose Tattoo*

Joseph C. Wright, art direction; Darrell Silvera, set decoration, *The Man With the Golden Arm*

COLOR
William Flannery and Jo Mielziner, art direction; Robert Priestley, set decoration, *Picnic*

Hal Pereira and Joseph McMillan Johnson, art direction; Sam Comer and Arthur Krams, set decoration, *To Catch a Thief*

Oliver Smith and Joseph C. Wright, art direction; Howard Bristol, set decoration, *Guys and Dolls*

Lyle Wheeler and George W. Davis, art direction; Walter M. Scott and Jack Stubbs, set decoration, *Love Is a Many Splendored Thing*

Lyle Wheeler and John DeCuir, art direction; Walter M. Scott and Paul S. Fox, set decoration, *Daddy Long Legs*

SOUND RECORDING
MGM Studio Sound Dept., *Love Me or Leave Me*

RCA Sound Department, *Not as a Stranger*

Todd-AO Sound Department, *Oklahoma!*

Twentieth Century-Fox Studio Sound Dept., *Love Is a Many Splendored Thing*

Warner Bros. Studio Sound Dept., *Mister Roberts*

MUSIC
SONG
"I'll Never Stop Loving You," *Love Me or Leave Me*, Nicholas Brodszky, music; Sammy Cahn, lyrics

"Love Is a Many Splendored Thing," *Love Is a Many Splendored Thing*, Sammy Fain, music; Paul Francis Webster, lyrics

"Something's Gotta Give," *Daddy Long Legs*, Johnny Mercer, music and lyrics

(Love Is) "The Tender Trap," *The Tender Trap*, James Van Heusen, music; Sammy Cahn, lyrics

"Unchained Melody," *Unchained*, Alex North, music; Hy Zaret, lyrics

SCORING OF A DRAMATIC OR COMEDY PICTURE
Elmer Bernstein, *The Man With the Golden Arm*

George Duning, *Picnic*

Alfred Newman, *Love Is a Many Splendored Thing*

Alex North, *The Rose Tattoo*

Max Steiner, *Battle Cry*

SCORING OF A MUSICAL PICTURE
Robert Russell Bennett, Jay Blackton and Adolph Deutsch, *Oklahoma!*

Jay Blackton and Cyril J. Mockridge, *Guys and Dolls*

Percy Faith and George Stoll, *Love Me or Leave Me*

Alfred Newman, *Daddy Long Legs*

André Previn, *It's Always Fair Weather*

FILM EDITING
Warren Low, *The Rose Tattoo*

Alma Macrorie, *The Bridges at Toko-Ri*

Charles Nelson and William A. Lyon, *Picnic*

Gene Ruggiero and George Boemler, *Oklahoma!*

Ferris Webster, *Blackboard Jungle*

COSTUME DESIGN
BLACK-AND-WHITE
Beatrice Dawson, *The Pickwick Papers*

Edith Head, *The Rose Tattoo*

Tadaoto Kainoscho, *Ugetsu*

Jean Louis, *Queen Bee*

Helen Rose, *I'll Cry Tomorrow*

COLOR
Edith Head, *To Catch a Thief*

Charles LeMaire, *Love Is a Many Splendored Thing*

Charles LeMaire and Mary Wills, *The Virgin Queen*

Helen Rose, *Interrupted Melody*

Irene Sharaff, *Guys and Dolls*

SPECIAL EFFECTS
The Bridges at Toko-Ri **(Paramount)**

The Dam Busters (Warner Bros.)

The Rains of Ranchipur (Twentieth Century-Fox)

SHORT SUBJECTS
CARTOON
Good Will to Men (*MGM Cartoon Series*) (Frederick Quimby, William Hanna and Joseph Barbera, producers; MGM)

The Legend of Rock-a-Bye Point (Walter Lantz Productions; Universal-International)

No Hunting (*Donald Duck Series*) (Walt Disney Productions; RKO Radio)

***Speedy Gonzales* (*Merrie Melodies Series*) (Warner Bros. Cartoons, Inc.; Warner Bros.)**

ONE-REEL
Gadgets Galore (*Warner Varieties Series*) (Robert Youngson, producer; Warner Bros.)

***Survival City* (*Movietone CinemaScope Series*) (Edmund Reek, producer; Twentieth Century-Fox)**

3rd Ave. El (Carson Davidson Productions; Ardee Films)

Three Kisses (*Topper Special Series*) (Justin Herman, producer; Paramount)

TWO-REEL
The Battle of Gettysburg (Dore Schary, producer; MGM)

***The Face of Lincoln* (University of Southern California Presentation; Cavalcade Pictures, Inc.)**

On The Twelfth Day . . . (United Kingdom Series) (Go Pictures, Inc.; George Brest and Associates)

Switzerland (*People and Places Series*) (Walt Disney Productions; Buena Vista)

24-Hour Alert (Cedric Francis, producer; Warner Bros.)

DOCUMENTARY
SHORT SUBJECT
The Battle of Gettysburg (Dore Schary, producer; MGM)

The Face of Lincoln (University of Southern California Presentation; Cavalcade Pictures, Inc.)

***Men Against the Arctic* (*People and Places Series*) (Walt Disney Productions; Buena Vista)**

FEATURE
Heartbreak Ridge (Rene Risacher Production; Tudor Pictures)

***Helen Keller in Her Story* (Nancy Hamilton, producer; Nancy Hamilton Presentation)**

HONORARY AWARD
To ***Samurai, The Legend of Musashi*** (Japan), best foreign language film first released in the United States during 1955

1956
BEST MOTION PICTURE
***Around the World in 80 Days*, Michael Todd, producer (United Artists)**

Friendly Persuasion, William Wyler, producer (Allied Artists)

Giant, George Stevens and Henry Ginsberg, producers (Warner Bros.)

The King and I, Charles Brackett, producer (Twentieth Century-Fox)

The Ten Commandments, Cecil B. DeMille, producer (Paramount)

Around the World in 80 Days

BEST ACTOR
Yul Brynner, *The King and I*

James Dean, *Giant*

Kirk Douglas, *Lust for Life*

Rock Hudson, *Giant*

Sir Laurence Olivier, *Richard III*

BEST ACTRESS
Carroll Baker, *Baby Doll*

Ingrid Bergman, *Anastasia*

Katharine Hepburn, *The Rainmaker*

Nancy Kelly, *The Bad Seed*

Deborah Kerr, *The King and I*

ACTOR IN A SUPPORTING ROLE
Don Murray, *Bus Stop*

Anthony Perkins, *Friendly Persuasion*

Anthony Quinn, *Lust for Life*

Mickey Rooney, *The Bold and the Brave*

Robert Stack, *Written on the Wind*

ACTRESS IN A SUPPORTING ROLE
Mildred Dunnock, *Baby Doll*

Eileen Heckart, *The Bad Seed*

Mercedes McCambridge, *Giant*

Patty McCormack, *The Bad Seed*

Dorothy Malone, *Written on the Wind*

DIRECTING
Michael Anderson, *Around the World in 80 Days*

Walter Lang, *The King and I*

George Stevens, *Giant*

King Vidor, *War and Peace*

William Wyler, *Friendly Persuasion*

WRITING
MOTION PICTURE STORY
Leo Katcher, *The Eddy Duchin Story*

Jean Paul Sartre, *The Proud and the Beautiful*

Dalton Trumbo, *The Brave One*

Cesare Zavattini, *Umberto D.*

SCREENPLAY, ADAPTED

Norman Corwin, *Lust for Life*

Fred Guiol and Ivan Moffat, *Giant*

James Poe, John Farrow and S.J. Perelman, *Around the World in 80 Days*

Tennessee Williams, *Baby Doll*

SCREENPLAY, ORIGINAL

Federico Fellini and Tullio Pinelli, *La Strada*

Albert Lamorisse, *The Red Balloon*

Robert Lewin, *The Bold and the Brave*

William Rose, *The Lady Killers*

Andrew L. Stone, *Julie*

CINEMATOGRAPHY

BLACK-AND-WHITE

Burnett Guffey, *The Harder They Fall*

Boris Kaufman, *Baby Doll*

Hal Rosson, *The Bad Seed*

Joseph Ruttenberg, *Somebody Up There Likes Me*

Walter Strenge, *Stagecoach to Fury*

COLOR

Jack Cardiff, *War and Peace*

Loyal Griggs, *The Ten Commandments*

Lionel Lindon, *Around the World in 80 Days*

Leon Shamroy, *The King and I*

Harry Stradling, *The Eddy Duchin Story*

ART DIRECTION

BLACK-AND-WHITE

Ross Bellah, art direction; William R. Kiernan and Louis Diage, set decoration, *The Solid Gold Cadillac*

Cedric Gibbons and Malcolm F. Brown, art direction; Edwin B. Willis and F. Keogh Gleason, set decoration, *Somebody Up There Likes Me*

Takashi Matsuyama, art direction and set decoration, *The Magnificent Seven*

Hal Pereira and A. Earl Hedrick, art direction; Samuel M. Comer and Frank R. McKelvy, set decoration, *The Proud and the Profane*

Lyle R. Wheeler and Jack Martin Smith, art direction; Walter M. Scott and Stuart A. Reiss, set decoration, *Teenage Rebel*

COLOR

Cedric Gibbons, Hans Peters and Preston Ames, art direction; Edwin B. Willis and F. Keogh Gleason, set decoration, *Lust for Life*

Boris Leven, art direction; Ralph S. Hurst, set decoration, *Giant*

Hal Pereira, Walter H. Tyler and Albert Nozaki, art direction; Sam M. Comer and Ray Moyer, set decoration, *The Ten Commandments*

James W. Sullivan and Ken Adam, art direction; Ross J. Dowd, set decoration, *Around the World in 80 Days*

Lyle R. Wheeler and John DeCuir, art direction; Walter M. Scott and Paul S. Fox, set decoration, *The King and I*

SOUND RECORDING

Columbia Studio Sound Dept., *The Eddy Duchin Story*

Paramount Studio Sound Dept., *The Ten Commandments*

RKO Radio Studio Sound Dept., *The Brave One*

Twentieth Century-Fox Studio Sound Dept., *The King and I*

Westrex Sound Services, Inc. and Samuel Goldwyn Studio Sound Dept., *Friendly Persuasion*

MUSIC

SONG

"Friendly Persuasion" (Thee I Love), *Friendly Persuasion*, Dimitri Tiomkin, music; Paul Francis Webster, lyrics

"Julie," *Julie*, Leith Stevens, music; Tom Adair, lyrics

"True Love," *High Society*, Cole Porter, music and lyrics

"Whatever Will Be, Will Be" (Que Será, Será), *The Man Who Knew Too Much*, Jay Livingston and Ray Evans, music and lyrics

"Written on the Wind," *Written on the Wind*, Victor Young, music; Sammy Cahn, lyrics

SCORING OF A DRAMATIC OR COMEDY PICTURE

Hugo Friedhofer, *Between Heaven and Hell*

Alfred Newman, *Anastasia*

Alex North, *The Rainmaker*

Dimitri Tiomkin, *Giant*

Victor Young, *Around the World in 80 Days*

SCORING OF A MUSICAL PICTURE

Johnny Green and Saul Chaplin, *High Society*

Alfred Newman and Ken Darby, *The King and I*

Lionel Newman, *The Best Things in Life Are Free*

George Stoll and Johnny Green, *Meet Me in Las Vegas*

Morris Stoloff and George Duning, *The Eddy Duchin Story*

FILM EDITING

Albert Akst, *Somebody Up There Likes Me*

Anne Bauchens, *The Ten Commandments*

William Hornbeck, Philip W. Anderson and Fred Bohanan, *Giant*

Gene Ruggiero and Paul Weatherwax, *Around the World in 80 Days*

Merrill G. White, *The Brave One*

COSTUME DESIGN

BLACK-AND-WHITE

Kohei Ezaki, *The Magnificent Seven*

Edith Head, *The Proud and the Profane*

Charles LeMaire and Mary Wills, *Teenage Rebel*

Jean Louis, *The Solid Gold Cadillac*

Helen Rose, *The Power and the Prize*

COLOR

Marie De Matteis, *War and Peace*

Edith Head, Ralph Jester, John Jensen, Dorothy Jeakins and Arnold Friberg, *The Ten Commandments*

Moss Mabry and Marjorie Best, *Giant*

Irene Sharaff, *The King and I*

Miles White, *Around the World in 80 Days*

SPECIAL EFFECTS

John Fulton, *The Ten Commandments*

A. Arnold Gillespie, Irving Ries and Wesley C. Miller, *Forbidden Planet*

SHORT SUBJECTS

CARTOON
Gerald McBoing-Boing on Planet Moo (*Jolly Frolics Series*) (United Productions of America; Columbia)

The Jay Walker (*UPA Special Series*) (United Productions of America; Columbia)

Mister Magoo's Puddle Jumper (*Mr. Magoo Series*) **(United Productions of America; Columbia)**

ONE-REEL
Crashing the Water Barrier (*The Sports Parade Series*) **(Konstantin Kalser, producer; Warner Bros.)**

I Never Forget a Face (*Warner Specials Series*) (Robert Youngson, producer; Warner Bros.)

Time Stood Still (*Scope Gems Series*) (Cedric Francis, producer; Warner Bros.)

TWO-REEL
The Bespoke Overcoat (Go Pictures, Inc.; Romulus Films)

Cow Dog (Walt Disney Productions; Buena Vista)

The Dark Wave (John Healy, producer; Twentieth Century-Fox)

Samoa (*People and Places Series*) (Walt Disney Productions; Buena Vista)

DOCUMENTARY

SHORT SUBJECT
A City Decides (Charles Guggenheim and Associates, Inc.)

The Dark Wave (John Healy, producer; Twentieth Century-Fox)

The House Without a Name (Valentine Davies, producer; Universal-International)

Man in Space (Walt Disney Productions; Buena Vista)

The True Story of the Civil War (Louis Clyde Stoumen, producer; Camera Eye Pictures, Inc.)

FEATURE
The Naked Eye (Camera Eye Pictures, Inc.; Film Representatives, Inc.)

The Silent World (Filmad-F.S.J.Y.C. Production; Columbia)

Where Mountains Float (Arno/Studios, Copenhagen; Brandon Films, Inc.)

FOREIGN LANGUAGE FILM
The Captain of Kopenick, Federal Republic of Germany – West

Gervaise, France

Harp of Burma, Japan

Qivitoq, Denmark

La Strada, Italy

IRVING G. THALBERG MEMORIAL AWARD
Buddy Adler

JEAN HERSHOLT HUMANITARIAN AWARD
(Not necessarily given each year)
Y. Frank Freeman

HONORARY AWARD
To **Eddie Cantor** for distinguished service to the film industry

1957

BEST MOTION PICTURE
The Bridge on the River Kwai, Sam Spiegel, producer (Columbia)

Peyton Place, Jerry Wald, producer (Twentieth Century-Fox)

Sayonara, William Goetz, producer (Warner Bros.)

12 Angry Men, Henry Fonda and Reginald Rose, producers (United Artists)

Witness for the Prosecution, Arthur Hornblow, Jr., producer (United Artists)

BEST ACTOR
Marlon Brando, *Sayonara*

Anthony Franciosa, *A Hatful of Rain*

Alec Guinness, The Bridge on the River Kwai

Charles Laughton, *Witness for the Prosecution*

Anthony Quinn, *Wild Is the Wind*

Joanne Woodward,
The Three Faces of Eve

BEST ACTRESS
Deborah Kerr, *Heaven Knows, Mr. Allison*

Anna Magnani, *Wild Is the Wind*

Elizabeth Taylor, *Raintree County*

Lana Turner, *Peyton Place*

Joanne Woodward, The Three Faces of Eve

ACTOR IN A SUPPORTING ROLE
Red Buttons, Sayonara

Vittorio de Sica, *A Farewell to Arms*

Sessue Hayakawa, *The Bridge on the River Kwai*

Arthur Kennedy, *Peyton Place*

Russ Tamblyn, *Peyton Place*

ACTRESS IN A SUPPORTING ROLE
Carolyn Jones, *The Bachelor Party*

Elsa Lanchester, *Witness for the Prosecution*

Hope Lange, *Peyton Place*

Miyoshi Umeki, Sayonara

Diane Varsi, *Peyton Place*

DIRECTING
David Lean, *The Bridge on the River Kwai*

Joshua Logan, *Sayonara*

Sidney Lumet, *12 Angry Men*

Mark Robson, *Peyton Place*

Billy Wilder, *Witness for the Prosecution*

WRITING

SCREENPLAY BASED ON MATERIAL FROM ANOTHER MEDIUM
Pierre Boulle, Michael Wilson and Carl Foreman, *The Bridge on the River Kwai*

John Michael Hayes, *Peyton Place*

John Lee Mahin and John Huston, *Heaven Knows, Mr. Allison*

Paul Osborn, *Sayonara*

Reginald Rose, *12 Angry Men*

STORY AND SCREENPLAY WRITTEN DIRECTLY FOR THE SCREEN
Federico Fellini, Ennio Flaiano and Tullio Pinelli, story; Federico Fellini and Ennio Flaiano, screenplay, *I Vitelloni*

Leonard Gershe, *Funny Face*

Barney Slater and Joel Kane, story; Dudley Nichols, screenplay, *The Tin Star*

George Wells, *Designing Woman*

Ralph Wheelright, story; R. Wright Campbell, Ivan Goff and Ben Roberts, screenplay, *Man of a Thousand Faces*

CINEMATOGRAPHY
Ellsworth Fredericks, *Sayonara*

Jack Hildyard, *The Bridge on the River Kwai*

Ray June, *Funny Face*

Milton Krasner, *An Affair to Remember*

William Mellor, *Peyton Place*

ART DIRECTION
Ted Haworth, art direction; Robert Priestley, set decoration, *Sayonara*

Walter Holscher, art direction; William Kiernan and Louis Diage, set decoration, *Pal Joey*

William A. Horning and Gene Allen, art direction; Edwin B. Willis and Richard Pefferle, set decoration, *Les Girls*

William A. Horning and Urie McCleary, art direction; Edwin B. Willis and Hugh Hunt, set decoration, *Raintree County*

Hal Pereira and George W. Davis, art direction; Sam Comer and Ray Moyer, set decoration, *Funny Face*

SOUND RECORDING
Columbia Studio Sound Dept., *Pal Joey*

MGM Studio Sound Dept., *Les Girls*

Paramount Studio Sound Dept., *Gunfight at the O.K. Corral*

Samuel Goldwyn Studio Sound Dept., *Witness for the Prosecution*

Warner Bros. Studio Sound Dept., *Sayonara*

MUSIC

SONG
"An Affair to Remember," *An Affair to Remember*, Harry Warren, music; Harold Adamson and Leo McCarey, lyrics

"All the Way," *The Joker Is Wild*, James Van Heusen, music; Sammy Cahn, lyrics

"April Love," *April Love*, Sammy Fain, music; Paul Francis Webster, lyrics

"Tammy," *Tammy and the Bachelor*, Ray Evans and Jay Livingston, music and lyrics

"Wild Is the Wind," *Wild Is the Wind*, Dimitri Tiomkin, music; Ned Washington, lyrics

SCORE
Malcolm Arnold, *The Bridge on the River Kwai*

Hugo Friedhofer, *An Affair to Remember*

Hugo Friedhofer, *Boy on a Dolphin*

Johnny Green, *Raintree County*

Paul Smith, *Perri*

FILM EDITING
Viola Lawrence and Jerome Thoms, *Pal Joey*

Warren Low, *Gunfight at the O.K. Corral*

Daniel Mandell, *Witness for the Prosecution*

Arthur P. Schmidt and Philip W. Anderson, *Sayonara*

Peter Taylor, *The Bridge on the River Kwai*

COSTUME DESIGN
Edith Head and Hubert de Givenchy, *Funny Face*

Charles LeMaire, *An Affair to Remember*

Jean Louis, *Pal Joey*

Orry-Kelly, *Les Girls*

Walter Plunkett, *Raintree County*

SPECIAL EFFECTS
Louis Lichtenfield, visual, *The Spirit of St. Louis*

Walter Rossi, audible, *The Enemy Below*

SHORT SUBJECTS

CARTOON
Birds Anonymous (*Tweety and Sylvester Series*) (Edward Selzer, producer; Warner Bros.)

One Droopy Knight (*Droopy Series*) (William Hanna and Joseph Barbera, producers; MGM)

Tabasco Road (*Speedy Gonzales Series*) (Edward Selzer, producer; Warner Bros.)

Trees and *Jamaica Daddy* (*Ham and Hattie Series*) (United Productions of America; Columbia)

The Truth About Mother Goose (Walt Disney Productions; Buena Vista)

LIVE ACTION SUBJECTS
A Chairy Tale (National Film Board of Canada; Kingsley International)

City of Gold (National Film Board of Canada; Kingsley International)

Foothold on Antarctica (World Wide Pictures; Lester A. Shoenfeld Films)

Portugal (*People and Places Series*) (Walt Disney Productions; Buena Vista)

The Wetback Hound (Walt Disney Productions; Buena Vista)

DOCUMENTARY

SHORT SUBJECT
No award given this year

FEATURE
Albert Schweitzer (Hill and Anderson Production; Louis de Rochemont Associates)

On the Bowery (Lionel Rogosin Productions; Film Representations, Inc.)

Torero! (Producciones Barbachano Ponce; Columbia)

FOREIGN LANGUAGE FILM

The Devil Came at Night, Federal Republic of Germany – West

Gates of Paris, France

Mother India, India

The Nights of Cabiria, Italy

Nine Lives, Norway

JEAN HERSHOLT HUMANITARIAN AWARD

Samuel Goldwyn

HONORARY AWARDS

To **Charles Brackett** for outstanding service to the academy

To **B. B. Kahane** for distinguished service to the motion picture industry

To **Gilbert M. "Broncho Billy" Anderson,** motion picture pioneer, for his contributions to the development of motion pictures as entertainment

To the **Society of Motion Picture and Television Engineers** for their contributions to the advancement of the motion picture industry

1958

BEST MOTION PICTURE

Auntie Mame (Warner Bros.)

Cat on a Hot Tin Roof, Lawrence Weingarten, producer (MGM)

The Defiant Ones, Stanley Kramer, producer (United Artists)

Gigi, Arthur Freed, producer **(MGM)**

Separate Tables, Harold Hecht, producer (United Artists)

BEST ACTOR

Tony Curtis, *The Defiant Ones*

Paul Newman, *Cat on a Hot Tin Roof*

David Niven, Separate Tables

Sidney Poitier, *The Defiant Ones*

Spencer Tracy, *The Old Man and the Sea*

BEST ACTRESS

Susan Hayward, I Want to Live!

Deborah Kerr, *Separate Tables*

Shirley MacLaine, *Some Came Running*

Rosalind Russell, *Auntie Mame*

Elizabeth Taylor, *Cat on a Hot Tin Roof*

ACTOR IN A SUPPORTING ROLE

Theodore Bikel, *The Defiant Ones*

Lee J. Cobb, *The Brothers Karamazov*

Burl Ives, The Big Country

Arthur Kennedy, *Some Came Running*

Gig Young, *Teacher's Pet*

ACTRESS IN A SUPPORTING ROLE

Peggy Cass, *Auntie Mame*

Wendy Hiller, Separate Tables

Gigi

Martha Hyer, *Some Came Running*

Maureen Stapleton, *Lonelyhearts*

Cara Williams, *The Defiant Ones*

DIRECTING

Richard Brooks, *Cat on a Hot Tin Roof*

Stanley Kramer, *The Defiant Ones*

Vincente Minnelli, Gigi

Mark Robson, *The Inn of the Sixth Happiness*

Robert Wise, *I Want to Live!*

WRITING

SCREENPLAY BASED ON MATERIAL FROM ANOTHER MEDIUM

Richard Brooks and James Poe, *Cat on a Hot Tin Roof*

Nelson Gidding and Don Mankiewicz, *I Want to Live!*

Alec Guinness, *The Horse's Mouth*

Alan Jay Lerner, *Gigi*

Terence Rattigan and John Gay, *Separate Tables*

STORY AND SCREENPLAY WRITTEN DIRECTLY FOR THE SCREEN

Paddy Chayefsky, *The Goddess*

James Edward Grant and William Bowers, *The Sheepman*

Fay and Michael Kanin, *Teacher's Pet*

Melville Shavelson and Jack Rose, *Houseboat*

Nedrick Young and Harold Jacob Smith, The Defiant Ones

CINEMATOGRAPHY

BLACK-AND-WHITE

Daniel L. Fapp, *Desire Under the Elms*

Charles Lang, Jr., *Separate Tables*

Sam Leavitt, The Defiant Ones

Lionel Lindon, *I Want to Live!*

Joe MacDonald, *The Young Lions*

COLOR

William Daniels, *Cat on a Hot Tin Roof*

James Wong Howe, *The Old Man and the Sea*

Joseph Ruttenberg, Gigi

Leon Shamroy, *South Pacific*

Harry Stradling, Sr., *Auntie Mame*

ART DIRECTION

Malcolm Bert, art direction; George James Hopkins, set decoration, *Auntie Mame*

William A. Horning and Preston Ames, art direction; Henry Grace and Keogh Gleason, set decoration, *Gigi*

Cary Odell, art direction; Louis Diage, set decoration, *Bell, Book and Candle*

Hal Pereira and Henry Bumstead, art direction; Sam Comer and Frank McKelvy, set decoration, *Vertigo*

Lyle R. Wheeler and John DeCuir, art direction; Walter M. Scott and Paul S. Fox, set decoration, *A Certain Smile*

SOUND

Paramount Studio Sound Dept., *Vertigo*

Samuel Goldwyn Studio Sound Dept., *I Want to Live!*

Todd-AO Sound Dept., *South Pacific*

Twentieth Century-Fox Studio Sound Dept., *The Young Lions*

Universal-International Studio Sound Dept., *A Time to Love and a Time to Die*

MUSIC

SONG

"Almost in Your Arms" (Love Song From *Houseboat*), *Houseboat*, Jay Livingston and Ray Evans, music and lyrics

"A Certain Smile," *A Certain Smile*, Sammy Fain, music; Paul Francis Webster, lyrics

"Gigi," *Gigi*, Frederick Loewe, music; Alan Jay Lerner, lyrics

"To Love and Be Loved," *Some Came Running*, James Van Heusen, music; Sammy Cahn, lyrics

"A Very Precious Love," *Marjorie Morningstar*, Sammy Fain, music; Paul Francis Webster, lyrics

SCORING OF A DRAMATIC OR COMEDY PICTURE

Hugo Friedhofer, *The Young Lions*

Jerome Moross, *The Big Country*

David Raksin, *Separate Tables*

Dimitri Tiomkin, *The Old Man and the Sea*

Oliver Wallace, *White Wilderness*

SCORING OF A MUSICAL PICTURE

Yuri Faier and G. Rozhdestvensky, *The Bolshoi Ballet*

Ray Heindorf, *Damn Yankees*

Alfred Newman and Ken Darby, *South Pacific*

Lionel Newman, *Mardi Gras*

André Previn, *Gigi*

FILM EDITING

Adrienne Fazan, *Gigi*

William Hornbeck, *I Want to Live!*

Frederick Knudtson, *The Defiant Ones*

William A. Lyon and Al Clark, *Cowboy*

William Ziegler, *Auntie Mame*

COSTUME DESIGN

BLACK-AND-WHITE OR COLOR

Cecil Beaton, *Gigi*

Ralph Jester, Edith Head and John Jensen, *The Buccaneer*

Charles LeMaire and Mary Wills, *A Certain Smile*

Jean Louis, *Bell, Book and Candle*

Walter Plunkett, *Some Came Running*

SPECIAL EFFECTS

A. Arnold Gillespie, visual; Harold Humbrock, audible, *Torpedo Run*

Tom Howard, visual, *tom thumb*

SHORT SUBJECTS

CARTOON

***Knighty Knight Bugs* (*Bugs Bunny Series*) (John W. Burton, producer; Warner Bros.)**

Paul Bunyan (Walt Disney Productions; Buena Vista)

Sidney's Family Tree (*Silly Sidney Series*) (Terrytoons; Twentieth Century-Fox)

LIVE ACTION

***Grand Canyon* (Walt Disney Productions; Buena Vista)**

Journey Into Spring (British Transport Films; Lester A. Schoenfeld Films)

The Kiss (Cohay Productions; Continental Distributing, Inc.)

Snows of Aorangi (New Zealand Screen Board; George Brest and Associates)

T Is for Tumbleweed (James A. Lebenthal Productions; Continental Distributing, Inc.)

DOCUMENTARY

SHORT SUBJECT

***AMA Girls* (*People and Places Series*) (Walt Disney Productions; Buena Vista)**

Employees Only (Kenneth G. Brown, producer; Hughes Aircraft Co.)

Journey Into Spring (British Transport Films; Lester A. Schoenfeld Films)

The Living Stone (Tom Daly, producer; National Film Board of Canada)

Overture (United Nations Film Services; Kingsley International Pictures)

FEATURE

Antarctic Crossing (World Wide Pictures; Lester A. Schoenfeld Films)

The Hidden World (Robert Snyder, producer; Small World Co.)

Psychiatric Nursing (Nathan Zucker, producer; Dynamic Films, Inc.)

***White Wilderness* (*True Life Adventure Series*) (Walt Disney Productions; Buena Vista)**

FOREIGN LANGUAGE FILM

Arms and the Man, Federal Republic of Germany – West

La Venganza, Spain

***My Uncle*, France**

The Road a Year Long, Yugoslavia

The Usual Unidentified Thieves, Italy

IRVING G. THALBERG MEMORIAL AWARD

Jack L. Warner

HONORARY AWARD

To **Maurice Chevalier** for his contributions to the world of entertainment over more than half a century

1959

BEST MOTION PICTURE

Anatomy of a Murder, Otto Preminger, producer (Columbia)

Ben-Hur, Sam Zimbalist, producer (MGM)

The Diary of Anne Frank, George Stevens, producer (Twentieth Century-Fox)

The Nun's Story, Henry Blanke, producer (Warner Bros.)

Room at the Top, John and James Woolf, producers (Continental)

BEST ACTOR

Laurence Harvey, *Room at the Top*

Charlton Heston, *Ben-Hur*

Jack Lemmon, *Some Like It Hot*

Paul Muni, *The Last Angry Man*

James Stewart, *Anatomy of a Murder*

Charlton Heston, *Ben-Hur*

BEST ACTRESS

Doris Day, *Pillow Talk*

Audrey Hepburn, *The Nun's Story*

Katharine Hepburn, *Suddenly, Last Summer*

Simone Signoret, *Room at the Top*

Elizabeth Taylor, *Suddenly, Last Summer*

ACTOR IN A SUPPORTING ROLE

Hugh Griffith, *Ben-Hur*

Arthur O'Connell, *Anatomy of a Murder*

George C. Scott, *Anatomy of a Murder*

Robert Vaughn, *The Young Philadelphians*

Ed Wynn, *The Diary of Anne Frank*

ACTRESS IN A SUPPORTING ROLE

Hermione Baddeley, *Room at the Top*

Susan Kohner, *Imitation of Life*

Juanita Moore, *Imitation of Life*

Thelma Ritter, *Pillow Talk*

Shelley Winters, *The Diary of Anne Frank*

DIRECTING

Jack Clayton, *Room at the Top*

George Stevens, *The Diary of Anne Frank*

Billy Wilder, *Some Like It Hot*

William Wyler, *Ben-Hur*

Fred Zinnemann, *The Nun's Story*

WRITING

SCREENPLAY BASED ON MATERIAL FROM ANOTHER MEDIUM

Robert Anderson, *The Nun's Story*

Wendell Mayes, *Anatomy of a Murder*

Neil Paterson, *Room at the Top*

Karl Tunberg, *Ben-Hur*

Billy Wilder and I. A. L. Diamond, *Some Like It Hot*

STORY AND SCREENPLAY WRITTEN DIRECTLY FOR THE SCREEN

Ingmar Bergman, *Wild Strawberries*

Ernest Lehman, *North by Northwest*

Russell Rouse and Clarence Greene, story; Stanley Shapiro and Maurice Richlin, screenplay, *Pillow Talk*

François Truffaut and Marcel Moussy, *The 400 Blows*

CINEMATOGRAPHY

BLACK-AND-WHITE

Charles Lang, Jr., *Some Like It Hot*

Joseph LaShelle, *Career*

Sam Leavitt, *Anatomy of a Murder*

William C. Mellor, *The Diary of Anne Frank*

Harry Stradling, Sr., *The Young Philadelphians*

COLOR

Daniel L. Fapp, *The Five Pennies*

Lee Garmes, *The Big Fisherman*

Franz Planer, *The Nun's Story*

Leon Shamroy, *Porgy and Bess*

Robert L. Surtees, *Ben-Hur*

ART DIRECTION

BLACK-AND-WHITE

Carl Anderson, art direction; William Kiernan, set decoration, *The Last Angry Man*

Ted Haworth, art direction; Edward G. Boyle, set decoration, *Some Like It Hot*

Oliver Messel and William Kellner, art direction; Scot Slimon, set decoration, *Suddenly, Last Summer*

Hal Pereira and Walter Tyler, art direction; Sam Comer and Arthur Krams, set decoration, *Career*

Lyle R. Wheeler and George W. Davis, art direction; Walter M. Scott and Stuart A. Reiss, set decoration, *The Diary of Anne Frank*

COLOR

John DeCuir, art direction; Julia Heron, set decoration, *The Big Fisherman*

William A. Horning, Robert Boyle and Merrill Pye, art direction; Henry Grace and Frank McKelvy, set decoration, *North by Northwest*

William A. Horning and Edward Carfagno, art direction; Hugh Hunt, set decoration, *Ben-Hur*

Richard H. Riedel, art direction; Russell A. Gausman and Ruby R. Levitt, set decoration, *Pillow Talk*

Lyle R. Wheeler, art direction, Franz Bachelin and Herman A. Blumenthal, set decoration; Walter M. Scott and Joseph Kish, *Journey to the Center of the Earth*

SOUND

MGM London Studio Sound Dept., *Libel!*

MGM Studio Sound Dept. *Ben-Hur*

Samuel Goldwyn Studio Sound Dept. and Todd-AO Sound Dept., *Porgy and Bess*

Twentieth Century-Fox Studio Sound Dept., *Journey to the Center of the Earth*

Warner Bros. Studio Sound Dept., *The Nun's Story*

MUSIC

SONG

"The Best of Everything," *The Best of Everything*, Alfred Newman, music; Sammy Cahn, lyrics

"The Five Pennies," *The Five Pennies*, Sylvia Fine, music and lyrics

"The Hanging Tree," *The Hanging Tree*, Jerry Livingston, music; Mack David, lyrics

"High Hopes," *A Hole in the Head*, James Van Heusen, music; Sammy Cahn, lyrics

"Strange Are the Ways of Love," *The Young Land*, Dimitri Tiomkin, music; Ned Washington, lyrics

SCORING OF A DRAMATIC OR COMEDY PICTURE

Frank DeVol, *Pillow Talk*

Ernest Gold, *On the Beach*

Miklos Rozsa, *Ben-Hur*

Franz Waxman, *The Nun's Story*

SCORING OF A MUSICAL PICTURE

George Bruns, *Sleeping Beauty*

Lionel Newman, *Say One for Me*

André Previn and Ken Darby, *Porgy and Bess*

Nelson Riddle and Joseph J. Lilley, *Li'l Abner*

Leith Stevens, *The Five Pennies*

FILM EDITING

Frederic Knudtson, *On the Beach*

Louis R. Loeffler, *Anatomy of a Murder*

Walter Thompson, *The Nun's Story*

George Tomasini, *North by Northwest*

Ralph E. Winters and John D. Dunning, *Ben-Hur*

COSTUME DESIGN

BLACK-AND-WHITE

Edith Head, *Career*

Charles LeMaire and Mary Wills, *The Diary of Anne Frank*

Orry-Kelly, *Some Like It Hot*

Helen Rose, *The Gazebo*

Howard Shoup, *The Young Philadelphians*

COLOR

Elizabeth Haffenden, *Ben-Hur*

Edith Head, *The Five Pennies*

Adele Palmer, *The Best of Everything*

Renie, *The Big Fisherman*

Irene Sharaff, *Porgy and Bess*

SPECIAL EFFECTS

L. B. Abbott and James B. Gordon, visual; Carl Faulkner, audible, *Journey to the Center of the Earth*

A. Arnold Gillespie and Robert MacDonald, visual; Milo Lory, audible, *Ben-Hur*

SHORT SUBJECTS

CARTOON

Mexicali Shmoes (*Speedy Gonzales Series*) (John W. Burton, producer; Warner Bros.)

Moonbird (Storyboard, Inc.; Edward Harrison)

Noah's Ark (Walt Disney Productions; Buena Vista)

The Violinist (Pintoff Productions; Kingsley International)

LIVE ACTION

Between the Tides (British Transport Films; Lester A. Schoenfeld Films)

The Golden Fish (Les Requins Associes; Columbia)

Mysteries of the Deep (Walt Disney Productions; Buena Vista)

The Running, Jumping and Standing-Still Film (Lion International Films; Kingsley-Union Films)

Skyscraper (Tishman Realty and Construction Co.; Burstyn Film Enterprises)

DOCUMENTARY

SHORT SUBJECT

Donald in Mathmagic Land (Walt Disney Productions; Buena Vista)

From Generation to Generation (Cullen Associates; Maternity Center Association)

Glass (Netherlands Government; George K. Arthur-Go Pictures, Inc.)

FEATURE

The Race for Space (David L. Wolper, producer; Wolper, Inc.)

Serengeti Shall Not Die (Okapia-Film GmbH Production; Transocean-Film)

FOREIGN LANGUAGE FILM

Black Orpheus, France

The Bridge, Federal Republic of Germany—West

The Great War, Italy

Paw, Denmark

The Village on the River, Netherlands

JEAN HERSHOLT HUMANITARIAN AWARD

Bob Hope

HONORARY AWARDS

To **Lee De Forest** for his pioneering inventions that brought sound to the motion picture

To **Buster Keaton** for his unique talents that brought immortal comedies to the screen

1960

BEST MOTION PICTURE

The Alamo, John Wayne, producer (United Artists)

The Apartment, Billy Wilder, producer (United Artists)

Elmer Gantry, Bernard Smith, producer (United Artists)

Sons and Lovers, Jerry Wald, producer (Twentieth Century-Fox)

The Sundowners, Fred Zinnemann, producer (Warner Bros.)

The Apartment

BEST ACTOR

Trevor Howard, *Sons and Lovers*

Burt Lancaster, *Elmer Gantry*

Jack Lemmon, *The Apartment*

Laurence Olivier, *The Entertainer*

Spencer Tracy, *Inherit the Wind*

BEST ACTRESS

Greer Garson, *Sunrise at Campobello*

Deborah Kerr, *The Sundowners*

Shirley MacLaine, *The Apartment*

Melina Mercouri, *Never on Sunday*

Elizabeth Taylor, *Butterfield 8*

ACTOR IN A SUPPORTING ROLE

Peter Falk, *Murder, Inc.*

Jack Kruschen, *The Apartment*

Sal Mineo, *Exodus*

Peter Ustinov, *Spartacus*

Chill Wills, *The Alamo*

ACTRESS IN A SUPPORTING ROLE

Glynis Johns, *The Sundowners*

Shirley Jones, *Elmer Gantry*

Shirley Knight, *The Dark at the Top of the Stairs*

Janet Leigh, *Psycho*

Mary Ure, *Sons and Lovers*

DIRECTING

Jack Cardiff, *Sons and Lovers*

Jules Dassin, *Never on Sunday*

Alfred Hitchcock, *Psycho*

Billy Wilder, *The Apartment*

Fred Zinnemann, *The Sundowners*

WRITING

SCREENPLAY BASED ON MATERIAL FROM ANOTHER MEDIUM

Richard Brooks, *Elmer Gantry*

James Kennaway, *Tunes of Glory*

Gavin Lambert and T. E. B. Clarke, *Sons and Lovers*

Isobel Lennart, *The Sundowners*

Nedrick Young and Harold Jacob Smith, *Inherit the Wind*

STORY AND SCREENPLAY WRITTEN DIRECTLY FOR THE SCREEN

Jules Dassin, *Never on Sunday*

Marguérite Duras, *Hiroshima, Mon Amour*

Richard Gregson and Michael Craig, story; Bryan Forbes, screenplay, *The Angry Silence*

Norman Panama and Melvin Frank, *The Facts of Life*

Billy Wilder and I. A. L. Diamond, *The Apartment*

CINEMATOGRAPHY

BLACK-AND-WHITE

Freddie Francis, *Sons and Lovers*

Charles B. Lang, Jr., *The Facts of Life*

Joseph LaShelle, *The Apartment*

Ernest Laszlo, *Inherit the Wind*

John L. Russell, *Psycho*

COLOR

William H. Clothier, *The Alamo*

Sam Leavitt, *Exodus*

Joe MacDonald, *Pepe*

Russell Metty, *Spartacus*

Joseph Ruttenberg and Charles Harten, *Butterfield 8*

ART DIRECTION

BLACK-AND-WHITE

Joseph Hurley and Robert Clatworthy, art direction; George Milo, set decoration, *Psycho*

Joseph McMillan Johnson and Kenneth A. Reid, art direction; Ross Dowd, set decoration, *The Facts of Life*

Tom Morahan, art direction; Lionel Couch, set decoration, *Sons and Lovers*

Hal Pereira and Walter Tyler, art direction; Sam Comer and Arthur Krams, set decoration, *Visit to a Small Planet*

Alexander Trauner, art direction; Edward G. Boyle, set decoration, *The Apartment*

COLOR

Edward Carrere, art direction; George James Hopkins, set decoration, *Sunrise at Campobello*

George W. Davis and Addison Hehr, art direction; Henry Grace, Hugh Hunt and Otto Siegel, set decoration, *Cimarron*

Alexander Golitzen and Eric Orbom, art direction; Russell A. Gausman and Julia Heron, set decoration, *Spartacus*

Ted Haworth, art direction; William Kiernan, set decoration, *Pepe*

Hal Pereira and Roland Anderson, art direction; Sam Comer and Arrigo Breschi, set decoration, *It Started in Naples*

SOUND

Columbia Studio Sound Dept., *Pepe*

MGM Studio Sound Dept., *Cimarron*

Samuel Goldwyn Studio Sound Dept. and Todd-AO Sound Dept., *The Alamo*

Samuel Goldwyn Studio Sound Dept., *The Apartment*

Warner Bros. Studio Sound Dept., *Sunrise at Campobello*

MUSIC

SONG

"The Facts of Life," *The Facts of Life*, Johnny Mercer, music and lyrics

"Faraway Part of Town," *Pepe*, André Previn, music; Dory Langdon, lyrics

"The Green Leaves of Summer," *The Alamo*, Dimitri Tiomkin, music; Paul Francis Webster, lyrics

"Never on Sunday," ***Never on Sunday***, **Manos Hadjidakis, music and lyrics**

"The Second Time Around," *High Time*, James Van Heusen, music; Sammy Cahn, lyrics

SCORING OF A DRAMATIC OR COMEDY PICTURE

Elmer Bernstein, *The Magnificent Seven*

Ernest Gold, ***Exodus***

Alex North, *Spartacus*

André Previn, *Elmer Gantry*

Dimitri Tiomkin, *The Alamo*

SCORING OF A MUSICAL PICTURE

Johnny Green, *Pepe*

Lionel Newman and Earle H. Hagen, *Let's Make Love*

André Previn, *Bells Are Ringing*

Nelson Riddle, *Can-Can*

Morris Stoloff and Harry Sukman, ***Song Without End***

FILM EDITING

Stuart Gilmore, *The Alamo*

Frederic Knudtson, *Inherit the Wind*

Robert Lawrence, *Spartacus*

Viola Lawrence and Al Clark, *Pepe*

Daniel Mandell, ***The Apartment***

COSTUME DESIGN

BLACK-AND-WHITE

Edith Head and Edward Stevenson, ***The Facts of Life***

Howard Shoup, *The Rise and Fall of Legs Diamond*

Bill Thomas, *Seven Thieves*

Deni Vachlioti, *Never on Sunday*

Marik Vos, *The Virgin Spring*

COLOR

Marjorie Best, *Sunrise at Campobello*

Edith Head, *Pepe*

Irene, *Midnight Lace*

Irene Sharaff, *Can-Can*

Bill Thomas and Valles, ***Spartacus***

SPECIAL EFFECTS

A.J. Lohman, visual, *The Last Voyage*

Gene Warren and Tim Baar, visual, ***The Time Machine***

SHORT SUBJECTS

CARTOON

Goliath II (Walt Disney Productions; Buena Vista)

High Note (*Looney Tune Series*) (Warner Bros.)

Mouse and Garden (*Sylvester the Cat Series*) (Warner Bros.)

Munro **(***Nooletoon Series***) (Rembrandt Films; Film Representations)**

A Place in the Sun (Frantisek Vystrecil, producer; George K. Arthur-Go Pictures)

LIVE ACTION

The Creation of Woman (Trident Films, Inc.; Sterling World Distributors)

Day of the Painter **(Little Movies; Kingsley-Union Films)**

Islands of the Sea (*True Life Adventure Series*) (Walt Disney Productions; Buena Vista)

A Sport Is Born (*Sports Illustrated Series*) (Leslie Winik, producer; Paramount)

DOCUMENTARY

SHORT SUBJECT

Beyond Silence (U.S. Information Agency)

A City Called Copenhagen (Statens Filmcentral; Danish Government Film Office)

George Grosz' Interregnum (Charles Carey and Altina Carey, producers; Educational Communications Corp.)

Giuseppina **(James Hill Production; Lester A. Schoenfeld Films)**

Universe (National Film Board of Canada; Lester A. Schoenfeld Films)

FEATURE

The Horse With the Flying Tail **(Walt Disney Productions; Buena Vista)**

Rebel in Paradise (Robert D. Fraser, producer; Tiare Co.)

FOREIGN LANGUAGE FILM

Kapo, Italy

La Verité, France

Macario, Mexico

The Ninth Circle, Yugoslavia

The Virgin Spring, **Sweden**

JEAN HERSHOLT HUMANITARIAN AWARD

Sol Lesser

HONORARY AWARDS

To **Gary Cooper** for his many memorable screen performances and the international recognition he, as an individual, has gained for the motion picture industry

To **Stan Laurel** for his creative pioneering in the field of cinema comedy

To **Hayley Mills** for *Pollyana*, the most outstanding juvenile performance during 1960

1961

BEST MOTION PICTURE

Fanny, Joshua Logan, producer (Warner Bros.)

The Guns of Navarone, Carl Foreman, producer (Columbia)

The Hustler, Robert Rossen, producer (Twentieth Century-Fox)

Judgment at Nuremberg, Stanley Kramer, producer (United Artists)

West Side Story, **Robert Wise, producer (United Artists)**

Rita Moreno, *West Side Story*

BEST ACTOR

Charles Boyer, *Fanny*

Paul Newman, *The Hustler*

Maximilian Schell, *Judgment at Nuremberg*

Spencer Tracy, *Judgment at Nuremberg*

Stuart Whitman, *The Mark*

BEST ACTRESS

Audrey Hepburn, *Breakfast at Tiffany's*

Piper Laurie, *The Hustler*

Sophia Loren, *Two Women*

Geraldine Page, *Summer and Smoke*

Natalie Wood, *Splendor in the Grass*

ACTOR IN A SUPPORTING ROLE

George Chakiris, *West Side Story*

Montgomery Clift, *Judgment at Nuremberg*

Peter Falk, *Pocketful of Miracles*

Jackie Gleason, *The Hustler*

George C. Scott, *The Hustler*

ACTRESS IN A SUPPORTING ROLE

Fay Bainter, *The Children's Hour*

Judy Garland, *Judgment at Nuremberg*

Lotte Lenya, *The Roman Spring of Mrs. Stone*

Una Merkel, *Summer and Smoke*

Rita Moreno, *West Side Story*

DIRECTING

Federico Fellini, *La Dolce Vita*

Stanley Kramer, *Judgment at Nuremberg*

Robert Rossen, *The Hustler*

J. Lee Thompson, *The Guns of Navarone*

Robert Wise and Jerome Robbins, *West Side Story*

WRITING

SCREENPLAY BASED ON MATERIAL FROM ANOTHER MEDIUM

George Axelrod, *Breakfast at Tiffany's*

Sidney Carroll and Robert Rossen, *The Hustler*

Carl Foreman, *The Guns of Navarone*

Ernest Lehman, *West Side Story*

Abby Mann, *Judgment at Nuremberg*

STORY AND SCREENPLAY WRITTEN DIRECTLY FOR THE SCREEN

Sergio Amidei, Diego Fabbri and Indro Montanelli, *General Della Rovere*

Federico Fellini, Tullio Pinelli, Ennio Flaiano and Brunello Rondi, *La Dolce Vita*

William Inge, *Splendor in the Grass*

Stanley Shapiro and Paul Henning, *Lover Come Back*

Valentin Yoshov and Grigori Chukhrai, *Ballad of a Soldier*

CINEMATOGRAPHY

BLACK-AND-WHITE

Edward Colman, *The Absent-Minded Professor*

Daniel L. Fapp, *One, Two, Three*

Ernest Laszlo, *Judgment at Nuremberg*

Franz F. Planer, *The Children's Hour*

Eugen Shuftan, *The Hustler*

COLOR

Jack Cardiff, *Fanny*

Daniel L. Fapp, *West Side Story*

Charles Lang, Jr., *One-Eyed Jacks*

Russell Metty, *Flower Drum Song*

Harry Stradling, Sr., *A Majority of One*

ART DIRECTION

BLACK-AND-WHITE

Fernando Carrere, art direction; Edward G. Boyle, set decoration, *The Children's Hour*

Carroll Clark, art direction; Emile Kuri and Hal Gausman, set decoration, *The Absent-Minded Professor*

Piero Gherardi, art direction and set decoration, *La Dolce Vita*

Harry Horner, art direction; Gene Callahan, set decoration, *The Hustler*

Rudolph Sternad, art direction; George Milo, set decoration, *Judgment at Nuremberg*

COLOR

Veniero Colasanti and John Moore, art direction and set decoration, *El Cid*

Alexander Golitzen and Joseph Wright, art direction; Howard Bristol, set decoration, *Flower Drum Song*

Boris Leven, art direction; Victor Gangelin, set decoration, *West Side Story*

Hal Pereira and Roland Anderson, art direction; Sam Comer and Ray Moyer, set decoration, *Breakfast at Tiffany's*

Hal Pereira and Walter Tyler, art direction; Sam Comer and Arthur Krams, set decoration, *Summer and Smoke*

SOUND

Revue Studio Sound Dept., Waldon O. Watson, sound director, *Flower Drum Song*

Samuel Goldwyn Studio Sound Dept., Gordon E. Sawyer, sound director, *The Children's Hour*

Shepperton Studio Sound Dept., John Cox, sound director, *The Guns of Navarone*

Todd-AO Sound Dept., Fred Hynes, sound director and Samuel Goldwyn Studio Sound Dept., Gordon E. Sawyer, sound director, *West Side Story*

Walt Disney Studio Sound Dept., Robert O. Cook, sound director, *The Parent Trap*

REFERENCE

MUSIC

SONG

"Bachelor in Paradise," *Bachelor in Paradise*, Henry Mancini, music; Mack David, lyrics

"Love Theme From *El Cid*" (The Falcon and the Dove), *El Cid*, Miklos Rozsa, music; Paul Francis Webster, lyrics

"Moon River," *Breakfast at Tiffany's*, Henry Mancini, music; Johnny Mercer, lyrics

"Pocketful of Miracles," *Pocketful of Miracles*, James Van Heusen, music; Sammy Cahn, lyrics

"Town Without Pity," *Town Without Pity*, Dimitri Tiomkin, music; Ned Washington, lyrics

SCORING OF A DRAMATIC OR COMEDY PICTURE

Elmer Bernstein, *Summer and Smoke*

Henry Mancini, *Breakfast at Tiffany's*

Miklos Rozsa, *El Cid*

Morris Stoloff and Harry Sukman, *Fanny*

Dimitri Tiomkin, *The Guns of Navarone*

SCORING OF A MUSICAL PICTURE

George Bruns, *Babes in Toyland*

Saul Chaplin, Johnny Green, Sid Ramin and Irwin Kostal, *West Side Story*

Duke Ellington, *Paris Blues*

Alfred Newman and Ken Darby, *Flower Drum Song*

Dimitri Shostakovich, *Khovanshchina*

FILM EDITING

Philip W. Anderson, *The Parent Trap*

Frederic Knudtson, *Judgment at Nuremberg*

Alan Osbiston, *The Guns of Navarone*

William H. Reynolds, *Fanny*

Thomas Stanford, *West Side Story*

COSTUME DESIGN

BLACK-AND-WHITE
Piero Gherardi, *La Dolce Vita*

Dorothy Jeakins, *The Children's Hour*

Jean Louis, *Judgment at Nuremberg*

Yoshiro Muraki, *Yojimbo*

Howard Shoup, *Claudelle Inglish*

COLOR
Edith Head and Walter Plunkett, *Pocketful of Miracles*

Jean Louis, *Back Street*

Irene Sharaff, *Flower Drum Song*

Irene Sharaff, *West Side Story*

Bill Thomas, *Babes in Toyland*

SPECIAL EFFECTS

Robert A. Mattey and Eustace Lycett, visual, *The Absent-Minded Professor*

Bill Warrington, visual; Vivian C. Greenham, audible, *The Guns of Navarone*

SHORT SUBJECTS

CARTOON
Aquamania (Walt Disney Productions; Buena Vista)

Beep Prepared (Roadrunner and Coyote Series) (Chuck Jones, producer; Warner Bros.)

Ersatz (The Substitute) (Zagreb Film; Herts-Lion International Corp.)

Nelly's Folly (Nelly the Giraffe Series) (Chuck Jones, producer; Warner Bros.)

Pied Piper of Guadalupe (Speedy Gonzalez and Sylvester Series) (Friz Freleng, producer; Warner Bros.)

LIVE ACTION
Ballon Vole (Play Ball!) (Ciné-Documents; Kingsley International)

The Face of Jesus (Jenga Productions; Harry Stern, Inc.)

Rooftops of New York (Musical Travelbook Series) (McCarty-Rush Production in association with Robert Gaffney; Columbia)

Seawards the Great Ships (Templar Film Studios; Lester A. Schoenfeld Films)

Very Nice, Very Nice (National Film Board of Canada; Kingsley International)

DOCUMENTARY

SHORT SUBJECT
Breaking the Language Barrier (Travel Adventure Series) (U.S. Air Force)

Cradle of Genius (Plough Productions; Irving M. Lesser Film Presentation)

Kahl (Dido Film GmbH; AEG-Filmdienst)

L'Uomo in Grigio (The Man in Gray) (Benedetto Benedetti, producer; Benedetto Benedetti Production)

Project Hope (MacManus, John and Adams, Inc./Klaeger Film Production; Ex-Cell-O Corp.)

FEATURE
La Grande Olimpiade (Olympic Games 1960) (Dell Istituto Nationale Luce, Comitato Organizzatore Del Giochi Della XVII Olimpiade; Cineriz)

Le Ciel et la Boue (Sky Above and Mud Beneath) (Ardennes Films and Michael Arthur Film Productions; Rank Films)

FOREIGN LANGUAGE FILM

Harry and the Butler, Denmark

Immortal Love, Japan

The Important Man, Mexico

Placido, Spain

Through a Glass Darkly, Sweden

IRVING G. THALBERG MEMORIAL AWARD
Stanley Kramer

JEAN HERSHOLT HUMANITARIAN AWARD
George Seaton

HONORARY AWARDS

To **William L. Hendricks** for his outstanding patriotic service in the conception, writing and production of the Marine Corps film, *A Force in Readiness*, which has brought honor to the Academy and the motion picture industry

To **Fred L. Metzler** for his dedication and outstanding service to the Academy of Motion Picture Arts and Sciences

To **Jerome Robbins** for his brilliant achievements in the art of choreography on film

1962

BEST PICTURE

Lawrence of Arabia, Sam Spiegel, producer (Columbia)

The Longest Day, Darryl F. Zanuck, producer (Twentieth Century-Fox)

Meredith Willson's the Music Man, Morton Da Costa, producer (Warner Bros.)

Mutiny on the Bounty, Aaron Rosenberg, producer (MGM)

To Kill a Mockingbird, Alan J. Pakula, producer (Universal-International)

BEST ACTOR

Burt Lancaster, Birdman of Alcatraz

Jack Lemmon, Days of Wine and Roses

Marcello Mastroianni, Divorce — Italian Style

Peter O'Toole, Lawrence of Arabia

Gregory Peck, To Kill a Mockingbird

BEST ACTRESS

Anne Bancroft, The Miracle Worker

Bette Davis, What Ever Happened to Baby Jane?

Katharine Hepburn, Long Day's Journey Into Night

Geraldine Page, Sweet Bird of Youth

Lee Remick, Days of Wine and Roses

ACTOR IN A SUPPORTING ROLE

Ed Begley, Sweet Bird of Youth

Victor Buono, What Ever Happened to Baby Jane?

Telly Savalas, Birdman of Alcatraz

Omar Sharif, Lawrence of Arabia

Terence Stamp, Billy Budd

ACTRESS IN A SUPPORTING ROLE

Mary Badham, To Kill a Mockingbird

Patty Duke, The Miracle Worker

Shirley Knight, Sweet Bird of Youth

Angela Lansbury, The Manchurian Candidate

Thelma Ritter, Birdman of Alcatraz

DIRECTING

Pietro Germi, Divorce — Italian Style

David Lean, Lawrence of Arabia

Robert Mulligan, To Kill a Mockingbird

Arthur Penn, The Miracle Worker

Frank Perry, David and Lisa

WRITING

SCREENPLAY BASED ON MATERIAL FROM ANOTHER MEDIUM
Robert Bolt, Lawrence of Arabia

Horton Foote, To Kill a Mockingbird

William Gibson, The Miracle Worker

Vladimir Nabokov, Lolita

Eleanor Perry, David and Lisa

STORY AND SCREENPLAY WRITTEN DIRECTLY FOR THE SCREEN
Ingmar Bergman, Through a Glass Darkly

Ennio de Concini, Alfredo Giannetti and Pietro Germi, Divorce — Italian Style

Charles Kaufman, story; Charles Kaufman and Wolfgang Reinhardt, screenplay, Freud

Alain Robbe-Grillet, Last Year at Marienbad

Stanley Shapiro and Nate Monaster, That Touch of Mink

CINEMATOGRAPHY

BLACK-AND-WHITE
Jean Bourgoin and Walter Wottitz, The Longest Day

Burnett Guffey, Birdman of Alcatraz

Ernest Haller, What Ever Happened to Baby Jane?

Russell Harlan, To Kill a Mockingbird

Ted McCord, Two for the Seesaw

COLOR
Russell Harlan, Hatari!

Harry Stradling, Sr., Gypsy

Robert L. Surtees, Mutiny on the Bounty

Paul C. Vogel, The Wonderful World of the Brothers Grimm

Fred A. Young, Lawrence of Arabia

ART DIRECTION

BLACK-AND-WHITE
George W. Davis and Edward Carfagno, art direction; Henry Grace and Dick Pefferle, set decoration, Period of Adjustment

Alexander Golitzen and Henry Bumstead, art direction; Oliver Emert, set decoration, To Kill a Mockingbird

Ted Haworth, Leon Barsacq and Vincent Korda, art direction; Gabriel Bechir, set decoration, The Longest Day

Hal Pereira and Roland Anderson, art direction; Sam Comer and Frank R. McKelvy, set decoration, The Pigeon That Took Rome

Joseph Wright, art direction; George James Hopkins, set decoration, Days of Wine and Roses

Gregory Peck, To Kill a Mockingbird

COLOR

John Box and John Stoll, art direction; Dario Simoni, set decoration, *Lawrence of Arabia*

George W. Davis and Edward Carfagno, art direction; Henry Grace and Dick Pefferle, set decoration, *The Wonderful World of the Brothers Grimm*

Alexander Golitzen and Robert Clatworthy, art direction; George Milo, set decoration, *That Touch of Mink*

Paul Groesse, art direction; George James Hopkins, set decoration, *Meredith Willson's The Music Man*

Hugh Hunt, set decoration, *Mutiny on the Bounty*

SOUND

Shepperton Studio Sound Dept., John Cox, sound director, *Lawrence of Arabia*

Universal City Studio Sound Dept., Waldon O. Watson, sound director, *That Touch of Mink*

Walt Disney Studio Sound Dept., Robert O. Cook, sound director, *Bon Voyage!*

Warner Bros. Studio Sound Dept. and Glen Glenn Sound Dept., Joseph Kelly, sound director, *What Ever Happened to Baby Jane?*

Warner Bros. Studio Sound Dept., George R. Groves, sound director, *Meredith Willson's The Music Man*

MUSIC

SONG

"Days of Wine and Roses," *Days of Wine and Roses*, Henry Mancini, music; Johnny Mercer, lyrics

"Love Song From *Mutiny on the Bounty*" (Follow Me), *Mutiny on the Bounty*, Bronislau Kaper, music; Paul Francis Webster, lyrics

"Song From *Two for the Seesaw*" (Second Chance), *Two for the Seesaw*, André Previn, music; Dory Langdon, lyrics

"Tender Is the Night," *Tender Is the Night*, Sammy Fain, music; Paul Francis Webster, lyrics

"Walk on the Wild Side," *Walk on the Wild Side*, Elmer Bernstein, music; Mack David, lyrics

MUSICAL SCORE, SUBSTANTIALLY ORIGINAL

Elmer Bernstein, *To Kill a Mockingbird*

Jerry Goldsmith, *Freud*

Maurice Jarre, *Lawrence of Arabia*

Bronislau Kaper, *Mutiny on the Bounty*

Franz Waxman, *Taras Bulba*

SCORING OF MUSIC, ADAPTATION OR TREATMENT

Leigh Harline, *The Wonderful World of the Brothers Grimm*

Ray Heindorf, *Meredith Willson's The Music Man*

Michel Magne, *Gigot*

Frank Perkins, *Gypsy*

George Stoll, *Billy Rose's Jumbo*

FILM EDITING

Samuel E. Beetley, *The Longest Day*

Anne Coates, *Lawrence of Arabia*

John McSweeney, Jr., *Mutiny on the Bounty*

Ferrris Webster, *The Manchurian Candidate*

William Ziegler, *Meredith Willson's The Music Man*

COSTUME DESIGN

BLACK-AND-WHITE

Don Feld, *Days of Wine and Roses*

Edith Head, *The Man Who Shot Liberty Valance*

Norma Koch, *What Ever Happened to Baby Jane?*

Ruth Morley, *The Miracle Worker*

Denny Vachlioti, *Phaedra*

COLOR

Edith Head, *My Geisha*

Dorothy Jeakins, *Meredith Willson's The Music Man*

Orry-Kelly, *Gypsy*

Bill Thomas, *Bon Voyage!*

Mary Wills, *The Wonderful World of the Brothers Grimm*

SPECIAL EFFECTS

A. Arnold Gillespie, visual; Milo Lory, audible, *Mutiny on the Bounty*

Robert MacDonald, visual; Jacques Maumont, audible, *The Longest Day*

SHORT SUBJECTS

CARTOON

***The Hole* (Storyboard, Inc.; Brandon Films)**

Icarus Montgolfier Wright (Format Films; United Artists)

Now Hear This (*Looney Tune Series*) (Warner Bros. Cartoons, Inc.; Warner Bros.)

Self-Defense — For Cowards (*Self-Help Series*) (Rembrandt Films; Film Representations)

Symposium on Popular Songs (Walt Disney Productions; Buena Vista)

LIVE ACTION

Big City Blues (Martina and Charles Huguenot van der Linden, producers; Mayfair Pictures)

The Cadillac (Robert Clouse Production; United Producers Releasing)

The Cliff Dwellers (Formerly titled *One Plus One*) (Group II Film Production; Lester A. Schoenfeld Films)

***Heureux Anniversaire* (*Happy Anniversary*) (C.A.P.A.C. Productions; Atlantic Pictures Corp.)**

Pan (Herman van der Horst Production; Mayfair Pictures)

DOCUMENTARY

SHORT SUBJECT

***Dylan Thomas* (TWW Ltd.; Janus Films)**

The John Glenn Story (U.S. Navy; Warner Bros.)

The Road to the Wall (CBS Films, Inc.; U.S. Department of Defense)

FEATURE

Alvorada (*Brazil's Changing Face*) (Hugo Niebeling, producer; MW Filmproduktion)

***Black Fox* (Image Productions, Inc.; Heritage Films, Inc.)**

FOREIGN LANGUAGE FILM

Electra, Greece

The Four Days of Naples, Italy

Keeper of Promises (*The Given Word*) Brazil

***Sundays and Cybèle*, France**

Tlayucan, Mexico

JEAN HERSHOLT HUMANITARIAN AWARD

Steve Broidy

1963

BEST PICTURE

America, America, Elia Kazan, producer (Warner Bros.)

Cleopatra, Walter Wanger, producer (Twentieth Century-Fox)

How the West Was Won, Bernard Smith, producer (MGM)

Lilies of the Field, Ralph Nelson, producer (United Artists)

Tom Jones, Tony Richardson, producer (United Artists-Lopert Pictures)

BEST ACTOR

Albert Finney, *Tom Jones*

Richard Harris, *This Sporting Life*

Rex Harrison, *Cleopatra*

Paul Newman, *Hud*

Sidney Poitier, Lilies of the Field

Sidney Poitier, *Lilies of the Field*

BEST ACTRESS

Leslie Caron, *The L-Shaped Room*

Shirley MacLaine, *Irma La Douce*

Patricia Neal, Hud

Rachel Roberts, *This Sporting Life*

Natalie Wood, *Love With the Proper Stranger*

ACTOR IN A SUPPORTING ROLE

Nick Adams, *Twilight of Honor*

Bobby Darin, *Captain Newman, M.D.*

Melvyn Douglas, Hud

Hugh Griffith, *Tom Jones*

John Huston, *The Cardinal*

ACTRESS IN A SUPPORTING ROLE

Diane Cilento, *Tom Jones*

Dame Edith Evans, *Tom Jones*

Joyce Redman, *Tom Jones*

Margaret Rutherford, The V.I.P.s

Lilia Skala, *Lilies of the Field*

DIRECTING

Federico Fellini, *Federico Fellini's 8-1/2*

Elia Kazan, *America, America*

Otto Preminger, *The Cardinal*

Tony Richardson, Tom Jones

Martin Ritt, *Hud*

WRITING

SCREENPLAY BASED ON MATERIAL FROM ANOTHER MEDIUM

Serge Bourguignon and Antoine Tudal, *Sundays and Cybèle*

Richard Breen, Phoebe Ephron and Henry Ephron, *Captain Newman, M.D.*

John Osborne, Tom Jones

James Poe, *Lilies of the Field*

Irving Ravetch and Harriet Frank, Jr., *Hud*

STORY AND SCREENPLAY WRITTEN DIRECTLY FOR THE SCREEN

Carlo Bernari, screenplay, *The Four Days of Naples*

Pasquale Festa Campanile, Massimo Franciosa, Vasco Pratolini and Nanni Loy, story; Pasquale Festa Campanile, Massimo Franciosa, Nanni Loy and James R. Webb, How the West Was Won

Federico Fellini, Ennio Flaiano, Tullio Pinelli and Brunello Rondi, *Federico Fellini's 8-1/2*

Elia Kazan, *America, America*

Arnold Schulman, *Love With the Proper Stranger*

CINEMATOGRAPHY

BLACK-AND-WHITE

Lucien Ballard, *The Caretakers*

George Folsey, *The Balcony*

Ernest Haller, *Lilies of the Field*

James Wong Howe, Hud

Milton Krasner, *Love With the Proper Stranger*

COLOR

William H. Daniels, Milton Krasner, Charles Lang, Jr. and Joseph LaShelle, *How the West Was Won*

Joseph LaShelle, *Irma La Douce*

Ernest Laszlo, *It's a Mad, Mad, Mad, Mad World*

Leon Shamroy, *The Cardinal*

Leon Shamroy, Cleopatra

ART DIRECTION

BLACK-AND-WHITE

Gene Callahan, art direction, America, America

George W. Davis and Paul Groesse, art direction; Henry Grace and Hugh Hunt, set decoration, *Twilight of Honor*

Piero Gherardi, art direction, *Federico Fellini's 8-1/2*

Hal Pereira and Tambi Larsen, art direction; Sam Comer and Robert Benton, set decoration, *Hud*

Hal Pereira and Roland Anderson, art direction; Sam Comer and Grace Gregory, set decoration, *Love With the Proper Stranger*

COLOR

Ralph Brinton, Ted Marshall and Jocelyn Herbert, art direction; Josie MacAvin, set decoration, *Tom Jones*

George W. Davis, William Ferrari and Addison Hehr, art direction; Henry Grace, Don Greenwood, Jr. and Jack Mills, set decoration, *How the West Was Won*

John DeCuir, Jack Martin Smith, Hilyard Brown, Herman Blumenthal, Elven Webb, Maurice Pelling and Boris Juraga, art direction; Walter M. Scott, Paul S. Fox and Ray Moyer, set decoration, *Cleopatra*

Hal Pereira and Roland Anderson, art direction; Sam Comer and James Payne, set decoration, *Come Blow Your Horn*

Lyle Wheeler, art direction; Gene Callahan, set decoration, *The Cardinal*

SOUND

Columbia Studio Sound Dept., *Bye Bye Birdie*

MGM Studio Sound Dept., *How the West Was Won*

Samuel Goldwyn Studio Sound Dept., *It's a Mad, Mad, Mad, Mad World*

Twentieth Century-Fox Studio Sound Dept. and Todd-AO Sound Dept., *Cleopatra*

Universal City Studio Sound Dept., *Captain Newman, M.D.*

MUSIC
SONG

"Call Me Irresponsible," *Papa's Delicate Condition*, James Van Heusen, music; Sammy Cahn, lyrics

"Charade," *Charade*, Henry Mancini, music; Johnny Mercer, lyrics

"It's a Mad, Mad, Mad, Mad World," *It's a Mad, Mad, Mad, Mad World*, Ernest Gold, music; Mack David, lyrics

"More," *Mondo Cane*, Riz Ortolani and Nino Oliviero, music; Norman Newell, lyrics

"So Little Time," *55 Days at Peking*, Dimitri Tiomkin, music; Paul Francis Webster, lyrics

MUSICAL SCORE, SUBSTANTIALLY ORIGINAL

John Addison, *Tom Jones*

Ernest Gold, *It's a Mad, Mad, Mad, Mad World*

Alfred Newman and Ken Darby, *How the West Was Won*

Alex North, *Cleopatra*

Dimitri Tiomkin, *55 Days at Peking*

SCORING OF MUSIC, ADAPTATION OR TREATMENT

George Bruns, *The Sword in the Stone*

John Green, *Bye Bye Birdie*

Maurice Jarre, *Sundays and Cybèle*

André Previn, *Irma La Douce*

Leith Stevens, *A New Kind of Love*

FILM EDITING

Frederic Knudtson, Robert C. Jones and Gene Fowler, Jr., *It's a Mad, Mad, Mad, Mad World*

Harold F. Kress, *How the West Was Won*

Louis R. Loeffler, *The Cardinal*

Dorothy Spencer, *Cleopatra*

Ferris Webster, *The Great Escape*

COSTUME DESIGN
BLACK-AND-WHITE

Piero Gherardi, *Federico Fellini's 8-1/2*

Edith Head, *Love With the Proper Stranger*

Edith Head, *Wives and Lovers*

Bill Thomas, *Toys in the Attic*

Travilla, *The Stripper*

COLOR

Donald Brooks, *The Cardinal*

Edith Head, *A New Kind of Love*

Walter Plunkett, *How the West Was Won*

Irene Sharaff, Vittorio Nino Novarese and Renie, *Cleopatra*

Piero Tosi, *The Leopard*

SPECIAL EFFECTS

Ub Iwerks, *The Birds*

Emil Kosa, Jr., *Cleopatra*

SOUND EFFECTS

(Not necessarily given each year)

Robert L. Bratton, *A Gathering of Eagles*

Walter G. Elliott, *It's a Mad, Mad, Mad, Mad World*

SHORT SUBJECTS
CARTOON

Automania 2000 (Halas and Batchelor Production; Pathé Contemporary Films)

The Critic (Pintoff-Crossbow Productions; Columbia)

The Game (Igra) (Zagreb Film; Rembrandt Films-Film Representations)

My Financial Career (National Film Board of Canada; Walter Reade-Sterling-Continental Distributing)

Pianissimo (Carmen D'Avino Production; Cinema 16)

LIVE ACTION

The Concert (James A. King Corp.; George K. Arthur-Go Pictures)

Home-Made Car, BP (North American) Ltd.; Lester A. Schoenfeld Films)

An Occurrence at Owl Creek Bridge (Films du Centaure-Filmartic; Cappagariff-Janus Films)

Six-Sided Triangle (Milesian Film Production, Ltd.; Lion International Films)

That's Me (Stuart Productions; Pathé Contemporary Films)

DOCUMENTARY
SHORT SUBJECT

Chagall (Auerbach Film Enterprises, Ltd.-Flag Films; Union Films)

The Five Cities of June (George Stevens, Jr., producer; U.S. Information Agency)

The Spirit of America (Algernon G. Walker, producer; Spotlight News, Inc.)

Thirty Million Letters (Edgar Anstey, producer; British Transport Films)

To Live Again (Wilding, Inc.; St. Barnabas Hospital, Bronx, N.Y.)

FEATURE

Robert Frost: A Lover's Quarrel With the World (WGBH Educational Foundation; Holt, Reinhart and Winston, Inc.)

Le Maillon et la Chaine (The Link and the Chain) (Paul de Roubaix, producer; Films Du Centaure-Filmartic)

Terminus (Edgar Anstey, producer; British Transport Films)

The Yanks Are Coming (Marshall Flaum, producer; David L. Wolper Productions)

FOREIGN LANGUAGE FILM

Federico Fellini's 8-1/2, Italy
Knife in the Water, Poland
Los Tarantos, Spain
The Red Lanterns, Greece
Twin Sisters of Kyoto, Japan

IRVING G. THALBERG MEMORIAL AWARD
Sam Spiegel

1964

BEST PICTURE

Becket, Hal B. Wallis, producer (Paramount)
Dr. Strangelove or: How I Learned to Stop Worrying and Love the Bomb, Stanley Kubrick, producer (Columbia)
Mary Poppins, Walt Disney and Bill Walsh, producers (Buena Vista)
My Fair Lady, Jack L. Warner, producer (Warner Bros.)
Zorba the Greek, Michael Cacoyannis, producer (International Classics)

BEST ACTOR

Richard Burton, *Becket*
Rex Harrison, *My Fair Lady*
Peter O'Toole, *Becket*
Anthony Quinn, *Zorba the Greek*
Peter Sellers, *Dr. Strangelove or: How I Learned to Stop Worrying and Love the Bomb*

My Fair Lady

BEST ACTRESS

Julie Andrews, *Mary Poppins*
Anne Bancroft, *The Pumpkin Eater*
Sophia Loren, *Marriage Italian Style*
Debbie Reynolds, *The Unsinkable Molly Brown*
Kim Stanley, *Seance on a Wet Afternoon*

ACTOR IN A SUPPORTING ROLE

John Gielgud, *Becket*
Stanley Holloway, *My Fair Lady*
Edmond O'Brien, *Seven Days in May*
Lee Tracy, *The Best Man*
Peter Ustinov, *Topkapi*

ACTRESS IN A SUPPORTING ROLE

Gladys Cooper, *My Fair Lady*
Dame Edith Evans, *The Chalk Garden*
Grayson Hall, *The Night of the Iguana*
Lila Kedrova, *Zorba the Greek*
Agnes Moorehead, *Hush . . . Hush, Sweet Charlotte*

DIRECTING

Michael Cacoyannis, *Zorba the Greek*
George Cukor, *My Fair Lady*
Peter Glenville, *Becket*
Stanley Kubrick, *Dr. Strangelove or: How I Learned to Stop Worrying and Love the Bomb*
Robert Stevenson, *Mary Poppins*

WRITING

SCREENPLAY BASED ON MATERIAL FROM ANOTHER MEDIUM
Edward Anhalt, *Becket*
Michael Cacoyannis, *Zorba the Greek*
Stanley Kubrick, Peter George and Terry Southern, *Dr. Strangelove or: How I Learned to Stop Worrying and Love the Bomb*
Alan Jay Lerner, *My Fair Lady*
Bill Walsh and Don DaGradi, *Mary Poppins*

STORY AND SCREENPLAY WRITTEN DIRECTLY FOR THE SCREEN
Age, Scarpelli and Mario Monicelli, *The Organizer*
S. H. Barnett, story; Peter Stone and Frank Tarloff, screenplay, *Father Goose*
Orville H. Hampton, story; Orville H. Hampton and Raphael Hayes, screenplay, *One Potato, Two Potato*
Alun Owen, *A Hard Day's Night*
Jean-Paul Rappeneau, Ariane Mnouchkine, Daniel Boulanger and Philippe De Broca, *That Man From Rio*

CINEMATOGRAPHY

BLACK-AND-WHITE
Joseph Biroc, *Hush . . . Hush, Sweet Charlotte*
Gabriel Figueroa, *The Night of the Iguana*
Milton Krasner, *Fate Is the Hunter*
Walter Lassally, *Zorba the Greek*
Philip H. Lathrop, *The Americanization of Emily*

COLOR
William H. Clothier, *Cheyenne Autumn*
Edward Colman, *Mary Poppins*
Daniel L. Fapp, *The Unsinkable Molly Brown*
Harry Stradling, *My Fair Lady*
Geoffrey Unsworth, *Becket*

ART DIRECTION

BLACK-AND-WHITE

George W. Davis, Hans Peters and Elliot Scott, art direction; Henry Grace and Robert R. Benton, set decoration, *The Americanization of Emily*

Vassilis Fotopoulos, *Zorba the Greek*

William Glasgow, art direction; Raphael Bretton, set decoration, *Hush . . . Hush, Sweet Charlotte*

Stephen Grimes, *The Night of the Iguana*

Cary Odell, art direction; Edward G. Boyle, set decoration, *Seven Days in May*

COLOR

Gene Allen and Cecil Beaton, art direction; George James Hopkins, set decoration, *My Fair Lady*

John Bryan and Maurice Carter, art direction; Patrick McLoughlin and Robert Cartwright, set decoration, *Becket*

Carroll Clark and William H. Tuntke, art direction; Emile Kuri and Hal Gausman, set decoration, *Mary Poppins*

George W. Davis and Preston Ames, art direction; Henry Grace and Hugh Hunt, set decoration, *The Unsinkable Molly Brown*

Jack Martin Smith and Ted Haworth, art direction; Walter M. Scott and Stuart A. Reiss, set decoration, *What a Way to Go!*

SOUND

MGM Studio Sound Dept., *The Unsinkable Molly Brown*

Shepperton Studio Sound Dept., *Becket*

Universal City Studio Sound Dept., *Father Goose*

Walt Disney Studio Sound Dept., *Mary Poppins*

Warner Bros. Studio Sound Dept., *My Fair Lady*

MUSIC

SONG

"Chim Chim Cher-ee," *Mary Poppins*, Richard M. Sherman and Robert B. Sherman, music and lyrics

"Dear Heart," *Dear Heart*, Henry Mancini, music; Jay Livingston and Ray Evans, lyrics

"Hush . . . Hush, Sweet Charlotte," *Hush . . . Hush, Sweet Charlotte*, Frank DeVol, music; Mack David, lyrics

"My Kind of Town," *Robin and the 7 Hoods*, James Van Heusen, music; Sammy Cahn, lyrics

"Where Love Has Gone," *Where Love Has Gone*, James Van Heusen, music; Sammy Cahn, lyrics

MUSICAL SCORE, SUBSTANTIALLY ORIGINAL

Frank DeVol, *Hush . . . Hush, Sweet Charlotte*

Henry Mancini, *The Pink Panther*

Laurence Rosenthal, *Becket*

Richard M. Sherman and Robert B. Sherman, *Mary Poppins*

Dimitri Tiomkin, *The Fall of the Roman Empire*

SCORING OF MUSIC, ADAPTATION OR TREATMENT

Robert Armbruster, Leo Arnaud, Jack Elliott, Jack Hayes, Calvin Jackson and Irwin Kostal, *Mary Poppins*

George Martin, *A Hard Day's Night*

André Previn, *My Fair Lady*

Nelson Riddle, *Robin and the 7 Hoods*

Leo Shuken, *The Unsinkable Molly Brown*

FILM EDITING

Anne Coates, *Becket*

Ted J. Kent, *Father Goose*

Michael Luciano, *Hush . . . Hush, Sweet Charlotte*

Cotton Warburton, *Mary Poppins*

William Ziegler, *My Fair Lady*

COSTUME DESIGN

BLACK-AND-WHITE

Edith Head, *A House Is Not a Home*

Rene Hubert, *The Visit*

Dorothy Jeakins, *The Night of the Iguana*

Norma Koch, *Hush . . . Hush, Sweet Charlotte*

Howard Shoup, *Kisses for My President*

COLOR

Cecil Beaton, *My Fair Lady*

Margaret Furse, *Becket*

Morton Haack, *The Unsinkable Molly Brown*

Edith Head and Moss Mabry, *What a Way to Go!*

Tony Walton, *Mary Poppins*

SPECIAL VISUAL EFFECTS

Jim Danforth, *7 Faces of Dr. Lao*

Peter Ellenshaw, Hamilton Luske and Eustace Lycett, *Mary Poppins*

SOUND EFFECTS

Robert L. Bratton, *The Lively Set*

Norman Wanstall, *Goldfinger*

SHORT SUBJECTS

CARTOON

Christmas Cracker (National Film Board of Canada; Favorite Films of California)

How to Avoid Friendship (Self-Help Series) (Rembrandt Films; Film Representations)

Nudnik #2 (Nudnik Series) (Rembrandt Films; Film Representations)

The Pink Phink (*Pink Panther Series*) (Mirisch-Geoffrey Productions; United Artists)

LIVE ACTION SUBJECT

Casals Conducts: 1964 (Thalia Films; Beckman Film Corp.)

Help! My Snowman's Burning Down (Carson Davidson Productions; Pathé Contemporary Films)

The Legend of Jimmy Blue Eyes (Robert Clouse Associates; Topaz Film Corp.)

DOCUMENTARY

SHORT SUBJECT

Breaking the Habit (American Cancer Society; Modern Talking Picture Service)

Children Without (Guggenheim Productions; National Education Association)

Kenojuak (National Film Board of Canada)

Nine From Little Rock (Guggenheim Productions; U.S. Information Agency)

140 Days Under the World (New Zealand National Film Unit; Rank Film Distributors of New Zealand)

FEATURE

The Finest Hours (Le Vien Films, Ltd.; Columbia)

Four Days in November (David L. Wolper Productions; United Artists)

The Human Dutch (Bert Haanstra, producer; Haanstra Filmproductie)

Jacques-Yves Cousteau's World Without Sun (Filmad Les Requins Associes-Orsay-CEIAP; Columbia)

Over There, 1914–18 (Zodiac Productions; Pathé Contemporary Films)

FOREIGN LANGUAGE FILM

Raven's End, Sweden

Sallah, Israel

The Umbrellas of Cherbourg, France

Woman in the Dunes, Japan

Yesterday, Today and Tomorrow, Italy

HONORARY AWARD

To **William Tuttle** for his outstanding makeup achievement for *7 Faces of Dr. Lao*

1965

BEST PICTURE

Darling, Joseph Janni, producer (Embassy Pictures Corp.)

Doctor Zhivago, Carlo Ponti, producer (MGM)

Ship of Fools, Stanley Kramer, producer (Columbia)

The Sound of Music, Robert Wise, producer (Twentieth Century-Fox)

A Thousand Clowns, Fred Coe, producer (United Artists)

The Sound of Music

BEST ACTOR

Richard Burton, *The Spy Who Came in From the Cold*

Lee Marvin, *Cat Ballou*

Laurence Olivier, *Othello*

Rod Steiger, *The Pawnbroker*

Oskar Werner, *Ship of Fools*

BEST ACTRESS

Julie Andrews, *The Sound of Music*

Julie Christie, *Darling*

Samantha Eggar, *The Collector*

Elizabeth Hartman, *A Patch of Blue*

Simone Signoret, *Ship of Fools*

ACTOR IN A SUPPORTING ROLE

Martin Balsam, *A Thousand Clowns*

Ian Bannen, *The Flight of the Phoenix*

Tom Courtenay, *Doctor Zhivago*

Michael Dunn, *Ship of Fools*

Frank Finlay, *Othello*

ACTRESS IN A SUPPORTING ROLE

Ruth Gordon, *Inside Daisy Clover*

Joyce Redman, *Othello*

Maggie Smith, *Othello*

Shelley Winters, *A Patch of Blue*

Peggy Wood, *The Sound of Music*

DIRECTING

David Lean, *Doctor Zhivago*

John Schlesinger, *Darling*

Hiroshi Teshigahara, *Woman in the Dunes*

Robert Wise, *The Sound of Music*

William Wyler, *The Collector*

WRITING

SCREENPLAY BASED ON MATERIAL FROM ANOTHER MEDIUM
Robert Bolt, *Doctor Zhivago*

Herb Gardner, *A Thousand Clowns*

Abby Mann, *Ship of Fools*

Stanley Mann and John Kohn, *The Collector*

Walter Newman and Frank R. Pierson, *Cat Ballou*

STORY AND SCREENPLAY WRITTEN DIRECTLY FOR THE SCREEN
Age, Scarpelli, Mario Monicelli, Tonino Guerra, Giorgio Salvioni and Suso Cecchi D'Amico, *Casanova 70*

Franklin Coen and Frank Davis, *The Train*

Jack Davies and Ken Annakin, *Those Magnificent Men in Their Flying Machines*

Jacques Demy, *The Umbrellas of Cherbourg*

Frederic Raphael, *Darling*

CINEMATOGRAPHY

BLACK-AND-WHITE
Robert Burks, *A Patch of Blue*

Loyal Griggs, *In Harm's Way*

Burnett Guffey, *King Rat*

Conrad Hall, *Morituri*

Ernest Laszlo, *Ship of Fools*

COLOR
Russell Harlan, *The Great Race*

Ted McCord, *The Sound of Music*

William C. Mellor and Loyal Griggs, *The Greatest Story Ever Told*

Leon Shamroy, *The Agony and the Ecstasy*

Freddie Young, *Doctor Zhivago*

ART DIRECTION

BLACK-AND-WHITE

Robert Clatworthy, art direction; Joseph Kish, set decoration, *Ship of Fools*

George W. Davis and Urie McCleary, art direction; Henry Grace and Charles S. Thompson, set decoration, *A Patch of Blue*

Hal Pereira, Tambi Larsen and Edward Marshall, art direction; Josie MacAvin, set decoration, *The Spy Who Came in From the Cold*

Hal Pereira and Jack Poplin, art direction; Robert Benton and Joseph Kish, set decoration, *The Slender Thread*

Robert Emmet Smith, art direction; Frank Tuttle, set decoration, *King Rat*

COLOR

John Box and Terry Marsh, art direction; Dario Simoni, set decoration, *Doctor Zhivago*

Robert Clatworthy, art direction; George James Hopkins, set decoration, *Inside Daisy Clover*

Richard Day, William Creber and David Hall, art direction; Ray Moyer, Fred MacLean and Norman Rockett, set decoration, *The Greatest Story Ever Told*

John DeCuir and Jack Martin Smith, art direction; Dario Simoni, set decoration, *The Agony and the Ecstasy*

Boris Leven, art direction; Walter M. Scott and Ruby Levitt, set decoration, *The Sound of Music*

SOUND

MGM British Studio Sound Dept. and MGM Studio Sound Dept., *Doctor Zhivago*

Twentieth Century-Fox Studio Sound Dept., *The Agony and the Ecstasy*

Twentieth Century-Fox Studio Sound Dept. and Todd-AO Sound Dept., *The Sound of Music*

Universal City Studio Sound Dept., *Shenandoah*

Warner Bros. Studio Sound Dept., *The Great Race*

MUSIC

SONG

"The Ballad of Cat Ballou," *Cat Ballou*, Jerry Livingston, music; Mack David, lyrics

"I Will Wait for You," *The Umbrellas of Cherbourg*, Michel Legrand, music; Jacques Demy, lyrics

"The Shadow of Your Smile," *The Sandpiper*, Johnny Mandel, music; Paul Francis Webster, lyrics

"The Sweetheart Tree," *The Great Race*, Henry Mancini, music; Johnny Mercer, lyrics

"What's New, Pussycat?," *What's New, Pussycat?*, Burt Bacharach, music; Hal David, lyrics

MUSICAL SCORE, SUBSTANTIALLY ORIGINAL

Jerry Goldsmith, *A Patch of Blue*

Maurice Jarre, *Doctor Zhivago*

Michel Legrand and Jacques Demy, *The Umbrellas of Cherbourg*

Alfred Newman, *The Greatest Story Ever Told*

Alex North, *The Agony and the Ecstasy*

SCORING OF MUSIC, ADAPTATION OR TREATMENT

DeVol, *Cat Ballou*

Irwin Kostal, *The Sound of Music*

Michel Legrand, *The Umbrellas of Cherbourg*

Lionel Newman and Alexander Courage, *The Pleasure Seekers*

Don Walker, *A Thousand Clowns*

FILM EDITING

Michael Luciano, *The Flight of the Phoenix*

Charles Nelson, *Cat Ballou*

William Reynolds, *The Sound of Music*

Norman Savage, *Doctor Zhivago*

Ralph E. Winters, *The Great Race*

COSTUME DESIGN

BLACK-AND-WHITE

Julie Harris, *Darling*

Edith Head, *The Slender Thread*

Moss Mabry, *Morituri*

Howard Shoup, *A Rage to Live*

Bill Thomas and Jean Louis, *Ship of Fools*

COLOR

Phyllis Dalton, *Doctor Zhivago*

Edith Head and Bill Thomas, *Inside Daisy Clover*

Dorothy Jeakins, *The Sound of Music*

Vittorio Nino Novarese, *The Agony and the Ecstasy*

Vittorio Nino Novarese and Marjorie Best, *The Greatest Story Ever Told*

SPECIAL VISUAL EFFECTS

J. McMillan Johnson, *The Greatest Story Ever Told*

John Stears, *Thunderball*

SOUND EFFECTS EDITING

Tregoweth Brown, *The Great Race*

Walter A. Rossi, *Von Ryan's Express*

SHORT SUBJECTS

CARTOON

Clay or the Origin of Species (Harvard University; Pathé Contemporary Films)

***The Dot and the Line* (Chuck Jones and Les Goldman, producers; MGM)**

The Thieving Magpie (*La Gazza Ladra*) (Giulio Gianni-Emanuele Luzzati; Allied Artists)

LIVE ACTION

***The Chicken (Le Poulet)* (Renn Productions; Pathé Contemporary Films)**

Fortress of Peace (Lothar Wolff Productions for Farner-Looser Films; Cinerama)

Skaterdater (Byway Productions; United Artists)

Snow (British Transport Films in association with Geoffrey Jones, Ltd.; Manson Distributing)

Time Piece (Muppets, Inc.; Pathé Contemporary Films)

DOCUMENTARY

SHORT SUBJECT

Mural on Our Street (Henry Street Settlement; Pathé Contemporary Films)

Ouverture (Mafilm Studios Production; Hungarofilm-Pathé Contemporary Films)

Point of View (Vision Associates Production; National
  Tuberculosis Association)

To Be Alive! (Francis Thompson, producer; Johnson Wax)

Yeats Country (Patrick Carey and Joe Mendoza, producers;
  Aengus Films for the Dept. of External Affairs of Ireland)

FEATURE
The Battle of the Bulge . . . The Brave Rifles (Laurence E.
  Mascott, producer; Mascott Productions)

**The Eleanor Roosevelt Story (Sidney Glazier Production;
  American International)**

The Forth Road Bridge (Random Film Productions; Shell-Mex
  and B.P. Film Library)

Let My People Go (Marshall Flaum, producer;
  David L. Wolper Productions)

To Die in Madrid (Ancinex Productions; Altura Films
  International)

FOREIGN LANGUAGE FILM
Blood on the Land, Greece

Dear John, Sweden

Kwaidan, Japan

Marriage Italian Style, Italy

The Shop on Main Street, Czechoslovakia

IRVING G. THALBERG MEMORIAL AWARD
William Wyler

JEAN HERSHOLT HUMANITARIAN AWARD
Edmond L. DePatie

HONORARY AWARD
To **Bob Hope** for unique and distinguished service to our
industry and the Academy

1966

BEST PICTURE
Alfie, Lewis Gilbert, producer (Paramount)

A Man for All Seasons, Fred Zinnemann, producer (Columbia)

The Russians Are Coming, The Russians Are Coming,
  Norman Jewison, producer (United Artists)

The Sand Pebbles, Robert Wise, producer (Twentieth
  Century-Fox)

Who's Afraid of Virginia Woolf? Ernest Lehman, producer
  (Warner Bros.)

BEST ACTOR
Alan Arkin, *The Russians Are Coming, The Russians Are
  Coming*

Richard Burton, *Who's Afraid of Virginia Woolf?*

Michael Caine, *Alfie*

Steve McQueen, *The Sand Pebbles*

Paul Scofield, A Man for All Seasons

BEST ACTRESS
Anouk Aimée, *A Man and a Woman*

Ida Kaminska, *The Shop on Main Street*

Lynn Redgrave, *Georgy Girl*

Vanessa Redgrave, *Morgan!*

Elizabeth Taylor, Who's Afraid of Virginia Woolf?

Elizabeth Taylor,
Who's Afraid of Virginia Woolf?

ACTOR IN A SUPPORTING ROLE
Mako, *The Sand Pebbles*

James Mason, *Georgy Girl*

Walter Matthau, The Fortune Cookie

George Segal, *Who's Afraid of Virginia Woolf?*

Robert Shaw, *A Man for All Seasons*

ACTRESS IN A SUPPORTING ROLE
Sandy Dennis, Who's Afraid of Virginia Woolf?

Wendy Hiller, *A Man for All Seasons*

Jocelyne Lagarde, *Hawaii*

Vivien Merchant, *Alfie*

Geraldine Page, *You're a Big Boy Now*

DIRECTING
Michelangelo Antonioni, *Blow-Up*

Richard Brooks, *The Professionals*

Claude Lelouch, *A Man and a Woman*

Mike Nichols, *Who's Afraid of Virginia Woolf?*

Fred Zinnemann, A Man for All Seasons

WRITING
**SCREENPLAY BASED ON MATERIAL
FROM ANOTHER MEDIUM**
Robert Bolt, A Man for All Seasons

Richard Brooks, *The Professionals*

Ernest Lehman, *Who's Afraid of Virginia Woolf?*

Bill Naughton, *Alfie*

William Rose, *The Russians Are Coming, The Russians
  Are Coming*

**STORY AND SCREENPLAY WRITTEN
DIRECTLY FOR THE SCREEN**
Michelangelo Antonioni, story; Michelangelo Antonioni,
  Tonino Guerra and Edward Bond, *Blow-Up*

Robert Ardrey, *Khartoum*

Clint Johnston and Don Peters, *The Naked Prey*

**Claude Lelouch, story; Pierre Uytterhoeven and Claude
  Lelouch, screenplay, A Man and a Woman**

Billy Wilder and I. A. L. Diamond, *The Fortune Cookie*

CINEMATOGRAPHY

BLACK-AND-WHITE
Marcel Grignon, *Is Paris Burning?*

Ken Higgins, *Georgy Girl*

James Wong Howe, *Seconds*

Joseph LaShelle, *The Fortune Cookie*

Haskell Wexler, *Who's Afraid of Virginia Woolf?*

COLOR
Conrad Hall, *The Professionals*

Russell Harlan, *Hawaii*

Ernest Laszlo, *Fanastic Voyage*

Joseph MacDonald, *The Sand Pebbles*

Ted Moore, *A Man for All Seasons*

ART DIRECTION

BLACK-AND-WHITE
George W. Davis and Paul Groesse, art direction; Henry Grace and Hugh Hunt, set decoration, *Mister Buddwing*

Willy Holt, art direction; Marc Frederix and Pierre Guffroy, set decoration, *Is Paris Burning?*

Robert Luthardt, art direction; Edward G. Boyle, set decoration, *The Fortune Cookie*

Luigi Scaccianoce, art direction, *The Gospel According to St. Matthew*

Richard Sylbert, art direction; George James Hopkins, set decoration, *Who's Afraid of Virginia Woolf?*

COLOR
Piero Gherardi, art direction, *Juliet of the Spirits*

Alexander Golitzen and George C. Webb, art direction; John McCarthy and John Austin, set decoration, *Gambit*

Boris Leven, art direction; Walter M. Scott, John Sturtevant and William Kiernan, set decoration, *The Sand Pebbles*

Hal Pereira and Arthur Lonergan, art direction; Robert Benton and James Payne, set decoration, *The Oscar*

Jack Martin Smith and Dale Hennesy, art direction; Walter M. Scott and Stuart A. Reiss, set decoration, *Fantastic Voyage*

SOUND
MGM Studio Sound Dept., *Grand Prix*

Samuel Goldwyn Studio Sound Dept., *Hawaii*

Twentieth Century-Fox Studio Sound Dept., *The Sand Pebbles*

Universal City Studio Sound Dept., *Gambit*

Warner Bros. Studio Sound Dept., *Who's Afraid of Virginia Woolf?*

MUSIC

SONG
"Alfie," *Alfie*, Burt Bacharach, music; Hal David, lyrics

"Born Free," *Born Free*, John Barry, music; Don Black, lyrics

"Georgy Girl," *Georgy Girl*, Tom Springfield, music; Jim Dale, lyrics

"My Wishing Doll," *Hawaii*, Elmer Bernstein, music; Mack David, lyrics

"A Time for Love," *An American Dream*, Johnny Mandel, music; Paul Francis Webster, lyrics

ORIGINAL MUSIC SCORE
John Barry, *Born Free*

Elmer Bernstein, *Hawaii*

Jerry Goldsmith, *The Sand Pebbles*

Toshiro Mayuzumi, *The Bible*

Alex North, *Who's Afraid of Virginia Woolf?*

SCORING OF MUSIC, ADAPTATION OR TREATMENT
Luis Enrique Bacalov, *The Gospel According to St. Matthew*

Elmer Bernstein, *Return of the Seven*

Al Ham, *Stop the World — I Want to Get Off*

Harry Sukman, *The Singing Nun*

Ken Thorne, *A Funny Thing Happened on the Way to the Forum*

FILM EDITING
Hal Ashby and J. Terry Williams, *The Russians Are Coming, The Russians Are Coming*

William B. Murphy, *Fantastic Voyage*

Sam O'Steen, *Who's Afraid of Virginia Woolf?*

William Reynolds, *The Sand Pebbles*

Fredric Steinkamp, Henry Berman, Stewart Linder and Frank Santillo, *Grand Prix*

COSTUME DESIGN

BLACK-AND-WHITE
Danilo Donati, *The Gospel According to St. Matthew*

Danilo Donati, *Mandragola*

Jocelyn Rickards, *Morgan!*

Helen Rose, *Mister Buddwing*

Irene Sharaff, *Who's Afraid of Virginia Woolf?*

COLOR
Piero Gherardi, *Juliet of the Spirits*

Elizabeth Haffenden and Joan Bridge, *A Man for All Seasons*

Edith Head, *The Oscar*

Dorothy Jeakins, *Hawaii*

Jean Louis, *Gambit*

SPECIAL VISUAL EFFECTS
Art Cruickshank, *Fantastic Voyage*

Linwood G. Dunn, *Hawaii*

SOUND EFFECTS
Gordon Daniel, *Grand Prix*

Walter Rossi, *Fantastic Voyage*

SHORT SUBJECTS

CARTOON
The Drag (National Film Board of Canada; Favorite Films of California)

Herb Alpert and the Tijuana Brass Double Feature (*I Feel Special Series*) (Hubley Studios; Paramount)

The Pink Blueprint (*Pink Panther Series*) (Mirisch-Geoffrey-DePatie-Freleng; United Artists)

LIVE ACTION
Turkey the Bridge (Samaritan Productions; Schoenfeld Films)

Wild Wings (British Transport Films; Manson Distributing)

The Winning Strain (*Sports in Action Series*) (Winik Films; Paramount)

DOCUMENTARY

SHORT SUBJECT
Adolescence (Marin Karmitz and Vladimir Forgency, producers; M.K. Productions)

Cowboy (Ahnemann /Schlosser Productions; U.S. Information Agency)

The Odds Against (Vision Associates Production; American Foundation Institute of Corrections)

Saint Matthew Passion (Mafilm Studios Production; Hungarofilm)

A Year Toward Tomorrow (Sun Dial Films, Inc.; Office of Economic Opportunity)

FEATURE
The Face of Genius (WBZ-TV, Group W, Boston)

Helicopter Canada (National Film Board of Canada Centennial Commission; National Film Board of Canada)

Le Volcan Interdit (*The Forbidden Volcano*) (Cine Documents Tazieff; Athos Films)

The Really Big Family (Alex Grasshoff, producer; David L. Wolper Production)

The War Game (BBC Production for the British Film Institute; Pathé Contemporary Films)

FOREIGN LANGUAGE FILM
The Battle of Algiers, Italy

Loves of a Blonde, Czechoslovakia

A Man and a Woman, France

Pharaoh, Poland

Three, Yugoslavia

IRVING G. THALBERG MEMORIAL AWARD
Robert Wise

JEAN HERSHOLT HUMANITARIAN AWARD
George Bagnall

HONORARY AWARDS
To **Y. Frank Freeman** for unusual and outstanding service to the Academy during his 30 years in Hollywood

To **Yakima Canutt** for achievements as a stuntman and for developing safety devices to protect stuntmen everywhere

1967

BEST PICTURE
Bonnie and Clyde, Warren Beatty, producer (Warner Bros.-Seven Arts)

Doctor Dolittle, Arthur P. Jacobs, producer (Twentieth Century-Fox)

The Graduate, Lawrence Turman, producer (Embassy Pictures)

Guess Who's Coming to Dinner?, Stanley Kramer, producer (Columbia)

In the Heat of the Night, Walter Mirisch, producer (United Artists)

BEST ACTOR
Warren Beatty, *Bonnie and Clyde*

Dustin Hoffman, *The Graduate*

Paul Newman, *Cool Hand Luke*

Rod Steiger, In the Heat of the Night

Spencer Tracy, *Guess Who's Coming to Dinner?*

BEST ACTRESS
Anne Bancroft, *The Graduate*

Faye Dunaway, *Bonnie and Clyde*

Dame Edith Evans, *The Whisperers*

Audrey Hepburn, *Wait Until Dark*

Katharine Hepburn, Guess Who's Coming to Dinner?

ACTOR IN A SUPPORTING ROLE
John Cassavetes, *The Dirty Dozen*

Gene Hackman, *Bonnie and Clyde*

Cecil Kellaway, *Guess Who's Coming to Dinner?*

George Kennedy, Cool Hand Luke

Michael J. Pollard, *Bonnie and Clyde*

ACTRESS IN A SUPPORTING ROLE
Carol Channing, *Thoroughly Modern Millie*

Mildred Natwick, *Barefoot in the Park*

Estelle Parsons, Bonnie and Clyde

Beah Richards, *Guess Who's Coming to Dinner?*

Katharine Ross, *The Graduate*

DIRECTING
Richard Brooks, *In Cold Blood*

Norman Jewison, *In the Heat of the Night*

Stanley Kramer, *Guess Who's Coming to Dinner?*

Mike Nichols, The Graduate

Arthur Penn, *Bonnie and Clyde*

WRITING
SCREENPLAY BASED ON MATERIAL FROM ANOTHER MEDIUM
Richard Brooks, *In Cold Blood*

Donn Pearce and Frank R. Pierson, *Cool Hand Luke*

Mike Nichols

Stirling Silliphant, *In the Heat of the Night*

Joseph Strick and Fred Haines, *Ulysses*

Calder Willingham and Buck Henry, *The Graduate*

STORY AND SCREENPLAY WRITTEN DIRECTLY FOR THE SCREEN

Robert Kaufman, story; Norman Lear, screenplay, *Divorce American Style*

David Newman and Robert Benton, *Bonnie and Clyde*

Frederic Raphael, *Two for the Road*

William Rose, *Guess Who's Coming to Dinner?*

Jorge Semprun, *La Guerre Est Finie*

CINEMATOGRAPHY

Burnett Guffey, *Bonnie and Clyde*

Conrad Hall, *In Cold Blood*

Richard H. Kline, *Camelot*

Robert Surtees, *Doctor Dolittle*

Robert Surtees, *The Graduate*

ART DIRECTION

Mario Chiari, Jack Martin Smith and Ed Graves, art direction; Walter M. Scott and Stuart A. Reiss, set decoration, *Doctor Dolittle*

Robert Clatworthy, art direction; Frank Tuttle, set decoration, *Guess Who's Coming to Dinner?*

Alexander Golitzen and George C. Webb, art direction; Howard Bristol, set decoration, *Thoroughly Modern Millie*

Renzo Mongiardino, John DeCuir, Elven Webb and Giuseppe Mariani, art direction; Dario Simoni and Luigi Gervasi, set decoration, *The Taming of the Shrew*

John Truscott and Edward Carrere, art direction; John W. Brown, set decoration, *Camelot*

SOUND

MGM Studio Sound Dept., *The Dirty Dozen*

Samuel Goldwyn Studio Sound Dept., *In the Heat of the Night*

Twentieth Century-Fox Studio Sound Dept., *Doctor Dolittle*

Universal City Studio Sound Dept., *Thoroughly Modern Millie*

Warner Bros.-Seven Arts Studio Sound Dept., *Camelot*

MUSIC

SONG

"The Bare Necessities," *The Jungle Book*, Terry Gilkyson, music and lyrics

"The Eyes of Love," *Banning*, Quincy Jones, music; Bob Russell, lyrics

"The Look of Love," *Casino Royale*, Burt Bacharach, music; Hal David, lyrics

"Talk to the Animals," *Doctor Dolittle*, Leslie Bricusse, music and lyrics

"Thoroughly Modern Millie," *Thoroughly Modern Millie*, James Van Heusen and Sammy Cahn, music and lyrics

ORIGINAL MUSIC SCORE

Richard Rodney Bennett, *Far From the Madding Crowd*

Elmer Bernstein, *Thoroughly Modern Millie*

Leslie Bricusse, *Doctor Dolittle*

Quincy Jones, *In Cold Blood*

Lalo Schifrin, *Cool Hand Luke*

SCORING OF MUSIC, ADAPTATION OR TREATMENT

DeVol, *Guess Who's Coming to Dinner?*

Alfred Newman and Ken Darby, *Camelot*

Lionel Newman and Alexander Courage, *Doctor Dolittle*

André Previn and Joseph Gershenson, *Thoroughly Modern Millie*

John Williams, *Valley of the Dolls*

FILM EDITING

Hal Ashby, *In the Heat of the Night*

Samuel E. Beetley and Marjorie Fowler, *Doctor Dolittle*

Robert C. Jones, *Guess Who's Coming to Dinner?*

Frank P. Keller, *Beach Red*

Michael Luciano, *The Dirty Dozen*

COSTUME DESIGN

Jean Louis, *Thoroughly Modern Millie*

Irene Sharaff and Danilo Donati, *The Taming of the Shrew*

Bill Thomas, *The Happiest Millionaire*

John Truscott, *Camelot*

Theadora Van Runkle, *Bonnie and Clyde*

SPECIAL VISUAL EFFECTS

L. B. Abbott, *Doctor Dolittle*

Howard A. Anderson, Jr. and Albert Whitlock, *Tobruk*

SOUND EFFECTS

John Poyner, *The Dirty Dozen*

James A. Richard, *In the Heat of the Night*

SHORT SUBJECTS

CARTOON

***The Box* (Murakami-Wolf Films; Brandon Films)**

Hypothese Beta (Films Orzeaux; Pathé Contemporary Films)

What on Earth! (National Film Board of Canada; Columbia)

LIVE ACTION

Paddle to the Sea (National Film Board of Canada; Favorite Films of California)

***A Place to Stand* (T.D.F. Production for the Ontario Department of Economics and Development; Columbia)**

Sky Over Holland (John Ferno Production for the Netherlands; Warner Bros.-Seven Arts)

Stop, Look and Listen (Len Janson and Chuck Menville, producers; MGM)

DOCUMENTARY

SHORT SUBJECT

Monument to the Dream (Charles E. Guggenheim, producer; Guggenheim Productions)

A Place to Stand (T.D.F. Production for the Ontario Department of Economics and Development; Columbia)

***The Redwoods* (Mark Harris and Trevor Greenwood, producers; King Screen Productions)**

See You at the Pillar (Robert Fitchett, producer; Associated British-Pathé Production)

While I Run This Race (Carl V. Ragsdale, producer; Sun Dial Films for VISTA)

FEATURE

***The Anderson Platoon* (French Broadcasting System)**

Festival (Patchke Productions)

Harvest (U.S. Information Agency)

A King's Story (Jack Le Vien Production)

A Time for Burning (Quest Productions for Lutheran Film Associates)

FOREIGN LANGUAGE FILM

***Closely Watched Trains,* Czechoslovakia**

El Amor Brujo, Spain

I Even Met Happy Gypsies, Yugoslavia

Live for Life, France

Portrait of Chieko, Japan

IRVING G. THALBERG MEMORIAL AWARD

Alfred Hitchcock

JEAN HERSHOLT HUMANITARIAN AWARD

Gregory Peck

HONORARY AWARD

To **Arthur Freed** for distinguished service to the Academy and the production of six top-rated Awards telecasts

1968

BEST PICTURE

Funny Girl, Ray Stark, producer (Columbia)

The Lion in Winter, Martin Poll, producer (Avco Embassy)

***Oliver!,* John Woolf, producer (Columbia)**

Rachel, Rachel, Paul Newman, producer (Warner Bros.-Seven Arts)

Romeo and Juliet, Anthony Havelock-Allan and John Brabourne, producers (Paramount)

BEST ACTOR

Alan Arkin, *The Heart Is a Lonely Hunter*

Alan Bates, *The Fixer*

Ron Moody, *Oliver!*

Peter O'Toole, *The Lion in Winter*

Cliff Robertson, *Charly*

BEST ACTRESS (TIE)

Katharine Hepburn, *The Lion in Winter*

Patricia Neal, *The Subject Was Roses*

Barbra Streisand, *Funny Girl*

Vanessa Redgrave, *Isadora*

Barbra Streisand, *Funny Girl*

Joanne Woodward, *Rachel, Rachel*

ACTOR IN A SUPPORTING ROLE

Jack Albertson, *The Subject Was Roses*

Seymour Cassel, *Faces*

Daniel Massey, *Star!*

Jack Wild, *Oliver!*

Gene Wilder, *The Producers*

ACTRESS IN A SUPPORTING ROLE

Lynn Carlin, *Faces*

Ruth Gordon, *Rosemary's Baby*

Sondra Locke, *The Heart Is a Lonely Hunter*

Kay Medford, *Funny Girl*

Estelle Parsons, *Rachel, Rachel*

DIRECTING

Anthony Harvey, *The Lion in Winter*

Stanley Kubrick, *2001: A Space Odyssey*

Gillo Pontecorvo, *The Battle of Algiers*

Carol Reed, *Oliver!*

Franco Zeffirelli, *Romeo and Juliet*

WRITING

SCREENPLAY BASED ON MATERIAL FROM ANOTHER MEDIUM
James Goldman, *The Lion in Winter*

Vernon Harris, *Oliver!*

Roman Polanski, *Rosemary's Baby*

Neil Simon, *The Odd Couple*

Stewart Stern, *Rachel, Rachel*

STORY AND SCREENPLAY WRITTEN DIRECTLY FOR THE SCREEN
Mel Brooks, *The Producers*

John Cassavetes, *Faces*

Stanley Kubrick and Arthur C. Clarke, *2001: A Space Odyssey*

Franco Solinas and Gillo Pontecorvo, *The Battle of Algiers*

Ira Wallach and Peter Ustinov, *Hot Millions*

CINEMATOGRAPHY

Pasqualino De Santis, *Romeo and Juliet*

Daniel L. Fapp, *Ice Station Zebra*

Ernest Laszlo, *Star!*

Oswald Morris, *Oliver!*

Harry Stradling, *Funny Girl*

ART DIRECTION

Mikhail Bogdanov and Gennady Myasnikov, art direction; G. Koshelev and V. Uvarov, set decoration, *War and Peace*

John Box and Terence Marsh, art direction; Vernon Dixon and Ken Muggleston, set decoration, *Oliver!*

George W. Davis and Edward Carfagno, art direction, *The Shoes of the Fisherman*

Boris Leven, art direction; Walter M. Scott and Howard Bristol, set decoration, *Star!*

Tony Masters, Harry Lange and Ernie Archer, art direction, *2001: A Space Odyssey*

SOUND

Columbia Studio Sound Dept., *Funny Girl*

Shepperton Studio Sound Dept., *Oliver!*

Twentieth Century-Fox Studio Sound Dept., *Star!*

Warner Bros.-Seven Arts Studio Sound Dept., *Bullitt*

Warner Bros.-Seven Arts Studio Sound Dept., *Finian's Rainbow*

MUSIC

SONG

"Chitty Chitty Bang Bang," *Chitty Chitty Bang Bang*, Richard M. Sherman and Robert B. Sherman, music and lyrics

"For Love of Ivy," *For Love of Ivy*, Quincy Jones, music; Bob Russell, lyrics

"Funny Girl," *Funny Girl*, Jule Styne, music; Bob Merrill, lyrics

"Star!," *Star!*, Jimmy Van Heusen, music; Sammy Cahn, lyrics

"The Windmills of Your Mind," *The Thomas Crown Affair*, Michel Legrand, music; Alan and Marilyn Bergman, lyrics

ORIGINAL SCORE FOR A MOTION PICTURE, NOT A MUSICAL

John Barry, *The Lion in Winter*

Jerry Goldsmith, *Planet of the Apes*

Michel Legrand, *The Thomas Crown Affair*

Alex North, *The Shoes of the Fisherman*

Lalo Schifrin, *The Fox*

SCORE OF A MUSICAL PICTURE, ORIGINAL OR ADAPTATION

John Green, *Oliver!*

Lennie Hayton, *Star!*

Ray Heindorf, *Finian's Rainbow*

Michel Legrand, music and adaptation; Jacques Demy, lyrics, *The Young Girls of Rochefort*

Walter Scharf, *Funny Girl*

FILM EDITING

Frank Bracht, *The Odd Couple*

Fred Feitshans and Eve Newman, *Wild in the Streets*

Frank P. Keller, *Bullitt*

Ralph Kemplen, *Oliver!*

Robert Swink, Maury Winetrobe and William Sands, *Funny Girl*

COSTUME DESIGN

Donald Brooks, *Star!*

Phyllis Dalton, *Oliver!*

Danilo Donati, *Romeo and Juliet*

Margaret Furse, *The Lion in Winter*

Morton Haack, *Planet of the Apes*

SPECIAL VISUAL EFFECTS

Stanley Kubrick, *2001: A Space Odyssey*

Hal Millar and J. McMillan Johnson, *Ice Station Zebra*

SHORT SUBJECTS

CARTOON

The House That Jack Built (National Film Board of Canada; Columbia)

The Magic Pear Tree (Murakami-Wolf Films; Bing Crosby Productions)

Windy Day (Hubley Studios; Paramount)

Winnie the Pooh and the Blustery Day (Walt Disney Productions; Buena Vista)

LIVE ACTION

The Dove (Coe-Davis Ltd.; Schoenfeld Films Distributing Co.)

Duo (National Film Board of Canada; Columbia)

Prelude (Prelude Co.; Excelsior Distributing)

Robert Kennedy Remembered (Guggenheim Productions; National General Pictures)

DOCUMENTARY

SHORT SUBJECT

The House That Ananda Built (Films Division, Government of India)

The Revolving Door (Vision Associates Production for the American Foundation Institute of Corrections)

A Space to Grow (Office of Economic Opportunity for Project Upward Bound)

A Way Out of the Wilderness (Dan E. Weisburd, producer; John Sutherland Productions)

Why Man Creates (Saul Bass, producer; Saul Bass and Associates)

FEATURE

A Few Notes on Our Food Problem (James Blue, producer; U.S. Information Agency)

Journey Into Self (Bill McGaw, producer; Western Behavioral Sciences Institute) (At the April 14, 1968, awards ceremony, *Young Americans* was announced as the Documentary Feature winner. On May 7, 1969, the film was disqualified because it played in October 1967, therefore ineligible for a 1968 award. Journey Into Self, the first runner-up was awarded the Oscar on May 8, 1969.)

The Legendary Champions (William Cayton, producer; Turn of the Century Fights)

Other Voices (David H. Sawyer, producer; DHS Films)

Young Americans (Robert Cohn and Alex Grasshoff, producers; The Young Americans Production)

FOREIGN LANGUAGE FILM

The Boys of Paul Street, Hungary

The Fireman's Ball, Czechoslovakia

The Girl With the Pistol, Italy

Stolen Kisses, France

War and Peace, U.S.S.R.

JEAN HERSHOLT HUMANITARIAN AWARD

Martha Raye

HONORARY AWARDS

To **John Chambers** for his outstanding makeup achievement for *Planet of the Apes*

To **Onna White** for her outstanding choreography achievement for *Oliver!*

1969

BEST PICTURE

Anne of the Thousand Days, Hal B. Wallis, producer (Universal)

Butch Cassidy and the Sundance Kid, John Foreman, producer (Twentieth Century-Fox)

Hello, Dolly!, Ernest Lehman, producer (Twentieth Century-Fox)

Midnight Cowboy, Jerome Hellman, producer (United Artists)

Z, Jacques Perrin and Hamed Rachedi, producers (Cinema V)

BEST ACTOR

Richard Burton, *Anne of the Thousand Days*

Dustin Hoffman, *Midnight Cowboy*

Peter O'Toole, *Goodbye, Mr. Chips*

Jon Voight, *Midnight Cowboy*

John Wayne, *True Grit*

BEST ACTRESS

Genevieve Bujold, *Anne of the Thousand Days*

Jane Fonda, *They Shoot Horses, Don't They?*

Liza Minnelli, *The Sterile Cuckoo*

Jean Simmons, *The Happy Ending*

Maggie Smith, *The Prime of Miss Jean Brodie*

ACTOR IN A SUPPORTING ROLE

Rupert Crosse, *The Reivers*

Elliott Gould, *Bob & Carol & Ted & Alice*

Jack Nicholson, *Easy Rider*

Anthony Quayle, *Anne of the Thousand Days*

Gig Young, *They Shoot Horses, Don't They?*

ACTRESS IN A SUPPORTING ROLE

Catherine Burns, *Last Summer*

Dyan Cannon, *Bob & Carol & Ted & Alice*

Goldie Hawn, *Cactus Flower*

Sylvia Miles, *Midnight Cowboy*

Susannah York, *They Shoot Horses, Don't They?*

DIRECTING

Costa-Gavras, *Z*

George Roy Hill, *Butch Cassidy and the Sundance Kid*

Arthur Penn, *Alice's Restaurant*

Sydney Pollack, *They Shoot Horses, Don't They?*

John Schlesinger, *Midnight Cowboy*

WRITING

SCREENPLAY BASED ON MATERIAL FROM ANOTHER MEDIUM

John Hale and Bridget Boland, screenplay; Richard Sokolove, adaptation, *Anne of the Thousand Days*

James Poe and Robert E. Thompson, *They Shoot Horses, Don't They?*

Waldo Salt, *Midnight Cowboy*

Arnold Schulman, *Goodbye, Columbus*

Jorge Semprun and Costa-Gavras, *Z*

STORY AND SCREENPLAY BASED ON MATERIAL NOT PREVIOUSLY PUBLISHED OR PRODUCED

Nicola Badalucco, story; Nicola Badalucco, Enrico Medioli and Luchino Visconti, screenplay, *The Damned*

Peter Fonda, Dennis Hopper and Terry Southern, *Easy Rider*

William Goldman, *Butch Cassidy and the Sundance Kid*

Walon Green and Roy N. Sickner, story; Walon Green and Sam Peckinpah, screenplay, *The Wild Bunch*

Paul Mazursky and Larry Tucker, *Bob & Carol & Ted & Alice*

Butch Cassidy and the Sundance Kid

CINEMATOGRAPHY

Daniel Fapp, *Marooned*

Conrad Hall, *Butch Cassidy and the Sundance Kid*

Arthur Ibbetson, *Anne of the Thousand Days*

Charles B. Lang, *Bob & Carol & Ted & Alice*

Harry Stradling, *Hello, Dolly!*

ART DIRECTION

Robert Boyle and George B. Chan, art direction; Edward Boyle and Carl Biddiscombe, set decoration, *Gaily, Gaily*

Maurice Carter and Lionel Couch, art direction; Patrick McLoughlin, set decoration, *Anne of the Thousand Days*

John DeCuir, Jack Martin Smith and Herman Blumenthal, art direction; Walter M. Scott, George Hopkins and Raphael Bretton, set decoration, *Hello, Dolly!*

Alexander Golitzen and George C. Webb, art direction; Jack D. Moore, set decoration, *Sweet Charity*

Harry Horner, art direction; Frank McKelvy, set decoration, *They Shoot Horses, Don't They?*

SOUND

John Aldred, *Anne of the Thousand Days*

William Edmundson and David Dockendorf, *Butch Cassidy and the Sundance Kid*

Les Fresholtz and Arthur Piantadosi, *Marooned*

Robert Martin and Clem Portman, *Gaily, Gaily*

Jack Solomon and Murray Spivack, *Hello, Dolly!*

MUSIC

SONG

"Come Saturday Morning," *The Sterile Cuckoo*, Fred Karlin, music; Dory Previn, lyrics

"Jean," *The Prime of Miss Jean Brodie*, Rod McKuen, music and lyrics

"Raindrops Keep Fallin' on My Head," *Butch Cassidy and the Sundance Kid*, Burt Bacharach, music; Hal David, lyrics

"True Grit," *True Grit*, Elmer Bernstein, music; Don Black, lyrics

"What Are You Doing the Rest of Your Life?," *The Happy Ending*, Michel Legrand, music; Alan and Marilyn Bergman, lyrics

ORIGINAL SCORE FOR A MOTION PICTURE, NOT A MUSICAL

Burt Bacharach, *Butch Cassidy and the Sundance Kid*

Georges Delerue, *Anne of the Thousand Days*

Jerry Fielding, *The Wild Bunch*

Ernest Gold, *The Secret of Santa Vittoria*

John Williams, *The Reivers*

SCORE OF A MUSICAL PICTURE, ORIGINAL OR ADAPTATION

Leslie Bricusse, music and lyrics; John Williams, score, *Goodbye, Mr. Chips*

Cy Coleman, *Sweet Charity*

John Green and Albert Woodbury, *They Shoot Horses, Don't They?*

Lennie Hayton and Lionel Newman, *Hello, Dolly!*

Nelson Riddle, *Paint Your Wagon*

FILM EDITING

Françoise Bonnot, *Z*

William Lyon and Earle Herdan, *The Secret of Santa Vittoria*

William Reynolds, *Hello, Dolly!*

Hugh A. Robertson, *Midnight Cowboy*

Fredric Steinkamp, *They Shoot Horses, Don't They?*

COSTUME DESIGN

Ray Aghayan, *Gaily, Gaily*

Donfeld, *They Shoot Horses, Don't They?*

Margaret Furse, *Anne of the Thousand Days*

Edith Head, *Sweet Charity*

Irene Sharaff, *Hello, Dolly!*

SPECIAL VISUAL EFFECTS

Eugene Lourie and Alex Weldon, *Krakatoa, East of Java*

Robbie Robertson, *Marooned*

SHORT SUBJECTS

CARTOON

***It's Tough to be a Bird* (Walt Disney Productions; Buena Vista)**

Of Men and Demons (Hubley Studios; Paramount)

Walking (National Film Board of Canada; Columbia)

LIVE ACTION

Blake (National Film Board of Canada; Vaudeo, Inc.)

***The Magic Machines* (Fly-By-Night Productions; Manson Distributing)**

People Soup (Pangloss Productions; Columbia)

DOCUMENTARY

SHORT SUBJECT

***Czechoslovakia 1968* (Sanders-Fresco Film Makers for the U.S. Information Agency)**

An Impression of John Steinbeck: Writer (Donald Wrye Productions for the U.S. Information Agency)

Jenny Is a Good Thing (A.C.I. Prod. for Project Head Start)

Leo Beuerman (Arthur H. Wolf and Russell A. Mosser, producers; Centron Production)

The Magic Machines (Fly-By-Night Productions; Manson Distributing)

FEATURE

***Arthur Rubinstein — The Love of Life* (Bernard Chevry, producer; Midem Production)**

Before the Mountain Was Moved (Robert K. Sharpe Productions for the Office of Economic Opportunity)

In the Year of the Pig (Emile de Antonio, producer; Emile de Antonio Production)

The Olympics in Mexico (Film Section of the Organizing Committee for the XIX Olympic Games)

The Wolf Men (Irwin Rosten, producer; MGM)

FOREIGN LANGUAGE FILM (TIE)

Adalen '31, Sweden

The Battle of Neretva, Yugoslavia

***The Brothers Karamazov,* U.S.S.R.**

My Night With Maud, France

Z, Algeria

JEAN HERSHOLT HUMANITARIAN AWARD

George Jessel

HONORARY AWARD

To **Cary Grant** for his unique mastery of the art of screen acting with the respect and affection of his colleagues

1970

BEST PICTURE

Airport, Ross Hunter, producer (Universal)

Five Easy Pieces, Bob Rafelson and Richard Wechsler, producers (Columbia)

Love Story, Howard G. Minsky, producer (Paramount)

*M*A*S*H,* Ingo Preminger, producer (Twentieth Century-Fox)

***Patton,* Frank McCarthy, producer (Twentieth Century-Fox)**

BEST ACTOR

Melvyn Douglas, *I Never Sang for My Father*

James Earl Jones, *The Great White Hope*

Jack Nicholson, *Five Easy Pieces*

Ryan O'Neal, *Love Story*

George C. Scott, *Patton*

Patton

BEST ACTRESS
Jane Alexander, *The Great White Hope*
Glenda Jackson, *Women in Love*
Ali MacGraw, *Love Story*
Sarah Miles, *Ryan's Daughter*
Carrie Snodgress, *Diary of a Mad Housewife*

ACTOR IN A SUPPORTING ROLE
Richard Castellano, *Lovers and Other Strangers*
Chief Dan George, *Little Big Man*
Gene Hackman, *I Never Sang for My Father*
John Marley, *Love Story*
John Mills, *Ryan's Daughter*

ACTRESS IN A SUPPORTING ROLE
Karen Black, *Five Easy Pieces*
Lee Grant, *The Landlord*
Helen Hayes, *Airport*
Sally Kellerman, *M*A*S*H*
Maureen Stapleton, *Airport*

DIRECTING
Robert Altman, *M*A*S*H*
Federico Fellini, *Fellini Satyricon*
Arthur Hiller, *Love Story*
Ken Russell, *Women in Love*
Franklin J. Schaffner, *Patton*

WRITING
SCREENPLAY BASED ON MATERIAL FROM ANOTHER MEDIUM
Robert Anderson, *I Never Sang for My Father*
Larry Kramer, *Women in Love*
Ring Lardner, Jr., *M*A*S*H*
George Seaton, *Airport*
Renee Taylor, Joseph Bologna and David Zelag Goodman, *Lovers and Other Strangers*

ORIGINAL SCREENPLAY
Francis Ford Coppola and Edmund H. North, *Patton*
Bob Rafelson and Adrien Joyce, story; Adrien Joyce, screenplay, *Five Easy Pieces*
Eric Rohmer, *My Night at Maud's*
Erich Segal, *Love Story*
Norman Wexler, *Joe*

CINEMATOGRAPHY
Fred Koenekamp, *Patton*
Ernest Laszlo, *Airport*
Charles F. Wheeler, Osami Furuya, Sinsaku Himeda and Masamichi Satoh, *Tora! Tora! Tora!*
Billy Williams, *Women in Love*
Freddie Young, *Ryan's Daughter*

ART DIRECTION
Alexander Golitzen and E. Preston Ames, art direction; Jack D. Moore and Mickey S. Michaels, set decoration, *Airport*
Tambi Larsen, art direction; Darrell Silvera, set decoration, *The Molly Maguires*

Terry Marsh and Bob Cartwright, art direction; Pamela Cornell, set decoration, *Scrooge*
Urie McCleary and Gil Parrondo, art direction; Antonio Mateos and Pierre-Louis Thevenet, set decoration, *Patton*
Mickey S. Michaels, set decoration, *Airport*
Jack Martin Smith, Yoshiro Muraki, Richard Day and Taizoh Kawashima, art direction; Walter M. Scott, Norman Rockett and Carl Biddiscombe, set decoration, *Tora! Tora! Tora!*

SOUND
Gordon K. McCallum and John Bramall, *Ryan's Daughter*
Ronald Pierce and David Moriarty, *Airport*
Murray Spivack and Herman Lewis, *Tora! Tora! Tora!*
Dan Wallin and Larry Johnson, *Woodstock*
Douglas Williams and Don Bassman, *Patton*

MUSIC
SONG
"For All We Know," *Lovers and Other Strangers*, Fred Karlin, music; Robb Royer and James Griffin, lyrics
"Pieces of Dreams," *Pieces of Dreams*, Michel Legrand, music; Alan and Marilyn Bergman, lyrics
"Thank You Very Much," *Scrooge*, Leslie Bricusse, music and lyrics
"Till Love Touches Your Life," *Madron*, Riz Ortolani, music; Arthur Hamilton, lyrics
"Whistling Away the Dark," *Darling Lili*, Henry Mancini, music; Johnny Mercer, lyrics

ORIGINAL SCORE
Frank Cordell, *Cromwell*
Jerry Goldsmith, *Patton*
Francis Lai, *Love Story*
Henry Mancini, *Sunflower*
Alfred Newman, *Airport*

ORIGINAL SONG SCORE
The Beatles, *Let It Be*
Leslie Bricusse, music and lyrics; Ian Fraser and Herbert W. Spencer, adaptation, *Scrooge*
Fred Karlin and Tylwyth Kymry, *The Baby Maker*
Henry Mancini, music; Johnny Mercer, lyrics, *Darling Lili*
Rod McKuen and John Scott Trotter, music; Rod McKuen, Bill Melendez and Al Shean, lyrics; Vince Guaraldi, adaptation score, *A Boy Named Charlie Brown*

FILM EDITING
Hugh S. Fowler, *Patton*
Stuart Gilmore, *Airport*
Danford B. Greene, *M*A*S*H*
James E. Newcom, Pembroke J. Herring and Inoue Chikaya, *Tora! Tora! Tora!*
Thelma Schoonmaker, *Woodstock*

COSTUME DESIGN
Donald Brooks and Jack Bear, *Darling Lili*
Margaret Furse, *Scrooge*
Edith Head, *Airport*
Nino Novarese, *Cromwell*
Bill Thomas, *The Hawaiians*

SPECIAL VISUAL EFFECTS

A. D. Flowers and L. B. Abbott, *Tora! Tora! Tora!*

Alex Weldon, *Patton*

SHORT SUBJECTS

CARTOON

The Further Adventures of Uncle Sam: Part Two (Haboush Company; Goldstone Films)

Is It Always Right to Be Right? (Stephen Bosustow Productions; Lester A. Schoenfeld Films)

The Shepherd (Cameron Guess and Associates; Brandon Films)

LIVE ACTION

The Resurrection of Broncho Billy (University of Southern California, Department of Cinema; Universal)

Shut Up . . . I'm Crying (Robert Siegler Productions; Lester A. Schoenfeld Films)

Sticky My Fingers . . . Fleet My Feet (American Film Institute; Lester A. Schoenfeld Films)

DOCUMENTARY

SHORT SUBJECT

The Gifts (Robert McBride, producer; Richter-McBride Productions for the Water Quality Office of the Environmental Protection Agency)

Interviews With My Lai Veterans (Joseph Strick, producer; Laser Film Corp.)

A Long Way From Nowhere (Bob Aller, producer; Robert Aller Productions)

Oisin (Vivien Carey and Patrick Carey, producers; Aengus Films)

Time Is Running Out (Horst Dallmayr and Robert Menegoz, producers; Gesellschaft für bildende Filme)

FEATURE

Chariots of the Gods (Dr. Harald Reinl, producer; Terra-Filmkunst GmbH)

Jack Johnson (Jim Jacobs, producer; The Big Fights)

King: A Filmed Record . . . Montgomery to Memphis (Ely Landau, producer; Commonwealth United Corporation Production)

Say Goodbye (David H. Vowell, producer; David L. Wolper Productions)

Woodstock (Wadleigh-Maurice Ltd.; Warner Bros.)

FOREIGN LANGUAGE FILM

First Love, Switzerland

Hoa-Binh, France

Investigation of a Citizen Above Suspicion, Italy

Paix Sur Les Champs, Belgium

Tristana, Spain

IRVING G. THALBERG MEMORIAL AWARD

Ingmar Bergman

JEAN HERSHOLT HUMANITARIAN AWARD

Frank Sinatra

HONORARY AWARDS

To **Lillian Gish** for superlative artistry and for distinguished contribution to the progress of motion pictures

To **Orson Welles** for superlative artistry and versatility in the creation of motion pictures

Gene Hackman,
The French Connection

1971

BEST PICTURE

A Clockwork Orange, Stanley Kubrick, producer (Warner Bros.)

Fiddler on the Roof, Norman Jewison, producer (United Artists)

The French Connection, Philip D'Antoni, producer (Twentieth Century-Fox)

The Last Picture Show, Stephen J. Friedman, producer (Columbia)

Nicholas and Alexandra, Sam Spiegel, producer (Columbia)

BEST ACTOR

Peter Finch, *Sunday Bloody Sunday*

Gene Hackman, *The French Connection*

Walter Matthau, *Kotch*

George C. Scott, *The Hospital*

Topol, *Fiddler on the Roof*

BEST ACTRESS

Julie Christie, *McCabe & Mrs. Miller*

Jane Fonda, *Klute*

Glenda Jackson, *Sunday Bloody Sunday*

Vanessa Redgrave, *Mary, Queen of Scots*

Janet Suzman, *Nicholas and Alexandra*

ACTOR IN A SUPPORTING ROLE

Jeff Bridges, *The Last Picture Show*

Leonard Frey, *Fiddler on the Roof*

Richard Jaeckel, *Sometimes a Great Notion*

Ben Johnson, *The Last Picture Show*

Roy Scheider, *The French Connection*

ACTRESS IN A SUPPORTING ROLE

Ellen Burstyn, *The Last Picture Show*

Barbara Harris, *Who Is Harry Kellerman and Why Is He Saying Those Terrible Things About Me?*

Cloris Leachman, *The Last Picture Show*

Margaret Leighton, *The Go-Between*

Ann-Margret, *Carnal Knowledge*

DIRECTING

Peter Bogdanovich, *The Last Picture Show*

William Friedkin, *The French Connection*

Norman Jewison, *Fiddler on the Roof*

Stanley Kubrick, *A Clockwork Orange*

John Schlesinger, *Sunday Bloody Sunday*

WRITING

SCREENPLAY BASED ON MATERIAL FROM ANOTHER MEDIUM

Bernardo Bertolucci, *The Conformist*

Stanley Kubrick, *A Clockwork Orange*

Larry McMurtry and Peter Bogdanovich, *The Last Picture Show*

Ugo Pirro and Vittorio Bonicelli, *The Garden of the Finzi-Continis*

Ernest Tidyman, *The French Connection*

ORIGINAL SCREENPLAY

Paddy Chayefsky, *The Hospital*

Penelope Gilliatt, *Sunday Bloody Sunday*

Andy Lewis and Dave Lewis, *Klute*

Elio Petri and Ugo Pirro, *Investigation of a Citizen Above Suspicion*

Herman Raucher, *Summer of '42*

CINEMATOGRAPHY

Oswald Morris, *Fiddler on the Roof*

Owen Roizman, *The French Connection*

Robert Surtees, *The Last Picture Show*

Robert Surtees, *Summer of '42*

Freddie Young, *Nicholas and Alexandra*

ART DIRECTION

John Box, Ernest Archer, Jack Maxsted and Gil Parrondo, art direction; Vernon Dixon, set decoration, *Nicholas and Alexandra*

Robert Boyle and Michael Stringer, art direction; Peter Lamont, set decoration, *Fiddler on the Roof*

Boris Leven and William Tuntke, art direction; Ruby Levitt, set decoration, *The Andromeda Strain*

John B. Mansbridge and Peter Ellenshaw, art direction; Emile Kuri and Hal Gausman, set decoration, *Bedknobs and Broomsticks*

Terence Marsh and Robert Cartwright, art direction; Peter Howitt, set decoration, *Mary, Queen of Scots*

SOUND

Bob Jones and John Aldred, *Mary, Queen of Scots*

Gordon K. McCallum and David Hildyard, *Fiddler on the Roof*

Gordon K. McCallum, John Mitchell and Alfred J. Overton, *Diamonds Are Forever*

Richard Portman and Jack Solomon, *Kotch*

Theodore Soderberg and Christopher Newman, *The French Connection*

MUSIC

SONG

"The Age of Not Believing," *Bedknobs and Broomsticks*, Richard M. Sherman and Robert B. Sherman, music and lyrics

"All His Children," *Sometimes a Great Notion*, Henry Mancini, music; Alan and Marilyn Bergman, lyrics

"Bless the Beasts and Children," *Bless the Beasts and Children*, Barry DeVorzon and Perry Botkin, Jr., music and lyrics

"Life Is What You Make It," *Kotch*, Marvin Hamlisch, music; Johnny Mercer, lyrics

"Theme From *Shaft*," *Shaft*, Isaac Hayes, music and lyrics

ORIGINAL DRAMATIC SCORE

John Barry, *Mary, Queen of Scots*

Richard Rodney Bennett, *Nicholas and Alexandra*

Jerry Fielding, *Straw Dogs*

Isaac Hayes, *Shaft*

Michel Legrand, *Summer of '42*

SCORING: ADAPTATION AND ORIGINAL SONG SCORE

Leslie Bricusse and Anthony Newley, song; Walter Scharf, adaptation, *Willy Wonka and the Chocolate Factory*

Peter Maxwell Davies and Peter Greenwell, *The Boy Friend*

Richard M. Sherman and Robert B. Sherman, song; Irwin Kostal, adaptation, *Bedknobs and Broomsticks*

Dimitri Tiomkin, *Tchaikovsky*

John Williams, *Fiddler on the Roof*

FILM EDITING

Folmar Blangsted, *Summer of '42*

Bill Butler, *A Clockwork Orange*

Stuart Gilmore and John W. Holmes, *The Andromeda Strain*

Jerry Greenberg, *The French Connection*

Ralph E. Winters, *Kotch*

COSTUME DESIGN

Yvonne Blake and Antonio Castillo, *Nicholas and Alexandra*

Margaret Furse, *Mary, Queen of Scots*

Morton Haack, *What's the Matter With Helen?*

Bill Thomas, *Bedknobs and Broomsticks*

Piero Tosi, *Death in Venice*

SPECIAL VISUAL EFFECTS

Jim Danforth and Roger Dicken, *When Dinosaurs Ruled the Earth*

Alan Maley, Eustace Lycett and Danny Lee, *Bedknobs and Broomsticks*

SHORT SUBJECTS

ANIMATED

***The Crunch Bird* (Maxwell-Petok-Petrovich Productions; Regency Film Distributing Corp.)**

Evolution (National Film Board of Canada; Columbia)

The Selfish Giant (Potterton Productions; Pyramid Films)

LIVE ACTION

Good Morning (E/G Films; Seymour Borde and Associates)

The Rehearsal (Cinema Verona Production; Schoenfeld Film Distributing Corp.)

***Sentinels of Silence* (Producciones Concord; Paramount)**

DOCUMENTARY

SHORT SUBJECT

Adventures in Perception (Hans van Gelder Filmproduktie; Netherlands Information Service)

Art Is . . . (Henry Strauss Associates; Sears, Roebuck Foundation)

The Numbers Start With the River (WH Picture; U.S. Information Agency)

Sentinels of Silence (Producciones Concord; Paramount)

Somebody Waiting (Snider Productions; University of California Medical Film Library)

FEATURE

Alaska Wilderness Lake (Alan Landsburg, producer; Alan Landsburg Productions)

The Hellstrom Chronicle (David L. Wolper Productions; Cinema 5, Ltd.)

On Any Sunday (Bruce Brown-Solar; Cinema 5, Ltd.)

The RA Expeditions (Swedish Broadcasting Company; Interwest Film Corp.)

The Sorrow and the Pity (Television Rencontre-Norddeutscher Rundfunk-Television Swiss Romande; Cinema 5, Ltd.)

FOREIGN LANGUAGE FILM

Dodes'Ka-Den, Japan

The Emigrants, Sweden

The Garden of the Finzi-Continis, Italy

The Policeman, Israel

Tchaikovsky, U.S.S.R.

HONORARY AWARD

To **Charles Chaplin** for the incalculable effect he has had in making motion pictures the art form of this century

1972

BEST PICTURE

Cabaret, Cy Feuer, producer (Allied Artists)

Deliverance, John Boorman, producer (Warner Bros.)

The Emigrants, Bengt Forslund, producer (Warner Bros.)

The Godfather, Albert S. Ruddy, producer (Paramount)

Sounder, Robert B. Radnitz, producer (Twentieth Century-Fox)

**Sacheen Littlefeather accepts
Marlon Brando's Best Actor Oscar**

BEST ACTOR

Marlon Brando, *The Godfather*

Michael Caine, *Sleuth*

Laurence Olivier, *Sleuth*

Peter O'Toole, *The Ruling Class*

Paul Winfield, *Sounder*

BEST ACTRESS

Liza Minelli, *Cabaret*

Diana Ross, *Lady Sings the Blues*

Maggie Smith, *Travels With My Aunt*

Cicely Tyson, *Sounder*

Liv Ullman, *The Emigrants*

ACTOR IN A SUPPORTING ROLE

Eddie Albert, *The Heartbreak Kid*

James Caan, *The Godfather*

Robert Duvall, *The Godfather*

Joel Grey, *Cabaret*

Al Pacino, *The Godfather*

ACTRESS IN A SUPPORTING ROLE

Jeannie Berlin, *The Heartbreak Kid*

Eileen Heckart, *Butterflies Are Free*

Geraldine Page, *Pete 'n' Tillie*

Susan Tyrrell, *Fat City*

Shelley Winters, *The Poseidon Adventure*

DIRECTING

John Boorman, *Deliverance*

Francis Ford Coppola, *The Godfather*

Bob Fosse, *Cabaret*

Joseph L. Mankiewicz, *Sleuth*

Jan Troell, *The Emigrants*

WRITING

SCREENPLAY BASED ON MATERIAL FROM ANOTHER MEDIUM

Jay Allen, *Cabaret*

Lonne Elder, III, *Sounder*

Julius J. Epstein, *Pete 'n' Tillie*

Mario Puzo and Francis Ford Coppola, *The Godfather*

Jan Troell and Bengt Forslund, *The Emigrants*

ORIGINAL SCREENPLAY

Luis Buñuel, story and screenplay in collaboration with Jean-Claude Carrière, *The Discreet Charm of the Bourgeoisie*

Carl Foreman, *Young Winston*

Jeremy Larner, *The Candidate*

Louis Malle, *Murmur of the Heart*

Terence McCloy, Chris Clark and Suzanne de Passe, *Lady Sings the Blues*

CINEMATOGRAPHY

Charles B. Lang, *Butterflies Are Free*

Douglas Slocombe, *Travels With My Aunt*

Harold E. Stine, *The Poseidon Adventure*

Harry Stradling, Jr., *1776*

Geoffrey Unsworth, *Cabaret*

ART DIRECTION

Carl Anderson, art direction; Reg Allen, set decoration, *Lady Sings the Blues*

Don Ashton, Geoffrey Drake, John Graysmark and William Hutchinson, art direction; Peter James, set decoration, *Young Winston*

John Box, Gil Parrondo and Robert W. Laing, art direction and set decoration, *Travels With My Aunt*

William Creber, art direction; Raphael Bretton, set decoration, *The Poseidon Adventure*

Rolf Zehetbauer and Jurgen Kiebach, art direction; Herbert Strabel, set decoration, *Cabaret*

SOUND

Bud Grenzbach, Richard Portman and Christopher Newman, *The Godfather*

Robert Knudson and David Hildyard, *Cabaret*

Arthur Piantadosi and Charles Knight, *Butterflies Are Free*

Richard Portman and Gene Cantamessa, *The Candidate*

Theodore Soderberg and Herman Lewis, *The Poseidon Adventure*

MUSIC

SONG

"Ben," *Ben*, Walter Scharf, music; Don Black, lyrics

"Come Follow, Follow Me," *The Little Ark*, Fred Karlin, music; Marsha Karlin, lyrics

"Marmalade, Molasses & Honey," *The Life and Times of Judge Roy Bean*, Maurice Jarre, music; Marilyn and Alan Bergman, lyrics

"The Morning After," *The Poseidon Adventure*, Al Kasha and Joel Hirschhorn, music and lyrics

"Strange Are the Ways of Love," *The Stepmother*, Sammy Fain, music; Paul Francis Webster, lyrics

ORIGINAL DRAMATIC SCORE

John Addison, *Sleuth*

Buddy Baker, *Napoleon and Samantha*

Charles Chaplin, Raymond Rasch and Larry Russell, *Limelight*

John Williams, *Images*

John Williams, *The Poseidon Adventure*

SCORING: ADAPTATION AND ORIGINAL SCORE

Gil Askey, *Lady Sings the Blues*

Ralph Burns, *Cabaret*

Laurence Rosenthal, *Man of La Mancha*

FILM EDITING

David Bretherton, *Cabaret*

Frank P. Keller and Fred W. Berger, *The Hot Rock*

Harold F. Kress, *The Poseidon Adventure*

Tom Priestley, *Deliverance*

William Reynolds and Peter Zinner, *The Godfather*

COSTUME DESIGN

Anna Hill Johnstone, *The Godfather*

Bob Mackie, Ray Aghayan and Norma Koch, *Lady Sings the Blues*

Anthony Mendleson, *Young Winston*

Anthony Powell, *Travels With My Aunt*

Paul Zastupnevich, *The Poseidon Adventure*

SHORT SUBJECTS

ANIMATED

***A Christmas Carol* (Richard Williams Production; American Broadcasting Company Film Services)**

Kama Sutra Rides Again (Bob Godfrey Films, Ltd.; Lion International Films)

Tup Tup (Zagreb Film-Corona Cinematografica Production; Manson Distributing)

LIVE ACTION

Frog Story (Gidron Productions; Lester A. Schoenfeld Films)

***Norman Rockwell's World . . . An American Dream* (Concepts Unlimited; Columbia)**

Solo (Pyramid Films; United Artists)

DOCUMENTARY

SHORT SUBJECT

Hundertwasser's Rainy Day (Argos Films-Peter Schamoni Film Production)

K-Z (Giorgio Treves, producer; Nexus Film S.r.l. Production)

Selling Out (Tadeusz Jaworski, producer; Unit Productions Film)

***This Tiny World* (Charles Huguenot van der Linden and Martina Huguenot van der Linden, producers; Charles Huguenot van der Linden Production)**

The Tide of Traffic (Humphrey Swingler, producer; BP-Greenpark Production)

FEATURE

Ape and Super-Ape (Bert Haanstra Film Production; Netherlands Ministry of Culture, Recreation and Social Welfare)

Malcolm X (Marvin Worth Production; Warner Bros.)

Manson (Robert Hendrickson and Laurence Merrick, producers; Merrick International Pictures)

***Marjoe* (Cinema X Production; Cinema 5, Ltd.)**

The Silent Revolution (Eckehard Munck, producer; Leonaris Film Production)

FOREIGN LANGUAGE FILM

The Dawns Here Are Quiet, U.S.S.R.

***The Discreet Charm of the Bourgeoisie*, France**

I Love You Rosa, Israel

My Dearest Señorita, Spain

The New Land, Sweden

JEAN HERSHOLT HUMANITARIAN AWARD

Rosalind Russell

HONORARY AWARDS

To **Charles S. Boren,** leader for 38 years of the industry's enlightened labor relations and architect of its policy of nondiscrimination

To **Edward G. Robinson** who achieved greatness as a player, a patron of the arts and a dedicated citizen . . . in sum, a Renaissance man

SPECIAL ACHIEVEMENT AWARD

(Not necessarily given each year)

VISUAL EFFECTS

L. B. Abbott and A. D. Flowers, *The Poseidon Adventure*

1973

BEST PICTURE

American Graffiti, Francis Ford Coppola, producer; Gary Kurtz, co-producer (Universal)

Cries and Whispers, Ingmar Bergman, producer (New World Pictures)

The Exorcist, William Peter Blatty, producer (Warner Bros.)

The Sting, Tony Bill, Michael Phillips and Julia Phillips, producers (Universal)

A Touch of Class, Melvin Frank, producer (Avco Embassy)

BEST ACTOR

Marlon Brando, *Last Tango in Paris*

Jack Lemmon, *Save the Tiger*

Jack Nicholson, *The Last Detail*

Al Pacino, *Serpico*

Robert Redford, *The Sting*

BEST ACTRESS

Ellen Burstyn, *The Exorcist*

Glenda Jackson, *A Touch of Class*

Marsha Mason, *Cinderella Liberty*

Barbra Streisand, *The Way We Were*

Joanne Woodward, *Summer Wishes, Winter Dreams*

ACTOR IN A SUPPORTING ROLE

Vincent Gardenia, *Bang the Drum Slowly*

Jack Gilford, *Save the Tiger*

John Houseman, *The Paper Chase*

Jason Miller, *The Exorcist*

Randy Quaid, *The Last Detail*

ACTRESS IN A SUPPORTING ROLE

Linda Blair, *The Exorcist*

Candy Clark, *American Graffiti*

Madeline Kahn, *Paper Moon*

Tatum O'Neal, *Paper Moon*

Sylvia Sidney, *Summer Wishes, Winter Dreams*

DIRECTING

Ingmar Bergman, *Cries and Whispers*

Bernardo Bertolucci, *Last Tango in Paris*

William Friedkin, *The Exorcist*

George Roy Hill, *The Sting*

George Lucas, *American Graffiti*

WRITING

SCREENPLAY BASED ON MATERIAL FROM ANOTHER MEDIUM

William Peter Blatty, *The Exorcist*

James Bridges, *The Paper Chase*

Waldo Salt and Norman Wexler, *Serpico*

Alvin Sargent, *Paper Moon*

Robert Towne, *The Last Detail*

ORIGINAL SCREENPLAY

Ingmar Bergman, *Cries and Whispers*

Melvin Frank and Jack Rose, *A Touch of Class*

George Lucas, Gloria Katz and Willard Huyck, *American Grafitti*

Steve Shagan, *Save the Tiger*

David S. Ward, *The Sting*

CINEMATOGRAPHY

Jack Couffer, *Jonathan Livingston Seagull*

Sven Nykvist, *Cries and Whispers*

Owen Roizman, *The Exorcist*

Harry Stradling, Jr., *The Way We Were*

Robert Surtees, *The Sting*

ART DIRECTION

Henry Bumstead, art direction; James Payne, set decoration, *The Sting*

Stephen Grimes, art direction; William Kiernan, set decoration, *The Way We Were*

Philip Jefferies, art direction; Robert de Vestel, set decoration, *Tom Sawyer*

Bill Malley, art direction; Jerry Wunderlich, set decoration, *The Exorcist*

Lorenzo Mongiardino and Gianni Quaranta, art direction; Carmelo Patrono, set decoration, *Brother Sun Sister Moon*

SOUND

Robert Knudson and Chris Newman, *The Exorcist*

Donald O. Mitchell and Lawrence O. Jost, *The Paper Chase*

Ronald K. Pierce and Robert Bertrand, *The Sting*

Richard Portman and Les Fresholtz, *Paper Moon*

Richard Portman and Lawrence O. Jost, *The Day of the Dolphin*

MUSIC

SONG

"All That Love Went to Waste," *A Touch of Class*, George Barrie, music; Sammy Cahn, lyrics

"Live and Let Die," *Live and Let Die*, Paul McCartney and Linda McCartney, music and lyrics

"Love," *Robin Hood*, George Bruns, music; Floyd Huddleston, lyrics

"Nice to Be Around," *Cinderella Liberty*, John Williams, music; Paul Williams, lyrics

"The Way We Were," *The Way We Were*, Marvin Hamlisch, music; Alan and Marilyn Bergman, lyrics

ORIGINAL DRAMATIC SCORE

John Cameron, *A Touch of Class*

Georges Delerue, *The Day of the Dolphin*

Jerry Goldsmith, *Papillon*

Marvin Hamlisch, *The Way We Were*

John Williams, *Cinderella Liberty*

SCORING: ORIGINAL SONG SCORE AND ADAPTATION OR SCORING: ADAPTATION

Marvin Hamlisch, *The Sting*

André Previn, Herbert Spencer and Andrew Lloyd Webber, *Jesus Christ Superstar*

Richard M. Sherman and Robert B. Sherman, song; John Williams, adaptation, *Tom Sawyer*

Tatum O'Neal, *Paper Moon*

FILM EDITING

Verna Fields and Marcia Lucas, *American Graffiti*

Frank P. Keller and James Galloway, *Jonathan Livingston Seagull*

Ralph Kemplen, *The Day of the Jackal*

Jordan Leondopoulos, Bud Smith, Evan Lottman and Norman Gay, *The Exorcist*

William Reynolds, *The Sting*

COSTUME DESIGN

Donfeld, *Tom Sawyer*

Edith Head, *The Sting*

Dorothy Jeakins and Moss Mabry, *The Way We Were*

Piero Tosi, *Ludwig*

Marik Vos, *Cries and Whispers*

SHORT SUBJECTS

ANIMATED

***Frank Film* (Frank Mouris, producer; Frank Mouris Production)**

The Legend of John Henry (Nick Bosustow and David Adams, producers; Bosustow-Pyramid Films Production)

Pulcinella (Emanuele Luzzati and Guilio Gianini, producers; Luzzati-Gianini Production)

LIVE ACTION

The Bolero (Allan Miller and William Fertik, producers; Allan Miller Production)

Clockmaker (Richard Gayer, producer; James Street Productions)

Life Times Nine (Pen Densham and John Watson, producers; Insight Productions)

DOCUMENTARY

SHORT SUBJECT

Background (Carmen D'Avino, producer; D'Avino and Fucci-Stone Productions)

Children at Work (*Paisti Ag Obair*) (Louis Marcus, producer; Gael-Linn Films)

Christo's Valley Curtain (Albert Maysles and David Maysles, producers; Maysles Films Production)

Four Stones for Kanemitsu (Terry Sanders and June Wayne, producers; Tamarind Production)

***Princeton: A Search for Answers* (Julian Krainin and DeWitt L. Sage, Jr., producers; Krainin-Sage Productions)**

FEATURE

Always a New Beginning (John D. Goodell, producer; Goodell Motion Pictures)

Battle of Berlin (Bengt von zur Muehlen, producer; Chronos Film GmbH)

***The Great American Cowboy* (Keith Merrill, producer; Keith Merrill Associates-Rodeo Film Productions)**

Journey to the Outer Limits (Alex Grasshoff, producer; National Geographic Society and Wolper Productions)

Walls of Fire (Gertrude Ross Marks and Edmund F. Penney, producers; Mentor Productions)

FOREIGN LANGUAGE FILM

Day for Night, France

The House of Chelouche Street, Israel

L'Invitation, Switzerland

The Pedestrian, Federal Republic of Germany – West

Turkish Delight, Netherlands

IRVING G. THALBERG MEMORIAL AWARD

Lawrence Weingarten

JEAN HERSHOLT HUMANITARIAN AWARD

Lew Wasserman

HONORARY AWARDS

To **Henri Langlois** for his devotion to the art of film, his massive contributions to preserving its past and his unswerving faith in its future

To **Groucho Marx** in recognition of his brilliant creativity and for the unequalled acheivements of the Marx Brothers in the art of motion picture comedy

1974

BEST PICTURE

Chinatown, Robert Evans, producer (Paramount)

The Conversation, Francis Ford Coppola, producer (Paramount)

***The Godfather Part II*, Francis Ford Coppola, producer; Gray Frederickson and Fred Roos, co-producers (Paramount)**

Lenny, Marvin Worth, producer (United Artists)

The Towering Inferno, Irwin Allen, producer (Twentieth Century-Fox/Warner Bros.)

BEST ACTOR

Art Carney, *Harry and Tonto*

Albert Finney, *Murder on the Orient Express*

Dustin Hoffman, *Lenny*

Jack Nicholson, *Chinatown*

Al Pacino, *The Godfather Part II*

BEST ACTRESS

Ellen Burstyn, *Alice Doesn't Live Here Anymore*

Diahann Carroll, *Claudine*

Faye Dunaway, *Chinatown*

Valerie Perrine, *Lenny*

Gena Rowlands, *A Woman Under the Influence*

Robert De Niro, *The Godfather Part II*

ACTOR IN A SUPPORTING ROLE

Fred Astaire, *The Towering Inferno*

Jeff Bridges, *Thunderbolt and Lightfoot*

Robert De Niro, *The Godfather Part II*

Michael V. Gazzo, *The Godfather Part II*

Lee Strasberg, *The Godfather Part II*

ACTRESS IN A SUPPORTING ROLE

Ingrid Bergman, *Murder on the Orient Express*

Valentina Cortese, *Day for Night*

Madeline Kahn, *Blazing Saddles*

Diane Ladd, *Alice Doesn't Live Here Anymore*

Talia Shire, *The Godfather Part II*

DIRECTING

John Cassavetes, *A Woman Under the Influence*

Francis Ford Coppola, *The Godfather Part II*

Bob Fosse, *Lenny*

Roman Polanski, *Chinatown*

François Truffaut, *Day for Night*

WRITING

ORIGINAL SCREENPLAY

Francis Ford Coppola, *The Conversation*

Robert Getchell, *Alice Doesn't Live Here Anymore*

Paul Mazursky and Josh Greenfeld, *Harry and Tonto*

Robert Towne, *Chinatown*

François Truffaut, Jean-Louis Richard and Suzanne Schiffman, *Day for Night*

SCREENPLAY ADAPTED FROM OTHER MATERIAL

Julian Barry, *Lenny*

Paul Dehn, *Murder on the Orient Express*

Francis Ford Coppola and Mario Puzo, *The Godfather Part II*

Mordecai Richler, screenplay; Lionel Chetwynd, adaptation, *The Apprenticeship of Duddy Kravitz*

Gene Wilder and Mel Brooks, *Young Frankenstein*

CINEMATOGRAPHY

John A. Alonzo, *Chinatown*

Fred Koenekamp and Joseph Biroc, *The Towering Inferno*

Philip Lathrop, *Earthquake*

Bruce Surtees, *Lenny*

Geoffrey Unsworth, *Murder on the Orient Express*

ART DIRECTION

William Creber and Ward Preston, art direction; Raphael Bretton, set decoration, *The Towering Inferno*

Peter Ellenshaw, John B. Mansbridge, Walter Tyler and Al Roelofs, art direction; Hal Gausman, set decoration, *The Island at the Top of the World*

Alexander Golitzen and E. Preston Ames, art direction; Frank McKelvy, set decoration, *Earthquake*

Richard Sylbert and W. Stewart Campbell, art direction; Ruby Levitt, set decoartion, *Chinatown*

Dean Tavoularis and Angelo Graham, art direction; George R. Nelson, set decoration, *The Godfather Part II*

SOUND

Bud Grenzbach and Larry Jost, *Chinatown*

Walter Murch and Arthur Rochester, *The Conversation*

Ronald Pierce and Melvin Metcalfe, Sr., *Earthquake*

Richard Portman and Gene Cantamessa, *Young Frankenstein*

Theodore Soderberg and Herman Lewis, *The Towering Inferno*

MUSIC

SONG

"Benji's Theme" (I Feel Love), *Benji*, Euel Box, music; Betty Box, lyrics

"Blazing Saddles," *Blazing Saddles*, John Morris, music; Mel Brooks, lyrics

"Little Prince," *The Little Prince*, Frederick Loewe, music; Alan Jay Lerner, lyrics

"We May Never Love Like This Again," *The Towering Inferno*, Al Kasha and Joel Hirschhorn, music and lyrics

"Wherever Love Takes Me," *Gold*, Elmer Bernstein, music; Don Black, lyrics

ORIGINAL DRAMATIC SCORE

Richard Rodney Bennett, *Murder on the Orient Express*

Jerry Goldsmith, *Chinatown*

Alex North, *Shanks*

Nino Rota and Carmine Coppola, *The Godfather Part II*

John Williams, *The Towering Inferno*

SCORING: ORIGINAL SONG SCORE AND ADAPTATION OR SCORING: ADAPTATION

Alan Jay Lerner and Frederick Loewe, song; Angela Morley and Douglas Gamley, adaptation, *The Little Prince*

Nelson Riddle, adaptation, *The Great Gatsby*

Paul Williams, song; George Aliceson Tipton and Paul Williams, adaptation, *Phantom of the Paradise*

FILM EDITING

John C. Howard and Danford Greene, *Blazing Saddles*

Harold F. Kress and Carl Kress, *The Towering Inferno*

Michael Luciano, *The Longest Yard*

Sam O'Steen, *Chinatown*

Dorothy Spencer, *Earthquake*

COSTUME DESIGN

Theoni V. Aldredge, *The Great Gatsby*

John Furness, *Daisy Miller*

Anthea Sylbert, *Chinatown*

Theadora Van Runkle, *The Godfather Part II*

Tony Walton, *Murder on the Orient Express*

SHORT FILMS

ANIMATED

***Closed Mondays* (Will Vinton and Bob Gardiner, producers; Lighthouse Productions)**

The Family That Dwelt Apart (Yvon Mallette and Robert Verrall, producers; National Film Board of Canada)

Hunger (Peter Foldes and René Jodoin, producers; National Film Board of Canada)

Voyage to Next (Faith Hubley and John Hubley, producers; Hubley Studios)

Winnie the Pooh and Tigger Too (Wolfgang Reitherman, producer; Walt Disney Productions)

LIVE ACTION

Climb (Dewitt Jones, producer; Dewitt Jones Productions)

The Concert (Julian and Claude Chagrin, producers; The Black and White Colour Film Company, Ltd.)

***One-Eyed Men Are Kings* (Paul Claudon and Edmond Sechan, producers; C.A.P.A.C. Productions)**

Planet Ocean (George V. Casey, producer; Graphic Films)

The Violin (Andrew Welsh and George Pastic, producers; Sincinkin, Ltd.)

DOCUMENTARY

SHORT SUBJECT

City Out of Wilderness (Francis Thompson, producer; Francis Thompson Inc.)

***Don't* (Robin Lehman, producer; R. A. Films)**

Exploratorium (Jon Boorstin, producer; Jon Boorstin Production)

John Muir's High Sierra (Dewitt Jones and Lesley Foster, producers; Dewitt Jones Productions)

Naked Yoga (Ronald S. Kass and Mervyn Lloyd, producers; Filmshop Production)

FEATURE

Antonia: A Portrait of the Woman (Judy Collins and Jill Godmilow, producers; Rocky Mountain Productions)

The Challenge . . . A Tribute to Modern Art (Herbert Kline, producer; World View Production)

The 81st Blow (Jacquot Ehrlich, David Bergman and Haim Gouri, producers; Ghetto Fighters House Film)

***Hearts and Minds* (Touchstone-Audjeff-BBS Production; Howard Zucker/Henry Jaglom-Rainbow Pictures Presentation)**

The Wild and the Brave (E.S.J. Productions in association with Tomorrow Entertainment Inc. and Jones/Howard Ltd.)

FOREIGN LANGUAGE FILM

***Amarcord*, Italy**

Cats' Play, Hungary

The Deluge, Poland

Lacombe, Lucien, France

The Truce, Argentina

JEAN HERSHOLT HUMANITARIAN AWARD

Arthur B. Krim

HONORARY AWARDS

To **Howard Hawks,** a master American filmmaker whose creative efforts hold a distinguished place in world cinema

To **Jean Renoir,** a genius who, with grace, responsibility and enviable devotion through silent film, sound film, feature, documentary and television, has won the world's admiration

SPECIAL ACHIEVEMENT AWARD

VISUAL EFFECTS

Frank Brendel, Glen Robinson and Albert Whitlock, *Earthquake*

1975

BEST PICTURE

Barry Lyndon, Stanley Kubrick, producer (Warner Bros.)

Dog Day Afternoon, Martin Bregman and Martin Elfand, producers (Warner Bros.)

Jaws, Richard D. Zanuck and David Brown, producers (Universal)

Nashville, Robert Altman, producer (Paramount)

***One Flew Over the Cuckoo's Nest*, Saul Zaentz and Michael Douglas, producers (United Artists)**

BEST ACTOR

Walter Matthau, *The Sunshine Boys*

Jack Nicholson, *One Flew Over the Cuckoo's Nest*

Al Pacino, *Dog Day Afternoon*

Maximilian Schell, *The Man in the Glass Booth*

James Whitmore, *Give 'em Hell, Harry!*

BEST ACTRESS

Isabelle Adjani, *The Story of Adele H.*

Louise Fletcher, *One Flew Over the Cuckoo's Nest*

Glenda Jackson, *Hedda*

Carol Kane, *Hester Street*

Ann-Margret, *Tommy*

**Jack Nicholson,
*One Flew Over the Cuckoo's Nest***

ACTOR IN A SUPPORTING ROLE
George Burns, *The Sunshine Boys*

Brad Dourif, *One Flew Over the Cuckoo's Nest*

Burgess Meredith, *The Day of the Locust*

Chris Sarandon, *Dog Day Afternoon*

Jack Warden, *Shampoo*

ACTRESS IN A SUPPORTING ROLE
Ronee Blakley, *Nashville*

Lee Grant, *Shampoo*

Sylvia Miles, *Farewell, My Lovely*

Lily Tomlin, *Nashville*

Brenda Vaccaro, *Jacqueline Susann's Once Is Not Enough*

DIRECTING
Robert Altman, *Nashville*

Federico Fellini, *Amarcord*

Milos Forman, *One Flew Over the Cuckoo's Nest*

Stanley Kubrick, *Barry Lyndon*

Sidney Lumet, *Dog Day Afternoon*

WRITING
ORIGINAL SCREENPLAY
Ted Allan, *Lies My Father Told Me*

Federico Fellini and Tonino Guerra, *Amarcord*

Claude Lelouch and Pierre Uytterhoeven, *And Now My Love*

Frank Pierson, *Dog Day Afternoon*

Robert Towne and Warren Beatty, *Shampoo*

SCREENPLAY ADAPTED FROM OTHER MATERIAL
Lawrence Hauben and Bo Goldman, *One Flew Over the Cuckoo's Nest*

John Huston and Gladys Hill, *The Man Who Would Be King*

Stanley Kubrick, *Barry Lyndon*

Ruggero Maccari and Dino Risi, *Scent of a Woman*

Neil Simon, *The Sunshine Boys*

CINEMATOGRAPHY
John Alcott, *Barry Lyndon*

Conrad Hall, *The Day of the Locust*

James Wong Howe, *Funny Lady*

Robert Surtees, *The Hindenburg*

Haskell Wexler and Bill Butler, *One Flew Over the Cuckoo's Nest*

ART DIRECTION
Ken Adam and Roy Walker, art direction; Vernon Dixon, set decoration, *Barry Lyndon*

Albert Brenner, art direction; Marvin March, set decoration, *The Sunshine Boys*

Edward Carfagno, art direction; Frank McKelvy, set decoration, *The Hindenburg*

Richard Sylbert and W. Stewart Campbell, art direction; George Gaines, set decoration, *Shampoo*

Alexander Trauner and Tony Inglis, art direction; Peter James, set decoration, *The Man Who Would Be King*

SOUND
Robert L. Hoyt, Roger Heman, Earl Madery and John Carter, *Jaws*

Leonard Peterson, John A. Bolger, Jr., John Mack and Don K. Sharpless, *The Hindenburg*

Arthur Piantadosi, Les Fresholtz, Richard Tyler and Al Overton, Jr., *Bite the Bullet*

Richard Portman, Don MacDougall, Curly Thirlwell and Jack Solomon, *Funny Lady*

Harry W. Tetrick, Aaron Rochin, William McCaughey and Roy Charman, *The Wind and the Lion*

MUSIC
ORIGINAL SONG
"How Lucky Can You Get," *Funny Lady*, Fred Ebb and John Kander, music and lyrics

"I'm Easy," *Nashville*, **Keith Carradine, music and lyrics**

"Now That We're in Love," *Whiffs*, George Barrie, music; Sammy Cahn, lyrics

"Richard's Window," *The Other Side of the Mountain*, Charles Fox, music; Norman Gimbel, lyrics

"Theme From *Mahogany*" (Do You Know Where You're Going To), *Mahogany*, Michael Masser, music; Gerry Goffin, lyrics

ORIGINAL SCORE
Gerald Fried, *Birds Do It, Bees Do It*

Jerry Goldsmith, *The Wind and the Lion*

Jack Nitzsche, *One Flew Over the Cuckoo's Nest*

Alex North, *Bite the Bullet*

John Williams, *Jaws*

SCORING: ORIGINAL SONG SCORE AND ADAPTATION OR SCORING: ADAPTATION
Peter Matz, *Funny Lady*

Leonard Rosenman, *Barry Lyndon*

Peter Townshend, *Tommy*

FILM EDITING
Dede Allen, *Dog Day Afternoon*

Richard Chew, Lynzee Klingman and Sheldon Kahn, *One Flew Over the Cuckoo's Nest*

Verna Fields, *Jaws*

Russell Lloyd, *The Man Who Would Be King*

Frederic Steinkamp and Don Guidice, *Three Days of the Condor*

COSTUME DESIGN
Ray Aghayan and Bob Mackie, *Funny Lady*

Yvonne Blake and Ron Talsky, *The Four Musketeers*

Edith Head, *The Man Who Would Be King*

Henny Noremark and Karin Erskine, *The Magic Flute*

Ulla-Britt Soderlund and Milena Canonero, *Barry Lyndon*

SHORT FILMS
ANIMATED
Great (Grantstern Ltd.; British Lion Films Ltd.)

Kick Me (Robert Swarthe, producer; Robert Swarthe Productions)

Monsieur Pointu (René Jodoin, Bernard Longpré and André Leduc, producers; National Film Board of Canada)

Sisyphus (Marcell Jankovics, producer; Hungarofilms)

LIVE ACTION

Angel and Big Joe **(Bert Salzman, producer; Bert Salzman Productions)**

Conquest of Light (Louis Marcus, producer; Louis Marcus Films Ltd.)

Dawn Flight (Lawrence M. Lansburgh and Brian Lansburgh, producers; Lawrence M. Lansburgh Productions)

A Day in the Life of Bonnie Consolo (Barry Spinello, producer; Barr Films)

Doubletalk (Alan Beattie, producer; Beattie Productions)

DOCUMENTARY

SHORT SUBJECT

Arthur and Lillie (Jon Else, Steven Kovacs and Kristine Samuelson, producers; Stanford University Department of Communication)

The End of the Game **(Claire Wilbur and Robin Lehman, producers; Opus Films Ltd.)**

Millions of Years Ahead of Man (Manfred Baier, producer; BASF)

Probes in Space (George V. Casey, producer; Graphic Films)

Whistling Smith (Barrie Howells and Michael Scott, producers; National Film Board of Canada)

FEATURE

The California Reich (Walter F. Parkes and Keith F. Critchlow, producers; Yasny Talking Pictures)

Fighting for Our Lives (Glen Pearcy, producer; Farm Worker Film)

The Incredible Machine (National Geographic Society and Wolper Productions)

The Man Who Skied Down Everest **(F. R. Crawley, James Hager and Dale Hartleben, producers; Crawley Films Presentation)**

The Other Half of the Sky: A China Memoir (Shirley MacLaine, producer; MacLaine Productions)

FOREIGN LANGUAGE FILM

Dersu Uzala, **U.S.S.R.**

Land of Promise, Poland

Letters From Marusia, Mexico

Sandakan No. 8, Japan

Scent of a Woman, Italy

IRVING G. THALBERG MEMORIAL AWARD

Mervyn LeRoy

JEAN HERSHOLT HUMANITARIAN AWARD

Dr. Jules C. Stein

HONORARY AWARD

To **Mary Pickford** in recognition of her unique contributions to the film industry and the development of film as an artistic medium

SPECIAL ACHIEVEMENT AWARDS

SOUND EFFECTS

Peter Berkos, *The Hindenburg*

VISUAL EFFECTS

Albert Whitlock and Glen Robinson, *The Hindenburg*

1976

BEST PICTURE

All the President's Men, Walter Coblenz, producer (Warner Bros.)

Bound for Glory, Robert F. Blumofe and Harold Leventhal, producers (United Artists)

Network, Howard Gottfried, producer (MGM/United Artists)

Rocky, **Irwin Winkler and Robert Chartoff, producers (United Artists)**

Taxi Driver, Michael Phillips and Julia Phillips, producers (Columbia)

BEST ACTOR

Robert De Niro, *Taxi Driver*

Peter Finch, *Network*

Giancarlo Giannini, *Seven Beauties*

William Holden, *Network*

Sylvester Stallone, *Rocky*

BEST ACTRESS

Marie-Christine Barrault, *Cousin, Cousine*

Faye Dunaway, *Network*

Talia Shire, *Rocky*

Sissy Spacek, *Carrie*

Liv Ullman, *Face to Face*

ACTOR IN A SUPPORTING ROLE

Ned Beatty, *Network*

Burgess Meredith, *Rocky*

Laurence Olivier, *Marathon Man*

Jason Robards, *All the President's Men*

Burt Young, *Rocky*

ACTRESS IN A SUPPORTING ROLE

Jane Alexander, *All the President's Men*

Jodie Foster, *Taxi Driver*

Lee Grant, *Voyage of the Damned*

Piper Laurie, *Carrie*

Beatrice Straight, *Network*

Rocky

DIRECTING

John G. Avildsen, *Rocky*

Ingmar Bergman, *Face to Face*

Sidney Lumet, *Network*

Alan J. Pakula, *All the President's Men*

Lina Wertmuller, *Seven Beauties*

WRITING

ORIGINAL SCREENPLAY

Walter Bernstein, *The Front*

Paddy Chayefsky, *Network*

Sylvester Stallone, *Rocky*

Jean-Charles Tacchella, story and screenplay; Daniele Thompson, adaptation, *Cousin, Cousine*

Lina Wertmuller, *Seven Beauties*

SCREENPLAY BASED ON MATERIAL FROM ANOTHER MEDIUM

Federico Fellini and Bernadino Zapponi, *Fellini's Casanova*

Robert Getchell, *Bound for Glory*

William Goldman, *All the President's Men*

Nicholas Meyer, *The Seven-Per-Cent Solution*

Steve Shagan and David Butler, *Voyage of the Damned*

CINEMATOGRAPHY

Richard H. Kline, *King Kong*

Ernest Laszlo, *Logan's Run*

Owen Roizman, *Network*

Robert Surtees, *A Star Is Born*

Haskell Wexler, *Bound for Glory*

ART DIRECTION

Robert F. Boyle, art direction; Arthur Jeph Parker, set decoration, *The Shootist*

Gene Callahan and Jack Collis, art direction; Jerry Wunderlich, set decoration, *The Last Tycoon*

Dale Hennesy, art direction; Robert de Vestel, set decoration, *Logan's Run*

George Jenkins, art direction; George Gaines, set decoration, *All the President's Men*

Elliot Scott and Norman Reynolds, art direction; Peter Howitt, set decoration, *The Incredible Sarah*

SOUND

Robert Knudson, Dan Wallin, Robert Glass and Tom Overton, *A Star Is Born*

Donald Mitchell, Douglas Williams, Richard Tyler and Hal Etherington, *Silver Streak*

Arthur Piantadosi, Les Fresholtz, Dick Alexander and Jim Webb, *All the President's Men*

Harry Warren Tetrick, William McCaughey, Aaron Rochin and Jack Solomon, *King Kong*

Harry Warren Tetrick, William McCaughey, Lyle Burbridge and Bud Alper, *Rocky*

MUSIC

ORIGINAL SONG

"Ave Satani," *The Omen*, Jerry Goldsmith, music and lyrics

"Come to Me," *The Pink Panther Strikes Again*, Henry Mancini, music; Don Black, lyrics

"Evergreen" (Love Theme From *A Star Is Born*), *A Star Is Born*, Barbra Streisand, music; Paul Williams, lyrics

"Gonna Fly Now," *Rocky*, Bill Conti, music; Carol Connors and Ayn Robbins, lyrics

"A World That Never Was," *Half a House*, Sammy Fain, music; Paul Francis Webster, lyrics

ORIGINAL SCORE

Jerry Fielding, *The Outlaw Josey Wales*

Jerry Goldsmith, *The Omen*

Bernard Herrmann, *Obsession*

Bernard Herrmann, *Taxi Driver*

Lalo Schifrin, *Voyage of the Damned*

ORIGINAL SONG SCORE AND ITS ADAPTATION OR ADAPTATION SCORE

Roger Kellaway, *A Star Is Born*

Leonard Rosenman, *Bound for Glory*

Paul Williams, *Bugsy Malone*

FILM EDITING

Richard Halsey and Scott Conrad, *Rocky*

Alan Heim, *Network*

Robert Jones and Pembroke J. Herring, *Bound for Glory*

Eve Newman and Walter Hannemann, *Two-Minute Warning*

Robert L. Wolfe, *All the President's Men*

COSTUME DESIGN

Alan Barrett, *The Seven-Per-Cent Solution*

Danilo Donati, *Fellini's Casanova*

Anthony Mendleson, *The Incredible Sarah*

William Theiss, *Bound for Glory*

Mary Wills, *The Passover Plot*

SHORT FILMS

ANIMATED

Dedalo (Manfredo Manfredi, producer; Cineteam Realizzazioni Production)

***Leisure* (Suzanne Baker, producer; Film Australia Production)**

The Street (Caroline Leaf and Guy Glover, producers; National Film Board of Canada)

LIVE ACTION

***In the Region of Ice* (Andre Guttfreund and Peter Werner, producers; American Film Institute)**

Kudzu (Marjorie Ann Short, producer; Short Productions)

The Morning Spider (Julian Chagrin and Claude Chagrin, producers; The Black and White Colour Film Company)

Nightlife (Claire Wilbur and Robin Lehman, producers; Opus Films Ltd.)

Number One (Dyan Cannon and Vince Cannon, producers; Number One Productions)

DOCUMENTARY

SHORT SUBJECT

American Shoeshine (Sparky Greene, producer; Titan Films)

Blackwood (Tony Ianzelo and Andy Thompson, producers; National Film Board of Canada)

The End of the Road (John Armstrong, producer; Pelican Films)

***Number Our Days* (Lynne Littman, producer; Community Television of Southern California)**

Universe (Lester Novros, producer; Graphic Films Corporation for NASA)

FEATURE

Harlan County, U.S.A. (Barbara Kopple, producer; Cabin Creek Films)

Hollywood on Trial (James Gutman and David Helpern, Jr., producers; October Films/Cinema Associates)

Off the Edge (Michael Firth, producer; Pentacle Films)

People of the Wind (Anthony Howarth and David Koff, producers; Elizabeth E. Rogers Productions)

Volcano: An Inquiry Into the Life and Death of Malcolm Lowry (Donald Brittain and Robert Duncan, producers; National Film Board of Canada)

FOREIGN LANGUAGE FILM

Black and White in Color, Ivory Coast

Cousin, Cousine, France

Jacob, the Liar, German Democratic Republic – East

Nights and Days, Poland

Seven Beauties, Italy

IRVING G. THALBERG MEMORIAL AWARD

Pandro S. Berman

SPECIAL ACHIEVEMENT AWARDS

VISUAL EFFECTS

Carlo Rambaldi, Glen Robinson and Frank Van der Veer, *King Kong*

VISUAL EFFECTS

L.B. Abbott, Glen Robinson and Matthew Yuricich, *Logan's Run*

1977

BEST PICTURE

Annie Hall, Charles H. Joffe, producer (United Artists)

The Goodbye Girl, Ray Stark, producer (MGM/Warner Bros.)

Julia, Richard Roth, producer (Twentieth Century-Fox)

Star Wars, Gary Kurtz, producer (Twentieth Century-Fox)

The Turning Point, Herbert Ross and Arthur Laurents, producers (Twentieth Century-Fox)

ACTOR IN A LEADING ROLE

Woody Allen, *Annie Hall*

Richard Burton, *Equus*

Richard Dreyfuss, *The Goodbye Girl*

Marcello Mastroianni, *A Special Day*

John Travolta, *Saturday Night Fever*

ACTRESS IN A LEADING ROLE

Anne Bancroft, *The Turning Point*

Jane Fonda, *Julia*

Diane Keaton, *Annie Hall*

Shirley MacLaine, *The Turning Point*

Marsha Mason, *The Goodbye Girl*

ACTOR IN A SUPPORTING ROLE

Mikhail Baryshnikov, *The Turning Point*

Peter Firth, *Equus*

Alec Guinness, *Star Wars*

Jason Robards, *Julia*

Maximilian Schell, *Julia*

ACTRESS IN A SUPPORTING ROLE

Leslie Browne, *The Turning Point*

Quinn Cummings, *The Goodbye Girl*

Melinda Dillon, *Close Encounters of the Third Kind*

Vanessa Redgrave, *Julia*

Tuesday Weld, *Looking for Mr. Goodbar*

DIRECTING

Woody Allen, *Annie Hall*

George Lucas, *Star Wars*

Herbert Ross, *The Turning Point*

Steven Spielberg, *Close Encounters of the Third Kind*

Fred Zinnemann, *Julia*

WRITING

ORIGINAL SCREENPLAY

Woody Allen and Marshall Brickman, *Annie Hall*

Robert Benton, *The Late Show*

Arthur Laurents, *The Turning Point*

George Lucas, *Star Wars*

Neil Simon, *The Goodbye Girl*

SCREENPLAY BASED ON MATERIAL FROM ANOTHER MEDIUM

Luis Buñuel and Jean-Claude Carrière, *That Obscure Object of Desire*

Larry Gelbart, *Oh, God!*

Gavin Lambert and Lewis John Carlino, *I Never Promised You a Rose Garden*

Alvin Sargent, *Julia*

Peter Shaffer, *Equus*

CINEMATOGRAPHY

William A. Fraker, *Looking for Mr. Goodbar*

Fred J. Koenekamp, *Islands in the Stream*

Douglas Slocombe, *Julia*

Robert Surtees, *The Turning Point*

Vilmos Zsigmond, *Close Encounters of the Third Kind*

Woody Allen

ART DIRECTION

Ken Adam and Peter Lamont, art direction; Hugh Scaife, set decoration, *The Spy Who Loved Me*

Joe Alves and Dan Lomino, art direction; Phil Abramson, set decoration, *Close Encounters of the Third Kind*

John Barry, Norman Reynolds and Leslie Dilley, art direction; Roger Christian, set decoration, *Star Wars*

Albert Brenner, art direction; Marvin March, set decoration, *The Turning Point*

George C. Webb, art direction; Mickey S. Michaels, set decoration, *Airport '77*

SOUND

Walter Goss, Dick Alexander, Tom Beckert and Robin Gregory, *The Deep*

Robert Knudson, Robert J. Glass, Don MacDougall and Gene S. Cantamessa, *Close Encounters of the Third Kind*

Robert Knudson, Robert J. Glass, Richard Tyler and Jean-Louis Ducarme, *Sorcerer*

Don MacDougall, Ray West, Bob Minkler and Derek Ball, *Star Wars*

Theodore Soderberg, Paul Wells, Douglas O. Williams and Jerry Jost, *The Turning Point*

MUSIC

ORIGINAL SONG

"Candle on the Water," *Pete's Dragon,* Al Kasha and Joel Hirschhorn, music and lyrics

"Nobody Does It Better," *The Spy Who Loved Me,* Marvin Hamlisch, music; Carole Bayer Sager, lyrics

"The Slipper and the Rose Waltz" (He Danced With Me/She Danced With Me), *The Slipper and the Rose — The Story of Cinderella,* Richard M. Sherman and Robert B. Sherman, music and lyrics

"Someone's Waiting for You," *The Rescuers,* Sammy Fain, music; Carol Connors and Ayn Robbins, lyrics

"You Light Up My Life," *You Light Up My Life,* Joseph Brooks, music and lyrics

ORIGINAL SCORE

Georges Delerue, *Julia*

Marvin Hamlisch, *The Spy Who Loved Me*

Maurice Jarre, *Mohammad — Messenger of God*

John Williams, *Close Encounters of the Third Kind*

John Williams, *Star Wars*

ORIGINAL SONG SCORE AND ITS ADAPTATION OR ADAPTATION SCORE

Al Kasha and Joel Hirschhorn, song; Irwin Kostal, adaptation, *Pete's Dragon*

Richard M. Sherman and Robert B. Sherman, song; Angela Morley, adaptation, *The Slipper and the Rose — The Story of Cinderella*

Jonathan Tunick, *A Little Night Music*

FILM EDITING

Walter Hannemann and Angelo Ross, *Smokey and the Bandit*

Paul Hirsch, Marcia Lucas and Richard Chew, *Star Wars*

Michael Kahn, *Close Encounters of the Third Kind*

Walter Murch, *Julia*

William Reynolds, *The Turning Point*

COSTUME DESIGN

Edith Head and Burton Miller, *Airport '77*

Florence Klotz, *A Little Night Music*

John Mollo, *Star Wars*

Irene Sharaff, *The Other Side of Midnight*

Anthea Sylbert, *Julia*

VISUAL EFFECTS

Roy Arbogast, Douglas Trumbull, Matthew Yuricich, Gregory Jein and Richard Yuricich, *Close Encounters of the Third Kind*

John Stears, John Dykstra, Richard Edlund, Grant McCune and Robert Blalack, *Star Wars*

SHORT FILMS

ANIMATED

The Bead Game (Ishu Patel, producer; National Film Board of Canada)

The Doonesbury Special (John Hubley, Faith Hubley and Garry Trudeau, producers; Hubley Studios)

Jimmy the C (James Picker, Robert Grossman and Craig Whitaker, producers; Motionpicker Production)

***The Sand Castle* (Co Hoedeman, producer; National Film Board of Canada)**

LIVE ACTION

The Absent-Minded Waiter (William E. McEuen, producer; Aspen Film Society)

Floating Free (Jerry Butts, producer; Trans World International)

***I'll Find a Way* (Beverly Shaffer and Yuki Yoshida, producers; National Film Board of Canada)**

Notes on the Popular Arts (Saul Bass, producer; Saul Bass Films)

Spaceborne (Philip Dauber, producer; Lawrence Hall of Science Production for the Regents of the University of California with the cooperation of NASA)

DOCUMENTARY

SHORT SUBJECT

Agueda Martinez: Our People, Our Country (Moctesuma Esparza, producer; Moctesuma Esparza Production)

First Edition (Helen Whitney and DeWitt L. Sage, Jr., producers; D.L. Sage Productions)

***Gravity Is My Enemy* (John Joseph and Jan Stussy, producers; John Joseph Production)**

Of Time, Tombs and Treasure (James R. Messenger and Paul N. Raimondi, producers; Charlie/Papa Productions, Inc.)

The Shetland Experience (Douglas Gordon, producer; Balfour Films)

FEATURE

The Children of Theatre Street (Robert Dornhelm and Earle Mack, producers; Mack-Vaganova Company)

High Grass Circus (Bill Brind, Torben Schioler and Tony Ianzelo, producers; National Film Board of Canada)

Homage to Chagall — The Colours of Love (Harry Rasky, producer; CBC Production)

Union Maids (James Klein, Julia Reichert and Miles Mogulescu, producers; Klein, Reichert, Mogulescu Production)

***Who Are the DeBolts? And Where Did They Get Nineteen Kids?* (Korty Films and Charles M. Schulz Creative Associates in association with Sanrio Films)**

FOREIGN LANGUAGE FILM
Iphigenia, Greece
Madame Rosa, France
Operation Thunderbolt, Israel
A Special Day, Italy
That Obscure Object of Desire, Spain

IRVING G. THALBERG MEMORIAL AWARD
Walter Mirisch

JEAN HERSHOLT HUMANITARIAN AWARD
Charlton Heston

HONORARY AWARDS
To **Margaret Booth** for her exceptional contribution to the art
of film editing in the motion picture industry

To **Gordon E. Sawyer** in appreciation for outstanding service
and dedication in upholding the high standards of the
Academy of Motion Picture Arts and Sciences

To **Sidney P. Solow** in appreciation for outstanding service
and dedication in upholding the high standards of the
Academy of Motion Picture Arts and Sciences

SPECIAL ACHIEVEMENT AWARDS
SOUND EFFECTS EDITING
Frank E. Warner, *Close Encounters of the Third Kind*

To **Benjamin Burtt, Jr.** for the creation of the alien, creature
and robot voices in *Star Wars*

1978

BEST PICTURE
Coming Home, Jerome Hellman, producer (United Artists)
The Deer Hunter, **Barry Spikings, Michael Deeley, Michael**
Cimino and John Peverall, producers (Universal)
Heaven Can Wait, Warren Beatty, producer (Paramount)
Midnight Express, Alan Marshall and David Puttnam,
producers (Columbia)
An Unmarried Woman, Paul Mazursky and Tony Ray,
producers (Twentieth Century-Fox)

ACTOR IN A LEADING ROLE
Warren Beatty, *Heaven Can Wait*
Gary Busey, *The Buddy Holly Story*
Robert De Niro, *The Deer Hunter*
Laurence Olivier, *The Boys From Brazil*
Jon Voight, Coming Home

ACTRESS IN A LEADING ROLE
Ingrid Bergman, *Autumn Sonata*
Ellen Burstyn, *Same Time, Next Year*
Jill Clayburgh, *An Unmarried Woman*
Jane Fonda, Coming Home
Geraldine Page, *Interiors*

Christopher Walken, *The Deer Hunter*

ACTOR IN A SUPPORTING ROLE
Bruce Dern, *Coming Home*
Richard Farnsworth, *Comes a Horseman*
John Hurt, *Midnight Express*
Christopher Walken, The Deer Hunter
Jack Warden, *Heaven Can Wait*

ACTRESS IN A SUPPORTING ROLE
Dyan Cannon, *Heaven Can Wait*
Penelope Milford, *Coming Home*
Maggie Smith, California Suite
Maureen Stapleton, *Interiors*
Meryl Streep, *The Deer Hunter*

DIRECTING
Woody Allen, *Interiors*
Hal Ashby, *Coming Home*
Warren Beatty and Buck Henry, *Heaven Can Wait*
Michael Cimino, The Deer Hunter
Alan Parker, *Midnight Express*

WRITING
SCREENPLAY WRITTEN DIRECTLY FOR THE
SCREEN
Woody Allen, *Interiors*
Ingmar Bergman, *Autumn Sonata*
Michael Cimino, Deric Washburn, Louis Garfinkle and
Quinn K. Redeker, story; Deric Washburn, screenplay,
The Deer Hunter
Nancy Dowd, story; Waldo Salt and Robert C. Jones,
screenplay, Coming Home
Paul Mazursky, *An Unmarried Woman*

SCREENPLAY BASED ON MATERIAL FROM
ANOTHER MEDIUM
Elaine May and Warren Beatty, *Heaven Can Wait*
Walter Newman, *Bloodbrothers*
Neil Simon, *California Suite*
Bernard Slade, *Same Time, Next Year*
Oliver Stone, Midnight Express

CINEMATOGRAPHY

Nestor Almendros, *Days of Heaven*
William A. Fraker, *Heaven Can Wait*
Oswald Morris, *The Wiz*
Robert Surtees, *Same Time, Next Year*
Vilmos Zsigmond, *The Deer Hunter*

ART DIRECTION

Mel Bourne, art direction; Daniel Robert, set decoration,
    Interiors
Albert Brenner, art direction; Marvin March, set decoration,
    California Suite
Paul Sylbert and Edwin O'Donovan, art direction; George
    Gaines, set decoration, *Heaven Can Wait*
Dean Tavoularis and Angelo Graham, art direction; George R.
    Nelson and Bruce Kay, set decoration, *The Brink's Job*
Tony Walton and Philip Rosenberg, art direction; Edward
    Stewart and Robert Drumheller, set decoration, *The Wiz*

SOUND

Robert Knudson, Robert J. Glass, Don MacDougall and
    Jack Solomon, *Hooper*
Gordon K. McCallum, Graham Hartstone, Nicholas Le
    Messurier and Roy Charman, *Superman*
Richard Portman, William McCaughey, Aaron Rochin and
    Darin Knight, *The Deer Hunter*
Tex Rudloff, Joel Fein, Curly Thirlwell and Willie Burton,
    The Buddy Holly Story
John K. Wilkinson, Robert W. Glass, Jr., John T. Reitz and
    Barry Thomas, *Days of Heaven*

MUSIC

ORIGINAL SONG

"Hopelessly Devoted to You," *Grease*, John Farrar, music
    and lyrics
"Last Dance," *Thank God It's Friday*, Paul Jabara, music
    and lyrics
"The Last Time I Felt Like This," *Same Time, Next Year*, Marvin
    Hamlisch, music; Alan and Marilyn Bergman, lyrics
"Ready to Take a Chance Again," *Foul Play*, Charles Fox,
    music; Norman Gimbel, lyrics
"When You're Loved," *The Magic of Lassie*, Richard M.
    Sherman and Robert B. Sherman, music and lyrics

ORIGINAL SCORE

Jerry Goldsmith, *The Boys From Brazil*
Dave Grusin, *Heaven Can Wait*
Giorgio Moroder, *Midnight Express*
Ennio Morricone, *Days of Heaven*
John Williams, *Superman*

ADAPTATION SCORE

Quincy Jones, *The Wiz*
Joe Renzetti, *The Buddy Holly Story*
Jerry Wexler, *Pretty Baby*

FILM EDITING

Stuart Baird, *Superman*
Gerry Hambling, *Midnight Express*
Robert E. Swink, *The Boys From Brazil*
Don Zimmerman, *Coming Home*
Peter Zinner, *The Deer Hunter*

COSTUME DESIGN

Renie Conley, *Caravans*
Patricia Norris, *Days of Heaven*
Anthony Powell, *Death on the Nile*
Tony Walton, *The Wiz*
Paul Zastupnevich, *The Swarm*

SHORT FILMS

ANIMATED

Oh My Darling (Nico Crama, producer; Nico Crama
    Productions)
Rip Van Winkle (Will Vinton, producer; Will Vinton Productions)
***Special Delivery* (Eunice Macaulay and John Weldon, pro-**
    ducers; National Film Board of Canada)

LIVE ACTION

A Different Approach (Jim Belcher and Fern Field, producers;
    Jim Belcher/Brookfield Production)
Mandy's Grandmother (Andrew Sugerman, producer;
    Illumination Films)
Strange Fruit (Seth Pinsker, producer; American Film Institute)
***Teenage Father* (Taylor Hackford, producer; New Visions Inc.**
    for the Children's Home Society of California)

DOCUMENTARY

SHORT SUBJECT

The Divided Trail: A Native American Odyssey (Jerry Aronson,
    producer; Jerry Aronson Production)
An Encounter With Faces (K. K. Kapil, producer; Films Division,
    Government of India)
***The Flight of the Gossamer Condor* (Jacqueline Phillips Shedd**
    and Ben Shedd, producers; Shedd Production)
Goodnight Miss Ann (August Cinquegrana, producer; August
    Cinquegrana Films Production)
Squires of San Quentin (J. Gary Mitchell, producer;
    J. Gary Mitchell Film Company)

FEATURE

The Lovers' Wind (Ministry of Culture and Arts of Iran)
Mysterious Castles of Clay (Survival Anglia Ltd. Production)
Raoni (Franco-Brazilian Production)
***Scared Straight!* (Golden West Television Production)**
*With Babies and Banners: Story of the Women's Emergency
    Brigade* (Women's Labor History Film Project Production)

FOREIGN LANGUAGE FILM

***Get Out Your Handkerchiefs*, France**
The Glass Cell, German Federal Republic – West
Hungarians, Hungary
Viva Italia!, Italy
White Bim Black Ear, U.S.S.R.

JEAN HERSHOLT HUMANITARIAN AWARD

Leo Jaffe

HONORARY AWARDS

To **Walter Lantz** for bringing joy and laughter to every part of
the world through his unique animated motion pictures

To **Laurence Olivier** for the full body of his work, for the unique
achievements of his entire career and his lifetime of contribution to the art of film

To **King Vidor** for his incomparable achievements as a cinematic creator and innovator

To the **Museum of Modern Art Department of Film** for the contribution it has made to the public's perception of movies as an art form

To **Linwood G. Dunn, Loren L. Ryder** and **Waldon O. Watson** in appreciation for outstanding service and dedication in upholding the high standards of the Academy of Motion Picture Arts and Sciences

SPECIAL ACHIEVEMENT AWARD
VISUAL EFFECTS
Les Bowie, Colin Chilvers, Denys Coop, Roy Field, Derek
   Meddings and Zoran Perisic, *Superman*

1979

BEST PICTURE
All That Jazz, Robert Alan Aurthur, producer (Twentieth
   Century-Fox)

Apocalypse Now, Francis Coppola, producer; Fred Roos,
   Gray Frederickson and Tom Sternberg, co-producers
   (United Artists)

Breaking Away, Peter Yates, producer (Twentieth Century-Fox)

Kramer vs. Kramer, Stanley R. Jaffe, producer (Columbia)

Norma Rae, Tamara Asseyev and Alex Rose, producers
   (Twentieth Century-Fox)

ACTOR IN A LEADING ROLE
Dustin Hoffman, *Kramer vs. Kramer*
Jack Lemmon, *The China Syndrome*
Al Pacino, . . . *And Justice for All*
Roy Scheider, *All That Jazz*
Peter Sellers, *Being There*

ACTRESS IN A LEADING ROLE
Jill Clayburgh, *Starting Over*
Sally Field, *Norma Rae*
Jane Fonda, *The China Syndrome*
Marsha Mason, *Chapter Two*
Bette Midler, *The Rose*

Kramer vs. Kramer

ACTOR IN A SUPPORTING ROLE
Melvyn Douglas, *Being There*
Robert Duvall, *Apocalypse Now*
Frederic Forrest, *The Rose*
Justin Henry, *Kramer vs. Kramer*
Mickey Rooney, *The Black Stallion*

ACTRESS IN A SUPPORTING ROLE
Jane Alexander, *Kramer vs. Kramer*
Barbara Barrie, *Breaking Away*
Candice Bergen, *Starting Over*
Mariel Hemingway, *Manhattan*
Meryl Streep, *Kramer vs. Kramer*

DIRECTING
Robert Benton, *Kramer vs. Kramer*
Francis Coppola, *Apocalypse Now*
Bob Fosse, *All That Jazz*
Edouard Molinaro, *La Cage aux Folles*
Peter Yates, *Breaking Away*

WRITING
SCREENPLAY WRITTEN DIRECTLY FOR THE SCREEN
Woody Allen and Marshall Brickman, *Manhattan*
Robert Alan Aurthur and Bob Fosse, *All That Jazz*
Valerie Curtin and Barry Levinson, . . . *And Justice for All*
Mike Gray, T.S. Cook and James Bridges, *The China Syndrome*
Steve Tesich, *Breaking Away*

SCREENPLAY BASED ON MATERIAL FROM ANOTHER MEDIUM
Robert Benton, *Kramer vs. Kramer*
Allan Burns, *A Little Romance*
John Milius and Francis Coppola, *Apocalypse Now*
Irving Ravetch and Harriet Frank, Jr., *Norma Rae*
Francis Veber, Edouard Molinaro, Marcello Danon and
   Jean Poiret, *La Cage Aux Folles*

CINEMATOGRAPHY
Nestor Almendros, *Kramer vs. Kramer*
William A. Fraker, *1941*
Frank Phillips, *The Black Hole*
Giuseppe Rotunno, *All That Jazz*
Vittorio Storaro, *Apocalypse Now*

ART DIRECTION
George Jenkins, art direction; Arthur Jeph Parker, set
   decoration, *The China Syndrome*

Harold Michelson, Joe Jennings, Leon Harris and John
   Vallone, art direction; Linda DeScenna, set decoration,
   Star Trek — The Motion Picture

**Philip Rosenberg and Tony Walton, art direction; Edward
   Stewart and Gary Brink, set decoration, *All That Jazz***

Michael Seymour, Les Dilley and Roger Christian, art direction;
   Ian Whittaker, set decoration, *Alien*

Dean Tavoularis and Angelo Graham, art direction; George R.
   Nelson, set decoration, *Apocalypse Now*

SOUND

Robert Knudson, Robert J. Glass, Don MacDougall and Gene S. Cantamessa, *1941*

William McCaughey, Aaron Rochin, Michael J. Kohut and Jack Solomon, *Meteor*

Walter Murch, Mark Berger, Richard Beggs and Nat Boxer, *Apocalypse Now*

Arthur Piantadosi, Les Fresholtz, Michael Minkler and Al Overton, *The Electric Horseman*

Theodore Soderberg, Douglas Williams, Paul Wells and Jim Webb, *The Rose*

MUSIC

ORIGINAL SONG

"I'll Never Say 'Goodbye'," *The Promise*, David Shire, music; Alan and Marilyn Bergman, lyrics

"It Goes Like It Goes," *Norma Rae*, music by David Shire; lyrics by Norman Gimbel

"It's Easy to Say," *10*, Henry Mancini, music; Robert Wells, lyrics

"The Rainbow Connection," *The Muppet Movie*, Paul Williams and Kenny Ascher, music and lyrics

"Through the Eyes of Love," *Ice Castles*, Marvin Hamlisch, music; Carole Bayer Sager, lyrics

ORIGINAL SCORE

Georges Delerue, *A Little Romance*

Jerry Goldsmith, *Star Trek — The Motion Picture*

Dave Grusin, *The Champ*

Henry Mancini, *10*

Lalo Schifrin, *The Amityville Horror*

ORIGINAL SONG SCORE AND ITS ADAPTATION OR ADAPTATION SCORE

Ralph Burns, *All That Jazz*

Patrick Williams, *Breaking Away*

Paul Williams and Kenny Ascher, song; Paul Williams, adaptation, *The Muppet Movie*

FILM EDITING

Robert Dalva, *The Black Stallion*

Jerry Greenberg, *Kramer vs. Kramer*

Alan Heim, *All That Jazz*

Richard Marks, Walter Murch, Gerald B. Greenberg and Lisa Fruchtman, *Apocalypse Now*

Robert L. Wolfe and C. Timothy O'Meara, *The Rose*

COSTUME DESIGN

Judy Moorcroft, *The Europeans*

Shirley Russell, *Agatha*

William Ware Theiss, *Butch and Sundance: The Early Days*

Piero Tosi and Ambra Danon, *La Cage aux Folles*

Albert Wolsky, *All That Jazz*

VISUAL EFFECTS

Peter Ellenshaw, Art Cruickshank, Eustace Lycett, Danny Lee, Harrison Ellenshaw and Joe Hale, *The Black Hole*

William A. Fraker, A. D. Flowers and Gregory Jein, *1941*

H.R. Giger, Carlo Rambaldi, Brian Johnson, Nick Allder and Denys Ayling, *Alien*

Derek Meddings, Paul Wilson and John Evans, *Moonraker*

Douglas Trumbull, John Dykstra, Richard Yuricich, Robert Swarthe, Dave Stewart and Grant McCune, *Star Trek — The Motion Picture*

SHORT FILMS

ANIMATED

Dream Doll (Bob Godfrey Films/Zagreb Films/Halas and Batchelor; FilmWright)

***Every Child* (Derek Lamb, producer; National Film Board of Canada)**

It's So Nice to Have a Wolf Around the House (Paul Fierlinger, producer; AR&T Productions for Learning Corporation of America)

LIVE ACTION

***Board and Care* (Sarah Pillsbury and Ron Ellis, producers; Ron Ellis Films)**

Bravery in the Field (Roman Kroitor and Stefan Wodoslawsky, producers; National Film Board of Canada)

Oh Brother, My Brother (Carol Lowell and Ross Lowell, producers; Pyramid Films, Inc.)

The Solar Film (Saul Bass and Michael Britton, producers; Wildwood Enterprises Inc.)

Solly's Diner (Harry Mathias, Jay Zukerman and Larry Hankin, producers; Mathias/Zukerman/Hankin Productions)

DOCUMENTARY

SHORT SUBJECT

Dae (Risto Teofilovski, producer; Vardar Film/Skopje)

Koryo Celadon (Donald A. Connolly and James R. Messenger, producers; Charlie/Papa Productions, Inc.)

Nails (Phillip Borsos, producer; National Film Board of Canada)

***Paul Robeson: Tribute to an Artist* (Saul J. Turell, producer; Janus Films, Inc.)**

Remember Me (Dick Young, producer; Dick Young Productions, Ltd.)

FEATURE

***Best Boy* (Ira Wohl, producer; Only Child Motion Pictures, Inc.)**

Generation on the Wind (David A. Vassar, producer; More Than One Medium)

Going the Distance (Paul Cowan and Jacques Bobet, producers; National Film Board of Canada)

The Killing Ground (Steve Singer and Tom Priestley, producers; ABC News Closeup Unit)

The War at Home (Glenn Silber and Barry Alexander Brown, producers; Catalyst Films/Madison Film Production Co.)

FOREIGN LANGUAGE FILM AWARD

The Maids of Wilko, Poland

Mama Turns a Hundred, Spain

A Simple Story, France

***The Tin Drum*, Federal Republic of Germany – West**

To Forget Venice, Italy

IRVING G. THALBERG MEMORIAL AWARD

Ray Stark

JEAN HERSHOLT HUMANITARIAN AWARD

Robert Benjamin

HONORARY AWARDS

To **Hal Elias** for his dedication and distinguished service to the Academy of Motion Picture Arts and Sciences

To **Alec Guinness** for advancing the art of screen acting through a host of memorable and distinguished performances

John O. Aalberg, Charles G. Clarke and **John G. Frayne** in appreciation for outstanding service and dedication in upholding the high standards of the Academy of Motion Picture Arts and Sciences

SPECIAL ACHIEVEMENT AWARD
SOUND EDITING
Alan Splet, *The Black Stallion*

1980

BEST PICTURE
Coal Miner's Daughter, Bernard Schwartz, producer (Universal)

The Elephant Man, Jonathan Sanger, producer (Paramount)

***Ordinary People*, Ronald L. Schwary, producer (Paramount)**

Raging Bull, Irwin Winkler and Robert Chartoff, producers (United Artists)

Tess, Claude Berri, producer; Timothy Burrill, co-producer (Columbia)

ACTOR IN A LEADING ROLE
Robert De Niro, *Raging Bull*
Robert Duvall, *The Great Santini*
John Hurt, *The Elephant Man*
Jack Lemmon, *Tribute*
Peter O'Toole, *The Stunt Man*

ACTRESS IN A LEADING ROLE
Ellen Burstyn, *Resurrection*
Goldie Hawn, *Private Benjamin*
Mary Tyler Moore, *Ordinary People*
Gena Rowlands, *Gloria*
Sissy Spacek, *Coal Miner's Daughter*

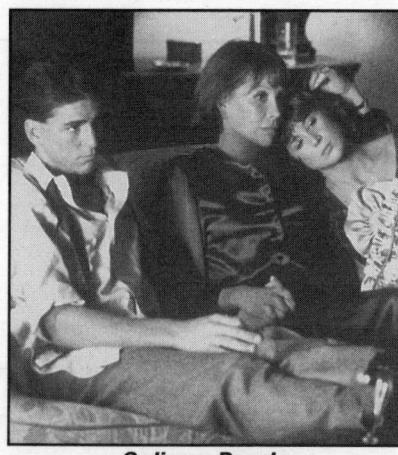

Ordinary People

ACTOR IN A SUPPORTING ROLE
Judd Hirsch, *Ordinary People*
Timothy Hutton, *Ordinary People*
Michael O'Keefe, *The Great Santini*
Joe Pesci, *Raging Bull*
Jason Robards, *Melvin and Howard*

ACTRESS IN A SUPPORTING ROLE
Eileen Brennan, *Private Benjamin*
Eva Le Gallienne, *Resurrection*
Cathy Moriarty, *Raging Bull*
Diana Scarwid, *Inside Moves*
Mary Steenburgen, *Melvin and Howard*

DIRECTING
David Lynch, *The Elephant Man*
Roman Polanski, *Tess*
Robert Redford, *Ordinary People*
Richard Rush, *The Stunt Man*
Martin Scorsese, *Raging Bull*

WRITING
SCREENPLAY WRITTEN DIRECTLY FOR THE SCREEN
Bo Goldman, *Melvin and Howard*
Christopher Gore, *Fame*
Jean Gruault, *Mon Oncle D'Amerique*
Nancy Meyers, Charles Shyer and Harvey Miller, *Private Benjamin*
W. D. Richter, screenplay; W. D. Richter and Arthur Ross, story, *Brubaker*

SCREENPLAY BASED ON MATERIAL FROM ANOTHER MEDIUM
Christopher DeVore, Eric Bergren and David Lynch, *The Elephant Man*
Jonathan Hardy, David Stevens and Bruce Beresford, *Breaker Morant*
Lawrence B. Marcus and Richard Rush, *The Stunt Man*
Tom Rickman, *Coal Miner's Daughter*
Alvin Sargent, *Ordinary People*

CINEMATOGRAPHY
Nestor Almendros, *The Blue Lagoon*
Ralf D. Bode, *Coal Miner's Daughter*
Michael Chapman, *Raging Bull*
James Crabe, *The Formula*
Geoffrey Unsworth and Ghislain Cloquet, *Tess*

ART DIRECTION
John W. Corso, art direction; John M. Dwyer, set decoration, *Coal Miner's Daughter*
Stuart Craig and Bob Cartwright, art direction; Hugh Scaife, set decoration, *The Elephant Man*
Pierre Guffroy and Jack Stephens, art direction, *Tess*
Yoshiro Muraki, art direction, *Kagemusha (The Shadow Warrior)*
Norman Reynolds, Leslie Dilley, Harry Lange and Alan Tomkins, art direction; Michael Ford, set decoration, *The Empire Strikes Back*

SOUND

Michael J. Kohut, Aaron Rochin, Jay M. Harding and Chris Newman, *Fame*

Donald O. Mitchell, Bill Nicholson, David J. Kimball and Les Lazarowitz, *Raging Bull*

Arthur Piantadosi, Les Fresholtz, Michael Minkler and Willie D. Burton, *Altered States*

Richard Portman, Roger Heman and Jim Alexander, *Coal Miner's Daughter*

Bill Varney, Steve Maslow, Gregg Landaker and Peter Sutton, *The Empire Strikes Back*

MUSIC

ORIGINAL SONG
"Fame," *Fame*, Michael Gore, music; Dean Pitchford, lyrics

"Nine to Five," *Nine to Five*, Dolly Parton, music and lyrics

"On the Road Again," *Honeysuckle Rose*, Willie Nelson, music and lyrics

"Out Here on My Own," *Fame*, Michael Gore, music; Lesley Gore, lyrics

"People Alone," *The Competition,* Lalo Schifrin, music; Wilbur Jennings, lyrics

ORIGINAL SCORE
John Corigliano, *Altered States*

Michael Gore, *Fame*

John Morris, *The Elephant Man*

Philippe Sarde, *Tess*

John Williams, *The Empire Strikes Back*

FILM EDITING

David Blewitt, *The Competition*

Anne V. Coates, *The Elephant Man*

Gerry Hambling, *Fame*

Arthur Schmidt, *Coal Miner's Daughter*

Thelma Schoonmaker, *Raging Bull*

COSTUME DESIGN

Jean-Pierre Dorleac, *Somewhere in Time*

Patricia Norris, *The Elephant Man*

Anthony Powell, *Tess*

Anna Senior, *My Brilliant Career*

Paul Zastupnevich, *When Time Ran Out*

SHORT FILMS

ANIMATED
All Nothing (Frédéric Back, producer; Société Radio Canada)

The Fly (Ferenc Rofusz, producer; Pannonia Film)

History of the World in Three Minutes Flat (Michael Mills, producer; Michael Mills Productions Ltd.)

DRAMATIC LIVE ACTION
The Dollar Bottom (Rocking Horse Films, Ltd.; Paramount)

Fall Line (Bob Carmichael and Greg Lowe, producers; Sports Imagery, Inc.)

A Jury of Her Peers (Sally Heckel, producer; Sally Heckel Productions)

DOCUMENTARY

SHORT SUBJECT
Don't Mess With Bill (John Watson and Pen Densham, producers; John Watson and Pen Densham's Insight Productions Inc.)

The Eruption of Mount St. Helens (George Casey, producer; Graphic Films Corporation)

It's the Same World (Dick Young, producer; Dick Young Productions, Ltd.)

Karl Hess: Toward Liberty (Roland Hallé and Peter W. Ladue, producers; Hallé/Ladue, Inc.)

Luther Metke at 94, U.C.L.A. (Richard Hawkins and Jorge Preloran, producers; U.C.L.A. Ethnographic Film Program)

FEATURE
Agee (Ross Spears, producer; James Agee Film Project)

The Day After Trinity (Jon Else, producer; Jon Else Productions)

From Mao to Mozart: Isaac Stern in China (Murray Lerner, producer; The Hopewell Foundation)

Front Line (David Bradbury, producer; David Bradbury Productions)

The Yellow Star — The Persecution of the Jews in Europe, 1933–45 (Bengt von zur Muehlen and Arthur Cohn, producers; Chronos Film GmbH)

FOREIGN LANGUAGE FILM

Confidence, Hungary

Kagemusha (*The Shadow Warrior*), Japan

The Last Metro, France

Moscow Does Not Believe in Tears, U.S.S.R.

The Nest, Spain

SPECIAL ACHIEVEMENT 1AWARD

VISUAL EFFECTS
Brian Johnson, Richard Edlund, Dennis Muren and Bruce Nicholson, *The Empire Strikes Back*

HONORARY AWARDS

To **Henry Fonda**, the consummate actor, in recognition of his brilliant accomplishments and enduring contribution to the art of motion pictures

To **Fred Hynes** in appreciation for outstanding service and dedication in upholding the high standards of the Academy of Motion Picture Arts and Sciences

1981

BEST PICTURE

Atlantic City, Denis Heroux and John Kemeny, producers (Paramount)

Chariots of Fire, David Puttnam, producer (The Ladd Co.; Warner Bros.)

On Golden Pond, Bruce Gilbert, producer (Universal)

Raiders of the Lost Ark, Frank Marshall, producer (Paramount)

Reds, Warren Beatty, producer (Paramount)

ACTOR IN A LEADING ROLE

Warren Beatty, *Reds*

Henry Fonda, *On Golden Pond*

Burt Lancaster, *Atlantic City*

Dudley Moore, *Arthur*

Paul Newman, *Absence of Malice*

ACTRESS IN A LEADING ROLE
Katharine Hepburn, *On Golden Pond*
Diane Keaton, *Reds*
Marsha Mason, *Only When I Laugh*
Susan Sarandon, *Atlantic City*
Meryl Streep, *The French Lieutenant's Woman*

ACTOR IN A SUPPORTING ROLE
James Coco, *Only When I Laugh*
John Gielgud, *Arthur*
Ian Holm, *Chariots of Fire*
Jack Nicholson, *Reds*
Howard E. Rollins, Jr., *Ragtime*

ACTRESS IN A SUPPORTING ROLE
Melinda Dillon, *Absence of Malice*
Jane Fonda, *On Golden Pond*
Joan Hackett, *Only When I Laugh*
Elizabeth McGovern, *Ragtime*
Maureen Stapleton, *Reds*

DIRECTING
Warren Beatty, *Reds*
Hugh Hudson, *Chariots of Fire*
Louis Malle, *Atlantic City*
Mark Rydell, *On Golden Pond*
Steven Spielberg, *Raiders of the Lost Ark*

WRITING
SCREENPLAY WRITTEN DIRECTLY FOR THE SCREEN
Warren Beatty and Trevor Griffiths, *Reds*
Steve Gordon, *Arthur*
John Guare, *Atlantic City*
Kurt Luedtke, *Absence of Malice*
Colin Welland, *Chariots of Fire*

SCREENPLAY BASED ON MATERIAL FROM ANOTHER MEDIUM
Jay Presson Allen and Sidney Lumet, *Prince of the City*
Harold Pinter, *The French Lieutenant's Woman*
Dennis Potter, *Pennies From Heaven*
Ernest Thompson, *On Golden Pond*
Michael Weller, *Ragtime*

CINEMATOGRAPHY
Miroslav Ondricek, *Ragtime*
Douglas Slocombe, *Raiders of the Lost Ark*
Vittorio Storaro, *Reds*
Alex Thomson, *Excalibur*
Billy Williams, *On Golden Pond*

ART DIRECTION
Assheton Gorton, art direction; Ann Mollo, set decoration, *The French Lieutenant's Woman*
John Graysmark, Patrizia Von Brandenstein and Anthony Reading; art direction; George de Titta, Sr., George de Titta, Jr. and Peter Howitt, set decoration, *Ragtime*
Tambi Larsen, art direction; Jim Berkey, set decoration, *Heaven's Gate*

Henry Fonda, *On Golden Pond*

Norman Reynolds and Leslie Dilley, art direction; **Michael Ford,** set decoration, *Raiders of the Lost Ark*
Richard Sylbert, art direction; Michael Seirton, set decoration, *Reds*

SOUND
Michael J. Kohut, Jay M. Harding, Richard Tyler and Al Overton, *Pennies From Heaven*
Richard Portman and David Ronne, *On Golden Pond*
Bill Varney, Steve Maslow, Gregg Landaker and Roy Charman, *Raiders of the Lost Ark*
Dick Vorisek, Tom Fleischman and Simon Kaye, *Reds*,
John K. Wilkinson, Robert W. Glass, Jr., Robert M. Thirlwell and Robin Gregory, *Outland*

MUSIC
ORIGINAL SONG
"Arthur's Theme (Best That You Can Do), *Arthur,* **Burt Bacharach, Carole Bayer Sager, Christopher Cross and Peter Allen,** music and lyrics
"Endless Love," *Endless Love,* Lionel Richie, music and lyrics
"The First Time It Happens," *The Great Muppet Caper,* Joe Raposo, music and lyrics
"For Your Eyes Only," *For Your Eyes Only,* Bill Conti, music; Mick Leeson, lyrics
"One More Hour," *Ragtime,* Randy Newman, music and lyrics

ORIGINAL SCORE
Dave Grusin, *On Golden Pond*
Randy Newman, *Ragtime*
Alex North, *Dragonslayer*
Vangelis, *Chariots of Fire*
John Williams, *Raiders of the Lost Ark*

FILM EDITING
Dede Allen and Craig McKay, *Reds*
John Bloom, *The French Lieutenant's Woman*
Michael Kahn, *Raiders of the Lost Ark*
Terry Rawlings, *Chariots of Fire*
Robert L. Wolfe, *On Golden Pond*

COSTUME DESIGN

Milena Canonero, *Chariots of Fire*

Tom Rand, *The French Lieutenant's Woman*

Bob Mackie, *Pennies From Heaven*

Anna Hill Johnstone, *Ragtime*

Shirley Russell, *Reds*

MAKEUP

Rick Baker, *An American Werewolf in London*

Stan Winston, *Heartbeeps*

VISUAL EFFECTS

Richard Edlund, Kit West, Bruce Nicholson and Joe Johnston, *Raiders of the Lost Ark*

Dennis Muren, Phil Tippett, Ken Ralston and Brian Johnson, *Dragonslayer*

SHORT FILMS

ANIMATION
***Crac* (Frédéric Back, producer; Société Radio Canada)**

The Creation (Will Vinton, producer; Will Vinton Productions)

The Tender Tale of Cinderella Penguin (Janet Perlman, producer; National Film Board of Canada)

LIVE ACTION
Couples and Robbers (Christine Oestreicher, producer; Flamingo Pictures Ltd.)

First Winter (John N. Smith, producer; National Film Board of Canada)

***Violet* (Paul Kemp and Shelley Levinson, producers; American Film Institute)**

DOCUMENTARY

SHORT SUBJECT
Americas in Transition (Obie Benz, producer; Americas in Transition, Inc.)

***Close Harmony* (Nigel Noble, producer; Noble Enterprise)**

Journey for Survival (Dick Young, producer; Dick Young Productions, Ltd.)

See What I Say (Linda Chapman, Pam LeBlanc and Freddi Stevens, producers; Michigan Women Filmmakers Productions)

Urge to Build (Roland Hallé and John Hoover, producers; Roland Hallé Productions, Inc.)

FEATURE
Against Wind and Tide: A Cuban Odyssey (Suzanne Bauman, Paul Neshamkin and Jim Burroughs, producers; Seven League Productions, Inc.)

Brooklyn Bridge (Ken Burns, producer; Florentine Films Production)

Eight Minutes to Midnight: A Portrait of Dr. Helen Caldicott (Mary Benjamin, Susanne Simpson and Boyd Estus, producers; The Caldicott Project)

El Salvador: Another Vietnam (Glenn Silber and Tete Vasconcellos, producers; Catalyst Media Productions)

***Genocide* (Arnold Schwartzman and Rabbi Marvin Hier, producers; Arnold Schwartzman Productions, Inc.)**

FOREIGN LANGUAGE FILM

The Boat Is Full, Switzerland

Man of Iron, Poland

***Mephisto*, Hungary**

Muddy River, Japan

Three Brothers, Italy

IRVING G. THALBERG AWARD
Albert R. Broccoli

JEAN HERSHOLT HUMANITARIAN AWARD
Danny Kaye

HONORARY AWARD
To **Barbara Stanwyck** for superlative creativity and unique contribution to the art of screen acting

SPECIAL ACHIEVEMENT AWARD
SOUND EFFECTS EDITING
Benjamin P. Burtt, Jr. and Richard L. Anderson, *Raiders of the Lost Ark*

1982

BEST PICTURE

E.T. the Extra-Terrestrial, Steven Spielberg and Kathleen Kennedy, producers (Universal)

***Gandhi*, Richard Attenborough, producer (Columbia)**

Missing, Edward Lewis and Mildred Lewis, producers (Universal)

Tootsie, Sydney Pollack and Dick Richards, producers (Columbia)

The Verdict, Richard D. Zanuck and David Brown, producers (Twentieth Century-Fox)

ACTOR IN A LEADING ROLE

Dustin Hoffman, *Tootsie*

Ben Kingsley, *Gandhi*

Jack Lemmon, *Missing*

Paul Newman, *The Verdict*

Peter O'Toole, *My Favorite Year*

ACTRESS IN A LEADING ROLE

Julie Andrews, *Victor/Victoria*

Jessica Lange, *Frances*

Ben Kingsley, *Gandhi*

Sissy Spacek, *Missing*

Meryl Streep, *Sophie's Choice*

Debra Winger, *An Officer and a Gentleman*

ACTOR IN A SUPPORTING ROLE

Charles Durning, *The Best Little Whorehouse in Texas*

Louis Gossett, Jr., *An Officer and a Gentleman*

John Lithgow, *The World According to Garp*

James Mason, *The Verdict*

Robert Preston, *Victor/Victoria*

ACTRESS IN A SUPPORTING ROLE

Glenn Close, *The World According to Garp*

Teri Garr, *Tootsie*

Jessica Lange, *Tootsie*

Kim Stanley, *Frances*

Lesley Ann Warren, *Victor/Victoria*

DIRECTING

Richard Attenborough, *Gandhi*

Sidney Lumet, *The Verdict*

Wolfgang Petersen, *Das Boot*

Sidney Pollack, *Tootsie*

Steven Spielberg, *E.T. the Extra-Terrestrial*

WRITING

SCREENPLAY WRITTEN DIRECTLY FOR THE SCREEN

John Briley, *Gandhi*

Larry Gelbart and Murray Schisgal, screenplay; Don McGuire and Larry Gelbart, story, *Tootsie*

Barry Levinson, *Diner*

Melissa Mathison, *E.T. the Extra-Terrestrial*

Douglas Day Stewart, *An Officer and a Gentleman*

SCREENPLAY BASED ON MATERIAL FROM ANOTHER MEDIUM

Blake Edwards, *Victor/Victoria*

Costa-Gavras and Donald Stewart, *Missing*

David Mamet, *The Verdict*

Alan J. Pakula, *Sophie's Choice*

Wolfgang Petersen, *Das Boot*

CINEMATOGRAPHY

Nestor Almendros, *Sophie's Choice*

Allen Daviau, *E.T. the Extra-Terrestrial*

Owen Roizman, *Tootsie*

Jost Vacano, *Das Boot*

Billy Williams and Ronnie Taylor, *Gandhi*

ART DIRECTION

Stuart Craig and Bob Laing, art direction; Michael Seirton, set decoration, *Gandhi*

Dale Hennesy, art direction; Marvin March, set decoration, *Annie*

Rodger Maus, Tim Hutchinson and William Craig Smith, art direction; Harry Cordwell, set decoration, *Victor/Victoria*

Lawrence G. Paull and David L. Snyder, art direction; Linda DeScenna, set decoration, *Blade Runner*

Franco Zeffirelli, art direction; Gianni Quaranta, set decoration, *La Traviata*

SOUND

Milan Bor, Trevor Pyke and Mike Le-Mare, *Das Boot*

Gerry Humphreys, Robin O'Donoghue, Jonathan Bates and Simon Kaye, *Gandhi*

Buzz Knudson, Robert Glass, Don Digirolamo and Gene Cantamessa, *E.T. the Extra-Terrestrial*

Michael Minkler, Bob Minkler, Lee Minkler and Jim La Rue, *Tron*

Arthur Piantadosi, Les Fresholtz, Dick Alexander and Les Lazarowitz, *Tootsie*

MUSIC

SONG

"Eye of the Tiger," *Rocky III*, Jim Peterik and Frankie Sullivan III, music and lyrics

"How Do You Keep the Music Playing?," *Best Friends*, Michel Legrand, music; Alan and Marilyn Bergman, lyrics

"If We Were in Love," *Yes, Giorgio*, John Williams, music; Alan and Marilyn Bergman, lyrics

"It Might Be You," *Tootsie*, Dave Grusin, music; Alan and Marilyn Bergman, lyrics

"Up Where We Belong," *An Officer and a Gentleman*, Jack Nitzsche and Buffy Sainte-Marie, music; Will Jennings, lyrics

ORIGINAL SCORE

Jerry Goldsmith, *Poltergeist*

Marvin Hamlisch, *Sophie's Choice*

Jack Nitzsche, *An Officer and a Gentleman*

Ravi Shankar and George Fenton, *Gandhi*

John Williams, *E.T. the Extra-Terrestrial*

ORIGINAL SONG SCORE AND ITS ADAPTATION OR ADAPTATION SCORE

Leslie Bricusse and Henry Mancini, *Victor/Victoria*

Ralph Burns, *Annie*

Tom Waits, *One From the Heart*

FILM EDITING

John Bloom, *Gandhi*

Carol Littleton, *E.T. the Extra-Terrestrial*

Hannes Nikel, *Das Boot*

Fredric Steinkamp and William Steinkamp, *Tootsie*

Peter Zinner, *An Officer and a Gentleman*

COSTUME DESIGN

Elois Jenssen and Rosanna Norton, *Tron*

John Mollo and Bhanu Athaiya, *Gandhi*

Patricia Norris, *Victor/Victoria*

Piero Tosi, *La Traviata*

Albert Wolsky, *Sophie's Choice*

MAKEUP

Sarah Monzani and Michèle Burke, *Quest for Fire*

Tom Smith, *Gandhi*

VISUAL EFFECTS

Richard Edlund, Michael Wood and Bruce Nicholson, *Poltergeist*

Carlo Rambaldi, Dennis Murren and Kenneth F. Smith, *E.T. the Extra-Terrestrial*

Douglas Trumbull, Richard Yuricich and David Dryer, *Blade Runner*

SOUND EFFECTS EDITING
Charles L. Campbell and Ben Burtt, *E.T. the Extra-Terrestrial*
Stephen Hunter Flick and Richard L. Anderson, *Poltergeist*
Mike Le-Mare, *Das Boot*

SHORT FILMS
ANIMATED
The Great Cognito (Will Vinton, producer; Will Vinton
    Productions)
The Snowman (John Coates, producer; Snowman
    Enterprises Ltd.)
**Tango (Zbigniew Rybczynski, producer; Film Polski
    Production)**

LIVE ACTION
Ballet Robotique (Bob Rogers, producer; Bob Rogers and Co.)
**A Shocking Accident (Christine Oestreicher, producer;
    Flamingo Pictures, Ltd.)**
The Silence (Michael Toshiyuki Uno and Joseph Benson,
    producers; American Film Institute)
Split Cherry Tree (Jan Saunders, producer; Learning
    Corporation of America)
Sredni Vashtar (Andrew Birkin, producer; Laurentic Film
    Productions, Ltd.)

DOCUMENTARY
SHORT SUBJECT
Gods of Metal (Robert Richter, producer; Richter Productions)
**If You Love This Planet (Edward Le Lorrain and Terri Nash,
    producers; National Film Board of Canada)**
The Klan: A Legacy of Hate in America (Charles Guggenheim
    and Werner Schumann, producers; Guggenheim
    Productions, Inc.)
To Live or Let Die (Freida Lee Mock, producer; American Film
    Foundation)
Traveling Hopefully (John G. Avildsen, producer; Arnuthfonyus
    Films, Inc.)

FEATURE
After the Axe (Sturla Gunnarsson and Steve Lucas, producers;
    National Film Board of Canada)
Ben's Mill (John Karol and Michel Chalufour, producers;
    Public Broadcasting Associates – ODYSSEY)
In Our Water (Meg Switzgable, producer; Foresight Films
    Production)
**Just Another Missing Kid (John Zaritsky, producer; Canadian
    Broadcasting Corp.)**
A Portrait of Giselle (ABC Video Enterprises, Inc. in association
    with Wishupon Productions)

FOREIGN LANGUAGE FILM
Alsino and the Condor, Nicaragua
Coup de Torchon (*Clean Slate*), France
The Flight of the Eagle, Sweden
Private Life, U.S.S.R.
Volver a Empezar (To Begin Again), Spain

JEAN HERSHOLT HUMANITARIAN AWARD
Walter Mirisch

HONORARY AWARD
To **Mickey Rooney** for 60 years of versatility in a variety of
memorable film performances

1983

BEST PICTURE
The Big Chill, Michael Shamberg, producer (Columbia)
The Dresser, Peter Yates, producer (Columbia)
The Right Stuff, Irwin Winkler and Robert Chartoff, producers
    (The Ladd Co. through Warner Bros.)
Tender Mercies, Philip S. Hobel, producer (Universal)
Terms of Endearment, James L. Brooks, producer (Paramount)

ACTOR IN A LEADING ROLE
Michael Caine, *Educating Rita*
Tom Conti, *Reuben, Reuben*
Tom Courtenay, *The Dresser*
Robert Duvall, Tender Mercies
Albert Finney, *The Dresser*

ACTRESS IN A LEADING ROLE
Jane Alexander, *Testament*
Shirley MacLaine, Terms of Endearment
Meryl Streep, *Silkwood*
Julie Walters, *Educating Rita*
Debra Winger, *Terms of Endearment*

ACTOR IN A SUPPORTING ROLE
Charles Durning, *To Be or Not to Be*
John Lithgow, *Terms of Endearment*
Jack Nicholson, Terms of Endearment
Sam Shepard, *The Right Stuff*
Rip Torn, *Cross Creek*

ACTRESS IN A SUPPORTING ROLE
Cher, *Silkwood*
Glenn Close, *The Big Chill*
Linda Hunt, The Year of Living Dangerously
Amy Irving, *Yentl*
Alfre Woodard, *Cross Creek*

DIRECTING
Bruce Beresford, *Tender Mercies*
Ingmar Bergman, *Fanny & Alexander*
James L. Brooks, Terms of Endearment
Mike Nichols, *Silkwood*
Peter Yates, *The Dresser*

WRITING
SCREENPLAY WRITTEN DIRECTLY FOR THE SCREEN
Ingmar Bergman, *Fanny & Alexander*
Nora Ephron and Alice Arlen, *Silkwood*
Horton Foote, Tender Mercies
Lawrence Kasdan and Barbara Benedek, *The Big Chill*
Lawrence Lasker and Walter F. Parkes, *WarGames*

SCREENPLAY BASED ON MATERIAL FROM ANOTHER MEDIUM
James L. Brooks, Terms of Endearment
Julius J. Epstein, *Reuben, Reuben*
Ronald Harwood, *The Dresser*

Harold Pinter, *Betrayal*

Willy Russell, *Educating Rita*

CINEMATOGRAPHY

Caleb Deschanel, *The Right Stuff*

William A. Fraker, *WarGames*

Sven Nykvist, *Fanny & Alexander*

Don Peterman, *Flashdance*

Gordon Willis, *Zelig*

ART DIRECTION

Anna Asp, art direction and set decoration, *Fanny & Alexander*

Geoffrey Kirkland, Richard J. Lawrence, W. Stewart Campbell and Peter Romero, art direction; Pat Pending and George R. Nelson, set decoration, *The Right Stuff*

Polly Platt and Harold Michelson, art direction; Tom Pedigo and Anthony Mondello, set decoration, *Terms of Endearment*

Norman Reynolds, Fred Hole and James Schoppe, art direction; Michael Ford, set decoration, *Return of the Jedi*

Roy Walker and Leslie Tomkins, art direction; Tessa Davies, set decoration, *Yentl*

SOUND

Mark Berger, Tom Scott, Randy Thom and David MacMillan, *The Right Stuff*

Ben Burtt, Gary Summers, Randy Thom and Tony Dawe, *Return of the Jedi*

Michael J. Kohut, Carlos de Larios, Aaron Rochin and Willie D. Burton, *WarGames*

Donald O. Mitchell, Rick Kline, Kevin O'Connell and Jim Alexander, *Terms of Endearment*

Alan R. Splet, Todd Boekelheide, Randy Thom and David Parker, *Never Cry Wolf*

MUSIC

SONG

"Flashdance . . . What a Feeling," *Flashdance*, Giorgio Moroder, music; Keith Forsey and Irene Cara, lyrics

"Maniac," *Flashdance*, Michael Sembello and Dennis Matkosky, music and lyrics

"Over You," *Tender Mercies*, Austin Roberts and Bobby Hart, music and lyrics

"Papa, Can You Hear Me?," *Yentl*, Michel Legrand, music; Alan and Marilyn Bergman, lyrics

"The Way He Makes Me Feel," *Yentl*, Michel Legrand, music; Alan and Marilyn Bergman, lyrics

ORIGINAL SCORE

Bill Conti, *The Right Stuff*

Jerry Goldsmith, *Under Fire*

Michael Gore, *Terms of Endearment*

Leonard Rosenman, *Cross Creek*

John Williams, *Return of the Jedi*

ORIGINAL SONG SCORE OR ADAPTATION SCORE

Elmer Bernstein, *Trading Places*

Michel Legrand, Alan and Marilyn Bergman, *Yentl*

Lalo Schifrin, *The Sting II*

FILM EDITING

Glenn Farr, Lisa Fruchtman, Stephen A. Rotter, Douglas Steward and Tom Rolf, *The Right Stuff*

Richard Marks, *Terms of Endearment*

Frank Morriss and Edward Abroms, *Blue Thunder*

Sam O'Steen, *Silkwood*

Bud Smith and Walt Mulconery, *Flashdance*

COSTUME DESIGN

Santo Loquasto, *Zelig*

Anne-Marie Marchand, *The Return of Martin Guerre*

Joe I. Tompkins, *Cross Creek*

Marik Vos, *Fanny & Alexander*

William Ware Theiss, *Heart Like a Wheel*

SOUND EFFECTS EDITING

Jay Boekelheide, *The Right Stuff*

Ben Burtt, *Return of the Jedi*

SHORT FILMS

ANIMATED

Mickey's Christmas Carol (Burny Mattinson, producer; Walt Disney Productions)

Sound of Sunshine — Sound of Rain (Eda Godel Hallinan, producer; Hallinan Plus! Production)

***Sundae in New York* (Jimmy Picker, producer; Motionpicker Productions)**

LIVE ACTION

***Boys and Girls* (Janice L. Platt, producer; Atlantis Films Ltd. Production)**

Goodie-Two-Shoes (Timeless Films Production; Paramount)

Overnight Sensation (Jon N. Bloom, producer; Bloom Film Production)

DOCUMENTARY

SHORT SUBJECT

Flamenco at 5:15 (Cynthia Scott and Adam Symansky, producers; National Film Board of Canada)

In the Nuclear Shadow: What Can the Children Tell Us? (Vivienne Verdon-Roe and Eric Thiermann, producers; Impact Production)

Shirley MacLaine, *Terms of Endearment*

Sewing Woman (Arthur Dong, producer; DeepFocus Productions)

Spaces: The Architecture of Paul Rudoph (Robert Eisenhardt, producer; Eisenhardt Productions)

You Are Free (*Ihr Zent Frei*) (Dea Brokman and Ilene Landis, producers; Brokman/Landis Production)

FEATURE
Children of Darkness (Richard Kotuk and Ara Chekmayan, producers; Children of Darkness Production)

First Contact (Bob Connolly and Robin Anderson, producers; Arundel Production)

He Makes Me Feel Like Dancin' (Emile Ardolino, producer; **Edgar J. Scherick Associates Production)**

The Profession of Arms, (*War Series Film #3*) (Michael Bryan and Tina Viljoen, producers; National Film Board of Canada)

Seeing Red (James Klein and Julia Reichert, producers; Heartland Production)

FOREIGN LANGUAGE FILM
Carmen, Spain

Entre Nous, France

Fanny & Alexander, Sweden

Job's Revolt, Hungary

Le Bal, Algeria

JEAN HERSHOLT HUMANITARIAN AWARD
M. J. Frankovich

HONORARY AWARD
To **Hal Roach** in recognition of his unparalleled record of distinguished contributions to the motion picture art form

SPECIAL ACHIEVEMENT AWARDS
VISUAL EFFECTS
Richard Edlund, Dennis Muren, Ken Ralston and Phil Tippett, *Return of the Jedi*

1984

BEST PICTURE
Amadeus, Saul Zaentz, producer (Orion)

The Killing Fields, David Puttnam, producer (Warner Bros.)

A Passage to India, John Brabourne and Richard Goodwin, producer (Columbia)

Places in the Heart, Arlene Donovan, producer (TriStar)

A Soldier's Story, Norman Jewison, Ronald L. Schwary and Patrick Palmer, producers (Columbia)

ACTOR IN A LEADING ROLE
F. Murray Abraham, *Amadeus*

Jeff Bridges, *Starman*

Albert Finney, *Under the Volcano*

Tom Hulce, *Amadeus*

Sam Waterston, *The Killing Fields*

ACTRESS IN A LEADING ROLE
Judy Davis, *A Passage to India*

Sally Field, *Places in the Heart*

Fanny & Alexander

Jessica Lange, *Country*

Vanessa Redgrave, *The Bostonians*

Sissy Spacek, *The River*

ACTOR IN A SUPPORTING ROLE
Adolph Caesar, *A Soldier's Story*

John Malkovich, *Places in the Heart*

Noriyuki "Pat" Morita, *The Karate Kid*

Haing S. Ngor, *The Killing Fields*

Ralph Richardson, *Greystoke: The Legend of Tarzan, Lord of the Apes*

ACTRESS IN A SUPPORTING ROLE
Peggy Ashcroft, *A Passage to India*

Glenn Close, *The Natural*

Lindsay Crouse, *Places in the Heart*

Christine Lahti, *Swing Shift*

Geraldine Page, *The Pope of Greenwich Village*

DIRECTING
Woody Allen, *Broadway Danny Rose*

Robert Benton, *Places in the Heart*

Milos Forman, *Amadeus*

Roland Joffe, *The Killing Fields*

David Lean, *A Passage to India*

WRITING
SCREENPLAY WRITTEN DIRECTLY FOR THE SCREEN
Woody Allen, *Broadway Danny Rose*

Robert Benton, *Places in the Heart*

Lowell Ganz, Babaloo Mandel and Bruce Jay Friedman, screenplay; Bruce Jay Friedman; screen story, *Splash*

Gregory Nava and Anna Thomas, *El Norte*

Daniel Petrie, Jr., screenplay; Danilo Bach and Daniel Petrie, Jr., story, *Beverly Hills Cop*

SCREENPLAY BASED ON MATERIAL FROM ANOTHER MEDIUM
Charles Fuller, *A Soldier's Story*

David Lean, *A Passage to India*

Bruce Robinson, *The Killing Fields*

Peter Shaffer, *Amadeus*

P.H. Vazak and Michael Austin, *Greystoke: The Legend of Tarzan, Lord of the Apes*

CINEMATOGRAPHY

Ernest Day, *A Passage to India*

Caleb Deschanel, *The Natural*

Chris Menges, *The Killing Fields*

Miroslav Ondricek, *Amadeus*

Vilmos Zsigmond, *The River*

ART DIRECTION

John Box and Leslie Tomkins, art direction; Hugh Scaife, set decoration, *A Passage to India*

Albert Brenner, art direction; Rick Simpson, set decoration, *2010*

Angelo Graham and Mel Bourne, James J. Murakami and Speed Hopkins, art direction; Bruch Weintraub, set decoration, *The Natural*

Richard Sylbert, art direction; George Gaines and Les Bloom, set decoration, *The Cotton Club*

Patrizia Von Brandenstein, art direction; Karel Cerny, set decoration, *Amadeus*

SOUND

Nick Alphin, Robert Thirwell, Richard Portman and David Ronne, *The River*

Mark Berger, Tom Scott, Todd Boekelheide and Chris Newman, *Amadeus*

Graham V. Hartstone, Nicolas Le Messurier, Michael A. Carter and John Mitchell, *A Passage to India*

Michael J. Kohut, Aaron Rochin, Carlos De Larios and Gene S. Cantamessa, *2010*

Bill Varney, Steve Maslow, Kevin O'Connell and Nelson Stoll, *Dune*

MUSIC

ORIGINAL SONG

"Against All Odds" (Take a Look at Me Now), *Against All Odds*, Phil Collins, music and lyrics

"Footloose," *Footloose*, Kenny Loggins and Dean Pitchford, music and lyrics

"Ghostbusters," *Ghostbusters*, Ray Parker, Jr., music and lyrics

"I Just Called to Say I Love You," *The Woman in Red*, Stevie Wonder, music and lyrics

"Let's Hear It for the Boy," *Footloose*, Dean Pitchford and Tom Snow, music and lyrics

ORIGINAL SCORE

Maurice Jarre, *A Passage to India*

Randy Newman, *The Natural*

Alex North, *Under the Volcano*

John Williams, *Indiana Jones and the Temple of Doom*

John Williams, *The River*

ORIGINAL SONG SCORE

Kris Kristofferson, *Songwriter*

Jeffrey Moss, *The Muppets Take Manhattan*

Prince, *Purple Rain*

FILM EDITING

Donn Cambern and Frank Morriss, *Romancing the Stone*

Jim Clark, *The Killing Fields*

Nena Danevic and Michael Chandler, *Amadeus*

David Lean, *A Passage to India*

Barry Malkin and Robert Q. Lovett, *The Cotton Club*

COSTUME DESIGN

Jenny Beavan and John Bright, *The Bostonians*

Judy Moorcroft, *A Passage to India*

Patricia Norris, *2010*

Theodor Pistek, *Amadeus*

Ann Roth, *Places in the Heart*

MAKEUP

Rick Baker and Paul Engelen, *Greystoke: The Legend of Tarzan, Lord of the Apes*

Paul LeBlanc and Dick Smith, *Amadeus*

Michael Westmore, *2010*

VISUAL EFFECTS

Richard Edlund, John Bruno, Mark Vargo and Chuck Gasper, *Ghostbusters*

Richard Edlund, Neil Krepela, George Jenson and Mark Stetson, *2010*

Dennis Muren, Michael McAlister, Lorne Peterson and George Gibbs, *Indiana Jones and the Temple of Doom*

SHORT FILMS

ANIMATED

***Charade* (Jon Minnis, producer; Sheridan College Production)**

Doctor De Soto (Morton Schindel and Michael Sporn, producers; Michael Sporn Animation, Inc.)

Paradise (Ishu Patel, producer; National Film Board of Canada)

LIVE ACTION

The Painted Door (Atlantis Films Ltd. in association with the National Film Board of Canada)

Tales of Meeting and Parting (Sharon Oreck and Lesli Linka Glatter, producers; American Film Institute — Directing Workshop for Women)

***Up* (Mike Hoover, producer; Pyramid Films)**

DOCUMENTARY

SHORT SUBJECT

The Children of Soong Ching Ling (Gary Bush and Paul T.K. Lin, producers; UNICEF and the Soong Ching Ling Foundation)

Code Gray: Ethical Dilemmas in Nursing (Ben Achtenberg and Joan Sawyer, producers; The Nursing Ethics Project/Fanlight Productions)

The Garden of Eden (Lawrence R. Hott and Roger M. Sherman, producers; Florentine Films Production)

Recollections of Pavlovsk (Irina Kalinina, producer; Leningrad Documentary Film Studio)

***The Stone Carvers* (Marjorie Hunt and Paul Wagner, producers, Paul Wagner Productions)**

FEATURE

High Schools (Charles Guggenheim and Nancy Sloss, producers; Guggenheim Productions)

In the Name of the People (Alex W. Drehsler and Frank Christopher, producers; Pan American Films)

Marlene (Zev Braun Pictures, Inc.; OKO Film Produktion)

Streetwise (Cheryl McCall, producer; Bear Creek Productions, Inc.)

The Times of Harvey Milk (Robert Epstein and Richard Schmiechen, producers; Black Sand Educational Productions, Inc.)

FOREIGN LANGUAGE FILM

Beyond the Walls, Israel

Camila, Argentina

***Dangerous Moves*, Switzerland**

Double Feature, Spain

Wartime Romance, U.S.S.R.

JEAN HERSHOLT HUMANITARIAN AWARD

David L. Wolper

HONORARY AWARDS

To the **National Endowment for the Arts** in recognition of its 20th anniversary and its dedication to fostering artistic and creative activity and excellence in every area of the arts

To **James Stewart** for 50 years of memorable performances and for his high ideals, both on and off the screen, with the respect and affection of his colleagues

SPECIAL ACHIEVEMENT AWARD

SOUND EFFECTS EDITING
Kay Rose, *The River*

1985

BEST PICTURE

The Color Purple, Steven Spielberg, Kathleen Kennedy, Frank Marshall and Quincy Jones, producers (Warner Bros.)

Kiss of the Spider Woman, David Weisman, producer (Island Alive)

***Out of Africa*, Sydney Pollack, producer (Universal)**

Prizzi's Honor, John Foreman, producer (Twentieth Century-Fox)

Witness, Edward S. Feldman, producer (Paramount)

ACTOR IN A LEADING ROLE

Harrison Ford, *Witness*

James Garner, *Murphy's Romance*

William Hurt, *Kiss of the Spider Woman*

Jack Nicholson, *Prizzi's Honor*

Jon Voight, *Runaway Train*

ACTRESS IN A LEADING ROLE

Anne Bancroft, *Agnes of God*

Whoopi Goldberg, *The Color Purple*

Jessica Lange, *Sweet Dreams*

Geraldine Page, *The Trip to Bountiful*

Meryl Streep, *Out of Africa*

ACTOR IN A SUPPORTING ROLE

Don Ameche, *Cocoon*

Klaus Maria Brandauer, *Out of Africa*

William Hickey, *Prizzi's Honor*

Robert Loggia, *Jagged Edge*

Eric Roberts, *Runaway Train*

Anjelica Huston, *Prizzi's Honor*

ACTRESS IN A SUPPORTING ROLE

Margaret Avery, *The Color Purple*

Anjelica Huston, *Prizzi's Honor*

Amy Madigan, *Twice in a Lifetime*

Meg Tilly, *Agnes of God*

Oprah Winfrey, *The Color Purple*

DIRECTING

Hector Babenco, *Kiss of the Spider Woman*

John Huston, *Prizzi's Honor*

Akira Kurosawa, *Ran*

Sydney Pollack, *Out of Africa*

Peter Weir, *Witness*

WRITING

SCREENPLAY WRITTEN DIRECTLY FOR THE SCREEN
Woody Allen, *The Purple Rose of Cairo*

Terry Gilliam, Tom Stoppard and Charles McKeown, *Brazil*

Luis Puenzo and Aida Bortnik, *The Official Story*

Earl W. Wallace and William Kelley, screenplay; William Kelley, Pamela Wallace and Earl W. Wallace, story, *Witness*

Robert Zemeckis and Bob Gale, *Back to the Future*

SCREENPLAY BASED ON MATERIAL FROM ANOTHER MEDIUM
Richard Condon and Janet Roach, *Prizzi's Honor*

Horton Foote, *The Trip to Bountiful*

Kurt Luedtke, *Out of Africa*

Menno Meyjes, *The Color Purple*

Leonard Schrader, *Kiss of the Spider Woman*

CINEMATOGRAPHY

Allen Daviau, *The Color Purple*

William A. Fraker, *Murphy's Romance*

Takao Saito, Masaharu Ueda and Asakazu Nakai, *Ran*

John Seale, *Witness*

David Watkin, *Out of Africa*

ART DIRECTION

Norman Garwood, art direction; Maggie Gray, set decoration, *Brazil*

Stephen Grimes, art direction; Josie MacAvin, set decoration, *Out of Africa*

Stan Jolley, art direction; John Anderson, set decoration, *Witness*

Yoshiro Muraki and Shinobu Muraki, art direction, *Ran*

J. Michael Riva and Robert W. Welch, art direction; Linda DeScenna, set decoration, *The Color Purple*

SOUND

Les Fresholtz, Dick Alexander, Vern Poore and Bud Alper, *Ladyhawke*

Chris Jenkins, Gary Alexander, Larry Stensvold and Peter Handford, *Out of Africa*

Donald O. Mitchell, Rick Kline, Kevin O'Connell and David Ronne, *Silverado*

Donald O. Mitchell, Michael Minkler, Gerry Humphreys and Chris Newman, *A Chorus Line*

Bill Varney, B. Tennyson Sebastian II, Robert Thirlwell and William B. Kaplan, *Back to the Future*

MUSIC
SONG

"Miss Celie's Blues" (Sister), *The Color Purple*, Quincy Jones and Rod Temperton, music; Quincy Jones, Rod Temperton and Lionel Richie, lyrics

"The Power of Love," *Back to the Future*, Chris Hayes and Johnny Colla, music; Huey Lewis, lyrics

"Say You, Say Me," *White Nights*, Lionel Richie, music and lyrics

"Love Theme From *White Nights*" (Separate Lives), *White Nights*, Stephen Bishop, music and lyrics

"Surprise, Surprise," *A Chorus Line*, Marvin Hamlisch, music; Edward Kleban, lyrics

ORIGINAL SCORE

John Barry, *Out of Africa*

Bruce Broughton, *Silverado*

Georges Delerue, *Agnes of God*

Quincy Jones, Jeremy Lubbock, Rod Temperton, Caiphus Semenya, Andrae Crouch, Chris Boardman, Jorge Calandrelli, Joel Rosenbaum, Fred Steiner, Jack Hayes, Jerry Hey and Randy Kerber, *The Color Purple*

Maurice Jarre, *Witness*

FILM EDITING

John Bloom, *A Chorus Line*

Rudi Fehr and Kaja Fehr, *Prizzi's Honor*

Thom Noble, *Witness*

Henry Richardson, *Runaway Train*

Fredric Steinkamp, William Steinkamp, Pembroke Herring and Sheldon Kahn, *Out of Africa*

COSTUME DESIGN

Milena Canonero, *Out of Africa*

Donfeld, *Prizzi's Honor*

Aggie Guerard Rodgers, *The Color Purple*

Emi Wada, *Ran*

Albert Wolksy, *The Journey of Natty Gann*

MAKEUP

Ken Chase, *The Color Purple*

Carl Fullerton, *Remo Williams: The Adventure Begins*

Michael Westmore and Zoltan Elek, *Mask*

VISUAL EFFECTS

Dennis Muren, Kit West, John Ellis and David Allen, *Young Sherlock Holmes*

Ken Ralston, Ralph McQuarrie, Scott Farrar and David Berry, *Cocoon*

Will Vinton, Ian Wingrove, Zoran Perisic and Michael Lloyd, *Return to Oz*

SOUND EFFECTS EDITING

Frederick J. Brown, *Rambo: First Blood Part II*

Charles L. Campbell and Robert Rutledge, *Back to the Future*

Bob Henderson and Alan Murray, *Ladyhawke*

SHORT FILMS
ANIMATED

***Anna & Bella* (Cilia Van Dijk, producer; Netherlands)**

The Big Snit (Richard Condie and Michael Scott, producers; National Film Board of Canada)

Second Class Mail (Alison Snowden, producer; National Film and Television School)

LIVE ACTION

Graffiti (Dianna Costello, producer; American Film Institute)

***Molly's Pilgrim* (Jeff Brown and Chris Pelzer, producers; Phoenix Films)**

Rainbow War (Bob Rogers, producer; Bob Rogers and Co.)

DOCUMENTARY
SHORT SUBJECT

The Courage to Care (Robert Gardner, producer; United Way)

Keats and His Nightingale: A Blind Date (Michael Crowley and James Wolpaw, producers; Rhode Island Committee for the Humanities)

Making Overtures — The Story of a Community Orchestra (Barbara Willis Sweete, producer; Rhombus Media, Inc.)

***Witness to War: Dr. Charlie Clements* (David Goodman, producer; Skylight Picture Production)**

The Wizard of the Strings (Alan Edelstein, producer; Seventh Hour Production)

FEATURE

***Broken Rainbow* (Maria Florio and Victoria Mudd, producers; Earthworks Films Production)**

Las Madres — The Mothers of Plaza de Mayo (Susana Muñoz and Lourdes Portillo, producers; Film Arts Foundation)

Soldiers in Hiding (Japhet Asher, producer; Filmworks, Inc. Production)

The Statue of Liberty (Ken Burns and Buddy Squires, producers; Florentine Films Production)

Unfinished Business (Steven Okazaki, producer; Mouchette Films Production)

FOREIGN LANGUAGE FILM

Angry Harvest, Federal Republic of Germany – West

Colonel Redl, Hungary

***The Official Story*, Argentina**

Three Men and a Cradle, France

When Father Was Away on Business, Yugoslavia

JEAN HERSHOLT HUMANITARIAN AWARD
Charles "Buddy" Rogers

HONORARY AWARDS

To **Paul Newman** in recognition of his many memorable and compelling screen performances and for his personal integrity and dedication to his craft

To **Alex North** in recognition of his brilliant artistry in the creation of memorable music for a host of distinguished motion pictures

To **John H. Whitney, Sr.** for cinematic pioneering

1986

BEST PICTURE

Children of a Lesser God, Burt Sugarman and Patrick Palmer, producers (Paramount)

Hannah and Her Sisters, Robert Greenhut, producer (Orion)

The Mission, Fernando Ghia and David Puttnam, producers (Warner Bros.)

***Platoon*, Arnold Kopelson, producer (Orion)**

A Room With a View, Ismail Merchant, producer (Cinecom. Pictures)

ACTOR IN A LEADING ROLE

Dexter Gordon, *'Round Midnight*

Bob Hoskins, *Mona Lisa*

William Hurt, *Children of a Lesser God*

Paul Newman, *The Color of Money*

James Woods, *Salvador*

ACTRESS IN A LEADING ROLE

Jane Fonda, *The Morning After*

Marlee Matlin, *Children of a Lesser God*

Sissy Spacek, *Crimes of the Heart*

Kathleen Turner, *Peggy Sue Got Married*

Sigourney Weaver, *Aliens*

ACTOR IN A SUPPORTING ROLE

Tom Berenger, *Platoon*

Michael Caine, *Hannah and Her Sisters*

Willem Dafoe, *Platoon*

Denholm Elliott, *A Room With a View*

Dennis Hopper, *Hoosiers*

ACTRESS IN A SUPPORTING ROLE

Tess Harper, *Crimes of the Heart*

Piper Laurie, *Children of a Lesser God*

Mary Elizabeth Mastrantonio, *The Color of Money*

Maggie Smith, *A Room With a View*

Dianne Wiest, *Hannah and Her Sisters*

DIRECTING

Woody Allen, *Hannah and Her Sisters*

James Ivory, *A Room With a View*

Roland Joffe, *The Mission*

David Lynch, *Blue Velvet*

Oliver Stone, *Platoon*

WRITING
SCREENPLAY WRITTEN DIRECTLY FOR THE SCREEN
Woody Allen, *Hannah and Her Sisters*

Paul Hogan, story; Paul Hogan, Ken Shadie and John Cornell, screenplay, *"Crocodile" Dundee*

Hanif Kureishi, *My Beautiful Laundrette*

Oliver Stone, *Platoon*

Oliver Stone and Richard Boyle, *Salvador*

SCREENPLAY BASED ON ANOTHER MEDIUM
Hesper Anderson and Mark Medoff, *Children of a Lesser God*

Raynold Gideon and Bruce A. Evans, *Stand By Me*

Beth Henley, *Crimes of the Heart*

Ruth Prawer Jhabvala, *A Room With a View*

Richard Price, *The Color of Money*

CINEMATOGRAPHY

Jordan Cronenweth, *Peggy Sue Got Married*

Chris Menges, *The Mission*

Don Peterman, *Star Trek IV: The Voyage Home*

Tony Pierce-Roberts, *A Room With a View*

Robert Richardson, *Platoon*

ART DIRECTION

Stuart Craig, art direction; Jack Stephens, set decoration, *The Mission*

Peter Lamont, art direction; Crispian Sallis, set decoration, *Aliens*

Boris Leven, art direction; Karen A. O'Hara, set decoration, *The Color of Money*

Gianni Quaranta and Brian Ackland-Snow, art direction; Brian Savegar and Elio Altramura, set decoration, *A Room With a View*

Stuart Wurtzel, art direction; Carol Joffe, set decoration, *Hannah and Her Sisters*

SOUND

Les Fresholtz, Dick Alexander, Vern Poore and William Nelson, *Heartbreak Ridge*

Graham V. Hartstone, Nicolas Le Messurier, Michael A. Carter and Roy Charman, *Aliens*

Donald O. Mitchell, Kevin O'Connell, Rick Kline and William B. Kaplan, *Top Gun*

Terry Porter, Dave Hudson, Mel Metcalfe and Gene S. Cantamessa, *Star Trek IV: The Voyage Home*

John Wilkinson, Richard Rogers, Charles "Bud" Grenzbach and Simon Kaye, *Platoon*

MUSIC
SONG
"Glory of Love," *The Karate Kid Part II*, Peter Cetera and David Foster, music; Peter Cetera and Diane Nini, lyrics

"Life in a Looking Glass," *That's Life*, Henry Mancini, music; Leslie Bricusse, lyrics

"Mean Green Mother From Outer Space," *Little Shop of Horrors*, Alan Menken, music; Howard Ashman, lyrics

"Somewhere Out There," *An American Tail*, James Horner and Barry Mann, music; Cynthia Weil, lyrics

"Take My Breath Away," *Top Gun*, Giorgio Moroder, music; Tom Whitlock, lyrics

ORIGINAL SCORE
Jerry Goldsmith, *Hoosiers*

Herbie Hancock, *'Round Midnight*

James Horner, *Aliens*

Ennio Morricone, *The Mission*

Leonard Rosenman, *Star Trek IV: The Voyage Home*

FILM EDITING
Jim Clark, *The Mission*

Ray Lovejoy, *Aliens*

Susan E. Morse, *Hannah and Her Sisters*

Claire Simpson, *Platoon*

Billy Weber and Chris Lebenzon, *Top Gun*

COSTUME DESIGN
Anna Anni and Maurizio Millenotti, *Otello*

Jenny Beaven and John Bright, *A Room With a View*

Anthony Powell, *Pirates*

Enrico Sabbatini, *The Mission*

Theadora Van Runkle, *Peggy Sue Got Married*

MAKEUP
Rob Bottin and Peter Robb-King, *Legend*

Chris Walas and Stephan Dupuis, *The Fly*

Michael G. Westmore and Michèle Burke, *The Clan of the Cave Bear*

VISUAL EFFECTS
Lyle Conway, Brian Ferren and Martin Gutteridge, *Little Shop of Horrors*

Richard Edlund, John Bruno, Garry Waller and William Neil, *Poltergeist II: The Other Side*

Robert Skotak, Stan Winston, John Richardson and Suzanne Benson, *Aliens*

SOUND EFFECTS EDITING
Cecelia Hall and George Watters II, *Top Gun*

Mark Mangini, *Star Trek IV: The Voyage Home*

Don Sharpe, *Aliens*

SHORT FILMS
ANIMATED
The Frog, the Dog and the Devil (Bob Stenhouse, producer; New Zealand National Film Unit)

***A Greek Tragedy* (Linda Van Tulden and Willem Thijssen producers; CineTe pvba)**

Luxo Jr. (John Lasseter and William Reeves, producers; Pixar Productions)

LIVE ACTION
Exit (Stefano Reali and Pino Quartullo, producers; Rai Radiotelevisione Italiana/RAI-UNO)

Love Struck (Fredda Weiss, producer; Rainy Day Productions)

***Precious Images* (Chuck Workman, producer; Calliope Films, Inc.)**

DOCUMENTARY
SHORT SUBJECT
Debonair Dancers (Alison Nigh-Strelich, producer; Alison Nigh-Strelich Production)

The Masters of Disaster (Sonya Friedman, producer; Indiana University Audio Visual Center)

Red Grooms: Sunflower in a Hothouse (Thomas L. Neff and Madeline Bell, producers; Polaris Entertainment Production)

Sam (Aaron D. Weisblatt Production)

***Women — for America, for the World* (Vivienne Verdon-Roe, producer; Educational Film & Video Project)**

FEATURE (TIE)
***Artie Shaw: Time Is All You've Got* (Brigitte Berman, producer; Bridge Film Production)**

Chile: Hasta Cuando? (David Bradbury, producer; David Bradbury Productions)

***Down and Out in America* (Joseph Feury and Milton Justice, producers; Joseph Feury Production)**

Isaac in America: A Journey With Isaac Bashevis Singer (Kirk Simon and Amram Nowak, producers; Amram Nowak Associates)

Witness to Apartheid (Sharon I. Sopher, producer; Production of Developing News, Inc.)

FOREIGN LANGUAGE FILM
The Assault, Netherlands

Betty Blue, France

The Decline of the American Empire, Canada

My Sweet Little Village, Czechoslovakia

"38", Austria

IRVING G. THALBERG MEMORIAL AWARD
Steven Spielberg

HONORARY AWARD
To **Ralph Bellamy** for his unique artistry and his distinguished service to the profession of acting

To **E.M. (Al) Lewis** in appreciation for outstanding service and dedication in upholding the high Academy standards

Steven Spielberg

The Last Emperor

1987

BEST PICTURE

Broadcast News, James L. Brooks, producer (Twentieth Century-Fox)

Fatal Attraction, Stanley R. Jaffe and Sherry Lansing, producers (Paramount)

Hope and Glory, John Boorman, producer (Columbia)

The Last Emperor, Jeremy Thomas, producer (Columbia)

Moonstruck, Patrick Palmer and Norman Jewison, producers (MGM)

ACTOR IN A LEADING ROLE

Michael Douglas, *Wall Street*

William Hurt, *Broadcast News*

Marcello Mastroianni, *Dark Eyes*

Jack Nicholson, *Ironweed*

Robin Williams, *Good Morning, Vietnam*

ACTRESS IN A LEADING ROLE

Cher, *Moonstruck*

Glenn Close, *Fatal Attraction*

Holly Hunter, *Broadcast News*

Sally Kirkland, *Anna*

Meryl Streep, *Ironweed*

ACTOR IN A SUPPORTING ROLE

Albert Brooks, *Broadcast News*

Sean Connery, *The Untouchables*

Morgan Freeman, *Street Smart*

Vincent Gardenia, *Moonstruck*

Denzel Washington, *Cry Freedom*

ACTRESS IN A SUPPORTING ROLE

Norma Aleandro, *Gaby — A True Story*

Anne Archer, *Fatal Attraction*

Olympia Dukakis, *Moonstruck*

Anne Ramsey, *Throw Momma From the Train*

Ann Sothern, *The Whales of August*

DIRECTING

Bernardo Bertolucci, *The Last Emperor*

John Boorman, *Hope and Glory*

Lasse Hallström, *My Life as a Dog*

Norman Jewison, *Moonstruck*

Adrian Lyne, *Fatal Attraction*

WRITING

SCREENPLAY WRITTEN DIRECTLY FOR THE SCREEN

Woody Allen, *Radio Days*

John Boorman, *Hope and Glory*

James L. Brooks, *Broadcast News*

Louis Malle, *Au Revoir les Enfants*

John Patrick Shanley, *Moonstruck*

SCREENPLAY BASED ON MATERIAL FROM ANOTHER MEDIUM

James Dearden, *Fatal Attraction*

Lasse Hallström, Reidar Jönsson, Brasse Brännström and Per Berglund, *My Life as a Dog*

Tony Huston, *The Dead*

Stanley Kubrick, Michael Herr and Gustav Hasford, *Full Metal Jacket*

Mark Peploe and Bernardo Bertolucci, *The Last Emperor*

CINEMATOGRAPHY

Michael Ballhaus, *Broadcast News*

Allen Daviau, *Empire of the Sun*

Philippe Rousselot, *Hope and Glory*

Vittorio Storaro, *The Last Emperor*

Haskell Wexler, *Matewan*

ART DIRECTION

Santo Loquasto, art direction; Carol Joffe, Les Bloom and George DeTitta, Jr., set decoration, *Radio Days*

Anthony Pratt, art direction; Joan Woolard, set decoration, *Hope and Glory*

Norman Reynolds, art direction; Harry Cordwell, set decoration, *Empire of the Sun*

Ferdinando Scarfiotti, art direction; Bruno Cesari and Osvaldo Desideri, set decoration, *The Last Emperor*

Patrizia Von Brandenstein and William A. Elliot, art direction; Hal Gausman, set decoration, *The Untouchables*

SOUND

Wayne Artman, Tom Beckert, Tom Dahl and Art Rochester, *The Witches of Eastwick*

Les Fresholtz, Dick Alexander, Vern Poore and Bill Nelson, *Lethal Weapon*

Robert Knudson, Don Digirolamo, John Boyde and Tony Dawe, *Empire of the Sun*

Michael J. Kohut, Carlos DeLarios, Aaron Rochin and Robert Wald, *RoboCop*

Bill Rowe and Ivan Sharrock, *The Last Emperor*

MUSIC

SONG

"Cry Freedom," *Cry Freedom*, George Fenton and Jonas Gwangwa, music and lyrics

"(I've Had) The Time of My Life," *Dirty Dancing*, Franke Previte, John DeNicola and Donald Markowitz, music; Franke Previte, lyrics

"Nothing's Gonna Stop Us Now," *Mannequin*, Albert Hammond and Diane Warren, music and lyrics

"Shakedown," *Beverly Hills Cop II*, Harold Faltermeyer and Keith Forsey, music; Harold Faltermeyer, Keith Forsey and Bob Seger, lyrics

"Storybook Love," *The Princess Bride*, Willy DeVille, music and lyrics

ORIGINAL SCORE

George Fenton and Jonas Gwangwa, *Cry Freedom*

Ennio Morricone, *The Untouchables*

Ryuichi Sakamoto, David Byrne and Cong Su, *The Last Emperor*

John Williams, *Empire of the Sun*

John Williams, *The Witches of Eastwick*

FILM EDITING

Gabriella Cristiani, *The Last Emperor*

Michael Kahn, *Empire of the Sun*

Michael Kahn and Peter E. Berger, *Fatal Attraction*

Richard Marks, *Broadcast News*

Frank J. Urioste, *RoboCop*

COSTUME DESIGN

James Acheson, *The Last Emperor*

Jenny Beavan and John Bright, *Maurice*

Dorothy Jeakins, *The Dead*

Bob Ringwood, *Empire of the Sun*

Marilyn Vance-Straker, *The Untouchables*

MAKEUP

Rick Baker, *Harry and the Hendersons*

Bob Laden, *Happy New Year*

VISUAL EFFECTS

Joel Hynek, Robert M. Greenberg, Richard Greenberg and Stan Winston, *Predator*

Dennis Muren, William George, Harley Jessup and Kenneth Smith, *Innerspace*

SHORT FILMS

ANIMATED

George and Rosemary (Eunice Macaulay, producer; National Film Board of Canada)

The Man Who Planted Trees (Frédéric Back, producer; Société Radio-Canada/Canadian Broadcasting Corporation)

Your Face (Bill Plympton, producer; Bill Plympton Productions)

LIVE ACTION

Making Waves (Ann Wingate, producer; The Production Pool Ltd.)

Ray's Male Heterosexual Dance Hall (Jonathan Sanger and Jana Sue Memel, producers; Chanticleer Films)

Shoeshine (Robert A. Katz, producer; Tom Abrams Productions)

DOCUMENTARY

SHORT SUBJECT

Frances Steloff: Memoirs of a Bookseller (Deborah Dickson, producer; Winterlude Films, Inc. Production)

In the Wee Wee Hours . . . (Dr. Frank Daniel and Izak Ben-Meir, producers; University of Southern California School of Cinema/Television)

Languge Says It All (Megan Williams, producer; Tripod Production)

Silver Into Gold (Lynn Mueller, producer; Stanford University Department of Communications)

Young at Heart (Sue Marx and Pamela Conn, producers; Sue Marx Films, Inc. Production)

FEATURE

Eyes on the Prize: America's Civil Rights Years/Bridge to Freedom 1965 (Callie Crossley and James A. DeVinney, producers; Blackside, Inc. Production)

Hellfire: A Journey From Hiroshima (John Junkerman and John W. Dower, producers; Muraki Film Project)

Radio Bikini (Robert Stone, producer; Crossroads Film Project, Ltd.)

A Stitch for Time (Barbara Herbich and Cyril Christo, producers; Peace Quilters Production Company, Inc.)

The Ten-Year Lunch: The Wit and Legend of the Algonquin Round Table (Aviva Slesin, producer; Aviva Films)

FOREIGN LANGUAGE FILM

Au Revoir les Enfants (*Goodbye, Children*), France

Babette's Feast, Denmark

Course Completed, Spain

The Family, Italy

Pathfinder, Norway

IRVING G. THALBERG MEMORIAL AWARD

Billy Wilder

SPECIAL ACHIEVEMENT AWARD

SOUND EFFECTS EDITING
Stephen Flick and John Pospisil, *RoboCop*

1988

BEST PICTURE

The Accidental Tourist, Lawrence Kasdan, Charles Okun and Michael Grillo, producers (Warner Bros.)

Dangerous Liaisons, Norma Heyman and Hank Moonjean, producers (Warner Bros.)

Mississippi Burning, Frederick Zollo and Robert F. Colesberry, producers (Orion)

Rain Man, Mark Johnson, producer (United Artists)

Working Girl, Douglas Wick, producer (Twentieth Century-Fox)

ACTOR IN A LEADING ROLE

Gene Hackman, *Mississippi Burning*

Tom Hanks, *Big*

Dustin Hoffman, *Rain Man*

Edward James Olmos, *Stand and Deliver*

Max von Sydow, *Pelle the Conqueror*

ACTRESS IN A LEADING ROLE

Glenn Close, *Dangerous Liaisons*

Jodie Foster, *The Accused*

Melanie Griffith, *Working Girl*

Meryl Streep, *A Cry in the Dark*

Sigourney Weaver, *Gorillas in the Mist*

ACTOR IN A SUPPORTING ROLE

Alec Guinness, *Little Dorrit*

Kevin Kline, *A Fish Called Wanda*

Martin Landau, *Tucker: The Man and His Dream*

River Phoenix, *Running on Empty*

Dean Stockwell, *Married to the Mob*

ACTRESS IN A SUPPORTING ROLE

Joan Cusack, *Working Girl*

Geena Davis, *The Accidental Tourist*

Frances McDormand, *Mississippi Burning*

Michelle Pfeiffer, *Dangerous Liaisons*

Sigourney Weaver, *Working Girl*

DIRECTING

Charles Crichton, *A Fish Called Wanda*

Barry Levinson, *Rain Man*

Mike Nichols, *Working Girl*

Alan Parker, *Mississippi Burning*

Martin Scorsese, *The Last Temptation of Christ*

WRITING

SCREENPLAY WRITTEN DIRECTLY FOR THE SCREEN

Ronald Bass and Barry Morrow, screenplay; Barry Morrow, story, *Rain Man*

John Cleese, screenplay; John Cleese and Charles Crichton, story, *A Fish Called Wanda*

Naomi Foner, *Running on Empty*

Gary Ross and Anne Spielberg, *Big*

Ron Shelton, *Bull Durham*

SCREENPLAY BASED ON MATERIAL FROM ANOTHER MEDIUM

Jean-Claude Carrière and Philip Kaufman, *The Unbearable Lightness of Being*

Christine Edzard, *Little Dorrit*

Frank Galati and Lawrence Kasdan, *The Accidental Tourist*

Christopher Hampton, *Dangerous Liaisons*

Anna Hamilton Phelan, screenplay; Anna Hamilton Phelan and Tab Murphy, story, *Gorillas in the Mist*

CINEMATOGRAPHY

Peter Biziou, *Mississippi Burning*

Dean Cundey, *Who Framed Roger Rabbit*

Conrad L. Hall, *Tequila Sunrise*

Sven Nykvist, *The Unbearable Lightness of Being*

John Seale, *Rain Man*

ART DIRECTION

Albert Brenner, art direction; Garrett Lewis, set decoration, *Beaches*

Stuart Craig, art direction; Gerard James, set decoration, *Dangerous Liaisons*

Ida Random, art direction; Linda DeScenna, set decoration, *Rain Man*

Elliot Scott, art direction; Peter Howitt, set decoration, *Who Framed Roger Rabbit*

Dean Tavoularis, art direction; Armin Ganz, set decoration, *Tucker: The Man and His Dream*

SOUND

Don Bassman, Kevin F. Cleary, Richard Overton and Al Overton, *Die Hard*

Les Fresholtz, Dick Alexander, Vern Poore and Willie D. Burton, *Bird*

Robert Knudson, John Boyd, Don Digirolamo and Tony Dawe, *Who Framed Roger Rabbit*

Robert Litt, Elliot Tyson, Rick Kline and Danny Michael, *Mississippi Burning*

Andy Nelson, Brian Saunders and Peter Handford, *Gorillas in the Mist*

MUSIC

SONG

"Calling You," *Bagdad Cafe*, Bob Telson, music and lyrics

"Let the River Run," *Working Girl*, Carly Simon, music and lyrics

"Two Hearts," *Buster*, Lamont Dozier, music; Phil Collins, lyrics

ORIGINAL SCORE

George Fenton, *Dangerous Liaisons*

Dave Grusin, *The Milagro Beanfield War*

Maurice Jarre, *Gorillas in the Mist*

John Williams, *The Accidental Tourist*

Hans Zimmer, *Rain Man*

FILM EDITING

Stuart Baird, *Gorillas in the Mist*

Gerry Hambling, *Mississippi Burning*

Stu Linder, *Rain Man*

Arthur Schmidt, *Who Framed Roger Rabbit*

Frank J. Urioste and John F. Link, *Die Hard*

COSTUME DESIGN

James Acheson, *Dangerous Liaisons*

Milena Canonero, *Tucker: The Man and His Dream*

Deborah Nadoolman, *Coming to America*

Patricia Norris, *Sunset*

Jane Robinson, *A Handful of Dust*

MAKEUP

Rick Baker, *Coming to America*

Tom Burman and Bari Dreiband-Burman, *Scrooged*

Ve Neill, Steve La Porte and Robert Short, *Beetlejuice*

VISUAL EFFECTS

Richard Edlund, Al DiSarro, Brent Boates and Thaine Morris, *Die Hard*

Dennis Muren, Michael McAlister, Phil Tippett and Chris Evans, *Willow*

Ken Ralston, Richard Williams, Edward Jones and George Gibbs, *Who Framed Roger Rabbit*

SOUND EFFECTS EDITING

Ben Burtt and Richard Hymns, *Willow*

Charles L. Campbell and Louis L. Edemann, *Who Framed Roger Rabbit*

Stephen H. Flick and Richard Shorr, *Die Hard*

SHORT FILMS

ANIMATION

The Cat Came Back (Cordell Barker, producer; National Film Board of Canada)

Technological Threat (Bill Kroyer and Brian Jennings, producers; Kroyer Films, Inc.)

Tin Toy (John Lasseter and William Reeves, producers; Pixar)

LIVE ACTION

The Appointments of Dennis Jennings (Dean Parisot and Steven Wright, producer; Schooner Productions, Inc.)

Cadillac Dreams (Matia Karrell and Abbee Goldstein, producers; Cadillac Dreams Production)

Gullah Tales (George deGolian and Gary Moss, producers; Georgia State University)

DOCUMENTARY

SHORT SUBJECT

The Children's Storefront (Karen Goodman, producer; Simon and Goodman Picture Company Production)

Family Gathering (Lise Yasui and Ann Tegnell, producers; Lise Yasui Production)

Gang Cops (Thomas B. Fleming and Daniel J. Marks, producers; University of Southern California Center for Visual Anthropology and the School of Cinema/Television)

Portrait of Imogen (Nancy Hale and Meg Partridge, producers; Pacific Pictures Production)

You Don't Have to Die (William Guttentag and Malcolm Clarke, producers; Tiger Rose Production in association with Filmworks, Inc.)

FEATURE

The Cry of Reason — Beyers Naude: An Afrikaner Speaks Out (Robert Bilheimer and Ronald Mix, producers; Worldwide Documentaries, Inc.)

Hotel Terminus: The Life and Times of Klaus Barbie (Marcel Ophuls, producer; The Memory Pictures Company)

Let's Get Lost (Bruce Weber and Nan Bush, producers; Little Bear Films, Inc.)

Promises to Keep (Ginny Durrin, producer; Durrin Productions, Inc.)

Who Killed Vincent Chin? (Renee Tajima and Christine Choy, producers; Film News Now Foundation and Detroit Educational Television Foundation Production)

FOREIGN LANGUAGE FILM

Hanussen, Hungary

The Music Teacher, Belgium

Pelle the Conqueror, Denmark

Salaam Bombay!, India

Women on the Verge of a Nervous Breakdown, Spain

SPECIAL ACHIEVEMENT AWARDS

ANIMATION DIRECTION
Richard Williams, *Who Framed Roger Rabbit*

HONORARY AWARDS

To the **National Film Board of Canada** in recognition of its 50th anniversary and its dedicated commitment to originate artistic, creative and technological activity and excellence in every area of filmmaking

To **Eastman Kodak Company** in recognition of the company's fundamental contributions to the art of motion pictures during the first century of film history

Denzel Washington, *Glory*

1989

BEST PICTURE

Born on the Fourth of July, A. Kitman Ho and Oliver Stone, producers (Universal)

Dead Poets Society, Steven Haft, Paul Junger Witt and Tony Thomas, producers (Buena Vista)

Driving Miss Daisy, Richard D. Zanuck and Lili Fini Zanuck, producers (Warner Bros.)

Field of Dreams, Lawrence Gordon and Charles Gordon, producers (Universal)

My Left Foot, Noel Pearson, producers (Miramax)

ACTOR IN A LEADING ROLE

Kenneth Branagh, *Henry V*

Tom Cruise, *Born on the Fourth of July*

Daniel Day-Lewis, *My Left Foot*

Morgan Freeman, *Driving Miss Daisy*

Robin Williams, *Dead Poets Society*

ACTRESS IN A LEADING ROLE

Isabelle Adjani, *Camille Claudel*

Pauline Collins, *Shirley Valentine*

Jessica Lange, *Music Box*

Michelle Pfeiffer, *The Fabulous Baker Boys*

Jessica Tandy, *Driving Miss Daisy*

ACTOR IN A SUPPORTING ROLE

Danny Aiello, *Do the Right Thing*

Dan Aykroyd, *Driving Miss Daisy*

Marlon Brando, *A Dry White Season*

Martin Landau, *Crimes and Misdemeanors*

Denzel Washington, *Glory*

ACTRESS IN A SUPPORTING ROLE

Brenda Fricker, *My Left Foot*

Anjelica Huston, *Enemies, A Love Story*

Lena Olin, *Enemies, A Love Story*

Julia Roberts, *Steel Magnolias*

Dianne Wiest, *Parenthood*

DIRECTING

Woody Allen, *Crimes and Misdemeanors*

Kenneth Branagh, *Henry V*

Jim Sheridan, *My Left Foot*

Oliver Stone, *Born on the Fourth of July*

Peter Weir, *Dead Poets Society*

WRITING

SCREENPLAY WRITTEN DIRECTLY FOR THE SCREEN

Woody Allen, *Crimes and Misdemeanors*

Nora Ephron, *When Harry Met Sally...*

Spike Lee, *Do the Right Thing*

Tom Schulman, *Dead Poets Society*

Steven Soderbergh, *sex, lies and videotape*

SCREENPLAY BASED ON MATERIAL FROM ANOTHER MEDIUM

Phil Alden Robinson, *Field of Dreams*

Jim Sheridan and Shane Connaughton, *My Left Foot*

Roger L. Simon and Paul Mazursky, *Enemies, A Love Story*

Oliver Stone and Ron Kovic, *Born on the Fourth of July*

Alfred Uhry, *Driving Miss Daisy*

CINEMATOGRAPHY

Michael Ballhaus, *The Fabulous Baker Boys*

Freddie Francis, *Glory*

Robert Richardson, *Born on the Fourth of July*

Mikael Salomon, *The Abyss*

Haskell Wexler, *Blaze*

ART DIRECTION

Leslie Dilley, art direction; Anne Kuljian, set decoration, *The Abyss*

Dante Ferretti, art direction; Francesca Lo Schiavo, set decoration, *The Adventures of Baron Munchausen*

Anton Furst, art direction; Peter Young, set decoration, *Batman*

Norman Garwood, art direction; Garrett Lewis, set decoration, *Glory*

Bruno Rubeo, art direction; Crispian Sallis, set decoration, *Driving Miss Daisy*

SOUND

Don Bassman, Kevin F. Cleary, Richard Overton and Lee Orloff, *The Abyss*

Ben Burtt, Gary Summers, Shawn Murphy and Tony Dawe, *Indiana Jones and the Last Crusade*

Michael Minkler, Gregory H. Watkins, Wylie Stateman and Tod A. Maitland, *Born on the Fourth of July*

Donald O. Mitchell, Kevin O'Connell, Greg P. Russell and Keith A. Wester, *Black Rain*

Donald O. Mitchell, Gregg C. Rudloff, Elliot Tyson and Russell Williams II, *Glory*

MUSIC

SONG

"After All," *Chances Are*, Tom Snow, music; Dean Pitchford, lyrics

"The Girl Who Used to Be Me," *Shirley Valentine*, Marvin Hamlisch, music; Alan and Marilyn Bergman, lyrics

Driving Miss Daisy

"I Love to See You Smile," *Parenthood*, Randy Newman, music and lyrics

"Kiss the Girl," *The Little Mermaid*, Alan Menken, music; Howard Ashman, lyrics

"Under the Sea," *The Little Mermaid*, Alan Menken, music; Howard Ashman, lyrics

ORIGINAL SCORE

David Grusin, *The Fabulous Baker Boys*

James Horner, *Field of Dreams*

Alan Menken, *The Little Mermaid*

John Williams, *Born on the Fourth of July*

John Williams, *Indiana Jones and the Last Crusade*

FILM EDITING

Noëlle Boisson, *The Bear*

David Brenner and Joe Hutshing, *Born on the Fourth of July*

Steven Rosenblum, *Glory*

William Steinkamp, *The Fabulous Baker Boys*

Mark Warner, *Driving Miss Daisy*

COSTUME DESIGN

Phyllis Dalton, *Henry V*

Elizabeth McBride, *Driving Miss Daisy*

Gabriella Pescucci, *The Adventures of Baron Munchausen*

Theodor Pistek, *Valmont*

Joe I. Tompkins, *Harlem Nights*

MAKEUP

Manlio Rocchetti, Lynn Barber and Kevin Haney, *Driving Miss Daisy*

Dick Smith, Ken Diaz and Greg Nelson, *Dad*

Maggie Weston and Fabrizio Sforza, *The Adventures of Baron Munchausen*

VISUAL EFFECTS

John Bruno, Dennis Muren, Hoyt Yeatman and Dennis Skotak, *The Abyss*

Richard Conway and Kent Houston, *The Adventures of Baron Munchausen*

Ken Ralston, Michael Lantieri, John Bell and Steve Gawley, *Back to the Future Part II*

SOUND EFFECTS EDITING

Milton C. Burrow and William L. Manger, *Black Rain*

Ben Burtt and Richard Hymns, *Indiana Jones and the Last Crusade*

Robert Henderson and Alan Robert Murray, *Lethal Weapon 2*

SHORT FILMS

ANIMATION

***Balance* (Christoph Lauenstein and Wolfgang Lauenstein, producers; Lauenstein Production)**

The Cow (Alexander Petrov, producer; The "Pilot" Co-op Animated Film Studio with VPTO Videofilm)

The Hill Farm (Mark Baker, producer; National Film and Television School)

LIVE ACTION

Amazon Diary (Robert Nixon, producer; Determined Productions, Inc.)

The Childeater (Jonathan Tammuz, producer; Stephen-Tammuz Productions, Ltd.)

***Work Experience* (James Hendrie, producer; North Inch Production Ltd.)**

DOCUMENTARY

SHORT SUBJECT

Fine Food, Fine Pastries, Open 6 to 9 (David Petersen, producer; David Petersen Productions)

***The Johnstown Flood* (Charles Guggenheim, producer; Guggenheim Productions)**

Yad Vashem: Preserving the Past to Ensure the Future (Ray Errol Fox, producer; Ray Errol Fox Production)

FEATURE

Adam Clayton Powell (Richard Killberg and Yvonne Smith, producers; RKB Productions)

***Common Threads: Stories From the Quilt* (Robert Epstein and Bill Couturie, producers; Telling Pictures and the Couturie Company Production)**

Crack USA: County Under Siege (Vince DiPersio and William Guttentag, producers; Half-Court Productions, Ltd.)

For All Mankind (Al Reinert and Betsy Broyles Breier, producers; Apollo Associates/FAM Productions Inc.)

Super Chief: The Life and Legacy of Earl Warren (Judith Leonard and Bill Jersey, producers; Quest Production)

FOREIGN LANGUAGE FILM

Camille Claudel, France

***Cinema Paradiso,* Italy**

Jesus of Montreal, Canada

Waltzing Regitze, Denmark

What Happened to Santiago, Puerto Rico

JEAN HERSHOLT HUMANITARIAN AWARD

Howard W. Koch

HONORARY AWARDS

To **Akira Kurosawa** for accomplishments that have inspired, delighted, enriched and entertained audiences and influenced filmmakers throughout the world

The Academy of Motion Picture Arts and Sciences' Board of Governors commends the contributions of the members of the engineering committees of **The Society of Motion Picture and Television Engineers (SMPTE).** By establishing industry standards, they have greatly contributed to making film a primary form of international communication.

1990

BEST PICTURE

Awakenings, Walter F. Parkes and Lawrence Lasker, producers (Columbia)

***Dances With Wolves,* Jim Wilson and Kevin Costner, producers (Orion)**

Ghost, Lisa Weinstein, producer (Paramount)

The Godfather Part III, Francis Ford Coppola, producer (Paramount)

GoodFellas, Irwin Winkler, producer (Warner Bros.)

ACTOR IN A LEADING ROLE

Kevin Costner, *Dances With Wolves*

Robert De Niro, *Awakenings*

Gérard Depardieu, *Cyrano de Bergerac*

Richard Harris, *The Field*

Jeremy Irons, *Reversal of Fortune*

ACTRESS IN A LEADING ROLE

Kathy Bates, *Misery*

Anjelica Huston, *The Grifters*

Julia Roberts, *Pretty Woman*

Meryl Streep, *Postcards From the Edge*

Joanne Woodward, *Mr. & Mrs. Bridge*

ACTOR IN A SUPPORTING ROLE

Bruce Davison, *Longtime Companion*

Andy Garcia, *The Godfather Part III*

Graham Greene, *Dances With Wolves*

Al Pacino, *Dick Tracy*

Joe Pesci, *GoodFellas*

ACTRESS IN A SUPPORTING ROLE

Annette Bening, *The Grifters*

Lorraine Bracco, *GoodFellas*

Whoopi Goldberg, *Ghost*

Diane Ladd, *Wild at Heart*

Mary McDonnell, *Dances With Wolves*

Dances With Wolves

DIRECTING

Francis Ford Coppola, *The Godfather Part III*

Kevin Costner, *Dances With Wolves*

Stephen Frears, *The Grifters*

Barbet Schroeder, *Reversal of Fortune*

Martin Scorsese, *GoodFellas*

WRITING

SCREENPLAY WRITTEN DIRECTLY FOR THE SCREEN

Woody Allen, *Alice*

Barry Levinson, *Avalon*

Bruce Joel Rubin, *Ghost*

Whit Stillman, *Metropolitan*

Peter Weir, *Green Card*

SCREENPLAY BASED ON MATERIAL FROM ANOTHER MEDIUM

Michael Blake, *Dances With Wolves*

Nicholas Kazan, *Reversal of Fortune*

Nicholas Pileggi and Martin Scorsese, *GoodFellas*

Donald E. Westlake, *The Grifters*

Steven Zaillian, *Awakenings*

CINEMATOGRAPHY

Allen Daviau, *Avalon*

Philippe Rousselot, *Henry & June*

Dean Semler, *Dances With Wolves*

Vittorio Storaro, *Dick Tracy*

Gordon Willis, *The Godfather Part III*

ART DIRECTION

Jeffrey Beecroft, art direction; Lisa Dean, set decoration, *Dances With Wolves*

Dante Ferretti, art direction; Francesca Lo Schiavo, set decoration, *Hamlet*

Ezio Frigerio, art direction; Jacques Rouxel, set decoration, *Cyrano de Bergerac*

Richard Sylbert, art direction; Rick Simpson, set decoration, *Dick Tracy*

Dean Tavoularis, art direction; Gary Fettis, set decoration, *The Godfather Part III*

SOUND

Don Bassman, Richard Overton, Kevin F. Cleary and Richard Bryce Goodman, *The Hunt for Red October*

Chris Jenkins, David E. Campbell, D. M. Hemphill and Thomas Causey, *Dick Tracy*

Michael J. Kohut, Carlos de Larios, Aaron Rochin and Nelson Stoll, *Total Recall*

Donald O. Mitchell, Rick Kline, Kevin O'Connell and Charles Wilborn, *Days of Thunder*

Jeffrey Perkins, Bill W. Benton, Greg Watkins and Russell Williams II, *Dances With Wolves*

MUSIC

SONG

"Blaze of Glory," *Young Guns II*, Jon Bon Jovi, music and lyrics

"I'm Checkin' Out," *Postcards From the Edge*, Shel Silverstein, music and lyrics

"Promise Me You'll Remember," *The Godfather Part III*, Carmine Coppola, music; John Bettis, lyrics

"Somewhere in My Memory," *Home Alone*, music by John Williams; lyrics by Leslie Bricusse

"Sooner Or Later" (I Always Get My Man), *Dick Tracy*, Stephen Sondheim, music and lyrics

ORIGINAL SCORE

John Barry, *Dances With Wolves*

David Grusin, *Havana*

Maurice Jarre, *Ghost*

Randy Newman, *Avalon*

John Williams, *Home Alone*

FILM EDITING

Barry Malkin, Lisa Fruchtman and Walter Murch, *The Godfather Part III*

Walter Murch, *Ghost*

Thelma Schoonmaker, *GoodFellas*

Neil Travis, *Dances With Wolves*

Dennis Virkler, John Wright, *The Hunt for Red October*

COSTUME DESIGN

Milena Canonero, *Dick Tracy*

Gloria Gresham, *Avalon*

Maurizio Millenotti, *Hamlet*

Franca Squarciapino, *Cyrano de Bergerac*

Elsa Zamparelli, *Dances With Wolves*

MAKEUP

Michèle Burke and Jean-Pierre Eychenne, *Cyrano de Bergerac*

John Caglione, Jr. and Doug Drexler, *Dick Tracy*

Ve Neill and Stan Winston, *Edward Scissorhands*

SOUND EFFECTS EDITING

Charles L. Campbell and Richard Franklin, *Flatliners*

Stephen H. Flick, *Total Recall*

Cecelia Hall and George Watters II, *The Hunt for Red October*

SHORT FILMS

ANIMATION

***Creature Comforts* (Nick Park, producer; Aardman Animations Ltd. Production)**

A Grand Day Out (Nick Park, producer; National Film and Television School)

Grasshoppers (Cavallette) (Bruno Bozzetto, producer; Bruno Bozzetto Production)

LIVE ACTION

Bronx Cheers (Raymond De Felitta and Matthew Gross, producers; American Film Institute)

Dear Rosie (Peter Cattaneo and Barnaby Thompson, producers; World's End Production)

***The Lunch Date* (Adam Davidson, producer; Adam Davidson Production)**

Senzeni Na? (What Have We Done?) (Bernard Joffa and Anthony E. Nicholas, producers; American Film Institute)

12:01 P.M. (Hillary Ripps and Jonathan Heap, producers; Chanticleer Films)

DOCUMENTARY

SHORT SUBJECT

Burning Down Tomorrow (Kit Thomas, producer; Interscope Communications Inc.)

Chimps: So Like Us (Karen Goodman and Kirk Simon, producers; Simon and Goodman Picture Company)

Days of Waiting (Steven Okazaki, producer; Mouchette Films Production)

Journey Into Life: The World of the Unborn (Derek Bromhall, producer; ABC/Kane Productions International, Inc.)

Rose Kennedy: A Life to Remember (Sanders and Mock Productions and American Film Foundation)

FEATURE

American Dream (Barbara Kopple and Arthur Cohn, producers; Cabin Creek Films)

Berkeley in the Sixties (Mark Kitchell, producer; Berkeley in the Sixties Production Partnership)

Building Bombs (Mark Mori and Susan Robinson, producers; Mori/Robinson Production)

Forever Activists: Stories From the Veterans of the Abraham Lincoln Brigade (Judith Montell, producer; Judith Montell Production)

Waldo Salt: A Screenwriter's Journey (Robert Hillmann and Eugene Corr, producers; Waldo Productions, Inc.)

FOREIGN LANGUAGE FILM

Cyrano de Bergerac, France

Journey of Hope, Switzerland

Ju Dou, People's Republic of China

The Nasty Girl, Germany

Open Doors, Italy

IRVING G. THALBERG MEMORIAL AWARD

David Brown and Richard D. Zanuck

SPECIAL ACHIEVEMENT AWARDS

VISUAL EFFECTS

Eric Brevig, Rob Bottin, Tim McGovern and Alex Funke, Total Recall

HONORARY AWARDS

To **Sophia Loren,** one of the genuine treasures of world cinema who, in a career rich with memorable performances, has added permanent luster to our art form

To **Myrna Loy,** in recognition of her extraordinary qualities both on screen and off, with appreciation for a lifetime's worth of indelible performances

To **Roderick T. Ryan, Don Trumbull** and **Geoffrey H. Williamson** in appreciation for outstanding service and dedication in upholding the high standards of the Academy of Motion Picture Arts and Sciences

1991

BEST PICTURE

Beauty and the Beast, Don Hahn, producer (Buena Vista)

Bugsy, Barry Levinson and Warren Beatty, producers (TriStar)

JFK, A. Kitman Ho and Oliver Stone, producers (Warner Bros.)

Anthony Hopkins,
The Silence of the Lambs

The Prince of Tides, Barbra Streisand and Andrew Karsch, producers (Columbia)

The Silence of the Lambs, Edward Saxon, Kenneth Utt and Ron Bozman, producers (Orion)

ACTOR IN A LEADING ROLE

Warren Beatty, *Bugsy*

Robert De Niro, *Cape Fear*

Anthony Hopkins, *The Silence of the Lambs*

Nick Nolte, *The Prince of Tides*

Robin Williams, *The Fisher King*

ACTRESS IN A LEADING ROLE

Geena Davis, *Thelma & Louise*

Laura Dern, *Rambling Rose*

Jodie Foster, *The Silence of the Lambs*

Bette Midler, *For the Boys*

Susan Sarandon, *Thelma & Louise*

ACTOR IN A SUPPORTING ROLE

Tommy Lee Jones, *JFK*

Harvey Keitel, *Bugsy*

Ben Kingsley, *Bugsy*

Michael Lerner, *Barton Fink*

Jack Palance, *City Slickers*

ACTRESS IN A SUPPORTING ROLE

Diane Ladd, *Rambling Rose*

Juliette Lewis, *Cape Fear*

Kate Nelligan, *The Prince of Tides*

Mercedes Ruehl, *The Fisher King*

Jessica Tandy, *Fried Green Tomatoes*

DIRECTING

Jonathan Demme, *The Silence of the Lambs*

Barry Levinson, *Bugsy*

Ridley Scott, *Thelma & Louise*

John Singleton, *Boyz N the Hood*

Oliver Stone, *JFK*

WRITING

SCREENPLAY WRITTEN DIRECTLY FOR THE SCREEN

Lawrence Kasdan and Meg Kasdan, *Grand Canyon*

Callie Khouri, *Thelma & Louise*

Richard LaGravenese, *The Fisher King*

John Singleton, *Boyz N the Hood*

James Toback, *Bugsy*

SCREENPLAY BASED ON MATERIAL PREVIOUSLY PRODUCED OR PUBLISHED

Pat Conroy and Becky Johnston, *The Prince of Tides*

Fannie Flagg and Carol Sobieski, *Fried Green Tomatoes*

Agnieszka Holland, *Europa Europa*

Oliver Stone and Zachary Sklar, *JFK*

Ted Tally, *The Silence of the Lambs*

CINEMATOGRAPHY

Adrian Biddle, *Thelma & Louise*

Allen Daviau, *Bugsy*

Stephen Goldblatt, *The Prince of Tides*

Adam Greenberg, *Terminator 2: Judgment Day*

Robert Richardson, *JFK*

ART DIRECTION

Mel Bourne, art direction; Cindy Carr, set decoration, *The Fisher King*

Norman Garwood, art direction; Garrett Lewis, set decoration, *Hook*

Dennis Gassner, art direction; Nancy Haigh, set decoration, *Barton Fink*

Dennis Gassner, art direction; Nancy Haigh, set decoration, *Bugsy*

Paul Sylbert, art direction; Caryl Heller, set decoration, *The Prince of Tides*

SOUND

Tom Fleischman and Christopher Newman, *The Silence of the Lambs*

Tom Johnson, Gary Rydstrom, Gary Summers and Lee Orloff, *Terminator 2: Judgment Day*

Michael Minkler, Gregg Landaker and Tod A. Maitland, *JFK*

Terry Porter, Mel Metcalfe, David J. Hudson and Doc Kane, *Beauty and the Beast*

Gary Summers, Randy Thom, Gary Rydstrom and Glenn Williams, *Backdraft*

MUSIC

SONG

"Beauty and the Beast," *Beauty and the Beast*, Alan Menken, music; Howard Ashman, lyrics

"Belle," *Beauty and the Beast*, Alan Menken, music; Howard Ashman, lyrics

"Be Our Guest," *Beauty and the Beast*, Alan Menken, music; Howard Ashman, lyrics

(Everything I Do) "I Do It for You," *Robin Hood: Prince of Thieves*, Michael Kamen, music; Bryan Adams and Robert John Lange, lyrics

"When You're Alone," *Hook*, John Williams, music; Leslie Bricusse, lyrics

ORIGINAL SCORE

George Fenton, *The Fisher King*

James Newton Howard, *The Prince of Tides*

Alan Menken, *Beauty and the Beast*

Ennio Morricone, *Bugsy*

John Williams, *JFK*

FILM EDITING

Conrad Buff, Mark Goldblatt and Richard A. Harris, *Terminator 2: Judgment Day*

Gerry Hambling, *The Commitments*

Joe Hutshing and Pietro Scalia, *JFK*

Craig McKay, *The Silence of the Lambs*

Thom Noble, *Thelma & Louise*

COSTUME DESIGN

Richard Hornung, *Barton Fink*

Corinne Jorry, *Madame Bovary*

Ruth Myers, *The Addams Family*

Anthony Powell, *Hook*

Albert Wolsky, *Bugsy*

MAKEUP

Michael Mills, Edward French and Richard Snell, *Star Trek VI: The Undiscovered Country*

Christina Smith, Monty Westmore and Greg Cannom, *Hook*

Stan Winston and Jeff Dawn, *Terminator 2: Judgment Day*

VISUAL EFFECTS

Eric Brevig, Harley Jessup, Mark Sullivan and Michael Lantieri, *Hook*

Dennis Muren, Stan Winston, Gene Warren, Jr. and Robert Skotak, *Terminator 2: Judgment Day*

Mikael Salomon, Allen Hall, Clay Pinney and Scott Farrar, *Backdraft*

SOUND EFFECTS EDITING

Gary Rydstrom and Gloria S. Borders, *Terminator 2: Judgment Day*

Gary Rydstrom and Richard Hymns, *Backdraft*

George Watters II and F. Hudson Miller, *Star Trek VI: The Undiscovered Country*

SHORT FILMS

ANIMATION

Blackfly (Christopher Hinton, producer; National Film Board of Canada)

***Manipulation* (Daniel Greaves, producer; Tandem Films Production)**

Strings (Wendy Tilby, producer; National Film Board of Canada)

LIVE ACTION

Birch Street Gym (Stephen Kessler and Thomas R. Conroy, producers; Chanticleer Films)

Last Breeze of Summer (David M. Massey, producer; American Film Institute)

***Session Man* (Seth Winston and Rob Fried, producers; Chanticleer Films)**

DOCUMENTARY

SHORT SUBJECT

Birdnesters of Thailand (*Shadow Hunters*) (Antenne 2/National Geographic Society/M.D.I./Wind Horse Production)

***Deadly Deception: General Electric, Nuclear Weapons and Our Environment* (Debra Chasnoff, producer; Women's Educational Media, Inc. Production)**

A Little Vicious (Immy Humes, producer; Film and Video Workshop, Inc. Production)

The Mark of the Maker (David McGowan, producer; McGowan Film and Video, Inc. Production)

Memorial: Letters From American Soldiers (Bill Couturie and Bernard Edelman, producers; Couturie Company Production)

FEATURE

Death on the Job (Vince DiPersio and William Guttentag, producers; Half-Court Pictures, Ltd. Production)

Doing Time: Life Inside the Big House (Alan Raymond and Susan Raymond, producers; Video Verité Production)

***In the Shadow of the Stars* (Allie Light and Irving Saraf, producers; Light-Saraf Films Production)**

The Restless Conscience (Hava Kohav Beller, producer; Hava Kohav Beller Production)

Wild by Law (Lawrence Hott and Diane Garey, producers; Florentine Films Production)

FOREIGN LANGUAGE FILM

Children of Nature, Iceland

The Elementary School, Czechoslovakia

***Mediterraneo,* Italy**

The Ox, Sweden

Raise the Red Lantern, Hong Kong

IRVING G. THALBERG MEMORIAL AWARD

George Lucas

HONORARY AWARDS

To **Satyajit Ray,** in recognition of his rare mastery of the art of motion pictures, and of his profound humanitarian outlook, which has had an indelible influence on filmmakers and audiences throughout the world

To **Pete Comandini, Richard T. Dayton, Donald Hagans** and **Richard T. Ryan** of YCM Laboratories for the creation and development of a motion picture film restoration process using liquid gate and registration correction on a contact printer

To **Richard J. Stumpf** and **Joseph Westheimer** for outstanding service and dedication in upholding the high standards of the Academy of Motion Picture Arts and Sciences

1992

BEST PICTURE

The Crying Game, Stephen Woolley, producer (Miramax)

A Few Good Men, David Brown, Rob Reiner and Andrew Scheinman, producers (Columbia)

Howards End, Ismail Merchant, producer (Sony Pictures Classics)

Scent of a Woman, Martin Brest, producer (Universal)

***Unforgiven,* Clint Eastwood, producer (Warner Bros.)**

Emma Thompson, *Howards End*

ACTOR IN A LEADING ROLE

Robert Downey, Jr., *Chaplin*

Clint Eastwood, *Unforgiven*

Al Pacino, *Scent of a Woman*

Stephen Rea, *The Crying Game*

Denzel Washington, *Malcolm X*

ACTRESS IN A LEADING ROLE

Catherine Deneuve, *Indochine*

Mary McDonnell, *Passion Fish*

Michelle Pfeiffer, *Love Field*

Susan Sarandon, *Lorenzo's Oil*

Emma Thompson, *Howards End*

ACTOR IN A SUPPORTING ROLE

Jaye Davidson, *The Crying Game*

Gene Hackman, *Unforgiven*

Jack Nicholson, *A Few Good Men*

Al Pacino, *Glengarry Glen Ross*

David Paymer, *Mr. Saturday Night*

ACTRESS IN A SUPPORTING ROLE

Judy Davis, *Husbands and Wives*

Joan Plowright, *Enchanted April*

Vanessa Redgrave, *Howards End*

Miranda Richardson, *Damage*

Marisa Tomei, *My Cousin Vinny*

DIRECTING

Robert Altman, *The Player*

Martin Brest, *Scent of a Woman*

Clint Eastwood, *Unforgiven*

James Ivory, *Howards End*

Neil Jordan, *The Crying Game*

WRITING

SCREENPLAY WRITTEN DIRECTLY FOR THE SCREEN

Woody Allen, *Husbands and Wives*

Neil Jordan, *The Crying Game*

George Miller and Nick Enright, *Lorenzo's Oil*

John Sayles, *Passion Fish*

David Webb Peoples, *Unforgiven*

SCREENPLAY BASED ON MATERIAL PREVIOUSLY PRODUCED OR PUBLISHED

Peter Barnes, *Enchanted April*

Richard Friedenberg, *A River Runs Through It*

Bo Goldman, *Scent of a Woman*

Ruth Prawer Jhabvala, *Howards End*

Michael Tolkin, *The Player*

CINEMATOGRAPHY

Stephen H. Burum, *Hoffa*

Robert Fraisse, *The Lover*

Jack N. Green, *Unforgiven*

Tony Pierce-Roberts, *Howards End*

Philippe Rousselot, *A River Runs Through It*

ART DIRECTION

Luciana Arrighi, art direction; Ian Whittaker, set decoration, *Howards End*

Henry Bumstead, art direction; Janice Blackie-Goodine, set decoration, *Unforgiven*

Stuart Craig, art direction; Chris A. Butler, set decoration, *Chaplin*

Thomas Sanders, art direction; Garrett Lewis, set decoration, *Bram Stoker's Dracula*

Ferdinando Scarfiotti, art direction; Linda DeScenna, set decoration, *Toys*

SOUND

Les Fresholtz, Vern Poore, Dick Alexander and Rob Young, *Unforgiven*

Chris Jenkins, Doug Hemphill, Mark Smith and Simon Kaye, *The Last of the Mohicans*

Don Mitchell, Frank A. Montano, Rick Hart and Scott Smith, *Under Siege*

Kevin O'Connell, Rick Kline and Bob Eber, *A Few Good Men*

Terry Porter, Mel Metcalfe, David J. Hudson and Doc Kane, *Aladdin*

MUSIC

SONG

"Beautiful Maria of My Soul," *The Mambo Kings*, Robert Kraft, music; Arne Glimcher, lyrics

"Friend Like Me," *Aladdin*, Alan Menken, music; Howard Ashman, lyrics

"I Have Nothing," *The Bodyguard*, David Foster, music; Linda Thompson, lyrics

"Run to You," *The Bodyguard*, Jud Friedman, music; Allan Rich, lyrics

"A Whole New World," *Aladdin*, Alan Menken, music; Tim Rice, lyrics

ORIGINAL SCORE

John Barry, *Chaplin*

Jerry Goldsmith, *Basic Instinct*

Mark Isham, *A River Runs Through It*

Alan Menken, *Aladdin*

Richard Robbins, *Howards End*

FILM EDITING

Joel Cox, *Unforgiven*

Robert Leighton, *A Few Good Men*

Kant Pan, *The Crying Game*

Geraldine Peroni, *The Player*

Frank J. Urioste, *Basic Instinct*

COSTUME DESIGN

Jenny Beavan and John Bright, *Howards End*

Ruth Carter, *Malcolm X*

Eiko Ishioka, *Bram Stoker's Dracula*

Sheena Napier, *Enchanted April*

Albert Wolsky, *Toys*

MAKEUP

Greg Cannom, Michèle Burke and Matthew W. Mungle, *Bram Stoker's Dracula*

Ve Neill, Greg Cannom and John Blake, *Hoffa*

Ve Neill, Ronnie Specter and Stan Winston, *Batman Returns*

VISUAL EFFECTS

Richard Edlund, Alec Gillis, Tom Woodruff, Jr. and George Gibbs, *Alien³*

Michael Fink, Craig Barron, John Bruno and Dennis Skotak, *Batman Returns*

Ken Ralston, Doug Chiang, Doug Smythe and Tom Woodruff, Jr., *Death Becomes Her*

SOUND EFFECTS EDITING

John Leveque and Bruce Stambler, *Under Siege*

Mark Mangini, *Aladdin*

Tom C. McCarthy and David E. Stone, *Bram Stoker's Dracula*

SHORT FILMS

ANIMATION

Adam (Peter Lord, producer; Aardman Animations Ltd. Production)

***Mona Lisa Descending a Staircase* (Joan C. Gratz, producer; Joan C. Gratz Production)**

Reci, Reci, Reci . . . (Words, Words, Words) (Michaela Pavlátová, producer; Krátky Film Production)

The Sandman (Paul Berry, producer; Batty Berry Mackinnon Production)

Screen Play (Barry J.C. Purves, producer; Bare Boards Film Production)

LIVE ACTION

Contact (Jonathan Darby and Jana Sue Memel, producers; Chanticleer Films)

Cruise Control (Matt Palmieri, producer; Palmieri Pictures Production)

The Lady in Waiting (Christian M. Taylor, producer; Taylor Made Films Production)

***Omnibus* (Sam Karmann, producer; Lazennec tout court/Le C.R.R.A.V. Production)**

Swan Song (Kenneth Branagh and David Parfitt, producers; Renaissance Film PLC Production)

DOCUMENTARY

SHORT SUBJECT

At the Edge of Conquest: The Journey of Chief Wai-Wai
(Geoffrey O'Connor, producer; Realis Pictures Inc.
Production)

Beyond Imagining: Margaret Anderson and the "Little Review"
(Wendy L. Weinberg, producer; Wendy L. Weinberg
Production)

The Colours of My Father: A Portrait of Sam Borenstein
(Imageries P.B. Ltd. Production in coproduction with the
National Film Board of Canada)

Educating Peter (Thomas C. Goodwin and Gerardine
Wurzburg, producers; State of the Art, Inc. Production)

When Abortion Was Illegal: Untold Stories (Dorothy Fadiman,
producer; Concentric Media Production)

FEATURE

Changing Our Minds: The Story of Dr. Evelyn Hooker (David
Haugland, producer; Intrepid Production)

Fires of Kuwait (Black Sun Films, Ltd./IMAX Corporation
Production)

Liberators: Fighting on Two Fronts in World War II (William
Miles and Nina Rosenblum, producers; Miles Educational
Film Productions, Inc.)

Music for the Movies: Bernard Herrmann (Alternate Current
Inc./Les Films d'Ici Production)

The Panama Deception (Barbara Trent and David Kasper,
producers; Empowerment Project Production)

FOREIGN LANGUAGE FILM

Close to Eden, Russia

Daens, Belgium

Indochine, France

A Place in the World, Uruguay (This film was declared
ineligible and removed from the final ballot because
it had insufficient Uruguayan artistic control.)

Schtonk, Germany

JEAN HERSHOLT HUMANITARIAN AWARD

Audrey Hepburn

Elizabeth Taylor

HONORARY AWARDS

To **Federico Fellini** in appreciation of one of the screen's
master storytellers

To **Petro Vlahos** in appreciation for outstanding service and
dedication in upholding the high standards of the Academy of
Motion Picture Arts and Sciences

1993

PICTURE

The Fugitive, Arnold Kopelson, producer (Warner Bros.)

In the Name of the Father, Jim Sheridan, producer (Universal)

The Piano, Jan Chapman, producer (Miramax)

The Remains of the Day, Mike Nichols, John Calley and Ismail
Merchant, producers (Columbia)

Schindler's List, Stephen Spielberg, Gerald R. Molen and
Branko Lustig, producers (Universal)

Holly Hunter and Anna Paquin,
The Piano

ACTOR IN A LEADING ROLE

Daniel Day-Lewis, *In the Name of the Father*

Laurence Fishburne, *What's Love Got to Do With It*

Tom Hanks, ***Philadelphia***

Anthony Hopkins, *The Remains of the Day*

Liam Neeson, *Schindler's List*

ACTRESS IN A LEADING ROLE

Angela Bassett, *What's Love Got to Do With It*

Stockard Channing, *Six Degrees of Separation*

Holly Hunter, ***The Piano***

Emma Thompson, *The Remains of the Day*

Debra Winger, *Shadowlands*

ACTOR IN A SUPPORTING ROLE

Leonardo DiCaprio, *What's Eating Gilbert Grape*

Ralph Fiennes, *Schindler's List*

Tommy Lee Jones, ***The Fugitive***

John Malkovich, *In the Line of Fire*

Pete Postlethwaite, *In the Name of the Father*

ACTRESS IN A SUPPORTING ROLE

Holly Hunter, *The Firm*

Anna Paquin, ***The Piano***

Rosie Perez, *Fearless*

Winona Ryder, *The Age of Innocence*

Emma Thompson, *In the Name of the Father*

DIRECTING

Robert Altman, *Short Cuts*

Jane Campion, *The Piano*

James Ivory, *The Remains of the Day*

Jim Sheridan, *In the Name of the Father*

Steven Spielberg, ***Schindler's List***

WRITING

SREENPLAY WRITTEN DIRECTLY
FOR THE SCREEN
Jane Campion, ***The Piano***

Nora Ephron, David S. Ward and Jeff Arch, screenplay;
Jeff Arch, story, *Sleepless in Seattle*

Jeff Maguire, *In the Line of Fire*

Ron Nyswaner, *Philadelphia*

Gary Ross, *Dave*

SCREENPLAY BASED ON MATERIAL PREVIOUSLY PRODUCED OR PUBLISHED

Jay Cocks and Martin Scorsese, *The Age of Innocence*

Terry George and Jim Sheridan, *In the Name of the Father*

Ruth Prawer Jhabvala, *The Remains of the Day*

William Nicholson, *Shadowlands*

Steven Zaillian, *Schindler's List*

CINEMATOGRAPHY

Gu Changwei, *Farewell My Concubine*

Michael Chapman, *The Fugitive*

Stuart Dryburgh, *The Piano*

Conrad L. Hall, *Searching for Bobby Fischer*

Janusz Kaminski, *Schindler's List*

ART DIRECTION

Ken Adam, art direction; Marvin March, set decoration, *Addams Family Values*

Luciana Arrighi, art direction; Ian Whittaker, set decoration, *The Remains of the Day*

Dante Ferretti, art direction; Robert J. Franco, set decoration, *The Age of Innocence*

Allan Starski, art direction; Ewa Braun, set decoration, *Schindler's List*

Ben Van Os and Jan Roelfs, art direction, *Orlando*

SOUND

Chris Carpenter, D. M. Hemphill, Bill W. Benton and Lee Orloff, *Geronimo: An American Legend*

Michael Minkler, Bob Beemer and Tim Cooney, *Cliffhanger*

Donald O. Mitchell, Michael Herbick, Frank A. Montaño and Scott D. Smith, *The Fugitive*

Andy Nelson, Steve Pederson, Scott Millan and Ron Judkins, *Schindler's List*

Gary Summers, Gary Rydstrom, Shawn Murphy and Ron Judkins, *Jurassic Park*

MUSIC

SONG

"Again," *Poetic Justice*, Janet Jackson, James Harris III and Terry Lewis, music and lyrics

"The Day I Fall in Love," *Beethoven's 2nd*, Carole Bayer Sager, James Ingram and Clif Magness, music and lyrics

"Philadelphia," *Philadelphia*, Neil Young, music and lyrics

"Streets of Philadelphia," *Philadelphia*, Bruce Springsteen, music and lyrics

"A Wink and a Smile," *Sleepless in Seattle*, Marc Shaiman, music; Ramsey McLean, lyrics

ORIGINAL SCORE

Elmer Bernstein, *The Age of Innocence*

Dave Grusin, *The Firm*

James Newton Howard, *The Fugitive*

Richard Robbins, *The Remains of the Day*

John Williams, *Schindler's List*

FILM EDITING

Anne V. Coates, *In the Line of Fire*

Gerry Hambling, *In the Name of the Father*

Veronika Jenet, *The Piano*

Michael Kahn, *Schindler's List*

Dennis Virkler, David Finfer, Dean Goodhill, Don Brochu, Richard Nord and Dov Hoenig, *The Fugitive*

COSTUME DESIGN

Jenny Beavan and John Bright, *The Remains of the Day*

Anna Biedrzycka-Sheppard, *Schindler's List*

Janet Patterson, *The Piano*

Gabriella Pescucci, *The Age of Innocence*

Sandy Powell, *Orlando*

MAKEUP

Greg Cannom, Ve Neill and Yolanda Toussieng, *Mrs. Doubtfire*

Carl Fullerton and Alan D'Angerio, *Philadelphia*

Christina Smith, Matthew Mungle and Judy Alexander Cory, *Schindler's List*

VISUAL EFFECTS

Pete Kozachik, Eric Leighton, Ariel Velasco Shaw and Gordon Baker, *The Nightmare Before Christmas*

Neil Krepela, John Richardson, John Bruno and Pamela Easley, *Cliffhanger*

Dennis Muren, Stan Winston, Phil Tippett and Michael Lantieri, *Jurassic Park*

SOUND EFFECTS EDITING

John Leveque and Bruce Stambler, *The Fugitive*

Gary Rydstrom and Richard Hymns, *Jurassic Park*

Wylie Stateman and Gregg Baxter, *Cliffhanger*

SHORT FILMS

ANIMATION

Blindscape (Stephen Palmer, producer; National Film and Television School)

The Mighty River (Frédéric Back and Hubert Tison, producers; Canadian Broadcasting Corporation/Société Radio-Canada Production)

Small Talk (Bob Godfrey and Kevin Baldwin, producers; Bob Godfrey Films, Ltd.)

The Village (Mark Baker, producer; Pizazz Pictures Production)

***The Wrong Trousers* (Nick Park, producer; Aardman Animations Limited Production)**

LIVE ACTION

***Black Rider (Schwarzfahrer)* (Pepe Danquart, producer; Trans-Film GmbH Production)**

Down on the Waterfront (Stacy Title and Jonathan Penner, producers; Stacy Title/Jonathan Penner Production)

The Dutch Master (Susan Seidelman and Jonathan Brett, producers; Regina Ziegler Film Production)

Partners (Peter Weller and Jana Sue Memel, producers; Chanticleer Films)

The Screw (La Vis) (Didier Flamand, producer; Perla Films Production)

OSCAR TRIVIA

CONSECUTIVE BEST ACTOR WINS

Spencer Tracy: *Captains Courageous* (1937) and *Boys Town* (1938)

Tom Hanks: *Philadelphia* (1993) and *Forrest Gump* (1994)

CONSECUTIVE BEST ACTRESS WINS

Luise Rainer: *The Great Ziegfeld* (1936) and *The Good Earth* (1937)

Katharine Hepburn: *Guess Who's Coming to Dinner* (1967) and *The Lion in Winter* (1968)

CONSECUTIVE DIRECTING WINS

John Ford: *The Grapes of Wrath* (1940) and *How Green Was My Valley* (1941)

Joseph L. Mankiewicz: *A Letter to Three Wives* (1949) and *All About Eve* (1950)

ONLY SILENT FILM TO WIN BEST PICTURE

Wings (1927–1928)

ONLY X-RATED FILM TO WIN BEST PICTURE

Midnight Cowboy (1969)

ONLY ANIMATED FILM NOMINATED FOR BEST PICTURE

Beauty and the Beast (1991)

MARRIED COUPLES WITH OSCARS

Laurence Olivier, *Hamlet* (1948) and **Vivien Leigh,** *A Streetcar Named Desire* (1951)

Paul Newman, *The Color of Money* (1986) and **Joanne Woodward,** *The Three Faces of Eve* (1957)

OLDEST OSCAR RECIPIENTS

George Burns was 80 when he won Best Actor honors for *The Sunshine Boys* (1975).

Jessica Tandy was also 80 when she won the Best Actress nod for *Driving Miss Daisy* (1989).

YOUNGEST OSCAR RECIPIENTS

Shirley Temple won a special award in 1934 at age five.

Tatum O'Neal was 10 when she won a Best Supporting Actress Oscar in 1973 for *Paper Moon.*

Source: Academy of Motion Picture Arts and Sciences

DOCUMENTARY

SHORT SUBJECT

Blood Ties: The Life and Work of Sally Mann (Steven Cantor and Peter Spirer, producers; Moving Target Production)

Chicks in White Satin (Elaine Holliman and Jason Schneider, producers; University of Southern California School of Cinema/Television)

***Defending Our Lives* (Margaret Lazarus and Renner Wunderlich, producers; Cambridge Documentary Films Production)**

FEATURE

The Broadcast Tapes of Dr. Peter (David Paperny and Arthur Ginsberg, producers; Canadian Broadcasting Corporation/HBO Films Production)

Children of Fate (Susan Todd and Andrew Young, producers; Young/Friedson Production)

For Better or for Worse (David Collier and Betsy Thompson, producers; David Collier Production)

***I Am a Promise: The Children of Stanton Elementary School* (Susan Raymond and Alan Raymond, Verité Films Production)**

The War Room (D. A. Pennebaker and Chris Hegedus, producers; R. J. Cutler/Wendy Ettinger/Frazer Pennebaker Production)

FOREIGN LANGUAGE FILM

***Belle Époque,* Spain**

Farewell My Concubine, Hong Kong

Hedd Wyn, United Kingdom

The Scent of Green Papaya, Vietnam

The Wedding Banquet, Republic of China on Taiwan

JEAN HERSHOLT HUMANITARIAN AWARD

Paul Newman

HONORARY AWARDS

To **Deborah Kerr** in appreciation for a full career's worth of elegant and beautifully crafted performances

1994

BEST PICTURE

***Forrest Gump,* Wendy Finerman, Steve Tisch and Steve Starkey, producers (Paramount)**

Four Weddings and a Funeral, Duncan Kenworthy, producer (Gramercy)

Pulp Fiction, Lawrence Bender, producer (Miramax)

Quiz Show, Robert Redford, Michael Jacobs, Julian Krainin and Michael Nozik, producers (Buena Vista)

The Shawshank Redemption, Niki Marvin, producer (Columbia)

ACTOR IN A LEADING ROLE

Morgan Freeman, *The Shawshank Redemption*

Tom Hanks, *Forrest Gump*

Nigel Hawthorne, *The Madness of King George*

Paul Newman, *Nobody's Fool*

John Travolta, *Pulp Fiction*

ACTRESS IN A LEADING ROLE

Jodie Foster, *Nell*

Jessica Lange, *Blue Sky*

Miranda Richardson, *Tom and Viv*

Winona Ryder, *Little Women*

Susan Sarandon, *The Client*

ACTOR IN A SUPPORTING ROLE

Samuel L. Jackson, *Pulp Fiction*

Martin Landau, *Ed Wood*

Chazz Palminteri, *Bullets Over Broadway*

Paul Scofield, *Quiz Show*

Gary Sinise, *Forrest Gump*

ACTRESS IN A SUPPORTING ROLE

Rosemary Harris, *Tom and Viv*

Helen Mirren, *The Madness of King George*

Uma Thurman, *Pulp Fiction*

Jennifer Tilly, *Bullets Over Broadway*

Dianne Wiest, *Bullets Over Broadway*

DIRECTING

Woody Allen, *Bullets Over Broadway*

Krzysztof Kieslowski, *Red*

Robert Redford, *Quiz Show*

Quentin Tarantino, *Pulp Fiction*

Robert Zemeckis, *Forrest Gump*

WRITING

SCREENPLAY WRITTEN DIRECTLY FOR THE SCREEN

Woody Allen and Douglas McGrath, *Bullets Over Broadway*

Richard Curtis, *Four Weddings and a Funeral*

Krzysztof Piesiewicz and Krzysztof Kieslowski, *Red*

Quentin Tarantino and Roger Avary, *Pulp Fiction*

Frances Walsh and Peter Jackson, *Heavenly Creatures*

SCREENPLAY BASED ON MATERIAL PREVIOUSLY PRODUCED OR PUBLISHED

Paul Attanasio, *Quiz Show*

Alan Bennett, *The Madness of King George*

Robert Benton, *Nobody's Fool*

Frank Darabont, *The Shawshank Redemption*

Eric Roth, *Forrest Gump*

CINEMATOGRAPHY

Don Burgess, *Forrest Gump*

Roger Deakins, *The Shawshank Redemption*

Owen Roizman, *Wyatt Earp*

Piotr Sobocinski, *Red*

John Toll, *Legends of the Fall*

ART DIRECTION

Ken Adam, art direction; Carolyn Scott, set decoration, *The Madness of King George*

Rick Carter, art direction; Nancy Haigh, set decoration, *Forrest Gump*

Dante Ferretti, art direction; Francesca Lo Schiavo, set decoration, *Interview With the Vampire*

Lilly Kilvert, art direction; Dorree Cooper, set decoration, *Legends of the Fall*

Santo Loquasto, art direction; Susan Bode, set decoration, *Bullets Over Broadway*

SOUND

Gregg Landaker, Steve Maslow, Bob Beemer and David R. B. MacMillan, *Speed*

Robert J. Litt, Elliot Tyson, Michael Herbick and Willie Burton, *The Shawshank Redemption*

Paul Massey, David Campbell, Christopher David and Douglas Ganton, *Legends of the Fall*

Donald O. Mitchell, Michael Herbick, Frank A. Montano and Arthur Rochester, *Clear and Present Danger*

Randy Thom, Tom Johnson, Dennis Dands and William B. Kaplan, *Forrest Gump*

MUSIC

SONG

"Can You Feel the Love Tonight," *The Lion King,* Elton John, music; Tim Rice, lyrics

"Circle of Life," *The Lion King,* Elton John, music; Tim Rice, lyrics

"Hakuna Matata," *The Lion King,* Elton John, music; Tim Rice, lyrics

"Look What Love Has Done," *Junior,* Carol Bayer Sager, James Newton Howard, James Ingram and Patty Smyth, music and lyrics

"Make Up Your Mind," *The Paper,* Randy Newman, music and lyrics

ORIGINAL SCORE

Elliot Goldenthal, *Interview With the Vampire*

Thomas Newman, *Little Women*

Thomas Newman, *The Shawshank Redemption*

Alan Silvestri, *Forrest Gump*

Hans Zimmer, *The Lion King*

FILM EDITING

Richard Francis-Bruce, *The Shawshank Redemption*

Frederick Marx, Steve James and Bill Haugse, *Hoop Dreams*

Sally Menke, *Pulp Fiction*

Arthur Schmidt, *Forrest Gump*

John Wright, *Speed*

COSTUME DESIGN

Colleen Atwood, *Little Women*

Moidele Bickel, *Queen Margot*

April Ferry, *Maverick*

Lizzy Gardiner and Tim Chappel, *The Adventures of Priscilla, Queen of the Desert*

Jeffrey Kurland, *Bullets Over Broadway*

MAKEUP

Rick Baker, Ve Neill and Yolanda Toussieng, *Ed Wood*

Daniel Parker, Paul Engelen and Carol Hemming, *Mary Shelley's Frankenstein*

Daniel C. Striepeke, Hallie D'Amore and Judith A. Cory, *Forrest Gump*

VISUAL EFFECTS

John Bruno, Thomas L. Fisher, Jacques Stroweis and Patrick McClung, *True Lies*

Ken Ralston, George Murphy, Stephen Rosenbaum and Allen Hall, *Forrest Gump*

Scott Squires, Steve Williams, Tom Bertino and John Farhat, *The Mask*

SOUND EFFECTS EDITING

Gloria S. Borders and Randy Thom, *Forrest Gump*

Stephen Hunter Flick, *Speed*

Bruce Stambler and John Leveque, *Clear and Present Danger*

SHORT FILMS

ANIMATION

The Big Story (Tim Watts and David Stoten, producers; Spitting Image Production)

Bob's Birthday (Alison Snowden and David Fine, producers; Channel Four/National Film Board of Canada Production)

The Janitor (Vanessa Schwartz, producer; Vanessa Schwartz Production)

The Monk and the Fish (Michael Dudok de Wit, producer; Folimage Valence Production)

Triangle (Erica Russell, producer; Gingco Ltd. Production)

LIVE ACTION

Franz Kafka's It's a Wonderful Life (Peter Capaldi and Ruth Kenley-Letts, producers; Conundrum Films Production)

Kangaroo Court (Sean Astin and Christine Astin, producers; Lava Entertainment Production)

On Hope (JoBeth Williams and Michele McGuire, producers; Chanticleer Films Production)

Syrup (Paul Unwin and Nick Vivian, producers; First Choice Production)

Trevor (Peggy Rajski and Randy Stone, producers; Rajski/Stone Production)

DOCUMENTARY

SHORT SUBJECT

Blues Highway (Vince DiPersio and Bill Guttentag, producers; Half Court Pictures, Ltd./National Geographic Society Production)

89MM od Europy (89MM From Europe) (Marcel Lozinski, producer; Studio Filmowe "Kalejdoskop"/Telewizja Polska Production)

School for the Americas Assassins (Robert Richter, producer; Richter Production)

Straight From the Heart (Dee Mosbacher and Frances Reid, producers; Woman Vision Production)

A Time for Justice (Charles Guggenheim, producer; Guggenheim Productions, Inc. Production)

FEATURE

Complaints of a Dutiful Daughter (Deborah Hoffmann, producer; D/D Production)

D-Day Remembered (Charles Guggenheim, producer; Guggenheim Productions, Inc. Production)

Freedom on My Mind (Connie Field and Marilyn Mulford, producers; Clarity Film Production)

A Great Day in Harlem (Jean Bach, producer; Jean Bach Production)

Maya Lin: A Strong Clear Vision (Freida Lee Mock and Terry Sanders, producers; American Film Foundation/Sanders and Mock Production)

FOREIGN LANGUAGE FILM

Before the Rain, The Former Yugoslav Republic of Macedonia

Burnt by the Sun, Russia

Eat Drink Man Woman, Republic of China on Taiwan

Farinelli: Il Castrato, Belgium

Strawberry and Chocolate, Cuba

IRVING G. THALBERG MEMORIAL AWARD

Clint Eastwood for a consistently high quality of motion picture production

JEAN HERSHOLT HUMANITARIAN AWARD

Quincy Jones

HONORARY AWARDS

Michelangelo Antonioni for lifetime achievement

Multiple Oscar Winners and Nominees

MULTIPLE WINNERS

BEST ACTOR

	Wins
Fredric March	2
Dustin Hoffman	2
Gary Cooper	2
Marlon Brando	2
Spencer Tracy	2
Tom Hanks	2

BEST ACTRESS

Katharine Hepburn	4
Ingrid Bergman	3
Jessica Lange	2

SUPPORTING ACTOR

Walter Brennan	3

SUPPORTING ACTRESS

Shelley Winters	2
Dianne Wiest	2

DIRECTING

John Ford	4
Frank Capra	3
William Wyler	3

MULTIPLE NOMINEES

BEST ACTOR

	Nominations
Laurence Olivier	10
Jack Nicholson	10
Spencer Tracy	9
Al Pacino	8
Paul Newman	8
Marlon Brando	8
Jack Lemmon	8
Robert De Niro	6
Dustin Hoffman	6

BEST ACTRESS

Katharine Hepburn	12
Bette Davis	10
Meryl Streep	9
Geraldine Page	8
Greer Garson	7
Ingrid Bergman	7
Jessica Lange	7
Vanessa Redgrave	6

DIRECTING

William Wyler	12
Billy Wilder	8
Robert Altman	4

Source: Academy of Motion Picture Arts and Sciences

Cannes Film Festival Winners

The Cannes International Film Festival, held annually in May on the French Riviera, attracts the glitterati for its parties as much as for its screenings. Directors, producers and agents work the crowds in pursuit of lucrative movie deals. The winners at Cannes often emerge as the year's most talked-about films.

1946

GRAND PRIX
The Red Earth, Lau Lauritzen (Denmark)
The Lost Weekend, Billy Wilder (United States)
Symphonie Pastorale, Jean Delannoy (France)
Brief Encounter, David Lean (United Kingdom)
Neecha Nagar, Chetan Anand (India)
Open City, Roberto Rossellini (Italy)
Maria Candelaria, Emilio Fernandez (Mexico)
The Prize, Alf Sjoberg (Sweden)
The Last Chance, Leopold Lindtberg (Switzerland)
Men Without Wings, M. Cap (Czechoslovakia)
The Great Turning Point, Friedrich Ermler (U.S.S.R.)

SPECIAL JURY PRIZE
Battle of the Rails, Rene Clement (France)

BEST ACTOR
Ray Milland, *The Lost Weekend* (United States)

BEST ACTRESS
Michele Morgan, *Symphonie Pastorale* (France)

DIRECTION
Rene Clement, *Battle of the Rails* (France)

SCREENPLAY
Tchirskov, *The Great Turning Point* (U.S.S.R.)

CINEMATOGRAPHY
Gabriel Figueroa, *Maria Candelaria* and *The Three Musketeers* (Mexico)

MUSIC
Georges Auric

COLOR
The Stone Flower, Alexander Ptouchko (U.S.S.R.)

DOCUMENTARY
Berlin, J. Raisman (U.S.S.R.)

ANIMATION
Make Mine Music, Walt Disney (United States)

GRAND PRIX FOR PEACE
The Last Chance, Leopold Lindtberg (Switzerland)

CIDALC PRIZE
Epaves, Jacques Yves Cousteau, Frederic Dumas, Philippe Tailliez and Roger Gary (France)

1947

PSYCHOLOGICAL AND LOVE FILM
Antoine et Antoinette, Jacques Becker (France)

The Lost Weekend

ADVENTURE AND DETECTIVE FILM
The Damned, Rene Clement (France)

SOCIAL FILM
Crossfire, Edward Dmytryk (United States)

MUSICAL
Ziegfeld Follies, Vincente Minnelli (United States)

ANIMATED FILM
Dumbo, Ben Sharpsteen for Walt Disney (United States)

1948

The festival was not held due to lack of funding.

1949

GRAND PRIX
The Third Man, Carol Reed (United Kingdom)

BEST ACTOR
Edward G. Robinson, *House of Strangers* (United States)

BEST ACTRESS
Isa Miranda, *The Walls of Malapaga* (France/Italy)

DIRECTION
Rene Clement, *The Walls of Malapaga* (France/Italy)

SCREENPLAY
Virginia Shaler and Eugene Ling, *Lost Boundaries* (United States)

MUSIC
Pueblerina, Emilio Fernandez (Mexico)

DECOR
Oh, Amelia, Claude Autant-Lara (France)

1950

The festival was not held due to lack of funds and other problems in France's film industry.

1951

GRAND PRIX
Miracle in Milan, Vittorio De Sica (Italy)
Miss Julie, Alf Sjoberg (Sweden)

SPECIAL JURY PRIZE
All About Eve, Joseph L. Mankiewicz (United States)

BEST ACTOR
Michael Redgrave, *The Browning Version* (United Kingdom)

BEST ACTRESS
Bette Davis, *All About Eve* (United States)

DIRECTION
Luis Buñuel, *Los Olvidados* (Mexico)

SCREENPLAY
Terence Rattigan, *The Browning Version* (United Kingdom)

CINEMATOGRAPHY
Luis-Maria Beltran, *La Caravelle Isabel Partira ce Soir* (Venezuela)

MUSIC
Joseph Kosma, *Juliette ou la Clef Des Songes* (France)

DECOR
Moussorgsky, Souvorov A. Veksler (U.S.S.R.)

SPECIAL PRIZE FOR ORIGINALITY OF LYRICAL ADAPTATION TO FILM
Tales of Hoffman, Michael Powell and Emeric Pressburger (United Kingdom)

SPECIAL AWARD
To the entire selection of films presented at the festival by Italy

1952

GRAND PRIX
Two Pennyworth of Hope, Renato Castellani (Italy)
Othello, Orson Welles (Morocco)

SPECIAL JURY PRIZE
We Are All Murderers, Andre Cayatte (France)

BEST ACTOR
Marlon Brando, *Viva Zapata!* (United States)

BEST ACTRESS
Lee Grant, *Detective Story* (United States)

DIRECTION
Christian-Jaque, *Fanfan la Tulipe* (France)

SCREENPLAY
Piero Fellini, *Cops and Robbers* (Italy)

PHOTOGRAPHY AND COMPOSITION
Kohei Sugiyama, *A Tale of Genji* (Japan)

MUSIC
Sven Skold, *One Summer of Happiness* (Sweden)

FILM LYRICISM
The Medium, Gian Carlo Menotti (United States)

1953

GRAND PRIX
The Wages of Fear, Henri-Georges Clouzot (France/Italy)

BEST ACTOR
Charles Vanel, *The Wages of Fear* (France/Italy)

BEST ACTRESS
Shirley Booth, *Come Back, Little Sheba* (United States)

SCREENPLAY
Luis Berlanga, *Bienvenido, Mister Marshall* (Spain)

MUSIC
O Cangaceiro, Lima Barreto (Spain)

ADVENTURE FILM
O Cangaceiro, Lima Barreto (Brazil)

ENTERTAINMENT FILM
Lili, Charles Walters (United States)

DRAMATIC FILM
Come Back Little Sheba, Daniel Mann (United States)

MYTHICAL FILM
The White Reindeer, Erik Blomberg (United States)

EXPLORATION FILM
Magia Verde, Gian Gaspare Napolitano (Italy)

COLOR FILM
Magia Verde, Gian Gaspare Napolitano (Italy)

PRIZE FOR GOOD HUMOR
Bienvenudo, Mister Marshall, Luis Berlanga (Spain)

LE MIEUX RACONTE PAR L'IMAGE
The Net, Emilio Fernandez (Mexico)

SPECIAL HOMAGE
To Walt Disney for the entire ensemble of his work
Duende y Misterio del Flamenco, Edgar Neville (Spain)

1954

GRAND PRIX
Gate of Hell, Teinosuke Kinugasa (Japan)

SPECIAL JURY PRIZE
Rene Clement, *Knave of Hearts* (United Kingdom)

INTERNATIONAL PRIZE
The Last Bridge, Helmut Kautner (Austria)
Maria Schell for her performance in *The Last Bridge* (Austria)

NATIONAL RECOGNITION AWARDS
The Living Desert, James Algar for Walt Disney (United States)
Avant le Deluge, Andre Cayatte (France)
Two Acres of Land, Bimal Roy (India)
Neapolitan Carousel, Ettore Giannini (Italy)
Chronicle of Poor Lovers, Carlo Lizzani (Italy)
Five Boys From Barska Street, Aleksander Ford (Poland)
The Great Adventure, Arne Sucksdorff (Sweden)
The Great Warrior, Skanderberg, Serge Youtkevitch (U.S.S.R.)

SPECIAL RECOGNITION PRIZE
From Here to Eternity, Fred Zinnemann (United States)

1955

PALME D'OR
Marty (United States)

  Particular praise for the following contributions to *Marty:*

  Paddy Chayevsky, screenplay
  Delbert Mann, direction
  Ernest Borgnine and Betsy Blair, performances

SPECIAL JURY PRIZE
The Lost Continent, Leonardo Bonzi, Mario Craveri, Enrico Gras, F. Lavagnino and G. Moser (Italy)

PERFORMANCES
Spencer Tracy, *Bad Day at Black Rock* (United States)

The ensemble of actors in *The Big Family,* Joseph Heifitz (U.S.S.R.)

DIRECTION
Sergei Vassiliev, *The Heroes of Shipka* (Bulgaria)

Jules Dassin, *Rififi* (France)

FILM LYRICISM
Romeo and Juliet, L. Arnchtam and L. Lavrovsky (U.S.S.R.)

DRAMATIC FILM
East of Eden, Elia Kazan (United States)

SPECIAL JURY MENTIONS
Baby Naaz, *Boot Polish* (India)

Haya Havarit, *Hill 24 Doesn't Answer* (Israel)

Ladislao Vajda, *Marcelino Pan y Vino* (Spain

1956

PALME D'OR
The Silent World, Jacques Yves Cousteau and Louis Malle (France)

SPECIAL JURY PRIZE
The Mystery of Picasso, Henri-Georges Clouzot (France)

BEST ACTRESS
Susan Hayward, *I'll Cry Tomorrow* (United States)

DIRECTION
Serge Youtkevitch, *Othello* (U.S.S.R.)

POETIC HUMOR FILM
Smiles of a Summer Night, Ingmar Bergman (Sweden)

HUMAN DOCUMENT
Pather Panchali, Satyajit Ray (India)

1957

PALME D'OR
Friendly Persuasion, William Wyler (United States)

SPECIAL JURY PRIZE
Kanal, Andrzej Wajda (Poland)

The Seventh Seal, Ingmar Bergman (Sweden)

SPECIAL PRIZE
The Forty-First, Grigori Chukhrai (U.S.S.R.)

BEST ACTOR
John Kitzmiller, *Valley of Faces* (Yugoslavia)

BEST ACTRESS
Giuletta Masina, *Nights of Cabiria* (Italy/France)

DIRECTION
Robert Bresson, *A Man Escaped* (France)

DOCUMENTARY
The Roof of Japan, Sadao Imamura (Japan)

Qivitoq, Erik Balling (Denmark)

SPECIAL MENTION
Gotoma the Buddha, Rajbans Khanna (India)

COUNTRY SELECTION: FRANCE
He Who Must Die, Jules Dassin

A Man Escaped, Robert Bresson

Toute la Memoire du Monde, Alain Resnais

Noik, Edmond Sechan

1958

PALME D'OR
The Cranes Are Flying, Mikhail Kalatozov with an Honorary Award to Tatiana Samoilova for her superb performance (U.S.S.R.)

SPECIAL JURY PRIZE
My Uncle, Jacques Tati (France)

BEST ACTOR
Paul Newman, *The Long Hot Summer* (United States)

BEST ACTRESS
Bibi Andersson, Eva Dahlbeck, Ingrid Thulin and Barbro Hiort-Af-Ornas for their combined performances in *Brink of Life* (Sweden)

DIRECTION
Ingmar Bergman, *Brink of Life* (Sweden)

ORIGINAL SCREENPLAY
Pier Paolo Pasolini, Massimo Franciosa and P. Festa Campanile, *Young Husbands* (Italy)

SPECIAL PRIZES
Goha, Jacques Baratier (Tunisia)

Bronze Faces, Bernard Taisant (Switzerland)

FIPRESCI AWARD
Vengeance, Juan Bardem (Spain)

1959

PALME D'OR
Black Orpheus, Marcel Camus (France)

SPECIAL JURY PRIZE
Stars, Konrad Wolf (Bulgaria)

INTERNATIONAL PRIZE
Nazarin, Luis Buñuel (Mexico)

BEST ACTOR
Dean Stockwell, Bradford Dillman and Orson Welles for their combined performances in *Compulsion* (United States)

BEST ACTRESS
Simone Signoret, *Room at the Top* (United Kingdom)

DIRECTION
The 400 Blows, François Truffaut (France)

La Dolce Vita

COMEDY
Policarpo, Mario Soldati (Italy)

SPECIAL MENTION
The White Heron, Teinosuke Kinugasa (Japan)

FIPRESCI AWARD
Hiroshima Mon Amour, Alain Resnais (France/Japan)

Araya, Margot Benaceraf (Venezuela)

CATHOLIC FILM OFFICE AWARD
The 400 Blows, François Truffaut (France)

FILM WRITERS AWARD
Margerite Duras and Alain Resnais, *Hiroshima Mon Amour*
(France/Japan)

1960

PALME D'OR
La Dolce Vita, Federico Fellini (Italy)

SPECIAL JURY PRIZES
Ballad of a Soldier, Grigori Chukrai (U.S.S.R.)

Lady With a Pet Dog, Josef Heifitz (U.S.S.R.)

Kagi, Kon Ichikawa (Japan)

L'Avventura, Michelangelo Antonioni (Italy)

BEST ACTRESS
Melina Mercouri, *Never on Sunday* (Greece)

Jeanne Moreau, *Moderato Cantabile* (France)

SPECIAL HOMAGE AWARDS
Ingmar Bergman, *The Virgin Spring* (Sweden)

Luis Buñuel, *The Young One* (Mexico)

1961

PALME D'OR
Viridiana, Luis Buñuel (Spain)

A Long Absence, Henri Colpi (France/Italy)

SPECIAL JURY PRIZE
Mother Joan of the Angels, Jerzy Kawalerowicz (Poland)

BEST ACTOR
Anthony Perkins, *Goodbye Again* (France/United States)

BEST ACTRESS
Sophia Loren, *Two Women* (France/Italy)

DIRECTION
Julia Solntzeva, *History of the Burning Years* (U.S.S.R.)

GARY COOPER AWARD FOR HUMAN VALUES
A Raisin in the Sun, Daniel Petrie (United States)

FIPRESCI AWARDS
Hands in the Trap, Leopoldo Torre Nilsson (Argentina)

Chronicle of a Summer, Jean Rouch (France)

CATHOLIC FILM OFFICE AWARD
The Hoodlum Priest, Irvin Kershner (United States)

NATIONAL SELECTION: ITALY
Nebbia, Raffaele Andreassi

Giovedì: Passeggiata, Vincenzo Gamma

Girl With a Suitcase, Valerio Zurlini

Che Gioia Vivere, Rene Clement

The Love Makers, Mauro Bolognini

1962

PALME D'OR
The Given Word, Anselmo Duarte (Brazil)

SPECIAL JURY PRIZE
The Trial of Joan of Arc, Robert Bresson (France)

L'Eclisse, Michelangelo Antonioni (Italy/France)

PERFORMANCES
The combined performances of Katharine Hepburn, Ralph
Richardson, Jason Robards, Jr. and Dean Stockwell in
Long Day's Journey Into Night (United States)

The combined performances of Rita Tushingham and Murray
Melvin in *A Taste of Honey* (United Kingdom)

ADAPTATION
Electra, Michael Cacoyannis (Greece)

COMEDY
Divorce — Italian Style, Pietro Germi (Italy)

FIPRESCI AWARD
The Exterminating Angel, Luis Buñuel (Mexico)

CATHOLIC FILM OFFICE AWARD
L'Eclisse, Michelangelo Antonioni (Italy/France)

1963

PALME D'OR
The Leopard, Luchino Visconti (France/Italy)

SPECIAL JURY PRIZE
Harakiri, Masaki Kobayashi (Japan)

A Cat, Vojtech Jasny (Czechoslovakia)

BEST ACTOR
Richard Harris, *This Sporting Life* (United Kingdom)

BEST ACTRESS
Marina Vlady, *The Conjugal Bed* (Italy)

SCREENPLAY
Yves Jamiaque, Dumuitru Carabat and Henri Colpi,
Codine (Romania)

EVOCATION D'UNWE EPOPEE REVOLUTIONNAIRE
The Optimistic Tragedy (U.S.S.R.)

GARY COOPER AWARD FOR HUMAN VALUES
To Kill a Mockingbird, Robert Mulligan (United States)

FIPRESCI AWARDS
This Sporting Life, Lindsay Anderson (United Kingdom)
Le Joli Mai, Chris Marker (France)

CATHOLIC FILM OFFICE AWARD
The Fiances, Ermanno Olmi (Italy)

1964

PALME D'OR
The Umbrellas of Cherbourg, Jacques Demy
(France/Germany)

SPECIAL JURY PRIZE
Woman of the Dunes, Hiroshi Teshigahara (Japan)

BEST ACTOR
Antal Pager, *Pacsirta* (Hungary)
Saro Urzi, *Seduced and Abandoned* (Italy)

BEST ACTRESS
Anne Bancroft, *The Pumpkin Eater* (United States)
Barbara Barrie, *One Potato-Two Potato* (United States)

SPECIAL HOMAGE
Andrzej Munk, *The Passenger* (Poland)

SPECIAL JURY MENTION
Jaromil Jires, *Krik* (Czechoslovakia)
Georgui Danelia, *Romance a Moscou* (U.S.S.R.)
Manuel Summers, *La Nina de Luto* (Spain)

FIPRESCI AWARD
The Passenger, Andrzej Munk (Poland)

CATHOLIC FILM OFFICE AWARD
The Umbrellas of Cherbourg, Jacques Demy (France)
Sterile Lives, Nelson Pereira dos Santos (Brazil)

1965

PALME D'OR
The Knack, Richard Lester (United Kingdom)

SPECIAL JURY PRIZE
Kwaidan, Masaki Kobayashi (Japan)

BEST ACTOR AND BEST ACTRESS
Samantha Eggar and Terence Stamp, *The Collector*
(United States)

DIRECTION
Liviu Ciulei, *The Lost Forest* (Romania)

SCREENPLAY
Ray Rigby, *The Hill* (United Kingdom)
Pierre Schoendoerffer, *317th Section* (France)

SPECIAL JURY MENTIONS
Josef Kroner (Czechoslovakia)
Ida Kaminska (Czechoslovakia)
Vera Kouznetsova (U.S.S.R.)

FIPRESCI PRIZE
Tarahumara, Luis Alcoriza (Mexico)

CATHOLIC FILM OFFICE AWARDS
Yoyo, Pierre Etaix (France)
Tokyo Olympics, Kon Ichikawa (Japan)

1966

PALME D'OR
A Man and a Woman, Claude Lelouch (France)
The Birds, the Bees and the Italians, Pietro Germi
(France/Italy)

SPECIAL JURY PRIZE
Alfie, Lewis Gilbert (United Kingdom)

BEST ACTOR
Per Oscarsson, *Hunger* (Denmark)

BEST ACTRESS
Vanessa Redgrave, *Morgan!* (United Kingdom)

DIRECTION
Serge Youtkevitch, *Portrait of Lenin* (U.S.S.R.)

DIRECTORIAL DEBUT
Rascoala, Mircea Muresan (Romania)

SPECIAL ACTING MENTION
Toto (Italy)

FIPRESCI PRIZE
Young Torless, Volker Schloendorff (Germany)
The War Is Over, Alain Resnais (France)

CATHOLIC FILM OFFICE AWARD
A Man and a Woman, Claude Lelouch (France)

20TH ANNIVERSARY TRIBUTE
To Orson Welles in recognition of his outstanding
contribution to cinema

1967

PALME D'OR
Blow-Up, Michelangelo Antonioni (United Kingdom/Italy)

Blow-Up

SPECIAL JURY PRIZE
Accident, Joseph Losey (United Kingdom)

I Even Met Happy Gypsies, Aleksandar Petrovic (Yugoslavia)

BEST ACTOR
Odded Kotler, *Three Days and a Child* (Israel)

BEST ACTRESS
Pia Degermark, *Elvira Madigan* (Denmark)

DIRECTION
Ferenc Kosa, *Ten Thousand Suns* (Hungary)

SCREENPLAY
Alain Jessua, *The Killing Game* (France)

Elio Petri and Ugo Pirro, *We Still Kill the Old Way* (Italy)

FILM DEBUT
Le Vent des Aures, Mohammed Lakhdar Hamina (Algeria)

SPECIAL HOMAGE AWARD
Robert Bresson

1968

The festival was canceled because of the unstable political climate in Paris.

1969

PALME D'OR
If, Lindsay Anderson (United Kingdom)

SPECIAL JURY PRIZE
Adalen 31, Bo Widerberg (Sweden)

BEST ACTOR
Jean-Louis Trintignant, *Z* (France)

BEST ACTRESS
Vanessa Redgrave, *Isadora* (United Kingdom)

DIRECTION
Antonio das Mortes, Glauber Rocha (Brazil)

All Good Citizens, Vojtech Jasny (Czechoslovakia)

FILM DEBUT
Easy Rider, Dennis Hopper (United States)

JURY PRIZE
Z, Constantin Costa-Gavras (France)

FIPRESCI PRIZE
Andrei Roublev, Andrei Tarkovsky (U.S.S.R.)

1970

PALME D'OR
*M*A*S*H,* Robert Altman (United States)

SPECIAL JURY PRIZE
Investigation of a Citizen Above Suspicion, Elio Petri (Italy)

BEST ACTOR
Marcello Mastroianni, *Drama of Jealousy* (Italy)

BEST ACTRESS
Ottavia Piccolo, *Metello* (Italy)

DIRECTION
John Boorman, *Leo the Last* (United Kingdom)

FILM DEBUT
Hoa-Binh, Raoul Coutard (France)

JURY PRIZES
The Falcons, Istvan Gal (Hungary)

The Strawberry Statement, Stuart Hagmann (United States)

1971

PALME D'OR
The Go-Between, Joseph Losey (United Kingdom)

SPECIAL JURY PRIZE
Taking Off, Milos Forman (United States)

Johnny Got His Gun, Dalton Trumbo (United States)

BEST ACTOR
Riccardo Cucciolla, *Sacco and Vanzetti* (Italy)

BEST ACTRESS
Kitty Winn, *Panic in Needle Park* (United States)

FILM DEBUT
By Grace Received, Nino Manfredi (Italy)

JURY PRIZE
Love, Karoly Makk with a special mention for
the performances of Lily Darvas and Mari Torocsik (Hungary)

Joe Hill, Bo Widerberg (Sweden)

25TH ANNIVERSARY PRIZE
To Luchino Visconti for *Death in Venice* (Italy) and his
complete oeuvre

1972

PALME D'OR
The Mattei Affair, Francesco Rosi with a Special Jury Mention
for the performance of Gian Maria Volonte (Italy)

The Working Class Go to Heaven, Elio Petri (Italy)

SPECIAL JURY PRIZE
Solaris, Andrei Tarkovsky (U.S.S.R.)

BEST ACTOR
Jean Yanne, *We Will Not Grow Old Together* (France)

BEST ACTRESS
Susannah York, *Images* (Ireland)

DIRECTION
Red Psalm, Miklos Jancso (Hungary)

JURY PRIZE
Slaughterhouse-Five, George Roy Hill (United States)

1973

PALME D'OR
Scarecrow, Jerry Schatzberg (United States)

The Hireling, Alan Bridges (United Kingdom)

SPECIAL JURY PRIZE
The Mother and the Whore, Jean Eustache (France)

BEST ACTOR
Giancarlo Giannini, *Love and Anarchy* (Italy)

BEST ACTRESS
Joanne Woodward, *The Effect of Gamma Rays on Man-in-the-Moon Marigolds* (United States)

SPECIAL PRIZE
La Planete Sauvage, Rene Laloux (France)

FILM DEBUT
Jeremy, Arthur Barron (United States)

JURY PRIZE
Hour Glass Sanatorium, Wojciech Has (Poland)
The Invitation, Claude Goretta (Switzerland)

FIPRESCI PRIZE
The Mother and the Whore, Jean Eustache (France)
La Grande Bouffe, Marco Ferreri (France)

1974

PALME D'OR
The Conversation, Francis Ford Coppola (United States)

SPECIAL JURY PRIZE
One Thousand and One Nights, Pier Paolo Pasolini (Italy)

BEST ACTOR
Jack Nicholson, *The Last Detail* (United States)

BEST ACTRESS
Marie-Jose Nat, *Les Violons du Bal* (France)

SCREENPLAY
Hal Barwood and Matthew Robbins, *The Sugarland Express* (United States)

TECHNIQUE
Mahler, Ken Russell (United Kingdom)

JURY PRIZE
Carlos Saura, *Cousin Angelica* (Spain)

SPECIAL TRIBUTE
To Charles Boyer for his portrayal in *Stavisky* (France)

FIPRESCI PRIZE
Lancelot of the Lake, Robert Bresson (France)
Fear Eats the Soul, Rainer Werner Fassbiner (Germany)

1975

PALME D'OR
Chronicle of the Burning Years, Mohammed Lakhdar-Hamina (Algeria)

SPECIAL JURY PRIZE
Every Man for Himself and God Against All, Werner Herzog (Germany)

BEST ACTOR
Vittorio Gassman, *Scent of a Woman* (Italy)

BEST ACTRESS
Valerie Perrine, *Lenny* (United States)

DIRECTION
Constantin Costa-Gavras, *Special Section* (France)
Michel Brault, *The Order* (Canada)

HONORABLE MENTION
Delphine Seyrig

FIPRESCI PRIZE
Every Man for Himself and God Against All, Werner Herzog (Germany)

Taxi Driver

ECUMENICAL PRIZE (MIXED CATHOLIC AND PROTESTANT JURY)
Every Man for Himself and God Against All, Werner Herzog (Germany)

1976

PALME D'OR
Taxi Driver, Martin Scorsese (United States)

SPECIAL JURY PRIZE
Cria Cuervos, Carlos Saura (Spain)
The Marquise of O, Eric Rohmer (Germany/France)

BEST ACTOR
José Luis Gomez, *Pascual Duarte* (Spain)

BEST ACTRESS
Dominique Sanda, *The Inheritance* (Italy)
Mari Toroscik, *Mrs. Dery, Where Are You?* (Hungary)

DIRECTION
Ettore Scola, *Ugly, Dirty, and Mean* (Italy)

FIPRESCI PRIZE
Ferdinand the Strongman, Alexander Kluge (Germany)
Kings of the Road, Wim Wenders (Germany)

1977

PALME D'OR
Padre Padrone, Paolo and Vittorio Taviani (Italy)

BEST ACTOR
Fernando Rey, *Elisa, My Love* (Spain)

BEST ACTRESS
Shelley Duvall, *Three Women* (United States)
Monique Mercure, *J. A. Martin, Photographer* (Canada)

MUSICAL SCORE
Norman Whitfield, *Car Wash* (United States)

FILM DEBUT
The Duellists, Ridley Scott (United Kingdom)

FIPRESCI PRIZE
Padre Padrone, Paolo and Vittorio Taviani (Italy)

ECUMENICAL AWARD (MIXED CATHOLIC AND PROTESTANT JURY)
The Lacemaker, Claude Goretta (Switzerland)

1978

PALME d'OR
The Tree of Wooden Clogs, Ermanno Olmi (Italy)

SPECIAL JURY PRIZE
Bye Bye Monkey, Marco Ferreri (Italy)
The Shout, Jerzy Skolimowski (United Kingdom)

BEST ACTOR
Jon Voight, *Coming Home* (United States)

BEST ACTRESS
Jill Clayburgh, *An Unmarried Woman* (United States)
Isabelle Huppert, *Violette* (France)

DIRECTION
Nagisa Oshima, *Empire of Passion* (Japan)

FIPRESCI PRIZE
Man of Marble, Andrzej Wajda (Poland)
Smell of Wild Flowers, Srdan Karanovic (Italy)

ECUMENICAL AWARD (MIXED CATHOLIC AND PROTESTANT JURY)
The Tree of Wooden Clogs, Ermanno Olmi (Italy)

1979

PALME d'OR
The Tin Drum, Volker Schloendorff (Germany)
Apocalypse Now, Francis Ford Coppola (United States)

SPECIAL JURY PRIZE
Siberaid, Andrei Mikhalkov Kontchalovksy (U.S.S.R.)

BEST ACTOR
Jack Lemmon, *The China Syndrome* (United States)

BEST ACTRESS
Sally Field, *Norma Rae* (United States)

DIRECTION
Terrence Malick, *Days of Heaven* (United States)

BEST SUPPORTING ACTOR
Stefano Madia, *Dear Papa* (Italy)

BEST SUPPORTING ACTRESS
Eva Mattes, *Woyzeck* (Germany)

CAMERA d'OR FOR FILM DEBUT
Northern Lights, John Hanson and Rob Nilsson (United States)

TECHNIQUE
Norma Rae, Martin Ritt (United States)

SPECIAL HOMAGE
Miklos Jancso in recognition of his ensemble of work

FIPRESCI PRIZE
COMPETING FILM
Apocalypse Now, Francis Ford Coppola (United States)
NON-COMPETING FILMS
Angi Vera, Pal Gabor (Hungary)
Black Jack, Ken Loach (United Kingdom)

ECUMENICAL AWARD (MIXED CATHOLIC AND PROTESTANT JURY)
Rough Treatment, Andrzej Wajda (Poland)

1980

PALME d'OR
Kagemusha, Akira Kurosawa (Japan)
All That Jazz, Bob Fosse (United States)

SPECIAL JURY PRIZE
Mon Oncle D'Amerique, Alain Resnais (France)

BEST ACTOR
Michel Piccoli, *Leap Into the Void* (Italy)

BEST ACTRESS
Anouk Aimée, *Leap Into the Void* (Italy)

SUPPORTING ACTOR
Jack Thompson, *Breaker Morant* (Austria)

SUPPORTING ACTRESS
Carla Gravina, *The Terrace* (Italy)
Milena Dravic, *Special Therapy* (Yugoslavia)

DIRECTION
Krzysztof Zanussi, *The Constant Factor* (Poland)

SCREENPLAY
Ettore Scola, Agenore Incrocci and Furio Scarpelli, *The Terrace* (Italy)

CAMERA d'OR FOR FILM DEBUT
Historie d'Adrien, Jean-Pierre Denis (France)

TECHNIQUE
Le Risque de Vivre, Gerald Calderon (France)

FIPRESCI PRIZE
Mon Oncle D'Amerique, Alain Resnais (France)
Provincial Actors, Agniezka Holland (Poland)

1981

PALME d'OR
Man of Iron, Andrzej Wajda (Poland)

SPECIAL JURY PRIZE
Light Years Away, Alain Tanner (France/Switzerland)

BEST ACTOR
Ugo Tognazzi, *The Tragedy of a Ridiculous Man* (Italy)

BEST ACTRESS
Isabelle Adjani, *Quartet* (United Kingdom/France) and *Possession* (France/Germany)

SUPPORTING ACTOR
Ian Holm, *Chariots of Fire* (United Kingdom)

SUPPORTING ACTRESS
Elena Solovei, *Blood Group Zero* (U.S.S.R.)

SCREENPLAY
Istvan Szabo and Peter Dobai, *Mephisto* (Hungary)

ARTISTIC CONTRIBUTION TO THE POETICS OF CINEMA
John Boorman, *Excalibur* (Ireland)

CAMERA d'OR FOR FILM DEBUT
Desperado City, Vadim Glowna (Germany)

TECHNIQUE
Les Uns et les Autres, Claude Lelouch (France)

CONTEMPORARY CINEMA
Looks and Smiles, Ken Loach (United Kingdom)
Neige, Juliet Berto and Jean-Henri Roger (France)

FIPRESCI PRIZE
Mephisto, Istvan Szabo (Hungary)

1982

PALME D'OR
Missing, Constantin Costa-Gavras (United States)
Yol, Yilmaz Guney (Turkey)

SPECIAL JURY PRIZE
Night of the Shooting Stars, Paolo and Vittorio Taviani (Italy)

BEST ACTOR
Jack Lemmon, *Missing* (United States)

BEST ACTRESS
Jadwiga Jankowska-Cieslak, *Another Way* (Hungary)

DIRECTION
Werner Herzog, *Fitzcarraldo* (Germany)

SCREENPLAY
Jerzy Skolimowski, *Moonlighting* (United Kingdom)

ARTISTIC CONTRIBUTION
For the photography of Bruno Nuytten in *Invitation au Voyage* (France)

CAMERA D'OR FOR FILM DEBUT
Mourir a Trente Ans, Romain Goupil (France)

TECHNIQUE
Passion, Raoul Coutard, photography (France)

FIPRESCI PRIZE
Yol, Yilmaz Guney (Turkey)

SPECIAL AWARDS
Another Way, Karoly Makk (Hungary)
Les Fleurs Sauvages (Canada)

SPECIAL 35TH ANNIVERSARY AWARD
Michelangelo Antonioni, *Identification of a Woman* (Italy)

1983

PALME D'OR
The Ballad of Narayama, Shohei Imamura (Japan)

SPECIAL JURY PRIZE
Monty Python — The Meaning of Life, Terry Jones (United Kingdom)

GRAND PRIX DU CINEMA DE CREATION
Robert Bresson, *L'Argent* (France)
Andrei Tarkovsky, *Nostalghia* (Italy)

BEST ACTOR
Gian Maria Volonte, *The Death of Mario Ricci* (Switzerland/France)

BEST ACTRESS
Hanna Schygulla, *The Story of Piera* (Italy)

ARTISTIC CONTRIBUTION
Carmen, Carlos Saura, screenplay (Spain)

CAMERA D'OR FOR FILM DEBUT
La Princesse, Pal Erdoss (Hungary)

TECHNIQUE
Carmen, Carlos Saura (Spain)

JURY PRIZE
Kharij, Mrinal Sen (India)

FIPRESCI PRIZE
Nostalghia, Andrei Tarkovsky (Italy)
Szerencses Daniel, Pal Sandor (Hungary)

1984

PALME D'OR
Paris, Texas, Wim Wenders (Germany)

SPECIAL JURY PRIZE
Naplo, Marta Meszaros (Hungary)

BEST ACTOR
Alfredo Landa and Francisco Rabal, *The Holy Innocents* (Spain)

BEST ACTRESS
Helen Mirren, *Cal* (Ireland)

DIRECTION
Bertrand Tavernier, *A Sunday in the Country* (France)

SCREENPLAY
Theo Angelopoulos, Theo Valtinos and Tonino Guerra, *Vovage to Cythera* (Greece)

ARTISTIC CONTRIBUTION
Peter Biziou for the cinematography of *Another Country* (United Kingdom)

CAMERA D'OR FOR FILM DEBUT
Stranger Than Paradise, Jim Jarmusch (United States)

TECHNIQUE
The Element of Crime, Lars von Trier (Denmark)

FIPRESCI PRIZE
Paris, Texas, Wim Wenders (Germany/France)
Voyage to Cythera, Theo Angelopoulos (Greece)

1985

PALME D'OR
When Father Was Away on Business, Emir Kusturica (Yugoslavia)

SPECIAL JURY PRIZE
Birdy, Alan Parker (United States)

BEST ACTOR
William Hurt, *Kiss of the Spider Woman* (United States/Brazil)

BEST ACTRESS
Norma Aleandro, *The Official Story* (Argentina)
Cher, *Mask* (United States)

DIRECTION
André Téchiné, *Rendez-vous* (France)

ARTISTIC CONTRIBUTION
John Bailey, visual concept; Eiko Ishioka, set design; and Philip Glass, music, *Mishima* (United States)

CAMERA D'OR FOR FILM DEBUT
Oriane, Fina Torres (Venezuela/France)

TECHNIQUE
Insignificance, Nicholas Roeg (United States)

JURY PRIZE
Colonel Redl, Istvan Szabo (Hungary/Germany/Austria)

PALME D'OR FOR SHORT FILM
Marriage, Slav Bakalov and Roman Petkov

FIPRESCI PRIZE
COMPETING FILM
When Father Was Away on Business, Emir Kusturica
   (Yugoslavia)

NON-COMPETING FILM
The Purple Rose of Cairo, Woody Allen (United States)

1986

PALME D'OR
The Mission, Roland Joffe (United Kingdom)

SPECIAL JURY PRIZE
The Sacrifice, Andrei Tarkovsky (Sweden)

BEST ACTOR
Michel Blanc, *Tenue de Soiree* (France)

Bob Hoskins, *Mona Lisa* (United Kingdom)

BEST ACTRESS
Barbara Sukowa, *Rosa Luxemburg* (Germany)

Fernanda Torres, *Speak to Me of Love* (Brazil)

DIRECTION
Martin Scorsese, *After Hours* (United States)

ARTISTIC CONTRIBUTION
Sven Nykvist, cinematographer, *The Sacrifice* (Sweden)

CAMERA D'OR FOR FILM DEBUT
Noir et Blanc, Claire Devers (France)

TECHNIQUE
The Mission, Roland Joffe (United Kingdom)

JURY PRIZE
Therésè, Alain Cavalier (France)

PALME D'OR FOR SHORT FILM
Peel, Jane Campion (Australia)

JURY PRIZE FOR SHORT FILM (ANIMATION)
Gaidouk, Y. Katsap and L. Gorokhov (U.S.S.R.)

JURY PRIZE FOR SHORT FILM (FICTION)
The Little Magicians, Vincent Mercier and Yves Robert
   (Switzerland)

1987

PALME D'OR
Under Satan's Sun, Maurice Pialat (France)

SPECIAL JURY PRIZE
Repentance, Tengiz Abuladze (U.S.S.R.)

BEST ACTOR
Marcello Mastroianni, *Dark Eyes* (Italy)

BEST ACTRESS
Barbara Hershey, *Shy People* (United States)

DIRECTION
Wim Wenders, *Wings of Desire* (Germany/France)

ARTISTIC CONTRIBUTION
Stanley Myers, music, *Prick Up Your Ears* (United Kingdom)

The Mission

CAMERA D'OR FOR FILM DEBUT
Nana Dzhordzhadze, *My English Grandfather* (U.S.S.R.)

TECHNIQUE
Le Cinema dans les Yeux, Gilles Jacob and Laurent Jacob
   (France)

JURY PRIZE
Souleymane Cisse, *Yeelen (La Lumière)* (Mali)

Rentaro Mikuni, *Shinran* (Japan)

PALME D'OR FOR SHORT FILM
Palisade, Laurie McInnes

40TH ANNIVERSARY PRIZE
Federico Fellini, *Intervista* (Italy)

1988

PALME D'OR
Pelle the Conqueror, Bille August (Denmark/Sweden)

SPECIAL JURY PRIZE
A World Apart, Chris Menges (United States)

BEST ACTOR
Forest Whitaker, *Bird* (United States)

BEST ACTRESS
Barbara Hershey, Jodhi May and Linda Mvusi, *A World Apart*
   (United States)

DIRECTION
Fernando E. Solanas, *The South* (Argentina)

ARTISTIC COLLABORATION
Peter Greenaway, *Drowning by Numbers* (United Kingdom)

CAMERA D'OR FOR FILM DEBUT
Salaam, Bombay!, Mira Nair (United Kingdom/India)

TECHNIQUE
Bird, Clint Eastwood (United States)

JURY PRIZE
Krzysztof Kieslowski, *Thou Shall Not Kill* (Poland)

PALME D'OR FOR SHORT FILM
Fioritures, Gary Bardine (U.S.S.R.)

JURY PRIZE FOR SHORT FILM (ANIMATION)
Ab Ovo/Traces de Sable, Ferenc Cako

JURY PRIZE FOR SHORT FILM (FICTION)
Physical Sculpture, Yann Piquer and Jean-Marie Maddeddu

FIPRESCI PRIZE
BEST OFFICIAL FILM
Thou Shall Not Kill, Krzysztof Kieslowski (Poland)

Hotel Terminus, Marcel Ophuls (France)

BEST UNOFFICIAL FILM
Distant Voices, Still Lives, Terence Davies (United Kingdom)

1989

PALME D'OR
sex, lies and videotape, Steven Soderbergh (United States)

SPECIAL JURY PRIZE
Trop Belle Pour Toi, Bertrand Blier (France)

Cinéma Paradiso, Giuseppe Tornatore (Italy/France)

BEST ACTOR
James Spader, s*ex, lies and videotape* (United States)

BEST ACTRESS
Meryl Streep, *A Cry in the Dark* (United States/Australia)

DIRECTION
Emir Kusturica, *Time of the Gypsies* (Yugoslavia)

ARTISTIC CONTRIBUTION
Jim Jarmusch, *Mystery Train* (United States)

CAMERA D'OR FOR FILM DEBUT
My Twentieth Century, Ildiko Enyedi (Hungary)

TECHNIQUE
Black Rain, Shohei Imamura (Japan)

JURY PRIZE
Jesus of Montreal, Denys Arcand (Canada/France)

PALME D'OR FOR SHORT FILM
50 Years, Gilles Carle, representing the continuing efforts of the National Film Board of Canada in the area of short film

1990

PALME D'OR
Wild at Heart, David Lynch (United States)

GRAND PRIX (TIE)
Shi no Toge, Kohei Oguri

Tilaï, Idrissa Ouedraogo (Burkina Faso/Switzerland/France)

BEST ACTOR
Gérard Depardieu, *Cyrano de Bergerac* (France)

BEST ACTRESS
Krystyna Janda, *Interrogation* (Poland)

DIRECTION
Pavel Lounguine, *Taxi Blues* (U.S.S.R./France)

ARTISTIC CONTRIBUTION
Gleb Panfilov, *Matj (Zaprechtchionnye Lioudi)* (U.S.S.R.)

CAMERA D'OR FOR FILM DEBUT
Freeze, Die, Come to Life, Vitali Kanevski (U.S.S.R.)

TECHNIQUE
Cyrano de Bergerac, Pierre Lhomme, director of photography (France)

JURY PRIZE
Hidden Agenda, Ken Loach (United Kingdom)

sex, lies and videotape

PALME D'OR FOR SHORT FILM
The Lunch Date, Adam Davidson

FIPRESCI PRIZE
Shi no Toge, Kohei Oguri (Japan)

FIPRESCI SPECIAL PRIZE
Manoel de Oliveira for his body of work

1991

PALME D'OR
Barton Fink, Joel Coen and Ethan Coen (United States)

GRAND PRIX
La Belle Noiseuse, Jacques Rivette (France)

BEST ACTOR
John Turturro, *Barton Fink* (United States)

BEST ACTRESS
Irène Jacob, *The Double Life of Veronique* (Poland/France)

DIRECTION
Joel Coen, *Barton Fink* (United States)

BEST SUPPORTING ROLE
Samuel Jackson, *Jungle Fever* (United States)

CAMERA D'OR FOR FILM DEBUT
Toto the Hero, Jaco van Dormael (Belgium/France/Germany)

TECHNIQUE
Europa, Lars von Trier (Denmark)

JURY PRIZE
Europa, Lars von Trier (Denmark)

Hors la Vie, Maroun Bagdadi (France/Italy/Germany)

PALME D'OR FOR SHORT FILM
Avec les Mains en l'Air, Mitko Panov (Yugoslavia)

JURY PRIZE FOR SHORT FILM
Push Comes to Shove, Bill Plympton (United States)

FIPRESCI PRIZE
The Double Life of Veronique, Krzysztof Kieslowski (Poland/France)

1992

PALME D'OR
The Best Intentions, Bille August (Sweden)

GRAND PRIX
Il Ladro di Bambini (Stolen Children), Gianni Amelio
(Italy/France)

BEST ACTOR
Tim Robbins, *The Player* (United States)

BEST ACTRESS
Pernilla August, *The Best Intentions* (Sweden)

DIRECTION
Robert Altman, *The Player* (United States)

CAMERA D'OR FOR FILM DEBUT
Mac, John Turturro (United States)

TECHNIQUE
El Viaje, Fernando Solanas (Argentina/France)

JURY PRIZE
El Sol Del Membrillo, Victor Erice (Spain)
An Independent Life, Vitali Kanevski (Russia)

PALME D'OR FOR SHORT FILM
Omnibus, Sam Karmann (France)

SPECIAL JURY PRIZE FOR SHORT FILM
La Sensation, Manuel Poutte (Belgium)

FIPRESCI PRIZE
El Sol del Membrillo, Victor Erice (Spain)

45TH ANNIVERSARY PRIZE
James Ivory, *Howards End* (United Kingdom)

1993

PALME D'OR
The Piano, Jane Campion (Australia/France)
Farewell, My Concubine, Chen Kaige (China/Hong Kong)

GRAND PRIX
Faraway, So Close!, Wim Wenders (Germany)

BEST ACTOR
David Thewlis, *Naked* (United Kingdom)

BEST ACTRESS
Holly Hunter, *The Piano* (Australia/France)

DIRECTION
Mike Leigh, *Naked* (United Kingdom)

CAMERA D'OR FOR FILM DEBUT
The Scent of Green Papaya, Tran Anh Hung (France/Vietnam)

TECHNIQUE
Mazeppa, Jean Gargonne and Vincent Arnardi (France)

JURY PRIZE
The Puppetmaster, Hou Hsiao Hsien (Taiwan)
Raining Stones, Ken Loach (United Kingdom)

SPECIAL MENTION
Friends, Elaine Proctor (South Africa)

PALME D'OR FOR SHORT FILM
Coffee and Cigarettes, Jim Jarmusch (United States)

FIPRESCI PRIZE
Farewell, My Concubine, Chen Kaige (China)

1994

PALME D'OR
Pulp Fiction, Quentin Tarantino (United States)

GRAND PRIZE
Burnt by the Sun, Nikita Mikhalkov (Russia/France)
To Live, Zhang Yimou (China/Hong Kong)

BEST ACTOR
Ge You, *To Live* (China/Hong Kong)

BEST ACTRESS
Virna Lisi, *Queen Margot* (France)

DIRECTION
Nanni Moretti, *Caro Diario* (Italy)

SCREENPLAY
Michel Blanc, *Grosse Fatigue* (France)

JURY PRIZE
Queen Margot, Patrice Chéreau (France)

CAMERA D'OR FOR FILM DEBUT
Petits Arrangements Avec les Morts, Pascale Ferran
(France)

SPECIAL MENTION
Les Silences du Palais, Moufida Tlatli (Tunisia)

TECHNIQUE
Grosse Fatigue, Pitof (France)

PALME D'OR FOR SHORT FILM
El Héroe, Carlos Carrera (Mexico)

SPECIAL JURY PRIZE FOR SHORT FILM
Lemming Aid, Grant Lahood

1995

PALME D'OR
Underground, Emir Kusturica (France, Germany and Hungary)

GRAND PRIZE
Ulysses' Gaze, Theo Angelopoulos (Greece, France and Italy)

BEST ACTOR
Jonathan Price, *Carrington*

BEST ACTRESS
Helen Mirren, *The Madness of King George*
(United Kingdom and United States)

DIRECTION
Hate, Matthieu Kassovitz (France)

SPECIAL JURY PRIZE
Carrington, Christopher Hampton
(United Kingdom and France)

JURY PRIZE
Don't Forget You're Going to Die, Xavier Beauvois (France)

CAMERA D'OR FOR FILM DEBUT
The White Balloon, Jafar Pahani (Iran)

SPECIAL MENTION
Denise Calls Up (United States)

TECHNIQUE
Shanghai Triad, Zhang Yimou (China)

PALME D'OR FOR SHORT FILM
Gagarine, Alexel Kharidiri (Russia)

SPECIAL JURY PRIZE FOR SHORT FILM
Swinger, Gregor Jordon (Australia)

Exhibitor Relations's Top 100 All-Time Box-Office Hits

Rank	Title/Year	Domestic Gross*
1.	E.T. (1982)	$399,804,539
2.	Jurassic Park (1993)	356,839,725
3.	Forrest Gump (1994)	329,690,974
4.	Star Wars (1977)	322,740,142
5.	The Lion King (1994)	312,855,561
6.	Home Alone (1990)	285,016,000
7.	Return of the Jedi (1983)	263,734,642
8.	Jaws (1975)	260,000,000
9.	Batman (1989)	251,188,924
10.	Raiders of the Lost Ark (1981)	242,374,454
11.	Beverly Hills Cop (1984)	234,760,478
12.	The Empire Strikes Back (1980)	222,674,266
13.	Ghostbusters (1984)	220,858,490
14.	Twister (1996)	219,558,165
15.	Mrs. Doubtfire (1993)	219,194,773
16.	Ghost (1990)	217,631,306
17.	Aladdin (1992)	217,350,219
18.	Back to the Future (1985)	210,609,762
19.	Terminator 2 (1991)	204,446,562
20.	Indiana Jones and the Last Crusade (1989)	197,171,806
21.	Gone With the Wind (1939)	193,597,756
22.	Toy Story (1995)	190,623,155
23.	Snow White (1937)	184,925,486
24.	Dances With Wolves (1990)	184,208,418
25.	Batman Forever (1995)	183,997,904
26.	The Fugitive (1993)	183,752,965
27.	Indiana Jones and the Temple of Doom (1984)	179,070,271
28.	Pretty Woman (1990)	170,406,280
29.	Tootsie (1982)	177,200,000
30.	Top Gun (1986)	176,781,728
31.	Crocodile Dundee (1986)	174,634,806
32.	Rain Man (1988)	172,825,435
33.	Home Alone II (1992)	172,667,450
34.	Apollo 13 (1995)	172,036,360
35.	Three Men and a Baby (1987)	167,780,960
36.	Close Encounters of the Third Kind (1977)	166,000,000
37.	Robin Hood: Prince of Thieves (1991)	165,493,908
38.	The Exorcist (1973)	165,000,000
39.	Mission: Impossible (1996)	164,266,086
40.	The Sound of Music (1965)	163,214,286
41.	Batman Returns (1992)	162,831,698
42.	The Sting (1973)	159,616,327
43.	The Firm (1993)	158,308,178
44.	Fatal Attraction (1987)	156,645,693
45.	Who Framed Roger Rabbit? (1988)	154,112,492
46.	Beverly Hills Cop 2 (1987)	153,665,036
47.	Grease (1978)	153,112,093
48.	101 Dalmations (1961)	152,551,111
49.	Rambo: First Blood Part 2 (1985)	150,415,432
50.	Gremlins (1984)	148,168,459
51.	Lethal Weapon 2 (1989)	$147,253,986
52.	True Lies (1994)	146,273,950
53.	The Santa Clause (1994)	144,000,357
54.	Beauty and the Beast (1991)	144,016,206
55.	Lethal Weapon 3 (1992)	144,731,527
56.	National Lampoon's Animal House (1978)	141,600,000
57.	Pocahontas (1995)	141,579,773
58.	A Few Good Men (1992)	141,340,178
59.	Look Who's Talking (1989)	140,088,813
60.	Sister Act (1992)	139,605,150
61.	Platoon (1986)	137,963,328
62.	Jungle Book (1967)	135,475,556
63.	Teenage Mutant Ninja Turtles (1990)	135,265,915
64.	Superman (1978)	134,218,018
65.	The Godfather (1972)	133,698,921
66.	Silence of the Lambs (1991)	130,742,922
67.	Honey, I Shrunk the Kids (1989)	130,742,172
68.	The Flintstones (1994)	130,531,710
69.	An Officer and a Gentleman (1982)	129,795,549
70.	Coming to America (1988)	128,152,301
71.	Rocky 4 (1985)	127,873,716
72.	Dumb and Dumber (1994)	127,169,057
73.	Smokey and the Bandit (1977)	126,737,428
74.	Sleepless in Seattle (1993)	126,551,583
75.	Good Morning, Vietnam (1987)	123,922,370
76.	City Slickers (1991)	123,534,798
77.	Rocky 3 (1982)	122,823,192
78.	The Birdcage (1996)	122,453,823
79.	Clear and Present Danger (1994)	122,010,252
80.	The Bodyguard (1992)	121,936,132
81.	Wayne's World (1992)	121,700,000
82.	Speed (1994)	121,221,190
83.	The Hunt for Red October (1990)	120,702,326
84.	The Mask (1994)	119,936,108
85.	Hook (1991)	119,654,823
86.	Blazing Saddles (1974)	119,500,000
87.	Total Recall (1990)	119,994,039
88.	On Golden Pond (1981)	119,285,432
89.	Back to the Future 2 (1989)	118,450,002
90.	Basic Instinct (1992)	117,727,224
91.	Die Hard 2 (1990)	117,323,878
92.	Rocky (1976)	117,235,147
93.	The Towering Inferno (1974)	116,000,000
94.	The Karate Kid 2 (1986)	115,103,979
95.	American Graffiti (1973)	115,000,000
96.	Big (1988)	113,883,454
97.	The Addams Family (1991)	113,379,166
98.	Ghostbusters 2 (1989)	112,494,738
99.	Twins (1988)	111,784,821
100.	Dr. Zhivago (1965)	111,721,910

*As of 7/1/96

National Film Registry

Each year, Librarian of Congress James H. Billington adds 25 films to the National Film Registry. The Library of Congress ensures that each film selected will be preserved in its original form. The films, which must be at least 10 years old, are chosen based on "their historical, cultural and aesthetic significance." Here are the films that have been added to the list since it was created in 1989.

Adam's Rib (1949)
The African Queen (1951)
All About Eve (1950)
All Quiet on the Western Front (1930)
An American in Paris (1951)
Annie Hall (1977)
The Apartment (1960)

Badlands (1973)
The Bank Dick (1940)
The Battle of San Pietro (1945)
The Best Years of Our Lives (1946)
Big Business (1929)
The Big Parade (1925)
The Birth of a Nation (1915)
The Black Pirate (1926)
Blade Runner (1982)
The Blood of Jesus (1941)
Bonnie and Clyde (1967)
Bringing Up Baby (1938)

Carmen Jones (1954)
Casablanca (1942)
Castro Street (1966)
Cat People (1942)
The Cheat (1915)
Chinatown (1974)
Chulas Fronteras (1976)
Citizen Kane (1941)
City Lights (1931)
The Cool World (1963)

A Corner in Wheat (1909)
The Crowd (1928)

David Holzman's Diary (1968)
Detour (1946)
Dodsworth (1936)
Dog Star Man (1964)
Double Indemnity (1944)
Dr. Strangelove or: How I Learned to Stop Worrying and Love the Bomb (1964)
Duck Soup (1933)

E.T. the Extra-Terrestrial (1982)
Eaux D'Artifice (1953)
The Exploits of Elaine (1914)

Fantasia (1940)
Footlight Parade (1933)
Force of Evil (1948)
Frankenstein (1931)
Freaks (1932)
The Freshman (1925)

The General (1927)
Gertie the Dinosaur (1914)
Gigi (1958)
The Godfather (1972)
The Godfather Part II (1974)
The Gold Rush (1925)
Gone With the Wind (1939)
The Grapes of Wrath (1940)
The Great Train Robbery (1903)
Greed (1924)

Dr. Strangelove

Harlan County, U.S.A. (1976)
Hell's Hinges (1916)
High Noon (1952)
High School (1968)
His Girl Friday (1940)
Hospital (1970)
How Green Was My Valley (1941)

I Am a Fugitive From a Chain Gang (1932)
Intolerance (1916)
Invasion of the Body Snatchers (1956)
It Happened One Night (1934)
It's a Wonderful Life (1946)
The Italian (1915)

MOVIE TIMELINE

1889

William Kennedy Laurie Dickson, commissioned by Thomas Alva Edison, builds the first motion-picture camera and names it the Kinetograph.

1894

The Edison Corporation establishes the first motion-picture studio, a Kinetograph production center nicknamed the Black Maria (slang for a police van).

The first Kinetoscope parlor opens at 1155 Broadway in New York City.

1895

In France, Auguste and Louis Lumière hold the first private screening. The brothers invent the Cinématograph, a combination camera and projector. The image of an oncoming train is said to have caused a stampede.

1903

Edison Corporation mechanic Edwin S. Porter turns cameraman, director and producer to make *The Great*

Train Robbery. With 14 shots cutting between simultaneous events, this 12-minute short establishes the shot as film's basic element and editing as a central narrative device. It is also the first Western.

1909

The New York Times publishes the first movie review, a report on D.W. Griffith's *Pippa Passes*.

Killer of Sheep (1977)
King Kong (1933)

The Lady Eve (1941)
Lassie Come Home (1943)
Lawrence of Arabia (1962)
The Learning Tree (1969)
Letter From an Unknown
  Woman (1948)
Louisiana Story (1948)
Love Me Tonight (1932)

Magical Maestro (1952)
The Magnificent Ambersons (1942)
The Maltese Falcon (1941)
The Manchurian Candidate (1962)
March of Time: Inside Nazi
  Germany — 1938 (1938)
Marty (1955)
Meet Me in St. Louis (1944)
Meshes of the Afternoon (1943)
Midnight Cowboy (1969)
Modern Times (1936)
Morocco (1930)
A Movie (1958)
Mr. Smith Goes to Washington (1939)
My Darling Clementine (1946)

Nanook of the North (1922)
Nashville (1975)
A Night at the Opera (1935)
The Night of the Hunter (1955)
Ninotchka (1939)
Nothing but a Man (1964)

On the Waterfront (1954)
One Flew Over the Cuckoo's Nest (1975)
Out of the Past (1947)

Paths of Glory (1957)
Pinocchio (1940)
A Place in the Sun (1951)
Point of Order (1964)
The Poor Little Rich Girl (1917)

Primary (1960)
The Prisoner of Zenda (1937)
Psycho (1960)

Raging Bull (1980)
Rebel Without a Cause (1955)
Red River (1948)
Ride the High Country (1962)
The River (1937)

Safety Last (1923)
Salesman (1969)
Salt of the Earth (1954)
Scarface (1932)
The Searchers (1956)
Shadow of a Doubt (1943)
Shadows (1959)
Shane (1953)
Sherlock, Jr. (1924)
Singin' in the Rain (1952)
Snow White (1933)
Snow White and the Seven
  Dwarfs (1937)
Some Like It Hot (1959)
Star Wars (1977)

Sullivan's Travels (1941)
Sunrise (1927)
Sunset Blvd. (1950)
Sweet Smell of Success (1957)

Tabu (1931)
Taxi Driver (1976)
Tevye (1939)
Top Hat (1935)
Touch of Evil (1958)
The Treasure of the Sierra Madre (1948)
Trouble in Paradise (1932)
2001: A Space Odyssey (1968)

Vertigo (1958)
What's Opera, Doc? (1957)

Where Are My Children? (1916)
The Wind (1928)
Within Our Gates (1920)
The Wizard of Oz (1939)
A Woman Under the Influence (1974)

Yankee Doodle Dandy (1942)

Zapruder Film (1963)

Sunset Blvd.

1911
The first feature film is released when the two reels of D.W. Griffith's *Enoch Arden* are screened together.

1912
Photoplay debuts as the first magazine for movie fans.

1915
D.W. Griffith's technically brilliant Civil War epic, *The Birth of a Nation*, introduces the narrative close-up, the flashback and other elements

that endure today as the structural principles of narrative filmmaking.

1927
Popular vaudevillian Al Jolson astounds audiences with his nightclub act in *The Jazz Singer*, the first feature-length talkie.

1935
Although a primitive, two-color process was first used in 1922, audiences weren't impressed by Technicolor until a three-color system appeared in *Becky Sharp*.

1941
In *Citizen Kane,* Orson Welles subordinates all previous technological and cinematic accomplishments to his own essentially cinematic vision. Using newly developed film stocks and a wider, faster lens, Welles pushes the boundaries of montage and mise-en-scène, as well as sound, redefining the medium.

1945
Roberto Rossellini's Neorealist ode to the Italian Resistance, *Rome, Open*

Motion Picture Producers and Distributors

Buena Vista Pictures Distribution
500 S. Buena Vista St.
Burbank, CA 91521
(818) 567-5000

Carolco Pictures Inc.
8800 Sunset Blvd.
Los Angeles, CA 90069
(310) 859-8800

Castle Hill Productions, Inc.
1414 Ave. of the Americas
New York, NY 10019
(212) 888-0080

Castle Rock Entertainment
335 N. Maple Drive, Suite 135
Beverly Hills, CA 90210
(310) 285-2300

Columbia Pictures
10202 W. Washington Blvd.
Culver City, CA 90232
(310) 280-8000

Walt Disney Pictures
500 S. Buena Vista St.
Burbank, CA 91521
(818) 560-1000

DreamWorks SKG
100 Universal Plaza, Building 601
Universal City, CA 91608
(818) 733-7000

Fine Line Features
888 Seventh Ave., 20th Floor
New York, NY 10106
(212) 649-4900

The Samuel Goldwyn Co.
10203 Santa Monica Blvd.
Los Angeles, CA 90067
(310) 552-2255

Gramercy Pictures
9247 Alden Drive
Beverly Hills, CA 90210
(310) 777-1960

Hemdale Home Video
1640 South Sepulveda Blvd., Suite 520
Los Angeles, CA 90025
(310) 473-7221

Home Box Office
1100 6th Ave.
New York, NY 10036
(212) 512-1000

Imagine Entertainment
1925 Century Park E., Suite 2300
Los Angeles, CA 90067
(310) 277-1665

Interscope
10900 Wilshire Blvd., Suite 1400
Los Angeles, CA 90024
(310) 208-8525

Largo Entertainment
2029 Century Park E., Suite 920
Los Angeles, CA 90067
(310) 203-0055

Merchant Ivory Productions
250 W. 57th St., Suite 1913A
New York, NY 10107
(212) 582-8049

MGM/UA
2500 Broadway St.
Santa Monica, CA 90404-3061
(310) 449-3000

Miramax Films Corp.
375 Greenwich St.
New York, NY 10013
(212) 941-3800

New Line Cinema Corp.
888 Seventh Ave., 20th Floor
New York, NY 10106
(212) 649-4900

October Films
65 Bleecker St., 2nd Floor
New York, NY 10012
(212) 539-4000

Orion Pictures Corp.
1888 Century Park East
Los Angeles, CA 90067
(310) 282-0550

Paramount Pictures
1515 Broadway, 3rd Floor
New York, NY 10019
(212) 846-1020

Republic Pictures Corp.
5700 Wilshire Blvd., Suite 525
Los Angeles, CA 90036
(213) 965-6900

Sony Pictures Entertainment, Inc.
10202 W. Washington Blvd.
Culver City, CA 90232
(310) 280-8000

City, presents an alternative to Hollywood with its use of street cinematography, grainy black-and-white stocks and untrained actors, lyrically capturing the despair and confusion of post-World War II Europe.

1948
The Hollywood Ten, a group of writers, producers and directors called as witnesses in the House Committee's Investigation of Un-American Activi-ties, are jailed for contempt of Congress when they refuse to disclose if they were or were not Communists.

1953
To counteract the threat of television, Hollywood thinks big and develops wide-screen processes such as CinemaScope, first seen in *The Robe.*

1955
70mm film is introduced with *Oklahoma!*

1959
Jean-Luc Godard's *Breathless,* typical of the French New Wave use of the jump cut, the hand-held camera and loose, improvised direction, is made for $90,000 in just four weeks. The jump cut's assault on seamless editing and the presumption of time continuity opens new possibilities for filmmakers.

1962
Government regulations force studios out of the talent agency business.

Touchstone Pictures
500 S. Buena Vista St.
Burbank, CA 91521
(818) 560-2785

TriStar Pictures
10202 W. Washington Blvd.
Culver City, CA 90232
(310) 280-7700

Troma, Inc.
733 Ninth Ave.
New York, NY 10019
(212) 757-4555

Twentieth Century-Fox
P.O. Box 900
Beverly Hills, CA 90213
(310) 277-2211

Universal Pictures
445 Park Ave.
New York, NY 10022
(212) 759-7500

Warner Bros.
Time Warner, Inc.
75 Rockefeller Plaza
New York, NY 10019
(212) 484-8000

Film Museums and Archives

Academy of Motion Picture Arts and Sciences
Center for Motion Picture Study
Academy Film Archive
333 S. La Cienega Blvd.
Beverly Hills, CA 90211
(310) 247-3000

American Museum of the Moving Image
3601 35th Ave.
Astoria, NY 11106
(718) 784-4520

American Cinematheque
Hollywood Roosevelt Hotel
7000 Hollywood Blvd., 3rd Floor
Hollywood, CA 90028
(213) 466-3456

American Film Institute/National Center for Film and Video Preservation
John F. Kennedy Center for the Performing Arts
Washington D.C. 20566
(202) 828-4000

George Eastman House
900 East Ave.
Rochester, NY 14607
(716) 271-3361

Harvard Film Archive
Carpenter Center for the Visual Arts
Harvard University
24 Quincy St.
Cambridge, MA 02138
(617) 495-4700

Library of Congress
Motion Picture, Broadcasting and Recorded Sound Division
Washington D.C. 20540-4690
(202) 707-5840

Museum of Modern Art
Department of Film and Video
11 W. 53rd St.
New York, NY 10019
(212) 708-9602

National Museum of Natural History/ Human Studies Film Archives
Smithsonian Institute,
Room E307, MRC 123
Washington D.C. 20560
(202) 357-3349, (202) 357-3356

Pacific Film Archive
University Art Museum
2625 Durant Ave.
Berkeley, CA 94720
(510) 642-1412

UCLA Film and Television Archive
302 E. Melnitz Hall
University of California
Box 951323
Los Angeles, CA 90095-1323
(310) 206-8013

Wisconsin Center for Film and Theater Research
Film and Photo Archive
816 State St.
Madison, WI 53706
(608) 264-6466

1964

Bonnie and Clyde and *Red Desert* make spectacular use of the recently perfected zoom lens, which increases the optical mobility of a shot and its expressive capacities.

1968

The motion picture rating system debuts with G, PG, R and X.

1969

Midnight Cowboy wins the Best Picture Oscar, the first and only time an X-rated movie received the honor.

1976

The Steadicam is used for the first time in *Rocky*.

1977

Saturday Night Fever sparks the disco inferno and the popularity of movie soundtracks.

1990

The X rating is replaced by NC-17 (no children under 17).

1993

Lost in Yonkers is edited on an Avid Media Composer system, the first non-linear editing system to allow viewing at film's required "real-time"-viewing rate of 24 frames per second. By converting film into digital bits, film can now be cut on a computer.

Movie Magazines and Journals

AFI Guide to College Courses in Film and Television
American Film Institute, Education Services
2021 N. Western Ave.
Los Angeles, CA 90027-1625
(213) 856-7600

American Cinematographer
A.S.C. Holding Corp.
1782 N. Orange Drive
Hollywood, CA 90028
(213) 876-5080

American Movie Classics Magazine
Working Media, Inc.
18 Shawmut St.
Boston, MA 02116
(800) 669-1002

Black Film Review
Sojourner Productions, Inc.
2025 Eye St. N.W.
Washington D.C. 20006
(202) 466-2753

Camera Obscura: A Journal of Feminism and Film Theory
Indiana University Press
601 N. Morton St.
Bloomington, IN 47404
(812) 855-9449

Cineaste
200 Park Ave. S., Suite 1601
New York, NY 10003
(212) 982-1241

Cinefantastique
P.O. Box 270
Oak Park, IL 60303
(708) 366-5566

Cinefex
Box 20027
Riverside, CA 92516-0027
(909) 781-1917

Director's Guild of America
Directors Guild of America, Inc.
7920 Sunset Blvd.
Hollywood, CA 90046-3388
(310) 289-2073

East-West Film Journal
University of Hawaii Press
2840 Kolowalu St.
Honolulu, HI 96822-1888
(808) 956-8833

Entertainment Weekly
1675 Broadway
New York, NY 10019
(212) 522-5600

Fangoria
Starlog Group
475 Park Ave. S.
New York, NY 10016-6989
(212) 689-2830

Film Comment
P.O. Box 3000
Denville, NJ 07834
(800) 783-4903

Filmfax
Box 1900
Evanston, IL 60204-1900
(708) 866-7155

Filmmaker Magazine
Independent Feature Project
110 West 57th St., 3rd Floor
New York, NY 10019
(212) 581-8080

Film Quarterly
University of California Press
2120 Berkeley Way
Berkeley, CA 94702
(510) 642-4247

Films in Review
P. O. Box 589
New York, NY 10021
(212) 628-1594

Film Threat Video Guide
Film Threat Video Inc.
2805 Magnolia Blvd.
Burbank, CA 91505
(818) 848-8971

Independent
Foundation for Independent Video and Film
304 Hudson St., 6th Floor N.
New York, NY 10013
(212) 807-1400

Millennium Film Journal
66 E. Fourth St.
New York, NY 10003
(212) 673-0090

Millimeter
Intertec Publishing
1775 Broadway, Suite 730
New York, NY 10019
(216) 641-5265

Movieline
1141 S. Beverly Drive
Los Angeles, CA 90035-1155
(619) 745-2809

Outré
3120 Oakton St.
Evanston, IL 60202
(847) 866-7155

Premiere
1633 Broadway, 41st Floor
New York, NY 10016
(212) 767-6000

Spectator-USC Journal of Film and Television Criticism
USC School of Cinema and TV
Division of Critical Studies
University of Southern California
Los Angeles, CA 90089-2211
(213) 740-3334

Velvet Light Trap
University of Texas Press
Box 7819
Austin, TX 78713-7819
(512) 471-4531

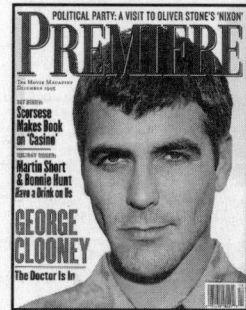

Movie Glossary

aspect ratio The width-to-height ratio of a movie frame and screen. Standard aspect ratio is 1.33 to 1; CinemaScope uses 2.35 to 1.

auteur A filmmaker, usually a director, with a recognizable, strong personal style.

best boy The chief assistant to the gaffer on a set.

boom A movable arm that holds a microphone over actors' heads during filming.

cineaste A film or movie enthusiast.

CinemaScope The trademark used for an anamorphic wide-screen process.

cinéma vérité A style of filmmaking that stresses unbiased realism and often contains unedited sequences.

coverage The shots, including close-ups and reverse angles, that a director takes in addition to the master shot.

cut 1. The instruction to stop the camera and the action in front of the camera. **2.** The process of editing a film or shortening a scene.

cutaway A brief shot that interrupts the continuity of the main action of a film, often used to depict related matter or indicate concurrent action.

day for night A shot filmed during the day, which appears on the screen as a night scene.

diffusion The reduction of the harshness or intensity of light achieved by using a screen, glass filter or smoke.

director of photography The movie photographer responsible for camera technique and lighting during production. Also called **cinematographer**.

dissolve The gradual transformation of one scene to the next by overlapping a fade-out with a fade-in.

dolly shot A moving shot that uses a wheeled camera platform known as a dolly.

editor The person often responsible for the final structure of a film.

fade-in A gradual transition from complete black to full exposure.

fade-out A gradual transition from full exposure to complete black.

frame An individual unit of movie film. The American standard film speed is 24 frames per second; there are 16 frames per foot of 35mm film.

freeze-frame A still picture during a movie, made by running a series of identical frames.

gaffer The main electrician and supervisor of lighting on a set.

grip The crew member who adjusts scenery, flags lights and often operates the camera cranes and dollies.

jump cut A cut made in the middle of a continuous shot rather than between shots, creating discontinuity in time and drawing attention to the film itself instead of its content.

key grip The head grip who supervises the grip crew and receives orders from the gaffer or the head lighting technician.

klieg light A powerful carbon-arc lamp producing an intense light that is commonly used in filmmaking. It is sometimes used outside Hollywood theaters to promote premieres. Named after **John H. Kliegl** (1869–1959) and his brother **Anton T. Kliegl** (1870–1970), German-born American lighting experts.

master shot A continuous take that covers the entire set or all of the action in a scene.

matte shot A partially opaque shot in the frame area. The shot can be printed with another frame, hiding unwanted content and permitting the addition of another scene on a reverse matte.

outtake A shot or scene that is shot but not used in the final print of the film.

pan A horizontal movement of the camera from a fixed point.

point of view A shot that depicts the outlook or position of a character.

postproduction A final stage in the production of a film or a television program, typically involving editing and the addition of soundtracks. Also called **post**.

preproduction The planning stage of a film or television program involving budgeting, scheduling, casting, design and location selection.

prescreen To see a movie before it is released for the public.

rush The print of the camera footage from one day's shooting. Also called **daily**.

scene A succession of shots that conveys a unified element of a movie's story.

sequence A succession of scenes that comprises a dramatic unit of film.

shooting script The final version of a script with the scenes arranged in proper sequence.

shot The basic building block of film narrative — the single unedited piece of film.

slate The digital board that is held in front of the camera and identifies shot number, director, cameraperson, studio and title. The data was originally written with chalk on a piece of slate. This footage is used in the laboratory and editing room to identify the shot.

sound stage A soundproof room or studio used in movie production.

SteadiCam A hydraulically-balanced apparatus that harnesses a camera to an operator's body providing smooth tracking shots without using a track.

storyboard The rough sketches depicting plot, action and characters in the sequential scenes of a film, television show or advertisement.

take The filming of a shot in a particular camera setup. The director usually films several takes before approving the shot.

tilt A vertical camera movement from a fixed position.

tracking shot A shot that moves in one plane by moving the camera dolly along fixed tracks.

trailer A short filmed preview or advertisement for a movie.

treatment A detailed synopsis of a movie's story, with action and character rendered in prose form.

voiceover The voice of an unseen narrator or of an onscreen character not seen speaking in a movie.

MUSIC

Grrrl, It's About Time

■ BY JOY PRESS

Joy Press is co-author of *The Sex Revolts: Gender Rebellion and Rock and Roll* **and a contributing writer and editor to many music publications.**

N THE PAST YEAR, GRUNGE FINALLY GOT STALE, THE ROCK AND ROLL Hall of Fame and Museum finally opened and all four Beatles finally reunited (although Lennon only made the gig through the miracles of modern technology). It was also the year that Hootie & the Blowfish cleaned up with their clean-cut rock'n'soul, Oasis invaded America with their Britpop anthems and Jerry Garcia passed to a higher plane.

Most of all, it has been the year of the Angry Young Woman in Rock — or at least the music industry figured out how to market a mainstream version of female rage that could be called Angry Young Woman Lite. The success of Courtney Love, Polly Jean Harvey and Liz Phair in previous years and the notoriety of the Riot Grrrl movement had opened record executives' eyes to something that rock fans already knew: Women were making some of the most interesting music around. "I want to be the girl with the most cake" was an oft-repeated lyric from Hole's song "Doll Parts," and it seemed representative of this new generation of female rocker that knows what it wants and how to get it. Even *Time* magazine agreed; Love made the magazine's list of the 25 Most Influential People of 1996.

MUSIC

In the wake of Love, Harvey and Phair came Alanis Morissette, a 22-year-old who had forged a career in Canada with bland, Debbie Gibson-style dance-pop. In 1995, she paired up with collaborator Glen Ballard (who previously had worked with slick mega-stars such as Paula Abdul and Michael Jackson) and constructed a new, angrier persona. Morissette took on the role of a betrayed lover and avenging angel in "You Oughta Know" ("I'm here to remind you of the mess you left when you went away"), unleashing a howl of rage that may have been cathartic but was not particularly feminist. As many critics pointed out, the sound and content of *Jagged Little Pill* is closer to Pat Benatar than to Bikini Kill, but that didn't stop this sanitized version of female rebellion from selling millions of copies. As her record soared to the top of the charts, the media rushed to document teenage girls' admiration for their new role model, and Morissette herself told the *New York Times:* "I wish I had me to listen to when I was fourteen." The mini-Morissettes recalled the Madonna wannabes of the '80s, which may have been more than a coincidence since *Jagged Little Pill* was released on Madonna's own Maverick label.

Other record companies, sensing gold in them thar girls, were also on the lookout for women with shrill vocals and pissed-off lyrics. Many female performers who had been kicking around for years were signed by major labels: former punks Penelope Houston, Seven Year Bitch and Ruby all benefited from this trend. The former wild woman singer for the punk band Silverfish, Ruby reinvented herself as a sultry, sinister chanteuse with blue hair and combat boots. Her album *Saltpeter* boasts electronic atmospherics and nasty lyrical tidbits such as: "You know I hate it when you cry/It makes me want to burn your eyes with a poker." Singer-songwriter Tracy Bonham's delightfully sarcastic MTV hit "Mother Mother" was among the best of this post-Alanis fashion for fury. "I'm starving/I'm bleeding to death,"

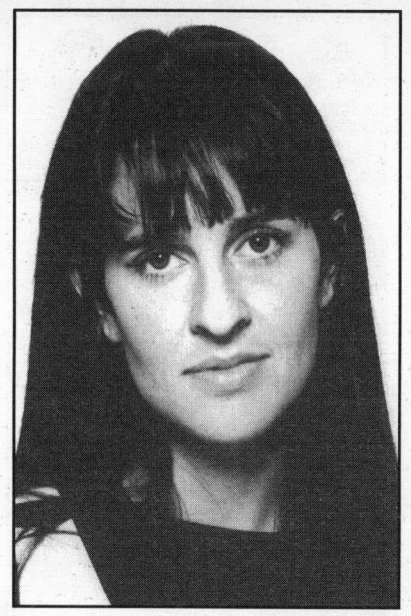

Tracy Bonham and Patti Smith

Bonham pleads sweetly to her impervious mother, before erupting in a blood-curdling screech seconds later: "Everything's fine!"

The multitude of female success stories in 1995 and 1996 proved that rock fans were ready for a diverse range of women's voices. Former Arrested Development singer Dionne Farris scored a hit with her funky, idiosyncratic blend of rap and R&B on *Wild Seed Wildflower*. And 24-year-old bluegrass singer/fiddler Alison Krauss finally got the attention she deserved with the release of *Now That I've Found You: A Collection,* which reached No. 2 on *Billboard*'s Country chart. Krauss, who likes to cover The Beatles and Bad Company songs as readily as old fiddle standards, won a whole new audience over to her pop-tinged version of bluegrass. With "One of Us," Joan Osborne became an overnight sensation — except, as usual, it was far from overnight. She'd been singing in blues clubs in and around New York City for years, part of the same scene that bred Blues Traveler. The song stirred up emotional controversy: Some listeners thought Osborne was a religious nut, while a number of Christian groups accused her of sacrilege.

This was a pretty good year for marginalized almost-legends, too: Both Patti Smith and Yoko Ono made comebacks. Smith emerged from semi-retirement to produce the elegiac album *Long Gone* and toured to sold-out houses; while Ono, long viewed as the dragon lady who destroyed The Beatles, attracted a new generation of fans with the album *Rising.* It was her most impressive record since her groundbreaking collaborations with John Lennon in the early '70s, once again infusing rock and roll with her avant-garde sensibility.

Just as women were finally becoming an indelible presence in the music world, some critics wondered why Joni Mitchell, one the most important rock artists of the '70s, failed to make it into the Rock and Roll Hall of Fame for the third year in a row, and why so few songs associated with female performers showed up on the Hall of Fame's list of the 500 most influential rock songs of all time. (Even The Monkees had two songs on the list, compared to Mitchell's one.) That wasn't the only controversy that greeted the Labor Day open-

Major Music Festivals

BEN & JERRY'S NEWPORT FOLK FESTIVAL
NEWPORT, RHODE ISLAND

The mother of all folk festivals returned in 1988 thanks to the sponsorship of the Vermont-based ice cream moguls. In 1996, the three-day lineup included such luminaries as Michelle Shocked, Suzanne Vega, John Hiatt, the Indigo Girls, Bruce Cockburn, Lisa Loeb, Clarence "Gatemouth" Brown and Cordelia's Dad. The festivities began on Friday, August 9, at the Hotel Viking, then spilled onto the sea-surrounded, expansive lawn of Fort Adams State Park on Saturday and Sunday. When the weather cooperates, this is a beautiful summer affair, with sailboats circling the concert grounds. And each year's festival has a special theme. In 1996, it was country and bluegrass, with the Nashville Bluegrass Band, Peter Rowan and Crucial Country and others performing. Despite a charming seacoast and its industrial-era mansions, downtown Newport is overrated, overpriced and overpopulated during the summer. — TED DROZDOWSKI

Ben & Jerry's Newport Folk Festival
P.O. Box 605
Newport, RI 02840
(401) 847-3700

CHICAGO BLUES FESTIVAL
CHICAGO, ILLINOIS

Held each year in late May or early June (1996's was May 31 to June 2) in Chicago's Grant Park on the shores of Lake Michigan, this is the country's largest blues festival. Throughout the event, there's plenty of hometown talent. This year, seven Chicago veterans, including guitarist Hubert Sumlin and sax player Eddie Shaw, honored the late Howlin' Wolf. Some of the deepest, most authentic performances occur on the Front Porch stage, where guitarist Honeyboy Edwards and David Bromberg's tribute to the Rev. Gary Davis highlighted each weekend day. When the performers take the main stage, some 360,000 listeners can flood the surrounding fields. Friday was the night to join the crowd this year as vocalist Wille Clayton opened the show for Texan Long John Hunter and the dark lord of voodoo blues, Screamin' Jay Hawkins. At night, as usual, Chicago's blues clubs are crawling with musicians and revelers. Recommended venues include Buddy Guy's Legends and the bars dotting Halstead Street, including the popular Kingston Mines and B.L.U.E.S. and Theresa's on the south side. — TD

Chicago Blues Festival
Mayor's Office of Special Events
City Hall
121 N. LaSalle St., Room 703
Chicago, IL 60602
(312) 744-3315 or (800) ITS-CHGO

Bush

ing of the Rock and Roll Hall of Fame and Museum in Cleveland. Amid the flurry of excitement, many rock fans were appalled that rock and roll was being officially institutionalized. It seemed impossible that the music could be penned into a museum just like any other staid, conventional artform and that rock, once about rebellion and the wrong side of the tracks, was being converted into a monument to baby-boomer memories.

But that's how it works — today's alternative is tomorrow's institution. The best rock artists try to stretch the boundaries to create music that is original and sometimes shocking. As soon as the shock is absorbed, that once-transgressive music begins to seem tame and the cycle starts all over again. Punk and other sub-genres of "alternative" rock, once considered outside the mainstream, have now become radio and MTV fodder. For the past five years, Lollapalooza had been a definitive symbol of alternative music. The 1996 traveling fest was a metal-heavy party, featuring Metallica, Soundgarden and Screaming

Trees. Unable to sustain the fiction of an alternative festival when the whole "alternative" genre is now little more than a marketing term, Perry Farrell gave up on the festival he founded and launched ENIT, a more techno-oriented cyber-hippy festival.

Four years since Nirvana's breakthrough album *Nevermind*, grunge still dominates the charts. But it's a new, watered-down grunge: Bands such as Silverchair, Bush, Sponge and Candlebox are as safe and predictable as the pretty-boy pop-metal groups (Poison, Skid Row, Slaughter) that grunge tried to replace. Instead of caked-on makeup and teased hair, though, these grungesters possess greasy locks and earnest, raspy voices. Dave Grohl from Nirvana took grunge in a poppy direction with his new band, Foo Fighters, as did ex-Nirvana producer Butch Vig with his band Garbage. (The latter also managed to capitalize on the Angry Woman craze courtesy of singer Shirley Manson's surly vocals and lyrics.) Meanwhile, Silverchair, three 16-year-olds from Australia, fooled more than a few Eddie Vedder fans with their Pearl Jam-soundalike hit "Tommorrow." *Rolling Stone* affectionately dubbed them the "grunge Menudo" and "Sound(kinder)garden."

British grunge stars Bush left their native land for the United States and beat us at our own game. Bush's doe-eyed singer Gavin Rossdale regularly graced the covers of American magazines and was said to be a Courtney Love confidant —

Foo Fighters

CHICAGO JAZZ FESTIVAL
CHICAGO, ILLINOIS

Each fall, visitors from all over the world attend this venerable event, one of the country's largest jazz festivals, which acknowledges the contributions of Chicago's strong jazz community and the African-American musical tradition in general. Local legends such as Lester Bowie, Joseph Jarman and other pillars of the AACM draw large crowds to Grant Park. And they're joined by many of the biggest names in jazz. In recent years neo-trad heroes such as Wynton Marsalis and Cyrus Chestnut have appeared, as have avant-grade major-leaguers, including Cecil Taylor and Don Byron, and aggressive generalists like David Murray. The 1996 festival ran from August 30 to September 1, and fans kept clubs such as local favorite Andy's and the more prestigious Jazz Showcase hopping throughout. — TD

> **Chicago Jazz Festival**
> **Mayor's Office of Special Events**
> **City Hall**
> **121 N. LaSalle St., Room 703**
> **Chicago, IL 60602**
> **(312) 744-3315 or (800) ITS-CHGO**

FAN FAIR
NASHVILLE, TENNESSEE

A 13-year-old singer wowed festival goers at the Country Music Association's and the Grand Ole Opry's 25th Fan Fair. LeAnn Rimes, whose "Blue" has topped the country charts, is billed as the reincarnation of Patsy Cline. Each year, an army of fans descend on the Tennessee State Fairground to catch dozens of live performances, get autographs signed by stars such as Garth Brooks, Shania Twain and Billy Ray Cyrus and devour junk food. There's camping, with enough trailers and mobile homes on site to earn a spot in the Guinness book. And the atmosphere's plain, middle-American crazy. Country music stars and their fans do have a genuine love affair, and each June, this is where they let it all hang out. Add the Country Music Hall of Fame, the Grand Ole Opry, Ryman Auditorium and the gift shops of the stars surrounding Hope and Commerce streets to the agenda while in town. — TD

> **Fan Fair**
> **2804 Opryland Drive**
> **Nashville, TN 37214**
> **(615) 889-7503**

CONTINUED ON NEXT PAGE ▶

◀ CONTINUED FROM PREVIOUS PAGE

FESTIVAL INTERNATIONAL DE JAZZ DE MONTREAL
MONTREAL, QUEBEC, CANADA

With bookings as richly international as Montreal itself, this 11-day multimedia extravaganza is a favorite of fest hoppers. Roots rock, R&B, fusion, folk music, salsa, African highlife and soukous all have room on the stages that dot the city's streets, parks, clubs and theaters for the world's largest festival. Each year a theme is built around a series of major performances. During the 1996 Festival, which ran from June 27 to July 7, festival organizers paid homage to trumpet great Louis Armstrong. New Orleans trumpet virtuoso Nicholas Payton, arguably the best at capturing Armstrong's tone, performed contemporary interpretations of the great one's classics. Particularly reminiscent of Armstrong's Crescent City Swing was Payton's and Ellis Marsalis's duet. Kevin Mahogany's rendition of "What a Wonderful World" was the perfect close to a smashingly successful festival. If 11 days of music seems overwhelming, there are the delights of Old Montreal — shops, fine restaurants and all the other amenities a truly world-class city offers. — TD

> Festival International de Jazz de Montreal
> 822 Rue Sherbrooke Est
> Montreal, Quebec
> Canada H2L 1K4
> (514) 523-3378

H.O.R.D.E FESTIVAL

Five years ago, John Popper of Blues Traveler created the H.O.R.D.E Festival (Horizons of Rock Developing Everywhere) as a summit for like-minded bands, such as Phish and Spin Doctors, with roots in the blues. While the tour was initially greeted as a neo-hippie alternative to Lollapalooza's moshing madness, it has since gathered a formidable following beyond the tie-dye and Birkenstock crowd. This year's lineup reflected efforts to wrap in more diverse sounds with funky Lenny Kravitz joining headliners Blues Travelers (of course) and Rusted Root for the nine-week, 41-city tour. The Dave Matthews Band, Natalie Merchant, Me'Shell Ndegéocello, King Crimson and Rickie Lee Jones took the stage for selected dates. In the Lollapalooza sideshow tradition, H.O.R.D.E. extends the festival experience to a concourse of counter-culture foods, crafts and political activism. — ALICIA POTTER

> H.O.R.D.E. Festival
> 154 West 57th St., Suite 828
> Carnegie Hall
> New York, NY 10019
> (212) 582-0228

but back in England, no one had even heard of his band. After all, grunge has long been eclipsed there by Britpop, a movement originally born out of resentment for the long-haired, fuzzy-guitared American invaders. In the hands of bands such as Oasis, Blur, Elastica and Pulp, Britpop was a return to Englishness, the rediscovery of a distinctively English heritage comprised of The Beatles and The Kinks as well as other bands that never made much of a dent in the United States, such as the Buzzcocks, the Stranglers, Wire and the Jam.

In a year when the three surviving Beatles reunited to release *Anthology* and record several new songs sung by John Lennon from beyond the grave (by using vocal tracks he'd recorded while alive), the Beatles-obsessed band Oasis became superstars in Britain with songs about being superstars. When they finally made it big in America with their second album *(What's the Story) Morning Glory?*, Oasis leaders Noel and Liam Gallagher's heads swelled to cosmic proportions. The British media pitted Oasis against Blur, and loose cannon Noel Gallagher publicly announced that he wished that Blur's singer and bassist would "catch AIDS and die." (He later apologized, of course.)

Blur didn't die, but they also didn't do so well in the United States. While Oasis's

Oasis

Pulp

songs were larger than life and universally catchy, Blur's aesthetic was too self-consciously clever and Anglo-centric to grab an American audience. By the end of the year, Blur had been overshadowed by Pulp, led by a gawky and charismatic singer Jarvis Cocker. Their album, *Different Class*, combines the tacky glamour of Roxy Music with the caustic wit of Elvis Costello and the sheen of Gloria Gaynor-style disco. "Common People," a huge hit in England, is a smart, perfect pop song about an upper-class girl who likes to slum by hanging out with working-class people, like Jarvis. The song successfully turned Cocker into the voice of the disenfranchised. He quickly solidified his status at the Brit Awards, the UK equivalent of the Grammys, where he impulsively leaped onstage during Michael Jackson's performance and mocked Jackson's overblown, Christ-like posturing. The Jackson camp accused him of injuring some of the children onstage, but the British public crowned him a working-class hero.

Britpop brims with optimism and catchy hooks, but some critics complained that it is too parochial, too safe, too nostalgic for the glory days of British rock — especially when compared with the innovative music spawned by rave culture, like trip-hop and jungle. Hatched during the early '90s, these two UK styles washed up on our shores in 1995. Trip-hop is a moody,

HOUSE OF BLUES SMOKIN' GROOVES TOUR

The inaugural tour bridges blues and contemporary urban beats with its eclectic R&B mix of hip-hop, alternative rap, funk and reggae. The summer festival stopped at 34 outdoor amphitheaters in 1996 with an impressive first-year lineup that included Lollapalooza alumnus Cypress Hill, the red-hot, socially-conscious Fugees, legendary Ziggy Marley and the Melody Makers, rapper Busta Rhymes, mellow hip-hoppers A Tribe Called Quest and the more avant-garde Spearhead.— AP

> **House of Blues Smokin' Grooves Tour**
> **8439 Sunset Blvd., Suite 306**
> **West Hollywood, CA 90069**
> **(213) 848-2583**

JVC JAZZ FESTIVAL NEW YORK CITY

This is the granddaddy of American jazz fests. It began in Newport, Rhode Island, in 1954, moved to New York in the '70s and by the '90s had satellite events in Chicago; Dallas; Atlanta; Concord and Hollywood, California; Saratoga, New York; and back at Newport. The big kahuna's in New York City, however, and attracts an international audience. The 1996 festival, held from June 21 to June 30, mixed outdoor shows with gigs at such historic sites as Avery Fisher and Carnegie halls. And the music offered bristling highs: At the Knitting Factory, bassist Charlie Haden and saxophonist Dewey Redman engaged in a mesmerizing duet and Redman and his quartet paid tribute to Ed Blackwell. But the performances aren't always sterling — an evening featuring the pianists Ahmad Jamal and Herbie Hancock never connected — but the activity all over the city makes for a primer on the current state of jazz. — TD

> **JVC Jazz Festival New York**
> **P.O. Box 1169**
> **Ansonia Station**
> **New York, NY 10023**
> **(212) 787-2020**

Charlie Haden

CONTINUED ON NEXT PAGE ▶

Everything but the Girl

CONTINUED FROM PREVIOUS PAGE

LOLLAPALOOZA

This traveling three-stage, summertime rock and roll circus is not what it once was and intended to be. In fact, original fest organizer Perry Farrell relinquished his supervisory role in 1996 because his loss of artistic control to music-industry executives led to a line-up anything but alternative. In response, Farrell started a new festival called ENIT that evokes those early days when alternative was alternative. This year, America's premier youth-culture event — with performances, films, galleries, artisans, technology, dance music and politics woven into its lively mix — went heavy and mainstream with Metallica headlining and Soundgarden, Screaming Trees, the Ramones and Rancid also appearing on the first stage. Farrell established the extravaganza in 1991 as a grand farewell tour for his band Jane's Addiction, and it has grown to embrace nearly every trend, from body piercing to virtual reality, but the main attraction is still the music. — TD

Information can be obtained through local promoters or via the Internet, at http://lollapalooza.com

MACINTOSH NEW YORK MUSIC FESTIVAL/GLOBAL INTERNET GATHERING NEW YORK CITY

In its second year, the Macintosh New York Music Festival moved beyond the metropolis's smoky clubs to the Internet, where it was reincarnated as the first Global Internet Gathering, or The Gig. Mixing music with multimedia, the weeklong (July 14–20) festival cybercast live video and audio performances from more than 30 clubs and festivals around the world, including Switzerland's Montreaux Jazz Festival and Tokyo's Electronic Cafe. The Website's "open mike" area encouraged musicians to post information about their live performances during the festival, while a "backstage" area networked fans from around the globe. Modem-less music lovers and those more inclined to sidle up to a stage than a computer could still make the rounds to 17 New York clubs to hear more than 450 artists, including such known commodities as Throwing Muses, Henry Rollins, Social Distortion, Frente! and Verve Pipe. Participating clubs ranged from hall-size venues such as the Irving Palace to such holes-in-the-wall as Brownie's. A 1996 festival pass cost $50. — AP

Macintosh New York Music Festival/Global Internet Gathering
285 W. Broadway, Suite 630
New York, NY 10013
(212) 343-9290
http://www.thegig.com

down-tempo version of hip-hop that features singing as often as rapping. The genre's leading lights, Portishead, Tricky and Massive Attack, all hail from Bristol, a sleepy port in the west of England.

Tricky's debut album *Maxinquaye,* a disturbing masterpiece, melds hip-hop, dub-reggae, funk, pop and blues with eerie, ambiguous lyrics. Every song is dense with aural surprises. Despite being almost as bleak, Portishead's album *Dummy* became a ubiquitous presence at cafes, boutiques and parties. With its cinematic atmospherics, low-key hip-hop beat, and the mellifluous torch song vocals of singer Beth Gibbons, *Dummy* was every hipster's mood music of choice.

If trip-hop is chill-out music, jungle is the most ferociously energizing offshoot of Britain's rave culture yet. Jungle speeds up hip-hop's funky breakbeat rhythms and combines them with thunderous reggae basslines and techno's futuristic textures. London's jungle scene developed underground, via a vast network of pirate radio stations, independent labels and clubs, but Americans finally caught on this year with the release of Goldie's *Timeless.* Goldie's larger-than-life personality made it easier for rock fans to put a face to jungle — especially after he married Björk, who released the wonderful, techno-influenced album *Post* this year.

Suddenly everyone wanted jungle artists to remix their songs. And as jungle took on a more mellow, sophisticated flavor, jazz-pop artists such as Everything but the Girl started integrating breakbeats into their own music. Everything but the Girl weren't just bandwagon-jumping, though; they had been immersing themselves in dance music for several years, and finally scored a huge American hit with Todd Terry's dance remix of "Missing," which took a year to climb into the Top 5.

In the world of hip-hop, the Fugees and Coolio represented the acceptable face of rap. Both topped the charts with songs that returned to the pop-soul of the '70s: the Fugees remade Roberta Flack's "Killing Me Softly" into a shuffling hip-hop jam, while Coolio filched the doomy chords and chorus of Stevie Wonder's "Past Time Paradise" for his "Gangsta's Paradise." On the West Coast, Eazy E protégés Bone Thugs-N-Harmony scored a No. 1 hit with their fluttery hybrid of rap and doowop. Meanwhile, down in the East Coast underground, the ruling sound was the paranoid, cinematic hip-hop style invented by the Wu Tang Clan and Gravediggaz a few years earlier. Solo albums by Wu Tang clansmen Method Man Raekwon, Ol' Dirty Bastard and Genius/GZA all went gold or platinum this year; Method Man even scored a No. 1 *Billboard* hit with his Mary J. Blige duet "I'll Be There for You/You're All I Need to Get

Fugees

MISSISSIPPI DELTA BLUES FESTIVAL
GREENVILLE, MISSISSIPPI

Each fall — after the summer heat has passed — the heart of the Delta opens up to accommodate as many as 100,000 fans for this event, which primarily draws its talent from home. The no-frills festival embraces artists from Jackson, Mississippi's big-selling Malaco Records stable, slicks such as Latimore and Vasti Jackson, to more obscure players like rough-as-a-cob Belzoni guitarist/singer Paul "Wine" Jones, whose daddy, K.C. Jones, was a juke joint operator and old running buddy of Sonny Boy Williamson. And Greenville itself, a literary center of the old South, offers plenty of affordable chain-hotels, mall shopping, museums and brown tap water — a legacy of life on the muddy Mississippi River. It's also the home of the original Doe's Eat Place, a downhome cookery with a two-item dinner menu: a pile of plump Gulf shrimp or a steak twice as big as your head. Both delicious. — TD

M.A.C.E.
119 S. Theobold
Greenville, Mississippi 38701
(601) 335-3523

NEW ORLEANS JAZZ AND HERITAGE FESTIVAL
NEW ORLEANS, LOUISIANA

From its humble beginnings as a daylong celebration of local music and culture in the French Quarter's Congo Square 26 years ago, the New Orleans Jazz and Heritage Festival has become the nation's premier musical and folk-culture event. Now spanning the last weekend in April and the first in May, it fills the sprawling New Orleans Fairgrounds with hundreds of artists performing concurrently on 10 stages, dozens of vendors providing regional delicacies and artisans and craftspeople selling their wares and offering workshops. The real treats are appearances of local R&B legends such as Allen Toussaint, Snooks Eaglin and Ernie K. Doe or the deep-swamp cajun, zydeco and old-time country musicians who come to the city for their annual day in the warm southern sun. But expect to see plenty of big names, too. The Neville Brothers, Joan Osborne, Van Morrison, the Dave Matthews Band, Buddy Guy and Bela Fleck and the Flecktones performed at the 1996 fest. At night, the festival spills into the city's many clubs and music halls, the best of which are the local landmark Tipitina's (named after Professor Longhair's signature song) in the warehouse district, the House of Blues on the edge of the French Quarter and the Mid-City Lanes, a.k.a. Rock 'n' Bowl, where live music, bowling and good 'n' greasy eats can be had simultaneously. Of course, there's enough time

CONTINUED ON NEXT PAGE ▶

◀ CONTINUED FROM PREVIOUS PAGE

between festival shlepping and club-hopping to enjoy the Crescent City's other delights, from boozing and decadence on Bourbon Street to the world-class cuisine. — TD

New Orleans Jazz and Heritage Festival
1205 N. Rampart St.
New Orleans, LA 70116
(504) 522-4786

SOUTH BY SOUTHWEST MUSIC AND MEDIA CONFERENCE AUSTIN, TEXAS

Even before the New York City-based New Music Seminar wheezed to its death in 1994, this five-day fête in hospitable Austin had become the must-attend annual event for smart music-biz insiders. It's a fan's haven as well for two reasons. First, a special pass gets you into nearly every club in Austin — from the Sixth Street strip to the suburbs — which the conference's wide embrace fills with everything from Tex-Mex border music to country to folk, grunge, jazz and meat-and-potatoes rock. Second, Austin is beautiful in springtime, with its rolling hills and appealing riverbeds, strong artists' community and world-class downhome eateries such as Threadgill's, where Janis Joplin used to sing for her supper, and La Zona Rosa, where fantastic Mexican fare is served along with great music and Day of the Dead decor. This year's SXSW began on March 14 with the Austin Music Awards, an opportunity to hear some true Texas blues and see many of the city's estimable talents. The award-show lineup included Ian Moore, psychedelic-rock cult hero Roky Erickson and an incredible rendition of Aretha Franklin's "(You Make Me Feel Like) "A Natural Woman" performed in collective harmony by Austin girl rockers Kris McKay, Kelly Willis, Abra Moore, Sara Hickman and Barbara K. Lou Reed performed simultaneously at the Austin Music Hall, but impressed no one. The biggest buzzes among fans and pros in 1996 were resurgent interest in lonesome, drag-ass country rock; local heroes Spoon, who hyped their disc and upcoming tour; a great set from Rosie Flores at the new Split Rail club; and the return of the Plimsouls. — TD

South By Southwest
P.O. Box 4999
Austin, TX 78765
(512) 467-7979

By." Alliances between British and American B-boys — Tricky working with the Gravediggaz, Goldie remixing Scarface — suggest that the next exciting wave of music may involve some fusion of these different strands of hip-hop innovation.

If Wu Tang-style rap, trip-hop and jungle have one thing in common, it's a mood: a sort of apocalyptic paranoia and dread, often fueled by heavy marijuana use. Method Man named his album *Tical,* after a slang term for the drug; Tricky sang in "Ponderosa" of smoking so much he saw demons in his living room; and one jungle outfit called itself the Ganja Crew. Cypress Hill, long-time advocates of the drug, even pranced onstage at Lollapalooza '95 with giant marijuana leaves. For white bohemian youth, though, heroin was the drug of choice. Within a year and a half of Kurt Cobain's death, Blind Melon singer Shannon Hoon, Hole bassist Kristen Pfaff and Smashing Pumpkins's touring keyboardist Jonathan Melvoin all died of overdoses, and Kelley Deal of the Breeders, Scott Weiland of Stone Temple Pilots, Pumpkins drummer Jimmy Chamberlain and Al

Scott Weiland

Dave Matthews Band

Jourgensen of Ministry were all busted for possession. After Hoon's death, the National Academy of Recording Arts and Sciences, concerned about the resurgence of heroin, held the first-ever industry-wide symposium on drugs and rock.

Although drugs threw a pall over the industry, mainstream radio was dominated by wholesome bands such as Hootie & the Blowfish, whose strongest addiction appears to be playing golf. When the Grateful Dead decided to call it a day, following Jerry Garcia's death, some critics suggested that Hootie and that other VH1 favorite, the Dave Matthews Band, were worthy successors. Like Phish and Blues Traveler, the Dave Matthews Band spend a lot of time on the road touring and their loose, rootsy jams have drawn some stray Deadheads. After years of paying their proverbial dues, the DMB finally cracked the charts with their major label debut, *Under the Table and Dreaming*.

What with the cuddly Everyman rock of Hootie and the angst-lite of Alanis and fourth-generation grunge bands holding sway over the charts, mainstream rock feels somewhat stagnant. History tells us that at similar moments in the past, it's time to scope out rock's margins and outerzones. That's where the new sounds and attitudes are being hatched. There you'll find the very sounds and attitudes that will replenish the mainstream in years to come, once again reviving and redefining the spirit of rock and roll. ■

TANGLEWOOD
LENOX, MASSACHUSETTS

Each July, the Boston Symphony Orchestra (BSO) packs up its French horns and timpanis and heads to Tanglewood, its summer home in Western Massachusetts's lush Berkshires. This area has been a haven for cultural activity since the first half of the 19th century, when residents of Boston and New York began to build summer estates in the region's rolling hills. The two-month festival offers weekend programs for music lovers of many tastes: concerts by the BSO, performances by popular artists, chamber music, the internationally recognized Festival of Contemporary Music, a long weekend of jazz, Tanglewood on Parade, recitals and two Boston Pops concerts. The 1996 season opened to a capacity crowd with renowned cellist Yo-Yo Ma joining music director Seiji Ozawa and the BSO for the music of Bernstein and Dvořák. Throughout the summer, Ozawa yielded the podium to several guest conductors, including André Previn and John Williams, but returned in late July to lead the 50th anniversary production of Benjamin Britten's opera, *Peter Grimes*. The production (originally conducted at Tanglewood by a youthful Leonard Bernstein) was staged with musicians and singers from the Tanglewood Music Center, an intensive, tuition-free training program for young musical talent. — AP

Tanglewood
Lenox, Massachusetts 01240
(413) 637-5100

VANS® WARPED TOUR

While Lollapalooza wrestled with its image as a sell-out showcase for "corporate rock," the Vans® Warped tour turned out to be the summer's hottest alternative package. The second annual festival combined skateboarding, climbing and other extreme sports activities with 14 acts from thrash, ska, punk and grunge circles, including Rocket From the Crypt, 311, CIV, surf-music legend Dick Dale and the Mighty Mighty Bosstones. — AP

Vans® Warped Tour
Nasty Little Man Publicity
72 Spring St., 11th Floor
New York, NY 10012
(212) 343-2314
www.warpedtour.com

1995 Billboard Chart Toppers

Each week, *Billboard* publishes music charts based on nationwide airplay and sales figures using a point system and information compiled by Broadcast Data Systems (airplay) and SoundScan (retail sales). Here are the recordings that topped the *Billboard* charts in 1995.

Top 100 Albums

1. **Cracked Rear View**
   Hootie & the Blowfish
   (Atlantic)

2. **The Hits**
   Garth Brooks
   (Capitol Nashville)

3. **II**
   Boyz II Men
   (Motown)

4. **Hell Freezes Over**
   Eagles
   (Geffen)

5. **CrazySexyCool**
   TLC
   (LaFace)

6. **Vitalogy**
   Pearl Jam
   (Epic)

7. **Dookie**
   Green Day
   (Reprise)

8. **Throwing Copper**
   Live
   (Radioactive)

9. **Miracles: The Holiday Album**
   Kenny G
   (Arista)

10. **The Lion King**
    Soundtrack
    (Walt Disney)

11. **Smash**
    Offspring
    (Epitaph)

12. **No Need to Argue**
    The Cranberries
    (Island)

13. **MTV Unplugged in New York**
    Nirvana
    (DGC)

Hootie & the Blowfish

14. **Jagged Little Pill**
    Alanis Morissette
    (Maverick/Reprise)

15. **Tuesday Night Music Club**
    Sheryl Crow
    (A&M)

16. **Wildflowers**
    Tom Petty
    (Warner Bros.)

17. **Dangerous Minds**
    Soundtrack
    (MCA Soundtracks)

18. **Yes I Am**
    Melissa Etheridge
    (Island)

19. **The Woman in Me**
    Shania Twain
    (Mercury Nashville)

20. **My Life**
    Mary J. Blige
    (Uptown)

21. **Merry Christmas**
    Mariah Carey
    (Columbia)

22. **Greatest Hits**
    Bob Seger and the Silver Bullet Band
    (Capitol)

23. **Pocahontas**
    Soundtrack
    (Walt Disney)

24. **Big Ones**
    Aerosmith
    (Geffen)

25. **Under the Table and Dreaming**
    Dave Matthews Band
    (RCA)

26. **Balance**
    Van Halen
    (Warner Bros.)

27. **John Michael Montgomery**
    John Michael Montgomery
    (Atlantic)

28. **Bedtime Stories**
    Madonna
    (Maverick/Sire)

29. **Four**
    Blues Traveler
    (A&M)

30. **Not a Moment Too Soon**
    Tim McGraw
    (Curb)

31. **Forrest Gump**
    Soundtrack
    (Epic Soundtrax)

Eric Clapton

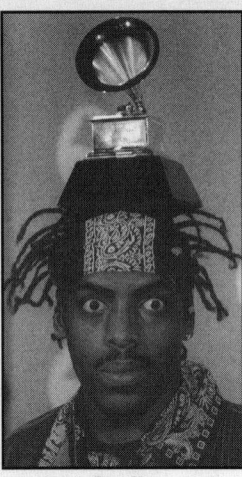

Coolio

81. *Breathless*
Kenny G
(Arista)

82. *I Ain't Movin'*
Des'ree
(550 Music)

83. *No Ordinary Man*
Tracy Byrd
(MCA)

84. *The Show*
Soundtrack
(Def Jam/RAL)

85. *Pulse*
Pink Floyd
(Columbia)

86. *Live Through This*
Hole
(DGC)

87. *Stones in the Road*
Mary Chapin Carpenter
(Columbia)

88. *Superunknown*
Soundgarden
(A&M)

89. *Made in England*
Elton John
(Rocket)

90. *Candy Rain*
Soul for Real
(Uptown)

91. *No Quarter*
Jimmy Page and
Robert Plant
(Atlantic)

92. *When Love Finds You*
Vince Gill
(MCA)

93. *Greatest Hits*
Tom Petty and the
Heartbreakers
(MCA)

94. *Metallica*
Metallica
(Elektra)

95. *From the Bottom Up*
Brownstone
(MJJ)

96. *Songs*
Luther Vandross
(LV)

97. *Let Your Dim Light Shine*
Soul Asylum
(Columbia)

98. *The Diary*
Scarface
(Rap-A-Lot)

99. *Third Rock From the Sun*
Joe Diffie
(Epic)

100. *House of Love*
Amy Grant
(A&M)

Hot 50 Singles

1. "Gangsta's Paradise"
(From the motion picture
Dangerous Minds)
Coolio featuring L.V.
(MCA Soundtracks)

2. "Waterfalls"
TLC
(LaFace)

3. "Creep"
TLC
(LaFace)

4. "Kiss From a Rose"
(From the motion picture
Batman Forever)
Seal
(ZTT/Sire)

5. "On Bended Knee"
Boyz II Men
(Motown)

6. "Another Night"
Real McCoy
(Arista)

7. "Fantasy"
Mariah Carey
(Columbia)

8. "Take a Bow"
Madonna
(Maverick/Sire)

9. "Don't Take It Personal (Just
One of Dem Days)"
Monica
(Rowdy)

10. "This Is How We Do It"
Montell Jordan
(PMP/RAL)

11. "I Know"
Dionne Farris
(Columbia)

12. "Water Runs Dry"
Boyz II Men
(Motown)

13. "Freak Like Me"
Adina Howard
(Mecca Don/EastWest)

14. "Run-Around"
Blues Traveler
(A&M)

15. "I Can Love You Like That"
All-4-One
(Blitzz)

16. "Have You Ever Really
Loved a Woman?"
Bryan Adams
(A&M)

17. "Always"
Bon Jovi
(Mercury)

18. "Boombastic/In the
Summertime"
Shaggy
(Virgin)

19. "Total Eclipse of the Heart"
Nicki French
(Critique)

20. "You Gotta Be"
Des'ree
(550 Music)

21. "You Are Not Alone"
Michael Jackson
(Epic)

22. "Hold My Hand"
Hootie & the Blowfish
(Atlantic)

23. "One More Chance/Stay
With Me"
The Notorious B.I.G.
(Bad Boy)

24. "Here Comes the Hotstepper
(From the motion picture
Ready to Wear)
Ini Kamoze
(Columbia)

Janet Jackson

Top 20 Hot Modern Rock Tracks

Mary J. Blige

7. **"December"**
Collective Soul
(Atlantic)

8. **"Molly"**
Sponge
(Work)

9. **"All Over You"**
Live
(Radioactive)

10. **"When I Come Around"**
Green Day
(Reprise)

11. **"In the Blood"**
Better Than Ezra
(Elektra)

12. **"Lump"**
The Presidents of the United
States of America
(Columbia)

13. **"Connection"**
Elastica
(DGC)

14. **"Say It Ain't So"**
Weezer
(DGC)

15. **"Little Things"**
Bush
(Trauma)

16. **"Hand in My Pocket"**
Alanis Morissette
(Maverick)

17. **"Everything Zen"**
Bush
(Trauma)

18. **"Carnival"**
Natalie Merchant
(Elektra)

19. **"Hold Me, Thrill Me, Kiss
Me, Kill Me"**
U2
(Island/Atlantic)

20. **"Sick of Myself"**
Matthew Sweet
(Zoo)

Top 20 Hot Album Rock Tracks

1. **"December"**
Collective Soul
(Atlantic)

2. **"Lightning Crashes"**
Live
(Radioactive)

3. **"Better Man"**
Pearl Jam
(Epic)

4. **"When I Come Around"**
Green Day
(Reprise)

5. **"And Fools Shine On"**
Brother Cane
(Virgin)

6. **"You Wreck Me"**
Tom Petty
(Warner Bros.)

7. **"All Over You"**
Live
(Radioactive)

8. **"Good"**
Better Than Ezra
(Elektra)

9. **"Tomorrow"**
Silverchair
(Epic)

10. **"Gel"**
Collective Soul
(Atlantic)

11. **"Everything Zen"**
Bush
(Trauma)

12. **"Can't Stop Lovin' You"**
Van Halen
(Warner Bros.)

13. **"Misery"**
Soul Asylum
(Columbia)

14. **"Hold Me, Thrill Me, Kiss
Me, Kill Me"**
U2
(Island/Atlantic)

15. **"Only Wanna Be With You"**
Hootie & the Blowfish
(Atlantic)

16. **"River of Deceit"**
Mad Season
(Columbia)

17. **"Don't Tell Me (What Love
Can Do)"**
Van Halen
(Warner Bros.)

18. **"Possum Kingdom"**
Toadies
(Interscope)

19. **"Interstate Love Song"**
Stone Temple Pilots
(Atlantic)

20. **"Little Things"**
Bush
(Trauma)

Top 50 R&B Albums

1. *My Life*
Mary J. Blige
(Uptown)

2. *CrazySexyCool*
TLC
(LaFace)

3. *Me Against the World*
2Pac
(Interscope)

4. *II*
Boyz II Men
(Motown)

5. *E. 1999 Eternal*
Bone Thugs-N-Harmony
(Ruthless)

Boyz II Men

285

These are the songs that topped the charts in the United Kingdom and Japan in June 1996.

TOP OF THE POPS

1. "Killing Me Softly," Fugees
2. "Mysterious Girl," Peter Andre featuring Bubbler Ranx
3. "Always Be My Baby," Mariah Carey
4. "Three Lions," Baddiel & Skinner and Lightning Seed
5. "Because You Loved Me," Celine Dion
6. "Don't Stop Movin'," Livin' Joy
7. "Make It With You," Let Loose
8. "Blurred," Pianoman
9. "The Day We Caught the Train," Ocean Colour Scene
10. "Nobody Knows," Tony Rich Project
11. We're in This Together," Simply Red
12. "Instinct," Crowded House
13. "Theme From *Mission: Impossible*," Adam Clayton and Larry Mullen
14. "Thank God It's Friday," R. Kelly
15. "That Girl," Maxi Priest featuring Shaggy
16. "She Said," Longpigs
17. "There's Nothing I Won't Do," JX
18. "Female of the Species," Space
19. "Purple Heather," Rod Stewart with The Scottish Euro '96 Squad
20. "Naked," Louise

Source: CIN Ltd.

BIG EAST

1. "Fast Love," George Michael
2. "You're the One," SWV
3. "The Only Thing That Looks Good on Me Is You," Bryan Adams
4. "Reach," Gloria Estefan
5. "How Crazy Are You," Meja
6. "For the Love of You," Jordan Hill
7. "Walking Wounded," Everything but the Girl
8. "Sing a Song," Take 6
9. "J'attendrai," Nadege
10. "Deeper and Deeper," Anna McMurphy
11. "La La La Love Song," Toshinobu Kubota with Naomi Campbell
12. "Because You Loved Me," Celine Dion
13. "Theme From *Mission: Impossible*," Adam Clayton and Larry Mullen
14. "Forever More," Puff Johnson
15. "When Love Comes Calling," George Benson
16. "Killing Me Softly," Fugees
17. "Give Me a Little More Time," Gabrielle
18. "Always Be My Baby," Mariah Carey
19. "North Shore Serenade," Na Leo
20. "Too Much," Dave Matthews Band

Source: J-Wave's Tokio Hot 100

Hot 50 R&B Singles

1. **"Creep"**
   TLC
   (LaFace)

2. **"This Is How We Do It"**
   Montell Jordan
   (PMP/RAL)

3. **"One More Chance/Stay With Me"**
   The Notorious B.I.G.
   (Bad Boy)

4. **"If You Love Me"**
   Brownstone
   (MJJ)

5. **"Candy Rain"**
   Soul for Real
   (Uptown)

6. **"Don't Take It Personal (Just One of Dem Days)"**
   Monica
   (Rowdy)

7. **"Freak Like Me"**
   Adina Howard
   (Mecca Don/EastWest)

8. **"Before I Let You Go"**
   Blackstreet
   (Interscope)

9. **"Boombastic/In the Summertime"**
   Shaggy
   (Virgin)

10. **"Baby"**
    Brandy
    (Atlantic)

11. **"Can't You See"**
    (From the motion picture *New Jersey Drive*)
    Total featuring The Notorious B.I.G.
    (Tommy Boy)

12. **"On Bended Knee"**
    Boyz II Men
    (Motown)

13. **"He's Mine"**
    MoKenStef
    (Outburst/RAL)

14. **"Fantasy"**
    Mariah Carey
    (Columbia)

15. **"I'll Be There for You/You're All I Need to Get By"**
    Method Man/Mary J. Blige
    (Def Jam/RAL)

16. **"Waterfalls"**
TLC
(LaFace)

17. **"Ask of You"**
(From the motion picture
Higher Learning)
Raphael Saadiq
(Epic Soundtrax/550 Music)

18. **"Someone to Love"**
Jon B. featuring Babyface
(Yab Yum/550 Music)

19. **"Freek'n You"**
Jodeci
(Uptown)

20. **"Practice What You Preach"**
Barry White
(A&M)

21. **"Big Poppa/Warning"**
The Notorious B.I.G.
(Bad Boy)

22. **"I Wanna Be Down"**
Brandy
(Atlantic)

23. **"Water Runs Dry"**
Boyz II Men
(Motown)

24. **"I Apologize"**
Anita Baker
(Elektra)

25. **"You Used to Love Me"**
Faith Evans
(Bad Boy)

26. **"Brown Sugar"**
D'Angelo
(EMI)

27. **"Dear Mama"**
2Pac
(Interscope)

28. **"I Like"**
Kut Klose
(Keia/Elektra)

29. **"Crazy Love"**
(From the motion picture
Jason's Lyric)
Brian McKnight
(Mercury)

30. **"Gangsta's Paradise"**
(From the motion picture
Dangerous Minds)
Coolio featuring L.V.
(MCA Soundtracks)

31. **"I Got 5 on It"**
Luniz
(Noo Trybe)

32. **"Red Light Special"**
TLC
(LaFace)

Shania Twain

33. **"You Are Not Alone"**
Michael Jackson
(Epic)

34. **"This Lil' Game We Play"**
Subway Featuring 702
(Biv 10)

35. **"'Til You Do Me Right"**
After 7
(Virgin)

36. **"Think of You"**
Usher
(LaFace)

37. **"Best Friend"**
Brandy
(Atlantic)

38. **"Tell Me"**
Groove Theory
(Epic)

39. **"Grapevyne"**
Brownstone
(MJJ)

40. **"Brokenhearted"**
Brandy
(Atlantic)

41. **"Be Happy"**
Mary J. Blige
(Uptown)

42. **"Keep Their Heads Ringin'"**
(From the motion picture
Friday)
Dr. Dre
(Priority)

43. **"For Your Love"**
Stevie Wonder
(Motown)

44. **"Feels So Good"**
Xscape
(So So Def)

45. **"We Must Be in Love"**
Pure Soul
(Step Sun)

46. **"Every Little Thing I Do"**
Soul for Real
(Uptown)

47. **"I Belong to You/How
Many Ways"**
Toni Braxton
(LaFace)

48. **"Heaven"**
Solo
(Perspective)

49. **"Here Comes the
Hotstepper"**
(From the motion picture
Ready to Wear)
Ini Kamoze
(Columbia)

50. **"Emotions"**
H-Town
(Luke)

Top 50 Country Albums

1. ***The Hits***
Garth Brooks
(Capitol Nashville)

2. ***The Woman in Me***
Shania Twain
(Mercury Nashville)

3. ***John Michael Montgomery***
John Michael Montgomery
(Atlantic)

4. ***Not a Moment Too Soon***
Tim McGraw
(Curb)

5. ***You Might Be a Redneck If ...***
Jeff Foxworthy
(Warner Bros.)

6. ***Now That I've Found You:
A Collection***
Alison Krauss
(Rounder)

7. ***The Tractors***
The Tractors
(Arista)

8. ***Who I Am***
Alan Jackson
(Arista)

9. **Games Rednecks Play**
Jeff Foxworthy
(Warner Bros.)

10. **Waitin' on Sundown**
Brooks & Dunn
(Arista)

11. **Lead On**
George Strait
(MCA)

12. **Read My Mind**
Reba McEntire
(MCA)

13. **Stones in the Road**
Mary Chapin Carpenter
(Columbia)

14. **No Ordinary Man**
Tracy Byrd
(MCA)

15. **When Love Finds You**
Vince Gill
(MCA)

16. **Third Rock From the Sun**
Joe Diffie
(Epic)

17. **All I Want**
Tim McGraw
(Curb)

18. **I See It Now**
Tracy Lawrence
(Atlantic)

19. **Kickin' It Up**
John Michael Montgomery
(Atlantic)

20. **Greatest Hits Vol. 3**
Alabama
(RCA)

21. **If I Could Make a Living**
Clay Walker
(Giant)

22. **What a Crying Shame**
The Mavericks
(MCA)

23. **Greatest Hits Volume Two**
Reba McEntire
(MCA)

24. **Blackhawk**
Blackhawk
(Arista)

25. **Thinkin' Problem**
David Ball
(Warner Bros.)

26. **One Emotion**
Clint Black
(RCA)

27. **Starting Over**
Reba McEntire
(MCA)

28. **Greatest Hits 1990–1995**
Sawyer Brown
(Curb)

29. **Thinkin' About You**
Trisha Yearwood
(MCA)

30. **When Fallen Angels Fly**
Patty Loveless
(Epic)

31. **The Greatest Hits Collection**
Alan Jackson
(Arista)

32. **Sweetheart's Dance**
Pam Tillis
(Arista)

33. **Old Enough to Know Better**
Wade Hayes
(Columbia)

34. **You Gotta Love That**
Neal McCoy
(Atlantic)

35. **Ten Feet Tall and Bulletproof**
Travis Tritt
(Warner Bros.)

36. **Boomtown**
Toby Keith
(Polydor Nashville)

37. **Pure Country** (Soundtrack)
George Strait
(MCA)

38. **Storm in the Heartland**
Billy Ray Cyrus
(Mercury Nashville)

39. **A Lot About Livin' (And a Little 'Bout Love)**
Alan Jackson
(Arista)

40. **Take Me as I Am**
Faith Hill
(Warner Bros.)

41. **Greatest Hits**
Lorrie Morgan
(BNA)

42. **Love a Little Stronger**
Diamond Rio
(Arista)

43. **Come On Come On**
Mary Chapin Carpenter
(Columbia)

44. **Kick a Little**
Little Texas
(Warner Bros.)

45. **John Berry**
John Berry
(Capitol Nashville)

46. **Greatest Hits — From the Beginning**
Travis Tritt
(Warner Bros.)

47. **Standing on the Edge**
John Berry
(Capitol Nashville)

48. **In Pieces**
Garth Brooks
(Capitol Nashville)

49. **Brand New Man**
Brooks & Dunn
(Arista)

50. **Hard Workin' Man**
Brooks & Dunn
(Arista)

Hot 50 Country Singles and Tracks

1. "Sold (The Grundy County Auction Incident)"
John Michael Montgomery
(Atlantic)

2. "Any Man of Mine"
Shania Twain
(Mercury Nashville)

3. "I Like It, I Love It"
Tim McGraw
(Curb)

4. "Summer's Comin'"
Clint Black
(RCA)

5. "I Can Love You Like That"
John Michael Montgomery
(Atlantic)

6. "Thinkin' About You"
Trisha Yearwood
(MCA)

7. "This Woman and This Man"
Clay Walker
(Giant)

8. "You Better Think Twice"
Vince Gill
(MCA)

9. "They're Playin' Our Song"
Neal McCoy
(Atlantic)

Clint Black

10. **"If the World Had a Front Porch"**
Tracy Lawrence
(Atlantic)

11. **"You Ain't Much Fun"**
Toby Keith
(Polydor Nashville)

12. **"Not on Your Love"**
Jeff Carson
(MCG Curb)

13. **"You're Gonna Miss Me When I'm Gone"**
Brooks & Dunn
(Arista)

14. **"Tell Me I Was Dreaming"**
Travis Tritt
(Warner Bros.)

15. **"Texas Tornado"**
Tracy Lawrence
(Atlantic)

16. **"One Boy, One Girl"**
Collin Raye
(Epic)

17. **"Little Miss Honky Tonk"**
Brooks & Dunn
(Arista)

18. **"What Mattered Most"**
Ty Herndon
(Epic)

19. **"Give Me One More Shot"**
Alabama
(RCA)

20. **"I'm Not Strong Enough to Say No"**
Blackhawk
(Arista)

21. **"The Heart Is a Lonely Hunter"**
Reba McEntire
(MCA)

22. **"Gonna Get a Life"**
Mark Chesnutt
(Decca)

23. **"I Didn't Know My Own Strength"**
Lorrie Morgan
(BNA)

24. **"And Still"**
Reba McEntire
(MCA)

25. **"For a Change"**
Neal McCoy
(Atlantic)

26. **"I Don't Even Know Your Name"**
Alan Jackson
(Arista)

27. **"A Little Bit of You"**
Lee Roy Parnell
(Career)

28. **"Darned if I Don't (Danged if I Do)"**
Shenandoah
(Capitol Nashville)

29. **"As Any Fool Can See"**
Tracy Lawrence
(Atlantic)

30. **"One Emotion"**
Clint Black
(RCA)

31. **"Party Crowd"**
David Lee Murphy
(MCA)

32. **"In Between Dances"**
Pam Tillis
(Arista)

33. **"Standing on the Edge of Goodbye"**
John Berry
(Capitol Nashville)

34. **"If I Were You"**
Collin Raye
(Epic)

35. **"My Kind of Girl"**
Collin Raye
(Epic)

36. **"Mi Vida Loca (My Crazy Life)"**
Pam Tillis
(Arista)

37. **"Dust on the Bottle"**
David Lee Murphy
(MCA)

38. **"Better Things to Do"**
Terri Clark
(Mercury Nashville)

39. **"Halfway Down"**
Patty Loveless
(Epic)

40. **"Till You Love Me"**
Reba McEntire
(MCA)

41. **"So Help Me Girl"**
Joe Diffie
(Epic)

42. **"You Can't Make a Heart Love Somebody"**
George Strait
(MCA)

43. **"Bend It Until It Breaks"**
John Anderson
(BNA)

44. **"Safe in the Arms of Love"**
Martina McBride
(RCA)

45. **"Should've Asked Her Faster"**
Ty England
(RCA)

46. **"Not a Moment Too Soon"**
Tim McGraw
(Curb)

47. **"I Think About It All the Time"**
John Berry
(Capitol Nashville)

48. **"She Ain't Your Ordinary Girl"**
Alabama
(RCA)

49. **"That's Just About Right"**
Blackhawk
(Arista)

50. **"Refried Dreams"**
Tim McGraw
(Curb)

Top 20 Jazz Albums

1. ***MTV Unplugged***
Tony Bennett
(Columbia)

2. ***The Bridges of Madison County***
Soundtrack
(Malpaso)

3. *Pearls*
David Sanborn
(Elektra)

4. *First Instrument*
Rachelle Ferrell
(Blue Note)

5. *Joe Cool's Blues*
Wynton Marsalis and Ellis
Marsalis
(Columbia)

6. *All My Tomorrows*
Grover Washington, Jr.
(Columbia)

7. *25*
Harry Connick, Jr.
(Columbia)

8. *Steppin' Out*
Tony Bennett
(Columbia)

9. *Mood Swing*
Joshua Redman Quartet
(Warner Bros.)

10. *Time After Time*
Etta James
(Private)

11. *Swing Kids*
Soundtrack
(Hollywood)

12. *Double Rainbow*
Joe Henderson
(Verve)

13. *Gershwin for Lovers*
Marcus Roberts
(Columbia)

14. *Mystery Lady*
Etta James
(Private)

15. *Here's to the Ladies*
Tony Bennett
(Columbia)

16. *The Best of the Songbooks*
Ella Fitzgerald
(Verve)

17. *Quiet After the Storm*
Dianne Reeves
(Blue Note)

18. *Billie's Best*
Billie Holiday
(Verve)

19. *Side by Side*
Perlman/Peterson
(Telarc)

20. *Afterglow*
Dr. John
(Blue Thumb)

Hot 25 Rap Singles

1. **"One More Chance/
Stay With Me"**
The Notorious B.I.G.
(Bad Boy)

2. **"I'll Be There for You/You're
All I Need to Get By"**
Method Man/Mary J. Blige
(Def Jam/RAL)

3. **"Big Poppa/Warning"**
The Notorious B.I.G.
(Bad Boy)

4. **"Gangsta's Paradise"**
(From the motion picture
Dangerous Minds)
Coolio Featuring L.V.
(MCA Soundtracks)

5. **"I Got 5 on It"**
Luniz
(Noo Trybe)

6. **"Dear Mama/Old School"**
2Pac
(Interscope)

7. **"Boombastic/In the
Summertime"**
Shaggy
(Virgin)

8. **"Keep Their Heads Ringin'"**
(From the motion picture
Friday)
Dr. Dre
(Priority)

9. **"Player's Anthem"**
Junior M.A.F.I.A.
(Undeas/Big Beat)

10. **"Sugar Hill"**
AZ
(EMI)

11. **"Get Down"**
Craig Mack
(Bad Boy)

12. **"Tootsee Roll"**
69 Boyz
(Rip-It)

13. **"Give It 2 You"**
Da Brat
(So So Def/Work)

14. **"Feel Me Flow"**
Naughty by Nature
(Tommy Boy)

15. **"How High"**
(From the motion picture
The Show)
Redman/Method Man
(Def Jam/RAL)

16. **"Flava in Ya Ear"**
Craig Mack
(Bad Boy)

17. **"1st of Tha Month"**
Bone Thugs-N-Harmony
(Ruthless)

18. **"Mad Izm"**
Channel Live
(Capitol)

19. **"I Never Seen a Man Cry
(I Seen a Man Die)"**
Scarface
(Rap-A-Lot)

20. **"Freak Me Baby"**
Dis 'N' Dat
(Epic Street)

21. **"Bring the Pain"**
Method Man
(Def Jam/RAL)

22. **"Brooklyn Zoo"**
Ol' Dirty Bastard
(Elektra)

23. **"Kitty Kitty"**
69 Boyz
(Rip-It)

24. **"Foe Life"**
Mack 10
(Priority)

25. **"Sprinkle Me"**
E-40 featuring Suga T
(Sick Wid' It)

Top 10 World Music Albums

1. *The Lion King: Rhythm of
the Pride Lands*
Lebo M
(Walt Disney)

2. *The Long Black Veil*
The Chieftains
(RCA Victor)

3. *Best Of*
Gipsy Kings
(Nonesuch)

4. *The Mask and Mirror*
Loreena McKennitt
(Warner Bros.)

The Three Tenors

Top 10 New Age Albums

1. ***Live at the Acropolis***
   Yanni
   (Private Music)

2. ***Shepherd Moons***
   Enya
   (Reprise)

3. ***Forest***
   George Winston
   (Windham Hill)

4. ***Live at Red Rocks***
   John Tesh
   (GTS)

5. ***Christmas in the Aire***
   Mannheim Steamroller
   (American Gramaphone)

6. ***In My Time***
   Yanni
   (Private Music)

7. ***A Family Christmas***
   John Tesh
   (GTS)

8. ***Nouveau Flamenco***
   Ottmar Liebert
   (Higher Octave)

9. ***Acoustic Planet***
   Craig Chaquico
   (Higher Octave)

10. ***By Heart***
    Jim Brickman
    (Windham Hill)

5. ***Alegria***
   Cirque Du Soleil
   (RCA Victor)

6. ***Celtic Legacy: A Global
   Celtic Journey***
   Various Artists
   (Narada)

7. ***Love and Liberté***
   Gipsy Kings
   (Elektra Musician)

8. ***Clannad Themes***
   Clannad
   (Celtic Heartbeat/Atlantic)

9. ***Celtic Heartbeat Collection***
   Various Artists
   (Celtic Heartbeat/Atlantic)

10. ***Banba***
    Clannad
    (Atlantic)

Top 15 Classical Albums

1. ***The Three Tenors in
   Concert 1994***
   Carreras, Domingo, Pavarotti
   (Mehta)
   (Atlantic)

2. ***Chant***
   Benedictine Monks of Santo
   Domingo de Silos
   (Angel)

3. ***Immortal Beloved***
   Soundtrack
   (Sony Classical)

4. ***Chant Noel***
   Benedictine Monks of Santo
   Domingo de Silos
   (Angel)

5. ***In Concert***
   Carreras, Domingo, Pavarotti
   (Mehta)
   (London)

6. ***Mozart Portraits***
   Cecilia Bartoli
   (London)

7. ***Officium***
   Jan Garbarek/Hilliard
   Ensemble
   (ECM)

8. ***Vivaldi: the Four Seasons***
   Gil Shaham
   (Deutsche Grammophon)

9. ***Paper Music***
   Saint Paul Chamber
   Orchestra (McFerrin)
   (Sony Classical)

10. ***A Carnegie Hall
    Christmas Concert***
    Battle, Von Stade, Marsalis
    (Previn)
    (Sony Classical)

11. ***Pavarotti in Central Park***
    Luciano Pavarotti
    (London)

12. ***Sensual Classics, Too***
    Various Artists
    (Teldec)

13. ***A Portrait***
    Cecilia Bartoli
    (London)

14. ***Adagio***
    Berlin Philharmonic
    (Karajan)
    (Deutsche Grammophon)

15. ***Farinelli***
    Soundtrack
    (Travelling)

Top 10 Gospel Albums

1. ***Kirk Franklin and the Family***
   Kirk Franklin and the Family
   (Gospo Centric)

2. ***The Live Experience***
   Helen Baylor
   (Word)

3. ***Show Up!***
   The New Life Community
   Choir featuring John P. Kee
   (Verity)

4. ***It's Our Time***
   GMWA Women of Worship
   (Aleho International
   Music/Tyscot)

Selena

5. **On Time God**
Dottie Peoples
(Atlanta International)

6. **Live in Atlanta at Morehouse College**
Hezekiah Walker/Fellowship Crusade Choir
(Benson)

7. **Broken**
William Becton and Friends
(Web)

8. **It Remains to Be Seen**
Mississippi Mass Choir
(Malaco)

9. **Live in Memphis**
The Canton Spirituals
(Blackberry)

10. **Africa to America: The Journey of the Drum**
Sounds of Blackness
(Perspective)

Top 10 Latin Albums

1. **Dreaming of You**
Selena
(EMI Latin/EMI)

2. **Amor Prohibido**
Selena
(EMI Latin)

3. **The Best of Gipsy Kings**
Gipsy Kings
(Nonesuch)

4. **Segundo Romance**
Luis Miguel
(WEA Latina)

5. **12 Super Éxitos**
Selena
(EMI Latin)

6. **Live!**
Selena
(EMI Latin)

7. **Entre a Mi Mundo**
Selena
(EMI Latin)

8. **Mi Tierra**
Gloria Estefan
(Epic)

9. **Abriendo Puertas**
Gloria Estefan
(Epic)

10. **Las Reinas Del Pueblo**
Selena y Graciela Beltrán
(EMI Latin)

Top 10 Reggae Albums

1. **Boombastic**
Shaggy
(Virgin)

2. **Natural Mystic**
Bob Marley and The Wailers
(Tuff Gong)

3. **Bad Boys**
Inner Circle
(Big Beat)

4. **Tougher Than Love**
Diana King
(Work)

5. **Here Comes the Hotstepper**
Ini Kamoze
(Columbia)

6. **Real Ting**
Mad Lion
(Weeded)

7. **Destination Brooklyn**
Vicious
(Epic Street)

8. **'Til Shiloh**
Buju Banton
(Loose Cannon)

9. **Promises and Lies**
UB40
(Virgin)

10. **A Mi Shabba**
Shabba Ranks
(Epic)

Top 10 Contemporary Christian Albums

1. **House of Love**
Amy Grant
(Myrrh)

2. **Kirk Franklin and The Family**
Kirk Franklin and The Family
(Gospo Centric)

3. **Heaven in the Real World**
Steven Curtis Chapman
(Sparrow)

4. **My Utmost for His Highest**
Various Artists
(Word)

5. **The Whole Truth**
Point of Grace
(Word)

6. **Going Public**
Newsboys
(Starsong)

7. **Show Up!**
New Life Community Choir featuring John P. Kee
(Verity)

8. **Free at Last**
DC Talk
(Forefront)

9. **First Decade 1983–1993**
Michael W. Smith
(Reunion)

10. **Find It on the Wings**
Sandi Patty
(Word)

Amy Grant

Top 20 Concert Grosses of 1995

Amusement Business annually ranks domestic and international concert grosses and touring acts. Here are 1995's top 20 concerts.

HEADLINER/ SUPPORTING ACT	GROSS TICKET SALES	TOTAL ATTENDANCE	TICKET SCALE	VENUE, CITY
1. **The Rolling Stones**	$27,613,380	285,294	$100, $70	Tokyo (Japan) Dome
2. **The Rolling Stones/ Las Pelotas/Ratones Paranoicas**	$19,796,750	344,144	$150, $25	River Plate Stadium, Buenos Aires, Argentina
3. **The Rolling Stones/ Caifanes**	$11,784,755	204,020	$295, $115, $57, $26.50	Hermanos Rodriguez Autodromo, Mexico City, Mexico
4. **The Rolling Stones/ The Black Crowes**	$8,666,640	207,340	$48.31, $40.26	Wembley Stadium, London, England
5. **The Rolling Stones/ Bon Jovi/Eric Lapointe**	$8,612,247	160,605	$139, $43.95	Longchamps Racetrack, Paris, France
6. **The Rolling Stones/ The Tragically Hip**	$6,222,222	140,000	$44.44	Festival Site, Werchter, Belgium
7. **The Rolling Stones**	$5,879,683	87,609	$69.65, $43.58	Cricket Ground, Melbourne, Australia
8. **The Rolling Stones/ The Black Crowes**	$5,561,673	98,955	$56.20	St. Jakob Stadium, Basel, Switzerland
9. **The Rolling Stones**	$5,237,710	78,187	$69.65, $43.58	Cricket Ground, Sydney, Australia
10. **The Rolling Stones/ Robert Cray Band**	$5,152,429	124,665	$41.33	Park De Goffert, Nijmegen, The Netherlands
11. **R.E.M./Blur/The Cranberries/Radiohead**	$4,796,364	130,000	$38.60	National Bowl, Milton Keynes, England
12. **The Rolling Stones/ Mango Groove**	$4,588,405	86,209	$70.57, $40.93	Ellis Park Stadium, Johannesburg, South Africa
13. **The Rolling Stones/ Runrig/Rudiger Hoffmann/ Big Country/Jimmy Barnes**	$4,584,171	84,896	$64.78, $53.98	Festival Site, Schuttorf, Germany
14. **The Rolling Stones/Red Baron/Rita Lee/Spin Doctors**	$4,527,556	131,253	$120, $18	Pacaembu Stadium, São Paulo, Brazil
15. **Elton John/ Billy Joel**	$4,385,725	103,694	$50, $25	Joe Robbie Stadium, Miami, Florida
16. **The Rolling Stones/ Big Country**	$4,372,814	93,959	$79.48, $41.33	Feyenoord Stadium, Rotterdam, The Netherlands
17. **The Rolling Stones/ Big Country**	$4,251,518	90,871	$53.98, $46.78	The Ring, Hockenheim, Germany
18. **The Rolling Stones**	$4,234,300	42,483	$100, $72	Fukuoka (Japan) Dome
19. **The Rolling Stones/ Big Country**	$4,210,752	90,000	$46.78	VW Festival Site, Wolfsburg, Germany
20. **The Rolling Stones/ Big Country**	$3,894,202	83,105	$53.98, $46.78	Fest Wiese, Leipzig, Germany

Significant Recordings of 1995–1996

These are the recordings (released in the United States between September 1995 and September 1996) that caught our ears. Our selections are alphabetical, unscientific and highly opinionated.

BARRIOS — DAVID RUSSELL, GUITAR
Music of Barrios
Telarc

Barrios is Agustin Barrios Mangore, the recently rediscovered composer-virtuoso born in Paraguay in 1885. Russell, a Scot raised in Spanish Menorca, finds Barrios's contemporary voice: keen harmonics, exacting balance between lines and a tonal palette that would make Steve Vai blush. Barrios spins tunes of the utmost rusticity into tightropes of technical demand, and Russell has both the fingers and the mind for the job. He thinks like a dancer, plays like a singer and gets six strings sounding like at least 50. — TIM RILEY

THE BEATLES
Anthology 1
Apple/Capitol

This was the record that brought everyone into the stores during a year marked by misery in record retailing. It's not often that the industry gets "event" records in these days of disposable divas and dispirited sounds. Well, did this ever get the build-up, with television specials, video releases, ubiquitous advertising and the debut of a reunion song, "Free as a Bird," compiled (and I use the word advisedly) around a John Lennon practice tape. For all three of you who weren't given the thing for the holidays, the first Anthology opens in Liverpool with the lads still calling themselves the Quarrymen and continues to the dawn of Beatlemania in 1964. Outtakes, snippets from TV interviews and alternate takes (some enlightening) of familiar songs fill the discs. Most of this was available in bootleg form for years, and that's probably the point. We'll take last year's Live at the B.B.C. recording for its revelation of our most beloved musical icons as bar-band bashers. Look for two more Anthologies and the release of the rumored acoustic version of The White Album. — ROBERT MOSES

THE BEAU HUNKS
The Beau Hunks Play the Original Little Rascals Music
Koch

With those Gershwin piano rolls and the opening of the Soviet recording archives, international musical sleuthing is enjoying a heyday. This renowned Dutch ensemble discovered the American composer Leroy Shield's cheeky scores for the Little Rascals comedies after playing a tribute to Laurel and Hardy music. The melodies are simple but deceptive; the arrangements and instrumentation are charmed. Using tape reconstructions of scores, culled from hundreds of Hal Roach Studio flicks, this "documentary orchestra" went so far as to use period instruments and recording techniques. If you didn't know, you'd swear this boundless collection of hooks was the real thing. — TR

BEETHOVEN — EUGENE ISTOMIN
Piano Sonatas: Moonlight, Waldstein, Opus 110 in A-Flat Major
Reference Recordings

Finally a title that doesn't pair the "Moonlight" with the "Appassionata"! For a working musical definition of "forward momentum," there's no better example than Istomin's relentless attack on the Waldstein sonata's first movement. The trick, of course, is holding back, of giving the illusion of cumulative force. Istomin is not as delicately shaded in the legato sections as some others, but the overall effect is thrilling. The tempo of the coda to the third movement is beautifully resigned in a way that shakes up a few assumptions about aging. The Opus 110, that sprawling meditation on music, piano playing and the nature of sound itself, is revelatory and about as good as late Beethoven gets. This is an autumnal release from the hands that supported Isaac Stern and Leonard Rose in the great trio recordings from the '60s, and its strength is a little baffling. Given his interpretive strengths, it makes you wonder why Istomin hasn't been a bigger presence on the concert scene. — TR

PAUL BLEY/EVAN PARKER/ BARRE PHILLIPS
Time Will Tell
ECM

Canadian pianist Bley, British saxophonist Parker and San Francisco-born bassist Phillips helped invent a form of spontaneous collective improvisation that's as strongly rooted in European chamber music as in American jazz. On the 17-minute "Poetic Justice," they squiggle along playing cat-and-mouse with one another's melodic lines, creating their own drummerless, tempo-less tension, gradually accumulating a density of exclamatory blips, dots-and-dashes of notes, slap-tongued reeds and bowed lines. If it's dreamlike noodling, it's noodling of a very high order, an equivalent of Japanese calligraphy: black mark to white ground, every stroke counts. Most of the selections here hover at around five minutes, and it's a tribute to the discipline and ears of these master improvisers that they're able to come up with a real piece every time, with nothing wasted and every note contributing to every other. — JON GARELICK

RORY BLOCK
When a Woman Gets the Blues
Rounder

Between shots at pandering to a pop audience, Block occasionally returns to her roots with a brilliant album. Dedi-cated to the grandly rough-hewn singer/guitarist Son House (Robert Johnson's inspiration), these are country blues and spirituals set to Block's acoustic guitar. Block binds the songs of House, Skip James, Charlie Patton, Blind Willie McTell and other forefathers to her own grace and fire. Her guitar echoes a simple authenticity sprung from intensive study of the masters, and her singing is its own bold, expressive creature. What's often best about her renditions, which include Hattie Hart's "I Let My Daddy Do That" and Louise Johnson's "On the Wall," is that they're reminders of the blues' long history of raw carnality and that a woman can work the most low-down double-entendre with the same aplomb as the music's grand old men. — TED DROZDOWSKI

JANE IRA BLOOM
The Nearness
Arabesque

The 41-year-old soprano saxophonist/composer gained much acclaim in recent years for her use of electronics in a jazz setting, including a NASA-commissioned set, *Art and Aviation* (Arabesque, 1993). Here she works with various combinations of a traditional jazz ensemble, all practiced hands: Kenny Wheeler (trumpet), Julian Priester (trombone), Fred Hersch (piano), Rufus Reid (bass) and Bobby Previte (drums). Her writing shows continuing mastery, juxtaposing knotty originals and venerable standards. On the whole, Bloom proves herself one of the bearers of the jazz soprano sax flame lit by Sidney Bechet and extended from her immediate predecessor, Steve Lacy. — JG

SHEILA CHANDRA
ABoneCroneDrone
Realworld

A one-woman rain forest of sounds, this third entry for Realworld shows off Chandra's futuristic way with the most minimalist form, the drone. You can hear this London-born Anglo-Indian woman on different levels: as an echo of her earlier incarnation as Britain's first mainstream Asian pop star (with Monsoon, and a 1982 song called "Every So Lonely"), as a kind of aural perfume (best heard in darkness) or as the most challenging internationalistic avant-garde possible within the space of a single note. The more you listen, the deeper it takes you. — TR

ALLAN CHASE QUARTET
Dark Clouds With Silver Linings
Accurate

Alto saxophonist Chase has a strong reputation from his work with Your Neighborhood Saxophone Quartet (who have distinguished themselves with, among others, a CD of Sun Ra covers). Nonetheless, the assurance of his album debut as a leader is stunning. This pianoless quartet conjures the famous precedents of Gerry Mulligan, Ornette Coleman and Charles Mingus. But the ensemble balance also recalls the Modern Jazz Quartet. The solo work is sterling (especially by trumpet/flugelhorn Ron Horton), but it's the interplay that makes the album. When Chase and Horton interweave simultaneously improvised lines along with the tug and nudge of bassist Tony Scherr and drummer Matt Wilson, foreground and background merge into one joyful dance. It helps that the covers (including, for example, two by Bud Powell, Horace Silver's "Yeah," Brooks Bowman's "East of the Sun" and the Gershwins's "Of Thee I Sing") are as unlikely as the originals are sturdy. — JG

SISI CHEN
Tides and Sand
Henry Street/Rounder

At 500, the Yanqin (YANG-tseen) is the baby of traditional Japanese instruments. And Chen is certainly its master: She turns this glistening instrument, somewhere between a harp and a dulcimer, often with straight diatonic harmonies your kids could sing, into a uniquely picturesque medium for modernism. Folk-song melodies and traditional tunes emerge as intricately woven patterns of impudence and intrigue, moments of crystalline beauty mixing with chilling reserve. It's enough to make you wonder if the present isn't just as mysterious and intimidating as the past. — TR

CHOPIN — MURRAY PERAHIA
Four Ballades (including Valses, Nocturnes, Etudes, Mazurkas)
Sony

You want warhorses? Perahia serves up four, played in his inimitable poetic style, with flourishes of heroism, sober defeat, unflinching realism and calm, modernist cynicism. On the big numbers, he pulls out all the stops without going over the edge. Some of this music is thrilling because of its restraint. On the smaller numbers, he gets away with murder: thick rubatos, luscious ritards, deeply felt pauses and playful witticisms. You may never have heard these staples sound so glorious, so passionate and so keenly controlled. — TR

CIBO MATTO
VIVA! La Woman
Warner Bros.

Those nutty Japanese and their queer affection for American trash — they took our car market, now they want our imaginations!? Cibo Matto is a girl group that takes the raw elements of post-modern pop and grinds it up into cheesy tofu music ("Beef Jerky," "White Pepper Ice Cream"). When you're not chasing after countless samples and associations, you're swayed by the singing (which can be arid but never grating) and the humor, which saves the day ("I know my chicken/You got to know your chicken..."). Nifty new trend: mock irony, as in "The Candy Man." — TR

CLARKSDALE, MISSISSIPPI: COAHOMA THE BLUES
Various Artists
Rooster

Most blues compilations are archival or roundups of whoever's currently signed to the issuing label. This one's a testament to the vitality of the music still being made in the Mississippi Delta. Featuring 13 un- or under-recorded artists from the musically fertile Clarksdale area, it embraces the full-blown electric antics of juke-crawlers Wesley Jefferson, Lorenzo Nicholson, David Porter, James "Super Chicken" Johnson, Arthneice "Gas Man" Jones and "Rip" Butler. These are the players who keep local watering holes like the Rivermont and Red's blasting on weekends. There's also room for acoustic weirdness such as Wade Walton (a.k.a. "the Blues Barber") and guitar powerhouse Big Jack Johnson duetting on razor-strop and six-string. The stingingly virtuosic Johnson is the best-known artist here through relentless touring and his two wonderful all-electric CDs on Earwig. But the legendary drums and harp team of Sam Carr and Frank Frost (who, when joined by Johnson, perform as the Jelly Roll Kings) also make an appearance, and there's Carr's plaintive recorded debut as a vocalist and guitarist. This is a labor of love for Rooster label owner Jim O'Neal and an opportunity for those of us who can't get to Clarksdale to feel the lively beat of the music's heartland. This collection is available only on cassette via the Delta Blues Museum, 114 Delta Ave., Clarksdale, MS 38614, and it benefits that modest shrine to a great cultural legacy. It's slated for national release on CD later in 1996. — TD

JOHN COLTRANE
The Heavyweight Champion: John Coltrane
The Complete Atlantic Recordings
Rhino

Most boxed sets are for completists and archivists only. Not so here. Call this Coltrane's early mature period (1959–61). There are the great original tunes ("Giant Steps," "Naima," "Cousin Mary," "Mr. P.C.") and his revolutionary cover of "My Favorite Things," whose modal scheme helped change not only the way jazz was played, but also the way we hear it. From the early, hard-bop sides with Modern Jazz Quartet vibist Milt Jackson through the first recordings with his "classic" quartet (McCoy Tyner, Jimmy Garrison, Elvin Jones) to the extended experiment of "Ole," this is one of the few boxed sets that's listenable as a whole, from beginning to end. — JG

COWBOY JUNKIES
Lay It Down
Geffen

Having opened the door for dreamy-voiced, disaffected female singers employing gauzy musical backdrops with their 1988 major-label debut, *The Trinity Session*, Cowboy Junkies toughened up their sound with their sophomore outing, *Black Eyed Man*. But that CD's rootsy grunge (imagine Crazy Horse fronted by a sweet, troubled girl) was considerably less intriguing than the quiet, elegant pathos to which the Junkies returned with *Lay It Down*. Singer Margot Timmins's soft-spoken style allows her to explore delicate nuances of emotion without straining her limited range. The lower volumes also give her multi-instrumentalist (and songwriter) brother Michael a chance to explore a wider palette than conventional alternative rock's premium on energy and overdriven guitar distortion permits. It's refreshing to hear a band that can take your breath away with a whisper rather than a sledgehammer. — TD

MILES DAVIS AND GIL EVANS
The Complete Columbia Studio Recordings
Columbia Jazz Legacy (6CDs);
Mosaic (vinyl, 11 LPs)

This latest edition in Columbia's Miles Davis reissue project is a must-have luxury. Simply put, composer/arranger Evans and soloist Davis represent one of the great collaborations in the history of the music. Their work on *Miles Ahead*, *Porgy and Bess* and *Sketches of Spain* is a touchstone for orchestral jazz (as opposed to "big band" music), Third Stream classical/jazz hybrids and what has been called "cool jazz." Evans fashions dramatic settings from the Gershwin classic and Joaquin Rodirigo's "Concierto De Aranjuez" for Davis to play both male and female roles, and his trumpet never sounded more expressive. The presence of rhythm-section stalwarts such as Paul Chambers and Art Taylor guarantee swing. Also included are the controversial *Quiet Nights* (which Davis renounced in his autobiography) and alternate and rehearsal takes that are revealing rather than pedantic. — JG

BO DIDDLEY
A Man Amongst Men
Code Blue/Atlantic

Bo Diddley's an architect of early rock and roll. But to hear him holler "that mule in your backyard, he's eatin' all your straw," a line ripe with double-entendre and backwoods imagery, is to understand that the blood in his 67-year-old heart is still drawn from his Mississippi Delta birthplace. Although this CD, his first for a major label since the '70s, includes duets with rapper Philosopher G ("Kids Don't Do It") and glitzy rock players such as guitarist Richie Sambora, it's mostly a blues outing replete with Diddley's famous self-aggrandizing raps and dissin' "dozens." Most of the guitar playing's left to a who's who of other hotshots, including Jimmie Vaughan, the late Johnny "Guitar" Watson and Stones Keith Richards and Ron Wood, but when Diddley weighs in, there's an earthy gravity to his six-stringing. At its best, as on the title tune, this CD sounds like a better-recorded update of his genre-defining Chess Records sound. — TD

RONNIE EARL AND THE BROADCASTERS
Blues Guitar Virtuoso Live in Europe
Bullseye Blues

Not content to be the world's finest blues guitarist, Earl is connecting the dots between blues and jazz with a command not seen since T-Bone Walker's late '40s and early '50s recordings. His playing is strong on melody and soulful emotionalism, wrapped in tight arrangements that share the spotlight with organ ace Bruce Katz and the rest of Earl's ironclad quartet. The tunes run the gamut from Freddie King's Texas gutbucket sting ("San-Ho-Zay," "The Stumble") to the guitarist's own exploratory writing ("Akos," "Rego Park Blues") and nods to tradition ("Thank You Mr. T-Bone"). Not only the best live album of 1995, but a textbook in how to build a musical personality from dynamics, tone, vibrato and signature licks. In these 14 transcendent instrumentals, Earl's guitar sings the blues as eloquently as Mahalia Jackson sang gospel. — TD

RICHARD EINHORN WITH ANONYMOUS 4
Voices of Light
Sony

Taking a cue from Carl Dreyer's moving film, *The Passion of Joan of Arc* (1928), Einhorn has come up with an unlikely fusion, a kind of contemporary Medievalism. The texts combine ancient writings of female medieval mystics with those of Joan herself. As the female Christ figure, Joan has always made for great material, but this is one setting for period instruments and voices that you don't have to be a historian to enjoy. Conductor Steve Mercurio brings a reverence for calm and quiet, urging strong, linear tones sung without vibrato. But there's also a huge dynamic range, from solo murmurs to chorus-wide tuttis — and the emotions range from naïveté to metaphysical dread. — TR

FLAMENCO
Caravan
Lyrichord

The bastard offspring of Spanish guitar, Middle Eastern modalities and gypsy dances, *flamenco* has become as much a world view as a style. Rodrigo and his singer, Remedios Flores, are one of southern Spain's hardest working acts. This disc explains why. "Brisas Ananluzas" is all you need to convince you of the genre's range, should you suspect that *flamenco* is all flash. And on "Malaguena Salerosa," Rodrigo himself does some very fine singing. His rhythmic acuity follows his guitar's nimbly insinuating bravura: what a helicopter might sound like if it could make music. — TR

GARBAGE
Garbage
Almo Sounds/Geffen

Three math-club studio wizards and a little woman with a reform-school sneer may be the oddball aggregation that finally makes some adult sense out of the musical scrawl called grunge. Butch Vig, the Garbage mastermind and producer of Nirvana's *Nevermind*, became associated with the buried, listless vocals and overdriven amps that launched a thousand luckless record-label signings of the "new Nirvana." With *Garbage*, Vig scratches his own legacy in the face of what he helped create. His palette is dense with samples, keyboards, percussion hits and a variety of beats, textures, tempos, rants and crooning. Screamer Shirley Manson, late of the never-lamented Angelfish, stomps and glides, full of petulance and a yearning for forgiveness. A perfect foil for the careful arrangements, she is pure energy opposing pure thought, a pink-tressed bird smashing into a plate-glass window. — RM

GOLDEN SMOG
Down by the Old Mainstream
Rykodisc

With only five days to write and record this album, Golden Smog achieved the kind of smart melodies and harmonies it takes years to perfect, and the playing's warm as a winter's fire. Think of the Byrds and the Stones shuffled together; more aptly, imagine an alterna-rock supergroup with Soul Asylum's Dan Murphy, Wilco's Jeff Tweedy, ex-Jayhawks Gary Louris and Marc Perlman, Kraig Johnson of noisy popsters Run Westy Run and drummer Noah Levy of Minneapolis's Honeydogs. Originally a side project for Murphy, Louris and Soul Asylum singer Dave Pirner (look for '92's EP *On Golden Smog*, on the tiny Crackpot label), the new Smog is amped on country-rock twang and the thrill of making spontaneous music. Their semi-acoustic palette embraces Dylanesque harmonica, mandolin, piano and lots of Murphy's red-blooded slide guitar. The best songs, including the album opener "V" and Murphy's Soul Asylum leftover "Ill Fated," are strong character portraits with flag-waving choruses, thickened by the brassy harmonies that are the group's trump card. — TD

GREEN DAY
Insomniac
Sire

Twenty years after its bloody birthing, punk rock progressed from blank-generation music to bank-generation music. Green Day's success had much to do with that, with *Dookie*'s multi-platinum sales signaling (at least for the record labels that went on a punk-signing spree) a new punk uprising. The most interesting aspect of *Insomniac* is that (like the previous three Green Day records) it *doesn't* strain the formula. Punk rock used to be the anti-formula. Now it is a reference wielded to shorthand a point, much like Green Day forefathers the Clash employed reggae or rockabilly to reach back to previous outlaw cultures. But music as cultural reference doesn't allow for much variety or growth: Shed the punk trappings and you've shrugged off the meaning. Does that concern Billie Joe and pals? Probably not much and why should it. They gleefully bash their way through another set of dead-end tales set to bouncing, loud pop that owes as much to Who-idolaters the Jam as to the Sex Pistols. But taken out of its original social context, the new punk rock smacks of a Stray Cat-like re-creation of an original inspiration. — RM

GUIDED BY VOICES
Under the Bushes Under the Stars
Matador

Now that these Akron, Ohio, pop supremacists have been acknowledged by the mainstream, they could have their pick of major labels. Instead, they stick with hip indie Matador with the same tenacity with which they've clung to their belief in melody and song structure for more than a decade. The results are beautiful. Tunes such as the acoustic-guitar strummer "Acorns & Orioles" and "Don't Stop Now" (which boasts cello and piano) host some of songwriter Robert Pollard's most charming vocals, full of rich, breathy phrasing. It's a pleasure to hear him tackle a number like "The Official Ironmen Rally Song," working the gentle melody, modulating his voice up for the second verse. It's a reminder of the way a good pop song was always meant to be sung. The irony of this band's underground-darlings status is their wholehearted embrace of '70s classic-rock songcraft. The joy is that, in their mid-30s, they've finally been able to quit their day jobs. — TD

ORUJ GUVENC & TUMATA
Ocean of Remembrance: Sufi Improvisations and Zhikrs
Interworld

Recorded in Western Massachusetts during a blizzard in February 1994, and while all the musicians were fasting for the month of Ramadan, this traditional Turkish Sufi music reaches uncommon depth of consciousness through repetition and improvisation. Zhikr means "remembrance" and involves the chanted recitation of God's names. Irregular cadences make for passages that are at once lulling and reflectively fascinating. With the sinuous flute improvising overhead, these voices and the unison strings and hushed drumming make for a timeless feel; its beauty is wrapped up in the repetitiveness. You can almost smell the incense. — TR

BUDDY GUY
Live! The Real Deal
Silvertone

Spitfire Guy's major-label career has been mixed in recent years. *Damn Right, I've Got the Blues* and *Slippin' In!* were gems; the crossover-heavy *Feels Like Rain* was dreadful. Here's the middle ground, recorded live at Guy's own Chicago club Legends. It's not the best Guy concert I've heard by a long shot, but it's good, especially when he dips into sweet-toned, vibrato-laden guitar solos like the one in "Sweet Black Angel" or uses his underappreciated, soulful voice to invoke the demons of passion that always seem just beneath the surface of his best work. It's probably quibbling to say more flexible, informed back-up than G.E. Smith's band could have been found. But rock-piano granddaddy Johnny Johnson lends aesthetic balance. Nonetheless, it's still a pleasure to see this veteran — a Chess studios MVP and one of the innovators who created the gritty, hot-wired urban strain of soul-blues that became synonymous with Chicago's West Side in the '60s — finally enjoy mainstream success in his mid-50s. — TD

1995 COUNTRY MUSIC ASSOCIATION AWARDS

The 29th annual Country Music Association Awards were presented on October 4, 1995, at the Grand Ole Opry House in Nashville, Tennessee.

Entertainer of the Year
Alan Jackson

Single of the Year
"When You Say Nothing at All," Alison Krauss and Union Station

Album of the Year
When Fallen Angels Fly, Patty Loveless

Song of the Year
"Independence Day," Gretchen Peters

Male Vocalist of the Year
Vince Gill

Female Vocalist of the Year
Alison Krauss

Vocal Group of the Year
The Mavericks

Vocal Duo of the Year
Brooks & Dunn

Vocal Event of the Year
"Somewhere in the Vicinity of the Heart,"
Alison Krauss and Shenandoah

Horizon Award
Alison Krauss

Musician of the Year
Mark O'Connor (fiddle)

Music Video of the Year
"Baby Likes to Rock It," Tractors

1995 INDUCTEES TO THE COUNTRY MUSIC HALL OF FAME

Jo Walker-Meador, former executive director of the Country Music Association

Roger Miller

Roger Miller

COREY HARRIS
Between Midnight and Day
Alligator
GUY DAVIS
Stomp Down Rider
Red House

These debut CDs are proof that the acoustic, country-blues tradition is still vital. Harris and Davis are both expert pickers, although *Stomp Down Rider*, a live recording made in 1993, doesn't capture Davis's new-found command of his six-string. Harris is the better singer; his slide dobro is nuanced as the charcoal shadings of his butterscotch voice, whether paying tribute to Robert Johnson or caressing his own tunes, which have an easy sense of swing and an often idiosyncratic rhythmic approach attributable to his formative years in Africa. At 40, some 15-odd years older than Harris, Davis seems a more mature stylist — a living gene-splice of Brownie McGhee and Sonny Terry. But Harris's Afro-centric flavors and Davis's hard-edged drive bring modernity to the Delta style. And they're both aiming somewhere deep. — TD

HOOTIE & THE BLOWFISH
Fairweather Johnson
Atlantic

What is it about Hootie that drives people — fans as well as sniping critics — crazy? Those who love Hootie & the Blowfish (and bought more than 12 million copies of 1994's *Cracked Rear View*), sway to the insistent, chugging rhythm, while their non-threatening personas make the band approachable. The songs are memorable, if only because they make shop-worn phrases like "I only want to be with you" repeat endlessly in your head despite your best efforts to shake them. Who does this hurt? Hootie takes heat from writers because their success is baffling (Why this band and not one of the thousand others in each town that Hootie visits during their constant touring?) and because they homogenize music that is held dear: Isn't this half-digested, R.E.M.-style strumming with a sunny disposition? It seems to me that years spent entertaining drunken Southern college students gave Darius Rucker et al. a pretty keen sense of the possible: Kids who buy records want new but not challenging. *Fairweather Johnson* is not challenging, though the songs are more introspective than *Cracked Rear View*. It is also not a disappointing pothole in the road to continuing Hootiemania, and it contains not one brooding moment of self-doubt or self-pity. Credit it for that at least. — RM

HANK JONES
Cheick-Tidiane Seck, Sarala
Verve

Here's the most unlikely jazz/world-music pairing you could imagine: bebop classicist Hank Jones meets Malian bandleader and multi-instrumentalist Cheick-Tidiane Seck. Seck has worked with Afro-pop superstars such as Salif Keita and Mory Kante (as well as Jimmy Cliff and jazzers Joe Zawinul and Graham Haynes). Jones, noted for his blues and standards work, meets Seck more than halfway here, working in the folkloric Mandingo plainsong tradition of Mali. Jones's legato touch on the keyboard meshes beautifully with the light, percussive textures of balafon (wood xylophone), kora (African lute or harp), and n'goni (a banjo-like lute). For his part, Seck contributes an American-style funk reference with a Hammond B-3 organ, and grainy, attractive vocals. Nothing feels out of place: not the electric guitars and bass, not the backing chorus of the Mandinkas and not the brilliant, hair-raising vocals of Manian Damba. — JG

KIDS
Original Motion Picture Soundtrack
London

Cult-hero Lou Barlow's mind was blown when he found he'd made a hit with the unstoppably catchy "Natural One" on this soundtrack, a project he undertook as a lark at the urging of *Kids* director Larry Clark. Recorded with Folk Implosion collaborator John Davis, the crisp sounding, major-label-budgeted song puts a bouncy hip-hop-derived shuffle under lyrics about a conniving slimeball. It sounds like little else in Barlow's catalog. Barlow defined his own genre with a legacy of lo-fi pop tunes, recorded with such indie bands as the Implosion, Sebadoh and Sentridoh, and often written from the perspective of love-struck, insecure youth. Seven more Folk Implosion numbers, a wilding rap by Lo-Down, two from indie-flake Daniel Johnston, a Sebadoh track, one from the Deluxx Folk Implosion (Davis and Barlow with two collaborators) and "Good Morning Captain" by defunct underground supergroup Slint complete this CD. But it's really a calling card for the talented Barlow, who may yet emerge from the alternative-rock squall of the '90s as the era's great, sensitive, romantic-pop songsmith. — TD

METALLICA
Load
Elektra

Metallica continue their de-evolution and are better off for it. Not that before their 1991 *Metallica* they weren't one of the most intriguing purveyors of heavy metal as thrash-infested, post-industrial grind. But that album's shift toward melodies and more disciplined song structures yielded their most accessible work to date without relinquishing their teeth-gnashing overdose of power. *Load*'s biggest surprise is "Mama Said," an Eagles-styled acoustic ballad spiced with country steel guitar. Elsewhere slide guitar appears and "Wasting My Hate" begins as an outright sojourn into blues-rock before smashing under the band's steely fist. In a field overcrowded with angst-filled songwriters, James Hetfield's genuine introspection and emotional embrace (he's a sensitive guy in wolf's clothing) actually make his lyrics worth deciphering. With *Load*, Metallica has become quite simply a rock band, dropping all but the crunch of their metal vestiges and writing the best, most diverse material of their career. — TD

MIGHTY SAM McCLAIN
Keep On Movin'
AudioQuest

McClain may be the last great red-clay soul singer America will produce. Yet there's more to his craft than echoes of past artists like Otis Redding, O.V. Wright and his idol Bobby Bland. Like Son House in pure country blues, McClain fuses the carnal and the spiritual in his songs — and his struggle to find a place with God and a place in the world is evident in much of his frequently autobiographical lyrics. Here he's leading a crack band, including deft guitarist Kevin Barry and B-3 wizard Bruce Katz, but he's always the star, accenting his words of loss and pain with deep-in-the-belly moans, soaring powerfully over the mix as he shouts out the need to keep on movin' through the trials of life. The highlights are his own soul-wrenching "I'm So Lonely," where the buttery purr of his vocal nuances detail emotional devastation, and the Ronnie Earl-authored "A Soul That's Been Abused," perhaps the best slow-blues tune of the last decade. — TD

ALANIS MORISSETTE
Jagged Little Pill
Maverick

Morissette's history as a mall-rat, dance-music teen-queen, her signing to Madonna's label and her collaboration with notorious L.A. song-doctor Glen Ballard have made her as popular as gonorrhea with critics. But plain ole folks love her. Why? This is a great album, packed with passionate and strange vocal twists, full of the kind of anger and frustration women are expected to quietly endure — and loaded with pop hooks.

Morissette's voice, now overexposed due to radio's slavish rotation of "You Oughta Know," "All I Really Want" and "You Learn," is the freshest to hit the charts since Sinéad O'Connor's 1987 debut. Her Canadian accent can turn abruptly chirpy and harsh, she leaps octaves impetuously and has a grating edge that snaps on and off. In short, she sounds like a real person, not a wind-up like Joan Osborne. And the arrangements, which lean toward a bright-eyed minimalism, give Morissette plenty of room without fading to wallpaper. This is an unforeseen artistic rebirth and one of 1995's best. — TD

GERRY MULLIGAN
Dragonfly
Telarc

The last studio recording by Gerry Mulligan before his death in January 1996 at 68 may sound at first like sweet jazz-pop, especially with Grover Washington's soprano saxophone the first solo voice on the opening track. But then Mulligan's baritone enters stage left, lithe and brawny at once. Washington picks up a tenor for "Brother Blues," digs into a meatier bebop vocabulary and then makes way for a typically understated Mulligan entrance: a four-bar break on the turn-around, the big horn swinging lightly behind the beat, giving its natural heft a singing, vocal eloquence. The dialogue between Mulligan and Webster is supplanted on succeeding tunes by more complex group conversations with vibist Dave Samuels, cornetist Warren Vachi, young trumpeter Ryan Kisor and guitarist John Scofield. A backing brass ensemble lends a little big-band effect, one familiar to Mulligan's fans from the time he helped Miles Davis reshape the language of jazz on what became known as the "Birth of the Cool" sessions. In the liner notes, Mulligan talks about the soloists walking a tightrope. As a composer and player for more than 40 years, no one secured and walked that line better than Mulligan. — JG

ME'SHELL NDEGÉOCELLO
Peace Beyond Passion
Maverick

What's Madonna, would-be pop Evita, trying to do: get pregnant, supervise Alanis's ascent and use her label, Maverick, to break her own world music sensation all in one year? Madonna may have met her match in Ndegéocello. This is the kind of world music audiences have been waiting for since *Graceland*. A sleek, soulful excursion, with sample-ready beats and attitude to spare, it links racism ("Deuteronomy: Niggerman") with homophobia ("Leviticus: Faggot"), adds a note about "Mary Magdalene" and goes out with a slow, tight grind that gives new meaning to the mother-daughter tango ("Make Me Wanna Holler"). The black Madonna? Nope: smarter, warmer and more of a true feminist threat. — TR

OASIS
(What's the Story) Morning Glory
Epic

Oasis presented itself on these shores as the reincarnation of The Kinks, with pretensions to artistic merit built on sub-Who power chords and complete with brawling brothers. Their 1994 release, *Definitely Maybe*, the fastest-selling debut record ever in England, augured a Brit Pop backlash against the American horde of slacker amp crankers and, well, H.O.R.D.E. Oasis's bid for stardom and enduring importance received a boost from *(What's the Story) Morning Glory* though their tiresome swaggering makes them all too easy to despise. Where the first record crashed and blasted, *Morning Glory* makes peace between singer Liam Gallagher's punkish prating and brother Noel's maturing musical craft, which shows an unabashed reverence for the Lennon-McCartney songbook. There are soft piano passages, neo-psychedelic washes and a single (the inescapable "Wonderwall") that jangled guitar strings instead of nerves. A step forward artistically. Now let's dispense with the made-for-*Tiger-Beat* battling brothers stories. — RM

ELIADES OCHOA & CUARTETO PATRIA
The Lion Is Loose
Corason

Ochoa is one of the masters of Cuban *trova* — a mix of *son, bolero* and *guarachas* song styles. He grew up in Santiago and starred on his own popular radio show beginning in 1963. Most of the love songs here are by Los Compadres (Lorenzo Hierrezuelo and Francisco Repilado), broken up by the subdued boleros of Eusebio Defin, Rosendo Ruiz, Rafael Hernandez and Miguel Matamoras. Where the instrumentation is simple (guitar, upright bass, congas), the rhythms are anything but. Dare yourself to find the downbeat in "Huellas del Pasado." And the bridge in "Desvelo de Amor" (track 9) is worthy of Lennon-McCartney, circa "I'll Be Back." Swerving expertly between sharp syncopations and straightforward call-and-response, Ochoa sings like a man hexed by this music's quiet strength. Melodically addictive. — TR

JOAN OSBORNE
Relish
Blue Gorilla/Mercury

With its mix of magic realism, blues, nursery rhymes and musky sexuality, this album should be a blood-stirring revelation. But it's tepid and spineless. Osborne's a capable singer with an often pleasing contralto, as the ironic radio hit "One of Us" reveals. But it sounds as if she couldn't be bothered to wake up for "Let's Just Get Naked" or her mind-numbingly horrible take on blues master Sonny Boy Williamson's "Help Me." In recent interviews, Osborne's taken to cautiously blaming producer Rick Chertoff and her collaborators, the songwriting multi-instrumentalists Eric Bazilian (who penned "One of Us") and Rob Hyman, for making a CD that doesn't show she can sing. Given *Relish*'s success, that's not gracious. But if she's passing the buck, at least it's going all the way to the bank. — TD

PEARL JAM
No Code
Epic

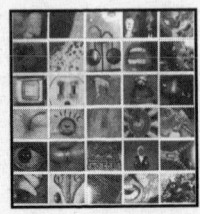

Pearl Jam is back from excursions with progenitor Neil Young (last year's *Mirror Ball*) and Eddie Vedder's duet with *qawwali* master Nusrat Fateh Ali Khan (on the soundtrack for *Dead Man Walking*) and, like all good travelers, they've incorporated worldly sights and sounds into their experience of home. Home isn't that far afield from Young territory and there are a couple of rousing would-be Crazy Horse numbers, "Smile" and "Off He Goes." The curious parts of the record come from the more distant journeys, the chant-like, near-world-beat murmurs of "Who You Are" and "I'm Open." You can still find the propulsive kick that made Pearl Jam a platinum commodity, but the beauty of *No Code* is in its exploration and surprise. An unexpected show of strength and confidence. — RM

DANILO PEREZ
PanaMonk
Impulse!

This album represents a breakthrough for the brilliant Panamanian pianist and former Dizzy Gillespie sideman. In the past, Perez has created strong work that was nonetheless generic Afro-Cuban bebop that followed in Gillespie's shoes, or, perhaps, post-Coltrane jazz with a Latin feel. Here he's liberated by Monk's compositions: The knotty rhythmic figures, dance-like schemes, inventive harmonies and blues grounding open a door for Perez to mix and match rhythms freely. Rather than individual genre pieces, we get one kaleidoscopic entry after another. In one instance, he plays two Monk pieces simultaneously, one in each hand ("Evidence" in the left and "Four in One" in the right). By digging so deeply into Monk, Perez is more himself than he's ever been. — JG

RACHMANINOV
Liturgy of St. John Chrysostom Opus 31
(Melodiya/BMG)

Inspired by the fall of communism and the Melodiya distribution deals it afforded (this recording was made in 1988), this CD is imbued with a bottomless melancholy that sounds distinctly Russian in its vastness, its largesse of spirit. Even though the text is from the ancient Russian liturgy, the religious (read: political) sounds profoundly personal here, as though it takes many souls to reveal the spirit of solitude. Rachmaninov's reputation as a pianist precedes and overshadows his talent as a composer and hearing RCA's 10-CD box collection of his playing, that's understandable. But his choral writing teems with layers — several distinct bass lines, for instance — that makes you wonder what kind of organist he might have made. — TR

MARCUS ROBERTS
Time and Circumstance
Columbia

Pianist Roberts has been a consistently thrilling live performer but, on record, somewhat studied. His refined touch and unlimited technique blossom here as they do in performance. This trio album is, according to Roberts's notes, a suite "about two people in a life-long love affair." But, like most programmatic schemes, that idea serves the composer more than the listener. For the rest of us, the album speaks about the elasticity of a good beat, about trio interplay and solo virtuosity, and about pianistic beauty. Roberts is one of the few jazz pianists who has a complete sense of his instrument, taking in its range from the highest highs to the most ominous, rumbling lows. With bassist David Grossman and drummer Jason Marsalis he explores New Orleans shuffles, Gershwin romanticism (he simultaneously released a Gershwin classical album) and blues feeling. The range of that feeling is indeed as rich as a love affair. — JG

SCARLATTI — SERGEI BABYAN
Sonatas
ProPiano Records

Armenian-born Babyan has been one of the Cleveland's regular soloists since he won the Casadesus International competition in 1989. Beginning with the peculiarly stirring "K8 in G Minor," this set puts him in the first rank of those few players who understand Scarlatti's range of feeling — from sublime to silly, with plenty of consolation and aching happiness in between. He doesn't dazzle like, say, Horowitz (who does?), but his cool polish gives these jewels a shine all their own. Half the pleasure comes from the precision of cleanly articulated lines meant for an instrument with a much swifter decay. Instead of trying to sound like a harpsichord, Babyan coaxes a similar delicate rakishness from a steel-cased modern piano designed for machine-age heft. A few minor quibbles: the recording is so closely miked you can hear the pedal's damper pressing and lifting on the strings. Also, Babyan has a way of sounding "poky" in some of the louder passages. But then, it's nice to hear a rising star who impresses more through nuance than bombast. — TR

SCHUBERT — ANDREAS SCHIFF
Complete Piano Sonatas and Impromptus and Moment Musiceaux
London

His technically polished and often fussy excursions into Bach behind him, the intrepid Hungarian moves on to the classical — and how. Schubert's piano writing bridges the tension between late classical and romantic in an entirely different way than Beethoven. Instead of breaking all the rules, he sounds like a romantic who's gone back to sonata-form school. Schubert treats his structures, with their coy transitions, supernatural developments, modest recapitulations, affectionately, in a way that's virtually nostalgic. With so many precious moments in these pieces, the best approach is to give the surface the sheen it deserves and let the poetic understatement spring forth where it will. Schiff, the most tonally imaginative pianist going, gives technically forbidding exercises like the third "Impromptu in G-Flat Major" a discreet balance of voices with just the right wistfulness. This guy's a poet. — TR

SCHUBERT — AX, FRANK, YOUNG, MA, MEYER
Quintet, Opus 114 (Trout with the "Arpeggione" Sonata, and "Die Forelle")
Sony

Superstar ensembles provide mixed pleasures. With their typically huge string sounds and diffident professionalism, it's sometimes fun to hunt for the odd inspired moment. But this group pits vets against youth: old hands Emmanuel Ax and Yo-Yo Ma pair up with the young Pamela Frank, a violinist whose tone is a scintillating match for Ma's, violist Rebecca Young, whose descant harmonies are fluid and gracious, and bassist Edgar Meyer, who knows whereof he bows. Tempos are appropriately fleet, and smart attention is paid to the pert dotted rhythms, ensemble attacks and cut-offs. Here the pleasures of trading off ornaments and detail finery is made to sound like a good romp. — TR

SHOSTAKOVICH — MAXIM SHOSTAKOVICH/USSR SYMPHONY ORCHESTRA
Symphony No. 5 in D Minor, Opus 47
Melodiya/RCA

Shostakovich mapped the psychological terrain of Stalinism. This sternly optimistic piece, written for Stalin in 1937 as atonement for his "vulgar" *Lady Macbeth of Mtsensk,* gains in irony after the fall. It's long been a myth that Maxim Shostakovich held the goods on this music, that he alone knew how his father wanted it performed. Pedigree rarely guarantees anything, especially in music, but darned if he doesn't pull it off. Recorded in 1977, and remastered for digital, this Fifth will displace your current favorite, even late-'50s Bernstein, though the Party's harps go out of tune. Whether it's the flute-horn duet in the first movement, the gloomy consternation of the third or the heady faux triumph of the last, these Soviets play with true Russian abandon, as if they always knew the secret, subversive meanings lurking inside this warhorse's genes. — TR

SMASHING PUMPKINS
Mellon Collie and the Infinite Sadness
Virgin

Now tainted by the heroin-induced death of their hired-hand tour keyboardist Jonathan Melvoin and the subsequent firing of drummer Jimmy Chamberlain, this album is nonetheless the definitive statement from these Chicago-based alt-rockers led by troubled spirit and singer-guitarist-songwriter Billy Corgan. At two CDs, it's fair to call this album Corgan's *Goodbye Yellow Brick Road.* Like Elton John's '70s masterpiece, which captured the crumbling of the '60s gentle, hopeful soul in its broad pop landscape, Corgan has caught the desperation of living in a decaying hyper-industrialized society. "Despite all my rage/I'm still just a rat in a cage," from the chorus of the hit "Bullet with Butterfly Wings," captures the frustration and anger that emanate from all corners of our culture in such a simple and direct fashion it's nearly off-putting. Then there's the music: mini-symphonies of feedback-dripping guitars, rhythms that alternate between a stroll and a jack-booted lockstep. Pummeling tides of grinding sonic distortion float out of stereo speakers like radio-signal noise or form monolithic walls that threaten to crumble the listener as they tumble. Heavy shit, indeed. — TD

PATTI SMITH
Gone Again
Arista

At its finest, this album gives us Patti Smith the poet, hurling lightning-bolt-and-rose-petal images against a shifting landscape engineered by her improv-minded band, which includes her old Patti Smith Group mates Lenny Kaye and Jay Dee Daugherty and Television's Tom Verlaine. The rock songs, however, lack the punch and hooks of her hits. Hence, this CD is doomed to a short chart-life. One surmises Smith was at a personal low writing this material, since multiple songs seem to deal with the death of her husband, Fred "Sonic" Smith (once the guitarist for the MC5), and "About a Boy" is a paean to infamous suicide Kurt Cobain. But the joy is in hearing Smith push her digestion of life's sweetness and bitter pills to its fullest, the textural playing and her stream-of-consciousness recitations teaching lessons about musical freedom, the denial of spiritual and creative limitations and the state of organic grace that a rock-marketed CD can assume if left to evolve without the cage of a wholly predetermined structure. — TD

SOUNDGARDEN
Down on the Upside
A&M

Nearly a decade after kick-starting the grunge revolution with their 1987 *Screaming Life* EP on Sub Pop, Soundgarden have graduated from Seattle underdogs to the pre-eminent lords of traditional heavy metal. Much like Led Zeppelin during their early '70s nadir, Soundgarden have a patented sound: riff-heavy rock driven by a thunderous rhythm section with a yowling vocalist pegging wistful/yearning lyrics over the top. Too bad that Chris Cornell sometimes sounds more like Ozzy Osbourne than Robert Plant, and that guitarist Kim Thayil hasn't got his own voice, either. His Jimmy Page turn alongside Cornell's effort at sliding his vowels à la Plant on "Rhinosaur" is bald-faced theft. That said, if you're going to copy someone, there's merit in copying the best. Which is why *Down on the Upside,* right down to the semi-acoustic, blues-rock, death-and-repentance-themed hit "Burden in My Hand" (which would comfortably fit the vibe of *Led Zeppelin III*) is fun to hear. But there's nothing resembling an original musical or lyrical statement. — TD

BRUCE SPRINGSTEEN
The Ghost of Tom Joad
Columbia

Springsteen may be the last of our national pop icons to seek inspiration and imagery from literary rather than televised sources. The promise his Oscar-winning "Streets of Philadelphia" held for reclaiming the soc-ially conscious pop song spins here into a painful journey back to the touchstone of American protest-folk music, Woody Guthrie, and the

Depression-era defiance of *The Grapes of Wrath* (also an inspiration for Guthrie). While the inspiration for *The Ghost of Tom Joad* is noble and the subject matter contemporary — Mexican laborers turned into drug makers, ex-cons struggling with life outside, meditations on the border and border crossings in everyone's life — the stark renditions give the record an anachronistic feel, as if the Smithsonian had just unearthed a previously unheralded Wobbly balladeer. Serious, sober narratives from a performer whose love for his country's people and feeling for their challenges and triumphs is unquestioned. — RM

NOLAN STRUCK AND KING EDWARD
Brother to Brother
Paula

Chestnuts like "Blues With Feeling" have been too often raked over by third-rate bands. But Nolan Struck does a fine needlepoint with the emotional fabric of the Little Walter classic. His lofty tenor makes syllables flutter like a palpitating heart, beating in a nervous rhythm of loneliness. He has a beautiful voice, employing a romantic purr seemingly made for the sanctified church. It's the voice of an angel, but one with a dirty face. Like his brother King Edward, with whom he shares a band, licks and lead vocals, Struck's a juking swamp dog, from the country near Lafayette, Louisiana. The 55-year-old sings lead on eight tunes, his arching vocals painting a blue rainbow. And 58-year-old King Edward's guitar is a noble foil, lapping at the edges of Struck's voice with phrases gleaned from B.B. King and the rocking zydeco/R&B of the late Clifton Chenier, who mentored him. When Edward sings the heart-pinning intensity ebbs — until his guitar speaks in a wise vocabulary built on notes spare as a picked-clean rib bone. Screw the guys in the fedoras and sunglasses: Nolan Struck and King Edward are the real Blues Brothers. — TD

DAVE THOMPSON
Little Dave and Big Love
Fat Possum

Dave Thompson's got something 99% of the fresh-faced aspirants to the blues guitar throne don't: Delta heart and soul. Thompson didn't hone his chops in rock clubs or just cop licks from records. Since he was 17, when he joined the band of Greenville, Mississippi's Roosevelt "Booby" Barnes, he's learned on the road and in the juke joints. And when he sings about hard times, he's not serving up fiction. This 24 year old's talking about his own life, raising a family in a small place on the poor side of the tracks in Leland with the few dollars he scratches out playing music. Thompson wears his guitar influences on his sleeve, bending strings like Albert King, soaring through volume-flooded licks like Stevie Ray Vaughan and taking strange melodic and harmonic turns that scream Jeff Beck. Yet there's a ragged aggression in his playing that translates every nuance into his own nasty voice. And Thompson never plays too many notes. As a singer, he makes hay with a limited range and a gentle delivery that keeps his songs earnest. Here's more proof that the Delta's still raising dynamic new artists with the potential to keep the music fresh and vital. — TD

CASSANDRA WILSON
New Moon Daughter
Blue Note

Wilson's preceding album, *Blue Light 'Til Dawn* (Blue Note, 1993), was a phenomenon. It mixed unorthodox cover material (blues saint Robert Johnson's

"Come On in My Kitchen" and "Hellhound on My Trail," Joni Mitchell's "Black Crow" and Van Morrison's "Tupelo Honey") with more typical standards ("You Don't Know What Love Is") and Wilson's idiosyncratic originals. Her moody, dramatic contralto was set to Brandon Ross's medium-to-slow tempo minimalist arrangements, most of them limned by his acoustic and steel-string guitar playing. It became a breakout hit. *New Moon Daughter* seeks to capitalize on this unlikely crossover hit. If anything, the choice of covers is even more eclectic: U2, Son House, Hoagy Carmichael, Hank Williams, Neil Young, "Strange Fruit" and "Last Train to Clarksville." In concept, Wilson can't be beat. Jazz sorely needs innovators willing to bend the music to a new repertoire of pop standards. And Wilson's own pen has grown more assured. But her relentlessly dirgey attack may strike some as a jagged little pill. — JG

Collecting Happens

■ BY BONNI MILLER

Collecting records happens to most of us by default. We buy the music we love and one day we wake up with — voila! — a collection. At the other end of the spectrum, there is, of course, those rare animals that collect records as if they were filling Blue Books with coins. One collector I know is gathering every 45 that ever charted in the United States. I don't want to demean another's pastime, but such habits of acquisition seem tiring. When it's all over and done with, what have you really got but a conversation piece?

But while most buyers would find such bean-counting about as exciting as collecting dust, this fellow is quite passionate about it. His knowledge is as vast and varied as his collection, and he's managed to parlay his accumulation into a successful career writing record-price guides.

Like what we collect, the physical state of our collections reflects our natures as well. Careful, tidy people still have all the sleeves their records came in, pristine and plastic-shrouded; their vinyl is immaculate and un-scratched (in  record-collector parlance, "mint"). The more careless, myself included, left stacks of uncased, naked and vulnerable discs lying about to slide against each other and, worse, to accumulate dust, resulting in a collection worth diddley squat. Hope-fully, you fall somewhere in between.

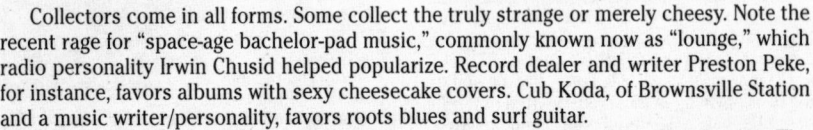

Collectors come in all forms. Some collect the truly strange or merely cheesy. Note the recent rage for "space-age bachelor-pad music," commonly known now as "lounge," which radio personality Irwin Chusid helped popularize. Record dealer and writer Preston Peke, for instance, favors albums with sexy cheesecake covers. Cub Koda, of Brownsville Station and a music writer/personality, favors roots blues and surf guitar.

But most people start out with a favorite artist or group, such as The Beatles, The Rolling Stones, Garth Brooks, Madonna and, of course, Elvis, and end up pursuing pertinent peripheral recordings.

Some collectors favor ragtime 78s, some fancy Blue Note jazz LPs, some go ape for soundtracks, some even prefer eight-tracks (really!), reel-to-reels and cassettes (and please, let's not get into the vinyl versus CD debate), but, to get back to the point, nearly all of us get ourselves into this mess because we love music.

We live in a golden age when virtually every kind of music imaginable is available to us, cheaply, readily and reliably. Before the 20th century, if you wanted music and were not a wealthy landowner, you made your own. And, if sheer love of music is your sole motivation, and you're not against new technology, you, like myself, get on your hands and knees every day and bow your head, thankful beyond measure for the CD-reissue revolution.

A few years ago, Columbia Records reissued a two-CD collection of Robert Johnson's seminal blues recordings. Johnson died young, recorded little and left behind a huge, mysterious legacy. If you wanted the original 78s, you'd have to pay thousands of dollars for each disc, assuming that you could find them. But some labels' entire catalogs have yet to be reissued. For example, the Cameo and Parkway archives are largely unreleased because the individual who owns the rights to these recordings hasn't yet seen fit to reissue them

The Beatles

(Allen Klein, if you're reading this, pretty please?). As a result, those vinyl recordings are in high demand.

Some audiophiles (I really did try to avoid this) avow vinyl's sound to be superior ("warmer" is the term most often used) to that of CDs (thin, tinny) and buy accordingly.

And, too, there are those of us who are now simply nostalgic for the big, black discs of our youth. (If you're a young reader, go ask your mom.) So, there are some who are willing to pay basketfuls of good American dollars to rebuild the trappings of what we remember as a time when music was melodic, danceable and we knew all the words.

Bob Dylan

(Careful and tidy people take note: That stack of pristine Motown LPs kicking around your closet has monetary value!) Hence, what is called a "secondary market" has grown to fill the demand. Nearly every town of size has a used record store. College towns host record "shows" where dealers — and a few collectors interested in becoming a bit more liquid — display on folding tables thousands of records of all sizes, shapes and colors, CDs and music memorabilia for nimble-fingered buyers to peruse. Mail-order dealers, some with shops and many without, advertise their wares in full-page ads in

---

THE TOP 10 MOST VALUABLE U.S. ROCK AND R&B RECORDINGS

According to Neal Umphred, author of *Goldmine's Price Guide to Collectible Record Albums,* the most valuable rock record released in this country is Bob Dylan's *The Freewheelin' Bob Dylan,* Columbia CS-8796, in stereo. The original pressing of this record contains four songs that are not on the legitimate second pressing: "Talkin' John Birch Blues," was deemed too problematic and, perhaps, libelous and was replaced along with three other songs ("Gamblin' Willie's Dead Man's Hand," "Rocks and Gravel" and "Let Me Die in My Footsteps").

The records containing the first four songs were pressed and waiting for the album sleeves when the decision was made to remaster the record and the release was pulled. Apparently some copies slipped through the net. All known copies of this record (and there are only two) have listed the songs on the inside label but not on the sleeve. In near mint condition, these records would be worth between $20,000 and $30,000.

The next nine most valuable rock and R&B records, according to Umphred, are as follows with their values:

The Beatles, *Introducing The Beatles* (title back cover) (Vee Jay) SR-1062, Stereo (originally released in 1963) $25,000

Billy Ward & the Dominoes, *Billy Ward & His Dominoes* (10-inch) (Federal) 295-94 (originally released in 1955) $20,000

Bob Dylan, *The Freewheelin' Bob Dylan* (mono) (Columbia) CL-1986 (1963) $15,000 (mono version of above)

The Midnighters, *The Midnighters: Their Greatest Hits* (10-inch) (Federal) 295-90 (1955) $15,000

Ike and Tina Turner, *River Deep-Mountain High* (stereo, no covers are known to exist) (Philles) PHLPS-4011 (1966) $13,000

The Beatles, *Introducing The Beatles* (ad back) (Vee Jay) SR-1062 (1963) $12,500

The Beatles/Frank Ifield, *On Stage* (portrait cover) (Vee Jay) LPS-1085 (1964) $12,500

The Beatles, *Hear The Beatles Tell All* (DJ copy, only one copy known to exist) (Vee Jay) PRO-202 (1964) $12,500

Elvis Presley, *Elvis' Christmas Album* (red vinyl) (RCA Victor) LOC-1035 (1957) $10,000

specialty record-collecting publications along with hordes of collectors who fill the classifieds with want lists and items for sale and trade.

All in all it amounts to, according to highly scientific market analysts, a bijillion dollar-a-year business. Impressive, eh?

And the craze shows no sign of slowing. Special, limited-edition vinyl continues to be pressed both for major acts on major labels and for unknown but potentially famous artists on small, independent labels. Publications continue to spring up, catering to the specialty collector. Savvy dealers travel world-wide to buy and sell merchandise. Fancy shmancy auction houses now deal in music memorabilia and recordings on the slow days when they aren't selling off Camelot.

And every day, another music lover awakens to a collection. But before you quit your day job and cash in on your vinyl, take note. Most records are worth about $2. Unless you were listening to records that none of your peers were hip enough to appreciate at the time and now like to pretend otherwise, you've probably got the same dreck that everyone else has and, therefore, nobody needs it any more than you do. As Neal Umphred, author of *Goldmine's Price Guide to Collectible Record Albums,* has so kindly pointed-ed out, it's simply a matter of supply and demand. For example: Big band and pop music 78s, which when issued were hugely popular, are, with few exceptions, traditionally worthless. Everybody alive when these records were issued has the same stuff. Big band, while still fairly popular (in fact, it has recently enjoyed a bit of a resurgence in popularity), is easily available in more user-friendly formats (Do you have a turntable that plays 78s? Do you even have a turntable?). Consequently, scores have found their way to the trash. Perhaps, some day, they'll be both rare and desired. At present, even in pristine condition, they're commonly found in antique and junk stores for no more than a few coins. At least they're still fun to listen to.

But, '70s soul and funk records, for example, are currently growing in popularity among collectors, with prices for quality vinyl in these genres showing some escalation in value in certain markets (mostly coastal, where trends are born). Classical music, as well, has shown increasing values, though the lack of a comprehensive price guide makes this a difficult area to knowledgeably explore.

Important note: Speculators, if you're reading this, my advice is to invest in a secure money-market fund. Or try some of those lovely painted plates that sell on late-night cable television or, better yet, just send your money to me. But if you're serious about getting into this, the key is to buy only mint-condition recordings and to buy them cheap. Stay away from recordings that were more popular when they came out than they are now, such as Michael Jackson's *Thriller*. And, most important, before you spend a dollar, educate yourself. Read music-collecting publications. Buy the ancillary price guides. Familiarize yourself with what people are buying and selling and learn to recognize first and limited pressings. And, by all means, unless you've got money to burn, buy music that you like. Your love of a genre or artist will teach you more about the value of the recordings than even the best publication will. And, besides, if you can't sell the darn things later, at least you will have a whole heap of good listening. ∎

Bonni Miller is a freelance writer and the former managing editor of Goldmine *magazine. She is available online at bandbinc@add-inc.com*

1996 Grammy Awards

The 38th Annual Grammy Awards were presented at Los Angeles's Shrine Auditorium on February 28, 1996.

Alanis Morissette

Record of the Year
"Kiss From a Rose," Seal

Album of the Year
Jagged Little Pill, Alanis Morissette
(Maverick/Reprise)

Song of the Year
"Kiss From a Rose," Seal, songwriter

Best New Artist
Hootie & the Blowfish

Best Pop Vocal Performance, Male
"Kiss From a Rose," Seal

Best Pop Vocal Performance, Female
"No More 'I Love You's,'" Annie Lennox

Best Pop Performance by a Duo or Group With Vocal
"Let Her Cry," Hootie & the Blowfish

Best Traditional Pop Vocal Performance
"Duets II," Frank Sinatra

Best Pop Instrumental Performance
"Mariachi Suite," Los Lobos

Best Pop Vocal Collaboration
"Have I Told You Lately That I Love You?,"
The Chieftains with Van Morrison

Best Pop Album
Turbulent Indigo, Joni Mitchell (Reprise)

Best Rock Album
Jagged Little Pill, Alanis Morissette
(Maverick/Reprise)

Best Rock Gospel Album
Lesson of Love, Ashley Cleveland (Reunion)

Best Rock Song
"You Oughta Know," Glen Ballard and
Alanis Morissette, songwriters

Best Rock Vocal Performance, Male
"You Don't Know How It Feels," Tom Petty

Best Rock Vocal Performance, Female
"You Oughta Know," Alanis Morissette

Best Rock Performance by a Duo or Group With Vocal
"Run-Around," Blues Traveler

Best Rock Instrumental Performance
"Jessica," The Allman Brothers Band

Best Hard Rock Performance
"Spin the Black Circle," Pearl Jam

Best Metal Performance
"Happiness Is Slavery," Nine Inch Nails

Best Alternative Music Performance
MTV Unplugged in New York, Nirvana (DGC)

Best Rhythm and Blues Album
CrazySexyCool, TLC (LaFace Records)

Best Rhythm and Blues Song
"For Your Love," Stevie Wonder, songwriter

Best Rhythm and Blues Vocal Performance, Male
"For Your Love," Stevie Wonder

Best Rhythm and Blues Vocal Performance, Female
"I Apologize," Anita Baker

Best Rhythm and Blues Performance by a Duo or Group With Vocal
"Creep," TLC

Best Rap Album
Poverty's Paradise, Naughty by Nature (Tommy Boy)

Best Rap Solo Performance
"Gangsta's Paradise," Coolio

Best Rap Performance by a Duo or Group
"I'll Be There for You"/"You're All I Need to Get By,"
Method Man/Mary J. Blige

Best Jazz Vocal Performance
"An Evening With Lena Horne," Lena Horne

Best Jazz Instrumental Solo
"Impressions," Michael Brecker

Best Jazz Instrumental Performance, Individual or Group
"Infinity," McCoy Tyner Trio featuring
Michael Brecker

Best Contemporary Jazz Performance
"We Live Here," Pat Metheny Group

Best Large Jazz Ensemble Performance
"All Blues," GRP All-Star Big Band and Tom Scott

Best Latin Jazz Performance
"Antônio Brasileiro," Antônio Carlos Jobim

Best Country Album
The Woman in Me, Shania Twain (Mercury Nashville)

Best Country Song
"Go Rest High on That Mountain," Vince Gill, songwriter

Best Country Vocal Performance, Male
"Go Rest High on That Mountain," Vince Gill

Best Country Vocal Performance, Female
"Baby, Now That I've Found You," Alison Krauss

Best Country Performance by a Duo or Group With Vocal
"Here Comes the Rain," The Mavericks

Best Country Vocal Collaboration
"Somewhere in the Vicinity of the Heart," Shenandoah with Alison Krauss

Best Country Instrumental Performance
"Hightower," Asleep at the Wheel featuring Bela Fleck and Johnny Gimble

Best Bluegrass Album
Unleashed, The Nashville Bluegrass Band (Sugar Hill)

Best Traditional Soul Gospel Album
Shirley Caesar Live ... He Will Come, Shirley Caesar (Word)

Best Contemporary Soul Gospel Album
Alone in His Presence, CeCe Winans (Sparrow Communications Group)

Best Pop/Contemporary Gospel Album
I'll Lead You Home, Michael W. Smith (Reunion)

Best Rock Gospel Album
Lesson of Love, Ashley Cleveland (Reunion)

Best Southern Gospel, Country Gospel or Bluegrass Gospel Album
Amazing Grace — A Country Salute to Gospel, various artists (Sparrow Communications Group)

Best Gospel Album by a Choir or Chorus
Praise Him ... Live!, The Brooklyn Tabernacle Choir (Warner Alliance)

Best Latin Pop Performance
"Amor," Jon Secada

Best Tropical Latin Performance
"Abriendo Puertas," Gloria Estefan

Best Mexican-American Performance
"Flaco Jimenez," Flaco Jimenez

Best Traditional Blues Album
Chill Out, John Lee Hooker (Point-Blank)

Best Contemporary Blues Album
Slippin' In, Buddy Guy (Silvertone)

Best Traditional Folk Album
South Coast, Ramblin' Jack Elliott (Red House)

Best Contemporary Folk Album
Wrecking Ball, Emmylou Harris (Asylum/Elektra)

Best Reggae Album
Boombastic, Shaggy (Virgin)

Best New Age Album
Forest, George Winston

Best World Music Album
Boheme, Deep Forest (Windham Hill)

Best Polka Album
I Love to Polka, Jimmy Sturr (Rounder)

Best Instrumental Arrangement
"Lament," Robert Farnon, arranger

Best Instrumental Arrangement With Accompanying Vocal(s)
"I Get a Kick out of You," Rob McConnell, arranger

Best Instrumental Composition
"A View From the Side," Bill Holman

Best Musical Show Album
Smokey Joe's Cafe — The Songs of Leiber and Stoller, Jerry Leiber, lyricist; Mike Stoller, composer (Atlantic Theater)

Best Instrumental Composition Written for a Motion Picture or for Television
"Crimson Tide," Hans Zimmer, composer

Best Song Written Specifically for a Motion Picture or for Television
"Colors of the Wind" (From *Pocahontas*), Alan Menken and Stephen Schwartz, songwriters

Best Classical Contemporary Composition
"Messiaen: Concert a Quatre," Olivier Messiaen, composer

Best Classical Album
Debussy: La Mer; Nocturnes; Jeux, etc. Pierre Boulez conducting the Cleveland Orchestra (Deutsche Grammophon)

Best Chamber Music Performance
Brahms/Beethoven/Mozart: Clarinet Trios, Emanuel Ax, piano; Yo-Yo Ma, cello; Richard Stoltzman, clarinet

Best Classical Performance, Instrumental Soloist(s) (With Orchestra)
The American Album (Works of Bernstein, Barber, Foss), Itzhak Perlman, violin (EMI Classics)

Best Classical Performance, Instrumental Soloist(s) (Without Orchestra)
Schubert: Piano Sonatas (B-Flat Major and A Major), Radu Lupu, piano (London Records)

Best Orchestral Performance
Debussy: La Mer, Nocturnes; Jeux, etc., Pierre
Boulez conducting the Cleveland Orchestra
(Deutsche Grammophon)

Best Opera Recording
Berlioz: Les Troyens, Charles Dutoit conducting the
Orchestre Symphonie de Montreal

Best Performance of a Choral Work
Brahms: Ein Deutsches Requiem, Herbert Blomstedt
conducting San Francisco Symphony, San
Francisco Symphony Chorus and various artists

Best Classical Vocal Performance
*The Echoing Air — The Music of Henry Purcell
(If Music Be the Food of Love; Sweeter Than
Roses, etc.),* Sylvia McNair, soprano

Best Spoken Comedy Album
Crank Calls, Jonathan Winters (Audio Select)

Best Spoken Word or Non-Musical Album
Phenomenal Woman, Maya Angelou
(Random House Audio Books)

Best Musical Album for Children
Sleepy Time Lullabys, Barbara Bailey Hutchison
(Jaba)

Best Spoken Word Album for Children
Prokofiev: Peter and the Wolf, Patrick Stewart
(Erato)

Best Recording Package
Turbulent Indigo, Robbie Cavolina and Joni Mitchell,
art directors (Reprise)

Best Recording Package—Boxed
Civilization Phaze III, Frank Zappa and Gail Zappa,
art directors (Barking Pumpkin)

Best Album Notes
*The Complete Stax/Volt Soul Singles, Volume 3:
1972–1975,* Rob Bowman, album notes writer
(Stax)

Best Historical Album
The Heifitz Collection (RCA Victor Gold Seal)

Best Music Video, Short Form
"Scream," Michael Jackson and Janet Jackson

Best Music Video, Long Form
"Secret World Live," Peter Gabriel

Best Engineered Album (Non-Classical)
Wildflowers, Dave Bianco, Richard Dodd,
Stephen McLaughlin and Jim Scott,
engineers (Warner Bros.)

Best Classical Engineered Recording
*Bartók: Concerto for Orchestra/Kossuth: Symphonic
Poem,* Michael Mailes and Jonathan Stokes,
engineers (London Records)

Producer of the Year (Non-Classical)
Babyface

Classical Producer of the Year
Steven Epstein

Small Changes

After years of not-so-subtle derision by music-industry insiders and music critics, as well as behind-the-scenes threats from labels to pull funding for the National Academy of Recording Arts and Sciences, Academy president Mike Greene tried to make the Grammys cool by changing the rules. Tried is the operative word. Give him a B for effort.

For years, the winners of Grammy's big four — Record of the Year, Album of the Year, Song of the Year and New Artist — reflected record sales and mainstream names rather than talent. Take, for example, Tony Bennett snaring the album trophy in 1994 for *MTV Unplugged,* Mariah Carey winning New Artist honors in 1990 and Whitney Houston walking away with three major awards in 1992. Last year, David Geffen of Geffen Records reportedly hit the roof when the Academy failed to recognize Courtney Love's band, Hole, after their album, *Live Through This,* topped major critics' polls as record of the year. Also oddly missing from Grammy's history books are Nirvana, Smashing Pumpkins and R.E.M. (Grammy considers them alternative). And who can forget the infamous Milli Vanilli incident in 1989?

David Geffen

In the past, NARAS members (8,000 musicians, songwriters and industry insiders) were polled and the top five vote getters in the big four became the nominees. The winners were then chosen in another round of voting. It has been rumored that many Academy members never heard any of the nominated recordings and voted solely on name recognition or label loyalty. This year, the democratic process was thrown out the window in favor of a vote by a secret panel of 25 that selected the five nominees from the top 20 vote getters in each category. The entire academy membership then chose the winner.

"I think we're going to see nominations much more based on excellence as opposed to the lowest common denominator," Greene said.

The outcome? Alanis Morissette ain't no Mariah Carey, but we certainly would have preferred PJ Harvey. — BETH ROWEN

Rolling Stone 1996 Music Awards

Each year *Rolling Stone* polls its readers and critics to illuminate the year's shining stars in contemporary music. Take note of the several "worst" categories added this year to accommodate Hootie & the Blowfish. Here's what they had to say.

Eddie Vedder

Smashing Pumpkins

READERS' PICKS

ARTIST OF THE YEAR
Live

BEST ALBUM
Mellon Collie and the Infinite Sadness, Smashing
    Pumpkins (Virgin)

WORST ALBUM
Cracked Rear View, Hootie & the Blowfish (Atlantic)

BEST SINGLE
"You Oughta Know," Alanis Morissette

WORST SINGLE
"Only Wanna Be With You," Hootie & the Blowfish

BEST BAND
R.E.M.

BEST NEW BAND
Foo Fighters

BEST MALE SINGER
Eddie Vedder, Pearl Jam

BEST FEMALE SINGER
Alanis Morissette

BEST TOUR
R.E.M.

BEST NEW MALE SINGER
Dave Grohl, Foo Fighters

BEST NEW FEMALE SINGER
Alanis Morissette

BEST SONGWRITER
Billy Corgan

BEST METAL BAND
White Zombie

BEST RAP ARTIST
Coolio

BEST R&B ARTIST
TLC

BEST INDIE-ROCK BAND
Rancid

BEST VIDEO
"Geek Stink Breath," Green Day

WORST VIDEO
"Only Wanna Be With You," Hootie & the Blowfish

BEST ALBUM COVER
Mellon Collie and the Infinite Sadness, Smashing
    Pumpkins

WORST ALBUM COVER
Cracked Rear View, Hootie & the Blowfish

BEST REISSUE ALBUM
The Ultimate Experience, Jimi Hendrix (MCA)

BEST TRIBUTE ALBUM
Encomium, Led Zeppelin (Atlantic)

WORST TRIBUTE ALBUM
Encomium, Led Zeppelin

BEST RADIO STATION, LARGE MARKET
WHTZ, New York, New York

BEST RADIO STATION, MEDIUM MARKET
WBRU, Providence, Rhode Island

BEST RADIO STATION, SMALL MARKET
WAPL, Appleton, Wisconsin

NEXT HOOTIE & THE BLOWFISH
Silverchair

CRITICS' PICKS

ARTIST OF THE YEAR
PJ Harvey

TEN BEST ALBUMS
1. *To Bring You My Love,* PJ Harvey (Island)
2. *Foo Fighters,* Foo Fighters (Roswell/Capitol)
3. *Maxinquaye,* Tricky (Island)
4. *Elastica,* Elastica (DGC/Geffen)
5. *Mellon Collie and the Infinite Sadness,*
   Smashing Pumpkins (Virgin)
6. *Mirror Ball,* Neil Young and Pearl Jam
   (Reprise/Warner Bros.)
7. *(What's the Story) Morning Glory?,* Oasis (Epic)
8. *Post,* Björk (Elektra)
9. *Trace,* Son Volt (Warner Bros.)
10. *Jesus Wept,* P.M. Dawn (Gee Street Records)

FIVE BEST SINGLES
1. "Gangsta's Paradise," Coolio
2. "A Girl Like You," Edwyn Collins
3. "You Oughta Know," Alanis Morissette
4. "Lump," The Presidents of the United States
   of America
5. "Wonderwall," Oasis

BEST BAND
R.E.M.

BEST NEW BAND
Elastica

BEST METAL BAND
White Zombie

BEST RAP ARTIST
Coolio

BEST R&B ARTIST
TLC

BEST COUNTRY ARTIST
Alison Krauss

BEST VIDEO
"It's Oh So Quite," Björk

BEST ALBUM COVER
Mellon Collie and the Infinite Sadness, Smashing
   Pumpkins

BEST TOUR
PJ Harvey

HYPE OF THE YEAR
Michael Jackson

MOST WELCOME COMEBACK
Patti Smith

LEAST WELCOME COMEBACK
The Beatles

Elastica

The Recording Industry Association of America's Top-Selling Albums of 1995

The RIAA certifies recordings that sell 500,000 or more copies as gold, those selling 1,000,000 or more as platinum and those with sales of 2,000,000 or more as multi-platinum. These are the RIAA's top-selling albums of 1995.

Aerosmith

11 million
Hootie & the Blowfish
Cracked Rear View
(Atlantic)

8 million
Garth Brooks
The Hits
(Capitol Nashville)

7 million
TLC
CrazySexyCool
(LaFace/Arista)

6 million
Boyz II Men
II (Motown)

5 million
Mariah Carey
Daydream
(Columbia)

Eagles
Hell Freezes Over
(Geffen)

Kenny G.
Miracles: The Holiday Album (Arista)

Pearl Jam
Vitalogy (Epic)

Live
Throwing Copper
(Radioactive/MCA)

Green Day
Dookie (Reprise)

Michael Jackson
HIStory: Past, Present and Future Book 1 (Epic)

4 million
Alanis Morissette
Jagged Little Pill
(Maverick/Reprise/
Warner Bros.)

Shania Twain
The Woman in Me
(Mercury)

The Cranberries
No Need to Argue (Island)

The Beatles
Live at the BBC (Capitol)

3 million
Aerosmith
Big Ones (Columbia)

Mary J. Blige
My Life (Uptown/MCA)

Garth Brooks
The Garth Brooks Collection
(Capitol Nashville)

Mannheim Steamroller
Christmas in the Aire
(American Gramaphone)

Nirvana
MTV Unplugged in New York
(DGC/Geffen)

Tom Petty
Wildflowers
(Warner Bros. Records)

Pocahontas
Soundtrack
(Walt Disney Records)

The Lion King
Soundtrack
(Walt Disney Records)

M2: MTV's Second Generation

■ BY DAVID KLEILER, JR.

Tears well in my eyes as veteran music-video director Alan Bernstein (B52's, Dead Milkmen, Frank Black) reminisces about the glory days of MTV. He refers to 1985–1986 as MTV's "Prague Spring." "It was a time when they sort of opened up their playlist to just about anything that was cool." At the time, Bernstein's quirky, low-budget They Might Be Giants video, "Put Your Hand Inside the Puppet Head," was on regular rotation while "the band did not have a record out." Bernstein pauses wistfully. "They did not have a record in stores."

As a music-video director in the 1990s, this story makes me weep. I find low-budget production creatively enriching and high in anecdote value. Paltry budgets and constant scrounging for work do not discourage me. What discourages me is only being able to view my work on local cable access stations, in the wee hours of Monday morning on MTV's supposedly hip *120 Minutes* or chopped-up during *Beavis and Butt-Head*. Video directors constantly work with unknown artists hoping that MTV will fancy the artist or the video and start showing the videos regularly. With music-industry pressure, slim playlists and hours of non-video programming, the idea that MTV in 1997 would put into rotation a video by a truly obscure indie band, let alone an unsigned band, is unthinkable. Or is it?

MUSIC VIDEO

Ten years after the supposed glory days of MTV, M2 arrives. The launch ends ongoing speculation over who will debut a music-video channel to compete head-to-head with MTV and silences complaints that currently MTV is sparse on videos and glutted with game and reality shows. M2 is MTV's own, commercial-free, satellite-only, mostly-music-video channel.

M2 targets an older, music-savvy audience. The station's slogan is "24 more hours of music." A whole posse of MTV programmers and producers pitch in to program all those extra video hours. Since programming M2 is a supplement to their regular programming chores, "It's almost as if we can do whatever we want," says M2 programmer Amy Finnerty, creating an atmosphere "like a college radio station." Finnerty quickly adds that this doesn't mean alterna-rock all the time and that MTV's usual blend of rock and hip-hop persists.

Finnerty explains that M2's programmers are distributing extensive lists of videos to musicians, allowing rockers to custom-program video hours that will have a text crawl on the bottom of the screen announcing "this hour was programmed by so and so." M2 also boasts interactive components, including the ability to be viewed via the Internet while receiving such information as tour dates, poll questions and artist bios. On August 1, 1996, the first video M2 beamed was Black Flag's "TV Party

Courtney Love of Hole

1996 MTV MUSIC VIDEO AWARDS

The 1996 MTV Music Video Awards were presented September 4, 1996, at New York City's Radio City Music Hall.

Video of the Year
"Tonight, Tonight," Smashing Pumpkins

Viewers' Choice Award
"Glycerine," Bush

Breakthrough Video
"Tonight, Tonight," Smashing Pumpkins

Best Male Video
"Where It's At," Beck

Best Female Video
"Ironic," Alanis Morissette

Best Group Video
"Big Me," Foo Fighters

Best Rap Video
"Gangsta's Paradise,"Coolio featuring LV

Best Dance Video
"1,2,3,4 (Sumpin' New)," Coolio

Best Hard Rock Video
"Until It Sleeps," Metallica

Best Alternative Video
"1979," Smashing Pumpkins

Best New Artist in a Video
"Ironic," Alanis Morissette

Best Video From a Film
"Gangsta's Paradise," Dangerous Minds, Coolio featuring LV

Best R&B Video
"Killing Me Softly," Fugees

Best Direction
Jonathan Dayton and Valerie Faris, "Tonight, Tonight," Smashing Pumpkins.

Best Choreography
Michael Rooney, "It's Oh So Quiet," Björk

Best Special Effects in a Video
Chris Staves, "Tonight, Tonight," Smashing Pumpkins

Best Art Direction in a Video
K.K. Barrett and Wayne White "Tonight, Tonight," Smashing Pumpkins

Best Editing in a Video
Scott Grey, "Ironic," Alanis Morissette

Best Cinematography in a Video
Declan Quinn "Tonight, Tonight"

Gary Young

Tonight," the second was by Hole, while the third video was Gary Young's "Plant Man."

Wait a minute? Gary Young? "Plant Man"?

Directed by Tom Surgal, an under-appreciated master of the low-budget video, "Plant Man," is a truly insane clip made for Young, the manic ex-drummer for Pavement. In the video, an addled Young blithely strums a ukelele wearing a special-ly-tailored Astro Turf suit. Absurd and won-derful, it's precisely the kind of video one wants to see regularly on a music-video channel. When Young's record was released in 1995, the video might have been played a handful of times during overnight time slots on MTV. And, after all, *Pavement* bare-ly gets played on MTV.

"We all love the 'Plant Man' video. We're going to play it all the time," says Finnerty. "We're going to call Big Cat, or Matador, or whoever puts out 'Plant Man' records and say, 'We're making this guy a star and there's nothing you can do about it.'" If this playful approach heralds M2's programming policy, there may be hope for low-budget video directors — and fans of music video — everywhere. ∎

David Kleiler, Jr. is a music-video director and co-author of an upcoming book on music video.

1995 Radio and Records Charts

Radio and Records magazine compiles year-end charts based on radio play. The country charts, however, are based on number of plays and market size. The following titles got the most play in 1995.

ADULT CONTEMPORARY (AC)

1. **"Love Will Keep Us Alive"**
   Eagles
   (Geffen)

2. **"Believe"**
   Elton John
   (Rocket/Island)

3. **"Take a Bow"**
   Madonna
   (Maverick/Sire/WB)

4. **"Have You Ever Really Loved a Woman?"**
   Bryan Adams
   (A&M)

5. **"In the House of Stone and Light"**
   Martin Page
   (Mercury)

6. **"Colors of the Wind"**
   Vanessa Williams
   (Hollywood)

7. **"I Can Love You Like That"**
   All-4-One
   (Blitzz/Atlantic)

8. **"Kiss From a Rose"**
   Seal
   (ZTT/Sire/WB)

9. **"As I Lay Me Down"**
   Sophie B. Hawkins
   (Columbia/CRG)

10. **"Water Runs Dry"**
    Boyz II Men
    (Motown)

11. **"The Sweetest Days"**
    Vanessa Williams
    (Mercury)

12. **"Until the End of Time"**
    Foreigner
    (Generama/Rhythm Safari/Priority)

13. **"You Gotta Be"**
    Des'ree
    (550 Music)

14. **"On Bended Knee"**
    Boyz II Men
    (Motown)

Vanessa Williams

15. **"House of Love"**
    Amy Grant and Vince Gill
    (A&M)

16. **"I Believe"**
    Blessid Union of Souls
    (EMI)

17. **"Back for Good"**
    Take That
    (Arista)

18. **"I Could Fall in Love"**
    Selena
    (EMI Latin)

19. **"Learn to Be Still"**
    Eagles
    (Geffen)

20. **"Forever Tonight"**
    Peter Cetera with Crystal Bernard
    (River North)

HOT AC

1. **"In the House of Stone and Light"**
   Martin Page
   (Mercury)

2. **"I Know"**
   Dionne Farris
   (Columbia/CRG)

3. **"Kiss From a Rose"**
   Seal
   (ZTT/Sire/WB)

4. **"Have You Ever Really Loved a Woman?"**
   Bryan Adams
   (A&M)

5. **"I'll Be There for You"**
   Rembrandts
   (EastWest/EEG)

6. **"Hold My Hand"**
   Hootie & the Blowfish
   (Atlantic)

7. **"Take a Bow"**
   Madonna
   (Maverick/Sire/WB)

8. **"You Gotta Be"**
   Des'ree
   (550 Music)

9. **"As I Lay Me Down"**
   Sophie B. Hawkins
   (Columbia/CRG)

10. **"Love Will Keep Us Alive"**
    Eagles
    (Geffen)

11. **"Believe"**
    Elton John
    (Rocket/Island)

12. **"Run-Around"**
    Blues Traveler
    (A&M)

13. **"House of Love"**
    Amy Grant and Vince Gill
    (A&M)

14. **"I Believe"**
    Blessid Union of Souls
    (EMI)

15. **"I Can Love You Like That"**
    All-4-One
    (Blitzz/Atlantic)

16. **"Let Her Cry"**
    Hootie & the Blowfish
    (Atlantic)

17. **"Only Wanna Be With You"**
    Hootie & the Blowfish
    (Atlantic)

18. **"Colors of the Wind"**
    Vanessa Williams
    (Hollywood)

19. **"I'm the Only One"**
    Melissa Etheridge
    (Island)

20. **"Water Runs Dry"**
    Boyz II Men
    (Motown)

CONTEMPORARY HIT RADIO (CHR)/POP

1. **"I Know"**
Dionne Farris
(Columbia/CRG)

2. **"Run-Around"**
Blues Traveler
(A&M)

3. **"Kiss From a Rose"**
Seal
(ZTT/Sire/WB)

4. **"I Believe"**
Blessid Union of Souls
(EMI)

5. **"Water Runs Dry"**
Boyz II Men
(Motown)

6. **"Let Her Cry"**
Hootie & the Blowfish
(Atlantic)

7. **"When I Come Around"**
Green Day
(Reprise)

8. **"I'll Be There for You"**
Rembrandts
(EastWest/EEG)

9. **"Waterfalls"**
TLC
(LaFace/Arista)

10. **"Take a Bow"**
Madonna
(Maverick/Sire/WB)

11. **"I Can Love You Like That"**
All-4-One
(Blitzz/Atlantic)

12. **"Hold My Hand"**
Hootie & the Blowfish
(Atlantic)

13. **"Strong Enough"**
Sheryl Crow
(A&M)

14. **"Only Wanna Be With You"**
Hootie & the Blowfish
(Atlantic)

15. **"Hold On"**
Jamie Walters
(Atlantic)

16. **"Another Night"**
Real McCoy
(Arista)

17. **"Total Eclipse of the Heart"**
Nicki French
(Critique)

18. **"Lightning Crashes"**
Live
(Radioactive)

19. **"Have You Ever Really Loved a Woman?"**
Bryan Adams
(A&M)

20. **"December"**
Collective Soul
(Atlantic)

CHR/ RHYTHMIC

1. **"Waterfalls"**
TLC
(LaFace/Arista)

2. **"This Is How We Do It"**
Montell Jordan
(PMP/RAL/Island)

3. **"Water Runs Dry"**
Boyz II Men
(Motown)

4. **"Freak Like Me"**
Adina Howard
(EastWest/EEG)

5. **"Don't Take It Personal (Just One of Dem Days)"**
Monica
(Rowdy/Arista)

6. **"Candy Rain"**
Soul for Real
(Uptown/MCA)

7. **"Red Light Special"**
TLC
(LaFace/Arista)

8. **"Creep"**
TLC
(LaFace/Arista)

9. **"Every Little Thing I Do"**
Soul for Real
(Uptown/MCA)

10. **"He's Mine"**
Mokenstef
(OutBurst/RAL/Island)

11. **"Someone to Love"**
Jon B. and Babyface
(Yab Yum/550 Music)

12. **"If You Love Me"**
Brownstone
(MJJ/Epic)

13. **"Fantasy"**
Mariah Carey
(Columbia/CRG)

14. **"You Are Not Alone"**
Michael Jackson
(Epic)

15. **"On Bended Knee"**
Boyz II Men
(Motown)

16. **"Baby"**
Brandy
(Atlantic)

17. **"This Lil' Game We Play"**
Subway
(Biv 10/Motown)

18. **"I Can Love You Like That"**
All-4-One
(Blitzz/Atlantic)

19. **"Take a Bow"**
Madonna
(Maverick/Sire/WB)

20. **"Gangsta's Paradise"**
Coolio
(MCA)

ROCK

1. **"December"**
Collective Soul
(Atlantic)

2. **"Lightning Crashes"**
Live
(Radioactive)

Van Halen

Live

3. **"Better Man"**
   Pearl Jam
   (Epic)

4. **"And Fools Shine On"**
   Brother Cane
   (Virgin)

5. **"You Wreck Me"**
   Tom Petty
   (Warner Bros.)

6. **"Can't Stop Lovin' You"**
   Van Halen
   (Warner Bros.)

7. **"When I Come Around"**
   Green Day
   (Reprise)

8. **"Good"**
   Better Than Ezra
   (Swell/Elektra/EEG)

9. **"Gel"**
   Collective Soul
   (Atlantic)

10. **"Tomorrow"**
    Silverchair
    (Epic)

11. **"All Over You"**
    Live
    (Radioactive)

12. **"What Would You Say"**
    Dave Matthews Band
    (RCA)

13. **"Only Wanna Be With You"**
    Hootie & the Blowfish
    (Atlantic)

14. **"Misery"**
    Soul Asylum
    (Columbia/CRG)

15. **"Run-Around"**
    Blues Traveler
    (A&M)

16. **"Possum Kingdom"**
    Toadies
    (Interscope)

17. **"River of Deceit"**
    Mad Season
    (Columbia/CRG)

18. **"Everything Zen"**
    Bush
    (Trauma/Interscope)

19. **"Comedown"**
    Bush
    (Trauma/Interscope)

20. **"Hold Me, Thrill Me, Kiss Me, Kill Me"**
    U2
    (Atlantic/Island)

ALTERNATIVE

1. **"Tomorrow"**
   Silverchair
   (Epic)

2. **"Name"**
   Goo Goo Dolls
   (Metal Blade/WB)

3. **"Good"**
   Better Than Ezra
   (Swell/Elektra/EEG)

4. **"Comedown"**
   Bush
   (Trauma/Interscope)

5. **"You Oughta Know"**
   Alanis Morissette
   (Maverick/Reprise)

Joan Osborne

6. **"Lump"**
   The Presidents of the United States of America
   (Columbia/CRG)

7. **"Lightning Crashes"**
   Live
   (Radioactive)

8. **"December"**
   Collective Soul
   (Atlantic)

9. **"All Over You"**
   Live
   (Radioactive)

10. **"Molly"**
    Sponge
    (Work/CRG)

11. **"Connection"**
    Elastica
    (DGC/Geffen)

12. **"In the Blood"**
    Better Than Ezra
    (Swell/Elektra/EEG)

13. **"Possum Kingdom"**
    Toadies
    (Interscope)

14. **"Hand in My Pocket"**
    Alanis Morissette
    (Maverick/Reprise)

15. **"Sick of Myself"**
    Matthew Sweet
    (Zoo)

16. **"Little Things"**
    Bush
    (Trauma/Interscope)

17. **"Say It Ain't So"**
    Weezer
    (DGC/Geffen)

18. **"Live Forever"**
    Oasis
    (Epic)

19. **"Hold Me, Thrill Me, Kiss Me, Kill Me"**
    U2
    (Atlantic/Island)

20. **"Carnival"**
    Natalie Merchant
    (Elektra/EEG)

ADULT ALTERNATIVE ALBUMS

1. ***Under the Table and Dreaming***
   Dave Matthews Band
   (RCA)

2. ***Cracked Rear View***
   Hootie & the Blowfish
   (Atlantic)

Annie Lennox

3. *Wildflowers*
Tom Petty
(Warner Bros.)

4. *Tigerlily*
Natalie Merchant
(Elektra/EEG)

5. *Forever Blue*
Chris Isaak
(Reprise)

6. *Relish*
Joan Osborne
(Mercury)

7. *Twisted*
Del Amitri
(A&M)

8. *Tomorrow the Green Grass*
Jayhawks
(American/Reprise)

9. *Empire Records Soundtrack*
Various Artists
(A&M)

10. *Greatest Hits*
Bruce Springsteen
(Columbia/CRG)

11. *A Day at the Beach*
Sonia Dada
(Capricorn)

12. *Days Like This*
Van Morrison
(Polydor/A&M)

13. *Boys on the Side
Soundtrack*
Various Artists
(Arista)

14. *Four*
Blues Traveler
(A&M)

15. *Medusa*
Annie Lennox
(Arista)

16. *Collective Soul*
Collective Soul
(Atlantic)

17. *Monster*
R.E.M.
(WB)

18. *Let Your Dim Light Shine*
Soul Asylum
(Columbia/CRG)

19. *Hot House*
Bruce Hornsby
(RCA)

20. *Good News From the Next
World*
Simple Minds
(Virgin)

NEW AC

1. "Walkin' to Freedom"
Jazzmasters
(JVC)

2. "M.L. in the Sunshine"
Count Basic
(Instinct)

3. "After the Fall"
Incognito
(Verve Forecast)

4. "Exotica"
Paul Taylor
(Countdown/Unity)

5. "Worlds Outside"
Chris Botti
(Verve Forecast)

6. "Here to Stay"
Pat Metheny
(Geffen)

7. "This Masquerade"
David Sanborn
(Elektra/EEG)

8. "90 Degrees in the Shade"
Heavy Shift
(Discovery)

9. "Ariana"
Spyro Gyra
(GRP)

10. "Grace"
Nelson Rangell
(GRP)

11. "For Your Love"
Stevie Wonder
(Motown)

12. "Angel Eyes"
Jim Brickman
(Windham Hill)

13. "Midnight Sun"
Brian Culbertson
(Mesa/Bluemoon)

14. "Celebration"
Kevin Toney
(Ichiban)

15. "Can't Stop My Heart From
Loving You"
Aaron Neville
(A&M)

16. "Smooth Operator"
Greg Adams
(Epic)

17. "Faith in Us"
Slim Man
(GES)

18. "Safari"
Keiko Matsui
(White Cat/Unity)

19. "Phat City"
Chieli Minucci
(JVC)

20. "When You Love Someone"
Anita Baker and James
Ingram
(Elektra/EEG)

NEW AC
ALBUMS

1. *Beat Street*
Rick Braun
(Mesa/Bluemoon)

2. *Modern Life*
Brian Culbertson
(Mesa/Bluemoon)

3. *We Live Here*
Pat Metheny
(Geffen)

4. *Jazzmasters II*
Jazzmasters
(JVC)

5. *Hidden Agenda*
Greg Adams
(Epic)

6. *The Sweetest Days*
Vanessa Williams
(Mercury)

7. *Night Creatures*
Tom Scott
(GRP)

8. *West Side Stories*
Jeff Lorber
(Verve Forecast)

9. *First Wish*
Chris Botti
(Verve Forecast)

10. *Destiny*
Nelson Rangell
(GRP)

11. *After Dark*
Richard Elliot
(Blue Note)

12. *Truth*
Warren Hill
(RCA)

13. *Pearls*
David Sanborn
(Elektra/EEG)

14. *100 Degrees and Rising*
Incognito
(Verve Forecast)

15. *On the Horn*
Paul Taylor
(Countdown/Unity)

16. *Love & Other Obsessions*
Spyro Gyra
(GRP)

17. *Larry & Lee*
Lee Ritenour and Larry
Carlton
(GRP)

18. *The Tattooed Heart*
Aaron Neville
(A&M)

19. *I'll Be Over You*
Larry Coryell
(CTI)

20. *Urban Knights*
Urban Knights
(GRP)

U R B A N

1. "This Is How We Do It"
Montell Jordan
(PMP/RAL/Island)

2. "Don't Take It Personal (Just
One of Dem Days)"
Monica
(Rowdy/Arista)

3. "Ask of You"
Raphael Saadiq
(550 Music/Epic ST)

4. "Waterfalls"
TLC
(LaFace/Arista)

Brandy

5. "He's Mine"
Mokenstef
(OutBurst/RAL/Island)

6. "Candy Rain"
Soul for Real
(Uptown/MCA)

7. "Best Friend"
Brandy
(Atlantic)

8. "Freak Like Me"
Adina Howard
(EastWest/EEG)

9. "Baby"
Brandy
(Atlantic)

10. "Grapevyne"
Brownstone
(MJJ/Epic)

11. "Water Runs Dry"
Boyz II Men
(Motown)

12. "If You Love Me"
Brownstone
(MJJ/Epic)

13. "Red Light Special"
TLC
(LaFace/Arista)

14. "I Like"
Kut Klose
(Elektra/EEG)

15. "Can't You See"
Total featuring The
Notorious B.I.G.
(Tommy Boy)

16. "Crazy Love"
Brian McKnight
(Mercury)

17. "Tell Me"
Groove Theory
(Epic)

18. "Someone to Love"
Jon B. and Babyface
(Yab Yum/550 Music)

19. "You Used to Love Me"
Faith Evans
(Bad Boy/Arista)

20. "You Are Not Alone"
Michael Jackson
(Epic)

C O U N T R Y

1. "Party Crowd"
David Lee Murphy
(MCA)

2. "Not on Your Love"
Jeff Carson
(MCG/Curb)

3. "Thinkin' About You"
Trisha Yearwood
(MCA)

4. "Someone Else's Star"
Bryan White
(Asylum/EEG)

5. "What Mattered Most"
Ty Herndon
(Epic)

6. "Tell Me I Was Dreaming"
Travis Tritt
(WB)

7. "In Between Dances"
Pam Tillis
(Arista)

8. "This Woman and
This Man"
Clay Walker
(Giant)

9. "I Can Love You Like That"
John Michael Montgomery
(Atlantic)

10. "That Ain't My Truck"
Rhett Akins
(Decca)

11. "I Didn't Know My Own
Strength"
Lorrie Morgan
(BNA)

12. "A Little Bit of You"
Lee Roy Parnell
(Career)

13. "If I Were You"
Collin Raye
(Epic)

14. "Sold (The Grundy County
Auction Incident)"
John Michael Montgomery
(Atlantic)

15. "Song for the Life"
Alan Jackson
(Arista)

16. "The Keeper of the Stars"
Tracy Byrd
(MCA)

17. "They're Playin' Our Song"
Neal McCoy
(Atlantic)

18. "Safe in the Arms of Love"
Martina McBride
(RCA)

19. "If the World Had a Front
Porch"
Tracy Lawrence
(Atlantic)

20. "Give Me One More Shot"
Alabama
(RCA)

Rock Comes of Age

■ BY BETH ROWEN

ROCK GREW UP ON SEPTEMBER 1, 1995, and some music fans and industry types are not pleased with its new maturity level. Long considered the voice of the rebellious, rock became an institution with the opening of Cleveland's $92-million Rock and Roll Hall of Fame and Museum.

Few can deny that rock has gone mainstream. But for some of rock's legends, it was painful to admit that it had become so commercialized and corporate. Bob Dylan, Van Morrison and the Sex Pistols' John Lydon openly embraced that sentiment, choosing to shun the weekend's festivities.

The Rock Hall of Fame and Museum

"It should be titled the Hall of Shame," said Lydon. "Institutionalized rock is something to be ashamed of. We're not here to be nice to the mums and dads. [Rock] is the only chance we get to say what we really mean."

But even the most ardent naysayers have to admit that the museum and its holdings are dazzling. Architect I. M. Pei designed the 150,000-square foot, 7-story futuristic structure that sits on the banks of Lake Erie. From the air, the museum resembles a record player complete with a turntable, tone arm and pile of 45s. From the ground, the structure is an imposing mass of geometric shapes that jut out in every direction.

The museum's constantly evolving exhibits chronicle the history of rock using state-of-the-art interactive and multimedia technology. One of the most enjoyable and educational is The Beat Goes On, a multimedia touchscreen exhibit that provides audio and video footage of artists and the musicians that influenced them. The Blank Generation exhibit explores punk's London and New York roots. Other exhibits highlight regional music that exploded into new genres — Detroit's Motown, San Francisco's psychedelic scene, New York's rap and Seattle's grunge.

Also among the 3,500 items on display are John Lennon's lime-green Sgt. Pepper's uniform; one of his early report cards that deemed him "hopeless;" a replica of Memphis's Sun Studios, where Elvis Presley recorded his first records; Michael Jackson's sequined jacket; and Janis Joplin's

1996 INDUCTEES TO THE ROCK AND ROLL HALL OF FAME

David Bowie

David Bowie
Jefferson Airplane
Gladys Knight and the Pips
Little Willie John
Pink Floyd
Shirelles
Velvet Underground

Nonperformer
Tom Donahue

Early Influence
Pete Seeger

Porsche. The top level of the museum, reached by conquering a towering spiral staircase, features a shrine-like tribute to the 130 Hall of Fame inductees. Engraved into a black wall is the signature of each honoree.

A weekend of nonstop events celebrating the museum's opening was highlighted by a seven-hour megaconcert attended by 67,000 fans who paid between $80 and $540 per ticket. Performers included Chuck Berry, Bruce Springsteen, James Brown, Melissa Etheridge, John Mellencamp, Aretha Franklin, Bruce Hornsby, Johnny Cash, Jon Bon Jovi, Martha and the Vendellas, Annie Lennox, Jerry Lee Lewis, Little Richard, John Fogerty and Robbie Robertson. Springsteen and Berry opened the superstar concert jamming on "Johnny B. Goode." Etheridge was the real crowd-pleaser, asking "Remember when rock 'n' roll wore a dress?" before belting out "Be My Baby." Lou Reed was in top form singing "Sweet Jane."

The opening culminated a long, often rocky trip. In 1983, *Rolling Stone* editor Jann Wenner and Ahmet Ertegun, president of Atlantic Records, formed the Rock and Roll Hall of Fame Foundation to recognize those figures who have contributed to the energy and evolution of rock music. They selected the first inductees in 1986 and in the same year chose Cleveland as the site over Memphis and New York. After 12 years, a three-year groundbreaking delay and three museum directors, their dream became reality. In the interim, the foundation conducted all of its business — organizing the nomination process, planning the annual induction event and dealing with the press — from a cramped New York office.

Why Cleveland? There are two reasons. Local DJ Alan Freed popularized the term rock and roll there in the 1950s. Though it sounds good, it wasn't the driving force behind the decision. It was the almighty buck. Cleveland raised somewhere around $65 million in public funds to finance the project.

For all the controversy surrounding the idea of a rock museum, in its first year it has drawn nearly one million music fans who have spent an average of four hours roaming, reading, listening and reminiscing. ∎

Visit the Rock and Roll Hall of Fame and Museum at its Web site: http://www.rockhall.com

1995 BLUES FOUNDATION HALL OF FAME INDUCTEES

Koko Taylor

Classics of Blues Recordings (Albums)
Boss of the Blues, Big Joe Turner (Atlantic)
Otis Spann Is the Blues, Otis Spann (Candid)

Classics of Blues Recordings (Singles)
"Wang Dang Doodle," Koko Taylor
"I'm a King Bee," Slim Harpo

Classics of Blues Literature
The Land Where the Blues Began, Alan Lomax
Searching for Robert Johnson, Peter Guralnick

Individuals: Performers
Jimmy Rogers

Individuals: Nonperformers
Leonard and Phil Chess

Inside the Rock and Roll Hall of Fame and Museum

500 Songs That Shaped Rock

James Henke, chief curator for the Rock and Roll Hall of Fame, with the help of music writers and critics, selected 500 songs (not only rock songs) that they believe have been most influential in shaping rock and roll. The list is alphabetical by artist.

A

AC/DC, **"Back in Black"**

AC/DC, **"Highway to Hell"**

Roy Acuff and the Smoky Mountain Boys, **"Wabash Cannonball"**

Aerosmith, **"Dream On"**

Aerosmith, **"Toys in the Attic"**

Afrika Bambaataa, **"Planet Rock"**

The Allman Brothers Band, **"Ramblin' Man"**

The Allman Brothers Band, **"Whipping Post"**

The Animals, **"The House of the Rising Sun"**

The Animals, **"We Gotta Get Out of This Place"**

Louis Armstrong, **"West End Blues"**

Arrested Development, **"Tennessee"**

B

The B-52's, **"Rock Lobster"**

LaVern Baker, **"Jim Dandy"**

Hank Ballard and the Midnighters, **"Work With Me Annie"**

The Band, **"The Night They Drove Old Dixie Down"**

The Band, **"The Weight"**

Beach Boys, **"California Girls"**

Beach Boys, **"Don't Worry Baby"**

Beach Boys, **"God Only Knows"**

Beach Boys, **"Good Vibrations"**

Beach Boys, **"Surfin' U.S.A."**

The Beastie Boys, **"(You Gotta) Fight for Your Right (to Party)"**

The Beatles, **"A Day in the Life"**

The Beatles, **"Help!"**

The B-52's

The Beatles, **"Hey Jude"**

The Beatles, **"I Want to Hold Your Hand"**

The Beatles, **"Norwegian Wood"**

The Beatles, **"Yesterday"**

The Beau Brummels, **"Laugh Laugh"**

Beck, **"Loser"**

Jeff Beck Group, **"Plynth (Water Down the Drain)"**

The Bee Gees, **"Stayin' Alive"**

Archie Bell and the Drells, **"Tighten Up"**

Chuck Berry, **"Johnny B. Goode"**

Chuck Berry, **"Maybelline"**

Chuck Berry, **"Rock and Roll Music"**

The Big Bopper, **"Chantilly Lace"**

Big Brother and the Holding Company, **"Piece of My Heart"**

Big Star, **"September Gurls"**

Black Sabbath, **"Iron Man"**

Black Sabbath, **"Paranoid"**

Bobby Blue Bland, **"Turn On Your Love Light"**

Blondie, **"Heart of Glass"**

Kurtis Blow, **"The Breaks"**

Gary U.S. Bonds, **"Quarter to Three"**

Booker T. & the M.G.'s, **"Green Onions"**

Boston, **"More Than a Feeling"**

David Bowie, **"Fame"**

David Bowie, **"Space Oddity"**

David Bowie, **"Ziggy Stardust"**

The Box Tops, **"The Letter"**

Charles Brown, **"Driftin' Blues"**

James Brown, **"I Got You (I Feel Good)"**

James Brown, **"Please, Please, Please"**

James Brown, **"Say It Loud—I'm Black and I'm Proud"**

Ruth Brown, **"Mama, He Treats Your Daughter Mean"**

Jackson Browne, **"Late for the Sky"**

Buffalo Springfield, **"For What It's Worth"**

Solomon Burke, **"Everybody Needs Somebody to Love"**

Johnny Burnette Trio, **"Train Kept a-Rollin'"**

The Byrds, **"Eight Miles High"**

The Byrds, **"Hickory Wind"**

The Byrds, **"Mr. Tambourine Man"**

C

Johnny Cash, **"Folsom Prison Blues"**

Johnny Cash, **"I Walk the Line"**

The Champs, **"Tequila"**

Gene Chandler, **"Duke of Earl"**

The Chantays, **"Pipeline"**

Ray Charles, **"Hallelujah I Love Her So"**

Ray Charles, **"I Got a Woman"**

Ray Charles, **"What'd I Say"**

Chubby Checker, **"The Twist"**

Chic, **"Le Freak"**

Charlie Christian with The Benny Goodman Orchestra, **"Solo Flight"**

Eric Clapton, **"After Midnight"**

Dave Clark Five, **"Glad All Over"**

The Clash, **"London Calling"**

Jimmy Cliff, **"Many Rivers to Cross"**

Jimmy Cliff, **"The Harder They Come"**

Patsy Cline, **"I Fall to Pieces"**

The Clovers, **"Love Potion No. 9"**

The Coasters, **"Yakety Yak"**

The Coasters, **"Young Blood"**

Eddie Cochran, **"C'mon Everybody"**

Eddie Cochran, **"Summertime Blues"**

Joe Cocker, **"With a Little Help From My Friends"**

The Contours, **"Do You Love Me"**

Sam Cooke, **"A Change Is Gonna Come"**

Sam Cooke, **"Bring It on Home to Me"**

Sam Cooke, **"You Send Me"**

Alice Cooper, **"I'm Eighteen"**

Elvis Costello, **"Pump It Up"**

The Count Five, **"Psychotic Reaction"**

Country Joe and the Fish, **"The Fish Cheer and I-Feel-Like-I'm Fixin'-to-Die Rag"**

Don Covay, **"Mercy Mercy"**

Cream, **"Crossroads"**

Cream, **"Sunshine of Your Love"**

Creedence Clearwater Revival, **"Fortunate Son"**

Creedence Clearwater Revival, **"Green River"**

Creedence Clearwater Revival, **"Proud Mary"**

Crosby, Stills and Nash, **"Suite: Judy Blue Eyes"**

Crosby, Stills, Nash and Young, **"Ohio"**

The Crows, **"Gee"**

The Crystals, **"Da Doo Ron Ron (When He Walked Me Home)"**

The Crystals, **"He's a Rebel"**

Culture Club, **"Time (Clock of the Heart)"**

D

Dick Dale and the Del-Tones, **"Let's Go Trippin'"**

The Damned, **"New Rose"**

Danny & the Juniors, **"At the Hop"**

Bobby Darin, **"Splish Splash"**

Spencer Davis Group, **"Gimme Some Lovin'"**

De La Soul, **"Me Myself and I"**

Deep Purple, **"Smoke on the Water"**

The Dell-Vikings, **"Come Go With Me"**

The Dells, **"Oh, What a Night"**

The Delmore Brothers, **"Hillbilly Boogie"**

Derek and the Dominos, **"Layla"**

Devo, **"Whip It"**

Bo Diddley, **"Bo Diddley"**

Dion and the Belmonts, **"A Teenager in Love"**

Dire Straits, **"Sultans of Swing"**

The Dixie Cups, **"Chapel of Love"**

The Dixie Hummingbirds, **"I'll Live Again"**

Bill Doggett, **"Honky Tonk"**

Fats Domino, **"Ain't That a Shame"**

Fats Domino, **"Blueberry Hill"**

The Dominoes, **"Sixty Minute Man"**

Lonnie Donegan, **"Rock Island Line"**

Donovan, **"Sunshine Superman"**

The Doors, **"Light My Fire"**

The Doors, **"The End"**

Dr. Dre, **"Nuthin' but a 'G' Thang"**

Dr. John, **"Right Place Wrong Time"**

The Drifters, **"Money Honey"**

The Drifters, **"There Goes My Baby"**

The Drifters, **"Up on the Roof"**

Duran Duran, **"Hungry Like the Wolf"**

Crosby, Stills and Nash

Bob Dylan, **"Blowin' in the Wind"**

Bob Dylan, **"Like a Rolling Stone"**

Bob Dylan, **"Subterranean Homesick Blues"**

Bob Dylan, **"Tangled Up in Blue"**

Bob Dylan, **"The Times They Are a-Changin'"**

E

The Eagles, **"Hotel California"**

The Eagles, **"Take It Easy"**

Duane Eddy, **"Rebel Rouser"**

Eurythmics, **"Sweet Dreams (Are Made of This)"**

The Everly Brothers, **"All I Have to Do Is Dream"**

The Everly Brothers, **"Bye Bye Love"**

F

The 5 Satins, **"In the Still of the Night"**

The Flamingos, **"I Only Have Eyes for You"**

Fleetwood Mac, **"Go Your Own Way"**

The Flying Burrito Brothers, **"Sin City"**

The 4 Seasons, **"Big Girls Don't Cry"**

The 4 Seasons, **"Walk Like a Man"**

The Four Tops, **"Baby I Need Your Loving"**

The Four Tops, **"Reach Out I'll Be There"**

Aretha Franklin, **"Chain of Fools"**

Aretha Franklin, **"I Never Loved a Man (the Way I Love You)"**

Aretha Franklin, **"Respect"**

Free, **"All Right Now"**

The Bobby Fuller Four, **"I Fought the Law"**

Lowell Fulson, **"Reconsider Baby"**

Funkadelic, **"One Nation Under a Groove"**

G

Peter Gabriel, **"Biko"**

Cecil Gant, **"We're Gonna Rock"**

Marvin Gaye, **"I Heard It Through the Grapevine"**

Marvin Gaye, **"Sexual Healing"**

Marvin Gaye, **"What's Going On"**

Gerry and the Pacemakers, **"How Do You Do It?"**

Gary Glitter, **"Rock 'n' Roll Part 2"**

Go-Go's, **"We Got the Beat"**

Golden Gate Quartet, **"Rock My Soul"**

Grand Funk Railroad, **"We're an American Band"**

Grandmaster Flash and the Furious Five, **"The Message"**

The Grateful Dead, **"Dark Star"**

The Grateful Dead, **"Uncle John's Band"**

Al Green, **"Let's Stay Together"**

Guitar Slim, **"The Things That I Used to Do"**

Guns N' Roses, **"Welcome to the Jungle"**

Woody Guthrie, **"Pastures of Plenty"**

Woody Guthrie, **"Pretty Boy Floyd"**

Woody Guthrie, **"This Land Is Your Land"**

H

Bill Haley and His Comets, **"(We're Gonna) Rock Around the Clock"**

Slim Harpo, **"Rainin' in My Heart"**

Wynonie Harris, **"Good Rockin' Tonight"**

Wilbert Harrison, **"Kansas City"**

Dale Hawkins, **"Suzy-Q"**

Screamin' Jay Hawkins, **"I Put a Spell on You"**

Richard Hell & the Voidoids, **"(I Belong to the) Blank Generation"**

Jimi Hendrix, **"All Along the Watchtower"**

Peter Gabriel

Jimi Hendrix, **"Purple Haze"**

Jimi Hendrix, **"Voodoo Child (Slight Return)"**

The Hollies, **"Bus Stop"**

Buddy Holly, **"Peggy Sue"**

Buddy Holly and The Crickets, **"That'll Be the Day"**

John Lee Hooker, **"Boogie Chillun"**

John Lee Hooker, **"Boom Boom"**

Howlin' Wolf, **"Smokestack Lightnin'"**

Howlin' Wolf, **"Spoonful"**

Howlin' Wolf, **"The Red Rooster"**

Human League, **"Don't You Want Me?"**

Mississippi John Hurt, **"Stack o' Lee Blues"**

Hüsker Dü, **"Turn on the News"**

I

The Impressions, **"People Get Ready"**

The Ink Spots, **"If I Didn't Care"**

Iron Butterfly, **"In-a-Gadda-da-Vida"**

The Isley Brothers, **"It's Your Thing"**

The Isley Brothers, **"Shout — Parts 1 & 2"**

J

Jackson 5, **"ABC"**

Jackson 5, **"I Want You Back"**

Mahalia Jackson, **"Move on Up a Little Higher"**

Michael Jackson, **"Beat It"**

Michael Jackson, **"Billie Jean"**

Elmore James, **"Dust My Broom"**

Elmore James, **"Shake Your Moneymaker"**

Etta James, **"Tell Mama"**

Rick James, **"Super Freak"**

Tommy James and the Shondells, **"Hanky Panky"**

Jan & Dean, **"Surf City"**

Jane's Addiction, **"Been Caught Stealin'"**

Jefferson Airplane, **"Somebody to Love"**

Jefferson Airplane, **"White Rabbit"**

Blind Lemon Jefferson, **"Matchbox Blues"**

Jethro Tull, **"Aqualung"**

Joan Jett and the Blackhearts, **"I Love Rock 'n' Roll"**

Billy Joel, **"Just the Way You Are"**

Elton John, **"Bennie and the Jets"**

Elton John, **"Your Song"**

Little Willie John, **"Fever"**

Blind Willie Johnson, **"Motherless Children"**

Robert Johnson, **"Crossroads Blues"**

Robert Johnson, **"Hell Hound on My Trail"**

Robert Johnson, **"Love in Vain"**

Robert Johnson, **"Sweet Home Chicago"**

Louis Jordan and His Tympany Five, **"Caldonia"**

Louis Jordan and His Tympany Five, **"Saturday Night Fish Fry"**

Joy Division, **"Love Will Tear Us Apart"**

K

Albert King, **"Born Under a Bad Sign"**

B.B. King, **"Sweet Little Angel"**

B.B. King, **"The Thrill Is Gone"**

Ben E. King, **"Spanish Harlem"**

Ben E. King, **"Stand by Me"**

Carole King, **"You've Got a Friend"**

Freddy King, **"Hide Away"**

The Kingsmen, **"Louie Louie"**

The Kinks, **"A Well Respected Man"**

The Kinks, **"Lola"**

The Kinks, **"You Really Got Me"**

Kiss, **"Rock and Roll All Nite"**

Buddy Knox, **"Party Doll"**

Kraftwerk, **"Autobahn"**

L

LL Cool J, **"Mama Said Knock You Out"**

Cyndi Lauper, **"Girls Just Want to Have Fun"**

Leadbelly, **"The Midnight Special"**

Led Zeppelin, **"Dazed and Confused"**

Led Zeppelin, **"Rock and Roll"**

Led Zeppelin, **"Stairway to Heaven"**

Led Zeppelin, **"Whole Lotta Love"**

The Left Banke, **"Walk Away Renee"**

John Lennon, **"Give Peace a Chance"**

John Lennon, **"Imagine"**

John Lennon, **"Instant Karma (We All Shine On)"**

Jerry Lee Lewis, **"Great Balls of Fire"**

Jerry Lee Lewis, **"Whole Lotta Shakin' Goin' On"**

Little Eva, **"The Loco-Motion"**

Little Feat, **"Dixie Chicken"**

Little Walter, **"Juke"**

Professor Longhair, **"Tipitina"**

The Lovin' Spoonful, **"Do You Believe in Magic"**

Frankie Lymon and the Teenagers, **"I'm Not a Juvenile Delinquent"**

Frankie Lymon and The Teenagers, **"Why Do Fools Fall in Love"**

Lynyrd Skynyrd, **"Free Bird"**

M

Madonna, **"Like a Virgin"**

The Mamas and the Papas, **"California Dreamin'"**

The Marcels, **"Blue Moon"**

Bob Marley and The Wailers, **"Lively Up Yourself"**

Bob Marley and The Wailers, **"No Woman, No Cry"**

Martha and the Vandellas, **"Dancing in the Street"**

Martha and the Vandellas, **"(Love Is Like a) Heat Wave"**

Curtis Mayfield, **"Superfly"**

M.C. Hammer, **"U Can't Touch This"**

Paul McCartney, **"Maybe I'm Amazed"**

Barry McGuire, **"Eve of Destruction"**

Don McLean, **"American Pie"**

Jackson Five

Blind Willie McTell, "Statesboro Blues"

John Cougar Mellencamp, "Authority Song"

Metallica, "Enter Sandman"

Midnight Oil, "Beds Are Burning"

Amos Milburn, "Let's Have a Party"

Steve Miller Band, "Fly Like an Eagle"

The Miracles, "Going to a Go-Go"

The Miracles, "The Tracks of My Tears"

The Miracles, "You've Really Got a Hold on Me"

Joni Mitchell, "Help Me"

Moby Grape, "Omaha"

The Monkees, "I'm a Believer"

The Monkees, "Last Train to Clarksville"

The Monotones, "Book of Love"

Bill Monroe, "Mule Skinner Blues"

The Moody Blues, "Nights in White Satin"

The Moonglows, "Sincerely"

Van Morrison, "Brown Eyed Girl"

Van Morrison, "Madame George"

Van Morrison, "Moondance"

The Mothers of Invention, "Brown Shoes Don't Make It"

Mott the Hoople, "All the Young Dudes"

N

Ricky Nelson, "Hello Mary Lou"

Aaron Neville, "Tell It Like It Is"

New York Dolls, "Personality Crisis"

Randy Newman, "Sail Away"

Nirvana, "Smells Like Teen Spirit"

O

O'Jays, "Love Train"

Phil Ochs, "I Ain't Marchin' Anymore"

Pink Floyd

Roy Orbison, "Oh, Pretty Woman"

The Orioles, "Crying in the Chapel"

Johnny Otis, "Willie and the Hand Jive"

P

Parliament, "Give Up the Funk (Tear the Roof off the Sucker)"

Les Paul and Mary Ford, "How High the Moon"

Pearl Jam, "Jeremy"

The Penguins, "Earth Angel (Will You Be Mine)"

Carl Perkins, "Blue Suede Shoes"

Carl Perkins, "Matchbox"

Pinetop Perkins, "Pinetop's Boogie Woogie"

Peter and Gordon, "A World Without Love"

Peter, Paul and Mary, "If I Had a Hammer (The Hammer Song)"

Tom Petty and the Heartbreakers, "American Girl"

Wilson Pickett, "In the Midnight Hour"

Pink Floyd, "Another Brick in the Wall, Part 2"

Pink Floyd, "Money"

Pink Floyd, "See Emily Play"

The Platters, "The Great Pretender"

The Police, "Every Breath You Take"

The Police, "Roxanne"

Elvis Presley, "Heartbreak Hotel"

Elvis Presley, "Jailhouse Rock"

Elvis Presley, "Love Me Tender"

Elvis Presley, "Mystery Train"

Elvis Presley, "Suspicious Minds"

Elvis Presley, "That's All Right"

The Pretenders, "Brass in Pocket"

Lloyd Price, "Lawdy Miss Clawdy"

Prince, "Little Red Corvette"

Prince, "When Doves Cry"

Procol Harum, "A Whiter Shade of Pale"

Public Enemy, "Fight the Power"

Q

Queen, "Bohemian Rhapsody"

Queen Latifah, "Ladies First"

Question Mark and the Mysterians, "96 Tears"

Quicksilver Messenger Service, "Who Do You Love"

R

R.E.M., "Losing My Religion"

R.E.M., "Radio Free Europe"

Ma Rainey and Her Tub Jug Washboard Band, "Prove It on Me Blues"

Bonnie Raitt, "Something to Talk About"

Ramones, "Sheena Is a Punk Rocker"

The Young Rascals, **"Groovin'"**

The Young Rascals, **"Good Lovin'"**

Red Hot Chili Peppers, **"Give It Away"**

Otis Redding, **"Shake"**

Otis Redding, **"(Sittin' on) The Dock of the Bay"**

Otis Redding, **"Try a Little Tenderness"**

Jimmy Reed, **"Big Boss Man"**

Jimmy Reed, **"Bright Lights, Big City"**

Lou Reed, **"Walk on the Wild Side"**

The Replacements, **"I Will Dare"**

Paul Revere and The Raiders, **"Just Like Me"**

Cliff Richard and the Shadows, **"Move It"**

Little Richard, **"Good Golly, Miss Molly"**

Little Richard, **"Long Tall Sally"**

Little Richard, **"Tutti Frutti"**

The Righteous Brothers, **"You've Lost That Lovin' Feelin'"**

Billy Riley and His Little Green Men, **"Red Hot"**

Jimmie Rodgers, **"Blue Yodel No. 9"**

The Rolling Stones, **"Honky Tonk Women"**

The Rolling Stones, **"(I Can't Get No) Satisfaction"**

The Rolling Stones, **"Jumpin' Jack Flash"**

The Rolling Stones, **"Miss You"**

The Rolling Stones, **"Sympathy for the Devil"**

The Rolling Stones, **"Time Is on My Side"**

The Ronettes, **"Be My Baby"**

Roxy Music, **"Love Is the Drug"**

Run-D.M.C., **"Walk This Way"**

Rush, **"The Spirit of Radio"**

Otis Rush, **"I Can't Quit You Baby"**

Mitch Ryder and the Detroit Wheels, **"Devil With a Blue Dress On/Good Golly Miss Molly"**

S

Sam and Dave, **"Soul Man"**

Sam the Sham and the Pharoahs, **"Wooly Bully"**

Santana, **"Black Magic Woman/Gypsy Queen"**

The Searchers, **"Needles and Pins"**

The Seeds, **"Pushin' Too Hard"**

Pete Seeger, **"Where Have All the Flowers Gone"**

Bob Seger and the Silver Bullet Band, **"Night Moves"**

Sex Pistols, **"Anarchy in the U.K."**

Sex Pistols, **"God Save the Queen"**

The Shadows of Knight, **"Gloria"**

The Shangri-Las, **"Leader of the Pack"**

Del Shannon, **"Runaway"**

Shirelles, **"Dedicated to the One I Love"**

Shirelles, **"Will You Love Me Tomorrow"**

Simon and Garfunkel, **"Bridge Over Troubled Water"**

Simon and Garfunkel, **"The Sounds of Silence"**

Paul Simon, **"Graceland"**

Sir Douglas Quintet, **"She's About a Mover"**

Sister Sledge, **"We Are Family"**

Percy Sledge, **"When a Man Loves a Woman"**

Sly and the Family Stone, **"Dance to the Music"**

Sly and the Family Stone, **"Thank You (Falettinme Be Mice Elf Agin)"**

Bessie Smith, **"Downhearted Blues"**

Huey "Piano" Smith & His Clowns, **"Rockin' Pneumonia and the Boogie-Woogie Flu"**

Patti Smith, **"Gloria (in Excelsis Deo)"**

The Smiths, **"Heaven Knows I'm Miserable Now"**

Sonic Youth, **"Teenage Riot"**

The Soul Stirrers, **"By and By"**

Bruce Springsteen, **"Born to Run"**

Bruce Springsteen, **"Dancing in the Dark"**

Bruce Springsteen, **"Rosalita (Come Out Tonight)"**

The Standells, **"Dirty Water"**

The Staple Singers, **"Respect Yourself"**

Edwin Starr, **"War"**

Steely Dan, **"Reelin' in the Years"**

Steppenwolf, **"Born to Be Wild"**

Rod Stewart, **"Maggie May"**

Iggy and The Stooges, **"Search and Destroy"**

The Stooges, **"I Wanna Be Your Dog"**

Stray Cats, **"Rock This Town"**

Barrett Strong, **"Money (That's What I Want)"**

The Sugarhill Gang, **"Rapper's Delight"**

Run-D.M.C.

The Who

Donna Summer, **"Love to Love You Baby"**

The Supremes, **"Stop! In the Name of Love"**

The Supremes, **"You Can't Hurry Love"**

The Surfaris, **"Wipe Out"**

Swinging Blue Jeans, **"Hippy Hippy Shake"**

T

T. Rex, **"Bang a Gong (Get It On)"**

Talking Heads, **"Life During Wartime"**

Talking Heads, **"Once in a Lifetime"**

James Taylor, **"Fire and Rain"**

Television, **"Little Johnny Jewel"**

The Temptations, **"Ain't Too Proud to Beg"**

The Temptations, **"My Girl"**

The Temptations, **"Papa Was a Rollin' Stone"**

Sister Rosetta Tharpe, **"This Train"**

Willie Mae **"Big Mama"** Thornton, **"Ball 'n' Chain"**

Willie Mae **"Big Mama"** Thornton, **"Hound Dog"**

Toots and the Maytals, **"Pressure Drop"**

Peter Tosh, **"Legalize It"**

Traffic, **"Dear Mr. Fantasy"**

The Trammps, **"Disco Inferno"**

The Troggs, **"Wild Thing"**

Big Joe Turner, **"Shake, Rattle and Roll"**

Ike and Tina Turner, **"River Deep, Mountain High"**

The Turtles, **"It Ain't Me Babe"**

U

U.T.F.O., **"Roxanne, Roxanne"**

U2, **"I Still Haven't Found What I'm Looking For"**

U2, **"Pride (In the Name of Love)"**

U2, **"Sunday Bloody Sunday"**

V

Ritchie Valens, **"La Bamba"**

Van Halen, **"Jump"**

Van Halen, **"Runnin' With the Devil"**

Stevie Ray Vaughan, **"Pride and Joy"**

Velvet Underground, **"Heroin"**

Velvet Underground, **"White Light/White Heat"**

The Ventures, **"Walk Don't Run"**

Gene Vincent and His Blue Caps, **"Be-Bop-a-Lula"**

W

The Wailers, **"Get Up Stand Up"**

The Wailers, **"I Shot the Sheriff"**

Jr. Walker and the All Stars, **"Shotgun"**

T-Bone Walker, **"Call It Stormy Monday"**

War, **"Slippin' Into Darkness"**

Clara Ward and the Ward Singers, **"How I Got Over"**

Dinah Washington, **"Am I Asking Too Much"**

Muddy Waters, **"Got My Mojo Working"**

Muddy Waters, **"Hoochie Coochie Man"**

Muddy Waters, **"Mannish Boy"**

Muddy Waters, **"Rollin' Stone"**

The Weavers, **"Goodnight Irene"**

Mary Wells, **"My Guy"**

The Who, **"Baba O'Riley"**

The Who, **"Go to the Mirror Boy"**

The Who, **"My Generation"**

Big Joe Williams, **"Baby Please Don't Go"**

Larry Williams, **"Bony Maronie"**

Marion Williams, **"Packing Up"**

Sonny Boy (John Lee) Williamson, **"Good Morning (Little) School Girl"**

Chuck Willis, **"C. C. Rider"**

Bob Wills and His Texas Playboys, **"Take Me Back to Tulsa"**

Jackie Wilson **"(Your Love Keeps Lifting Me) Higher and Higher"**

Stevie Wonder, **"Living for the City"**

Stevie Wonder, **"Master Blaster (Jammin')"**

Stevie Wonder, **"Superstition"**

Stevie Wonder, **"Uptight (Everything's Alright)"**

Link Wray, **"Rumble"**

X

X, **"Los Angeles"**

Y

Jimmy Yancey, **"Midnight Stomp"**

The Yardbirds, **"Shapes of Things"**

Yes, **"Roundabout"**

Neil Young, **"Down by the River"**

Neil Young, **"Heart of Gold"**

Neil Young, **"My My Hey Hey (Out of the Blue)"**

Z

ZZ Top, **"Legs"**

1995 Down Beat Readers Poll

The results of *Down Beat*'s Readers Poll appeared in the December 1995 issue of the magazine. "Beyond" categories honor performers outside the jazz world.

Jazz Musician of the Year
Joe Lovano

Jazz Album of the Year
Rush Hour, Joe Lovano and
   Gunther Schuller
   (Blue Note)

Jazz Acoustic Group
Charlie Haden/Quartet West

Jazz Electric Group
John Scofield

Jazz Big Band
McCoy Tyner

Composer
Henry Threadgill

Arranger
Toshiko Akiyoshi

Soprano Saxophone
Steve Lacy

Alto Saxophone
Phil Woods

Tenor Saxophone
Joe Lovano

Baritone Saxophone
Gerry Mulligan

Clarinet
Don Byron

Flute
James Newton

Trumpet
Roy Hargrove

Trombone
J.J. Johnson

Synthesizer
Herbie Hancock

Acoustic Piano
Tommy Flanagan

Organ
Jimmy Smith

Acoustic Guitar
John McLaughlin

Acoustic Bass
Charlie Haden

Electric Guitar
John Scofield

1995 JAZZ HALL OF FAME

1995 Readers Poll
J.J. Johnson

1995 Critics Poll
Julius Hemphill

Electric Bass
Steve Swallow

Drums
Elvin Jones

Percussion
Airto Moriera

Vibes
Milt Jackson

Violin
Stephane Grappelli

Miscellaneous Instrument
Toots Thielemans (harmonica)

Male Singer
Joe Williams

Female Singer
Cassandra Wilson

Vocal Group
Take 6

Blues/Soul/Rhythm and Blues Album of the Year
Slippin' In, Buddy Guy
   (Silvertone)

Blues/Soul/Rhythm and Blues Musician of the Year
Buddy Guy

Blues/Soul/Rhythm and Blues Group
B.B. King

Beyond Album of the Year
Palmas, Eddie Palmieri
   (Elektra/Nonesuch)

Beyond Musician of the Year
Dr. John

Beyond Group
Jerry Gonzalez Fort Apache Band

Joe Lovano

1996 Down Beat Critics Poll

The results of *Down Beat*'s Critics Poll appeared in the August 1996 issue of the magazine. TDWR indicates Talent Deserving Wider Recognition. "Beyond" categories honor performers outside the jazz world.

Jazz Artist of the Year
Joe Lovano
TDWR
James Carter

Jazz Album of the Year
Keith Jarrett Standards
Trio, *Keith Jarrett at
the Blue Note* (ECM)

Reissue of the Year
Miles Davis, *Complete
Live at the Plugged
Nickel* (Columbia)

Male Vocalist
Joe Williams
TDWR
Kevin Mahogany

Female Vocalist
Cassandra Wilson
TDWR
Diana Krall

Vocal Jazz Group
Take 6
TDWR
Sweet Honey in the
Rock

Acoustic Jazz Group
Charlie Haden's
Quartet West
TDWR
8 Bold Souls
Jacky Terrasson

Electric Jazz Group
John Scofield
TDWR
Medeski, Martin and
Wood

Big Band
Mingus Big Band
TDWR
Either/Orchestra

Arranger
Toshiko Akiyoshi
TDWR
Maria Schneider

Composer
Randy Weston
TDWR
Maria Schneider

Soprano Saxophone
Steve Lacy
TDWR
Jane Bunnett

Alto Saxophone
Phil Woods
TDWR
Kenny Garrett

Tenor Saxophone
Sonny Rollins
TDWR
James Carter

Baritone Saxophone
Hamiet Bluiett
TDWR
James Carter

Clarinet
Don Byron
TDWR
Ken Peplowski

Flute
James Newton
TDWR
Jane Bunnett

Trumpet
Tom Harrell
TDWR
Nicholas Payton

Trombone
J.J. Johnson
TDWR
Frank Ku-umba Lacy

Piano
Keith Jarrett
TDWR
Jacky Terrasson

Organ
Jimmy Smith
TDWR
Barbara Dennerlein

Electric Keyboard
Herbie Hancock
TDWR
John Medeski

Guitar
Bill Frisell
TDWR
Howard Alden

Acoustic Bass
Charlie Haden
TDWR
Christian McBride

Electric Bass
Steve Swallow
TDWR
Eberhard Weber

Drums
Elvin Jones
TDWR
Leon Parker

Percussion
Trilok Gurtu
TDWR
Steve Berrios

Vibes
Milt Jackson
TDWR
Steve Nelson

Violin
Stephane Grappelli
TDWR
Regina Carter

**Miscellaneous
Instrument**
Toots Thielemans,
harmonica
TDWR
Howard Johnson, tuba

Blues Artist of the Year
B.B. King
TDWR
Lucky Peterson

Blues Album of the Year
Ronnie Earl, *Grateful
Heart* (Bullseye Blues)

Blues Group
Roomful of Blues
TDWR
Ronnie Earl and the
Broadcasters

**Beyond Artist of the
Year**
Cesaria Evora
TDWR
Cachao

**Beyond Album of the
Year (tie)**
Cachao, *Master
Sessions Volume II*
(Crescent Moon/Epic)
Los Lobos, *Colossal
Head* (Warner Bros.)

Beyond Group
Los Lobos
TDWR
Wayne Horvitz's
Pigpen

**Record Label of the
Year**
Verve

Record Producer
Michael Cuscuna
TDWR
Craig Street

1995 Gramophone Awards

The 1995 Gramophone Awards were presented on October 4, 1995, at London's Savoy Hotel and were listed in the November 1995 issue of the magazine.

CONCERTO (RECORD OF THE YEAR)
Prokofiev and Shostakovich, *Violin Concertos No. 1,* Mstislav Rostropovich conducting London Symphony Orchestra; solo: Vengerov (EMI)

BAROQUE VOCAL
Rameau, *Les Grands Motets,* William Christie conducting Les Arts Florissants (Erato)

BAROQUE NON-VOCAL
Biber, *Violin Sonatas,* Romanesca (Harmonia Mundi)

CHAMBER
Fauré, *Piano Quintets nos. 1–2,* Domus with Anthony Marwood (Hyperion)

CHORAL
Szymanowski, *Stabat Mater, Litany to the Virgin Mary, Symphony No. 3,* Sir Simon Rattle conducting City of Birmingham Symphony Orchestra and Chorus; solos: Szmytka, Quivar, Garrison and Connell (EMI Classics)

CONTEMPORARY
Ligeti, *Concertos for Cello, Violin, Piano,* Pierre Boulez conducting Ensemble InterContemporain; solos: Queyras, Gawriloff and Aimard (Deutsche Grammophon)

EARLY MUSIC
Fayrfax, *Missa O Quam Glorifica,* etc. The Cardinall's Musick/Andrew Carwood (ASV Gaudemus)

EARLY OPERA
Purcell, *King Arthur,* William Christie conducting Les Arts Florissants (Erato)

ENGINEERING
Szymanowski, *Stabat Mater, Litany to the Virgin Mary, Symphony No. 3,* Sir Simon Rattle conducting City of Birmingham Symphony Orchestra and Chorus; solos: Szmytka, Quivar, Garrison and Connell (EMI Classics)

HISTORIC VOCAL
Ravel, *L'Enfant et les Sortilèges,* Ernest Bour conducting French Radio National Chorus and Orchestra; solos: Sautereau, Scharley, Michel, Turba-Rabier, Verneuil, Vessières, Hadour, Peyron, Angelici, Legouhy and Prigent (Testament)

HISTORIC NON-VOCAL
Beethoven, *Symphony No. 9,* Lucerne Festival Chorus; Wilhelm Furtwängler conducting Philharmonia Orchestra; solos: Schwartzkopf, Haefliger and Edelmann (Tahra)

INSTRUMENTAL
Chopin, *Four Ballades,* Murray Perahia (Sony Classical)

MUSIC THEATER
I Wish It So, Dawn Upshaw (Elektra Nonesuch)

OPERA
Walton, *Troilus and Cressida,* Richard Hickox conducting Chorus of Opera North and English Northern Philharmonia; solos: Howarth, Davies, Bayley, Robson, Opie, Thornton, Owen-Lewis and Howard (Chandos)

ORCHESTRAL
Schoenberg, *Chamber Symphony No. 1,* Erwartung, Variations for Orchestra, Sir Simon Rattle conducting City of Birmingham Symphony Orchestra; solo: Bryn-Julson (EMI)

SOLO VOCAL
Schubert, *An Die Musik,* Bryn Terfel (Deutsche Grammophon)

VIDEO
The Art of Conducting/Great Conductors of the Past, Sir John Barbirolli, Sir Thomas Beecham, Leonard Bernstein, Fritz Busch, Wilhelm Furtwängler, Herbert von Karajan, Otto Klemperer, Serge Koussevitzky, Artur Nikisch, Fritz Reiner, Leopold Stokowski, Richard Strauss, George Szell, Arturo Toscanini, Bruno Walter and Felix Weingartner (Teldec)

BEST-SELLING RECORD
The Three Tenors in Concert, 1994, José Carreras, Plácido Domingo and Luciano Pavarotti; Zubin Mehta conducting Los Angeles Music Center Opera Chorus and Philharmonic Orchestra (EMI)

SPECIAL ACHIEVEMENT
Decca Entartete Musik project

ARTIST OF THE YEAR
Pierre Boulez

YOUNG ARTIST OF THE YEAR
Maxim Vengerov

LIFETIME ACHIEVEMENT
Sir Michael Tippett

Must-Have Recordings

One of the pleasures in life in the post-CD era is reassessing your record collection. The enormous volume of back-catalog recordings being released and compilations being assembled on disc means that music fans can more easily explore new types of music.

To help in that exploration, we've assembled a list of recordings you should consider. There have been literally millions of musical performances recorded since the advent of audio tape, and thousands are worthy of your attention. Our list is meant to suggest genres, time periods and artists that should be represented in your CD collection. The list is historical; we assume you're keeping up with current artists (and you've already read our survey of this year's significant recordings). Many of the artists have had their work compiled into greatest hits collections that you may want to purchase. We've avoided them (except when a collection is the most commonly available or desirable form) in order to suggest interesting periods in the artists' development.

CLASSICAL

Various, *Ancient Music for a Modern Age*, Sequentia (RCA Red Label)

Pachelbel, Handel, Vivaldi, Gluck, *Various Compositions,* Academy of Ancient Music/Christopher Hogwood (L'Oiseau Lyre)

Bach, *Goldberg Variations* (1955), Glenn Gould (Columbia)

Bach, *Brandenburg Concertos*, Amsterdam Baroque Orchestra/Tom Koopman (Erato)

Bach, *Unaccompanied Cello Suites,* Yo-Yo Ma (Columbia)

Mozart, *Don Giovanni*, Wachter, Sutherland, others; Philharmonia Orchestra and Chorus/Carlo Maria Giulini (EMI)

Mozart, *Requiem*, Academy of St. Martin's-in-the-Fields/Neville Marriner (London)

Beethoven, **Nine Symphonies** (complete cycle), Academy of Ancient Music/Christopher Hogwood (L'Oiseau Lyre) (This is a period instruments reading; classicists may want to consider the redoubtable Bruno Walter/Columbia 1959 cycle.)

Beethoven, **The Late String Quartets,** Guarneri Quartet (RCA Victor Gold Seal)

Schubert, *Symphony No. 8 (Unfinished)*, Royal Concertgebouw Orchestra/Leonard Bernstein (Deutsche Grammophon)

Brahms, *Symphony No. 1*, Berlin Philharmonic/Claudio Abbado (Deutsche Grammophon)

Bellini, *Norma*, Sutherland, Pavarotti, Caballe, Chorus and Orchestra of the Welsh National Opera/Bonynge (London)

Louis Armstrong

Verdi, *Falstaff*, Bruson, Ricciarelli, Nucci, Los Angeles Philharmonic/Giulini (Deutsche Grammophon)

Wagner, *Tristan und Isolde*, Nilsson, Ludwig, Wachter, Chorus and Orchestra of the Bayreuth Festival/Bohm (Deutsche Grammophon)

Puccini, *Turandot*, Pavarotti, Sutherland, Caballe, London Philharmonic Orchestra/Mehta (London)

Stravinsky, *The Rite of Spring*, Cleveland Orchestra/Boulez (CBS Masterworks)

Schoenberg, *Verklarte Nacht*, Juilliard Quartet With Yo-Yo Ma (Sony Classical)

Weill, *The Threepenny Opera*, Ute Lemper, Berlin Sinfonietta (London)

Barber, *Complete Songs*, Thomas Hampson, Cheryl Studer, Emerson String Quartet (Deutsche Grammophon)

Ives, *Three Places in New England*, Boston Symphony Orchestra/Thomas (Deutsche Grammophon)

Gershwin, *Rhapsody in Blue*, Columbia Symphony/Bernstein (CBS Masterworks)

Reich, *Music for 18 Musicians*, Steve Reich Ensemble (ECM)

Glass, *Einstein on the Beach (1993)*, Philip Glass Ensemble (Elektra Nonesuch)

Pärt, *Tabula Rasa*, Gidon Kremer (ECM)

Gorecki, *Symphony No. 3*, London Sinfonietta with Dawn Upshaw/Zinman (Elektra Nonesuch)

JAZZ/BLUES

Louis Armstrong, *Hot Fives and Sevens 1927–1928* (Columbia)

Fats Waller, *The Complete Fats Waller, vols. 1–4* (Bluebird/RCA)

Duke Ellington, *The Blanton-Webster Band 1940–1942* (Bluebird)

Billie Holiday, *The Quintessential Billie Holiday 1940–1942* (Columbia)

Charlie Parker, *The Complete Charlie Parker Savoy Studio Sessions* (Savoy)

Charlie Parker, *Bird: The Complete Charlie Parker on Verve* (Verve)

Thelonious Monk, *The Genius of Modern Music 1947–1952* (Blue Note)

Miles Davis, *Kind of Blue* (Columbia)

Dave Brubeck, *Time Out* (Columbia)

Duke Ellington, *The Far East Suite: Special Mix* (Bluebird)

John Coltrane, *A Love Supreme* (Impulse)

John Coltrane, *My Favorite Things* (Impulse)

Ornette Coleman, *The Shape of Jazz to Come* (Atlantic)

Chet Baker, *Best of Chet Baker Sings* (Pacific Jazz)

Frank Sinatra, *Songs for Swinging Lovers* (Capitol)

Ella Fitzgerald, *The Best of the Songbooks* (Verve)

Charles Mingus, *Mingus Ah-Um* (Columbia)

Miles Davis, *Bitches Brew* (Columbia)

Wynton Marsalis, *Hot House Flowers* (Columbia)

Robert Johnson, *The Complete Recordings* (Columbia)

Charlie Patton, *Founder of the Delta Blues* (Yazoo)

Son House, *Son House* (Arhoolie)

Bessie Smith, *The Complete Recordings* (Columbia)

Muddy Waters, *Folksinger* (Chess/MCA)

Muddy Waters, *The Chess Box* (Chess/MCA)

Professor Longhair, *Rock 'n' Roll Gumbo* (A&M)

John Lee Hooker, *John Lee Hooker Plays and Sings the Blues* (Chess/MCA)

Albert King, *Born Under a Bad Sign* (Atlantic)

ROCK

Elvis Presley, *Elvis Presley* (RCA)

Sam Cooke, *The Man and His Music* (RCA)

Chuck Berry, *St. Louis to Liverpool* (Chess)

The Drifters, *1959–1965 All-Time Greatest Hits and More* (Atlantic)

Buddy Holly, *The Complete Buddy Holly* (MCA)

Phil Spector/Various, *Back to Mono* (ABKCO)

The Beatles, *Revolver* (Capitol)

The Beatles, *Sgt. Pepper's Lonely Hearts Club Band* (Capitol)

The Rolling Stones, *High Tide and Green Grass* (ABKCO)

Beach Boys, *Pet Sounds* (Capitol)

The Byrds, *The Byrds* (Columbia)

Bob Dylan, *Blonde on Blonde* (Columbia)

Simon and Garfunkel, *Parsley, Sage, Rosemary and Thyme* (Columbia)

Jefferson Airplane, *Surrealistic Pillow* (RCA)

Big Brother and the Holding Company, *Cheap Thrills* (Columbia)

Cream, *Disraeli Gears* (Polydor)

Jimi Hendrix, *Are You Experienced?* (Reprise)

Funkadelic, *Cosmic Slop* (Westbound)

James Brown, *Star Time* (Polydor)

Van Morrison, *Astral Weeks* (Warner Bros.)

The Four Tops, *Anthology* (Motown)

The Supremes, *Anthology* (Motown)

The Band, *The Band* (Capitol)

Creedance Clearwater Revival, *Willie and the Poor Boys* (Fantasy)

The Rolling Stones

Sex Pistols

Elvis Presley, *Elvis (TV Special)* (RCA)

Neil Young, *After the Gold Rush* (Reprise)

The Allman Brothers, *At Fillmore East* (Capricorn)

Derek and the Dominoes, *Layla and Other Assorted Love Songs* (RSO)

Aerosmith, *Toys in the Attic* (CBS)

The Rolling Stones, *Exile on Main Street* (Rolling Stones)

The Who, *Live at Leeds* (MCA)

The Doors, *Morrison Hotel* (Elektra)

David Bowie, *Hunky Dory* (Rykodisc)

The Stooges, *Fun House* (Elektra)

Stevie Wonder, *Songs in the Key of Life* (Motown)

Marvin Gaye, *Let's Get It On* (Tamla)

Al Green, *Let's Stay Together* (Motown)

Sex Pistols, *Never Mind the Bollocks, Here's the Sex Pistols* (Warner Bros.)

The Clash, *London Calling* (Epic)

Buzzcocks, *Singles Going Steady* (IRS)

Talking Heads, *Talking Heads '77* (Sire)

Elvis Costello, *Get Happy!* (Columbia)

Wire, *Chairs Missing* (Restless reissue)

Gang of Four, *Entertainment!* (Warner Bros.)

Blondie, *Plastic Letters* (Chrysalis)

Devo, *Q: Are We Not Men? A: We Are Devo* (Warner Bros.)

X, *Los Angeles* (Slash)

The Gun Club, *Fire of Love* (Ruby)

Tom Petty and the Heartbreakers, *Damn the Torpedoes* (MCA)

AC/DC, *Back in Black* (Atlantic)

U2, *The Joshua Tree* (Island)

R.E.M., *Murmur* (IRS)

Peter Gabriel, *So* (Geffen)

Tom Waits, *Swordfish Trombones* (Island)

Bruce Springsteen, *Greetings From Asbury Park* or *Darkness at the Edge of Town* (Columbia)

Nirvana, *Nevermind* (DGC)

FOLK/COUNTRY

Jimmie Rodgers, *The Early Years 1928–1929* (Rounder)

The Carter Family, *My Clinch Mountain Home* (Rounder)

Bill Monroe, *The Original Bluegrass Band* (Rounder)

Hank Williams, eight-volume Polydor reissue (Polydor)

Patsy Cline, *The Patsy Cline Collection* (MCA)

George Jones, *The Best of George Jones* (Rhino)

Johnny Cash, *Johnny Cash at Folsom Prison* (Columbia)

R.E.M.

Joni Mitchell

Woody Guthrie

Merle Haggard, *Sing Me Back Home* (Capitol)

Emmylou Harris, *Luxury Liner* (Warner Bros.)

Woody Guthrie, *The Greatest Songs of Woody Guthrie* (Vanguard)

Leadbelly, *Midnight Special, Gwine Dig a Hole to Put the Devil In* or *Let It Shine on Me* (three CDs; Rounder)

Doc Watson, *The Doc Watson Family* (Smithsonian/Folkways)

Various, *Jubilation Volume: Great Gospel Performances* (Rhino)

Phil Ochs, *Phil Ochs in Concert* (Elektra)

Clifton Chenier, *Bogalusa Boogie* (Arhoolie)

Joan Baez, *Joan Baez 5* (Vanguard)

Joni Mitchell, *Blue* (Reprise)

Tim Hardin, *Reason to Believe* (Polydor)

WORLD MUSIC

Planxty, *Planxty* (Shanachie)

The Bothy Band, *The Best of the Bothy Band* (Green Linnet)

The Chieftains, *The Long Black Veil* (RCA)

Altan, *Island Angel* (Green Linnet)

De Dannan, *De Dannan* (Shanachie)

Ewan MacColl, *Black and White* (Green Linnet)

The Oyster Band, *From Little Rock to Leipzig* (Rykodisc)

Kate and Anna McGarrigle, *French Record* (Hannibal)

Various, *Rai Rebels* (Earthworks)

Paco de Lucia, *Almoraima* (Philips)

Don Byron, *Don Byron Plays the Music of Mickey Katz* (Nonesuch)

Nusrat Fatah Ali Khan, *En Concert à Paris* (Harmonia Mundi)

Sabri Brothers, *Ya Habib* (Real World)

Ustad Ali Akbar Khan, *Signature Series Vol.1* (AMMP)

Dr. L. Subramaniam, *Raga Hemavati* (Nimbus)

Ramnad Krishnan, *Vidwan — Songs of the Carnatic Tradition* (Nonesuch)

Youssou N'Dour, *Eyes Open* (Columbia)

King Sunny Ade, *Juju Music* (Island)

Various, *Juju Roots 1930s–1950s* (Rounder)

Various, *The Indestructible Beat of Soweto* (Earthworks)

Mahlatini and the Mahotella Queens, *The Lion Roars* (Shanachie)

Various, *Zimbabwe Frontline* (Earthworks)

Thomas Mapfumo, *The Chimurenga Singles* (Shanachie)

The Bhundu Boys, *Jit Jive* (Mango)

Bob Marley and The Wailers, *Natty Dread* (Tuff Gong)

Gamelan of Pura Pakualaman, *Javanese Court Gamelan* (Nonesuch)

Various, *Bali: Gamelan and Kecak* (Nonesuch)

Fong Naam, *The Hang Hong Suite* (Nimbus)

Kohachiro Miyata, *Shakuhachi — The Japanese Flute* (Nonesuch)

Various, *Cuba Classics Vol. 1–3* (Luaka Bop)

Los Munequitos de Matanzas, *Rumba Caliente* (Qbadisc)

Various, *Konbit: Burning Rhythms of Haiti* (A&M)

Various, *Zouk Attack* (Rounder)

Los Pinguinos del Norte, *Conjuntos Nortenos* (Arhoolie)

Steve Jordan, *The Many Sounds of Steve Jordan* (Arhoolie)

Various, *Beliza Tropical: Brazil Classics* (Luaka Bop)

Various, *O Samba: Brazil Classics* (Luaka Bop)

Joao Gilberto, *Joao Gilberto* (Polygram)

Astor Piazzolla, *Zero Hour* (American Clave)

Various, *Vintage Hawaiian Music: Steel Guitar Masters 1928–1934* (Rounder)

The Chieftains

The Grammy Awards

The Grammy Awards, presented annually by the National Academy of Recording Arts and Sciences (NARAS), are considered the most coveted of the many contemporary music awards. Despite the honor the awards carry and the ratings success of the televised awards show, many industry insiders consider the Grammys to be merely a reflection of mainstream commercial success.

Count Basie

1958

Record of the Year
"Nel Blu Dipinto di Blu" (Volare), Domenico Modugno

Album of the Year
The Music From Peter Gunn, Henry Mancini (RCA)

Song of the Year
"Nel Blu Dipinto di Blu," Domenico Modugno, songwriter

Best Vocal Performance, Male
"Catch a Falling Star," Perry Como

Best Vocal Performance, Female
Ella Fitzgerald Sings the Irving Berlin Song Book,
Ella Fitzgerald

Best Performance by a Vocal Group or Chorus
"That Old Black Magic," Louis Prima and Keely Smith

Best Rhythm and Blues Performance
"Tequila," Champs

Best Jazz Performance, Individual
Ella Fitzgerald Sings the Duke Ellington Song Book,
Ella Fitzgerald

Best Jazz Performance, Group
Basie, Count Basie

Best Performance by a Dance Band
Basie, Count Basie

Best Country and Western Performance
"Tom Dooley," Kingston Trio

Best Performance by an Orchestra
Billy May's Big Fat Brass, Billy May

Best Arrangement
The Music From Peter Gunn, Henry Mancini, arranger

Best Musical Composition First Recorded and Released in 1958 (More Than Five Minutes)
"Cross Country Suite," Nelson Riddle, composer

Best Original Cast Album, Broadway or Television
The Music Man, Meredith Willson (Capitol)

Best Soundtrack Album, Dramatic Picture Score or Original Cast
Gigi, André Previn (MGM)

Best Classical Performance, Orchestra
Gaîté Parisienne, Felix Slatkin conducting Hollywood Bowl
Symphony Orchestra

Best Classical Performance, Chamber Music (Including Chamber Orchestra)
Beethoven, *Quartet 130,* Hollywood String Quartet

Best Classical Performance, Instrumental (With Concerto Scale Accompaniment)
Tchaikovsky, *Concerto No. 1 in B-Flat Minor, Op. 23,* Van
Cliburn, pianist; Kiril Kondrashin Symphony Orchestra

Best Classical Performance, Instrumental (Other Than Concerto Scale)
Segovia Golden Jubilee, Andrés Segovia

Best Classical Performance, Operatic or Choral
Virtuoso, Roger Wagner Chorale

Best Classical Performance, Vocal Soloist (With or Without Orchestra)
Operatic Recital, Renata Tebaldi

Best Comedy Performance
"The Chipmunk Song," David Seville

Best Performance, Documentary or Spoken Word
The Best of the Stan Freberg Shows, Stan Freberg

Best Recording for Children
"The Chipmunk Song," David Seville (Liberty)

Best Album Cover
Only the Lonely, Frank Sinatra (Capitol)

1959

Record of the Year
"Mack the Knife," Bobby Darin

Album of the Year
Come Dance With Me, Frank Sinatra (Capitol)

Song of the Year
"The Battle of New Orleans," Jimmy Driftwood, songwriter

Best Artist of 1959
Bobby Darin

Best Performance by a "Top 40" Artist
"Midnight Flyer," Nat King Cole

Best Vocal Performance, Male
Come Dance With Me, Frank Sinatra

Best Vocal Performance, Female
"But Not for Me," Ella Fitzgerald

Best Performance by a Chorus
"Battle Hymn of the Republic," Mormon Tabernacle Choir

Best Rhythm and Blues Performance
"What a Diff'rence a Day Makes," Dinah Washington

Best Jazz Performance, Soloist
Ella Swings Lightly, Ella Fitzgerald

Best Jazz Performance, Group
I Dig Chicks, Jonah Jones

Best Performance by a Dance Band
Anatomy of a Murder, Duke Ellington

Best Country and Western Performance
"The Battle of New Orleans," Johnny Horton

Best Performance, Folk
The Kingston Trio at Large, Kingston Trio

Best Performance by an Orchestra
Like Young, David Rose and His Orchestra With André Previn

Best Arrangement
Come Dance With Me, Billy May, arranger

Best Musical Composition First Recorded and Released in 1959 (More Than Five Minutes)
Anatomy of a Murder, Duke Ellington, composer

Best Broadway Show Album (tie)
Gypsy, Ethel Merman (Columbia)
Redhead, Gwen Verdon (RCA)

Best Soundtrack Album, Original Cast, Motion Picture or Television
Porgy and Bess, André Previn and Ken Darby (Columbia)

Best Soundtrack Album, Background Score From Motion Picture or Television
Anatomy of a Murder, Duke Ellington (Columbia)

Best Classical Performance, Orchestra
Debussy, *Images for Orchestra,* Charles Munch conducting Boston Symphony Orchestra

Best Classical Performance, Chamber Music (Including Chamber Orchestra)
Beethoven, *Sonata No. 21 in C, Op. 53; Waldstein Sonata No. 18 in E-Flat, Op. 31, No. 3,* Artur Rubinstein, pianist

Best Classical Performance, Concerto or Instrumental Soloist (Full Orchestra)
Rachmaninoff, *Piano Concerto No. 3,* Van Cliburn, pianist; Kiril Kondrashin conducting Symphony of the Air

Best Classical Performance, Instrumental Soloist (Other Than Full Orchestral Accompaniment)
Beethoven, *Sonata No. 21 in C, Op. 53; Waldstein Sonata No. 18 in E-Flat, Op. 31, No. 3,* Artur Rubinstein, pianist

Best Classical Performance, Opera Cast or Choral
Mozart, *The Marriage of Figaro,* Erich Leinsdorf conducting Vienna Philharmonic Orchestra

Best Classical Performance, Vocal Soloist (With or Without Orchestra)
Björling in Opera, Jussi Björling

Best Comedy Performance, Spoken Word
Inside Shelley Berman, Shelley Berman

Best Comedy Performance, Musical
The Battle of Kookamonga, Homer and Jethro

Best Performance, Documentary or Spoken Word (Other Than Comedy)
A Lincoln Portrait, Carl Sandburg

Best Recording for Children
Peter and the Wolf, Peter Ustinov, narrating; Herbert von Karajan conducting Philharmonia Orchestra (Angel)

Best Album Cover
Shostakovich, *Symphony No. 5,* Robert M. Jones, art director (RCA)

1960

Record of the Year
"Theme From *A Summer Place,*" Percy Faith

Album of the Year
Button Down Mind, Bob Newhart (Warner Bros.)

Song of the Year
"Theme From *Exodus,*" Ernest Gold, songwriter

Best New Artist of 1960
Bob Newhart

Best Performance by a Pop Single Artist
"Georgia on My Mind," Ray Charles

Best Vocal Performance Single Record or Track, Male
"Georgia on My Mind," Ray Charles (ABC)

Best Vocal Performance Single Record or Track, Female
"Mack the Knife," Ella Fitzgerald (Verve)

Best Vocal Performance, Album, Male
Genius of Ray Charles, Ray Charles (Atlantic)

Best Vocal Performance, Album, Female
Mack the Knife — Ella in Berlin, Ella Fitzgerald (Verve)

Best Performance by a Vocal Group
"We Got Us," Eydie Gormé and Steve Lawrence

Best Performance by a Chorus
Songs of the Cowboy, Norman Luboff Choir

Best Rhythm and Blues Performance
"Let the Good Times Roll," Ray Charles

Best Jazz Performance, Solo or Small Group
West Side Story, André Previn

Best Jazz Performance, Large Group
Blues and the Beat, Henry Mancini

Best Jazz Composition of More Than Five Minutes
Sketches of Spain, Miles Davis and Gil Evans, composers

Best Performance by a Band for Dancing
Dance With Basie, Count Basie

Best Country and Western Performance
"El Paso," Marty Robbins

Best Performance, Folk
"Swing Dat Hammer," Harry Belafonte

Best Performance by an Orchestra
Mr. Lucky, Henry Mancini

Best Arrangement
Mr. Lucky, Henry Mancini, arranger

Best Show Album (Original Cast)
The Sound of Music, Richard Rodgers and Oscar Hammerstein, composers (Columbia)

Best Soundtrack Album or Recording of Music Score From Motion Picture or Television
Exodus, Ernest Gold, composer (RCA)

Best Soundtrack Album or Recording of Original Cast From Motion Picture or Television
Can-Can, Cole Porter, composer (Capital)

Best Classical Performance, Orchestra
Bartók, *Music for Strings, Percussion and Celeste,* Fritz Reiner conducting Chicago Symphony

Best Classical Performance, Vocal or Instrumental Chamber Music
Conversations With the Guitar, Laurindo Almeida

Best Classical Performance, Concerto or Instrumental Soloist
Brahms, *Piano Concerto No. 2 in B-Flat,* Sviatoslav Richter; Erich Leinsdorf conducting Chicago Symphony

Best Classical Performance, Instrumental Soloist or Duo (Other Than Orchestral)
The Spanish Guitars of Laurindo Almeida, Laurindo Almeida

Best Classical Opera Production
Puccini, *Turandot,* Erich Leinsdorf conducting Rome Opera House Chorus and Orchestra; solos: Tebaldi, Nilsson, Björling and Tozzi

Best Classical Performance, Choral (Including Oratorio)
Handel, *The Messiah,* Sir Thomas Beecham conducting Royal Philharmonic Orchestra and Chorus

Best Classical Performance, Vocal Soloist
A Program of Song, Leontyne Price

Best Contemporary Classical Composition
Orchestral Suite From Tender Land Suite, Aaron Copland, composer

Best Comedy Performance (Spoken Word)
Button Down Mind Strikes Back, Bob Newhart

Best Comedy Performance (Musical)
Jonathan and Darlene Edwards in Paris, Jo Stafford and Paul Weston

Best Performance, Documentary or Spoken Word (Other Than Comedy)
F.D.R. Speaks, Robert Bialek

Best Album Created for Children
Let's All Sing With the Chipmunks, David Seville (Liberty)

Best Album Cover
Latin a la Lee, Marvin Schwartz, art director (Capitol)

1961

Record of the Year
"Moon River," Henry Mancini

Album of the Year
Judy at Carnegie Hall, Judy Garland (Capitol)

Song of the Year
"Moon River," Henry Mancini and Johnny Mercer, songwriters

Henry Mancini

Best New Artist of 1961
Peter Nero

Best Solo Vocal Performance, Male
"Lollipops and Roses," Jack Jones

Best Solo Vocal Performance, Female
Judy at Carnegie Hall, Judy Garland

Best Performance by a Vocal Group
High Flying, Lambert, Hendricks and Ross

Best Performance by a Chorus
Great Band With Great Voices, Johnny Mann Singers and Si Zentner Orchestra

Best Rock and Roll Recording
Let's Twist Again, Chubby Checker (Parkway)

Best Rhythm and Blues Recording
Hit the Road Jack, Ray Charles (ABC/Paramount)

Best Jazz Performance, Soloist or Small Group (Instrumental)
André Previn Plays Harold Arlen, André Previn

Best Jazz Performance, Large Group
West Side Story, Stan Kenton

Best Original Jazz Composition
"African Waltz," Galt MacDermott, composer

Best Country and Western Recording
Big Bad John, Jimmy Dean (Columbia)

Best Gospel or Other Religious Recording
Everytime I Feel the Spirit, Mahalia Jackson (Columbia)

Best Folk Recording
Belafonte Folk Singers at Home and Abroad, Belafonte Folk Singers (RCA)

Best Performance by an Orchestra for Dancing
Up a Lazy River, Si Zentner

Best Performance by an Orchestra for Other Than Dancing
Breakfast at Tiffany's, Henry Mancini

Best Arrangement
"Moon River," Henry Mancini, arranger

Best Instrumental Theme or Instrumental Version of a Song
"African Waltz," Galt MacDermott, composer

Best Original Cast Show Album
How to Succeed in Business Without Really Trying, Frank Loesser, composer (RCA)

Best Soundtrack Album or Recording of Score From a Motion Picture or Television
Breakfast at Tiffany's, Henry Mancini (RCA)

Best Soundtrack Album or Recording of Original Cast From a Motion Picture or Television
West Side Story, Johnny Green, Saul Chaplin, Sid Ramin and Irwin Kostal (Columbia)

Album of the Year, Classical
Stravinsky Conducts, 1960: Le Sacre du Printemps; Petrouchka, Igor Stravinsky conducting Columbia Symphony (Columbia)

Best Classical Performance, Orchestra
Ravel, *Daphnis et Chloe,* Charles Munch conducting Boston Symphony Orchestra

Best Classical Performance, Chamber Music
Beethoven, *Serenade, Op. 8;* Kodaly, *Duo for Violin and Cello, Op. 7,* Jascha Heifetz, Gregor Piatigorsky and William Primrose

Best Classical Performance, Instrumental Soloist (With Orchestra)
Bartók, *Concerto No. 1 for Violin and Orchestra,* Isaac Stern; Eugene Ormandy conducting Philharmonic Orchestra

Best Classical Performance, Instrumental Soloist or Duo (Without Orchestra)
Reverie for Spanish Guitars, Laurindo Almeida

Best Opera Recording
Puccini, *Madame Butterfly,* Gabriele Santini conducting Rome Opera Chorus and Orchestra (Capitol)

Best Classical Performance, Choral
Bach, *B Minor Mass,* Robert Shaw conducting Robert Shaw Chorale

Best Classical Performance, Vocal Soloist
The Art of the Prima Donna, Joan Sutherland; Francesco Molinari-Pradelli conducting Royal Opera House Orchestra

Best Contemporary Classical Composition (tie)
Discantus, Laurindo Almeida, composer
Movements for Piano and Orchestra, Igor Stravinsky, composer

Best Comedy Performance
An Evening With Mike Nichols and Elaine May, Mike Nichols and Elaine May

Best Documentary or Spoken Word Recording (Other Than Comedy)
Humor in Music, Leonard Bernstein conducting New York Philharmonic Symphony (Columbia)

Best Recording for Children
Prokofiev, *Peter and the Wolf,* Leonard Bernstein conducting New York Philharmonic Orchestra (Columbia)

Best Album Cover
Judy at Carnegie Hall, Jim Silke, art director (Capitol)

Best Album Cover, Classical
Puccini, *Madame Butterfly,* Marvin Schwartz, art director (Angel)

1962

Record of the Year
"I Left My Heart in San Francisco," Tony Bennett

Album of the Year
The First Family, Vaughn Meader (Cadence)

Song of the Year
"What Kind of Fool Am I," Leslie Bricusse and Anthony Newley, songwriters

Best New Artist of 1962
Robert Goulet

Best Solo Vocal Performance, Male
I Left My Heart in San Francisco, Tony Bennett

Best Solo Vocal Performance, Female
Ella Swings Brightly With Nelson Riddle, Ella Fitzgerald

Best Performance by a Vocal Group
"If I Had a Hammer," Peter, Paul and Mary

Best Performance by a Chorus
Presenting the New Christy Minstrels, New Christy Minstrels

Best Rock and Roll Recording
"Alley Cat," Bent Fabric (Atco)

Best Rhythm and Blues Recording
"I Can't Stop Loving You," Ray Charles (ABC)

Best Jazz Performance, Soloist or Small Group (Instrumental)
"Desafinado," Stan Getz

Best Jazz Performance, Large Group (Instrumental)
Adventures in Jazz, Stan Kenton

Best Original Jazz Composition
"Cast Your Fate to the Winds," Vince Guaraldi, composer

Best Country and Western Recording
"Funny Way of Laughin'," Burl Ives (Decca)

Best Gospel or Other Religious Recording
Great Songs of Love and Faith, Mahalia Jackson (Columbia)

Best Folk Recording
"If I Had a Hammer," Peter, Paul and Mary (Warner Bros.)

Best Performance by an Orchestra for Dancing
Fly Me to the Moon Bossa Nova, Joe Harnell

Best Performance by an Orchestra or Instrumentalist With Orchestra, Not for Jazz or Dancing
The Colorful Peter Nero, Peter Nero

Best Instrumental Arrangement
"Baby Elephant Walk," Henry Mancini, arranger

Best Background Arrangement
"I Left My Heart in San Francisco," Marty Manning, arranger

Best Instrumental Theme
"A Taste of Honey," Bobby Scott and Ric Marlow, composers

Best Original Cast Show Album
No Strings, Richard Rodgers, composer (Capitol)

Album of the Year, Classical
Columbia Records Presents Vladimir Horowitz, Vladimir Horowitz (Columbia)

Best Classical Performance, Orchestra
Stravinsky, *The Firebird Ballet,* Igor Stravinsky conducting Columbia Symphony

Best Classical Performance, Chamber Music
The Heifetz-Piatigorsky Concerts With Primrose, Pennario and Guests, Jascha Heifetz, Gregor Piatigorsky and William Primrose

Best Classical Performance, Instrumental Soloist(s) (With Orchestra)
Stravinsky, *Concerto in D for Violin,* Isaac Stern; Igor Stravinsky conducting Columbia Symphony

Best Classical Performance, Instrumental Soloist or Duo (Without Orchestra)
Columbia Records Presents Vladimir Horowitz, Vladimir Horowitz

Best Opera Recording
Verdi, *Aïda,* Georg Solti conducting Rome Opera House Orchestra and Chorus; solos: Price, Vickers, Gorr, Merrill and Tozzi (RCA)

Best Classical Performance, Choral
Bach, *St. Matthew Passion,* Philharmonia Choir, Wilhelm Pitz, choral director; Otto Klemperer conducting Philharmonic Orchestra

Best Classical Performance, Vocal Soloist (With or Without Orchestra)
Wagner, *Götterdamerung Brunnhilde's Immolation Scene;* Wesendonck, *Songs,* Eileen Farrell; Leonard Bernstein conducting New York Philharmonic

Best Classical Composition by Contemporary Composer
The Flood, Igor Stravinsky, composer

Best Comedy Performance
The First Family, Vaughn Meader

Best Documentary or Spoken Word Recording (Other Than Comedy)
The Story-Teller: A Session With Charles Laughton, Charles Laughton (Capitol)

Best Recording for Children
Saint-Saëns, *Carnival of the Animals;* Britten, *Young Person's Guide to the Orchestra,* Leonard Bernstein (Columbia)

Best Album Cover
Lena . . . Lovely and Alive, Robert Jones, art director (RCA)

Best Album Cover, Classical
The Intimate Bach, Marvin Schwartz, art director (Capitol)

1963

Record of the Year
"The Days of Wine and Roses," Henry Mancini

Album of the Year
The Barbra Streisand Album, Barbra Streisand (Columbia)

Song of the Year
"The Days of Wine and Roses," Henry Mancini and Johnny Mercer, composers

Best New Artist of 1963
Swingle Singers

Best Vocal Performance, Male
"Wives and Lovers, " Jack Jones

Best Vocal Performance, Female
The Barbra Streisand Album, Barbra Streisand

Best Performance by a Vocal Group
"Blowin' in the Wind," Peter, Paul and Mary

Best Performance by a Chorus
Bach's Greatest Hits, Swingle Singers

Best Rock and Roll Recording
"Deep Purple," Nino Tempo and April Stevens (Atco)

Best Rhythm and Blues Recording
"Busted," Ray Charles (ABC/Paramount)

Best Instrumental Jazz Performance, Soloist or Small Group
Conversations With Myself, Bill Evans

Best Instrumental Jazz Performance, Large Group
Encore: Woody Herman, 1963, Woody Herman Band

Best Original Jazz Composition
"Gravy Waltz," Steve Allen and Ray Brown, composers

Best Country and Western Recording
"Detroit City," Bobby Bare (RCA)

Best Gospel or Other Religious Recording (Musical)
"Dominique," Soeur Sourire (The Singing Nun) (Philips)

Best Folk Recording
"Blowin' in the Wind," Peter, Paul and Mary (Warner Bros.)

Best Performance by an Orchestra for Dancing
This Time by Basie! Hits of the '50s and '60s, Count Basie

Best Performance by an Orchestra or Instrumentalist With Orchestra, Not for Jazz or Dancing
"Java," Al Hirt

Best Instrumental Arrangement
"I Can't Stop Loving You," Quincy Jones, arranger

Best Background Arrangement
"The Days of Wine and Roses," Henry Mancini, arranger

Best Instrumental Theme
"More" (Theme From *Mondo Cane*), Norman Newell, Nino Oliviero and Riz Ortolani, composers

Best Original Score From a Motion Picture or Television Show
Tom Jones, John Addison, composer

Best Score From an Original Cast Show Album
She Loves Me, Jerry Bock and Sheldon Harnick, composers (MGM)

Album of the Year, Classical
Britten, *War Requiem,* Benjamin Britten conducting London Symphony Orchestra and Chorus (London)

Most Promising New Classical Recording Artist
André Watts, pianist

Best Classical Performance, Orchestra
Bartók, *Concerto for Orchestra,* Erich Leinsdorf conducting Boston Symphony Orchestra

Best Classical Performance, Chamber Music
Evening of Elizabethan Music, Julian Bream Consort

Best Classical Performance, Instrumental Soloist(s) (With Orchestra)
Tchaikovsky, *Concerto No. 1 in B-Flat Minor for Piano and Orchestra,* Artur Rubinstein; Erich Leinsdorf conducting Boston Symphony Orchestra

Best Classical Performance, Instrumental Soloist or Duo (Without Orchestra)
The Sound of Horowitz, Vladimir Horowitz

Best Opera Recording
Puccini, *Madama Butterfly,* Erich Leinsdorf conducting RCA Italiana Opera Orchestra and Chorus; solos: Price, Tucker and Elias (RCA)

Best Classical Performance, Choral
Britten, *War Requiem,* David Willcocks directing Bach Choir; Edward Chapman directing Highgate School Choir; Benjamin Britten conducting London Symphony Orchestra and Chorus

Best Classical Performance, Vocal Soloist (With or Without Orchestra)
Great Scenes From Gershwin's Porgy and Bess, Leontyne Price

Best Classical Composition by Contemporary Composer
War Requiem, Benjamin Britten, composer

Best Comedy Performance
Hello Mudduh, Hello Faddah, Allan Sherman

Best Documentary, Spoken Word or Drama Recording (Other Than Comedy)
Who's Afraid of Virginia Woolf?, Edward Albee (Warner Bros.)

Best Recording for Children
Bernstein Conducts for Young People, Leonard Bernstein conducting New York Philharmonic (Columbia)

Best Album Cover, Other Than Classical
The Barbra Streisand Album, John Berg, art director (Columbia)

Best Album Cover, Classical
Puccini, *Madama Butterfly,* Robert Jones, art director (RCA)

Best Album Notes
The Ellington Era, Stanley Dance and Leonard Feather, annotators (Columbia)

1964

Record of the Year
"The Girl From Ipanema," Stan Getz and Astrud Gilberto

Album of the Year
Getz/Gilberto, Stan Getz and Joao Gilberto (Verve)

Song of the Year
"Hello, Dolly!," Jerry Herman, songwriter

Best New Artist of 1964
The Beatles

Most Promising New Recording Artist
Marilyn Horne

Best Vocal Performance, Male
"Hello, Dolly!," Louis Armstrong

Best Vocal Performance, Female
"People," Barbra Streisand

Best Performance by a Vocal Group
A Hard Day's Night, The Beatles

Best Performance by a Chorus
The Swingle Singers Going Baroque, Swingle Singers

Best Rock and Roll Recording
"Downtown," Petula Clark (Warner Bros.)

Best Rhythm and Blues Recording
"How Glad I Am," Nancy Wilson (Capitol)

Best Instrumental Jazz Performance, Small Group or Soloist With Small Group
Getz/Gilberto, Stan Getz

Best Instrumental Jazz Performance, Large Group or Soloist With Large Group
Guitar From Ipanema, Laurindo Almeida

Best Original Jazz Composition
"The Cat," Lalo Schifrin, composer

Best Country and Western Single
"Dang Me," Roger Miller

Best Country and Western Album
Dang Me/Chug-a-Lug, Roger Miller (Smash)

Best Country and Western Song
"Dang Me," Roger Miller, songwriter

Best Country and Western Vocal Performance, Male
"Dang Me," Roger Miller

Best Country and Western Vocal Performance, Female
"Here Comes My Baby," Dottie West

Best New Country and Western Artist of 1964
Roger Miller

Best Gospel or Other Religious Recording (Musical)
Great Gospel Songs, Tennessee Ernie Ford (Capitol)

Best Folk Recording
We'll Sing in the Sunshine, Gale Garnett (RCA)

Best Instrumental Arrangement
"*The Pink Panther* Theme," Henry Mancini, arranger

Best Accompaniment Arrangement for Vocalist(s) or Instrumentalist(s)
"People," Peter Matz, arranger

The Beatles

Best Instrumental Composition (Other Than Jazz)
"*The Pink Panther* Theme," Henry Mancini, composer

Best Instrumental Performance, Non-Jazz
"*The Pink Panther* Theme," Henry Mancini

Best Score From an Original Cast Show Album
Funny Girl, Jule Styne and Bob Merrill, composers (Capitol)

Best Original Score Written for a Motion Picture or Television Show
Mary Poppins, Richard M. Sherman and Robert B. Sherman, composers

Music by Mail

Here are some places to turn if you can't find a recording at your local store.

Alternative Press
6516 Detroit Ave., Suite 5
Cleveland, OH 44102
(216) 631-1212

Arhoolie
Arhoolie Productions, Inc.
10341 San Pablo Ave.
El Cerrito, CA 94530
(510) 525-2129

Cadence Magazine
600 Harrison St.
San Francisco, CA 94107
(415) 905-2200

Classics
P.O. Box 64502
St. Paul, MN 55164-0502
(800) 949-9999

Footlight Records
113 E. 12th St.
New York, NY 10003
(212) 533-1572

Grateful Dead Catalog and Newsletter
Grateful Dead Mercantile Co.
P.O. Box 2139
Novato, CA 94948
(800) 225-3323

Pulse! Magazine
2500 Del Monte St.
Building C
West Sacramento, CA 95691-3820
(916) 373-2450

Rara Avis
77 Wittenberg Road
Bearsville, NY 12409
(914) 679-1054

Request Magazine
7500 Excelsior Blvd.
Minneapolis, MN 55426
(612) 932-7740

Rhino
P.O. Box 60062
Tampa, FL 33660
(800) 432-0020

Rounder Mail Order
1 Camp St.
Cambridge, MA 02140
(800) 443-4727

Wireless Audio
P.O. Box 64454
St. Paul, MN 55164-0422
(800) 726-8742

Album of the Year, Classical
Bernstein, *Symphony No. 3 ("Kaddish"),* Leonard Bernstein conducting New York Philharmonic Orchestra (Columbia)

Best Classical Performance, Orchestra
Mahler, *Symphony No. 5 in C-Sharp Minor;* Berg, *"Wozzeck" Excerpts,* Erich Leinsdorf conducting Boston Symphony

Best Chamber Performance, Instrumental
Beethoven, *Trio No. 1 in E-Flat, Op. 1, No. 1,* Jascha Heifetz and Gregor Piatigorsky; Jacob Lateiner, pianist

Best Chamber Music Performance, Vocal
It Was a Lover and His Lass, Morley, Byrd and others; Noah Greenberg conducting New York Pro Musica

Best Classical Performance, Instrumental Soloist(s) (With Orchestra)
Prokofiev, *Concerto No. 1 in D Major for Violin,* Isaac Stern; Eugene Ormandy conducting Philadelphia Orchestra

Best Performance, Instrumental Soloist (Without Orchestra)
Vladimir Horowitz Plays Beethoven, Debussy, Chopin (Beethoven, *Sonata No. 8 "Pathetique;"* Debussy, *Preludes;* Chopin, *Etudes and Scherzos 1–4),* Vladimir Horowitz

Best Opera Recording
Bizet, *Carmen,* Herbert von Karajan conducting Vienna Philharmonic Orchestra and Chorus; solos: Price, Corelli, Merrill and Freni (RCA)

Best Classical Choral Performance (Other Than Opera)
Britten, *A Ceremony of Carols,* Robert Shaw conducting Robert Shaw Chorale

Best Classical Vocal Soloist Performance (With or Without Orchestra)
Berlioz, *Nuits d'Ete Falla: El Amor Brujo,* Leontyne Price; Fritz Reiner conducting Chicago Symphony

Best Classical Composition by a Contemporary Composer
Samuel Barber, *Concerto*

Best Comedy Performance
I Started Out as a Child, Bill Cosby

Best Documentary, Spoken Word or Drama Recording (Other Than Comedy)
BBC Tribute to John F. Kennedy, That Was the Week That Was, cast (Decca)

Best Recording for Children
Mary Poppins, Julie Andrews and Dick Van Dyke (Buena Vista)

Best Album Cover
People, Robert Cato, art director; Don Bronstein, photographer (Columbia)

Best Album Cover, Classical
Saint-Saëns, *Carnival of the Animals;* Britten, *Young Person's Guide to the Orchestra,* Robert Jones, art director; Jan Balet, graphic artist (RCA)

Best Album Notes
Mexico (Legacy Collection), Stanton Catlin and Carleton Beals, annotators (Columbia)

1965

Record of the Year
"A Taste of Honey," Herb Alpert and the Tijuana Brass

Album of the Year
September of My Years, Frank Sinatra (Reprise)

Song of the Year
"The Shadow of Your Smile" (Love Theme From *The Sandpiper*), Paul Francis Webster and Johnny Mandel, songwriters

Best New Artist
Tom Jones

Most Promising New Recording Artist
Peter Serkin, pianist

Best Vocal Performance, Male
"It Was a Very Good Year," Frank Sinatra

Best Vocal Performance, Female
My Name Is Barbra, Barbra Streisand

Best Performance by a Vocal Group
We Dig Mancini, Anita Kerr Singers

Best Performance by a Chorus
Anyone for Mozart?, Swingle Singers

Best Contemporary (Rock and Roll) Single
"King of the Road," Roger Miller

Best Contemporary (Rock and Roll) Vocal Performance, Male
"King of the Road," Roger Miller

Best Contemporary (Rock and Roll) Vocal Performance, Female
"I Know a Place," Petula Clark

Best Contemporary (Rock and Roll) Performance Group (Vocal or Instrumental)
"Flowers on the Wall," Statler Brothers

Best Rhythm and Blues Recording
"Papa's Got a Brand New Bag," James Brown (King)

Best Instrumental Jazz Performance, Small Group or Soloist With Small Group
The "In" Crowd, Ramsey Lewis Trio

Best Instrumental Jazz Performance, Large Group or Soloist With Large Group
Ellington '66, Duke Ellington Orchestra

Best Original Jazz Composition
Jazz Suite on the Mass Texts, Lalo Shifrin, composer

Best Country and Western Single
"King of the Road," Roger Miller

Best Country and Western Album
The Return of Roger Miller, Roger Miller (Smash)

Best Country and Western Song
"King of the Road," Roger Miller, songwriter

Best Country and Western Vocal Performance, Male
"King of the Road," Roger Miller

Best Country and Western Vocal Performance, Female
"Queen of the House," Jody Miller

Best New Country and Western Artist
Statler Brothers

Best Gospel or Other Religious Recording (Musical)
Southland Favorites, George Beverly Shea and the Anita Kerr Quartet (RCA)

Best Folk Recording
An Evening With Belafonte/Makeba, Harry Belafonte and Miriam Makeba (RCA)

Best Instrumental Arrangement
"A Taste of Honey," Herb Alpert, arranger

Best Arrangement Accompanying a Vocalist or Instrumentalist
"It Was a Very Good Year," Gordon Jenkins, arranger

Best Instrumental Performance, Non-Jazz
"A Taste of Honey," Herb Alpert and the Tijuana Brass

Best Score From an Original Show Album
On a Clear Day, Alan Lerner and Burton Lane (RCA)

Best Original Score Written for a Motion Picture or Television Show
The Sandpiper, Johnny Mandel, composer (Mercury)

Album of the Year, Classical
Horowitz at Carnegie Hall, An Historic Return, Vladimir Horowitz (Columbia)

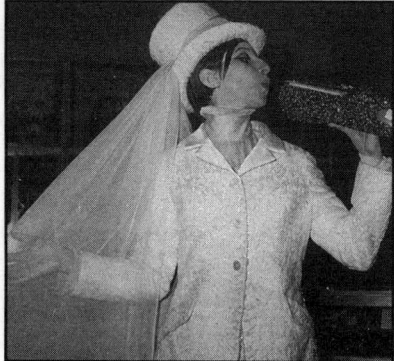

Barbra Streisand

Best Classical Performance, Orchestra
Ives, *Symphony No. 4,* Leopold Stokowski conducting American Symphony Orchestra

Best Classical Chamber Music Performance, Instrumental or Vocal
Bartók, *The Six String Quartets,* Juilliard String Quartet

Best Classical Performance, Instrumental Soloist(s) (With Orchestra)
Beethoven, *Concerto No. 4 in G Major for Piano and Orchestra,* Artur Rubinstein; Erich Leinsdorf conducting Boston Symphony

Best Classical Performance, Instrumental Soloist (Without Orchestra)
Horowitz at Carnegie Hall, An Historic Return, Vladimir Horowitz

Best Opera Recording
Berg, *Wozzeck,* Karl Bohm conducting Orchestra of German Opera, Berlin; solos: Fisher-Dieskau, Lear and Wunderlich (Deutsche Grammophon)

Best Classical Choral Performance (Other Than Opera)
Stravinsky, *Symphony of Psalms; Poulenc, Gloria,* Robert Shaw conducting Robert Shaw Chorale and RCA Victor Symphony Orchestra

Best Classical Vocal Performance, With or Without Orchestra
Strauss, *Salome ("Dance of the Seven Veils," Interlude, Final Scene); The Egyptian Helen (Awakening Scene),* Leontyne Price

Best Composition by a Contemporary Classical Composer
Symphony No. 4, Charles Ives, composer

Best Comedy Performance
Why Is There Air?, Bill Cosby

Best Spoken Word or Drama Recording
John F. Kennedy: As We Remember Him (Columbia)

Best Recording for Children
Dr. Seuss Presents "Fox in Sox" and "Green Eggs and Ham," Marvin Miller (RCA)

Best Album Cover, Graphic Arts
Bartók, *Concerto No. 2 for Violin;* Stravinsky, *Concerto for Violin,* James Alexander, graphic artist; George Estes, art director (RCA)

Best Album Cover, Photography
Jazz Suite on the Mass Texts, Ken Whitmore, photographer; Bob Jones, art director (RCA)

Best Album Notes
September of My Years, Stan Cornyn, annotator (Reprise)

1966

Record of the Year
"Strangers in the Night," Frank Sinatra

Album of the Year
Sinatra: A Man and His Music, Frank Sinatra (Reprise)

Song of the Year
"Michelle," John Lennon and Paul McCartney, songwriters

Best Vocal Performance, Male
"Strangers in the Night," Frank Sinatra

Best Vocal Performance, Female
"If He Walked Into My Life," Eydie Gormé

Best Performance by a Vocal Group
"A Man and a Woman," Anita Kerr Singers

Best Performance by a Chorus
"Somewhere, My Love" (Lara's Theme From *Dr. Zhivago*), Ray Conniff and Singers

Best Contemporary (Rock and Roll) Recording
"Winchester Cathedral," New Vaudeville Band (Fontana)

Best Contemporary (Rock and Roll) Solo Vocal Performance, Male or Female
"Eleanor Rigby," Paul McCartney

Best Contemporary (Rock and Roll) Group Performance, Vocal or Instrumental
"Monday, Monday," Mamas and the Papas

Best Rhythm and Blues Recording
"Crying Time," Ray Charles (ABC/Paramount)

Best Rhythm and Blues Solo Vocal Performance, Male or Female
"Crying Time," Ray Charles

Best Rhythm and Blues Group, Vocal or Instrumental
"Hold It Right There," Ramsey Lewis

Best Instrumental Jazz Performance, Group or Soloist With Group
"Goin' Out of My Head," Wes Montgomery

Best Original Jazz Composition
"In the Beginning God," Duke Ellington, composer

Best Country and Western Song
"Almost Persuaded," Billy Sherrill and Glenn Sutton, songwriters

Best Country and Western Recording
"Almost Persuaded," David Houston (Epic)

Best Country and Western Vocal Performance, Male
"Almost Persuaded," David Houston

Best Country and Western Vocal Performance, Female
"Don't Touch Me," Jeannie Seely

Best Sacred Recording (Musical)
Grand Old Gospel, Porter Wagoner and the Blackwood Brothers (RCA)

Best Folk Recording
Blues in the Street, Cortelia Clark (RCA)

Best Instrumental Arrangement
"What Now My Love," Herb Alpert, arranger

Best Arrangement Accompanying a Vocalist or Instrumentalist
"Strangers in the Night," Ernie Freeman, arranger

Best Instrumental Theme
"*Batman* Theme," Neal Hefti, composer

Best Instrumental Performance (Other Than Jazz)
"What Now My Love," Herb Alpert and the Tijuana Brass

Best Score From an Original Cast Show Album
Mame, Jerry Herman, composer (Columbia)

Best Original Score Written for a Motion Picture or Television Show
Dr. Zhivago, Maurice Jarre, composer

Album of the Year, Classical
Ives, *Symphony No. 1 in D Minor,* Morton Gould conducting Chicago Symphony (RCA)

Best Classical Performance, Orchestra
Mahler, *Symphony No. 6 in A Minor,* Erich Leinsdorf conducting Boston Symphony

Best Chamber Music Performance, Instrumental or Vocal
Boston Symphony Chamber Players, Boston Symphony Chamber Players

Best Classical Music Performance, Instrumental Soloist(s) (With or Without Orchestra)
Baroque Guitar, Julian Bream

Best Opera Recording
Wagner, *Die Walkure,* Georg Solti conducting Vienna Philharmonic; solos: Nilsson, Crespin, Ludwig, King and Hotter (London)

Best Classical Choral Performance (Other Than Opera) (tie)
Handel, *Messiah,* Robert Shaw conducting Robert Shaw Chorale and Orchestra

Ives, *Music for Chorus,* Gregg Smith conducting Columbia Chamber Orchestra, Gregg Smith Singers and Ithaca College Concert Choir; George Bragg conducting Texas Boys Choir

Best Classical Vocal Soloist Performance (With or Without Orchestra)
Prima Donna, Leontyne Price; Francesco Molinari-Pradelli conducting RCA Italiana Opera Orchestra

Best Comedy Performance
Wonderfulness, Bill Cosby

Best Spoken Word, Documentary or Drama Recording
Edward R. Murrow: A Reporter Remembers — Vol. I The War Years, Edward R. Murrow (Columbia)

Best Recording for Children
Dr. Seuss Presents: "If I Ran the Zoo" and "Sleep Book," Marvin Miller (RCA)

Best Album Cover, Graphic Arts
Revolver, Klaus Voormann, graphic artist (Capitol)

Best Album Cover, Photography
Confessions of a Broken Man, Les Leverette, photographer; Robert Jones, art director (RCA)

Best Album Notes
Sinatra at the Sands, Stan Cornyn, annotator (Reprise)

1967

Record of the Year
"Up, Up and Away," 5th Dimension

Album of the Year
Sgt. Pepper's Lonely Hearts Club Band, The Beatles (Capitol)

Song of the Year
"Up, Up and Away," Jimmy L. Webb, songwriter

Best New Artist
Bobbie Gentry

Best Vocal Performance, Male
"By the Time I Get to Phoenix," Glen Campbell

Best Vocal Performance, Female
"Ode to Billie Joe," Bobbie Gentry

Best Performance by a Vocal Group (Two to Six Persons)
"Up, Up and Away," 5th Dimension

Best Performance by a Chorus (Seven or More Persons)
"Up, Up and Away," Johnny Mann Singers

Duke Ellington

Best Contemporary Single
"Up, Up and Away," 5th Dimension

Best Contemporary Album
Sgt. Pepper's Lonely Hearts Club Band, The Beatles (Capitol)

Best Contemporary Male Solo Vocal Performance
"By the Time I Get to Phoenix," Glen Campbell

Best Contemporary Female Solo Vocal Performance
"Ode to Billie Joe," Bobbie Gentry

Best Contemporary Group Performance, Vocal or Instrumental
"Up, Up and Away," 5th Dimension

Best Rhythm and Blues Recording
"Respect," Aretha Franklin (Atlantic)

Best Rhythm and Blues Solo Vocal Performance, Male
"Dead End Street," Lou Rawls

Best Rhythm and Blues Solo Vocal Performance, Female
"Respect," Aretha Franklin

Best Rhythm and Blues Group Performance, Vocal or Instrumental (Two or More)
"Soul Man," Sam and Dave

Best Instrumental Jazz Performance, Small Group or Soloist With Small Group
Mercy, Mercy, Mercy, Cannonball Adderley Quintet

Best Instrumental Jazz Performance, Large Group or Soloist With Large Group
"Far East Suite," Duke Ellington

Best Country and Western Song
"Gentle on My Mind" John Hartford, songwriter

Best Country and Western Recording
"Gentle on My Mind," Glen Campbell (Capitol)

Best Country and Western Solo Vocal Performance, Male
"Gentle on My Mind," Glen Campbell

Best Country and Western Solo Vocal Performance, Female
"I Don't Wanna Play House," Tammy Wynette

Best Country and Western Performance, Duet, Trio or Group (Vocal or Instrumental)
"Jackson," Johnny Cash and June Carter

Best Gospel Performance
More Grand Old Gospel, Porter Wagoner and the Blackwood Brothers

Best Sacred Performance
How Great Thou Art, Elvis Presley

Best Folk Performance
"Gentle on My Mind," John Hartford

Best Instrumental Arrangement
Alfie, Burt Bacharach, arranger

Best Arrangement Accompanying Vocalist(s) or Instrumentalist(s)
"Ode to Billie Joe," Jimmie Haskell, arranger

Best Instrumental Theme
"Mission: Impossible," Lalo Schifrin, composer

Best Instrumental Performance
"Chet Atkins Picks the Best," Chet Atkins

Best Score From an Original Cast Show Album
Cabaret, Fred Ebb and John Kander, composers (Columbia)

Best Original Score Written for a Motion Picture or Television Show
"Mission: Impossible," Lalo Schifrin, composer

Album of the Year, Classical (tie)
Berg, *Wozzeck,* Pierre Boulez conducting Paris National Opera; solos: Berry, Strauss, Uhl and Doench (Columbia)

Mahler, *Symphony No. 8 in E-Flat Major ("Symphony of a Thousand"),* Leonard Bernstein conducting London Symphony Orchestra (Columbia)

Best Classical Performance, Orchestra
Stravinsky, *Firebird and Petrouchka Suites,* Igor Stravinsky conducting Columbia Symphony

Best Chamber Music Performance
West Meets East, Ravi Shankar and Yehudi Menuhin

Best Classical Performance, Instrumental Soloist(s) (With or Without Orchestra)
Horowitz in Concert, Vladimir Horowitz

Best Opera Recording
Berg, *Wozzeck,* Pierre Boulez conducting Paris National Opera; solos: Berry, Strauss, Uhl and Doench (Columbia)

Best Classical Choral Performance (tie)
Mahler, *Symphony No. 8 in E-Flat Major ("Symphony of a Thousand"),* Leonard Bernstein conducting London Symphony Orchestra

Orff, *Catulli Carmina,* Robert Page conducting Temple University Chorus; Eugene Ormandy conducting Philadelphia Orchestra

Best Classical Vocal Soloist Performance
Prima Donna, Vol. 2, Leontyne Price; Francesco Molinari-Pradelli conducting RCA Italiana Opera Orchestra

Best Comedy Recording
Revenge, Bill Cosby (Warner Bros.-Seven Arts)

Best Spoken Word, Documentary or Drama Recording
Gallant Men, Sen. Everett M. Dirksen (Capitol)

Best Recording for Children
Dr Seuss: How the Grinch Stole Christmas, Boris Karloff (MGM)

Best Album Cover, Graphic Arts
Sgt. Pepper's Lonely Hearts Club Band, Peter Blake and Jann Haworth, art directors (Capitol)

Best Album Cover, Photography
Bob Dylan's Greatest Hits, Roland Scherman, photographer; John Berg and Bob Cato, art directors (Columbia)

Best Album Notes
Suburban Attitudes in Country Verse, John D. Loudermilk, annotator (RCA)

1968

Record of the Year
"Mrs. Robinson," Simon and Garfunkel

Album of the Year
By the Time I Get to Phoenix, Glen Campbell (Capitol)

Song of the Year
"Little Green Apples," Bobby Russell, songwriter

Best New Artist of 1968
José Feliciano

Best Contemporary Pop Vocal Performance, Male
"Light My Fire," José Feliciano

Best Contemporary Pop Vocal Performance, Female
"Do You Know the Way to San Jose," Dionne Warwick

Best Contemporary Pop Vocal Performance, Duo or Group
"Mrs. Robinson," Simon and Garfunkel

Best Contemporary Pop Performance, Chorus
"Mission Impossible/Norwegian Wood" (medley), Alan Copeland Singers

Best Contemporary Pop Performance, Instrumental
"Classical Gas," Mason Williams

Best Rhythm and Blues Song
(Sittin' On) "The Dock of the Bay," Otis Redding and Steve Cropper, songwriters

Best Rhythm and Blues Vocal Performance, Male
(Sittin' On) "The Dock of the Bay," Otis Redding

Best Rhythm and Blues Vocal Performance, Female
"Chain of Fools," Aretha Franklin

Best Rhythm and Blues Performance by a Duo or Group, Vocal or Instrumental
"Cloud Nine," The Temptations

Best Instrumental Jazz Performance, Small Group or Soloist With Small Group
Bill Evans at the Montreux Jazz Festival, Bill Evans Trio

Best Instrumental Jazz Performance, Large Group or Soloist With Large Group
"And His Mother Called Him Bill," Duke Ellington

Best Country Song
"Little Green Apples," Bobby Russell, songwriter

Best Country Vocal Performance, Male
"Folsom Prison Blues," Johnny Cash

Best Country Vocal Performance, Female
"Harper Valley P.T.A.," Jeannie C. Riley

Best Country Performance, Duo or Group Vocal or Instrumental
"Foggy Mountain Breakdown," Flatt and Scruggs

Best Sacred Performance
"Beautiful Isle of Somewhere," Jack Hess

Best Gospel Performance
The Happy Gospel of the Happy Goodmans, Happy Goodman Family

Best Soul Gospel Performance
"The Soul of Me," Dottie Rambo

Best Folk Performance
"Both Sides Now," Judy Collins

Best Instrumental Arrangement
"Classical Gas," Mike Post, arranger

Best Arrangement Accompanying Vocalist(s)
"MacArthur Park," Jimmy L. Webb, arranger

Best Instrumental Theme
"Classical Gas," Mason Williams, composer

Best Score From an Original Cast Show Album
Hair, Gerome Ragni, James Rado and Galt MacDermott, composers (RCA)

Best Original Score Written for a Motion Picture or a Television Special
The Graduate, Paul Simon and Dave Grusin, composers

Best Classical Performance, Orchestra
Boulez Conducts Debussy, Pierre Boulez conducting New Philharmonia Orchestra

Best Chamber Music Performance
Gabrieli, *Canzoni for Brass, Winds, Strings and Organ,*
E. Power Biggs with Edward Tarr Ensemble and Gabrieli
Consort; Vittorio Negri, conductor

Best Classical Performance, Instrumental Soloist(s) (With or Without Orchestra)
Horowitz on Television, Vladimir Horowitz

Best Opera Recording
Mozart, *Cosi fan Tutte,* Erich Leinsdorf conducting New
Philharmonia Orchestra and Ambrosian Opera Chorus; solos:
Price, Raskin, Troyanos, Milnes, Shirley and Flagello (RCA)

Best Choral Performance (Other Than Opera)
The Glory of Gabrieli, Vittorio Negri conducting Gregg Smith
Singers and Texas Boys Choir; George Bragg directing
Edward Tarr Ensemble with E. Power Biggs

Best Classical Vocal Soloist Performance
Rossini Rarities, Montserrat Caballe; Carlo Felice Cillario conducting RCA Italiana Opera Orchestra and Chorus

Best Comedy Recording
To Russell, My Brother, Whom I Slept With, Bill Cosby (Warner
Bros.)

Best Spoken Word Recording
Lonesome Cities, Rod McKuen (Warner Bros.-Seven Arts)

Best Album Cover
Underground, John Berg and Richard Mantel, art directors
(Columbia)

Best Album Notes
Johnny Cash at Folsom Prison, Johnny Cash, annotator

1969

Record of the Year
"Aquarius/Let the Sunshine In," 5th Dimension

Album of the Year
Blood, Sweat and Tears, Blood, Sweat and Tears (Columbia)

Song of the Year
"Games People Play," Joe South, songwriter

Best New Artist of 1969
Crosby, Stills and Nash

Best Contemporary Song
"Games People Play," Joe South, songwriter

Best Contemporary Vocal Performance, Male
"Everybody's Talkin'," Harry Nilsson

Best Contemporary Vocal Performance, Female
"Is That All There Is," Peggy Lee

Best Contemporary Vocal Performance by a Group
"Aquarius/Let the Sunshine In," 5th Dimension

Best Contemporary Performance by a Chorus
"Love Theme From *Romeo and Juliet,*" Percy Faith Orchestra
and Chorus

Best Contemporary Instrumental Performance
"Variations on a Theme by Eric Satie," Blood, Sweat and Tears

Best Rhythm and Blues Song
"Color Him Father," Richard Spencer, songwriter

Best Rhythm and Blues Vocal Performance, Male
"The Chokin' Kind," Joe Simon

Best Rhythm and Blues Vocal Performance, Female
"Share Your Love With Me," Aretha Franklin

Best Rhythm and Blues Vocal Performance by a Group or Duo
"It's Your Thing," Isley Brothers

Best Rhythm and Blues Instrumental Performance
"Games People Play," King Curtis

Best Instrumental Jazz Performance, Small Group or Soloist With Small Group
Willow Weep for Me, Wes Montgomery

Best Instrumental Jazz Performance, Large Group or Soloist With Large Group
"Walking in Space," Quincy Jones

Best Country Song
"A Boy Named Sue," Shel Silverstein, songwriter

Best Country Vocal Performance, Male
"A Boy Named Sue," Johnny Cash

Best Country Vocal Performance, Female
Stand by Your Man, Tammy Wynette

Best Country Performance by a Duo or Group
"MacArthur Park," Waylon Jennings and the Kimberlys

Best Country Instrumental Performance
*The Nashville Brass Featuring Danny Davis Play More
Nashville Sounds,* Danny Davis and the Nashville Brass

Best Gospel Performance
"In Gospel Country," Porter Wagoner and the Blackwood
Brothers

Best Soul Gospel Performance
Oh Happy Day, Edwin Hawkins Singers

Best Sacred Performance
"Ain't That Beautiful Singing," Jake Hess

Best Folk Performance
Clouds, Joni Mitchell

Best Instrumental Arrangement
"Love Theme From *Romeo and Juliet,*" Henry Mancini, arranger

Best Arrangement Accompanying Vocalist(s)
"Spinning Wheel," Fred Lipsius, arranger

Best Instrumental Theme
Midnight Cowboy, John Barry, composer

Best Score From an Original Cast Show Album
Promises, Promises, Burt Bacharach and Hal Davis, composers (Liberty)

Best Original Score Written for Motion Picture or Television
Butch Cassidy and the Sundance Kid, Burt Bacharach,
composer

Album of the Year, Classical
Switched-On Bach, Walter Carlos (Columbia)

Best Classical Performance, Orchestra
Boulez Conducts Debussy, Vol. 2 "Images Pour Orchestre,"
Pierre Boulez conducting Cleveland Orchestra

Best Chamber Music Performance
Gabrieli, *Antiphonal Music of Gabrieli (Canzoni for Brass
Choirs),* the Philadelphia, Cleveland and Chicago Brass
ensembles

Best Classical Performance, Instrumental Soloist(s) (With or Without Orchestra)
Switched-On Bach, Walter Carlos

Best Opera Recording
Wagner, *Siegfried,* Herbert von Karajan conducting Berlin
Philharmonic; solos: Thomas, Stewart, Stolze, Dernesch,
Keleman, Dominguez, Gayer and Ridderbusch (Deutsche
Grammophon)

Best Choral Performance (Other Than Opera)
Berio, *Sinfonia,* Swingle Singers; Ward Swingle, choral master;
Luciano Berio conducting New York Philharmonic

Best Vocal Soloist Performance, Classical
Barber, *Two Scenes From "Antony and Cleopatra";* Knoxville,
Summer of 1915, Leontyne Price; Thomas Schippers con-
ducting New Philharmonia

Best Comedy Recording
Bill Cosby, Bill Cosby (Uni)

Best Spoken Word Recording
We Love You, Call Collect, Art Linkletter and Diane
(Word/Capitol)

Best Recording for Children
Peter, Paul and Mommy, Peter, Paul and Mary (Warner Bros.)

Best Album Cover
America the Beautiful, Evelyn J. Kelbish, painting; David
Stahlberg, graphics (Skye)

Best Album Notes
Nashville Skyline, Johnny Cash, annotator (Columbia)

1970

Record of the Year
"Bridge Over Troubled Water," Simon and Garfunkel

Album of the Year
Bridge Over Troubled Water, Simon and Garfunkel (Columbia)

Song of the Year
"Bridge Over Troubled Water," Paul Simon, songwriter

Best New Artist of the Year
Carpenters

Best Contemporary Song
"Bridge Over Troubled Water," Paul Simon, songwriter

Best Contemporary Vocal Performance, Male
"Everything Is Beautiful," Ray Stevens

Best Contemporary Vocal Performance, Female
I'll Never Fall in Love Again, Dionne Warwick

Best Contemporary Vocal Performance by a Group
"Close to You," Carpenters

Best Contemporary Instrumental Performance
Theme From Z and Other Film Music, Henry Mancini

Best Rhythm and Blues Song
"Patches," Ronald Dunbar and General Johnson, songwriters

Best Rhythm and Blues Vocal Performance, Male
"The Thrill Is Gone," B.B. King

Best Rhythm and Blues Vocal Performance, Female
"Don't Play That Song," Aretha Franklin

Best Rhythm and Blues Vocal Performance by a Duo or Group
"Didn't I (Blow Your Mind This Time)," Delfonics

Best Jazz Performance, Small Group or Soloist With Small Group
Alone, Bill Evans

Best Jazz Performance, Large Group or Soloist With Large Group
Bitches Brew, Miles Davis

Best Country Song
"My Woman, My Woman, My Wife," Marty Robbins,
songwriter

Best Country Vocal Performance, Male
"For the Good Times," Ray Price

Best Country Vocal Performance, Female
"Rose Garden," Lynn Anderson

Best Country Performance by a Duo or Group
"If I Were a Carpenter," Johnny Cash and June Carter

Best Country Instrumental Performance
Me and Jerry, Chet Atkins and Jerry Reed

Best Gospel Performance (Other Than Soul Gospel)
"Talk About the Good Times," Oak Ridge Boys

Best Soul Gospel Performance
"Every Man Wants to Be Free," Edwin Hawkins Singers

Best Sacred Performance
"Everything Is Beautiful," Jake Hess

Aretha Franklin

Best Ethnic or Traditional Recording
"Good Feelin'," T-Bone Walker (Polydor)

Best Instrumental Arrangement
"Theme From *Z,*" Henry Mancini, arranger

Best Arrangement Accompanying Vocalist(s)
"Bridge Over Troubled Water," Paul Simon, Arthur Garfunkel,
Jimmie Haskell, Ernie Freeman and Larry Knechtel,
arrangers

Best Instrumental Composition
"*Airport* Love Theme," Alfred Newman, composer

Best Score From an Original Cast Show Album
Company, Stephen Sondheim, composer (Columbia)

Best Original Score Written for a Motion Picture or Television Special
Let It Be, John Lennon, Paul McCartney, George Harrison and
Ringo Starr, composers

Album of the Year, Classical
Berlioz, *Les Troyens,* Colin Davis conducting Royal Opera
House Orchestra and Chorus; solos: Vickers, Veasey and
Lindholm (Philips)

Best Classical Performance, Orchestra
Stravinsky, *Le Sacre du Printemps,* Pierre Boulez conducting
Cleveland Orchestra

Best Chamber Music Performance
Beethoven, *The Complete Piano Trios,* Eugene Istomin, Isaac
Stern and Leonard Rose

Best Classical Performance, Instrumental Soloist(s) (With or Without Orchestra)
Brahms, *Double Concerto (Concerto in A Minor for Violin and
Cello),* David Oistrakh and Mstislav Rostropovich

Best Choral Performance (Other Than Opera)
New Music of Charles Ives, Gregg Smith conducting Gregg
Smith Singers and Columbia Chamber Ensemble

Best Opera Recording
Berlioz, *Les Troyens,* Colin Davis conducting Royal Opera
House Orchestra and Chorus; solos: Vickers, Veasey and
Lindholm (Philips)

Best Vocal Soloist Performance, Classical
Schubert, *Lieder,* Dietrich Fischer-Dieskau

Best Comedy Recording
The Devil Made Me Buy This Dress, Flip Wilson (Little David)

Best Spoken Word Recording
Why I Oppose the War in Vietnam, Dr. Martin Luther King, Jr.
(Black Forum)

Best Recording for Children
Sesame Street, Sesame Street cast (Columbia)

Best Album Cover
Indianola Mississippi Seeds, Robert Lockart, cover design; Ivan Nagy, photography (ABC)

Best Album Notes
The World's Greatest Blues Singer, Chris Albertson, annotator (Columbia)

1971

Record of the Year
"It's Too Late," Carole King

Album of the Year
Tapestry, Carole King (Ode)

Song of the Year
"You've Got a Friend," Carole King, songwriter

Best New Artist of the Year
Carly Simon

Best Pop Vocal Performance, Male
"You've Got a Friend," James Taylor

Best Pop Vocal Performance, Female
Tapestry, Carole King

Best Pop Vocal Performance by a Group
Carpenters, Carpenters

Best Pop Instrumental Performance
Smackwater Jack, Quincy Jones

Best Rhythm and Blues Song
"Ain't No Sunshine," Bill Withers, songwriter

Best Rhythm and Blues Vocal Performance, Male
"A Natural Man," Lou Rawls

Best Rhythm and Blues Vocal Performance, Female
"Bridge Over Troubled Water," Aretha Franklin

Best Rhythm and Blues Vocal Performance by a Group
"Proud Mary," Ike and Tina Turner

Best Jazz Performance by a Soloist
The Bill Evans Album, Bill Evans

Best Jazz Performance by a Group
The Bill Evans Album, Bill Evans Trio

Best Jazz Performance by a Big Band
"New Orleans Suite," Duke Ellington

Best Country Song
"Help Me Make It Through the Night," Kris Kristofferson, songwriter

Best Country Vocal Performance, Male
"When You're Hot, You're Hot," Jerry Reed

Best Country Vocal Performance, Female
"Help Me Make It Through the Night," Sammi Smith

Best Country Vocal Performance by a Group
"After the Fire Is Gone," Conway Twitty and Loretta Lynn

Best Country Instrumental Performance
"Snowbird," Chet Atkins

Best Gospel Performance (Other Than Soul Gospel)
"Let Me Live," Charley Pride

Best Soul Gospel Performance
Put Your Hand in the Hand of the Man From Galilee, Shirley Caesar

Best Sacred Performance
Did You Think to Pray, Charley Pride

Best Ethnic or Traditional Recording
They Call Me Muddy Waters, Muddy Waters (Chess)

Best Instrumental Arrangement
"Theme From *Shaft,*" Isaac Hayes and Johnny Allen, arrangers

Carole King

Best Arrangement Accompanying Vocalist(s)
"Uncle Albert/Admiral Halsey," Paul McCartney, arranger

Best Instrumental Compostion
"Theme From *Summer of '42,*" Michel Legrand, composer

Best Score From an Original Cast Show Album
Godspell, Stephen Schwartz, composer and producer (Bell)

Best Original Score Written for a Motion Picture or Television Special
Shaft, Isaac Hayes, composer

Album of the Year, Classical
Horowitz Plays Rachmaninoff, Vladimir Horowitz (Columbia)

Best Classical Performance, Orchestra
Mahler, *Symphony No. 1 in D Major,* Carlo Maria Giulini conducting Chicago Symphony Orchestra

Best Chamber Music Performance
Debussy, *Quartet in G Minor,* Ravel, *Quartet in F Major,* Juilliard Quartet

Best Classical Performance, Instrumental Soloist(s) (With Orchestra)
Villa-Lobos, *Concerto for Guitar,* Julian Bream; André Previn conducting London Symphony

Best Classical Performance, Instrumental Soloist(s) (Without Orchestra)
Horowitz Plays Rachmaninoff, Vladimir Horowitz

Best Opera Recording
Verdi, *Aïda,* Erich Leinsdorf conducting London Symphony Orchestra; solos: Price, Domingo, Milnes, Bumbry and Raimondi (RCA)

Best Choral Performance, Classical (Other Than Opera)
Berlioz, *Requiem,* Colin Davis conducting London Symphony Orchestra; Russell Burgess conducting Wandsworth School Boys Choir; Arthur Oldham conducting London Symphony Chorus

Best Classical Vocal Soloist Performance
Leontyne Price Sings Robert Schumann, Leontyne Price

Best Comedy Recording
This Is a Recording, Lily Tomlin (Polydor)

Best Spoken Word Recording
Desiderata, Les Crane (Warner Bros.)

Best Recording for Children
Bill Cosby Talks to Kids About Drugs, Bill Cosby (Uni)

Best Album Cover
Pollution, Dean O. Torrance, album design; Gene Brownell, art director (Prophesy)

Best Album Notes
Sam, Hard and Heavy, Sam Samudio, annotator (Atlantic)

1972

Record of the Year
"The First Time Ever I Saw Your Face," Roberta Flack

Album of the Year
The Concert for Bangla Desh, George Harrison, Ravi Shanker, Bob Dylan, Leon Russell, Ringo Starr, Billy Preston, Eric Clapton and Klaus Voormann (Apple)

Song of the Year
"The First Time Ever I Saw Your Face," Ewan MacColl, songwriter

Best New Artist of the Year
America

Best Pop Vocal Performance, Male
"Without You," Nilsson

Best Pop Vocal Performance, Female
"I Am Woman," Helen Reddy

Best Pop Vocal Performance by a Duo, Group or Chorus
"Where Is the Love," Roberta Flack and Donny Hathaway

Best Pop Instrumental Performance by an Instrumental Performer
"Outa-Space," Billy Preston

Best Pop Instumental Performance With Vocal Coloring
Black Moses, Isaac Hayes

Best Rhythm and Blues Song
"Papa Was a Rolling Stone," Barrett Strong and Norman Whitfield, songwriters

Best Rhythm and Blues Vocal Performance, Male
"Me and Mrs. Jones," Billy Paul

Best Rhythm and Blues Vocal Performance, Female
Young, Gifted and Black, Aretha Franklin

Best Rhythm and Blues Vocal Performance by a Duo, Group, or Chorus
"Papa Was a Rolling Stone," Temptations

Best Jazz Performance by a Soloist
"Alone at Last," Gary Burton

Best Jazz Performance by a Group
"First Light," Freddie Hubbard

Best Jazz Performance by a Big Band
"Toga Brava Suite," Duke Ellington

Best Country Vocal Performance, Female
"Happiest Girl in the Whole USA," Donna Fargo

Best Country Vocal Performance, Male
Charley Pride Sings Heart Songs, Charley Pride

Best Country Vocal Performance by a Duo or Group
"Class of '57," Statler Brothers

Best Country Instrumental Performance
Charlie McCoy/The Real McCoy, Charlie McCoy

Best Country Song
"Kiss an Angel Good Mornin'," Ben Peters, songwriter

Best Gospel Performance
L-O-V-E, Blackwood Brothers

Best Soul Gospel Performance
"Amazing Grace," Aretha Franklin

Best Inspirational Performance
He Touched Me, Elvis Presley

Best Ethnic or Traditional Recording
The London Muddy Waters Session, Muddy Waters (Chess)

Best Instrumental Arrangement
"Theme From *The French Connection,*" Don Ellis, arranger

Best Arrangement Accompanying Vocalist
"What Are You Doing the Rest of Your Life," Michel Legrand, arranger

Best Instrumental Composition
"Brian's Song," Michel Legrand, composer

Best Score From an Original Cast Show Album
Don't Bother Me, I Can't Cope, Micki Grant, composer (Polydor)

Best Original Score Written for a Motion Picture or a Television Special
The Godfather, Nino Rota, composer

Album of the Year, Classical
Mahler, *Symphony No. 8 in E-Flat Major (Symphony of a Thousand),* Sir Georg Solti conducting Chicago Symphony Orchestra, Vienna Boys Choir, Vienna State Opera Chorus, Vienna Singverein Chorus and Soloists (London)

Best Classical Performance, Orchestra
Mahler, *Symphony No. 7 in E Minor,* Sir Georg Solti conducting Chicago Symphony Orchestra

Best Chamber Music Performance
Julian and John, Julian Bream and John Williams

Best Instrumental Soloist Performance, Classical (With Orchestra)
Brahms, *Concerto No. 2,* Artur Rubinstein

Best Instrumental Soloist Performance, Classical (Without Orchestra)
Horowitz Plays Chopin, Vladimir Horowitz

Best Opera Recording
Berlioz, *Benvenuto Cellini,* Colin Davis conducting BBC Symphony and Chorus of Covent Garden (Philips)

Best Choral Performance, Classical
Mahler, *Symphony No. 8 in E-Flat Major (Symphony of a Thousand),* Sir Georg Solti conducting Chicago Symphony Orchestra, Vienna Boys Choir, Vienna State Opera Chorus, Vienna Singverein Chorus and Soloists

[9]**Best Vocal Soloist Performance, Classical**
Brahms, *Die Schöne Magelone,* Dietrich Fischer-Dieskau

Best Comedy Recording
FM and AM, George Carlin (Little David)

Best Spoken Word Recording
Lenny, Original Cast (Blue Thumb)

Best Recording for Children
The Electric Company, Lee Chamberlin, Bill Cosby and Rita Moreno (Warner Bros.)

Best Album Cover
The Siegel Schwall Band, Acy Lehman, art director; Harvey Dinnerstein, artist (Wooden Nickel)

Best Album Notes
Tom T. Hall's Greatest Hits, Tom T. Hall, annotator (Mercury)

Best Album Notes, Classical
Williams, *Symphony No. 2,* James Lyons, annotator (RCA)

1973

Record of the Year
"Killing Me Softly With His Song," Roberta Flack

Album of the Year
Innervisions, Stevie Wonder (Tamla/Motown)

Song of the Year
"Killing Me Softly With His Song," Norman Gimbel and Charles Fox, songwriters

Roberta Flack

Best New Artist of the Year
Bette Midler

Best Pop Vocal Performance, Male
"You Are the Sunshine of My Life," Stevie Wonder

Best Pop Vocal Performance, Female
"Killing Me Softly With His Song," Roberta Flack

Best Pop Vocal Performance by a Duo, Group or Chorus
"Neither One of Us" (Wants to Be the First to Say Goodbye), Gladys Knight and the Pips

Best Pop Instrumental Performance
"Also Sprach Zarathustra (2001)," Eumir Deodato

Best Rhythm and Blues Song
"Superstition," Stevie Wonder, songwriter

Best Rhythm and Blues Vocal Performance, Male
"Superstition," Stevie Wonder

Best Rhythm and Blues Vocal Performance, Female
"Master of Eyes," Aretha Franklin

Best Rhythm and Blues Vocal Performance by a Duo, Group or Chorus
"Midnight Train to Georgia," Gladys Knight and the Pips

Best Rhythm and Blues Instrumental Performance
"Hang on Sloopy," Ramsey Lewis

Best Jazz Performance by a Soloist
God Is in the House, Art Tatum

Best Jazz Performance by a Group
Supersax Plays Bird, Supersax

Best Jazz Performance by a Big Band
Giant Steps, Woody Herman

Best Country Song
"Behind Closed Doors," Kenny O'Dell, songwriter

Best Country Vocal Performance, Male
"Behind Closed Doors," Charlie Rich

Best Country Vocal Performance, Female
"Let Me Be There," Olivia Newton-John

Best Country Vocal Performance by a Duo or Group
"From the Bottle to the Bottom," Kris Kristofferson and Rita Coolidge

Best Country Instrumental Performance
"Dueling Banjos," Eric Weissberg and Steve Mandell

Best Gospel Performance
Release Me (From My Sin), Blackwood Brothers

Best Soul Gospel Performance
"Loves Me Like a Rock," Dixie Hummingbirds

Best Inspirational Performance
Let's Just Praise the Lord, Bill Gaither Trio

Best Ethnic or Traditional Recording
Then and Now, Doc Watson (United Artists)

Best Instrumental Arrangement
"Summer in the City," Quincy Jones, arranger

Best Arrangement Accompanying Vocalist
"Live and Let Die," George Martin, arranger

Best Instrumental Composition
"Last Tango in Paris," Gato Barbieri, composer

Best Score From an Original Cast Show Album
A Little Night Music, Stephen Sondheim, composer

Best Original Score Written for a Motion Picture or a Television Special
Jonathan Livingston Seagull, Neil Diamond, composer

Album of the Year, Classical
Bartók, *Concerto for Orchestra,* Pierre Boulez conducting New York Philharmonic Orchestra (Columbia)

Best Classical Performance, Orchestra
Bartók, *Concerto for Orchestra,* Pierre Boulez conducting New York Philharmonic Orchestra

Best Chamber Music Performance
Joplin, *The Red Back Book,* Gunther Schuller and the New England Conservatory Ragtime Ensemble

Best Classical Performance, Instrumental Soloist (With Orchestra)
Beethoven, *Concerti (5) for Piano and Orchestra,* Vladimir Ashkenazy; Sir Georg Solti conducting Chicago Symphony

Best Classical Performance, Instrumental Soloist (Without Orchestra)
Scriabin, *Horowitz Plays Scriabin,* Vladimir Horowitz

Best Opera Recording
Bizet, *Carmen,* Leonard Bernstein conducting The Metropolitan Opera Orchestra and Manhattan Opera Chorus; solos: Horne, McCracken, Maliponte and Krause (Deutsche Grammophon/Polydor)

Best Choral Performance, Classical
Walton, *Belshazzar's Feast,* André Previn conducting London Symphony Orchestra; Arthur Oldham conducting London Symphony Orchestra Chorus

Best Classical Vocal Soloist Performance
Puccini, *Heroines (La Boheme, Tosca, Manon Lescaut),* Leontyne Price; Downes conducting New Philharmonia

Best Comedy Recording
Los Cochinos, Cheech and Chong (Ode)

Best Spoken Word Recording
Jonathan Livingston Seagull, Richard Harris (Columbia)

Best Recording for Children
Sesame Street Live, Sesame Street cast (Columbia)

Best Album Package
Tommy, Wilkes and Braun, Inc., art director (Ode)

Best Album Notes
God Is in the House, Dan Morgenstern, annotator (Onyx)

Best Album Notes, Classical
Hindemith, *Sonatas for Piano (Complete),* Glenn Gould, annotator (Columbia)

1974

Record of the Year
"I Honestly Love You," Olivia Newton-John

Album of the Year
Fulfillingness' First Finale, Stevie Wonder (Tamla/Motown)

Song of the Year
"The Way We Were," Marilyn and Alan Bergman and Marvin Hamlisch, songwriters

Best New Artist of the Year
Marvin Hamlisch

Best Pop Vocal Performance, Male
Fulfillingness' First Finale, Stevie Wonder

Best Pop Vocal Performance, Female
"I Honestly Love You," Olivia Newton-John

Best Pop Vocal Performance by a Duo, Group or Chorus
"Band on the Run," Paul McCartney and Wings

Best Pop Instrumental Performance
"The Entertainer," Marvin Hamlisch

Best Rhythm and Blues Song
"Living for the City," Stevie Wonder, songwriter

Best Rhythm and Blues Vocal Performance, Male
"Boogie on Reggae Woman," Stevie Wonder

Best Rhythm and Blues Vocal Performance, Female
"Ain't Nothing Like the Real Thing," Aretha Franklin

Best Rhythm and Blues Vocal Performance by a Duo, Group or Chorus
"Tell Me Something Good," Rufus

Best Rhythm and Blues Instrumental Performance
"TSOP" (The Sound of Philadelphia), MFSB

Best Jazz Performance by a Soloist
First Recordings!, Charlie Parker

Best Jazz Performance by a Group
The Trio, Oscar Peterson, Joe Pass and Niels Pedersen

Best Jazz Performance by a Big Band
Thundering Herd, Woody Herman

Best Country Song
"A Very Special Love Song," Norris Wilson and Billy Sherrill, songwriters

Best Country Vocal Performance, Male
"Please Don't Tell Me How the Story Ends," Ronnie Milsap

Best Country Vocal Performance, Female
Love Song, Anne Murray

Best Country Vocal Performance by a Duo or Group
"Fairytale," Pointer Sisters

Best Country Instrumental Performance
The Atkins-Travis Traveling Show, Chet Atkins and Merle Travis

Best Gospel Performance
"The Baptism of Jesse Taylor," Oak Ridge Boys

Best Soul Gospel Performance
In the Ghetto, James Cleveland and the Southern California Community Choir

Best Inspirational Performance
"How Great Thou Art," Elvis Presley

Best Ethnic or Traditional Recording
Two Days in November, Doc and Merle Watson

Best Instrumental Arrangement
"Threshold," Pat Williams, arranger

Best Arrangement Accompanying Vocalists
"Down to You," Joni Mitchell and Tom Scott, arrangers

Best Instrumental Composition
"Tubular Bells" (Theme From *The Exorcist*), Mike Oldfield, composer

Best Score From an Original Cast Show Album
Raisin, Judd Woldin and Robert Britten, composers (Columbia)

Album of Best Original Score Written for a Motion Picture or a Television Special
The Way We Were, Marvin Hamlisch and Alan and Marilyn Bergman, composers (Columbia)

Album of the Year, Classical
Berlioz, *Symphonie Fantastique,* Sir Georg Solti conducting Chicago Symphony (London)

Best Classical Performance, Orchestra
Berlioz, *Symphonie Fantastique,* Sir Georg Solti conducting Chicago Symphony

Best Chamber Music Performance
Brahms and Schumann Trios, Artur Rubinstein, Henryk Szeryng and Pierre Fournier

Best Classical Performance, Instrumental Soloist(s) (With Orchestra)
Shostakovich, *Violin Concerto No. 1,* David Oistrakh

Best Classical Performance, Instrumental Soloist(s) (Without Orchestra)
Albeniz, *Iberia,* Alicia de Larrocha

Best Opera Recording
Puccini, *La Boheme,* Sir Georg Solti conducting London Philharmonic; solos: Caballé, Domingo, Milnes, Blegen and Raimondi (RCA)

Best Choral Performance, Classical (Other Than Opera)
Berlioz, *The Damnation of Faust,* Colin Davis conducting London Symphony Orchestra and Chorus, Ambrosian Singers and Wandsworth School Boys' Choir; solos: Gedda, Bastin, Veasey and Van Allen

Best Classical Vocal Soloist Performance
Leontyne Price Sings Richard Strauss, Leontyne Price

Best Comedy Recording
That Nigger's Crazy, Richard Pryor (Partee/Stax)

Best Spoken Word Recording
Good Evening, Peter Cook and Dudley Moore (Island)

Best Recording for Children
Winnie the Pooh and Tigger Too, Sebastian Cabot, Sterling Holloway and Paul Winchell (Disneyland)

Best Album Package
Come and Gone, Ed Thrasher and Christopher Whorf, art directors (Warner Bros.)

Best Album Notes (tie)
For the Last Time, Charles R. Townsend, annotator (United Artists)

The Hawk Flies, Dan Morgenstern, annotator (Milestone)

Best Album Notes, Classical
The Classic Erich Wolfgang Korngold, Rory Guy, annotator (Angel)

Best Producer of the Year
Thom Bell

1975

Record of the Year
"Love Will Keep Us Together," Captain and Tennille

Album of the Year
Still Crazy After All These Years, Paul Simon (Columbia)

Song of the Year
"Send in the Clowns," Stephen Sondheim, songwriter

Best New Artist of the Year
Natalie Cole

Best Pop Vocal Performance, Male
Still Crazy After All These Years, Paul Simon

Best Pop Vocal Performance, Female
"At Seventeen," Janis Ian

Best Pop Vocal Performance by a Duo, Group or Chorus
"Lyin' Eyes," Eagles

Best Pop Instrumental Performance
"The Hustle," Van McCoy and the Soul City Symphony

Best Rhythm and Blues Song
"Where Is the Love," Harry Wayne Casey, Richard Finch,
    Willie Clarke and Betty Wright, songwriters

Best Rhythm and Blues Vocal Performance, Male
"Living for the City," Ray Charles

Best Rhythm and Blues Vocal Performance, Female
"This Will Be," Natalie Cole

Best Rhythm and Blues Vocal Performance by a Duo, Group or Chorus
"Shining Star," Earth, Wind and Fire

Best Rhythm and Blues Instrumental Performance
"Fly, Robin, Fly," Silver Convention

Best Jazz Performance by a Soloist
Oscar Peterson and Dizzy Gillespie, Dizzy Gillespie

Best Jazz Performance by a Group
No Mystery, Chick Corea and Return to Forever

Best Jazz Performance by a Big Band
Images, Phil Woods with Michel Legrand and His Orchestra

Best Country Song
(Hey Won't You Play) "Another Somebody Done Somebody
    Wrong Song," Chips Moman and Larry Butler,
    songwriters

Best Country Vocal Performance, Male
"Blue Eyes Crying in the Rain," Willie Nelson

Best Country Vocal Performance, Female
"I Can't Help It" (If I'm Still in Love With You), Linda Ronstadt

Best Country Vocal Performance by a Duo or Group
"Lover Please," Kris Kristofferson and Rita Coolidge

Best Country Instrumental Performance
"The Entertainer," Chet Atkins

Best Gospel Performance
No Shortage, Imperials

Best Soul Gospel Performance
Take Me Back, Andrae Crouch and the Disciples

Best Latin Recording
Sun of Latin Music, Eddie Palmieri (Coco)

Best Inspirational Performance
Jesus, We Just Want to Thank You, Bill Gaither Trio

Best Ethnic or Traditional Recording
The Muddy Waters Woodstock Album, Muddy Waters (Chess)

Best Instrumental Arrangement
"The Rockford Files," Mike Post and Pete Carpenter, arrangers

Best Arrangement Accompanying Vocalists
"Misty," Ray Stevens, arranger

Captain and Tennille

Best Instrumental Composition
"Images," Michel Legrand, composer

Best Cast Show Album
The Wiz, Charlie Smalls, composer (Atlantic)

Album of Best Original Score Written for a Motion Picture or a Television Special
Jaws, John Williams, composer (MCA)

Album of the Year, Classical
Beethoven, *Symphonies Complete,* Sir Georg Solti conducting
    Chicago Symphony Orchestra (London)

Best Classical Performance, Orchestra
Ravel, *Daphnis et Chloë (Complete Ballet),* Pierre Boulez con-
    ducting New York Philharmonic

Best Chamber Music Performance (Instrumental or Vocal)
Schubert, *Trios nos. 1 in B-Flat Major, ops. 99 and 2 in E-Flat
    Major, Op. 11 (The Piano Trios),* Artur Rubinstein, Henryk
    Szeryng and Pierre Fournier

Best Classical Performance, Instrumental Soloist (With Orchestra)
Ravel, *Concerto for Left Hand and Concerto for Piano in G
    Major;* Fauré, *Fantaisie for Piano and Orchestra,* Alicia de
    Lorrocha; De Burgos and Foster conducting London
    Philharmonic

Best Classical Performance, Instrumental Soloist (Without Orchestra)
Bach, *Sonatas and Partitas for Violin Unaccompanied,* Nathan
    Milstein

Best Opera Recording
Mozart, *Cosi fan Tutte,* Colin Davis conducting Royal Opera
    House, Covent Garden; principle solos: Caballé, Baker,
    Gedda, Ganzarolli, Van Allan and Cotrubas (Philips)

Best Choral Performance, Classical
Orff, *Carmina Burana,* Robert Page directing the Cleveland
    Orchestra Chorus and Boys Choir; Michael Tilson Thomas
    conducting Cleveland Orchestra; soloists: Blegen, Binder
    and Riegel

Best Classical Vocal Soloist Performance
Mahler, *Kindertotenlieder,* Janet Baker; Leonard Bernstein
    conducting Israel Philharmonic

Best Comedy Recording
Is It Something I Said?, Richard Pryor (Reprise)

Best Spoken Word Recording
Give 'Em Hell Harry, James Whitmore (United Artists)

Best Recording for Children
The Little Prince, Richard Burton, narrator (RIP)

Best Album Package
Honey, Jim Ladwig, art director (Mercury)

Best Album Notes (Non-Classical)
Blood on the Tracks, Pete Hamill, annotator (Columbia)

Best Album Notes, Classical
Footlifters, Gunther Schuller, annotator (Columbia)

Best Producer of the Year
Arif Mardin

1976

Record of the Year
"This Masquerade," George Benson

Album of the Year
Songs in the Key of Life, Stevie Wonder (Tamla/Motown)

Song of the Year
"I Write the Songs," Bruce Johnston, songwriter

Best New Artist of the Year
Starland Vocal Band

Best Pop Vocal Performance, Male
Songs in the Key of Life, Stevie Wonder

Best Pop Vocal Performance, Female
Hasten Down the Wind, Linda Ronstadt

Best Pop Vocal Performance by a Duo, Group or Chorus
"If You Leave Me Now," Chicago

Best Pop Instrumental Performance
Breezin', George Benson

Best Rhythm and Blues Song
"Lowdown," Boz Scaggs and David Paich, songwriters

Best Rhythm and Blues Vocal Performance, Male
"I Wish," Stevie Wonder

Best Rhythm and Blues Vocal Performance, Female
"Sophisticated Lady" (She's a Different Lady), Natalie Cole

Best Rhythm and Blues Vocal Performance by a Duo, Group or Chorus
"You Don't Have to Be a Star" (To Be in My Show), Marilyn McCoo and Billy Davis, Jr.

Best Rhythm and Blues Instrumental Performance
"Theme From *Good King Bad*," George Benson

Best Jazz Vocal Performance
Fitzgerald & Pass Again, Ella Fitzgerald

Best Jazz Performance by a Soloist
Basie and Zoot, Count Basie

Best Jazz Performance by a Big Band
The Ellington Suites, Duke Ellington

Best Country Song
"Broken Lady," Larry Gatlin, songwriter

Best Country Vocal Performance, Male
(I'm a) "Stand By My Woman Man," Ronnie Milsap

Best Country Vocal Performance, Female
Elite Hotel, Emmylou Harris

Best Country Vocal Performance by a Duo or Group
"The End Is Not in Sight" (The Cowboy Tune), Amazing Rhythm Aces

Best Country Instrumental Performance
Chester and Lester, Chet Atkins and Les Paul

Best Gospel Performance
"Where the Soul Never Dies," Oak Ridge Boys

Best Soul Gospel Performance
How I Got Over, Mahalia Jackson

Best Latin Recording
Unfinished Masterpiece, Eddie Palmieri (Coco)

Best Inspirational Performance
The Astonishing, Outrageous, Amazing, Incredible, Unbelievable, Different World of Gary S. Paxton, Gary S. Paxton

Best Ethnic or Traditional Recording
Mark Twang, John Hartford (Flying Fish)

Best Instrumental Arrangement
"Leprechaun's Dream," Chick Corea, arranger

Best Arrangement Accompanying Vocalists
"If You Leave Me Now," Jimmy Haskell and James William Guercio, arrangers

Best Arrangement for Voices
"Afternoon Delight," Starland Vocal Band, arrangers

Best Instrumental Composition
Bellavia, Chuck Mangione, composer

Best Cast Show Album
Bubbling Brown Sugar, various composers (H&L)

Album of Best Original Score Written for a Motion Picture or a Television Special
Car Wash, Norman Whitfield, composer (MCA)

Album of the Year, Classical
Beethoven, *Five Piano Concertos*, Artur Rubinstein; Daniel Barenboim conducting London Philharmonic (RCA)

Best Classical Orchestral Performance
Strauss, *Also Sprach Zarathustra*, Sir Georg Solti conducting Chicago Symphony

Best Chamber Music Performance
The Art of Courtly Love, David Munrow conducting Early Music Consort of London

Best Classical Performance, Instrumental Soloist (With Orchestra)
Beethoven, *The Five Piano Concertos*, Artur Rubinstein; Daniel Barenboim conducting London Philharmonic

Best Classical Performance, Instrumental Soloist (Without Orchestra)
Horowitz Concerts 1975/76, Vladimir Horowitz

Best Opera Recording
Gershwin, *Porgy and Bess*, Lorin Maazel conducting Cleveland Orchestra and Chorus (London)

Best Choral Performance, Classical
Rachmaninoff, *The Bells*, Arthur Oldham, Chorus master of London Symphony Chorus; André Previn conducting London Symphony Orchestra

Best Classical Vocal Soloist Performance
Music of Victor Herbert, Beverly Sills

Best Comedy Recording
Bicentennial Nigger, Richard Pryor (Warner Bros.)

Best Spoken Word Recording
Great American Documents, Orson Welles, Henry Fonda, Helen Hayes and James Earl Jones (CBS)

Best Recording for Children
Prokofiev, *Peter and the Wolf*; Saint-Saëns, *Carnival of the Animals*, Hermione Gingold, narrator; Karl Bohm, conductor (Deutsche Grammophon)

Best Album Package
Chicago X, John Berg, art director (Columbia)

Best Album Notes
The Changing Face of Harlem, the Savoy Sessions, Dan Morgenstern, annotator (Savoy)

Best Producer of the Year
Stevie Wonder

1977

Record of the Year
"Hotel California," Eagles

Album of the Year
Rumours, Fleetwood Mac (Warner Bros.)

Song of the Year (tie)
"Love Theme From *A Star Is Born*" (Evergreen), Barbra
Streisand and Paul Williams, songwriters

"You Light Up My Life," Joe Brooks, songwriter

Best New Artist of the Year
Debby Boone

Best Pop Vocal Performance, Male
"Handy Man," James Taylor

Best Pop Vocal Performance, Female
"Love Theme From *A Star Is Born*" (Evergreen), Barbra
Streisand

Best Pop Vocal Performance by a Duo, Group or Chorus
"How Deep Is Your Love," Bee Gees

Best Pop Instrumental Performance
Star Wars, John Williams conducting London Symphony
Orchestra

Best Rhythm and Blues Song
"You Make Me Feel Like Dancing," Leo Sayer and Vini Poncia,
songwriters

Best Rhythm and Blues Vocal Performance, Male
Unmistakably Lou, Lou Rawls

Best Rhythm and Blues Vocal Performance, Female
"Don't Leave Me This Way," Thelma Houston

**Best Rhythm and Blues Vocal Performance by a Duo, Group or
Chorus**
"Best of My Love," Emotions

Best Rhythm and Blues Instrumental Performance
"Q," Brothers Johnson

Best Jazz Vocal Performance
Look to the Rainbow, Al Jarreau

Best Jazz Performance by a Soloist
The Giants, Oscar Peterson

Vladimir Horowitz

Best Jazz Performance by a Group
The Phil Woods Six — Live From the Showboat, Phil Woods

Best Jazz Performance by a Big Band
Prime Time, Count Basie and His Orchestra

Best Country Song
"Don't It Make My Brown Eyes Blue," Richard Leigh,
songwriter

Best Country Vocal Performance, Male
"Lucille," Kenny Rogers

Best Country Vocal Performance, Female
"Don't It Make My Brown Eyes Blue," Crystal Gayle

Best Country Vocal Performance by a Duo or Group
"Heaven's Just a Sin Away," The Kendalls

Best Country Instrumental Performance
Country Instrumentalist of the Year, Hargus "Pig" Robbins

Best Gospel Performance, Contemporary or Inspirational
Sail On, Imperials

Best Gospel Performance, Traditional
"Just a Little Talk With Jesus," Oak Ridge Boys

Best Soul Gospel Performance, Contemporary
Wonderfull, Edwin Hawkins and the Edwin Hawkins Singers

Best Soul Gospel Performance, Traditional
James Cleveland Live at Carnegie Hall, James Cleveland

Best Latin Recording
Dawn, Mongo Santamaria (Vaya)

Best Inspirational Performance
Home Where I Belong, B.J. Thomas

Best Ethnic or Traditional Recording
Hard Again, Muddy Waters (Blue Sky/CBS)

Best Instrumental Arrangement
"Nadia's Theme" (The Young and the Restless), Harry Betts,
Perry Botkin, Jr. and Barry De Vorzon, arrangers

Best Arrangement Accompanying Vocalist(s)
"Love Theme From *A Star Is Born*" (Evergreen), Ian Freebairn-
Smith, arranger

Best Arrangement for Voices
"New Kid in Town," Eagles, arrangers

Best Instrumental Composition
"Main Title From *Star Wars,*" John Williams, composer

Best Cast Show Album
Annie, Charles Strouse and Martin Charnin, composers (Columbia)

**Best Original Score Written for a Motion Picture or
Television Special**
Star Wars, John Williams, composer (20th Century)

Album of the Year, Classical
Concert of the Century, Leonard Bernstein, Vladimir Horowitz,
Isaac Stern, Mstislav Rostropovich, Dietrich Fischer-
Dieskau, Yehudi Menuhin and Lyndon Woodside
(Columbia)

Best Classical Orchestral Performance
Mahler, *Symphony No. 9,* Carlo Maria Giulini conducting
Chicago Symphony Orchestra

Best Chamber Music Performance
Schoenberg, *Quartets for Strings,* Juilliard Quartet

**Best Classical Performance, Instrumental Soloist(s)
(With Orchestra)**
Vivaldi, *The Four Seasons,* Itzhak Perlman, violin; Itzhak
Perlman conducting London Philharmonic Orchestra

**Best Classical Performance Instrumental Soloist(s)
(Without Orchestra)**
Beethoven, *Sonata for Piano No. 18;* Schumann,
Fantasiestücke, Artur Rubinstein, piano

Best Opera Recording
Gershwin, *Porgy and Bess,* John De Main conducting Sherwin M. Goldman Houston Grand Opera Production; solos: Albert, Dale, Smith, Shakesnider, Lane, Brice and Smalls (RCA)

Best Choral Performance, Classical (Other Than Opera)
Verdi, *Requiem,* Sir Georg Solti conducting Chicago Symphony Orchestra; Margaret Hillis, choral director of the Chicago Symphony Chorus

Best Classical Vocal Soloist Performance
Bach, *Arias,* Janet Baker; Neville Marriner conducting Academy of St. Martin-in-the-Fields

Best Comedy Recording
Let's Get Small, Steve Martin (Warner Bros.)

Best Spoken Word Recording
The Belle of Amherst, Julie Harris (Credo)

Best Recording for Children
Aren't You Glad You're You, Sesame Street cast and Muppets (Sesame Street)

Best Album Package
Simple Dreams, Kosh, art director (Asylum)

Best Album Notes
Bing Crosby: A Legendary Performer, George T. Simon, annotator (RCA)

Best Producer of the Year
Peter Asher

1978

Record of the Year
"Just the Way You Are," Billy Joel

Album of the Year
Saturday Night Fever, Bee Gees, David Shire, Yvonne Elliman, Tevares, Kool and the Gang, K.C. and the Sunshine Band, MFSB, Trammps, Walter Murphy and Ralph MacDonald (RSO)

Song of the Year
"Just the Way You Are," Billy Joel, songwriter

Best New Artist of the Year
A Taste of Honey

Best Pop Vocal Performance, Male
"Copacabana" (At the Copa), Barry Manilow

Best Pop Vocal Performance, Female
"You Needed Me," Anne Murray

Best Pop Vocal Performance by a Duo, Group or Chorus
Saturday Night Fever, Bee Gees

Best Pop Instrumental Performance
Children of Sanchez, Chuck Mangione Group

Best Rhythm and Blues Song
"Last Dance," Paul Jabara, songwriter

Best Rhythm and Blues Vocal Performance, Male
"On Broadway," George Benson

Best Rhythm and Blues Vocal Performance, Female
"Last Dance," Donna Summer

Best Rhythm and Blues Vocal Performance by a Duo, Group or Chorus
All 'n All, Earth, Wind and Fire

Best Rhythm and Blues Instrumental Performance
"Runnin'," Earth, Wind and Fire

Best Jazz Vocal Performance
All Fly Home, Al Jarreau

Best Jazz Instrumental Performance, Soloist
Montreux '77 Oscar Peterson Jam, Oscar Peterson

Best Jazz Instrumental Performance, Group
Friends, Chick Corea

Best Jazz Instrumental Performance, Big Band
Live in Munich, Thad Jones and Mel Lewis

Best Country Song
"The Gambler," Don Schlitz, songwriter

Best Country Vocal Performance, Male
"Georgia on My Mind," Willie Nelson

Best Country Vocal Performance, Female
Here You Come Again, Dolly Parton

Best Country Vocal Performance by a Duo or Group
"Mamas Don't Let Your Babies Grow Up to Be Cowboys," Waylon Jennings and Willie Nelson

Best Country Instrumental Performance
"One O'Clock Jump," Asleep at the Wheel

Best Gospel Performance, Contemporary or Inspirational
"What a Friend," Larry Hart

Best Gospel Performance, Traditional
Refreshing, Happy Goodman Family

Best Soul Gospel Performance, Contemporary
Live in London, Andrae Crouch and the Disciples

Best Soul Gospel Performance, Traditional
Live and Direct, Mighty Clouds of Joy

Best Latin Recording
Homenaje a Beny Moré, Tito Puente (Tico)

Best Inspirational Performance
Happy Man, B.J. Thomas

Best Ethnic or Traditional Recording
I'm Ready, Muddy Waters (Blue Sky)

Best Instrumental Arrangement
"Main Title" (Overture Part One, *The Wiz* Original Soundtrack), Quincy Jones and Robert Freedman, arrangers

Best Arrangement Accompanying Vocalist(s)
"Got to Get You Into My Life," Maurice White, arranger

Best Arrangement for Voices
"Stayin' Alive," Bee Gees, arrangers

Best Instrumental Composition
"Theme From *Close Encounters of the Third Kind,*" John Williams, composer

Best Cast Show Album
Ain't Misbehavin', Thomas "Fats" Waller and others, composers (RCA Red Seal)

Best Album of Original Score Written for a Motion Picture or a Television Special
Close Encounters of the Third Kind, John Williams, composer (Arista)

Album of the Year, Classical
Brahms, *Concerto for Violin in D Major,* Itzhak Perlman; Carlo Maria Giulini conducting Chicago Symphony (Angel)

Best Classical Orchestral Performance
Beethoven, *Symphonies (Complete),* Herbert von Karajan conducting Berlin Philharmonic

Best Chamber Music Performance
Beethoven, *Sonatas for Violin and Piano (Complete),* Itzhak Perlman and Vladimir Ashkenazy

Best Classical Performance, Instrumental Soloist(s) (With Orchestra)
Rachmaninoff, *Concerto No. 3 in D Minor for Piano (Horowitz Golden Jubilee),* Vladimir Horowitz; Eugene Ormandy conducting Philadelphia Orchestra

Best Classical Performance, Instrumental Soloist(s) (Without Orchestra)
The Horowitz Concerts 1977/78, Vladimir Horowitz

Best Opera Recording
Lehar, *The Merry Widow,* Julius Rudel conducting New York City Opera Orchestra and Chorus; solos: Sills and Titus (Angel)

Best Choral Performance, Classical (Other Than Opera)
Beethoven, *Missa Solemnis,* Sir Georg Solti, conductor and Margaret Hillis, choral director, Chicago Symphony Orchestra and Chorus

Best Classical Vocal Soloist Performance
Luciano Pavarotti — Hits From Lincoln Center, Luciano Pavarotti

Best Comedy Recording
A Wild and Crazy Guy, Steve Martin (Warner Bros.)

Best Spoken Word Recording
Citizen Kane (Original Motion Picture Soundtrack), Orson Welles (Mark 56)

Best Recording for Children
The Muppet Show, Jim Henson (Arista)

Best Album Package
Boys in the Trees, Johnny Lee and Tony Lane, art directors (Elektra)

Best Album Notes
A Bing Crosby Collection, vols. I and II, Michael Brooks, annotator (Columbia)

Best Historical Repackage Album
Lester Young Story Vol. 3 (Columbia)

Best Producers of the Year
Bee Gees, Albhy Galuten and Karl Richardson

1979

Record of the Year
"What a Fool Believes," Doobie Brothers

Album of the Year
52nd Street, Billy Joel (Columbia)

Song of the Year
"What a Fool Believes," Kenny Loggins and Michael McDonald, songwriters

Best New Artist
Rickie Lee Jones

Best Pop Vocal Performance, Male
52nd Street, Billy Joel

Best Pop Vocal Performance, Female
"I'll Never Love This Way Again," Dionne Warwick

Best Pop Vocal Performance by a Duo, Group or Chorus
Minute by Minute, Doobie Brothers

Best Pop Instrumental Performance
"Rise," Herb Alpert

Best Rock Vocal Performance, Male
"Gotta Serve Somebody," Bob Dylan

Best Rock Vocal Performance, Female
"Hot Stuff," Donna Summer

Best Rock Vocal Performance by a Duo or Group
"Heartache Tonight," Eagles

Best Rock Instrumental Performance
"*Rockestra* Theme," Wings

Best Rhythm and Blues Song
"After the Love Has Gone," David Foster, Jay Graydon and Bill Champlin, songwriters

Best Rhythm and Blues Vocal Performance, Male
"Don't Stop 'Til You Get Enough," Michael Jackson

Best Rhythm and Blues Vocal Performance, Female
"Deja Vu," Dionne Warwick

Gloria Gaynor

Best Rhythm and Blues Vocal Performance by a Duo, Group or Chorus
"After the Love Has Gone," Earth, Wind and Fire

Best Rhythm and Blues Instrumental Performance
"Boogie Wonderland," Earth, Wind and Fire

Best Disco Recording
"I Will Survive," Gloria Gaynor (Polydor)

Best Jazz Vocal Performance
Fine and Mellow, Ella Fitzgerald

Best Jazz Instrumental Performance, Soloist
Jousts, Oscar Peterson

Best Jazz Instrumental Performance, Group
Duet, Gary Burton and Chick Corea

Best Jazz Instrumental Performance, Big Band
At Fargo, 1940 Live, Duke Ellington

Best Jazz Fusion Performance, Vocal or Instrumental
8:30, Weather Report

Best Country Song
"You Decorated My Life," Debbie Hupp and Bob Morrison, songwriters

Best Country Vocal Performance, Male
"The Gambler," Kenny Rogers

Best Country Vocal Performance, Female
Blue Kentucky Girl, Emmylou Harris

Best Country Vocal Performance by a Duo or Group
"The Devil Went Down to Georgia," Charlie Daniels Band

Best Country Instrumental Performance
"Big Sandy/Leather Britches," Doc and Merle Watson

Best Gospel Performance, Contemporary or Inspirational
Heed the Call, Imperials

Best Gospel Performance, Traditional
Lift Up the Name of Jesus, Blackwood Brothers

Best Soul Gospel Performance, Contemporary
I'll Be Thinking of You, Andrae Crouch

Best Soul Gospel Performance, Traditional
Changing Times, Mighty Clouds of Joy

Best Latin Recording
Irakere, Irakere (Columbia)

Best Inspirational Performance
You Gave Me Love (When Nobody Gave Me a Prayer), B.J. Thomas

Best Ethnic or Traditional Recording
Muddy "Mississippi" Waters Live, Muddy Waters (Sky/CBS)

Best Instrumental Arrangement
"Soulful Strut," Claus Ogerman, arranger

Best Arrangement Accompanying Vocalist(s)
"What a Fool Believes," Michael McDonald, arranger

Best Instrumental Composition
"Main Title Theme From *Superman*," John Williams, composer

Best Cast Show Album
Sweeney Todd, Stephen Sondheim, composer and lyricist (RCA)

Best Album of Original Score Written for a Motion Picture or a Television Special
Superman, John Williams, composer (Warner Bros.)

Best Classical Album
Brahms, *Symphonies Complete,* Sir Georg Solti conducting Chicago Symphony Orchestra (London)

Best Classical Orchestral Recording
Brahms, *Symphonies Complete,* Sir Georg Solti conducting Chicago Symphony Orchestra (London)

Best Chamber Music Performance
Copland, *Appalachian Spring,* Dennis Russell Davies conducting St. Paul Chamber Orchestra

Best Classical Performance, Instrumental Soloist(s) (With Orchestra)
Bartók, *Concertos for Piano nos. 1 and 2,* Maurizio Pollini; Abbado conducting Chicago Symphony Orchestra

Best Classical Performance, Instrumental Soloist(s) (Without Orchestra)
The Horowitz Concerts 1978/79, Vladimir Horowitz

Best Opera Recording
Britten, *Peter Grimes,* Colin Davis conducting Orchestra and Chorus of the Royal Opera House, Covent Garden; solos: Vickers, Harper and Summers (Philips)

Best Choral Performance, Classical (Other Than Opera)
Brahms, *A German Requiem,* Sir Georg Solti, conductor and Margaret Hillis, choral director, Chicago Symphony Chorus and Orchestra

Best Classical Vocal Soloist Performance
O Sole Mio, Luciano Pavarotti

Best Comedy Recording
Reality . . . What a Concept, Robin Williams (Casablanca)

Best Spoken Word, Documentary or Drama Recording
Ages of Man (Readings From Shakespeare), Sir John Gielgud (Caedmon)

Best Recording for Children
The Muppet Movie, Jim Henson, creator (Atlantic)

Best Album Package
Breakfast in America, Mike Doud and Mick Haggerty, art directors (A&M)

Best Album Notes
Charlie Parker: The Complete Savoy Sessions, Bob Porter and James Patrick, annotators (Savoy)

Best Historical Reissue
Billie Holiday (Giants of Jazz) (Time Life)

Producer of the Year (Non-Classical)
Larry Butler

Classical Producer of the Year
James Mallinson

1980

Record of the Year
"Sailing," Christopher Cross

Album of the Year
Christopher Cross, Christopher Cross (Warner Bros.)

Song of the Year
"Sailing," Christopher Cross, songwriter

Best New Artist
Christopher Cross

Best Pop Vocal Performance, Male
"This Is It," Kenny Loggins

Best Pop Vocal Performance, Female
"The Rose," Bette Midler

Best Pop Performance by a Duo or Group With Vocal
"Guilty," Barbra Streisand and Barry Gibb

Best Pop Instrumental Performance
One on One, Bob James and Earl Klugh

Best Rock Vocal Performance, Male
Glass Houses, Billy Joel

Best Rock Vocal Performance, Female
Crimes of Passion, Pat Benatar

Best Rock Performance by a Duo or Group With Vocal
Against the Wind, Bob Seger and the Silver Bullet Band

Best Rock Instrumental Performance
"Reggatta de Blanc," Police

Best Rhythm and Blues Song
"Never Knew Love Like This Before," Reggie Lucas and James Mtume, songwriters

Best Rhythm and Blues Performance, Male
Give Me the Night, George Benson

Best Rhythm and Blues Vocal Performance, Female
"Never Knew Love Like This Before," Stephanie Mills

Best Rhythm and Blues Performance by a Duo or Group With Vocal
"Shining Star," Manhattans

Best Rhythm and Blues Instrumental Performance
"Off Broadway," George Benson

Best Jazz Vocal Performance, Male
"Moody's Mood," George Benson

Best Jazz Vocal Performance, Female
A Perfect Match/Ella and Basie, Ella Fitzgerald

Best Jazz Instrumental Performance, Soloist
I Will Say Goodbye, Bill Evans

Best Jazz Instrumental Performance, Group
We Will Meet Again, Bill Evans

Best Jazz Instrumental Performance, Big Band
On the Road, Count Basie and Orchestra

Best Jazz Fusion Performance, Vocal or Instrumental
"Birdland," Manhattan Transfer

Best Country Song
"On the Road Again," Willie Nelson, songwriter

Best Country Vocal Performance, Male
"He Stopped Loving Her Today," George Jones

Best Country Vocal Performance, Female
"Could I Have This Dance," Anne Murray

Best Country Performance by a Duo or Group With Vocal
"That Lovin' You Feelin' Again," Roy Orbison and Emmylou Harris

Best Country Instrumental Performance
"Orange Blossom Special/Hoedown," Gilley's Urban Cowboy Band

Best Gospel Performance, Contemporary or Inspirational
The Lord's Prayer, Reba Rambo, Dony McGuire, B.J. Thomas, Andrae Crouch, the Archers, Walter and Tramiane Hawkins and Cynthia Clawson

Best Gospel Performance, Traditional
We Come to Worship, Blackwood Brothers

Best Soul Gospel Performance, Contemporary
Rejoice, Shirley Caesar

Best Soul Gospel Performance, Traditional
Lord, Let Me Be an Instrument, James Cleveland and the Charles Fold Singers

Best Latin Recording
La Onda Va Bien, Cal Tjader (Concord Jazz)

Best Inspirational Performance
With My Song I Will Praise Him, Debby Boone

Best Ethnic or Traditional Recording
Rare Blues, Dr. Isaiah Ross, Maxwell Street Jimmy, Big Joe Williams, Son House, Rev. Robin Wilkins, Little Brother Montgomery and Sunnyland Slim (Takoma)

Best Instrumental Arrangement
"Dinorah, Dinorah," Quincy Jones and Jerry Hey, arrangers

Best Arrangement Accompanying Vocalist(s)
"Sailing," Michael Omatian and Christopher Cross, arrangers

Best Arrangement for Voices
"Birdland," Janis Siegel, arranger

Best Instrumental Composition
The Empire Strikes Back, John Williams, composer

Best Cast Show Album
Evita — Premier American Recording, Andrew Lloyd Webber, composer; Tim Rice, lyricist (MCA)

Best Album of Original Score Written for a Motion Picture or a Television Special
The Empire Strikes Back, John Williams, composer (RSO)

Best Classical Album
Berg, *Lulu (Complete Version),* Pierre Boulez conducting Orchestre de l'Opera de Paris; solos: Stratas, Minton, Mazura and Blankenheim (Deutsche Grammophon)

Best Classical Orchestral Recording
Bruckner, *Symphony No. 6 in A Major,* Sir Georg Solti conducting Chicago Symphony Orchestra (London)

Best Chamber Music Performance
Music for Two Violins (Moszkowski, *Suite for Two Violins;* Shostakovich, *Duets;* Prokofiev, *Sonata for Two Violins*), Itzhak Perlman and Pinchas Zukerman

Best Classical Performance, Instrumental Soloist(s) (With Orchestra) (tie)
Berg, *Concerto for Violin and Orchestra;* Stravinsky, *Concerto in D Major for Violin and Orchestra,* Itzhak Perlman; Seiji Ozawa conducting Boston Symphony Orchestra

Brahms, *Concerto in A Minor for Violin and Cello (Double Concerto),* Itzhak Perlman and Mstislav Rostropovich; Bernard Haitink conducting Concertgebouw Orchestra

Best Classical Performance Instrumental Soloist(s) (Without Orchestra)
The Spanish Album, Itzhak Perlman

Best Opera Recording
Berg, *Lulu (Complete Version),* Pierre Boulez conducting Orchestre de l'Opera de Paris; solos: Stratas, Minton, Mazura and Blankenheim

Best Choral Performance, Classical (Other Than Opera)
Mozart, *Requiem,* Carlo Maria Giulini, conductor and Norbert Balatsch, chorus master, Philharmonia Chorus and Orchestra (Deutsche Grammophon)

Best Classical Vocal Soloist Performance
Prima Donna, Volume 5 Great Soprano Arias From Handel to Britten, Leontyne Price; Henry Lewis conducting Philharmonia Orchestra

Best Comedy Recording
No Respect, Rodney Dangerfield (Casablanca)

Best Spoken Word, Documentary or Drama Recording
Gertrude Stein, Gertrude Stein, Gertrude Stein, Pat Carroll (Caedmon)

Best Recording for Children
In Harmony/A Sesame Street Record, Doobie Brothers, James Taylor, Carly Simon, Bette Midler, Muppets, Al Jarreau, Linda Ronstadt, Wendy Waldman, Libby Titus and Dr. John, Livingston Taylor, George Benson and Pauline Wilson, Lucy Simon, Kate Taylor and the Simon/Taylor Family (Sesame Street/Warner Bros.)

Best Album Package
Against the Wind, Roy Kohara, art director (Capitol)

Best Album Notes
Trilogy: Past, Present and Future, David McClintick, annotator (Reprise/Warner Bros.)

Best Historical Reissue Album
Segovia — The EMI Recordings 1927–39 (Angel)

Producer of the Year (Non-Classical)
Phil Ramone

Classical Producer of the Year
Robert Woods

1981

Record of the Year
"Bette Davis Eyes," Kim Carnes

Album of the Year
Double Fantasy, John Lennon and Yoko Ono (Warner Bros./Geffen)

Song of the Year
"Bette Davis Eyes," Donna Weiss and Jackie DeShannon, songwriters

Best New Artist
Sheena Easton

Best Pop Vocal Performance, Male
Breakin Away, Al Jarreau

Best Pop Vocal Performance, Female
Lena Horne: The Lady and Her Music Live On Broadway, Lena Horne

Best Pop Vocal Performance by a Duo or Group With Vocal
"Boy From New York City," Manhattan Transfer

Best Pop Instrumental Performance
"The Theme From *Hill Street Blues,*" Mike Post featuring Larry Carlton

Best Rock Vocal Performance, Male
"Jessie's Girl," Rick Springfield

Best Rock Vocal Performance, Female
"Fire and Ice," Pat Benatar

Best Rock Performance by a Duo or Group With Vocal
"Don't Stand So Close to Me," Police

Best Rock Instrumental Performance
"Behind My Camel," Police

Best Rhythm and Blues Song
"Just the Two of Us," Bill Withers, William Salter and Ralph MacDonald, songwriters

Best Rhythm and Blues Performance, Male
"One Hundred Ways," James Ingram

Best Rhythm and Blues Vocal Performance, Female
"Hold On I'm Comin'," Aretha Franklin

Best Rhythm and Blues Performance by a Duo or Group With Vocal
The Dude, Quincy Jones

Best Rhythm and Blues Instrumental Performance
"All I Need Is You," David Sanborn

Best Jazz Vocal Performance, Male
"Blue Rondo a la Turk," Al Jarreau

Yoko Ono and John Lennon

Best Jazz Vocal Performance, Female
Digital III at Montreux, Ella Fitzgerald

Best Jazz Vocal Performance, Duo or Group
"Until I Met You" (Corner Pocket), Manhattan Transfer

Best Jazz Instrumental Performance, Soloist
Bye Bye Blackbird, John Coltrane

Best Jazz Instrumental Performance, Group
*Chick Corea and Gary Burton in Concert, Zurich, October 28,
1979,* Chick Corea and Gary Burton

Best Jazz Instrumental Performance, Big Band
Walk on the Water, Gerry Mulligan and His Orchestra

Best Jazz Fusion Performance, Vocal or Instrumental
Winelight, Grover Washington, Jr.

Best Country Song
"9 to 5," Dolly Parton, songwriter

Best Country Vocal Performance, Male
(There's) "No Gettin' Over Me," Ronnie Milsap

Best Country Vocal Performance, Female
"9 to 5," Dolly Parton

Best Country Performance by a Duo or Group With Vocal
"Elvira," Oak Ridge Boys

Best Country Instrumental Performance
Country, After All These Years, Chet Atkins

Best Gospel Performance, Contemporary or Inspirational
Priority, Imperials

Best Gospel Performance, Traditional
The Masters V, J.D. Sumner, James Blackwood, Hovie Lister,
Rosie Rozell and Jake Hess

Best Soul Gospel Performance, Contemporary
Don't Give Up, Andrae Crouch

Best Soul Gospel Performance, Traditional
The Lord Will Make a Way, Al Green

Best Latin Recording
"Guajira Pa la Jeva," Clare Fischer (Pausa)

Best Inspirational Performance
Amazing Grace, B.J. Thomas

Best Ethnic or Traditional Recording
There Must Be a Better World Somewhere, B.B. King (MCA)

Best Arrangement of an Instrumental Recording
"Velas," Quincy Jones and Johnny Mandel, arrangers

Best Instrumental Arrangement Accompanying Vocal(s)
"Ai No Corrida," Quincy Jones and Jerry Hey, arrangers

Best Vocal Arrangement for Two or More Voices
"A Nightingale Sang in Berkeley Square," Gene Puerling,
arranger

Best Instrumental Composition
"The Theme From *Hill Street Blues,*" Mike Post, composer

Best Cast Show Album
Lena Horne: The Lady and Her Music Live on Broadway, various composers and lyricists (Qwest/Warner Bros.)

**Best Album of Original Score Written for a Motion Picture or
a Television Special**
Raiders of the Lost Ark, John Williams, composer
(Columbia/CBS)

Best Classical Album
Mahler, *Symphony No. 2 in C Minor,* Sir Georg Solti conducting
Chicago Symphony Orchestra and Chorus (London)

Best Classical Orchestral Recording
Mahler, *Symphony No. 2 in C Minor,* Sir Georg Solti conducting
Chicago Symphony Orchestra and Chorus (London)

Best Chamber Music Performance
Tchaikovsky, *Piano Trio in A Minor,* Itzhak Perlman, Lynn
Harrell and Vladimir Ashkenazy

**Best Classical Performance, Instrumental Soloist(s)
(With Orchestra)**
Isaac Stern 60th Anniversary Celebration, Isaac Stern, Itzhak
Perlman and Pinchas Zukerman; Zubin Mehta conducting
New York Philharmonic Orchestra

**Best Classical Performance, Instrumental Soloist(s)
(Without Orchestra)**
The Horowitz Concerts 1979/80, Vladimir Horowitz

Best Opera Recording
Janácek, *From the House of the Dead,* Sir Charles Mackerras
conducting Vienna Philharmonic; solos: Zahradnicek,
Zitek and Zidek (London)

Best Choral Performance (Other Than Opera)
Haydn, *The Creation,* Neville Marriner conducting Chorus of
Academy of St. Martin-in-the-Fields

Best Classical Vocal Soloist Performance
Live From Lincoln Center, Sutherland-Horne-Pavarotti, Joan
Sutherland, Marilyn Horne and Luciano Pavarotti

Best Comedy Recording
Rev. Du Rite, Richard Pryor (Laff)

Best Spoken Word, Documentary or Drama Recording
Donovan's Brain, Orson Welles (Radiola)

Best Recording for Children
Sesame Country, Muppets, Glen Campbell, Crystal Gayle,
Loretta Lynn, Tanya Tucker; Jim Henson (Sesame Street)

Best Album Package
Tatoo You, Peter Corriston, art director (Rolling
Stones/Atlantic)

Best Album Notes
Erroll Garner, Master of the Keyboard, Dan Morgenstern,
annotator (Book-of-the-Month Records)

Best Historical Album
Hoagy Carmichael: From "Star Dust" to "Ole Buttermilk Sky"
(Book-of-the-Month Records)

Video of the Year
"Michael Nesmith in Elephant Parts," Michael Nesmith

Producer of the Year (Non-Classical)
Quincy Jones

Classical Producer of the Year
James Mallinson

1982

Record of the Year
"Rosanna," Toto

Album of the Year
Toto IV, Toto (Columbia)

Song of the Year
"Always on My Mind," Johnny Christopher, Mark James and Wayne Carson, songwriters

Best New Artist
Men at Work

Best Pop Vocal Performance, Male
"Truly," Lionel Richie

Best Pop Vocal Performance, Female
"You Should Hear How She Talks About You," Melissa Manchester

Best Pop Performance by a Duo or Group With Vocal
"Up Where We Belong," Joe Cocker and Jennifer Warnes

Best Pop Instrumental Performance
"*Chariots of Fire* Theme" (dance version), Ernie Watts

Best Rock Vocal Performance, Male
"Hurts So Good," John Cougar

Best Rock Vocal Performance, Female
"Shadows of the Night," Pat Benatar

Best Rock Performance by a Duo or Group With Vocal
"Eye of the Tiger," Survivor

Best Rock Instrumental Performance
"D.N.A.," A Flock of Seagulls

Best Rhythm and Blues Song
"Turn Your Love Around," Jay Graydon, Steve Lukather and Bill Champlin, songwriters

Best Rhythm and Blues Vocal Performance, Male
"Sexual Healing," Marvin Gaye

Best Rhythm and Blues Performance, Female
"And I Am Telling You I'm Not Going," Jennifer Holliday

Best Rhythm and Blues Performance by a Duo or Group With Vocal (tie)
"Let It Whip," Dazz Band
"Wanna Be With You," Earth, Wind and Fire

Best Rhythm and Blues Instrumental Performance
"Sexual Healing," Marvin Gaye

Best Jazz Vocal Performance, Male
An Evening With George Shearing and Mel Tormé, Mel Tormé

Best Vocal Jazz Performance, Female
Gershwin Live!, Sarah Vaughan

Best Jazz Vocal Performance, Duo or Group
"Route 66," Manhattan Transfer

Best Jazz Instrumental Performance, Soloist
We Want Miles, Miles Davis

Best Jazz Instrumental Performance, Group
"More" Live, Phil Woods Quartet

Best Jazz Instrumental Performance, Big Band
Warm Breeze, Count Basie and His Orchestra

Best Jazz Fusion Performance, Vocal or Instrumental
Offramp, Pat Metheny Group

Best Country Song
"Always on My Mind," Johnny Christopher, Mark James and Wayne Carson, songwriters

Best Country Vocal Performance, Male
"Always on My Mind," Willie Nelson

Best Country Vocal Performance, Female
"Break It to Me Gently," Juice Newton

Best Country Performance by a Duo or Group With Vocal
Mountain Music, Alabama

Best Country Instrumental Performance
"Alabama Jubilee," Roy Clark

Best Gospel Performance, Contemporary
Age to Age, Amy Grant

Best Gospel Performance, Traditional
I'm Following You, Blackwood Brothers

Best Soul Gospel Performance, Contemporary
Higher Plane, Al Green

Best Soul Gospel Performance, Traditional
Precious Lord, Al Green

Best Latin Recording
Machito and His Salsa Big Band '82, Machito (Timeless)

Best Inspirational Performance
He Set My Life to Music, Barbara Mandrell

Best Traditional Blues Recording
Alright Again, Clarence Gatemouth Brown (Rounder)

Best Ethnic or Traditional Folk Recording
Queen Ida and the Bon Temps Zydeco Band on Tour, Queen Ida (GNR/Crescendo)

Best Arrangement on an Instrumental Recording
"Flying," John Williams, arranger

Best Instrumental Arrangement Accompanying Vocal(s)
"Rosanna," Jerry Hey, David Paich and Jeff Porcaro, arrangers

Best Vocal Arrangement for Two or More Voices
"Rosanna," David Paich, arranger

Best Instrumental Composition
"Flying" (Theme From *E.T. the Extra-Terrestrial*), John Williams, composer

Best Cast Show Album
Dreamgirls, Henry Krieger, composer; Tom Eyen, lyricist (Geffen/Warner Bros.)

Best Album of Original Score Written for a Motion Picture or a Television Special
E.T. the Extra-Terrestrial, John Williams, composer (MCA)

Best Classical Album
Bach, *The Goldberg Variations,* Glenn Gould (CBS)

Best Classical Orchestral Recording
Mahler, *Symphony No. 7 in E Minor,* James Levine conducting Chicago Symphony Orchestra (RCA)

Best Chamber Music Performance
Brahms, *The Sonatas for Clarinet and Piano, Op. 120,* Richard Stoltzman and Richard Goode

Best Classical Performance, Instrumental Soloist(s) (With Orchestra)
Elgar, *Concerto for Violin in B Minor,* Itzhak Perlman; Daniel Barenboim conducting Chicago Symphony

Best Classical Performance, Instrumental Soloist(s) (Without Orchestra)
Bach, *The Goldberg Variations,* Glenn Gould

Best Opera Recording
Wagner, *Der Ring des Nibelungen,* Pierre Boulez conducting Bayreuth Festival Orchestra; solos: Jones, Altmeyer, Wenkel, Hofmann, Jung, Jerusalem, Zednik, McIntrye, Salminen and Becht (Philips)

Best Choral Performance (Other Than Opera)
Berlioz, *La Damnation de Faust,* Sir Georg Solti conducting Chicago Symphony Orchestra; Margaret Hillis, chorus director, Chicago Symphony Chorus

Best Classical Vocal Soloist Performance
Leontyne Price Sings Verdi, Leontyne Price; Zubin Mehta conducting Israel Philharmonic Orchestra

Michael Jackson

Best Comedy Recording
Live on the Sunset Strip, Richard Pryor (Warner Bros.)

Best Spoken Word, Documentary or Drama Recording
Raiders of the Lost Ark: The Movie on Record (Columbia)

Best Recording for Children
In Harmony 2, Billy Joel, Bruce Springsteen, James Taylor, Kenny Loggins, Carly and Lucy Simon, Teddy Pendergrass, Crystal Gayle, Lou Rawls, Deniece Williams, Janis Ian and Dr. John (CBS)

Best Album Package
Get Closer, Kosh and Ron Larson, art directors (Elektra/Asylum)

Best Album Notes
Bunny Berigan (Giants of Jazz), John Chilton and Richard Sudhalter, art directors (Time Life)

Best Historical Album
The Tommy Dorsey/Frank Sinatra Sessions vols. 1, 2 and 3 (RCA)

Video of the Year
"Olivia Physical," Olivia Newton-John

Producer of the Year (Non-Classical)
Toto

Classical Producer of the Year
Robert Woods

1983

Record of the Year
"Beat It," Michael Jackson

Album of the Year
Thriller, Michael Jackson (Epic/CBS)

Song of the Year
"Every Breath You Take," Sting, songwriter

Best New Artist
Culture Club

Best Pop Vocal Performance, Male
Thriller, Michael Jackson

Hard-to-Find Classical Recordings

Having trouble locating a classical title? The following stores accept mail and telephone orders.

A Classical Record
547 W. 27th St.
New York, NY 10001
(212) 675-8010

Academy Record Store
12 W. 18th St.
New York, NY 10011
(212) 242-3000

Acoustic Sounds
Box 2043
Salina, KS 67402-2043
(800) 525-1630

Benedikt & Salmon
3020 Meade Ave.
San Diego, CA 92116
(619) 281-3345

Briggs & Briggs
1270 Massachusetts Ave.
Cambridge, MA 02138
(617) 547-2007

Canterbury Records
805 E. Colorado Blvd.
Pasadena, CA 91101
(818) 792-7184

Encore Productions
P.O. Box 2240
Stamford, CT 06906-0240
(800) 546-2968

Footlight Records
113 E. 12th St.
New York, NY 10003
(212) 533-1572

H & B Recordings Direct
12037 Starcrest
San Antonio, TX 78247
(800) 222-6872

Harvey Gilman Rediscoveries
243 W. 76th St.
New York, NY 10023
(212) 496-1681

Music for All
2908 E. Third Ave.
Denver, CO 80206
(303) 388-0487

Music Revolution
4055 S. Dale Mabry
Tampa, FL 33611
(813) 831-8889

Nathan Muchnick Inc.
1725 Chesnut St.
Philadelphia, PA 19103
(800) 373-9873

Opera World
P.O. Box 800
Concord, MA 01742
(800) 996-7372

Parnassus Records
56 Parnassus Lane
Saugerties, NY 12477
(914) 246-3332

Rara Avis
77 Wittenberg Road
Bearsville, NY 12409
(914) 679-1054

SKR Classical
539 E. Liberty
Ann Arbor, MI 48104
(800) 272-4506

Tower Records
Tower Records Mail Order
22 E. Fourth St., Suite 302
New York, NY 10003
(800) 648-4844

Yankee Music Search
P.O. Box 1143
Flushing, NY 11354
(718) 463-1702

Best Pop Vocal Performance, Female
"Flashdance: What a Feeling," Irene Cara

Best Pop Performance by a Duo or Group With Vocal
"Every Breath You Take," Police

Best Pop Instrumental Performance
"Being With You," George Benson

Best Rock Vocal Performance, Male
"Beat It," Michael Jackson

Best Rock Vocal Performance, Female
"Love Is a Battlefield," Pat Benatar

Best Rock Performance by a Duo or Group With Vocal
Synchronicity, Police

Best New Rhythm and Blues Song
"Billie Jean," Michael Jackson, songwriter

Best Rhythm and Blues Vocal Performance, Male
"Billie Jean," Michael Jackson

Best Rhythm and Blues Vocal Performance, Female
Chaka Khan, Chaka Khan

Best Rhythm and Blues Vocal Performance by a Duo or Group With Vocal
"Ain't Nobody," Rufus and Chaka Khan

Best Rhythm and Blues Instrumental Performance
"Rockit," Herbie Hancock

Best Jazz Vocal Performance, Male
Top Drawer, Mel Tormé

Best Jazz Vocal Performance, Female
The Best Is Yet to Come, Ella Fitzgerald

Best Jazz Vocal Performance, Duo or Group
"Why Not!," Manhattan Transfer

Best Jazz Instrumental Performance, Soloist
Think of One, Wynton Marsalis

Best Jazz Instrumental Performance, Group
At the Vanguard, Phil Woods Quartet

Best Jazz Instrumental Performance, Big Band
All in Good Time, Rob McConnell and the Boss Brass

Best Jazz Fusion Performance, Vocal or Instrumental
Travels, Pat Metheny Group

Best New Country Song
"Stranger in My House," Mike Reid, songwriter

Best Country Vocal Performance, Male
"I.O.U.," Lee Greenwood

Best Country Vocal Performance, Female
"A Little Good News," Anne Murray

Best Country Performance by a Duo or Group With Vocal
The Closer You Get, Alabama

Best Country Instrumental Performance
"Fireball," New South (Ricky Skaggs, Jerry Douglas, Tony Rice, J.D. Crowe and Todd Phillips)

Best Gospel Performance, Male
Walls of Glass, Russ Taff

Best Gospel Performance, Female
"Ageless Medley," Amy Grant

Best Gospel Performance by a Duo or Group
"More Than Wonderful," Sandi Patti and Larnelle Harris

Best Soul Gospel Performance, Male
I'll Rise Again, Al Green

Best Soul Gospel Performance, Female
We Sing Praises, Sandra Crouch

Best Soul Gospel Performance by a Duo or Group
"I'm So Glad I'm Standing Here Today," Bobby Jones with Barbara Mandrell

Best Latin Pop Performance
Me Enamore, José Feliciano

Best Tropical Latin Performance
On Broadway, Tito Puente and His Latin Ensemble

Best Inspirational Performance
"He's a Rebel," Donna Summer

Best Traditional Blues Recording
Blues 'n Jazz, B.B. King (MCA)

Best Mexican-American Performance
"Anselma," Los Lobos

Best Ethnic or Traditional Folk Recording
I'm Here, Clifton Chenier and His Red Hot Louisiana Band (Alligator)

Best Arrangement on an Instrumental
"Summer Sketches '82," Dave Grusin, arranger

Best Instrumental Arrangement Accompanying Vocal(s)
"What's New," Nelson Riddle, arranger

Best Vocal Arrangement for Two or More Voices
"Be Bop Medley," Arif Mardin and Chaka Khan, arrangers

Best Instrumental Composition
"Love Theme From *Flashdance,*" Giorgio Moroder, composer

Best Cast Show Album
Cats (Complete Original Broadway Cast Recording), Andrew Lloyd Webber, producer (Geffen/Warner Bros.)

Best Album of Original Score Written for a Motion Picture or a Television Special
Flashdance, Giorgio Moroder, Keith Forsey, Irene Cara, Shandi Sinnamon, Ronald Magness, Douglas Cotler, Richard Gilbert, Michael Boddicker, Jerry Hey, Phil Ramone, Michael Sembello, Kim Carnes, Duane Hitchings, Craig Krampf and Dennis Matkosky, songwriters (Casablanca/Polygram)

Best Classical Album
Mahler, *Symphony No. 9 in D Major,* Sir Georg Solti conducting Chicago Symphony Orchestra and Chorus (London)

Best Classical Orchestral Recording
Mahler, *Symphony No. 9 in D Major,* Sir Georg Solti conducting Chicago Symphony Orchestra (London)

Best Chamber Music Performance
Brahms, *Sonata for Cello and Piano in E Minor, Op. 38 and Sonata in F Major, Op. 99,* Mstislav Rostropovich and Rudolf Serkin

Best Classical Performance, Instrumental Soloist(s) (With Orchestra)
Haydn, *Concerto for Trumpet and Orchestra in E-Flat Major;* L. Mozart, *Concerto for Trumpet and Orchestra in D Major;* Hummel, *Concerto for Trumpet and Orchestra in E-Flat Major,* Wynton Marsalis; Raymond Leppard conducting National Philharmonic Orchestra

Best Classical Performance, Instrumental Soloist(s) (Without Orchestra)
Beethoven, *Sonata for Piano No. 12 in A-Flat Major, Op. 26 and No. 13 in E-Flat Major, Op. 27, No. 1,* Glenn Gould

Best Opera Recording (tie)
Mozart, *Le Nozzi de Figaro,* Sir Georg Solti conducting London Philharmonic; solos: Kanawa, Popp, Ramey, Allen, Moll and von Stade (London)

Verdi, *La Traviata* (Original Soundtrack), James Levine conducting The Metropolitan Opera Orchestra and Chorus; solos: Stratas, Domingo and MacNeil (Elektra)

Best Choral Performance (Other Than Opera)
Haydn, *The Creation,* Sir Georg Solti conducting Chicago Symphony Orchestra; Margaret Hillis, choral director, Chicago Symphony Chorus

Best Classical Vocal Soloist Performance
Leontyne Price and Marilyn Horne in Concert at The Met, Leontyne Price and Marilyn Horne; James Levine conducting The Metropolitan Opera Orchestra

Best Comedy Recording
Eddie Murphy, Comedian, Eddie Murphy (The Entertainment Co./Columbia)

Best Spoken Word or Non-Musical Recording
Copland, *A Lincoln Portrait,* William Warfield (Mercury/Philips)

Best Recording for Children
E.T. the Extra-Terrestrial, Michael Jackson, narration and vocals (MCA)

Best Album Package
Speaking in Tongues, Robert Rauschenberg, art director (Sire/Warner Bros.)

Best Album Notes
The "Interplay" Sessions, Orrin Keepnews, annotator (Milestone)

Best Historical Album
The Greatest Recordings of Arturo Toscanini Symphonies Vol. I, Arturo Toscanini (Franklin Mint)

Best Video, Short Form
"Girls on Film/Hungry Like the Wolf," Duran Duran

Producers of the Year (Non-Classical)
Quincy Jones and Michael Jackson

Classical Producers of the Year
Marc J. Aubort and Joanna Nickrenz

1984

Record of the Year
"What's Love Got to Do With It," Tina Turner

Album of the Year
Can't Slow Down, Lionel Richie (Motown)

Song of the Year
"What's Love Got to Do With It," Graham Lyle and Terry Britten, songwriters

Best New Artist
Cyndi Lauper

Best Pop Vocal Performance, Male
"Against All Odds (Take a Look at Me Now)," Phil Collins

Best Pop Vocal Performance, Female
"What's Love Got to Do With It," Tina Turner

Best Pop Performance by a Duo or Group With Vocal
"Jump (For My Love)," Pointer Sisters

Best Pop Instrumental Performance
"Ghostbusters" (instrumental version), Ray Parker, Jr.

Best Rock Vocal Performance, Male
"Dancing in the Dark," Bruce Springsteen

Best Rock Vocal Performance, Female
"Better Be Good to Me," Tina Turner

Best Rock Performance by a Duo or Group With Vocal
Purple Rain — Music From the Motion Picture, Prince and the Revolution

Best Rock Instrumental Performance
"Cinema," Yes

Best New Rhythm and Blues Song
"I Feel for You," Prince, songwriter

Best Rhythm and Blues Vocal Performance, Male
"Caribbean Queen (No More Love on the Run)," Billy Ocean

Best Rhythm and Blues Vocal Performance, Female
"I Feel for You," Chaka Khan

Best Rhythm and Blues Performance by a Duo or Group With Vocal
"Yah Mo B There," James Ingram and Michael McDonald

Best Rhythm and Blues Instrumental Performance
Sound-System, Herbie Hancock

Best Jazz Vocal Performance
Nothin' but the Blues, Joe Williams

Best Jazz Instrumental Performance, Soloist
Hot House Flowers, Wynton Marsalis

Best Jazz Instrumental Performance, Group
"New York Scene," Art Blakey

Best Jazz Instrumental Performance, Big Band
88 Basie Street, Count Basie and His Orchestra

Best Jazz Fusion Performance, Vocal or Instrumental
First Circle, Pat Metheny Group

Best Country Song
"City of New Orleans," Steve Goodman, songwriter

Best Country Vocal Performance, Male
"That's the Way Love Goes," Merle Haggard

Best Country Vocal Performance, Female
"In My Dreams," Emmylou Harris

Best Country Performance by a Duo or Group With Vocal
"Mama He's Crazy," Judds

Best Country Instrumental Performance
"Wheel Hoss," Ricky Skaggs

Best Gospel Performance, Male
Michael W. Smith, Michael W. Smith

Best Gospel Performance, Female
"Angels," Amy Grant

Best Gospel Performance by a Duo or Group
"Keep the Flame Burning," Debby Boone and Phil Driscoll

Best Soul Gospel Performance, Male
"Always Remember," Andrae Crouch

Best Soul Gospel Performance, Female
Sailin', Shirley Caesar

Best Soul Gospel Performance by a Duo or Group
"Sailin' on the Sea of Your Love," Shirley Caeser and Al Green

Best Latin Pop Performance
Always in My Heart (Siempre en mi Corazón), Placido Domingo

Best Tropical Latin Performance
Palo Pa Rumba, Eddie Palmieri

Best Mexican/American Performance
"Me Gustas Tal Como Eres," Sheena Easton and Luis Miguel

Best Inspirational Performance
"Forgive Me," Donna Summer

Bruce Springsteen

Best Traditional Blues Recording
Blues Explosion, John Hammond, Stevie Ray Vaughan and Double Trouble, Sugar Blue, Koko Taylor and the Blues Machine, Luther "Guitar Junior" Johnson and J.B. Hutto and the New Hawks (Atlantic)

Best Ethnic or Traditional Folk Recording
Elizabeth Cotten Live!, Elizabeth Cotten (Arhoolie)

Best Reggae Recording
Anthem, Black Uhuru (Island)

Best Arrangement on an Instrumental
"Grace" (Gymnastics Theme), Quincy Jones and Jeremy Lubbock, arrangers

Best Instrumental Arrangement Accompanying Vocal(s)
"Hard Habit to Break," David Foster and Jeremy Lubbock, arrangers

Best Vocal Arrangement for Two or More Voices
"Automatic," Pointer Sisters, arrangers

Best Instrumental Composition (tie)
"The Natural," Randy Newman, composer

"Olympic Fanfare and Theme," John Williams, composer

Best Cast Show Album
Sunday in the Park With George, Stephen Sondheim, composer and lyricist (RCA)

Best Album of Original Score Written for a Motion Picture or a Television Special
Purple Rain, Prince, John L. Nelson, Lisa and Wendy, songwriters (Warner Bros.)

Best New Classical Composition
Antony and Cleopatra, Samuel Barber, composer

Best Classical Album
Amadeus (Original Soundtrack), Neville Marriner conducting the Academy of St. Martin-in-the-Fields; Ambrosian Opera Chorus; Choristers of Westminster Abbey (Fantasy)

Best Classical Orchestral Recording
Prokofiev, *Symphony No. 5 in B-Flat, Op. 100,* Leonard Slatkin conducting Saint Louis Symphony (RCA)

Best Chamber Music Performance
Beethoven, *The Late String Quartets,* Juilliard String Quartet

Best Classical Performance, Instrumental Soloist(s) (With Orchestra)
Wynton Marsalis, Edita Gruberova: Handel, Purcell, Torelli, Fasch, Molter, Wynton Marsalis and Edita Gruberova; Raymond Leppard conducting English Chamber Orchestra

Best Classical Performance, Instrumental Soloist(s) (Without Orchestra)
Bach, *The Unaccompanied Cello Suites,* Yo-Yo Ma

Best Opera Recording
Bizet, *Carmen* (Original Soundtrack), Lorin Maazel conducting Orchestre National de France; Choeurs et Maitrise de Radio France; solos: Johnson, Esham, Domingo and Raimondi (Erato)

Best Choral Performance (Other Than Opera)
Brahms, *A German Requiem,* James Levine conducting Chicago Symphony Orchestra; Margaret Hillis, choral director, Chicago Symphony Chorus

Best Classical Vocal Soloist Performance
Ravel, *Songs of Maurice Ravel,* Jessye Norman, Jose Van Dam and Heather Harper; Pierre Boulez conducting the Members of Ensemble Intercontemporain and BBC Symphony Orchestra

Best Comedy Recording
Eat It, "Weird Al" Yankovic (Rock & Roll)

Best Spoken Word or Non-Musical Recording
The Words of Gandhi, Ben Kingsley (Caedmon)

Best Recording for Children
Where the Sidewalk Ends, Shel Silverstein (Columbia)

Best Album Package
She's So Unusual, Janet Perr, art director (Portrait/CBS)

Best Album Notes
Big Band Jazz, Gunther Schuller and Martin Williams, songwriters (Smithsonian)

Best Historical Album
Big Band Jazz, Paul Whiteman, Fletcher Henderson, Chick Webb, Tommy Dorsey, Count Basie, Benny Goodman and others (Smithsonian)

Best Video, Short Form
"David Bowie," David Bowie

Best Video Album
Making Michael Jackson's Thriller, Michael Jackson (Vestron Music Video)

Producers of the Year (Non-Classical) (tie)
David Foster

Lionel Richie and James Anthony Carmichael

Classical Producer of the Year
Steven Epstein

1985

Record of the Year
"We Are the World," USA for Africa

Album of the Year
No Jacket Required, Phil Collins (Atlantic)

Song of the Year
"We Are the World," Michael Jackson and Lionel Richie, songwriters

Best New Artist
Sade

Best Pop Vocal Performance, Male
No Jacket Required, Phil Collins

Best Pop Vocal Performance, Female
"Saving All My Love for You," Whitney Houston

Best Pop Performance by a Duo or Group With Vocal
"We Are the World," USA for Africa

Phil Collins

Best Pop Instrumental Performance
"Miami Vice Theme," Jan Hammer

Best Rock Vocal Performance, Male
"The Boys of Summer," Don Henley

Best Rock Vocal Performance, Female
"One of the Living," Tina Turner

Best Rock Performance by a Duo or Group With Vocal
"Money for Nothing,' Dire Straits

Best Rock Instrumental Performance
"Escape," Jeff Beck

Best Rhythm and Blues Song
"Freeway of Love," Narada Michael Walden and Jeffrey
Cohen, songwriters

Best Rhythm and Blues Vocal Performance, Male
In Square Circle, Stevie Wonder

Best Rhythm and Blues Vocal Performance, Female
"Freeway of Love," Aretha Franklin

**Best Rhythm and Blues Performance by a Duo or Group
With Vocal**
"Nightshift," Commodores

Best Rhythm and Blues Instrumental Performance
Musician, Ernie Watts

Best Jazz Vocal Performance, Male
"Another Night in Tunisia," Jon Hendricks and Bobby
McFerrin

Best Jazz Vocal Performance, Female
Cleo at Carnegie (The 10th Anniversary Concert), Cleo Laine

Best Jazz Vocal Performance, Duo or Group
Vocalese, Manhattan Transfer

Best Jazz Instrumental Performance, Soloist
Black Codes From the Underground, Wynton Marsalis

Best Jazz Instrumental Performance, Group
Black Codes From the Underground, Wynton Marsalis Group

Best Jazz Instrumental Performance, Big Band
The Cotton Club — Original Motion Picture Soundtrack, John
Barry and Bob Wilber

Best Jazz Fusion Performance, Vocal or Instrumental
Straight to the Heart, David Sanborn

Best Country Song
"Highwayman," Jimmy L. Webb, songwriter

Best Country Vocal Performance, Male
"Lost in the Fifties Tonight" (In the Still of the Night), Ronnie Milsap

Best Country Vocal Performance, Female
"I Don't Know Why You Don't Want Me," Rosanne Cash

Best Country Performance by a Duo or Group With Vocal
Why Not Me, Judds

Best Country Instrumental Performance
"Cosmic Square Dance," Chet Atkins and Mark Knopfler

Best Gospel Performance, Male
"How Excellent Is Thy Name," Larnelle Harris

Best Gospel Performance, Female
Unguarded, Amy Grant

Best Soul Gospel Performance, Male
"Bring Back the Days of Yea and Nay," Marvin Winans

Best Soul Gospel Performance, Female
"Martin," Shirley Caesar

Best Soul Gospel Performance by a Duo or Group
Tomorrow, Winans

Best Latin Pop Performance
Ec Facil Amar, Lani Hall

Best Tropical Latin Performance (tie)
Mambo Diablo, Tito Puente and His Latin Ensemble

Solito, Eddie Palmieri

Best Mexican/American Performance
Simplemente Mujer, Vikki Carr

Best Inspirational Performance
"Come Sunday," Jennifer Holliday

Best Traditional Blues Recording
"My Guitar Sings the Blues," B.B. King (MCA)

Best Ethnic or Traditional Folk Recording
"My Toot Toot," Rockin' Sidney (Maison De Soul)

Best Reggae Recording
Cliff Hanger, Jimmy Cliff (Columbia/CBS)

Best Polka Recording
70 Years of Hits, Frank Yankovic (Cleveland International/CBS)

Best Arrangement on an Instrumental
"Early a.m. Attitude," Dave Grusin and Lee Ritenour, arrangers

Best Instrumental Arrangement Accompanying Vocal(s)
"Lush Life," Nelson Riddle, arranger

Best Vocal Arrangement for Two or More Voices
"Another Night in Tunisia," Cheryl Bentyne and Bobby
McFerrin, arrangers

Best Instrumental Composition
"Miami Vice Theme," Jan Hammer, composer

Best Cast Show Album
West Side Story, Stephen Sondheim, lyricist; Leonard
Bernstein, composer (Deutsche Grammophone)

**Best Album of Original Score Written for a Motion Picture or
Television Special**
Beverly Hills Cop, Sharon Robinson, Jon Gilutin, Bunny Hull,
Hawk, Howard Hewett, Micki Free, Sue Sheridan, Howie
Rice, Keith Forsey, Harold Faltermeyer, Allee Willis, Dan
Sembello, Marc Benno and Richard Theisen, composers
and songwriters (MCA)

Best Contemporary Composition
Requiem, Andrew Lloyd Webber, composer (Angel)

Best Classical Album
Berlioz, *Requiem,* Robert Shaw conducting Atlanta Symphony
Orchestra and Chorus; solo: Aler (Telarc)

Best New Classical Artist
Chicago Pro Musica

Best Classical Orchestral Recording
Fauré, *Pelléas et Mélisande,* Robert Shaw conducting Atlanta
Symphony Orchestra

Best Chamber Music Performance
Brahms, *Cello and Piano Sonatas in E Minor and F Major,*
Emanuel Ax and Yo-Yo Ma

**Best Classical Performance, Instrumental Soloist(s)
(With Orchestra)**
Elgar, *Cello Concerto, Op. 85;* Walton, *Concerto for Cello and
Orchestra,* Yo-Yo Ma; André Previn conducting London
Symphony Orchestra

**Best Classical Performance, Instrumental Soloist(s)
(Without Orchestra)**
Ravel, *Gaspard de la Nuit, Pavane Pour Une Infant Defunte,
Valses Nobles et Sentimentales,* Vladimir Ashkenazy

Best Opera Recording
Schoenberg, *Moses und Aron,* Sir Georg Solti conducting
Chicago Symphony Orchestra and Chorus; solos: Mazura
and Langridge (London)

Best Choral Performance (Other Than Opera)
Berlioz, *Requiem,* Robert Shaw conducting Atlanta Symphony
Chorus and Orchestra

Best Classical Vocal Soloist Performance
Berlioz, *Requiem,* John Aler; Robert Shaw conducting Atlanta
Symphony Orchestra and Chorus

Best Comedy Recording
Whoopi Goldberg (Original Broadway Show Recording), Whoopi Goldberg (Geffen)

Best Spoken Word or Non-Musical Recording
Ma Rainey's Black Bottom, Original Broadway cast (Manhattan)

Best Recording for Children
Follow That Bird (Original Motion Picture Soundtrack), Jim Henson's Muppets and the Sesame Street cast (RCA)

Best Album Package
Lush Life, Kosh and Ron Larson, art directors (Asylum)

Best Album Notes
Sam Cooke Live at the Harlem Square Club, 1963, Peter Guralnick, annotator (RCA)

Best Historical Album
RCA/MET — 100 Singers-100 Years, Melba, Schumann-Heink, Caruso, Price, Verrett, Domingo and 94 others (RCA Red Seal)

Best Music Video, Short Form
"We Are the World, the Video Event," USA for Africa

Best Music Video, Long Form
"Huey Lewis and the News: The Heart of Rock 'n Roll," Huey Lewis and the News

Producers of the Year (Non-Classical)
Phil Collins and Hugh Padgham

Classical Producer of the Year
Robert Woods

1986

Record of the Year
"Higher Love," Steve Winwood

Album of the Year
Graceland, Paul Simon (Warner Bros.)

Song of the Year
"That's What Friends Are For," Burt Bacharach and Carole Bayer Sager, songwriters

Best New Artist
Bruce Hornsby and the Range

Best Pop Vocal Performance, Male
"Higher Love," Steve Winwood

Best Pop Vocal Performance, Female
The Broadway Album, Barbra Streisand

Best Pop Performance by a Duo or Group With Vocal
"That's What Friends Are For," Dionne Warwick and Friends Featuring Elton John, Gladys Knight and Stevie Wonder

Best Pop Instrumental Performance (Orchestra, Group or Soloist)
"*Top Gun* Anthem," Harold Faltermeyer and Steve Stevens

Best Rock Vocal Performance, Male
"Addicted to Love," Robert Palmer

Best Rock Vocal Performance, Female
"Back Where You Started," Tina Turner

Best Rock Performance by a Duo or Group With Vocal
"Missionary Man," Eurythmics

Best Rock Instrumental Performance (Orchestra, Group or Soloist)
"Peter Gunn," Art of Noise featuring Duane Eddy

Best Rhythm and Blues Song
"Sweet Love," Anita Baker, Louis A. Johnson and Gary Bias, songwriters

Best Rhythm and Blues Vocal Performance, Male
"Living in America," James Brown

Best Rhythm and Blues Vocal Performance, Female
Rapture, Anita Baker

Best Rhythm and Blues Performance by a Duo or Group With Vocal
"Kiss," Prince and the Revolution

Best Rhythm and Blues Instrumental Performance (Orchestra, Group or Soloist)
"And You Know That," Yellowjackets

Best Jazz Vocal Performance, Male
"Round Midnight," Bobby McFerrin

Best Jazz Vocal Performance, Female
Timeless, Diane Schuur

Best Jazz Vocal Performance, Duo or Group
Free Fall, 2 + 2 Plus (Clare Fischer and His Latin Jazz Sextet)

Best Jazz Instrumental Performance, Soloist
Tutu, Miles Davis

Best Jazz Instrumental Performance, Group
J Mood, Wynton Marsalis

Best Jazz Instrumental Performance, Big Band
The Tonight Show Band With Doc Severinsen, The Tonight Show Band With Doc Severinsen

Best Jazz Fusion Performance, Vocal or Instrumental
Double Vision, Bob James and David Sanborn

Best Country Song
"Grandpa (Tell Me 'Bout the Good Old Days)," Jamie O'Hara, songwriter

Best Country Vocal Performance, Male
Lost in the Fifties Tonight, Ronnie Milsap

Best Country Vocal Performance, Female
"Whoever's in New England," Reba McEntire

Best Country Performance by a Duo or Group With Vocal
"Grandpa (Tell Me 'Bout the Good Old Days)," Judds

Best Country Instrumental Performance (Orchestra, Group or Soloist)
"Raisin' the Dickens," Ricky Skaggs

Best Gospel Performance, Male
Triumph, Philip Bailey

Best Gospel Performance, Female
Morning Like This, Sandi Patti

Best Gospel Performance by a Duo or Group, Choir or Chorus
"They Say," Sandi Patti and Deniece Williams

Best Soul Gospel Performance, Male
"Going Away," Al Green

Best Soul Gospel Performance, Female
"I Surrender All," Deniece Williams

Best Soul Gospel Performance by a Duo or Group, Choir or Chorus
Let My People Go, Winans

Best Latin Pop Performance
"Lelolai," José Feliciano

Best Tropical Latin Performance
Escenas, Ruben Blades

Best Mexican/American Performance
Ay Te Dejo en San Antonio, Flaco Jimenez

Best Traditional Blues Recording
Showdown!, Albert Collins, Robert Cray and Johnny Copeland (Alligator)

Best Traditional Folk Recording
Riding the Midnight Train, Doc Watson (Sugar Hill)

Best Contemporary Folk Recording
Tribute to Steve Goodman, Arlo Guthrie, John Hartford, Richie Havens, Bonnie Koloc, Nitty Gritty Dirt Band, John Prine and others (Red Pajamas)

Best Reggae Recording
Babylon the Bandit, Steel Pulse (Elektra)

Best New Age Recording
Down to the Moon, Andreas Vollenweider (FM/CBS)

Best Polka Recording (tie)
Another Polka Celebration, Eddie Blazonczyk's Versatones (Bel Aire)

I Remember Warsaw, Jimmy Sturr and His Orchestra (Starr)

Best Arrangement on an Instrumental
"Suite Memories," Patrick Williams, arranger

Best Instrumental Arrangement Accompanying Vocal(s)
"Somewhere," David Foster, arranger

Best Instrumental Composition
Out of Africa (Original Motion Picture Soundtrack), John Barry, composer

Best Musical Cast Show Album
Follies in Concert (RCA)

Best Classical Album
Horowitz: The Studio Recordings, New York 1985, Vladimir Horowitz (Deutsche Grammophon)

Best Contemporary Composition
Symphony No. 3, Witold Lutoslawski, composer

Best Classical Orchestral Recording
Liszt, *A Faust Symphony,* Sir Georg Solti conducting the Chicago Symphony Orchestra (London)

Best Chamber Music Performance, Instrumental or Vocal
Beethoven, *Cello and Piano Sonata No. 4 in C Major and Variations,* Yo-Yo Ma and Emanuel Ax

Best Classical Performance, Instrumental Soloist(s) (With or Without Orchestra)
Horowitz, *The Studio Recordings, New York 1985,* Vladimir Horowitz

Best Opera Recording
Bernstein, *Candide,* John Mauceri conducting New York City Opera Chorus and Orchestra; solos: Mills, Eisler, Lankston, Castle, Reeve, Harrold, Billings and Clement (New World)

Best Choral Performance (Other Than Opera)
Orff, *Carmina Burana,* James Levine conducting Chicago Symphony Orchestra and Chorus

Best Classical Vocal Soloist Performance
Mozart, *Kathleen Battle Sings Mozart,* Kathleen Battle

Best Comedy Recording
Those of You With or Without Children, You'll Understand, Bill Cosby (Geffen)

Best Spoken Word or Non-Musical Recording
Interviews From the Class of '55 Recording Sessions, Carl Perkins, Jerry Lee Lewis, Roy Orbison, Johnny Cash, Sam Phillips, Rick Nelson and Chips Moman (America Record Corp.)

Best Recording for Children
The Alphabet, Sesame Street Muppets; Jim Henson (Golden Books)

Best Album Package
Tutu, Eiko Ishioka, art director (Warner Bros.)

Best Album Notes
The Voice, the Columbia Years 1943–1952, Gary Giddins, Wilfrid Sheed, Jonathan Schwartz, Murray Kempton, Andrew Sarris, Stephen Holden and Frank Conroy, annotators (Columbia/CBS)

Best Historical Album
Atlantic Rhythm and Blues 1947–1974 vols. 1–7, various artists (Atlantic)

Best Music Video, Short Form (VHS)
"Dire Straits Brothers in Arms," Dire Straits

Best Music Video, Short Form (VHS) (Beta) (Disk)
"Bring on the Night," Sting

Producers of the Year (Non-Classical)
Jimmy Jam and Terry Lewis

Classical Producer of the Year
Thomas Frost

1987

Record of the Year
"Graceland," Paul Simon

Album of the Year
Joshua Tree, U2 (Island)

Song of the Year
"Somewhere Out There," James Horner, Barry Mann and Cynthia Weil, songwriters

Best New Artist
Jody Watley

Best Pop Vocal Performance, Male
Bring on the Night, Sting

Best Pop Vocal Performance, Female
"I Wanna Dance With Somebody (Who Loves Me)," Whitney Houston

Best Pop Performance by a Duo or Group With Vocal
"(I've Had) The Time of My Life," Bill Medley and Jennifer Warnes

Best Pop Instrumental Performance (Orchestra, Group or Soloist)
"Minute by Minute," Larry Carlton

Best Rock Vocal Performance, Solo
Tunnel of Love, Bruce Springsteen

Best Rock Performance by a Duo or Group With Vocal
The Joshua Tree, U2

Best Rock Instrumental Performance (Orchestra, Group or Soloist)
Jazz From Hell, Frank Zappa

Sting

Best Rhythm and Blues Song
"Lean on Me," Bill Withers, songwriter

Best Rhythm and Blues Vocal Performance, Male
"Just to See Her," Smokey Robinson

Best Rhythm and Blues Vocal Performance, Female
Aretha, Aretha Franklin

Best Rhythm and Blues Performance by a Duo or Group With Vocal
"I Knew You Were Waiting (For Me)", Aretha Franklin and George Michael

Best Rhythm and Blues Instrumental Performance (Orchestra, Group or Soloist)
"Chicago Song," David Sanborn

Best Jazz Vocal Performance, Male
"What Is This Thing Called Love," Bobby McFerrin

Best Jazz Vocal Performance, Female
Diane Schuur and the Count Basie Orchestra, Diane Schuur

Best Jazz Instrumental Performance, Soloist
The Other Side of Round Midnight, Dexter Gordon

Best Jazz Instrumental Performance, Group
Marsalis Standard Time, Volume 1, Wynton Marsalis

Best Jazz Instrumental Performance, Big Band
Digital Duke, Duke Ellington Orchestra conducted by Mercer Ellington

Best Jazz Fusion Performance, Vocal or Instrumental
Still Life (Talking), Pat Metheny Group

Best Country Song
"Forever and Ever, Amen," Paul Overstreet and Don Schlitz, songwriters

Best Country Vocal Performance, Male
Always and Forever, Randy Travis

Best Country Vocal Performance, Female
"'80's Ladies," K.T. Oslin

Best Country Performance by a Duo or Group With Vocal
Trio, Dolly Parton, Linda Ronstadt and Emmylou Harris

Best Country Vocal Performance, Duet
"Make No Mistake, She's Mine," Ronnie Milsap and Kenny Rogers

Best Country Instrumental Performance (Orchestra, Group or Soloist)
"String of Pars," Asleep at the Wheel

Best Gospel Performance, Male
The Father Hath Provided, Larnelle Harris

Best Gospel Performance, Female
"I Believe in You," Deniece Williams

Best Gospel Performance by a Duo, Group, Choir or Chorus
Crack the Sky, Mylon LeFevre and Broken Heart

Best Soul Gospel Performance, Male
"Everything's Gonna Be Alright," Al Green

Best Soul Gospel Performance, Female
"For Always," CeCe Winans

Best Soul Gospel Performance by a Duo, Group, Choir or Chorus
"Ain't No Need to Worry," Winans and Anita Baker

Best Latin Pop Performance
Un Hombre Solo, Julio Iglesias

Best Tropical Latin Performance
La Verdad — The Truth, Eddie Palmieri

Best Mexican/American Performance
Gracias! America sin Fronteras, Los Tigres Del Norte

Best Traditional Blues Recording
Houseparty New Orleans Style, Professor Longhair (Rounder)

Best Contemporary Blues Recording
Strong Persuader, Robert Cray Band (Mercury/Hightone)

Best Traditional Folk Recording
Shaka Zulu, Ladysmith Black Mambazo (Warner Bros.)

Best Contemporary Folk Recording
Unfinished Business, Steve Goodman (Red Pajamas)

Best Reggae Recording
No Nuclear War, Peter Tosh (EMI-America)

Best New Age Performance
Yusef Lateef's Little Symphony, Yusef Lateef

Best Polka Recording
A Polka Just for Me, Jimmy Sturr and His Orchestra (Starr)

Best Arrangement on an Instrumental
"Take the "A" Train," Bill Holman, arranger

Best Instrumental Arrangement Accompanying Vocal(s)
"Deedle's Blues," Frank Foster, arranger

Best Instrumental Composition
"Call Sheet Blues," Dexter Gordon, Wayne Shorter, Herbie Hancock, Ron Carter and Billy Higgins, composers

Best Musical Cast Show Album
Les Miserables (Geffen)

Best Album of Original Instrumental Background Score Written for a Motion Picture or Television
The Untouchables (Original Motion Picture Soundtrack), Ennio Morricone, composer (A&M)

Best Song Written Specifically for a Motion Picture or Television
"Somewhere Out There" (From the animated movie *An American Tale*), James Horner, Barry Mann and Cynthia Weil, songwriters

Best Contemporary Composition
Cello Concerto No. 2, Krzysztof Penderecki, composer

Best Classical Album
Horowitz in Moscow, Vladimir Horowitz (Deutsche Grammophon)

Best Orchestral Recording
Beethoven, *Symphony No. 9 in D Minor (Choral),* Sir Georg Solti conducting Chicago Symphony Orchestra (London)

Best Chamber Music Performance, Instrumental or Vocal
Beethoven, *The Complete Piano Trios,* Itzhak Perlman, Lynn Harrell and Vladimir Ashkenazy

Best Classical Performance, Instrumental Soloist(s) (With Orchestra)
Mozart, *Violin Concertos nos. 2 and 4 in D,* Itzhak Perlman; James Levine conducting Vienna Philarmonic

Best Classical Performance, Instrumental Soloist(s) (Without Orchestra)
Horowitz in Moscow, Vladimir Horowitz, piano

Best Opera Recording
Strauss, *Ariadne auf Naxos,* James Levine conducting Vienna Philharmonic; solos: Tomowa-Sintow, Battle, Baltsa, Lakes and Prey (Deutsche Grammophon)

Best Choral Performance (Othen Than Opera)
Hindemith, *When Lilacs Last in the Dooryard Bloom'd (A Requiem for Those We Love);* Robert Shaw conducting Atlanta Symphony Chorus and Orchestra

Best Classical Vocal Soloist Performance
Kathleen Battle, Salzburg Recital, Kathleen Battle; James Levine, accompanist

Best Comedy Recording
A Night at The Met, Robin Williams (Columbia/CBS)

Best Spoken Word or Non-Musical Recording
Lake Wobegon Days, Garrison Keillor (PHC)

Best Recording for Children
The Elephant's Child, Jack Nicholson, narrator; Bobby McFerrin, music (Windham Hill)

Best Album Package
King's Record Shop, Bill Johnson, art director (Columbia/CBS)

Best Album Notes
Thelonious Monk, the Complete Riverside Recordings, Orrin Keepnews, annotator (Riverside)

Best Historical Album
Thelonious Monk, the Complete Riverside Recordings, Thelonious Monk (Riverside)

Best Performance Music Video
The Prince's Trust All-Star Rock Concert, Elton John, Tina Turner, Sting and others

Best Concept Music Video
"Land of Confusion," Genesis

Producer of the Year (Non-Classical)
Narada Michael Walden

Classical Producer of the Year
Robert Woods

1988

Record of the Year
"Don't Worry Be Happy," Bobby McFerrin

Album of the Year
Faith, George Michael (Columbia/CBS)

Song of the Year
"Don't Worry Be Happy," Bobby McFerrin, songwriter

Best New Artist
Tracy Chapman

Best Pop Vocal Performance, Male
"Don't Worry Be Happy," Bobby McFerrin

Best Pop Vocal Performance, Female
"Fast Car," Tracy Chapman

Best Pop Vocal Performance by a Duo or Group With Vocal
Brasil, Manhattan Transfer

Best Pop Instrumental Performance (Orchestra, Group or Soloist)
Close-up, David Sanborn

Best Rock Vocal Performance, Male
"Simply Irresistible," Robert Palmer

Best Rock Vocal Performance, Female
Tina Live in Europe, Tina Turner

Best Rock Instrumental Performance by a Duo or Group With Vocal
"Desire," U2

Best Rock Instrumental Performance (Orchestra, Group or Soloist)
Blues for Salvador, Carlos Santana

Best Hard Rock/Metal Performance, Vocal or Instrumental
Crest of a Knave, Jethro Tull

Best Rhythm and Blues Song
"Giving You the Best That I Got," Anita Baker, Skip Scarborough and Randy Holland, songwriters

Best Rhythm and Blues Vocal Performance, Male
Introducing the Hardline According to Terence Trent D'Arby, Terence Trent D'Arby

Best Rhythm and Blues Vocal Performance, Female
"Giving You the Best That I Got," Anita Baker

Best Rhythm and Blues Performance by a Duo or Group With Vocal
"Love Overboard," Gladys Knight and the Pips

Best Rhythm and Blues Instrumental Performance (Orchestra, Group or Soloist)
"Light Years," Chick Corea

Robert Palmer

Best Rap Performance
"Parents Just Don't Understand," D.J. Jazzy Jeff and the Fresh Prince

Best Jazz Vocal Performance, Male
Brothers, Bobby McFerrin

Best Jazz Vocal Performance, Female
Look What I Got!, Betty Carter

Best Jazz Vocal Performance, Duo or Group
"Spread Love," Take 6

Best Jazz Instrumental Performance, Soloist on a Jazz Recording
Don't Try This at Home, Michael Brecker

Best Jazz Instrumental Performance, Group
Blues for Coltrane, A Tribute to John Coltrane, McCoy Tyner, Pharoah Sanders, David Murray, Cecil McBee and Roy Haynes

Best Jazz Instrumental Performance, Big Band
Bud and Bird, Gil Evans and the Monday Night Orchestra

Best Jazz Fusion Performance
Politics, Yellowjackets

Best Country Song
"Hold Me," K.T. Oslin, songwriter

Best Country Vocal Performance, Male
Old 8 x 10, Randy Travis

Best Country Vocal Performance, Female
"Hold Me," K.T. Oslin

Best Country Performance by a Duo or Group With Vocal
"Give a Little Love," Judds

Best Country Vocal Collaboration
"Crying," Roy Orbison and k.d. lang

Best Country Instrumental Performance (Orchestra, Group or Soloists)
"Sugarfoot Rag," Asleep at the Wheel

Best Bluegrass Recording (Vocal or Instrumental)
Southern Flavor, Bill Monroe (MCA)

Best Gospel Performance, Male
Christmas, Larnelle Harris

Best Gospel Performance, Female
Lead Me On, Amy Grant

Best Gospel Performance by a Duo or Group, Choir or Chorus
The Winans Live at Carnegie Hall, Winans

Best Soul Gospel Performance, Male
"Abundant Life," BeBe Winans

Best Soul Gospel Performance, Female
One Lord, One Faith, One Baptism, Aretha Franklin

Best Soul Gospel Performance by a Duo or Group, Choir or Chorus
Take Six, Take 6

Best Latin Pop Performance
Roberto Carlos, Roberto Carlos

Best Tropical Latin Performance
Antecedente, Rubén Blades

Best Mexican/American Performance
Canciones de Mi Padre, Linda Ronstadt

Best Traditional Blues Recording
Hidden Charms, Willie Dixon (Bug/Capitol)

Best Contemporary Blues Recording
"Don't Be Afraid of the Dark," Robert Cray Band (Mercury)

Best Traditional Folk Recording
Folkways: A Vision Shared — A Tribute to Woody Guthrie and Leadbelly, various artists (Columbia/CBS)

Best Contemporary Folk Recording
Tracy Chapman, Tracy Chapman (Elektra)

Best Reggae Recording
Conscious Party, Ziggy Marley and the Melody Makers (Virgin)

Best New Age Performance
Folksongs for a Nuclear Village, Shadowfax

Best Polka Recording
Born to Polka, Jimmy Sturr and His Orchestra (Starr)

Best Arrangement on an Instrumental
"Memos From Paradise," Roger Kellaway, arranger

Best Instrumental Arrangement Accompanying Vocal(s)
"No One Is Alone," Jonathan Tunick, arranger

Best Instrumental Composition
"The Theme From *L.A. Law,*" Mike Post, composer

Best Musical Cast Show Album
Into the Woods, Stephen Sondheim, composer and lyricist (RCA)

Best Album of Original Instrumental Background Score Written for a Motion Picture or Television
The Last Emperor, Ryuichi Sakamoto, David Byrne and Cong Su, composers (Virgin)

Best Song Written Specifically for a Motion Picture or Television
"Two Hearts" (From the motion picture *Buster*), Phil Collins and Lamont Dozier, songwriters (Atlantic)

Best Contemporary Composition
Nixon in China, John Adams, composer

Best Classical Album
Verdi, *Requiem and Operatic Choruses,* Robert Shaw conducting Atlanta Symphony Orchestra and Chorus (Telarc)

Best Orchestral Recording
Rorem, *String Symphony; Sunday Morning, Eagles*; Robert Shaw conducting Atlanta Symphony Orchestra: *String Symphony*; Louis Lane conducting Atlanta Symphony Orchestra: *Sunday Morning* and *Eagles* (New World)

Best Chamber Music Performance (Instrumental or Vocal)
Bartók, *Sonata for Two Pianos and Percussion;* Brahms, *Variation on a Theme by Joseph Haydn for Two Pianos,* Murray Perahia and Sir Georg Solti, pianos; David Corkhill and Evelyn Glennie, percussion

Best Classical Performance, Instrumental Soloist(s) (With Orchestra)
Mozart, *Piano Concerto No. 23 in A,* Vladimir Horowitz, piano; Giulini conducting LaScala Opera Orchestra

Best Classical Performance, Instrumental Soloist(s) (Without Orchestra)
Albéniz, *Iberia; Navarra; Suite Espagnola,* Alicia de Larrocha

Best Opera Recording
Wagner, *Lohengrin,* Sir Georg Solti conducting Vienna State Opera Choir and Vienna Philharmonic; solos: Domingo, Norman, Randova, Nimsgern, Sotin and Fischer-Dieskau (London)

Best Choral Performance (Other Than Opera)
Verdi, *Requiem and Operatic Choruses,* Robert Shaw conducting Atlanta Symphony Chorus and Orchestra

Best Classical Vocal Soloist Performance
Luciano Pavarotti in Concert, Luciano Pavarotti

Best Comedy Recording
Good Morning Vietnam, Robin Williams (A&M)

Best Spoken Word or Non-Musical Recording
"Speech by Rev. Jesse Jackson (July 27)," Rev. Jesse Jackson (Arista)

Best Recording for Children
Pecos Bill, Robin Williams, narrator; Ry Cooder, music (Windham Hill)

Best Album Package
Tired of Runnin', Bill Johnson, art director (Columbia/CBS)

Best Album Notes
Crossroads, Anthony DeCurtis, annotator (Polydor)

Best Historical Album
Crossroads, Eric Clapton (Polydor)

Best Performance Music Video
"Where the Streets Have No Name," U2

Best Concept Music Video
"Fat," "Weird Al" Yankovic

Producer of the Year (Non-Classical)
Neil Dorfsman

Classical Producer of the Year
Robert Woods

1989

Record of the Year
"Wind Beneath My Wings," Bette Midler

Album of the Year
Nick of Time, Bonnie Raitt (Capitol)

Song of the Year
"Wind Beneath My Wings," Larry Henley and Jeff Silbar, songwriters

Best Pop Vocal Performance, Male
"How Am I Supposed to Live Without You," Michael Bolton

Best Pop Vocal Performance, Female
"Nick of Time," Bonnie Raitt

Best Pop Performance by a Duo or Group With Vocal
"Don't Know Much," Linda Ronstadt and Aaron Neville

Best Pop Instrumental Performance
"Healing Chant," Neville Brothers

Best Rock Vocal Performance, Male
The End of the Innocence, Don Henley

Best Rock Vocal Performance, Female
Nick of Time, Bonnie Raitt

Best Rock Performance by a Duo or Group With Vocal
Traveling Wilburys Volume One, Traveling Wilburys

Best Rock Instrumental Performance
Jeff Beck's Guitar Shop With Terry Bozzio and Tony Hymas, Jeff Beck, Terry Bozzio and Tony Hymas

Best Hard Rock Performance
"Cult of Personality," Living Colour

Best Metal Performance
"One," Metallica

Bonnie Raitt

Best Rhythm and Blues Song
"If You Don't Know Me by Now," Kenny Gamble and Leon Huff, songwriters

Best Rhythm and Blues Vocal Performance, Male
"Every Little Step," Bobby Brown

Best Rhythm and Blues Vocal Performance, Female
Giving You the Best That I Got, Anita Baker

Best Rhythm and Blues Performance by a Duo or Group With Vocal
"Back to Life," Soul II Soul featuring Caron Wheeler

Best Rhythm and Blues Instrumental Performance
"African Dance," Soul II Soul

Best Rap Performance
"Bust a Move," Young MC

Best Jazz Vocal Performance, Male
When Harry Met Sally, Harry Connick, Jr.

Best Jazz Vocal Performance, Female
Blues on Broadway, Ruth Brown

Best Jazz Vocal Performance, Duo or Group
"Makin' Whoopee," Dr. John and Rickie Lee Jones

Best Jazz Instrumental Performance, Soloist on a Jazz Recording
Aura, Miles Davis (Columbia/CBS)

Best Jazz Instrumental Performance, Group
Chick Corea Akoustic Band, Chick Corea Akoustic Band

Best Jazz Instrumental Performance, Big Band
Aura, Miles Davis

Best Jazz Fusion Performance
Letter From Home, Pat Metheny Group

Best Country Song
"After All This Time," Rodney Crowell, songwriter

Best Country Vocal Performance, Male
Lyle Lovett and His Large Band, Lyle Lovett

Best Country Vocal Performance, Female
Absolute Torch and Twang, k.d. lang

Best Country Performance by a Duo or Group With Vocal
Will the Circle Be Unbroken Volume Two, Nitty Gritty Dirt Band

Best Country Vocal Collaboration
"There's a Tear in My Beer," Hank Williams, Jr. and Hank Williams, Sr.

Best Country Instrumental Performance
"Amazing Grace," Randy Scruggs

Best Bluegrass Recording
"The Valley Road," Bruce Hornsby and the Nitty Gritty Dirt Band (Universal)

Best Gospel Vocal Performance, Male
"Meantime," BeBe Winans

Best Gospel Vocal Performance, Female
"Don't Cry," CeCe Winans

Best Gospel Vocal Performance by a Duo or Group, Choir or Chorus
"The Savior Is Waiting," Take 6

Best Soul Gospel Vocal Performance, Male or Female
"As Long as We're Together," Al Green

Best Soul Gospel Vocal Performance by a Duo or Group, Choir or Chorus
"Let Brotherly Love Continue," Daniel Winans and Choir

Best Latin Pop Performance
"Cielito Lindo," José Feliciano

Best Tropical Latin Performance
Ritmo en el Corazon, Celia Cruz and Ray Barretto

Best Mexican/American Performance
La Pistola y el Corazon, Los Lobos

Best Traditional Blues Recording
"I'm in the Mood," John Lee Hooker and Bonnie Raitt (Chameleon Music Group)

Best Contemporary Blues Recording
In Step, Stevie Ray Vaughan and Double Trouble (Epic)

Best Traditional Folk Recording
Le Mystère des Voix Bulgares, Vol. II, Bulgarian State Female Vocal Choir (Elektra/Nonesuch)

Best Contemporary Folk Recording
Indigo Girls, Indigo Girls (Epic)

Best Reggae Recording
One Bright Day, Ziggy Marley and the Melody Makers (Virgin)

Best New Age Performance
Passion (Music from *The Last Temptation of Christ*), Peter Gabriel

Best Polka Recording
All in My Love for You, Jimmy Sturr and His Orchestra (Starr)

Best Arrangement on an Instrumental
"Suite From *The Milagro Beanfield War*," Dave Grusin, arranger

Best Instrumental Arrangement Accompanying Vocal(s)
"My Funny Valentine," Dave Grusin, arranger

Best Instrumental Composition
"The *Batman* Theme," Danny Elfman, composer

Best Musical Cast Show Album
Jerome Robbins' Broadway, Jason Alexander, Debbie Shapiro and Robert La Fasse (RCA Victor)

Best Album of Original Instrumental Background Score Written for a Motion Picture or Television
The Fabulous Baker Boys, Dave Grusin, composer (GRP)

Best Song Written Specifically for a Motion Picture or Television
Let the River Run (From the motion picture *Working Girl*), Carly Simon, composer (Arista)

Best Contemporary Composition
Different Trains, Steve Reich, composer

Best Classical Album
Bartók, *6 String Quartets,* Emerson String Quartet (Deutsche Grammophon)

Best Orchestral Performance
Mahler, *Symphony No. 3 in D Minor,* Leonard Bernstein and the
New York Philharmonic

Best Chamber Music Performance
Bartók, *6 String Quartets,* Emerson String Quartet

**Best Classical Performance, Instrumental Soloist(s)
(With Orchestra)**
Barber, *Cello Concerto, Op. 22;* Britten, *Symphony for Cello and
Orchestra, Op. 68,* Yo-Yo Ma, cellist; David Zinman con-
ducting Baltimore Symphony Orchestra

**Best Classical Performance, Instrumental Soloist(s)
(Without Orchestra)**
Bach, *English Suites, BMV 806–11,* Andras Schiff, pianist

Best Opera Recording
Wagner, *Die Walkuere,* James Levine conducting Metropolitan
Opera Orchestra; solos: Lakes, Moll, Morris, Norman,
Behrens and Ludwig (Deutsche Grammophon)

Best Choral Performance (Other Than Opera)
Britten, *War Requiem,* Robert Shaw conducting Atlanta
Symphony Orchestra and Chorus and Atlanta Boys Choir

Best Classical Vocal Soloist Performance
Knoxville, *Summer of 1915 (Music of Barber, Menott, Harbison
and Stravinsky),* Dawn Upshaw, soprano; David Zinman
conducting Orchestra of St. Luke's

Best Comedy Recording
P.D.Q. Bach, *1712 Overture and Other Musical Assaults,*
Professor Peter Schickele (Telarc)

Best Spoken Word or Non-Musical Recording
It's Always Something, Gilda Radner (Simon & Schuster Audio)

Best Recording for Children
The Rock-a-Bye Collection Vol. I, Tanya Goodman (Jaba)

Best Album Package
Sound + Vision, Roger Gorman, art director (Rykodisc)

Best Album Notes
Bird: The Complete Charlie Parker on Verve, Phil Schaap,
annotator (Verve)

Best Historical Album
Chuck Berry — The Chess Box, Chuck Berry (Chess/MCA)

Best Music Video, Short Form
"Leave Me Alone," Michael Jackson

Best Music Video, Long Form
"Rhythm Nation 1814," Janet Jackson

Producer of the Year (Non-Classical)
Peter Asher

Classical Producer of the Year
Robert Woods

1990

Record of the Year
"Another Day in Paradise," Phil Collins

Album of the Year
Back on the Block, Quincy Jones (Qwest/Warner Bros.)

Song of the Year
"From a Distance," Julie Gold, songwriter

Best New Artist
Mariah Carey

Best Pop Vocal Performance, Male
"Oh Pretty Woman," Roy Orbison

Best Pop Vocal Performance, Female
"Vision of Love," Mariah Carey

Best Pop Performance by a Duo or Group With Vocal
"All My Life," Linda Ronstadt with Aaron Neville

Ella Fitzgerald

Best Pop Instrumental Performance
"Twin Peaks Theme," Angelo Badalamenti

Best Rock/Contemporary Gospel Album
Beyond Belief, Petra (Dayspring/Word)

Best Rock Vocal Performance, Male
"Bad Love," Eric Clapton

Best Rock Vocal Performance, Female
"Black Velvet," Alannah Myles

Best Pop Performance by a Duo or Group With Vocal
"Janie's Got a Gun," Aerosmith

Best Rock Instrumental Performance
"D/FW," Vaughan Brothers

Best Hard Rock Performance
Time's Up, Living Colour

Best Metal Performance
"Stone Cold Crazy," Metallica

Best Alternative Music Performance
I Do Not Want What I Haven't Got, Sinead O'Connor

Best Rhythm and Blues Song
"U Can't Touch This," Rick James, Alonzo Miller and M.C.
Hammer, songwriters

Best Rhythm and Blues Vocal Performance, Male
"Here and Now," Luther Vandross

Best Rhythm and Blues Vocal Performance, Female
Compositions, Anita Baker

**Best Rhythm and Blues Performance by a Duo or Group
With Vocal**
"I'll Be Good to You," Ray Charles and Chaka Khan

Best Rap Solo Performance
"U Can't Touch This," M.C. Hammer

Best Rap Performance by a Duo or Group
"Back on the Block," Ice T, Melle Mel, Big Daddy Kane, Kool
Moe Dee, Quincy D. III and Quincy Jones

Best Jazz Vocal Performance, Male
We Are in Love, Harry Connick, Jr.

Best Jazz Vocal Performance, Female
All That Jazz, Ella Fitzgerald

Best Jazz Instrumental Performance, Soloist
The Legendary Oscar Peterson Trio Live at the Blue Note,
Oscar Peterson

Best Jazz Instrumental Performance, Group
The Legendary Oscar Peterson Trio Live at the Blue Note,
Oscar Peterson Trio

Best Jazz Instrumental Performance, Big Band
"Basie's Bag," George Benson featuring the Count Basie
Orchestra

Best Jazz Fusion Performance
"Birdland," Quincy Jones

Best Country Song
"Where've You Been," Jon Vezner and Don Henry, songwriters

Best Country Vocal Performance, Male
"When I Call Your Name," Vince Gill

Best Country Vocal Performance, Female
"Where've You Been," Kathy Mattea

Best Country Performance by a Duo or Group With Vocal
Pickin' on Nashville, Kentucky Headhunters

Best Country Vocal Collaboration
"Poor Boy Blues," Chet Atkins and Mark Knopfler

Best Country Instrumental Performance
"So Soft, Your Goodbye," Chet Atkins and Mark Knopfler

Best Bluegrass Recording
I've Got That Old Feeling, Alison Krauss (Rounder)

Best Traditional Soul Gospel Album
Tramaine Hawkins Live, Tramaine Hawkins (Sparrow Corp.)

Best Contemporary Soul Gospel Album
So Much 2 Say, Take 6 (Reprise/Warner/Alliance)

Best Pop Gospel Album
Another Time . . . Another Place, Sandi Patti (A&M/Word)

Best Southern Gospel Album
The Great Exchange, Bruce Carroll (Word)

Best Gospel Album by a Choir or Chorus
Having Church, Rev. James Cleveland (Savoy)

Best Latin Pop Performance
"Por Que Te Tengo Que Olvidar?," José Feliciano

Best Tropical Latin Performance
"Lambada Timbales," Tito Puente

Best Mexican/American Performance
"Soy de San Luis," Texas Tornados

Best Traditional Blues Recording
Live at San Quentin, B.B. King (MCA)

Best Contemporary Blues Recording
Family Style, Vaughan Brothers (Epic Associated)

Best Traditional Folk Recording
On Praying Ground, Doc Watson (Sugar Hill)

Best Contemporary Folk Recording
Steady On, Shawn Colvin (Columbia/CBS)

Best Reggae Recording
Time Will Tell — A Tribute to Bob Marley, Bunny Wailer
(Shanachie)

Best New Age Performance
Mark Isham, Mark Isham

Best Polka Recording
When It's Polka Time at Your House, Jimmy Sturr and His
Orchestra (Starr)

Best Arrangement on an Instrumental
"Birdland," Quincy Jones, Ian Prince, Rod Temperton and
Jerry Hey, arrangers

Best Instrumental Arrangement Accompanying Vocal(s)
"The Places You Find Love," Jerry Hey, Glen Ballard, Clif
Magness and Quincy Jones, arrangers

Best Instrumental Composition
"Change of Heart" Pat Metheny, composer

Best Musical Cast Show Album
Les Miserables, The Complete Symphonic Recording (Relativity)

**Best Instrumental Composition Written for a Motion Picture or
for Television**
Glory, James Horner, composer (Virgin)

**Best Song Written Specifically for a Motion Picture or for
Television**
"Under the Sea" (From *The Little Mermaid*), Alan Menken and
Howard Ashman, composers

Best Contemporary Composition
Arias and Barcarolles, Leonard Bernstein, composer

Best Classical Album
Ives, *Symphony No. 2 and Three Short Works,* Leonard
Bernstein conducting New York Philharmonic (Deutsche
Grammophon)

Best Chamber Music or Other Small Ensemble Performance
Brahms, *The Three Violin Sonatas,* Itzhak Perlman, violinist;
Daniel Barenboim, pianist

**Best Classical Performance, Instrumental Soloist(s)
(With Orchestra)**
Shostakovich, *Violin Concerto No. 1;* Glazunov, *Violin Concerto,*
Itzhak Perlman, violinist; Zubin Mehta conducting Israel
Philharmonic

**Best Classical Performance, Instrumental Soloist(s)
(Without Orchestra)**
The Last Recording (Chopin, Haydn, Liszt and Wagner),
Vladimir Horowitz

Best Opera Recording
Wagner, *Das Rheingold,* James Levine conducting The
Metropolitan Opera Orchestra; solos: Morris, Ludwig,
Jerusalem, Wlaschiha, Moll, Zednik and Rootering
(Deutsche Grammophon)

Best Choral Performance (Other Than Opera)
Walton, *Belshazzar's Feast;* Bernstein, *Chichester Psalms,
Missa Brevis,* Robert Shaw conducting Atlanta Symphony
Orchestra and Chorus

Best Classical Vocal Performance
Carreras, Domingo and Pavarotti in Concert, José Carreras,
Placido Domingo and Luciano Pavarotti, tenors; Zubin
Mehta conducting Orchestra del Maggio Musicale
Fiorentino and Orchestra del teatro dell'Opera di Roma

Best Comedy Recording
P.D.Q. Bach, *Oedipus Tex and Other Choral Calamities,*
Professor Peter Schickele (Telarc)

Best Spoken Word or Non-Musical Recording
Gracie: A Love Story, George Burns (Simon & Schuster Audio)

Best Recording for Children
The Little Mermaid — Original Motion Picture Soundtrack,
Howard Ashman and Alan Menken, composers
(Disneyland Records)

Best Album Package
Days of Open Hand (Special Edition Hologram Digapack), Len
Peltier, Jeffrey Gold and Suzanne Vega, art directors
(A&M)

Best Album Notes
Brownie: The Complete Emarcy Recordings of Clifford Brown,
Dan Morgenstern, annotator (Emarcy)

Best Historical Album
Robert Johnson: The Complete Recordings, Robert Johnson
(Columbia/CBS)

Best Music Video, Short Form
"Opposites Attract," Paula Abdul

Best Music Video, Long Form
"Please Hammer Don't Hurt 'Em the Movie," M.C. Hammer

Producer of the Year (Non-Classical)
Quincy Jones

Classical Producer of the Year
Adam Stern

Natalie Cole

1991

Record of the Year
"Unforgettable," Natalie Cole with Nat King Cole

Album of the Year
Unforgettable, Natalie Cole with Nat King Cole (Elektra)

Song of the Year
"Unforgettable," Irving Gordon, songwriter

Best New Artist
Marc Cohn

Best Pop Vocal Performance, Male
"When a Man Loves a Woman," Michael Bolton

Best Pop Vocal Performance, Female
"Something to Talk About," Bonnie Raitt

Best Pop Performance by a Duo or Group With Vocal
"Losing My Religion," R.E.M.

Best Pop Instrumental Performance
Robin Hood: Prince of Thieves, Michael Kamen conducting Greater Los Angeles Orchestra

Best Rock/Contemporary Gospel Album
Under Their Influence, Russ Taff (Myrrh)

Best Rock Song
"Soul Cages," Sting, songwriter

Best Rock Vocal Performance, Solo
Luck of the Draw, Bonnie Raitt

Best Rock Performance by a Duo or Group With Vocal
"Good Man, Good Woman," Bonnie Raitt and Delbert McClinton

Best Rock Instrumental Performance
"Cliffs of Dover," Eric Johnson

Best Hard Rock Performance With Vocal
For Unlawful Carnal Knowledge, Van Halen

Best Metal Performance With Vocal
Metallica, Metallica

Best Alternative Music Album
Out of Time, R.E.M. (Warner Bros.)

Best Rhythm and Blues Song
"Power of Love/Love Power," Luther Vandross, Marcus Miller and Teddy Vann, songwriters

Best Rhythm and Blues Vocal Performance, Male
Power of Love, Luther Vandross

Best Rhythm and Blues Vocal Performance, Female (tie)
Burnin', Patti LaBelle
"How Can I Ease the Pain," Lisa Fischer

Best Rhythm and Blues Performance by a Duo or Group With Vocal
Cooleyhigh Harmony, Boyz II Men

Best Rap Solo Performance
"Mama Said Knock You Out," L.L. Cool J

Best Rap Performance by a Duo or Group
"Summertime," D.J. Jazzy Jeff and the Fresh Prince

Best Jazz Vocal Performance
He Is Christmas, Take 6

Best Jazz Instrumental, Solo
"I Remember You," Stan Getz

Best Jazz Instrumental Performance, Group
Saturday Night at the Blue Note, Oscar Peterson Trio

Best Large Jazz Ensemble Performance
Live at the Royal Festival Hall, Dizzy Gillespie and the United Nation Orchestra

Best Contemporary Jazz Performance
"Sassy," Manhattan Transfer

Best Country Song
"Love Can Build a Bridge," Naomi Judd, John Jarvis and Paul Overstreet, songwriters

Best Country Vocal Performance, Male
Ropin' the Wind, Garth Brooks

Best Country Vocal Performance, Female
"Down at the Twist and Shout," Mary Chapin Carpenter

Best Country Performance by a Duo or Group With Vocal
"Love Can Build a Bridge," Judds

Best Country Vocal Collaboration
"Restless," Steve Wariner, Ricky Skaggs and Vince Gill

Best Country Instrumental Performance
The New Nashville Cats, Mark O'Conner

Best Bluegrass Album
Spring Training, Carl Jackson and John Starling (and the Nash Ramblers) (Sugar Hill)

Best Pop Gospel Album
For the Sake of the Call, Steven Curtis Chapman (Sparrow)

Best Traditional Soul Gospel Album
Pray for Me, Mighty Clouds of Joy (Word)

Best Contemporary Soul Gospel Album
Different Lifestyles, BeBe and CeCe Winans (Capitol/Sparrow)

Best Southern Gospel Album
Homecoming, Gaither Vocal Band (Star Song)

Best Gospel Album by a Choir or Chorus
The Evolution of Gospel, Sounds of Blackness; Gary Hines, choir director (Perspective/A&M)

Best Latin Pop Album
Cosas del Amor, Vikki Carr (Sony Discos International)

Best Tropical Latin Album
Bachata Rosa, Juan Luis Guerra 4.40 (Karen)

Best Mexican/American Album
16 de Septiembre, Little Joe (Sony Discos International)

Best Traditional Blues Album
Live at the Apollo, B.B. King (GRP)

Best Contemporary Blues Album
Damn Right, I've Got the Blues, Buddy Guy (Silvertone)

Best Traditional Folk Album
The Civil War (Original Soundtrack), various artists (Elektra/Nonesuch)

Best Contemporary Folk Album
The Missing Years, John Prine (Oh Boy)

Best Reggae Album
As Raw as Ever, Shabba Ranks (Epic)

Best New Age Album
Fresh Aire 7, Mannheim Steamroller (American Gramaphone)

Best World Music Album
Planet Drum, Mickey Hart (Rykodisc)

Best Polka Album
Live! At Gilley's, Jimmy Sturr and His Orchestra (Starr)

Best Arrangement on an Instrumental
"Medley: Bess You Is My Woman/I Love You Porgy," Dave Grusin, arranger

Best Instrumental Arrangement Accompanying Vocal(s)
"Unforgettable," Johnny Mandel, arranger

Best Instrumental Composition
"Basque," Elton John, composer

Best Musical Show Album
The Will Rogers Follies (Original Broadway Cast Album), Keith Carradine and cast (Columbia)

Best Instrumental Composition Written Specifically for a Motion Picture or for Television
Dances With Wolves, John Barry, composer

Best Song Written Specifically for a Motion Picture or for Television
"(Everything I Do) I Do It for You" (From *Robin Hood: Prince of Thieves*), Bryan Adams, Robert John "Mutt" Lange and Michael Kamen, songwriters (A&M/Morgan Creek)

Best Contemporary Composition
Symphony No. 1, John Corigliano, composer

Best Classical Album
Bernstein, *Candide,* Leonard Bernstein conducting London Symphony Orchestra; solos: Hadley, Anderson, Ludwig, Green, Gedda and Jones (Deutsche Grammophon)

Best Orchestral Performance
Corigliano, *Symphony No. 1,* Daniel Barenboim conducting Chicago Symphony Orchestra

Best Chamber Music Performance
Brahms, *Piano Quartets,* Isaac Stern and Jamime Laredo, violinists; Yo-Yo Ma, cellist; Emanuel Ax, pianist

Best Classical Performance, Instrumental Soloist(s) (With Orchestra)
Barber, *Piano Concertos,* John Browning, pianist; Leonard Slatkin conducting St. Louis Symphony Orchestra

Best Classical Performance, Instrumental Soloist(s) (Without Orchestra)
Granados, *Goyescas, Allegro de Concierto, Danza Lenta,* Alicia de Larrocha, pianist

Best Opera Recording
Wagner, *Götterdammerung,* James Levine conducting The Metropolitan Opera Orchestra and Choir; solos: Behrens, Studer, Schwartz, Goldberg, Weikl, Wlaschiha and Salminen (Deutsche Grammophon)

Best Performance of a Choral Work
Bach, *Mass in B Minor,* Sir Georg Solti conducting Chicago Symphony Chorus and Orchestra; Margaret Hills, choral director

Best Classical Vocal Performance
The Girl With Orange Lips, De Falla, Ravel, Kim, Stravinsky and Delage; Dawn Upshaw, soprano

Best Comedy Album
P.D.Q. Bach, *WTWP Classical Talkity-Talk Radio,* Professor Peter Schickele (Telarc)

Best Spoken Word or Non-Musical Album
The Civil War (Geoffrey Ward With Rick Burns and Ken Burns), Ken Burns (Sound Editions)

Best Album for Children
A Cappella Kids, Marantha! Kids (Marantha)

Best Album Package
Billie Holiday, The Complete Decca Recordings, Vartan, art director (GRP)

Best Album Notes
Star Time, James Brown, Cliff White, Harry Weinger, Nelson George and Alan M. Leeds, annotators (Polydor)

Best Historical Album
Billie Holiday, The Complete Decca Recordings, Billie Holiday (GRP)

Best Music Video, Short Form
"Losing My Religion," R.E.M.

Best Music Video, Long Form
Madonna: Blonde Ambition World Tour Live, Madonna

Producer of the Year (Non-Classical)
David Foster

Classical Producer of the Year
James Mallinson

1992

Record of the Year
"Tears in Heaven," Eric Clapton

Album of the Year
Unplugged, Eric Clapton (Reprise)

Song of the Year
"Tears in Heaven," Eric Clapton, songwriter

Best New Artist
Arrested Development

Best Pop Vocal Performance, Male
"Tears in Heaven," Eric Clapton

Best Pop Vocal Performance, Female
"Constant Craving," k.d. lang

Best Pop Performance by a Duo or Group With Vocal
"Beauty and the Beast," Celine Dion and Peabo Bryson

Best Traditional Pop Vocal Performance
Perfectly Frank, Tony Bennett

Best Pop Instrumental Performance
"Beauty and the Beast," Richard Kaufman conducting Nurenberg Symphony Orchestra

Eric Clapton

Best Rock/Contemporary Gospel Album
Unseen Power, Petra (Dayspring)

Best Rock Song
"Layla," Eric Clapton and Jim Gordon, songwriters

Best Rock Vocal Performance, Male
Unplugged, Eric Clapton

Best Rock Vocal Performance, Female
"Ain't It Heavy," Melissa Etheridge

Best Rock Performance by a Duo or Group With Vocal
Achtung Baby, U2

Best Rock Instrumental Performance
"Little Wing," Stevie Ray Vaughan and Double Trouble

Best Hard Rock Performance With Vocal
"Give It Away," Red Hot Chili Peppers

Best Metal Performance With Vocal
"Wish," Nine Inch Nails

Best Alternative Music Album
Bone Machine, Tom Waits (Island)

Best Rhythm and Blues Song
"End of the Road," L.A. Reid, Babyface and Daryl Simmons, songwriters

Best Rhythm and Blues Vocal Performance, Male
Heaven and Earth, Al Jarreau

Best Rhythm and Blues Vocal Performance, Female
The Woman I Am, Chaka Khan

Best Rhythm and Blues Performance by a Duo or Group With Vocal
"End of the Road," Boys II Men

Best Rhythm and Blues Instrumental Performance
Doo-Bop, Miles Davis

Best Rap Solo Performance
"Baby Got Back," Sir Mix-A-Lot

Best Rap Performance by a Duo or Group
"Tennessee," Arrested Development

Best Jazz Vocal Performance
"'Round Midnight," Bobby McFerrin

Best Jazz Instrumental Performance, Solo
"Lush Life," Joe Henderson

Best Jazz Instrumental Performance, Individual or Group
I Heard You Twice the First Time, Branford Marsalis

Best Large Jazz Ensemble Performance
The Turning Point, McCoy Tyner Big Band

Best Contemporary Jazz Performance, Instrumental
Secret Story, Pat Metheny

Best Country Song
"I Still Believe in You," Vince Gill and John Barlow Jarvis, songwriters

Best Country Vocal Performance, Male
I Still Believe in You, Vince Gill

Best Country Vocal Performance, Female
"I Feel Lucky," Mary Chapin Carpenter

Best Country Performance by a Duo or Group With Vocal
Emmylou Harris and the Nash Ramblers at the Ryman, Emmylou Harris and the Nash Ramblers at the Ryman

Best Country Vocal Collaboration
"The Whiskey Ain't Workin'," Travis Tritt and Marty Stuart

Best Country Instrumental Performance
Sneakin' Around, Chet Atkins and Jerry Reed

Best Bluegrass Album
Every Time You Say Goodbye, Alison Krauss and Union Station (Rounder)

Best Traditional Soul Gospel Album
He's Working It Out for You, Shirley Caesar (Word)

Best Contemporary Soul Gospel Album
Handel's Messiah — A Soulful Celebration, various artists (Reprise)

Best Pop Gospel Album
The Great Adventure, Steven Curtis Chapman (Sparrow)

Best Southern Gospel Album
Sometimes Miracles Hide, Bruce Carroll (Word)

Best Gospel Album by a Choir or Chorus
Edwin Hawkins Music and Arts Seminar Mass Choir — Recorded Live in Los Angeles, Music and Arts Seminar Mass Choir; Edwin Hawkins, choir director (Fixit)

Best Latin Pop Album
Otro Dia Mas Sin Verte, Jon Secada (Capitol-EMI-Latin)

Best Tropical Latin Album
Frenesi, Linda Ronstadt (Elektra Entertainment)

Best Mexican/American Album
Mas Canciones, Linda Ronstadt (Elektra)

Best Traditional Blues Album
Goin' Back to New Orleans, Dr. John (Warner Bros.)

Best Contemporary Folk Album
Another Country, Chieftains (RCA Victor)

Best Contemporary Blues Album
The Sky Is Crying, Stevie Ray Vaughan and Double Trouble (Epic)

Best Traditional Folk Album
An Irish Evening Live at the Grand Opera House, Belfast, Chieftains (RCA Victor)

Best Reggae Album
X-Tra Naked, Shabba Ranks (Epic)

Best New Age Album
Shepherd Moons, Enya (Reprise)

Best World Music Album
Brasileiro, Sergio Mendes (Elektra Entertainment)

Best Polka Album
35th Anniversary, Walter Ostanek (World Renowned Sounds)

Best Arrangement on an Instrumental
"Strike Up the Band," Rob McConnell, arranger

Best Instrumental Arrangement Accompanying Vocal(s)
"Here's to Life," Johnny Mandel, arranger

Best Instrumental Composition
"Harlem Renaissance Suite," Benny Carter, composer

Best Musical Show Album
Guys and Dolls — The New Broadway Cast Recording, New Broadway cast (RCA Victor)

Best Instrumental Composition Written for a Motion Picture or for Television
Beauty and the Beast, Alan Menken, composer

Best Song Written Specifically for a Motion Picture or for Television
"Beauty and the Beast," Howard Ashman and Alan Menken, songwriters

Best Contemporary Composition
The Lovers, Samuel Barber, composer

Best Classical Album
Mahler, *Symphony No. 9*, Leonard Bernstein conducting Berlin Philharmonic Orchestra (Deutsche Grammophon)

Best Orchestral Performance
Mahler, *Symphony No. 9*, Leonard Bernstein conducting Berlin Philharmonic Orchestra

Best Chamber Music Performance
Brahms, *Sonatas for Cello and Piano*, Yo-Yo Ma, cello; Emanuel Ax, piano

Best Classical Performance, Instrumental Soloist(s) (With Orchestra)
Prokofiev, *Sinfonia Concertante*; Tchaikovsky, *Variations on a Rococo Theme*, Yo-Yo Ma, cello; Lorin Maazel conducting Pittsburgh Symphony Orchestra

Best Classical Performance, Instrumental Soloist(s) (Without Orchestra)
Horowitz — Discovered Treasures (Chopin, Clementi, Liszt, Scarlatti and Scriabin), Vladimir Horowitz, piano

Best Opera Recording
Strauss, *Die Frau Ohne Schatten*, Sir Georg Solti conducting Vienna Philharmonic; solos: Domingo, Varady, Van Dam, Behrens, Runkel and Jo (London)

Best Performance of a Choral Work
Orff, *Carmina Burana*, Herbert Blomstedt conducting San Francisco Girls and Boys Chorus, SFS Chorus and San Francisco Symphony Orchestra

Best Classical Vocal Performance
Kathleen Battle at Carnegie Hall (Handel, Mozart, Liszt, Strauss, Charpentier, etc.), Kathleen Battle, soprano; Margo Garrett, accompanist

Best Comedy Album
P.D.Q. Bach, *Music for an Awful Lot of Winds and Percussion*, Professor Peter Schickele (Telarc)

Best Spoken Word or Non-Musical Album
What You Can Do to Avoid AIDS, Earvin "Magic" Johnson and Robert O'Keefe (Random House Audiobooks)

Best Album for Children
Beauty and the Beast — Original Motion Picture Soundtrack, various artists (Walt Disney)

Best Album Package
Spellbound — Compact (Special Package), Melanie Nissen, art director (Capitol/Virgin)

Best Album Notes
Queen of Soul — The Atlantic Recordings, Dave Marsh, Jerry Wexler, David Ritz, Thulani Davis, Ahmet Ertegun, Tom Dowd and Arif Mardin, annotators (Rhino)

Best Historical Album
The Complete Capitol Recordings of the Nat King Cole Trio, Nat King Cole Trio (Mosaic)

Best Music Video, Short Form
"Digging in the Dirt," Peter Gabriel

Best Music Video, Long Form
"Diva," Annie Lennox

Producers of the Year (Non-Classical) (tie)
Daniel Lanois and Brian Eno
L.A. Reid and Babyface

Classical Producer of the Year
Michael Fine

1993

Record of the Year
"I Will Always Love You," Whitney Houston

Album of the Year
The Bodyguard — Original Soundtrack Album, Whitney Houston (Arista)

Song of the Year
"A Whole New World" (Theme From *Aladdin*), Alan Menken and Tim Rice, songwriters

Best New Artist
Toni Braxton

Best Pop Vocal Performance, Male
"If I Ever Lose My Faith in You," Sting

Whitney Houston

Best Pop Vocal Performance, Female
"I Will Always Love You," Whitney Houston

Best Pop Performance by a Duo or Group With Vocal
"A Whole New World" (Theme From *Aladdin*), Peabo Bryson and Regina Belle

Best Traditional Pop Vocal Performance
Steppin' Out, Tony Bennett

Best Pop Instrumental Performance
"Barcelona Mona," Bruce Hornsby and Branford Marsalis

Best Rock Gospel Album
Free at Last, DC Talk (ForeFront)

Best Rock Song
"Runaway Train," David Pirner, songwriter

Best Rock Vocal Performance, Solo
"I'd Do Anything for Love" (But I Won't Do That), Meat Loaf

Best Rock Performance by a Duo or Group With Vocal
"Livin' on the Edge," Aerosmith

Best Rock Instrumental Performance
"Sofa," Zappa's Universe Rock Group Featuring Steve Vai

Best Hard Rock Performance With Vocal
"Plush," Stone Temple Pilots

Best Metal Performance With Vocal
"I Don't Want to Change the World," Ozzy Osbourne

Best Alternative Music Album
Zooropa, U2 (Island)

Best Rhythm and Blues Song
"That's the Way Love Goes," Janet Jackson, James Harris III and Terry Lewis, songwriters

Best Rhythm and Blues Vocal Performance, Male
"A Song for You," Ray Charles

Best Rhythm and Blues Vocal Performance, Female
"Another Sad Love Song," Toni Braxton

Best Rhythm and Blues Performance by a Duo or Group With Vocal
"No Ordinary Love," Sade

Best Rap Solo Performance
"Let Me Ride," Dr. Dre

Best Rap Performance by a Duo or Group
"Rebirth of Slick" (Cool Like Dat), Digable Planets

Best Jazz Vocal Performance
Take a Look, Natalie Cole

Best Jazz Instrumental Solo
"Miles Ahead," Joe Henderson

Best Jazz Instrumental Performance, Individual or Group
So Near, So Far (Musings for Miles), Joe Henderson

Best Contemporary Jazz Performance (Instrumental)
The Road to You, Pat Metheny Group

Best Large Jazz Ensemble Performance
Miles and Quincy Live at Montreux, Miles Davis and Quincy Jones

Best Country Song
"Passionate Kisses," Lucinda Williams, songwriter

Best Country Vocal Performance, Male
"Ain't That Lonely Yet," Dwight Yoakam

Best Country Vocal Performance, Female
"Passionate Kisses," Mary Chapin Carpenter

Best Country Performance by a Duo or Group With Vocal
"Hard Workin' Man," Brooks and Dunn

Best Country Vocal Collaboration
"Does He Love You," Reba McEntire and Linda Davis

Best Country Instrumental Performance
"Red Wing," Asleep at the Wheel featuring Eldon Shamblin, Johnny Gimble, Chet Atkins, Vince Gill, Marty Stuart and Reuben "Lucky Oceans" Gosfield

Best Bluegrass Album
Waitin' for the Hard Times to Go, Nashville Bluegrass Band (Sugar Hill)

Best Traditional Soul Gospel Album
Stand Still, Shirley Caesar (Word Record and Music)

Best Contemporary Soul Gospel Album
All Out, Winans (Qwest/Warner Alliance)

Best Pop/Contemporary Gospel Album
The Live Adventure, Steven Curtis Chapman (Sparrow)

Best Southern Gospel, Country Gospel or Bluegrass Gospel Album
Good News, Kathy Mattea (Mercury)

Best Gospel Album by a Choir or Chorus
Live . . . We Come Rejoicing, Brooklyn Tabernacle Choir; Carol Cymbala, choir director (Warner Alliance)

Best Latin Pop Album
Aries, Luis Miguel (WEA Latina)

Best Tropical Latin Album
Mi Tierra, Gloria Estefan (Epic)

Best Mexican/American Album
Live, Selena (Capitol/EMI Latin)

Best Traditional Blues Album
Blues Summit, B.B. King (MCA)

Best Contemporary Blues Album
Feels Like Rain, Buddy Guy (Silvertone)

Best Traditional Folk Album
The Celtic Harp, Chieftains (RCA Victor)

Best Contemporary Folk Album
Other Voices/Other Rooms, Nanci Griffith (Elektra)

Best Reggae Album
Bad Boys, Inner Circle (Big Beat/Atlantic)

Best New Age Album
Spanish Angel, Paul Winter Consort (Living Music)

Best World Music Album
A Meeting by the River, Ry Cooder and V.M. Bhatt (Walter Lily Acoustics)

Best Polka Album
Accordionly Yours, Walter Ostanek and His Band (WRS)

Best Arrangement on an Instrumental
"Mood Indigo," Dave Grusin, arranger

Best Instrumental Arrangement Accompanying Vocal(s)
"When I Fall in Love," Jeremy Lubbock and David Foster, arrangers

Best Instrumental Composition
"Forever in Love," Kenny G, composer

Best Musical Show Album
The Who's Tommy — Original Cast Recording, original cast (RCA Victor)

Best Instrumental Composition Written for a Motion Picture or for Television
Aladdin, Alan Menken, composer

Best Song Written for a Motion Picture or for Television
"A Whole New World" (Theme From *Aladdin)*, Alan Menken and Tim Rice, songwriters

Best Contemporary Composition
Violin Concerto, Elliott Carter, composer

Best Classical Album
Bartók, *The Wooden Prince and Cantata Profana*, Pierre Boulez conducting Chicago Symphony Orchestra and Chorus; John Aler, tenor; John Tomlinson, baritone (Deutsche Grammophon)

Best Chamber Music Performance
Ives, *String Quartets nos. 1 and 2;* Barber *String Quartet Op. 11 (American Originals)*, Emerson String Quartet

Best Classical Performance, Instrumental Soloist(s) (With Orchestra)
Berg, *Violin Concerto;* Rihm, *Time Chant,* Anne-Sophie Mutter, violinist; James Levine conducting Chicago Symphony Orchestra

Best Classical Performance, Instrumental Soloist(s) (Without Orchestra)
Barber, *The Complete Solo Piano Music*, John Browning, pianist

Best Orchestral Performance
Bartók, *The Wooden Prince*, Pierre Boulez conducting Chicago Symphony

Best Opera Recording
Handel, *Semele*, John Nelson conducting English Chamber Orchestra and Ambrosian Opera Chorus; solos: Battle, Horne, Ramey, Aler, McNair, Chance, Mackie and Doss (Deutsche Grammophon)

Best Performance of a Choral Work
Bartók, *Cantata Profana*, Pierre Boulez conducting Chicago Symphony Orchestra and Chorus; Margaret Hillis, choral director

Best Classical Vocal Performance
The Art of Arleen Auger (Works of Larsen, Purcell, Schumann, Mozart), Arleen Auger, soprano; Joel Revzen, accompanist

Best Spoken Comedy Album
Jammin' in New York, George Carlin (Eardrum/Atlantic)

Best Spoken Word or Non-Musical Album
On the Pulse of Morning, Maya Angelou (Random House Audio Books)

Best Musical Album for Children
Aladdin (Original Motion Picture Soundtrack), various artists (Walt Disney Records)

Best Spoken Word Album for Children
Audrey Hepburn's Enchanted Tales, Audrey Hepburn (Dove Audio)

Best Recording Package
The Complete Billie Holiday on Verve 1945–1959, David Lau, art director (Verve)

Best Album Notes
The Complete Billie Holiday on Verve 1945–1959, Buck Clayton, Phil Schaap and Joel E. Siegel, annotators (Verve)

Best Historical Album
The Complete Billie Holiday on Verve 1945–1959, Billie Holiday (Verve)

Best Music Video, Short Form
"Steam," Peter Gabriel

Best Music Video, Long Form
"Ten Summoner's Tales," Sting

Producer of the Year (Non-Classical)
David Foster

Classical Producer of the Year
Judith Sherman

1994

Record of the Year
"All I Wanna Do," Sheryl Crow

Album of the Year
MTV Unplugged, Tony Bennett (Columbia)

Song of the Year
"Streets of Philadelphia" (Theme from Philadelphia), Bruce
    Springsteen, songwriter

Best New Artist
Sheryl Crow

Best Pop Vocal Performance, Male
"Can You Feel the Love Tonight," Elton John

Best Pop Vocal Performance, Female
"All I Wanna Do," Sheryl Crow

Best Pop Performance by a Duo or Group With Vocal
"I Swear," All-4-One

Best Traditional Pop Vocal Performance
MTV Unplugged, Tony Bennett

Best Pop Instrumental Performance
"Cruisin'," Booker T and the MG's

Best Pop Vocal Collaboration
"Funny How Time Slips Away," Al Green and
    Lyle Lovett

Best Pop Album
Longing in Their Hearts, Bonnie Raitt (Capitol)

Best Rock Album
Voodoo Lounge, The Rolling Stones (Virgin)

Best Rock Gospel Album
Wake-Up Call, Petra (Dayspring)

Best Rock Song
"Streets of Philadelphia," Bruce Springsteen,
    songwriter

Best Rock Vocal Performance, Male
"Streets of Philadelphia," Bruce Springsteen

Best Rock Vocal Performance, Female
"Come to My Window," Melissa Etheridge

Best Rock Performance by a Duo or Group With Vocal
"Crazy," Aerosmith

Best Rock Instrumental Performance
"Marooned," Pink Floyd

Best Hard Rock Performance
"Black Hole Sun," Soundgarden

Best Metal Performance
"Spoonman," Soundgarden

Best Alternative Music Performance
Dookie, Green Day

Best Rhythm and Blues Album
II, Boyz II Men (Motown)

Best Rhythm and Blues Song
"I'll Make Love to You," Babyface, songwriter

Best Rhythm and Blues Vocal Performance, Male
"When Can I See You," Babyface

Best Rhythm and Blues Vocal Performance, Female
"Breathe Again," Toni Braxton

**Best Rhythm and Blues Performance by a Duo or Group
With Vocal**
"I'll Make Love to You," Boyz II Men

Best Rap Solo Performance
"U.N.I.T.Y.," Queen Latifah

Best Rap Performance by a Duo or Group
"None of Your Business," Salt-N-Pepa

Best Jazz Vocal Performance
Mystery Lady (Songs of Billie Holiday), Etta James

Best Jazz Instrumental Solo
"Prelude to a Kiss," Benny Carpenter

Best Jazz Instrumental Performance, Individual or Group
A Tribute to Miles, Ron Carter, Herbie Hancock, Wallace
    Roney, Wayne Shorter and Tony Williams

Best Contemporary Jazz Performance
"Out of the Loop," Brecker Brothers

Best Large Jazz Ensemble Performance
"Journey," McCoy Tyner Big Band

Best Latin Jazz Performance
"Danzon," Arturo Sandoval

Best Country Album
Stones in the Road, Mary Chapin Carpenter (Columbia)

Best Country Song
"I Swear," Gary Baker and Frank J. Meyers, songwriters

Best Country Vocal Performance, Male
"When Love Finds You," Vince Gill

Best Country Vocal Performance, Female
"Shut Up and Kiss Me," Mary Chapin Carpenter

Best Country Performance by a Duo or Group With Vocal
"Blues for Dixie," Asleep at the Wheel with Lyle Lovett

Best Country Vocal Collaboration
"I Fall to Pieces," Aaron Neville and Trisha Yearwood

Best County Instrumental Performance
"Young Thing," Chet Atkins

Best Bluegrass Album
The Great Dobro Sessions, various artists (Sugar Hill)

Best Traditional Soul Gospel Album
Songs of the Church — Live in Memphis, Albertina Walker
    (Benson)

Best Contemporary Soul Gospel Album
Join the Band, Take 6 (Reprise/Warner Alliance)

Best Pop/Contemporary Gospel Album
Mercy, Andrae Crouch (Qwest/Warner Alliance)

**Best Southern Gospel, Country Gospel or Bluegrass Gospel
Album**
I Know Who Holds Tomorrow, Alison Krauss and the Cox
    Family (Rounder)

Best Gospel Album by a Choir or Chorus (tie)
Through God's Eyes, Thompson Community Singers; Rev.
    Milton Brunson, choir director (Word)

Live in Atlanta at Morehouse College, Love Fellowship
    Crusade Choir; Hezekiah Walker, choir director (Benson)

Best Latin Pop Performance
"Segundo Romance," Luis Miguel

Best Tropical Latin Performance
Master Sessions Volume 1, Chachao

Best Mexican-American Performance
"Recuerdo a Javier Solis," Vikki Carr

Best Traditional Blues Album
From the Cradle, Eric Clapton (Reprise)

MULTIPLE GRAMMY WINNERS

	Wins			Wins
1. Sir Georg Solti	30	9.	Ella Fitzgerald	13
2. Quincy Jones	26		Leontyne Price	13
3. Vladimir Horowitz	25		Robert Shaw (including Robert Shaw Chorale)	13
4. Henry Mancini	20	10.	Chet Atkins	12
5. Stevie Wonder	17		Ray Charles	12
6. Leonard Bernstein	16		David Foster	12
Paul Simon (including Simon and Garfunkel)	16		Michael Jackson	12
7. Aretha Franklin	15		Thomas Z. Shepard	12
John Williams	15		Sting (including Police)	12
8. Pierre Boulez	14			
Itzhak Perlman	14			

Source: National Academy of Recording Arts and Sciences

Best Contemporary Blues Album
Father Father, Pops Staples (Pointblank)

Best Traditional Folk Album
World Gone Wrong, Bob Dylan (Columbia)

Best Contemporary Folk Album
American Recordings, Johnny Cash
(American Recordings)

Best Reggae Album
Crucial! Roots Classics, Bunny Wailer (Shanachie)

Best New Age Album
Prayer for the Wild Things, Paul Winter (Living Music Records)

Best World Music Album
Talking Timbuktu, Ali Farka Toure with Ry Cooder (Hannibal)

Best Polka Album
Music & Friends, Walter Ostanek Band (WRS)

Best Instrumental Arrangement
"Three Cowboy Songs," Dave Grusin, arranger

Best Instrumental Arrangement With Accompanying Vocal(s)
"Circle of Life," Lebo Morake and Hans Zimmer, arrangers

Best Instrumental Composition
"African Skies," Michael Brecker, composer

Best Musical Show Album
Passion, Original Broadway cast (Angel)

Best Instrumental Composition Written for a Motion Picture or for Television
Schindler's List, John Williams, composer

Best Song Written Specifically for a Motion Picture or for Television
"Streets of Philadelphia" (From *Philadelphia*), Bruce Springsteen, songwriter

Best Classical Contemporary Composition
"Cello Concerto," Stephen Albert, composer

Best Classical Album
Bartok, *Concerto for Orchestra; Four Orchestral Pieces, Op. 12*,
Pierre Boulez conducting Chicago Symphony Orchestra
(Deutsche Grammophon)

Best Chamber Music Performance
Beethoven and Mozart, *Quintets*, Daniel Barenboim, piano;
Dale Clevenger, horn; Larry Combs, clarinet; Daniele
Damiano, bassoon; Hansjorg Schellenberger, oboe

**Best Classical Performance, Instrumental Soloist(s)
(With Orchestra)**
The New York Album (Works of Albert, Bartok and Bloch),
David Zinman conducting Baltimore Symphony Orchestra;
Yo-Yo Ma, cellist and alto violinist

**Best Classical Performance, Instrumental Soloist(s)
(Without Orchestra)**
Haydn, *Piano Sonatas nos. 32, 47, 53 and 59*, Emmanuel Ax,
pianist

Best Orchestral Performance
Bartok, *Concerto for Orchestra; Four Orchestral Pieces, Op. 12*,
Pierre Boulez, conducting Chicago Symphony Orchestra

Best Opera Recording
Floyd, *Susannah*, Kent Nagano conducting Orchestra and
Chorus of Opera de Lyon; solos: Studer, Hadley, Ramey
and Chester (Virgin Classics)

Best Performance of a Choral Work
Berlioz, *Messe Solennelle*, John Eliot Gardiner, choir director,
the Monteverdi Choir, Orchestra Revolutionnaire et
Romantique and various artists

Best Classical Vocal Performance
The Impatient Lover (Italian Songs by Beethoven, Schubert,
Mozart, etc.), Cecilia Bartoli, mezzo-soprano; Andras
Schiff, piano

Best Spoken Comedy Album
Live From Hell, Sam Kinison (Priority Records)

Best Spoken Word or Non-Musical Album
Get in the Van: On the Road With Black Flag, Henry Rollins
(Time Warner Audiobooks)

Best Musical Album for Children
The Lion King — Original Motion Picture Soundtrack, various
artists (Walt Disney Records)

Best Spoken Word Album for Children
The Lion King Read-Along, original cast (Walt Disney Records)

Best Recording Package
Tribute to the Music of Bob Willis and the Texas Playboys,
Buddy Jackson, art director (Liberty)

Best Recording Package—Boxed
The Complete Ella Fitzgerald Song Books, Chris Thompson, art
director (Verve)

Best Album Notes
*Louis Armstrong: Portrait of the Artist as a Young Man,
1923–1934*, Dan Morgenstern and Loren Schoenberg,
album notes writers (Columbia/Legacy/Smithsonian)

Best Historical Album
The Complete Ella Fitzgerald Song Books on Verve (Verve)

Best Music Video, Short Form
"Love Is Strong," The Rolling Stones

Best Music Video, Long Form
Zoo TV: Live From Sydney, U2

Producer of the Year (Non-Classical)
Don Was

Classical Producer of the Year
Andrew Cornall

Country Music Association Awards

The Country Music Association Awards, presented annually in October, are considered the most prestigious awards in the country-music industry. Voting is limited to current CMA members, who select winners in a two-round balloting process.

1967

Entertainer of the Year
Eddy Arnold

Single of the Year
"There Goes My Everything," Jack Greene

Album of the Year
There Goes My Everything, Jack Greene (Decca)

Song of the Year (Songwriter's Award)
"There Goes My Everything," Dallas Frazier

Male Vocalist of the Year
Jack Greene

Female Vocalist of the Year
Loretta Lynn

Vocal Group of the Year
The Stoneman Family

Instrumental Group of the Year
The Buckaroos

Comedian of the Year
Don Bowman

Musician of the Year
Chet Atkins

1968

Entertainer of the Year
Glen Campbell

Single of the Year
"Harper Valley P.T.A.," Jeannie C. Riley

Album of the Year
Johnny Cash at Folsom Prison, Johnny Cash (Columbia)

Song of the Year (Songwriter's Award)
"Honey," Bobby Russell

Male Vocalist of the Year
Glen Campbell

Female Vocalist of the Year
Tammy Wynette

Vocal Group of the Year
Porter Wagoner and Dolly Parton

Instrumental Group of the Year
The Buckaroos

Comedian of the Year
Ben Colder

Musician of the Year
Chet Atkins

Loretta Lynn

1969

Entertainer of the Year
Johnny Cash

Single of the Year
"A Boy Named Sue," Johnny Cash

Album of the Year
Johnny Cash at San Quentin Prison, Johnny Cash (Columbia)

Song of the Year (Songwriter's Award)
"Carroll County Accident," Bob Ferguson

Male Vocalist of the Year
Johnny Cash

Female Vocalist of the Year
Tammy Wynette

Vocal Group of the Year
Johnny Cash and June Carter

Instrumental Group of the Year
Danny Davis and the Nashville Brass

Comedian of the Year
Archie Campbell

Musician of the Year
Chet Atkins

1970

Entertainer of the Year
Merle Haggard

Single of the Year
"Okie From Muskogee," Merle Haggard

Album of the Year
Okie From Muskogee, Merle Haggard (Capitol)

Song of the Year (Songwriter's Award)
"Sunday Morning Coming Down," Kris Kristofferson

Male Vocalist of the Year
Merle Haggard

Female Vocalist of the Year
Tammy Wynette

Vocal Group of the Year
The Glaser Brothers

Vocal Duo of the Year
Porter Wagoner and Dolly Parton

Instrumental Group of the Year
Danny Davis and the Nashville Brass

Comedian of the Year
Roy Clark

Musician of the Year
Jerry Reed

1971

Entertainer of the Year
Charley Pride

Single of the Year
"Help Me Make It Through the Night," Sammi Smith

Album of the Year
I Won't Mention It Again, Ray Price (Columbia)

Song of the Year (Songwriter's Award)
"Easy Loving," Freddie Hart

Male Vocalist of the Year
Charley Pride

Female Vocalist of the Year
Lynn Anderson

Vocal Group of the Year
The Osborne Brothers

Vocal Duo of the Year
Porter Wagoner and Dolly Parton

Instrumental Group of the Year
Danny Davis and the Nashville Brass

Musician of the Year
Jerry Reed

1972

Entertainer of the Year
Loretta Lynn

Single of the Year
"The Happiest Girl in the Whole U.S.A.,"
Donna Fargo

Album of the Year
Let Me Tell You About a Song, Merle
Haggard (Capitol)

Song of the Year (Songwriter's Award)
"Easy Loving," Freddie Hart

Male Vocalist of the Year
Charley Pride

Female Vocalist of the Year
Loretta Lynn

Vocal Group of the Year
Statler Brothers

Vocal Duo of the Year
Conway Twitty and Loretta Lynn

Instrumental Group of the Year
Danny Davis and the Nashville Brass

Musician of the Year
Charlie McCoy

1973

Entertainer of the Year
Roy Clark

Single of the Year
"Behind Closed Doors," Charlie Rich

Album of the Year
Behind Closed Doors, Charlie Rich
(Epic)

Song of the Year (Songwriter's Award)
"Behind Closed Doors," Kenny O'Dell

Male Vocalist of the Year
Charlie Rich

Female Vocalist of the Year
Loretta Lynn

Vocal Group of the Year
Statler Brothers

Vocal Duo of the Year
Conway Twitty and Loretta Lynn

Instrumental Group of the Year
Danny Davis and the Nashville Brass

Musician of the Year
Charlie McCoy

1974

Entertainer of the Year
Charlie Rich

Single of the Year
"Country Bumpkin," Cal Smith

Album of the Year
A Very Special Love Song, Charlie Rich
(Epic)

Song of the Year (Songwriter's Award)
"Country Bumpkin," Don Wayne

Male Vocalist of the Year
Ronnie Milsap

Female Vocalist of the Year
Olivia Newton-John

Vocal Group of the Year
Statler Brothers

Vocal Duo of the Year
Conway Twitty and Loretta Lynn

Instrumental Group of the Year
Danny Davis and the Nashville Brass

Musician of the Year
Don Rich

1975

Entertainer of the Year
John Denver

Single of the Year
"Before the Next Teardrop Falls,"
Freddy Fender

Album of the Year
A Legend in My Time, Ronnie Milsap
(RCA)

Song of the Year (Songwriter's Award)
"Back Home Again," John Denver

Male Vocalist of the Year
Waylon Jennings

Female Vocalist of the Year
Dolly Parton

Vocal Group of the Year
Statler Brothers

Vocal Duo of the Year
Conway Twitty and Loretta Lynn

Instrumental Group of the Year
Roy Clark and Buck Trent

Musician of the Year
Johnny Gimble

1976

Entertainer of the Year
Mel Tillis

Single of the Year
"Good Hearted Woman," Waylon
Jennings and Willie Nelson

Album of the Year
Wanted — The Outlaws, Waylon
Jennings, Willie Nelson, Tompall
Glaser and Jesse Colter (RCA)

Song of the Year (Songwriter's Award)
"Rhinestone Cowboy," Larry Weiss

Male Vocalist of the Year
Ronnie Milsap

Female Vocalist of the Year
Dolly Parton

Vocal Group of the Year
Statler Brothers

Vocal Duo of the Year
Waylon Jennings and Willie Nelson

Instrumental Group of the Year
Roy Clark and Buck Trent

Musician of the Year
Hargus "Pig" Robbins

1977

Entertainer of the Year
Ronnie Milsap

Single of the Year
"Lucille," Kenny Rogers

Album of the Year
Ronnie Milsap Live, Ronnie Milsap
(RCA)

Song of the Year (Songwriter's Award)
"Lucille," Roger Bowling and Hal Bynum

Male Vocalist of the Year
Ronnie Milsap

Female Vocalist of the Year
Crystal Gayle

Vocal Group of the Year
Statler Brothers

Vocal Duo of the Year
Jim Ed Brown and Helen Cornelius

Instrumental Group of the Year
The Original Texas Playboys

Musician of the Year
Roy Clark

1978

Entertainer of the Year
Dolly Parton

Single of the Year
"Heaven's Just a Sin Away," The
Kendalls

Album of the Year
It Was Almost Like a Song, Ronnie
Milsap (RCA)

Song of the Year (Songwriter's Award)
"Don't It Make My Brown Eyes Blue,"
Richard Leigh

Male Vocalist of the Year
Don Williams

Female Vocalist of the Year
Crystal Gayle

Vocal Group of the Year
Oak Ridge Boys

Vocal Duo of the Year
Kenny Rogers and Dottie West

Instrumental Group of the Year
Oak Ridge Boys

Musician of the Year
Roy Clark

1979

Entertainer of the Year
Willie Nelson

Willie Nelson

Single of the Year
"The Devil Went Down to Georgia,"
Charlie Daniels Band

Album of the Year
The Gambler, Kenny Rogers (United
Artists)

**Song of the Year (Songwriter's
Award)**
"The Gambler," Don Schlitz

Male Vocalist of the Year
Kenny Rogers

Female Vocalist of the Year
Barbara Mandrell

Vocal Group of the Year
Statler Brothers

Vocal Duo of the Year
Kenny Rogers and Dottie West

Instrumental Group of the Year
Charlie Daniels Band

Musician of the Year
Charlie Daniels

1980

Entertainer of the Year
Barbara Mandrell

Single of the Year
"He Stopped Loving Her Today," George
Jones

Album of the Year
*Coal Miner's Daughter — Original
Motion Picture Soundtrack* (MCA)

Song of the Year (Songwriter's Award)
"He Stopped Loving Her Today," Bobby
Braddock and Curly Putman

Male Vocalist of the Year
George Jones

Female Vocalist of the Year
Emmylou Harris

Vocal Group of the Year
Statler Brothers

Vocal Duo of the Year
Moe Bandy and Joe Stampley

Instrumental Group of the Year
Charlie Daniels Band

Musician of the Year
Roy Clark

1981

Entertainer of the Year
Barbara Mandrell

Single of the Year
"Elvira," Oak Ridge Boys

Album of the Year
I Believe in You, Don Williams (MCA)

Song of the Year (Songwriter's Award)
"He Stopped Loving Her Today," Bobby
Braddock and Curly Putman

Male Vocalist of the Year
George Jones

Female Vocalist of the Year
Barbara Mandrell

Vocal Group of the Year
Alabama

Barbara Mandrell

Vocal Duo of the Year
David Frizzell and Shelly West

Instrumental Group of the Year
Alabama

Horizon Award
Terri Gibbs

Musician of the Year
Chet Atkins

1982

Entertainer of the Year
Alabama

Single of the Year
"Always on My Mind," Willie Nelson

Album of the Year
Always on My Mind, Willie Nelson
(Columbia)

Song of the Year (Songwriter's Award)
"Always on My Mind," Johnny
Christopher, Wayne Carson and
Mark James

Male Vocalist of the Year
Ricky Skaggs

Female Vocalist of the Year
Janie Frickie

Vocal Group of the Year
Alabama

Vocal Duo of the Year
David Frizzell and Shelly West

Instrumental Group of the Year
Alabama

Horizon Award
Ricky Skaggs

Musician of the Year
Chet Atkins

1983

Entertainer of the Year
Alabama

Single of the Year
"Swingin'," John Anderson

Album of the Year
The Closer You Get, Alabama (RCA)

Song of the Year (Songwriter's Award)
"Always on My Mind," Johnny
Christopher, Wayne Carson and
Mark James

Male Vocalist of the Year
Lee Greenwood

Female Vocalist of the Year
Janie Frickie

Vocal Group of the Year
Alabama

Vocal Duo of the Year
Merle Haggard and Willie Nelson

Instrumental Group of the Year
The Ricky Skaggs Band

Horizon Award
John Anderson

Musician of the Year
Chet Atkins

1984

Entertainer of the Year
Alabama

Single of the Year
"A Little Good News," Anne Murray

Album of the Year
A Little Good News, Anne Murray
(Capitol)

Song of the Year (Songwriter's Award)
"Wind Beneath My Wings," Larry
Henley and Jeff Silbar

Male Vocalist of the Year
Lee Greenwood

Female Vocalist of the Year
Reba McEntire

Vocal Group of the Year
Statler Brothers

Vocal Duo of the Year
Willie Nelson and Julio Iglesias

Instrumental Group of the Year
The Ricky Skaggs Band

Horizon Award
Judds

Musician of the Year
Chet Atkins

1985

Entertainer of the Year
Ricky Skaggs

Single of the Year
"Why Not Me," Judds

Album of the Year
Does Fort Worth Ever Cross Your Mind,
George Strait (MCA)

Song of the Year (Songwriter's Award)
"God Bless the U.S.A.," Lee Greenwood

Male Vocalist of the Year
George Strait

Female Vocalist of the Year
Reba McEntire

Vocal Group of the Year
Judds

Vocal Duo of the Year
Anne Murray and Dave Loggins

Instrumental Group of the Year
The Ricky Skaggs Band

Horizon Award
Sawyer Brown

Musician of the Year
Chet Atkins

Music Video of the Year
"All My Rowdy Friends Are Coming Over Tonight," Hank Williams, Jr.

1986

Entertainer of the Year
Reba McEntire

Single of the Year
"Bop," Dan Seals

Album of the Year
Lost in the Fifties Tonight, Ronnie Milsap (RCA)

Song of the Year (Songwriter's Award)
"On the Other Hand," Paul Overstreet and Don Schlitz

Male Vocalist of the Year
George Strait

Female Vocalist of the Year
Reba McEntire

Vocal Group of the Year
Judds

Vocal Duo of the Year
Dan Seals and Marie Osmond

Instrumental Group of the Year
Oak Ridge Boys

Horizon Award
Randy Travis

Musician of the Year
Johnny Gimble

Music Video of the Year
"Who's Gonna Fill Their Shoes," George Jones

1987

Entertainer of the Year
Hank Williams, Jr.

Single of the Year
"Forever and Ever, Amen," Randy Travis

Album of the Year
Always and Forever, Randy Travis (Warner Bros.)

Song of the Year (Songwriter's Award)
"Forever and Ever, Amen," Paul Overstreet and Don Schlitz

Male Vocalist of the Year
Randy Travis

Female Vocalist of the Year
Reba McEntire

Vocal Group of the Year
Judds

Vocal Duo of the Year
Ricky Skaggs and Sharon White

Horizon Award
Holly Dunn

Reba McEntire

Musician of the Year
Johnny Gimble

Music Video of the Year
"My Name Is Bocephus," Hank Williams, Jr.

1988

Entertainer of the Year
Hank Williams, Jr.

Single of the Year
"Eighteen Wheels and a Dozen Roses," Kathy Mattea

Album of the Year
Born to Boogie, Hank Williams, Jr. (Warner Bros.)

Song of the Year (Songwriter's Award)
'80's Ladies," K.T. Oslin

Male Vocalist of the Year
Randy Travis

Female Vocalist of the Year
K.T. Oslin

Vocal Group of the Year
Highway 101

Vocal Duo of the Year
Judds

Vocal Event of the Year
Trio, Dolly Parton, Emmylou Harris and Linda Ronstadt

Horizon Award
Ricky Van Shelton

Musician of the Year
Chet Atkins

1989

Entertainer of the Year
George Strait

Single of the Year
"I'm No Stranger to the Rain," Keith Whitley

Album of the Year
Will the Circle Be Unbroken Volume II, Nitty Gritty Dirt Band (Universal)

Song of the Year (Songwriter's Award)
"Chiseled in Stone," Max D. Barnes and Vern Gosdin

Male Vocalist of the Year
Ricky Van Shelton

Female Vocalist of the Year
Kathy Mattea

Vocal Group of the Year
Highway 101

Vocal Duo of the Year
Judds

Vocal Event of the Year
"There's a Tear in My Beer," Hank Williams, Jr. and Hank Williams, Sr.

Horizon Award
Clint Black

Musician of the Year
Johnny Gimble

Music Video of the Year
"There's a Tear in My Beer," Hank Williams, Jr.

1990

Entertainer of the Year
George Strait

Single of the Year
"When I Call Your Name," Vince Gill

Album of the Year
Pickin' on Nashville, Kentucky HeadHunters (Mercury)

Song of the Year (Songwriter's Award)
"Where've You Been," Jon Vezner and Don Henry

Male Vocalist of the Year
Clint Black

Female Vocalist of the Year
Kathy Mattea

Vocal Group of the Year
Kentucky HeadHunters

Vocal Duo of the Year
Judds

Vocal Event of the Year
"Till a Tear Becomes a Rose," Lorrie Morgan and Keith Whitley

Horizon Award
Garth Brooks

Musician of the Year
Johnny Gimble

Music Video of the Year
"The Dance," Garth Brooks

1991

Entertainer of the Year
Garth Brooks

Single of the Year
"Friends in Low Places," Garth Brooks

Album of the Year
No Fences, Garth Brooks (Capitol Nashville)

Song of the Year (Songwriter's Award)
"When I Call Your Name," Vince Gill and Tim DuBois

Male Vocalist of the Year
Vince Gill

Female Vocalist of the Year
Tanya Tucker

Vocal Group of the Year
Kentucky HeadHunters

Vocal Duo of the Year
Judds

Vocal Event of the Year
Mark O'Connor and the New Nashville Cats, Mark O'Connor and the New Nashville Cats (featuring Vince Gill, Ricky Skaggs and Steve Wariner)

Horizon Award
Travis Tritt

Musician of the Year
Mark O'Connor

Music Video of the Year
"The Thunder Rolls," Garth Brooks

1992

Entertainer of the Year
Garth Brooks

Single of the Year
"Achy Breaky Heart," Billy Ray Cyrus

Album of the Year
Ropin' the Wind, Garth Brooks (Liberty)

Song of the Year (Songwriter's Award)
"Look at Us," Vince Gill and Max D. Barnes

Male Vocalist of the Year
Vince Gill

Female Vocalist of the Year
Mary Chapin Carpenter

Vocal Group of the Year
Diamond Rio

Vocal Duo of the Year
Brooks & Dunn

Vocal Event of the Year
"The Whiskey Ain't Workin'," Marty Stuart and Travis Tritt

Horizon Award
Suzy Bogguss

Musician of the Year
Mark O'Connor

Music Video of the Year
"Midnight in Montgomery," Alan Jackson

1993

Entertainer of the Year
Vince Gill

Single of the Year
"Chattahoochee," Alan Jackson

Album of the Year
I Still Believe in You, Vince Gill (MCA)

Song of the Year (Songwriter's Award)
"I Still Believe in You," Vince Gill

Male Vocalist of the Year
Vince Gill

Female Vocalist of the Year
Mary Chapin Carpenter

Vocal Group of the Year
Diamond Rio

Vocal Duo of the Year
Brooks & Dunn

Vocal Event of the Year
"I Don't Need Your Rocking Chair," George Jones with Vince Gill, Mark Chesnutt, Garth Brooks, Travis Tritt, Joe Diffie, Alan Jackson, Pam Tillis, T. Graham Brown, Patty Loveless and Clint Black

Horizon Award
Mark Chesnutt

Musician of the Year
Mark O'Connor

Music Video of the Year
"Chattahoochee," Alan Jackson

1994

Entertainer of the Year
Vince Gill

Single of the Year
"I Swear," John Michael Montgomery

Album of the Year
Common Thread: The Songs of the Eagles, John Anderson, Clint Black, Suzy Bogguss, Brooks & Dunn, Billy Dean, Diamond Rio, Vince Gill, Alan Jackson, Little Texas, Lorrie Morgan, Travis Tritt, Tanya Tucker and Trisha Yearwood (Giant)

Song of the Year (Songwriter's Award)
"Chattahoochee," Alan Jackson

Male Vocalist of the Year
Vince Gill

Female Vocalist of the Year
Pam Tillis

Vocal Group of the Year
Diamond Rio

Vocal Duo of the Year
Brooks & Dunn

Vocal Event of the Year
"Does He Love You," Reba McEntire and Linda Davis

Horizon Award
John Michael Montgomery

Musician of the Year
Mark O'Connor

Music Video of the Year
"Independence Day," Martina McBrde

Garth Brooks

Down Beat Critics Poll and Hall of Fame

Each year, *Down Beat* magazine polls a group of international music critics to recognize those who have achieved excellence in the jazz world. The critics annually nominate inductees to the Jazz Hall of Fame, which appears in the August issue of the magazine with the poll. Talent Deserving Wider Recognition (TDWR) allows critics to cite young, emerging talent and overlooked established talent. Here are the past winners.

Critics Poll

1953

Male Singer
Louis Armstrong
TDWR
Jackie Paris

Female Singer
Ella Fitzgerald
TDWR (tie)
Annie Ross
Jeri Southern

Combo
Dave Brubeck

Big Band
Duke Ellington

Alto Saxophone
Charlie Parker
TDWR
Paul Desmond

Tenor Saxophone
Stan Getz
TDWR
Paul Quinichette

Baritone Saxophone
Harry Carney
TDWR
Gerry Mulligan

Clarinet
Buddy DeFranco
TDWR
Tony Scott

Trumpet
Louis Armstrong
TDWR
Chet Baker

Trombone
Bill Harris
TDWR (tie)
Bob Brookmeyer
Carl Fontana
Frank Rosolino

Acoustic Piano
Oscar Peterson
TDWR
Billy Taylor

Guitar
Barney Kessel
TDWR
Johnny Smith

Acoustic Bass
Oscar Pettiford
TDWR (tie)
Charles Mingus
Red Mitchell

Drums
Buddy Rich
TDWR
Art Blakey

1954

Male Singer
Louis Armstrong
TDWR
Clancy Hayes

Female Singer
Ella Fitzgerald
TDWR
Carmen McRae

Combo
Modern Jazz Quartet

Big Band
Count Basie

Alto Saxophone
Charlie Parker
TDWR
Bud Shank

Tenor Saxophone
Stan Getz
TDWR
Frank Wess

Baritone Saxophone
Harry Carney
TDWR
Lars Gullin

Clarinet
Buddy DeFranco
TDWR
Sam Most

Trumpet
Dizzy Gillespie
TDWR
Clifford Brown

Louis Armstrong

Trombone
Bill Harris
TDWR
Urbie Green

Acoustic Piano
Art Tatum
TDWR
Horace Silver

Guitar
Jimmy Raney
TDWR
Tal Farlow

Acoustic Bass
Ray Brown
TDWR
Percy Heath

Drums
Buddy Rich
TDWR
Osie Johnson

Vibes
Lionel Hampton
TDWR
Teddy Charles

1955

Male Singer
Louis Armstrong
TDWR
Joe Williams

Female Singer
Ella Fitzgerald
TDWR
Teddi King

Combo
Modern Jazz Quartet

Big Band
Count Basie

Alto Saxophone
Benny Carter
TDWR
Herb Geller

Tenor Saxophone
Stan Getz
TDWR
Bill Perkins

Baritone Saxophone
Gerry Mulligan
TDWR
Bob Gordon

Clarinet
Tony Scott
TDWR
Jimmy Giuffre

Trumpet (tie)
Dizzy Gillespie
Miles Davis
TDWR
Ruby Braff

Trombone
J. J. Johnson
TDWR
Jimmy Cleveland

Acoustic Piano
Art Tatum
TDWR
Randy Weston

Guitar
Jimmy Raney
TDWR
Howard Roberts

Acoustic Bass
Oscar Pettiford
TDWR
Wendell Marshall

Drums
Art Blakey
TDWR
Joe Morello

Vibes
Milt Jackson
TDWR
Cal Tjader

1956

Male Singer
Louis Armstrong
TDWR
Joe Turner

Female Singer
Ella Fitzgerald
TDWR
Barbara Lea

Combo
Modern Jazz Quartet

Big Band
Count Basie

Alto Saxophone
Benny Carter
TDWR
Phil Woods

Tenor Saxophone
Lester Young
TDWR
Bobby Jaspar

Baritone Saxophone
Harry Carney
TDWR
Jimmy Giuffre

Clarinet
Benny Goodman
TDWR
Buddy Collette

Trumpet
Dizzy Gillespie
TDWR
Thad Jones

Trombone
J. J. Johnson
TDWR
Benny Powell

Acoustic Piano
Art Tatum
TDWR
Hampton Hawes

Guitar
Tal Farlow
TDWR
Dick Garcia

Acoustic Bass
Oscar Pettiford
TDWR
Paul Chambers

Drums
Jo Jones
TDWR
Chico Hamilton

Vibes
Milt Jackson
TDWR
Terry Pollard

1957

Male Singer
Frank Sinatra

Female Singer
Ella Fitzgerald

Combo
Modern Jazz Quartet

Big Band
Count Basie

Alto Saxophone
Lee Konitz
TDWR
Art Pepper

Tenor Saxophone
Stan Getz
TDWR
Sonny Rollins

Baritone Saxophone
Gerry Mulligan
TDWR
Pepper Adams

Clarinet
Tony Scott

Trumpet
Dizzy Gillespie
TDWR
Donald Byrd

Trombone
J. J. Johnson
TDWR
Frank Rehak

Acoustic Piano
Erroll Garner
TDWR
Eddie Costa

Guitar
Tal Farlow
TDWR
Kenny Burrell

Acoustic Bass
Oscar Pettiford
TDWR
Leroy Vinnegar

Drums
Max Roach
TDWR
Philly Joe Jones

Vibes
Milt Jackson
TDWR
Eddie Costa

1958

Male Singer
Jimmy Rushing
TDWR
Ray Charles

Female Singer
Ella Fitzgerald

Combo
Modern Jazz Quartet

Big Band
Duke Ellington

Alto Saxophone
Lee Konitz

Tenor Saxophone
Stan Getz
TDWR
Benny Golson

Baritone Saxophone
Gerry Mulligan
TDWR
Tony Scott

Clarinet
Tony Scott

Trumpet
Miles Davis
TDWR
Art Farmer

Trombone
J. J. Johnson
TDWR
Jimmy Knepper

Acoustic Piano
Thelonious Monk
TDWR
Bill Evans

Guitar
Freddie Green
TDWR
Jim Hall

Acoustic Bass
Ray Brown
TDWR
Wilbur Ware

Drums
Max Roach

Vibes
Milt Jackson
TDWR
Victor Feldman

1959

Male Singer
Jimmy Rushing
TDWR
Jon Hendricks

Female Singer
Ella Fitzgerald
TDWR
Ernestine Anderson

Combo
Modern Jazz Quartet
TDWR
Mastersounds

Big Band
Duke Ellington
TDWR
Maynard Ferguson

Arranger/Composer
Duke Ellington
TDWR
Benny Golson

Alto Saxophone
Johnny Hodges
TDWR
Cannonball Adderley

Tenor Saxophone
Coleman Hawkins
TDWR
Benny Golson

Baritone Saxophone
Harry Carney
TDWR
Ronnie Ross

Clarinet
Tony Scott
TDWR
Bob Wilber

Trumpet
Miles Davis
TDWR
Lee Morgan

Trombone
J. J. Johnson
TDWR
Curtis Fuller

Acoustic Piano
Thelonious Monk
TDWR
Bill Evans

Guitar
Barney Kessel
TDWR
Charlie Byrd

Acoustic Bass
Ray Brown
TDWR
Scott LaFaro

Drums
Max Roach
TDWR (tie)
Elvin Jones
Ed Thigpen

Vibes
Milt Jackson
TDWR
Buddy Montgomery

Miscellaneous Instrument
Frank Wess, Flute

1960

Male Singer
Jimmy Rushing
TDWR
Bill Henderson

Female Singer
Ella Fitzgerald

Vocal Group
Lambert, Hendricks and Ross

Combo
Modern Jazz Quartet
TDWR (tie)
Art Farmer
Benny Golson

Big Band
Duke Ellington
TDWR
Quincy Jones

Arranger/Composer
Duke Ellington
TDWR
Quincy Jones

Alto Saxophone
Cannonball Adderley
TDWR
Ornette Coleman

Tenor Saxophone
Coleman Hawkins
TDWR
Johnny Griffin

Baritone Saxophone
Gerry Mulligan

Clarinet
Buddy DeFranco
TDWR
Pete Fountain

Flute
Frank Wess
TDWR
Les Spann

Trumpet
Dizzy Gillespie
TDWR
Nat Adderley

Trombone
J. J. Johnson
TDWR
Al Grey

Acoustic Piano
Thelonious Monk
TDWR
Ray Bryant

Guitar
Kenny Burrell
TDWR
Wes Montgomery

Acoustic Bass
Ray Brown
TDWR
Sam Jones

Drums
Max Roach
TDWR
Billy Higgins

Vibes
Milt Jackson
TDWR
Lem Winchester

Miscellaneous Instrument
Julius Watkins, French Horn
TDWR
Steve Lacy, Soprano
   Saxophone

1961

Male Singer
Ray Charles
TDWR
Jimmy Witherspoon

Duke Ellington

Female Singer
Ella Fitzgerald
TDWR
Aretha Franklin

Vocal Group
Lambert, Hendricks and Ross
TDWR
Double Six

Combo
Modern Jazz Quartet
TDWR
John Coltrane

Big Band
Duke Ellington
TDWR
Gerry Mulligan

Arranger/Composer
Duke Ellington
TDWR
George Russell

Alto Saxophone
Cannonball Adderley
TDWR
Eric Dolphy

Tenor Saxophone
John Coltrane
TDWR
Charlie Rouse

Baritone Saxophone
Gerry Mulligan
TDWR
Sahib Shihab

Clarinet
Buddy DeFranco
TDWR
Rolf Kuhn

Flute
Frank Wess
TDWR
Leo Wright

Trumpet
Dizzy Gillespie
TDWR
Freddie Hubbard

Trombone
J. J. Johnson
TDWR
Julian Priester

Acoustic Piano
Thelonious Monk
TDWR
Junior Mance

Guitar
Wes Montgomery
TDWR
Les Spann

Acoustic Bass
Ray Brown
TDWR
Charlie Haden

Drums
Max Roach
TDWR
Louis Hayes

Vibes
Milt Jackson
TDWR
Mike Mainieri

Miscellaneous Instrument
Julius Watkins, French Horn
TDWR
John Coltrane, Soprano
   Saxophone

1962

Male Singer
Ray Charles
TDWR
Lightnin' Hopkins

Female Singer
Ella Fitzgerald
TDWR
Abbey Lincoln

Vocal Group
Lambert, Hendricks and
   Ross
TDWR
Staple Singers

Combo
Miles Davis
TDWR (tie)
Al Grey
Billy Mitchell

Big Band
Duke Ellington
TDWR
Terry Gibbs

Arranger/Composer
Duke Ellington
TDWR
Oliver Nelson

Alto Saxophone
Johnny Hodges
TDWR
Leo Wright

Tenor Saxophone
Sonny Rollins
TDWR
Wayne Shorter

Baritone Saxophone
Gerry Mulligan
TDWR
Cecil Payne

Clarinet
Pee Wee Russell
TDWR
Jimmy Hamilton

Flute
Frank Wess
TDWR
Eric Dolphy

Trumpet
Dizzy Gillespie
TDWR
Don Ellis

Trombone
J. J. Johnson
TDWR (tie)
Dave Baker
Slide Hampton

Acoustic Piano
Bill Evans
TDWR
Cecil Taylor

Guitar
Wes Montgomery
TDWR
Grant Green

Acoustic Bass
Ray Brown
TDWR
Art Davis

Drums
Philly Joe Jones
TDWR (tie)
Roy Haynes
Mel Lewis

Vibes
Milt Jackson
TDWR
Walt Dickerson

Miscellaneous Instrument
John Coltrane, Soprano
Saxophone
TDWR
Roland Kirk, Manzello and
Stritch

1963

Male Singer
Ray Charles
TDWR
Mark Murphy

Female Singer
Ella Fitzgerald
TDWR
Sheila Jordan

Vocal Group
Lambert, Hendricks and
Bavan
TDWR
Stars of Faith

Combo
Miles Davis
TDWR (tie)
Clark Terry
Bobby Brookmeyer

Big Band
Duke Ellington
TDWR
Gerald Wilson

Arranger/Composer
Duke Ellington
TDWR
Gary McFarland

Alto Saxophone
Johnny Hodges
TDWR
Jackie McLean

Tenor Saxophone
Sonny Rollins
TDWR
Dexter Gordon

Baritone Saxophone
Gerry Mulligan
TDWR
Jay Cameron

Clarinet
Pee Wee Russell
TDWR
Phil Woods

Flute
Frank Wess
TDWR
Roland Kirk

Trumpet
Dizzy Gillespie
TDWR
Don Cherry

Trombone
J. J. Johnson
TDWR
Roswell Rudd

Acoustic Piano
Bill Evans
TDWR
McCoy Tyner

Guitar (tie)
Jim Hall
Wes Montgomery
TDWR
Joe Pass

Acoustic Bass
Charles Mingus
TDWR
Gary Peacock

Drums
Elvin Jones
TDWR
Pete LaRoca

Vibes
Milt Jackson
TDWR
Dave Pike

Miscellaneous Instrument
John Coltrane, Soprano
Saxophone
TDWR
Eric Dolphy, Bass Clarinet

1964

Male Singer
Ray Charles
TDWR
Muddy Waters

Female Singer
Ella Fitzgerald
TDWR (tie)
Nancy Wilson
Jeanne Lee

Vocal Group
Double Six
TDWR
Swingle Singers

Combo
Thelonious Monk
TDWR
Art Farmer

Big Band
Duke Ellington
TDWR
Henry James

CONTINUED ON NEXT PAGE ▶

Down Beat Jazz Hall of Fame

Max Roach

1961
Coleman Hawkins

1962
Bix Beiderbecke

1963
Jelly Roll Morton

1964
Art Tatum

1965
Earl Hines

1966
Charlie Christian

1967
Bessie Smith

1968
Sidney Bechet/Fats Waller

1969
Pee Wee Russell/Jack
Teagarden

1970
Johnny Hodges

1971
Roy Eldridge/Django
Reinhardt

1972
Clifford Brown

1973
Fletcher Henderson

1974
Ben Webster

1975
Cecil Taylor

1976
King Oliver

1977
Benny Carter

1978
Rahsaan Roland Kirk

1979
Lennie Tristano

1980
Max Roach

1981
Bill Evans

1982
Fats Navarro

1983
Albert Ayler

1984
Sun Ra

1985
Zoot Sims

1986
Gil Evans

1987
Johnny Dodds

1988
Kenny Clarke

1989
Chet Baker

1990
Mary Lou Williams

1991
John Carter

1992
James P. Johnson

1993
Edward Blackwell

1994
Frank Zappa

1995
Julius Hemphill

Arranger/Composer
Duke Ellington
TDWR (tie)
Cecil Taylor
Gerald Wilson

Alto Saxophone
Johnny Hodges
TDWR
Jimmy Woods

Tenor Saxophone
John Coltrane
TDWR
Booker Ervin

Baritone Saxophone
Gerry Mulligan
TDWR
Charles Davis

Clarinet
Pee Wee Russell
TDWR
Bill Smith

Flute
Frank Wess
TDWR
Yusef Lateef

Trumpet
Miles Davis
TDWR
Carmell Jones

Trombone
J. J. Johnson
TDWR
Grachan Moncur III

Acoustic Piano
Bill Evans
TDWR
Don Friedman

Organ
Jimmy Smith
TDWR
Freddie Roach

Guitar
Jim Hall
TDWR
Gabor Szabo

Acoustic Bass
Charles Mingus
TDWR
Steve Swallow

Drums
Elvin Jones
TDWR
Tony Williams

Vibes
Milt Jackson
TDWR
Bobby Hutcherson

Miscellaneous Instrument
Roland Kirk, Manzello and
Stritch
TDWR
Yusef Lateef, Oboe

1965

Record of the Year
John Coltrane, *A Love
Supreme* (MCA/Impulse)

Male Singer
Louis Armstrong
TDWR
Johnny Hartman

Female Singer
Ella Fitzgerald
TDWR
Cleo Laine

Vocal Group
Double Six

Combo
Miles Davis
TDWR
Al Cohn and Zoot Sims

Big Band
Duke Ellington
TDWR
Johnny Dankworth

Arranger
Gil Evans
TDWR
Clare Fischer

Composer
Duke Ellington
TDWR
Ornette Coleman

Alto Saxophone
Johnny Hodges
TDWR
Charlie Marlano

Tenor Saxophone
John Coltrane
TDWR
Archie Shepp

Baritone Saxophone
Harry Carney
TDWR
Jerome Richardson

Clarinet
Pee Wee Russell
TDWR
Paul Horn

Flute
Roland Kirk
TDWR
James Moody

Trumpet
Miles Davis
TDWR
Johnny Coles

Trombone
J. J. Johnson
TDWR
Albert Mangelsdorff

Acoustic Piano
Bill Evans
TDWR
Andrew Hill

Organ
Jimmy Smith
TDWR
John Patton

Guitar
Jim Hall
TDWR
Bola Sete

Acoustic Bass
Charles Mingus
TDWR
Ron Carter

Drums
Elvin Jones
TDWR (tie)
Alan Dawson
Dannie Richmond

Vibes
Milt Jackson
TDWR
Gary Burton

Miscellaneous Instrument
Roland Kirk, Manzello and
Stritch
TDWR
Stuff Smith, Violin

1966

Record of the Year
Ornette Coleman, *At the
Golden Circle Vol. 1* (Blue
Note)

Reissue of the Year
Billie Holiday, *The Golden
Years Vol. 2* (Columbia)

Male Singer
Louis Armstrong
TDWR
Lou Rawls

Female Singer
Ella Fitzgerald
TDWR
Carol Sloane

Vocal Group
Double Six

Combo
Miles Davis
TDWR
Denny Zeitlin

Big Band
Duke Ellington
TDWR
Thad Jones and Mel Lewis

Arranger
Gil Evans
TDWR
Rod Levitt

Composer
Duke Ellington
TDWR
Carla Bley

Alto Saxophone
Johnny Hodges
TDWR (tie)
John Handy
John Tchicai

Tenor Saxophone
John Coltrane
TDWR
Charles Lloyd

Baritone Saxophone
Harry Carney
TDWR
Ronnie Cuber

Clarinet
Pee Wee Russell
TDWR
Edmond Hall

Flute
Roland Kirk
TDWR
Charles Lloyd

Trumpet
Miles Davis
TDWR
Ted Curson

Trombone
J. J. Johnson
TDWR
Buster Cooper

Acoustic Piano
Earl Hines
TDWR
Jaki Byard

Organ
Jimmy Smith
TDWR
Larry Smith

Guitar
Wes Montgomery
TDWR
Rene Thomas

Acoustic Bass
Charles Mingus
TDWR
Richard Davis

Drums
Elvin Jones
TDWR
Sonny Murray

Vibes
Milt Jackson
TDWR
Roy Ayres

Miscellaneous Instrument
Roland Kirk, Manzello and
Stritch
TDWR
Jean-Luc Ponty, Violin

1967

Record of the Year (tie)
Duke Ellington, *The Popular
Ellington* (RCA)
Miles Davis, *Miles Smiles*
(Columbia)

Reissue of the Year
Johnny Hodges and Rex
Stewart, *Things Ain't
What They Used To Be*
(Victrola)

Male Singer
Louis Armstrong
TDWR
Richard Boone

Female Singer
Ella Fitzgerald
TDWR
Lorez Alexandria

Combo
Miles Davis
TDWR
Charles Lloyd

Big Band
Duke Ellington
TDWR
Don Ellis

Arranger
Duke Ellington
TDWR
Thad Jones

Composer
Duke Ellington
TDWR
Herbie Hancock

Alto Saxophone
Ornette Coleman
TDWR
Charles McPherson

Tenor Saxophone
Sonny Rollins
TDWR
Joe Henderson

Baritone Saxophone
Harry Carney
TDWR
Pepper Adams

Clarinet
Pee Wee Russell
TDWR
Perry Robinson

Flute
James Moody
TDWR
Jeremy Steig

Trumpet
Miles Davis
TDWR
Jimmy Owens

Trombone
J. J. Johnson
TDWR
Garnett Brown

Acoustic Piano
Earl Hines
TDWR
Keith Jarrett

Organ
Jimmy Smith
TDWR
Don Patterson

Guitar
Wes Montgomery
TDWR
George Benson

Acoustic Bass
Richard Davis
TDWR
David Izenson

Drums
Elvin Jones
TDWR
Milford Graves

Vibes
Milt Jackson
TDWR
Tommy Vig

Miscellaneous Instrument
Roland Kirk, Manzello and
   Stritch
TDWR
Michael White, Violin

Rock/Blues Group
The Beatles
TDWR
Supremes

1968

Record of the Year
Duke Ellington, *Far East
   Suite* (Bluebird)

Reissue of the Year
Johnny Hodges, *Hodge
   Podge* (Encore)

Male Singer (tie)
Louis Armstrong
Ray Charles
TDWR
Jimmy Witherspoon

Female Singer
Ella Fitzgerald
TDWR
Aretha Franklin

Combo
Miles Davis
TDWR
Gary Burton

Big Band
Duke Ellington
TDWR
Buddy Rich

Arranger
Duke Ellington
TDWR
Tom McIntosh

Composer
Duke Ellington
TDWR
Wayne Shorter

Alto Saxophone
Johnny Hodges
TDWR
Sonny Criss

Tenor Saxophone
Sonny Rollins
TDWR
Joe Farrell

Baritone Saxophone
Harry Carney
TDWR
Cecil Payne

Clarinet
Pee Wee Russell
TDWR
Eddie Daniels

Flute
James Moody
TDWR
Hubert Laws

Trumpet
Miles Davis
TDWR
Charles Tolliver

Trombone
J. J. Johnson
TDWR
Carl Fontana

Acoustic Piano
Bill Evans
TDWR
Roger Kellaway

Organ
Jimmy Smith
TDWR (tie)
Odell Brown
Eddy Louiss

Guitar
Kenny Burrell
TDWR
Larry Coryell

Acoustic Bass
Richard Davis
TDWR
Eddie Gomez

Drums
Elvin Jones
TDWR
Billy Higgins

Vibes
Milt Jackson
TDWR
Karl Berger

Miscellaneous Instrument
Jean-Luc Ponty, Violin
TDWR
Howard Johnson, Tuba

Rock/Blues Group
Muddy Waters
TDWR
Jr. Wells

Ray Charles

1969

Record of the Year
Duke Ellington, *. . . And His
   Mother Called Him Bill*
   (Bluebird)

Reissue of the Year
Louis Armstrong, *V.S.O.P.
   Vol. 1* (Encore)

Male Singer
Ray Charles
TDWR
Jon Hendricks

Female Singer
Ella Fitzgerald
TDWR
Karin Krog

Combo
Miles Davis
TDWR
Elvin Jones Trio

Big Band
Duke Ellington
TDWR
Kenny Clarke and Francy
   Boland

Arranger
Duke Ellington
TDWR
Francy Boland

Composer
Duke Ellington
TDWR
Mike Westbrook

Soprano Saxophone
Lucky Thompson
TDWR
John Surman

Alto Saxophone
Johnny Hodges
TDWR
Lee Konitz

Tenor Saxophone
Sonny Rollins
TDWR
Albert Ayler

Baritone Saxophone
Harry Carney
TDWR
John Surman

Clarinet
Jimmy Hamilton
TDWR
Roland Kirk

Flute
James Moody
TDWR
Joe Farrell

Trumpet
Miles Davis
TDWR
Randy Brecker

Trombone
J. J. Johnson
TDWR
Lester Lashley

Acoustic Piano
Earl Hines
TDWR
Chick Corea

Organ
Jimmy Smith
TDWR
Lonnie Smith

Guitar
Kenny Burrell
TDWR
Pat Martino

Acoustic Bass
Richard Davis
TDWR
Niels-Henning Ørsted
  Pedersen

Drums
Elvin Jones
TDWR
Daniel Humair

Vibes
Bobby Hutcherson
TDWR
Red Norvo

Miscellaneous Instrument
Jean-Luc Ponty, Violin
TDWR
Ray Nance, Violin

Rock/Blues Group
Muddy Waters
TDWR (tie)
Canned Heat
J. B. Hutto

1970

Record of the Year
Miles Davis, *Bitches Brew*
  (Columbia Jazz
  Masterpieces)

Reissue of the Year
Various artists, *Blue Note's
  Three Decades of Jazz,
  Vol. 1* (Blue Note)

Male Singer
Louis Armstrong
TDWR
Leon Thomas

Female Singer
Ella Fitzgerald
TDWR
Jeanne Lee

Combo
Miles Davis
TDWR
Phil Woods' European
  Rhythm Machine

Big Band
Duke Ellington
TDWR
Mike Westbrook

Arranger
Duke Ellington
TDWR
Duke Pearson

Composer
Duke Ellington
TDWR
Mike Gibbs

Soprano Saxophone
Wayne Shorter
TDWR
Tom Scott

Alto Saxophone
Phil Woods
TDWR
Eric Kloss

Tenor Saxophone
Sonny Rollins
TDWR (tie)
Paul Gonsalves
  Pharoah Sanders

Baritone Saxophone
Harry Carney
TDWR
Nick Brignola

Clarinet
Russell Procope
TDWR (tie)
Frank Chase
Bob Wilber

Flute
James Moody
TDWR
Norris Turney

Trumpet
Miles Davis
TDWR (tie)
Woody Shaw
Kenny Wheeler

Trombone
J. J. Johnson
TDWR (tie)
Malcolm Griffiths
Eje Thelin

Acoustic Piano
Earl Hines
TDWR
Stanley Cowell

Organ
Jimmy Smith
TDWR
Lou Bennett

Guitar
Kenny Burrell
TDWR
Sonny Sharrock

Acoustic Bass
Richard Davis
TDWR
Miroslav Vitous

Drums
Elvin Jones
TDWR
Jack DeJohnette

Vibes
Milt Jackson
TDWR
Dave Pike

Miscellaneous Instrument
Jean-Luc Ponty, Violin
TDWR
Stephane Grappelli, Violin

Rock/Blues Group
B. B. King
TDWR
Ike and Tina Turner

1971

Record of the Year
Duke Ellington, *New Orleans
  Suite* (Atlantic)

Reissue of the Year
Bessie Smith series of
  reissues on Columbia

Male Singer
Louis Armstrong
TDWR
Richard Boone

Female Singer
Ella Fitzgerald
TDWR
Betty Carter

Organ
Miles Davis
TDWR
Art Ensemble of Chicago

Big Band
Duke Ellington
TDWR
Sun Ra

Arranger
Duke Ellington
TDWR
Herbie Hancock

Composer
Duke Ellington
TDWR
Carla Bley

Soprano Saxophone
Wayne Shorter
TDWR
Budd Johnson

Alto Saxophone
Phil Woods
TDWR
Frank Strozier

Tenor Saxophone
Dexter Gordon
TDWR
Harold Ashby

Baritone Saxophone
Harry Carney
TDWR
Pat Patrick

Clarinet
Russell Procope
TDWR
Bob Wilber

Flute
James Moody
TDWR
Norris Turney

Trumpet
Dizzy Gillespie
TDWR
Roy Eldridge

Miles Davis

Trombone
Vic Dickenson
TDWR (tie)
Vic Dickenson
Bill Watrous

Acoustic Piano
Earl Hines
TDWR (tie)
Jaki Byard
Tommy Flanagan

Organ
Jimmy Smith
TDWR
Eddy Louis

Guitar
Kenny Burrell
TDWR
Dennis Budimir

Acoustic Bass
Richard Davis
TDWR
Miroslav Vitous

Drums
Elvin Jones
TDWR
Gus Johnson

Vibes
Bobby Hutcherson
TDWR (tie)
Roy Ayers
Karl Berger

Violin
Jean-Luc Ponty
TDWR
Michael White

Miscellaneous Instrument
Rahsaan Roland Kirk,
    Manzello and Stritch
TDWR
Russ Whitman, Bass
    Saxophone

Rock/Blues Group
B.B. King
TDWR
Soft Machine

1972

Record of the Year
Jimmy Rushing, *The You and
    Me That Used to Be*
    (Bluebird)

Reissue of the Year
*Genius of Louis Armstrong,
Vol. 1* (Columbia)

Male Singer
Jimmy Rushing
TDWR
Richard Boone

Female Singer
Ella Fitzgerald
TDWR (tie)
Dee Dee Bridgewater
Asha Puthli

Combo
World's Greatest Jazz Band
TDWR
JPJ Quartet

Big Band
Duke Ellington
TDWR
Sun Ra

Arranger
Duke Ellington
TDWR
Alan Broadbent

Composer
Duke Ellington
TDWR
Carla Bley

Soprano Saxophone
Wayne Shorter
TDWR
Joseph Jarman

Alto Saxophone
Ornette Coleman
TDWR
Gary Bartz

Tenor Saxophone
Sonny Rollins
TDWR
Gato Barbieri

Baritone Saxophone
Harry Carney
TDWR
Ronnie Cuber

Clarinet
Russell Procope
TDWR
Bob Wilber

Flute
James Moody
TDWR
Norris Turney

Trumpet
Dizzy Gillespie
TDWR
Lester Bowie

Trombone
Vic Dickenson
TDWR
Bill Watrous

Acoustic Piano
Earl Hines
TDWR
Randy Weston

Organ
Jimmy Smith
TDWR
Eddy Louiss

Guitar
Kenny Burrell
TDWR (tie)
Tiny Grimes
Pat Martino

Acoustic Bass
Richard Davis
TDWR
Dave Holland

Drums
Elvin Jones
TDWR
Harold Jones

Vibes
Gary Burton
TDWR
Roy Ayers

Violin
Jean-Luc Ponty
TDWR
Michael White

Miscellaneous Instrument
Rahsaan Roland Kirk,
    Manzello and Stritch
TDWR
Airto Moreira, Percussion

Rock/Blues Group
B.B. King
TDWR
Mahavishnu Orchestra

1973

Record of the Year (tie)
McCoy Tyner, *Sahara*
    (Fantasy/OJC)
Sonny Stitt, *Constellation*
    (Muse)

Reissue of the Year
Art Tatum, *God Is in the
    House* (Onyx)

Male Singer
Ray Charles
TDWR
Joe Lee Wilson

Female Singer
Sarah Vaughan
TDWR
Anita O'Day

Combo
Mahavishnu Orchestra
TDWR
Art Ensemble of Chicago

Big Band
Duke Ellington
TDWR
Gil Evans

Arranger
Duke Ellington
TDWR
Sy Oliver

Composer
Duke Ellington
TDWR
Chick Corea

Soprano Saxophone
Wayne Shorter
TDWR
Kenny Davern

Alto Saxophone
Ornette Coleman
TDWR
Anthony Braxton

Tenor Saxophone
Sonny Rollins
TDWR
John Klemmer

Baritone Saxophone
Harry Carney
TDWR
Howard Johnson

Clarinet
Russell Procope
TDWR
Bobby Jones

Flute
James Moody
TDWR
Jeremy Steig

Trumpet
Dizzy Gillespie
TDWR
Bill Hardman

Trombone
Vic Dickenson
TDWR
Dicky Wells

Acoustic Piano
Earl Hines
TDWR
Jan Hammer

Organ
Jimmy Smith
TDWR
Eddy Louiss

Guitar
Kenny Burrell
TDWR (tie)
George Benson
Attila Zoller

Acoustic Bass
Richard Davis
TDWR
Stanley Clarke

Drums
Elvin Jones
TDWR
Oliver Jackson

Vibes
Milt Jackson
TDWR
David Friedman

Violin
Jean-Luc Ponty
TDWR
Michael White

Miscellaneous Instrument
Rahsaan Roland Kirk,
    Manzello and Stritch
TDWR
Howard Johnson, Tuba

Rock/Blues Group
B.B. King
TDWR
War

1974

Record of the Year
Keith Jarrett, *Solo Concerts*
    (ECM)

Reissue of the Year
*Thelonious Monk and John
    Coltrane* (Fantasy/OJC)

Male Singer
Joe Williams
TDWR (tie)
Roy Eldridge
Stevie Wonder

Dizzy Gillespie

Female Singer
Ella Fitzgerald
TDWR
Flora Purim

Vocal Group
Pointer Sisters
TDWR
Pointer Sisters

Combo
McCoy Tyner
TDWR
Ruby Braff and George Barnes

Big Band
Thad Jones and Mel Lewis
TDWR
Gil Evans

Arranger
Gil Evans
TDWR
Bill Stapleton

Composer
Duke Ellington
TDWR
McCoy Tyner

Soprano Saxophone
Wayne Shorter
TDWR
Gerry Niewood

Alto Saxophone
Ornette Coleman
TDWR
Anthony Braxton

Tenor Saxophone
Sonny Rollins
TDWR
Billy Harper

Baritone Saxophone
Gerry Mulligan
TDWR
Howard Johnson

Clarinet
Rahsaan Roland Kirk
TDWR
Kalaparusha Ara Difda

Flute
James Moody
TDWR
Jeremy Steig

Trumpet
Dizzy Gillespie
TDWR
Jon Faddis

Trombone
Vic Dickenson
TDWR
Garnett Brown

Acoustic Piano (tie)
Keith Jarrett
McCoy Tyner
TDWR
Muhal Richard Abrams

Organ
Jimmy Smith
TDWR
Eddy Louiss

Guitar
Jim Hall
TDWR
Ralph Towner

Acoustic Bass
Richard Davis
TDWR
Stanley Clarke

Electric Bass
Stanley Clarke
TDWR
Stanley Clarke

Drums
Elvin Jones
TDWR
Billy Hart

Percussion
Airto Moreira
TDWR
Dom Um Romao

Vibes
Gary Burton
TDWR
Karl Berger

Violin
Jean-Luc Ponty
TDWR
Leroy Jenkins

Miscellaneous Instrument
Rahsaan Roland Kirk,
  Manzello and Stritch
TDWR
Howard Johnson, Tuba

Rock/Blues Group
B.B. King
TDWR
Jimmy Dawkins

1975

Record of the Year
Cecil Taylor, *Silent Tongues*
  (Arista/Freedom)

Reissue of the Year (tie)
Charlie Parker, *First
  Recordings* (Onyx)
Art Tatum, *Solo
  Masterpieces* (Pablo)

Male Singer
Joe Williams
TDWR
Eddie Jefferson

Female Singer
Sarah Vaughan
TDWR
Dee Dee Bridgewater

Vocal Group
Jackie and Roy
TDWR
Jackie and Roy

Combo
McCoy Tyner
TDWR
Oregon

Big Band
Thad Jones and Mel Lewis
TDWR
Clark Terry

Arranger
Gil Evans
TDWR
Michael Gibbs

Composer
Keith Jarrett
TDWR
Randy Weston

Soprano Saxophone
Wayne Shorter
TDWR
Gerry Niewood

Alto Saxophone
Phil Woods
TDWR
Sonny Fortune

Tenor Saxophone
Sonny Rollins
TDWR
Billy Harper

Baritone Saxophone
Gerry Mulligan
TDWR (tie)
John Surman
Pat Patrick

Clarinet
Rahsaan Roland Kirk
TDWR
Perry Robinson

Flute
Hubert Laws
TDWR
Sam Rivers

Trumpet
Dizzy Gillespie
TDWR
Jon Faddis

Trombone
Roswell Rudd
TDWR
Bruce Fowler

Synthesizer
Sun Ra
TDWR
George Duke

Piano
Keith Jarrett
TDWR
Dollar Brand

Organ
Jimmy Smith
TDWR
Sun Ra

Guitar
Joe Pass
TDWR
John Abercrombie

Acoustic Bass
Ron Carter
TDWR
George Mraz

Electric Bass
Stanley Clarke
TDWR
Steve Swallow

Drums
Elvin Jones
TDWR
Billy Higgins

Percussion
Airto Moreira
TDWR
Joe Evans

Vibes
Gary Burton
TDWR (tie)
Karl Berger
Dave Friedman

Violin
Jean-Luc Ponty
TDWR
Michal Urbaniak

Miscellaneous Instrument
Rahsaan Roland Kirk,
  Manzello and Stritch
TDWR
Howard Johnson, Tuba

Blues/R&B Group
B.B. King
TDWR (tie)
Blackbyrds
Otis Rush

1976

Record of the Year
Oscar Peterson and Dizzy Gillespie (Pablo)

Reissue of the Year
Herbie Nichols, *The Third World* (Blue Note)

Male Singer (tie)
Mel Tormé
Joe Williams
TDWR
Joe Lee Wilson

Female Singer
Sarah Vaughan
TDWR
Betty Carter

Vocal Group
Jackie and Roy
TDWR
Novi Singers

Combo
McCoy Tyner
TDWR
Lookout Farm

Big Band
Thad Jones and Mel Lewis
TDWR
Toshiko Akiyoshi and Lew Tabackin

Arranger
Gil Evans
TDWR
Toshiko Akiyoshi

Composer
Charles Mingus
TDWR
Michael Gibbs

Soprano Saxophone
Wayne Shorter
TDWR
Jan Garbarek

Alto Saxophone
Phil Woods
TDWR
Sonny Fortune

Tenor Saxophone
Sonny Rollins
TDWR
Jan Garbarek

Baritone Saxophone
Gerry Mulligan
TDWR
Howard Johnson

Clarinet
Benny Goodman
TDWR
Perry Robinson

Flute
Hubert Laws
TDWR
Sam Rivers

Trumpet
Dizzy Gillespie
TDWR (tie)
Jon Faddis

Trombone
Bill Watrous
TDWR
George Lewis

Synthesizer
Joe Zawinul
TDWR
Jan Hammer

Acoustic Piano
McCoy Tyner
TDWR
Don Pullen

Electric Piano
Chick Corea
TDWR
George Duke

Organ
Jimmy Smith
TDWR
Shirley Scott

Guitar
Jim Hall
TDWR
John Abercrombie

Acoustic Bass
Ron Carter
TDWR
Niels-Henning Ørsted

Electric Bass
Stanley Clarke
TDWR
Jaco Pastorius

Drums
Elvin Jones
TDWR
Philip Wilson

Percussion
Airto Moreira
TDWR
Guilherme Franco

Vibes
Milt Jackson
TDWR
Karl Berger

Violin
Jean-Luc Ponty
TDWR
Michal Urbaniak

Miscellaneous Instrument
Rahsaan Roland Kirk, Manzello and Stritch
TDWR
Paul McCandless, Oboe

Soul/R&B Artist
Stevie Wonder
TDWR
Bob Marley and the Wailers

Record Label of the Year
Pablo

Record Producer of the Year
Manfred Eicher (ECM)

1977

Record of the Year
Anthony Braxton, *Creative Orchestra Music 1976* (Arista)

Reissue of the Year
Lester Young, *Lester Young Story, Vol. 1* (Columbia)

Male Singer
Joe Williams
TDWR
Joe Lee Wilson

Female Singer
Sarah Vaughan
TDWR
Sheila Jordan

Vocal Group
Jackie and Roy
TDWR
Jackie and Roy

Combo
McCoy Tyner
TDWR
Air

Big Band
Thad Jones and Mel Lewis
TDWR
Toshiko Akiyoshi and Lew Tabackin

Arranger
Gil Evans
TDWR
Toshiko Akiyoshi

Composer
Charles Mingus
TDWR
Toshiko Akiyoshi

Soprano Saxophone
Wayne Shorter
TDWR
Zoot Sims

Alto Saxophone
Phil Woods
TDWR
Art Pepper

Tenor Saxophone
Dexter Gordon
TDWR
Billy Harper

Baritone Saxophone
Gerry Mulligan
TDWR
Henry Threadgill

Clarinet
Anthony Braxton
TDWR
Perry Robinson

Flute
Hubert Laws
TDWR
Sam Rivers

Trumpet
Dizzy Gillespie
TDWR
Woody Shaw

Trombone
Bill Watrous
TDWR
George Lewis

Synthesizer
Jan Hammer
TDWR
Richard Teitelbaum

Acoustic Piano
McCoy Tyner
TDWR
Don Pullen

Electric Piano
Joe Zawinul
TDWR
Patrice Rushen

Organ
Jimmy Smith
TDWR
Shirley Scott

Guitar
Jim Hall
TDWR
Derek Bailey

Acoustic Bass
Ron Carter
TDWR
Malachi Favors

Electric Bass
Stanley Clarke
TDWR
Steve Swallow

Drums
Elvin Jones
TDWR
Steve McCall

Percussion
Airto Moreira
TDWR
Don Moye

Vibes
Milt Jackson
TDWR
Karl Berger

Violin
Joe Venuti
TDWR
Michal Urbaniak

Miscellaneous Instrument
Howard Johnson, Tuba
TDWR
Anthony Braxton, Contrabass Saxophone

Soul/R&B Artist
Stevie Wonder
TDWR
Son Seals

Record Label of the Year
Pablo

Record Producer of the Year
Norman Granz

1978

Record of the Year (tie)
Toshiko Akiyoshi and Lew
Tabackin, *Insights* (RCA)
Ornette Coleman, *Dancing in
Your Head* (Horizon)
Dexter Gordon, *Sophisticated
Giant* (Columbia)
Dexter Gordon, *Homecoming*
(Columbia)
Roscoe Mitchell, *Nonaah*
(Nessa)

Reissue of the Year
Lester Young, *The Lester
Young Story vols. II and III*
(Columbia)

Male Singer
Joe Williams
TDWR
Joe Lee Wilson

Female Singer
Sarah Vaughan
TDWR
Sheila Jordan

Vocal Group
Jackie and Roy
TDWR
Wild Tchoupitoulas

Combo
Weather Report
TDWR
Air

Big Band
Thad Jones and Mel Lewis
TDWR
Gil Evans

Arranger
Gil Evans
TDWR
Michael Gibbs

Composer
Charles Mingus
TDWR
Carla Bley

Soprano Saxophone
Wayne Shorter
TDWR
Jan Garbarek

Alto Saxophone
Phil Woods
TDWR
Oliver Lake

Tenor Saxophone
Dexter Gordon
TDWR
Scott Hamilton

Baritone Saxophone
Gerry Mulligan
TDWR
John Surman

Clarinet
Anthony Braxton
TDWR
Perry Robinson

Flute
Hubert Laws
TDWR
Sam Rivers

Trumpet
Dizzy Gillespie
TDWR
Kenny Wheeler

Trombone
Roswell Rudd
TDWR
George Lewis

Synthesizer
Joe Zawinul
TDWR
Brian Eno

Acoustic Piano
Cecil Taylor
TDWR (tie)
Jimmie Rowles
Randy Weston

Electric Piano
Joe Zawinul
TDWR
Kenny Barron

Organ
Jimmy Smith
TDWR
Jasper Van't Hof

Guitar
Joe Pass
TDWR
Pat Metheny

Acoustic Bass
Ron Carter
TDWR
Fred Hopkins

Electric Bass
Jaco Pastorius
TDWR
Eberhard Weber

Drums
Elvin Jones
TDWR
Barry Altschul

Percussion
Airto Moreira
TDWR
Don Moye

Vibes
Milt Jackson
TDWR
Gunter Hampel

Violin
Stephane Grappelli
TDWR
Michal Urbaniak

Miscellaneous Instrument
Howard Johnson, Tuba
TDWR
Paul McCandless, Oboe and
English Horn

Soul/R&B Artist
Stevie Wonder
TDWR
Otis Rush

Record Label of the Year
Columbia

Record Producer of the Year
Norman Granz

1979

Record of the Year
Charles Mingus, *Cumbia and
Jazz Fusion* (Atlantic)

Reissue of the Year
Charlie Parker, *The Savoy
Sessions* (Arista/Savoy)

Jazz Group
Phil Woods Quartet
TDWR
Air

Male Singer
Mel Torme
TDWR
Eddie Jefferson

Female Singer
Sarah Vaughan
TDWR (tie)
Norma Winstone
Helen Humes

Vocal Group
Jackie and Roy
TDWR
Anita Kerr Singers

Big Band
Toshiko Akiyoshi and Lew
Tabackin
TDWR
Carla Bley

Arranger
Toshiko Akiyoshi
TDWR
Michael Gibbs

Composer
Charles Mingus
TDWR
Carla Bley

Soprano Saxophone
Wayne Shorter
TDWR
Jan Garbarek

Alto Saxophone
Phil Woods
TDWR
Arthur Blythe

Tenor Saxophone
Dexter Gordon
TDWR
Scott Hamilton

Baritone Saxophone
Pepper Adams
TDWR
Henry Threadgill

Clarinet
Anthony Braxton
TDWR
Perry Robinson

Flute
Sam Rivers
TDWR
James Newton

Trumpet
Dizzy Gillespie
TDWR
Kenny Wheeler

Trombone
Roswell Rudd
TDWR
Jimmy Knepper

Synthesizer
Joe Zawinul
TDWR
Richard Teitelbaum

Acoustic Piano
Cecil Taylor
TDWR
Joanne Brackeen

Electric Piano
Chick Corea
TDWR
Kenny Barron

Organ
Jimmy Smith
TDWR
Richard Tee

Guitar
Jim Hall
TDWR
Philip Catherine

Acoustic Bass
Ron Carter
TDWR
David Friesen

Electric Bass
Jaco Pastorius
TDWR
Eberhard Weber

Drums
Elvin Jones
TDWR
Steve McCall

Percussion
Airto Moreira
TDWR (tie)
Nana Vasconcelos
Collin Walcott

Vibes
Milt Jackson
TDWR
David Friedman

Violin
Stephane Grappelli
TDWR
L. Shankar

Miscellaneous Instrument
Toots Thielemans, Harmonica
TDWR
Bob Stewart, Tuba

Soul/R&B Artist
Stevie Wonder
TDWR
Junior Wells

Record Label of the Year
Inner City

Record Producer
Michael Cuscuna

Sarah Vaughan

1980

Record of the Year
Air, *Air Lore* (Arista/Novus)

Reissue of the Year
Charles Mingus, *Mingus at Antibes* (Atlantic)

Jazz Group
Art Ensemble of Chicago
TDWR
World Saxophone Quartet

Male Singer
Joe Williams
TDWR
Joe Lee Wilson

Female Singer
Sarah Vaughan
TDWR
Sheila Jordan

Vocal Group
Manhattan Transfer
TDWR
Manhattan Transfer

Big Band
Toshiko Akiyoshi and Lew Tabackin
TDWR
Globe Unity Orchestra

Arranger
Gil Evans
TDWR
Slide Hampton

Composer
Carla Bley
TDWR
Roscoe Mitchell

Soprano Saxophone
Steve Lacy
TDWR
John Surman

Alto Saxophone
Art Pepper
TDWR
Arthur Blythe

Tenor Saxophone
Sonny Rollins
TDWR
Chico Freeman

Baritone Saxophone
Pepper Adams
TDWR
Ronnie Cuber

Clarinet
Anthony Braxton
TDWR
Perry Robinson

Flute
Lew Tabackin
TDWR
James Newton

Trumpet
Dizzy Gillespie
TDWR
Leo Smith

Trombone
Albert Mangelsdorff
TDWR
George Lewis

Synthesizer
Joe Zawinul
TDWR
Denny Zeitlin

Acoustic Piano
Cecil Taylor
TDWR
Anthony Davis

Electric Piano
Chick Corea
TDWR (tie)
Kenny Barron
Richard Belrach
Paul Bley

Organ
Jimmy Smith
TDWR
Amina Claudine Myers

Guitar
Joe Pass
TDWR
James "Blood" Ulmer

Acoustic Bass
Charlie Haden
TDWR
Fred Hopkins

Electric Bass
Jaco Pastorius
TDWR
Jamaaladeen Tacuma

Drums
Max Roach
TDWR
Billy Hart

Percussion
Airto Moreira
TDWR
Nana Vasconcelos

Vibes
Milt Jackson
TDWR
Jay Hoggard

Violin
Stephane Grappelli
TDWR
John Blake

Miscellaneous Instrument
Toots Thielemans, Harmonica
TDWR
Abdul Wadud, Cello

Soul/R&B Artist
Stevie Wonder
TDWR
Jimmy Johnson

Record Label (tie)
ECM
Inner City

Record Producer
Michael Cuscuna

1981

Lifetime Achievement Award
John Hammond

Record of the Year (tie)
Art Ensemble of Chicago, *Full Force* (ECM)
Archie Shepp and Horace Parlan, *Trouble in Mind* (SteepleChase)
Cecil Taylor, *One Too Many Salty Swift and Not Goodbye* (hat Hut)

Reissue of the Year
Lennie Tristano, *Requiem* (Atlantic)

Jazz Group
Art Ensemble of Chicago
TDWR
World Saxophone Quartet

Male Singer
Joe Williams

Female Singer
Sarah Vaughan
TDWR
Carol Sloane

Vocal Group
Manhattan Transfer
TDWR
Hendricks Family

Big Band
Toshiko Akiyoshi and Lew Tabackin
TDWR
Globe Unity

Arranger
Gil Evans
TDWR
Jimmy Knepper

Composer
Toshiko Akiyoshi
TDWR
Kenny Wheeler

Soprano Saxophone
Steve Lacy
TDWR
John Surman

Alto Saxophone
Phil Woods
TDWR
Arthur Blythe

Tenor Saxophone
Dexter Gordon
TDWR
Ricky Ford

Baritone Saxophone
Pepper Adams
TDWR
Henry Threadgill

Clarinet
Anthony Braxton
TDWR
John Carter

Flute
Lew Tabackin
TDWR
James Newton

Trumpet
Dizzy Gillespie
TDWR
Wynton Marsalis

Trombone
Jimmy Knepper
TDWR
Ray Anderson

Synthesizer
Joe Zawinul
TDWR
George Lewis

Acoustic Piano
Cecil Taylor
TDWR
Anthony Davis

Electric Piano
Joe Zawinul
TDWR
Kenny Barron

Cecil Taylor

Organ
Jimmy Smith
TDWR
Amina Claudine Myers

Guitar
Joe Pass
TDWR
James "Blood" Ulmer

Acoustic Bass
Niels-Henning Ørsted
TDWR
Aladar Pege

Electric Bass
Jaco Pastorius
TDWR
Jamaaladeen Tacuma

Drums
Max Roach
TDWR
Billy Hart

Percussion
Airto Moreira
TDWR
Nana Vasconcelos

Vibes
Milt Jackson
TDWR
Jay Hoggard

Violin
Stephane Grappelli
TDWR
Billy Bang

Miscellaneous Instrument
Toots Thielemans, Harmonica
TDWR
Abdul Wadud, Cello

Soul/R&B Artist
Stevie Wonder
TDWR
Otis Rush

Record Label
Concord

Record Producer
Michael Cuscuna

1982

Lifetime Achievement Award
George Theodore Wein

Record of the Year
Old and New Dreams,
 Playing (ECM)

Reissue of the Year (tie)
Steve Lacy, Evidence
 (Prestige)
Charles Mingus,
 Pithecanthropus Erectus
 (Atlantic)
Ben Webster, Giants of Jazz
 (Time-Life)

Jazz Group
Art Ensemble of Chicago
TDWR
Old and New Dreams

Male Singer
Joe Williams
TDWR
Joe Lee Wilson

Female Singer
Sarah Vaughan
TDWR
Sheila Jordan

Vocal Group
Manhattan Transfer
TDWR
Hendricks Family

Big Band
Toshiko Akiyoshi and Lew
 Tabackin
TDWR
Globe Unity

Arranger
Toshiko Akiyoshi
TDWR
Muhal Richard Abrams

Composer
Toshiko Akiyoshi
TDWR
Muhal Richard Abrams

Soprano Saxophone
Steve Lacy
TDWR
Ira Sullivan

Alto Saxophone
Phil Woods
TDWR
Richie Cole

Tenor Saxophone
Archie Shepp
TDWR
Ricky Ford

Baritone Saxophone
Pepper Adams
TDWR
Henry Threadgill

Clarinet
Anthony Braxton
TDWR
John Carter

Flute
James Newton
TDWR
Ira Sullivan

Trumpet
Lester Bowie
TDWR
Wynton Marsalis

Trombone
Jimmy Knepper
TDWR
Ray Anderson

Synthesizer
Joe Zawinul
TDWR
George Lewis

Acoustic Piano
Cecil Taylor
TDWR
JoAnne Brackeen

Electric Piano
Chick Corea
TDWR
Lyle Mays

Organ
Sun Ra
TDWR
Amina Claudine Myers

Guitar
Jim Hall
TDWR
Emily Remler

Acoustic Bass
Charlie Haden
TDWR
Fred Hopkins

Electric Bass
Steve Swallow
TDWR
Jamaaladeen Tacuma

Drums
Max Roach
TDWR
Ronald Shannon Jackson

Percussion
Airto Moreira
TDWR
Famoudou Don Moye

Vibes
Milt Jackson
TDWR
Jay Hoggard

Violin
Stephane Grappelli
TDWR
Billy Bang

Miscellaneous Instrument
Toots Thielemans, Harmonica
TDWR
John Clark, French Horn

Soul/R&B Artist
Stevie Wonder
TDWR (tie)
Clifton Chenier
Otis Rush

Record Label (tie)
Concord Jazz
hat Hut

Record Producer (tie)
Giovanni Bonandrini (Black
 Saint/Soul Note)
Carl Jefferson (Concord Jazz)

1983

Lifetime Achievement Award
Leonard Feather

Record of the Year
Muhal Richard Abrams, Blues
 Forever (Black Saint)

Reissue of the Year
Pee Wee Russell, Pied Piper
 of Jazz (Columbia)

Acoustic Jazz Group
Art Blakey
TDWR
Air

Electric Jazz Group
Weather Report
TDWR
Ronald Shannon Jackson

Male Singer
Joe Williams
TDWR
Bobby McFerrin

Female Singer
Sarah Vaughan
TDWR
Sheila Jordan

Vocal Group
Manhattan Transfer
TDWR
Rare Silk

Big Band
Toshiko Akiyoshi and Lew
 Tabackin
TDWR
Muhal Richard Abrams

Arranger
Gil Evans
TDWR
Rob McConnell

Composer
Carla Bley
TDWR
Anthony Davis

Soprano Saxophone
Steve Lacy
TDWR
Jane Ira Bloom

Alto Saxophone
Phil Woods
TDWR
Paquito D'Rivera

Tenor Saxophone
Sonny Rollins
TDWR
Ricky Ford

Baritone Saxophone
Pepper Adams
TDWR
John Surman

Clarinet
Anthony Braxton
TDWR
Alvin Batiste

Flute
James Newton
TDWR
Ira Sullivan

Trumpet
Wynton Marsalis
TDWR
Olu Dara

Trombone
Jimmy Knepper
TDWR
Ray Anderson

Synthesizer
Joe Zawinul
TDWR
Lyle Mays

Acoustic Piano
Cecil Taylor
TDWR
John Hicks

Electric Piano
Joe Zawinul
TDWR
Lyle Mays

Organ
Jimmy Smith
TDWR
Amina Claudine Myers

Guitar
Jimmy Hall
TDWR (tie)
Bruce Forman
Emily Remler

Acoustic Bass (tie)
Charlie Haden
Fred Hopkins

Electric Bass (tie)
Steve Swallow
Bill Laswell

Drums
Max Roach
TDWR
Ronald Shannon Jackson

Percussion
Nana Vasconcelos
TDWR
Famoudou Don Moye

Vibes
Gary Burton
TDWR
Walt Dickerson

Violin
Stephane Grappelli
TDWR
John Blake

Miscellaneous Instrument
Howard Johnson, Tuba
TDWR
Abdul Wadud, Cello

Pop/Rock Artist
Donald Fagan
TDWR
King Sunny Adé

Soul/R&B Artist
Ray Charles
TDWR
Johnny Copeland

Record Label
Elektra Musician

Record Producer
Giovanni Bonandrini

1984

Lifetime Achievement Award
Dr. Billy Taylor

Record of the Year
Charlie Haden, *The Ballad of the Fallen* (ECM)

Reissue of the Year
Thelonious Monk, *The Complete Blue Note Recordings of Thelonious Monk* (Mosaic)

Acoustic Jazz Group
Art Blakey
TDWR
Sphere

Electric Jazz Group
Weather Report
TDWR
Ronald Shannon Jackson

Male Singer
Joe Williams
TDWR
Bobby McFerrin

Female Singer
Sarah Vaughan
TDWR
Tania Maria

Vocal Group
Manhattan Transfer
TDWR
Rare Silk

Big Band
Count Basie
TDWR
Vienna Art Orchestra

Arranger
Gil Evans
TDWR (tie)
Bob Moses
David Murray
Mathias Rüegg

Composer
Carla Bley
TDWR
Anthony Davis

Soprano Saxophone
Steve Lacy
TDWR
Jane Ira Bloom

Alto Saxophone
Phil Woods
TDWR
Eddie "Cleanhead" Vinson

Tenor Saxophone
Sonny Rollins
TDWR
Branford Marsalis

Baritone Saxophone
Pepper Adams
TDWR
John Surman

Clarinet
John Carter
TDWR
Perry Robinson

Flute
James Newton
TDWR
Henry Threadgill

Trumpet
Wynton Marsalis
TDWR
Olu Dara

Trombone
Jimmy Knepper
TDWR
Craig Harris

Synthesizer
Joe Zawinul
TDWR
Lyle Mays

Acoustic Piano
Cecil Taylor
TDWR
Michel Petrucciani

Electric Piano
Joe Zawinul
TDWR
Jasper Van't Hof

Organ
Jimmy Smith
TDWR
Amina Claudine Myers

Guitar
Joe Pass
TDWR
Emily Remler

Acoustic Bass
Charlie Haden
TDWR
Fred Hopkins

Electric Bass
Steve Swallow
TDWR (tie)
Bill Laswell
Jamaaladeen Tacuma

Drums
Max Roach
TDWR
Ronald Shannon Jackson

Percussion
Nana Vasconcelos
TDWR
Mino Cinelu

Vibes
Milt Jackson
TDWR
Jay Hoggard

Violin
Stephane Grappelli
TDWR
John Blake

Miscellaneous Instrument
Toots Thielemans, Harmonica
TDWR (tie)
Andy Narell, Steel Drums
Abdul Wadud, Cello

Pop/Rock Artist
Police
TDWR
UB40

Soul/R&B Artist
Ray Charles
TDWR
Buddy Guy

Record Label
Black Saint/Soul Note

Record Producer
Giovanni Bonandrini

1985

Lifetime Achievement Award
Dr. Lawrence Berk

Record of the Year
Various artists, *That's the Way I Feel Now (A Tribute to Thelonious Monk)* (A&M)

Reissue of the Year
Clifford Brown, *The Complete Blue Note and Pacific Jazz Recordings* (Mosaic)

Acoustic Jazz Group
Art Ensemble of Chicago
TDWR
Henry Threadgill Sextet

Electric Jazz Group
Miles Davis
TDWR
Ronald Shannon Jackson and Decoding Society

Male Singer
Joe Williams
TDWR
Bobby McFerrin

Female Singer
Sarah Vaughan
TDWR
Sheila Jordan

Vocal Group
Manhattan Transfer
TDWR
Rare Silk

Big Band
Sun Ra
TDWR
Vienna Art Orchestra

Arranger
Gil Evans
TDWR
Mathias Rüegg

Composer
Carla Bley
TDWR
Anthony Davis

Soprano Saxophone
Steve Lacy
TDWR
Branford Marsalis

Alto Saxophone
Phil Woods
TDWR (tie)
Paquito D'Rivera
Donald Harrison

Tenor Saxophone
Sonny Rollins
TDWR
Branford Marsalis

Baritone Saxophone
Pepper Adams
TDWR
John Surman

Clarinet
John Carter
TDWR
Alvin Batiste

Flute
James Newton
TDWR
Ira Sullivan

Trumpet
Wynton Marsalis
TDWR
Terence Blanchard

Trombone
Jimmy Knepper
TDWR
Craig Harris

Synthesizer
Joe Zawinul
TDWR
John Surman

Acoustic Piano
Cecil Taylor
TDWR
Kenny Kirkland

Electric Piano
Chick Corea
TDWR
Jasper Van't Hof

Organ
Jimmy Smith
TDWR
Amina Claudine Myers

Guitar
Jim Hall
TDWR
Emily Remler

Acoustic Bass
Charlie Haden
TDWR
Fred Hopkins

Electric Bass
Steve Swallow
TDWR
Jamaaladeen Tacuma

Drums
Max Roach
TDWR
Marvin "Smitty" Smith

Percussion
Nana Vasconcelos
TDWR
Günter Sommer

Vibes
Milt Jackson
TDWR
Walt Dickerson

Violin
Stephane Grappelli
TDWR
John Blake

Miscellaneous Instrument
Toots Thielemans, Harmonica
TDWR
Abdul Wadud, Cello

Pop/Rock Group
Stevie Wonder
TDWR
Los Lobos

Soul/R&B Artist
Ray Charles
TDWR
Neville Brothers

Record Label
Black Saint/Soul Note

Record Producer
Giovanni Bonandrini

1986

Lifetime Achievement Award
Orrin Keepnews

Record of the Year
James Newton, *The African Flower* (Blue Note)

Reissue of the Year (tie)
Charles Mingus, *The Complete Candid Recordings* (Mosaic)
Ben Webster, *The Complete Ben Webster on EmArcy* (EmArcy/PolyGram)

Acoustic Jazz Group
Art Blakey's Jazz Messengers
TDWR
Adams/Pullen Quintet

Electric Jazz Group
Miles Davis
TDWR
Jamaaladeen Tacuma

Male Singer
Joe Williams
TDWR
Dave Frishberg

Female Singer
Sarah Vaughan
TDWR
Sheila Jordan

Vocal Group
Manhattan Transfer
TDWR
The Nylons

Big Band
Count Basie
TDWR
Willem Breuker Kollektief

Arranger
Gil Evans
TDWR
Mathias Rüegg

Composer
Carla Bley
TDWR
Henry Threadgill

Soprano Saxophone
Steve Lacy
TDWR
Jane Ira Bloom

Alto Saxophone
Ornette Coleman
TDWR
Steve Coleman

Tenor Saxophone
Sonny Rollins
TDWR
Bennie Wallace

Baritone Saxophone
Pepper Adams
TDWR
John Surman

Clarinet
John Carter
TDWR
Kenny Davern

Flute
James Newton
TDWR
Ira Sullivan

Trumpet
Lester Bowie
TDWR
Terence Blanchard

Trombone
Jimmy Knepper
TDWR
Ray Anderson

Synthesizer
Joe Zawinul
TDWR
John Surman

Acoustic Piano
Cecil Taylor
TDWR
Geri Allen

Electric Piano
Chick Corea
TDWR
Lyle Mays

Organ
Jimmy Smith
TDWR
Amina Claudine Myers

Guitar
John Scofield
TDWR
Bill Frisell

Acoustic Bass
Charlie Haden
TDWR
Cecil McBee

Electric Bass
Steve Swallow
TDWR
Gerald Veasley

Drums
Max Roach
TDWR
Marvin "Smitty" Smith

Percussion
Nana Vasconcelos
TDWR
Famoudou Don Moye

Vibes
Milt Jackson
TDWR
Walt Dickerson

Violin
Stephane Grappelli
TDWR
John Blake

Miscellaneous Instrument
Toots Thielemans, Harmonica
TDWR
Andy Narell, Steel Drums

Pop/Rock Group
Stevie Wonder
TDWR
Laurie Anderson

Soul/R&B Group
Ray Charles
TDWR
Neville Brothers

Record Label
Black Saint/Soul Note

Record Producer
Michael Cuscuna

1987

Lifetime Achievement Award
David Baker

Record of the Year
Pat Metheny and Ornette Coleman, *Song X* (Geffen)

Reissue of the Year (tie)
Duke Ellington, *The Blanton/Webster Years* (RCA/Bluebird)
Thelonious Monk, *The Complete Riverside Recordings* (Riverside)

Acoustic Jazz Group
Art Blakey's Jazz Messengers
TDWR
Blanchard/Harrison Quintet

Electric Jazz Group
Ornette Coleman and Prime Time
TDWR
Bass Desires

Male Singer
Bobby McFerrin
TDWR
Dave Frishberg

Female Singer
Sarah Vaughan
TDWR
Sheila Jordan

Vocal Group
Manhattan Transfer
TDWR
Sweet Honey in the Rock

Big Band
Gil Evans
TDWR
Willem Breuker Kollektief

Arranger
Gil Evans
TDWR
Mathias Rüegg

Composer
Carla Bley
TDWR
Henry Threadgill

Soprano Saxophone
Steve Lacy
TDWR
Jane Ira Bloom

Alto Saxophone
Ornette Coleman
TDWR
Steve Coleman

Tenor Saxophone
Sonny Rollins
TDWR
Bennie Wallace

Baritone Saxophone
Gerry Mulligan
TDWR
John Surman

Clarinet
John Carter
TDWR
Eddie Daniels

Flute
James Newton
TDWR
Henry Threadgill

Trumpet
Lester Bowie
TDWR
Tom Harrell

Trombone (tie)
Ray Anderson
Jimmy Knepper
TDWR
Steve Turre

Synthesizer
Sun Ra
TDWR
John Surman

Acoustic Piano
Cecil Taylor
TDWR
Geri Allen

Electric Piano
Chick Corea
TDWR
Lyle Mays

Organ
Jimmy Smith
TDWR
Amina Claudine Myers

Guitar
Jim Hall
TDWR (tie)
Bill Frisell
Stanley Jordan

Acoustic Bass
Charlie Haden
TDWR
Charnett Moffett

Electric Bass
Steve Swallow
TDWR
Marcus Miller

Drums
Max Roach
TDWR
Marvin "Smitty" Smith

Percussion
Nana Vasconcelos
TDWR
Han Bennink

Vibes
Milt Jackson
TDWR
Jay Haggard

Violin
Stephane Grappelli
TDWR
Didier Lockwood

Miscellaneous Instrument
Toots Thielemans, Harmonica
TDWR
David Murray, Bass Clarinet

Pop/Rock Group
Paul Simon
TDWR
Brave Combo

Soul/R&B Group
Ray Charles
TDWR
Neville Brothers

Record Label
Black Saint/Soul Note

Record Producer
Giovanni Bonandrini

1988

Lifetime Achievement Award
Congressman John Conyers, Jr.

Record of the Year
Ornette Coleman, *In All Languages* (Caravan of Dreams)

Reissue of the Year
Herbie Nichols, *The Complete Blue Note Recordings* (Mosaic)

Acoustic Jazz Group
Phil Woods Quintet
TDWR
Henry Threadgill Sextet

Electric Jazz Group
Ornette Coleman and Prime Time
TDWR
Bass Desires

Male Singer
Bobby McFerrin
TDWR
Dave Frishberg

Female Singer
Sarah Vaughan
TDWR
Cassandra Wilson

Vocal Group
Manhattan Transfer
TDWR
Ladysmith Black Mambazo

Big Band
Sun Ra
TDWR
Willem Breuker Kollektief

Arranger
Gil Evans
TDWR
Willem Breuker Kollektief

Composer
Henry Threadgill
TDWR
Willem Breuker Kollektief

Soprano Saxophone
Steve Lacy
TDWR
Jane Ira Bloom

Alto Saxophone
Phil Woods
TDWR
Frank Morgan

Tenor Saxophone
Sonny Rollins
TDWR
Ricky Ford

Baritone Saxophone
Gerry Mulligan
TDWR
John Surman

Clarinet
John Carter
TDWR
Jimmy Hamilton

Flute
James Newton
TDWR
Sam Rivers

Trumpet
Wynton Marsalis
TDWR
Wallace Roney

Sun Ra

Trombone
Ray Anderson
TDWR
Steve Turre

Synthesizer
Joe Zawinul
TDWR
John Surman

Acoustic Piano
Cecil Taylor
TDWR
Mulgrew Miller

Electric Piano
Chick Corea
TDWR
Lyle Mays

Organ
Jimmy Smith
TDWR
Amina Claudine Myers

Guitar
Jim Hall
TDWR
Bill Frisell

Acoustic Bass
Charlie Haden
TDWR
Charnett Moffett

Electric Bass
Steve Swallow
TDWR
Gerald Veasley

Drums
Max Roach
TDWR
Terri Lynn Carrington

Percussion
Nana Vasconcelos
TDWR
Mino Cinelu

Vibes
Milt Jackson
TDWR
Khan Jamal

Violin
Stephane Grappelli
TDWR
Claude Williams

Miscellaneous Instrument
Toots Thielemans, Harmonica
TDWR
John Surman, Bass Clarinet

Pop/Rock Group
Sting
TDWR
Ladysmith Black Mambazo

Soul/R&B Group
Ray Charles
TDWR
Kinsey Report

Record Label
Black Saint/Soul Note

Record Producer
Giovanni Bonandrini

1989

Lifetime Achievement Award
Norman Granz

Record of the Year (tie)
Jack DeJohnette, *Audio Visualscapes* (Impulse!)
Charlie Haden, Paul Motian and Geri Allen, *Etudes* (Soul Note)

Reissue of the Year
Charlie Parker, *The Complete Charlie Parker on Verve* (Verve)

Acoustic Jazz Group
Phil Woods
TDWR
8 Bold Souls

Electric Jazz Group
Miles Davis
TDWR
Bass Desires

Male Singer
Joe Williams
TDWR
Dave Frishberg

Female Singer
Betty Carter
TDWR
Cassandra Wilson

Vocal Group
Manhattan Transfer
TDWR
Take 6

Big Band
Sun Ra
TDWR
Willem Breuker Kollektief

Arranger
Benny Carter
TDWR
John Zorn

Composer
Henry Threadgill
TDWR
Henry Threadgill

Soprano Saxophone
Steve Lacy
TDWR
Jane Ira Bloom

Alto Saxophone
Phil Woods
TDWR
Bobby Watson

Tenor Saxophone
Sonny Rollins
TDWR (tie)
Courtney Pine
George Adams

Baritone Saxophone
Gerry Mulligan
TDWR
John Surman

Clarinet
John Carter
TDWR
Jimmy Hamilton

Wynton Marsalis

Flute
James Newton
TDWR
Sam Rivers

Trumpet
Wynton Marsalis
TDWR
Tom Harrell

Trombone
Ray Anderson
TDWR
Robin Eubanks

Synthesizer
Sun Ra
TDWR
John Surman

Acoustic Piano
Cecil Taylor
TDWR
Marcus Roberts

Organ
Jimmy Smith
TDWR
Amina Claudine Myers

Guitar
John Scofield
TDWR
Emily Remler

Acoustic Bass
Charlie Haden
TDWR
Charnett Moffett

Electric Bass
Steve Swallow
TDWR
Marcus Miller

Drums
Max Roach
TDWR
Marvin "Smitty" Smith

Percussion
Nana Vasconcelos
TDWR
Mino Cinelu

Vibes
Milt Jackson
TDWR
Steve Nelson

Violin
Stephane Grappelli
TDWR
Claude Williams

Miscellaneous Instrument
Toots Thielemans, Harmonica
TDWR
Hank Roberts, Cello

Pop/Rock Group
Sting
TDWR
Ray Charles

Soul/R&B Group
Ray Charles
TDWR
Jeannie Cheatham

Record Label
Black Saint/Soul Note

Record Producer
Giovanni Bonandrini

1990

Lifetime Achievement Award
Rudy Van Gelder

Jazz Album of the Year
Cecil Taylor, *In Berlin* (FMP)

Reissue of the Year
Clifford Brown, *Brownie: The Complete Emarcy Recordings* (Emarcy)

Acoustic Jazz Group
Phil Woods Quintet
TDWR
Harper Brothers

Electric Jazz Group
Ornette Coleman's Prime Time
TDWR
John Zorn's Naked City

Male Jazz Singer
Joe Williams
TDWR
Mark Murphy

Male Non-Jazz Singer
Aaron Neville
TDWR
Harry Connick, Jr.

Female Jazz Singer
Betty Carter
TDWR
Cassandra Wilson

Female Non-Jazz Singer
Bonnie Raitt
TDWR
Sinead O'Connor

Vocal Jazz Group
Take 6
TDWR
Ladysmith Black Mambazo

Big Band
Sun Ra and His Arkestra
TDWR
Willem Breuker Kollektief

Arranger
Toshiko Akiyoshi
TDWR
Don Sickler

Composer
Henry Threadgill
TDWR
Bobby Previte

Soprano Saxophone
Steve Lacy
TDWR
Jane Ira Bloom

Alto Saxophone
Phil Woods
TDWR
Bobby Watson

Tenor Saxophone
Sonny Rollins
TDWR
Ralph Moore

Baritone Saxophone
Hamiet Bluiett
TDWR
John Surman

Clarinet
John Carter
TDWR
Don Byron

Flute
James Newton
TDWR
Frank Wess

Trumpet
Lester Bowie
TDWR
Wallace Roney

Trombone
Ray Anderson
TDWR
Robin Eubanks

Synthesizer
Sun Ra
TDWR
John Surman

Acoustic Piano
Cecil Taylor
TDWR
Geri Allen

Organ
Jimmy Smith
TDWR
Barbara Dennerlein

Acoustic Guitar
Jim Hall
TDWR
Emily Remler

Electric Guitar
Bill Frisell
TDWR
Sonny Sharrock

Acoustic Bass
Charlie Haden
TDWR
Fred Hopkins

Electric Bass
Steve Swallow
TDWR
Bill Laswell

Drums
Max Roach
TDWR
Marvin "Smitty" Smith

Percussion
Nana Vasconcelos
TDWR
Marilyn Mazur

Vibes
Milt Jackson
TDWR
Jay Hoggard

Violin
Stephane Grappelli
TDWR
Terry Jenoure

Miscellaneous Instrument
Toots Thielemans, Harmonica
TDWR
Hank Roberts, Cello

Rock Artist of the Year
Elvis Costello
TDWR
John Hiatt

Rock Group
Rolling Stones
TDWR
Living Colour

R&B Soul Artist of the Year
Ray Charles
TDWR
Barrence Whitfield

R&B/Soul Group
Neville Brothers
TDWR
Barrence Whitfield and the Savages

Blues Group
Kinsey Report
TDWR
Saffire

Rap Artist/Group of the Year
Public Enemy
TDWR
Jon Faddis

World Beat Artist of the Year
Youssou N'Dour
TDWR
Nusrat Fateh Ali Khan

Record Label
Blue Note

Record Producer
Michael Cuscuna
TDWR
Willem Breuker Kollektief

1991

Lifetime Achievement Award
Bill Cosby

Jazz Artist of the Year
Wynton Marsalis
TDWR
Geri Allen

Jazz Album of the Year
Charlie Haden and the Liberation Music Orchestra, *Dream Keeper* (Blue Note)

Reissue of the Year
Robert Johnson, *The Complete Recordings* (Columbia/Legacy)

Acoustic Jazz Group
Phil Woods
TDWR
Harper Brothers

Electric Jazz Group
John Scofield Group
TDWR
Steve Coleman and Five Elements

Male Jazz Singer
Joe Williams
TDWR
Harry Connick, Jr.

Male Non-Jazz Singer
Aaron Neville
TDWR
Harry Connick, Jr.

Female Jazz Singer
Betty Carter
TDWR
Cassandra Wilson

Female Non-Jazz Singer
Aretha Franklin
TDWR
Tracy Chapman

Vocal Jazz Group
Take 6
TDWR (tie)
New York Voices
Sweet Honey in the Rock

Big Band
Count Basie Orchestra
TDWR
Peter Apfelbaum and the Hieroglyphics Ensemble

Arranger
Carla Bley
TDWR
John Zorn

Composer
Henry Threadgill
TDWR
Ed Wilkerson, Jr.

Soprano Saxophone
Steve Lacy
TDWR
Jane Ira Bloom

Alto Saxophone
Frank Morgan
TDWR
Bobby Watson

Tenor Saxophone
Sonny Rollins
TDWR
Joe Lovano

Bill Cosby

Baritone Saxophone
Hamiet Bluiett
TDWR
John Surman

Clarinet
John Carter
TDWR
Don Byron

Flute
James Newton
TDWR
Kent Jordan

Trumpet
Wynton Marsalis
TDWR
Roy Hargrove

Trombone
Ray Anderson
TDWR
Robin Eubanks

Synthesizer
Sun Ra
TDWR
John Surman

Acoustic Piano
Cecil Taylor
TDWR
Geri Allen

Organ
Jimmy Smith
TDWR
Barbara Dennerlein

Acoustic Guitar
Jim Hall
TDWR
Egberto Gismonti

Electric Guitar
John Scofield
TDWR (tie)
Kevin Eubanks
Sonny Sharrock

Acoustic Bass
Charlie Haden
TDWR
Ray Drummond

Electric Bass
Steve Swallow
TDWR
Bill Laswell

Drums
Max Roach
TDWR
Marvin "Smitty" Smith

Percussion
Nana Vasconcelos
TDWR
Jerry Gonzalez

Vibes
Milt Jackson
TDWR
Steve Nelson

Violin
Stephane Grappelli
TDWR
Terry Jenoure

Miscellaneous Instrument
Toots Thielemans, Harmonica
TDWR
Steve Turre, Conch Shells

Rock Artist of the Year
Paul Simon
TDWR
Richard Thompson

Rock Album of the Year
Neil Young and Crazy Horse,
    Ragged Glory (Reprise)

Rock Group
Living Colour
TDWR
Fishbone

R&B/Soul Artist of the Year
Ray Charles
TDWR
Maceo Parker

R&B/Soul Album of the Year
Maceo Parker, *Roots
    Revisited* (Verve)

R&B/Soul Group
Neville Brothers
TDWR
J. B. Horns

Blues Artist of the Year
B.B. King
TDWR
Joe Louis Walker

Blues Album of the Year
Charles Brown, *All My Life*
    (Bullseye Blues/Rounder)

Blues Group
Kinsey Report
TDWR
Lil' Ed and the Blues Imperials

**World Beat Artist of the
    Year**
Milton Nascimento
TDWR
Jerry Gonzalez

**World Beat Album of the
    Year**
Paul Simon, *The Rhythm of the
    Saints* (Warner Bros.)

World Beat Group
Mahlathini and the
    Mahotella Queens
TDWR
Jerry Gonzalez and the Fort
    Apache Band

Record Label of the Year
Blue Note

Record Producer
Michael Cuscuna
TDWR
Delfeayo Marsalis

1992

**Lifetime Achievement
Award**
Rich Matteson

Jazz Artist of the Year
Joe Henderson
TDWR
Don Byron

Jazz Album of the Year
Joe Henderson, *Lush Life*
    (Verve)

Reissue of the Year
Nat King Cole, *The Complete
    Capitol Recordings of the
    Nat King Cole Trio*
    (Mosaic)

Acoustic Jazz Group
Wynton Marsalis
TDWR
Ralph Peterson Fo'tet

Electric Jazz Group
Ornette Coleman
TDWR
Naked City

Male Jazz Singer
Joe Williams
TDWR
David Frishberg

Male Non-Jazz Singer
Aaron Neville
TDWR
Lyle Lovett

Female Jazz Singer
Betty Carter
TDWR
Cassandra Wilson

Female Non-Jazz Singer
Bonnie Raitt
TDWR
Diamanda Galas

Vocal Jazz Group
Take 6
TDWR
New York Voices

Big Band
Sun Ra Arkestra
TDWR (tie)
Willem Breuker Kollektief
George Gruntz Concert Band

Arranger
Carla Bley
TDWR
Bob Belden

Composer
Muhal Richard Abrams
TDWR
Ed Wilkerson

Soprano Saxophone
Steve Lacy
TDWR
Jane Bunnett

Alto Saxophone
Phil Woods
TDWR
Bobby Watson

Tenor Saxophone
Joe Henderson
TDWR
Ralph Moore

Baritone Saxophone
Hamiet Bluiett
TDWR
Nick Brignola

Clarinet
Don Byron
TDWR
Don Byron

Flute
James Newton
TDWR
Kent Jordan

Trumpet
Wynton Marsalis
TDWR
Roy Hargrove

Trombone
Ray Anderson
TDWR
Robin Eubanks

Synthesizer
Sun Ra
TDWR
Wayne Horvitz

Acoustic Piano
Tommy Flanagan
TDWR
Geri Allen

Betty Carter

Billie Holiday

Organ
Jimmy Smith
TDWR
Don Pullen

Acoustic Guitar
John McLaughlin
TDWR
Howard Alden

Electric Guitar
John Scofield
TDWR
Sonny Sharrock

Acoustic Bass
Charlie Haden
TDWR
Anthony Cox

Electric Bass
Steve Swallow
TDWR
Gerald Veasley

Drums
Max Roach
TDWR
Ralph Peterson, Jr.

Percussion
Airto Moriera
TDWR
Poncho Sanchez

Vibes
Milt Jackson
TDWR
Steve Nelson

Violin
Stephane Grappelli
TDWR
Claude Williams

Miscellaneous Instrument
Toots Thielemans,
   Harmonica
TDWR
Diedre Murray, Cello

Rock Artist of the Year
Neil Young
TDWR
Dave Alvin

Rock Album of the Year
Neil Young, *Arc/Weld*
   (Reprise)

Rock Group
Grateful Dead
TDWR
NRBQ

R&B/Soul Artist of the Year
Ray Charles
TDWR
Charles Brown

R&B/Soul Album of the Year
Prince, *Diamonds and
   Pearls* (Paisley
   Park/Warner Bros.)

R&B/Soul Group
Neville Brothers

Blues Artist of the Year
B.B. King
TDWR
Joe Louis Walker

Blues Album of the Year
Buddy Guy, *Damn Right I Got
   the Blues* (Silvertone)

Blues Group
B.B. King
TDWR
Holmes Brothers

**World Beat Artist of the
   Year**
Milton Nascimento
TDWR
Margareth Menezes

**World Beat Album of the
   Year**
Mickey Hart, *Planet Drum*
   (Rykodisc)

World Beat Group
Ladysmith Black Mambazo
TDWR
Jerry Gonzalez and the Fort
   Apache Band

Record Label of the Year
Blue Note

Record Producer
Michael Cuscuna
TDWR
Delfeayo Marsalis

1993

Lifetime Achievement Award
Gunther Schuller

Jazz Artist of the Year
Joe Henderson
TDWR
Joe Lovano

Jazz Album of the Year
Joe Henderson, *So Near, So
   Far (Musings for Miles)*
   (Verve)

Reissue Album of the Year
Billie Holiday, *The Complete
   Billie Holiday on Verve*
   (Verve)

Male Jazz Singer
Joe Williams
TDWR
Mark Murphy

Male Non-Jazz Singer
Aaron Neville
TDWR
Harry Connick, Jr.

Female Jazz Singer
Betty Carter
TDWR
Cassandra Wilson

Female Non-Jazz Singer
Bonnie Raitt
TDWR
Lucinda Williams

Vocal Jazz Group
Take 6
TDWR
Sweet Honey in the Rock

Acoustic Jazz Group
Wynton Marsalis
TDWR
Bobby Watson

Electric Jazz Group
John Scofield
TDWR
Sonny Sharrock

Big Band
Count Basie
TDWR
Either/Orchestra

Arranger
Carla Bley
TDWR
Bob Belden

Composer
Muhal Richard Abrams
TDWR
Bobby Watson

Soprano Saxophone
Steve Lacy
TDWR
Jane Bunnett

Alto Saxophone
Jackie McLean
TDWR
Kenny Garrett

Tenor Saxophone
Joe Henderson
TDWR
Joshua Redman

Baritone Saxophone
Hamiet Bluiett
TDWR
Gary Smulyan

Clarinet
Don Byron
TDWR
Marty Ehrlich

Flute
James Newton
TDWR
Dave Valentin

Trumpet (tie)
Lester Bowie
Wynton Marsalis
TDWR
Roy Hargrove

Trombone
J. J. Johnson
TDWR
Frank Lacy

Acoustic Piano
Kenny Barron
TDWR (tie)
Geri Allen
Gonzalo Rubalcaba

Organ
Jimmy Smith
TDWR
Barbara Dennerlein

Acoustic Guitar
John McLaughlin
TDWR
Howard Alden

Electric Guitar
John Scofield
TDWR
Mike Stern

Acoustic Bass
Charlie Haden
TDWR
Christian McBride

Electric Bass
Steve Swallow
TDWR
Gerald Vessiey

Drums
Max Roach
TDWR
Lewis Nash

Percussion
Airto Moriera
TDWR
Jerry Gonzalez

Vibes
Milt Jackson
TDWR
Steve Nelson

Marian McPartland

Violin
Stephane Grappelli
TDWR
Regina Carter

Miscellaneous Instrument
Toots Thielemans, Harmonica
TDWR
Don Byron, Bass Clarinet

Blues Artist of the Year
B.B. King
TDWR
Lil' Ed

Blues Album of the Year
John Lee Hooker, *Boom Boom*
(Pointblank/Virgin)

Blues Group
B.B. King
TDWR
Little Charlie and the Nightcats

Beyond Artist of the Year
Tom Waits
TDWR
Lyle Lovett

Beyond Album of the Year
Mario Bauza, *Tanga*
(Messidor)

Beyond Group (tie)
Kronos Quartet
Los Lobos
TDWR
Greg Osby

Record Label of the Year
Verve

Record Producer
Michael Cuscuna
TDWR
Delfeayo Marsalis

1994

**Lifetime Achievement
Award**
Marian McPartland

Jazz Artist of the Year
Wynton Marsalis
TDWR
Joshua Redman

Jazz Album of the Year
Charlie Haden, *Always Say
Goodbye* (Verve)

Reissue of the Year
Ornette Coleman, *Beauty Is
a Rare Thing: The
Complete Atlantic
Recordings*
(Rhino/Atlantic)

Male Jazz Singer
Joe Williams
TDWR
Kevin Mahogany

Male Non-Jazz Singer
Aaron Neville
TDWR
Salif Keita

Female Jazz Singer
Betty Carter
TDWR
Cassandra Wilson

Female Non-Jazz Singer
Aretha Franklin
TDWR
Jane Siberry

Vocal Jazz Group
Take 6
TDWR
New York Voices

Acoustic Jazz Group
Wynton Marsalis
TDWR
Bobby Watson

Electric Jazz Group
John Scofield
TDWR
Naked City

Big Band
Count Basie
TDWR
Maria Schneider

Arranger
Carla Bley
TDWR
Bob Belden

Composer
Randy Weston
TDWR
Bobby Watson

Soprano Saxophone
Steve Lacy
TDWR
Jane Bunnett

Alto Saxophone
Jackie McLean
TDWR
Vincent Herring

Tenor Saxophone
Joe Henderson
TDWR
Joshua Redman

Baritone Saxophone
Gerry Mulligan
TDWR
Mwata Bowden

Clarinet
Don Byron
TDWR
Ken Peplowski

Flute
James Newton
TDWR
Kent Jordan

Trumpet
Wynton Marsalis
TDWR
Nicholas Payton

Trombone
J. J. Johnson
TDWR
Frank Lacy

Acoustic Piano
Tommy Flanagan
TDWR
Geri Allen

Organ
Jimmy Smith
TDWR
Joey DeFrancesco

Electric Keyboard
Joe Zawinul
TDWR
Lyle Mays

Acoustic Guitar
John McLaughlin
TDWR
Fareed Haque

Electric Guitar
John Scofield
TDWR
Mike Stern

Acoustic Bass
Charlie Haden
TDWR
Christian McBride

Electric Bass
Steve Swallow
TDWR
Bill Laswell

Drums
Max Roach
TDWR
Lewis Nash

Percussion
Trilok Gurtu
TDWR
Giovanni Hidalgo

Vibes
Milt Jackson
TDWR
Steve Nelson

Violin
Stephane Grappelli
TDWR
Mark Feldman

Miscellaneous Instrument
Toots Thielemans,
Harmonica
TDWR
Steve Turre, Conch Shells

Blues Artist of the Year
B.B. King
TDWR
Lucky Peterson

Blues Album of the Year
B.B. King, *Blues Summit*
(MCA)

Blues Group
B.B. King
TDWR
Cheatham's Sweet Baby
Blues Band

Beyond Artist of the Year
George Clinton
TDWR
Salif Keita

Beyond Album of the Year
A. F. Toure and Ry Cooder,
Talking Timbuktu
(Hannibal)

Beyond Group
Neville Brothers
TDWR
Morphine

Record Label of the Year
Verve

Record Producer
Michael Cuscuna
TDWR
Hal Willner

1995

Jazz Artist of the Year
Joe Lovano
TDWR
James Carter

Jazz Album of the Year
Joe Lovano and Gunther
Schuller, *Rush Hour*
(Blue Note)

Reissue of the Year
Bud Powell, *The Complete
Bud Powell on Verve*
(Verve)

Male Vocalist
Joe Williams
TDWR
Kevin Mahogany

Female Jazz Singer
Betty Carter
TDWR
Patricia Barber

Vocal Jazz Group
Take 6
TDWR
Zap Mama

Acoustic Jazz Group
Charlie Haden's Quartet
West
TDWR
Joshua Redman

Electric Jazz Group
John Scofield
TDWR
Medeski Martin and Wood

Big Band
McCoy Tyner Big Band
TDWR
Either/Orchestra

Arranger
Toshiko Akiyosha
TDWR
Maria Schneider

Composer
Henry Threadgill
TDWR
Ed Wilkerson

Soprano Saxophone
Steve Lacy
TDWR
Jane Bunnett

Alto Saxophone
Jackie McLean
TDWR
Sonny Simmons

Tenor Saxophone
Sonny Rollins
TDWR
James Carter

Baritone Saxophone
Gerry Mulligan
TDWR
James Carter

Clarinet
Don Byron
TDWR
Ken Peplowski

Flute
James Newton
TDWR
Kent Jordan

Trumpet
Wynton Marsalis
TDWR
Nicholas Payton

Trombone
J. J. Johnson
TDWR
Robin Eubanks

Piano
Tommy Flanagan
TDWR
Cyrus Chestnut

Organ
Jimmy Smith
TDWR
Amina Claudine Myers

Aaron Neville

Electric Keyboard
Herbie Hancock
TDWR
Wayne Horvitz

Acoustic Guitar
John McLaughlin
TDWR
Howard Alden

Electric Guitar
John Scofield
TDWR
Mark Whitfield

Acoustic Bass
Charlie Haden
TDWR
Christian McBride

Electric Bass
Steve Swallow
TDWR
Bill Laswell

Drums
Elvin Jones
TDWR
Leon Parker

Percussion
Trilok Gurtu
TDWR
Kahil El'Zabar

Vibes
Milt Jackson
TDWR
Steve Nelson

Violin
Stephane Grappelli
TDWR
Mark Feldman

Miscellaneous Instrument
Toots Thielemans,
Harmonica
TDWR
Howard Johnson, Tuba

Blues Artist of the Year
Buddy Guy
TDWR
R. L. Burnside

Blues Album of the Year
Buddy Guy, *Slippin' In*
(Silvertone)

Blues Group
B.B. King
TDWR
Lucky Peterson

Beyond Artist of the Year
Eddie Palmieri
TDWR
Steve Tibbetts

Beyond Album of the Year
Maleem Mahmoud Ghania
and Pharoah Sanders,
*The Trance of Seven
Colors* (Axiom)

Beyond Group
Jerry Gonzalez Fort Apache
Band
TDWR
Wayne Horvitz's Pigpen

Record Label of the Year
Verve

Record Producer
Michael Cuscuna
TDWR
Delfeayo Marsalis

Stephane Grappelli

Pulitzer Prizes in Music

Aaron Copland

1943
Secular Cantata No. 2,
A Free Song, William Schuman

1944
Symphony No. 4 (Op. 34), Howard
Hanson

1945
Appalachian Spring, Aaron Copland

1946
The Canticle of the Sun, Leo Sowerby

1947
Symphony No. 3, Charles Ives

1948
Symphony No. 3, Walter Piston

1949
Louisiana Story Music, Virgil Thomson

1950
The Consul, Gian Carlo Menotti

1951
Music for Opera Giants
in the Earth, Douglas Stuart Moore

1952
Symphony Concertante, Gail Kubik

1953
No award

1954
Concerto for Two Pianos and
Orchestra, Quincy Porter

1955
The Saint of Bleecker Street,
Gian Carlo Menotti

1956
Symphony No. 3, Ernst Toch

1957
Meditations on Ecclesiastes,
Norman Dello Joio

1958
Vanessa, Samuel Barber

1959
Concerto for Piano and Orchestra,
John La Montaine

1960
Second String Quartet, Elliott Carter

1961
Symphony No. 7, Walter Piston

1962
The Crucible, Robert Ward

1963
Piano Concerto No. 1, Samuel Barber

1964
No award

1965
No award

1966
Variations for Orchestra, Leslie
Bassett

1967
Quartet No. 3, Leon Kirchner

1968
Echoes of Time and the River, George
Crumb

1969
String Quartet No. 3, Karel Husa

1970
Time's Encomium, Charles Wuorinen

1971
Synchronisms No. 6 for Piano and
Electronic Sound, Mario
Davidowsky

1972
Windows, Jacob Druckman

1973
String Quartet No. 3, Elliott Carter

1974
Notturno, Donald Martino

1975
From the Diary of Virginia Woolf,
Dominick Argento

1976
Air Music, Ned Rorem

1977
Visions of Terror and Wonder,
Richard Wernick

1978
Deja Vu for Percussion Quartet and
Orchestra, Michael Colgrass

1979
Aftertones of Infinity, Joseph
Schwantner

1980
In Memory of a Summer Day, David
Del Tredici

1981
No award

1982
Concerto for Orchestra, Roger
Sessions

1983
Three Movements for Orchestra,
Ellen T. Zwilich

1984
Canti del Sole, Bernard Rands

1985
Symphony RiverRun, Stephen Albert

1986
Wind Quintet IV, George Perle

1987
The Flight Into Egypt, John Harbison

1988
12 New Etudes for Piano, William
Bolcom

1989
Whispers Out of Time, Roger
Reynolds

1990
Duplicates: A Concerto for Two
Pianos and Orchestra,
Mel Powell

1991
Symphony, Shulamit Ran

1992
The Face of the Night, the Heart
of the Dark, Wayne Peterson

1993
Trombone Concerto, Christopher
Rouse

1994
Of Reminiscences and
Reflections, Gunther Schuller

1995
String Music, Morton Gould

Samuel Barber

Gramophone Awards

The *Gramophone* Awards are widely regarded as the most important and influential classical music awards in the world. *Gramophone* critics select nominees from a pool of more than 2,000 reviews that have appeared in the magazine throughout the year and choose the winners after a two-round balloting process. Each year a Record of the Year is selected from the list of winners.

1977

CHAMBER
Shostakovich, *String Quartets nos. 4 and 12,* Fitzwilliam Quartet (Decca)

CHORAL
Elgar, *Coronation Ode;* Parry, *I Was Glad,* Philip Ledger conducting Kings College Choir and New Philharmonia Orchestra (EMI)

CONCERTO
Mozart, *Piano Concerto No. 22,* Neville Marriner conducting Academy of St. Martin-in-the-Fields; solo: Brendel (Philips)

CONTEMPORARY
Berio, *Concerto for Two Pianos,* Pierre Boulez conducting London Symphony Orchestra and Luciano Berio conducting BBC Symphony Orchestra (RCA Red Seal)

EARLY MUSIC
Dowland, *Lute Works,* Julian Bream (RCA Red Seal)

HISTORICAL
Various artists, *Record of Singing,* various artists (HMV)

INSTRUMENTAL
Beethoven, *Piano Sonatas nos. 27–32,* Maurizio Pollini (Deutsche Grammophon)

OPERATIC (RECORD OF THE YEAR)
Janácek, *Kata Kabanova,* Charles Mackerras conducting Vienna State Opera and Vienna Philharmonic Orchestra (Decca)

ORCHESTRAL
Elgar, *Symphony No. 1,* Sir Adrian Boult conducting London Philharmonic Orchestra (EMI)

SOLO VOCAL
Shostakovich, *Suite, Six Songs to Lyrics, etc.,* Maxim Shostakovich conducting Moscow Radio Symphony Orchestra (HMV Melodiya)

1978

CHAMBER
Bartók, *Sonata for 2 Pianos;* Debussy, *En Blanc;* Mozart, *Andante With 5 Variations for Piano,* Martha Argerich, Stephen Bishop-Kovacevich, Willy Goudswaard and Michael de Roo (Philips)

CHORAL
Handel, *Dixit Dominus,* John Eliot Gardiner conducting Monteverdi Choir and Orchestra (Erato)

Ludwig van Beethoven

CONCERTO
Prokofiev, *Piano Concerto No. 1,* Simon Rattle conducting London Symphony Orchestra; solo: Gavrilov (EMI Studio Plus)

CONTEMPORARY
Webern, *Complete Works,* Pierre Boulez conducting Juilliard String Quartet and London Symphony Orchestra (Sony)

EARLY MUSIC
Handel, *Acis and Galatea,* John Eliot Gardiner conducting English Baroque Soloists (Archiv)

HISTORICAL
Gluck, *Orfeo ed Euridice,* Charles Bruck conducting Netherlands Opera Chorus and Orchestra (EMI)

INSTRUMENTAL
Liszt, *Piano Works,* Alfred Brendel (Philips)

OPERATIC (RECORD OF THE YEAR)
Puccini, *La Fanciulla del West,* Zubin Mehta conducting Royal Opera House Choir and Orchestra (Deutsche Grammophon)

ORCHESTRAL
Mozart, *Symphonies nos. 25 and 29,* Benjamin Britten conducting English Chamber Orchestra (Decca)

SOLO VOCAL
Chausson, *Poeme;* Duparc, *Melodies,* André Previn conducting London Symphony Orchestra; solo: Baker (HMV)

1979

CHAMBER (RECORD OF THE YEAR)
Haydn, *Piano Trios*, Beaux Arts Trio (Philips)

CHORAL
Schoenberg, *Gurrelieder*, Seiji Ozawa conducting Tanglewood Festival Chorus and Boston Symphony Orchestra (Philips)

CONCERTO
Bartók, *Piano Concertos nos. 1 and 2*, Claudio Abbado conducting Chicago Symphony Orchestra; solo: Pollini (Deutsche Grammophon)

CONTEMPORARY
Maxwell Davies, *Symphony No. 1*, Simon Rattle conducting Philharmonia Orchestra (Decca)

EARLY MUSIC
Mozart, *Symphonies Vol. 3*, Christopher Hogwood conducting Academy of Ancient Music (L'Oiseau-Lyre)

ENGINEERING
Debussy, *Images, Prélude à l'après-midi*, André Previn conducting London Symphony Orchestra (EMI)

HISTORICAL
Various artists, *Record of Singing Vol. 2*, various artists (HMV)

INSTRUMENTAL
Bach, *Organ Works Vol. 3*, Peter Hurford (Argo)

OPERATIC
Berg, *Lulu*, Pierre Boulez conducting Paris Opera Orchestra (Deutsche Grammophon)

ORCHESTRAL
Debussy, *Images, Prélude à l'après-midi*, André Previn conducting London Symphony Orchestra (EMI)

SOLO VOCAL
Grechaninov, etc., *Five Children's Songs*, Elisabeth Söderström and Vladimir Ashkenazy (Decca)

1980

CHAMBER
Brahms, *Piano Quintet*, Quartetto Italiano; solo: Pollini (Deutsche Grammophon)

CHORAL
Handel, *L'Allegro, il Penseroso*, John Eliot Gardiner conducting Monteverdi Choir (Erato)

CONCERTO
Ravel, *Piano Concerto in G*, Lorin Maazel conducting French National Orchestra; solo: Collard (HMV)

CONTEMPORARY
Birtwistle, *Punch and Judy*, David Atherton conducting London Sinfonietta (Etcetera)

EARLY MUSIC
C.P.E. Bach, *Sinfonias*, Trevor Pinnock conducting The English Concert (Archiv)

ENGINEERING
Debussy, *Nocturnes, Jeux*, Bernard Haitink conducting Concertgebouw Orchestra (Philips)

HISTORICAL VOCAL
Various artists, *Gramophone Co. Recordings*, Fernando de Lucia (Rubini)

HISTORICAL NON-VOCAL
Bartók, *Contrasts for Clarinet, Violin and Piano*, Bela Bartók, Joseph Szigeti and Benny Goodman (Sony)

INSTRUMENTAL
Brahms, *Piano Sonatas nos. 1 and 2*, Krystian Zimerman (Deutsche Grammophon)

OPERATIC (RECORD OF THE YEAR)
Janácek, *From the House of the Dead*, Sir Charles Mackerras conducting Vienna State Opera and Vienna Philharmonic Orchestra (Decca)

ORCHESTRAL
Debussy, *Nocturnes, Jeux*, Bernard Haitink conducting Concertgebouw Orchestra (Philips)

SOLO VOCAL
Various artists, *A Shropshire Lad*, Graham Trew and Roger Vignoles (Meridian)

1981

CHAMBER
Bartók, *String Quartets nos. 1–6*, Tokyo Quartet (Deutsche Grammophon)

CHORAL
Delius, *Fenby Legacy*, Eric Fenby conducting Royal Philharmonia Orchestra (Unicorn-Kanchan)

CONCERTO
Beethoven, *Violin Concerto in D Minor*, Carlo Maria Giulini conducting Philharmonia; solo: Perlman (EMI)

CONTEMPORARY
Tippett, *King Priam*, David Atherton conducting London Sinfonietta (Decca)

Johannes Brahms

EARLY MUSIC
Various artists, *German Chamber Music,* Cologne Music
    Antiqua (Archiv)

ENGINEERING
Massenet, *Werther,* Sir Colin Davis conducting Royal Opera
    House Orchestra (Philips)

HISTORICAL VOCAL
Various artists, *Hugo Wolf Society Lieder,* various artists
    (HMV)

HISTORICAL NON-VOCAL
Brahms, *Chamber Works,* Busch Quartet, Rudolf Serkin,
    Reginald Kell and Aubrey Brain (World Records)

INSTRUMENTAL
Liszt, *Piano Works,* Alfred Brendel (Philips)

OPERATIC (RECORD OF THE YEAR)
Wagner, *Parsifal,* Herbert von Karajan conducting Deutsche
    Oper and Berlin Philharmonic Orchestra (Deutsche
    Grammophon)

ORCHESTRAL
Mahler, *Symphony No. 9,* Herbert von Karajan conducting
    Berlin Philharmonic Orchestra (Deutsche Grammophon)

SOLO VOCAL
Liszt, *Lieder,* Dietrich Fischer-Dieskau and Daniel Barenboim
    (Deutsche Grammophon)

1982–1983

CHAMBER
Borodin, *String Quartets nos. 1 and 2,* Borodin Quartet (EMI)

CHORAL
Bach, *Mass in B Minor,* Joshua Rifkin conducting Bach
    Ensemble (Elektra-Nonesuch)

CONCERTO (RECORD OF THE YEAR)
Tippett, *Triple Concerto,* Sir Colin Davis conducting London
    Symphony Orchestra (Philips)

CONTEMPORARY
Boulez, *Pli Selon Pli,* Pierre Boulez conducting BBC Symphony
    Orchestra; solo: Bryn-Jolson (Erato)

EARLY-BAROQUE
Charpentier, *Acteon,* William Christie conducting Les Arts
    Florissants Vocal (Harmonia Mundi)

EARLY-MEDIEVAL
Hildegard of Binge, *Sequences and Hymns,* Christopher Page
    conducting Gothic Voices (Hyperion)

ENGINEERING
Shostakovich, *Symphony No. 5,* Bernard Haitink conducting
    Concertgebouw Orchestra (Decca)

HISTORICAL VOCAL
Schubert, *Historical Recordings of Lieder,* various artists
    (HMV)

HISTORICAL NON-VOCAL
Bartók, *At the Piano Vol. 1,* Béla Bartók (Hungaraton)

INSTRUMENTAL
Liszt, *Piano Sonata in B Minor,* Alfred Brendel (Philips)

OPERATIC
Janácek, *Cunning Little Vixen,* Sir Charles Mackerras
    conducting Vienna State Opera and Vienna Philharmonic
    Orchestra (Decca)

Gustav Mahler

ORCHESTRAL
Strauss, *Metamorphosen,* Herbert von Karajan conducting
    Berlin Philharmonic Orchestra (Deutsche Grammophon)

SOLO VOCAL
Brahms, *Lieder,* Kurt Masur conducting Leipzig Gewandhaus
    Orchestra; solo: Norman (Philips)

1984

CHAMBER
Beethoven, *String Quartets nos. 12–16,* Lindsay Quartet (ASV)

CHORAL
Mozart, *Requiem,* Peter Schreier conducting Staatskapelle
    Dresden (Philips)

CONCERTO
Mozart, *Piano Concertos nos. 15 and 16,* Murray Perahia
    conducting English Chamber Orchestra (CBS Master)

CONTEMPORARY
Carter and Harvey, *String Quartets,* Arditti Quartet (RCA Red Seal)

EARLY-BAROQUE
Bach, *Chamber Works,* Reinhard Goebel conducting Cologne
    Musica Antiqua (Archiv)

EARLY-MEDIEVAL
Dunstable, *Motets,* Paul Hillier conducting Hilliard Ensemble
    (HMV)

ENGINEERING
Bax, *Symphony No. 4, Tintagel,* Bryden Thomson conducting
    Ulster Orchestra (Chandos)

HISTORICAL VOCAL
Brahms and Schumann, *Historical Recordings of Lieder,*
    various artists (HMV)

HISTORICAL NON-VOCAL
Beethoven, *Piano Sonatas nos. 30–32,* Egon Petri (dell'Arte)

INSTRUMENTAL
Beethoven, *Piano Sonata No. 29,* Emil Gilels (Deutsche
    Grammophon)

OPERATIC
Janácek, *Jenufa,* Sir Charles Mackerras conducting Vienna State Opera and Vienna Philharmonic Orchestra (Decca)

ORCHESTRAL (RECORD OF THE YEAR)
Mahler, *Symphony No. 9,* Herbert von Karajan conducting Berlin Philharmonic Orchestra (Deutsche Grammophon)

SOLO VOCAL
Strauss, *Four Last Songs,* Kurt Masur conducting Leipzig Gewandhaus Orchestra; solo: Norman (Philips)

1985

CHAMBER
Beethoven, *String Quartets nos. 12–16,* Alban Berg Quartet (EMI)

CHORAL
Fauré, *Requiem,* John Rutter conducting Cambridge Singers and City of London Sinfonia members (Collegium)

CONCERTO (RECORD OF THE YEAR)
Elgar, *Violin Concerto in B Minor,* Vernon Handley conducting London Philharmonic Orchestra; solo: Kennedy (EMI)

CONTEMPORARY
Kurtag, *Messages*; Birtwistle, *. . . agm . . .*, Pierre Boulez conducting John Alldis Choir (Erato)

EARLY-BAROQUE
Charpentier, *Medée,* William Christie conducting Arts Florissants Chorus and Orchestra (Harmonia Mundi)

EARLY-MEDIEVAL
Victoria, *Masses and Motets,* David Hill conducting Westminster Cathedral Choir (Hyperion)

ENGINEERING
Ravel, *Ma Mère l'Oye,* Charles Dutoit conducting Montreal Symphony Orchestra (Decca)

HISTORICAL VOCAL
Various artists, *Opera Arias and Songs,* Claudio Muzio, Molajoli and Refice (EMI Références)

HISTORICAL NON-VOCAL
Nielsen, *Symphonies nos. 1–6,* Erik Tuxen and Thomas Jensen conducting Danish Radio Symphony (Danacord)

INSTRUMENTAL
Liszt, *Années de Pèlerinage,* Jorge Bolet (Decca)

OPERATIC
Mozart, *Don Giovanni,* Bernard Haitink conducting Glyndebourne Choir and London Philharmonic Orchestra (EMI)

ORCHESTRAL
Prokofiev, *Symphony No. 6,* Neeme Järvi conducting Scottish National Orchestra (Chandos)

SOLO VOCAL
Sibelius, *Songs,* Elisabeth Söderström and Vladimir Ashkenazy (Argo)

1986

CHAMBER
Fauré, *Piano Quartets nos. 1 and 2,* Domus (Hyperion)

CHORAL
Janácek, *Glagolitic Mass,* Sir Charles Mackerras conducting Czech Philharmonic Orchestra and Choir (Supraphon)

CONCERTO
Beethoven, *Piano Concertos nos. 3 and 4,* Bernard Haitink conducting Concertgebouw Orchestra; solo: Perahia (CBS Masterworks)

CONTEMPORARY
Lutoslawski, *Symphony No. 3,* Esa-Pekka Salonen conducting Los Angeles Philharmonic Orchestra; solo: Shirley-Quirk (CBS Masterworks)

EARLY-BAROQUE
Bach, *Art of Fugue,* Davitt Moroney (Harmonia Mundi)

EARLY-MEDIEVAL
Various artists, *Chansons de Toile,* Esther Lamandier (Alienor)

ENGINEERING
Respighi, *Belkis, Queen of Sheba,* Geoffrey Simon conducting Philharmonia Orchestra (Chandos)

HISTORICAL VOCAL
Various artists, *Record of Singing Vol. 3,* various artists (HMV)

HISTORICAL NON-VOCAL
Beethoven, *String Quartets nos. 9, 11–12 and 15,* Busch Quartet (HMV)

INSTRUMENTAL
Mozart, *Sonata for 2 Pianos*; Schubert, *Fantasia,* Murray Perahia and Radu Lupu (Sony)

OPERATIC (RECORD OF THE YEAR)
Rossini, *Il Viaggio a Reims,* Claudio Abbado conducting Prague Philharmonic Chorus and Chamber Orchestra Europe (Deutsche Grammophon)

ORCHESTRAL
Williams, *Sinfonia Antartica,* Bernard Haitink conducting London Philharmonic Orchestra; solo: Armstrong (EMI)

RE-MASTERED CD
Britten, *Peter Grimes,* Benjamin Britten conducting Royal Opera House Chorus and Orchestra (Decca)

SOLO VOCAL
Schubert, *Winterreise,* Peter Schreier and Sviatoslav Richter (Philips)

1987

CHAMBER
Chausson, *Concerto for Piano, etc.,* Muir Quartet; solos: Collard and Dumay (EMI)

CHORAL
Handel, *Athalia,* Christopher Hogwood conducting Academy of Ancient Music and New College Choir Oxford (L'Oiseau-Lyre)

CONCERTO
Hummel, *Piano Concertos in A Minor and B Minor,* Bryden Thomson conducting English Chamber Orchestra; solo: Hough (Chandos)

CONTEMPORARY
Tippett, *Mask of Time,* Andrew Davis conducting BBC Symphony Orchestra and Chorus (EMI)

EARLY MUSIC (RECORD OF THE YEAR)
Desprez, *Masses,* Peter Phillips conducting Tallis Scholars (Gimell)

ENGINEERING
Holst, *Planets,* Charles Dutoit conducting Montreal Symphony Orchestra (Decca)

HISTORICAL VOCAL
Various artists, *Art of Tito Schipa,* Tito Schipa (EMI Treasury)

HISTORICAL NON-VOCAL
Schubert, *String Quartets, Piano Trio, etc.,* Busch Quartet; solo: Serkin (EMI)

INSTRUMENTAL
Haydn, *Complete Piano Sonatas,* Alfred Brendel (Philips)

OPERATIC
Verdi, *La Forza del Destino,* Guiseppe Sinopoli conducting Philharmonia Orchestra and Ambrosian Opera Chorus (Deutsche Grammophon)

ORCHESTRAL
Mahler, *Symphony No. 8,* Klaus Tennstedt conducting London Philharmonic Orchestra and Choir (EMI)

PERIOD PERFORMANCE
Beethoven, *Symphonies nos. 2 and 8,* Roger Norrington conducting London Classical Players (EMI)

RE-MASTERED CD
Delius, *Beecham Conducts Delius,* Sir Thomas Beecham conducting Royal Philharmonic Orchestra (EMI)

SOLO VOCAL
Liszt and Strauss, *Lieder,* Brigitte Fassbaender and Irwin Gage (Deutsche Grammophon)

1988

CHAMBER
Mendelssohn, *Violin Sonatas in F Major and F Minor,* Shlomo Mintz and Paul Ostrovsky (Deutsche Grammophon)

CHORAL
Verdi, *Messa da Requiem, Choruses,* Robert Shaw conducting Atlanta Symphony Orchestra and Choir (Telarc)

CONCERTO
Tchaikovsky, *Piano Concerto No. 2,* Rudolf Barshai conducting Bournemouth Symphony Orchestra; solo: Donohoe (EMI)

CONTEMPORARY
Birtwistle, *Carmen Arcadiae Mechanicae,* Elgar Howarth conducting London Sinfonietta (Etcetera)

EARLY-BAROQUE
Leclair, *Scylla et Glaucus,* John Eliot Gardiner conducting Monteverdi Choir (Erato)

EARLY-MEDIEVAL
Various artists, *Service of Venus and Mars,* Christopher Page conducting Gothic Voices (Hyperion)

ENGINEERING (RECORD OF THE YEAR)
Mahler, *Symphony No. 2,* Simon Rattle conducting City of Birmingham Symphony Orchestra (EMI)

HISTORICAL VOCAL
Various artists, *Feodor Chaliapin,* Feodor Chaliapin (EMI Treasury)

HISTORICAL NON-VOCAL
Brahms and Sibelius, *Violin Concertos,* Walter Susskind conducting Philharmonia Orchestra; solo: Neveu (EMI Références)

INSTRUMENTAL
Poulenc, *Piano Works,* Pascal Rogé (Decca)

OPERATIC
Britten, *Paul Bunyan,* Philip Brunelle conducting Plymouth Choir and Orchestra (Virgin Classics)

ORCHESTRAL (RECORD OF THE YEAR)
Mahler, *Symphony No. 2,* Simon Rattle conducting City of Birmingham Symphony Orchestra (EMI)

PERIOD PERFORMANCE
Haydn, *Mass in D Minor, etc.,* Trevor Pinnock conducting The English Concert and Choir (Archiv)

RE-MASTERED CD
Strauss, *Der Rosenkavalier,* Herbert von Karajan conducting Philharmonia Orchestra (EMI)

SOLO VOCAL
Schubert, *Die Schöne Müllerin,* Olaf Bär and Geoffrey Parsons (EMI)

1989

CHAMBER (RECORD OF THE YEAR)
Bartók, *String Quartets nos. 1–6,* Emerson Quartet (Deutsche Grammophon)

CHORAL
Handel, *Jephtha,* John Eliot Gardiner conducting Monteverdi Choir and English Baroque Soloists (Philips)

CONCERTO
Nielsen and Sibelius, *Violin Concertos,* Esa-Pekka Salonen conducting Swedish Radio Symphony Orchestra; solo: Lin (Sony)

CONTEMPORARY
Simpson, *Symphony No. 9,* Vernon Handley conducting Bournemouth Symphony Orchestra (Hyperion)

EARLY-BAROQUE
Corelli, *12 Concerti Grossi,* Trevor Pinnock conducting The English Concert (Archiv)

EARLY-MEDIEVAL
Various artists, *A Song for Francesca,* Christopher Page conducting Gothic Voices (Hyperion)

ENGINEERING
Tubin, *Symphonies nos. 3 and 8,* Neeme Järvi conducting Swedish Radio Symphony Orchestra (Bis)

Benjamin Britten

HISTORICAL VOCAL
Various artists, *Record of Singing Vol. 4*, various artists (EMI)

HISTORICAL NON-VOCAL
Mahler, *Symphony No. 9*, Bruno Walter conducting Vienna
    Philharmonic Orchestra (EMI Références)

INSTRUMENTAL
Mozart, *Complete Piano Sonatas*, Mitsuko Uchida (Philips)

MUSIC THEATRE
Kern and Hammerstein, *Show Boat*, John McGlinn conducting
    London Sinfonietta (EMI)

OPERATIC
Gershwin, *Porgy and Bess*, Simon Rattle conducting London
    Philharmonic Orchestra and Glyndebourne Chorus (EMI)

ORCHESTRAL
Schubert, *Symphonies nos. 1–6, 8 and 9*, Claudio Abbado
    conducting Chamber Orchestra of Europe (Deutsche
    Grammophon)

RE-MASTERED CD
Ravel, *L'enfant et les Sortilèges*, Lorin Maazel conducting
    French Radio National Orchestra (Deutsche
    Grammophon)

SOLO VOCAL
Schubert, *Lieder Vol. 1*, Dame Janet Baker and Graham
    Johnson (Hyperion)

1990

BAROQUE VOCAL
Bach, *St. Matthew Passion*, John Eliot Gardiner conducting
    Monteverdi Choir and English Baroque Soloists (Archiv)

BAROQUE NON-VOCAL
Bach, *Orchestral Suites*, Ton Koopman conducting Amsterdam
    Baroque Orchestra (DHM)

CHAMBER
Respighi, *Violin Sonata in B Minor*, Kyung-Wha Chung and
    Krystian Zimerman (Deutsche Grammophon)

Johann Sebastian Bach

CHORAL
Shumann, *Das Paradise und die Peri*, Armin Jordan
    conducting Suisse Romande Chamber Choir and
    Orchestra (Erato)

CONCERTO
Shostakovich, *Violin Concertos nos. 1 and 2*, Neeme Järvi
    conducting Scottish National Orchestra; solo:
    Mordkovitch (Chandos)

CONTEMPORARY
Benjamin, *Antara*; Boulez, *Dérive, etc.*, George Benjamin
    conducting London Sinfonietta (Nimbus)

EARLY MUSIC
Giovanni and Andrea Gabrieli, *A Venetian Coronation*, Paul
    McCreesh conducting Gabrieli Consort and Players
    (Virgin Classics)

ENGINEERING
Britten, *Prince of the Pagodas*, Oliver Knussen conducting
    London Sinfonietta (Virgin Classics)

HISTORICAL VOCAL
Massenet, *Werther*, Elie Cohen conducting Paris Opéra-
    Comique (EMI Références)

HISTORICAL NON-VOCAL
Delius, *Orchestral Works*, Sir Thomas Beecham conducting
    London Philharmonic Orchestra (Beecham Trust)

INSTRUMENTAL
Debussy, *Piano Works*, Zoltan Kocsis (Philips)

MUSIC THEATRE
Porter, *Anything Goes*, John McGlinn conducting Ambrosian
    Chorus and London Symphony Orchestra (EMI)

OPERA (RECORD OF THE YEAR)
Prokofiev, *The Love for Three Oranges*, Kent Nagano
    conducting Lyon Opera and Orchestra (Virgin Classics)

ORCHESTRAL
Williams, *A Sea Symphony*, Bernard Haitink conducting
    London Philharmonic Orchestra (EMI)

SOLO VOCAL
Schubert, *Schwanengesang*, Peter Schreier and Andras Schiff
    (Decca)

SPECIAL ACHIEVEMENT
Bach, *Sacred Cantatas vols. 1–45*, Nikolaus Harnoncourt and
    Gustav Leonhardt (Teldec)

1991

BAROQUE VOCAL
Handel, *Susanna*, Nicholas McGegan conducting Philharmonia
    Baroque Orchestra (Harmonia Mundi)

BAROQUE NON-VOCAL
Biber, *Mystery Sonatas*, Tragicomedia, John Holloway and
    Davitt Moroney (Virgin Classics)

CHAMBER
Brahms, *Piano Quartets nos. 1–3*, Isaac Stern, Jamie Laredo,
    Yo-Yo Ma and Emanuel Ax (Sony Classical)

CHORAL (RECORD OF THE YEAR)
Beethoven, *Missa Solemnis*, John Eliot Gardiner conducting
    Monteverdi Choir (Archiv)

CONCERTO
Sibelius, *Violin Concerto*, Osmo Vänskä conducting Lahti
    Symphony Orchestra; solo: Kavakos (Bis)

CONTEMPORARY
Casken, *Golem,* Richard Bernas conducting Music Projects London (Virgin Classics)

EARLY MUSIC
Palestrina, *Masses and Motets,* Peter Phillips conducting The Tallis Scholars (Gimell)

ENGINEERING
Wordsworth, *Symphonies nos. 2 and 3,* Nicholas Braithwaite conducting London Philharmonic Orchestra (Lyrita)

HISTORICAL VOCAL
Fauré and Chausson, *French Songs,* Gerard Souzay and Jaqueline Bonneau (Decca)

HISTORICAL NON-VOCAL
Berg, *Violin Concerto, Lyric Suite,* Fritz Busch conducting BBC Symphony Orchestra and Galimir Quartet; solo: Krasner (Continuum)

INSTRUMENTAL
Shostakovich, *24 Preludes and Fugues,* Tatyana Nikolaieva (Hyperion)

MUSIC THEATRE
Sondheim, *Into the Woods,* Original London cast (RCA Red Seal)

OPERA
Mozart, *Idomeneo,* John Eliot Gardiner conducting English Baroque Soloists and Monteverdi Choir (Archiv)

ORCHESTRAL
Nielsen, *Symphionies nos. 2 and 3,* Herbert Blomstedt conducting San Francisco Symphony Orchestra (Decca)

SOLO VOCAL
Schubert, *Die Schöne Müllerin,* Peter Schreier and Andras Schiff (Decca)

SPECIAL ACHIEVEMENT
Mozart, *Complete Edition,* various artists (Philips)

1992

BAROQUE VOCAL
Handel, *Giulio Cesare,* Rene Jacobs conducting Concerto Cologne (Harmonia Mundi)

BAROQUE NON-VOCAL
Rameau, *Harpsichord Works,* Christophe Rousset (L'Oiseau-Lyre)

CHAMBER
Szymanowski, *String Quartets nos. 1 and 2,* Carmina Quartet (Denon)

CHORAL
Britten, *War Requiem,* Richard Hickox conducting London Symphony Orchestra and St. Paul's Cathedral Choir (Chandos)

CONCERTO
Medtner, *Piano Concertos nos. 2 and 3,* Nikolai Demidenko and Jerzy Maksymiuk, (Hyperion)

CONTEMPORARY
Tavener, *Protecting Veil,* Gennadi Rozhdestvensky conducting London Symphony Orchestra; solo: Isserlis (Virgin Classics)

EARLY MUSIC
Various artists, *Rose and the Ostrich Feather,* Harry Christophers conducting The Sixteen (Collins Classics)

George Frederick Handel

ENGINEERING
Britten, *War Requiem,* Richard Hickox conducting St. Paul's Cathedral Choir and London Symphony Orchestra (Chandos)

HISTORICAL VOCAL
Various artists, *Covent Garden on Record,* various artists (Pearl)

HISTORICAL NON-VOCAL
Elgar, *Elgar Edition Vol. 1,* Sir Edward Elgar conducting London Symphony Orchestra and Royal Albert Hall Orchestra (EMI)

INSTRUMENTAL
Alkan, *25 Preludes;* Shostakovich, *24 Preludes,* Olli Mustonen (Decca)

MUSIC THEATRE
Bernstein, *Candide,* Leonard Bernstein conducting London Symphony Orchestra (Deutsche Grammophon)

OPERA
Strauss, *Die Frau Ohne Schatten,* Sir Georg Solti conducting Vienna State Opera and Vienna Philharmonic Orchestra (Decca)

ORCHESTRAL (RECORD OF THE YEAR)
Beethoven, *Symphonies nos. 1–9,* Nikolaus Harnoncourt conducting Chamber Orchestra of Europe (Teldec)

SOLO VOCAL
Schubert, *Lieder,* Brigitte Fassbaender and Aribert Reimann (Deutsche Grammophon)

1993

BAROQUE VOCAL
Stradella, *San Giovanni Battista,* Marc Minkowski conducting Louvre Musiciens du Louvre (Erato)

BAROQUE NON-VOCAL
Heinichen, *Dresden Concertos,* Reinhard Goebel conducting Musica Antiqua Köln (Archiv)

CHAMBER
Haydn, *String Quartets,* Quator Mosaïques (Astrée Auvidis)

CHORAL
Mendelssohn, *Elijah,* Kurt Masur conducting Israel
Philharmonic Orchestra (Teldec)

CONCERTO
Brahms, *Piano Concerto No. 1,* Wolfgang Sawallisch
conducting London Philharmonic Orchestra; solo:
Kovacevich (EMI)

CONTEMPORARY
MacMillan, *Confession of Isabel Gowdie,* Jerzy Maksymiuk
conducting BBC Scottish Symphony (Koch Schwann)

EARLY MUSIC
Various artists, *Venetian Vespers,* Paul McCreesh conducting
Gabrieli Consort and Players (Archiv)

ENGINEERING
Debussy, *Le Martyr de Saint Sébastien,* Michael Tilson Thomas
conducting London Symphony Orchestra (Sony Classical)

HISTORICAL VOCAL
Various artists, *Singers of Imperial Russia vols. 1–4,* various
artists (Pearl)

HISTORICAL NON-VOCAL
Rachmaninov, *Complete Recordings,* Sergei Rachmaninov
(RCA)

INSTRUMENTAL
Various artists, *80th Birthday Carnegie Hall,* Shura Cherkassky
(Decca)

MUSIC THEATRE
Gershwin, *Lady, Be Good!,* Eric Stern (Elektra Nonesuch)

OPERA
Poulenc, *Dialogues des Carmelites,* Kent Nagano conducting
Opera de Lyon Chorus and Orchestra (Virgin Classics)

ORCHESTRAL
Hindemith, *Kammermusik,* Riccardo Chailly conducting Royal
Concertgebouw Orchestra (Decca)

SOLO VOCAL (RECORD OF THE YEAR)
Grieg, *Songs,* Anne Sofie von Otter and Bengt Forsberg
(Deutsche Grammophon)

1994

INSTRUMENTAL (RECORD OF THE YEAR)
Debussy, *Préludes,* Krystian Zimerman (Deutsche
Grammophon)

BAROQUE VOCAL
Monteverdi, *Quarto Libro dei Madrigali,* Concerto Italiano /
Rinaldo Alessandrini (Opus 111)

BAROQUE NON-VOCAL
Bach, *Goldberg Variations,* Pierre Hantaï (Opus 111)

CHAMBER
Tchaikovsky, *String Quartets nos. 1–3,* Borodin Quartet (Teldec)

CHORAL
Delius, *Sea Drift, Songs of Sunset, etc.,* Richard Hickox
conducting Bournemouth Symphony Orchestra; solos:
Terfel and Burgess (Chandos)

CONCERTO
Bartók, *Violin Concerto No. 2,* Simon Rattle conducting City of
Birmingham Symphony Orchestra; solo: Chung (EMI)

CONTEMPORARY
Holloway, *Second Concerto for Orchestra,* Oliver Knussen
conducting BBC Symphony Orchestra (NMC)

EARLY MUSIC
Rore, *Missa Praeter Rerum Seriem,* Peter Phillips conducting
the Tallis Scholars (Gimell)

ENGINEERING
Dutilleux, *Symphonies 1 and 2,* Yan Pascal Tortelier conducting
BBC Philharmonic Orchestra (Chandos)

HISTORIC VOCAL
Britten, Peter Grimes, *Rape of Lucretia, Folksong
Arrangements,* Reginald Goodall conducting
Benjamin Britten Orchestra; solos: Cross, Pears,
Evans and Wyss (EMI)

HISTORIC NON-VOCAL
Schubert, Schoenberg, *Verklärte Nacht, String Quartet,* Kurt
Reher, Hollywood String Quartet (Testament)

MUSIC THEATER AND VIDEO
Leonard Bernstein, *On the Town,* Michael Tilson Thomas
conducting London Symphony Orchestra and London
Voices (DG)

OPERA
Britten, *Gloriana,* Charles Mackerras conducting Welsh
National Opera Chorus and Orchestra (Argo)

ORCHESTRAL
Koechlin, *Jungle Book,* David Zinman conducting Berlin Radio
Symphony Orchestra (RCA)

SOLO VOCAL
Barber, *Complete Songs,* Emerson String Quartet; solos:
Studer, Hampson and Browning (DG)

BEST-SELLING RECORD
Canto Gregoriano, *Coro del Monasterio Benedictino de Santo
Domingo de Silos* (EMI)

SPECIAL ACHIEVEMENT
Richter, *The Authorized Recordings,* Richter (Philips)

ARTIST OF THE YEAR
John Eliot Gardiner

YOUNG ARTIST OF THE YEAR
Maxim Vengerov

LIFETIME ACHIEVEMENT
Klaus Tennstedt

Leonard Bernstein

Radio and Records All-Time Charts

Until 1995, *Radio and Records* used a mathematical system that considered the number of radio plays and market size to compile its charts. Now, the charts, except for the country category, which still reflect both, are based solely on the number of plays.

1975

POP

1. **"Love Will Keep Us Together"**
   Captain and Tennille
   (A&M)

2. **"Another Somebody Done Somebody Wrong"**
   B.J. Thomas
   (ABC)

3. **"Wildfire"**
   Michael Murphey
   (Epic)

4. **"Rhinestone Cowboy"**
   Glen Campbell
   (Capitol)

5. **"Feelings"**
   Morris Albert
   (RCA)

6. **"The Hustle"**
   Van McCoy
   (Avco)

7. **"Calypso and I'm Sorry"**
   John Denver
   (RCA)

8. **"My Eyes Adored You"**
   Frankie Valli
   (Private Stock)

9. **"The Last Farewell"**
   Roger Whittaker
   (RCA)

10. **"Have You Never Been Mellow"**
    Olivia Newton-John
    (MCA)

ROCK

1. **"Love Will Keep Us Together"**
   Captain and Tennille
   (A&M)

2. **"Philadelphia Freedom"**
   Elton John
   (MCA)

3. **"Have You Never Been Mellow"**
   Olivia Newton-John
   (MCA)

4. **"Jive Talkin'"**
   Bee Gees
   (RSO)

5. **"Mandy"**
   Barry Manilow
   (Arista)

6. **"That's the Way (I Like It)"**
   KC and the Sunshine Band
   (TK)

7. **"Island Girl"**
   Elton John
   (MCA)

8. **"Bad Blood"**
   Neil Sedaka
   (Rocket)

9. **"Get Down Tonight"**
   KC and the Sunshine Band
   (TK)

10. **"Black Water"**
    Doobie Brothers
    (Warner Bros.)

ALBUM-ORIENTED ROCK (AOR) ALBUMS

1. *Red Octopus*
   Jefferson Starship
   (Grunt)

2. *Fleetwood Mac*
   Fleetwood Mac
   (Warner Bros.)

3. *One of These Nights*
   Eagles
   (Asylum)

4. *Captain Fantastic*
   Elton John
   (MCA)

5. *Physical Graffiti*
   Led Zeppelin
   (Swan Song)

6. *Born to Run*
   Bruce Springsteen
   (Columbia)

7. *Original Soundtrack*
   10cc
   (Mercury)

8. *Wish You Were Here*
   Pink Floyd
   (Columbia)

Elton John

9. *Fandango*
   ZZ Top
   (London)

10. *Straight Shooter*
    Bad Company
    (Swan Song)

COUNTRY

1. **"Before the Next Teardrop Falls"**
   Freddy Fender
   (ABC/Dot)

2. **"Rhinestone Cowboy"**
   Glen Campbell
   (Capitol)

3. **"Blue Eyes Crying in the Rain"**
   Willie Nelson
   (Columbia)

4. **"Blanket on the Ground"**
   Billie Jo Spears
   (UA)

5. **"I'm Not Lisa"**
   Jessie Colter
   (Capitol)

6. **"Linda on My Mind"**
   Conway Twitty
   (MCA)

7. **"You're My Best Friend"**
   Don Williams
   (ABC/Dot)

8. **"Wasted Days and Wasted Nights"**
   Freddy Fender
   (ABC/Dot)

9. **"Feelin's"**
   Loretta Lynn and Conway Twitty
   (MCA)

10. **"Daydreams About Night Things"**
    Ronnie Milsap
    (RCA)

1976

POP ADULT

1. **"Afternoon Delight"**
   Starland Vocal Band
   (Windsong)

2. **"I'd Really Love to See You"**
   England Dan and J.F. Coley
   (Big Tree)

3. **"If You Leave Me Now"**
   Chicago
   (Columbia)

Peter Frampton

4. "Let Your Love Flow"
   Bellamy Brothers
   (Warner Bros.)

5. "Don't Go Breaking My
   Heart"
   Elton John and Kiki Dee
   (Rocket)

6. "You'll Never Find
   Another Love"
   Lou Rawls
   (Phil./Int.)

7. "Nadia's Theme"
   DeVorzon & Botkin
   (A&M)

8. "Moonlight Feels
   Right"
   Starbuck
   (Private Stock)

9. "December 1963"
   Four Seasons
   (Warner Bros.)

10. "Silly Love Songs"
    Wings
    (Capitol)

TOP 40

1. "If You Leave Me Now"
   Chicago
   (Columbia)

2. "Don't Go Breaking My
   Heart"
   Elton John and Kiki Dee
   (Rocket)

3. "Afternoon Delight"
   Starland Vocal Band
   (Windsong)

4. "Silly Love Songs"
   Wings
   (Capitol)

5. "Play That Funky
   Music"
   Wild Cherry
   (Epic)

6. "December 1963"
   Four Seasons
   (Warner Bros.)

7. "Theme From S.W.A.T."
   Rhythm Heritage
   (ABC)

8. "Boogie Fever"
   Sylvers
   (Capitol)

9. "Kiss and Say
   Goodbye"
   Manhattans
   (Columbia)

10. "Rock 'N Me"
    Steve Miller
    (Capitol)

ALBUM AIRPLAY

1. *Comes Alive*
   Peter Frampton
   (A&M)

2. *Silk Degrees*
   Boz Scaggs
   (Columbia)

3. *Fly Like an Eagle*
   Steve Miller
   (Capitol)

4. *Dreamboat Annie*
   Heart
   (Mushroom)

5. *A Night on the Town*
   Rod Stewart
   (Warner Bros.)

6. *Fleetwood Mac*
   Fleetwood Mac
   (Warner Bros.)

7. *At the Speed of Sound*
   Wings
   (Capitol)

8. *The Royal Scam*
   Steely Dan
   (ABC)

9. *Spitfire*
   Jefferson Starship
   (Grunt)

10. *Takin' It to the Streets*
    Doobie Brothers
    (Warner Bros.)

COUNTRY

1. "I'll Get Over You"
   Crystal Gayle
   (UA)

2. "Good Hearted
   Woman"
   Waylon & Willie
   (RCA)

3. "One Piece at a Time"
   Johnny Cash
   (Columbia)

4. "Teddy Bear"
   Red Sovine
   (Starday)

5. "Golden Ring"
   George Jones and
   Tammy Wynette
   (Epic)

6. "Till the Rivers All Run
   Dry"
   Don Williams
   (ABC/Dot)

7. "All These Things"
   Joe Stampley
   (ABC/Dot)

8. "Stranger"
   Johnny Duncan
   (Columbia)

9. "You and Me"
   Tammy Wynette
   (Epic)

10. "El Paso City"
    Marty Robbins
    (Columbia)

1977

POP/ADULT

1. "Theme From A Star is
   Born"
   Barbra Streisand
   (Columbia)

2. "Looks Like We
   Made It"
   Barry Manilow
   (Arista)

3. "Handy Man"
   James Taylor
   (Columbia)

4. "Southern Nights"
   Glen Campbell
   (Capitol)

5. "Nobody Does It
   Better"
   Carly Simon
   (Elektra)

6. "Higher and Higher"
   Rita Coolidge
   (A&M)

7. "Right Time of the
   Night"
   Jennifer Warnes
   (Arista)

8. "Don't It Make My
   Brown Eyes Blue"
   Crystal Gayle
   (UA)

9. "Don't Give Up on Us"
   David Soul
   (Private Stock)

10. "You Light Up My Life"
    Debby Boone
    (Warner Bros./Curb)

TOP 40

1. "You Light Up My Life"
   Debby Boone
   (Warner Bros.)

2. "When I Need You"
   Leo Sayer
   (Warner Bros.)

3. "I Just Want to Be Your
   Everything"
   Andy Gibb
   (RSO)

4. "Dreams"
   Fleetwood Mac
   (Warner Bros.)

5. "Undercover Angel"
   Alan O'Day
   (Pacific)

6. "Theme From A Star Is
   Born"
   Barbra Streisand
   (Columbia)

7. "Hotel California"
   Eagles
   (Asylum)

8. "Rich Girl"
   Daryl Hall and John
   Oates
   (RCA)

9. "Star Wars"
   Meco
   (Millennium)

10. "Best of My Love"
    Emotions
    (Columbia)

ALBUM AIRPLAY

1. *Rumours*
   Fleetwood Mac
   (Warner Bros.)

2. *Hotel California*
   Eagles
   (Asylum)

3. *Foreigner*
   Foreigner
   (Atlantic)

4. *Book of Dreams*
   Steve Miller
   (Capitol)

5. *Crosby Stills and Nash*
   Crosby Stills and Nash
   (Atlantic)

6. *I Robot*
   Alan Parsons
   (Arista)

7. *Little Queen*
   Heart
   (Portrait)

8. *Rock & Roll Alternative*
   Atlanta Rhythm Section
   (Polydor)

9. *Night Moves*
   Bob Seger
   (Capitol)

10. *Even in the Quietest Moments*
    Supertramp
    (A&M)

COUNTRY

1. "It Was Almost Like a Song"
   Ronnie Milsap
   (RCA)

2. "Luckenbach Texas"
   Waylon Jennings
   (RCA)

3. "Don't It Make My Brown Eyes Blue"
   Crystal Gayle
   (UA)

4. "Heaven's Just a Sin Away"
   The Kendalls
   (Ovation)

5. "Lucille"
   Kenny Rogers
   (UA)

6. "Way Down/Pledging My Love"
   Elvis Presley
   (RCA)

7. "Rollin' With the Flow"
   Charlie Rich
   (Epic)

8. "Southern Nights"
   Glen Campbell
   (Capitol)

9. "Daytime Friends"
   Kenny Rogers
   (UA)

10. "Blue Bayou"
    Linda Ronstadt
    (Asylum)

1978

POP ADULT

1. "Can't Smile Without You"
   Barry Manilow
   (Arista)

2. "You Needed Me"
   Anne Murray
   (Capitol)

3. "Just the Way You Are"
   Billy Joel
   (Columbia)

4. "Reminiscing"
   Little River Band
   (Harvest)

5. "Feels So Good"
   Chuck Mangione
   (A&M)

6. "Goodbye Girl"
   David Gates
   (Elektra)

7. "Three Times a Lady"
   Commodores
   (Motown)

8. "Hopelessly Devoted to You"
   Olivia Newton-John
   (RSO)

9. "You Belong to Me"
   Carly Simon
   (Elektra)

10. "The Closer I Get to You"
    Roberta Flack and D. Hathaway
    (Atlantic)

TOP 40

1. "Night Fever"
   Bee Gees
   (RSO)

2. "Stayin' Alive"
   Bee Gees
   (RSO)

3. "Kiss You All Over"
   Exile
   (Warner Bros./Curb)

4. "Three Times a Lady"
   Commodores
   (Motown)

5. "Shadow Dancing"
   Andy Gibb
   (RSO)

6. "Baker Street"
   Gerry Rafferty
   (UA)

7. "Hot Child in the City"
   Nick Gilder
   (Chrysalis)

8. "With a Little Luck"
   Wings
   (Capitol)

9. "Emotion"
   Samantha Sang
   (Private Stock)

10. "Can't Smile Without You"
    Barry Manilow
    (Arista)

AOR ALBUMS

1. *Some Girls*
   Rolling Stones
   (Rolling Stones)

2. *Stranger in Town*
   Bob Seger
   (Capitol)

3. *Double Vision*
   Foreigner
   (Atlantic)

4. *Running on Empty*
   Jackson Browne
   (Asylum)

5. *Earth*
   Jefferson Starship
   (Grunt/RCA)

6. *Slow Hand*
   Eric Clapton
   (RSO)

7. *But Seriously Folks*
   Joe Walsh
   (Asylum)

8. *Stranger*
   Billy Joel
   (Columbia)

9. *City to City*
   Gerry Rafferty
   (United Artists)

10. *Darkness on the Edge of Town*
    Bruce Springsteen
    (Columbia)

COUNTRY

1. "Mamas Don't Let Your Babies Grow Up to Be Cowboys"
   Waylon & Willie
   (RCA)

2. "Talking in Your Sleep"
   Crystal Gayle
   (UA)

3. "Heartbreaker"
   Dolly Parton
   (RCA)

4. "Love or Something Like It"
   Kenny Rogers
   (UA)

5. "You Don't Love Me Anymore"
   Eddie Rabbitt
   (Elektra)

6. "Someone Loves You Honey"
   Charley Pride
   (RCA)

7. "Everytime Two Fools Collide"
   Kenny Rogers and Dottie West
   (UA)

8. "Don't Break the Heart That Loves You"
   Margo Smith
   (Warner Bros.)

9. "Georgia on My Mind"
   Willie Nelson
   (Columbia)

10. "I've Always Been Crazy"
    Waylon Jennings
    (RCA)

1979

POP ADULT

1. "Rise"
   Herb Alpert
   (A&M)

2. "I'll Never Love This Way Again"
   Dionne Warwick
   (Arista)

3. "I Just Fell in Love Again"
   Anne Murray
   (Capitol)

4. "She Believes in Me"
   Kenny Rogers
   (UA)

5. "The Main Event/Fight"
   Barbra Streisand
   (Columbia)

6. "Lead Me On"
   Maxine Nightingale
   (Windsong)

7. "Just When I Needed You Most"
   Randy Vanwarmer
   (Bearsville)

8. "Music Box Dancer"
   Frank Mills
   (Polydor)

9. "Reunited"
   Peaches and Herb
   (Polydor)

10. "Sad Eyes"
    Robert John
    (EMI America)

TOP 40

1. "Do Ya Think I'm Sexy"
   Rod Stewart
   (Warner Bros.)

2. "What a Fool Believes"
   Doobie Brothers
   (Warner Bros.)

3. "Reunited"
   Peaches and Herb
   (Polydor)

4. "Sail On"
   Commodores
   (Motown)

5. "Lonesome Loser"
   Little River Band
   (Capitol)

6. "Heartache Tonight"
   Eagles
   (Asylum)

7. "Sad Eyes"
   Robert John
   (EMI America)

8. "My Sharona"
   Knack
   (Capitol)

9. "Heart of Glass"
   Blondie
   (Chrysalis)

10. "Tragedy"
    Bee Gees
    (RSO)

AOR ALBUMS

1. *Breakfast in America*
   Supertramp
   (A&M)

2. *Minute by Minute*
   Doobie Brothers
   (Warner Bros.)

3. *Desolation Angels*
   Bad Company
   (Swan Song)

4. *Candy-O*
   Cars
   (Elektra)

5. *Get the Knack*
   Knack
   (Capitol)

6. *Dire Straits*
   Dire Straits
   (Warner Bros.)

7. *Van Halen II*
   Van Halen
   (Warner Bros.)

8. *Blondes Have More Fun*
   Rod Stewart
   (Warner Bros.)

9. *At Budokan*
   Cheap Trick
   (Epic)

10. *Rickie Lee Jones*
    Rickie Lee Jones
    (Warner Bros.)

COUNTRY

1. "She Believes in Me"
   Kenny Rogers
   (UA)

2. "I Just Fell in Love Again"
   Anne Murray
   (Capitol)

3. "It Must Be Love"
   Don Williams
   (MCA)

4. "Amends"
   Waylon Jennings
   (RCA)

5. "All I Ever Need Is You"
   Kenny Rogers and Dottie West
   (UA)

6. "You Decorated My Life"
   Kenny Rogers
   (UA)

7. "Back on My Mind Again"
   Ronnie Milsap
   (RCA)

8. "Shadows in the Moonlight"
   Anne Murray
   (Capitol)

9. "You're the Only One"
   Dolly Parton
   (RCA)

10. "The Devil Went Down to Georgia"
    Charlie Daniels Band
    (Epic)

1980

POP ADULT

1. "All Out of Love"
   Air Supply
   (Arista)

2. "Lost in Love"
   Air Supply
   (Arista)

3. "Magic"
   Olivia Newton-John
   (MCA)

4. "Sailing"
   Christopher Cross
   (Warner Bros.)

5. "The Rose"
   Bette Midler
   (Atlantic)

6. "Women in Love"
   Barbra Streisand
   (Columbia)

7. "Longer"
   Dan Fogelberg
   (Full Moon/Epic)

8. "Little Jeannie"
   Elton John
   (MCA)

9. "September Morn"
   Neil Diamond
   (Columbia)

10. "Let Me Love You Tonight"
    Pure Prairie League
    (Casablanca)

CONTEMPORARY HIT RADIO (CHR)/POP

1. "Call Me"
   Blondie
   (Chrysalis)

2. "It's Still Rock and Roll to Me"
   Billy Joel
   (Columbia)

3. "Sailing"
   Christopher Cross
   (Warner Bros.)

4. "Woman in Love"
   Barbra Streisand
   (Columbia)

5. "Another Brick in the Wall"
   Pink Floyd
   (Columbia)

6. "Biggest Part of Me"
   Ambrosia
   (Warner Bros.)

7. "Magic"
   Olivia Newton-John
   (MCA)

8. "Crazy Little Thing Called Love"
   Queen

Blondie

(Elektra)

9. "Longer"
   Dan Fogelberg
   (Full Moon/Epic)

10. "Ride Like the Wind"
    Christopher Cross
    (Warner Bros.)

AOR ALBUMS

1. *Against the Wind*
   Bob Seger and the Silver Bullet Band
   (Capitol)

2. *The Wall*
   Pink Floyd
   (Columbia)

3. *Emotional Rescue*
   Rolling Stones
   (Rolling Stones)

4. *Empty Glass*
   Pete Townshend
   (Atco)

5. *Hold Out*
   Jackson Browne
   (Asylum)

6. *Duke*
   Genesis
   (Atlantic)

7. *The Game*
   Queen
   (Elektra)

8. *Glass Houses*
   Billy Joel
   (Columbia)

9. *Pretenders*
   Pretenders
   (Sire)

10. *Crimes of Passion*
    Pat Benatar
    (Chrysalis)

COUNTRY

1. "Drivin' My Life Away"
   Eddie Rabbitt
   (Elektra)
2. "I Believe in You"
   Don Williams
   (MCA)
3. "Lookin' for Love"
   Johnny Lee
   (Full Moon/Asylum)
4. "Smoky Mountain Rain"
   Ronnie Milsap
   (RCA)
5. "On the Road Again"
   Willie Nelson
   (Columbia)
6. "He Stopped Loving Her Today"
   George Jones
   (Epic)
7. "Don't Fall in Love With a Dreamer"
   Kenny Rogers with Kim Carnes
   (UA)
8. "Stand by Me"
   Mickey Gilley
   (Full Moon/Asylum)
9. "It's Like We Never Said Goodbye"
   Crystal Gayle
   (Columbia)
10. "Coward of the County"
    Kenny Rogers
    (UA)

1981

ADULT CONTEMPORARY(AC)

1. "Endless Love"
   Diana Ross and Lionel Richie
   (Motown)
2. "I Don't Need You"
   Kenny Rogers
   (Liberty)
3. "Hard to Say"
   Dan Fogelberg
   (Full Moon/Epic)
4. "The One That You Love"
   Air Supply
   (Arista)
5. "Her Town Too"
   James Taylor and J.D. Souther
   (Columbia)
6. "Arthur's Theme (Best That You Can Do)"
   Christopher Cross
   (Warner Bros.)
7. "What Are We Doing in Love"
   Dottie West
   (Liberty)
8. "(There's) No Gettin' Over Me"
   Ronnie Milsap
   (RCA)
9. "Woman"
   John Lennon
   (Geffen/Warner Bros.)
10. "Theme From Greatest American Hero"
    Joey Scarbury
    (Elektra)

CHR/POP

1. "Bette Davis Eyes"
   Kim Carnes
   (EMI America)
2. "Endless Love"
   Diana Ross and Lionel Richie
   (Motown)
3. "Arthur's Theme (Best That You Can Do)"
   Christopher Cross
   (Warner Bros.)
4. "The One That You Love"
   Air Supply
   (Arista)
5. "Who's Crying Now"
   Journey
   (Columbia)
6. "The Best of Times"
   Styx
   (A&M)
7. "Woman"
   John Lennon
   (Geffen/Warner Bros.)
8. "Private Eyes"
   Daryl Hall and John Oates
   (RCA)
9. "Keep on Loving You"
   REO Speedwagon
   (Epic)
10. "Slow Hand"
    Pointer Sisters
    (Planet/Elektra-Asylum)

AOR ALBUMS

1. Tattoo You
   Rolling Stones
   (Rolling Stones/Atco)
2. 4
   Foreigner
   (Atlantic)
3. Don't Say No
   Billy Squier
   (Capitol)
4. Hi Infidelity
   REO Speedwagon
   (Epic)
5. Escape
   Journey
   (Columbia)
6. Face Value
   Phil Collins
   (Atlantic)
7. Arc of a Diver
   Steve Winwood
   (Island/Warner Bros.)
8. Paradise Theater
   Styx
   (A&M)
9. Hard Promises
   Tom Petty and the Heartbreakers
   (Backstreet/MCA)
10. Long Distance Voyager
    Moody Blues
    (Threshold/PG)

COUNTRY

1. "Step by Step"
   Eddie Rabbitt
   (Elektra)
2. "Party Time"
   T.G. Sheppard
   (Warner Bros./Curb)
3. "Takin' It Easy"
   Lacy J. Dalton
   (Columbia)
4. "(There's) No Gettin' Over Me"
   Ronnie Milsap
   (RCA)
5. "Wish You Were Here"
   Barbara Mandrell
   (MCA)
6. "I Don't Need You"
   Kenny Rogers
   (EMI/Liberty)
7. "Elvira"
   Oak Ridge Boys
   (MCA)
8. "Feels So Right"
   Alabama
   (RCA)
9. "You Don't Know Me"
   Mickey Gilley
   (Epic)
10. "Too Many Lovers"
    Crystal Gayle
    (Columbia)

1982

AC

1. "Ebony and Ivory"
   Paul McCartney and Stevie Wonder
   (Columbia)
2. "Hard to Say I'm Sorry"
   Chicago
   (Full Moon/ Warner Bros.)
3. "Love Will Turn You Around"
   Kenny Rogers
   (Liberty)
4. "Chariots of Fire"
   Vangelis
   (Polydor/PolyGram)
5. "Even the Nights Are Better"
   Air Supply
   (Arista)
6. "Wasted on the Way"
   Crosby Stills and Nash
   (Atlantic)
7. "Always on My Mind"
   Willie Nelson
   (Columbia)
8. "Key Largo"
   Bertie Higgins
   (Kat Family/CBS)
9. "Any Day Now"
   Ronnie Milsap
   (RCA)
10. "The One You Love"
    Glenn Frey
    (Asylum)

CHR

1. "Open Arms"
   Journey
   (Columbia)
2. "Hard to Say I'm Sorry"
   Chicago
   (Full Moon/Warner Bros.)
3. "Don't Talk to Strangers"
   Rick Springfield
   (RCA)
4. "Rosanna"
   Toto
   (Columbia)
5. "Ebony and Ivory"
   Paul McCartney and Stevie Wonder
   (Columbia)
6. "Eye of the Tiger"
   Survivor
   (Scotti Bros./CBS)
7. "Jack and Diane"
   John Cougar
   (Riva/PolyGram)
8. "I Keep Forgettin' (Every Time You're Near)"
   Michael McDonald
   (Warner Bros.)
9. "Hold Me"
   Fleetwood Mac
   (Warner Bros.)

10. **"That Girl"**
Stevie Wonder
(Tamla/Motown)

AOR ALBUMS

1. *Asia*
Asia
(Geffen)

2. *American Fool*
John Cougar
(Riva/PolyGram)

3. *Get Lucky*
Loverboy
(Columbia)

4. *I Love Rock and Roll*
Joan Jett and the
Blackhearts
(Boardwalk)

5. *Special Forces*
.38 Special
(A&M)

6. *Aldo Nova*
Aldo Nova
(Portrait/CBS)

7. *Business as Usual*
Men at Work
(Columbia)

8. *Standing Hampton*
Sammy Hagar
(Geffen)

9. *Freeze-Frame*
J. Geils Band
(EMI America)

10. *Emotions in Motion*
Billy Squier
(Capitol)

URBAN

1. **"That Girl"**
Stevie Wonder
(Tamla/Motown)

2. **"Jump to It"**
Aretha Franklin
(Arista)

3. **"Love Come Down"**
Evelyn King
(RCA)

4. **"I Really Don't Need
No Light"**
Jeffrey Osborne
(A&M)

5. **"Early in the Morning"**
Gap Band
(Total Experience/
PolyGram)

6. **"Do I Do"**
Stevie Wonder
(Tamla/Motown)

7. **"Let It Whip"**
Dazz Band
(Motown)

8. **"Tell Me Tomorrow"**
Smokey Robinson
(Tamla/Motown)

9. **"It's Gonna Take a
Miracle"**
Deniece Williams
(ARC/Columbia)

10. **"Forget Me Nots"**
Patrice Rushen
(Elektra)

COUNTRY

1. **"The Clown"**
Conway Twitty
(Elektra)

2. **"Love Will Turn You
Around"**
Kenny Rogers
(Liberty)

3. **"I Don't Think She's in
Love"**
Charley Pride
(RCA)

4. **"Another Sleepless
Night"**
Anne Murray
(Capitol)

5. **"What's Forever For"**
Michael Murphey
(Liberty)

6. **"Just to Satisfy You"**
Waylon & Willie
(RCA)

7. **"'Til You're Gone"**
Barbara Mandrell
(MCA)

8. **"Nobody"**
Sylvia
(RCA)

9. **"Same Ole Me"**
George Jones
(Epic)

10. **"Big City"**
Merle Haggard
(Epic)

1983

AC

1. **"Never Gonna Let
You Go"**
Sergio Mendes
(A&M)

2. **"You Are"**
Lionel Richie
(Motown)

3. **"It Might Be You"**
(theme from *Tootsie*)
Stephen Bishop
(Warner Bros.)

4. **"True"**
Spandau Ballet
(Chrysalis)

5. **"My Love"**
Lionel Richie
(Motown)

6. **"Every Breath You
Take"**
Police
(A&M)

7. **"Islands in the Stream"**
Kenny Rogers with
Dolly Parton
(RCA)

8. **"Make Love Stay"**
Dan Fogelberg
(Full Moon/Epic)

9. **"I Won't Hold You
Back"**
Toto
(Columbia)

10. **"All Night Long (All
Night)"**
Lionel Richie
(Motown)

CHR/POP

1. **"Every Breath You
Take"**
Police
(A&M)

2. **"Flashdance ... (What a
Feeling)"**
Irene Cara
(Casablanca/PolyGram)

3. **"Total Eclipse of the
Heart"**
Bonnie Tyler (Columbia)

4. **"Billie Jean"**
Michael Jackson
(Epic)

5. **"Maniac"**
Michael Sembello
(Casablanca/PolyGram)

6. **"Jeopardy"**
Greg Kihn Band
(Beserkley/E-A)

7. **"Beat It"**
Michael Jackson
(Epic)

8. **"You Are"**
Lionel Richie
(Motown)

9. **"Overkill"**
Men at Work
(Columbia)

10. **"Down Under"**
Men at Work
(Columbia)

AOR/HOT TRACKS

1. **"King of Pain"**
Police
(A&M)

2. **"Photograph"**
Def Leppard
(Mercury/PolyGram)

3. **"One Thing Leads to
Another"**
Fixx
(MCA)

4. **"Rock of Ages"**
Def Leppard
(Mercury/PolyGram)

5. **"She's a Beauty"**
Tubes
(Capitol)

6. **"Every Breath You
Take"**
Police
(A&M)

7. **"The One Thing"**
INXS
(Atco)

8. **"Burning Down the
House"**
Talking Heads
(Sire/Warner Bros.)

9. **"Synchronicity II"**
Police
(A&M)

10. **"Gimme All Your
Lovin'"**
ZZ Top
(Warner Bros.)

AOR ALBUMS

1. *Pyromania*
Def Leppard
(Mercury/PolyGram)

2. *Synchronicity*
Police
(A&M)

3. *Cuts Like a Knife*
Bryan Adams
(A&M)

4. *Eliminator*
ZZ Top
(Warner Bros.)

5. *Reach the Beach*
Fixx
(MCA)

6. *Let's Dance*
David Bowie
(EMI America)

7. *Frontiers*
Journey
(Columbia)

8. *The Wild Heart*
Stevie Nicks
(Modern/Atco)

9. *War*
U2
(Island/Atco)

10. *Metal Health*
Quiet Riot
(Pasha/CBS)

URBAN

1. **"Billie Jean"**
Michael Jackson
(Epic)

2. **"Save the Overtime for Me"**
Gladys Knight and the Pips
(Columbia)

3. **"All Night Long (All Night)"**
Lionel Richie
(Motown)

4. **"Just Be Good to Me"**
S.O.S. Band
(Tabu/CBS)

5. **"Cold Blooded"**
Rick James
(Gordy/Motown)

6. **"Inside Love (So Personal)"**
George Benson
(Warner Bros.)

7. **"Don't You Get So Mad"**
Jeffrey Osborne
(A&M)

8. **"Ain't Nobody"**
Rufus and Chaka Khan
(Warner Bros.)

9. **"I Just Gotta Have You (Lover Turn Me On)"**
Kashif
(Arista)

10. **"Fall in Love With Me"**
Earth Wind & Fire
(Columbia)

COUNTRY

1. **"Islands in the Stream"**
Kenny Rogers and Dolly Parton
(RCA)

2. **"He's a Heartache"**
Janie Fricke
(Columbia)

3. **"Dixieland Delight"**
Alabama
(RCA)

4. **"Hey Bartender"**
Johnny Lee
(Full Moon/Warner Bros.)

5. **"Pancho and Lefty"**
Willie Nelson and Merle Haggard
(Epic)

6. **"Common Man"**
John Conlee
(MCA)

7. **"Lost in the Feeling"**
Conway Twitty
(Warner Bros.)

8. **"Night Games"**
Charley Pride
(RCA)

9. **"Our Love Is on the Faultline"**
Crystal Gayle
(Warner Bros.)

10. **"Fool for Your Love"**
Mickey Gilley
(Epic)

1984

AC

1. **"Hello"**
Lionel Richie
(Motown)

2. **"Stuck on You"**
Lionel Richie
(Motown)

3. **"I Just Called to Say I Love You"**
Stevie Wonder
(Motown)

4. **"If Ever You're in My Arms Again"**
Peabo Bryson
(Elektra)

5. **"Time After Time"**
Cyndi Lauper
(Portrait/CBS)

6. **"Against All Odds (Take a Look at Me Now)"**
Phil Collins
(Atlantic)

7. **"Drive"**
Cars
(Elektra)

8. **"Sad Songs (Say So Much)"**
Elton John
(Geffen)

9. **"Leave a Tender Moment Alone"**
Billy Joel
(Columbia)

10. **"The Longest Time"**
Billy Joel
(Columbia)

CHR/POP

1. **"Jump"**
Van Halen
(Warner Bros.)

2. **"Against All Odds (Take a Look at Me Now)"**
Phil Collins
(Atlantic)

3. **"Footloose"**
Kenny Loggins
(Columbia)

4. **"When Doves Cry"**
Prince
(Warner Bros.)

The Cars

5. **"Let's Go Crazy"**
Prince
(Warner Bros.)

6. **"Missing You"**
John Waite
(EMI America)

7. **"Hello"**
Lionel Richie
(Motown)

8. **"Time After Time"**
Cyndi Lauper
(Portrait/CBS)

9. **"Ghostbusters"**
Ray Parker, Jr.
(Arista)

10. **"Let's Hear It for the Boy"**
Deniece Williams
(Columbia)

AOR/HOT TRACKS

1. **"Cover Me"**
Bruce Springsteen
(Columbia)

2. **"Panama"**
Van Halen
(Warner Bros.)

3. **"Magic"**
Cars
(Elektra)

4. **"I'll Wait"**
Van Halen
(Warner Bros.)

5. **"Drive"**
Cars
(Elektra)

6. **"Missing You"**
John Waite
(EMI America)

7. **"Round and Round"**
Ratt
(Atlantic)

8. **"Dancing in the Dark"**
Bruce Springsteen
(Columbia)

9. **"The Warrior"**
Scandal featuring Patty Smyth
(Columbia)

10. **"Rock You Like a Hurricane"**
Scorpions
(Mercury/PG)

AOR ALBUMS

1. *Heartbeat City*
Cars
(Elektra)

2. *Sports*
Huey Lewis and the News
(Chrysalis)

3. *Born in the U.S.A.*
Bruce Springsteen
(Columbia)

4. *1984*
Van Halen
(Warner Bros.)

5. *Midnight Madness*
Night Ranger
(Camel/MCA)

6. *Rebel Yell*
Billy Idol
(Chrysalis)

7. *90125*
Yes
(Atco)

8. *Love at First Sting*
Scorpions
(Mercury/PG)

9. *Street Talk*
Steve Perry
(Columbia)

10. *No Brakes*
John Waite
(EMI America)

URBAN

1. **"When Doves Cry"**
Prince
(Warner Bros.)

2. **"I Feel for You"**
Chaka Khan
(Warner Bros.)

3. **"She's Strange"**
Cameo
(Atlanta Artists/PG)

4. **"Somebody's Watching Me"**
Rockwell
(Motown)

5. **"If Only You Knew"**
Patti Labelle
(Phil. Int./CBS)

6. **"Hello"**
Lionel Richie
(Motown)

7. **"Cool It Now"**
New Edition
(MCA)

8. **"Let's Hear It for the Boy"**
Deniece Williams
(Columbia)

9. **"What's Love Got to Do With It?"**
Tina Turner
(Capitol)

10. **"Caribbean Queen (No More Love on the Run)"**
Billy Ocean
(Jive/Arista)

COUNTRY

1. **"Roll On (Eighteen Wheeler)"**
Alabama
(RCA)

2. **"When We Make Love"**
Alabama
(RCA)

3. **"That's the Thing About Love"**
Don Williams
(MCA)

4. **"I Don't Know a Thing About Love"**
Conway Twitty
(Warner Bros.)

5. **"I've Been Around Enough to Know"**
John Schneider
(MCA)

6. **"Somebody's Needin' Somebody"**
Conway Twitty
(Warner Bros.)

7. **"Somewhere Down the Line"**
T.G. Sheppard
(Warner Bros./Curb)

8. **"City of New Orleans"**
Willie Nelson
(Columbia)

9. **"Long Hard Road"**
Nitty Gritty Dirt Band
(Warner Bros.)

10. **"You're Gettin' to Me Again"**
Jim Glaser
(Noble Vision)

1985

AC

1. **"Cherish"**
Kool and the Gang
(De-Lite/PG)

2. **"Careless Whisper"**
Wham!
(Columbia)

3. **"Everytime You Go Away"**
Paul Young
(Columbia)

4. **"One More Night"**
Phil Collins
(Atlantic)

5. **"The Search Is Over"**
Survivor
(Scotti Bros./CBS)

6. **"Suddenly"**
Billy Ocean
(Jive/Arista)

7. **"Part-Time Lover"**
Stevie Wonder
(Tamla/Motown)

8. **"Crazy for You"**
Madonna
(Geffen)

9. **"Saving All My Love for You"**
Whitney Houston
(Arista)

10. **"Who's Holding Donna Now"**
DeBarge
(Gordy/Motown)

CHR (CHR/POP)

1. **"Crazy for You"**
Madonna
(Geffen)

2. **"Can't Fight This Feeling"**
REO Speedwagon
(Epic)

3. **"Power of Love"**
Huey Lewis and the News
(Chrysalis)

4. **"Take On Me"**
A-Ha
(Reprise/Warner Bros.)

Alabama

5. **"St. Elmo's Fire"**
John Parr
(Atlantic)

6. **"Money for Nothing"**
Dire Straits
(Warner Bros.)

7. **"Careless Whisper"**
Wham!
(Columbia)

8. **"Everytime You Go Away"**
Paul Young
(Columbia)

9. **"I Want to Know What Love Is"**
Foreigner
(Atlantic)

10. **"Everybody Wants to Rule the World"**
Tears for Fears
(Mercury/PG)

AOR TRACKS

1. **"Money for Nothing"**
Dire Straits
(Warner Bros.)

2. **"Fortress Around Your Heart"**
Sting
(A&M)

3. **"That Was Yesterday"**
Foreigner
(Atlantic)

4. **"Rock and Roll Girls"**
John Fogerty
(Warner Bros.)

5. **"Don't You (Forget About Me)"**
Simple Minds
(A&M)

6. **"Broken Wings"**
Mr. Mister
(RCA)

7. **"Everybody Wants to Rule the World"**
Tears for Fears
(Mercury/PG)

8. **"All She Wants to Do Is Dance"**
Don Henley
(Geffen)

9. **"Don't Lose My Number"**
Phil Collins
(Atlantic)

10. **"Small Town"**
John C. Mellencamp
(Riva/PG)

AOR ALBUMS

1. *Reckless*
Bryan Adams
(A&M)

2. *Brothers in Arms*
Dire Straits
(Warner Bros.)

3. *Songs From the Big Chair*
Tears for Fears
(Mercury/PG)

4. *No Jacket Required*
Phil Collins
(Atlantic)

5. *Building the Perfect Beast*
Don Henley
(Geffen)

6. *The Dream of the Blue Turtles*
Sting
(A&M)

7. *Born in the U.S.A.*
Bruce Springsteen
(Columbia)

8. *Centerfield*
John Fogerty
(Warner Bros.)

9. **Southern Accents**
Tom Petty and the
Heartbreakers
(MCA)

10. **Agent Provocateur**
Foreigner
(Atlantic)

URBAN

1. **"Part-Time Lover"**
Stevie Wonder
(Tamla/Motown)

2. **"Saving All My Love
for You"**
Whitney Houston
(Arista)

3. **"You Give Good Love"**
Whitney Houston
(Arista)

4. **"Freeway of Love"**
Aretha Franklin
(Arista)

5. **"Rock Me Tonight (For
Old Times' Sake)"**
Freddie Jackson
(Capitol)

6. **"You Are My Lady"**
Freddie Jackson
(Capitol)

7. **"Missing You"**
Diana Ross
(RCA)

8. **"Rhythm of the Night"**
DeBarge
(Gordy/Motown)

9. **"Who's Zoomin' Who"**
Aretha Franklin
(Arista)

10. **"Mr. Telephone Man"**
New Edition
(MCA)

COUNTRY

1. **"There's No Way"**
Alabama
(RCA)

2. **"Lost in the Fifties
Tonight"**
Ronnie Milsap
(RCA)

3. **"She Keeps the Home
Fires Burnin'"**
Ronnie Milsap
(RCA)

4. **"Love Is Alive"**
Judds
(RCA/Curb)

5. **"Dixie Road"**
Lee Greenwood
(MCA)

6. **"Real Love"**
Dolly Parton with
Kenny Rogers
(RCA)

7. **"Can't Keep a Good
Man Down"**
Alabama
(RCA)

8. **"Forty Hour Week (For
a Livin')"**
Alabama
(RCA)

9. **"I'll Never Stop Loving
You"**
Gary Morris
(Warner Bros.)

10. **"Forgiving You Was
Easy"**
Willie Nelson
(Columbia)

1986
AC

1. **"Your Wildest Dreams"**
Moody Blues
(Polydor/PG)

2. **"Glory of Love"**
Peter Cetera
(Full Moon/Warner
Bros.)

3. **"There'll Be Sad Songs
(To Make You Cry)"**
Billy Ocean
(Jive/Arista)

4. **"Stuck With You"**
Huey Lewis and the
News
(Chrysalis)

5. **"Words Get in
the Way"**
Miami Sound Machine
(Epic)

6. **"Sweet Love"**
Anita Baker
(Elektra)

7. **"No One Is to Blame"**
Howard Jones
(Elektra)

8. **"These Dreams"**
Heart
(Capitol)

9. **"Sara"**
Starship
(Grunt/RCA)

10. **"I'll Be Over You"**
Toto
(Columbia)

AOR TRACKS

1. **"In Your Eyes"**
Peter Gabriel
(Geffen)

2. **"Love Walks In"**
Van Halen
(Warner Bros.)

3. **"Throwing It All Away"**
Genesis
(Atlantic)

4. **"Rough Boy"**
ZZ Top
(Warner Bros.)

5. **"Land of Confusion"**
Genesis
(Atlantic)

6. **"Sledgehammer"**
Peter Gabriel
(Geffen)

7. **"One Hit (To the Body)"**
Rolling Stones
(Rolling Stones/
Columbia)

8. **"Dreams"**
Van Halen
(Warner Bros.)

9. **"Higher Love"**
Steve Winwood
(Island/Warner Bros.)

10. **"Stages"**
ZZ Top
(Warner Bros.)

AOR ALBUMS

1. **Afterburner**
ZZ Top
(Warner Bros.)

2. **5150**
Van Halen
(Warner Bros.)

3. **So**
Peter Gabriel
(Geffen)

4. **Scarecrow**
John Cougar
Mellencamp
(Riva/PG)

5. **Invisible Touch**
Genesis
(Atlantic)

6. **Like a Rock**
Bob Seger and the
Silver Bullet Band
(Capitol)

7. **Back in the High Life**
Steve Winwood
(Island/Warner Bros.)

8. **Listen Like Thieves**
INXS
(Atlantic)

9. **Tuff Enuff**
Fabulous Thunderbirds
(CBS Associated)

10. **Once Upon a Time**
Simple Minds
(Virgin/A&M)

URBAN

1. **"Kiss"**
Prince
(Warner Bros.)

2. **"On My Own"**
Patti Labelle/Michael
McDonald
(MCA)

3. **"What Have You Done
for Me Lately"**
Janet Jackson
(A&M)

4. **"I Can't Wait"**
Nu Shooz
(Atlantic)

5. **"Rumors"**
Timex Social Club
(Jay)

6. **"Do Me Baby"**
Meli'sa Morgan
(Capitol)

7. **"Word Up"**
Cameo
(Atl. Art/PG)

8. **"I've Learned to
Respect the Power
of Love"**
Stephanie Mills
(MCA)

9. **"There'll Be Sad Songs
(To Make You Cry)"**
Billy Ocean
(Jive/Arista)

10. **"The Finest"**
SOS Band
(Tabu/CBS)

COUNTRY

1. **"It'll Be Me"**
Exile
(Epic)

2. **"Happy Happy Birthday
Baby"**
Ronnie Milsap
(RCA)

3. **"In Love"**
Ronnie Milsap
(RCA)

4. **"Hearts Aren't Made to
Break"**
Lee Greenwood
(MCA)

5. **"Grandpa"**
Judds
(RCA/Curb)

6. **"Little Rock"**
Reba McEntire
(MCA)

7. **"We've Got a Good Fire
Goin'"**
Don Williams
(Capitol)

8. "Just Another Love"
Tanya Tucker
(Capitol)

9. "Everything That
Glitters"
Dan Seals
(EMI America)

10. "She and I"
Alabama
(RCA)

1987

AC

1. "Will You Still Love
Me?"
Chicago
(Warner Bros.)

2. "Mandolin Rain"
Bruce Hornsby and the
Range
(RCA)

3. "Can't We Try?"
Dan Hill
(Columbia)

4. "Just to See Her"
Smokey Robinson
(Motown)

5. "I Wanna Dance With
Somebody (Who Loves
Me)"
Whitney Houston
(Arista)

6. "Didn't We Almost
Have It All"
Whitney Houston
(Arista)

7. "Nothing's Gonna Stop
Us Now"
Starship
(Grunt/RCA)

8. "You Got It All"
Jets
(MCA)

9. "Ballerina Girl"
Lionel Richie
(Motown)

10. "Back in the High Life
Again"
Steve Winwood
(Island/Warner Bros.)

CHR/POP

1. "I Wanna Dance With
Somebody (Who Loves
Me)" Whitney Houston
(Arista)

2. "Livin' on a Prayer"
Bon Jovi
(Mercury/PolyGram)

3. "Alone"
Heart
(Capitol)

4. "With or Without You"
U2
(Island)

5. "Nothing's Gonna Stop
Us Now"
Starship
(Grunt/RCA)

6. "Shakedown"
Bob Seger
(MCA)

7. "Here I Go Again"
Whitesnake
(Geffen)

8. "Jacob's Ladder"
Huey Lewis and the
News
(Chrysalis)

9. "(I Just) Died in Your
Arms"
Cutting Crew
(Virgin)

10. "Open Your Heart"
Madonna
(Sire/Warner Bros.)

Bon Jovi

AOR TRACKS

1. "I Still Haven't Found
What I'm Looking For"
U2
(Island)

2. "Where the Streets
Have No Name"
U2
(Island)

3. "Here I Go Again"
Whitesnake
(Geffen)

4. "Who Will You Run To"
Heart
(Capitol)

5. "Midnight Blue"
Lou Gramm
(Atlantic)

6. "Seven Wonders"
Fleetwood Mac
(Warner Bros.)

7. "The One I Love"
R.E.M.
(IRS/MCA)

8. "Touch of Grey"
The Grateful Dead
(Arista)

9. "Don't Mean Nothing"
Richard Marx
(EMI-Manhattan)

10. "Livin' on a Prayer"
Bon Jovi
(Mercury/PolyGram)

AOR ALBUMS

1. *The Joshua Tree*
U2
(Island)

2. *Whitesnake*
Whitesnake
(Geffen)

3. *Slippery When Wet*
Bon Jovi
(Mercury PolyGram)

4. *Tango in the Night*
Fleetwood Mac
(Warner Bros.)

5. *Into the Fire*
Bryan Adams
(A&M)

6. *August*
Eric Clapton
(Duck/Warner Bros.)

7. *I'm No Angel*
Gregg Allman Band
(Epic)

8. *Ready or Not*
Lou Gramm
(Atlantic)

9. *Richard Marx*
Richard Marx
(EMI-Manhattan)

10. *Strong Persuader*
Robert Cray Band
(Mercury/PolyGram)

URBAN

1. "Always"
Atlantic Starr
(Warner Bros.)

2. "Looking for a New
Love"
Jody Watley
(MCA)

3. "Don't Disturb This
Groove"
System
(Atlantic)

4. "Show Me the Way"
Regina Belle
(Columbia)

5. "I Feel Good All Over"
Stephanie Mills
(MCA)

6. "Casanova"
Levert
(Atlantic)

7. "Diamonds"
Herb Alpert
(A&M)

8. "Just to See Her"
Smokey Robinson
(Motown)

9. "Have You Ever Loved
Somebody"
Freddie Jackson
(Capitol)

10. "Happy"
Surface
(Columbia)

COUNTRY

1. "Forever and Ever
Amen"
Randy Travis
(Warner Bros.)

2. "Rose in Paradise"
Waylon Jennings
(MCA)

3. "The Way We Make a
Broken Heart"
Rosanne Cash
(Columbia)

4. "Why Does It Have to
Be Wrong or Right"
Restless Heart
(RCA)

5. "Ocean Front Property"
George Strait
(MCA)

6. "It Takes a Little Rain"
Oak Ridge Boys
(MCA)

7. **"To Know Him Is to Love Him"**
Dolly Parton, Linda Ronstadt and Emmylou Harris
(Warner Bros.)

8. **"This Crazy Love"**
Oak Ridge Boys
(MCA)

9. **"Fishin' in the Dark"**
Nitty Gritty Dirt Band
(Warner Bros.)

10. **"Kids of the Baby Boom"**
Bellamy Brothers
(MCA/Curb)

1988

AC

1. **"I'll Always Love You"**
Taylor Dayne
(Arista)

2. **"I Don't Wanna Go on With You Like That"**
Elton John
(MCA)

3. **"Kokomo"**
Beach Boys
(Elektra)

4. **"Make It Real"**
Jets
(MCA)

5. **"Hands to Heaven"**
Breathe
(A&M)

6. **"Endless Summer Nights"**
Richard Marx
(EMI)

7. **"Don't You Know What the Night Can Do"**
Steve Winwood
(Virgin)

8. **"Anything for You"**
Gloria Estefan & Miami Sound Machine
(Epic)

9. **"Never Gonna Give You Up"**
Rick Astley
(RCA)

10. **"I Don't Wanna Live Without You"**
Chicago
(Full Moon/Reprise)

CHR/POP

1. **"Get Outta My Dreams Get Into My Car"**
Billy Ocean
(Jive/Arista)

2. **"Roll With It"**
Steve Winwood
(Virgin)

3. **"One More Try"**
George Michael
(Columbia)

4. **"Man in the Mirror"**
Michael Jackson
(Epic)

5. **"The Flame"**
Cheap Trick
(Epic)

6. **"Father Figure"**
George Michael
(Columbia)

7. **"Anything for You"**
Gloria Estefan & Miami Sound Machine
(Epic)

7. **"Could've Been"**
Tiffany
(MCA)

9. **"Never Gonna Give You Up"**
Rick Astley
(RCA)

9. **"Foolish Beat"**
Debbie Gibson
(Atlantic)

AOR TRACKS

1. **"Finish What Ya Started"**
Van Halen
(Warner Bros.)

2. **"Ship of Fools"**
Robert Plant
(Es Paranza/Atlantic)

3. **"Beds Are Burning"**
Midnight Oil
(Columbia)

4. **"Tall Cool One"**
Robert Plant
(Es Paranza/Atlantic)

5. **"Sweet Child O' Mine"**
Guns n' Roses
(Geffen)

6. **"When It's Love"**
Van Halen
(Warner Bros.)

7. **"Under the Milky Way"**
Church
(Arista)

8. **"Look Out Any Window"**
Bruce Hornsby & the Range
(RCA)

9. **"Devil Inside"**
INXS
(Atlantic)

10. **"I Wish I Had a Girl Like That"**
Henry Lee Summer
(CBS Associated)

AOR ALBUMS

1. **Kick**
INXS
(Atlantic)

2. **Now and Zen**
Robert Plant
(Es Paranza/Atlantic)

3. **OU812**
Van Halen
(Warner Bros.)

4. **Hysteria**
Def Leppard
(Mercury)

5. **Roll With It**
Steve Winwood
(Virgin)

6. **The Lonesome Jubilee**
John Cougar Mellencamp
(Mercury)

7. **Inside Information**
Foreigner
(Atlantic)

8. **Cloud Nine**
George Harrison
(Dark Horse)

9. **Diesel and Dust**
Midnight Oil
(Columbia)

10. **Scenes From the Southside**
Bruce Hornsby & the Range
(RCA)

URBAN

1. **"Nice 'N' Slow"**
Freddie Jackson
(Capitol)

2. **"Girlfriend"**
Pebbles
(MCA)

3. **"I Want Her"**
Keith Sweat
(Vintertainment/Elektra)

4. **"She's on the Left"**
Jeffrey Osborne
(A&M)

5. **"Giving You the Best That I Got"**
Anita Baker
(Elektra)

6. **"The Way You Love Me"**
Karyn White
(Warner Bros.)

7. **"Joy"**
Teddy Pendergrass
(Elektra)

7. **"Troop"**
Mamacita
(Atlantic)

9. **"Any Love"**
Luther Vandross
(Epic)

10. **"Wishing Well"**
Terence Trent D'Arby
(Columbia)

COUNTRY

1. **"Don't Close Your Eyes"**
Keith Whitley
(RCA)

2. **"If You Change Your Mind"**
Rosanne Cash
(Columbia)

3. **"Bluest Eyes in Texas"**
Restless Heart
(RCA)

4. **"New Shade of Blue"**
Southern Pacific
(Warner Bros.)

5. **"Fallin' Again"**
Alabama
(RCA)

6. **"Darlene"**
T. Graham Brown
(Capitol)

7. **"Strong Enough to Bend"**
Tanya Tucker
(Capitol)

8. **"Too Gone Too Long"**
Randy Travis
(Warner Bros.)

9. **"Baby Blue"**
George Strait
(MCA)

10. **"Joe Knows How to Live"**
Eddy Raven
(RCA)

1989

AC

1. **"Second Chance"**
.38 Special
(A&M)

2. **"Soul Provider"**
Michael Bolton
(Columbia)

3. **"The End of the Innocence"**
Don Henley
(Geffen)

Tom Petty

4. **"Right Here Waiting"**
Richard Marx
(EMI)

5. **"Living Years"**
Mike and the
Mechanics
(Atlantic)

6. **"Dreamin'"**
Vanessa Williams
(Wing/Polydor)

7. **"You Got It"**
Roy Orbison
(Virgin)

8. **"After All"**
Cher and Peter Cetera
(Geffen)

9. **"Wind Beneath My
Wings"**
Bette Midler
(Atlantic)

10. **"Miss You Like Crazy"**
Natalie Cole
(EMI)

CHR/POP

1. **"Miss You Much"**
Janet Jackson
(A&M)

2. **"Cold Hearted"**
Paula Abdul
(Virgin)

3. **"Forever Your Girl"**
Paula Abdul
(Virgin)

4. **"I'll Be Loving You
Forever"**
New Kids on the Block
(Columbia)

5. **"If You Don't Know Me
by Now"**
Simply Red
(Elektra)

6. **"Lost in Your Eyes"**
Debbie Gibson
(Atlantic)

7. **"Don't Wanna Lose
You"**
Gloria Estefan
(Epic)

8. **"Straight Up"**
Paula Abdul
(Virgin)

9. **"Listen to Your Heart"**
Roxette
(EMI)

10. **"Like a Prayer"**
Madonna
(Sire/Warner Bros.)

AOR TRACKS

1. **"Runnin' Down a
Dream"**
Tom Petty
(MCA)

2. **"Free Fallin'"**
Tom Petty
(MCA)

3. **"Patience"**
Guns n' Roses (Geffen)

4. **"Let the Day Begin"**
Call
(MCA)

5. **"I Will Not Go Quietly"**
Don Henley
(Geffen)

6. **"Crossfire"**
Stevie Ray Vaughan
and Double Trouble
(Epic)

7. **"Rock and a Hard
Place"**
Rolling Stones
(Columbia)

8. **"Once Bitten Twice
Shy"**
Great White
(Capitol)

9. **"Working on It"**
Chris Rea
(Geffen)

10. **"I'll Be You"**
Replacements
(Sire/Reprise)

AOR ALBUMS

1. *Full Moon Fever*
Tom Petty
(MCA)

2. *The End of the
Innocence*
Don Henley
(Geffen)

3. *Green*
R.E.M.
(Warner Bros.)

4. *Rattle & Hum*
U2
(Island)

5. *Traveling Wilburys*
Traveling Wilburys
(Wilbury/Warner Bros.)

6. *New Jersey*
Bon Jovi
(Mercury)

7. *Sonic Temple*
Cult
(Sire/Reprise)

8. *Dirty Rotten Filthy
Stinking Rich*
Warrant
(Columbia)

9. *In Step*
Stevie Ray Vaughan
and Double Trouble
(Epic)

10. *Twice Shy*
Great White
(Capitol)

URBAN

1. **"Baby Come to Me"**
Regina Belle
(Columbia)

2. **"Congratulations"**
Vesta
(A&M)

3. **"Something in the Way
(You Make Me Feel)"**
Stephanie Mills
(MCA)

4. **"Don't Take It
Personal"**
Jermaine Jackson
(Arista)

5. **"Miss You Much"**
Janet Jackson
(A&M)

6. **"Start of a Romance"**
Skyy
(Atlantic)

7. **"It's No Crime"**
Babyface
(Solar/Epic)

8. **"Real Love"**
Jody Watley
(MCA)

9. **"You Are My
Everything"**
Surface
(Columbia)

10. **"Love Saw It"**
Karyn White
(Warner Bros.)

COUNTRY

1. **"Better Man"**
Clint Black
(RCA)

2. **"Killin' Time"**
Clint Black
(RCA)

3. **"Above and Beyond"**
Rodney Crowell
(Columbia)

4. **"What's Going on in
Your World"**
George Strait
(MCA)

4. **"Living Proof"**
Ricky van Shelton
(Columbia)

6. **"I'm No Stranger to
the Rain"**
Keith Whitley
(RCA)

7. **"Cathy's Clown"**
Reba McEntire
(MCA)

8. **"Lovin' Only Me"**
Ricky Skaggs
(Epic)

9. **"Love Out Loud"**
Earl Thomas Conley
(RCA)

10. **"Let Me Tell You About
Love"**
Judds
(Curb/RCA)

1990

AC

1. **"Oh Girl"**
Paul Young
(Columbia)

2. **"I Don't Have the Heart"**
James Ingram
(Warner Bros.)

3. **"Release Me"**
   Wilson Phillips
   (SBK)

4. **"Club at the End of the Street"**
   Elton John
   (MCA)

5. **"Vision of Love"**
   Mariah Carey
   (Columbia)

6. **"Do You Remember"**
   Phil Collins
   (Atlantic)

7. **"Cuts Both Ways"**
   Gloria Estefan
   (Epic)

8. **"It Must Have Been Love"**
   Roxette
   (EMI)

9. **"Hold On"**
   Wilson Phillips
   (SBK)

10. **"Here We Are"**
    Gloria Estefan
    (Epic)

CHR/POP

1. **"Vision of Love"**
   Mariah Carey
   (Columbia)

2. **"Escapade"**
   Janet Jackson
   (A&M)

3. **"Hold On"**
   Wilson Phillips
   (SBK)

4. **"U Can't Touch This"**
   M.C. Hammer
   (Capitol)

5. **"It Must Have Been Love"**
   Roxette
   (EMI)

6. **"Vogue"**
   Madonna
   (Sire/Warner Bros.)

7. **"She Ain't Worth It"**
   Glenn Medeiros featuring Bobby Brown
   (Amherst/MCA)

8. **"Release Me"**
   Wilson Phillips
   (SBK)

9. **"Nothing Compares 2 U"**
   Sinead O'Connor
   (Chrysalis)

10. **"Love Will Lead You Back"**
    Taylor Dayne
    (Arista)

AOR TRACKS

1. **"What It Takes"**
   Aerosmith
   (Geffen)

2. **"Jealous Again"**
   Black Crowes
   (Def American/Geffen)

3. **"Cliffs of Dover"**
   Eric Johnson
   (Capitol)

4. **"Baby It's Tonight"**
   Jude Cole
   (Reprise)

5. **"Black Velvet"**
   Alannah Myles
   (Atlantic)

6. **"Coming of Age"**
   Damn Yankees
   (Warner Bros.)

7. **"The Other Side"**
   Aerosmith
   (Geffen)

8. **"Cradle of Love"**
   Billy Idol
   (Chrysalis)

9. **"Bad Love"**
   Eric Clapton
   (Reprise)

10. **"Holy Water"**
    Bad Company
    (Atco)

AOR ALBUMS

1. *Journeyman*
   Eric Clapton
   (Reprise)

2. *Pump*
   Aerosmith
   (Geffen)

3. *Damn Yankees*
   Damn Yankees
   (Warner Bros.)

4. *Shake Your Moneymaker*
   Black Crowes
   (Def American/Geffen)

5. *The End of the Innocence*
   Don Henley
   (Geffen)

6. *Holy Water*
   Bad Company
   (Atco)

7. *Brigade*
   Heart
   (Capitol)

8. *Manic Nirvana*
   Robert Plant
   (Es Paranza/Atlantic)

9. *Dr. Feelgood*
   Motley Crue
   (Elektra)

10. *Full Moon Fever*
    Tom Petty
    (MCA)

ALTERNATIVE

1. *Violator*
   Depeche Mode
   (Sire/Reprise)

2. *I Do Not Want What I Haven't Got*
   Sinead O'Connor
   (Chrysalis)

3. *Blue Sky Mining*
   Midnight Oil
   (Columbia)

4. *Deep*
   Peter Murphy
   (Beggars Banquet/RCA)

5. *Ritual de lo Habitual*
   Jane's Addiction
   (Warner Bros.)

6. *Brick by Brick*
   Iggy Pop
   (Virgin)

7. *Automatic*
   Jesus and Mary Chain
   (Warner Bros.)

8. *Bloodletting*
   Concrete Blonde
   (IRS)

9. *Some Friendly*
   Charlatans U.K.
   (Beggars Banquet/RCA)

10. *Goodbye Jumbo*
    World Party
    (Chrysalis)

URBAN

1. **"B.B.D. (I Thought It Was Me)?"**
   Bell Biv Devoe
   (MCA)

2. **"Giving You the Benefit of the Doubt"**
   Pebbles
   (MCA)

3. **"My Kinda Girl"**
   Babyface
   (Solar/Epic)

4. **"Lies"**
   En Vogue
   (Atlantic)

5. **"Feels Good"**
   Tony! Toni! Tone!
   (Wing/Polydor)

6. **"Ready or Not"**
   After 7
   (Virgin)

7. **"Under New Managment"**
   Miki Howard
   (Atlantic)

8. **"All Around the World"**
   Lisa Stansfield
   (Arista)

9. **"Crazy"**
   Boys
   (Motown)

10. **"Everything You Touch"**
    Smokey Robinson
    (Motown)

COUNTRY

1. **"The Dance"**
   Garth Brooks
   (Capitol)

2. **"Walkin' Away"**
   Clint Black
   (RCA)

3. **"Home"**
   Joe Diffie
   (Epic)

4. **"Here in the Real World"**
   Alan Jackson
   (Arista)

5. **"Not Counting You"**
   Garth Brooks
   (Capitol)

6. **"He Walked on Water"**
   Randy Travis
   (Warner Bros.)

7. **"Holdin' a Good Hand"**
   Lee Greenwood
   (Capitol)

8. **"Love Without End Amen"**
   George Strait
   (MCA)

9. **"Love on Arrival"**
   Dan Seals
   (Capitol)

10. **"When I Call Your Name"**
    Vince Gill
    (MCA)

1991

AC

1. **"(Everything I Do) I Do It For You"**
   Bryan Adams
   (A&M/Morgan Creek)

2. **"Coming Out of the Dark"**
   Gloria Estefan
   (Epic)

3. **"Cry for Help"**
   Rick Astley
   (RCA)

4. **"All the Man That I Need"**
   Whitney Houston
   (Arista)

Bryan Adams

5. **"Baby Baby"**
Amy Grant
(A&M)

6. **"Rush Rush"**
Paula Abdul
(Captive/Virgin)

7. **"You're in Love"**
Wilson Phillips
(SBK)

8. **"I Don't Wanna Cry"**
Mariah Carey
(Columbia)

9. **"Love Is a Wonderful Thing"**
Michael Bolton
(Columbia)

10. **"Can't Forget You"**
Gloria Estefan
(Epic)

CHR/POP

1. **"(Everything I Do) I Do It For You"**
Bryan Adams
(A&M/Morgan Creek)

2. **"Rush Rush"**
Paula Abdul
(Captive/Virgin)

3. **"Baby Baby"**
Amy Grant
(A&M)

4. **"Someday"**
Mariah Carey
(Columbia)

5. **"Romantic"**
Karyn White
(Warner Bros.)

6. **"Adore Mi Amor"**
Color Me Badd
(Giant/Reprise)

7. **"Don't Wanna Cry"**
Mariah Carey
(Columbia)

8. **"More Than Words"**
Extreme
(A&M)

9. **"Touch Me (All Night Long)"**
Cathy Dennis
(Polydor/PLG)

10. **"Every Heartbeat"**
Amy Grant
(A&M)

AOR TRACKS

1. **"Silent Lucidity"**
Queensryche
(EMI)

2. **"Wind of Change"**
Scorpions
(Mercury)

3. **"Hole Hearted"**
Extreme
(A&M)

4. **"Losing My Religion"**
R.E.M.
(Warner Bros.)

5. **"She Talks to Angels"**
Black Crowes
(Def American)

6. **"Runaround"**
Van Halen
(Warner Bros.)

7. **"Top of the World"**
Van Halen
(Warner Bros.)

8. **"Out in the Cold"**
Tom Petty and the Heartbreakers
(MCA)

9. **"Lift Me Up"**
Yes
(Arista)

10. **"Jet City Woman"**
Queensryche
(EMI)

AOR ALBUMS

1. *Empire*
Queensryche
(EMI)

2. *Crazy World*
Scorpions
(Mercury)

3. *Shake Your Moneymaker*
Black Crowes
(Def American)

4. *Out of Time*
R.E.M.
(Warner Bros.)

5. *Into the Great Wide Open*
Tom Petty and the Heartbreakers
(MCA)

6. *For Unlawful Carnal Knowledge*
Van Halen
(Warner Bros.)

7. *Extreme II Pornograffitti*
Extreme
(A&M)

8. *Holy Water*
Bad Company
(Atco)

9. *Ah Via Musicom*
Eric Johnson
(Capitol)

10. *Union*
Yes
(Arista)

ALTERNATIVE

1. *Out of Time*
R.E.M.
(Warner Bros.)

2. *Schubert Dip*
EMF
(EMI)

3. *Doubt*
Jesus Jones
(SBK)

4. *The Globe*
Big Audio Dynamite II
(Columbia)

5. *Electronic*
Electronic
(Warner Bros.)

6. *Superstition*
Siouxsie and the Banshees
(Geffen)

7. *Woodface*
Crowded House
(Capitol)

8. *World Outside*
Psychedelic Furs
(Columbia)

9. *La's*
La's
(Go!Discs/London/PLG)

10. *Perspex Island*
Robyn Hitchcock and the Egyptians
(A&M)

URBAN

1. **"Tender Kisses"**
Tracie Spencer
(Capitol)

2. **"Can You Stop the Rain"**
Peabo Bryson
(Columbia)

3. **"Written All Over Your Face"**
Rude Boys
(Atlantic)

4. **"Miracle"**
Whitney Houston
(Arista)

5. **"Men"**
Gladys Knight
(MCA)

6. **"Wrap My Body Tight"**
Johnny Gill
(Motown)

7. **"I Can't Wait Another Minute"**
Hi-Five
(Jive/RCA)

8. **"How Can I Ease the Pain"**
Lisa Fischer
(Elektra)

9. **"Do Me Again"**
Freddie Jackson
(Capitol)

10. **"Addictive Love"**
Bebe & Cece Winans
(Capitol)

COUNTRY

1. **"Small Town Saturday Night"**
Hal Ketchum
(Curb)

2. **"Fallin' Out of Love"**
Reba McEntire
(MCA)

3. **"We Both Walk"**
Lorrie Morgan
(RCA)

4. **"Mirror Mirror"**
Diamond Rio
(Arista)

5. **"I Am a Simple Man"**
Ricky Van Shelton
(Columbia)

6. **"Down to My Last Teardrop"**
Tanya Tucker
(Capitol)

7. **"Brand New Man"**
Brooks & Dunn
(Arista)

8. **"The Walk"**
Sawyer Brown
(Curb)

9. **"Meet in the Middle"**
Diamond Rio
(Arista)

10. **"Somewhere in My Broken Heart"**
Billy Dean
(SBK/Capitol)

1992

AC

1. **"The One"**
Elton John
(MCA)

2. **"Restless Heart"**
Peter Cetera
(Warner Bros.)

3. **"Save the Best for Last"**
Vanessa Williams
(Wing/Mercury)

4. **"Sometimes Love Just Ain't Enough"**
Patty Smyth with Don Henley
(MCA)

5. **"Hold on My Heart"**
Genesis
(Atlantic/AG)

6. **"Just Another Day"**
Jon Secada
(SBK/ERG)

7. **"If You Asked Me To"**
Celine Dion
(Epic)

8. **"Tears in Heaven"**
Eric Clapton
(Reprise)

9. **"Hazard (The River)"**
Richard Marx
(Capitol)

10. **"Constant Craving"**
k.d. lang
(Sire/Warner Bros.)

CHR/POP

1. **"End of the Road"**
Boyz II Men
(Motown)

2. **"Save the Best for Last"**
Vanessa Williams
(Wing/Mercury)

3. **"Sometimes Love Just Ain't Enough"**
Patty Smyth with Don Henley
(MCA)

4. **"I'll Be There"**
Mariah Carey
(Columbia)

5. **"Baby Baby Baby"**
TLC
(LaFace/Arista)

6. **"My Lovin'(You're Never Gonna Get It)"**
En Vogue
(EastWest/AG)

7. **"Under the Bridge"**
Red Hot Chili Peppers
(Warner Bros.)

8. **"Just Another Day"**
Jon Secada
(SBK/ERG)

9. **"If You Asked Me To"**
Celine Dion
(Epic)

10. **"Remember the Time"**
Michael Jackson
(Epic)

AOR TRACKS

1. **"Come As You Are"**
Nirvana
(DGC)

2. **"Even Flow"**
Pearl Jam
(Epic Associated)

3. **"Thorn in My Pride"**
Black Crowes
(Def American/Reprise)

4. **"Little Miss Can't Be Wrong"**
Spin Doctors
(Epic)

5. **"Mama I'm Coming Home"**
Ozzy Osbourne
(Epic Associated)

6. **"Under the Bridge"**
Red Hot Chili Peppers
(Warner Bros.)

7. **"Life Is a Highway"**
Tom Cochrane
(Capitol)

8. **"One"**
U2
(Island/PLG)

9. **"Living in a Dream"**
Arc Angels
(DGC)

10. **"What You Give"**
Tesla
(Geffen)

AOR ALBUMS

1. *Achtung Baby*
U2
(Island/PLG)

2. *The Southern Harmony and Musical Companion*
Black Crowes
(Def American/Reprise)

3. *Ten*
Pearl Jam
(Epic Associated)

4. *Whenever We Wanted*
John Mellencamp
(Mercury)

5. *No More Tears*
Ozzy Osbourne
(Epic Associated)

6. *Nevermind*
Nirvana
(DGC)

7. *Adrenalize*
Def Leppard
(Mercury)

8. *Psychotic Supper*
Tesla
(Geffen)

9. *Arc Angels*
Arc Angels
(DGC)

10. *We Can't Dance*
Genesis
(Atlantic/AG)

ALTERNATIVE

1. *Achtung Baby*
U2
(Island/PLG)

2. *Wish*
Cure
(Fiction/Elektra)

3. *Your Arsenal*
Morrissey
(Sire/Reprise)

4. *Welcome to Wherever You Are*
INXS
(Atlantic/AG)

5. *Good Stuff*
B-52's
(Reprise)

6. *Somewhere Between Heaven and Hell*
Social Distortion
(Epic)

7. *Between 10th and 11th*
Charlatans U.K.
(Beggars Bqt/RCA)

8. *Cracker*
Cracker
(Virgin)

MUSIC TIMELINE

c. 500 B.C.
Pythagoras describes musical intervals.

325
Constantine declares Christianity the official religion of the Roman Empire. The spread of Christianity in the western world spurred the development of European music.

600
Pope Gregory the Great codifies and collects the chant, which is used in Roman Catholic services and is named the Gregorian chant in his honor.

c. 850
Western music begins to move from monophony to polyphony with the vocal parts in church music moving in parallel intervals.

c. 1030
Guido of Arezzo, an Italian monk, develops a system for learning music by ear. Voice students often use the system, called solfège, to memorize their vocal exercises. In the 19th century, solfège developed into the tonic sol-fa system used today.

1163–1182
Master Léonin assembles the *Magnus Liber Organi*, the Great Book of Organum, which was written for Paris's Notre Dame Cathedral and

9. *Nevermind*
Nirvana
(DGC)

10. *Hotwired*
Soup Dragons
(Big Life/Mercury)

URBAN

1. "Somebody Loves You Baby"
Patti LaBelle
(MCA)

2. "Honey Love"
R. Kelly and Public Announcement
(Jive)

3. "Here I Go Again"
Glenn Jones
(Atlantic/AG)

4. "Love Me"
Tracie Spencer
(Capitol)

5. "Remember the Time"
Michael Jackson
(Epic)

6. "Sweet November"
Troop
(Atlantic/AG)

7. "Goodbye"
Tevin Campbell
(Qwest/Warner Bros.)

8. "Why Me Baby"
Keith Sweat with L. L. Cool J.
(Elektra)

9. "Games"
Chuckii Booker
(Atlantic/AG)

10. "Ain't Nobody Like You"
Miki Howard
(Giant/Reprise)

COUNTRY

1. "Norma Jean Riley"
Diamond Rio
(Arista)

2. "Ships That Don't Come In"
Joe Diffie
(Epic)

3. "Sacred Ground"
McBride and the Ride
(MCA)

4. "The Woman Before Me"
Trisha Yearwood
(MCA)

5. "Rock My Baby"
Shenandoah
(RCA)

6. "When It Comes to You"
John Anderson
(BNA Entertainment)

7. "Take Your Memory With You"
Vince Gill
(MCA)

8. "Neon Moon"
Brooks & Dunn
(Arista)

9. "Is There Life Out There"
Reba McEntire
(MCA)

10. "Dallas"
Alan Jackson
(Arista)

1993

AC

1. "Love Is"
Vanessa Williams and Brian McKnight
(Giant/Reprise)

2. "Tell Me What You Dream"
Restless Heart featuring Warren Hill
(RCA)

3. "Forever in Love"
Kenny G
(Arista)

4. "The River of Dreams"
Billy Joel
(Columbia)

5. "A Whole New World"
Peabo Bryson and Regina Belle
(Columbia)

6. "By the Time This Night Is Over"
Kenny G with Peabo Bryson
(Arista)

7. "Don't Take Away My Heaven"
Aaron Neville
(A&M)

8. "Reason to Believe"
Rod Stewart
(Warner Bros.)

9. "I'll Never Get Over You"
Expose
(Arista)

10. "Hopelessly"
Rick Astley
(RCA)

CHR

1. "Dreamlover"
Mariah Carey
(Columbia)

2. "That's the Way Love Goes"
Janet Jackson
(Virgin)

3. "Can't Help Falling in Love"
UB40
(Virgin)

4. "Weak"
SWV
(RCA)

5. "Looking Through Patient Eyes"
PM Dawn
(Gee St/Isl/PLG)

6. "Love Is"
Vanessa Williams and Brian McKnight
(Giant/Reprise)

7. "I Have Nothing"
Whitney Houston
(Arista)

8. "Two Princes"
Spin Doctors
(Epic)

9. "If I Had No Loot"
Tony Toni Tone
(Wing/Mercury)

10. "If"
Janet Jackson
(Virgin)

AOR TRACKS

1. "Plush"
Stone Temple Pilots
(Atlantic/AG)

2. "Got No Shame"
Brother Cane
(Virgin)

3. "Are You Gonna Go My Way"
Lenny Kravitz
(Virgin)

4. "Cryin'"
Aerosmith
(Geffen)

5. "No Rain"
Blind Melon
(Capitol)

6. "Peace Pipe"
Cry of Love
(Columbia)

7. "Hey Jealousy"
Gin Blossoms
(A&M)

8. "Two Princes"
Spin Doctors
(Epic)

9. "Runaway Train"
Soul Asylum
(Columbia)

10. "Black"
Pearl Jam
(Epic Associated)

---

contained music for the entire church year.

c. 1180

Troubadours appear in Germany and call themselves *minnesingers,* "singers about love."

1430

The Renaissance begins. This rebirth favors the simplistic virtues of Greek and Roman Classic styles, moves from polyphony to one harmonized melody and sees the increased importance and popularity of secular music. Josquin Desprez, often called the Prince of Music, is a leading composer of the Renaissance. He worked for ducal courts in Italy and France, at the Sistine Chapel and for kings Louis XI and Louis XII.

1562

In Pope Pius IV's Counter-Reformation, he restores church music to its pure vocal form by eliminating all instruments except the organ, any evidence of secularism, harmony and folk melody. Giovanni Da Palestrina satisfies the pope's rigid requirements and creates a new spiritual style that legend says "saved polyphony" when he writes *Pope Marcellus Mass,* his most famous and enchanting piece.

1565

Castration emerges as a way of preserving the sound of a woman's voice in Italian music. St. Paul's dictum prohibited women from singing on stage and in churches. The practice becomes commonplace by 1574.

Soul Asylum

AOR ALBUMS

1. *Grave Dancers Union*
   Soul Asylum
   (Columbia)

2. *Get a Grip*
   Aerosmith
   (Geffen)

3. *Core*
   Stone Temple Pilots
   (Atlantic/AG)

4. *Are You Gonna Go My Way*
   Lenny Kravitz
   (Virgin)

5. *Pocket Full of Kryptonite*
   Spin Doctors
   (Epic)

6. *Coverdale/Page*
   Coverdale/Page
   (Geffen)

7. *Automatic for the People*
   R.E.M.
   (Warner Bros.)

8. *Sister Sweetly*
   Big Head Todd and the Monsters
   (Giant/Reprise)

9. *Jackyl*
   Jackyl
   (Geffen)

10. *Brother Cane*
    Brother Cane
    (Virgin)

ALTERNATIVE

1. *Songs of Faith and Devotion*
   Depeche Mode
   (Sire/Reprise)

2. *Zooropa*
   U2
   (Island/PLG)

3. *Republic*
   New Order
   (Qwest/Warner Bros.)

4. *Earth and Sun and Moon*
   Midnight Oil
   (Columbia)

5. *Star*
   Belly
   (4AD/Sire/Reprise)

6. *Everybody Else Is Doing It So Why Can't We*
   The Cranberries
   (Island/PLG)

7. *Elemental*
   Tears for Fears
   (Mercury)

8. *Porno for Pyros*
   Porno for Pyros
   (Warner Bros.)

9. *Automatic for the People*
   R.E.M.
   (Warner Bros.)

10. *Ten Summoner's Tales*
    Sting
    (A&M)

URBAN

1. "So Alone"
   Men at Large
   (EastWest/AG)

2. "Something's Goin' On"
   U.N.V.
   (Maverick/Sire/Warner Bros.)

3. "Another Sad Love Song"
   Toni Braxton
   (LaFace/Arista)

4. "Girl U For Me"
   Silk
   (Elektra)

5. "Seems You're Much Too Busy"
   Vertical Hold
   (A&M)

6. "One Last Cry"
   Brian McKnight
   (Mercury)

7. "Something in Your Eyes"
   Bell Biv Devoe
   (MCA)

8. "Good Ol' Days"
   Levert
   (Atlantic/AG)

9. "Kiss of Life"
   Sade
   (Epic)

10. "One Woman"
    Jade
    (Giant/Reprise)

COUNTRY

1. "No Future in the Past"
   Vince Gill
   (MCA)

2. "Can't Break It To My Heart"
   Tracy Lawrence
   (Atl. Nash/AG)

3. "What's It To You"
   Clay Walker
   (Giant)

4. "Ain't That Lonely Yet"
   Dwight Yoakam
   (Reprise)

5. "That Was a River"
   Collin Raye
   (Epic)

6. "What Might Have Been"
   Little Texas
   (Warner Bros.)

7. "Blame It On Your Heart"
   Patty Loveless
   (Epic)

8. "Tonight I Climbed the Wall"
   Alan Jackson
   (Arista)

9. "In the Heart of a Woman"
   Billy Ray Cyrus
   (Mercury)

10. "Should've Been a Cowboy"
    Toby Keith
    (Mercury)

1994

AC

1. "Now and Forever"
   Richard Marx
   (Capitol)

2. "You Mean the World to Me"
   Toni Braxton
   (LaFace/Arista)

3. "Everyday"
   Phil Collins
   (Atlantic/AG)

4. "If You Go"
   Jon Secada
   (SBK/ERG)

5. "Can You Feel the Love Tonight"
   Elton John
   (Hollywood)

1588

The English Madrigal School is firmly established. The movement, led by Thomas Morley, produces some of the most delightful secular music ever heard. Madrigals often told stories of love or grief.

1590–1604

A group of musicians and intellectuals gather in Count Giovanni de Bardi's camerata (salon) and discuss and experiment with music drama. It is during this period that opera is born. Jacopo Peri's *Dafne*, the first Italian opera, is produced in 1598 and *Euridice* in 1600.

c. 1600

The Baroque period, characterized by strict musical forms and highly ornamental works, begins in Europe. This period signals the end of the Renaissance.

1607

Italian master composer Claudio Monteverdi writes the opera *Orfeo, Favola in Musica*, a work deemed to be a prime example of the early Baroque musical form.

1625

Francesca Caccini, who most historians say is the first female composer, finishes the opera-ballet *La Liberazione di Ruggiero*, which is performed at a reception for Wladyslaw IV of Poland.

6. **"The Power of Love"**
Celine Dion
(550 Music/Epic)

7. **"Beautiful in My Eyes"**
Joshua Kadison
(SBK/ERG)

8. **"Breathe Again"**
Toni Braxton
(LaFace/Arista)

9. **"I'll Remember"**
Madonna
(Maverick/Sire/Warner Bros.)

10. **"Without You"**
Mariah Carey
(Columbia)

CHR/POP

1. **"I'll Make Love to You"**
Boyz II Men
(Motown)

2. **"The Sign"**
Ace of Base
(Arista)

3. **"I Swear"**
All-4-One
(Blitzz/AG)

4. **"Don't Turn Around"**
Ace of Base
(Arista)

5. **"The Most Beautiful Girl in the World"**
Prince
(N.P.G./Bellmark)

6. **"Stay (I Missed You)"**
Lisa Loeb
(RCA)

7. **"Mr. Jones"**
Counting Crows
(DGC)

8. **"You Mean the World to Me"**
Toni Braxton
(LaFace/Arista)

9. **"Baby I Love Your Way"**
Big Mountain
(RCA)

10. **"When Can I See You"**
Babyface
(Epic)

ROCK TRACKS

1. **"Interstate Love Affair"**
Stone Temple Pilots
(Atlantic/AG)

2. **"Shine"**
Collective Soul
(Atlantic/AG)

3. **"Keep Talking"**
Pink Floyd
(Columbia)

4. **"Black Hole Sun"**
Soundgarden
(A&M)

5. **"No Excuses"**
Alice in Chains
(Columbia)

6. **"Vasoline"**
Stone Temple Pilots
(Atlantic/AG)

7. **"Backwater"**
Meat Puppets
(London/PLG)

8. **"Far Behind"**
Candlebox
(Maverick/Sire/Warner Bros.)

9. **"Big Empty"**
Stone Temple Pilots
(Atlantic/AG)

10. **"Dissident"**
Pearl Jam
(Epic Associated)

ALTERNATIVE

1. **"Selling the Drama"**
Live
(Radioactive/A&M)

2. **"Daughter"**
Pearl Jam
(Epic)

3. **"The More You Ignore Me the Closer I Get"**
Morrissey
(Sire/Reprise)

4. **"Fall Down"**
Toad the Wet Sprocket
(Columbia)

5. **"Basket Case"**
Green Day
(Reprise)

6. **"Mmm Mmm Mmm Mmm"**
Crash Test Dummies
(Arista)

7. **"Black Hole Sun"**
Soundgarden
(A&M)

8. **"Longview"**
Green Day
(Reprise)

9. **"What's the Frequency, Kenneth?"**
R.E.M.
(Warner Bros.)

10. **"Zombie"**
The Cranberries
(Island)

URBAN

1. **"I'll Make Love To You"**
Boyz II Men
(Motown)

2. **"Your Body's Callin'"**
R. Kelly
(Jive)

3. **"I Miss You"**
Aaron Hall
(Silas/MCA)

4. **"I'm Ready"**
Tevin Campbell
(Qwest/Warner Bros.)

5. **"You Mean the World to Me"**
Toni Braxton
(LaFace/Arista)

6. **"Always in My Heart"**
Tevin Campbell
(Qwest/Warner Bros.)

7. **"Any Time Any Place"**
Janet Jackson
(Virgin)

8. **"Back & Forth"**
Aaliyah
(BlackGround/Jive)

9. **"Sending My Love"**
Zhane'
(Illtown/Motown)

10. **"At Your Best (You Are Love)"**
Aaliyah
(BlackGround/Jive)

COUNTRY

1. **"I Swear"**
John Michael Montgomery
(Atl. Nash/AG)

2. **"Tryin' to Get Over You"**
Vince Gill
(MCA)

3. **"I'm Holding My Own"**
Lee Roy Parnell
(Arista)

4. **"Every Once in a While"**
Blackhawk
(Arista)

5. **"Foolish Pride"**
Travis Tritt
(Warner Bros.)

6. **"I Can't Reach Her Anymore"**
Sammy Kershaw
(Mercury)

7. **"Little Rock"**
Collin Raye
(Epic)

8. **"He Thinks He'll Keep Her"**
Mary Chapin Carpenter
(Columbia)

9. **"Your Love Amazes Me"**
John Berry
(Liberty)

10. **"Wink"**
Neal McCoy
(Atlantic/AG)

1631
Professional female singers appear for the first time on the English stage in the production of *Chloridia*, a court masque produced by Ben Jonson and Inigo Jones.

1637
The world's first public opera house, The Teatro San Cassiano, opens in Venice.

1639
The first comic opera, *Chi Soffre Speri* by Virgilio Mazzocchi and Marco Marazzoli, premieres in Rome.

1656
Henry Lawes and Matthew Locke add music to William Davenant's libretto *The Siege of Rhodes*, which is performed at the Rutland House in London. Davenant helps make the opera-masque a form of public entertainment.

1666
The first signed Stradivarius violins emerge from Antonio Stradivari's workshop in Cremona, Italy.

1675
Matthew Locke composes *Psyche*, the first surviving English opera.

1685
Johann Sebastian Bach and George Frederick Handel are born. They become principle classical composers of the Baroque period. Bach,

The Recording Industry Association of America's Top-Selling Certified Albums of All Time

The RIAA certifies recordings that sell 500,000 or more copies as gold, those selling 1,000,000 or more as platinum and those selling 2,000,000 or more as multi-platinum.

24 MILLION

Thriller
Michael Jackson (Epic)

22 MILLION

Eagles — Their Greatest Hits 1971–1975
Eagles (Elektra)

17 MILLION

Rumours
Fleetwood Mac (Warner Bros.)

16 MILLION

Led Zeppelin IV
Led Zeppelin (Swan Song)

15 MILLION

Born in the U.S.A.
Bruce Springsteen (Columbia)

Boston
Boston (Epic)

The Bodyguard Soundtrack
Whitney Houston (Arista)

14 MILLION

Hotel California
Eagles (Elektra)

13 MILLION

Appetite for Destruction
Guns 'N Roses (Geffen)

Greatest Hits
Elton John (Rockett)

No Fences
Garth Brooks (Liberty)

The Dark Side of the Moon
Pink Floyd (Capitol)

12 MILLION

Back in Black
AC/DC (Atco)

Bat Out of Hell
Meat Loaf (Epic)

Bruce Springsteen & E Street Band Live 1975–'85 (Box set)
Bruce Springsteen (Columbia)

Cracked Rear View
Hootie & the Blowfish (Atlantic)

Slippery When Wet
Bon Jovi (Mercury)

Whitney Houston
Whitney Houston (Arista)

11 MILLION

Dirty Dancing
Soundtrack (RCA)

Hysteria
Def Leppard (Mercury)

II
Boyz II Men (Motown)

Purple Rain Soundtrack
Prince and the Revolution (Warner Bros.)

Ropin' the Wind
Garth Brooks (Liberty)

Saturday Night Fever Soundtrack
Bee Gees (RSO)

10 MILLION

Breathless
Kenny G (Arista)

Can't Slow Down
Lionel Richie (Motown)

Michael Jackson

Greatest Hits
Elton John (MCA)

Live Shit: Binge and Purge (Video box set)
Metallica (Warnervision Entertainment)

Please Hammer Don't Hurt 'Em
M. C. Hammer (Capitol)

Tapestry
Carole King (Ode)

The Joshua Tree
U2 (Island)

The Lion King
Soundtrack (Walt Disney)

The Wall
Pink Floyd (Columbia)

---

who fathers 20 children, explores musical forms associated with the church and Handel works as a dramatic composer.

1689

Henry Purcell's *Dido and Aeneas* opens in London.

1703

Vivaldi becomes violin master at Venice's La Pieta orphanage. He writes more then 400 concertos for La Pieta in his 35-year service there.

1705

Reinhard Keiser uses French horns for the first time in opera in his production of *Octavia*.

1725

Vivaldi writes *The Four Seasons*.

1733

The comic opera, *La Serva Padrona*, from Battista Pergolesi's serious opera *Il Prigionier Superbo*, wows Europe with its humorous story and enchanting music.

1735

Handel produces his last great operatic success, *Alcina*, which features dancer Marie Salle.

1742

Handel's *Messiah* premieres in Dublin to an enthusiastic audience.

1750

Bach dies. The end of the Baroque period is often seen in conjunction with his death. The highly ornate style of the Baroque period gives

9 MILLION

Abbey Road
The Beatles (Capitol)

CooleyHighHarmony
Boyz II Men (Motown)

Escape
Journey (Columbia)

Faith
George Michael (Columbia)

Hi Infidelity
R.E.O. Speedwagon (Epic)

Like a Virgin
Madonna (Sire)

Music Box
Mariah Carey (Columbia)

Pyromania
Def Leppard (Mercury)

Ten
Pearl Jam (Epic)

The Stranger
Billy Joel (Columbia)

Whitney
Whitney Houston (Arista)

8 MILLION

Aerosmith's Greatest Hits
Aerosmith (Columbia)

Bad
Michael Jackson (Epic)

CrazySexyCool
TLC (Laface)

Dookie
Green Day (Reprise)

Footloose
Soundtrack (Columbia)

Grease Soundtrack
Olivia Newton-John and John Travolta (RSO)

Greatest Hits
Journey (Columbia)

Greatest Hits Vol. I and II
Billy Joel (Columbia)

Hangin' Tough
New Kids on the Block (Columbia)

Mariah Carey

Mariah Carey
Mariah Carey (Columbia)

Metallica
Metallica (Elektra)

Sergeant Pepper's Lonely Hearts Club Band
The Beatles (Capitol)

Some Gave All
Billy Ray Cyrus (Mercury)

The Hits
Garth Brooks (Capitol Nashville)

The Sign
Ace of Base (Arista)

Time, Love and Tenderness
Michael Bolton (Columbia)

Van Halen
Van Halen (Warner Bros.)

Whitesnake
Whitesnake (Geffen)

7 MILLION

1984
Van Halen (Warner Bros.)

52nd Street
Billy Joel (Columbia)

Achtung Baby
U2 (Island)

An Innocent Man
Billy Joel (Columbia)

Best of the Doobies
Doobie Brothers (Warner Bros.)

Brothers in Arms
Dire Straits (Warner Bros.)

Deja Vu
Crosby, Stills, Nash and Young (Atlantic)

Don't Be Cruel
Bobby Brown (MCA)

Eagles Greatest Hits Vol. II
Eagles (Elektra)

Eliminator
ZZ Top (Warner Bros.)

Forever Your Girl
Paula Abdul (Virgin)

Get a Grip
Aerosmith (Geffen)

Glass Houses
Billy Joel (Columbia)

James Taylor's Greatest Hits
James Taylor (Warner Bros.)

Nevermind
Nirvana (DGC)

No Jacket Required
Phil Collins (Atlantic)

Off the Wall
Michael Jackson (Epic)

Pump
Aerosmith (Geffen)

Sports
Lewis, Huey and the News (Chrysalis)

The Beatles
The Beatles (Capitol)

The Lion King
Soundtrack (Disneyland)

Time Pieces/Best of Eric Clapton
Eric Clapton (Polydor)

To the Extreme
Vanilla Ice (SBK)

Toni Braxton
Toni Braxton (Arista)

Top Gun
Soundtrack (Columbia)

---

rise to the more simple, clarified styles of the Classical period, which sees the emergence of symphonies and string quartets.

1761

Franz Joseph Haydn becomes Vice-Kapellmeister to the Esterhazy family and Kapellmeister in 1766. Though living virtually as a slave to the family, he had at his disposal an impressive orchestra. During his 30-year service to the family, he completes 108 symphonies, 68 string quartets,

47 piano sonatas, 26 operas, 4 oratorios and hundreds of smaller pieces.

1762

Christoph Willibald von Glück sets out to reform opera with his *Orfeo ed Euridice*. He wants to restore opera to what the original composers intended it to be — an art form marked by high drama, few recitatives and orchestral set-pieces.

1786

Mozart's *The Marriage of Figaro* premieres in Vienna.

1787

Mozart's *Don Giovanni* debuts in Prague.

1797

Franz Peter Schubert is born in Vienna. Though many musicians make Vienna their home, Schubert is the only one to be born there.

1803

Beethoven produces his third symphony, *Eróica*. This piece marks the beginning of the Romantic period, in

True Blue
Madonna (Sire)

Unplugged
Eric Clapton (Reprise)

6 MILLION

4
Foreigner (Atlantic)

A Lot About Livin' (And a Little 'Bout Love)
Alan Jackson (Arista)

August and Everything After
Counting Crows (Geffen)

Business as Usual
Men at Work (Columbia)

Dangerous
Michael Jackson (Epic)

Daydream
Mariah Carey (Columbia)

Don't Look Back
Boston (Epic)

Frampton Comes Alive!
Peter Frampton (A&M)

Garth Brooks
Garth Brooks (Liberty)

Girl You Know It's True
Milli Vanilli (Arista)

Goodbye Yellow Brick Road
Elton John (Rockett)

Greatest Hits
Patsy Cline (MCA)

Greatest Hits 1974–1978
Steve Miller Band (Capitol)

Hell Freezes Over
Eagles (Geffen)

HIStory: Past, Present and Future Book I
(Box set)
Michael Jackson (Epic)

Houses of the Holy
Led Zeppelin (Swan Song)

Janet
Janet Jackson (Virgin)

Led Zeppelin II
Led Zeppelin (Swan Song)

Make It Big
Wham! (Columbia)

Metal Health
Quiet Riot (Epic)

New Jersey
Bon Jovi (Mercury)

No Fences
Garth Brooks (Capitol)

Rhythm Nation 1814
Janet Jackson (A&M)

Ropin' the Wind
Garth Brooks (Capitol)

Simon and Garfunkel's Greatest Hits
Simon and Garfunkel (Columbia)

So Far
Crosby, Stills, Nash and Young (Atlantic)

Soul Provider
Michael Bolton (Columbia)

The Cars
The Cars (Elektra)

The Chase
Garth Brooks (Liberty)

The Immaculate Collection
Madonna (Sire)

Throwing Copper
Live (Radioactive)

Toys in the Attic
Aerosmith (Columbia)

Use Your Illusion I
Guns 'n Roses (Geffen)

Use Your Illusion II
Guns 'n Roses (Geffen)

Vs.
Pearl Jam (Epic)

5 MILLION

5150
Van Halen (Warner Bros.)

A Fresh Aire Christmas
Mannheim Steamroller (American Gramaphone)

Air Supply Greatest Hits
Air Supply (Arista)

Back in Black
AC/DC (Atlantic)

Bad Company
Bad Company (Swan Song)

Bat Out of Hell II: Back Into Hell
Meat Loaf (MCA)

Brand New Man
Brooks & Dunn (Arista)

Bridge Over Troubled Water
Simon and Garfunkel (Columbia)

Chicago 17
Chicago (Warner Bros.)

Chicago IX — Chicago's Greatest Hits
Chicago (Columbia)

Control
Janet Jackson (A&M)

Double Vision
Foreigner (Atlantic)

Duotones
Kenny G (Arista)

Elvis' Golden Records, Vol. I
Elvis Presley (RCA)

Flashdance
Soundtrack (Casablanca)

Fleetwood Mac
Fleetwood Mac (Reprise)

Forrest Gump
Soundtrack (Epic)

Elvis Presley

---

which the formality of the Classical period is replaced by subjectivity.

1807

Beethoven completes his *Symphony No. 5,* which many consider to be the most popular classical work ever written.

1810

Robert Schumann is born in Germany.

c. 1815

A new invention, the valve, makes all brass instruments chromatic. Prior to this, the instruments were limited to the harmonic series.

Schubert writes "Der Erlkönig," his first public success and most famous song.

1816

Gioacchino Rossini's *The Barber of Seville,* based on Pierre Beaumarchais's play, debuts in Rome. His *Otello* opens in Naples.

1818

Beethoven's hearing has deteriorated so badly that he no longer can hear the piano and must communicate with conversation books.

1821

Carl Maria von Weber's *Der Freischutz* debuts in Berlin, and he becomes the master of German opera.

Frontiers
Journey (Columbia)

G 'n R Lies
Guns 'n Roses (Geffen)

Gonna Make You Sweat
C&C Music Factory (Columbia)

Goodbye Yellow Brick Road
Elton John (MCA)

Graceland
Paul Simon (Warner Bros.)

Greatest Hits
Linda Ronstadt (Asylum)

Greatest Hits Vol. II
Barbra Streisand (Columbia)

Guilty
Barbra Streisand (Columbia)

Heart
Heart (Capitol)

In Pieces
Garth Brooks (Liberty)

In Through the Out Door
Led Zeppelin (Swan Song)

Invisible Touch
Genesis (Atlantic)

Jagged Little Pill
Alanis Morissette (Maverick)

Legend
Bob Marley and The Wailers (Island)

Licensed to Ill
Beastie Boys (Columbia)

Luck of the Draw
Bonnie Raitt (Capitol)

Magical Mystery Tour
The Beatles (Capitol)

Mannheim Steamroller Christmas
Mannheim Steamroller (American Gramaphone)

Meet The Beatles!
The Beatles (Capitol)

Miracles
Kenny G (Arista)

More of The Monkees
The Monkees (Rhino)

Night Moves
Bob Seger and the Silver Bullet Band (Capitol)

No Need to Argue
The Cranberries (Island)

Open Up and Say ... Ahh
Poison (Capitol)

Permanent Vacation
Aerosmith (Geffen)

Pocket Full of Kryptonite
Spin Doctors (Epic)

Private Dancer
Tina Turner (Capitol)

Pure Country
George Strait (MCA)

Rapture
Anita Baker (Elektra)

Rattle and Hum
U2 (Island)

Reckless
Bryan Adams (A&M)

Shake Your Money Maker
The Black Crowes (American)

She's So Unusual
Cyndi Lauper (Epic)

Silk Degrees
Boz Scaggs (Columbia)

Skid Row
Skid Row (Atlantic)

Smash
Offspring (Epitaph)

Songs From the Big Chair
Tears for Fears (Mercury)

Stranger in Town
Bob Seger and the Silver Bullet Band (Capitol)

The Beatles 1962–1966
The Beatles (Capitol)

The Beatles 1967–1970
The Beatles (Capitol)

The End of the Innocence
Don Henley (Geffen)

The Hits
Garth Brooks (Liberty)

Bob Marley

The Jazz Singer Soundtrack
Neil Diamond (Capitol)

The Monkees
The Monkees (Rhino)

Tuesday Night Music Club
Sheryl Crow (A&M)

Unforgettable
Natalie Cole (Elektra)

Very Necessary
Salt 'n Pepa (London)

Vitalogy
Pearl Jam (Epic)

Wilson Phillips
Wilson Phillips (SBK)

Wish You Were Here
Pink Floyd (Columbia)

Yes I Am
Melissa Etheridge (Island)

1826

Mendelssohn writes the overture to *A Midsummer Night's Dream,* which debuts in Stettin in 1827.

1832

Schumann's career as a pianist is over as one of his fingers becomes paralyzed.

1839

The New York Philharmonic is established.

1841

Adolphe Sax invents the saxophone.

1851

Verdi's *Rigoletto* debuts in Venice.

1853

Steinway is founded in New York.

Richard Wagner publishes the librettos to *Der Ring des Nibelungen (The Ring Cycle): Das Rheingold, Die Walküre, Seigfried* and *Die Götterdämerung. The Ring Cycle* is

considered one of the most ambitious musical projects ever undertaken by a single person.

1854

Liszt conducts the first performance of his symphonic poems in Weimar. The symphonic poem is an orchestral work, often in one movement, and is usually based on a literary idea. Liszt is credited with creating the genre. His symphonic poems include *Orpheus, Les Preludes* and *Mazeppa.*

Blues Foundation Hall of Fame

The Blues Foundation, established in 1980 in Memphis, Tennessee, promotes and preserves blues music. The Blues Hall of Fame, also founded in 1980, recognizes artists and individuals for their "contribution and perpetuation of the blues." Here are the inductees.

HALL OF FAME HONOR ROLL

Bill "Hoss" Allen
Chuck Berry
Blind Blake
Bobby "Blue" Bland
Big Bill Broonzy
Roy Brown
Leroy Carr
Ray Charles
Clifton Chenier
Albert Collins
Arthur "Big Boy" Crudup
Willie Dixon
Champion Jack Dupree
Sleepy John Estes
Lowell Fulson
Buddy Guy

Chuck Berry

Slim Harpo
Wynonie Harris
John Lee Hooker
Lightnin' Hopkins
Big Walter Horton
Son House
Howlin' Wolf
J.B. Hutto
Elmore James
Skip James
Blind Lemon Jefferson
Lonnie Johnson
Robert Johnson
Tommy Johnson
Louis Jordan
Albert King

B.B. King
Freddie King
Leadbelly
Robert Jr. Lockwood
Alan Lomax
John Lomax
Little Milton
Little Walter
Magic Sam
Percy Mayfield
Fred McDowell
Jay McShann
Blind Willie McTell
Memphis Minnie
Memphis Slim
Mississippi John Hurt
Muddy Waters
Robert Nighthawk

Howlin' Wolf

Ma Rainey

c. 1860

The slave trade introduces West African rhythms, work songs, chants and spirituals to America, which strongly influence blues and jazz.

Gustav Mahler is born in Bohemia.

1871

Verdi's *Aïda* premieres in Cairo.

1874

Verdi's *Requiem,* his most respected work, premieres in Milan.

Wagner finishes the score for *The Ring Cycle.*

1876

Tchaikovsky completes *Swan Lake*. It opens in 1877 at Moscow's Bolshoi Theatre.

Wagner's *The Ring Cycle* is performed in full at the Bayreuth Festival. The opera house was built to accomodate Wagner's works.

Johannes Brahms completes his *First Symphony.* Twenty years in the making, the symphony received mixed reviews but would become one of the most popular ever written.

1877

Thomas Edison invents sound recording.

Camille Saint-Saëns' *Samson et Dalila* debuts in Weimar.

1878

Thomas Edison patents the phonograph.

Bessie Smith

Muddy Waters

Gene Nobles
Charley Patton
Professor Longhair
Ma Rainey
Jimmy Reed
John "R" Richbourg
Otis Rush
Johnny Shines
Bessie Smith
Otis Spann
Tampa Red
Eddie Taylor
Hound Dog Taylor
Sonny Terry
Big Momma Thornton
Big Joe Turner
T-Bone Walker
Bukka White
Big Joe Williams
Sonny Boy Williamson #1
   (John Lee Williamson)
Sonny Boy Williamson #2
   (Rice Miller)
Johnny Minter

CLASSICS OF BLUES LITERATURE

Blues and Gospel Records 1902–1942, J. Godrich and R.M.W. Dixon

Blues Unlimited (magazine)

Chicago Breakdown (Chicago Blues), Mike Rowe

Living Blues (magazine)

Country Blues, Sam Charters

Nothing but the Blues, Lawrence Cohn

Blues Records 1943–1966, Mike Leadbetter and Neil Slaven

Blues Who's Who, Sheldon Harris

Deep Blues, Robert Palmer

Conversation With the Blues, Paul Oliver

The Story of the Blues, Paul Oliver

Feel Like Going Home, Peter Guralnick

Big Bill Blues, Big Bill Broonzy and Yannick Bruynoghe

Big Road Blues, Dr. David Evans

I Am the Blues, Willie Dixon and Don Snowden

Urban Blues, Charles Keil

CLASSICS OF BLUES RECORDINGS (SINGLES/ALBUM TRACKS)

"Worried Life Blues," Big Maceo

"The Things That I Used to Do," Guitar Slim

"Boogie Chillun," John Lee Hooker

"Dust My Broom," Elmore James

"Hell Hound on My Trail," Robert Johnson

"Help Me," Sonny Boy Williamson #2

"The Sky Crying," Elmore James

"Reconsider Baby," Lowell Fulson

"Big Road Blues," Tommy Johnson

"Juke," Little Walter

"Got My Mojo Working," Muddy Waters

"I'm Your Hoochie Coochie Man," Muddy Waters

"Call It Stormy Monday," T-Bone Walker

"Smokestack Lightning," Howlin' Wolf

"Rocket 88," Jackie Brenson

"Crossroad Blues," Robert Johnson

"Sweet Home Chicago," Robert Johnson

1880
John Paine's symphony, *In Spring,* debuts in Cambridge, Massachusetts. It is the first American symphony published in the United States.

Tchaikovsky writes the *1812 Overture,* commemorating Russia's defeat of Napoleon.

1881
The Boston Symphony Orchestra is established.

1882
The Berlin Philharmonic is established.

1883
The Metropolitan Opera House opens in New York.

1885
Gilbert and Sullivan finish *The Mikado,* which premieres in London.

1888
Strauss writes the symphonic poem, *Don Juan,* which brings him international fame.

1890
Tchaikovsky's *The Sleeping Beauty* debuts in St. Petersburg.

1891
Carnegie Hall opens in New York.

1893
Dvorak composes his best and most popular work, *From the New World.*

"The Thrill Is Gone," B.B. King

"Please Send Me Someone to Love," Percy Mayfield

"I'm Ready," Muddy Waters

"Mannish Boy," Muddy Waters

"Nine Below Zero," Sonny Boy Williamson #2

"Long Distance Call," Muddy Waters

"Come on in My Kitchen," Robert Johnson

"Driftin' Blues," Charles Brown

"Big Boss Man," Jimmy Reed

"Good Morning Little School Girl," John Lee "Sonny Boy" Williamson and Big Joe Williams

"Terraplane Blues," Robert Johnson

"The Killing Floor," Howlin' Wolf

"Baby Please Don't Go," Big Joe Williams

"Statesboro Blues," Blind Willie McTell

"I Can't Quit You Baby," Otis Rush

Jimmy Reed

CLASSICS OF BLUES RECORDINGS (ALBUMS)

The Best of Bobby "Blue" Bland, Bobby "Blue" Bland (Duke)

Ice Pickin', Albert Collins (Alligator)

A.K.A. Howlin' Wolf, Howlin' Wolf (Chess)

Born Under a Bad Sign/Livewire Blues Power, Albert King (Stax)

Hideaway, Freddie King (King)

Live at the Regal, B.B. King (ABC)

I Am the Blues, Willie Dixon (Columbia)

Blues Before Sunrise, Leroy Carr (Columbia)

King of the Delta Blues Singers, vols. I and II, Robert Johnson (Columbia)

Bass Blues Harmonica, Little Walter (Chess)

West Side Soul, Magic Sam (Delmark)

Hoodoo Man Blues, Junior Wells (Delmark)

Founder of the Delta Blues, Charley Patton (Yazoo)

The Best of Muddy Waters and McKinley Morganfield/A.K.A. Muddy Waters, Muddy Waters (Chess)

Chicago Bound, Jimmy Rogers

Showdown, Albert Collins, Robert Cray and Johnny Copeland (Alligator)

Live on Maxwell Street 1964, Robert Nighthawk (Rounder)

Right Place, Wrong Time, Otis Rush (Hightone)

The World's Greatest Blues Singer, Bessie Smith (Columbia)

Black Magic, Magic Sam (Delmark)

The Chess Box, Willie Dixon (MCA)

The Complete 1931 Session, Skip James (Yazoo)

The Muddy Waters Box, Muddy Waters (MCA/Chess)

T-Bone Walker

The Best of Little Walter, Little Walter (MCA/Chess)

Chicago, The Blues Today, various artists (Vanguard)

Robert Johnson, The Complete Recordings, Robert Johnson (Columbia)

Blues From the Gutter, Champion Jack Dupree (Atlantic)

Father of Folk Blues, Son House (Columbia)

Parchman Farm, Bukka White (Columbia)

The Complete T-Bone Walker 1940–1954, T-Bone Walker (Cobra)

1896

Ragtime, a combination of West Indian rhythm and European musical form, is born.

1900

Jean Sibelius's *Finlandia* premieres in Helsinki.

1901

Mahler's *Fourth Symphony,* his most popular, debuts in Munich.

1902

Debussy's *Pelleas et Melisande* debuts in Paris and brings him international fame.

1904

The London Symphony Orchestra is established.

1908

A major change in classical-music style comes about with the release of Arnold Schoenberg's *Book of Hanging Gardens.* The harmony and tonality characteristic of classical music are replaced by dissonance, creating what many listeners consider to be noise.

1910

Igor Stravinsky completes *The Firebird* for Sergei Diaghilev's Ballets Russes. Stravinsky will become one of the greatest composers of the 20th century.

1911

Strauss's *Der Rosenkavalier* premieres in Dresden.

The Rock and Roll Hall of Fame

The Rock and Roll Hall of Fame honors musicians and music-industry figures who have contributed to the energy and evolution of rock music. To be eligible for inclusion, musicians and bands must have released a record at least 25 years prior to the year of induction. A committee of 29 music historians and critics nominates 15 contenders, and a group of 600 music-industry figures makes the final cut.

Bob Dylan

The Beatles

1986
Chuck Berry
James Brown
Ray Charles
Sam Cooke
Fats Domino
The Everly Brothers
Buddy Holly
Jerry Lee Lewis
Elvis Presley
Little Richard

Nonperformers
Alan Freed
Sam Phillips

Early Influences
Robert Johnson
Jimmie Rodgers
Jimmy Yancey

Lifetime Achievement
John Hammond

1987
The Coasters
Eddie Cochran
Bo Diddley
Aretha Franklin
Marvin Gaye
Bill Haley
B.B. King
Clyde McPhatter
Ricky Nelson
Roy Orbison
Carl Perkins
Smokey Robinson
Joe Turner
Muddy Waters
Jackie Wilson

Nonperformers
Leonard Chess
Ahmet Ertegun
Jerry Leiber and Mike Stoller
Jerry Wexler

Early Influences
Louis Jordan
T-Bone Walker
Hank Williams

1988
Beach Boys
The Beatles
The Drifters
Bob Dylan
The Supremes

Nonperformer
Berry Gordy, Jr.

Early Influences
Woody Guthrie
Leadbelly
Les Paul

1989
Dion
Otis Redding
The Rolling Stones
The Temptations
Stevie Wonder

1916
Charles Ives finishes his *Fourth Symphony,* his defining piece.

1919
After moving from its southern rural roots, jazz establishes Chicago as its capital. The city will become home to such jazz greats as trumpeter Louis Armstrong and pianist Jelly Roll Morton.

1923
"Queen of the Blues" Bessie Smith records her first song, "Down Hearted Blues," which becomes an immediate success.

1924
The Juilliard School opens in New York.

Maurice Ravel's *Bolero* opens in Paris.

George Gershwin's *Rhapsody in Blue* premieres in New York.

1925
Alban Berg's *Wozzeck* opens in Berlin.

1932
Jazz composer Duke Ellington writes "It Don't Mean a Thing, If It Ain't Got That Swing," a song that presaged the swing era of the 1930s and 1940s.

1933
Laurens Hammond introduces his Hammond organ.

Nonperformer
Phil Spector

Early Influences
The Ink Spots
Bessie Smith
The Soul Stirrers

1990

Hank Ballard
Bobby Darin
The Four Seasons
The Four Tops
The Kinks
The Platters
Simon and Garfunkel
The Who

Nonperformers
Gerry Goffin and Carole King
Brian Holland, Eddie Holland and
    Lamont Dozier

Early Influences
Louis Armstrong
Charlie Christian
Ma Rainey

Jimi Hendrix

1991

LaVern Baker
The Byrds
John Lee Hooker
The Impressions
Wilson Pickett
Jimmy Reed
Ike and Tina Turner

Nonperformers
Dave Bartholomew
Ralph Bass

Early Influence
Howlin' Wolf

Lifetime Achievement
Nesuhi Ertegun

1992

Bobby "Blue" Bland
Booker T. and the MG's
Johnny Cash
Jimi Hendrix Experience
The Isley Brothers
Sam and Dave
The Yardbirds

Nonperformers
Leo Fender
Bill Graham
Doc Pomus

Early Influences
Elmore James
Professor Longhair

1993

Ruth Brown
Cream
Creedence Clearwater Revival
The Doors
Etta James
Frankie Lymon and the Teenagers
Van Morrison
Sly and the Family Stone

Nonperformers
Dick Clark
Milt Gabler

Early Influence
Dinah Washington

Janis Joplin

1994

The Animals
The Band
Duane Eddy
The Grateful Dead
Elton John
John Lennon
Bob Marley
Rod Stewart

Nonperformer
Johnny Otis

Early Influence
Willie Dixon

1995

The Allman Brothers Band
Al Green
Janis Joplin
Led Zeppelin
Martha and the Vandellas
Neil Young
Frank Zappa

Nonperformer
Paul Ackerman

Early Influence
The Orioles

1936
Electric guitars debut.

1937
Bela Bartok's masterpiece, *Music for Strings, Percussion and Celesta*, premieres in Basel.

1938
Roy Acuff joins the Grand Ole Opry and brings national recognition to the Nashville-based radio program.

1945
Benjamin Britten's *Peter Grimes* premieres in London, which signals the rebirth of British opera.

1948
Columbia Records introduces the 33 1/3 LP ("long playing") record at New York's Waldorf-Astoria Hotel. It allows listeners to enjoy an unprecedented 25 minutes of music per side, compared to the four minutes per side of the standard 78 rpm record.

1951
In an effort to introduce rhythm and blues to a broader white audience, which was hesitant to embrace "black music," disc jockey Alan Freed uses the term rock 'n' roll to describe R&B.

Elliott Carter composes his *String Quartet No. 1* and becomes a leading avant-garde composer of the 20th century.

The Country Music Hall of Fame

The Country Music Hall of Fame, founded in 1961 by the Country Music Association, is located on Nashville's Music Row. Inductees are selected annually by an anonymous panel of 200 electors, each of whom has been an active participant in the music business for at least 15 years and has made a major contribution to the industry.

1961
Jimmie Rodgers
Fred Rose
Hank Williams

1962
Roy Acuff

1963
Elections were held but no candidate received enough votes to qualify for induction.

1964
Tex Ritter

1965
Ernest Tubb

1966
Eddy Arnold
James R. Denny
George D. Hay
Uncle Dave Macon

1967
Red Foley
J.L. Frank
Jim Reeves
Stephen H. Sholes

1968
Bob Wills

1969
Gene Autry

1970
Original Carter Family
Bill Monroe

1971
Arthur Edward Satherley

1972
Jimmie H. Davis

1973
Chet Atkins
Patsy Cline

1974
Owen Bradley
Frank "Pee Wee" King

1975
Minnie Pearl

1976
Paul Cohen
Kitty Wells

1977
Merle Travis

1978
Grandpa Jones

1979
Hubert Long
Hank Snow

1980
Connie B. Gay
Johnny Cash
Original Sons of the Pioneers

1981
Vernon Dalhart
Grant Turner

1982
Lefty Frizzell
Ray Horton
Marty Robbins

Merle Haggard

1983
Little Jimmy Dickens

1984
Ralph Sylvester Peer
Floyd Tillman

1985
Lester Flatt and Earl Scruggs

1986
Whitey Ford
Wesley H. Rose

1987
Rod Brasfield

1988
Loretta Lynn
Roy Rogers

1989
Jack Stapp
Cliffie Stone
Hank Thompson

1990
Tennessee Ernie Ford

1991
Boudleaux and Felice Bryant

1992
George Jones
Frances Williams Preston

1993
Willie Nelson

1994
Merle Haggard

1954
Bill Haley and the Comets begin writing hit songs. As a white band using black-derived forms, they venture into rock 'n' roll.

Pierre Boulez completes *Le Marteau Sans Maître (The Hammer Without a Master)*.

1956
With many hit singles (including "Heartbreak Hotel"), Elvis Presley emerges as one of the world's first rock stars. The gyrating rocker

enjoys fame on the stages of the Milton Berle, Steve Allen and Ed Sullivan shows, as well as in the first of his many movies, *Love Me Tender*.

1957
Leonard Bernstein completes *West Side Story*.

1959
The National Academy of Recording Arts and Sciences sponsors the first Grammy Award ceremony for music recorded in 1958.

1960
John Coltrane forms his own quartet and becomes the voice of jazz's New Wave movement.

1961
Patsy Cline releases "I Fall to Pieces" and "Crazy." The success of the songs help her cross over from country to pop.

1963
A wave of Beatlemania hits the U.K. The Beatles, a British band com-

Major Record Labels

A & M Records
1416 N. LaBrea Ave.
Hollywood, CA 90028
(213) 469-2411

American Recordings
3500 W. Olive Ave.
Suite 1550
Burbank, CA 91505
(818) 973-4545

Angel/Virgin Classics
810 Seventh Ave.
New York, NY 10019
(212) 603-8600

Arista Records
6 W. 57th St.
New York, NY 10019
(212) 489-7400

Atlantic Records
75 Rockefeller Plaza
New York, NY 10019
(212) 275-2000

Blue Note
1290 Sixth Ave.
New York, NY 10104
(212) 492-1200

BMG/RCA Records
1540 Broadway, 9th Floor
New York, NY 10036
(212) 930-4000

Capitol Records
1750 N. Vine St.
Hollywood, CA 90028
(213) 462-6252

Chrysalis Records
1290 Ave. of the Americas
New York, NY 10104
(212) 492-1200

Columbia Records
550 Madison Ave.
New York, NY 10022
(212) 833-8000

East/West Records
75 Rockefeller Plaza
New York, NY 10019
(212) 275-2500

Elektra Entertainment
75 Rockefeller Plaza
New York, NY 10019
(212) 275-4000

EMI Records
1290 Sixth Ave.
New York, NY 10104
(212) 492-1200

Epic Records
550 Madison Ave.
New York, NY 10022
(212) 833-7442

Geffen Record Co. (DGC)
9130 Sunset Blvd.
Los Angeles, CA 90069
(310) 278-9010

Gramophone Records
P.O. Box 910
Beverly Hills, CA 90213
(213) 276-2726

Interscope Records
10900 Wilshire Blvd.
Suite 1230
Los Angeles, CA 90024
(310) 208-6547

**Island Records
(Polygram Label)**
825 Eighth Ave.
New York, NY 10019
(212) 333-8000

Mammoth Records
101 B St.
Carrboro, NC 27510
(919) 932-1882

Matador Records
676 Broadway
New York, NY 10012
(212) 995-5882

Maverick Music Co.
8000 Beverly Blvd.
Los Angeles, CA 90048
(213) 852-1177

MCA Records
70 Universal City Plaza
Universal City, CA 91608
(818) 777-4000

Mercury Records
825 Eighth Ave.
New York, NY 10019
(212) 333-8000

Motown Record Co.
5750 Wilshire Blvd.
Suite 300
Los Angeles, CA 90036
(213) 634-3500

Nonesuch Records
590 Fifth Ave., 16th Floor
New York, NY 10036
(212) 575-6720

Polygram Label Group
825 Eighth Ave.
New York, NY 10019
(212) 333-8000

Reprise Records
3300 Warner Blvd.
Burbank, CA 91510
(818) 846-9090

Revolution Records
8900 Wilshire Blvd.
Beverly Hills, CA 90211
(310) 289-5500

Rhino Entertainment Co.
10635 Santa Monica Blvd.
2nd Floor
Los Angeles, CA 90025
(310) 474-4778

Rounder Records
1 Camp St.
Cambridge, MA 02140
(617) 354-0700

Rykodisc
Shetland Posk
27 Congress St.
Salem, MA 01970
(508) 744-7678

Sire Records
75 Rockefeller Plaza
New York, NY 10019
(212) 275-4220

Verve Records
825 Eighth Ave.
New York, NY 10019
(212) 333-8000

Virgin Records
338 N. Foothill Road
Beverly Hills, CA 90210
(310) 278-1181

Warner Bros. Records
3300 Warner Blvd.
Burbank, CA 91505
(818) 846-9090

Windham Hill
75 Willow Road
Menlo Park, CA 94025
(415) 329-0647

---

posed of John Lennon, George Harrison, Ringo Starr and Paul McCartney, take Britain by storm.

The Rolling Stones emerge as the anti-Beatles, with an aggressive, blues-derived style.

1964

Folk musician Bob Dylan becomes increasingly popular during this time of social protest with songs expressing objection to the condition of American society. Psychedelic bands such as The Grateful Dead

and Jefferson Airplane also enjoy great success with songs celebrating the counterculture of the '60s.

1967

The Beatles release their breakthrough concept album, *Sergeant Pepper's Lonely Hearts Club Band*.

1969

In August, more than half a million people gather in the small, upstate New York town of Woodstock for four days of rain, sex, drugs and rock 'n' roll. Performers include Janis

Joplin, Jimi Hendrix, The Who, Joan Baez, Crosby, Stills, Nash and Young, Jefferson Airplane and Sly and the Family Stone.

A Rolling Stones fan is killed at the group's Altamont, California, concert by members of Hell's Angels.

1973

The Jamaican film *The Harder They Come*, starring Jimmy Cliff, launches the popularity of reggae music in the United States.

Music Magazines and Journals

The Acoustic Guitar
String Letter Press
Box 767
San Anselmo, CA 94979-0767
(415) 485-6946

Alternative Press
6516 Detroit Ave., Suite 5
Cleveland, OH 44102
(216) 631-1212

The American Organist
American Guild of Organists
475 Riverside Drive, #1260
New York, NY 10115-0122
(212) 870-2310

Bass Player
Miller Freeman Publications
600 Harrison St.
San Francisco, CA 94107
(415) 905-2200

Billboard
Billboard Publications, Inc.
1515 Broadway, 14th Floor
New York, NY 10036-8986
(212) 764-7300

Bluegrass Unlimited
P.O. Box 111
Broad Run, VA 22014-0111
(540) 349-8181

Blues Access
1455 Chestnut Place
Boulder, CO 80304-3153
(303) 443-7245

**Buddy, The Original Texas Music
Magazine**
Buddy, Inc.
501 N. Good Latimer Expressway
Dallas, TX 75204-5899
(214) 484-9010

CD Review
Connell Communications, Inc.
86 Elm St.
Peterborough, NH 03458
(603) 924-7271

CMJ New Music Report
College Media Inc.
11 Middle Neck Road, Suite 400
Great Neck, NY 11021
(516) 466-6000

Cadence: The Review of Jazz and Blues
Cadence Building
Redwood, NY 13679
(315) 287-2852

Computer Music Journal
MIT Press
55 Hayward St.
Cambridge, MA 02142
(617) 253-2889

Country America
Meredith Corp.
1716 Locust St.
Des Moines, IA 50309
(515) 284-3790

Down Beat
102 N. Haven
Elmhurst, IL 60126
(708) 941-2030

Electronic Musician (Polyphony)
6400 Hollis St., #12
Emeryville, CA 94608
(510) 653-3307

Entertainment Weekly
1675 Broadway
New York, NY 10019
(212) 522-5600

Ethnomusicology
Society for Ethnomusicology
Morrison Hall 005
Bloomington, IN 47405-2501
(812) 855-6672

Fanfare
P. O. Box 720
Tenafly, NY 07670
(201) 567-3908

Goldmine
Krause Publications, Inc.
700 E. State St.
Iola, WI 54990-0001
(715) 445-2214

Guitar Player
Miller Freeman Publication
600 Harrison St.
San Francisco, CA 94107
(415) 905-2200

Guitar for the Practicing Musician
Cherry Lane Music Co.
10 Midland Ave.
Port Chester, NY 10573
(914) 935-5200

1974

Patti Smith releases what is considered to be the first punk rock single, "Hey Joe." Punk roars out of Britain during the late-'70s, with bands such as the Sex Pistols and the Clash expressing nihilistic and anarchistic views in response to a lack of opportunity in Britain, boredom and antipathy for the bland music of the day.

1976

Philip Glass completes *Einstein on the Beach,* the first widely known example of minimalist composition.

1977

Saturday Night Fever sparks the disco inferno.

1979

The Sugar Hill Gang releases the first commercial rap hit, "Rapper's Delight," bringing rap off the New York streets and into the popular

music scene. Rap originated in the mid 1970s as rhyme spoken over an instrumental track provided by snatches of music from records. Over the decades, rap becomes one of the most important commercial and artistic branches of pop music.

1981

MTV goes on the air running around the clock music videos, debuting with "Video Killed the Radio Star."

Guitar World
Harris Publications, Inc.
1115 Broadway, 8th Floor
New York, NY 10010
(212) 807-7100

Hot Wire: Journal of Women's Music & Culture
Empty Closet Enterprises
5210 N. Wayne
Chicago, IL 60640-2223
(312) 769-9009

Jazz Times (Radio Free Jazz)
7961 Eastern Ave., Suite 303
Silver Spring, MD 20910
(301) 588-4114

Jazziz Magazine
Mylore Entertainment
3620 N.W. 43rd St.
Gainesville, FL 32606
(352) 375-3705

Keyboard (Contemporary Keyboard)
Miller Freeman, Inc.
1515 Broadway
New York, NY 10036
(408) 446-1105

Living Blues
Southern Culture Publications
301 Hill Hall
University, MS 38677
(601) 232-5742

Mix, The Recording Industry Magazine
6400 Hollis St., #12
Emeryville, CA 94608-1028
(510) 653-3307

Modern Drummer
12 Old Bridge Road
Cedar Grove, NJ 07009
(201) 239-4140

Music City News
50 Music Square W., #601
Nashville, TN 37203
(615) 329-2200

Musician
Billboard Publications, Inc.
1515 Broadway
New York, NY 10036
(800) 347-6969

New Schwann Record and Tape Guide
Schwann Publications
440 Cerrillos Road, Suite C
Santa Fe, NM 87501-2644
(505) 988-2045

Option: Music Alternatives
1522 B Clover Field Blvd.
Santa Monica, CA 90404
(310) 449-0120

Pollstar
4697 W. Jacqueline Ave.
Fresno, CA 93722-6413
(209) 271-7900

Pulse! Magazine
2500 Del Monte St.
Building C
West Sacramento, CA 95691-3820
(916) 373-2450

Raygun
2812 Santa Monica Blvd., Suite 204
Santa Monica, CA 90404
(310) 828-0522

Relix
P.O. Box 94
Brooklyn, NY 11229
(718) 258-0009

Rolling Stone
1290 Ave. of the Americas
New York, NY 10104
(212) 484-1616

Schwann "Opus"
Schwann Publications
440 Cerrillos Road, Suite C
Santa Fe, NM 87501-2644
(505) 988-2045

Schwann "Spectrum"
Schwann Publications
440 Cerrillos Road, Suite C
Santa Fe, NM 87501-2644
(505) 988-2045

Sing Out! The Folk Song Magazine
P.O. Box 5253
Bethlehem, PA 18015-0253
(610) 865-5366

The Source
594 Broadway, Suite 510
New York, NY 10012
(212) 274-0464

Spin Magazine
6 W. 18th St.
New York, NY 10011
(212) 633-8200

Stereo Review Compact Disc Buyers Guide
Hachette Filipacchi Magazines, Inc.
1633 Broadway, 42nd Floor
New York, NY 10019
(212) 767-6000

Vibe
205 Lexington Ave.
3rd Floor
New York, NY 10016
(212) 522-7092

THE DEAD Weir, Lesh and Hart Talk About Life After Garcia

LIVE

SMASHING PUMPKINS (ALBUM)
R.E.M. (BAND) FOO FIGHTERS (NEW BAND)

WINNERS

PJ HARVEY, ELASTICA,
COOLIO, WHITE ZOMBIE

1982
Michael Jackson releases *Thriller,* which sells more than 24 million copies, becoming the biggest-selling album in history.

1983
With the introduction of noise-free compact discs, the vinyl record begins a steep decline.

1987
Though African, Latin American and other genres of international music have been around for centuries, a group of small, London-based labels coin the term "world music," which helps record sellers find rack space for the eclectic music.

1991
Seattle band Nirvana releases the song "Smells Like Teen Spirit" on the LP *Nevermind* and enjoys national success. With Nirvana's hit comes the grunge movement, which is characterized by distorted guitars, dispirited vocals and lots of flannel.

1992
Compact discs surpass cassette tapes as the preferred medium for recorded music.

1996
Janet Jackson becomes the highest paid musician in history when she signs an $80-million deal with Virgin Records.

Popular Music Glossary

acid rock Rock music with a repetitive beat and lyrics that suggest psychedelic experiences.

alternative Guitar-based rock with desultory male vocalists or chirpy female vocalists. It grew in response to the last gasp of dinosaur bands from the 1970s and from the commercial success of bands such as Nirvana and Pearl Jam. Also known as **modern rock**.

bluegrass An early form of country music that combines the gospel-tinged vocals of the Blue Ridge Mountain region with folk melodies. Instrumentation generally includes guitars, banjos, mandolins and fiddles.

blues A style of music that evolved from southern African-American secular songs and is usually characterized by slow tempo and flatted thirds and sevenths. Blues influenced the development of rock, rhythm and blues and country music.

boogie-woogie A style of jazz piano characterized by a repeated rhythmic and melodic pattern in the bass and a series of improvised variations in the treble.

bop A style of jazz characterized by rhythmic and harmonic complexity, improvised solo performances and a virtuoso execution.

Calypso A type of music that originated in the West Indies and is characterized by humorous, improvised lyrics often on topical subjects.

doo-wop A style of music popularized in the 1950s with words and nonsense syllables sung in harmony by small groups.

folk music 1. Music that originates among the common people of a nation or region and is spread about or passed down orally. It is characterized by simple melodies. **2.** Contemporary music based on traditional folk that often contains political or satirical lyrics.

funk A type of popular music combining elements of jazz, blues and soul and characterized by syncopated rhythm and a heavy, repetitive bass line.

gangsta rap A form of rap music characterized by violent, often degrading lyrics.

grunge The label applied to a rock form featuring distorted guitars, whining vocals and flannel-shirt-wearing band members. Popularized by and associated primarily with Seattle bands such as Nirvana and Alice in Chains.

heavy metal A ponderous rock form characterized by brittle, flashy guitar work, unnaturally high-pitched male vocals and an adolescent fascination with the darker side of human experience. Born in the late 1960s of bands such as Deep Purple and Black Sabbath, heavy metal is currently associated with bands such as Metallica and Soundgarden. Also called **metal** and **speed metal**.

hip-hop The cultural context of rap music found in the urban style of dress, speech and art.

jazz American music born in the early part of the century from African rhythms and slave chants. It has spread from its African-American roots to a worldwide audience. Jazz developed from early ensemble improvisation to big band swing to the soloing brilliance of bop to thorny atonality and back to the current rearticulation of melody and harmony.

New Age Modern music characterized by quiet improvisation on the acoustic piano, guitar and synthesizer and a dreamy, relaxing sound.

new wave An emotionally detached style of rock music characterized by a synthesized sound and a repetitive beat.

punk A rock form characterized by aggressive volume, short, angry vocals and often bitter political or hopeless emotional content. It was born as a reaction to the bland, corporate rock of the 1970s. Early exponents of punk include Sex Pistols, The Clash, Ramones and Buzzcocks. Punk's recent revival is attributed to the dominance of sound-alike "alternative" bands.

raga A traditional form in Hindu music, consisting of a theme that expresses an aspect of religious feeling and sets forth a tonal system on which variations are improvised within a framework of progressions, melodic formulas and rhythmic patterns.

ragtime A style of jazz with elaborately syncopated rhythm in the melody and a steadily accented accompaniment.

rap Urban, typically African-American music that features spoken lyrics, often reflecting current social or political issues, over a background of sampled sounds or scratched records.

reggae Popular music of Jamaican origin having elements of Calypso, soul and rock and characterized by a strongly accentuated offbeat.

rhythm and blues The all-encompassing term used to describe the African-American wellspring of postwar popular music. From rhythm and blues has come rock, soul, funk, rap and regional and stylistic offshoots. Critics consider rhythm and blues's birth to coincide with the decline of big bands and jazz's turn toward the bop emphasis on soloing. Rhythm and blues retained an emphasis on vocals while adding a more pronounced beat characteristic of the blues.

rock Perhaps the most popular form of 20th-century music, a combination of African-American rhythms, urban blues, folk and country music of the rural South. It has developed since the early 1950s into hundreds of subgenres, each with its own audience, record labels and radio formats.

salsa A popular form of Latin-American dance music, characterized by Afro-Caribbean rhythms, Cuban big-band dance melodies and elements of jazz and rock.

ska A brisk form of Jamaican-born rock derived from reggae and rock energy. It was popularized in the early 1980s by British "black-and-white" multiracial bands that formed a lighter faction of the punk movement.

soca A West-Indian style of music that is a blend of soul and Calypso.

soul The name for a type of rhythm and blues built on elements of gospel and spiritual music. Often, practitioners such as Sam Cooke maintained two careers simultaneously in soul and popular music.

zydeco Music of Louisiana's bayous that blends Cajun rhythms with rhythm and blues. Instrumentation includes washboards and accordions, though more generally, electric instruments.

BROAD-CASTING

Empty Season

■ BY LEWIS GROSSBERGER

Media Person,
aka Lewis
Grossberger,
writes a weekly
column for
MediaWeek
magazine and is
the author of
*Read My Clips:
Media Person
Cuts Up.*

F MEDIA PERSON HAD BEEN A NETWORK TELEVISION EXECUTIVE IN 1995-1996 (and thank God he wasn't), at some point the terrifying thought would have crossed his mind: What if we throw a season and no one comes?

The potential was there. Whatever magic that conjures up hit series seemed to have abandoned the big-four networks. Perhaps the viewers became confused and dismayed by the sheer number of new shows (42!) introduced in the fall of '95 and the frantic shuffling of old shows in the network lineups. Or perhaps viewers just thought the new stuff stank.

Either way, they continued tiptoeing off to cable, exacerbating a trend that has been giving network moguls ulcers for some time. Basic cable's overall audience rose 16 percent. And when summer came around, viewers were fleeing the network reruns like panicked extras in *Independence Day*.

TELEVISION

Of the new network offerings, the only major hit in all of prime time was *3rd Rock From the Sun,* a silly comedy about a team of eccentric space aliens who land in Ohio disguised as humans in order to study the human race, though why the species merits any serious scientific attention Media Person has no idea.

Naturally, *3rd Rock* appeared on NBC, the only network that lately has seemed able to do anything right. (Even better for NBC, the show's success embarrassed one of its rivals, ABC, which had had the first shot at *3rd Rock* and passed it up.) NBC's established hits such as *ER, Seinfeld* and *Friends* kept rolling greenly along, and, on top of that, the General-Electric-owned network also televised the lucrative Summer Olympics and signed a $2.3-billion contract to go on televising them until 2008. It also made a deal with Bill Gates's Microsoft software empire to collaborate on a new venture that combines a new 24-hour news channel with an interactive on-line computer news service, which launched in July 1996.

3rd Rock From the Sun

Bill Gates and NBC executives announce the launch of MSNBC

Ted Turner

It would not be, however, the only new news channel. Suddenly, every media mogul in the land seemed to want one of his very own. You'd think that television watchers were clamoring for all news, all the time. For years, the other network owners had been casting covetous glances at Ted Turner with his pioneering Cable News Network. Now, out of the blue, big deals were being cooked up and reporters were being yanked into press conferences left and right. Rupert Murdoch, mighty megamogul of all media, proclaimed a 24-hour Fox news network. Roone Arledge announced an all-news network at ABC. Last but loudest came the joint NBC-Microsoft trumpet blast heralding their trendy new partnership, MSNBC. The announcement was made in appropriate high-tech fashion with an international electronic press conference featuring NBC executives in New York, NBC anchor Tom Brokaw from Germany and Microsoft's Gates from Hong Kong, where he was busy buying Asia or something.

And that wasn't all the news news, either. ESPN announced an all-sports news channel and Turner announced a new business news channel to compete with NBC's CNBC and, teaming up with *Sports Illustrated*, a new sports news channel to compete with ESPN. Even amidst all the alphabetic thrills, critics were asking sticky questions. Who would watch all this endless news? Were there really enough viewers to go around? (Indeed, a new survey found that viewership of the three network nightly newscasts was significantly down, and, among viewers under 30, it had dropped more than a third in the last year.) And with cable-system operators already out of channel space, where on the TV dial would these new networks fit?

It wasn't long before the competition began thinning out a bit. ABC waved the white flag, announcing that its grandiose news channel was being "indefinitely postponed." The network blamed Rupert Murdoch, darn him, for driving up the cost of news by offering to pay cable operators a fee of up to $10 per subscriber to carry his new channel.

Meanwhile, the players still in the game were going on the offensive. Ted Turner let it be known that CNN's 10-year-old policy of nurturing homegrown talent was over; he wouldn't be averse to stealing away news stars such as NBC's Brokaw. Instead, CBS went after one of his stars, crack foreign correspondent Christiane Amanpour. A Solomon-like compromise was worked out whereby Amanpour was split in two, with CNN having to share her with CBS's *60 Minutes*.

For the most part, CBS had an exceedingly miserable year. It disgorged the season's most spectacular flop, *Central Park West*, which had been hyped as an entertaining prime-time soap taking advantage of a sophisticated New York City setting. Instead, it was a screaming embarrassment. CBS quickly yanked the turkey but later revamped it, making it an older show with the addition of Raquel Welch and Gerald McRaney, and sneaked it back onto the screen in the summer disguised as a brand new show under the title *CPW*.

Central Park West

CBS's only bright spot was the comeback of its old classic, *60 Minutes*. Facing brisk competition from *Dateline NBC*, crusty producer Mike Hewitt actually started making changes in his 28-year-old show, which, after decades of glory, had been sliding in the ratings. Morale at *60 Minutes* had not been helped when tremulous network big shots pulled an interview with a former tobacco executive for fear of incurring a lawsuit, a move denounced on the show by an extremely peeved Mike Wallace. Hewitt ordered his minions to work harder and closer to deadline, covering more breaking news. Another Hewitt maneuver, adding three sharp voices from the print world, Molly Ivins, Stanley Crouch and P.J. O'Rourke, to do commentary, flopped and was summarily deleted. But the other changes seemed to revitalize the show and viewers noticed. Its ratings shot back toward the top again.

Mike Wallace

Sometimes an entire genre can flop. It happened in daytime television and the cries of "Good riddance!" could be heard echoing from all over the country. Sleazoid confessionals, also known as talk shows, had dominated daytime for years but finally reached a point where every possible combination of perversion and stupidity had been aired. Ratings of all but a few plunged and mass cancellations followed. Trash pioneer Geraldo Rivera killed his own show, *Geraldo*, admitting that he himself was "sick of the garbage that is on."

Even the white-haired father of the genre called it a career. Presaging the whole "interactive" computer craze, Phil Donahue had invented the give-the-audience-a-voice format, alternating earnest town-hall-style political debates with let-your-hair-down-and-cry personal dramas. "Talk shows are the last platform of the powerless," said Donahue, loyally defending his beleaguered calling as he bowed out after 29 years of nonstop blab.

With near-perfect timing, the brash and personable comedian and actress Rosie O'Donnell chose this season to debut *Rosie*, a new kind of talk show that actually was an old kind but seemed fresh and fragrant compared to the swamp of misery that daytime had become. On one level it was just an updating of the easy-going, afternoon variety formats once run by affable schmoozers such as Merv Griffin and Mike Douglas. But O'Donnell brought to the mix a confident urban wit and a sharp eye for deflating stale show-biz conventions as well as a happy, earthy knack for connecting with the TV audience. She was so at home from the outset it seemed as though she had been born at a talk-show desk.

There was also a hit channel, one that surprised everybody. The History Channel, launched on cable in January 1995, suddenly found itself with high ratings as an estimated 18 million homes tuned to it. Alternating between historical documentaries and movies dealing with the past, the channel made money by ignoring the young audiences so desperately sought by the networks and concentrating on older viewers. The strategy may have been noticed by the increasingly desperate CBS, which decided that for the fall 1996 season, it would shift its emphasis to attract-

Phil Donahue

ing slightly older folk and bring back such golden oldies as Bill Cosby and Ted Danson in new shows.

As 1996 was, unfortunately, an election year, politics began butting its ugly head into the world of television. After years of commotion by politicians and citizens over television sex and violence, Congress passed the Telecommunications Act, which, among other things, forced manufacturers to install the so-called V-Chip (V for violence) into all new television sets by 1998. This would supposedly enable parents to use technology to block out programming deemed unsuitable for their children.

Which of course raised the sticky question of what, exactly, was unsuitable and who, exactly, would decide it.

For years, the television industry had resisted any government control of TV content, considering it unconstitutional interference with freedom of the press. What happened now, though, was that the government told the television industry: Either you do it yourselves or we'll do it to you. The industry hastily gave in. As CNN's Turner sarcastically put it, "We're voluntarily having to comply." Working under the threat of government intervention, television executives came up with an agreement to institute a ratings system by January 1997. It promised to be, in the understated words of Jack Valenti, the father of Hollywood's movie-rating system and chair of the panel making up the new TV ratings, "a daunting, mammoth, monumental task."

Illustrative of the difficulties involved in rating programs was an exchange that took place in the White House, where President Clinton had invited (a euphemism for "summoned") 31 top television executives to discuss the issue. When one of the industry leaders asserted that television drama had come a long way since the days of dumb, violent shows like *Starsky and Hutch*, Clinton interjected, "I'm someone who has a deep emotional attachment to *Starsky and Hutch*." It was a joke, Media Person assumes, but one that inadvertently spoke to the question: How can a committee decide what is suitable or unsuitable

1995 GOLDEN GLOBE AWARDS

The 53rd Golden Globe Awards honoring excellence in film and television were presented on January 21, 1996, at Los Angeles's Beverly Hilton. Here are the television awards.

Party of Five

Best Series, Drama
 Party of Five (Fox)

Best Actor in a Drama
 Jimmy Smits, *NYPD Blue*

Best Actress in a Drama
 Jane Seymour, *Dr. Quinn, Medicine Woman*

Best Series, Musical or Comedy
 Cybill (CBS)

Best Actor in a Musical or Comedy
 Kelsey Grammer, *Frasier*

Best Actress in a Musical or Comedy
 Cybill Shepherd, *Cybill*

Best Miniseries or Movie Made for Television
 Indictment: The McMartin Trial (HBO)

Best Actor in a Miniseries or Movie Made for Television
 Gary Sinise, *Truman*

Best Actress in a Miniseries or Movie Made for Television
 Jessica Lange, *A Streetcar Named Desire*

Best Supporting Actor in a Series, Miniseries or Movie Made for Television
 Donald Sutherland, *Citizen X*

Best Supporting Actress in a Series, Miniseries or Movie Made for Television
 Shirley Knight, *Indictment: The McMartin Trial*

The Peabody Awards, administered by the University of Georgia's Henry W. Grady College of Journalism and Mass Communications, honor excellence in both radio and television broadcasting.

RADIO AWARDS

Blind Justice: Who Killed Janie Fray? (WJR Radio, Detroit, MI)

Kevin's Sentence (Canadian Broadcasting Corporation, Toronto, Canada)

St. Paul Sunday (Minnesota Public Radio, St. Paul, MN)

Oscar Brand (WNYC, New York, NY)

COMBINED RADIO AND TELEVISION AWARD

Wynton Marsalis: Making the Music/Marsalis on Music (National Public Radio, Washington D.C., and Sony Classical Film and Video for PBS)

TELEVISION

The Peavy Investigation (WFAA-TV, Dallas, TX)

Truth on Trial (ABC News *20/20*, New York, NY)

Target Seven: Armed and Angry (WXYZ-TV, Detroit, MI)

New York City School Corruption (WCBS-TV, New York, NY)

50 Years After the War (Television Broadcasts Ltd., Kowloon, Hong Kong)

Hoop Dreams (Kartemquin Educational Films and KTCA-TV, St. Paul, MN, presented on PBS)

The Dying Rooms (A Cinemax Reel Life Presentation of a Lauderdale Production for Channel 4, London, England, and Cinemax, New York)

Road Scholar (Public Policy Productions Inc. in association with Thirteen/WNET, New York, NY, presented on PBS)

Rock & Roll (WGBH-TV, Boston MA, and BBC Bristol, UK)

Peter Jennings Reporting: Hiroshima: Why the Bomb Was Dropped (ABC News, New York, NY)

Yugoslavia: Death of a Nation (A Discovery Journal Special, Discovery Channel, Bethesda, MD and Brian Lapping Associates for BBC London, England)

CBS Reports: In the Killing Fields of America (CBS News, New York)

Complaints of a Dutiful Daughter (P.O.V./Deborah Hoffman, New York, presented on PBS)

for individual viewers, be they adults, children or members of Congress?

This question also applies to the FCC's new regulation that requires networks to broadcast at least three hours of educational children's programming each week. Who's to decide what's educational? Does the *Jetsons* qualify as educational?

As the 1996 election campaigns heated up, waves of political advertising — much of it nastily negative — began hitting the nation's television screens with Democrats and Republicans spending millions of dollars, and there was no P-chip in sight to rescue the poor viewer. America's anchorman emeritus Walter Cronkite turned up in a *New York Times* advertisement co-signed by other distinguished citizens demanding that commercial television networks give free air time to the major presidential candidates. Fox's Murdoch had announced previously that he would do so independently, and CBS, Cronkite's former employer, said it was working on a plan, too. Why any of these people thought that large numbers of Americans would actually sit in front of their screens and watch politicians emitting gassy verbiage without challenge from opponents or journalists was a question for which Media Person has no answer.

But politicians did not constitute the only threat to the delicate purity of television art. There was also the usual snake under the bed, corporate encroachment. Sponsors have never exactly been shy in videoland, but lately they are bursting forth in creative new ways. Commercials are no longer enough. Pepsico, the giant food company, made a deal with ABC to work the names of its various products into the title of a new comedy series starring impressionist Dana Carvey. Thus it premiered as *The Taco Bell Dana Carvey Show*. Hilariously, the sponsor got so upset over the show's raunchy satire that it pulled out after the first installment and the show itself didn't last much longer.

But that was just the beginning. The History Channel was forced to cancel a new series grandly titled *Spirit of Enterprise* when newspaper critics began grousing that the show, featuring profiles of corporations like DuPont and AT&T, was being

Friends

sponsored, as well as controlled by — guess who?— corporations such as DuPont and AT&T. Then IBM cut a deal with CNBC for a new fall series titled *Scan* that would show how technology — such as IBM computers — is changing our lives.

On and on went the spirit of enterprise. The entire greedy cast of *Friends* was hired by Diet Coke to star in an ad in which they played their characters in the show. Elizabeth Taylor, hawking her new perfume, Black Pearls, showed up on four different CBS sitcoms on the same night, inventing a new form, the cameomercial. On another evening, one of the four, *Murphy Brown*, gave John F. Kennedy, Jr. a guest shot so he could plug his new magazine, *George*. The Fox network frequently made characters in its series work tag lines for advertising campaigns into the shows.

And looming over all of these individual intrusions was a larger problem, the growing prospect of news and information monopoly. With the corporate mega-mergers of the past few years, the majority of TV information and news will soon be under the control of four companies: General Electric, which owns NBC; Westinghouse, owner of CBS; Disney, parent company of ABC; and Time Warner, now in the process of acquiring Turner Broadcasting, owner of CNN. Ironically, we will have more news channels to watch but whether in the future any of them will be granted enough independence or the budgets to present much beyond bland, noncontroversial pap is a question Media Person leaves to your imagination. Don't worry, it won't require very much. ∎

Hank Aaron: Chasing the Dream (Turner Original Productions, Tollin/Robbins and Mundy Lane in association with Television Production Partners)

The Private Life of Plants (Turner Original Productions and BBC Natural History, London, England)

Coming Out Under Fire (DeepFocus Productions, Los Angeles, presented on PBS)

Wallace & Gromit (Aardman Animations in association with Wallace & Gromit Ltd., BBC Children's International, BBC Bristol and BBC Lionheart)

Frontline: Waco — The Inside Story (Frontline/WGBH-TV, Boston, MA)

CBS coverage of the assassination of Yitzhak Rabin (CBS News, New York)

The television news stations of Oklahoma City for coverage of the Murrah Building bombing (KFOR-TV, KOCO-TV and KWTV-TV, Oklahoma City, OK)

The Politician's Wife (The Producers Films for Channel 4, London, England)

The Tuskegee Airmen (An HBO Pictures Presentation of a Price Entertainment Production, Home Box Office, New York)

Homicide: Life on the Street (NBC, Baltimore Pictures, Reeves Entertainment SL/TMF Productions in association with NBC Productions)

The Boys of St. Vincent (Les Productions Tele-Action Inc. in association with the National Film Board of Canada, Canadian Broadcasting Corp. and Telefilm Canada, presented on the Arts & Entertainment Television Network, New York)

August Wilson's The Piano Lesson (A Hallmark Hall of Fame Presentation; CBS, Craig Anderson Productions Inc. in association with Hallmark Hall of Fame Productions Inc.)

Serving in Silence: The Margarethe Cammermeyer Story (NBC, Barwood Films Ltd., Story Line Productions Inc. and Trillium Productions Inc. in association with TriStar Television)

The Journey of Christopher Reeve (ABC News 20/20, New York, NY)

Oprah Winfrey

Fall 1995 Season*

The X-Files

Friends

Melrose Place

DAY	NETWORK	8:00-8:30
M	ABC	The Marshal———————
	CBS	The Nanny
	NBC	Fresh Prince of Bel Air
	FOX	Melrose Place———————
	UPN	Star Trek: Voyager———————
T	ABC	Roseanne
	CBS	The Client———————
	NBC	Wings
	FOX	Fox Tuesday Night Movie———————
	UPN	Deadly Games———————
W	ABC	Ellen
	CBS	Bless This House
	NBC	seaQuest 2032———————
	FOX	Beverly Hills, 90210———————
	WB	Sister, Sister
TH	ABC	Charlie Grace———————
	CBS	Murder, She Wrote———————
	NBC	Friends
	FOX	Living Single
F	ABC	Family Matters
	CBS	Dweebs
	NBC	Unsolved Mysteries———————
	FOX	Strange Luck———————
SAT	ABC	The Jeff Foxworthy Show
	CBS	Dr. Quinn, Medicine Woman ———————
	NBC	JAG———————
	FOX	Martin

DAY	NETWORK	7:00-7:30	7:30-8:00	
SUN	ABC	America's Funniest Videos Hour—————>		Lois and Clark———————
	CBS	60 Minutes——————————————>		Cybill
	NBC	Brotherly Love	Minor Adjustments	Mad About You
	FOX	Space: Above and Beyond—————————>		The Simpsons
	WB	Pinky and the Brain	Sister, Sister	Kirk

8:30-9:00	9:00-9:30	9:30-10:00	10:00-11:00
→	Monday Night Football —————————————————————————→		
Can't Hurry Love	Murphy Brown	If Not for You	Chicago Hope
In the House	NBC Monday Night Movie ——————————————————→		
→	Partners	Ned and Stacey	
→	Nowhere Man ——————————————→		
Hudson Street	Home Improvement	Coach	NYPD Blue
→	CBS Tuesday Night Movie ——————————————————→		
NewsRadio	Frasier	Pursuit of Happiness	Dateline NBC
→		→	
→	Live Shot ——————————————→		
The Drew Carey Show	Grace Under Fire	The Naked Truth	PrimeTime Live
Dave's World	Central Park West ——————————→	Courthouse	
→	Dateline NBC ——————————→	Law & Order	
→	Party of Five ——————————→		
The Parent 'Hood	The Wayans Bros.	Unhappily Ever After	
→	The Monroes ———————————————————→	Murder One	
→	New York News ———————————————————→	48 Hours	
The Single Guy	Seinfeld	Caroline in the City	ER
The Crew	New York Undercover ——————————→		
Boy Meets World	Step by Step	Hangin' With Mr. Cooper	20/20
The Bonnie Hunt Show	Picket Fences ——————————→	American Gothic	
→	Dateline NBC ——————————→	Homicide: Life on the Street	
→	The X-Files ——————————→		
Maybe This Time	ABC Saturday Night Movie ——————————————————→		
→	Touched by an Angel ——————————→	Walker, Texas Ranger	
→	John Larroquette Show	The Home Court	Sisters
The Preston Episodes	Cops	America's Most Wanted	
→	ABC Sunday Night Movie ——————————————————————————→		
Almost Perfect	CBS Sunday Night Movie ——————————————————————————→		
Hope and Gloria	NBC Sunday Night Movie ——————————————————————————→		
Too Something	Married . . . With Children	Misery Loves Company ——————————→	
Simon	First Time Out	Cleghorne!	

*This schedule reflects how the season started.
For changes in lineup, see show descriptions beginning on page 462.

Spring 1996 Season*

Lois and Clark

Beverly Hills, 90210

Seinfeld

Day	Network	8:00-8:30
M	ABC	Second Noah ———————
	CBS	The Nanny
	NBC	Fresh Prince of Bel Air
	FOX	Melrose Place ———————
	UPN	Star Trek: Voyager ————
T	ABC	Roseanne
	CBS	The Client ———————
	NBC	Wings
	FOX	Fox Tuesday Night Movie ———
	UPN	Moesha
W	ABC	Ellen
	CBS	Dave's World
	NBC	seaQuest 2032 ———————
	FOX	Beverly Hills, 90210 ———————
	UPN	The Sentinel ———————
	WB	Sister, Sister
Th	ABC	World's Funniest Videos
	CBS	Murder, She Wrote ————
	NBC	Friends
	FOX	Living Single
F	ABC	Family Matters
	CBS	Due South ———————
	NBC	Unsolved Mysteries ———————
	FOX	Strange Luck ———————
Sat	ABC	The Jeff Foxworthy Show
	CBS	Dr. Quinn, Medicine Woman ———
	NBC	JAG ———————
	FOX	Cops

Day	Network	7:00-7:30	7:30-8:00	
Sun	ABC	America's Funniest Videos Hour ——————>		Lois and Clark ———
	CBS	60 Minutes ———————————>		Cybill
	NBC	Dateline NBC ———————————>		Mad About You
	FOX	Space: Above and Beyond ——————>		The Simpsons
	WB	Pinky and the Brain	Simon	Sister, Sister

8:30–9:00	9:00–9:30	9:30–10:00	10:00–11:00
→	No permanent programming →		Murder One
Can't Hurry Love	Murphy Brown	High Society	Chicago Hope
In the House	NBC Monday Night Movie →		→
→	Ned and Stacey	Partners	
→	Nowhere Man →		
Hudson Street	Home Improvement	Champs	NYPD Blue
→	CBS Tuesday Night Movie →		→
3rd Rock From the Sun	Frasier	John Larroquette Show	Dateline NBC
Minor Adjustments	Live Shot →		
The Drew Carey Show	Grace Under Fire	The Naked Truth	PrimeTime Live
The Louie Show	Matt Waters →		American Gothic
→	Dateline NBC →		Law & Order
→	Party of Five →		
→	Swift Justice →		
The Parent 'Hood	The Wayans Bros.	Unhappily Ever After	
Before They Were Stars	ABC Thursday Night Movie →		→
→	No permanent programming →		48 Hours
The Single Guy	Seinfeld	Caroline in the City	ER
The Crew	New York Undercover →		
Boy Meets World	Step by Step	Hangin' With Mr. Cooper	20/20
→	Diagnosis Murder →		Picket Fences
→	Dateline NBC →		Homicide: Life on the Street
→	The X-Files →		
Maybe This Time	ABC Saturday Night Movie →		→
→	Touched by an Angel →		Walker, Texas Ranger
→	Hope and Gloria	The Home Court	Sisters
Cops	America's Most Wanted →		
→	ABC Sunday Night Movie →		→
Almost Perfect	CBS Sunday Night Movie →		→
NewsRadio	NBC Sunday Night Movie →		→
Martin	Married . . . With Children	No permanent programming	
Kirk	Savannah →		

*This schedule reflects how the season started.
For changes in lineup, see show descriptions beginning on page 460.

1995–1996 Broadcast Premieres

The constantly shifting television season is difficult to track accurately because the networks adjust their schedules to find the most effective (profitable) show placements. Sweeps periods (usually in February, May, July and November) are particularly tumultuous, as programming executives schedule movies and miniseries and juggle their lineups to win viewers. Below are the shows that premiered during the 1995–1996 season. If a show moved from its debut to a different timeslot but later returned to its original time, only the debuting time is given. If a show permanently changed positions, the beginning and final slots appear. Midseason replacements replace canceled shows, and midseason debuts temporarily replace shows that later return. Midseason debuts are usually in tryout, and ratings determine if the shows will return the following season.

ALIENS IN THE FAMILY

ABC
Spring Midseason Debut
Friday 9:00–9:30 p.m.; canceled after two episodes
Cast: John Bedford Lloyd, Margaret Trigg, Chris Marquette, Adam Brody and Paige Tiffany
Abducted by a spacecraft, Doug Brody (Lloyd), a father of two, falls in love with Cookie (Trigg), an alien with three extraterrestrial kids. Doug, Cookie and her kids return to Earth, Doug and Cookie marry and they live as a family. Cookie's youngest, Bobut, is Emperor of the Universe and has supernatural powers that prove to be both a help and a hindrance to the family. An otherworldly spin on the *Brady Bunch*.

ALMOST PERFECT

CBS
Fall Debut
Sunday 8:30–9:00 p.m.; moved to Monday 8:30–9:00 p.m. spring midseason
Cast: Nancy Travis and Kevin Kilner
Careerist Kim Cooper (Travis), a harried television producer, longs for a relationship but doesn't have time to pursue one. She tries to make room in her schedule for a personal life when she meets Mike Ryan (Kilner), a district attorney, who is as devoted to his job as Cooper is to hers. The series is meant to be funny and sometimes it succeeds.

AMERICAN GOTHIC

CBS
Fall Debut
Friday 10:00–11:00 p.m.; moved to Wednesday 10:00–11:00 p.m. spring season; on hiatus spring season
Cast: Gary Cole, Nicholas Searcy, Jake Weber, Paige Turco and Lucas Black
Trinity, South Carolina, seems to be a picture-perfect rural community, but its appearance is deceptive. Sheriff Lucas Buck's (Cole) corruption threatens the citizens of Trinity. Deputy Healy (Searcy), Dr. Crower (Weber) and Gail Emory (Turco) collaborate to control the demonic sheriff.

American Gothic

BEFORE THEY WERE STARS

ABC
Spring Midseason Replacement
Thursday 8:30–9:00 p.m.
Host: Scott Baio
Baio hosts this look at early performances of today's hottest stars. A fun look back at moments the celebrities would likely prefer to forget.

BLESS THIS HOUSE

CBS
Fall Debut
Wednesday 8:00–8:30 p.m.; moved to 8:30–9:00 p.m. fall season; canceled spring season
Cast: Andrew Clay, Cathy Moriarty, Reagan Kotz, Molly Price, Don Stark and Sam Gifaldi
Working-class couple Burt (Clay) and Alice (Moriarty) Clayton certainly know how to fight and how to make up. Though they don't agree on much, they do see eye-to-eye when it comes to their children and their dream of buying their own home. Intriguing casting that never jelled.

THE BONNIE HUNT SHOW

CBS
Fall Debut
Friday 8:30–9:00 p.m.; on hiatus; returned spring midseason Sunday 8:30–9:00 p.m. as *Bonnie*
Cast: Bonnie Hunt

Adjusting to her high-profile job as a Chicago broadcast reporter, Bonnie Kelly (Hunt) struggles to put aside her small-town ways in order to succeed in the big city. This comedy combines scripted and improvisational material shot in real time without retakes.

BOSTON COMMON

NBC
Spring Midseason Debut
Thursday 8:30–9:00 p.m.
Cast: Anthony Clark, Hedy Burress, Traylor Howard, Steve Paymer, Tasha Smith and Vincent Ventresca

Wyleen Pritchett (Burress) sees college as an escape from her small southern town. Wyleen's hopes are soon dashed when her protective brother, Boyd (Clark), escorts her to Boston's Randolph Harrington College and accepts a handyman job in the school's student union. Boyd falls hard for doctoral candidate Joy Byrnes (Howard), who is already involved with a professor (Ventresca). The show's ratings success owed much to NBC's hammocking it between *Friends* and *Seinfeld*.

BROTHERLY LOVE

NBC
Fall Debut
Sunday 7:00–7:30 p.m.; canceled fall season
Cast: Joey Lawrence, Matthew Lawrence, Andy Lawrence, Melinda Culea and Mike McShane

After the death of his father, Joe (Joey Lawrence) sacrifices his dream of becoming a Daytona racecar driver so he can provide for his stepbrothers (including two of Lawrence's real-life siblings, Matthew and Andy) as a mechanic in the family garage.

Caroline in the City

BUDDIES

ABC
Spring Midseason Debut
Wednesday 9:30–10:00 p.m.; canceled
Cast: Dave Chappelle, Christopher Gartin, Tanya Wright, Paula Cale, Judith Ivey and Richard Roundtree

Two best friends, single African American Dave (Chappelle) and married white guy John (Gartin) own a fledgling video-and-film business. The two don't have a problem with race, but their families do. John's mother-in-law (Ivey), the "white-trash queen," doesn't trust Dave, and Dave's father (Roundtree) believes in the motto, "black owned, black operated." A benign look at racism and race relations.

CAN'T HURRY LOVE

CBS
Fall Debut
Monday 8:30–9:00 p.m.
Cast: Nancy McKeon, Mariska Hargitay and Louis Mandylor

Annie (McKeon), a placement coordinator at a New York personnel agency, her crude co-worker (Mandylor) and her best friend (Hargitay) confront the ups and downs of romance while searching for the perfect mate.

CAROLINE IN THE CITY

NBC
Fall Debut
Thursday 9:30–10:00 p.m.
Cast: Lea Thompson, Eric Lutes, Malcolm Gets and Amy Pietz

New York cartoonist Caroline Duffy (Thompson) has a hard time keeping her personal life out of her comic strip. It's understandable considering her social circle, which includes her assistant, Richard (Gets), her on-again-off-again boyfriend and boss, Dell (Lutes), and her loopy neighbor Annie (Pietz).

CENTRAL PARK WEST

CBS
Fall Debut
Wednesday 9:00–10:00 p.m.; on hiatus; returned in the summer as *CPW*
Cast: Mariel Hemingway, Lauren Hutton, Raquel Welch, Madchen Amick, John Barrowman, Melissa Errico, Justin Lazard, Michael Michele and Tom Verica

From the creators of *Melrose Place* and *Beverly Hills, 90210,* this urban drama follows the intense lives of a group of glamorous young New Yorkers — a stockbroker, a Soho art gallery owner, the editor of a slick monthly magazine, a district attorney and a tabloid journalist. True to nighttime soap format, there's plenty of romance, scandal and backstabbing. Producers hoped for an East Coast *Melrose Place,* but scratched their heads as the show failed to find an audience.

CableACE Awards

The CableACE Awards, which recognize excellence in cable television, were presented in Los Angeles on three separate occasions: November 8, 1995 (an announcement of the craft and international categories winners), December 1, 1995, at the House of Blues and December 2, 1995, at the Wiltern Theater in a televised ceremony.

Movie or Miniseries
  Citizen X (HBO)

Actor in a Movie or Miniseries
  Raul Julia, *The Burning Season*

Actress in a Movie or Miniseries
  Linda Hamilton, *A Mother's Prayer*

Supporting Actor in a Movie or Miniseries
  Jeffrey DeMunn, *Citizen X*

Supporting Actress in a Movie or Miniseries
  Jean Marsh, *Fatherland*

Directing a Movie or Miniseries
  John Frankenheimer, *The Burning Season*

Writing a Movie or Miniseries
  Stanley Price, *Genghis Cohn*

Cinematography in a Movie or Miniseries
  Alexander Gruszynski, *Kingfish: The Story of Huey P. Long*

Art Direction in a Dramatic Special or Series, Theatrical Special, Movie or Miniseries
  Keith Wilson, Alistair Kay and Jim Harkin, *The Old Curiosity Shop*

Editing a Dramatic Special or Series, Theatrical Special, Movie or Miniseries
  Richard Harris, *Indictment: The McMartin Trial*

Costume Design
  Lainey Keogh, *Picture Windows:* "Two Nudes Bathing"

Makeup
  Bernard Eichholz, Donna Henderson, Justin Henderson, Timothy P. Huizing, David P. Matherly, Scott W. Patton, Ashlee Petersen, James A. Roland and Todd Masters, *Tales From the Crypt*

International Dramatic Special or Series, Movie or Miniseries
  Band of Gold (HBO)

Comedy Special
  HBO Comedy Hour: "Kathy & Mo: The Dark Side" (HBO)

Standup Comedy Special or Series
  Full Frontal Comedy (Showtime)

Champs
ABC
Spring Midseason Replacement
Tuesday 9:30–10:00 p.m.; canceled
Cast: Timothy Busfield, Ashley Crow, Ed Marinaro, Kevin Nealon, Ron McLarty, Paul McCrane, Libby Winters and Danny Pritchett
Much more was expected from DreamWorks's first television series, *Champs.* Tom McManus (Busfield) heads two families: one includes his wife (Crow) and two children (Winters and Pritchett), and the other is a group of his old buddies, who were all members of the same championship high-school basketball team. The men spend much of their free time playing poker at McManus's house, reminiscing about the good-ole days and complaining about their personal lives.

Charlie Grace
ABC
Fall Debut
Thursday 8:00–9:00 p.m.; canceled fall season
Cast: Mark Harmon, Cindy Katz, Robert Costanzo and Leelee Sobieski
Charlie Grace (Harmon), a street-smart Los Angeles private investigator, has a tough time balancing his work and single parenthood. His 12-year-old daughter, Jenny (Sobieski), is the only thing that keeps him going when things get out of hand.

Cleghorne!
WB
Fall Debut
Sunday 9:30–10:00 p.m.; canceled fall season
Cast: Ellen Cleghorne, Cerita Monet Bickelmann, Garrett Morris, Alaina Reed Hall, Sherri Shepherd and Michael Ralph
Based on the real-life experiences of *Saturday Night Live*'s Cleghorne, the comedy centers on the travails of the single working mother.

The Client
CBS
Fall Debut
Tuesday 8:00–9:00 p.m.
Cast: JoBeth Williams, John Heard, Ossie Davis, Polly Holliday and Raphael Sbarge
Based on the novel by John Grisham
Reggie Love (Williams), an attorney and recovering alcoholic, uses her specialty in family law to help kids in trouble and continue her fight to regain custody of her own children, whom she lost when she was drinking. Love has allies in her mother (Holliday), who shelters Reggie's wayward clients, and Judge Roosevelt (Davis), her advocate in the court system.

COURTHOUSE

CBS
Fall Debut
Wednesday 10:00–11:00 p.m.; canceled fall season
Cast: Patricia Wettig, Robin Givens, Brad Johnson, Annabeth Gish, Bob Gunton, Michael Lerner, Jennifer Lewis and Jeffrey Sams

In a world of shrinking budgets, overcrowded calendars, clashing philosophies and passionate attorneys, big-city judges struggle to administer justice in a system on the verge of self-destruction.

THE CREW

Fox
Fall Debut
Thursday 8:30–9:00 p.m.
Cast: Rose Jackson, Kristen Bauer, Charles Esten, David Burke, Christine Estabrook and Lane Davies

As they wait hand and foot on the passengers of Imperial Air, four young, sexy flight attendants — Jess (Jackson), Maggie (Bauer), Randy (Esten) and Paul (Burke) — deal with their whiny charges in their own, often outrageous, ways. Off duty, their lives are just as chaotic as they are in the air.

THE DANA CARVEY SHOW

ABC
Spring Midseason Debut
Tuesday 9:30–10:00 p.m.; canceled
Cast: Dana Carvey

The former *Saturday Night Live* star spoofs corporate-sponsored programming in this sketch comedy. Each episode has has a corporate sponsor, whose name was worked into the title. For example, the debut show was called "The Taco Bell Dana Carvey Show." The show gained notoriety when advertisers pulled out after being mercilessly tweaked. A grand satirical experiment that failed.

The Client

Performance in a Comedy Special
Mo Gaffney and Kathy Najimy, *HBO Comedy Hour:* "Kathy & Mo: The Dark Side"

Directing a Comedy Special
Anthony Morina, *The Clinic*

Writing an Entertainment Special
Jeff Cesario, Ed Driscoll, David Feldman, Eddie Feldmann, Greg Greenburg and Kevin Rooney, *Dennis Miller Live*

Entertainment Host
Garry Shandling, *HBO Comedy Hour:* "The 1995 Young Comedians Special Hosted by Garry Shandling"

Comedy Series
The Larry Sanders Show (HBO)

Actor in a Comedy Series
Garry Shandling, *The Larry Sanders Show*

Actress in a Comedy Series
Wendie Malick, *Dream On*

Directing a Comedy Series
Todd Holland, *The Larry Sanders Show:* "Doubt of the Benefit"

Writing a Comedy Series
Drake Sather, Garry Shandling and Peter Tolan, *The Larry Sanders Show:* "Doubt of the Benefit"

Art Direction in a Comedy or Music Special or Series
Ricardo Morin, Leslie Rollins, Tom Walsh and Tom Wilkin, *In Search of Dr. Seuss*

Editing a Comedy or Music Special or Series
Nancy Morrison, *Dream On:* "I Never Promised You Charoses, Martin"

Direction of Photography and/or Lighting Direction in a Comedy or Music Special or Series
Peter Sinclair, *Peter Gabriel's Secret World*

International Comedy Special or Series
Whose Line Is It Anyway? (Comedy Central)

Sports Information Special
Sonny Liston: *The Mysterious Life and Death of a Champion* (HBO)

Sports Information Series
MTV Sports (MTV)

Sports Event Coverage, Special
Discover Card Stars on Ice (TBS)

Sports Events Coverage Series
Sunday Night NFL (ESPN)

Sports News Series
NFL Game Day (ESPN)

CONTINUED ON NEXT PAGE ▶

Sports Host
Keith Olbermann, *SportsCenter*

Sports Play-by-Play Announcer
Marv Albert, New York Knicks Basketball
(Madison Square Garden Network)

Sports Commentator/Analyst
Dick Schaap, *The Sports Reporters*

Directing a Live Sports Event, Special or Series
Douglas Holmes, ESPN's 1995 Stanley Cup
Finals

Children's Special or Series, Six and Younger
Dr. Seuss Daisy-Head Mayzie (TNT)

Children's Special, Seven and Older
Eagle Scout: The Story of Henry Nicols (HBO)

Children's Series, Seven and Older
The Adventures of Pete & Pete (Nickelodeon)

Children's Educational or Informational Special or Series
Beakman's World (Learning Channel)

Animated Programming, Special or Series
Dr. Katz: Professional Therapist (Comedy Central)

Writing a Children's Special or Series
Pauline Le Bel, *The Song Spinner*

Dramatic Series
The Outer Limits (Showtime)

Actor in a Dramatic Special or Series
John Hurt, *Picture Windows:* "Two Nudes Bathing"

Actress in a Dramatic Special or Series
Paula Jai Parker, *Cosmic Slop:* "Tang"

Directing a Dramatic Special or Series
Stuart Gillard, *The Outer Limits:* "Sandkings"

Writing a Dramatic Special or Series
Patricia Resnik, *The Showtime 30-Minute Movie:* "Grandpa's Funeral"

Dramatic or Theatrical Special
Cosmic Slop: "Space Traders" (HBO)

Music Special or Series
Eagles: Hell Freezes Over (MTV)

Performance in a Music Special or Series
Elton John, *A Special Evening With Elton John*

Directing a Music Special or Series
Beth McCarthy, *Eagles: Hell Freezes Over*

Performing Arts Special or Series
South Bank Show: Marilyn Horne (Bravo)

International Cultural, Performing Arts, Theatrical, Music Special or Series
Peter & the Wolf (A&E)

DEADLY GAMES
UPN
Fall Debut
Tuesday 8:00–9:00 p.m.; canceled fall season
Cast: Cynthia Gibb, Christopher Lloyd, James Calvert
and Stephen T. Kay
Young, innovative scientist Dr. Gus Lloyd
(Calvert) is horrified when the characters in the
video game he created come to life after a freak
lab accident.

THE DREW CAREY SHOW
ABC
Fall Debut
Wednesday 8:30–9:00 p.m.
Cast: Drew Carey, Dietrich Bader, Ryan Stiles and
Christa Miller
Friends since high school, Drew (Carey), Oswald
(Bader), Lewis (Stiles) and Kate (Miller) share
career, romantic and financial troubles in working-
class Cleveland. Carey's deadpan delivery and feel
for middle America made the show a modest hit.

DWEEBS
CBS
Fall Debut
Friday 8:00–8:30 p.m.; canceled fall season
Cast: Farrah Forke, Peter Scolari, Stephen
Tobolowsky, Corey Feldman, David Kaufman, Adam
Biesk and Holly Fulger
When computer illiterate Carey (Forke) accepts
a job as office manager of Cyberbyte, Inc., she is
surrounded by a group of brilliant technogeeks.
Though she can't talk to them about computers
or networks, she can teach them social skills,
especially dating basics.

THE FACULTY
ABC
Spring Midseason Debut
Wednesday 8:30–9:00 p.m.
Cast: Meredith Baxter, Constance Shulman, Peter
Michael Goetz, Nancy Lenehan, Peter MacKenzie
and Jenica Bergere
Though part of her would love to resign, Flynn
Sullivan (Baxter) can't drag herself away from
her position as vice principal of Hamilton
Middle School. She's had it with apathetic teach-
ers and students and the annual budgetary
restrictions, but she is a devoted educator. Her
co-workers include the principal (Goetz), her
best friend (Shulman), the office secretary
(Lenehan) and neophyte teacher (Bergere).

FIRST TIME OUT
WB
Fall Debut
Sunday 9:00–9:30 p.m.; canceled fall season
Cast: Jackie Guerra, Mia Cottet, Leah Remini and
Craig Anton

Though unsuccessful in their pursuit of love, three young, female roommates (Guerra, Cottet and Remini) living in Los Angeles have otherwise full lives and chaotic social schedules.

GOOD COMPANY
CBS
Spring Midseason Debut
Monday 9:30–10:00 p.m.
Cast: Jason Beghe, Seymour Cassel, Timothy Fall, Lauren Graham, Terry Kiser, Wendie Malick, Elizabeth Anne Smith and Jon Tenney
A comic inside look at office politics and the day-to-day chaos of a Manhattan advertising agency. Will (Tenney) leads his creative team of copy writers with compassion and charm, qualities lacking in careerist creative director Zoe (Malick).

High Incident

HIGH INCIDENT
ABC
Spring Midseason Debut
Monday 9:00–10:00 p.m.
Cast: David Keith, Cole Hauser, Matt Craven and Catherine Kelner
Another police drama, but it's set in the suburbs rather than an urban environment. The cops cruise the pristine streets, confronting crime that ranges from minor misdemeanors to felonies. Personal dramas also unfold, as the men and women in blue include a three-time divorcé (Keith), a devoted family man (Craven) and Gayle Van Camp (Kelner), who works a little too hard to be one of the boys.

HIGH SOCIETY
CBS
Fall Midseason Replacement
Monday 9:30–10:00 p.m.
Cast: Jean Smart, Mary McDonnell, Faith Prince and Dan O'Donahue

Original Song
Carly Simon, "Touched by the Sun," *Carly Simon: Live at Grand Central*

Original Score
Marco Frisina, *Joseph*

Entertainment/Cultural Documentary
Inside the Dream Factory (Turner Classic Movies)

Environmental/Nature Documentary Special
Investigative Reports: "Plague Monkeys" (A&E)

Documentary Special
Anne Frank Remembered (Disney Channel)

Documentary Series
Desmond Morris' The Human Animal (Learning Channel)

International Documentary Special or Series
Charles Manson: The Man Who Killed the Sixties (Learning Channel)

Informational or Documentary Host
James Burke, *Connections 2* (Learning Channel)

Directing a Documentary Special
Kary Antholis, *One Survivor Remembers*

Writing a Documentary Special
Frank Deford, *Arthur Ashe: Citizen of the World*

Editing a Documentary Special or Series
Chuck Workman, *The First 100 Years: A Celebration of American Movies*

News Special or Series
Rwanda: Cry Justice (CNN International)

Extended News or Public Affairs Coverage
CNN's Coverage of the Oklahoma City Bombing (CNN)

Magazine Show or Special Series
National Geographic Explorer (TBS)

Magazine Host
Ian Wright, *Lonely Planet: "Morocco"* (Travel Channel)

Public Affairs Special or Series
The Transplant Trade (Discovery Channel)

International Informational Special or Series
France's Forgotten Shame (Discovery Channel)

Business or Consumer Programming Special or Series
TBS Network Earth (TBS)

Educational or Instructional Special or Series
One Survivor Remembers (HBO)

Talk Show Series
Politically Incorrect With Bill Maher (HBO)

CONTINUED ON NEXT PAGE ▶

◀ CONTINUED FROM PREVIOUS PAGE

Program Interviewer
Jane Wallace, *Under Scrutiny With Jane Wallace* (FX)

Variety Special or Series
Dennis Miller Live (HBO)

Fictional Short-Form Programming Special or Series
Short Films by Short People — Foil Man (Nickelodeon)

Nonfictional Short-Form Programming Special or Series
Hate Rock (CNN)

Recreation and Leisure Special or Series
Lonely Planet: "Morocco" (Travel Channel)

Game Show Special or Series
The News Hole With Harry Shearer (Comedy Central)

1995–1996 DAYTIME EMMY AWARDS

The 1995–1996 Daytime Emmy Awards were presented on May 22, 1996, at New York's Radio City Music Hall. Here is a partial list of winners.

Outstanding Children's Series
Reading Rainbow (PBS)

Outstanding Children's Special
Stand Up (CBS)

Outstanding Animated Program
Animaniacs (WB)

Outstanding Game/Audience Participation Show
The Price Is Right (CBS)

Outstanding Talk Show
Oprah Winfrey Show (Syndicated)

Outstanding Service Show
In Julia's Kitchen With Master Chefs (PBS)

Reading Rainbow

High Society offers some hope to the foundering network's weak lineup. This sitcom about super-chic/gaudy Ellie (Smart), a romance novelist, and her best friend and publisher, Dott (McDonnell), a divorced mother, works in a clean, *Absolutely Fabulous* sort of way.

THE HOME COURT
NBC
Fall Debut
Saturday 9:30–10:00 p.m.
Cast: Pamela Reed, Breckin Meyer, Meghann Haldeman, Robert Gorman, Phillip Glenn Van Dyke, Dennis Arndt and Meagen Fay
As a Chicago family-court judge, Sydney J. Solomon (Reed) intimidates even the toughest prosecuting attorney and the most flagrant offenders, but there's one group over which she can't exercise full control — her four children. As a single parent, her kids present more challenges than she faces on the bench.

HUDSON STREET
ABC
Fall Debut
Tuesday 8:30–9:00 p.m.; moved to Saturday 8:00–8:30 p.m. spring season; on hiatus spring season
Cast: Tony Danza, Lori Loughlin, Shareen Mitchell, Frank J. Galasso, Jerry Adler, Christine Dunford and Tom Gallop
Sparks fly between chauvinistic, hard-line detective Tony Canetti (Danza) and idealistic, liberal crime reporter Melanie Clifford (Loughlin). Divorced dad Tony shares custody of his 10-year-old son (Galasso) with his ex-wife, Lucy (Mitchell), who is still a big part of Tony's life.

IF NOT FOR YOU
CBS
Fall Debut
Monday 9:30–10:00 p.m.; canceled fall season
Cast: Elizabeth McGovern and Hank Azaria
Jessie Kent (McGovern) and Craig Schaeffer (Azaria) are engaged to the wrong people. She is betrothed to a depressed architect who is obsessed with the fat content in food and he to a neurotic recording artist. Fate brings them together, and they realize that the solution to their disastrous engagements is each other.

JAG
NBC
Fall Debut
Saturday 8:00–9:00 p.m.; moved to Wednesday 8:00–9:00 p.m. spring midseason
Cast: David James Elliott, Andrea Parker, Terry O'Quinn and Kevin Dunn
Judge Advocate General (JAG) officer/jet-fighter pilot, Lt. Harmon Rabb, Jr. (Elliott) investigates and tries high-profile cases for the Navy. Television's go at *A Few Good Men* and *Top Gun.*

THE JEFF FOXWORTHY SHOW

ABC
Fall Debut
Saturday 8:00–8:30 p.m.; on hiatus spring season
Cast: Jeff Foxworthy, Anita Barone, Kelsey
Mulrooney and Shawna Duling
Jeff (Foxworthy), full of Southern charm and a
common-sense perspective (translation: he's a
redneck), and his wife, Lisa (Barone), are hap-
pily married parents with two daughters, Jessica
(Mulrooney) and Chloe (Duling). Foxworthy has
an audience in the canebrake, but the show
doesn't deliver his good-ole-boyness.

KINDRED: THE EMBRACED

Fox
Spring Midseason Debut
Wednesday 9:00–10:00 p.m.
Cast: Mark Frankel, C. Thomas Howell, Kelly Rutherford, Stacy Haiduk, Jeff Kober and Channon Roe
Five modern vampire clans, headed by the Prince
of the City Julian Luna (Frankel), lead double lives
in San Francisco. They masquerade as humans,
careful to keep their real identities secret.

KIRK

WB
Fall Debut
Sunday 8:00–8:30 p.m.; moved to 8:30–9:00 p.m.
spring season
Cast: Kirk Cameron, Chelsea Noble, Debra Mooney,
Will Estes, Taylor Fry and Courtland Mead
A 24-year-old aspiring artist (Cameron) suddenly
becomes responsible for his three younger sib-
lings and tries to maintain a personal life while
minding his new charges.

LIVE SHOT

UPN
Fall Debut
Tuesday 9:00–10:00 p.m.; canceled fall season
Cast: David Birney, Wanda De Jesus, Hill Harper,
Spencer Klein, Cheryl Pollak, Rebecca Staab,
Michael Watson and Jeff Yagher
Alex Rydell (Yagher), a television news director,
has his hands full with a staff of backstabbing
reporters, egotistical anchors and frenzied tech-
nicians.

LOCAL HEROES

Fox
Spring Midseason Debut
Sunday 9:30–10:00 p.m.
Cast: Ken Hudson Campbell, Jason Kristofer, Jay
Mohr, Justin Louis, Rhoda Gemignani, Tricia Vessey,
Kristen Datillo-Hayward and Paula Cale
Four working-class guys (Campbell, Kristofer,
Mohr and Louis) living in Philadelphia aren't
quite ready to forget their high-school days and
face adulthood. They stick together as they face
mounting responsibilities, such as jobs, family
and relationships.

THE LOUIE SHOW

CBS
Spring Midseason Replacement
Wednesday 8:30–9:00 p.m.
Cast: Louie Anderson, Bryan Cranston, Paul Fieg and
Kate Hodge
Anderson is not the next Jerry Seinfeld. Louie
(Anderson), a Duluth, Minnesota, therapist, enter-
tains and counsels his circle of friends, which
includes police detective Curt (Cranston), colleague
Jake (Fieg) and loony roommate Gretchen (Hodge).

MALIBU SHORES

NBC
Spring Midseason Debut
Saturday 8:00–9:00 p.m.
Cast: Keri Russell, Tony Lucca, Katie Wright,
Christian Campbell, Essence Atkins, Randy Spelling,
Greg Vaughan and Charisma Carpenter
Aaron Spelling is at it again. It's not surprising
since *The Guinness Book of World Records* lists
him as television's most productive producer, an
easy feat when you build from the same blueprint over and over again. His latest, set in
California with many beautiful young people, features two sets of high-school students from different sides of the track. The paths of Malibu's
rich and San Fernando Valley's working-class
kids cross and clash as romances, friendships
and animosity develop between the two groups.

MATT WATERS

CBS
Spring Midseason Replacement
Wednesday 9:00–10:00 p.m.
Cast: Montel Williams, Richard Chevolleau,
Nathaniel Marston, Cyndi Cartagena, Felix A. Pire,
Amy Hargreaves, Sam McMurray and Kristen
Wilson
Navy Seal Matt Waters (Williams) retires from
the military to become a high-school teacher at
his alma mater, Bayview High School. He finds
things have changed quite a bit since he was a
student. Waters takes an unconventional but
effective approach in dealing with his students
and their problems, which include teen pregnancy, racism, gangs, abuse, poverty and illiteracy.

MAYBE THIS TIME

ABC
Fall Debut
Saturday 8:30–9:00 p.m.
Cast: Marie Osmond, Ashley Johnson and Betty
White
One year after her divorce, Julia (Osmond) gives
up on love and focuses her attention on her precocious daughter (Johnson), her mother (White)
and the family cafe. Julia's daughter and mother
work hard to convince her to give romance
another chance.

MINOR ADJUSTMENTS

NBC
Fall Debut
Sunday 7:30–8:00 p.m.
NBC canceled the series, and UPN picked it up as a spring midseason replacement in the Tuesday 8:30–9:00 p.m. slot.
Cast: Rondell Sheridan, Wendy Raquel Robinson, Bobby E. McAdams II, Camille Winbush, Linda Kash, Mitchell Whitfield and Sara Rue
Despite his special way with children, child psychologist Dr. Ron Aimes (Sheridan) finds that it takes much more to be a good parent than simply being a good psychologist.

MISERY LOVES COMPANY

Fox
Fall Debut
Sunday 9:30–10:00 p.m.; canceled fall season
Cast: Dennis Boutsikaris, Julius Carry, Stephen Furst and Lorraine Tessaint
In this comic look at divorce and marriage from the male perspective, four friends with love woes, three of whom are in the middle of bitter divorces, carouse and sympathize with each other.

Moesha

MOESHA

UPN
Spring Midseason Replacement
Tuesday 8:00–8:30 p.m.
Cast: Brandy Norwood, Sheryl Lee Ralph, William Allen Young, Countess Vaughn, Marcus T. Paulk, Lamont Bentley and Yvette Wilson
Moesha (Norwood) isn't pleased when her father (Young) marries Dee (Ralph), who replaces Moesha as female head of the house. Despite her resentment of Dee, Moesha looks to her new stepmother for advice and support.

THE MONROES

ABC
Fall Debut
Thursday 9:00–10:00 p.m.; canceled fall season
Cast: William Devane, Susan Sullivan, David Andrews, Steven Eckholdt, Cecil Hoffmann, Tracy Griffith, Tristan Tait, Darryl Theirse, Lynn Clark and Vince Grant
John Monroe (Devane), patriarch of his rich and powerful family, aspires to be president, but when a scandal foils his political career, he quickly makes other plans that involve his children. This larger-than-life family wields power and betrayal as they plunge into international intrigue.

MUPPETS TONIGHT!

ABC
Spring Midseason Debut
Friday 8:30–9:00 p.m.
They're back, and they're hipper than ever. Clifford, a new addition to the Muppet team, hosts the puppets' variety show, which is broadcast on KMUP. Each episode features musical numbers, comedy sketches, backstage antics and a big-name guest (Michelle Pfeiffer and Garth Brooks, for example).

MURDER ONE

ABC
Fall Debut
Thursday 10:00–11:00 p.m.; moved to Monday 10:00–11:00 p.m. spring season
Cast: Daniel Benzali and Stanley Tucci
Los Angeles attorney Ted Hoffman (Benzali) defends Richard Cross (Tucci), a wealthy entrepreneur implicated in the murder of his mistress's teenage sister, in this behind-the-scenes look at a police investigation and the legal process. Throughout the entire season, *Murder One* follows the progress of this one case.

MY GUYS

CBS
Spring Midseason Debut
Wednesday 8:30–9:00 p.m.
Cast: Michael Rispoli, Mike Damus, Francis Capra, Marisol Nichols and Sherie Scott
Recent widower Sonny Demarco (Rispoli) tries to cope with the loss of his wife, his struggling limousine business, his two sons (Damus and Capra) and the prospect of dating again — after 17 years.

THE NAKED TRUTH

ABC
Fall Debut
Wednesday 9:30–10:00 p.m.
Cast: Téa Leone, Jonathan Penner and Holland Taylor
Nora Wilde (Leone) walked away from her philandering, media-mogul husband confident that with hard work, she could regain her former status as a

respected photojournalist. She soon finds that her ex-husband has blackballed her from every reputable paper in the country, and she must resort to shooting pictures for a trashy tabloid.

NASH BRIDGES
CBS
Spring Midseason Debut
Friday 10:00–11:00 p.m.
Cast: Don Johnson, Cary-Hiroyuki Tagawa, Annette O'Toole, Serena Scott Thomas, Jeff Perry, Jaime Gomez, Cheech Marin and Jodi Lynn O'Keefe
Johnson returns to television as a hotshot cop who always gets his man and looks like a million bucks. No, it's not a continuation of *Miami Vice* (though it very well could be). He's Nash Bridges, lead inspector of San Francisco's Special Investigators Bureau, twice divorced and the father of 16-year-old Cassidy (O'Keefe).

NED AND STACEY
Fox
Fall Debut
Monday 9:30–10:00 p.m.; moved to 9:00–9:30 p.m. spring season
Cast: Thomas Haden Church and Deborah Messing
An ambitious advertising executive (Church) needs the perfect wife for a promotion, and a socially conscious journalist (Messing) is looking for a reason to get out of her parents' house. The solution? A marriage of convenience.

NEW YORK NEWS
CBS
Fall Debut
Thursday 9:00–10:00 p.m.; canceled fall season
Cast: Mary Tyler Moore, Melina Kanakaredes, Madeline Kahn, Joe Morton and Gregory Harrison
Emotions run high in the newsroom of New York's *Reporter*, and expectations ran equally high at CBS. Iron-fisted Louise "The Dragon Lady" Felcott (Moore) presides over the newsroom, and her staff includes Angela Villanova (Kanakaredes), a young reporter who will stop at nothing to get a story, and veteran gossip columnist Nan Chase (Kahn), who has clawed her way to the top.

NOWHERE MAN
UPN
Fall Debut
Monday 9:00–10:00 p.m.
Cast: Bruce Greenwood, Mary Gregory and Megan Gallagher
Documentary photographer Thomas Veil's (Greenwood) whole life has been erased, leaving no trace of his existence. His mother (Gregory), wife (Gallagher) and close friends are involved in the scheme. Veil desperately tries to figure out what happened to his former life.

1995 ALFRED I. duPONT — COLUMBIA UNIVERSITY AWARDS IN TELEVISION AND RADIO JOURNALISM

The Alfred I. duPont Awards, administered by Columbia University, recognize excellence in television and radio broadcasting. The awards were announced January 25, 1996.

GOLD BATON
> **Daniel Schorr,** senior news analyst for National Public Radio

SILVER BATONS
TELEVISION AWARDS
> ABC News, *Turning Point:* "Of Human Bondage: Slavery Today"
>
> *The American Experience:* "The Battle of the Bulge, FDR and the Way West" (PBS)
>
> The Center for Investigative Reporting and Telesis Productions, *Frontline,* "School Colors" (PBS)
>
> ABC News, *World News Tonight:* "American Agenda: Medicine Man; Vanishing Breed; Political Waters"

MAJOR MARKET TELEVISION
> *Target 7: Michigan's Secret Soldiers* (WXYZ-TV, Detroit, MI)

MEDIUM MARKET TELEVISION
> WTVJ, Miami, Florida, and Kerry Sanders for coverage of Haiti

SMALL MARKET TELEVISION
> No award

INDEPENDENT TELEVISION PRODUCTION
> Billy Golfus and David E. Simpson, *When Billy Broke His Head . . . and Other Tales of Wonder*
>
> Blackside, Inc., *America's War on Poverty*
>
> Deborah Hoffman and P.O.V., *Complaints of a Dutiful Daughter*

CABLE TELEVISION
> Brian Lapping Associates, London, *Watergate* (The Discovery Channel)

RADIO AWARDS
> *American History — The Disney Version* (WMAL-AM, Washington D.C.)
>
> National Public Radio for political coverage

PARTNERS

Fox
Fall Debut
Monday 9:00–9:30 p.m.; moved to 9:30–10:00 p.m.
spring season
Cast: Jon Cryer, Tate Donovan and Maria Pitillo
An architect (Donovan) finds himself in the middle of a tug-of-war battle between his fiancée (Pitillo) and his neurotic best friend (Cryer), who fight for his attention.

PINKY AND THE BRAIN

WB
Fall Debut
Sunday 7:00–7:30 p.m.
A spinoff of *Steven Spielberg Presents Animaniacs*, Pinky and the Brain, two industrious mice from Acme Labs, relentlessly try to take control of the world.

THE PRESTON EPISODES

Fox
Fall Debut
Saturday 8:30–9:00 p.m.; canceled fall season
Cast: David Alan Grier
A recently divorced English professor (Grier) harbors high hopes of becoming a Pulitzer Prize-winning journalist and abandons his academic career for a position as a cub reporter at a less-than-reputable tabloid.

PROFIT

Fox
Spring Midseason Debut
Monday 9:00–10:00 p.m.
Cast: Adrian Pasdar, Lisa Zane, Keith Szarabajka, Jack Gwaltney, Allison Hossack, Lisa Darr and Lisa Blount
Jim Profit (Pasdar) won't let anything slow his climb up the corporate ladder at Gracen & Gracen, a Fortune 100 company. The only person at the company onto his scheming is the head of corporate security (Zane), but she always remains a step behind the deviantly cunning Profit. Critics praised *Profit* as one of the few high points of the season, but Fox never gave it a chance to find an audience, limiting its run to a few episodes.

PURSUIT OF HAPPINESS

NBC
Fall Debut
Tuesday 9:30–10:00 p.m.; canceled fall season
Cast: Tom Amandes, Meredith Scott Lynn, Melinda McGraw, Larry Miller, Brad Garrett and Maxine Stuart
Chicago lawyer Steve Gerard (Amandes) suddenly faces several heavy issues: His careerist wife (McGraw) has recently lost her job, his scatter-brained brother-in-law (Miller) is moving in, his grandmother (Stuart) is losing her mind and his partner/best friend (Garrett) has just come out of the closet.

SAVANNAH

WB
Spring Midseason Replacement
Sunday 9:00–10:00 p.m.
Cast: Robyn Lively, Jamie Luner, Shannon Sturges, David Gail, Paul Satterfield, Beth Toussaint and Ray Wise
Aaron Spelling produces *Savannah*, WB's first dramatic series, so need more be said? Here's a brief lowdown: Set in Savannah, Georgia, the bond between three belles is tested by adultery, fraud, conspiracy and murder.

SECOND NOAH

ABC
Spring Midseason Replacement
Monday 8:00–9:00 p.m.
Cast: Daniel Hugh Kelly and Betsy Brantley
There's never a dull moment at the Beckett house. Noah (Kelly) and Jesse (Brantley) have eight adopted children, ranging in age from two to 17 years, and 37 pets. The Becketts endure their parenting problems by remaining optimistic and maintaining a sense of humor.

THE SENTINEL

UPN
Spring Debut
Wednesday 8:00–9:00 p.m.
Cast: Richard Burgi and Garrett Maggert
After surviving a helicopter crash, which left him stranded in a Peruvian jungle for 18 months, detective James Ellison (Burgi) discovers he has developed exceptional sensory powers. With the help of anthropologist Blair Sandburg (Maggert), Ellison learns to use his newfound skill to solve crimes.

THE SHOW

Fox
Spring Midseason Debut
Sunday 8:30–9:00 p.m.
Cast: Sam Seder and Mystro Clark
Black comedian Wilson Lee (Clark) hires white comedy writer Tom Delaney (Seder) as head writer of the all-black *Wilson Lee Show* because "young white males are a desirable demographic." Lee's other three writers are less than happy about answering to a white guy.

SIMON

WB
Fall Debut
Sunday 8:30–9:00 p.m.; moved to 7:30–8:00 p.m.
spring season
Cast: Harland Williams, Jason Bateman, Paxton Whitehead, Clifton Powell, Patrick Breen and Andrea Bendeald
A young, wide-eyed optimist (Williams) loves his job working for a New York television network but living with his cynical brother is another story.

The Single Guy

THE SINGLE GUY

NBC
Fall Debut
Thursday 8:30–9:00 p.m.
Cast: Jonathan Silverman, Joey Slotnick, Ming-Na Wen, Jessica Hecht, Mark Moses and Ernest Borgnine
Thirtysomething novelist Jonathan (Silverman) feels as if he's the last bachelor. His closest friends are married and assist him in his search for the perfect mate. The matchmaking entourage includes his best friend, Sam (Slotnick), Sam's wife, Trudy (Wen), longtime platonic friend Janeane (Hecht) and her husband (Moses).

SISTER, SISTER

WB
Fall Debut
Sunday 7:30–8:00 p.m.; moved to 8:00–8:30 p.m. spring season
WB acquired the show from ABC.
Cast: Tia Mowry, Tamera Mowry, Jackee Harry, Tim Reid and Marques Houston
Identical twins (Tia and Tamera Mowry) who were separated at birth are unexpectedly reunited when they meet in a clothing store. Their single parents move in together so the girls can live under one roof. Happens all the time, right?

SPACE: ABOVE AND BEYOND

Fox
Fall Debut
Sunday 7:00–8:00 p.m.
Cast: Morgan Weisser, Rodney Rowland, Kristin Cloke, Lanei Chapman, Joel De LaFuente and James Morrison
A Marine unit is unexpectedly dispatched to the frontlines of an intergalactic war after Earth's most elite fighting squadron is decimated in an attack by a previously unknown alien race.

STRANGE LUCK

Fox
Fall Debut
Friday 8:00–9:00 p.m.

Cast: D.B. Sweeney, Pamela Gidley and Frances Fisher
Ever since he survived a plane crash as a child, strange luck — both good and bad — has followed photojournalist Chance (Sweeney). Wherever he goes, something odd occurs, which, given his profession, always proves interesting.

SWIFT JUSTICE

UPN
Spring Debut
Wednesday 9:00–10:00 p.m.
Cast: James McCaffrey and Gary Dourdan
Ex-New York cop Matt Swift (McCaffrey) works outside the system and takes cases that the NYPD can't or won't handle. Detective Wendell Sims (Dourdan) sends Swift the hot cases.

3RD ROCK FROM THE SUN

NBC
Spring Midseason Replacement
Tuesday 8:30–9:00 p.m.
Cast: John Lithgow, Jane Curtin, Simbi Khali, Kristen Johnson, French Stewart, Joseph Gordon-Levitt and Elmarie Wendel
The biggest surprise of the 1995–1996 season came as a replacement. Four aliens posing as humans land on Earth with a mission: They must find out everything they can about the planet. The leader of the pack, Dick Solomon (Lithgow), becomes a physics professor and falls for a colleague (Curtin). The sometimes clever writing gets just the boost it needs from a fine cast.

TOO SOMETHING

Fox
Fall Debut
Sunday 8:30–9:00 p.m.
Cast: Eric Schaeffer and Donal Lardner Ward
Based on the film *My Life's in Turnaround*
Best friends Eric (Schaeffer) and Donny (Ward) work together in the mailroom of an investment bank while pursuing their career dreams: Eric wants to be a writer, and Donny hopes to be an astronaut.

WHAT'S SO FUNNY

Fox
Fall Midseason Replacement
Sunday 9:30–10:00 p.m.; canceled fall season
Host: Nick Bakay
What's So Funny features humorous outtakes from local and network newscasts, prime-time television shows, sports footage, feature films, standup comedy routines, commercials and home videos.

WORLD'S FUNNIEST VIDEOS

ABC
Spring Midseason Replacement
Thursday 8:00–8:30 p.m.
Hosts: Eva LaRue and Dave Coulier
The latest installment in the *Funniest Videos* series features an international selection of comical, though often unbelievable, home videos.

Fall 1996 Season

Suddenly Susan

Spin City

Townies

Day	Network	8:00–8:30
M	ABC	Dangerous Minds———
	CBS	Cosby
	NBC	The Jeff Foxworthy Show
	FOX	Melrose Place———
	UPN	In the House
	WB	7th Heaven———
T	ABC	Roseanne
	CBS	Home of the Brave———
	NBC	Mad About You
	FOX	Fox Tuesday Night Movie———
	UPN	Moesha
W	ABC	Ellen
	CBS	The Nanny
	NBC	Wings
	FOX	Beverly Hills, 90210———
	UPN	The Sentinel———
	WB	Sister, Sister
TH	ABC	High Incident———
	CBS	Diagnosis Murder———
	NBC	Friends
	FOX	Martin
F	ABC	Family Matters
	CBS	Dave's World
	NBC	Unsolved Mysteries———
	FOX	Sliders———
SAT	ABC	Second Noah———
	CBS	Dr. Quinn, Medicine Woman ———
	NBC	Dark Skies———
	FOX	Cops

Day	Network	7:00–7:30	7:30–8:00	8:00–8:30
SUN	ABC	America's Funniest Home Videos	America's Funniest Home Videos	Lois and Clark———
	CBS	60 Minutes——————————→		Touched by an Angel———
	NBC	Dateline NBC——————————→		3rd Rock From the Sun
	FOX	L.A. Firefighters——————→		The Simpsons
	WB	Kirk	Brotherly Love	The Parent 'Hood

8:30–9:00	9:00–9:30	9:30–10:00	10:00–11:00
	Monday Night Football ———————————————→		
Ink	Murphy Brown	Cybill	Chicago Hope
Mr. Rhodes	NBC Monday Night Movie ——————→		
	Party Girl	Lush Life	
Malcolm & Eddie	Goode Behavior	Sparks	
	Savannah ——————————————→		
Life's Work	Home Improvement	Spin City	NYPD Blue
	CBS Tuesday Night Movie ——————→		
Something So Right	Frasier	Caroline in the City	Dateline NBC
Homeboys in Outer Space	The Burning Zone ——————→		
Townies	Grace Under Fire	The Drew Carey Show	PrimeTime Live
Pearl	Almost Perfect	Public Morals	EZ Streets
John Larroquette Show	NewsRadio	Men Behaving Badly	Law & Order
	Party of Five ——————————→		
	Star Trek: Voyager ——————→		
Nick Freno: Licensed Teacher	The Wayans Bros.	The Jamie Foxx Show	
	Murder One ————————————→		Turning Point
	Moloney ——————————————→		48 Hours
The Single Guy	Seinfeld	Suddenly Susan	ER
Living Single	New York Undercover ——————→		
Sabrina, the Teenage Witch	Clueless	Boy Meets World	20/20
Everybody Loves Raymond	Mr. and Mrs. Smith ——————→		Nash Bridges
	Dateline NBC ——————————→		Homicide: Life on the Street
	Millennium ————————————→		
	Coach	Common Law	Relativity
	Early Edition ——————————→		Walker, Texas Ranger
	The Pretender ——————————→		Profiler
Cops	Married . . . With Children	Come Fly With Me	
	ABC Sunday Night Movie ———————————————————→		
	CBS Sunday Night Movie ———————————————————→		
Boston Common	NBC Sunday Night Movie ———————————————→		
Ned and Stacey	The X-Files ——————————→		
The Steve Harvey Show	Unhappily Ever After	Life With Roger	

1996 Broadcast Premieres

BROTHERLY LOVE
WB
Sunday 7:30–8:00 p.m.
WB picked up the show from NBC.
See page 463 for description

THE BURNING ZONE
UPN
Tuesday 9:00–10:00 p.m.
Cast: Jeffrey Dean Morgan, Dennis Arndt, Tamlyn
Tomita and James Black
Dr. Edward Marcase (Morgan) and his talented
team of virologists work against the clock to kill
a virus that threatens the population as it nears
the "burning zone."

CLUELESS
ABC
Friday 9:00–10:00 p.m.
Cast: Rachel Blanchard, Stacey Dash, Elisa
Donovan, Donald Faison, Sean Holland, Michael
Lerner, Wallace Shawn and Twink Caplan
Based on the 1995 film
Beverly Hills teens Cher (Blanchard), her side-
kick, Dionne (Dash), and their brat pack continue
to shop, gossip and matchmake in a big way even
though they've been reduced to the small screen.

COME FLY WITH ME
Fox
Saturday 9:30–10:00 p.m.
Cast: Patricia Healy and Tony Denison
Working-class couple April (Healy) and Jack
(Denison) Nardini struggle to make ends meet
and care for their three children. Their new
neighbors, the Beggs, seem like the Cleavers
compared to the Nardinis. Through all the tough
times, April and Jack manage to maintain their
newlywed passion for each other.

COMMON LAW
ABC
Saturday 9:30–10:00 p.m.
Cast: Greg Giraldo, Megyn Price and Gregory Sierra
John Alvarez (Giraldo) doesn't exactly fit in at his
high-powered, conservative Manhattan law firm
— he's Hispanic, wears an earring and has a
beard. He does hit it off with one colleague, Nancy
Slate (Price). They secretly move in together,
keeping their relationship under wraps at the
firm, which discourages interoffice romance.

Cosby

COSBY
CBS
Monday 8:00–8:30 p.m.
Cast: Bill Cosby, Phylicia Rashad and Madeline Kahn
Based on the British sitcom *One Foot in the Grave*
Cosby and Rashad reunite as a husband-and-wife
sitcom team, though this outing is nothing like
The Cosby Show. No longer the easygoing doctor
with a sense of humor, he's a grumpy aging man
who feels he's the last sane person on earth.
Forced to retire from his job, he can't handle
another annoyance and needs to lash out.
Believe it or not, this is a comedy.

DANGEROUS MINDS
ABC
Monday 8:00–9:00 p.m.
Cast: Annie Potts, Greg Serano and Tamala Jones
Based on the 1995 film, which was based on the
memoir *My Posse Don't Do Homework* by LouAnne
Johnson
There are no limits to what former Marine
LouAnne Johnson (Potts) will do for her stu-
dents at East Palo Alto High School. During the
day she ensures they get and enjoy an education
and after school hours she tries to keep them off
the streets.

DARK SKIES
NBC
Saturday 8:00–9:00 p.m.
Cast: Eric Close and Megan Ward
The 1995–1996 season was the year of *Friends*
clones, and 1996–1997 seems to be shaping up as

the year of *The X-Files* rip-offs. Invaded by extraterrestrial beings, a terrified young couple on the run (Close and Ward) relive historical events, from assassinations to wars, of the past four decades.

EARLY EDITION
CBS
Saturday 9:00–10:00 p.m.
Cast: Kyle Chandler, Shanesia Davis and Fisher Stevens
Gary Hobson (Chandler) receives a special delivery each morning: the next day's newspaper. Hobson and his friend Marissa (Davis) try to prevent the bad news from happening.

EVERYBODY LOVES RAYMOND
CBS
Friday 8:30–9:00 p.m.
Cast: Ray Romano, Patricia Heaton, Doris Roberts, Peter Boyle and Brad Garrett
Ray Barone (Romano) knows the true meaning of chaos. He has a 5-year-old daughter, twin 20-month-old sons and a wife who is beginning to feel claustrophobic as a homemaker. To make matters worse, his parents and brother consider his house their home away from home.

EZ STREETS
CBS
Wednesday 10:00–11:00 p.m.
Cast: Ken Olin, Jason Gedrick, Joe Pantoliano and Debrah Farentino
Detective Cameron Quinn (Olin) is on a mission to prove that his dead partner wasn't corrupt. Ex-con Danny Rooney (Gedrick) is out to prove he was incarcerated for a crime he didn't commit. The two pair up and attempt to set the record straight.

GOODE BEHAVIOR
UPN
Monday 9:00–9:30 p.m.
Cast: Sherman Hemsley, Dorien Wilson, Alex Datcher, Bianca Lawson, Scott Grimes and Joseph Maher
Newly paroled con artist Willie Goode (Hemsley) unexpectedly arrives at his estranged son's home with plans to move in and live there under house arrest. Franklin (Wilson), dean of humanities at Chapel Hill University, hesitatingly obliges, and his wife (Datcher) and daughter (Lawson) try to reconcile father and son.

HOMEBOYS IN OUTER SPACE
UPN
Tuesday 8:30–9:00 p.m.
Cast: Flex, Darryl M. Bell, Mel Jackson, Rhona Bennett, Kevin M. Richardson and John Webber
Twenty-third century homeboys Ty (Flex) and Morris (Bell) hop from one galaxy to another in their intergalactic vehicle, Space Hoopty, doing odd jobs. During slow times, they camp out in a corner of Jupiter Too, a futuristic tavern.

HOME OF THE BRAVE
CBS
Tuesday 8:00–9:00 p.m.
Cast: Gerald McRaney, Wendy Phillips, Austin O'Brien and Sara Schaub
A spinoff of *Touched by an Angel*
After Russell Greene (McRaney) loses his job, he and his family pack up their belongings and hit the road in search of work. They learn a lot about life in their travels, enriching themselves and the people they meet along the way.

INK
CBS
Monday 8:30–9:00 p.m.
Cast: Ted Danson and Mary Steenburgen
Jack (Danson) and Carrie (Steenburgen), a divorced couple who work together at the New York *Sun*, both still harbor romantic feelings for each other. When Carrie becomes Jack's editor, any hope of reconciliation is soon dashed. In a last-minute move, CBS shelved the first four episodes of the show and had to produce replacements at $1 million each. Sources said CBS would not settle for a mediocre product.

IN THE HOUSE
UPN
Monday 8:00–8:30 p.m.
Cast: Debbie Allen, LL Cool J, Lisa Arrindell, Maia Campbell, Jeffrey Woodard and Aura Holt
UPN picked up the series from NBC.
A mother of two (Allen), forced back to work after her husband cleans her out in a messy divorce, relies on her football-star landlord (Cool) to babysit her children.

THE JAMIE FOXX SHOW
WB
Wednesday 9:30–10:00 p.m.
Cast: Jamie Foxx, Garrett Morris, Ellia English, Garcelle Beauvais and Christopher B. Duncan
Jamie King (Foxx), determined to make it as a big

Ink

star, moves to L.A. to pursue his dream. While waiting for his big break, he works in his aunt's (English) and uncle's (Morris) run-down hotel and tries to breathe some life into the foundering establishment. Foxx also plays many of the hotel guests.

THE JEFF FOXWORTHY SHOW
NBC
Monday 8:00–8:30 p.m.
NBC picked up the show from ABC.
See page 469 for description

L.A. FIREFIGHTERS
Fox
Sunday 7:00–8:00 p.m.
Cast: Jarrod Emick, Christine Elise, Alexandra Hedison, Kane Picoy, Carlton Wilborn, Brian Leckner and Miquel Sandoval
There isn't room on the networks for another hospital- or cop-ensemble drama, so Fox offers up the next best thing: a look at the public servants who risk their lives battling fires. Jack Malloy (Emick) leads the firefighters of Station 132 with unmatched dedication. Erin Coffey (Elise) is out to prove she can do the job as well as any man. Also on the crew is a Jesus freak (Leckner) and a coward (Picoy). Away from the flames, passions burn and lives entangle.

LIFE'S WORK
ABC
Tuesday 8:30–9:00 p.m.
Cast: Lisa Ann Walter and Michael O'Keefe
Lisa Hunter (Walter) spent seven grueling years attending law school at night while raising her children. She thought things would get easier when she landed a job as assistant state's attorney in Baltimore. However, she soon finds that she has to fight for the respect of her boss and colleagues, and her husband (O'Keefe) has a hard time dealing with the family's new lifestyle.

LIFE WITH ROGER
WB
Sunday 9:00–9:30 p.m.
Cast: Mike O'Malley and Maurice Godin
Jason (Godin) can't stand his new best friend, Roger (O'Malley), but he owes him a lot considering Roger saved him from marrying the wrong woman. Jason accepts Roger's need for a friend, and the two share wild adventures.

LUSH LIFE
Fox
Monday 9:30–10:00 p.m.
Cast: Lori Petty, Karyn Parsons, Sullivan Walker, John Ortiz, Fab Filippo, Khalil Kain and Concetta Tomei
Carefree George Sanders (Petty) takes in her childhood friend, Margot Hines (Parsons), when she leaves her philandering husband. George, a struggling artist who likes the finer things, and Margot,

Men Behaving Badly

who has big dreams but no plans, spend many nights in George's favorite bar.

MALCOLM & EDDIE
UPN
Monday 8:30–9:00 p.m.
Cast: Malcolm-Jamal Warner and Eddie Griffin
New to Kansas City, unlikely roommates Malcolm (Warner), an aspiring sports commentator, and Eddie (Griffin), a tow-truck driver, look to each other for companionship and support. They live over a bar and spend much of their free time there flirting and freeloading.

MEN BEHAVING BADLY
NBC
Wednesday 9:30–10:00 p.m.
Cast: Rob Schneider, Ron Eldard, Justine Bateman and Anna Gunn
There are few whom politically incorrect buddies Jamie (Schneider) and Kevin (Eldard) don't offend. Kevin, manager of a security-systems company, barely maintains a relationship with his girlfriend, nurse Sarah (Bateman). Jamie, an unemployed photographer, relentlessly pursues his neighbor, Michelle (Gunn), a professor who has absolutely no interest in the stumblebum.

MILLENNIUM
Fox
Friday 9:00–10:00 p.m.
Cast: Lance Henriksen, Megan Gallagher, Brittany Tiplady and Bill Smitrovich
Retired FBI agent Frank Black (Henriksen) has the ability to enter the minds of homicidal criminals. His crime-solving gift helped him amass a nearly perfect track record for the FBI, and he hopes to continue that success as the leader of an underground task force that pursues society's most nefarious criminals. Fox hopes *Millennium* will attract *The X-Files* fans. The show was created by *The X-Files* writer and producer, Chris Carter.

MOLONEY

CBS

Thursday 9:00–10:00 p.m.

Cast: Peter Strauss

Police psychiatrist Dr. Nick Moloney (Strauss) treats clients who range from corrupt cops to serial killers but manages to maintain a calm, cool demeanor as he attempts to control the uncontrollable.

MR. AND MRS. SMITH

CBS

Friday 9:00–10:00 p.m.

Cast: Scott Bakula, Maria Bello and Roy Dotrice

Mr. Smith (Bakula) works as a detective for a mysterious detection/protection agency. When he teams up with a beautiful spy (Bello), the pair pass themselves off as a married couple and sparks fly.

MR. RHODES

NBC

Monday 8:30–9:00 p.m.

Cast: Tom Rhodes, Farrah Forke, Stephen Tobolowsky, Ron Glass and Jessica Stone

Failed New York author Tom Rhodes (Rhodes), a great-looking hipster, leaves the big city for a teaching job in his hometown, thinking he's going to be the teacher that all the students love. He encounters obstacles in the school's headmaster (Tobolowsky), who discourages Rhodes's frivolous style, and history teacher Ronald Felcher (Glass), who has few positive things to say about kids. He does hit it off with the school's guidance counselor (Forke).

Mr. Rhodes

NICK FRENO: LICENSED TEACHER
WB
Wednesday 8:30–9:00 p.m.
Cast: Mitch Mullany, Reggie Hayes and Lisa Thornhill
The teachers at Gerald R. Ford Middle School certainly don't have their students' interests at heart. The exceptions are former actor Nick Freno (Mullany), Mezz Crosby (Hayes) and Sheryl Sutherland (Thornhill). The three thumb their noses at bureaucracy and bypass the stodgy assistant principal.

PARTY GIRL
Fox
Monday 9:00–9:30 p.m.
Cast: Christine Taylor, John Cameron Mitchell, Bumper Robinson, Sasha Von Scherier and Merrin Dungey
Based on the 1995 film
Mary (Taylor), the ultimate party girl, spends her nights club hopping in search of fun and excitement. Her days are a different story. She works with her bookish godmother/boss (Von Scherier) at the New York Public Library where mastering the Dewey decimal system proves onerous.

PEARL
CBS
Wednesday 8:30–9:00 p.m.
Cast: Rhea Perlman and Malcolm McDowell
Widowed working mother Pearl Caraldo (Perlman) enrolls in an elite Eastern university and gives her uppity professor (McDowell) a dose of much-needed, down-to-earth candor.

THE PRETENDER
NBC
Saturday 9:00–10:00 p.m.
Cast: Michael T. Weiss, Patrick Bauchau and Andrea Parker
Genius Jarod (Weiss) was raised at the Centre, a secret research institute, under the supervision of psychiatrist Sydney (Bauchau), who sold the services of Jarod's computer-like mind. Jarod escapes from the Centre as an adult and uses his intelligence in his quest for justice and to evade Centre operatives who tail him.

PROFILER
NBC
Saturday 10:00–11:00 p.m.
Cast: Ally Walker, Robert Davi, Caitlin Wachs and Erica Gimpel
FBI forensic "profiler" Samantha Waters (Walker), an agent who examines a crime scene and then develops a profile of the suspect, retired from the bureau after a case pushed her over the edge. At the urging of former colleague Bailey Malone (Davi), she returns to help with the toughest cases.

Pearl

PUBLIC MORALS
CBS
Wednesday 9:30–10:00 p.m.
Cast: Julianne Christie, Jana Marie Hupp, Donal Logue, Larry Romano, Joseph Latimore, Peter Gerety and Justin Lois
Steven Bochco, known for his hard-hitting dramas, goes the comedy route in his latest outing. New York City's vice squad cops go after the Johns and Janes that do their business on the city's street corners. Though it's not always pretty, they get the job done. Some affiliates threatened to drop the show if Bochco didn't tone down the raunchy content.

RELATIVITY
ABC
Saturday 10:00–11:00 p.m.
Cast: Kimberly Williams, David Conrad and Randall Batinkoff
Isabel (Williams) and Leo (Conrad) meet in Europe, discover they're from the same town, fall instantly in love and make plans for a future together. There are a few problems though. Isabel is engaged to another man (Batinkoff), and Leo is ashamed of his blue-collar background and dysfunctional family.

SABRINA, THE TEENAGE WITCH
ABC
Friday 8:30–9:00 p.m.
Cast: Melissa Joan Hart, Caroline Rhea, Beth Broderick, Nate Richert, Michelle Beaudoin and Jenna Leigh Green
Based on the Showtime movie
It's hard enough being the new girl in town, but imagine being a witch from the big city who is sent to live with two odd aunts (Rhea and Broderick) in a small town. Sabrina (Hart) does her best and tries to live a normal adolescent life while honing her supernatural powers.

7TH HEAVEN
WB
Monday 8:00–8:30 p.m.
Cast: Stephen Collins, Catherine Hicks, Barry Watson, Jessica Biel and Beverley Mitchell

Eric (Collins) isn't your everyday minister; he's just as comfortable at the pulpit as he is shooting pool at the local bar. In addition to his calling, he's busy at home with his wife, Annie (Hicks), and their five children, who range in age from 3 to 16.

SOMETHING SO RIGHT
NBC
Tuesday 8:30–9:00 p.m.
Cast: Mel Harris, Jere Burns, Billy L. Sullivan, Marne Patterson and Emily Ann Lloyd
Twice-divorced mom Carly Davis (Harris) and divorced dad Jack Farrell (Burns) give marriage another try and form a family with their three children. Things aren't easy, though, as Davis has a hard time balancing her high-pressure career with the demands of being a wife and mother, and Farrell, a high-school English teacher, must cope with the hormones of Carly's 14-year-old son (Sullivan), who has a crush on his 16-year-old stepsister (Patterson).

SPARKS
UPN
Monday 9:30–10:00 p.m.
Cast: James Avery, Robin Givens, Miguel Nunez, Terrence Howard, Kym Whitley and Arif Kinchen
Alonzo Sparks (Avery) would love to retire from his law firm, Sparks, Sparks and Sparks, but his two sons, Greg (Howard) and Maxey (Nunez), would probably kill each other if left alone. Greg is a scrupulous attorney, while Maxey chases ambulances and hustles clients. They do have one thing in common: an attraction to associate Wilma Cuthbert (Givens).

Public Morals

SPIN CITY
ABC
Tuesday 9:30–10:00 p.m.
Cast: Michael J. Fox, Barry Bostwick, Carla Gugino, Alan Ruck, Richard Kind and Alexander Gaberman
The deputy mayor of New York (Fox) has his hands full presiding over his combative staff, dealing with the unrelenting press and maintaining the mayor's (Bostwick) image. As if his life isn't

Sparks

stressful enough, his girlfriend Ashley (Gugino) is a reporter who covers the mayor, forcing him to play politics in his personal as well as professional life.

THE STEVE HARVEY SHOW
WB
Sunday 8:30–9:00 p.m.
Cast: Steve Harvey and Cedric the Entertainer
Musician Steve Hightower (Harvey) gives up clubs for the classroom and gives his students lessons in music and life. The jazzman thought gigging was hard work, but he had no idea how challenging teaching inner-city kids would be. He has an ally in gym teacher Cedric James (the Entertainer).

SUDDENLY SUSAN
NBC
Thursday 9:30–10:00 p.m.
Cast: Judd Nelson, Brooke Shields, Kathy Griffin, Nestor Carbonelli and David Strickland
Magazine writer Susan (Shields) is going through a rough period in her life. She and her fiancé recently ended their relationship, she's playing the dating game again and she doesn't always see eye-to-eye with her boss (Nelson), who is her ex-boyfriend's brother. *Suddenly Susan* underwent a last-minute overhaul that changed the setting from a publishing house to a hip San Francisco magazine and replaced almost the entire supporting cast.

TOWNIES
ABC
Wednesday 8:30–9:00 p.m.
Cast: Molly Ringwald, Jenna Elfman, Lauren Graham, Rob Livingston, Billy Burr, Joseph Reitman, Lee Garlington, Dion Anderson and Conchata Ferrell
A group of twentysomething New Englanders have no plans to abandon their hometown. Instead, they work hard, play hard and devotedly follow the local hockey scene.

1995–1996 Emmy Awards

The 48th Annual Emmy Awards were presented in two ceremonies, one untelevised on September 7, 1996, and the other televised on September 8, 1996, from the Pasadena Civic Auditorium.

Outstanding Drama Series
ER (NBC)

Outstanding Lead Actor in a Drama Series
Dennis Franz, NYPD Blue

Outstanding Lead Actress in a Drama Series
Kathy Baker, Picket Fences

Outstanding Supporting Actor in a Drama Series
Ray Walston, Picket Fences

Outstanding Supporting Actress in a Drama Series
Tyne Daly, Christy

Outstanding Guest Actor in a Drama Series
Peter Boyle, The X-Files: "Clyde Bruckman's Final Repose"

Outstanding Guest Actress in a Drama Series
Amanda Plummer, Outer Limits: "A Stitch in Time"

Outstanding Directing for a Drama Series
Jeremy Kagan, Chicago Hope: "Leave of Absence"

Outstanding Writing for a Drama Series
Darin Morgan, The X-Files: "Clyde Bruckman's Final Repose"

Outstanding Comedy Series
Frasier (NBC)

Outstanding Lead Actor in a Comedy Series
John Lithgow, 3rd Rock From the Sun

Outstanding Lead Actress in a Comedy Series
Helen Hunt, Mad About You

Outstanding Supporting Actor in a Comedy Series
Rip Torn, The Larry Sanders Show

Outstanding Supporting Actress in a Comedy Series
Julia Louis-Dreyfus, Seinfeld

Outstanding Guest Actor in a Comedy Series
Tim Conway, Coach: "The Gardener"

Outstanding Guest Actress in a Comedy Series
Betty White, John Larroquette Show: "Here We Go Again"

Outstanding Directing for a Comedy Series
Michael Lembeck, Friends: "The One After the Superbowl"

Outstanding Writing for a Comedy Series
Joe Keenan, Christopher Lloyd, Rob Greenberg, Jack Burditt, Chuck Ranberg, Anne Flett-Giordano, Linda Morris and Vic Rauseo, Frasier: "Moon Dance"

Outstanding Variety, Music or Comedy Series
Dennis Miller Live (HBO)

Outstanding Individual Performance in a Variety or Music Program
Tony Bennett, Tony Bennett Live by Request: A Valentine Special

Outstanding Directing in a Variety or Music Program
Louis J. Horvitz, The Kennedy Center Honors

Outstanding Writing for a Variety or Music Program
Dennis Miller, Eddie Feldmann, David Feldman, Mike Gandolfi, Tom Hertz, Leah Krinsky and Rick Overton, Dennis Miller Live

Outstanding Variety, Music or Comedy Special
The Kennedy Center Honors (CBS)

Outstanding Miniseries
Gulliver's Travels (NBC)

Outstanding Lead Actor in a Miniseries or Special
Alan Rickman, Rasputin

Outstanding Lead Actress in a Miniseries or Special
Helen Mirren, Prime Suspect: "Scent of Darkness"

Outstanding Supporting Actor in a Miniseries or Special
Tom Hulce, The Heidi Chronicles

Outstanding Supporting Actress in a Miniseries or Special
Greta Scacchi, Rasputin

Outstanding Directing for a Miniseries or a Special
John Frankenheimer, Andersonville

Outstanding Writing for a Miniseries or a Special
Simon Moore, Gulliver's Travels

Outstanding Made for Television Movie
Truman (HBO)

Outstanding Informational Series
Time Life's Lost Civilizations (NBC)

Outstanding Informational Special
Survivors of the Holocaust (TBS)

Outstanding Cultural Music or Dance Program
Great Performances: Itzhak Perlman: In the Fiddler's House (PBS)

Outstanding Children's Program
Peter and the Wolf (ABC)

Outstanding Animated Program
A Pinky and the Brain Christmas Special (WB)

The President's Award
Blacklist: Hollywood on Trial (American Movie Classics)

1995—1996 Prime-Time Nielsen Ratings

OVERALL 1995–1996 RATINGS

ER

Seinfeld

RANK	SHOW	NETWORK	RATING*
1.	*ER*.	NBC	22.0
2.	*Seinfeld*.	NBC	21.2
3.	*Friends*	NBC	18.7
4.	*Caroline in the City*	NBC	17.9
5.	*NFL Monday Night Football*	ABC	17.1
6.	*The Single Guy*.	NBC	16.7
7.	*Home Improvement*	ABC	16.2
8.	*Boston Common*.	NBC	15.6
9.	*60 Minutes*.	CBS	14.2
10.	*NYPD Blue*	ABC	14.1
11.	*Frasier*.	NBC	13.6
11.	*20/20*.	ABC	13.6
13.	*Grace Under Fire*	ABC	13.2
14.	*Coach*.	ABC	12.9
14.	*NBC Monday Night Movie*	NBC	12.9
16.	*Roseanne*	ABC	12.5
17.	*The Nanny*.	CBS	12.4
18.	*Murphy Brown*	CBS	12.3
18.	*PrimeTime Live*.	ABC	12.3
18.	*Walker, Texas Ranger*	CBS	12.3
21.	*Champs*	ABC	12.2
21.	*NBC Sunday Night Movie*	NBC	12.2
23.	*3rd Rock From the Sun*	NBC	12.1
24.	*Chicago Hope*	CBS	11.9
25.	*Can't Hurry Love*	CBS	11.4

RANK	SHOW	NETWORK	RATING*
25.	*CBS Sunday Movie*	CBS	11.4
25.	*Law & Order*	NBC	11.4
25.	*The Naked Truth*.	ABC	11.4
29.	*America's Funniest Home Videos 2*	ABC	11.3
29.	*Dateline NBC* (Tuesday)	NBC	11.3
29.	*Dateline NBC* (Wednesday)	NBC	11.3
32.	*The Dana Carvey Show*	ABC	11.2
32.	*Fox NFL Sunday Postgame Show 2*.	FOX	11.2

Chicago Hope

RANK	SHOW	NETWORK	RATING*
34.	*Touched by an Angel*	CBS	11.1
35.	*Wings*	NBC	11.0
36.	*If Not for You*	CBS	10.9
37.	*Mad About You*	NBC	10.8
38.	*Hudson Street*	ABC	10.7
39.	*ABC Sunday Night Movie*	ABC	10.6
39.	*Ellen*	ABC	10.6
39.	*NewsRadio*	NBC	10.6
42.	*Family Matters*	ABC	10.5
42.	*John Larroquette Show*	NBC	10.5
44.	*Dateline NBC* (Friday)	NBC	10.3
44.	*Lois and Clark*	ABC	10.3
46.	*ABC Monday Night Movie*	ABC	10.2
46.	*High Society*	CBS	10.2
48.	*Boy Meets World*	ABC	10.1
48.	*The Drew Carey Show*	ABC	10.1
50.	*Cybill*	CBS	10.0
50.	*Pursuit of Happiness*	NBC	10.0
50.	*The X-Files*	FOX	10.0
53.	*Beverly Hills, 90210*	FOX	9.8
54.	*Step by Step*	ABC	9.7
55.	*CBS Tuesday Movie*	CBS	9.6
55.	*Dr. Quinn, Medicine Woman*	CBS	9.6
55.	*Fresh Prince of Bel Air*	NBC	9.6
58.	*Murder, She Wrote*	CBS	9.5
59.	*In the House*	NBC	9.4
59.	*Unsolved Mysteries*	NBC	9.4
61.	*The Faculty*	ABC	9.3
61.	*Hangin' With Mr. Cooper*	ABC	9.3
61.	*Melrose Place*	FOX	9.3

Picket Fences

RANK	SHOW	NETWORK	RATING*
64.	*Buddies*	ABC	9.1
65.	*Almost Perfect*	CBS	9.0
66.	*Good Company*	CBS	8.9
66.	*Homicide: Life on the Street*	NBC	8.9
66.	*Murder One*	ABC	8.9
69.	*Diagnosis Murder*	CBS	8.8
70.	*America's Funniest Home Videos*	ABC	8.7
70.	*CBS Wednesday Movie*	CBS	8.7
70.	*Dave's World*	CBS	8.7
73.	*Nash Bridges*	CBS	8.6
74.	*Bonnie*	CBS	8.4
74.	*High Incident*	ABC	8.4
74.	*Muppets Tonight!*	ABC	8.4
77.	*The Simpsons*	FOX	8.3
78.	*Married ... With Children*	FOX	8.2
79.	*JAG*	NBC	8.1
79.	*Second Noah*	ABC	8.1
81.	*Aliens in the Family*	ABC	8.0
82.	*The Client*	CBS	7.9
83.	*48 Hours*	CBS	7.8
84.	*ABC Thursday Night Movie*	ABC	7.7
84.	*Rescue: 911*	CBS	7.7
86.	*The Louie Show*	CBS	7.6
87.	*Bless This House*	CBS	7.5
87.	*Day One*	ABC	7.5
87.	*Matt Waters*	CBS	7.5
90.	*Before They Were Stars* (Thursday)	ABC	7.4
90.	*Dateline NBC* (Sunday)	NBC	7.4
90.	*World's Funniest Videos*	ABC	7.4

Profit

RANK	SHOW	NETWORK	RATING*
93.	*Cops 2*	FOX	7.3
94.	*Due South*	CBS	7.2
94.	*The Marshal*	ABC	7.2
96.	*The Jeff Foxworthy Show*	ABC	7.1
96.	*Party of Five*	FOX	7.1
98.	*Fox Tuesday Night Movie*	FOX	7.0
98.	*Hope and Gloria*	NBC	7.0
98.	*Picket Fences*	CBS	7.0
98.	*Saturday Night at the Movies*	ABC	7.0
102.	*New York Undercover*	FOX	6.9
103.	*Sisters*	NBC	6.8
104.	*America's Most Wanted*	FOX	6.7
104.	*Brotherly Love*	NBC	6.7
104.	*Martin*	FOX	6.7
104.	*NBC Saturday Night Movie*	NBC	6.7
108.	*American Gothic*	CBS	6.6
108.	*Charlie Grace*	ABC	6.6
108.	*Maybe This Time*	ABC	6.6
111.	*The Crew*	FOX	6.5
111.	*Living Single*	FOX	6.5
113.	*New York News*	CBS	6.3
113.	*Space: Above and Beyond*	FOX	6.3
115.	*Central Park West*	CBS	6.2
115.	*What's So Funny?*	FOX	6.2
117.	*Cops*	FOX	6.1
117.	*Courthouse*	CBS	6.1
117.	*seaQuest 2032*	NBC	6.1
117.	*Strange Luck*	FOX	6.1

RANK	SHOW	NETWORK	RATING*
121.	*Ned and Stacey*	FOX	6.0
122.	*Dweebs*	CBS	5.9
122.	*Misery Loves Company*	FOX	5.9
122.	*Sliders*	FOX	5.9
122.	*Too Something*	FOX	5.9
126.	*Kindred: The Embraced*	FOX	5.6
126.	*The Monroes*	ABC	5.6
126.	*The Show*	FOX	5.6
129.	*The Bonnie Hunt Show*	CBS	5.5
129.	*Local Heroes*	FOX	5.5
131.	*Malibu Shores*	NBC	5.4
131.	*Partners*	FOX	5.4
133.	*My Guys*	CBS	5.3
134.	*The Home Court*	NBC	5.1
134.	*NBC Baseball Night*	NBC	5.1
134.	*Star Trek: Voyager*	UPN	5.1
134.	*Time-Lost Civilizations*	NBC	5.1
138.	*Profit*	FOX	4.9
139.	*Minor Adjustments*	NBC	4.8
140.	*The Preston Episodes*	FOX	4.1
141.	*Moesha*	UPN	3.5
142.	*The Parent 'Hood*	WB	3.0
142.	*Sister, Sister*	WB	3.0
144.	*Savannah*	WB	2.9
144.	*The Wayans Bros.*	WB	2.9
146.	*The Sentinel*	UPN	2.8
147.	*Minor Adjustments*	UPN	2.7
148.	*Nowhere Man*	UPN	2.6
148.	*Sister, Sister* (Sunday)	WB	2.6
150.	*Swift Justice*	UPN	2.5
150.	*Unhappily Ever After*	WB	2.5
152.	*Kirk*	WB	2.2
152.	*The Paranormal Borderline*	UPN	2.2
154.	*Cleghorne!*	WB	2.1
154.	*Deadly Games*	UPN	2.1
156.	*The Parent 'Hood* (Sunday)	WB	1.8
156.	*Pinky and the Brain*	WB	1.8
158.	*First Time Out*	WB	1.6
158.	*Live Shot*	UPN	1.6
160.	*Simon*	WB	1.5

Each rating point represents 959,000 households using television

Brotherly Love

The Emmy® Awards

The Emmy Awards have evolved over the years to keep pace with the growth of the television industry. During the 1976–1977 season, the television academy split into two entities: the Academy of Television Arts and Sciences, which administers the prime-time awards, and the National Academy of Television Arts and Sciences, which presents the daytime awards. The awards are now featured in two ceremonies, prime-time in the fall and daytime in the spring.

1948

Most Popular Television Program
Pantomime Quiz Time (KTLA)

Most Outstanding Television Personality
Shirley Dinsdale and her puppet Judy Splinters

Best Film Made for Television
The Necklace

1949

Best Live Show
Ed Wynn (KTTV)

Most Outstanding Live Personality
Ed Wynn

Best Kinescope Show
Texaco Star Theatre (KNBH, NBC)

Most Outstanding Kinescoped Personality
Milton Berle

Best Film Made for and Viewed on Television in 1949
Life of Riley (KNBH)

Best Public Service, Cultural or Educational Program
Crusade in Europe (KECA-TV, KTTV)

Best Sports Coverage
Wrestling (KTLA)

Best Children's Show
Time for Beany (KTLA)

1950

Best Dramatic Show
Pulitzer Prize Playhouse (KECA-TV)

Best Actor
Alan Young

Best Actress
Gertrude Berg

Most Outstanding Personality
Groucho Marx

Best Variety Show
The Alan Young Show (KTTV, CBS)

Best Game and Audience Participation Show
Truth or Consequences (KTTV, CBS)

Best Public Service
City at Night (KTLA)

Edward R. Murrow

Best News Program
KTLA Newsreel

Best Sports Program
Rams Football (KNBH)

Best Cultural Show
Campus Chorus and Orchestra (KTSL)

Best Educational Show
KFI-TV University (KFI-TV)

Best Children's Show
Time for Beany (KTLA)

1951

Best Dramatic Show
Studio One (CBS)

Best Actor
Sid Caesar

Best Actress
Imogene Coca

Best Comedy Show
Red Skelton Show (NBC)

Best Comedian or Comedienne
Red Skelton

Best Variety Show
Your Show of Shows (NBC)

1952

Best Dramatic Program
Robert Montgomery Presents (NBC)

Best Actor
Thomas Mitchell

Best Actress
Helen Hayes

Most Outstanding Personality
Bishop Fulton J. Sheen

Best Situation Comedy
I Love Lucy (CBS)

Best Comedian
Jimmy Durante

Best Comedienne
Lucille Ball

Best Variety Program
Your Show of Shows (NBC)

Best Mystery, Action or Adventure Program
Dragnet (NBC)

Best Public Affairs Program
See It Now (CBS)

Best Children's Program
Time for Beany (KTLA)

Best Audience Participation, Quiz or Panel Program
What's My Line? (CBS)

1953

Best Dramatic Program
U.S. Steel Hour (ABC)

Best Male Star of a Regular Series
Donald O'Connor, *Colgate Comedy Hour*

Best Female Star of a Regular Series
Eve Arden, *Our Miss Brooks*

Best Series Supporting Actor
Art Carney, *Jackie Gleason Show*

Best Series Supporting Actress
Vivian Vance, *I Love Lucy*

Most Outstanding Personality
Edward R. Murrow

Best New Program (tie)
Make Room for Daddy (ABC)
U.S. Steel Hour (ABC)

Best Situation Comedy
I Love Lucy (CBS)

Best Variety Program
Omnibus (CBS)

Best Mystery, Action or Adventure Program
Dragnet (NBC)

Best Public Affairs Program
Victory at Sea (NBC)

Best Program of News or Sports
See It Now (CBS)

Best Children's Program
Kukla, Fran and Ollie (NBC)

Best Audience Participation, Quiz or Panel Program (tie)
This Is Your Life (NBC)
What's My Line? (CBS)

1954

Best Dramatic Series
U.S. Steel Hour (ABC)

Best Actor Starring in a Regular Series
Danny Thomas, *Make Room for Daddy*

Best Actress Starring in a Regular Series
Loretta Young, *Loretta Young Show*

Best Supporting Actor in a Regular Series
Art Carney, *Jackie Gleason Show*

Best Supporting Actress in a Regular Series
Audrey Meadows, *Jackie Gleason Show*

Best Individual Program of the Year
Operation Undersea (ABC)

Best Actor in a Single Performance
Robert Cummings, *Studio One: Twelve Angry Men*

Best Actress in a Single Performance
Judith Anderson, *Hallmark Hall of Fame: Macbeth*

Best Direction
Franklin Schaffner, *Studio One: Twelve Angry Men*

Best Written Dramatic Material
Reginald Rose, *Twelve Angry Men*

Most Outstanding New Personality
George Gobel

Best Situation Comedy Series
Make Room for Daddy (ABC)

Best Written Comedy Material
James Allardice, Jack Douglas, Hal Kanter and
Harry Winkler, *George Gobel Show*

Best Variety Series, Including Musical Varieties
Disneyland (ABC)

Best Mystery or Intrigue Series
Dragnet (NBC)

Best Western or Adventure Series
Stories of the Century (Syndicated)

Best Cultural, Religious or Educational Program
Omnibus (CBS)

Best News Reporter or Commentator
John Daly

Best Sports Program
Gillette Cavalcade of Sports (NBC)

Best Children's Program
Lassie (CBS)

Best Audience, Guest Participation or Panel Program
This Is Your Life (NBC)

1955

Best Dramatic Series
Producers' Showcase (NBC)

Best Actor, Continuing Performance
Phil Silvers, *Phil Silvers Show, You'll Never Get Rich*

Best Actress, Continuing Performance
Lucille Ball, *I Love Lucy*

Best Actor in a Supporting Role
Art Carney, *The Honeymooners*

Best Actress in a Supporting Role
Nanette Fabray, *Caesar's Hour*

Best Single Program of the Year
Producers' Showcase: Peter Pan (NBC)

Best Actor, Single Performance
Lloyd Nolan, *Ford Star Jubilee: Caine Mutiny Court Martial*

Best Actress, Single Performance
Mary Martin, *Producers' Showcase: Peter Pan*

Best Television Adaptation
Paul Gregory and Franklin Schaffner, *Caine Mutiny Court Martial* by Herman Wouk

Best Director, Film Series
Nat Hiken, *Phil Silvers Show, You'll Never Get Rich*

Best Director, Live Series
Franklin Schaffner, *Caine Mutiny Court Martial*

Best Original Teleplay Writing
Rod Serling, *Kraft TV Theatre: Patterns*

Best Comedy Series
Phil Silvers Show, You'll Never Get Rich (CBS)

Best Comedian
Phil Silvers

Best Comedienne
Nanette Fabray

Best Comedy Writing
Nat Hiken, Barry Blitser, Arnold Auerbach, Harvey Orkin, Vincent Bogert, Arnold Rosen, Coleman Jacoby, Tony Webster and Terry Ryan, *Phil Silvers Show, You'll Never Get Rich*

Best Variety Series
Ed Sullivan Show (CBS)

Best Music Series
Your Hit Parade (NBC)

Best Action or Adventure Series
Disneyland (ABC)

Best Documentary Program, Religious, Informational, Educational or Interview
Omnibus (CBS)

Best News Commentator or Reporter
Edward R. Murrow

Best Children's Series
Lassie (CBS)

Best Audience Participation Series (Quiz, Panel, etc.)
$64,000 Question (CBS)

Best Specialty Act, Single or Group
Marcel Marceau

Best MC or Program Host, Male or Female
Perry Como

1956

Best Series, Half Hour or Less
Phil Silvers Show (CBS)

Best Series, One Hour or More
Caesar's Hour (NBC)

Best Continuing Performance by an Actor in a Dramatic Series
Robert Young, *Father Knows Best*

Best Continuing Performance by an Actress in a Dramatic Series
Loretta Young, *Loretta Young Show*

Best Supporting Performance by an Actor
Carl Reiner, *Caesar's Hour*

Best Supporting Performance by an Actress
Pat Carroll, *Caesar's Hour*

Best Direction, Half Hour or Less
Sheldon Leonard, *Danny Thomas Show: "Danny's Comeback"*

Best Teleplay Writing, Half Hour or Less
James P. Cavanagh, *Alfred Hitchcock Presents: "Fog Closing In"*

Best Direction, One Hour or More
Ralph Nelson, *Playhouse 90: Requiem for a Heavyweight*

Best Teleplay Writing, One Hour or More
Rod Serling, *Playhouse 90: Requiem for a Heavyweight*

Best Male Personality, Continuing Performance
Perry Como

Best Female Personality, Continuing Performance
Dinah Shore

Best New Program Series
Playhouse 90 (CBS)

Best Single Program of the Year
Playhouse 90: Requiem for a Heavyweight (CBS)

Best Single Performance by an Actor
Jack Palance, *Playhouse 90: Requiem for a Heavyweight*

Best Single Performance by an Actress
Claire Trevor, *Producers' Showcase: Dodsworth*

Best Continuing Performance by a Comedian in a Series
Sid Caesar, *Caesar's Hour*

Best Continuing Performance by a Comedienne in a Series
Nanette Fabray, *Caesar's Hour*

Best Comedy Writing, Variety or Situation Comedy
Nat Hiken, Billy Friedberg, Tony Webster, Leonard Stern, Arnold Rosen and Coleman Jacoby, *Phil Silvers Show*

Best Public Service Series
See It Now (CBS)

Best News Commentator
Edward R. Murrow

1957

Best Dramatic Series With Continuing Characters
Gunsmoke (CBS)

Best Dramatic Anthology Series
Playhouse 90 (CBS)

Actor, Best Single Performance, Lead or Support
Peter Ustinov, *Omnibus: The Life of Samuel Johnson*

Actress, Best Single Performance, Lead or Support
Polly Bergen, *Playhouse 90: Helen Morgan Story*

Best Single Program of the Year
Playhouse 90: The Comedian (CBS)

Best New Program Series of the Year
Seven Lively Arts (CBS)

Best Comedy Series
Phil Silvers Show (CBS)

Best Continuing Performance by an Actor in a Leading Role in a Dramatic or Comedy Series
Robert Young, *Father Knows Best*

Best Continuing Performance by an Actress in a Leading Role in a Dramatic or Comedy Series
Jane Wyatt, *Father Knows Best*

Best Continuing Supporting Performance by an Actor in a Dramatic or Comedy Series
Carl Reiner, *Caesar's Hour*

Best Continuing Supporting Performance by an Actress in a Dramatic or Comedy Series
Ann B. Davis, *Bob Cummings Show*

Best Comedy Writing
Nat Hiken, Billy Friedberg, Phil Sharp, Terry Ryan, Coleman Jacoby, Arnold Rosen, Sidney Zelinka, A.J. Russell and Tony Webster, *Phil Silvers Show*

Best Musical, Variety, Audience Participation or Quiz Series
Dinah Shore Chevy Show (NBC)

Best Continuing Performance (Male) in a Series by a Comedian, Singer, Host, Dancer, MC, Announcer, Narrator, Panelist or Any Person Who Essentially Plays Himself
Jack Benny, *Jack Benny Show*

Best Continuing Performance (Female) in a Series by a Comedienne, Singer, Hostess, Dancer, MC, Announcer, Narrator, Panelist or Any Person Who Essentially Plays Herself
Dinah Shore, *Dinah Shore Chevy Show*

Best Direction, Half Hour or Less
Robert Stevens, *Alfred Hitchcock Presents:* "The Glass Eye"

Best Teleplay Writing, Half Hour or Less
Paul Monash, *Schlitz Playhouse of Stars:* "The Lonely Wizard"

Best Direction, One Hour or More
Bob Banner, *Dinah Shore Chevy Show*

Best Teleplay Writing, One Hour or More
Rod Serling, *Playhouse 90: The Comedian*

Best Public Service Program or Series
Omnibus (ABC, NBC)

Best News Commentary
Edward R. Murrow

1958—1959

Best Dramatic Series, Less Than One Hour
Alcoa-Goodyear Theatre (NBC)

Best Dramatic Series, One Hour or Longer
Playhouse 90 (CBS)

Best Actor in a Leading Role (Continuing Character) in a Dramatic Series
Raymond Burr, *Perry Mason*

Best Actress in a Leading Role (Continuing Character) in a Dramatic Series
Loretta Young, *Loretta Young Show*

Best Supporting Actor (Continuing Character) in a Dramatic Series
Dennis Weaver, *Gunsmoke*

Best Supporting Actress (Continuing Character) in a Dramatic Series
Barbara Hale, *Perry Mason*

Best Direction of a Single Program of a Dramatic Series, Less Than One Hour
Jack Smight, *Alcoa-Goodyear Theatre:* "Eddie"

Best Writing of a Single Program of a Dramatic Series, Less Than One Hour
Alfred Brenner and Ken Hughes, *Alcoa-Goodyear Theatre:* "Eddie"

Best Special Dramatic Program, One Hour or Longer
Hallmark Hall of Fame: Little Moon of Alban (NBC)

Best Direction of a Single Dramatic Program, One Hour or Longer
George Schaefer, *Hallmark Hall of Fame: Little Moon of Alban*

Best Writing of a Single Dramatic Program, One Hour or Longer
James Costigan, *Hallmark Hall of Fame: Little Moon of Alban*

Most Outstanding Single Program of the Year
An Evening With Fred Astaire (NBC)

Best Single Performance by an Actor
Fred Astaire, *An Evening With Fred Astaire*

Best Single Performance by an Actress
Julie Harris, *Hallmark Hall of Fame: Little Moon of Alban*

Best Comedy Series
Jack Benny Show (CBS)

Best Actor in a Leading Role (Continuing Character) in a Comedy Series
Jack Benny, *Jack Benny Show*

Best Actress in a Leading Role (Continuing Character) in a Comedy Series
Jane Wyatt, *Father Knows Best*

Best Supporting Actor (Continuing Character) in a Comedy Series
Tom Poston, *Steve Allen Show*

Best Supporting Actress (Continuing Character) in a Comedy Series
Ann B. Davis, *Bob Cummings Show*

Best Direction of a Single Program of a Comedy Series
Peter Tewksbury, *Father Knows Best:* "Medal for Margaret"

Best Writing of a Single Program of a Comedy Series
Sam Perrin, George Balzer, Hal Goldman and Al Gordon, *Jack Benny Show:* "Jack Benny Show With Ernie Kovacs"

Best Musical or Variety Series
Dinah Shore Chevy Show (NBC)

Best Performance by an Actor (Continuing Character) in a Musical or Variety Series
Perry Como, *Perry Como Show*

Loretta Young, *Loretta Young Show*

Jack Benny Show

Best Performance by an Actress (Continuing Character) in a Musical or Variety Series
Dinah Shore, *Dinah Shore Chevy Show*

Best Special Musical or Variety Program, One Hour or Longer
An Evening With Fred Astaire (NBC)

Best Direction of a Single Musical or Variety Program
Bud Yorkin, *An Evening With Fred Astaire*

Best Writing of a Single Musical or Variety Program
Bud Yorkin and Herbert Baker, *An Evening With Fred Astaire*

Best Western Series
Maverick (ABC)

Best Public Service Program or Series
Omnibus (NBC)

Best News Reporting Series
Huntley-Brinkley Report (NBC)

Best Special News Program
Face of Red China (CBS)

Best News Commentator or Analyst
Edward R. Murrow

Best Panel, Quiz or Audience Participation Series
What's My Line? (CBS)

1959—1960

Outstanding Program Achievement in the Field of Drama
Playhouse 90 (CBS)

Outstanding Performance by an Actor in a Series (Lead or Support)
Robert Stack, *The Untouchables*

Outstanding Performance by an Actress in a Series (Lead or Support)
Jane Wyatt, *Father Knows Best*

Outstanding Directorial Achievement in Drama
Robert Mulligan, *The Moon and Sixpence*

Outstanding Writing Achievement in Drama
Rod Serling, *Twilight Zone*

Outstanding Single Performance by an Actor (Lead or Support)
Laurence Olivier, *The Moon and Sixpence*

Outstanding Single Performance by an Actress (Lead or Support)
Ingrid Bergman, *Ford Startime: The Turn of the Screw*

Outstanding Program Achievement in the Field of Humor
Art Carney Special (NBC)

Outstanding Directorial Achievement in Comedy
Ralph Levy and Bud Yorkin, *Jack Benny Hour* specials

Outstanding Writing Achievement in Comedy
Sam Perrin, George Balzer, Al Gordon and Hal Goldman, *Jack Benny Show*

Outstanding Program Achievement in the Field of Variety
Fabulous Fifties (CBS)

Outstanding Performance in a Variety or Musical Program or Series
Harry Belafonte, *Revlon Revue: Tonight With Belafonte*

Outstanding Achievement in the Field of Music
Leonard Bernstein and the New York Philharmonic (CBS)

Outstanding Program Achievement in the Field of Public Affairs and Education
Twentieth Century (CBS)

Outstanding Program Achievement in the Field of News
Huntley-Brinkley Report (NBC)

Outstanding Writing Achievement in the Documentary Field
Howard K. Smith and Av Westin, *The Population Explosion*

Outstanding Achievement in the Field of Children's Programming
Huckleberry Hound (Syndicated)

1960—1961

Outstanding Program Achievement in the Field of Drama
Hallmark Hall of Fame: Macbeth (NBC)

Outstanding Performance by an Actor in a Series (Lead)
Raymond Burr, *Perry Mason*

Outstanding Performance by an Actress in a Series (Lead)
Barbara Stanwyck, *Barbara Stanwyck Show*

Outstanding Performance in a Supporting Role by an Actor or Actress in a Series
Don Knotts, *The Andy Griffith Show*

Outstanding Directorial Achievement in Drama
George Schaefer, *Hallmark Hall of Fame: Macbeth*

Outstanding Writing Achievement in Drama
Rod Serling, *The Twilight Zone*

The Program of the Year
Hallmark Hall of Fame: Macbeth (NBC)

Outstanding Single Performance by an Actor in a Leading Role
Maurice Evans, *Hallmark Hall of Fame: Macbeth*

Outstanding Single Performance by an Actress in a Leading Role
Judith Anderson, *Hallmark Hall of Fame: Macbeth*

Outstanding Performance in a Supporting Role by an Actor or Actress in a Single Program
Roddy McDowall, *Equitable's American Heritage: Not Without Honor*

Outstanding Program Achievement in the Field of Humor
Jack Benny Show (CBS)

Outstanding Directorial Achievement in Comedy
Sheldon Leonard, *The Danny Thomas Show*

Outstanding Writing Achievement in Comedy
Sherwood Schwartz, Dave O'Brien, Al Schwartz, Martin Ragaway and Red Skelton, *Red Skelton Show*

Outstanding Program Achievement in the Field of Variety
Astaire Time (NBC)

Outstanding Performance in a Variety or Musical Program or Series
Fred Astaire, *Astaire Time*

Outstanding Program Achievement in the Field of Public Affairs and Education
The Twentieth Century (CBS)

Outstanding Program Achievement in the Field of News
Huntley-Brinkley Report (NBC)

Outstanding Writing Achievement in the Documentary Field
Victor Wolfson, *Winston Churchill, The Valiant Years*

Outstanding Achievement in the Field of Children's Programming
Young People's Concert: Aaron Copland's Birthday Party (CBS)

1961–1962

Outstanding Program Achievement in the Field of Drama
The Defenders (CBS)

Outstanding Continued Performance by an Actor in a Series (Lead)
E.G. Marshall, *The Defenders*

Outstanding Continued Performance by an Actress in a Series (Lead)
Shirley Booth, *Hazel*

Outstanding Performance in a Supporting Role by an Actor
Don Knotts, *The Andy Griffith Show*

Outstanding Performance in a Supporting Role by an Actress
Pamela Brown, *Hallmark Hall of Fame: Victoria Regina*

Outstanding Directorial Achievement in Drama
Franklin Schaffner, *The Defenders:* various episodes

Outstanding Writing Achievement in Drama
Reginald Rose, *The Defenders:* various episodes

The Program of the Year
Hallmark Hall of Fame: Victoria Regina (NBC)

Outstanding Single Performance by an Actor in a Leading Role
Peter Falk, *Dick Powell Show:* "The Price of Tomatoes"

Outstanding Single Performance by an Actress in a Leading Role
Julie Harris, *Hallmark Hall of Fame: Victoria Regina*

Outstanding Program Achievement in the Field of Humor
Bob Newhart Show (NBC)

Outstanding Directorial Achievement in Comedy
Nat Hiken, *Car 54, Where Are You?*

Outstanding Writing Achievement in Comedy
Carl Reiner, *Dick Van Dyke Show*

Outstanding Program Achievements in the Fields of Variety and Music
VARIETY
Garry Moore Show (CBS)
MUSIC
Leonard Bernstein and the New York Philharmonic in Japan (CBS)

Outstanding Performance in a Variety or Musical Program or Series
Carol Burnett, *Garry Moore Show*

Outstanding Program Achievement in the Field of Educational and Public Affairs Programming
David Brinkley's Journal (NBC)

Outstanding Program Achievement in the Field of News
Huntley-Brinkley Report (NBC)

Outstanding Writing Achievement in the Documentary Field
Lou Hazam, *Vincent Van Gogh: A Self Portrait*

Outstanding Program Achievement in the Field of Children's Programming
New York Philharmonic Young People's Concerts With Leonard Bernstein (CBS)

1962–1963

Outstanding Program Achievement in the Field of Drama
The Defenders (CBS)

Outstanding Continued Performance by an Actor in a Series (Lead)
E.G. Marshall, *The Defenders*

Outstanding Continued Performance by an Actress in a Series (Lead)
Shirley Booth, *Hazel*

Outstanding Performance in a Supporting Role by an Actor
Don Knotts, *The Andy Griffith Show*

Outstanding Performance in a Supporting Role by an Actress
Glenda Farrell, *Ben Casey:* "A Cardinal Act of Mercy"

Outstanding Directorial Achievement in Drama
Stuart Rosenberg, *The Defenders:* "The Madman"

Outstanding Writing Achievement in Drama
Robert Thom and Reginald Rose, *The Defenders:* "The Madman"

The Program of the Year
The Tunnel (NBC)

Outstanding Single Performance by an Actor in a Leading Role
Trevor Howard, *Hallmark Hall of Fame: The Invincible Mr. Disraeli*

Outstanding Single Performance by an Actress in a Leading Role
Kim Stanley, *Ben Casey:* "A Cardinal Act of Mercy"

Outstanding Program Achievement in the Field of Humor
The Dick Van Dyke Show (CBS)

Outstanding Directorial Achievement in Comedy
John Rich, *The Dick Van Dyke Show*

Outstanding Writing Achievement in Comedy
Carl Reiner, *The Dick Van Dyke Show*

Outstanding Program Achievement in the Field of Variety
The Andy Williams Show (NBC)

Outstanding Program Achievement in the Field of Music
Julie and Carol at Carnegie Hall (CBS)

Outstanding Performance in a Variety or Musical Program or Series
Carol Burnett, *Julie and Carol at Carnegie Hall*

Outstanding Program Achievement in the Field of News Commentary or Public Affairs
David Brinkley's Journal (NBC)

Outstanding Program Achievement in the Field of News
Huntley-Brinkley Report (NBC)

Outstanding Achievement in the Field of Documentary Programs
The Tunnel (NBC)

Outstanding Program Achievement in the Field of Children's Programming
Walt Disney's Wonderful World of Color (NBC)

Outstanding Program Achievement in the Field of Panel, Quiz or Audience Participation
G-E College Bowl (CBS)

1963–1964

Outstanding Program Achievement in the Field of Drama
The Defenders (CBS)

Outstanding Continued Performance by an Actor in a Series (Lead)
Dick Van Dyke, *The Dick Van Dyke Show*

Outstanding Continued Performance by an Actress in a Series (Lead)
Mary Tyler Moore, *The Dick Van Dyke Show*

Outstanding Performance in a Supporting Role by an Actor
Albert Paulsen, *Bob Hope Presents the Chrysler Theatre: One Day in the Life of Ivan Denisovich*

Outstanding Performance in a Supporting Role by an Actress
Ruth White, *Hallmark Hall of Fame: Little Moon of Alban*

Outstanding Directorial Achievement in Drama
Tom Gries, *East Side/West Side*: "Who Do You Kill?"

Outstanding Writing Achievement in Drama, Original
Ernest Kinoy, *The Defenders*: "Blacklist"

Outstanding Writing Achievement in Drama, Adaptation
Rod Serling, *Bob Hope Presents the Chrysler Theatre: It's Mental Work*, from the story by John O'Hara

The Program of the Year
The Making of the President 1960 (ABC)

Outstanding Single Performance by an Actor in a Leading Role
Jack Klugman, *The Defenders*: "Blacklist"

Outstanding Single Performance by an Actress in a Leading Role
Shelley Winters, *Bob Hope Presents the Chrysler Theatre: Two Is the Number*

Outstanding Program Achievement in the Field of Comedy
The Dick Van Dyke Show (CBS)

Outstanding Directorial Achievement in Comedy
Jerry Paris, *The Dick Van Dyke Show*

Outstanding Writing Achievement in Comedy or Variety
Carl Reiner, Sam Denoff and Bill Persky, *The Dick Van Dyke Show*: various episodes

Outstanding Program Achievement in the Field of Variety
The Danny Kaye Show (CBS)

Outstanding Program Achievement in the Field of Music
Bell Telephone Hour (NBC)

Outstanding Performance in a Variety or Musical Program or Series
Danny Kaye, *The Danny Kaye Show*

Outstanding Directorial Achievement in Variety or Music
Robert Scheerer, *The Danny Kaye Show*

Outstanding Program Achievement in the Field of News Commentary or Public Affairs
Cuba, parts I and II — The Bay of Pigs and *The Missile Crisis* (NBC)

Outstanding Program Achievement in the Field of News Reports
Huntley-Brinkley Report (NBC)

Outstanding Achievement in the Field of Documentary Programs
The Making of the President 1960 (ABC)

Outstanding Program Achievement in the Field of Children's Programming
Discovery '63–'64 (ABC)

1964–1965

Outstanding Program Achievements in Entertainment
The Dick Van Dyke Show (CBS)

Hallmark Hall of Fame: The Magnificent Yankee (NBC)

My Name is Barbra (CBS)

New York Philharmonic Young People's Concerts With Leonard Bernstein: "What Is Sonata Form?" (CBS)

Outstanding Individual Achievements in Entertainment
ACTORS AND PERFORMERS
Leonard Bernstein, *New York Philharmonic Young People's Concerts With Leonard Bernstein*

Lynn Fontanne, *Hallmark Hall of Fame: The Magnificent Yankee*

Alfred Lunt, *Hallmark Hall of Fame: The Magnificent Yankee*

Barbra Streisand, *My Name Is Barbra*

Dick Van Dyke, *The Dick Van Dyke Show*

DIRECTOR
Paul Bogart, *The Defenders:* "The 700-Year-Old Gang"

WRITER
David Karp, *The Defenders:* "The 700-Year-Old Gang"

Outstanding Program Achievements in News, Documentaries, Information and Sports
Saga of Western Man: I, Leonardo Da Vinci (ABC)

The Louvre (NBC)

Outstanding Individual Achievements in News, Documentaries, Information and Sports
NARRATORS
Richard Basehart, *Let My People Go*

Charles Boyer, *The Louvre*

DIRECTOR
John J. Sughrue, *The Louvre*

WRITER
Sidney Carroll, *The Louvre*

1965–1966

Outstanding Dramatic Series
The Fugitive (ABC)

Outstanding Continued Performance by an Actor in a Leading Role in a Dramatic Series
Bill Cosby, *I Spy*

Outstanding Continued Performance by an Actress in a Leading Role in a Dramatic Series
Barbara Stanwyck, *The Big Valley*

Outstanding Performance by an Actor in a Supporting Role in a Drama
James Daly, *Hallmark Hall of Fame: Eagle in a Cage*

Outstanding Performance by an Actress in a Supporting Role in a Drama
Lee Grant, *Peyton Place*

Outstanding Directorial Achievement in Drama
Sydney Pollack, *Bob Hope Presents the Chrysler Theatre: The Game*

Outstanding Writing Achievement in Drama
Millard Lampell, *Hallmark Hall of Fame: Eagle in a Cage*

The Dick Van Dyke Show

Outstanding Dramatic Program
Ages of Man (CBS)

Outstanding Single Performance by an Actor in a Leading Role in a Drama
Cliff Robertson, *Bob Hope Presents the Chrysler Theatre: The Game*

Outstanding Single Performance by an Actress in a Leading Role in a Drama
Simone Signoret, *Bob Hope Presents the Chrysler Theatre: A Small Rebellion*

Outstanding Comedy Series
The Dick Van Dyke Show (CBS)

Outstanding Continued Performance by an Actor in a Leading Role in a Comedy Series
Dick Van Dyke, *The Dick Van Dyke Show*

Outstanding Continued Performance by an Actress in a Leading Role in a Comedy Series
Mary Tyler Moore, *The Dick Van Dyke Show*

Outstanding Performance by an Actor in a Supporting Role in a Comedy
Don Knotts, *The Andy Griffith Show:* "The Return of Barney Fife"

Outstanding Performance by an Actress in a Supporting Role in a Comedy
Alice Pearce, *Bewitched*

Outstanding Directorial Achievement in Comedy
William Asher, *Bewitched*

Outstanding Writing Achievement in Comedy
Bill Persky and Sam Denoff, *The Dick Van Dyke Show:* "Coast to Coast Big Mouth"

Outstanding Variety Series
The Andy Williams Show (NBC)

Outstanding Variety Special
Chrysler Presents the Bob Hope Christmas Special (NBC)

Outstanding Musical Program
Frank Sinatra: A Man and His Music (NBC)

Outstanding Directorial Achievement in Variety or Music
Alan Handley, *The Julie Andrews Show*

Outstanding Writing Achievement in Variety
Al Gordon, Hal Goldman and Sheldon Keller, *An Evening With Carol Channing*

Program Achievements in News and Documentaries
American White Paper: United States Foreign Policy (NBC)

CBS Reports: KKK — The Invisible Empire (CBS)

Senate Hearings on Vietnam (NBC)

Program Achievements in Sports
ABC Wide World of Sports (ABC)

CBS Golf Classic (CBS)

Shell's Wonderful World of Golf (NBC)

Outstanding Children's Program
A Charlie Brown Christmas (CBS)

1966–1967

Outstanding Dramatic Series
Mission: Impossible (CBS)

Outstanding Continued Performance by an Actor in a Leading Role in a Dramatic Series
Bill Cosby, *I Spy*

Outstanding Continued Performance by an Actress in a Leading Role in a Dramatic Series
Barbara Bain, *Mission: Impossible*

Outstanding Performance by an Actor in a Supporting Role in a Drama
Eli Wallach, *Xerox Special: The Poppy Is Also a Flower*

Outstanding Performance by an Actress in a Supporting Role in a Drama
Agnes Moorehead, *Wild, Wild West:* "Night of the Vicious Valentine"

Outstanding Directorial Achievement in Drama
Alex Segal, *Death of a Salesman*

Outstanding Writing Achievement in Drama
Bruce Geller, *Mission: Impossible*

Outstanding Dramatic Program
Death of a Salesman (CBS)

Outstanding Single Performance by an Actor in a Leading Role in a Drama
Peter Ustinov, *Hallmark Hall of Fame: Barefoot in Athens*

Outstanding Single Performance by an Actress in a Leading Role in a Drama
Geraldine Page, *ABC Stage 67: A Christmas Memory*

Outstanding Comedy Series
The Monkees (NBC)

Outstanding Continued Performance by an Actor in a Leading Role in a Comedy Series
Don Adams, *Get Smart!*

Outstanding Continued Performance by an Actress in a Leading Role in a Comedy Series
Lucille Ball, *The Lucy Show*

Outstanding Performance by an Actor in a Supporting Role in a Comedy
Don Knotts, *The Andy Griffith Show:* "Barney Comes to Mayberry"

Outstanding Performance by an Actress in a Supporting Role in a Comedy
Frances Bavier, *The Andy Griffith Show*

Outstanding Directorial Achievement in Comedy
James Frawley, *The Monkees:* "Royal Flush"

Outstanding Writing Achievement in Comedy
Buck Henry and Leonard Stern, *Get Smart!:* "Ship of Spies"

Outstanding Variety Series
The Andy Williams Show (NBC)

Outstanding Variety Special
The Sid Caesar, Imogene Coca, Carl Reiner and Howard Morris Special (CBS)

Outstanding Musical Program
Brigadoon (ABC)

Outstanding Directorial Achievement in Variety or Music
Fielder Cook, *Brigadoon*

Outstanding Writing Achievement in Variety
Mel Brooks, Sam Denoff, Bill Persky, Carl Reiner and Mel Tolkin, *The Sid Caesar, Imogene Coca, Carl Reiner and Howard Morris Special*

Program Achievements in News and Documentaries
China: The Roots of Madness (Syndicated)

Hall of Kings (ABC)

The Italians (CBS)

Program Achievement in Sports
ABC's Wide World of Sports (ABC)

Outstanding Children's Program
Jack and the Beanstalk (NBC)

1967–1968

Outstanding Dramatic Series
Mission: Impossible (CBS)

Outstanding Continued Performance by an Actor in a Leading Role in a Dramatic Series
Bill Cosby, *I Spy*

Outstanding Continued Performance by an Actress in a Leading Role in a Dramatic Series
Barbara Bain, *Mission: Impossible*

Outstanding Performance by an Actor in a Supporting Role in a Drama
Milburn Stone, *Gunsmoke*

Outstanding Performance by an Actress in a Supporting Role in a Drama
Barbara Anderson, *Ironside*

Outstanding Directorial Achievement in Drama
Paul Bogart, *CBS Playhouse: Dear Friends*

Outstanding Writing Achievement in Drama
Loring Mandel, *CBS Playhouse: Do Not Go Gentle Into That Good Night*

Outstanding Dramatic Program
Hallmark Hall of Fame: Elizabeth the Queen (NBC)

Outstanding Single Performance by an Actor in a Leading Role in a Drama
Melvyn Douglas, *CBS Playhouse: Do Not Go Gentle Into That Good Night*

Outstanding Single Performance by an Actress in a Leading Role in a Drama
Maureen Stapleton, *Among the Paths to Eden*

Outstanding Comedy Series
Get Smart! (NBC)

Outstanding Continued Performance by an Actor in a Leading Role in a Comedy Series
Don Adams, *Get Smart!*

Outstanding Continued Performance by an Actress in a Leading Role in a Comedy Series
Lucille Ball, *The Lucy Show*

Outstanding Performance by an Actor in a Supporting Role in a Comedy
Werner Klemperer, *Hogan's Heroes*

Mission: Impossible

Outstanding Performance by an Actress in a Supporting Role in a Comedy
Marion Lorne, *Bewitched*

Outstanding Directorial Achievement in Comedy
Bruce Bilson, *Get Smart!:* "Maxwell Smart, Private Eye"

Outstanding Writing Achievement in Comedy
Allan Burns and Chris Hayward, *He and She:* "The Coming Out Party"

Outstanding Musical or Variety Series
Rowan and Martin's Laugh-In (NBC)

Outstanding Musical or Variety Program
Rowan and Martin's Laugh-In Special (NBC)

Outstanding Directorial Achievement in Music or Variety
Jack Haley, Jr., *Movin' With Nancy*

Outstanding Writing Achievement in Music or Variety
Chris Beard, Phil Hahn, Jack Hanrahan, Coslough Johnson, Paul Keyes, Marc London, Allan Manings, David Panich, Hugh Wedlock and Digby Wolfe, *Rowan and Martin's Laugh-In*

Outstanding Program Achievement Within Regularly Scheduled News Programs
Public Broadcast Laboratory: Crisis in the Cities (NET)

Outstanding Program Achievements in News Documentaries
Africa (ABC)

Summer '67: What We Learned (NBC)

Other News and Documentary Program Achievements
The 21st Century (CBS)

CBS News Special: Science and Religion: Who Will Play God? (CBS)

Outstanding Program Achievements in Cultural Documentaries
CBS News Special: Eric Hoffer: The Passionate State of Mind (CBS)

CBS News Special: Gauguin in Tahiti: The Search for Paradise (CBS)

John Steinbeck's America and Americans (NBC)

NET Festival: Dylan Thomas: The World I Breathe (NET)

Outstanding Achievement in Sports Programming
ABC's Wide World of Sports (ABC)

Outstanding Achievements in Children's Programming
He's Your Dog Charlie Brown (CBS)

Mister Rogers's Neighborhood (NET)

You're in Love, Charlie Brown (CBS)

1968–1969

Outstanding Dramatic Series
NET Playhouse (NET)

Outstanding Continued Performance by an Actor in a Leading Role in a Dramatic Series
Carl Betz, *Judd for the Defense*

Outstanding Continued Performance by an Actress in a Leading Role in a Dramatic Series
Barbara Bain, *Mission: Impossible*

Outstanding Continued Performance by an Actor in a Supporting Role in a Series
Werner Klemperer, *Hogan's Heroes*

Outstanding Continued Performance by an Actress in a Supporting Role in a Series
Susan Saint James, *The Name of the Game*

Outstanding Directorial Achievement in Drama
David Green, *CBS Playhouse: The People Next Door*

Outstanding Writing Achievement in Drama
JP Miller, *CBS Playhouse: The People Next Door*

Outstanding Dramatic Program
Hallmark Hall of Fame: Teacher, Teacher (NBC)

Outstanding Single Performance by an Actor in a Leading Role
Paul Scofield, *Prudential's On Stage: Male of the Species*

Outstanding Single Performance by an Actress in a Leading Role
Geraldine Page, *The Thanksgiving Visitor*

Outstanding Single Performance by an Actor in a Supporting Role
No award presented

Outstanding Single Performance by an Actress in a Supporting Role
Anna Calder-Marshall, *Prudential's On Stage: Male of the Species*

Outstanding Comedy Series
Get Smart! (NBC)

Outstanding Continued Performance by an Actor in a Leading Role in a Comedy Series
Don Adams, *Get Smart!*

Outstanding Continued Performance by an Actress in a Leading Role in a Comedy Series
Hope Lange, *The Ghost and Mrs. Muir*

Outstanding Variety or Musical Series
Rowan and Martin's Laugh-In (NBC)

Outstanding Variety or Musical Program
The Bill Cosby Special (NBC)

Outstanding Directorial Achievement in Comedy, Variety or Music
No award presented

Outstanding Writing Achievement in Comedy, Variety or Music
Allan Blye, Bob Einstein, Murray Roman, Carl Gottlieb, Jerry Music, Steve Martin, Cecil Tuck, Paul Wayne, Cy Howard and Mason Williams, *The Smothers Brothers Comedy Hour*

Outstanding Achievement Within Regularly Scheduled News Programs
The Huntley-Brinkley Report: "Coverage of Hunger in the United States" (NBC)

Outstanding News Documentary Program Achievements
CBS News Hour: "Hunger in America" (CBS)

Public Broadcast Laboratory: Law and Order (NET)

Outstanding Cultural Documentary and "Magazine-Type" Program or Series Achievements
CBS News Hour: "Don't Count the Candles" (CBS)

CBS News Hour: "Justice Black and the Bill of Rights" (CBS)

Bell Telephone Hour: "Man Who Dances: Edward Villella" (NBC)

CBS News Hour: "The Great American Novel" (CBS)

Outstanding Achievement in Sports Programming
19th Summer Olympics Games (ABC)

Outstanding Achievement in Children's Programming
Mister Rogers's Neighborhood (NET)

1969–1970

Outstanding Dramatic Series
Marcus Welby, M.D. (ABC)

Outstanding Continued Performance by an Actor in a Leading Role in a Dramatic Series
Robert Young, *Marcus Welby, M.D.*

Outstanding Continued Performance by an Actress in a Leading Role in a Dramatic Series
Susan Hampshire, *The Forsyte Saga*

Outstanding Performance by an Actor in a Supporting Role in Drama
James Brolin, *Marcus Welby, M.D.*

Outstanding Performance by an Actress in a Supporting Role in Drama
Gail Fisher, *Mannix*

Outstanding Directorial Achievement in Drama
Paul Bogart, *CBS Playhouse: Shadow Game*

Outstanding Writing Achievement in Drama
Richard Levinson and William Link, *My Sweet Charlie*

Outstanding Dramatic Program
Hallmark Hall of Fame: A Storm in Summer (NBC)

Outstanding Single Performance by an Actor in a Leading Role
Peter Ustinov, *Hallmark Hall of Fame: A Storm in Summer*

Outstanding Single Performance by an Actress in a Leading Role
Patty Duke, *My Sweet Charlie*

Outstanding New Series
Room 222 (ABC)

Outstanding Comedy Series
My World and Welcome to It (NBC)

Outstanding Continued Performance by an Actor in a Leading Role in a Comedy Series
William Windom, *My World and Welcome to It*

Outstanding Continued Performance by an Actress in a Leading Role in a Comedy Series
Hope Lange, *The Ghost and Mrs. Muir*

Outstanding Performance by an Actor in a Supporting Role in Comedy
Michael Constantine, *Room 222*

Outstanding Performance by an Actress in a Supporting Role in Comedy
Karen Valentine, *Room 222*

Outstanding Variety or Musical Series
The David Frost Show (Syndicated)

Outstanding Variety or Musical Program Variety and Popular Music
Annie, The Women in the Life of a Man (CBS)

Classical Music
NET Festival: Cinderella, National Ballet of Canada (NET)

Outstanding Directorial Achievement in Comedy, Variety or Music
Dwight A. Hemion, *Kraft Music Hall: The Sound of Burt Bacharach* (NBC)

Outstanding Writing Achievement in Comedy, Variety or Music
Gary Belkin, Peter Bellwood, Herb Sargent, Thomas Meehan and Judith Viorst, *Annie, The Women in the Life of a Man*

Outstanding Achievements Within Regularly Scheduled News Programs
The Huntley-Brinkley Report: "An Investigation of Teenage Drug Addiction — Odyssey House" (NBC)

CBS Evening News With Walter Cronkite: "Can the World Be Saved?" (CBS)

Outstanding Achievement in News Documentary Programming
NET Journal: "Hospital" (NET)

Outstanding Achievement in Magazine-Type Programming
Black Journal (NET)

Outstanding Achievements in Cultural Documentary Programming
Artur Rubinstein (NBC)

CBS News Hour: "Fathers and Sons" (CBS)

CBS News Hour: "The Japanese" (CBS)

Outstanding Achievement in Sports Programming
The NFL Games (CBS)

Outstanding Achievement in Children's Programming
Sesame Street (NET)

1970–1971

Outstanding Series, Drama
The Bold Ones: The Senator (NBC)

Outstanding Continued Performance by an Actor in a Leading Role in a Dramatic Series
Hal Holbrook, *The Bold Ones: The Senator*

Outstanding Continued Performance by an Actress in a Leading Role in a Dramatic Series
Susan Hampshire, *Masterpiece Theatre: The First Churchills*

Outstanding Performance by an Actor in a Supporting Role in Drama
David Burns, *Hallmark Hall of Fame: The Price*

Outstanding Performance by an Actress in a Supporting Role in Drama
Margaret Leighton, *Hallmark Hall of Fame: Hamlet*

Outstanding Directorial Achievement in Drama (Single Program of a Series)
Daryl Duke, *The Bold Ones: The Senator:* "The Day the Lion Died"

Outstanding Writing Achievement in Drama (Single Program of a Series)
Joel Oliansky, *The Bold Ones: The Senator:* "To Taste of Death but Once"

Outstanding Single Program, Drama or Comedy
Hollywood Television Theatre: The Andersonville Trial (PBS)

Outstanding Single Performance by an Actor in a Leading Role
George C. Scott, *Hallmark Hall of Fame: The Price*

Outstanding Single Performance by an Actress in a Leading Role
Lee Grant, *NBC Monday Night at the Movies: The Neon Ceiling*

Outstanding Directorial Achievement in Drama (Single Program)
Fielder Cook, *Hallmark Hall of Fame: The Price*

Outstanding Writing Achievement in Drama, Original Teleplay
Tracy Keenan Wynn and Marvin Schwartz, *Movie of the Week on ABC: Tribes*

Outstanding Writing Achievement in Drama, Adaptation
Saul Levitt, *Hollywood Television Theatre: The Andersonville Trial*

Outstanding New Series
All in the Family (CBS)

Outstanding Series, Comedy
All in the Family (CBS)

Outstanding Continued Performance by an Actor in a Leading Role in a Comedy Series
Jack Klugman, *The Odd Couple*

Outstanding Continued Performance by an Actress in a Leading Role in a Comedy Series
Jean Stapleton, *All in the Family*

Outstanding Performance by an Actor in a Supporting Role in Comedy
Edward Asner, *The Mary Tyler Moore Show*

Outstanding Performance by an Actress in a Supporting Role in Comedy
Valerie Harper, *The Mary Tyler Moore Show*

Outstanding Directorial Achievement in Comedy
Jay Sandrich, *The Mary Tyler Moore Show:* "Toulouse Lautrec Is One of My Favorite Artists"

Outstanding Writing Achievement in Comedy
James L. Brooks and Allan Burns, *The Mary Tyler Moore Show:* "Support Your Local Mother"

Outstanding Variety Series, Musical
The Flip Wilson Show (NBC)

Outstanding Variety Series, Talk
The David Frost Show (Syndicated)

Outstanding Directorial Achievement in Variety or Music
Mark Warren, *Rowan and Martin's Laugh-In* (with Orson Welles)

Outstanding Writing Achievement in Variety or Music
Herbert Baker, Hal Goodman, Larry Klein, Bob Weiskopf, Bob Schiller, Norman Steinberg and Flip Wilson, *The Flip Wilson Show* (with Lena Horne and Tony Randall)

Outstanding Single Program, Variety or Musical Variety and Popular Music
Singer Presents Burt Bacharach (CBS)

Classical Music
NET Festival: Leopold Stokowski (PBS)

Outstanding Directorial Achievement in Comedy, Variety or Music (Single Program)
Sterling Johnson, *Timex Presents Peggy Fleming at Sun Valley*

All in the Family

Outstanding Writing Achievement in Comedy, Variety or Music (Single Program)
Bob Ellison and Marty Farrell, *Singer Presents Burt Bacharach*

Outstanding Achievement Within Regularly Scheduled News Programs
NBC Nightly News: "Five Part Investigation of Welfare" (NBC)

Outstanding Achievements in News Documentary Programming
CBS News: "The Selling of the Pentagon" (CBS)

CBS News: "The World of Charlie Company" (CBS)

NBC News: NBC White Paper: Pollution is a Matter of Choice (NBC)

Outstanding Achievements in Magazine-Type Programming
60 Minutes: "Gulf of Tonkin Segment" (CBS)

The Great American Dream Machine (PBS)

Outstanding Achievements in Cultural Documentary Programming
NBC News: The Everglades (NBC)

The Making of Butch Cassidy and the Sundance Kid (NBC)

Arthur Penn, 1922–: Themes and Variants (PBS)

Outstanding Achievement in Sports Programming
ABC's Wide World of Sports (ABC)

Outstanding Achievement in Children's Programming
Sesame Street (PBS)

1971–1972

Outstanding Series, Drama
Masterpiece Theatre: Elizabeth R (PBS)

Outstanding Continued Performance by an Actor in a Leading Role in a Dramatic Series
Peter Falk, *NBC Mystery Movie: Columbo*

Outstanding Continued Performance by an Actress in a Leading Role in a Dramatic Series
Glenda Jackson, *Masterpiece Theatre: Elizabeth R*

Outstanding Performance by an Actor in a Supporting Role in Drama
Jack Warden, *Movie of the Week: Brian's Song*

Outstanding Performance by an Actress in a Supporting Role in Drama
Jenny Agutter, *Hallmark Hall of Fame: The Snow Goose*

Outstanding Directorial Achievement in Drama (Single Program of a Series)
Alexander Singer, *The Bold Ones: The Lawyers:* "The Invasion of Kevin Ireland"

Outstanding Writing Achievement in Drama (Single Program of a Series)
Richard L. Levinson and William Link, *NBC Mystery Movie: Colombo: Death Lends a Hand*

Outstanding Single Program, Drama or Comedy
Movie of the Week: Brian's Song (ABC)

Outstanding Single Performance by an Actor in a Leading Role
Keith Michell, *The Six Wives of Henry VIII: Catherine Howard*

Outstanding Single Performance by an Actress in a Leading Role
Glenda Jackson, *Masterpiece Theatre: Elizabeth R:* "Shadow in the Sun"

Outstanding Directorial Achievement in Drama (Single Program)
Tom Gries, *The New CBS Friday Night Movies: The Glass House*

The Carol Burnett Show

Outstanding Writing Achievement in Drama, Original Teleplay
Allan Sloane, *To All My Friends on Shore*

Outstanding Writing Achievement in Drama, Adaptation
William Blinn, *Movie of the Week: Brian's Song*

Outstanding New Series
Masterpiece Theatre: Elizabeth R (PBS)

Outstanding Series, Comedy
All in the Family (CBS)

Outstanding Continued Performance by an Actor in a Leading Role in a Comedy Series
Carroll O'Connor, *All in the Family*

Outstanding Continued Performance by an Actress in a Leading Role in a Comedy Series
Jean Stapleton, *All in the Family*

Outstanding Performance by an Actor in a Supporting Role in Comedy
Edward Asner, *The Mary Tyler Moore Show*

Outstanding Performance by an Actress in a Supporting Role in a Comedy (tie)
Valerie Harper, *The Mary Tyler Moore Show*

Sally Struthers, *All in the Family*

Outstanding Directorial Achievement in Comedy
John Rich, *All in the Family:* "Sammy's Visit"

Outstanding Writing Achievement in Comedy
Burt Styler, *All in the Family:* "Edith's Problem"

Outstanding Variety Series, Musical
The Carol Burnett Show (CBS)

Outstanding Variety Series, Talk
The Dick Cavett Show (ABC)

Outstanding Achievement by a Performer in Music or Variety
Harvey Korman, *The Carol Burnett Show*

Outstanding Directorial Achievement in Variety or Music
Art Fisher, *The Sonny and Cher Comedy Hour* (with Tony Randall)

Outstanding Writing Achievement in Variety or Music
Don Hinkley, Stan Hart, Larry Siegel, Woody Kling, Roger Beatty, Art Baer, Ben Joelson, Stan Burns, Mike Marmer and Arnie Rosen, *The Carol Burnett Show* (with Tim Conway and Ray Charles)

Outstanding Single Program, Variety or Musical
VARIETY AND POPULAR MUSIC
Bell System Family Theatre: Jack Lemmon in 'S Wonderful, 'S Marvelous, 'S Gershwin (NBC)

CLASSICAL MUSIC
Beethoven's Birthday: A Celebration in Vienna With Leonard Bernstein (CBS)

Outstanding Directorial Achievement in Comedy, Variety or Music (Special Program)
Walter C. Miller and Martin Charnin, *Bell System Family Theatre: Jack Lemmon in 'S Wonderful, 'S Marvelous, 'S Gershwin*

Outstanding Writing Achievement in Comedy, Variety or Music (Special Program)
Anne Howard Bailey, *NET Opera Theatre: The Trial of Mary Lincoln*

Outstanding Achievement Within Regularly Scheduled News Programs
NBC Nightly News: "Defeat of Dacca" (NBC)

Outstanding Achievements for Regularly Scheduled Magazine-Type Programs
Chronolog (NBC)

The Great American Dream Machine (PBS)

Outstanding Documentary Program Achievements
CURRENT SIGNIFICANCE
CBS Reports: "A Night in Jail, A Day in Court" (CBS)

This Child Is Rated X: An NBC News White Paper on Juvenile Justice (NBC)

CULTURAL
The Monday Night Special: Hollywood: The Dream Factory (ABC)

The Undersea World of Jacques Cousteau: A Sound of Dolphins (ABC)

The Undersea World of Jacques Cousteau: The Unsinkable Sea Otter (ABC)

Outstanding Achievement in Sports Programming
ABC's Wide World of Sports (ABC)

Outstanding Achievement in Children's Programming
Sesame Street (PBS)

Special Classification of Outstanding Program Achievement
GENERAL PROGRAMMING
PBS Special: The Pentagon Papers (PBS)

DOCU-DRAMA
The Search for the Nile, parts I–VI (NBC)

1972–1973

Outstanding Drama Series, Continuing
The Waltons (CBS)

Outstanding Continued Performance by an Actor in a Leading Role in a Drama
Richard Thomas, *The Waltons* (CBS)

Outstanding Continued Performance by an Actress in a Leading Role in a Drama
Michael Learned, *The Waltons* (CBS)

Outstanding Performance by an Actor in a Supporting Role in Drama
Scott Jacoby, *Wednesday Movie of the Week: That Certain Summer*

Outstanding Performance by an Actress in a Supporting Role in Drama
Ellen Corby, *The Waltons*

Outstanding Directorial Achievement in Drama (Single Program of a Series)
Jerry Thorpe, *Kung Fu:* "An Eye for an Eye"

Outstanding Writing Achievement in Drama (Single Program of a Series)
John McGreevey, *The Waltons:* "The Scholar"

Outstanding Single Program, Drama or Comedy
The New CBS Tuesday Night Movies: A War of Children (CBS)

Outstanding Single Performance by an Actor in a Leading Role
Laurence Olivier, *Long Day's Journey Into Night* (ABC)

Outstanding Single Performance by an Actress in a Leading Role
Cloris Leachman, *Tuesday Movie of the Week: A Brand New Life* (ABC)

Outstanding Directorial Achievement in Drama (Single Program)
Joseph Sargent, *The CBS Thursday Night Movies: The Marcus-Nelson Murders*

Outstanding Writing Achievement in Drama, Original Teleplay
Abby Mann, *The CBS Thursday Night Movies: The Marcus-Nelson Murders*

Outstanding Writing Achievement in Drama, Adaptation
Eleanor Perry, *The House Without a Christmas Tree*

Outstanding New Series
America (NBC)

Outstanding Comedy Series
All in the Family (CBS)

Outstanding Continued Performance by an Actor in a Leading Role in a Comedy Series
Jack Klugman, *The Odd Couple*

Outstanding Continued Performance by an Actress in a Leading Role in a Comedy Series
Mary Tyler Moore, *The Mary Tyler Moore Show*

Outstanding Performance by an Actor in a Supporting Role in Comedy
Ted Knight, *The Mary Tyler Moore Show*

Outstanding Performance by an Actress in a Supporting Role in Comedy
Valerie Harper, *The Mary Tyler Moore Show*

Outstanding Directorial Achievement in Comedy
Jay Sandrich, *The Mary Tyler Moore Show:* "It's Whether You Win or Lose"

Outstanding Writing Achievement in Comedy
Michael Ross, Bernie West and Lee Kalcheim, *All in the Family:* "The Bunkers and the Swingers"

Outstanding Variety Musical Series
The Julie Andrews Hour (ABC)

Outstanding Achievement by a Supporting Performer in Music or Variety
Tim Conway, *The Carol Burnett Show*

Outstanding Directorial Achievement in Variety or Music
Bill Davis, *The Julie Andrews Hour* (with "Liza Doolittle" and "Mary Poppins")

Outstanding Writing Achievement in Variety or Music
Stan Hart, Larry Siegel, Gail Parent, Woody Kling, Roger Beatty, Tom Patchett, Jay Tarses, Robert Hilliard, Arnie Kogen, Bill Angelos and Buz Kohan, *The Carol Burnett Show* (with Steve Lawrence and Lili Tomlin)

Outstanding Single Program, Variety and Popular Music
Singer Presents Liza With a 'Z' (NBC)

Outstanding Single Program, Classical Music
The Sleeping Beauty (PBS)

Outstanding Directorial Achievement in Comedy, Variety or Music (Special Program)
Bob Fosse, *Singer Presents Liza With a 'Z'*

Outstanding Writing Achievement in Comedy, Variety or Music (Special Program)
Renée Taylor and Joseph Bologna, *Acts of Love — And Other Comedies*

Outstanding Drama/Comedy, Limited Episodes
Masterpiece Theatre: Tom Brown's Schooldays, parts I–V (PBS)

Outstanding Continued Performance by an Actor in a Leading Role in a Drama or Comedy, Limited Episodes
Anthony Murphy, *Masterpiece Theatre: Tom Brown's Schooldays,* parts I–V (PBS)

Outstanding Continued Performance by an Actress in a Leading Role in a Drama or Comedy, Limited Episodes
Susan Hampshire, *Masterpiece Theatre: Vanity Fair,* parts I–V

Outstanding Achievement Within Regularly Scheduled News Programs
CBS Evening News With Walter Cronkite: "The US/Soviet Wheat Deal: Is There a Scandal?" (CBS)

Outstanding Achievements for Regularly Scheduled Magazine-Type Programs
60 Minutes: "The Poppy Fields of Turkey — The Heroin Labs of Marseilles — The N.Y. Connection" (CBS)

60 Minutes: "The Selling of Colonel Herbert" (CBS)

60 Minutes (CBS)

Outstanding Documentary Program Achievements
CURRENT SIGNIFICANCE
NBC News White Paper: The Blue Collar Trap (NBC)

CBS Reports: "The Mexican Connection" (CBS)

NBC Reports: "One Billion Dollar Weapon and Now the War Is Over: The American Military in the '70s" (NBC)

CULTURAL
America (NBC)

Jane Goodall and the World of Animal Behavior: The Wild Dogs of Africa (ABC)

Outstanding Achievements in Sports Programming
ABC's Wide World of Sports (ABC)

1972 Summer Olympic Games (ABC)

Outstanding Achievements in Children's Programming
ENTERTAINMENT/FICTIONAL
Sesame Street (PBS)

Zoom (PBS)

INFORMATION/FACTUAL
The ABC Afterschool Special: Last of the Curlews (ABC)

Special Classification of Outstanding Program Achievements
The Advocates (PBS)

Special of the Week: "VD Blues" (PBS)

1973–1974

Actor of the Year, Series
Alan Alda, *M*A*S*H*

Actress of the Year, Series
Mary Tyler Moore, *The Mary Tyler Moore Show*

Supporting Actor of the Year
Michael Moriarty, *The Glass Menagerie*

Supporting Actress of the Year
Joanna Miles, *The Glass Menagerie*

Director of the Year, Series
Robert Butler, *The Blue Knight, Part III*

Writer of the Year, Series
Treva Silverman, *The Mary Tyler Moore Show:* "The Lou and Edie Story"

Actor of the Year, Special
Hal Holbrook, *ABC Theatre: Pueblo*

Actress of the Year, Special
Cicely Tyson, *The Autobiography of Miss Jane Pittman*

Director of the Year, Special
Dwight Hemion, *Barbra Streisand . . . And Other Musical Instruments*

Writer of the Year, Special
Fay Kanin, *GE Theater: Tell Me Where It Hurts*

Outstanding Drama Series
Masterpiece Theatre: Upstairs, Downstairs (PBS)

Best Lead Actor in a Drama Series
Telly Savalas, *Kojak*

Best Lead Actress in a Drama Series
Michael Learned, *The Waltons*

Best Lead Actor in a Drama (for a Special Program, Comedy or Drama or a Single Appearance in a Drama or Comedy Series)
Hal Holbrook, *ABC Theatre: Pueblo*

Best Lead Actress in a Drama (for a Special Program, Comedy or Drama or a Single Appearance in a Drama or Comedy Series)
Cicely Tyson, *The Autobiography of Miss Jane Pittman*

Best Supporting Actor in Drama (for a Special Program, a One-Time Appearance in a Series or a Continuing Role)
Michael Moriarty, *The Glass Menagerie*

Best Supporting Actress in Drama (for a Special Program, a One-Time Appearance in a Series or a Continuing Role)
Joanna Miles, *The Glass Menagerie*

Best Directing in a Drama (Single Program of a Series)
Robert Butler, *The Blue Knight, Part III*

Best Writing in Drama (Single Program of a Series)
Joanna Lee, *The Waltons:* "The Thanksgiving Story"

Best Writing in Drama, Original Teleplay
Fay Kanin, *GE Theater: Tell Me Where It Hurts*

Best Writing in Drama, Adaptation
Tracy Keenan Wynn, *The Autobiography of Miss Jane Pittman*

Outstanding Special, Comedy or Drama
The Autobiography of Miss Jane Pittman (CBS)

Alan Alda, *M*A*S*H*

Best Directing in Drama (Single Program, Comedy or Drama)
John Korty, *The Autobiography of Miss Jane Pittman*

Outstanding Comedy Series
*M*A*S*H* (CBS)

Best Lead Actor in a Comedy Series
Alan Alda, *M*A*S*H*

Best Lead Actress in a Comedy Series
Mary Tyler Moore, *The Mary Tyler Moore Show*

Best Supporting Actor in Comedy
Rob Reiner, *All in the Family*

Best Supporting Actress in Comedy
Cloris Leachman, *The Mary Tyler Moore Show:*
"The Lars Affair"

Best Directing in Comedy
Jack Cooper, *M*A*S*H:* "Carry On, Hawkeye"

Best Writing in Comedy
Treva Silverman, *The Mary Tyler Moore Show:* "The Lou and
Edie Story"

Outstanding Music-Variety Series
The Carol Burnett Show (CBS)

Best Supporting Actor in Comedy-Variety, Variety or Music
Harvey Korman, *The Carol Burnett Show*

Best Supporting Actress in Comedy-Variety, Variety or Music
Brenda Vaccaro, *The Shape of Things*

Best Directing in Variety or Music
Dave Powers, *The Carol Burnett Show:*
"The Australia Show"

Best Writing in Variety or Music
Ed Simmons, Gary Belkin, Roger Beatty, Arnie Kogen,
Bill Richmond, Gene Perret, Rudy DeLuca,
Barry Levinson, Dick Clair, Jenna McMahon
and Barry Harman, *The Carol Burnett Show*
(with Tim Conway and Bernadette Peters)

Outstanding Comedy-Variety, Variety or Music Special
Lily (CBS)

**Best Directing in Comedy-Variety, Variety or Music
(Special Program)**
Dwight Hemion, *Barbra Streisand . . . And Other Musical
Instruments*

**Best Writing in Comedy-Variety, Variety or Music
(Special Program)**
Herb Sargent, Rosalyn Drexler, Lorne Michaels,
Richard Pryor, Jim Rusk, James R. Stein,
Robert Illes, Lily Tomlin, George Yanok, Jane Wagner,
Rod Warren, Ann Elder and Karyl Geld, *Lily*

Outstanding Limited Series
NBC Sunday Mystery Movie: Columbo (NBC)

Best Lead Actor in a Limited Series
William Holden, *The Blue Knight*

Best Lead Actress in a Limited Series
Mildred Natwick, *NBC Tuesday Mystery Movie: The
Snoop Sisters*

**Outstanding Achievements Within Regularly Scheduled
News Programs**
CBS Evening News With Walter Cronkite: "Coverage of the
October War From Israel's Northern Front" (CBS)

CBS Evening News With Walter Cronkite: "The Agnew
Resignation" (CBS)

CBS Evening News With Walter Cronkite: "The Key
Biscayne Bank Charter Struggle" (CBS)

NBC Nightly News: "Reports on World Hunger" (NBC)

Outstanding Television News Broadcaster (tie)
Harry Reasoner, *ABC News*

Bill Moyers, *Bill Moyers' Journal:* "Essay on Watergate"

**Outstanding Achievements for Regularly Scheduled
Magazine-Type Programs**
First Tuesday: "America's Nerve Gas Arsenal" (NBC)

Behind the Lines: "The Adversaries" (PBS)

Bill Moyers' Journal: "A Question of Impeachment" (PBS)

Outstanding Interview Program (tie)
CBS News Special: "Solzhenitsyn" (CBS)

Bill Moyers' Journal: "Henry Steele Commager" (PBS)

Outstanding Documentary Program Achievements
CURRENT SIGNIFICANCE
ABC News Close Up: Fire! (ABC)

*CBS News Special Report: The Senate and the
Watergate Affair* (CBS)

CULTURAL
Journey to the Outer Limits (ABC)

The World at War (Syndicated)

CBS Reports: The Rockefellers (CBS)

**Outstanding Achievement in News and
Documentary Directing**
ABC News Close-up: Fire! (ABC)

Outstanding Children's Special
*Marlo Thomas and Friends in Free to Be . . .
You and Me* (ABC)

Outstanding Informational Children's Series (Prime Time)
Make a Wish (ABC)

Outstanding Informational Children's Special (Prime Time)
The Runaways (ABC)

Outstanding Children's Entertainment Series (Daytime)
Zoom (PBS)

Outstanding Children's Entertainment Special (Daytime)
The ABC Afterschool Special: Rookie of the Year (ABC)

**Outstanding Instructional Children's
Programming**
Inside/Out (Syndicated)

Outstanding Game Show
Password (ABC)

Outstanding Talk, Service or Variety Series
The Merv Griffin Show (Syndicated)

1974–1975

Outstanding Drama Series
Masterpiece Theatre: Upstairs, Downstairs (PBS)

Outstanding Lead Actor in a Drama Series
Robert Blake, *Baretta* (ABC)

Outstanding Lead Actress in a Drama Series
Jean Marsh, *Masterpiece Theatre: Upstairs, Downstairs*

**Outstanding Continuing Performance by a Supporting Actor
in a Drama Series**
Will Geer, *The Waltons*

**Outstanding Continuing Performance by a Supporting Actress
in a Drama Series**
Ellen Corby, *The Waltons*

**Outstanding Single Performance by a Supporting Actor
in a Comedy or Drama Series**
Patrick McGoohan, *NBC Sunday Mystery Movie: Columbo:
By Dawn's Early Light*

**Outstanding Single Performance by a Supporting Actress
in a Comedy or Drama Series (tie)**
Cloris Leachman, *The Mary Tyler Moore Show:*
"Phyllis Whips Inflation"

Zohra Lampert, *Kojak:* "Queen of the Gypsies"

Valerie Harper, *Rhoda*

Outstanding Directing in a Drama Series
Bill Bain, *Masterpiece Theatre: Upstairs, Downstairs:*
 "A Sudden Storm"

Outstanding Writing in a Drama Series
Howard Fast, *Benjamin Franklin:* "The Ambassador"

Outstanding Special, Drama or Comedy
The Law (NBC)

**Outstanding Lead Actor in a Special Program,
Drama or Comedy**
Laurence Olivier, *ABC Theatre: Love Among the Ruins*

**Outstanding Lead Actress in a Special Program,
Drama or Comedy**
Katharine Hepburn, *ABC Theatre: Love Among the Ruins*

**Outstanding Single Performance by a Supporting Actor in a
Comedy or Drama Special**
Anthony Quale, *ABC Movie Special: QB VII,* parts 1 and 2

**Outstanding Single Performance by a Supporting Actress
in a Comedy or Drama Special**
Juliet Mills, *ABC Movie Special: QB VII,* parts 1 and 2

**Outstanding Directing in a Special Program,
Drama or Comedy**
George Cukor, *ABC Theatre: Love Among the Ruins*

**Outstanding Writing in a Special Program,
Drama or Comedy, Original Teleplay**
James Costigan, *ABC Theatre: Love Among the Ruins*

**Outstanding Writing in a Special Program,
Drama or Comedy, Adaptation**
David W. Rintels, *IBM Presents Clarence Darrow*

Outstanding Comedy Series
The Mary Tyler Moore Show (CBS)

Outstanding Lead Actor in a Comedy Series
Tony Randall, *The Odd Couple*

Outstanding Lead Actress in a Comedy Series
Valerie Harper, *Rhoda*

**Outstanding Continuing Performance by a Supporting Actor
in a Comedy Series**
Ed Asner, *The Mary Tyler Moore Show*

**Outstanding Continuing Performance by a Supporting Actress
in a Comedy Series**
Betty White, *The Mary Tyler Moore Show*

Outstanding Directing in a Comedy Series
Gene Reynolds, *M*A*S*H*

Outstanding Writing in a Comedy Series
Ed Weinberger and Stan Daniels, *The Mary Tyler Moore
 Show:* "Mary Richards Goes to Jail"

Outstanding Comedy-Variety or Music Series
The Carol Burnett Show (CBS)

**Outstanding Continuing or Single Performance by a
Supporting Actor in Variety or Music**
Jack Albertson, *Cher*

**Outstanding Continuing or Single Performance by a
Supporting Actress in Variety or Music**
Cloris Leachman, *Cher*

Outstanding Directing in a Comedy-Variety or Music Series
Dave Powers, *The Carol Burnett Show* (with Alan Alda)

Outstanding Writing in a Comedy-Variety or Music Series
Ed Simmons, Gary Belkin, Roger Beatty, Arnie Kogen,
 Bill Richmond, Gene Perret, Rudy DeLuca, Barry
 Levinson, Dick Clair and Jenna McMahon,
 The Carol Burnett Show (with Alan Alda)

Outstanding Special, Comedy-Variety or Music
An Evening With John Denver (ABC)

Outstanding Directing in a Comedy-Variety or Music Special
Bill Davis, *An Evening With John Denver*

Outstanding Writing in a Comedy-Variety or Music Special
Bob Wells, John Bradford and Cy Coleman, *Shirley MacLaine:
 If They Could See Me Now*

Outstanding Limited Series
Benjamin Franklin (CBS)

Outstanding Lead Actor in a Limited Series
Peter Falk, *NBC Sunday Night Mystery Movie: Columbo*

Outstanding Lead Actress in a Limited Series
Jessica Walter, *NBC Sunday Mystery Movie: Amy Prentiss*

Outstanding Sports Program
Wide World of Sports (ABC)

Outstanding Children's Special (Prime Time)
Yes, Virginia, There Is a Santa Claus (ABC)

Outstanding Entertainment Children's Series (Daytime)
Star Trek (NBC)

Outstanding Entertainment Children's Special (Daytime)
The CBS Festival of Lively Arts for Young People: Harlequin
 (CBS)

Outstanding Game or Audience Participation Show
Hollywood Squares (NBC)

Outstanding Talk, Service or Variety Series
Dinah! (Syndicated)

Special Classification of Outstanding Program Achievement
The American Film Institute Salute to James Cagney (CBS)

1975–1976

Outstanding Drama Series
Police Story (NBC)

Outstanding Lead Actor in a Drama Series
Peter Falk, *NBC Sunday Mystery Movie: Columbo*

Outstanding Lead Actress in a Drama Series
Michael Learned, *The Waltons*

**Outstanding Continuing Performance by a Supporting Actor
in a Drama Series**
Anthony Zerbe, *Harry O*

**Outstanding Continuing Performance by a Supporting Actress
in a Drama Series**
Ellen Corby, *The Waltons*

Outstanding Lead Actor for a Single Appearance in a Drama or Comedy Series
Edward Asner, *Rich Man, Poor Man*

Outstanding Lead Actress for a Single Appearance in a Drama or Comedy Series
Kathryn Walker, *The Adams Chronicles:* "John Adams, Lawyer"

Outstanding Single Performance by a Supporting Actor in a Comedy or Drama Series
Gordon Jackson, *Masterpiece Theatre: Upstairs, Downstairs:* "The Beastly Hun"

Outstanding Single Performance by a Supporting Actress in a Comedy or Drama Series
Fionnuala Flanagan, *Rich Man, Poor Man*

Outstanding Directing in a Drama Series
David Greene, *Rich Man, Poor Man,* Episode 8

Outstanding Writing in a Drama Series
Sherman Yellen, *The Adams Chronicles:* "John Adams, Lawyer"

Outstanding Special, Drama or Comedy
ABC Theatre: Eleanor and Franklin (ABC)

Outstanding Lead Actor in a Drama or Comedy Special
Anthony Hopkins, *The Lindbergh Kidnapping Case*

Outstanding Lead Actress in a Drama or Comedy Special
Susan Clark, *Babe*

Outstanding Single Performance by a Supporting Actor in a Comedy or Drama Special
Ed Flanders, *ABC Theatre: A Moon for the Misbegotten*

Outstanding Single Performance by a Supporting Actress in a Comedy or Drama Special
Rosemary Murphy, *ABC Theatre: Eleanor and Franklin*

Outstanding Directing in a Special Program, Drama or Comedy
Daniel Petrie, *ABC Theatre: Eleanor and Franklin*

Outstanding Writing in a Special Program, Drama or Comedy, Original Teleplay
James Costigan, *ABC Theatre: Eleanor and Franklin*

Outstanding Writing in a Special Program, Drama or Comedy, Adaptation
David W. Rintels, *Fear on Trial*

Outstanding Comedy Series
The Mary Tyler Moore Show (CBS)

Outstanding Lead Actor in a Comedy Series
Jack Albertson, *Chico and the Man*

Outstanding Lead Actress in a Comedy Series
Mary Tyler Moore, *The Mary Tyler Moore Show*

Outstanding Continuing Performance by a Supporting Actor in a Comedy Series
Ted Knight, *The Mary Tyler Moore Show*

Outstanding Continuing Performance by a Supporting Actress in a Comedy Series
Betty White, *The Mary Tyler Moore Show*

Outstanding Directing in a Comedy Series
Gene Reynolds, *M*A*S*H:* "Welcome to Korea"

Outstanding Writing in a Comedy Series
David Lloyd, *The Mary Tyler Moore Show:* "Chuckles Bites the Dust"

Outstanding Comedy-Variety or Music Series
NBC's Saturday Night (NBC)

Outstanding Continuing or Single Performance by a Supporting Actor in Variety or Music
Chevy Chase, *NBC's Saturday Night*

Outstanding Continuing or Single Performance by a Supporting Actress in Variety or Music
Vicki Lawrence, *The Carol Burnett Show*

Outstanding Directing in a Comedy-Variety or Music Series
Dave Wilson, *NBC's Saturday Night* (with Paul Simon)

Outstanding Writing in a Comedy-Variety or Music Series
Anne Beatts, Chevy Chase, Al Franken, Tom Davis, Lorne Michaels, Marilyn Suzanne Miller, Michael O'Donoghue, Herb Sargent, Tom Schiller, Rosie Shuster and Alan Zweibel, *NBC's Saturday Night* (with Elliott Gould)

Outstanding Special, Comedy-Variety or Music
Gypsy in My Soul (CBS)

Outstanding Directing in a Comedy-Variety or Music Special
Dwight Hemion, *Steve and Eydie: Our Love Is Here to Stay*

Outstanding Writing in a Comedy-Variety or Music Special
Jane Wagner, Lorne Michaels, Ann Elder, Christopher Guest, Earl Pomerantz, Jim Rusk, Lily Tomlin, Rod Warren and George Yanok, *Lily Tomlin*

Outstanding Limited Series
Masterpiece Theatre: Upstairs, Downstairs (PBS)

Outstanding Lead Actor in a Limited Series
Hal Holbrook, *Sandburg's Lincoln*

Outstanding Lead Actress in a Limited Series
Rosemary Harris, *Masterpiece Theatre: Notorious Woman*

Outstanding Live Sports Series
NFL Monday Night Football (ABC)

Outstanding Live Sports Special
1975 World Series (NBC)

Outstanding Edited Sports Series
ABC's Wide World of Sports (ABC)

Outstanding Edited Sports Special
XII Winter Olympic Games (ABC)

Outstanding Children's Special (Prime Time) (tie)
You're a Good Sport, Charlie Brown (CBS)

Huckleberry Finn (ABC)

Triumph and Tragedy . . . The Olympic Experience (ABC)

Outstanding Entertainment Children's Series (Daytime)
Big Blue Marble (Syndicated)

Outstanding Entertainment Children's Special (Daytime)
The CBS Festival of Lively Arts for Young People: Danny Kaye's Look-In at the Metropolitan Opera (CBS)

Outstanding Informational Children's Series (Daytime)
Go (NBC)

Outstanding Informational Children's Special (Daytime)
Happy Anniversary, Charlie Brown (CBS)

Outstanding Instructional Children's Programming, Series and Specials (Daytime)
Grammar Rock (ABC)

James Garner, *The Rockford Files*

Outstanding Daytime Game or Audience Participation Show
The $20,000 Pyramid (ABC)

Outstanding Daytime Talk, Service or Variety Series
Dinah! (Syndicated)

Special Classification of Outstanding Program Achievement (tie)
Bicentennial Minutes (CBS)

The Tonight Show Starring Johnny Carson (NBC)

1976–1977

Outstanding Drama Series
Masterpiece Theatre: Upstairs, Downstairs (PBS)

Outstanding Lead Actor in a Drama Series
James Garner, *The Rockford Files*

Outstanding Lead Actress in a Drama Series
Lindsay Wagner, *The Bionic Woman*

Outstanding Continuing Performance by a Supporting Actor in a Drama Series
Gary Frank, *Family*

Outstanding Continuing Performance by a Supporting Actress in a Drama Series
Kristy McNichol, *Family*

Outstanding Lead Actor for a Single Appearance in a Drama or Comedy Series
Louis Gossett, Jr., *Roots, Part 2*

Outstanding Lead Actress for a Single Appearance in a Drama or Comedy Series
Beulah Bondi, *The Waltons:* "The Pony Cart"

Outstanding Single Performance by a Supporting Actor in a Comedy or Drama Series
Edward Asner, *Roots, Part 1*

Outstanding Single Performance by a Supporting Actress in a Comedy or Drama Series
Olivia Cole, *Roots, Part 8*

Outstanding Directing in a Drama Series
David Greene, *Roots, Part 1*

Outstanding Writing in a Drama Series
Ernest Kinoy and William Blinn, *Roots, Part 2*

Outstanding Special, Drama or Comedy
ABC Theatre: Eleanor and Franklin: The White House Years (ABC)

Outstanding Lead Actor in a Drama or Comedy Special
Ed Flanders, *Harry S. Truman: Plain Speaking*

Outstanding Lead Actress in a Drama or Comedy Special
Sally Field, *Sybil*

Outstanding Performance by a Supporting Actor in a Comedy or Drama Special
Burgess Meredith, *Tail Gunner Joe*

Outstanding Performance by a Supporting Actress in a Comedy or Drama Special
Diana Hyland, *The ABC Friday Night Movie: The Boy in the Plastic Bubble*

Outstanding Directing in a Special Program, Drama or Comedy
Daniel Petrie, *ABC Theatre: Eleanor and Franklin: The White House Years*

Outstanding Writing in a Special Program, Drama or Comedy, Original Teleplay
Lane Slate, *Tail Gunner Joe*

Outstanding Writing in a Special Program, Drama or Comedy, Adaptation
Stewart Stern, *Sybil*

Outstanding Comedy Series
The Mary Tyler Moore Show (CBS)

Outstanding Lead Actor in a Comedy Series
Carroll O'Connor, *All in the Family*

Outstanding Lead Actress in a Comedy Series
Beatrice Arthur, *Maude*

Outstanding Continuing Performance by a Supporting Actor in a Comedy Series
Gary Burghoff, *M*A*S*H*

Outstanding Continuing Performance by a Supporting Actress in a Comedy Series
Mary Kay Place, *Mary Hartman, Mary Hartman*

Outstanding Directing in a Comedy Series
Alan Alda, *M*A*S*H:* "Dear Sigmund"

Outstanding Writing in a Comedy Series
Allan Burns, James L. Brooks, Ed Weinberger, Stan Daniels, David Lloyd and Bob Ellison, *The Mary Tyler Moore Show:* "The Last Show"

Outstanding Comedy-Variety or Music Series
Van Dyke and Company (NBC)

Outstanding Continuing or Single Performance by a Supporting Actor in Variety or Music
Tim Conway, *The Carol Burnett Show,* entire series

Outstanding Continuing or Single Performance by a Supporting Actress in Variety or Music
Rita Moreno, *The Muppet Show*

Outstanding Directing in a Comedy-Variety or Music Series
Dave Powers, *The Carol Burnett Show* (with Eydie Gormé)

Outstanding Writing in a Comedy-Variety or Music Series
Anne Beatts, Dan Aykroyd, Al Franken, Tom Davis, James Downey, Lorne Michaels, Marilyn Suzanne Miller, Michael O'Donoghue, Herb Sargent, Tom Schiller, Rosie Shuster, Alan Zweibel, John Belushi and Bill Murray, *NBC's Saturday Night* (with Sissy Spacek)

Outstanding Special, Comedy-Variety or Music
The Barry Manilow Special (ABC)

Outstanding Directing in a Comedy-Variety or Music Special
Dwight Hemion, *America Salutes Richard Rodgers: The Sound of His Music*

Outstanding Writing in a Comedy-Variety or Music Special
Alan Buz Kohan and Ted Strauss, *America Salutes Richard Rodgers: The Sound of His Music*

Outstanding Limited Series
ABC Novel for Television: Roots (ABC)

Outstanding Lead Actor in a Limited Series
Christopher Plummer, *NBC World Premiere: The Moneychangers*

Outstanding Lead Actress in a Limited Series
Patty Duke Astin, *NBC's Best Seller: Captains and the Kings*

Outstanding Children's Special (Prime Time)
Piccadilly Circus: Ballet Shoes (PBS)

Outstanding Children's Entertainment Series (Daytime)
Zoom (PBS)

Outstanding Children's Entertainment Special (Daytime)
Special Treat: Big Henry and the Polka Dot Kid (NBC)

Outstanding Children's Informational Series (Daytime)
The Electric Company (PBS)

Outstanding Children's Informational Special (Daytime)
ABC Afterschool Special: My Mom's Having a Baby (ABC)

Outstanding Children's Instructional Programming, Series and Specials (Daytime)
Sesame Street (PBS)

Outstanding Game or Audience Participation Show (Daytime or Prime Time)
Family Feud (ABC)

Outstanding Daytime Talk, Service or Variety Series
The Merv Griffin Show (Syndicated)

Special Classification of Outstanding Program Achievement
The Tonight Show Starring Johnny Carson (NBC)

1977—1978

Outstanding Drama Series
The Rockford Files (NBC)

Outstanding Lead Actor in a Drama Series
Edward Asner, *Lou Grant*

Outstanding Lead Actress in a Drama Series
Sada Thompson, *Family*

Outstanding Continuing Performance by a Supporting Actor in a Drama Series
Robert Vaughn, *Washington: Behind Closed Doors*

Outstanding Continuing Performance by a Supporting Actress in a Drama Series
Nancy Marchand, *Lou Grant*

Outstanding Lead Actor for a Single Appearance in a Drama or Comedy Series
Barnard Hughes, *Lou Grant*

Outstanding Lead Actress for a Single Appearance in a Drama or Comedy Series
Rita Moreno, *The Rockford Files:* "The Paper Palace"

Outstanding Single Performance by a Supporting Actor in a Comedy or Drama Series
Ricardo Montalban, *How the West Was Won, Part II*

Outstanding Single Performance by a Supporting Actress in a Comedy or Drama Series
Blanche Baker, *Holocaust, Part I*

Outstanding Directing in a Drama Series
Marvin J. Chomsky, *Holocaust,* entire series

Outstanding Writing in a Drama Series
Gerald Green, *Holocaust,* entire series

Outstanding Special, Drama or Comedy
The Gathering (ABC)

Outstanding Lead Actor in a Drama or Comedy Special
Fred Astaire, *A Family Upside Down*

Outstanding Lead Actress in a Drama or Comedy Special
Joanne Woodward, *GE Theater: See How She Runs*

Outstanding Performance by a Supporting Actor in a Comedy or Drama Special
Howard Da Silva, *Great Performances: Verna: USO Girl*

Outstanding Performance by a Supporting Actress in a Drama or Comedy Special
Eva LeGallienne, *The Royal Family*

Outstanding Directing in a Special Program, Drama or Comedy
David Lowell Rich, *The Defection of Simas Kudirka*

Outstanding Writing in a Special Program, Drama or Comedy, Original Teleplay
George Rubino, *The Last Tenant*

Outstanding Writing in a Special Program, Drama or Comedy, Adaptation
Caryl Ledner, *Mary White*

Outstanding Comedy Series
All in the Family (CBS)

Outstanding Lead Actor in a Comedy Series
Carroll O'Connor, *All in the Family*

Outstanding Lead Actress in a Comedy Series
Jean Stapleton, *All in the Family*

Outstanding Continuing Performance by a Supporting Actor in a Comedy Series
Rob Reiner, *All in the Family*

Outstanding Continuing Performance by a Supporting Actress in a Comedy Series
Julie Kavner, *Rhoda*

Outstanding Directing in a Comedy Series
Paul Bogart, *All in the Family:* "Edith's 50th Birthday"

Outstanding Writing in a Comedy Series
Bob Weiskopf and Bob Schiller, *Teleplay*

Outstanding Comedy-Variety or Music Series
The Muppet Show (Syndicated)

Outstanding Continuing or Single Performance by a Supporting Actor in Variety or Music
Tim Conway, *The Carol Burnett Show*

Outstanding Continuing or Single Performance by a Supporting Actress in Variety or Music
Gilda Radner, *NBC's Saturday Night Live*

Outstanding Directing in a Comedy-Variety or Music Series
Dave Powers, *The Carol Burnett Show* (with Steve Martin and Betty White)

Outstanding Writing in a Comedy-Variety or Music Series
Ed Simmons, Roger Beatty, Rick Hawkins, Liz Sage, Robert Illes, James Stein, Franelle Silver, Larry Siegel, Tim Conway, Bill Richmond, Gene Perret, Dick Clair and Jenna McMahon, *The Carol Burnett Show* (with Steve Martin and Betty White)

Outstanding Special, Comedy-Variety or Music
Bette Midler — Ol' Red Hair Is Back (NBC)

Outstanding Directing in a Comedy-Variety or Music Special
Dwight Hemion, *The Sentry Collection Presents Ben Vereen — His Roots*

Outstanding Writing in a Comedy-Variety or Music Special
Lorne Michaels, Paul Simon, Chevy Chase, Tom Davis, Al Franken, Charles Grodin, Lily Tomlin and Alan Zweibel, *The Paul Simon Special*

Outstanding Limited Series
Holocaust (NBC)

Outstanding Lead Actor in a Limited Series
Michael Moriarty, *Holocaust*

Outstanding Lead Actress in a Limited Series
Meryl Streep, *Holocaust*

Outstanding Informational Series
The Body Human (CBS)

Outstanding Informational Special
National Geographic: The Great Whales (PBS)

Outstanding Children's Special (Prime Time)
Halloween Is Grinch Night (ABC)

Outstanding Children's Entertainment Series (Daytime)
Captain Kangaroo (CBS)

Outstanding Children's Entertainment Special (Daytime)
ABC Afterschool Special: Hewitt's Just Different (ABC)

Outstanding Children's Informational Series (Daytime)
Animals Animals Animals (ABC)

Outstanding Children's Informational Special (Daytime)
ABC Afterschool Special: Very Good Friends (ABC)

Outstanding Children's Instructional Series (Daytime)
Schoolhouse Rock (ABC)

Outstanding Game or Audience Participation Show
The Hollywood Squares (NBC)

Outstanding Talk, Service or Variety Series
Donahue (Syndicated)

Special Classification of Outstanding Program Achievement
The Tonight Show Starring Johnny Carson (NBC)

Ed Asner, *Lou Grant*

1978–1979

Outstanding Drama Series
Lou Grant (CBS)

Outstanding Lead Actor in a Drama Series
Ron Leibman, *Kaz*

Outstanding Lead Actress in a Drama Series
Mariette Hartley, *The Incredible Hulk:* "Married"

Outstanding Supporting Actor in a Drama Series
Stuart Margolin, *The Rockford Files*

Outstanding Supporting Actress in a Drama Series
Kristy McNichol, *Family*

Outstanding Directing in a Drama Series
Jackie Cooper, *The White Shadow:* Pilot

Outstanding Writing in a Drama Series
Michele Gallery, *Lou Grant:* "Dying"

Outstanding Drama or Comedy Special
Friendly Fire (ABC)

Outstanding Comedy Series
Taxi (ABC)

Outstanding Lead Actor in a Comedy Series
Carroll O'Connor, *All in the Family*

Outstanding Lead Actress in a Comedy Series
Ruth Gordon, *Taxi:* "Sugar Mama"

Outstanding Supporting Actor in a Comedy or Comedy-Variety or Music Series
Robert Guillaume, *Soap*

Outstanding Supporting Actress in a Comedy or Comedy-Variety or Music Series
Sally Struthers, *All in the Family:* "California Here We Are"

Outstanding Directing in a Comedy or Comedy-Variety or Music Series
Noam Pitlik, *Barney Miller:* "The Harris Incident"

Outstanding Writing in a Comedy or Comedy-Variety or Music Series
Alan Alda, *M*A*S*H:* "Inga"

Outstanding Comedy-Variety or Music Program
Steve and Eydie Celebrate Irving Berlin (NBC)

Outstanding Limited Series
Roots: The Next Generations (ABC)

Outstanding Lead Actor in a Limited Series or a Special
Peter Strauss, *The Jericho Mile*

Outstanding Lead Actress in a Limited Series or a Special
Bette Davis, *Strangers: The Story of a Mother and Daughter*

Outstanding Supporting Actor in a Limited Series or a Special
Marlon Brando, *Roots: The Next Generations,* Episode Seven

Outstanding Supporting Actress in a Limited Series or a Special
Esther Rolle, *Summer of My German Soldier*

Outstanding Directing in a Limited Series or a Special
David Greene, *Friendly Fire*

Outstanding Writing in a Limited Series or a Special
Patrick Nolan and Michael Mann, *The Jericho Mile*

Outstanding Informational Program
Scared Straight! (Syndicated)

Outstanding Children's Program (Prime Time)
Christmas Eve on Sesame Street (PBS)

Outstanding Children's Entertainment Series (Daytime)
Kids Are People Too (ABC)

Outstanding Children's Entertainment Special (Daytime)
The Tap Dance Kid (NBC)

Outstanding Children's Informational Series (Daytime)
Big Blue Marble (Syndicated)

Outstanding Children's Informational Special (Daytime)
Razzmatazz (CBS)

Outstanding Children's Instructional Series (Daytime)
Science Rock (ABC)

Outstanding Animated Program
The Lion, the Witch and the Wardrobe (CBS)

Outstanding Game or Audience Participation Show
The Hollywood Squares (NBC)

Outstanding Talk, Service or Variety Series
Donahue (Syndicated)

Outstanding Program Achievement, Special Class
The Tonight Show Starring Johnny Carson (NBC)

1979–1980

Outstanding Drama Series
Lou Grant (CBS)

Outstanding Lead Actor in a Drama Series
Ed Asner, *Lou Grant*

Outstanding Lead Actress in a Drama Series
Barbara Bel Geddes, *Dallas*

Outstanding Supporting Actor in a Drama Series
Stuart Margolin, *The Rockford Files*

Outstanding Supporting Actress in a Drama Series
Nancy Marchand, *Lou Grant*

Outstanding Directing in a Drama Series
Roger Young, *Lou Grant:* "Cop"

Outstanding Writing in a Drama Series
Seth Freeman, *Lou Grant:* "Cop"

Outstanding Drama or Comedy Special
The Miracle Worker (NBC)

Outstanding Comedy Series
Taxi (ABC)

Outstanding Lead Actor in a Comedy Series
Richard Mulligan, *Soap*

Outstanding Lead Actress in a Comedy Series
Cathryn Damon, *Soap*

Outstanding Supporting Actor in a Comedy or Variety or Music Series
Harry Morgan, *M*A*S*H*

Outstanding Supporting Actress in a Comedy or Variety or Music Series
Loretta Swit, M*A*S*H

Outstanding Directing in a Comedy Series
James Burrows, Taxi: "Louie and the Nice Girl"

Outstanding Writing in a Comedy Series
Bob Colleary, Barney Miller: "Photographer"

Outstanding Variety or Music Program
IBM Presents Baryshnikov on Broadway (ABC)

Outstanding Writing in a Variety or Music Program
Buz Kohan, Shirley MacLaine . . . 'Every Little Movement'

Outstanding Directing in a Variety or Music Program
Dwight Hemion, IBM Presents Baryshnikov on Broadway

Outstanding Limited Series
Edward and Mrs. Simpson (Syndicated)

Outstanding Lead Actor in a Limited Series or a Special
Powers Booth, Guyana Tragedy: The Story of Jim Jones

Outstanding Lead Actress in a Limited Series or a Special
Patty Duke Astin, The Miracle Worker

Outstanding Supporting Actor in a Limited Series or a Special
George Grizzard, The Oldest Living Graduate

Outstanding Supporting Actress in a Limited Series or a Special
Mare Winningham, Amber Waves

Outstanding Directing in a Limited Series or a Special
Marvin J. Chomsky, Attica

Outstanding Writing in a Limited Series or a Special
David Chase, Off the Minnesota Strip

Outstanding Informational Program
The Body Human: The Magic Sense (CBS)

Outstanding Children's Program (Prime Time)
Benji at Work (ABC)

Outstanding Children's Entertainment Series (Daytime)
Hot Hero Sandwich (NBC)

Outstanding Children's Entertainment Special (Daytime)
ABC Afterschool Special: The Late Great Me: Story of a Teenage Alcoholic (ABC)

Outstanding Children's Anthology/Dramatic Programming (Daytime) (tie)
CBS Library: Animal Talk (CBS)

ABC Weekend Special: The Gold Bug (ABC)

Once Upon a Classic: Leatherstocking Tales (PBS)

CBS Library: Once Upon a Midnight Dreary (CBS)

Outstanding Children's Informational Instructional Series/Specials (Daytime) (tie)
Sesame Street (PBS)

30 Minutes (CBS)

CBS Festival of Lively Arts for Young People: Why a Conductor? (CBS)

Outstanding Children's Informational/Instructional Programming, Short Format (Daytime) (tie)
Schoolhouse Rock (ABC)

Dr. Henry's Emergency Lessons for People (ABC)

In the News (CBS)

Outstanding Animated Program
Carlton Your Doorman (CBS)

Outstanding Game or Audience Participation Show (tie)
The Hollywood Squares (NBC)

The $20,000 Pyramid (ABC)

Outstanding Talk, Service or Variety Series
Donahue (Syndicated)

Outstanding Program Achievement, Special Class
Fred Astaire: Change Partners and Dance (PBS)

1980–1981

Outstanding Drama Series
Hill Street Blues (NBC)

Outstanding Lead Actor in a Drama Series
Daniel J. Travanti, Hill Street Blues

Outstanding Lead Actress in a Drama Series
Barbara Babcock, Hill Street Blues: "Fecund Hand Rose"

Outstanding Supporting Actor in a Drama Series
Michael Conrad, Hill Street Blues

Outstanding Supporting Actress in a Drama Series
Nancy Marchand, Lou Grant

Outstanding Directing in a Drama Series
Robert Butler, Hill Street Blues: "Hill Street Station"

Outstanding Writing in a Drama Series
Michael Kozoll and Steven Bochco, Hill Street Blues

Outstanding Drama Special
Playing for Time (CBS)

Outstanding Comedy Series
Taxi (ABC)

Outstanding Lead Actor in a Comedy Series
Judd Hirsch, Taxi

Outstanding Lead Actress in a Comedy Series
Isabel Sanford, The Jeffersons

Outstanding Supporting Actor in a Comedy or Variety or Music Series
Danny DeVito, Taxi

Outstanding Supporting Actress in a Comedy or Variety or Music Series
Eileen Brennan, Private Benjamin

Outstanding Directing in a Comedy Series
James Burrows, Taxi: "Elaine's Strange Triangle"

Outstanding Writing in a Comedy Series
Michael Leeson, Taxi: "Tony's Sister and Jim"

Outstanding Variety, Music or Comedy Program
Lily: Sold Out (CBS)

Outstanding Writing in a Variety, Music or Comedy Program
Jerry Juhl, David Odell and Chris Langham,
The Muppet Show (with Carol Burnett)

Outstanding Directing in a Variety, Music or Comedy Program
Don Mischer, The Kennedy Center Honors: A National Celebration of the Performing Arts

Outstanding Limited Series
Shogun (NBC)

Outstanding Lead Actor in a Limited Series or a Special
Anthony Hopkins, The Bunker

Outstanding Lead Actress in a Limited Series or a Special
Vanessa Redgrave, Playing for Time

Outstanding Supporting Actor in a Limited Series or a Special
David Warner, Masada

Outstanding Supporting Actress in a Limited Series or a Special
Jane Alexander, Playing for Time

Outstanding Directing in a Limited Series or a Special
James Goldstone, Kent State

Outstanding Writing in a Limited Series or a Special
Arthur Miller, Playing for Time

Outstanding Informational Series
Steve Allen's Meeting of Minds (PBS)

Outstanding Informational Special
The Body Human: The Bionic Breakthrough (CBS)

Outstanding Children's Program (Prime Time)
Donahue and Kids: Project Peacock (NBC)

Outstanding Children's Entertainment Series (Daytime) (tie)
Captain Kangaroo (CBS)

Once Upon a Classic: A Tale of Two Cities (PBS)

Outstanding Children's Entertainment Special (Daytime)
ABC Afterschool Special: A Matter of Time (ABC)

Outstanding Children's Informational/Instructional Series (Daytime)
30 Minutes (CBS)

Outstanding Children's Informational/Instructional Special (Daytime)
The CBS Festival of Lively Arts for Young People: Julie Andrews' Invitation to the Dance With Rudolf Nureyev (CBS)

Outstanding Animated Program
Life is a Circus, Charlie Brown (CBS)

Outstanding Game or Audience Participation Show
The $20,000 Pyramid (ABC)

Outstanding Talk/Service Series
Donahue (Syndicated)

1981–1982

Outstanding Drama Series
Hill Street Blues (NBC)

Outstanding Lead Actor in a Drama Series
Daniel J. Travanti, *Hill Street Blues*

Outstanding Lead Actress in a Drama Series
Michael Learned, *Nurse*

Outstanding Supporting Actor in a Drama Series
Michael Conrad, *Hill Street Blues*

Outstanding Supporting Actress in a Drama Series
Nancy Marchand, *Lou Grant*

Outstanding Directing in a Drama Series
Harry Harris, *Fame:* "To Soar and Never Falter"

Outstanding Writing in a Drama Series
Steven Bochco, Anthony Yerkovich, Jeffrey Lewis and Michael Wagner, teleplay; Michael Kozoll and Steven Bochco, story, *Hill Street Blues:* "Freedom's Last Stand"

Outstanding Drama Special
A Woman Called Golda (Syndicated)

Outstanding Comedy Series
Barney Miller (ABC)

Outstanding Lead Actor in a Comedy Series
Alan Alda, *M*A*S*H*

Outstanding Lead Actress in a Comedy Series
Carol Kane, *Taxi:* "Simka Returns"

Outstanding Supporting Actor in a Comedy or Variety or Music Series
Christopher Lloyd, *Taxi*

Outstanding Supporting Actress in a Comedy or Variety or Music Series
Loretta Swit, *M*A*S*H*

Outstanding Directing in a Comedy Series
Alan Rafkin, *One Day at a Time:* "Barbara's Crisis"

Outstanding Writing in a Comedy Series
Ken Estin, *Taxi:* "Elegant Iggy"

Outstanding Variety, Music or Comedy Program
Night of 100 Stars (ABC)

Outstanding Directing in a Variety or Music Program
Dwight Hemion, *Goldie and Kids . . . Listen to Us*

Outstanding Writing in a Variety or Music Program
John Candy, Joe Flaherty, Eugene Levy, Andrea Martin, Rick Moranis, Catherine O'Hara, Dave Thomas, Dick Blasucci, Paul Flaherty, Bob Dolman, John McAndrew, Doug Steckler, Mert Rich, Jeffrey Barron, Michael Short, Chris Cluess, Stuart Kreisman and Brian McConnachie, *SCTV Network: Moral Majority Show*

Outstanding Limited Series
Marco Polo (NBC)

Outstanding Lead Actor in a Limited Series or a Special
Mickey Rooney, *Bill*

Outstanding Lead Actress in a Limited Series or a Special
Ingrid Bergman, *A Woman Called Golda*

Outstanding Supporting Actor in a Limited Series or a Special
Laurence Olivier, *Brideshead Revisited*

Outstanding Supporting Actress in a Limited Series or a Special
Penny Fuller, *The Elephant Man*

Outstanding Directing in a Limited Series or a Special
Marvin J. Chomsky, *Inside the Third Reich*

Outstanding Writing in a Limited Series or a Special
Corey Blechman, teleplay; Barry Morrow, story, *Bill*

Outstanding Informational Series
Creativity with Bill Moyers (PBS)

Outstanding Informational Special
Making of Raiders of the Lost Ark (PBS)

Outstanding Children's Program (Prime Time)
The Wave (ABC)

Outstanding Children's Entertainment Series (Daytime)
Captain Kangaroo (CBS)

Outstanding Children's Entertainment Special (Daytime)
ABC Afterschool Special: Starstruck (ABC)

Outstanding Children's Informational/Instructional Series (Daytime)
30 Minutes (CBS)

Outstanding Informational/Instructional Programming, Short Format
In the News (CBS)

Outstanding Children's Informational/Instructional Special (Daytime)
Kathy (PBS)

Outstanding Animated Program
The Grinch Grinches the Cat in the Hat (ABC)

Globe Photos, Inc.

Hill Street Blues

Outstanding Game or Audience Participation Show
Password Plus (NBC)

Outstanding Talk or Service Series
The Richard Simmons Show (Syndicated)

1982–1983

Outstanding Drama Series
Hill Street Blues (NBC)

Outstanding Lead Actor in a Drama Series
Ed Flanders, *St. Elsewhere*

Outstanding Lead Actress in a Drama Series
Tyne Daly, *Cagney and Lacey*

Outstanding Supporting Actor in a Drama Series
James Coco, *St. Elsewhere:* "Cora and Arnie"

Outstanding Supporting Actress in a Drama Series
Doris Roberts, *St. Elsewhere:* "Cora and Arnie"

Outstanding Directing in a Drama Series
Jeff Bleckner, *Hill Street Blues:* "Life in the Minors"

Outstanding Writing in a Drama Series
David Milch, *Hill Street Blues:* "Trial by Fury"

Outstanding Drama Special
Special Bulletin (NBC)

Outstanding Comedy Series
Cheers (NBC)

Outstanding Lead Actor in a Comedy Series
Judd Hirsch, *Taxi*

Outstanding Lead Actress in a Comedy Series
Shelley Long, *Cheers*

Outstanding Supporting Actor in a Comedy, Variety or Music Series
Christopher Lloyd, *Taxi*

Outstanding Supporting Actress in a Comedy, Variety or Music Series
Carol Kane, *Taxi*

Outstanding Directing in a Comedy Series
James Burrows, *Cheers:* "Showdown, Part 2"

Outstanding Writing in a Comedy Series
Glen Charles and Les Charles, *Cheers:* "Give Me a Ring Sometime"

Outstanding Variety, Music or Comedy Program
Motown 25: Yesterday, Today, Forever (NBC)

Outstanding Directing in a Variety or Music Program
Dwight Hemion, *Sheena Easton . . . Act One*

Outstanding Writing in a Variety or Music Program
John Candy, Joe Flaherty, Eugene Levy, Andrea Martin, Martin Short, Dick Blasucci, Paul Flaherty, John McAndrew, Doug Steckler, Bob Dolman, Michael Short and Mary Charlotte Wilcox, *SCTV Network: The Energy Ball/Sweeps Week*

Outstanding Individual Performance in a Variety or Music Program
Leontyne Price, *Live From Lincoln Center, Leontyne Price, Zubin Mehta and the New York Philharmonic*

Outstanding Limited Series
Nicholas Nickleby (Syndicated)

Outstanding Lead Actor in a Limited Series or a Special
Tommy Lee Jones, *The Executioner's Song*

Outstanding Lead Actress in a Limited Series or a Special
Barbara Stanwyck, *The Thorn Birds, Part 1*

Outstanding Supporting Actor in a Limited Series or a Special
Richard Kiley, *The Thorn Birds, Part 1*

Outstanding Supporting Actress in a Limited Series or a Special
Jean Simmons, *The Thorn Birds*

Outstanding Directing in a Limited Series or a Special
John Erman, *Who Will Love My Children?*

Outstanding Writing in a Limited Series or a Special
Marshall Herskovitz, teleplay; Edward Zwick and Marshall Herskovitz, story, *Special Bulletin*

Outstanding Informational Series
The Barbara Walters Specials (ABC)

Outstanding Informational Special
The Body Human: The Living Code (CBS)

Outstanding Children's Program (Prime Time)
Big Bird in China (NBC)

Outstanding Children's Entertainment Series (Daytime)
Smurfs (NBC)

Outstanding Children's Entertainment Special (Daytime)
ABC Afterschool Special: The Woman Who Willed a Miracle (ABC)

Outstanding Children's Informational/Instructional Series (Daytime)
Sesame Street (PBS)

Outstanding Children's Informational/Instructional Special (Daytime)
Winners (Syndicated)

Outstanding Informational/Instructional Programming, Short Form (Daytime)
In the News (CBS)

Outstanding Animated Program
Ziggy's Gift (ABC)

Outstanding Game or Audience Participation Show
The New $25,000 Pyramid (CBS)

Outstanding Talk/Service Series
This Old House (PBS)

1983–1984

Outstanding Drama Series
Hill Street Blues (NBC)

Outstanding Lead Actor in a Drama Series
Tom Selleck, *Magnum, P.I.*

Outstanding Lead Actress in a Drama Series
Tyne Daly, *Cagney and Lacey*

Outstanding Supporting Actor in a Drama Series
Bruce Weitz, *Hill Street Blues*

Outstanding Supporting Actress in a Drama Series
Alfre Woodard, *Hill Street Blues:* "Doris in Wonderland"

Outstanding Directing in a Drama Series
Corey Allen, *Hill Street Blues:* "Goodbye, Mr. Scripps"

Outstanding Writing in a Drama Series
John Ford Noonan, teleplay; John Masius and Tom Fontana, story, *St. Elsewhere:* "The Women"

Outstanding Drama/Comedy Special
An ABC Theatre Presentation: Something About Amelia (ABC)

Outstanding Comedy Series
Cheers (NBC)

Outstanding Lead Actor in a Comedy Series
John Ritter, *Three's Company*

Outstanding Lead Actress in a Comedy Series
Jane Curtin, *Kate and Allie*

Outstanding Supporting Actor in a Comedy Series
Pat Harrington, Jr., *One Day at a Time*

Cheers

Outstanding Supporting Actress in a Comedy Series
Rhea Perlman, *Cheers*

Outstanding Directing in a Comedy Series
Bill Persky, *Kate and Allie:* "A Very Loud Family"

Outstanding Writing in a Comedy Series
David Angell, *Cheers:* "Old Flames"

Outstanding Variety, Music or Comedy Program
The 6th Annual Kennedy Center Honors: A Celebration of the Performing Arts (CBS)

Outstanding Individual Performance in a Variety or Music Program
Cloris Leachman, *Screen Actors Guild 50th Anniversary Celebration*

Outstanding Directing in a Variety or Music Program
Dwight Hemion, *Here's Television Entertainment*

Outstanding Writing in a Variety or Music Program
Steve O'Donnell, Gerard Mulligan, Sanford Frank, Joseph E. Toplyn, Christopher Elliott, Matt Wickline, Jeff Martin, Ted Greenberg, David Yazbek, Merrill Markoe and David Letterman, *Late Night With David Letterman, Show #312*

Outstanding Limited Series
American Playhouse: Concealed Enemies (PBS)

Outstanding Lead Actor in a Limited Series or a Special
Laurence Olivier, *Laurence Olivier's King Lear*

Outstanding Lead Actress in a Limited Series or a Special
Jane Fonda, *An ABC Theatre Presentation: The Dollmaker*

Outstanding Supporting Actor in a Limited Series or a Special
Art Carney, *An ITT Theatre Special: Terrible Joe Moran*

Outstanding Supporting Actress in a Limited Series or Special
Roxana Zal, *An ABC Theatre Presentation: Something About Amelia*

Outstanding Directing in a Limited Series or a Special
Jeff Bleckner, *American Playhouse: Concealed Enemies, Part 3: Investigation*

Outstanding Writing in a Limited Series or a Special
William Hanley, *An ABC Theatre Presentation: Something About Amelia*

Outstanding Informational Series
A Walk Through the 20th Century With Bill Moyers (PBS)

Outstanding Informational Special
America Remembers John F. Kennedy (Syndicated)

Outstanding Children's Program (Prime Time)
He Makes Me Feel Like Dancin' (NBC)

Outstanding Children's Entertainment Series (Daytime)
Captain Kangaroo (CBS)

Outstanding Children's Entertainment Specials
ABC Afterschool Special: The Great Love Experiment (ABC)

Outstanding Children's Informational/Instructional Special
Dead Wrong: The John Evans Story (CBS)

Outstanding Children's Informational/Instructional Programming, Short Form
Just Another Stupid Kid (Syndicated)

Outstanding Children's Informational/Instructional Programming
The ABC Weekend Special (ABC)

Outstanding Animated Program (Prime Time)
Garfield on the Town (CBS)

Outstanding Game or Audience Participation Show
The $25,000 Pyramid (CBS)

Outstanding Talk or Service Series
Woman to Woman (Syndicated)

1984–1985

Outstanding Drama Series
Cagney and Lacey (CBS)

Outstanding Lead Actor in a Drama Series
William Daniels, *St. Elsewhere*

Outstanding Lead Actress in a Drama Series
Tyne Daly, *Cagney and Lacey*

Outstanding Supporting Actor in a Drama Series
Edward James Olmos, *Miami Vice*

Outstanding Supporting Actress in a Drama Series
Betty Thomas, *Hill Street Blues*

Outstanding Directing in a Drama Series
Karen Arthur, *Cagney and Lacey:* "Heat"

Outstanding Writing in a Drama Series
Patricia Green, *Cagney and Lacey:* "Who Said It's Fair, Part II"

Outstanding Drama/Comedy Special
Do You Remember Love (CBS)

Outstanding Comedy Series
The Cosby Show (NBC)

Outstanding Lead Actor in a Comedy Series
Robert Guillaume, *Benson*

Outstanding Lead Actress in a Comedy Series
Jane Curtin, *Kate and Allie*

Outstanding Supporting Actor in a Comedy Series
John Larroquette, *Night Court*

Outstanding Supporting Actress in a Comedy Series
Rhea Perlman, *Cheers*

Outstanding Directing in a Comedy Series
Jay Sandrich, *The Cosby Show:* "The Younger Woman"

Outstanding Writing in a Comedy Series
Ed Weinberger and Michael Leeson, *The Cosby Show: Premiere Episode*

Outstanding Individual Performance in a Variety or Music Program
George Hearn, *Great Performances: Sweeney Todd*

Outstanding Variety, Music or Comedy Program
Motown Returns to the Apollo (NBC)

Outstanding Directing in a Variety or Music Program
Terry Hughes, *Great Performances: Sweeney Todd*

Outstanding Writing in a Variety or Music Program
Gerard Mulligan, Sandy Frank, Joe Toplyn, Chris Elliott, Matt Wickline, Jeff Martin, Eddie Gorodetsky, Randy Cohen, Larry Jacobson, Kevin Curran, Fred Graver, Merrill Markoe and David Letterman, *Late Night With David Letterman:* "Christmas With the Lettermans"

Outstanding Limited Series
Masterpiece Theatre: The Jewel in the Crown (PBS)

Outstanding Lead Actor in a Limited Series or a Special
Richard Crenna, *An ABC Theater Presentation: The Rape of Richard Beck*

Outstanding Lead Actress in a Limited Series or a Special
Joanne Woodward, *Do You Remember Love*

Outstanding Supporting Actor in a Limited Series or a Special
Karl Malden, *Fatal Vision*

Outstanding Supporting Actress in a Limited Series or a Special
Kim Stanley, *American Playhouse: Cat on a Hot Tin Roof*

Outstanding Directing in a Limited Series or a Special
Lamont Johnson, *Wallenberg: A Hero's Story*

Outstanding Writing in a Limited Series or a Special
Vickie Patik, *Do You Remember Love*

Outstanding Informational Series
The Living Planet: A Portrait of the Earth (PBS)

Outstanding Informational Special
Cousteau: Mississippi (Syndicated)

Outstanding Children's Program (Prime Time)
American Playhouse: Displaced Person (PBS)

Outstanding Children's Series (Daytime)
Sesame Street (PBS)

Outstanding Children's Special (Daytime)
All the Kids Do It (CBS)

Outstanding Animated Program (Daytime)
Jim Henson's Muppet Babies (CBS)

Outstanding Animated Program (Prime Time)
Garfield in the Rough (CBS)

Outstanding Game/Audience Participation Show
The $25,000 Pyramid (CBS)

Outstanding Talk or Service Series
Donahue (Syndicated)

1985–1986

Outstanding Drama Series
Cagney and Lacey (CBS)

Outstanding Lead Actor in a Drama Series
William Daniels, *St. Elsewhere*

Outstanding Lead Actress in a Drama Series
Sharon Gless, *Cagney and Lacey*

Outstanding Supporting Actor in a Drama Series
John Karlen, *Cagney and Lacey*

Outstanding Supporting Actress in a Drama Series
Bonnie Bartlett, *St. Elsewhere*

Outstanding Guest Performer in a Drama Series
John Lithgow, *Amazing Stories:* "The Doll"

Outstanding Directing in a Drama Series
George Stanford Brown, *Cagney and Lacy:* "Parting Shots"

Outstanding Writing in a Drama Series
Tom Fontana, John Tinker and John Masius, *St. Elsewhere:* "Time Heals"

Outstanding Drama/Comedy Special
Hallmark Hall of Fame: Love Is Never Silent (NBC)

Outstanding Comedy Series
The Golden Girls (NBC)

Outstanding Lead Actor in a Comedy Series
Michael J. Fox, *Family Ties*

Outstanding Lead Actress in a Comedy Series
Betty White, *The Golden Girls*

Outstanding Supporting Actress in a Comedy Series
Rhea Perlman, *Cheers*

Outstanding Supporting Actor in a Comedy Series
John Larroquette, *Night Court*

Outstanding Guest Performer in a Comedy Series
Roscoe Lee Browne, *The Cosby Show:* "The Card Game"

Outstanding Directing in a Comedy Series
Jay Sandrich, *The Cosby Show:* "Denise's Friend"

Outstanding Writing in a Comedy Series
Barry Fanaro and Mort Nathan, *The Golden Girls:* "A Little Romance"

Outstanding Variety, Music or Comedy Program
The Kennedy Center Honors: A Celebration of the Performing Arts (CBS)

Outstanding Individual Performance in a Variety or Music Program
Whitney Houston, *The 28th Annual Grammy Awards*

Outstanding Directing in a Variety or Music Program
Waris Hussein, *Copacabana*

Outstanding Writing in a Variety or Music Program
David Letterman, Steve O'Donnell, Sandy Frank, Joe Toplyn, Chris Elliott, Matt Wickline, Jeff Martin, Gerard Mulligan, Randy Cohen, Larry Jacobson, Kevin Curran, Fred Graver and Merrill Markoe, *Late Night With David Letterman, Fourth Anniversary Special*

Outstanding Miniseries
Peter the Great (NBC)

Outstanding Lead Actor in a Miniseries or a Special
Dustin Hoffman, *Death of a Salesman*

Outstanding Lead Actress in a Miniseries or a Special
Marlo Thomas, *Nobody's Child*

Outstanding Supporting Actor in a Miniseries or a Special
John Malkovich, *Death of a Salesman*

Outstanding Supporting Actress in a Miniseries or a Special
Colleen Dewhurst, *Between Two Women*

Outstanding Directing in a Miniseries or a Special
Joseph Sargent, *Hallmark Hall of Fame: Love Is Never Silent*

Outstanding Writing in a Miniseries or a Special
Ron Cowen and Daniel Lipman, teleplay; Sherman Yellen, story, *An Early Frost*

Outstanding Informational Series (tie)
Great Performances: Laurence Olivier — A Life (PBS)

Planet Earth (PBS)

Outstanding Informational Special
W. C. Fields Straight Up (PBS)

Outstanding Children's Program (Prime Time)
Anne of Green Gables (PBS)

Outstanding Children's Series (Daytime)
Sesame Street (PBS)

Outstanding Children's Special (Daytime)
CBS Schoolbreak Special: The War Between the Classes (CBS)

Outstanding Animated Program (Daytime)
Jim Henson's Muppet Babies (CBS)

Outstanding Animated Program (Prime Time)
Garfield's Halloween Adventure (CBS)

Outstanding Game/Audience Participation Show
The $25,000 Pyramid (CBS)

Outstanding Talk/Service Program
Donahue (Syndicated)

1986–1987

Outstanding Drama Series
L.A. Law (NBC)

Outstanding Lead Actor in a Drama Series
Bruce Willis, *Moonlighting*

Outstanding Lead Actress in a Drama Series
Sharon Gless, *Cagney and Lacey*

Outstanding Supporting Actor in a Drama Series
John Hillerman, *Magnum, P.I.*

Outstanding Supporting Actress in a Drama Series
Bonnie Bartlett, *St. Elsewhere*

Outstanding Guest Performer in a Drama Series
Alfre Woodard, *L.A. Law: Pilot*

Outstanding Directing in a Drama Series
Gregory Hoblit, *L.A. Law: Pilot*

Outstanding Writing in a Drama Series
Steven Bochco and Terry Louise Fisher, *L.A. Law:
 "Venus Butterfly"*

Outstanding Drama/Comedy Special
Hallmark Hall of Fame: Promise (CBS)

Outstanding Comedy Series
The Golden Girls (NBC)

Outstanding Lead Actor in a Comedy Series
Michael J. Fox, *Family Ties*

Outstanding Lead Actress in a Comedy Series
Rue McClanahan, *The Golden Girls*

Outstanding Supporting Actor in a Comedy Series
John Larroquette, *Night Court*

Outstanding Supporting Actress in a Comedy Series
Jackee Harry, *227*

Outstanding Guest Performer in a Comedy Series
John Cleese, *Cheers: "Simon Says"*

Outstanding Directing in a Comedy Series
Terry Hughes, *The Golden Girls: "Isn't It Romantic"*

Outstanding Writing in a Comedy Series
Gary David Goldberg and Alan Uger, *Family Ties: "'A,' My
 Name Is Alex"*

Outstanding Variety, Music or Comedy Program
The 1987 Tony Awards (CBS)

Outstanding Individual Performance in a Variety or Music Program
Robin Williams, *A Carol Burnett Special: Carol, Carl,
 Whoopi and Robin*

Outstanding Directing in a Variety or Music Program
Don Mischer, *The Kennedy Center Honors: A Celebration
 of the Performing Arts*

Outstanding Writing in a Variety or Music Program
Steve O'Donnell, Sandy Frank, Joe Toplyn, Chris Elliott, Matt
 Wickline, Jeff Martin, Gerard Mulligan, Randy Cohen,
 Larry Jacobson, Kevin Curran, Fred Graver, Adam
 Resnick and David Letterman, *Late Night With David
 Letterman: Fifth Anniversary Special*

Outstanding Miniseries
A Year in the Life (NBC)

Outstanding Lead Actor in a Miniseries or Special
James Woods, *Hallmark Hall of Fame: Promise*

Outstanding Lead Actress in Miniseries or a Special
Gena Rowlands, *The Betty Ford Story*

The Golden Girls

Outstanding Supporting Actor in a Miniseries or a Special
Dabney Coleman, *Sworn to Silence*

Outstanding Supporting Actress in a Miniseries or a Special
Piper Laurie, *Hallmark Hall of Fame: Promise*

Outstanding Directing in a Miniseries or a Special
Glenn Jordan, *Hallmark Hall of Fame: Promise*

Outstanding Writing in a Miniseries or a Special
Richard Friedenberg, teleplay; Kenneth Blackwell,
 Tennyson Flowers and Richard Friedenberg,
 story, *Hallmark Hall of Fame: Promise*

Outstanding Informational Series (tie)
Smithsonian World (PBS)

American Masters: Unknown Chaplin (PBS)

Outstanding Informational Special
*Great Performances: Dance in America: Agnes, the
 Indomitable DeMille* (PBS)

Outstanding Children's Program (Prime Time)
Jim Henson's the Story Teller: Hans My Hedgehog (NBC)

Outstanding Children's Series (Daytime)
Sesame Street (PBS)

Outstanding Children's Special (Daytime)
ABC Afterschool Special: Wanted: The Perfect Guy (ABC)

Outstanding Animated Program (Daytime)
Jim Henson's Muppet Babies (CBS)

Outstanding Animated Program (Prime Time)
Cathy (CBS)

Outstanding Game/Audience Participation Show
The $25,000 Pyramid (CBS)

Outstanding Talk/Service Show
The Oprah Winfrey Show (Syndicated)

1987–1988

Outstanding Drama Series
thirtysomething (ABC)

Outstanding Lead Actor in a Drama Series
Richard Kiley, *A Year in the Life*

Outstanding Lead Actress in a Drama Series
Tyne Daly, *Cagney and Lacey*

thirtysomething

Outstanding Supporting Actor in a Drama Series
Larry Drake, *L.A. Law*

Outstanding Supporting Actress in a Drama Series
Patricia Wettig, *thirtysomething*

Outstanding Guest Performer in a Drama Series
Shirley Knight, *thirtysomething:* "The Parents Are Coming"

Outstanding Directing in a Drama Series
Mark Tinker, *St. Elsewhere:* "Weigh In, Way Out"

Outstanding Writing in a Drama Series
Paul Haggis and Marshall Herskovitz, *thirtysomething:*
"Business as Usual" ("Michael's Father's Death")

Outstanding Drama/Comedy Special
AT&T Presents: Inherit the Wind (NBC)

Outstanding Comedy Series
The Wonder Years (ABC)

Outstanding Lead Actor in a Comedy Series
Michael J. Fox, *Family Ties*

Outstanding Lead Actress in a Comedy Series
Beatrice Arthur, *The Golden Girls*

Outstanding Supporting Actor in a Comedy Series
John Larroquette, *Night Court*

Outstanding Supporting Actress in a Comedy Series
Estelle Getty, *The Golden Girls*

Outstanding Guest Performer in a Comedy Series
Beah Richards, *Frank's Place:* "The Bridge"

Outstanding Directing in a Comedy Series
Gregory Hoblit, *Hooperman:* Pilot

Outstanding Writing in a Comedy Series
Hugh Wilson, *Frank's Place:* "The Bridge"

Outstanding Variety, Music or Comedy Program
Irving Berlin's 100th Birthday Celebration (CBS)

Outstanding Individual Performance in a Variety or Music Program
Robin Williams, *ABC Presents a Royal Gala*

Outstanding Directing in a Variety or Music Program
Patricia Birch and Humphrey Burton, *Great Performances:*
Celebrating Gershwin

Outstanding Writing in a Variety or Music Program
Jackie Mason, *Jackie Mason on Broadway*

Outstanding Miniseries
The Murder of Mary Phagan (NBC)

Outstanding Lead Actor in a Miniseries or a Special
Jason Robards, *AT&T Presents: Inherit the Wind*

Outstanding Lead Actress in a Miniseries or a Special
Jessica Tandy, *Hallmark Hall of Fame: Foxfire*

Outstanding Supporting Actor in a Miniseries or a Special
John Shea, *An ABC Circle Film: Baby M*

Outstanding Supporting Actress in a Miniseries or a Special
Jane Seymour, *Onassis: The Richest Man in the World*

Outstanding Directing in a Miniseries or a Special
Lamont Johnson, *Gore Vidal's Lincoln*

Outstanding Writing in a Miniseries or a Special
William Hanley, *General Foods Golden Showcase: The Attic:*
The Hiding of Anne Frank

Outstanding Informational Series
American Masters: Buster Keaton: A Hard Act to Follow (PBS)

Outstanding Informational Special
Dear America: Letters Home From Vietnam (HBO)

Outstanding Children's Program (Prime Time)
Hallmark Hall of Fame: The Secret Garden (CBS)

Outstanding Children's Series (Daytime)
Sesame Street (PBS)

Outstanding Children's Special (Daytime)
CBS Schoolbreak Special: Never Say Goodbye (CBS)

Oustanding Animated Program (Daytime)
Jim Henson's Muppet Babies (CBS)

Outstanding Animated Program (Prime Time)
A Claymation Christmas Celebration (CBS)

Outstanding Game/Audience Participation Show
The Price Is Right (CBS)

Outstanding Talk/Service Show
The Oprah Winfrey Show (Syndicated)

1988–1989

Outstanding Drama Series
L.A. Law (NBC)

Outstanding Lead Actor in a Drama Series
Carroll O'Connor, *In the Heat of the Night*

Outstanding Lead Actress in a Drama Series
Dana Delany, *China Beach*

Outstanding Supporting Actor in a Drama Series
Larry Drake, *L.A. Law*

Outstanding Supporting Actress in a Drama Series
Melanie Mayron, *thirtysomething*

Outstanding Guest Actor in a Drama Series
Joe Spano, *Midnight Caller:* "The Execution
of John Saringo"

Outstanding Guest Actress in a Drama Series
Kay Lenz, *Midnight Caller:* "After It Happened . . ."

Outstanding Directing in a Drama Series
Robert Altman, *Tanner '88:* "The Boiler Room"

Outstanding Writing in a Drama Series
Joseph Dougherty, *thirtysomething:* "First Day/Last Day"

Outstanding Drama/Comedy Special
AT&T Presents: Day One (CBS)

Outstanding Comedy Series
Cheers (NBC)

Outstanding Lead Actor in a Comedy Series
Richard Mulligan, *Empty Nest*

Outstanding Lead Actress in a Comedy Series
Candice Bergen, *Murphy Brown*

Outstanding Supporting Actor in a Comedy Series
Woody Harrelson, *Cheers*

Outstanding Supporting Actress in a Comedy Series
Rhea Perlman, *Cheers*

Outstanding Guest Actor in a Comedy Series
Cleavon Little, *Stand By Your Man*

Outstanding Guest Actress in a Comedy Series
Colleen Dewhurst, *Murphy Brown:* "Mama Said"

Outstanding Directing in a Comedy Series
Peter Baldwin, *The Wonder Years:* "Our Miss White"

Outstanding Writing in a Comedy Series
Diane English, *Murphy Brown:* "Respect"

Outstanding Variety, Music or Comedy Program
The Tracey Ullman Show (Fox)

Outstanding Individual Performance in a Variety or Music Program
Linda Ronstadt, *Great Performances: Canciones de Mi Padre*

Outstanding Directing in a Variety or Music Program
Jim Henson, *The Jim Henson Hour:* "Dog City"

Outstanding Writing in a Variety or Music Program
James Downey, head writer; John Bowman, A. Whitney
Brown, Gregory Daniels, Tom Davis, Al Franken,
Shannon Gaughan, Jack Handey, Phil Hartman,
Lorne Michaels, Mike Myers, Conan O'Brien,
Bob Odenkirk, Herb Sargent, Tom Schiller,
Robert Smigel, Bonnie Turner, Terry Turner and
Christine Zander, writers; George Meyer,
additional sketches, *Saturday Night Live*

Outstanding Miniseries
War and Remembrance (NBC)

Outstanding Lead Actor in a Miniseries or Special
James Woods, *Hallmark Hall of Fame: My Name Is Bill W.*

Outstanding Lead Actress in a Miniseries or a Special
Holly Hunter, *Roe vs. Wade*

Outstanding Supporting Actor in a Miniseries or Special
Derek Jacobi, *Hallmark Hall of Fame: The Tenth Man*

Outstanding Supporting Actress in a Miniseries or Special
Colleen Dewhurst, *Those She Left Behind*

Outstanding Directing in a Miniseries or a Special
Simon Wincer, *Lonesome Dove*

Outstanding Writing in a Miniseries or a Special
Abby Mann, Robin Vote and Ron Hutchinson, *Murderers
Among Us: The Simon Wiesenthal Story*

Outstanding Informational Series
Nature (PBS)

Outstanding Informational Special
American Masters: Lillian Gish: The Actor's Life for Me (PBS)

Outstanding Performance in Informational Programming
Hal Holbrook, *Portrait of America: Alaska*

Outstanding Directing in Informational Programming
Linda Otto, *Destined To Live*

Outstanding Writing in Informational Programming
John Heminway, *The Mind*

Outstanding Children's Program (Prime Time)
Free to Be . . . a Family (ABC)

Outstanding Children's Series (Daytime)
Newton's Apple (PBS)

Outstanding Children's Special (Daytime)
ABC Afterschool Special: Taking a Stand (ABC)

Outstanding Animated Program (Daytime)
The New Adventures of Winnie the Pooh (ABC)

**Outstanding Animated Program (Prime Time, for
Programming Less Than One Hour)**
Garfield: Babes and Bullets (CBS)

**Outstanding Animated Program (Prime Time, for
Programming More Than One Hour)**
Disney's Ducktales: Super Ducktales (NBC)

Outstanding Game/Audience Participation Show
The $25,000 Pyramid (CBS)

Outstanding Talk/Service Program
The Oprah Winfrey Show (Syndicated)

1989–1990

Outstanding Drama Series
L.A. Law (NBC)

Outstanding Lead Actor in a Drama Series
Peter Falk, *Columbo*

Outstanding Lead Actress in a Drama Series
Patricia Wettig, *thirtysomething*

Outstanding Supporting Actor in a Drama Series
Jimmy Smits, *L.A. Law*

Outstanding Supporting Actress in a Drama Series
Marg Helgenberger, *China Beach*

Outstanding Guest Actor in a Drama Series
Patrick McGoohan, *Columbo:* "Agenda for Murder"

Outstanding Guest Actress in a Drama Series
Viveca Lindfors, *Life Goes On:* "Save the Last Dance for Me"

Outstanding Directing in a Drama Series
Thomas Carter, *Equal Justice:* "Promises to Keep"

Outstanding Writing in a Drama Series
David E. Kelley, *L.A. Law:* "Blood, Sweat and Fears"

Outstanding Drama/Comedy Special
Hallmark Hall of Fame: Caroline? (CBS)

Outstanding Comedy Series
Murphy Brown (CBS)

Outstanding Lead Actor in a Comedy Series
Ten Danson, *Cheers*

Outstanding Lead Actress in a Comedy Series
Candice Bergen, *Murphy Brown*

Outstanding Supporting Actor in a Comedy Series
Alex Rocco, *The Famous Teddy Z*

Outstanding Supporting Actress in a Comedy Series
Bebe Neuwirth, *Cheers*

Outstanding Guest Actor in a Comedy Series
Jay Thomas, *Murphy Brown:* "Heart of Gold"

Outstanding Guest Actress in a Comedy Series
Swoosie Kurtz, *Carol and Company:* "Reunion"

Outstanding Directing in a Comedy Series
Michael Dinner, *The Wonder Years:* "Good-Bye"

Outstanding Writing in a Comedy Series
Bob Brush, *The Wonder Years:* "Good-Bye"

Outstanding Variety, Music or Comedy Series
In Living Color (Fox)

Outstanding Variety, Music or Comedy Special
Sammy Davis, Jr.'s 60th Anniversary Celebration (ABC)

Outstanding Individual Performance in a Variety or Music Program
Tracey Ullman, *The Best of the Tracey Ullman Show*

Outstanding Directing in a Variety or Music Program
Dwight Hemion, *The Kennedy Center Honors: A Celebration of the Performing Arts*

Outstanding Writing in a Variety or Music Program
Billy Crystal, *Billy Crystal: Midnight Train to Moscow*

Outstanding Miniseries
Drug Wars: The Camarena Story (NBC)

Outstanding Lead Actor in a Miniseries or a Special
Hume Cronyn, *Age-Old Friends*

Outstanding Lead Actress in a Miniseries or a Special
Barbara Hershey, *A Killing in a Small Town*

Outstanding Supporting Actor in a Miniseries or a Special
Vincent Gardenia, *Age-Old Friends*

Outstanding Supporting Actress in a Miniseries or a Special
Eva Marie Saint, *People Like Us*

Outstanding Directing in a Miniseries or a Special
Joseph Sargent, *Hallmark Hall of Fame: Caroline?*

Outstanding Writing in a Miniseries or a Special
Terrence McNally, *American Playhouse: Andre's Mother*

Outstanding Informational Series
Smithsonian World (PBS)

Outstanding Informational Special
Great Performances: Dance in America: Bob Fosse Steam Heat (PBS)

Outstanding Performance in Informational Programming
George Burns, *A Conversation With . . .*

Outstanding Directing in Informational Programming
Gene Lasko, *American Masters: Photography Made Difficult*

Outstanding Writing in Informational Programming
Steve Lawson, *American Masters: Broadway's Dreamers: The Legacy of the Group Theatre*

Outstanding Children's Program (Prime Time)
The Magical World of Disney: A Mother's Courage: The Mary Thomas Story (NBC)

Outstanding Children's Series (Daytime)
Reading Rainbow (PBS)

Outstanding Children's Special (Daytime)
CBS Schoolbreak Special: A Matter of Conscience (CBS)

Outstanding Animated Program (Daytime) (tie)
Beetlejuice (ABC)

The New Adventures of Winnie the Pooh (ABC)

Outstanding Animated Program (Prime Time, for Programming One Hour or Less)
The Simpsons (Fox)

Outstanding Game/Audience Participation Show
Jeopardy! (Syndicated)

Outstanding Talk/Service Show
Sally Jessy Raphael (Syndicated)

1990–1991

Outstanding Drama Series
L.A. Law (NBC)

Outstanding Lead Actor in a Drama Series
James Earl Jones, *Gabriel's Fire*

Outstanding Lead Actress in a Drama Series
Patricia Wettig, *thirtysomething*

Outstanding Supporting Actor in a Drama Series
Timothy Busfield, *thirtysomething*

Outstanding Supporting Actress in a Drama Series
Madge Sinclair, *Gabriel's Fire*

Outstanding Guest Actor in a Drama Series
David Opatoshu, *Gabriel's Fire:* "A Prayer for the Goldsteins"

Outstanding Guest Actress in a Drama Series
Peggy McCay, *The Trials of Rosie O'Neill:* "State of Mind"

Outstanding Directing in a Drama Series
Thomas Carter, *Equal Justice:* "In Confidence"

Outstanding Writing in a Drama Series
David E. Kelley, *L.A. Law:* "On the Toad Again"

Outstanding Comedy Series
Cheers (NBC)

Outstanding Lead Actor in a Comedy Series
Burt Reynolds, *Evening Shade*

Outstanding Lead Actress in a Comedy Series
Kirstie Alley, *Cheers*

Outstanding Supporting Actor in a Comedy Series
Jonathan Winters, *Davis Rules*

Outstanding Supporting Actress in a Comedy Series
Bebe Neuwirth, *Cheers*

Outstanding Guest Actor in a Comedy Series
Jay Thomas, *Murphy Brown:* "Gold Rush"

Outstanding Guest Actress in a Comedy Series
Colleen Dewhurst, *Murphy Brown:* "Bob and Murphy and Ted and Avery"

Outstanding Directing in a Comedy Series
James Burrows, *Cheers*

Outstanding Writing in a Comedy Series
Gary Dontzig and Steven Peterman, *Murphy Brown:* "Jingle Hell, Jingle Hell, Jingle All the Way"

Outstanding Variety, Music or Comedy Program
The 63rd Annual Academy Awards (ABC)

Outstanding Individual Performance in a Variety or Music Program
Billy Crystal, *The 63rd Annual Academy Awards*

Outstanding Directing in a Variety or Music Program
Hal Gurnee, *Late Night With David Letterman, Show #1425*

Outstanding Writing in a Variety or Music Program
Hal Kanter and Buz Kohan, writers; Billy Crystal, David Steinberg, Bruce Vilanch and Robert Wuhl, special material, *The 63rd Annual Academy Awards*

Outstanding Drama/Comedy Special and Miniseries
A General Motors Mark of Excellence Presentation: Separate but Equal (ABC)

Outstanding Lead Actor in a Miniseries or a Special
John Gielgud, *Masterpiece Theatre: Summer's Lease*

Outstanding Lead Actress in a Miniseries or a Special
Lynn Whitfield, *The Josephine Baker Story*

Outstanding Supporting Actor in a Miniseries or a Special
James Earl Jones, *Heat Wave*

Outstanding Supporting Actress in a Miniseries or a Special
Ruby Dee, *Hallmark Hall of Fame: Decoration Day*

The Simpsons

Outstanding Directing in a Miniseries or a Special
Brian Gibson, *The Josephine Baker Story*

Outstanding Writing in a Miniseries or a Special
Andrew Davies, *Masterpiece Theatre: House of Cards*

Outstanding Informational Series
*A General Motors Mark of Excellence Presentation:
The Civil War* (PBS)

Outstanding Informational Special
Edward R. Murrow, *American Masters: This Reporter*

Outstanding Directing in Informational Programming
Peter Gelb, Susan Froemke, Albert Maysles and Bob Eisenhardt,
Soldiers of Music: Rostropovich Returns to Russia

Outstanding Writing in Informational Programming
Geoffrey C. Ward, Ric Burns and Ken Burns,
*A General Motors Mark of Excellence
Presentation: The Civil War*

Outstanding Children's Program (Prime Time)
A 3-2-1 Contact Extra: You Can't Grow Home Again (PBS)

Outstanding Children's Series (Daytime)
Sesame Street (PBS)

Outstanding Children's Special (Daytime)
Lost in the Barrens (Disney Channel)

Outstanding Animated Program (Daytime)
Tiny Toon Adventures (Syndicated)

**Outstanding Animated Program (Prime Time, for Programming
One Hour or Less)**
The Simpsons (Fox)

**Outstanding Animated Program (Prime Time for Programming
One Hour or More)**
Disney's Tale Spin: Plunder and Lightning (Syndicated)

Outstanding Game/Audience Participation Show
Jeopardy! (Syndicated)

Outstanding Talk/Service Show
The Oprah Winfrey Show (Syndicated)

1991–1992

Outstanding Drama Series
Northern Exposure (CBS)

Outstanding Lead Actor in a Drama Series
Christopher Lloyd, *Avonlea*

Outstanding Lead Actress in a Drama Series
Dana Delany, *China Beach*

Outstanding Supporting Actor in a Drama Series
Richard Dysart, *L.A. Law*

Outstanding Supporting Actress in a Drama Series
Valerie Mahaffey, *Northern Exposure*

**Outstanding Individual Achievement in Directing
in a Drama Series**
Eric Laneuville, *I'll Fly Away:* "All God's Children"

**Outstanding Individual Achievement in Writing
in a Drama Series**
Andrew Schneider, *Northern Exposure:* "Seoul Mates"

Outstanding Comedy Series
Murphy Brown (CBS)

Outstanding Lead Actor in a Comedy Series
Craig T. Nelson, *Coach*

Outstanding Lead Actress in a Comedy Series
Candice Bergen, *Murphy Brown*

Outstanding Supporting Actor in a Comedy Series
Michael Jeter, *Evening Shade*

Outstanding Supporting Actress in a Comedy Series
Laurie Metcalf, *Roseanne*

**Outstanding Individual Achievement in Directing
in a Comedy Series**
Barnet Kellman, *Murphy Brown:* "Birth 101"

**Outstanding Individual Achievement in Writing
in a Comedy Series**
Elaine Pope, *Seinfeld:* "The Fix Up"

Outstanding Variety, Music or Comedy Program (Series)
The Tonight Show Starring Johnny Carson (NBC)

Outstanding Variety, Music or Comedy Program (Special)
Cirque du Soleil II: A New Experience (HBO)

**Outstanding Individual Performance in a Variety or Music
Program**
Bette Midler, *The Tonight Show Starring Johnny Carson*

**Outstanding Individual Achievement in Directing
in a Variety or Music Program**
Patricia Birch, *Great Performances: Unforgettable, With Love:
Natalie Cole Sings the Songs of Nat King Cole*

**Outstanding Individual Achievement in Writing
in a Variety or Music Program**
Hal Kanter and Buz Kohan, writers; Billy Crystal, Marc Shaiman,
David Steinberg, Robert Wuhl and Bruce Vilanch, special
material, *The 64th Annual Academy Awards*

Outstanding Miniseries
A Woman Named Jackie (NBC)

Outstanding Lead Actor in a Miniseries or Special
Beau Bridges, *Without Warning: The James Brady Story*

Outstanding Lead Actress in a Miniseries or a Special
Gena Rowlands, *Face of a Stranger*

Outstanding Supporting Actor in a Miniseries or Special
Hume Cronyn, *Neil Simon's Broadway Bound*

Outstanding Supporting Actress in a Miniseries or Special
Amanda Plummer, *Hallmark Hall of Fame: Miss Rose White*

**Outstanding Individual Achievement in Directing for a
Miniseries or a Special**
Daniel Petrie, *Mark Twain and Me*

**Outstanding Individual Achievement in Writing in a
Miniseries or a Special**
John Falsey and Joshua Brand, *I'll Fly Away:* Pilot

Outstanding Made for Television Movie
Hallmark Hall of Fame: Miss Rose White (NBC)

Outstanding Informational Series
MGM: When the Lion Roars (TNT)

Outstanding Informational Special
Abortion: Desperate Choices (HBO)

Outstanding Individual Achievement in Informational Programming, Directing
George Hickenlooper, Fax Bahr and Eleanor Coppola, *Hearts of Darkness: A Filmmaker's Apocalypse*

Outstanding Individual Achievement in Informational Programming, Writing
Fax Bahr and George Hickenlooper, *Hearts of Darkness: A Filmmaker's Apocalypse*

Outstanding Children's Program (Prime Time)
Mark Twain and Me (Disney Channel)

Outstanding Children's Series (Daytime)
Sesame Street (Syndicated)

Outstanding Children's Special (Daytime)
Vincent and Me (Disney Channel)

Outstanding Animated Program (Daytime)
Rugrats (Nickelodeon)

Outstanding Animated Program (Prime Time, for Programming One Hour or Less)
A Claymation Easter (CBS)

Outstanding Game/Audience Participation Show
Jeopardy! (Syndicated)

Outstanding Talk/Service Show
The Oprah Winfrey Show (Syndicated)

Michael Richards, *Seinfeld*

1992–1993

Outstanding Drama Series
Picket Fences (CBS)

Outstanding Lead Actor in a Drama Series
Tom Skerritt, *Picket Fences*

Outstanding Lead Actress in a Drama Series
Kathy Baker, *Picket Fences*

Outstanding Supporting Actor in a Drama Series
Chad Lowe, *Life Goes On*

Outstanding Supporting Actress in a Drama Series
Mary Alice, *I'll Fly Away*

Outstanding Guest Actor in a Drama Series
Laurence Fishburne, *Tribeca:* "The Box"

Outstanding Guest Actress in a Drama Series
Elaine Stritch, *Law & Order:* "Point of View"

Outstanding Individual Achievement in Directing in a Drama Series
Barry Levinson, *Homicide: Life on the Street:* "Gone for Goode"

Outstanding Individual Achievement in Writing in a Drama Series
Tom Fontana, *Homicide: Life on the Street:* "Three Men and Adena"

Outstanding Comedy Series
Seinfeld (NBC)

Outstanding Lead Actor in a Comedy Series
Ted Danson, *Cheers*

Outstanding Lead Actress in a Comedy Series
Roseanne Arnold, *Roseanne*

Outstanding Supporting Actor in a Comedy Series
Michael Richards, *Seinfeld*

Outstanding Supporting Actress in a Comedy Series
Laurie Metcalf, *Roseanne*

Outstanding Guest Actor in a Comedy Series
David Clennon, *Dream On:* "For Peter's Sake"

Outstanding Guest Actress in a Comedy Series
Tracey Ullman, *Love and War:* "The Prima Dava"

Outstanding Individual Achievement in Directing in a Comedy Series
Betty Thomas, *Dream On:* "For Peter's Sake"

Outstanding Individual Achievement in Writing in a Comedy Series
Larry David, *Seinfeld:* "The Contest"

Outstanding Variety, Music or Comedy Series
Saturday Night Live (NBC)

Outstanding Individual Performance in a Variety or Music Program
Dana Carvey, *Saturday Night Live: Saturday Night Live's Presidential Bash*

Outstanding Individual Achievement in Directing in a Variety or Music Program
Walter C. Miller, *The 1992 Tony Awards*

Outstanding Individual Achievement in Writing in a Variety or Music Program
Judd Apatow, Robert Cohen, David Cross, Brent Forrester, Jeff Kahn, Bruce Kirschbaum, Bob Odenkirk, Sultan Pepper, Dino Stamatopoulos and Ben Stiller, *The Ben Stiller Show*

Outstanding Variety, Music or Comedy Special
Bob Hope: The First 90 Years (NBC)

Outstanding Miniseries
Mystery: Prime Suspect 2 (PBS)

Outstanding Lead Actor in a Miniseries or Special
Robert Morse, *American Playhouse: Tru*

Outstanding Lead Actress in a Miniseries or a Special
Holly Hunter, *The Positively True Adventures of the Alleged Texas Cheerleader-Murdering Mom*

Outstanding Supporting Actor in a Miniseries or a Special
Beau Bridges, *The Positively True Adventures of the Alleged Texas Cheerleader-Murdering Mom*

Outstanding Supporting Actress in a Miniseries or Special
Mary Tyler Moore, *Stolen Babies*

Outstanding Individual Achievement in Directing for a Miniseries or a Special
James Sadwith, *Sinatra*

Outstanding Individual Achievement in Writing in a Miniseries or a Special
Jane Anderson, *The Positively True Adventures of the Alleged Texas Cheerleader-Murdering Mom*

Outstanding Made for Television Movie
Barbarians at the Gate (HBO)

Outstanding Informational Series
Healing and the Mind With Bill Moyers (PBS)

Outstanding Informational Special
Lucy and Desi: A Home Movie (NBC)

Outstanding Children's Program (Prime Time)
Avonlea (Disney Channel)

Outstanding Children's Series (Daytime)
Reading Rainbow (PBS)

Outstanding Children's Special (Daytime)
ABC Afterschool Special: Shades of a Single Protein (ABC)

Outstanding Animated Program (Daytime)
Tiny Toon Adventures (Fox)

Outstanding Animated Program (Prime Time, for Programming One Hour or Less)
Batman: The Series (Fox)

Outstanding Game/Audience Participation Show
Jeopardy! (Syndicated)

Outstanding Talk/Service Show
Good Morning America (ABC)

1993–1994

Outstanding Drama Series
Picket Fences (CBS)

Outstanding Lead Actor in a Drama Series
Dennis Franz, *NYPD Blue*

Outstanding Lead Actress in a Drama Series
Sela Ward, *Sisters*

Outstanding Supporting Actor in a Drama Series
Fyvush Finkel, *Picket Fences*

Outstanding Supporting Actress in a Drama Series
Leigh Taylor-Young, *Picket Fences*

Outstanding Guest Actor in a Drama Series
Richard Kiley, *Picket Fences:* "Buried Alive"

Outstanding Guest Actress in a Drama Series
Faye Dunaway, *Columbo:* "It's All in the Game"

Outstanding Individual Achievement in Directing in a Drama Series
Daniel Sackheim, *NYPD Blue:* "Tempest in a C-Cup"

Outstanding Individual Achievement in Writing in a Drama Series
Ann Biderman, teleplay/story, *NYPD Blue:* "Steroid Roy"

Outstanding Comedy Series
Frasier (NBC)

Outstanding Lead Actor in a Comedy Series
Kelsey Grammer, *Frasier*

Outstanding Lead Actress in a Comedy Series
Candice Bergen, *Murphy Brown*

Outstanding Supporting Actor in a Comedy Series
Michael Richards, *Seinfeld*

Outstanding Supporting Actress in a Comedy Series
Laurie Metcalf, *Roseanne*

Outstanding Guest Actor in a Comedy Series
Martin Sheen, *Murphy Brown:* "Angst for the Memories"

Outstanding Guest Actress in a Comedy Series
Eileen Heckart, *Love and War:* "You Make Me Feel So Young"

Outstanding Individual Achievement in Directing in a Comedy Series
James Burrows, *Frasier:* "The Good Son"

Outstanding Individual Achievement in Writing in a Comedy Series
David Angell, *Frasier:* "The Good Son"

Outstanding Variety, Music or Comedy Series
Late Show With David Letterman (CBS)

Outstanding Individual Performance in a Variety or Music Program
Tracey Ullman, *Tracey Ullman — Takes on New York*

Outstanding Individual Achievement in Directing in a Variety or Music Program
Walter C. Miller, *The Tony Awards*

Outstanding Individual Achievement in Writing in a Variety or Music Program
Jeff Cesario, Mike Dugan, Eddie Feldmann, Gregory Greenberg, Dennis Miller and Kevin Rooney, *Dennis Miller Live*

Outstanding Variety, Music or Comedy Special
The Kennedy Center Honors (CBS)

Outstanding Miniseries
Mystery: Prime Suspect 3 (PBS)

Outstanding Lead Actor in a Miniseries or Special
Hume Cronyn, *Hallmark Hall of Fame: To Dance With the White Dog*

Outstanding Lead Actress in a Miniseries or a Special
Kirstie Alley, *David's Mother*

Outstanding Supporting Actor in a Miniseries or Special
Michael Goorjian, *David's Mother*

Outstanding Supporting Actress in a Miniseries or a Special
Cicely Tyson, *Oldest Living Confederate Widow Tells All,* parts 1 and 2

Outstanding Individual Achievement in Directing for a Miniseries or a Special
John Frankenheimer, *Against the Wall*

Outstanding Individual Achievement in Writing in a Miniseries or a Special
Bob Randall, *David's Mother*

Outstanding Made for Television Movie
And the Band Played On (HBO)

Outstanding Informational Series
Later With Bob Costas (NBC)

Outstanding Information Special
I Am a Promise: The Children of Stanton Street Elementary School (HBO)

Outstanding Cultural Program
Vladimir Horowitz: A Reminiscence (PBS)

Outstanding Children's Program (Prime Time)
Kids Killing Kids/Kids Saving Kids (CBS, Fox)

Outstanding Children's Series (Daytime)
Sesame Street (PBS)

Outstanding Children's Special (Daytime)
Dead Drunk: The Kevin Tunell Story (HBO)

Outstanding Animated Children's Program (Daytime)
Rugrats (Nickelodeon)

Outstanding Animated Program (Prime Time, for Programming One Hour or Less)
The Roman City (PBS)

Outstanding Game/Audience Participation Show
Jeopardy! (Syndicated)

Outstanding Service Show
This Old House (PBS)

Outstanding Talk Show
The Oprah Winfrey Show (Syndicated)

1994–1995

Outstanding Drama Series
NYPD Blue (ABC)

Outstanding Lead Actor in a Drama Series
Mandy Patinkin, *Chicago Hope*

Outstanding Lead Actress in a Drama Series
Kathy Baker, *Picket Fences*

Outstanding Supporting Actor in a Drama Series
Ray Walston, *Picket Fences*

Outstanding Supporting Actress in a Drama Series
Julianna Margulies, *ER*

Outstanding Guest Actor in a Drama Series
Paul Winfield, *Picket Fences*: "Enemy Lines"

Outstanding Guest Actress in a Drama Series
Shirley Knight, *NYPD Blue*: "Large Mouth Bass"

Outstanding Individual Achievement in Directing in a Drama Series
Mimi Leder, *ER*: "Love's Labor Lost"

Outstanding Individual Achievement in Writing in a Drama Series
Lance A. Gentile, *ER*: "Love's Labor Lost"

Outstanding Comedy Series
Frasier (NBC)

Outstanding Lead Actor in a Comedy Series
Kelsey Grammer, *Frasier*

Outstanding Lead Actress in a Comedy Series
Candice Bergen, *Murphy Brown*

Outstanding Supporting Actor in a Comedy Series
David Hyde Pierce, *Frasier*

Outstanding Supporting Actress in a Comedy Series
Christine Baranski, *Cybill*

Outstanding Guest Actor in a Comedy Series
Carl Reiner, *Mad About You*: "The Alan Brady Show"

Outstanding Guest Actress in a Comedy Series
Cyndi Lauper, *Mad About You*: "Money Changes Everything"

Outstanding Individual Achievement in Directing in a Comedy Series
David Lee, *Frasier*: "The Matchmaker"

Outstanding Individual Achievement in Writing in a Comedy Series
Chuck Ranberg and Anne Flett-Giordano, *Frasier*: "An Affair to Remember"

Outstanding Variety, Music or Comedy Series
The Tonight Show With Jay Leno (NBC)

Outstanding Individual Performance in a Variety or Music Program
Barbra Streisand, *Barbra Streisand: The Concert*

Outstanding Individual Achievement in Directing in a Variety or Music Program
Jeff Margolis, *The 67th Annual Academy Awards*

Outstanding Individual Achievement in Writing in a Variety or Music Program
Eddie Feldmann, writing supervisor; Jeff Cesario, Ed Driscoll, David Feldman, Gregory Greenberg, Dennis Miller and Kevin Rooney, writers, *Dennis Miller Live*

Outstanding Variety, Music or Comedy Special
Barbra Streisand: The Concert (HBO)

Outstanding Miniseries
Joseph (TNT)

Outstanding Lead Actor in a Miniseries or Special
Raul Julia, *The Burning Season*

Outstanding Lead Actress in a Miniseries or a Special
Glenn Close, *Serving in Silence: The Margarethe Cammermeyer Story*

Outstanding Supporting Actor in a Miniseries or Special
Donald Sutherland, *Citizen X*

Outstanding Supporting Actress in a Miniseries or a Special (tie)
Judy Davis, *Serving in Silence: The Margarethe Cammermeyer Story*

Shirley Knight, *Indictment: The McMartin Trial*

Outstanding Individual Achievement in Directing in a Miniseries or a Special
John Frankenheimer, *The Burning Season*

Outstanding Individual Achievement in Writing in a Miniseries or a Special
Alison Cross, writer, *Serving in Silence: The Margarethe Cammermeyer Story*

Outstanding Made for Television Movie
Indictment: The McMartin Trial (HBO)

Outstanding Informational Series (tie)
Baseball (PBS)

TV Nation (NBC)

Outstanding Information Special
Taxicab Confessions (HBO)

Outstanding Cultural Program
Verdi's La Traviata — With the New York City Opera (PBS)

Outstanding Children's Program (Prime Time)
The World Wildlife Fund Presents — Going, Going, Almost Gone! Animals in Danger (HBO)

Outstanding Animated Program (for Programming One Hour or Less)
The Simpsons (Fox)

Outstanding Children's Series
Nick News (Nickelodeon)

Outstanding Children's Special
A Child Betrayed: The Calvin Mire Story (HBO)

Outstanding Animated Program
Where on Earth Is Carmen Sandiego? (PBS)

Outstanding Game/Audience Participation Show
Jeopardy (Syndicated)

Outstanding Talk/Service Show
Oprah Winfrey Show (Syndicated)

Kelsey Grammer, *Frasier*

All-Time Top Emmy Winners and Nominees

MOST EMMYS WON BY INDIVIDUALS

MOST EMMYS WON BY A MALE PERFORMER

MOST EMMYS WON BY A FEMALE PERFORMER

MOST EMMYS WON BY A SERIES

MOST EMMYS WON BY A MINISERIES

MOST EMMYS WON BY A MOVIE OF THE WEEK

MOST EMMYS WON IN A SINGLE YEAR BY A NETWORK

The Mary Tyler Moore Show

MOST EMMYS WON BY A SERIES IN ITS FIRST SEASON

MOST EMMYS WON BY A SERIES IN A SINGLE SEASON

MOST EMMY WINS AS BEST DRAMA SERIES

MOST EMMY WINS AS BEST COMEDY SERIES

MOST NOMINATIONS FOR AN INDIVIDUAL

MOST NOMINATIONS FOR A PROGRAM

Source: Academy of Television Arts and Sciences

Television Hall of Fame

Each year, the Academy of Television Arts and Sciences inducts up to seven people or programs to the Television Hall of Fame. Here are the past inductees honored for their outstanding and lasting contribution to television.

Johnny Carson

Ed Sullivan

Oprah Winfrey

1984
Lucille Ball
Milton Berle
Paddy Chayefsky
Norman Lear
Edward R. Murrow
William S. Paley
David Sarnoff

1985
Carol Burnett
Sid Caesar
Walter Cronkite
Joyce Hall
Rod Serling
Ed Sullivan
Sylvester (Pat) Weaver

1986
Steve Allen
Fred Coe
Walt Disney
Jackie Gleason
Mary Tyler Moore
Frank Stanton
Burr Tillstrom

1987
Johnny Carson
Jacques-Yves Cousteau
Leonard Goldenson
Jim Henson
Bob Hope
Ernie Kovacs
Eric Sevareid

1988
Jack Benny
George Burns and Gracie Allen
Chet Huntley and David Brinkley
Red Skelton
David Susskind
David Wolper

1989
Roone Arledge
Fred Astaire
Perry Como
Joan Ganz Cooney
Don Hewitt
Carroll O'Connor
Barbara Walters

1990
Desi Arnaz
Leonard Bernstein

James Garner
I Love Lucy
Danny Thomas
Mike Wallace

1991
Bill Cosby
Andy Griffith
Ted Koppel
Sheldon Leonard
Dinah Shore
Ted Turner

1992
Dick Clark
John Chancellor
Phil Donahue
Mark Goodson
Bob Newhart
Agnes Nixon
Jack Webb

1993
Alan Alda
Howard Cosell
Barry Diller
Fred Friendly
Bill Hanna and Joseph Barbera
Oprah Winfrey

What We Watched

Nielsen Media Research tracks the shows we watch each television season. The networks use the ratings to plan programming strategy and to determine how much to charge advertisers for commercials. Here are the most popular television programs since 1950.

October 1950 – April 1951

1. The Texaco Star Theater .... NBC
2. Fireside Theatre .... NBC
3. Your Show of Shows .... NBC
4. Philco Television Playhouse................. NBC
5. The Colgate Comedy Hour................... NBC
6. Gillette Cavalcade of Sports .... NBC
7. Arthur Godfrey's Talent Scouts .... CBS
8. Mama .... CBS
9. Robert Montgomery Presents .... NBC
10. Martin Kane, Private Eye .... NBC
11. Man Against Crime........................ CBS
12. Somerset Maugham Playhouse .... NBC
13. Kraft Television Theatre.................... NBC
14. The Toast of the Town..................... CBS
15. The Aldrich Family .... NBC
16. You Bet Your Life.......................... NBC
17. Armstrong Circle Theatre .... NBC
18. Big Town .... CBS
19. Lights Out................................. NBC
20. The Alan Young Show .... CBS

October 1951 – April 1952

1. Arthur Godfrey's Talent Scouts .... CBS
2. The Texaco Star Theater .... NBC
3. I Love Lucy................................. CBS
4. The Red Skelton Show...................... NBC
5. The Colgate Comedy Hour................... NBC
6. Fireside Theatre .... NBC

I Love Lucy

7. The Jack Benny Program.................... CBS
8. Your Show of Shows .... NBC
9. You Bet Your Life........................... NBC
10. Arthur Godfrey and His Friends.............. CBS
11. Mama .... CBS
12. Philco Television Playhouse.................. NBC
13. Amos 'n' Andy .... CBS
14. Big Town .... CBS
15. Pabst Blue Ribbon Bouts .... CBS
16. Gillette Cavalcade of Sports................. NBC
17. The Alan Young Show .... CBS
18. The All Star Revue .... NBC
19. Dragnet.................................... NBC
20. Kraft Television Theatre...................... NBC

October 1952 – April 1953

1. I Love Lucy................................. CBS
2. Arthur Godfrey's Talent Scouts .... CBS
3. Arthur Godfrey and His Friends............... CBS
4. Dragnet.................................... NBC
5. The Texaco Star Theater .... NBC
6. The Buick Circus Hour...................... NBC
7. The Colgate Comedy Hour................... NBC
8. Gangbusters .... NBC
9. You Bet Your Life........................... NBC
10. Fireside Theatre .... NBC
11. The Red Buttons Show...................... CBS
12. The Jack Benny Show .... CBS
13. Life With Luigi .... CBS
14. Pabst Blue Ribbon Bouts .... CBS
15. Goodyear Playhouse .... NBC
16. The Life of Riley .... NBC
17. Mama .... CBS
18. Your Show of Shows .... NBC
19. What's My Line? .... CBS
20. Strike It Rich .... CBS

October 1953 – April 1954

1. I Love Lucy................................. CBS
2. Dragnet .... NBC
3. Arthur Godfrey's Talent Scouts .... CBS
4. You Bet Your Life........................... NBC
5. The Bob Hope Show........................ NBC
6. The Milton Berle Show .... NBC
7. Arthur Godfrey and His Friends............. CBS
8. The Ford Show .... NBC
9. The Jackie Gleason Show................... CBS

10.	Fireside Theatre	NBC
11.	The Colgate Comedy Hour	NBC
12.	This Is Your Life	NBC
13.	The Red Buttons Show	CBS
14.	The Life of Riley	NBC
15.	Our Miss Brooks	CBS
16.	Treasury Men in Action	NBC
17.	All-Star Revue	NBC
18.	The Jack Benny Show	CBS
19.	Gillette Cavalcade of Sports	NBC
20.	Philco Television Playhouse	NBC

October 1954 – April 1955

1.	I Love Lucy	CBS
2.	The Jackie Gleason Show	CBS
3.	Dragnet	NBC
4.	You Bet Your Life	NBC
5.	Toast of the Town	CBS
6.	Disneyland	ABC
7.	The Bob Hope Show	NBC
8.	The Jack Benny Show	CBS
9.	The Martha Raye Show	NBC
10.	The George Gobel Show	NBC
11.	Ford Theatre	NBC
12.	December Bride	CBS
13.	The Buick-Berle Show	NBC
14.	This Is Your Life	NBC
15.	I've Got a Secret	CBS
16.	Two for the Money	CBS
17.	Your Hit Parade	NBC
18.	The Millionaire	CBS
19.	General Electric Theater	CBS
20.	Arthur Godfrey's Talent Scouts	CBS

October 1955 – April 1956

1.	The $64,000 Question	CBS
2.	I Love Lucy	CBS
3.	The Ed Sullivan Show	CBS
4.	Disneyland	ABC
5.	The Jack Benny Show	CBS
6.	December Bride	CBS
7.	You Bet Your Life	NBC
8.	Dragnet	NBC
9.	I've Got a Secret	CBS
10.	General Electric Theater	CBS
11.	Private Secretary	CBS
12.	Ford Theatre	NBC
13.	The Red Skelton Show	CBS
14.	The George Gobel Show	NBC
15.	The $64,000 Challenge	CBS
16.	Two for the Money	CBS
17.	Your Hit Parade	NBC
18.	The Millionaire	CBS
19.	General Electric Theater	CBS
20.	Arthur Godfrey's Talent Scouts	CBS

October 1956 – April 1957

1.	I Love Lucy	CBS
2.	The Ed Sullivan Show	CBS
3.	General Electric Theater	CBS
4.	The $64,000 Question	CBS
5.	December Bride	CBS
6.	Alfred Hitchcock Presents	CBS
7.	I've Got a Secret	CBS
8.	Gunsmoke	CBS
9.	The Perry Como Show	NBC
10.	The Jack Benny Show	CBS
11.	Dragnet	NBC
12.	Arthur Godfrey's Talent Scouts	CBS
13.	The Millionaire	CBS
14.	Disneyland	ABC
15.	Shower of Stars	CBS
16.	The Lineup	CBS
17.	The Red Skelton Show	CBS
18.	You Bet Your Life	NBC
19.	Wyatt Earp	ABC
20.	Private Secretary	CBS

October 1957 – April 1958

1.	Gunsmoke	CBS
2.	The Danny Thomas Show	CBS
3.	Tales of Wells Fargo	NBC
4.	Have Gun, Will Travel	CBS
5.	I've Got a Secret	CBS
6.	The Life and Legend of Wyatt Earp	ABC
7.	General Electric Theater	CBS
8.	The Restless Gun	NBC
9.	December Bride	CBS
10.	You Bet Your Life	NBC
11.	Alfred Hitchcock Presents	CBS
12.	Cheyenne	ABC
13.	The Ford Show	NBC
14.	The Red Skelton Show	CBS
15.	Wagon Train	NBC
16.	Sugarfoot	ABC
17.	Father Knows Best	CBS
18.	Twenty-One	NBC
19.	The Ed Sullivan Show	CBS
20.	The Jack Benny Show	CBS

October 1958 – April 1959

1.	Gunsmoke	CBS
2.	Wagon Train	NBC
3.	Have Gun, Will Travel	CBS
4.	The Rifleman	ABC
5.	The Danny Thomas Show	CBS
6.	Maverick	ABC
7.	Wells Fargo	NBC
8.	The Real McCoys	ABC
9.	I've Got a Secret	CBS
10.	The Life and Legend of Wyatt Earp	ABC

11.	*The Price Is Right*	NBC
12.	*The Red Skelton Show*	CBS
13.	*Zane Grey Theater*	CBS
14.	*Father Knows Best*	CBS
15.	*The Texan*	CBS
16.	*Wanted: Dead or Alive*	CBS
17.	*Peter Gunn*	NBC
18.	*Cheyenne*	ABC
19.	*Perry Mason*	CBS
20.	*The Tennessee Ernie Ford Show*	NBC

October 1959 – April 1960

1.	*Gunsmoke*	CBS
2.	*Wagon Train*	NBC
3.	*Have Gun, Will Travel*	CBS
4.	*The Danny Thomas Show*	CBS
5.	*The Red Skelton Show*	CBS
6.	*Father Knows Best*	CBS
7.	*77 Sunset Strip*	ABC
8.	*The Price Is Right*	NBC
9.	*Wanted: Dead or Alive*	CBS
10.	*Perry Mason*	CBS
11.	*The Real McCoys*	ABC
12.	*The Ed Sullivan Show*	CBS
13.	*The Bing Crosby Show*	ABC
14.	*Rifleman*	ABC
15.	*The Ford Show*	NBC
16.	*The Lawman*	ABC
17.	*Dennis the Menace*	CBS
18.	*Cheyenne*	ABC
19.	*Rawhide*	CBS
20.	*Maverick*	ABC

October 1960 – April 1961

1.	*Gunsmoke*	CBS
2.	*Wagon Train*	NBC
3.	*Have Gun, Will Travel*	CBS
4.	*The Andy Griffith Show*	CBS
5.	*The Real McCoys*	ABC

Gunsmoke

6.	*Rawhide*	CBS
7.	*Candid Camera*	CBS
8.	*The Untouchables*	ABC
9.	*The Price Is Right*	NBC
10.	*The Jack Benny Show*	CBS
11.	*Dennis the Menace*	CBS
12.	*The Danny Thomas Show*	CBS
13.	*My Three Sons*	ABC
14.	*77 Sunset Strip*	ABC
15.	*The Ed Sullivan Show*	CBS
16.	*Perry Mason*	CBS
17.	*Bonanza*	NBC
18.	*The Flintstones*	ABC
19.	*The Red Skelton Show*	CBS
20.	*Alfred Hitchcock Presents*	CBS

October 1961 – April 1962

1.	*Wagon Train*	NBC
2.	*Bonanza*	NBC
3.	*Gunsmoke*	CBS
4.	*Hazel*	NBC
5.	*Perry Mason*	CBS
6.	*The Red Skelton Show*	CBS
7.	*The Andy Griffith Show*	CBS
8.	*The Danny Thomas Show*	CBS
9.	*Dr. Kildare*	NBC
10.	*Candid Camera*	CBS
11.	*My Three Sons*	ABC
12.	*The Garry Moore Show*	CBS
13.	*Rawhide*	CBS
14.	*The Real McCoys*	ABC
15.	*Lassie*	CBS
16.	*Sing Along With Mitch*	NBC
17.	*Dennis the Menace*	CBS
18.	*Gunsmoke*	CBS
19.	*Ben Casey*	ABC
20.	*The Ed Sullivan Show*	CBS

October 1962 – April 1963

1.	*The Beverly Hillbillies*	CBS
2.	*Candid Camera*	CBS
3.	*The Red Skelton Show*	CBS
4.	*Bonanza*	NBC
5.	*The Lucy Show*	CBS
6.	*The Andy Griffith Show*	CBS
7.	*Ben Casey*	ABC
8.	*The Danny Thomas Show*	CBS
9.	*The Dick Van Dyke Show*	CBS
10.	*Gunsmoke*	CBS
11.	*Dr. Kildare*	NBC
12.	*The Jack Benny Show*	CBS
13.	*What's My Line*	CBS
14.	*The Ed Sullivan Show*	CBS
15.	*Hazel*	NBC
16.	*I've Got a Secret*	CBS
17.	*The Jackie Gleason Show*	CBS

Rowan and Martin's Laugh-In

19.	*The Defenders*	CBS
20.	*The Garry Moore Show*	CBS
20.	*To Tell the Truth*	CBS

October 1963 – April 1964

1.	*The Beverly Hillbillies*	CBS
2.	*Bonanza*	NBC
3.	*The Dick Van Dyke Show*	CBS
4.	*Petticoat Junction*	CBS
5.	*The Andy Griffith Show*	CBS
6.	*The Lucy Show*	CBS
7.	*Candid Camera*	CBS
8.	*The Ed Sullivan Show*	CBS
9.	*The Danny Thomas Show*	CBS
10.	*My Favorite Martian*	CBS
11.	*The Red Skelton Show*	CBS
12.	*I've Got a Secret*	CBS
13.	*Lassie*	CBS
14.	*The Jack Benny Show*	CBS
15.	*The Jackie Gleason Show*	CBS
16.	*The Donna Reed Show*	ABC
17.	*The Virginian*	NBC
18.	*The Patty Duke Show*	ABC
19.	*Dr. Kildare*	NBC
20.	*Gunsmoke*	CBS

October 1964 – April 1965

1.	*Bonanza*	NBC
2.	*Bewitched*	ABC
3.	*Gomer Pyle, U.S.M.C.*	CBS
4.	*The Andy Griffith Show*	CBS
5.	*The Fugitive*	ABC
6.	*The Red Skelton Hour*	CBS
7.	*The Dick Van Dyke Show*	CBS
8.	*The Lucy Show*	CBS
9.	*Peyton Place (II)*	ABC
10.	*Combat*	ABC
11.	*Walt Disney's Wonderful World of Color*	NBC
12.	*The Beverly Hillbillies*	CBS
13.	*My Three Sons*	ABC
14.	*Branded*	NBC
15.	*Petticoat Junction*	CBS
16.	*The Ed Sullivan Show*	CBS
17.	*Lassie*	CBS
18.	*The Munsters*	CBS
19.	*Gilligan's Island*	CBS
20.	*Peyton Place (V)*	ABC

October 1965 – April 1966

1.	*Bonanza*	NBC
2.	*Gomer Pyle, U.S.M.C.*	CBS
3.	*The Lucy Show*	CBS
4.	*The Red Skelton Hour*	CBS
5.	*Batman* (Thursday)	ABC
6.	*The Andy Griffith Show*	CBS
7.	*Bewitched*	ABC
8.	*The Beverly Hillbillies*	CBS
9.	*Hogan's Heroes*	CBS
10.	*Batman* (Wednesday)	ABC
11.	*Green Acres*	CBS
12.	*Get Smart*	NBC
13.	*The Man From U.N.C.L.E.*	NBC
14.	*Daktari*	CBS
15.	*My Three Sons*	CBS
16.	*The Dick Van Dyke Show*	CBS
17.	*Walt Disney's Wonderful World of Color*	NBC
18.	*The Ed Sullivan Show*	CBS
19.	*The Lawrence Welk Show*	ABC
20.	*I've Got a Secret*	CBS

October 1966 – April 1967

1.	*Bonanza*	NBC
2.	*The Red Skelton Hour*	CBS
3.	*The Andy Griffith Show*	CBS
4.	*The Lucy Show*	CBS
5.	*The Jackie Gleason Show*	CBS
6.	*Green Acres*	CBS
7.	*Daktari*	CBS
8.	*Bewitched*	ABC
9.	*The Beverly Hillbillies*	CBS
10.	*Gomer Pyle, U.S.M.C.*	CBS
11.	*The Virginian*	NBC
12.	*The Lawrence Welk Show*	ABC
13.	*The Ed Sullivan Show*	CBS
14.	*The Dean Martin Show*	CBS
15.	*Family Affair*	CBS
16.	*The Smothers Brothers Comedy Hour*	CBS
17.	*The CBS Friday Night Movie*	CBS
18.	*Hogan's Heroes*	CBS
19.	*Walt Disney's Wonderful World of Color*	NBC
20.	*Saturday Night at the Movies*	NBC

October 1967 – April 1968

1. *The Andy Griffith Show* .... CBS
2. *The Lucy Show* .... CBS
3. *Gomer Pyle, U.S.M.C.* .... CBS
4. *Gunsmoke* .... CBS
5. *Family Affair* .... CBS
6. *Bonanza* .... NBC
7. *The Red Skelton Show* .... CBS
8. *The Dean Martin Show* .... NBC
9. *The Jackie Gleason Show* .... CBS
10. *Saturday Night at the Movies* .... NBC
11. *Bewitched* .... ABC
12. *The Beverly Hillbillies* .... CBS
13. *The Ed Sullivan Show* .... CBS
14. *The Virginian* .... NBC
15. *The CBS Friday Night Movie* .... CBS
16. *Green Acres* .... CBS
17. *Lawrence Welk* .... ABC
18. *The Smothers Brothers Show* .... CBS
19. *Gentle Ben* .... CBS
20. *Tuesday Night at the Movies* .... NBC

October 1968 – April 1969

1. *Rowan and Martin's Laugh-In* .... NBC
2. *Gomer Pyle, U.S.M.C.* .... CBS
3. *Bonanza* .... NBC
4. *Mayberry R.F.D.* .... CBS
5. *Family Affair* .... CBS
6. *Gunsmoke* .... CBS
7. *Julia* .... NBC
8. *The Dean Martin Show* .... NBC
9. *Here's Lucy* .... CBS
10. *The Beverly Hillbillies* .... CBS
11. *Mission: Impossible* .... CBS
12. *Bewitched* .... ABC
13. *The Red Skelton Hour* .... CBS
14. *My Three Sons* .... CBS
15. *The Glen Campbell Goodtime Hour* .... CBS
16. *Ironside* .... NBC
17. *The Virginian* .... NBC
18. *The F.B.I.* .... ABC
19. *Green Acres* .... CBS
20. *Dragnet* .... NBC

October 1969 – April 1970

1. *Rowan and Martin's Laugh-In* .... NBC
2. *Gunsmoke* .... CBS
3. *Bonanza* .... NBC
4. *Mayberry R.F.D.* .... CBS
5. *Family Affair* .... CBS
6. *Here's Lucy* .... CBS
7. *The Red Skelton Hour* .... CBS
8. *Marcus Welby, M.D.* .... ABC
9. *The Wonderful World of Disney* .... NBC
10. *The Doris Day Show* .... CBS

11. *The Bill Cosby Show* .... NBC
12. *The Jim Nabors Hour* .... CBS
13. *The Carol Burnett Show* .... CBS
14. *The Dean Martin Show* .... NBC
15. *My Three Sons* .... CBS
16. *Ironside* .... NBC
17. *The Johnny Cash Show* .... ABC
18. *The Beverly Hillbillies* .... CBS
19. *Hawaii Five-O* .... CBS
20. *The Glen Campbell Goodtime Hour* .... CBS

October 1970 – April 1971

1. *Marcus Welby, M.D.* .... ABC
2. *The Flip Wilson Show* .... NBC
3. *Here's Lucy* .... CBS
4. *Ironside* .... NBC
5. *Gunsmoke* .... CBS
6. *ABC Movie of the Week* .... ABC
7. *Hawaii Five-O* .... CBS
8. *Medical Center* .... CBS
9. *Bonanza* .... NBC
10. *The F.B.I.* .... ABC
11. *The Mod Squad* .... ABC
12. *Adam-12* .... NBC
13. *Rowan and Martin's Laugh-In* .... NBC
14. *The Wonderful World of Disney* .... NBC
15. *Mayberry R.F.D.* .... CBS
16. *Hee Haw* .... CBS
17. *Mannix* .... CBS
18. *The Men From Shiloh* .... NBC
19. *My Three Sons* .... CBS
20. *The Doris Day Show* .... CBS

October 1971 – April 1972

1. *All in the Family* .... CBS
2. *The Flip Wilson Show* .... NBC
3. *Marcus Welby, M.D.* .... ABC
4. *Gunsmoke* .... CBS

All in the Family

5.	ABC Movie of the Week	ABC
6.	Sanford and Son	NBC
7.	Mannix	CBS
8.	Funny Face	CBS
9.	Adam-12	NBC
10.	The Mary Tyler Moore Show	CBS
11.	Here's Lucy	CBS
12.	Hawaii Five-O	CBS
13.	Medical Center	CBS
14.	NBC Mystery Movie	NBC
15.	Ironside	NBC
16.	The Partridge Family	ABC
17.	The F.B.I.	ABC
18.	The New Dick Van Dyke Show	CBS
19.	The Wonderful World of Disney	NBC
20.	Bonanza	NBC

October 1972 – April 1973

1.	All in the Family	CBS
2.	Sanford and Son	NBC
3.	Hawaii Five-O	CBS
4.	Maude	CBS
5.	Bridget Loves Bernie	CBS
6.	Sunday Mystery Movie	NBC
7.	The Mary Tyler Moore Show	CBS
8.	Gunsmoke	CBS
9.	The Wonderful World of Disney	NBC
10.	Ironside	NBC
11.	Adam-12	NBC
12.	The Flip Wilson Show	NBC
13.	Marcus Welby, M.D.	ABC
14.	Cannon	CBS
15.	Here's Lucy	CBS
16.	The Bob Newhart Show	CBS
17.	Tuesday Movie of the Week	ABC
18.	ABC NFL Football	ABC
19.	The Partridge Family	ABC
20.	The Waltons	CBS

September 1973 – April 1974

1.	All in the Family	CBS
2.	The Waltons	CBS
3.	Sanford and Son	NBC
4.	M*A*S*H	CBS
5.	Hawaii Five-O	CBS
6.	Maude	CBS
7.	Kojak	CBS
8.	The Sonny and Cher Comedy Hour	CBS
9.	The Mary Tyler Moore Show	CBS
10.	Cannon	CBS
11.	The Six Million Dollar Man	ABC
12.	The Bob Newhart Show	CBS
13.	The Wonderful World of Disney	NBC
14.	NBC Sunday Mystery Movie	NBC
15.	Gunsmoke	CBS
16.	Happy Days	ABC

17.	Good Times	CBS
18.	Barnaby Jones	CBS
19.	ABC Monday Night Football	ABC
20.	CBS Friday Night Movie	CBS

September 1974 – April 1975

1.	All in the Family	CBS
2.	Sanford and Son	NBC
3.	Chico and the Man	NBC
4.	The Jeffersons	CBS
5.	M*A*S*H	CBS
6.	Rhoda	CBS
7.	Good Times	CBS
8.	The Waltons	CBS
9.	Maude	CBS
10.	Hawaii Five-O	CBS
11.	The Mary Tyler Moore Show	CBS
12.	The Rockford Files	NBC
13.	Little House on the Prairie	NBC
14.	Kojak	CBS
15.	Police Woman	NBC
16.	S.W.A.T.	ABC
17.	The Bob Newhart Show	CBS
18.	The Wonderful World of Disney	NBC
19.	The Rookies	ABC
20.	Mannix	CBS

September 1975 – April 1976

1.	All in the Family	CBS
2.	Rich Man, Poor Man	ABC
3.	Laverne and Shirley	ABC
4.	Maude	CBS
5.	The Bionic Woman	ABC
6.	Phyllis	CBS
7.	Sanford and Son	NBC
8.	Rhoda	CBS
9.	The Six Million Dollar Man	ABC
10.	ABC Monday Night Movie	ABC
11.	Happy Days	ABC
12.	One Day at a Time	CBS
13.	ABC Sunday Night Movie	ABC
14.	The Waltons	CBS
15.	M*A*S*H	CBS
16.	Starsky and Hutch	ABC
17.	Good Heavens	ABC
18.	Welcome Back, Kotter	ABC
19.	The Mary Tyler Moore Show	CBS
20.	Kojak	CBS

September 1976 – April 1977

1.	Happy Days	ABC
2.	Laverne and Shirley	ABC
3.	ABC Monday Night Movie	ABC
4.	M*A*S*H	CBS
5.	Charlie's Angels	ABC
6.	The Big Event	NBC

Happy Days

7. The Six Million Dollar Man . . . . ABC
8. ABC Sunday Night Movie . . . . ABC
9. Baretta . . . . ABC
10. One Day at a Time . . . . CBS
11. Three's Company . . . . ABC
12. All in the Family . . . . CBS
13. Welcome Back, Kotter . . . . ABC
14. The Bionic Woman . . . . ABC
15. The Waltons . . . . CBS
16. Little House on the Prairie . . . . NBC
17. Barney Miller . . . . ABC
18. 60 Minutes . . . . CBS
19. Hawaii Five-O . . . . CBS
20. NBC Monday Night Movie . . . . NBC

September 1977 – April 1978

1. Laverne and Shirley . . . . ABC
2. Happy Days . . . . ABC
3. Three's Company . . . . ABC
4. 60 Minutes . . . . CBS
5. Charlie's Angels . . . . ABC
6. All in the Family . . . . CBS
7. Little House on the Prairie . . . . NBC
8. Alice . . . . CBS
9. M*A*S*H . . . . CBS
10. One Day at a Time . . . . CBS
11. How the West Was Won . . . . ABC
12. Eight Is Enough . . . . ABC
13. Soap . . . . ABC
14. The Love Boat . . . . ABC
15. NBC Monday Night Movie . . . . NBC
16. Monday Night Football . . . . ABC
17. Fantasy Island . . . . ABC
18. Barney Miller . . . . ABC
19. The Amazing Spider-Man . . . . CBS
20. Project U.F.O. . . . . NBC

September 1978 – April 1979

1. All in the Family . . . . CBS
2. Three's Company . . . . ABC
3. Happy Days . . . . ABC
4. Mork and Mindy . . . . ABC
5. Angie . . . . ABC
6. M*A*S*H . . . . CBS
7. 60 Minutes . . . . CBS
8. All in the Family . . . . CBS
9. The Ropers . . . . ABC
10. Taxi . . . . ABC
11. Charlie's Angels . . . . ABC
12. Eight Is Enough . . . . ABC
13. Alice (8:30) . . . . CBS
14. What's Happening (Thursday) . . . . ABC
15. One Day at a Time (Monday) . . . . CBS
16. One Day at a Time . . . . CBS
17. Little House on the Prairie . . . . NBC
18. ABC Sunday Night Movie . . . . ABC
19. Barney Miller . . . . ABC
20. Alice . . . . CBS

September 1979 – April 1980

1. 60 Minutes . . . . CBS
2. Three's Company . . . . ABC
3. That's Incredible . . . . ABC
4. M*A*S*H . . . . CBS
5. Alice . . . . CBS
6. Dallas . . . . CBS
7. Flo . . . . CBS
8. The Jeffersons . . . . CBS
9. The Dukes of Hazzard . . . . CBS
10. One Day at a Time . . . . CBS
11. WKRP in Cincinnati (9:30) . . . . CBS
12. Goodtime Girls (Tuesday) . . . . ABC
13. Archie Bunker's Place . . . . CBS
14. Taxi . . . . ABC
15. Eight Is Enough . . . . ABC
16. Little House on the Prairie . . . . NBC
17. House Calls . . . . CBS
18. Real People . . . . NBC
19. CHiPs (Saturday) . . . . NBC
20. Happy Days . . . . ABC

September 1980 – April 1981

1. Dallas . . . . CBS
2. 60 Minutes . . . . CBS
3. The Dukes of Hazzard . . . . CBS
4. Private Benjamin . . . . CBS
5. M*A*S*H . . . . CBS
6. The Love Boat . . . . ABC
7. The NBC Tuesday Night Movie . . . . NBC
8. House Calls . . . . CBS
9. The Jeffersons . . . . CBS
10. Little House on the Prairie . . . . NBC
11. The Two of Us . . . . CBS

The Bill Cosby Show

12.	Alice	CBS
13.	Three's Company	ABC
14.	Real People	NBC
15.	One Day at a Time	CBS
16.	The NBC Movie of the Week	NBC
17.	Too Close for Comfort	ABC
18.	Magnum, P.I.	CBS
19.	NFL Monday Night Football	ABC
20.	Diff'rent Strokes	NBC

September 1981 – April 1982

1.	Dallas	CBS
2.	Dallas (10:00)	CBS
3.	60 Minutes	CBS
4.	Three's Company	ABC
5.	CBS NFL Football Post 2	CBS
6.	The Jeffersons	CBS
7.	Joanie Loves Chachi	ABC
8.	The Dukes of Hazzard (9:00)	CBS
9.	Alice	CBS
10.	The Dukes of Hazzard	CBS
11.	The ABC Monday Night Movie	ABC
12.	Too Close for Comfort	ABC
13.	M*A*S*H	CBS
14.	One Day at a Time	CBS
15.	NFL Monday Night Football	ABC
16.	Falcon Crest	CBS
17.	Archie Bunker's Place	CBS
18.	The Love Boat	ABC
19.	Hart to Hart	ABC
20.	Trapper John, M.D.	CBS

September 1982 – April 1983

1.	60 Minutes	CBS
2.	Dallas	CBS
3.	M*A*S*H	CBS
4.	Magnum, P.I.	CBS
5.	Dynasty	ABC
6.	Three's Company	ABC
7.	Simon and Simon	CBS
8.	Falcon Crest	CBS
9.	NFL Monday Night Football	ABC
10.	The Love Boat	ABC
11.	One Day at a Time (Sunday)	CBS
12.	Newhart (Monday)	CBS
13.	The A-Team	NBC
12.	The Jeffersons	CBS
15.	The Fall Guy (9:00)	ABC
16.	Newhart (9:30)	CBS
17.	The Mississippi	CBS
18.	9 to 5	ABC
19.	The Fall Guy	ABC
20.	The ABC Monday Night Movie	ABC

September 1983 – April 1984

1.	Dallas	CBS
2.	Dynasty	ABC
3.	The A-Team	NBC
4.	60 Minutes	CBS
5.	Simon and Simon	CBS
6.	Magnum, P.I.	CBS
7.	Falcon Crest	CBS
8.	Kate and Allie	CBS
9.	Hotel	ABC
10.	Cagney and Lacey	CBS
11.	Knots Landing	CBS
12.	The ABC Sunday Night Movie	ABC
13.	The ABC Monday Night Movie	ABC
14.	TV's Bloopers and Practical Jokes	NBC
15.	After M*A*S*H	CBS
16.	The Fall Guy	ABC
17.	Four Seasons (8:00)	CBS
18.	The Love Boat	ABC
19.	Riptide	NBC
20.	The Jeffersons	CBS

September 1984 – April 1985

1.	Dynasty	ABC
2.	Dallas	CBS
3.	The Bill Cosby Show	NBC
4.	60 Minutes	CBS
5.	Family Ties	NBC
6.	Simon and Simon	CBS
7.	The A-Team	NBC
8.	Knots Landing	CBS
9.	Murder, She Wrote	CBS
10.	Crazy Like a Fox	CBS
11.	Falcon Crest	CBS
12.	Hotel	ABC
13.	Cheers	NBC
14.	Who's the Boss?	ABC
15.	Riptide	NBC
16.	Magnum, P.I.	CBS

17.	*Hail to the Chief*	ABC
18.	*Newhart*	CBS
19.	*Kate and Allie*	CBS
20.	*NBC Monday Night Movies*	NBC

September 1985 – April 1986

1.	*The Bill Cosby Show*	NBC
2.	*Family Ties*	NBC
3.	*Murder, She Wrote*	CBS
4.	*60 Minutes*	CBS
5.	*Cheers*	NBC
6.	*Dallas*	CBS
7.	*Dynasty*	ABC
8.	*The Golden Girls*	NBC
9.	*Miami Vice*	NBC
10.	*Who's the Boss?*	ABC
11.	*Perfect Strangers*	ABC
12.	*Night Court*	NBC
13.	*The CBS Sunday Night Movie*	CBS
14.	*Highway to Heaven*	NBC
15.	*Kate and Allie*	CBS
16.	*NFL Monday Night Football*	ABC
17.	*Newhart*	CBS
18.	*Knots Landing*	CBS
19.	*Growing Pains*	ABC
20.	*227*	NBC

September 1986 – April 1987

1.	*The Bill Cosby Show*	NBC
2.	*Family Ties*	NBC
3.	*Cheers*	NBC
4.	*Murder, She Wrote*	CBS
5.	*Night Court* (Thursday)	NBC
6.	*The Golden Girls*	NBC
7.	*60 Minutes*	CBS
8.	*Growing Pains*	ABC
9.	*Moonlighting*	ABC
10.	*Who's the Boss?*	ABC
11.	*Dallas*	CBS

Roseanne

12.	*Nothing in Common*	NBC
13.	*Newhart*	CBS
14.	*Amen*	NBC
15.	*227*	NBC
16.	*The CBS Sunday Movie*	CBS
17.	*Matlock*	NBC
18.	*NBC Monday Night Movies*	NBC
19.	*Kate and Allie*	CBS
20.	*NFL Monday Night Football*	ABC

September 1987 – April 1988

1.	*The Bill Cosby Show*	NBC
2.	*A Different World*	NBC
3.	*Cheers*	NBC
4.	*Growing Pains* (Tuesday)	ABC
5.	*Night Court* (Thursday)	NBC
6.	*The Golden Girls*	NBC
7.	*Who's the Boss?*	ABC
8.	*60 Minutes*	CBS
9.	*Murder, She Wrote*	CBS
10.	*The Wonder Years*	ABC
11.	*Alf*	NBC
12.	*Moonlighting*	ABC
13.	*L.A. Law*	NBC
14.	*NFL Monday Night Football*	ABC
15.	*Matlock*	NBC
16.	*Growing Pains* (Wednesday)	ABC
17.	*Amen*	NBC
18.	*Family Ties*	NBC
19.	*Hunter* (Saturday)	NBC
20.	*The CBS Sunday Night Movie*	CBS

September 1988 – April 1989

1.	*Roseanne*	ABC
2.	*The Bill Cosby Show*	NBC
3.	*A Different World*	NBC
4.	*Roseanne* (8:30)	ABC
5.	*Cheers*	NBC
6.	*60 Minutes*	CBS
7.	*The Golden Girls*	NBC
8.	*Who's the Boss?*	ABC
9.	*The Wonder Years*	ABC
10.	*Murder, She Wrote*	CBS
11.	*Empty Nest*	NBC
12.	*Anything but Love*	ABC
13.	*Dear John*	NBC
14.	*Growing Pains*	ABC
15.	*Alf*	NBC
16.	*L.A. Law*	NBC
17.	*Matlock*	NBC
18.	*Hunter*	NBC
19.	*Unsolved Mysteries*	NBC
20.	*In the Heat of the Night*	NBC

Murphy Brown

September 1989 – April 1990

1. *Roseanne* . . . . ABC
2. *The Bill Cosby Show* . . . . NBC
3. *Cheers* . . . . NBC
4. *A Different World* . . . . NBC
5. *America's Funniest Home Videos* . . . . ABC
6. *The Golden Girls* . . . . NBC
7. *60 Minutes* . . . . CBS
8. *The Wonder Years* . . . . ABC
9. *Empty Nest* . . . . NBC
10. *Chicken Soup* . . . . ABC
11. *NFL Monday Night Football* . . . . ABC
12. *Unsolved Mysteries* . . . . NBC
13. *Who's the Boss?* . . . . ABC
14. *L.A. Law* . . . . NBC
15. *Murder, She Wrote* . . . . CBS
16. *Grand* . . . . NBC
17. *In the Heat of the Night* . . . . NBC
18. *Dear John* . . . . NBC
19. *Coach* . . . . ABC
20. *Matlock* . . . . NBC

September 1990 – April 1991

1. *Cheers* . . . . NBC
2. *60 Minutes* . . . . CBS
3. *Roseanne* . . . . ABC
4. *A Different World* . . . . NBC
5. *The Bill Cosby Show* . . . . NBC
6. *NFL Monday Night Football* . . . . ABC
7. *America's Funniest Home Videos* . . . . ABC
8. *Murphy Brown* . . . . CBS
9. *America's Funniest People* . . . . ABC
10. *Designing Women* . . . . CBS
11. *Empty Nest* . . . . NBC
12. *The Golden Girls* . . . . NBC
13. *Murder, She Wrote* . . . . CBS
14. *Unsolved Mysteries* . . . . NBC
15. *Full House* . . . . ABC
16. *Family Matters* . . . . ABC
17. *Coach* . . . . ABC
18. *Matlock* . . . . NBC
19. *In the Heat of the Night* . . . . NBC
20. *Major Dad* . . . . CBS

September 1991 – April 1992

1. *60 Minutes* . . . . CBS
2. *Roseanne* . . . . ABC
3. *Murphy Brown* . . . . CBS
4. *Cheers* . . . . NBC
5. *Home Improvement* . . . . ABC
6. *Designing Women* . . . . CBS
7. *Coach* . . . . ABC
8. *Full House* . . . . ABC
9. *Murder, She Wrote* . . . . CBS
10. *Unsolved Mysteries* . . . . NBC
11. *Major Dad* . . . . CBS
12. *NFL Monday Night Football* . . . . ABC
13. *Room for Two* . . . . ABC
14. *The CBS Sunday Night Movie* . . . . CBS
15. *Evening Shade* . . . . CBS

BROADCASTING TIMELINE

1897
K.F. Braun invents the cathode-ray tube.

1906
Reginald Fessenden invents wireless telephony, a means for radio waves to carry signals a significant distance.

1912
The Radio Act of 1912 assigns three- and four-letter codes to radio stations and limits broadcasting to the 360m wavelength, which jams signals.

1920
KDKA, a Philadelphia Westinghouse station, transmits the first commercial radio broadcast.

1922
Reacting to problems posed by the Radio Act of 1912, the Commerce Department allows powerful stations to use the 400m wavelength as long as they only broadcast live music.

1923
Russian immigrant Vladimir Kosma Zworykin patents the iconoscope, the first television transmission tube. He patents the first color tube in 1925.

A.C. Nielsen Company is founded and provides measurements of radio audiences for advertisers.

1925
Radio's *The Smith Family* introduces the soap opera format.

16.	*Northern Exposure*	CBS
17.	*A Different World*	NBC
18.	*The Bill Cosby Show*	NBC
19.	*Wings*	NBC
20.	*America's Funniest Home Videos*	ABC

September 1992 – April 1993

1.	*60 Minutes*	CBS
2.	*Roseanne*	ABC
3.	*Home Improvement*	ABC
4.	*Murphy Brown*	CBS
5.	*Murder, She Wrote*	CBS
6.	*Coach*	ABC
7.	*NFL Monday Night Football*	ABC
8.	*The CBS Sunday Night Movie*	CBS
9.	*Cheers*	NBC
10.	*Full House*	ABC
11.	*Northern Exposure*	CBS
12.	*Rescue 911*	CBS
13.	*20/20*	ABC
14.	*The CBS Tuesday Night Movie*	CBS
15.	*Love and War*	CBS
16.	*Fresh Prince of Bel Air*	NBC
17.	*Hangin' With Mr. Cooper*	ABC
18.	*The Jackie Thomas Show*	ABC
19.	*Evening Shade*	CBS
20.	*Hearts Afire*	CBS

September 1993 – April 1994

1.	*Home Improvement*	ABC
2.	*60 Minutes*	CBS
3.	*Seinfeld*	NBC
4.	*Roseanne*	ABC
5.	*Ellen*	ABC
6.	*Grace Under Fire*	ABC
7.	*Frasier*	NBC
8.	*Coach*	ABC

9.	*Murder, She Wrote*	CBS
10.	*NFL Monday Night Football*	ABC
11.	*Murphy Brown*	CBS
12.	*The CBS Sunday Movie*	CBS
13.	*Thunder Alley*	ABC
14.	*20/20*	ABC
15.	*Love and War*	CBS
16.	*Northern Exposure*	CBS
17.	*Wings*	NBC
18.	*Full House*	ABC
19.	*PrimeTime Live*	ABC
20.	*Dave's World*	CBS

September 1994 – April 1995

1.	*Seinfeld*	NBC
2.	*ER*	NBC
3.	*Home Improvement*	ABC
4.	*Grace Under Fire*	ABC
5.	*NFL Monday Night Football*	ABC
6.	*60 Minutes*	CBS
7.	*NYPD Blue*	ABC
8.	*Friends*	NBC
9.	*Roseanne*	ABC
9.	*Murder, She Wrote*	CBS
11.	*Mad About You,* (Thursday)	NBC
12.	*Madman of the People*	NBC
13.	*Ellen*	ABC
14.	*Hope and Gloria*	NBC
15.	*Frasier*	NBC
16.	*Murphy Brown*	CBS
17.	*20/20*	ABC
18.	*CBS Sunday Night Movie*	CBS
19.	*NBC Monday Night Movie*	NBC
20.	*Dave's World*	CBS

1926

RCA, General Electric and Westinghouse establish NBC, which operates two national radio networks.

1928

John Baird beams a television image from England to the United States.

GE introduces a television set with a 3" x 4" screen.

The first television is sold — a Daven for $75.

1930

Crossley Inc. tabulates the first formal ratings system.

1933

Edwin Armstrong introduces Frequency Modulation (FM), a static-free method of transmission.

1934

The Communications Act of 1934 creates the Federal Communications Commission, which regulates broadcasting.

1936

The British Broadcasting Corporation (BBC) debuts the world's first television service with three hours of programming a day.

1938

Orson Welles broadcasts his adaptation of H.G. Wells's *War of the Worlds* on October 30, creating a nationwide panic as listeners believe that aliens have landed in New Jersey.

Broadcast and Cable Television Networks

ABC
77 W. 66th St.
New York, NY 10023-6298
(212) 456-7777

A&E Network
235 E. 45th St.
New York, NY 10017
(212) 210-1328
Comedy, drama, documentaries and performing-arts programming

American Movie Classics (AMC)
150 Crossways Park W.
Woodbury, NY 11797
(516) 364-2222
Uninterrupted classic movies from Hollywood's golden age and original classic-movie-related programming

Animal Planet
7700 Wisconsin Ave.
Bethesda, MD 20814
(301) 986-1999
Natural history programming including series and comedy from the Discovery Channel

Black Entertainment Television (BET)
1232 31st St. N.W.
Washington D.C. 20007
(202) 337-5260
African-American family programming, including music, sports, children's entertainment, news, public affairs and specials

The Box
12000 Biscayne Blvd.
Miami, FL 33181
(305) 674-5000
Interactive-music television programmed by viewers

Bravo
150 Crossways Park W.
Woodbury, NY 11797
(516) 364-2222
Foreign and independent films and performing-arts programming

CBS Inc.
51 W. 52nd St.
New York, NY 10019
(212) 975-4321

Canal de Noticias NBC/ NBC News Channel
925 Wood Ridge Center Drive
Charlotte, NC 28217
(704) 329-8706
Spanish-language news service

Cartoon Network
Box 105264
1050 Techwood Drive N.W.
Atlanta, GA 30318
(404) 827-1717
Colorful animated entertainment from the Turner Entertainment Co. and Hanna-Barbera cartoon libraries

Cinemax
1100 Ave. of the Americas
New York, NY 10036
(212) 512-1000
Films and movie-based original programming (pay service)

Classic Sports Network
35 E. 21st St.
New York, NY 10010
(212) 529-8000
Great moments in sports history and original programming

CMT: Country Music Television
Group W Satellite Communications
250 Harbor Drive, Box 10210
Stamford, CT 06904
(203) 965-6000
Country-music videos, interviews and specials

CNBC
2200 Fletcher Ave.
Fort Lee, NJ 07024
(201) 585-2622
Fast-breaking business and market news, consumer information and talk shows

CNN (Cable News Network)
P.O. Box 105366
One CNN Center
Atlanta, GA 30348-5366
(404) 827-1500
News and information programming

CNNfn
P.O. Box 105366
One CNN Center
Atlanta, GA 30348-5366
(404) 827-1500
Financial news 12 hours each day using CNN's resources

Comedy Central
1775 Broadway
New York, NY 10019
(212) 767-8600
Stand-up routines, movies, talk shows, sitcoms, specials and classic series

Courtroom Television Network
600 Third Ave., 2nd Floor
New York, NY 10016
(212) 973-2800
Legal news, live and taped coverage of trials and commentary

1940

CBS demonstrates color television in New York.

WNBT, the first regularly operating television station, debuts in New York with an estimated 10,000 viewers.

1944

The first instance of network censorship occurs. The sound is cut off on the Eddie Cantor and Nora Martin duet, "We're Having a Baby, My Baby and Me."

The DuMont network goes on the air. Paramount Pictures backs the startup enterprise, but its lack of affiliated radio networks leads to its early demise in 1956.

1945

The orthicon tube, developed by RCA, improves light sensitivity a hundredfold.

The FCC creates the commercial broadcasting spectrum of 13 channels, and 130 applications for broadcast licenses follow.

1946

Faraway Hill, what many television historians consider to be the first network soap opera, debuts on the DuMont network.

1947

The Yankees beat the Dodgers in seven games in the first televised World Series.

Meet the Press debuts on NBC. The first news show will become television's longest-running program.

C-SPAN/C-SPAN 2 (Cable Satellite Public Affairs Network)
400 N. Capitol St. N.W., Suite 650
Washington D.C. 20001
(202) 737-3220
Live gavel-to-gavel coverage of the U.S. House of Representatives (C-SPAN) and Senate (C-SPAN 2)

The Discovery Channel
7700 Wisconsin Ave.
Bethesda, MD 20814
(301) 986-1999
Nonfiction programming in science, nature, history, adventure and world exploration

Disney Channel
3800 W. Alameda Ave.
Burbank, CA 91505
(818) 569-7500
Family entertainment, including movies and specials (pay service)

E! Entertainment Television
5670 Wilshire Blvd.
Los Angeles, CA 90036-3709
(213) 954-2400
Interviews, news and media-savvy features from the entertainment world

Encore!
4700 S. Syracuse Parkway, Suite 1000
Denver, CO 80237-2721
(303) 771-7700
Uncut, unedited movies from 1960 to 1980 (pay service)

ESPN/ESPN 2
ESPN Plaza
Bristol, CT 06010
(203) 585-2000
Sports events, news and information

Family Channel
1000 Centerville Turnpike
Virginia Beach, VA 23463
(804) 523-7301
Family entertainment including original films, dramatic and comedy series, classic Westerns and inspirational programs

FiT TV
1000 Centerville Turnpike
Virginia Beach, VA 23463
(804) 523-7301
Fitness programming including workouts, nutritional information and home shopping

Fox Broadcasting Company
10201 W. Pico Blvd.
Los Angeles, CA 90035
(213) 203-3266

f/X
10201 W. Pico
Los Angeles, CA 90035
(310) 203-3474
Movies, television series and original programming from Fox Broadcasting and Twentieth Century-Fox

Galavision
6701 Center Drive W., 6th Floor
Los Angeles, CA 90045
(3001) 348-3640
Spanish-language programming including serials, music, movies and sports

Game Show Channel
3801 S. Sheridan
Tulsa, OK 74145
(918) 665-6690
Game shows and interactive games

The Golf Channel
7580 Commerce Center Drive
Orlando, FL 32819
(407) 363-4653
Live tournament coverage, instructional programs, news and classic tournaments

HBO (Home Box Office)
1100 Ave. of the Americas
New York, NY 10036
(212) 512-1000
Movies, comedy specials, documentaries, sports, original movies and comedy series (pay service)

Headline News
Turner Broadcasting System
One CNN Center
Atlanta, GA 30348
(404) 827-1500
News and information programming in half-hour intervals

The History Channel
235 E. 45th St.
New York, NY 10017
(212) 661-4500
Documentaries, movies and original programming highlighting historical American events

Home and Garden Television
P.O. Box 50970
Knoxville, TN 37950
(615) 694-2700
Tips and how-to advice for the home and garden

Home Shopping Network
Box 9090
Clearwater, FL 34618-9090
(813) 572-8585
Televised shopping

Independent Film Channel
150 Crossways Park W.
Woodbury, NY 11797
(516) 364-2222
Films produced outside the Hollywood studio system

International Channel
12401 West Olympic Blvd.
Los Angeles, CA 90064
(310) 826-2429
Foreign-language news, sports, drama and comedy from around the world

The Learning Channel
7700 Wisconsin Ave.
Bethesda, MD 20814-3539
(301) 986-1999
Adult learning and enrichment programs, documentaries and educational series

---

1949

Cable television brings better reception to rural areas where the conventional television signal is weak.

These Are My Children, a live, 15-minute show, premieres on NBC. It is the first continuing daytime drama.

1950

Saturday morning children's programming begins.

Phonevision, the first pay-per-view service, becomes available.

For the first time, a nationwide program airs. Edward R. Murrow, in the first broadcast of his *See It Now* series, tells viewers, as he looks into the split-screen image of the Golden Gate and Brooklyn bridges, that they for the first time are able to see the Atlantic and Pacific oceans simultaneously.

1952

Leonard Nimoy appears in a science fiction series. No, not that one. In *Zombies of the Stratosphere,* Nimoy

portrays the Martian Narab.

Television's first magazine-format program, the *Today* show, debuts on NBC with Dave Garroway hosting.

1953

Loretta Young abandons Hollywood for her stylish debut on the small screen.

The first issue of *TV Guide* magazine hits the newsstands on April 3 in 10 cities with a circulation of 1,560,000.

Lifetime
Lifetime Astoria Studios
36-12 35th Ave.
Astoria, NY 11106
(718) 482-4000
Contemporary programming of interest to women

Mind Extension University (ME/U)
9697 E. Mineral Ave.
Englewood, CO 80155
(303) 792-5808
Innovative use of interactive distance-learning for college- and graduate-level education

MOR Music
11500 Ninth St. N.
St. Petersburg, FL 33716
(813) 579-4600
Videos and music shopping

The Movie Channel (TMC)
1633 Broadway, 37th Floor
New York, NY 10019
(212) 708-1600
Movies and movie-related programming (pay service)

MSNBC
2200 Fletcher Ave.
Fort Lee, NJ 07024
(201) 583-5000
Joint venture between Microsoft and NBC that provides a 24-hour news service and on-line news

MTV (Music Television)
1515 Broadway
New York, NY 10036
(212) 258-7800
Music videos, music news, interviews and original programming

Much Music
150 Crossways Park W.
Woodbury, NY 11797
(516) 364-2222
Music videos and more

NBC
30 Rockefeller Plaza
New York, NY 10112
(212) 664-4444

NASA Select Television
400 Maryland Ave., S.W.
Washington D.C. 20546
(202) 453-8425
Lift-off-to-landing coverage of NASA missions, plus press conferences and public-affairs programming

Nickelodeon/Nick at Night
1515 Broadway
New York, NY 10036
(212) 258-8000
Programming for children during the day, and classic television at night

Nick at Nite's TV Land
1515 Broadway
New York, NY 10036
(212) 258-8000
Classic television and even classic commercials

Odyssey
305 Madison Ave.
New York, NY 10165
(212) 599-2760
Family and interfaith programming including dramas, documentaries and children's shows

Outdoor Life
250 Harbor Drive, 2nd Floor
Stamford, CT 06904
(203) 965-6000
Information and news about fishing, kayaking, hiking, conservation issues and other outdoor activities.

Playboy Channel
9242 Beverly Blvd.
Beverly Hills, CA 90210
(310) 246-4000
Adult entertainment especially for men (pay service)

Popcorn Channel
1120 Sixth Ave., 6th Floor
New York, NY 10036
(212) 302-8800
Full-length trailers for current and upcoming movies and local theater listings

Prevue Networks
3801 S. Sheridan
Tulsa, OK 74145
(918) 664-5566
Listing of basic, pay and pay-per-view programming

Prime Sports Channel Networks
150 Crossways Park W.
Woodbury, NY 11797
(516) 364-2222
National cable service that distributes sports programming to regional networks

Public Broadcasting Service
1320 Braddock Place
Alexandria, VA 22314-1698
(703) 739-5000

QVC Network
Goshen Corporate Park
1365 Enterprise Drive
West Chester, PA 19380
(215) 430-1000
Televised shopping

Sci-Fi Channel
1230 Ave. of the Americas
New York, NY 10020
(212) 408-9100
Science-fiction, fantasy and horror programming

The Sega Channel
1633 Broadway, 40th Floor
New York, NY 10019
(212) 767-4600
Video games on demand (pay service)

Showtime
1633 Broadway, 37th Floor
New York, NY 10019
(212) 708-1600
Movies, variety and comedy series, sports and original movies and specials (pay service)

SportsChannel
150 Crossways Park W.
Woodbury, NY 11797
(516) 364-2222
Sports programming;. regional networks feature local teams

1954

The revenue for television broadcasters finally surpasses that of radio broadcasters. Gross revenue for television is $593 million.

NBC broadcasts the World Series in color for the first time.

The first watch is tested for durability on camera. And it is a Bulova, not a Timex. The timepiece is attached to a ball and hurled over Niagara Falls.

1956

Gone With the Wind is broadcast on television for the first time. Fifty-two percent of television households watch.

1959

Rumors of cheating on quiz shows erupt into a national scandal.

1960

Seventy million people watch the presidential debate between Sen. John F. Kennedy and Vice President Richard Nixon.

1962

The first transatlantic television transmission occurs via the Telestar Satellite, making worldwide television and cable networks a reality.

Sundance Film Channel
1633 Broadway, 37th Floor
New York, NY 10019
(212) 708-1600
Independent film programming

TBS (Turner Broadcasting System)
P.O. Box 105366
One CNN Center
Atlanta, GA 30348-1947
(404) 827-1700
Original documentaries, exclusive sports,
specials, comedy series and movies

TCM (Turner Classic Movies)
P.O. Box 105366
One CNN Center
Atlanta, GA 30348-1947
(404) 827-1700
Classic movies from the MGM/UA library

TNN: The Nashville Network
Box 10210
250 Harbor Plaza Drive
Stamford, CT 06904-2210
(203) 965-6000
Country music entertainment, auto and
outdoor sports, news and country-
lifestyle programming

TNT: Turner Network Television
1050 Techwood Drive N.W.
Atlanta, GA 30318
(404) 885-2402
Classic movies, original movies and
miniseries, sports and children's
programming

Travel Channel
2690 Cumberland Parkway, Suite 500
Atlanta, GA 30339
(404) 801-2400
A look at worldwide destinations and
travel news

Trinity Broadcasting Network (TBN)
2528 US 31 South
Greenwood, IN 46143
(317) 535-5542
Around-the-clock religious and inspirational programming

TV Food Network
1177 Ave. of the Americas, 31st Floor
New York, NY 10036
(212) 398-8836
Food and food-related programming including nutrition, health and fitness shows

Univision
605 Third Ave.
New York, NY 10158
(212) 455-5200
Spanish-language programming featuring movies, novellas, sports and news

UPN (United Paramount Network)
11800 Wilshire Blvd.
Los Angeles, CA 90025
(310) 575-7000

USA Network
1230 Ave. of the Americas
New York, NY 10020
(212) 408-9100
Movies and television series, teen and
children's programming and sports
specials

VH1
1515 Broadway
New York, NY 10036
(212) 258-7860
Music videos, lifestyle news and specials

Video Jukebox
12000 Biscayne Blvd.
Miami, FL 33181
(305) 899-9000
Music videos programmed by local
viewers

WB (Warner Bros. Television Network)
4000 Warner Blvd.
Building 34R
Burbank, CA 91522
(818) 977-5000

Weather Channel
2600 Cumberland Parkway
Atlanta, GA 30339
(404) 434-6800
Around-the-clock updates on local,
national and worldwide conditions

WGN
3801 S. Sheridan Blvd.
Tulsa, OK 74145
(918) 665-6690
Chicago superstation with sports,
movies and television series

WPIX
3801 S. Sheridan Blvd.
Tulsa, OK 74145
(918) 665-6690
New York superstation with sports,
movies and television series

WWOR/EMI Communications Corp.
P.O. Box 4872
Syracuse, NY 13221
(315) 433-0022
Programming from the 1960s and 1970s
and coverage of the New York Mets

ZTV Music Network
15 E. Ohio Ave.
Lake Helen, FL 32744
(904) 228-1000
Christian music videos

1963
Viewers tuned into NBC witness
Jack Ruby shoot Lee Harvey Oswald
on camera — the first live telecast of
a murder.

1964
Peyton Place premieres on ABC and
is the first prime-time soap opera.

Color television makes its way into
U.S. homes.

1966
The first *Star Trek* episode, "The Man
Trap," is broadcast on September 8.
The plot concerns a creature that
sucks salt from human bodies.

1967
Congress creates PBS.

1968
60 Minutes airs on CBS, beginning its
reign as the longest-running prime-
time newsmagazine.

1969
The FCC bans all cigarette advertising on television and radio.

Children's Television Workshop introduces *Sesame Street*.

1970
FCC regulations require separate
ownership of television networks and
studios.

CONTINUED ON PAGE 538

National Public Radio U.S. Member Stations

STATION	CITY	FREQUENCY
ALABAMA		
WBHM-FM	Birmingham	90.3
WRWA-FM	Dothan	88.7
WSGN-FM	Gadsden	91.5
WLRH-FM	Huntsville	89.3
WLJS-FM	Jacksonville	91.9
WTSU-FM	Montgomery/Troy	89.9
WQPR-FM	Muscle Shoals	88.7
WJAB-FM	Normal	90.9
WUAL-FM	Tuscaloosa	91.5
ALASKA		
KSKA-FM	Anchorage	91.1
KBRW-AM	Barrow	680
KYUK-AM	Bethel	640
KUAC-FM	Fairbanks	104.7
KIYU-AM	Galena	910
KHNS-FM	Haines	102.3
KBBI-AM	Homer	890
KTOO-FM	Juneau	104.3
KCZP-FM	Kenai	91.9
KRBD-FM	Ketchikan	105.9
KMXT-FM	Kodiak	100.1
KFSK-FM	Petersburg	100.9
KCAW-FM	Sitka	104.7
KTNA-FM	Talkeetna	88.5
KCHU-AM	Valdez	770
ARIZONA		
KNAU-FM	Flagstaff	88.7
KJZZ-FM	Phoenix	91.5
KBAQ-FM	Mesa	89.5
KGHR-FM	Tuba City	91.5
KUAT-AM	Tucson	1550
KUAZ-FM	Tucson	89.1
KAWC-AM	Yuma	1320
KAWC-FM	Yuma	88.9
ARKANSAS		
KBSA-FM	El Dorado	90.9
KUAF-FM	Fayetteville	91.3
KUAR-FM	Little Rock	89.1
KLRE-FM	Little Rock	90.5
KASU-FM	State University	91.9
CALIFORNIA		
KHSU-FM	Arcata	90.5
KPRX-FM	Bakersfield	89.1
KNCA-FM	Burney	89.7
KCHO-FM	Chico	91.7
KUBO-FM	Fresno	88.7
KVPR-FM	Fresno	89.3
KXSR-FM	Groveland	91.7
KCRY-FM	Indio	89.3

STATION	CITY	FREQUENCY
KNSQ-FM	Mt. Shasta	88.1
KCRU-FM	Oxnard	89.1
KPCC-FM	Pasadena	89.3
KZYX-FM	Philo	90.7
KFPR-FM	Redding	88.9
KXPR-FM	Sacramento	90.9
KXJZ-FM	Sacramento	88.9
KVCR-FM	San Bernardino	91.9
KPBS-FM	San Diego	89.5
KALW-FM	San Francisco	91.7
KQED-FM	San Francisco	88.5
KCBX-FM	San Luis Obispo	90.1
KUSP-FM	Santa Cruz	88.9
KCRW-FM	Santa Monica	89.9
KUOP-FM	Stockton	91.3
COLORADO		
KRZA-FM	Alamosa	88.7
KAJX-FM	Aspen	91.5
KGNU-FM	Boulder	88.5
KDNK-FM	Carbondale	90.5
KRCC-FM	Colorado Springs	91.5
KSJD-FM	Cortez	91.5
KBUT-FM	Crested Butte	90.3
KUVO-FM	Denver	89.3
KCFR-FM	Denver	90.1
KPRN-FM	Grand Junction	89.5
KUNC-FM	Greeley	91.5
KSUT-FM	Ignacio	91.3
KVNF-FM	Paonia	90.9
KOTO-FM	Telluride	91.7
CONNECTICUT		
WSHU-FM	Fairfield	91.1
WPKT-FM	Hartford	90.5
WNPR-FM	Norwich	89.1
WEDW-FM	Stamford	88.5
WECS-FM	Willimantic	90.1
DISTRICT OF COLUMBIA		
WAMU-FM	Washington	88.5
WDCU-FM	Washington	90.1
WETA-FM	Arlington, VA	90.9
FLORIDA		
WSFP-FM	Fort Myers	90.1
WQCS-FM	Fort Pierce	88.9
WUFT-FM	Gainesville	89.1
WJCT-FM	Jacksonville	89.9
WLRN-FM	Miami	91.3
WUCF-FM	Orlando	89.9
WMFE-FM	Orlando	90.7
WKGC-FM	Panama City	90.7
WKGC-AM	Panama City	1480

STATION	CITY	FREQUENCY
WUWF-FM	Pensacola	88.1
WFSU-FM	Tallahassee	88.9
WFSQ-FM	Tallahassee	91.5
WUSF-FM	Tampa	89.7
WXEL-FM	West Palm Beach	90.7

GEORGIA

STATION	CITY	FREQUENCY
WUNV-FM	Albany	91.7
WUGA-FM	Athens	91.7
WCLK-FM	Atlanta	91.9
WABE-FM	Atlanta	90.1
WJSP-FM	Atlanta	88.1
WACG-FM	Augusta	90.7
WWIO-FM	Brunswick	89.1
WTJB-FM	Columbus	91.7
WJWV-FM	Ft. Gaines	90.9
WDCO-FM	Macon	89.7
WSVH-FM	Savannah	91.1
WABR-FM	Tifton	91.1
WWET-FM	Valdosta	91.7
WXVS-FM	Waycross	90.1

HAWAII

STATION	CITY	FREQUENCY
KHPR-FM	Honolulu	88.1
KIPO-FM	Honolulu	89.3
KIFO-AM	Pearl City	1380
KKUA-FM	Wailuku	90.7

IDAHO

STATION	CITY	FREQUENCY
KBSU-FM	Boise	90.3
KBSU-AM	Boise	730
KBSX-FM	Boise	91.5
KNWO-FM	Cottonwood	90.1
KBSM-FM	McCall	91.7
KRFA-FM	Moscow	91.7
KRIC-FM	Rexburg	100.5
KBSW-FM	Twin Falls	91.7

ILLINOIS

STATION	CITY	FREQUENCY
WSIU-FM	Carbondale	91.9
WBEZ-FM	Chicago	91.5
WNIU-FM	DeKalb	89.5
WSIE-FM	Edwardsville	88.7
WIUM-FM	Macomb	91.3
WGLT-FM	Normal	89.1
WUSI-FM	Olney	90.3
WCBU-FM	Peoria	89.9
WIPA-FM	Pittsfield	89.3
WQUB-FM	Quincy	90.3
WVIK-FM	Rock Island	90.3

STATION	CITY	FREQUENCY
WNIJ-FM	Rockford	90.5
WSSU-FM	Springfield	91.9
WILL-FM	Urbana	90.9
WILL-AM	Urbana	580

INDIANA

STATION	CITY	FREQUENCY
WFIU-FM	Bloomington	103.7
WVPE-FM	Elkhart	88.1
WNIN-FM	Evansville	88.3
WBNI-FM	Fort Wayne	89.1
WFYI-FM	Indianapolis	90.1
WBST-FM	Muncie	92.1
WBKE-FM	North Manchester	89.5
WVXR-FM	Richmond	89.3

IOWA

STATION	CITY	FREQUENCY
WOI-FM	Ames	90.1
WOI-AM	Ames	640
KUNI-FM	Cedar Falls	90.9
KCCK-FM	Cedar Rapids	88.3
KIWR-FM	Council Bluffs	89.7
KLNI-FM	Decorah	88.7
KTPR-FM	Fort Dodge	91.1
WSUI-AM	Iowa City	910
KUNY-FM	Mason City	91.5
KWIT-FM	Sioux City	90.3

KANSAS

STATION	CITY	FREQUENCY
KANZ-FM	Garden City	91.1
KHCT-FM	Great Bend	90.9
KZNA-FM	Hill City	90.5
KHCC-FM	Hutchinson	90.1
KANU-FM	Lawrence	91.5
KRPS-FM	Pittsburg	89.9
KHCD-FM	Salina	89.5
KMUW-FM	Wichita	89.1

KENTUCKY

STATION	CITY	FREQUENCY
WKYU-FM	Bowling Green	88.9
WKUE-FM	Elisabethtown	90.9
WEKH-FM	Hazard	90.9
WKPB-FM	Henderson	89.5
WNKU-FM	Highland Heights	89.7
WUKY-FM	Lexington	91.3
WFPL-FM	Louisville	89.3
WMKY-FM	Morehead	90.3
WKMS-FM	Murray	91.3
WEKU-FM	Richmond	88.9
WDCL-FM	Somerset	89.7

NATIONAL PUBLIC RADIO SUPPLIERS

National Public Radio
635 Massachusetts Ave. N.W.
Washington D.C. 20001-3753
(202) 414-2000

Pacifica
2390 Champlain Ave., N.W.
Washington D.C. 20009
(202) 588-0999

Public Radio International
100 N. Sixth St., Suite 900A
Minneapolis, MN 55403
(612) 338-5000

STATION	CITY	FREQUENCY
LOUISIANA		
KLSA-FM	Alexandria	90.7
WBRH-FM	Baton Rouge	90.3
WRKF-FM	Baton Rouge	89.3
KRVS-FM	Lafayette	88.7
KEDM-FM	Monroe	90.3
WWNO-FM	New Orleans	89.9
KDAQ-FM	Shreveport	89.9
MAINE		
WMEH-FM	Bangor	90.9
WMED-FM	Calais	89.7
WMEA-FM	Portland	90.1
WMEM-FM	Presque Isle	106.1
WMEW-FM	Waterville	91.3
MARYLAND		
WEAA-FM	Baltimore	88.9
WJHU-FM	Baltimore	88.1
WETH-FM	Hagerstown	89.1
WESM-FM	Princess Anne	91.3
WSCL-FM	Salisbury	89.5
MASSACHUSETTS		
WFCR-FM	Amherst	88.5
WKKL-FM	Barnstable	90.7
WGBH-FM	Boston	89.7
WBUR-FM	Boston	90.9
WAMQ-FM	Gt. Barrington	105.1
WCCT-FM	Harwich	90.3
WSDH-FM	Sandwich	91.5
WICN-FM	Worcester	90.5
MICHIGAN		
WCML-FM	Alpena	91.7
WUOM-FM	Ann Arbor	91.7
WUCX-FM	Bay City	90.1
WDET-FM	Detroit	101.9
WIZY-FM	East Jordan	100.9
WKAR-AM	East Lansing	870
WKAR-FM	East Lansing	90.5
WFUM-FM	Flint	91.1
WGVU-AM	Grand Rapids	1480

STATION	CITY	FREQUENCY
WGVU-FM	Grand Rapids	88.5
WVGR-FM	Grand Rapids	104.1
WGGL-FM	Houghton	91.1
WCMW-FM	Harbor Springs	103.9
WIAA-FM	Interlochen	88.7
WMUK-FM	Kalamazoo	102.1
WNMU-FM	Marquette	90.1
WCMU-FM	Mount Pleasant	89.5
WCMZ-FM	Sault Sainte Marie	98.3
WBLV-FM	Twin Lake	90.3
WEMU-FM	Ypsilanti	89.1
MINNESOTA		
KRSU-FM	Appleton	91.3
KMSK-FM	Austin	91.3
KCRB-FM	Bimidji	88.5
KBPR-FM	Brainerd	90.7
WIRR-FM	Buhl	90.9
KNSR-FM	Collegeville	88.9
WSCN-FM	Duluth	100.9
KAXE-FM	Grand Rapids	91.7
KXLC-FM	La Crescent	91.1
KMSU-FM	Mankato	89.7
KNOW-FM	Minneapolis/St. Paul	91.1
WCAL-FM	Minneapolis/St. Paul	89.3
KCCD-FM	Moorhead	90.3
KZSE-FM	Rochester	90.7
KNGA-FM	St. Peter	91.5
KNTN-FM	Thief River Falls	102.7
KRSW-FM	Worthington	91.7
MISSISSIPPI		
WMAH-FM	Biloxi	90.3
WMAE-FM	Booneville	89.5
WMAU-FM	Bude	88.9
WMAO-FM	Greenwood	90.9
WURC-FM	Holly Springs	88.1
WJSU-FM	Jackson	88.5
WMPN-FM	Jackson	91.3
WPRL-FM	Lorman	91.7
WMAW-FM	Meridian	88.1
WMAB-FM	Mississippi State	89.9
WMAV-FM	Oxford	90.3
WNJC-FM	Senatobia	88.9

◀ CONT. FROM PAGE 535

1971

All in the Family debuts on CBS and introduces a trend in socially conscious programming.

1972

Time Inc. transmits HBO, the first pay cable network.

The National Institute of Mental Health and the surgeon general issue a report that claims exposure to violence on television fosters aggression in children.

1975

ABC, CBS and NBC agree to create a "family hour," an early evening time slot that is free of violence and sex.

1981

The Supreme Court rules to allow television cameras in the courtroom.

1986

Barry Diller, head of News Corp., creates Fox, the fourth television network. Fox offers 10 hours of prime-time programming a week.

The Television Bureau of Advertising announces that the average American household watches television for more than seven hours a day.

STATION	CITY	FREQUENCY
MISSOURI		
KRCU-FM	Cape Girardeau	90.9
KBIA-FM	Columbia	91.3
KCUR-FM	Kansas City	89.3
KXCV-FM	Maryville	90.5
KCOZ-FM	Pt. Lookout	90.5
KUMR-FM	Rolla	88.5
KSMU-FM	Springfield	91.1
KWMU-FM	St. Louis	90.7
KCMW-FM	Warrensburg	90.9
MONTANA		
KEMC-FM	Billings	91.7
KBMC-FM	Bozeman	102.1
KGPR-FM	Great Falls	89.9
KNMC-FM	Havre	90.1
KECC-FM	Miles City	90.7
KUFM-FM	Missoula	89.1
NEBRASKA		
KTNE-FM	Alliance	91.1
KMNE-FM	Bassett	90.3
KCNE-FM	Chadron	91.9
KHNE-FM	Hastings	89.1
KLNE-FM	Lexington	88.7
KUCV-FM	Lincoln	90.9
KRNE-FM	Merriman	91.5
KXNE-FM	Norfolk	89.3
KPNE-FM	North Platte	91.7
KIOS-FM	Omaha	91.5
NEVADA		
KNCC-FM	Elko	91.5
KNPR-FM	Las Vegas	89.5
KCEP-FM	Las Vegas	88.1
KLNR-FM	Panaca	91.7
KUNR-FM	Reno	88.7
KTPH-FM	Tonopah	91.7
NEW HAMPSHIRE		
WEVO-FM	Concord	89.1
WEVH-FM	Hanover	91.3
NEW JERSEY		
WBGO-FM	Newark	88.3

STATION	CITY	FREQUENCY
NEW MEXICO		
KUNM-FM	Albuquerque	89.9
KGLP-FM	Gallup	91.7
KRWG-FM	Las Cruces	90.7
KMTH-FM	Maljamar	98.7
KTDB-FM	Pine Hill	89.7
KENW-FM	Portales	89.5
NEW YORK		
WAMC-FM	Albany	90.3
WALF-FM	Alfred	89.7
WSKG-FM	Binghamton	89.3
WXLH-FM	Blue Mountain Lake	89.9
WNED-AM	Buffalo	970
WBFO-FM	Buffalo	88.7
WOLN-FM	Buffalo	91.3
WCAN-FM	Canajoharie	93.3
WSLU-FM	Canton	89.5
WEOS-FM	Geneva	89.7
WSQG-FM	Ithaca	90.9
WJFF-FM	Jeffersonville	90.5
WAMK-FM	Kingston	90.9
WSLO-FM	Malone	90.9
WOSR-FM	Middletown	91.7
WNYC-AM	New York	820
WNYC-FM	New York	93.9
WSQC-FM	Oneonta	91.7
WRVO-FM	Oswego	89.9
WXLU-FM	Peru	88.3
WCFE-FM	Plattsburgh	91.9
WRHV-FM	Poughkeepsie	88.7
WXXI-AM	Rochester	1370
WSLL-FM	Saranac Lake	90.5
WMHT-FM	Schenectady	89.1
WCNY-FM	Syracuse	91.3
WAER-FM	Syracuse	88.3
WANC-FM	Ticonderoga	103.9
WRVN-FM	Utica	91.9
WUNY-FM	Utica	89.5
WJNY-FM	Watertown	90.9
WRVJ-FM	Watertown	91.7
WSLJ-FM	Watertown	88.5

1988

Ninety-eight percent of U.S. households have at least one television set.

1990

Ninety-nine percent of U.S. households have at least one radio, with the average owning five.

1991

Fox Broadcasting is the first network to permit condom advertising on television.

1992

There are 900 million television sets in use around the world; 201 million are in the United States.

1994

Ninety-five million viewers watch O.J. Simpson and Al Cowlings drive along Los Angeles freeways in history's most exciting low-speed chase.

1996

President Bill Clinton signs legislation that significantly deregulates telecommunications, creating almost limitless opportunities for broadcasters and cable companies.

Pressured by the Federal Communications Commission, television broadcasters agree to include three hours a week of educational children's programming into their schedule.

STATION	CITY	FREQUENCY
NORTH CAROLINA		
WCQS-FM	Asheville	88.1
WUNC-FM	Chapel Hill	91.5
WFAE-FM	Charlotte	90.7
WFSS-FM	Fayetteville	89.1
WFQS-FM	Franklin	91.3
WTEB-FM	New Bern	89.3
WESQ-FM	Rocky Mount	90.9
WNCW-FM	Spindale	88.7
WHQR-FM	Wilmington	91.3
WFDD-FM	Winston-Salem	88.5
NORTH DAKOTA		
KEYA-FM	Belcourt	88.5
KCND-FM	Bismarck	90.5
KDPR-FM	Dickinson	89.9
KDSU-FM	Fargo	91.9
KFJM-FM	Grand Forks	89.3
KFJM-AM	Grand Forks	1370
KMPR-FM	Minot	88.9
KPPR-FM	Williston	89.5
KPRJ-FM	Ypsilanti	93.5
OHIO		
WOUB-FM	Athens	91.3
WOUB-AM	Athens	1340
WOUC-FM	Cambridge	89.1
WOUH-FM	Chillicothe	91.9
WVXC-FM	Chillicothe	89.3
WVXU-FM	Cincinnati	91.7
WGUC-FM	Cincinnati	90.9
WCPN-FM	Cleveland	90.3
WOSU-AM	Columbus	820
WCBE-FM	Columbus	90.5
WOUL-FM	Ironton	89.1
WKSU-FM	Kent	89.7
WGLE-FM	Lima	90.7
WMUB-FM	Oxford	88.5
WGTE-FM	Toledo	91.3
WVXM-FM	West Union	89.5
WKRW-FM	Wooster	89.3
WYSO-FM	Yellow Springs	91.3
WYSU-FM	Youngstown	88.5
WOUZ-FM	Zanesville	90.1
OKLAHOMA		
KCCU-FM	Lawton	89.3
KGOU-FM	Norman	106.3
KROU-FM	Oklahoma City	105.7
KOSU-FM	Stillwater	91.7
KWGS-FM	Tulsa	89.5
OREGON		
KSMF-FM	Ashland	89.1
KSOR-FM	Ashland	90.1
KMUN-FM	Astoria	91.9
KOAB-FM	Bend	91.3
KSBA-FM	Coos Bay	88.5
KLCC-FM	Eugene	89.7
KAGI-AM	Grants Pass	930
KSKF-FM	Klamath Falls	90.9
KLCO-FM	Newport	90.5

STATION	CITY	FREQUENCY
KRBM-FM	Pendleton	90.9
KOAC-AM	Portland	550
KOPB-FM	Portland	91.5
KBPS-AM	Portland	1450
KSRS-FM	Roseburg	91.5
PENNSYLVANIA		
WQLN-FM	Erie	91.3
WITF-FM	Harrisburg	89.5
WJAZ-FM	Harrisburg	91.7
WRTY-FM	Mt. Pocono	91.1
WRTI-FM	Philadelphia	90.1
WHYY-FM	Philadelphia	90.9
WDUQ-FM	Pittsburgh	90.5
WVIA-FM	Scranton	89.9
WPSU-FM	State College	91.9
SOUTH CAROLINA		
WLJK-FM	Aiken	89.1
WJWJ-FM	Beaufort	89.9
WSCI-FM	Charleston	89.3
WLTR-FM	Columbia	91.3
WHMC-FM	Conway	90.1
WEPR-FM	Greenville/Clemson	90.1
WSSB-FM	Orangeburg	90.3
WNSC-FM	Rock Hill	88.9
WRJA-FM	Sumter	88.1
SOUTH DAKOTA		
KESD-FM	Brookings	88.3
KPSD-FM	Faith	97.1
KQSD-FM	Lowry	91.9
KZSD-FM	Martin	102.5
KDSD-FM	Pierpont	90.9
KBHE-FM	Rapid City	89.3
KTSD-FM	Reliance	91.1
KRSD-FM	Sioux Falls	88.1
KCSD-FM	Sioux Falls	90.9
KUSD-AM	Vermillion	690
KUSD-FM	Vermillion	89.7
TENNESSEE		
WUTC-FM	Chattanooga	88.1
WSMC-FM	Collegedale	90.5
WKNQ-FM	Dyersberg	90.7
WKNP-FM	Jackson	90.1
WETS-FM	Johnson City	89.5
WUOT-FM	Knoxville	91.9
WKNO-FM	Memphis	91.1
WMOT-FM	Murfreesboro	89.5
WPLN-FM	Nashville	90.3
TEXAS		
KACU-FM	Abilene	89.7
KUT-FM	Austin	90.5
KVLU-FM	Beaumont	91.3
KAMU-FM	College Station	90.9
KEDT-FM	Corpus Christi	90.3
KERA-FM	Dallas	90.1
KTEP-FM	El Paso	88.5
KMBH-FM	Harlingen	88.9
KUHF-FM	Houston	88.7

STATION	CITY	FREQUENCY
KOHM-FM	Lubbock	89.1
KHID-FM	McAllen	88.1
KOCV-FM	Odessa	91.3
KLDN-FM	Redland	88.9
KSTX-FM	San Antonio	89.1
KTXK-FM	Texarkana	91.5

UTAH

STATION	CITY	FREQUENCY
KUSU-FM	Logan	91.5
KPCW-FM	Park City	91.9
KBYU-FM	Provo	89.1
KUER-FM	Salt Lake City	90.1
KCPW-FM	Salt Lake City	88.3

VERMONT

STATION	CITY	FREQUENCY
WVPS-FM	Burlington	107.9
WRVT-FM	Rutland	88.7
WVPR-FM	Colchester	89.5

VIRGINIA

STATION	CITY	FREQUENCY
WVTU-FM	Charlottesville	89.3
WMRA-FM	Harrisonburg	90.7
WMRL-FM	Lexington	89.9
WVTR-FM	Marion	91.9
WHRV-FM	Norfolk	89.5
WHRO-FM	Norfolk	90.3
WCVE-FM	Richmond	88.9
WVTF-FM	Roanoke	89.1

WASHINGTON

STATION	CITY	FREQUENCY
KZAZ-FM	Bellingham	91.7
KNWR-FM	Ellensburg	90.7
KWSU-AM	Pullman	1250
KFAE-FM	Richland	89.1
KUOW-FM	Seattle	94.9
KPBX-FM	Spokane	91.1
KPLU-FM	Tacoma	88.5
KNWY-FM	Yakima	90.3

WEST VIRGINIA

STATION	CITY	FREQUENCY
WVPB-FM	Beckley	91.7
WVPW-FM	Buckhannon	88.9
WVPN-FM	Charleston	88.5
WVWV-FM	Huntington	89.9
WVEP-FM	Martinsburg	88.9
WVPM-FM	Morgantown	90.9
WVPG-FM	Parkersburg	90.3
WVNP-FM	Wheeling	89.9

WISCONSIN

STATION	CITY	FREQUENCY
WLFM-FM	Appleton	91.1
WLBL-AM	Auburndale	930
WHSA-FM	Brule	89.9
WHAD-FM	Delafield	90.7
WUEC-FM	Eau Claire	89.7
WGBW-FM	Green Bay	91.5
WPNE-FM	Green Bay	89.3
WOJB-FM	Hayward	88.9
WHHI-FM	Highland	91.3
WGTD-FM	Kenosha	91.1
WLSU-FM	La Crosse	88.9
WHLA-FM	La Crosse	90.3
WHA-AM	Madison	970
WERN-FM	Madison	88.7
WHWC-FM	Menomonee	88.3
WVSS-FM	Menomonee	90.7
WUWM-FM	Milwaukee	89.7
WRST-FM	Oshkosh	90.3
WHBM-FM	Park Falls	90.3
WXPR-FM	Rhinelander	91.7
KUWS-FM	Superior	91.3
WHRM-FM	Wausau	90.9

WYOMING

STATION	CITY	FREQUENCY
KUWJ-FM	Jackson	90.3
KUWR-FM	Laramie	91.9

National Radio Networks

ABC
Capital Cities/ABC Inc.
77 W. 66th St.
New York, NY 10023-6298
(212) 456-7777

ABC Radio Network
13725 Montfort Drive
Dallas, TX 75240
(214) 991-9200
(800) 527-4892

American Urban Radio Networks
463 Seventh Ave., 6th Floor
New York, NY 10018
(212) 714-1000

Associated Press Network News
Associated Press
Broadcast Division
1825 K St. N.W.
Washington D.C. 20006-1253
(800) 821-4747
(202) 736-1100

Bloomberg Business News Radio Network
499 Park Ave.
New York, NY 10022
(800) 448-5678

Business News Network
5025 Centennial Blvd.
Colorado Springs, CO 80919
(719) 528-7040

CBS Radio Network
51 W. 52nd St.
New York, NY 10019
(212) 975-4468

CNN Radio Network
One CNN Center
Box 105366
Atlanta, GA 30348-5366
(404) 827-2750

United Press International
1400 Eye St. N.W., 8th Floor
Washington D.C. 20005
(202) 898-8000
(800) 492-6924

USA Radio Network
2290 Springlake Road,
Suite 107
Dallas, TX 75234
(214) 484-3900
(800) 829-8111

Wall Street Journal Radio Network/Dow Jones Radio Network
World Financial Center
200 Liberty St., 14th Floor
New York, NY 10281
(212) 416-2116

Westwood One
9540 Washington Blvd.
Culver City, CA 90232
(310) 204-5000

What Do They Look Like?

The voices of NPR have inspired, informed and charmed many of us, becoming as welcome and reassuring as family members. Now you have a face to go with the voice.

Robert Siegel, Linda Wertheimer and Noah Adams
Hosts, *All Things Considered*

Maria Hinojosa
Host, *Latino USA*

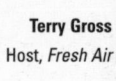

Terry Gross
Host, *Fresh Air*

George Collinet
Host, *Afropop Worldwide*

Cokie Roberts
Senior News Analyst

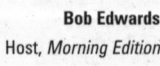

Bob Edwards
Host, *Morning Edition*

Scott Simon
Host, *Weekend Edition*

Nina Totenberg
Legal Affairs
Correspondent

Susan Stamberg
Special Correspondent

Daniel Zwerdling
Weekend Host,
All Things Considered

Ray Suarez
Host, *Talk of the Nation*

Ann Taylor
Newscaster

Corey Flintoff
Newscaster

Tom and Ray Magliozzi
Hosts, *Car Talk*

Radio Format Classifications

As the music and broadcast industries evolve, so do radio-programming formats. Arbitron and M Street Radio Directory, companies that monitor the radio industry, occasionally amend radio classifications and their definitions to reflect current trends. Here is the set of format classifications the companies now use.

AC (Adult Contemporary) Adult-oriented pop or rock, includes no hard rock, possibly some non-rock music and often a greater emphasis on non-current music.

AC-OL A version of **AC** that mostly plays gold-certified oldies.

AH (Adult Hits) An up-tempo version of the **CH** format but includes no hard rock or rap. Also called **Hot AC** and **Adult CH.**

AP (Album Progressive) Eclectic-rock, often featuring wide variations in musical style. Also called **AAA (Adult Album Alternative), Progressive** and **Rock AC.**

AR (Album Rock) Mainstream rock; can include guitar-oriented heavy metal.

AS (Adult Standards) Non-rock popular music from 1940 to 1980 and softer, current popular music.

BG (Black Gospel) Black gospel music.

CH (Contemporary Hit) Current popular music; often includes a variety of rock styles. Also called **CHR (Contemporary Hit Radio)** and **Top 40.**

CH-AR Rock-based **CH.**

CH-NR New rock- or modern rock-based **CH.**

CH-RB Dance music-based **CH.**

Classical See **FA.**

CR (Classic Rock) Rock-oriented oldies; often mixes hits of the '60s, '70s and '80s. Also called **Classic Hits.**

CW (Country) Country music, including contemporary and traditional styles.

CW-OL Country oldies.

DR (Drama) Radio dramas, often featuring pre-1950 programs.

ET (Ethnic) Programs primarily in languages other than English. Often brokered and/or block-programmed.

EZ (Easy Listening) Mainly instrumental cover versions of popular songs; can be combined with "Smooth Jazz" or **AS** programming.

FA (Fine Arts) Classical music, often including opera, theater and/or culture-oriented news and talk programming. Also called **Classical.**

FF (French) French-language programming.

HA Comedy programming.

JZ (Jazz) Mostly instrumental music, often mixed with **SA;** includes both traditional jazz and what is called "Smooth Jazz" or "New AC."

MT (Money Talk) All financial or money-talk programming.

NR (New Rock) Modern-rock music.

NX (News) All news, either local or network.

FX Farm news.

Hot AC Also called **AH.**

OL (Oldies) Popular music, usually rock, with 80 percent or more non-current music programming.

Progressive Also called **AP.**

PT (Preteen) Music, drama or readings intended primarily for a preteen audience.

RB-OL Rhythm and blues oldies.

RB (Rhythm and Blues — Urban) Covers a wide range of musical styles, including rap, R&B and urban music. Also called **Urban Contemporary.**

RC (Religious Contemporary) Modern and rock-based religious music.

RG (Religious Gospel) Traditional religious music that can also be classified as **BG** or **SG.**

RL (Religion) Local or syndicated religious programming that is sometimes mixed with music.

Rock AC Also called **AP.**

SA (Soft Adult Contemporary) A cross between **AC** and **EZ.** Primarily non-current, soft rock that can be mixed with **AS** or "Smooth Jazz."

SB (Soft Urban Contemporary) A mix of soft rhythm and blues and **JZ,** often heavy in oldies.

SG (Southern Gospel) Country-flavored gospel music that includes Christian-country programming.

SS (Spanish) Spanish-language programming. Spanish-language formats include SS-RA (ranchero music); SS-AC (modern music); SS-TP (salsa, tropical); SS-TJ *(tejano);* SS-MX (regional Mexican); and the English-language equivalents SS-VA (Variety); SS-EZ (Easy Listening); SS-NX (News); and SS-TK (Talk).

SX (Sports) The label is used only if all programming, a substantial block or an entire broadcast day is devoted to play-by-play, sports news, interviews or telephone talk.

TK (Talk) A talk-radio station, either local or network in origin.

Top 40 See **CH.**

Urban Contemporary Also called **RB.**

VA (Variety) A station that incorporates three or more distinct formats, either block-programmed or a simultaneous combination.

Television and Radio Magazines and Journals

A&E Monthly
235 E. 45th St.
New York, NY 10017
(212) 661-1500, (212) 210-9722

American Movie Classics Magazine
Working Media, Inc.
18 Shawmut St.
Boston, MA 02116
(800) 669-1002

Billboard
Billboard Publications, Inc.
1515 Broadway, 14th Floor
New York, NY 10036
(212) 764-7300

Broadcasting and Cable Yearbook
R.R. Bowker
121 Chanlon Road
New Providence, NJ 07974-1541
(908) 464-6800

The Cable Guide
(Cable Today/The Cable Guide)
TVSM
309 Lakeside Drive
Horsham, PA 19044-2313
(215) 443-9300

Daytime T.V.
Sterling's Magazines, Inc.
233 Park Ave. S.
New York, NY 10003
(212) 780-3500

Discover
(The Discovery Channel magazine)
Discovery Communications Inc.
7700 Wisconsin Ave.
Bethesda, MD 20814-3578
(800) 769-5908

Disney Channel Magazine
3800 W. Alameda Ave.
Burbank, CA 91505-4398
(818) 569-7797

Entertainment Weekly
1675 Broadway
New York, NY 10019
(212) 522-5600

Multichannel News
Capital Cities/ABC Inc.
825 Seventh Ave.
New York, NY 10019
(212) 887-8387

Radio and Records
10100 Santa Monica Blvd., 5th Floor
Los Angeles, CA 90067
(310) 553-4330

Satellite Orbit
(Satellite Direct)
Commtek Communications Corp.
8330 Boone Blvd., Suite 600
Vienna, VA 22182-2624
(703) 827-0511

Satellite TV Week
Fortuna Communications
140 S. Fortuna Blvd.
Fortuna, CA 95540
(707) 725-6951

Sci-Fi Entertainment
Sovereign Media Company
457 Carlisle Drive
Herndon, VA 22070
(800) 933-6407

Soap Opera Digest
45 W. 25th St.
New York, NY 10010
(212) 229-8400

Soap Opera Weekly
41 W. 25th St.
New York, NY 10010
(212) 645-2100

Total TV/Pay-Per-View
TVSM
309 Lakeside Drive
Horsham, PA 19044-2313
(215) 443-9300

TV Guide
News America Publications
100 Matson Ford Road, Building 4
Radnor, PA 19088
(800) 866-1400

Variety
5700 Wilshire Blvd., Suite 120
Los Angeles, CA 90036
(213) 857-6600

Broadcasting Glossary

addressable converter A cable television box that can be supplied with programming by a cable system, providing pay-per-view events.

bandwidth The numerical difference between the upper and lower frequencies of a band of electromagnetic radiation, especially an assigned range of radio frequencies.

blanking The brief period in the television scanning process when the electron beam returns from the right to left or from the bottom to top of the screen, rendering the video signal invisible. It is during the blanking interval that closed-captioning and teletext occurs.

blind spot An area where radio reception is weak or nonexistent.

canned The term to describe material that is recorded for repeated use on television or radio.

channel surfing The practice of scanning a series of television channels to find something that catches the eye or to avoid commercials. Made possible by the remote control, it now occupies some viewers for entire evenings, wreaking havoc on advertisers and programmers. Surfing is one reason programming practices such as seamless transitions from one show to the next and splitting 30-second commercials into two 15-second halves have become prevalent.

closed-captioned A program that is broadcast with captions seen only on a specially equipped receiver.

DBS (Direct Broadcast Satellite) The programming services that are available to home satellite-dish owners. The services include RCA's DSS small-dish service, PrimeStar and Full View TV.

dead spot A zone within the range of a radio transmitter where little or no radio signal can be received.

double pumping The programming tactic of presenting the same program twice in one night or twice in one week.

family hour The time slot, typically between 6 P.M. and 8 P.M., during which television and radio programs are free of violence and sex.

fin-syn regulations The laws passed by the Federal Communications Commission limiting the networks' ownership of the programming they broadcast. The laws prohibit networks from acquiring a financial interest in the program's producers and from distributing the programs in syndication, except overseas. The regulations were repealed because of increased competition from cable and other forms of home entertainment. The repeal has led to the phenomenon of one network producing programming that appears on another network.

hammock The programming slot between two hit shows, often used to launch a new program.

HDTV (high definition television) The broadcast standard that offers greater resolution by increasing the number of scan lines. Currently available in Japan, the format is expected to be available in the United States by the fall of 1996.

HUTs and **PUTs** Two measures of statistics used by analysts of Nielsen Media Research that denote houses using television and people using television.

infotainment A television program that combines news and entertainment features, such as interviews, commentaries and reviews.

kidvid Children's television programs or videotapes.

kinescope A film of a transmitted television program.

letterbox A technique for showing wide-screen movies on television that preserves the original aspect ratio by filling the top and bottom parts of the screen with black bars.

newsmagazine The genre of television programming that covers current events and topical issues.

Nielsen Media Research Television audience research conducted by the A.C. Nielsen Co. that provides the most widely accepted measure of television viewership. **Nielsen Ratings** determine what the networks and cable channels charge advertisers for commercials. A combination of viewing diaries and people meters in television sets measures the ratings. The company was founded in 1923 to provide advertisers measurements of radio audiences.

pilot A television program produced as a prototype of a series being considered a network. The success or failure of the pilot usually determines if the network picks up the series.

Q rating A measure by TVQ/Marketing Evaluations Co. that attempts to determine the familiarity of performers, products, athletes and other public figures. The recognizability of these personalities influences casting decisions and product endorsements.

stunt A programming maneuver that moves a show from its usual time slot to a more advantageous slot or multiple time periods in order to boost ratings or introduce a new program. It also refers to unusual or sensational programming designed to grab attention during sweeps periods. See **hammock** and **double pumping**.

sweeps The monthlong periods, usually in February, May, July and November, when Nielsen Media Research measures audiences in all television markets. These periods are important to local stations because they provide comparative ratings across the nation and important to networks because they provide an in-depth view of their audience. Advertising sales for the upcoming programming season are heavily affected by the outcome of the sweeps.

teaser An attention-getting highlight of a television show presented before the show begins. It is intended to draw viewers to the program.

TelePrompTer A trademark used for the device that shows an actor or a speaker an enlarged line-by-line reproduction of a script, unseen by the audience.

teletext An electronic communications system in which printed text is broadcast by television signal to sets equipped with decoders.

tent pole A hit program of such strength that its audience will stay with the network for the rest of the evening.

transponder The device in a communications satellite that receives signals from an uplink on earth and transmits it back to earth (downlink). It is used by cable programmers to deliver signals to local cable systems.

HOME ENTERTAINMENT

'Net Impact

■ BY ANDREW KANTOR

Andrew Kantor is senior editor of *Internet World* magazine. He can be reached at andrew@kantor.com.

SOMEWHERE, OUT THERE, THERE'S THIS INTERNET THING. YOU'VE heard about it — it's impossible to avoid. Business cards have E-mail addresses. Toyota commercials flash Web addresses. The 'Net appears in movie plots, sometimes as a main character. But is it really that important? Is the whole 'Net thing going to change the world, or is it just the defining fad of the '90s? Like religion or politics, it depends whom you ask.

On one side you've got the people — half of them on Wall Street — who sing the praises of the 'Net: The Internet will change the fabric of society! Everything will be online — books, entertainment, news, sex! Television networks will

GETTING WIRED

crumble before the onslaught of the Internet! Newspapers will fold! Magazines will go digital! It's gonna be a 16-lane mondo-info super-data-highway!

On another side you have the naysayers such as Cliff Stoll, author of *Silicon Snake Oil: Second Thoughts on the Information Highway* (Doubleday), who think that the 'Net is just today's media darling, the KC and the Sunshine Band of the 1990s. Yeah, E-mail is pretty useful, they say, but this World Wide Web thing is just a passing craze. Why shop online when you can just drive to the mall? What's the use of information on the Web if you can't trust the source? Why read something on the 'Net if you can hold a real, paper book instead?

Then, unless you count people like my parents ("Can you call the Internet and find out what to take for a headache?"), you have the last group. My group. We're the ones who think this Internet thing is pretty darned cool. It's not going to topple governments, but it's going to change a lot of things — the way we get information, the way we work together and the way we do business. It's not a fleeting fad, but it will, hopefully, pass out of the public eye the same way the telephone has. It will just be there, lurking behind the scenes, connecting us and being useful.

And that's the key word: useful. If the 'Net was just a bunch of computer geeks and *Star Trek* fans, most people wouldn't have anything to do with it. But something happened recently: The Internet became a thing for regular folks.

The Internet for Regular Folks pulled itself up by its own bootstraps, so to speak, over the last two years. The more information that became available for the everyman (and everywoman) on the 'Net, the more people got online. And the more who came online, the more information they made available for their own kind. It snowballed. So now, alongside "James T. Kirk vs. Jean-Luc Picard," we have everything from recipe archives to discussions about rebuilding the engine of a '69 Chevy 396 engine. From the latest CNN news to Civil War timelines. From the complete works of Shakespeare to live country music.

How can the Internet do all this? It is a hybrid of telephones, television and printed material. It's communications

Cliff Stoll

The Net

and information wrapped together. It has the strengths of those other media, but few of the weaknesses. Admittedly, it has its downside (anyone who's waited six minutes for a Web page to display knows that), but it *will* change more things than the naysayers think.

It already has. Having an E-mail address on a business card has passed from the cutting edge to the fashionable to the mundane. Web pages in print and TV ads are almost at that stage. And, thankfully, Hollywood is getting movies about the Internet out of its system. From newspapers to television, from banks to the halls of government, the Internet has already had a profound impact on the world. And it's going to have an even greater one.

Start with what the 'Net best provides: information. If you want it quickly but without much detail, turn to radio or television. If you want some more detail and you can wait for it, pick up a newspaper or magazine. If you want it both quickly and in detail, turn to the 'Net.

The Internet is nothing if not immediate. The very nature of Web sites means not only that they *can* be updated at a moment's notice, but also they *must* be, or they become stale and ignored. From the bombing in Oklahoma City to the O.J. Simpson trial, the most immediate information was available online. Sure, *ABC News* Special Reports can be just as immediate, but they are, thankfully, infrequent. And CNN can cover breaking news, but not *all* the breaking news.

The Internet also has them beat for coverage because the 'Net isn't a single entity like a newspaper or TV network. It's made up of thousands of separate people who can each make his or her information and opinion available. A *CBS News* reporter can interview a few people, true. But the 'Net lets many more people speak out. Yes, you have to separate the wheat from the chaff (and there's plenty of chaff), but if you trust everything you hear from ABC, CNN or the *Washington Post*, let me offer you some Florida swampland.

Traditional media, for the average person in the average place, is four or five television stations, a newspaper or two and a few magazines. The Internet adds thousands of sources and more information than you can find anywhere else. People who use the 'Net regularly learn that TV is a great place to get the basics, but if you want the real stories behind the story, jack in.

The 'Net's impact on publishing is yet another way it's shaken things up. Face it: Until the 'Net came along, a very small number of companies controlled a very large percentage of the information most people could obtain. But the Internet — the World Wide Web in particular — can make *anyone* a publisher. Even online services such as CompuServe and

America Online, which do a decent job of making information available, pale in comparison to the Internet when it comes to letting Joe on the street have his say.

Cliché, but true: The Web is a great equalizer. For about $35 a month, you can have a Web site as large as that of any corporation. Yes, you have to put something on it, but the storefront is the same size. And if what you have to say is interesting, people will find you; search engines like Alta Vista and Excite will see to that — look up "Wal-Mart" and you'll find not only what the company has to say, but also what other people have to say about it.

Political candidates' spin doctors have more to worry about now, thanks to the 'Net. They used to spend their time "spinning" a few networks and some major papers. Now they have 20 million to 50 million 'Net users to think about, almost any one of whom might publish information on the Web about the pols.

In 1996, this became even more apparent. Clinton and Dole each had an "official" Web site. But a search on either of their names yielded hundreds of unofficial sites — some pro, some con and some very slick parodies. Millions of people hear everything the candidates say and every promise they make, and now those millions can share and check information more easily than ever, thanks to the Internet. Truth, gossip and innuendo all make it to the Web. Certainly libel laws apply online as much as in print, but that was never the problem: Outright lies tend to be exposed on or off the 'Net; It's the truth getting out that these people are worried about. Ask former House Speaker Tom Foley, who was ousted, in part, thanks to an Internet-based campaign against him. Was he on his way out already? Certainly. But it's impossible to discount the effect the still-new Internet had back then. And there are a lot more people online today.

Traditional publishers have learned to beware. The Internet is here, and, like the printing press in the 15th and 16th centuries, it's revolutionizing the way information is being made available. Politics to poetry, dog-grooming tips to job-hunting guides, it's being published — online.

The 'Net is also changing the way people work. From relaying medical information from hospital to hospital, to helping police share information to catch a bad guy, to ushering in the age of telecommuting, the Internet was there this year.

As with anything that receives a lot of attention, there are those around who'd like to knock the Internet down a few notches. To some — specifically, the United States Congress — the 'Net's come too far, too fast.

It's like this: A few members of Congress — notably Sen. James Exon of Nebraska and Rep. Dianne Feinstein of California — discovered that, if you looked, you could find pictures of naked people on the Internet. (Never mind that you could more easily find pictures of naked people in your local bookstore or at night on HBO.) In 1995, this led to the drafting of the Communications Decency Act (CDA), and the much-ballyhooed cry of "Protect the children!" The CDA said, essentially, that people could not transmit "obscene" material over the Internet. Of course, much of this material was perfectly legal in print and even on cable TV but never mind that. The First Amendment would have to take a back seat to protecting the children, at least on the Internet.

In February 1996, President Clinton signed the Telecommunications Act, which contained the CDA, saying almost literally that although the act was unconstitutional, it was a still good thing. On June 12, 1996, a three-judge panel on

Rep. Dianne Feinstein

President Clinton

a federal court in Philadelphia ruled otherwise, calling the CDA "unconstitutional on its face," and essentially overturned the bill. A few weeks later, another court (this one in New York) ruled similarly. Internet, 2; overzealous opponents, 0. Despite this, there are still cries to have the government regulate the 'Net somehow. "Pornographers might use it!" they say. (They are more likely to use the U.S. Mail.) Terrorists might use it! (They probably use telephones more often.) You can find all sorts of horrible information! (It was in books a long time before the 'Net came around.) What about child porn?! (It's already illegal.)

To add insult to injury, the countries with the strictest regulations on the Internet are not the ones whose example we'd normally want to follow: China, Singapore, Turkey, Iraq and Germany all passed laws in 1996 limiting freedom of expression online. The 'Net effect (so to speak)? Little. Have something that's illegal in Germany? Put it on a computer in the States. Illegal in France? Try Canada. It's a big 'Net, and the law of one country doesn't often apply to another.

As for the future, the 'Net will continue to grow simply because we are training a generation to expect it to be there. Five, 10, 20 years down the line, the Internet will be as ubiquitous — and invisible — as the telephone or television. Checking E-mail will be as common as checking postal mail (if not more so). Many of us are already there, waiting for everyone else to catch up. One way or another, we'll see you on the 'Net. ■

1995 Billboard Video and Laserdisc Charts

Each year *Billboard* compiles video and laserdisc statistics based on SoundScan sales data and awards points to titles for each week they appear on the charts. The following titles accumulated the most points in 1995.

Billboard Top 20 Video Rentals

1. **The Shawshank Redemption**
   (Columbia TriStar Home Video)
2. **True Lies**
   (FoxVideo)
3. **Disclosure**
   (Warner Home Video)
4. **Speed**
   (FoxVideo)
5. **The Client**
   (Warner Home Video)
6. **Clear and Present Danger**
   (Paramount Home Video)
7. **When a Man Loves a Woman**
   (Buena Vista Home Video)
8. **Dumb and Dumber**
   (Turner Home Entertainment)
9. **Just Cause**
   (Warner Home Video)
10. **Outbreak**
    (Warner Home Video)
11. **Stargate**
    (Live Home Video)
12. **The Specialist**
    (Warner Home Video)
13. **Guarding Tess**
    (Columbia TriStar Home Video)
14. **Quiz Show**
    (Buena Vista Home Video)
15. **Blown Away**
    (MGM/UA Home Video)
16. **Legends of the Fall**
    (Columbia TriStar Home Video)
17. **It Could Happen to You**
    (Columbia TriStar Home Video)
18. **Color of Night**
    (Buena Vista Home Video)
19. **The River Wild**
    (Uni Distribution Corp.)
20. **Forrest Gump**
    (Paramount Home Video)

Billboard Top 20 Video Sales

1. **The Lion King**
   (Buena Vista Home Video)
2. **Forrest Gump**
   (Paramount Home Video)
3. **Speed**
   (FoxVideo)
4. **Jurassic Park**
   (Uni Distribution Corp.)
5. **The Mask**
   (Turner Home Entertainment)

6. **Playboy: The Best of Pamela Anderson**
   (Uni Distribution Corp.)
7. **Snow White and the Seven Dwarfs**
   (Buena Vista Home Video)
8. **The Crow**
   (Buena Vista Home Video)
9. **Pink Floyd: Pulse**
   (Sony Music Video)
10. **Yanni: Live at the Acropolis**
    (BMG Video)
11. **The Land Before Time II**
    (Uni Distribution Corp.)
12. **The Little Rascals**
    (Uni Distribution Corp.)
13. **The Flintstones**
    (Uni Distribution Corp.)
14. **Reservoir Dogs**
    (LIVE Home Video)
15. **Four Weddings and a Funeral**
    (PolyGram Video)
16. **Star Wars Trilogy**
    (FoxVideo)
17. **Angels in the Outfield**
    (Buena Vista Home Video)
18. **Playboy: The Girls of Hawaiian Tropic**
    (Uni Distribution Corp.)

19. *True Lies*
(FoxVideo)

20. *Tombstone*
(Buena Vista Home Video)

Billboard Top 20 Laserdisc Sales

1. *Speed*
(Image Entertainment)

2. *True Lies*
(Image Entertainment)

3. *Jurassic Park*
(Uni Distribution Corp.)

4. *Stargate*
(Pioneer Entertainment USA L.P.)

5. *Forrest Gump*
(Pioneer Entertainment USA L.P.)

6. *Interview With the Vampire*
(Warner Home Video)

7. *Snow White and the Seven Dwarfs*
(Image Entertainment)

8. *Clear and Present Danger*
(Pioneer Entertainment USA L.P.)

9. *Star Trek Generations*
(Pioneer Entertainment USA L.P.)

10. *The Mask*
(Image Entertainment)

11. *Aladdin*
(Image Entertainment)

12. *The Professional*
(Columbia TriStar Home Video)

13. *The Shawshank Redemption*
(Columbia TriStar Home Video)

14. *The Specialist*
(Warner Home Video)

15. *Total Recall*
(Pioneer Entertainment USA L.P.)

16. *Legends of the Fall*
(Columbia TriStar Home Video)

17. *Pink Floyd: Pulse*
(Sony Music Video)

18. *Natural Born Killers*
(Warner Home Video)

19. *The Shadow*
(Uni Distribution Corp.)

20. *Tombstone*
(Image Entertainment)

Billboard Top Music Videos

1. **Barbra — The Concert**
Barbra Streisand (Sony Music Video)

2. **Live at the Acropolis**
Yanni (BMG Video)

3. **Hell Freezes Over**
Eagles (Uni Distribution Corp.)

4. **The 3 Tenors in Concert 1994**
Carreras, Domingo and Pavarotti (WarnerVision Entertainment)

5. **Pulse**
Pink Floyd (Sony Music Video)

6. **Video Greatest Hits — HIStory**
Michael Jackson (Sony Music Video)

7. **Live! Tonight! Sold Out!!**
Nirvana (Uni Distribution Corp.)

8. **Murder Was the Case**
Snoop Doggy Dogg (WarnerVision Entertainment)

9. **Woodstock '94**
Various Artists (PolyGram Video)

10. **You Might Be a Redneck If. . .**
Jeff Foxworthy (Warner Reprise Video)

11. *Our First Video*
Mary-Kate and Ashley Olsen (WarnerVision Entertainment)

12. *Live*
Ray Stevens (Curb Video)

13. *Boyz II Men Then II Now*
Boyz II Men (PolyGram Video)

14. *Janet*
Janet Jackson (Virgin Music Video)

15. *Big Ones You Can Look At*
Aerosmith (Uni Distribution Corp.)

16. *Live Shit: Binge and Purge*
Metallica (Elektra Entertainment)

17. *Live Concert Home Video*
Sade (Sony Music Video)

18. *The Gate to the Mind's Eye*
Thomas Dolby (BMG Video)

19. *Cross Road*
Bon Jovi (PolyGram Video)

20. *Comedy Video Classics*
Ray Stevens (Curb Video)

Billboard Top 20 Health and Fitness Videos

1. *Your Personal Best With Elle Macpherson*
(Buena Vista Home Video)

2. *Ali MacGraw's Yoga Mind and Body*
(Warner Home Video)

3. *Kathy Smith's New Yoga*
(WarnerVision
Entertainment)

4. *Yoga Practice for Beginners*
(Healing Arts)

5. *Abs of Steel With Tamilee
Webb*
(WarnerVision
Entertainment)

6. *Cindy Crawford/The Next
Challenge*
(GoodTimes Home Video)

7. *Cindy Crawford/Shape Your
Body Workout*
(GoodTimes Home Video)

8. *Kathy Smith: Power Step
Workout*
(WarnerVision
Entertainment)

9. *The Grind Workout Hip-Hop
Aerobics*
(Sony Music Video)

10. *Abs of Steel 2 With Tamilee
Webb*
(WarnerVision
Entertainment)

11. *Step Reebok: The Power
Workout*
(PolyGram Video)

12. *Men of Steel: Abs of Steel*
(WarnerVision
Entertainment)

13. *Reebok Aerostep*
(PolyGram Video)

14. *Step Reebok: The Video*
(PolyGram Video)

15. *Karen Voight: Strong and
Smooth Moves*
(ABC Video)

16. *Kathy Ireland: Total Fitness
Video*
(UAV Entertainment)

17. *Kathy Smith's New Yoga
Basics*
(WarnerVision
Entertainment)

18. *Reebok Winning Body
Workout*
(PolyGram Video)

19. *Lucky Vanous: Ultimate Fat
Burning Workout*
(FoxVideo CBS/Fox)

20. *Buns of Steel 3 With
Tamilee Webb*
(WarnerVision
Entertainment)

Billboard Top 25 Kid Videos

1. *Snow White and the Seven
Dwarfs*
(Buena Vista Home Video)

2. *The Lion King*
(Buena Vista Home Video)

3. *Aladdin*
(Buena Vista Home Video)

4. *Disney's Sing Along Songs:
Circle of Life*
(Buena Vista Home Video)

5. *The Land Before Time II*
(Uni Distribution Corp.)

6. *The Pagemaster*
(FoxVideo)

7. *Beavis and Butt-Head:
There Goes the
Neighborhood*
(Sony Music Video)

8. *The Return of Jafar*
(Buena Vista Home Video)

9. *The Adventures of Mary-
Kate and Ashley: The Case
of Sea World*
(WarnerVision
Entertainment)

10. *Beavis and Butt-Head: Work
Sucks!*
(Sony Music Video)

11. *Disney's Sing Along Songs:
Pocahontas*
(Buena Vista Home Video)

12. *Beavis and Butt-Head: The
Final Judgement*
(Sony Music Video)

13. *The Adventures of Mary-
Kate and Ashley: The Case
of the Mystery Cruise*
(WarnerVision
Entertainment)

14. *The Fox and the Hound*
(Buena Vista Home Video)

15. *The Adventures of Mary-
Kate and Ashley: The Case
of Logical I Ranch*
(WarnerVision
Entertainment)

16. *Dumbo*
(Buena Vista Home Video)

17. *The Swan Princess*
(Turner Home Entertainment)

18. *A Goofy Movie*
(Buena Vista Home Video)

19. *A Troll in Central Park*
(Warner Home Video)

20. *Barney: Live in
New York City*
(The Lyons Group)

21. *Barney's Imagination Island*
(The Lyons Group)

22. *The Adventures of Mary-
Kate and Ashley: The Case
of Thorn Mansion*
(WarnerVision
Entertainment)

23. *Thumbelina*
(Warner Home Video)

24. *Mortal Kombat — The
Animated Video*
(Turner Home Entertainment)

25. *Pinocchio*
(Buena Vista Home Video)

50 Significant Videos of 1995—1996

From feature film to instructional, kids to music, here are the home-video releases from September 1995 through the summer of 1996 that caught our eye. Look for classic and foreign films on pages 568 and 569. "Rental pricing" means higher than you're willing to pay; wait for the "previously viewed" sale at your video store or just rent.

THE AMERICAN PRESIDENT
Columbia TriStar; rental pricing
Feature; PG-13
Director: Rob Reiner
Cast: Michael Douglas, Annette Bening and Michael J. Fox
See page 43

APOLLO 13
MCA/Universal; $22.98
Feature; PG
Director: Ron Howard
Cast: Tom Hanks, Kevin Bacon, Bill Paxton and Gary Sinise
A great video watch since we're used to seeing moon shots on the small screen anyway. In April 1970, the crew of Apollo 13 left Earth for a week-long adventure that included a walk on the moon. Things went wrong, and the crew nearly died in space. Howard manages to load the movie with suspense, quite a feat since we already know the ending before pushing play.

THE ARISTOCATS
Disney; $26.99
Children's; G
Voices: Eva Gabor, Phil Harris, Sterling Holloway and Scatman Crothers
The last of Disney's classic animated tales before the dawn of its blockbuster era. A cat named Duchess inherits a fortune from her late mistress and becomes the target of a greedy butler. Debonair star Maurice Chevalier came out of retirement to sing the film's title song.

BABE
MCA/Universal; $22.98
Feature; G
Director: Chris Noonan
Cast: James Cromwell and Magda Szubanski
Video renters clamored for this release after the story about a talking pig received a lot of attention at awards time. Babe, a homesick piglet who is awarded to an affable farmer at the county fair, sees his new farmmate, a sheepdog, as his surrogate mother. Realizing he must prove his worth or end up as Christmas dinner, the little pig learns to herd sheep better than any pooch.

BATMAN FOREVER
Warner; $19.95
Feature; PG-13
Director: Joel Schumacher
Cast: Val Kilmer, Jim Carrey, Tommy Lee Jones and Nicole Kidman
The video transfer is much better than one would expect, and the color fares best. There were some big changes in the third *Batman* installment, with Schumacher taking over helming duties from Tim Burton and Val Kilmer replacing Michael Keaton in the title role. The result was impressive, especially Carrey as The Riddler, who teams up with Two-Face to outwit the Caped Crusader.

THE BOYS OF ST. VINCENT
New Yorker; rental pricing
Feature; NR
Director: John N. Smith
Cast: Johnny Morina and Henry Czerny
Actual events inspired this remarkable three-hour film about the sexual abuse of boys in a Newfoundland orphanage. The dark, well-acted portrait of horror and its sensitive subject matter make this a good choice for video.

BRAVEHEART
Paramount; rental pricing
Feature; R
Director: Mel Gibson
Cast: Mel Gibson, Sophie Marceau and Patrick McGoohan

Typically the words "epic" and "home video" don't go together, and Gibson's sweeping, Oscar-winning look at the bloody, muddy 13th-century uprisings between the Scots and English is no exception. Unfortunately, scenes that were breathtakingly panoramic and powerful on the big screen just don't fare well on TV. But for the squeamish, video does offer the option of fast-forwarding through the stomach-turning carnage on the front lines.

THE BRIDGES OF MADISON COUNTY

Warner; rental pricing
Feature; PG-13
Director: Clint Eastwood
Cast: Clint Eastwood and Meryl Streep
Thankfully, Eastwood has managed to remove the purple prose from this celluloid version of Robert James Waller's best selling novel. Photographer Robert Kinkaid (Eastwood) and Francesca Johnson (Streep) fall in love and spend four amorous days together in Johnson's farmhouse. Sentimentality aside, it's a good curl-up-on-the-couch-together date movie.

THE BROTHERS McMULLEN

FoxVideo; rental pricing
Feature; R
Director: Ed Burns
Cast: Ed Burns and Maxine Bahns
Burns became director du jour after he won the top prize at the 1995 Sundance Film Festival with this story of three love-dazed Irish-Catholic brothers on New York's Long Island.

CASINO

MCA/Universal; rental pricing
Feature; R
Director: Martin Scorsese
Cast: Robert De Niro, Sharon Stone and Joe Pesci
See page 50

CINDERELLA

Walt Disney; $26.99
Children's; G
Voices of: Ilene Woods, William Phipps and Eleanor Audley
Though a bit politically incorrect, this restored classic Disney rags-to-riches fairy tale, complete with evil stepmother and fairy godmother, deserves another look.

CLOCKERS

MCA/Universal; rental pricing
Feature; R
Director: Spike Lee
Cast: Harvey Keitel, John Turturro, Delroy Lindo, Mekhi Phifer and Isaiah Washington
See page 51

CLUELESS

Paramount; $14.95
Feature; PG-13
Director: Amy Heckerling
Cast: Alicia Silverstone, Stacey Dash and Brittany Murphy
Surprisingly entertaining for teens and adults. Cher and her best friend, Dionne, both named "after great singers who now do infomercials," bring their cellular phones to school so they don't miss a beat and take on a protégée who wasn't blessed at birth with their looks and locks.

CRUMB

Columbia TriStar; rental pricing
Documentary; R
Director: Terry Zwigoff
Find out why so many moviegoers grumbled when this master portrait of underground cartoonist Robert Crumb didn't get nominated for the Best Documentary Oscar. An arresting look at the difficult comic genius and the dysfunctional family that spawned him.

DEAD MAN WALKING

PolyGram; rental pricing
Feature; R
Director: Tim Robbins
Cast: Sean Penn and Susan Sarandon
See page 54

DOLORES CLAIBORNE

Columbia TriStar; $19.95
Feature; R
Director: Taylor Hackford
Cast: Kathy Bates and Jennifer Jason Leigh
Unfortunately, *Dolores Claiborne* didn't fare well at the box office, and that's probably because Stephen King fans are used to supernatural thrillers, not psychological dramas. While under investigation for killing her boss, Claiborne relives her husband's murder, which she was also accused of committing. As if that isn't enough, she reunites with her estranged daughter, who is also confronting her troubled past.

FREE WILLY 2: THE ADVENTURE HOME

Warner Home Video; $22.98
Feature; PG
Director: Dwight Little
Cast: Jason James Richter and Michael Madsen
Video doesn't do the scenery justice, but this is a great choice for parents looking for ways to keep the young ones entertained on a rainy day. *Free Willy 2*, though loaded with subplots, manages to surpass its successful predecessor.

GEORGIA
Buena Vista; rental pricing
Feature; R
Director: Ulu Grosbard
Cast: Jennifer Jason Leigh and Mare Winningham
See page 62

GHOST IN THE SHELL
Polygram; $19.95
Feature; NR
Director: Mamoru Oshii
In this nihilistic animated feature from Japan, heroine Major Kusanagi, an android supercop, fights to keep an artificial intelligence from downloading in her neck.

A GREAT DAY IN HARLEM
Capital Cities/ABC Video Publishing; $19.95
Documentary
Narration: Quincy Jones
Interviews with: Art Kane, Dizzy Gillespie, Art Blakey, Sonny Rollins and others
A 1958 photo shoot for *Esquire* magazine is the focus of this nostalgic tribute to three generations of jazz greats. Interspersed with live footage of the 1958 event are interviews, bios and performances.

HOME FOR THE HOLIDAYS
PolyGram; rental pricing
Feature; PG-13
Director: Jodie Foster
Cast: Holly Hunter and Robert Downey, Jr.

A perfect choice for when you're stuffed with turkey and pumpkin pie and crazy Uncle Oscar has finally gone home. Jodie Foster's slice-of-life ode to the Thanksgiving ritual captures that all-too-familiar blend of dysfunction and love that makes the holidays the holidays and us thankful they only come once a year.

THE INDIAN IN THE CUPBOARD
Columbia TriStar; $22.95
Feature; PG
Director: Frank Oz
Cast: Hal Scardino and Litefoot
For his birthday, Omri receives a small plastic American Indian and a cupboard. The young boy soon discovers that the cupboard brings the Indian to life, and his adventure begins. Omri must feed and shelter the Iroquis brave Little Bear and keep him a secret, which takes some creativity. A great family rental.

KIDS
Vidmark; rental pricing
Feature; NR
Director: Larry Clark
Cast: Leo Fitzpatrick, Chloe Sevigny, Justin Pierce and Rosario Dawson

This disturbing film dives into New York's teen culture, finding loveless sex, aimless wandering and random violence. The story and style are stark and terrifying and originally earned *Kids* an NC-17 rating, making it one of 1995's most controversial films.

A LITTLE PRINCESS
Warner; $24.94
Feature; G
Director: Alfonso Cuaron
Cast: Eleanor Bron, Liam Cunningham, Lomax Study and Liesel Matthews
This critically acclaimed film about a young British girl left behind in a New York boarding school failed to attract audiences to theaters. In an unusual marketing strategy, Warner Bros. pulled the film shortly after its first theatrical release and re-released it later in the summer hoping for better box-office results. The plan produced disappointing returns, and the distributor is hoping video sales will prove more profitable. It should — this is a must for children and parents.

LADYBIRD, LADYBIRD
Evergreen; rental pricing
Feature; R
Director: Ken Loach
Cast: Crissy Rock and Vladimir Vega
Loach, known for his riveting, real-life dramas, made this compelling (but not widely seen) film about a British single mother who loses her children to the government's social services and finds a gentle man to love.

LEAVING LAS VEGAS
MGM/UA; rental pricing
Feature; R
Director: Mike Figgis
Cast: Nicolas Cage and Elisabeth Shue
This incredibly poignant and haunting story of an alcoholic Hollywood screenwriter on a suicidal drinking binge and the hooker who comforts him nabbed Cage an Oscar and freed Shue from her girl-next-door image.

THE MADNESS OF KING GEORGE

Hallmark; rental pricing
Feature; R
Director: Nicholas Hytner
Cast: Nigel Hawthorne and Helen Mirren

Hawthorne's performance as the ailing monarch King George III earned him a Best Actor Oscar nomination, and Mirren garnered a Best Actress nod at the 1995 Cannes Film Festival for her portrayal of George's loving wife. As George struggles with his condition and his grip on reality, his sons and political adversaries scheme for the throne.

MIGHTY APHRODITE

Buena Vista; rental pricing
Feature; R
Director: Woody Allen
Cast: Woody Allen, Mira Sorvino and Helena Bonham Carter

Catch Sorvino's Oscar-winning turn as the monotone, squeaky-voiced prostitute with a kind heart in Allen's most recent look at love, sex and relationships in New York City.

THE MONKEES: THE COLLECTOR'S EDITION

Rhino; rental pricing
NR
Cast: Davy Jones, Peter Tork, Mickey Dolenz and Mike Nesmith

Hey, hey, it's the largest boxed set in video history. This limited-edition, 21-cassette, 58-episode tribute to the made-for-TV Beatles features the 1966 pilot episode and other rarities including commercials starring the goofy but groovy quartet.

MURIEL'S WEDDING

Miramax; rental pricing
Feature; R
Director: P.J. Hogan
Cast: Toni Collette, Bill Hunter and Rachel Griffiths

Those who didn't catch this charming comedy in theaters can now find out what all the buzz was about. Plain, large and giddy Muriel leaves behind her small town and heads for metropolitan Sydney, where her vacation becomes permanent and she gains confidence, a new name and an outrageous adventure.

MUTE WITNESS

Columbia TriStar; rental pricing
Feature; R
Director: Anthony Waller
Cast: Marina Sudina and Fay Ripley

This low-budget film didn't make a big splash at the box office, but its twisting, suspenseful plot translates well to video, as it may demand some rewinding. A mute special-effects technician witnesses a snuff film being made on the set of the horror movie her American crew is making in Russia. That's not all: There's a subplot involving a missing computer disc.

NATURAL BORN KILLERS: THE DIRECTOR'S CUT

Vidmark; rental pricing
Feature; NR
Director: Oliver Stone
Cast: Woody Harrelson and Juliette Lewis

This version of Stone's controversial, graphic film about two mass murderers on the lam features unseen footage that the Motion Picture Arts of America nixed from the theatrical release.

NIXON

Hollywood; rental pricing
Feature; R
Director: Oliver Stone
Cast: Anthony Hopkins and Joan Allen

Be sure you've grabbed the letterbox version of Stone's gripping portrait of the disgraced ex-president. The alternative pan-and-scan edition cuts the wide-screen shots practically in half.

O.J. SIMPSON: THE INTERVIEW

H&K; $29.95 plus shipping and handling
To put it simply: the most talked-about video release of the year.

POCAHONTAS

Disney; $26.99
Animation; G
Directors: Mike Gabriel and Eric Goldberg
Voices of: Irene Bedard, Judy Kuhn, Mel Gibson and David Ogden Stiers

The mighty Disney marketing machine rolled out its love story between the Native American princess and scout John Smith to millions of families. Immediately, amidst cries of "Can we watch it again, mommy?" the film topped sales and rental charts. Unless you want to fork over your life savings on Disney merchandise, fastforward through the barrage of commercials at the tape's start.

PRIEST

Miramax; rental pricing
Feature; R
Director: Antonia Bird
Cast: Linus Roache, Tom Wilkinson, Cathy Tyson and Robert Carlyle

One of 1995's most controversial films and fodder for right-wing attacks against the entertainment industry, this portrait of a gay cleric struggling to reconcile his active sexuality with his Catholic faith is movingly acted. Unfortunately, Miramax played it safe and released the edited U.S. version, not the full European cut that includes erotic scenes involving the cleric and another man.

PULP FICTION

Miramax; $19.99
Feature; R
Director: Quentin Tarantino
Cast: John Travolta, Samuel L. Jackson, Uma Thurman, Ving Rhames and Bruce Willis

The hit of 1994 comes to video in two versions: pan-and-scan transfer, which fills a television screen but upsets some scenes, and letterbox, which preserves Tarantino's original work. Three stories link the characters, who include two hitmen, a mob boss, his wife and a palooka.

SAFE

Columbia TriStar; rental pricing
Feature; R
Director: Todd Haynes
Cast: Julianne Moore, Xander Berkeley and James LeGros

Many missed this film during its original art-house run, and that's too bad. A California housewife is convinced her undiagnosed malady is an environmental illness and checks into a New Age spa to find comfort among others who share her allergy to the 20th century.

THE SANTA CLAUSE

Walt Disney; $19.99
Feature; PG
Director: John Pasquin
Cast: Tim Allen, Judge Reinhold, Wendy Crewson and Eric Lloyd

The surprise hit of 1994 propelled Allen from sit-com success to motion-picture stardom. After Santa Claus is injured from a fall from a roof, divorced dad Scott Calvin dons the red suit and assumes Santa's responsibilities.

THE SECRET OF ROAN INISH

Columbia TriStar; rental pricing
Feature; PG
Director: John Sayles
Cast: Jeni Courtney and Richard Sheridan

The breathtaking Irish landscape and the sentiment will brighten up a dismal afternoon. A young Irish girl tries to convince her grandparents that her baby brother, who was carried out to sea and never found, is living in the ocean with friendly seals.

SENSE AND SENSIBILITY

Columbia TriStar; rental pricing
Feature; PG
Director: Ang Lee
Cast: Emma Thompson, Kate Winslet, Hugh Grant and Alan Rickman

While the rolling English countryside loses some of its lushness on the video screen, Jane Austen's charming tale of the Dashwood sisters and their beaux is a must-rent for those who somehow missed the award-winning film in theaters. Of course, the video release also gives those who loved the flawless period piece on the big screen the chance to watch the drama unfold again. And again.

SEVEN

New Line; rental pricing
Feature; R
Director: David Fincher
Cast: Morgan Freeman, Brad Pitt and Gwyneth Paltrow
See page 89

SHOWGIRLS

MGM/UA; rental pricing
Feature; R/NC-17
Director: Paul Verhoeven
Cast: Elizabeth Berkley, Gina Gershon and Kyle MacLachlan

This overhyped tale of one stripper's naked ambition sparked a ratings controversy when major chains such as Blockbuster demanded a tamer R-rated show. Both home-video versions quickly do away with the pasties and g-strings, with the NC-17 cut delivering an extra 61 seconds of campy erotica.

SMOKE

Miramax; rental pricing
Feature; R
Director: Wayne Wang
Cast: Harvey Keitel, William
Hurt and Stockard Channing

Unhappy relationships are
exposed and introduced
among tobacconist Auggie
and his customers. Auggie
learns he and a former girlfriend have an 18-year-old
crack-addicted, pregnant
daughter, and one of his customers befriends a
young black man who is in town to track down
his long-lost father.

STAR WARS TRILOGY

FoxVideo; $49.98 boxed set; $19.98 each
Feature; PG
Director: George Lucas
Cast: Mark Hamill, Harrison Ford and Carrie Fisher
Whether or not the release of this boxed set is a
marketing ploy to ready the public for the trio of
prequels due out sometime near the millennium,
the three *Star Wars* movies are timeless and
remind us about what a science fiction/thriller
was like before Schwarzenegger. Included with
each tape is a five-minute interview with
Leonard Maltin and director Lucas.

TAMILEE WEBB: TONING MIND & BODY

WarnerVision; $12.95
Exercise
High-impact heroine Tamilee Webb targets the
mind-body connection with a routine that combines nonimpact toning exercises with strength-
ening moves.

TO DIE FOR

Columbia TriStar; rental pricing
Feature; R
Director: Gus Van Sant
Cast: Nicole Kidman and Matt
Dillon

Nicole Kidman gives a
career-making performance
in this slick satire of
America's obsession with
the cult of celebrity. Her
portrayal of a small-town
newscaster who sets her
sights on television fame is a crackling combination of sex appeal, naivete and ambition. A perfect
choice for the small screen.

UNSTRUNG HEROES

Hollywood; rental pricing
Feature; PG
Director: Diane Keaton
Cast: Andie MacDowell, John Turturro, Michael
Richards and Nathan Watt
See page 97

UNZIPPED

Miramax; rental pricing
Documentary; R
Director: Douglas Keeves
With: Isaac Mizrahi, Sarah Mizrahi, Kate Moss,
Christy Turlington and Naomi Campbell
This documentary on the fashion industry suc-
cessfully captures the catwalk crowd and one of
its top designers as he prepares for the premiere
of a new line. Mizrahi and his models speak can-
didly about the industry and themselves.

WAITING TO EXHALE

FoxVideo; rental pricing
Feature; R
Director: Forest Whitaker
Cast: Whitney Houston,
Angela Bassett, Lela Rochon
and Loretta Devine
See page 98

WATERWORLD

MCA/Universal; $19.95
Feature; PG-13
Director: Kevin Reynolds
Cast: Kevin Costner, Jeanne Tripplehorn, Dennis
Hopper and Tina Majorino
This futuristic epic surprisingly kept its head
above box-office water after critics scoffed that it
would sink faster than the *Titanic.* While some of
the film's soggy grandeur is lost on video, the tale
of post-apocalypse survivors searching for land in
a water-logged world is worth the rental just to
see what a $175 million movie — the most expen-
sive ever made — looks like.

THE X-FILES

FoxVideo; $14.98 each
NR
Cast: David Duchovny and Gillian Anderson
Just in case you've caught *The X-Files* paranor-
mal trend a little late, FoxVideo has released six
early episodes on three tapes. A six-minute intro
by creator Chris Carter reveals some little-
known X-trivia about the development of the
creepy series and the casting of Duchovny and
Anderson as the cult fav's unlikely sex symbols.
The collection, which includes the pilot episode,
plays well on video — rewind to follow an unexpected plot twist or decipher some techno-talk.

Home Video Library

The ongoing transfer of 100 years of film history to videocassette and laserdisc means that it is possible to treat cinema as we do books. This alphabetical list is meant to suggest time periods, genres, actors and directors that you should consider for a home-video library. Your list of meaningful movies, just like your library of books, will represent your own taste, but this section may be a helpful guide or at least a rental reminder if you've missed any of these classics.

THE ADVENTURES OF ROBIN HOOD (1938)

Directors: Michael Curtiz and William Keighley
Cast: Errol Flynn, Claude Rains and Olivia de Havilland
Flynn is in his element here, playing the archetypal swashbuckler with ease and elegance, flair and bravura in this entertaining and artful classic.

AIRPLANE! (1980)

Director: Jim Abrahams
Cast: Leslie Nielsen, Lloyd Bridges and David Zucker
This hilarious spoof of those melodramatic '70s disaster flicks never relents with its sight gags, bad puns and sly innuendo. The first of the "you-know-it's-dumb-but-you-can't-help-laughing" films, *Airplane!* demands repeat viewings, since many of its jokes are tucked away in the background.

ALL ABOUT EVE (1950)

Director: Joseph L. Mankiewicz
Cast: Bette Davis, Anne Baxter, George Sanders and Marilyn Monroe
All About Eve is a witty, sophisticated study of Broadway backstage life, made all the more intriguing by its parallels with Davis's own off-screen reputation as one difficult diva. A sparkling script and consummate acting earned the film six Academy Awards.

ANNIE HALL (1977)

Director: Woody Allen
Cast: Woody Allen, Diane Keaton and Tony Roberts
Allen's bittersweet chronicle of a love affair makes sharp observations of mid-1970s culture, and is a once-a-year must-see for those with a romantic streak.

APOCALYPSE NOW (1979)

Director: Francis Ford Coppola
Cast: Martin Sheen, Marlon Brando, Robert Duvall, Dennis Hopper, Harrison Ford and Lawrence Fishburne
Based on Joseph Conrad's *Heart of Darkness*, this controversial, disturbing film grapples with the ghosts of Vietnam through a surreal and cerebral journey into Cambodia.

BEN-HUR (1959)

Director: William Wyler
Cast: Charlton Heston, Hugh Griffith, Stephen Boyd and Martha Scott
The epic of all biblical epics, *Ben-Hur* tells the story of Christ with conviction and authority and is at times thrilling, moving and melancholy. Watch for the daring and fast-paced chariot race, which was choreographed so realistically that it left one stuntman dead. The film won a record 11 Oscars, including Best Picture, Director, Actor, Supporting Actor and Cinematography.

BEAUTY AND THE BEAST (1991)

Directors: Gary Trousdale and Kirk Wise
Voices of: Paige O'Hara, Robby Benson, Jerry Orbach, Angela Lansbury, Richard White and David Ogden Stiers
The first animated feature nominated for a Best Picture Oscar captures the dazzling details of the original masterpiece. Here, the bookish Belle and the Beast fall in love while the Beast holds the beauty captive in his deserted castle.

THE BEST YEARS OF OUR LIVES (1946)

Director: William Wyler
Cast: Fredric March, Myrna Loy, Teresa Wright, Dana Andrews and Harold Russell
Upon returning home from WWII, servicemen face an uncertain future. A fine depiction of its moment in time, it set the stage for the postwar cinema of anxiety.

BREAKFAST AT TIFFANY'S (1961)
Director: Blake Edwards
Cast: Audrey Hepburn, George Peppard and Patricia Neal

With her little black Givenchys and a cat named Cat, Hepburn turned Manhattan partygirl Holly Golightly into one of film's most heartbreaking, unforgettable heroines.

BREATHLESS (1959)
Director: Jean-Luc Godard
Cast: Jean-Paul Belmondo and Jean Seberg
In the hands of Godard, this typical tale of an on-the-lam gangster with a weakness for an American girl became a cornerstone of New Wave film.

BRINGING UP BABY (1938)
Director: Howard Hawks

Cast: Cary Grant, Katharine Hepburn, Charlie Ruggles and May Robson
The very definition of screwball comedy, this lightning-fast farce exhibits the characteristic absent-minded hero, madcap heiress and frantic chases, romantic and otherwise.

BUTCH CASSIDY AND THE SUNDANCE KID (1969)
Director: George Roy Hill
Cast: Paul Newman and Robert Redford
Newman and Redford make this the buddy movie of all time. Even if you can't stand Westerns, the outlaws' smart-ass dialogue and comic crime spree will win you over.

CASABLANCA (1942)
Director: Michael Curtiz
Cast: Humphrey Bogart, Ingrid Bergman, Claude Rains and Peter Lorre
Considered by many to be Hollywood's greatest moment, *Casablanca* immortalized Bogart, Bergman and "As Time Goes By." This suspenseful saga of a nightclub owner, his old flame and her underground-leader husband is required watching for every film fan.

CHINATOWN (1974)
Director: Roman Polanski
Cast: Jack Nicholson, Faye Dunaway and John Huston

An homage to the 1930s' grim gumshoe films, *Chinatown* elicited career-defining performances from Nicholson, Dunaway and Huston and immersed moviegoers in a twisted, complex mystery that set the standard for its genre. Watch for the director's cameo as a knife-packing hood.

CITIZEN KANE (1941)
Director: Orson Welles
Cast: Orson Welles, Joseph Cotten, Agnes Moorehead and Everett Sloane
Considered by many to be the finest film of all time, the narrative complexity of Kane's story and the richness of the film technique make it a must for the shelf.

THE CONFORMIST (1970)
Director: Bernardo Bertolucci
Cast: Jean-Louis Trintignant, Stefania Sandrelli, Dominique Sanda and Pierre Clementi
With its stylish blend of social criticism and suspense/chase movie, the film's fluid structure made its mark on 1970s cinema.

DIRTY HARRY (1971)
Director: Don Siegel
Cast: Clint Eastwood, Reni Santoni, Harry Guardino and Andy Mitchum
Dirty Harry catapulted Eastwood to iconoclastic stardom as the flinty San Francisco cop and ushered in a slew of violent action pictures, including three sequels, that shocked moviegoers away from the mellow movies of the '60s.

DO THE RIGHT THING (1989)
Director: Spike Lee
Cast: Spike Lee, Danny Aiello and John Turturro
This film exposed the deep chasms undermining race relations in America and defined Lee as a provocative, honest and expressive filmmaker. Packed with gutsy, memorable moments, innovative camerawork and stellar acting, the slice-of-life drama erupts into one of cinema's most-talked-about endings.

DRACULA (1931)
Director: Tod Browning
Cast: Bela Lugosi, David Manners and Dwight Frye

FRANKENSTEIN (1931)
Director: James Whale
Cast: Boris Karloff, Colin Clive, Mae Clarke and Dwight Frye
How does one choose between Universal's twin pillars of fright? Don't bother trying; both are essential Halloween treats.

Dr. Zhivago (1965)

Director: David Lean
Cast: Omar Sharif, Julie Christie and Alec Guinness
This sweeping historical epic spans decades and wars, political transitions and romances. Visually lush and brilliantly directed.

Easy Rider (1969)

Director: Dennis Hopper
Cast: Peter Fonda, Dennis Hopper, Jack Nicholson and Karen Black
This gutsy, low-budget road film features inspired performances, good writing, expressive camera work and a rocking soundtrack. With time *Easy Rider* has added to its cult status recognition as an important film of its era.

Fanny & Alexander (1982)

Director: Ingmar Bergman
Cast: Pernilla Allwin, Bertil Guve, Erland Josephson and Harriet Andersson
Not the dark ruminations on failed love and impending death associated with Bergman's earlier films, this saga of family has a valedictory feel that brings the many threads of Bergman's work together in one fulfilling film.

From Russia With Love (1963)

Director: Terence Young
Cast: Sean Connery, Daniela Bianchi and Robert Shaw
The second James Bond film is considered by many to be the best in the 007 series. Sent to Istanbul to secure a top-secret Russian decoding machine, Bond falls for a Russian agent, nearly meets death by a poisonous switchblade (protruding from the shoes of a female assassin) and dukes it out with the deadly killer played by Shaw.

The Godfather (1972)
The Godfather Part II (1974)
The Godfather Part III (1990)

Director: Francis Ford Coppola
Cast: Al Pacino, Robert De Niro, Robert Duvall, Marlon Brando, Diane Keaton, James Caan and Talia Shire
The story of a gangland family extended over three feature films aptly portrays the 20th-century American experience. The three features are available as a set. Re-evaluate the controversial third chapter after seeing the reassembled cut available on video.

Gone With the Wind (1939)

Director: Victor Fleming
Cast: Vivien Leigh, Clark Gable and Olivia de Havilland
Considered one of the greatest movies ever made, the epic is really nothing more than a Civil War soap opera, but that's why we love it so much. Producer David O. Selznick, spent two-and-one-half years looking for the perfect Scarlett, which he found in Leigh. Winner of eight Oscars including Best Picture, Best Actress and Director.

The Graduate (1967)

Director: Mike Nichols
Cast: Dustin Hoffman, Anne Bancroft and Katharine Ross

The defining comedy of the 1960s, *The Graduate* is timeless in its treatment of youthful angst and surreal suburbia. Superb acting, especially by Hoffman in his first major role, Nichols's Oscar-winning direction and the Simon and Garfunkel score make this film a cultural landmark.

Grand Illusion (1937)

Director: Jean Renoir
Cast: Jean Gabin, Pierre Fresnay, Eric von Stroheim and Marcel Dalio
Renoir's examination of the waning influence of the aristocracy is set as a WWI prisoner-of-war drama. It earned international recognition as a movie milestone as well as a powerful story.

Intolerance (1916)

Director: D.W. Griffith
Cast: Lillian Gish, Mae Marsh and Constance Talmadge
Griffith responded to the outcry over *The Birth of a Nation* with *Intolerance*, and in the process created one of the most ambitious epics of the silent era.

It Happened One Night (1934)

Director: Frank Capra
Cast: Clark Gable, Claudette Colbert and Ward Bond
Though often overshadowed by Capra's later classic *It's a Wonderful Life*, this deserving picture has all the makings of a masterpiece. The trend-setting romantic comedy about a reporter falling in love with a runaway heiress remains timelessly entertaining. The first picture to sweep the five major Oscar categories: Picture, Actor, Actress, Director and Screenplay.

Jaws (1975)

Director: Steven Spielberg
Cast: Roy Scheider and Richard Dreyfuss
The thriller that made an entire generation think twice before taking a dip. This tale of a great white shark terrorizing a New England resort town propelled Spielberg to super-stardom and inspired three sequels.

KISS ME DEADLY (1955)
Director: Robert Aldrich
Cast: Ralph Meeker, Albert Dekker and Cloris Leachman
This wild, skittish blend of paranoia, brutality and intrigue makes just the right mix for a darkly cynical film noir.

KRAMER VS. KRAMER (1979)
Director: Robert Benton
Cast: Dustin Hoffman, Meryl Streep, Jane Alexander and Justin Henry
An insightful, intelligent look at the wrenching effects of divorce on one Manhattan family. The film swept the 1980 Oscars, winning Best Picture, Actor, Screenplay, Director and Supporting Actress.

LA DOLCE VITA (1960)
Director: Federico Fellini
Cast: Marcello Mastroianni, Anita Ekberg and Anouk Aimée
Fellini's masterpiece has endured as one of the icons of the 1960s, both in the cinema and in how it captured the existential ennui of the time — but a fun watch as well.

THE LADY EVE (1941)
Director: Preston Sturges
Cast: Henry Fonda, Barbara Stanwyck, Charles Coburn and Eugene Pallette
Sturges's observations on the romantic clash of men and women improves with age, with Fonda succumbing not once but twice to a wily Stanwyck.

THE LAST PICTURE SHOW (1971)
Director: Peter Bogdanovich
Cast: Timothy Bottoms, Jeff Bridges, Ben Johnson, Cybill Shepherd, Cloris Leachman, Sam Bottoms and Randy Quaid

Heightened by starkly beautiful black-and-white cinematography, this somber look at small-town life in 1950s America pays homage to a bygone era of filmmaking and the naivete of youth.

L'ECLISSE (1962)
Director: Michelangelo Antonioni
Cast: Monica Vitti and Alain Delon
The aimless drift of romantic attachment, the inevitability of missed connections, the emptiness of life: brooding 1960s existentialism perhaps, but this portrayal manages to be as magnificent as it is despairing.

THE LION KING (1994)
Directors: Roger Allers and Rob Minkoff
Voices of: Jonathan Taylor Thomas, James Earl Jones, Whoopi Goldberg, Matthew Broderick and Jeremy Irons
Disney's animated tale of the jungle wowed critics, parents and children and topped 1994's box-office charts, grossing nearly $300 million. Considered the most popular children's film of all time, *The Lion King's* skillful combination of high drama and hip comedy makes it a fun watch for the whole family.

THE MALTESE FALCON (1941)
Director: John Huston
Cast: Humphrey Bogart, Mary Astor, Peter Lorre and Sydney Greenstreet
Considered one of the first and best noir detective films. First-time director Huston interprets Dashiell Hammett's complex tale with scrutinous attention to detail and dead-on casting — Bogart's hard-boiled Spade, Astor as the quintessential femme fatale and the supporting ensemble of requisite shady characters.

MARY POPPINS (1964)
Director: Robert Stevenson
Cast: Julie Andrews and Dick Van Dyke
This tale of the beloved "nearly perfect nanny" blends charming animation, heel-kicking dance numbers and a whimsical score for timeless family entertainment. Besides introducing "supercalifragilisticexpalidocious" into our vocabulary, the film took home a carpetbag of Oscars, including Best Actress for Andrews's film debut.

METROPOLIS (1926)
Director: Fritz Lang
Cast: Brigitte Helm and Alfred Abel
The ageless vision of a dehumanized future is still relevant and great fun to look at. Be sure to avoid the tinted 1984 edition with its execrable score.

MODERN TIMES (1936)
Director: Charlie Chaplin
Cast: Charlie Chaplin and Paulette Goddard
As with Metropolis, this film centers on a fear of a mechanized world but with Chaplin's winning humanity — and even a score written by the director. *The Tramp* with a social conscience.

MONKEY BUSINESS (1931)
Director: Norman Z. MacLeod
Cast: Marx Brothers and Thelma Todd
The first Marx Brothers vehicle written for the movies (co-scripted by S.J. Perelman) features the boys on a luxury liner. In one of the most memorable scenes, the brothers all pretend to be Maurice Chevalier to get off the ship.

Mr. Hulot's Holiday (1953)

Director: Jacques Tati
Cast: Jacques Tati and Nathalie Pascaud

Silent but for sound effects, Tati's *Mr. Hulot* is an inimitable comic creation and a crowd-pleaser on the order of Chaplin. The intricate gags never go stale.

My Darling Clementine (1946)

Director: John Ford
Cast: Henry Fonda, Linda Darnell, Victor Mature, Walter Brennan and Ward Bond

Though Ford's *Stagecoach* (1939) redefined the Western, this contemplative consideration of frontier life (with the O.K. Corrall shootout hovering menacingly in the background) continues to reward repeated viewing.

Nashville (1975)

Director: Robert Altman
Cast: Henry Gibson, Karen Black, Ronee Blakley, Keith Carradine, Geraldine Chaplin, Lily Tomlin and many more

Altman's defining film, set in America's country-music capital, follows 24 characters as their paths intersect during a weekend-long political rally. The film perfectly captures the political and cultural turmoil of the 1970s.

Network (1976)

Director: Sidney Lumet
Cast: William Holden, Faye Dunaway and Peter Finch

Paddy Chayefsky's prescient script satirizing broadcast journalism packs an even more powerful punch in our current era of tabloid television and the 10-second soundbite. Executives at a foundering network are willing to air anything, no matter how profane or outrageous, to boost ratings.

Out of the Past (1947)

Director: Jacques Tourneur
Cast: Robert Mitchum, Kirk Douglas, Jane Greer and Rhonda Fleming

The classic example of film noir. Though reference to noir seems to be considered *de rigeur* among today's young filmmakers, a glance at this corrosive film reveals the genuine article. Avoid the colorized version.

The Philadelphia Story (1940)

Director: George Cukor
Cast: James Stewart, Cary Grant and Katharine Hepburn

Three of the greatest screen performers of all time at the peak of their power and appeal in this classic that touches on divorce, class distinctions and the durability of true love.

The Quiet Man (1952)

Director: John Ford
Cast: John Wayne, Maureen O'Hara and Victor McLaglen

Ford digresses from his dusty trademark Westerns with this spirited love story set in lush Ireland. And what a rewarding digression it is. This stunning labor of love earned Ford an Oscar, and its beautiful scenery and score were also recognized with statuettes.

Raging Bull (1980)

Director: Martin Scorsese
Cast: Robert De Niro, Cathy Moriarty and Joe Pesci

Formal brilliance and heart-stopping performances make this one of the finest works of a director with many memorable films.

Rear Window (1954)

Director: Alfred Hitchcock
Cast: James Stewart, Grace Kelly, Wendell Corey and Thelma Ritter

This may seem an idiosyncratic pick of Hitchcock's work, but many film lovers respond to the metaphor of voyeurism in this story of murder observed. And it features a stylish, luminescent Kelly.

Rebel Without a Cause (1955)

Director: Nicholas Ray
Cast: James Dean, Natalie Wood, Sal Mineo and Dennis Hopper

Oh, to be young and on the fringe. Dean first made it cool in this classic melodrama about alienation and set the tone for every teen angst-fest thereafter. With its rich hues, distinguished Method acting and evocative cinematography, the film easily earns a place among America's most important cinematic milestones.

The Red Shoes (1948)

Directors: Michael Powell and Emeric Pressburger
Cast: Anton Walbrook, Marius Goring and Moira Shearer

Considered Powell and Pressburger's magnum opus, *The Red Shoes* is a well-crafted fairy tale about a ballerina caught between two domineering, creative men. Unusual for its seamless integration of dance sequences in the narrative, this film departs from more traditional musicals, which often separate the choreography from the story.

ROCKY (1976)

Director: John G. Avildsen
Cast: Sylvester Stallone, Talia Shire, Burt Young, Carl Weathers and Burgess Meredith

Stallone's intense portrayal of the punk fighter with a once-in-a-lifetime shot at the world heavyweight title carried this classic rags-to-ringside tale to a Best Picture Oscar and four sequels and handily established Sly's star power.

ROMEO AND JULIET (1968)

Director: Franco Zeffirelli
Cast: Leonard Whiting and Olivia Hussey

More is always more in a Zeffirelli production. The Italian film, stage and opera director's baroque sensibility make a perfect marriage with Shakespeare's tale of first love. By casting unknown teenagers Hussey and Whiting and his use of nudity and authentic locations, Zeffirelli endows the film with a primal, compelling air that will enchant even the most Shakespeare-resistant.

SATURDAY NIGHT FEVER (1977)

Director: John Badham
Cast: John Travolta, Karen Lynn Gorney, Barry Miller, Joseph Call and Paul Page

The white polyester suit. The pulsing Bee Gees soundtrack. The electric moves. Travolta strutted into stardom, all attitude and sexuality, to define the disco era in this dark tale of a working-class kid who finds escapism in dancing.

SCHINDLER'S LIST (1993)

Director: Steven Spielberg
Cast: Liam Neeson, Ben Kingsley and Ralph Fiennes

Undeniably one of the best films of the 1990s. Veering from his trademark high-tech blockbuster, Spielberg directed (and won his first Oscar for the effort) the black-and-white historical epic. Neeson is outstanding as the WWII profiteer who saved thousands of Jews by employing them in his factory and went broke in the process.

THE SEVEN SAMURAI (1954)

Director: Akira Kurosawa
Cast: Toshiro Mifune and Takashi Shimura

The Western of the East. Ironically, this Japanese film influenced many other Westerns, including the American remake, John Sturges's *The Magnificent Seven*. A group of villagers hire seven samurai to protect their property from bandits. Groundbreaking action sequences.

SHANE (1953)

Director: George Stevens
Cast: Alan Ladd, Jean Arthur, Van Heflin, Jack Palance and Brandon de Wilde

Breathtaking vistas and the classic squatters-versus-cattle-herders plot make this the ultimate Western. Jack Palance as the hired "black hat" turns in an unforgettably icy performance.

SINGIN' IN THE RAIN (1952)

Directors: Gene Kelly and Stanley Donen
Cast: Gene Kelly, Debbie Reynolds, Donald O'Connor and Cyd Charisse

One of the most innovative of film musicals — and among the cheeriest — this is a treat for eyes and ears.

SOME LIKE IT HOT (1959)

Director: Billy Wilder
Cast: Jack Lemmon, Tony Curtis and Marilyn Monroe

This hilarious gender-bender about two musicians who don wigs and heels to escape the mob is genius Wilder at his crackling best. The laughs never let up until the credits roll — and beyond, considering the legend that surrounds the film's funny final line.

THE SOUND OF MUSIC (1965)

Director: Robert Wise
Cast: Julie Andrews, Christopher Plummer and Angela Cartwright

The Sound of Music remains entertaining to this day, bolstered by its lush composition and charming score. Based on the true story of the Von Trapp family, who escaped Nazi-ruled Austria in 1938, this film dominated the 1965 Academy Awards, winning Oscars for Best Picture, Director, Score Adaptation and Editing.

STAGECOACH (1939)

Director: John Ford
Cast: John Wayne, John Carradine and Thomas Mitchell

This revolutionary Wayne cowboy adventure downplays elements typical of the genre and instead focuses on carefully-etched character studies. Marked by deft and efficient editing, as well as remarkable camera work, *Stagecoach* transcends the traditional shoot-'em-up.

STAIRWAY TO HEAVEN (1946)

Directors: Michael Powell and Emeric Pressburger
Cast: David Niven, Kim Hunter, Raymond Massey and Roger Livesy

Probably not the first choice of many to represent the work of Powell and Pressburger, but this meditation on the line between life and death is a beguiling mix of fantasy and reality, a specialty of the two influential directors.

A Streetcar Named Desire (1951)

Director: Elia Kazan
Cast: Marlon Brando, Karl Malden, Vivien Leigh and Kim Hunter
This definitive adaptation of Tennessee Williams's play takes a dark look at daily life in a steamy New Orleans tenement slum. Broodingly sensual Brando made his mark with this film, bellowing his signature, "Stelllla!!," Ironically, he was the only actor of the four leads not to win an Oscar.

Sunrise (1927)

Director: F.W. Murnau
Cast: George O'Brien, Janet Gaynor and Margaret Livingston
The story of a farmer planning to murder his wife for another woman, though a simple story, is a fine example of the influence of German Expressionism on Hollywood and one of film's greatest cinematic love stories.

The Thin Man (1934)

Director: W.S. Van Dyke
Cast: William Powell, Myrna Loy and Maureen O'Sullivan
Powell and Loy define screen chemistry in the best example of romantic comedy/mystery. This is the first entry in a series of romps that established Powell's roguish wit and Loy's exasperated vivacity.

Throne of Blood (1957)

Director: Akira Kurosawa
Cast: Toshiro Mifune and Isuzu Yamada
Set in the milieu of a samurai film, this is arguably one of the greatest movie settings of *Macbeth*.

To Kill a Mockingbird (1962)

Director: Robert Mulligan
Cast: Gregory Peck, Mary Badham and Robert Duvall
Purely a sentimental pick, this is a film parents will want to show their children both for its moral sense and because it so lovingly captures a child's point of view.

Top Hat (1935)

Director: Mark Sandrich
Cast: Fred Astaire, Ginger Rogers, Edward Everett Horton and Eric Blore
Though it's difficult to select one Astaire/Rogers song-and-dance masterpiece, this one features the lovely "Cheek to Cheek."

12 Angry Men (1957)

Director: Sidney Lumet
Cast: Henry Fonda, Lee J. Cobb, Jack Warden, Ed Begley, E.G. Marshall and Jack Klugman
Lumet's brilliant feature-film debut about one man who tries to convince 11 other jurors to reconsider their conviction makes an enduring, provocative statement about the American justice system. Completely dialogue-driven, this psychological drama features several actors on the brink of major stardom.

2001: A Space Odyssey (1968)

Director: Stanley Kubrick
Cast: Keir Dullea, William Sylvester and Gary Lockwood
Now considered a masterwork, this futuristic tale was probably the single most cryptic and daring film to come out of Hollywood in its day. Notorious for its extended use of fixed camera and non-dialogue sequences, the visually stunning picture is an ambitious meditation on the evolution of humankind across the milleniums.

Willy Wonka and the Chocolate Factory (1971)

Director: Mel Stuart
Cast: Gene Wilder, Jack Albertson, Peter Ostrum, Roy Kinnear and Aubrey Woods
Wonka's guided tour through the mysterious Chocolate Factory is as enduring as, well, an Everlasting Gobstopper. From the bratty histrionics of Veruca Salt to the creepy yet sage Oompa-Loompas, the film offers surreal satire for adults and a fantastical allegory for kids.

The Wizard of Oz (1939)

Director: Victor Fleming
Cast: Judy Garland, Ray Bolger, Jack Haley, Bert Lahr, Margaret Hamilton and Billie Burke

If you must have just one of MGM's (and Fleming's!) color colossi of 1939, then this is the one. Even more so than *Gone With the Wind*, this charmer remains fresh and continues to appeal to audiences young and old.

Woman of the Year (1942)

Director: George Stevens
Cast: Katharine Hepburn and Spencer Tracy
This is where it all began, the debut of the Hepburn/Tracy team that collaborated (on- and offscreen) for 25 years until Tracy's death in 1967. Hepburn, a high-brow foreign-affairs reporter, falls for colleague Tracy, a low-key sportswriter. Their unlikely marriage survives Hepburn's commitment to her career and noncommital homemaking.

Classic Movies on Video

Home video distributors are emptying the movie archives to supply a seemingly endless demand for movie videos, giving home audiences the chance to see some of the timeless work of cinema's first century. Here are some of the classic movie tapes released between September 1995 and August 1996 that we enjoyed this year.

THE BLACK PIRATE (1926)

Kino; $24.95 (NR)
Director: Albert Parker
Cast: Douglas Fairbanks, Billie Dove, Donald Crisp and Sam DeGrasse
One of the first feature films shot entirely in an early form of Technicolor, this 1926 silent showcases the dashing Fairbanks as a mysterious swashbuckler out for revenge. Gorgeous cinematography and a classic vehicle for Hollywood's first heartthrob.

FOR WHOM THE BELL TOLLS (1943)

MCA/Universal; $19.98 (NR)
Director: Sam Wood
Cast: Gary Cooper and Ingrid Bergman

The classic Hemingway story of an American demolitions expert sent to Spain during the Spanish Civil War to blow up a bridge for the Loyalist guerillas comes with restored footage, overtures and intermission music.

A HARD DAY'S NIGHT (1964)

MPI; $19.98 (G)
Director: Richard Lester
Cast: Paul McCartney, John Lennon, Ringo Starr and George Harrison
This special edition, re-release of the 1964 day in the life of the Fab Four is a must-have for any movie and Beatle fan.

IT'S A WONDERFUL LIFE 50TH ANNIVERSARY DELUXE EDITION (1946)

Republic Pictures Home Video; $79.98 (NR)
Director: Frank Capra
Cast: James Stewart and Donna Reed
For those who can take another viewing, the Christmas chestnut has been digitally upgraded and includes the original 1946 trailer, a theatrical poster, a 365-page book and a short making-of documentary.

JAWS (1975)

MCA/Universal; $19.98 (PG)
Director: Steven Spielberg
Cast: Roy Scheider, Richard Dreyfuss and Robert Shaw
Celebrating *Jaws*'s 20th anniversary, MCA/Universal has released on video the first video letterboxed edition of the film and included 10 minutes of interviews with the cast and Spielberg. The re-release couldn't have come at a better time as most of the original tapes in video stores are beaten up almost beyond recognition.

THE OLD DARK HOUSE (1932)

Kino; $24.95 (NR)
Director: Jame Whale
Cast: Boris Karloff, Melvyn Douglas, Charles Laughton and Gloria Stuart

This follow-up to Whale's 1931 Frankenstein delivers an unshakable case of the creeps. While the plot is familiar — lost travelers stranded in an eerie mansion — the house's inhabitants are anything but expected: Boris Karloff as a mute butler and actress Elspeth Dudgeon as the household's 102-year-old patriarch (yes, patriach).

THE PHANTOM OF THE OPERA (1929)

Kino; $24.95 (NR)
Directors: Rupert Julian, Edward Sedgwick and Ernst Laemmle
Cast: Lon Chaney and Mary Philbin
One of the most famous horror movies ever created has finally made it to video in this restored, tinted version. Chaney is unforgettable as the masked villainous composer in love with his understudy. The new score does pose a problem: The arias don't work with the silent film.

Foreign Films on Video

Home video releases let us see some of the foreign films that have a limited big-screen release in this country. Here's what got our attention between September 1995 and August 1996.

BEFORE THE RAIN

PolyGram; rental pricing (NR)
Director: Milcho Manchevski
Cast: Katrin Cartlidge, Rade Seerbedzija, Gregoire Colin and Labina Mitevska
The Former Yugoslav Republic of Macedonia

Three seemingly unrelated stories overlap forming a heart-wrenching drama of violence, hatred and war that was nominated for a Best Foreign Language Film Oscar. In "Words," a monk harbors an Albanian girl; a British woman contemplates leaving her husband for a photographer in "Faces"; and in "Pictures" the photographer returns to his war-torn Macedonian village.

BELLE DE JOUR

Miramax; rental pricing (R)
Director: Luis Buñuel
Cast: Catherine Deneuve and Jean Sorel
France
Elusive Severine is outwardly passive and distant, even with her adoring husband. Inwardly, she is beset by complex, intense sexual fantasies, which eventually draw her to afternoon prostitution in a brothel. A ruthless young gangster becomes obsessed with her, and the resulting tragedy brings further fantasies. The most elegant of Buñuel's surreal masterpieces.

BURNT BY THE SUN

Columbia TriStar; rental pricing (NR)
Director: Nikita Mikhalkov
Cast: Nikita Mikhalkov and Ingeborga Dapkunaite
Russia
Set in 1936 Russia, the Kotov family enjoy an idyllic Sunday in the beautiful countryside. The tranquility will not last as Stalin begins his brutal rule. This film won the 1994 Academy Award for Best Foreign Language Film.

THE CITY OF LOST CHILDREN

Columbia TriStar; rental pricing (R)
Director: Jean-Pierre Jeunet
Cast: Ron Perlman, Dominique Pinon, Daniel Emilfork and Judith Vittet
France

In this surreal fantasy, a brilliant but mad scientist is aging prematurely because he can't dream. To stay alive, he resorts to capturing children to steal their dreams. Creeepy.

EXOTICA

Miramax; rental pricing (R)
Director: Atom Egoyaan
Cast: Mia Kirshner, Don McKellar and Elias Koteas
Canada

This is what *Showgirls* wasn't — a quality film about strip clubs and their personnel. A stripper is involved with the club owner and also has a spiritual relationship with a tragic club regular, who is an auditor investigating a gay exotic-bird smuggler.

FARINELLI

Columbia TriStar; rental pricing (R)
Director: Gérard Corbiau
Cast: Stéfano Dionisi, Enrico Lo Verso, Elsa Zylberstein and Jeroen Krabbe
Belgium
The madcap travels of four very different brothers — one's a veritable Pavarotti, the other's an opera hack, the third's a gorgeous castrato who has the last brother, er, finish what he starts. Set in 18th-century Europe, this amusing romp of three Italian stallions and one gelding is an artfully original take on the powers of seduction.

HEIMAT

Facets Multimedia, Inc.; rental pricing (NR)
Director: Edgar Reitz
Cast: Getrud Bredel, Marita Breuer and Dieter Schaad
France
This massive chronicle of small-town life in Germany from 1919 to 1982 is an extraordinary film experience. Set aside a weekend to watch it — at nearly 16 hours long, the rich drama made history as the longest film ever when it debuted in 1984.

I Am Cuba

Milestone; rental pricing (NR)
Director: Mikhail Kalatozov
Cast: José Gallardo and Luz Maria Collazo
Cuba/Russia
This exquisitely filmed production collected dust in an archive for 30 years before Martin Scorsese and Francis Ford Coppola arranged to bring it stateside. The Communist kitsch-fest explores the struggles of a prostitute, a down-on-his-luck sharecropper and student activists under Fulgencio Batista's tyrannical reign.

Love After Love

Orion; rental pricing (NR)
Director: Diane Kurys
Cast: Isabelle Huppert and Bernard Giraudeau
France
Certainly not a sugar-coated Hollywood love story. Novelist Lola is involved in a love triangle, complicated by the fact that the two men she is involved with both have families. Given the short end of the stick by both beaux, Lola manages to have the last word.

Lyrical Nitrate

Kino; rental pricing (NR)
Director: Peter Delpeut
Netherlands
This Dutch experimental documentary weaves together unrelated fragments from vintage silent films discovered in a delapitated Amsterdam theater. The result is an unexpectedly touching, visually captivating nod to the past.

The Mystery of Rampo

Evergreen; rental pricing (NR)
Director: Kazuyoshi Okuyama
Cast: Naoto Takenaka and Michiko Hada
Japan
This imaginative thriller combines superb acting and psychedelic computer animation to explore the inner workings of a writer's mind. Rampo, a mystery novelist, falls in love with one of his characters, a stunning creation but every bit the femme fatale.

Once Were Warriors

New Line Home Video; rental pricing (R)
Director: Lee Tamahori
Cast: Rena Owen, Temuera Morrison and Mamaengaroa Kerr-Bell
New Zealand
This powerful study of a New Zealand Maori mother fighting to keep her kin together explodes into a disturbing commentary on a troubled culture and modern family life.

Red Firecracker, Green Firecracker

Evergreen; rental pricing (NR)
Director: He Ping
Cast: Ning Jing and Wu Gang
China
A sweet tale of love. Orphan Chun Zhi heads her family's firecracker empire and falls in love with an adventurous artist. Before Chun Zhi's father died, he forbade her from ever marrying, fearing that the business would fall into the wrong hands. Insanely jealous, her chief assistant is willing to do anything to end the affair.

Shanghai Triad

Columbia TriStar; rental pricing (R)
Director: Zhang Yimou
Cast: Gong Li, Wang Xiao and Li Boatian
China
See page 89

Son of the Shark

Fox Lorber; rental pricing (NR)
Director: Agnes Merlet
Cast: Ludovic Vandendaele and Erick Da Silva
France
This shocking French film follows two unruly brothers as they compulsively vandalize their town. After the older brother is sent away to reformatory school, he escapes and travels for miles to reunite with his sibling for an unforgettable crime spree.

Strawberry and Chocolate

Miramax; rental pricing (R)
Directors: Tomás Guitiérrez Alea and Juan Carlos Tabio
Cast: Vladimir Cruz, Jorge Perugorría and Mirta Ibarra
Cuba
A virginal, heterosexual man involved in Cuba's Communist League becomes the object of a homosexual's desires, and the two men develop a platonic relationship. Things get really interesting when a suicidal woman makes the pair a triangle.

Significant Laserdiscs of 1995–1996

With greater image and audio fidelity and the addition of scenes, directors' cuts and behind-the-scenes footage, laserdiscs are fast becoming the cinephile's choice of home-theater format. These are some of the laserdiscs that we noticed between September 1995 and August 1996.

ABSOLUTELY FABULOUS

FoxVideo; three-disc boxed set $99.98
From the television series; NR
Cast: Jennifer Saunders and Joanna Lumley

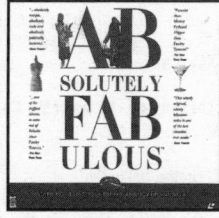

The British sitcom that gained a cult following in the United States on cable's Comedy Central is even more fabulous on disc with superior sound and picture quality. Twelve episodes are included in the set, but an entire season is missing, which makes the set not quite absolutely fabulous.

AMADEUS

Pioneer; $44.95
Feature; PG
Director: Milos Forman
Cast: F. Murray Abraham and Tom Hulce

The Oscar-winning foppery transfers well to this limited edition disc that features a new letterbox version, enhanced audio, a two-CD soundtrack and a copy of Peter Shaffer's 1980 play. A documentary with six restored scenes and director Forman's amusing tidbits about the frisky forefathers of classical music round out the bonuses.

THE ART OF BUSTER KEATON

Kino; vols. 1 and 3, $99.99; vol. 2, $139.99
Feature; NR

Well worth the investment for fans of the silent era's master actor and director, this collector's edition features 10 discs in three boxed-set volumes. All 11 of Keaton's independent features and 19 of his shorts are included in this high-quality transfer.

THE BICYCLE THIEF

Corinth/Image; $39.99
Feature; NR
Director: Vittorio De Sica
Cast: Lamberto Magiorani and Enzo Staiola

One of the most heartbreaking films of all time, this 1948 neorealist drama follows an Italian laborer's search through post-World War II Rome to find the stolen bicycle he needs to support his family. The laserdisc version offers superior black-and-white picture quality and easy-to-read bright yellow subtitles, while the analog soundtrack contains a well-dubbed track in English.

A BOY AND HIS DOG

Lumivision; $39.95
Feature; R
Director: L.Q. Jones
Cast: Don Johnson, Susan Benton and Jason Robards

This study of life after World War IV didn't make a big splash — or make its young star, Don Johnson, a sensation — when it premiered in 1975. But more than 20 years later, the film has attained cult status through midnight movie screenings and college film festivals. The new widescreen transfer is crisp (though there is a frame or two missing) and features insightful commentary by director Jones, cinematographer John Morrill and film critic Charles Champlin on the sci-fi favorite's much-discussed symbolism.

THE CABINET OF DR. CALIGARI

Image; $49.99
Feature; NR
Director: Robert Wiene
Cast: Werner Krauss and Conrad Veidt

The disc version of the original 1919 art-house horror film features speed correction, color tinting and, as a rare treat for the classic movie lover, the original hand-rendered title cards. This is where the German expressionist movement began.

CLERKS

Miramax/Image; $39.99
Feature; R
Director: Kevin Smith
Cast: Brian O'Halloran and Jeff Anderson

One may wonder what the low-budget, critically acclaimed, black-and-white film about a day in the life of two clerks could gain on laserdisc — not much in sound or visual quality, but the bogus original ending that has one of the clerks killed in a robbery and the running commentary make this disc worth having.

BEST-SELLING SOFTWARE OF 1996

The following list reflects software hits for the first half of 1996:

CD-ROM TITLES

1. **Microsoft Windows '95 Upgrade** (Microsoft)
2. **Turbo Tax Deluxe — Final** (Intuit)
3. **Warcraft II** (Davidson)
4. **Corel Printhouse** (Corel)
5. **Myst** (Brøderbund)

HOME EDUCATION TITLES FOR MS-DOS, WINDOWS AND WINDOWS '95

1. **Toy Story Animated Storybook** (Disney)
2. **Math Blaster: In Search of Spot** (Davidson)
3. **Pocahontas Animated Storybook** (Disney)
4. **Mathematics Box Set** (SofSource)
5. **Lion King Activity Center** (Disney)

HOME EDUCATION TITLES FOR MACINTOSH

1. **Mavis Beacon Teaches Typing** (Mindscape)
2. **Lion King Activity Center** (Disney)
3. **Pocahontas Animated Storybook** (Disney)
4. **Winnie the Pooh** (Disney)
5. **Kid's Mac Pack** (Palladium Interactive)

GAMES FOR MS-DOS, WINDOWS AND WINDOWS '95

1. **Warcraft II** (Davidson)
2. **Myst** (Brøderbund)
3. **Civilization 2** (MicroProse)
4. **Microsoft Flight Simulator** (Microsoft)
5. **Duke Nukem 3D** (Formgen)

MACINTOSH GAMES

1. **Myst** (Brøderbund)
2. **Top Ten Pack** (Electronic Arts)
3. **Warcraft II** (Davidson)
4. **Links Pro** (Access)
5. **X-Wing Collector's CD** (LucasArts)

Source: PC Data

COOL HAND LUKE

Warner; $39.98
Feature; NR
Director: Stuart
Rosenberg
Cast: Paul Newman
and George Kennedy
While this film has
not proved as time-
less as other Newman
outings, the classic
star is still memo-

rable as the tough-guy loner sent to a chain-gang camp. The infamous "egg scene," as well as a parade of now-famous faces — Harry Dean Stanton, Dennis Hopper, Joe Don Baker and Wayne Rogers — make this a good buy for loyal Newman fans.

DO THE RIGHT THING

Voyager; $124.95
Feature; R
Director: Spike Lee
Cast: Danny Aiello, John Turturro and Spike Lee
Lee's commentary on the racial divide is even more appropriate in the post-O.J. era than it was in 1989 when the movie was first released. A wide-screen transfer, a narrative by director of photography Ernest Dickerson, a making-of documentary and Lee's own videos shot on the set make this three-disc set a satisfying buy.

THE DOORS COLLECTION

MCA/Universal; $69.95
Music; NR
This two-disc package rocks with remastered performance compilations, revealing commentary from the surviving band members and two of keyboardist Ray Manzarek's student films from his bohemian days at UCLA.

THE GENE KELLY COLLECTION

MGM/UA; $124.98
Feature; NR
The breathtaking, athletic dances take center stage in this four-disc set. Three complete movies — 1949's *On the Town*, 1954's *Brigadoon* and 1955's *It's Always Fair Weather* — and plenty of studio outtakes make this collector's edition a tribute to cherish.

GOLDFINGER: THE DELUXE COLLECTOR'S EDITION

MGM/UA; $99.98
Feature; PG
Director: Guy Hamilton
Cast: Sean Connery
and Gert Frobe

The golden babe. The slick car. It's all here in a new letterbox version that includes two making-of documentaries narrated by '60s TV Bond Patrick Macnee. There are enough interviews and supplemental material here to fill both analog tracks and two sides of a third disc. A must for 007 fans.

GUNGA DIN

Turner/Image; $59.99
Feature; NR
Director: George Stevens
Cast: Cary Grant and Victor McLaglen

Perhaps still the best Hollywood action/adventure story, certainly much more entertaining than any Stallone or Seagal outing, *Gunga Din* gets even better on laserdisc. This version, from a fully restored print, includes home movies Stevens shot during production and an audio track that has William Goldman calling *Gunga Din* the best film ever made.

HENRY V

Voyager; $69.95
Feature; NR
Director: Laurence Olivier
Cast: Laurence Olivier, Robert Newton, Leslie Banks and Renee Asherson

Olivier's directing debut earned him a special Academy Award for "his outstanding achievement as actor, producer and director in bringing *Henry V* to the screen." The original was beautifully shot, capturing the flavor of the Globe Theatre in the 1500s, and the laserdisc is even more visually stunning.

HIS GIRL FRIDAY

Columbia TriStar; $39.95
Feature; NR
Director: Howard Hawks
Cast: Cary Grant and Rosalind Russell

This was a must-see even before it was released on laserdisc. Understandably many were turned off by the video, which was washed out and cacophonous. The soundtrack was cleaned up for laser release and looks as close to the 1940 original as one could ever hope. Grant is the scheming editor who tries to keep his star reporter (and former wife) on the job and prevent her from remarrying.

THE INNOCENTS

FoxVideo; $39.98
Feature; NR
Director: Jack Clayton
Cast: Deborah Kerr and Michael Redgrave

It's unfortunate that *The Innocents* never really found an audience; it's a great horror film. This

THE BEST-SELLING VIDEO GAME SOFTWARE OF 1995

1. **Donkey Kong Country,** Super Nintendo (Nintendo of America)

2. **Mortal Kombat III,** Super Nintendo (Williams Entertainment)

3. **Killer Instinct,** Super Nintendo (Nintendo of America)

4. **Mortal Kombat III,** Sega Genesis (Williams Entertainment)

5. **Donkey Kong Land,** Gameboy (Nintendo of America)

6. **Donkey Kong Country,** Super Nintendo (Nintendo of America)

7. **Yoshi's Island,** Super Nintendo (Nintendo of America)

8. **Madden NFL '96,** Sega Genesis (Electronic Arts)

9. **NBA Jam Tournament Edition,** Sega Genesis (Acclaim Entertainment)

10. **NBA Jam Tournament Edition,** Super Nintendo (Acclaim Entertainment)

11. **Mortal Kombat II,** Sega Genesis (Acclaim Entertainment)

12. **Lion King,** Super Nintendo (Virgin Interactive Entertainment)

13. **NBA Live '96,** Sega Genesis (Electronic Arts)

14. **'96 NHL,** Sega Genesis (Electronic Arts)

15. **Super Mario Land,** Gameboy (Nintendo of America)

Source: The NPD Group, Inc.

video debut on letterboxed laserdisc provides another opportunity. Based on Henry James's *The Turn of the Screw*, Kerr plays a governess at Redgrave's country estate who is convinced his children are possessed, and she sees apparitions that further evidence her suspicions. Repressed sexuality in the film was a big departure from typical films of the late 1950s and early '60s.

THE LION KING

Walt Disney/Image; $29.95
Feature/Animation; G
Director: Roger Allen and Rob Minkoff
Voices of: Jonathan Taylor Thomas, James Earl Jones, Whoopi Goldberg, Matthew Broderick and Jeremy Irons
The Disney classic has already made millions with the theatrical and video releases, and now it is destined for the record books again with the laserdisc release. With good reason. The package is loaded with a making-of documentary, commentary by the directors and producer and two discs that outline in great detail the character development process. A true gem.

A NIGHTMARE ON ELM STREET

Elite; $99.95
Feature; R
Director: Wes Craven
Cast: Heather Langenkamp and Robert Englund
Horror fans who caught every installment of Freddie Krueger's slashfests will rejoice at this letterboxed edition of the original featuring the first stereo soundtrack (imagine what those finger knives sound like now!) and commentary by Craven and the cast. As if that weren't enough, hear rejection letters from Hollywood bigwigs who probably experienced a few nightmares of their own after passing on Craven's lucrative screenplay.

THE ODD COUPLE

Paramount; $39.98
Feature; G
Director: Gene Saks
Cast: Jack Lemmon and Walter Matthau
See the Grumpy Old Men in their prime with this letterboxed version of the witty Neil Simon comedy. Fans who have found themselves as testy as Felix and Oscar over the poor video transition (the transfer from wide-screen often left only one of the mismatched roommates visible at a time) will cheer the laserdisc's reunion of the two onscreen.

RE-ANIMATOR

Elite; $49.95
Feature; NR
Director: Stuart Gordon
Cast: Jeffrey Combs and Bruce Abbott
Gordon goes over the edge in a few scenes, but the gore qualifies as a guilty pleasure, especially on laserdisc. The letterbox transfer, running commentary and unused footage make this classic horror flick unforgettable. The story: A medical student invents a serum to bring the dead back to life.

THE ROCKY HORROR PICTURE SHOW — 20TH ANNIVERSARY SPECIAL EDITION

FoxVideo; $124.98
Music; R
Director: Jim Sharman
Cast: Tim Curry, Susan Sarandon and Meat Loaf
Gather your friends, toast and newspapers and get ready to do the Time Warp. This deluxe, letterboxed edition of the king of all cult movies is chock full of extras, including a soundtrack CD with unreleased music, numerous outtakes, two musical sequences that didn't make the final cut, a documentary on the film's fan subculture, a book by its fan-club president, original trailers and a new audience-participation track recorded at two California theaters.

THE USUAL SUSPECTS

PolyGram; $34.95
Feature; R
Director: Bryan Singer
Cast: Gabriel Byrne, Kevin Spacey, Kevin Pollak, Chazz Palminteri and Stephen Baldwin
Director Singer and writer Christopher McQuarrie lead viewers through the twisting, stylish crime saga on an alternate soundtrack, pointing out parts that confused even them. They also discuss the casting of Byrne as one of the five career criminals who have united to carry out a mysterious crime lord's commands. You still might not get who Kaiser Sosé is, but you will notice a crisper and cleaner picture quality on this transfer.

Nitecrawler

■ BY PAULINA BORSOOK

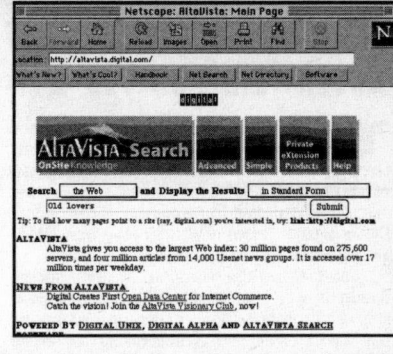

Past 2 a.m., raining. There was no one to E-mail, no one to talk to, simply the company of my own indwelling self-doubt monsters and longings ill-becoming my station. What there was, was to hit Alta Vista and get into trouble.

Of course, I wanted to trick the machine, skeptical it could do anything for me. I gave it a string that I was sure it couldn't find, that of my Great Lost Love (elsewhere referred to as Dirk Van Hooeven, whose absence is always present, much like the red-shift of receding stars). I typed in Dirk's name and waited for Alta Vista to stall. As far as I knew, Dirk, a high-ranking officer in the cabals of global finance, had nothing to do with the Net land-grab or the silliness of personal Web pages or anything tasteless or technologically off-point, ever.

CYBERLIFE

But the infernal machine came up with nine matches — my jaw would have dropped if there had been a human interpreter to see it.

Ghost traces of Dirk in HTML, he existed in the form of portfolio-management conference proceedings, official bios and agendas. Business-to-business marketing on the Web had placed him within my grasp for sicko late-night lonesome cowgirl inspections.

And if I wanted to, right then and there in the privacy of my own home, I could have ordered a two-hour tape of Dirk talking (about the latest in barely legal financial chicanery, no doubt. No matter.). For only $30 I could have delivered by snailmail, in plain brown businessy wrapping, his patented chesty rumble that had always made me go mush. I thought about making the purchase — but I couldn't do it.

Too humiliating, too akin to my feeling about sex toys — sad and shoddy phantasms of Genuine Contact. I scanned the rest of the listings. I could tell he'd moved back to New York from L.A., changed jobs. If I wanted to, I could now call him at his to-me new Manhattan office and say, "Hey, Dirk, play 'Misty' for me!"

I logged off, aghast and *encoeure*. I hadn't meant to, yet in using Alta Vista I had become a snoop, stalking Dirk online. And I knew that from now on, I would probably be able to trace his whereabouts, his career — better and faster and cheaper than the use of any private detective. Unless Dirk ceased from being a financial double-alpha, as business went more and more online, it would be easier and easier to be up-to-date on his life.

I had done something really sickening.

Nevertheless I couldn't help myself. Having seen what Alta Vista could do with Dirk, who didn't really belong in cyberspace, I wanted to see what it would do with Wretch, who did.

Wretch, my first date in two years and head technologist for an entertainment combine (call it FlameBoyCo). Wretch was much inclined to giving good quote about better business practices on the 'Net. And while nothing had ever really happened between me and Wretch, like a splinter under the skin, he was a foreign body my system of psychoneuro-immunology was taking a long time to dissolve.

Since Wretch, unlike Dirk, did have a vanilla, probably-would-score-Web-hits-in-the-thousands kinda name — let's say "Charles Forbes" — I did a search on "Charles Forbes and FlameBoy."

Sure enough, Alta Vista was happy to show me Wretch, sounding like his usual charismatic/flake self. I could just imagine his intonations, his moues, his practiced aw-shucks-knock'em-dead force, as I read the transcript of a radio interview with him and another Net-

You can just picture it: Ad execs hunched around a conference-room table, anxiously chewing on the ends of their horn-rimmed glasses and tapping their pens against their leather Filofaxes. There had to be some way to conquer the fertile, uncharted territory of the World Wide Web. Imagine the demographics!

Imagine they did, and onto the Web sprung hundreds of electronic billboards, cyber-sponsorships and corporate home pages. How successful has Madison Avenue been in courting this on-line area notorious for its guard against commercialism? We asked Michael Schrage, *Adweek* editor at large and a contributor to *Wired* magazine.

GOOD-BYE "BROCHURE-WARE"

Many companies rushed to secure their slice of cyberia by converting four-color brochures to HTML and slapping them up on the Web. These static billboards were not particularly effective or interesting, but, hey, at least you could say they were there, or so went the twisted rationale. No more, says Schrage, who gladly recognizes the early extinction of "brochure-ware."

"In the last year, advertisers began to get it that the Internet is another medium, that the World Wide Web is a platform for media just like radio and TV," he said. "Smart companies are not using it as another outlet to dump their marketing materials."

With the introduction of multimedia software such as Shockwave and Java, many companies began spicing up their Web pages in 1995 with more interactive content and actually made them useful by adding order forms and other direct-mail functions.

THE FUTURE

"Why can't the Web be more like TV?" cried the bewildered advertisers. Schrage observes that, in fact, the marketing and advertising industries are slowly getting their way. He expects to soon see an online hybrid commercial that plays like a 15-second TV spot but which allows surfers to purchase the advertised product through their computers.

Schrage also anticipates the often sacred line between advertising and editorial will begin to blur. "If I post an article on the Web that mentions Fidelity Investments and then has a hyperlink to Fidelity's home page for more information, is that promotional?" he asked. "I don't know."

Never mind journalistic ethics. What about all those hard-core 'Netheads still moaning about the online barrage of corporate logos and promotional pitches? Schrage shrugs off the grumbling: "No matter where they are, ads are going to be annoying." — ALICIA POTTER

business-expert guy. It brought Wretch back vividly; a shameful flareup of the infatuation I had tamped down months before.

Still, I was into it. I had to go for it.

I re-engaged with the accursed Alta Vista, called up his listings again. And then the strangest damned thing happened: I was directed to a bunch of queer websites. Hunh? I skimmed them with increasing dismay — until I ran across the mention of the outing of Forbes and Flameboy. Flameboy, the eponymous founder of the company Wretch worked for, was famously gay in Hollywood.

I logged off again. Was that what it had been? That Wretch, in spite of his statements ("I'm not gay") and actions (bragging about how much money he made had appeared to be a typical Regular Guy display to impress a female he wanted to bed) to the contrary, was gay? I'd had reasons to wonder, and it would be much nicer to ascribe his herkyjerky/hotcold behavior to sexual indeterminacy. Better a closet case than (as a friend said), "a lovely turd." I thought about what had the look and feel of an unwanted discovery. At the very least, it didn't seem right that the Web should be the means for outing a former potential object of desire.

I sat at my computer, motionless, the screen still carrying evidence of this latest adventure in data-mining, apparently so incriminating of Wretch. Nauseated at what could be retrieved by anyone about anyone, or what could appear to be retrieved; totally thrown by what maybe it seemed I had come across (being lied to, a closet life). Then it came to me: Alta Vista in its machine literal-mindness had approximated my Charles Forbes with the outed Malcolm Forbes (a close, not exact, match).

And though I was able to salvage my mate-hunting amourpropre (and maintain the historic good hit-rate of my hyper-sensitive Martian perceptual apparati), I remained disturbed that it was so easy to have drawn the wrong conclusions, extracted the wrong "information," done research assumed to be correct because done by computer, when because of the ways humans fill in the spaces in between — it was wrong.

With some relief, Wretch slipped back into the category I had constructed for him with much will and reluctance months before — like the Doubtful Case in Camus's *The Plague,* Wretch remained ambivalent for damned sure, but probably not about the gender of those he wanted to toy with.

By 4 A.M., I finally finished my network antics, after trying out the name of my ex-husband, the name of the second guy I'd slept with (a draft-dodger I had fallen in love with when I had been a 15-year-old runaway), and the first of my smooth-talking good-looking SOBs (an erratically brilliant CalTech undergrad who had gone down in history as my first encounter with my weakness for polymath sociopaths). Thank goddess none of them was there.

And Dirk wouldn't know, and Wretch wouldn't know, that I had been sidling up to them for hours.

Yet when I logged out for the last time, I was afraid of E-mail that might await me from Wretch or Dirk. Somehow, through the genius of magical thinking, my scare at getting caught lead me to fear they might link back to me through my linking to their names on the Web.

The guilt about acting furtive was about as rational as the atavistic fear of contagion that erupted as I had held the hand of my best friend as he lay dying of AIDS in San Francisco General Ward 5A. Though I knew better, I had still gotten tested a few months later. So it was with assuming my lost subjects-for-limerance would be able to tell I had been pawing at them electronically, like a possum or chipmunk scrabbling through papers on their desks. I was afraid of little trackmarks or scuffles, signs of (tele)presence.

It had become clear even before the sun came up that I could be updated on the World Wide Web life of Dirk and Wretch as each week Alta Vista enhanced and refreshed itself. And I knew I would not do it. The gesture was sneaky and unclean. Unrequited love should more honorably be left where it's always belonged: in the body — the head and the heart — and not in discorporated electronic pulses of intelligent agents — of those who pine. ∎

TOP WORLD WIDE WEB ADVERTISING SITES

Total advertising revenue for the first half of 1996 was an estimated $71.7 million. These sites raked in the most advertising dollars:

1. Netscape
2. InfoSeek
3. Yahoo!
4. Lycos
5. Excite
6. CNET
7. ZD Net
8. NewsPage
9. ESPNET SportsZone
10. WebCrawler

Source: Jupiter Communications

TOP WORLD WIDE WEB ADVERTISERS

These companies spent the most on Web advertising for the first half of 1996:

1. Microsoft
2. InfoSeek
3. Excite
4. McKinley Group
5. Netscape
6. Yahoo!
7. Lycos
8. AT&T
9. CNET
10. NYNEX

Source: Jupiter Communications

Recommended Internet Sites

Here's a selection of cool and useful Web sites the editors of *The Entertainment Almanac* came across while surfing the Internet.

Addicted to Noise
http://www.addicted.com
This slick Webzine with neon-bright, pop-art graphics dishes daily buzz about the alternative-music scene. In-depth interviews with current chart-toppers, as well as bands on the cusp of stardom, make this on-line read as addicting as the music it follows.

The All-Music Guide
http://thenewage.com
A humongous searchable database of fair-minded music reviews from all genres. Trace music history by following each artist's hyperlinks to related and influential performers. A must-visit on your Internet itinerary.

@tlas
http://atlas.organic.com
This stylish on-line 'zine blends international photography, intense graphics and thoughtful journalism for a cerebral digital read.

AudioNet
http://www.audionet.com
The Internet's definitive broadcast network, this site uses real-time sound technology, RealAudio, to deliver a variety of radio-style programming, from sports and current events to concerts and business, as well as links to other RealAudio stations online. Well worth a look and a listen.

BookWire
http://www.bookwire.com
For surfers who love to read, BookWire presents a comprehensive guide to book-related sources on the Internet, including bestseller lists, book reviews and a calendar of events.

Classical Music Online
http://www.crl.com/~virtualv/cmo
Though a bit highbrow, CMO is quite thorough, providing artist, agent and composer information; a classified section; music school and college listings; news (with contributions from *Gramophone*, *Opera News* and *CD Review* writers); and international performance dates.

Dance Directory
http://www.cyberspace.com/vandehay/dance.html
This site is no more than a list of links, but what a list it is, covering everything from the lindy and ballet to folk and modern dance.

Dear Doc
http://deardoc.artifex.net/
This useful, well-designed site features a candid physician (with a degree from McGill University) who explains rumors, statistics and historical facts in lay language. Search for a topic, post a query or cruise separate forums dedicated to men's, women's and teens' health issues.

Electronic Frontier Foundation
http://www.eff.org/
The nonprofit civil liberties organization working to protect privacy and free expression online provides calls to arms and legislative updates.

Film Music
http://www.filmmusic.com
From Vangelis to Williams to Conti, this site lists 6,300 movie soundtracks with links to reviews, sound clips and fan sites. For those looking to add a couple of blockbuster scores to their CD collection, there's also a connection to purchase memorable (and obscure) film soundtracks.

Firefly
http://www.ffly.com
Build an online personal music-preference profile that suggests what artists you might enjoy based on your current tastes, or chat with other music lovers to find out what they recommend. There's also plenty of record reviews and artists' bios to peruse.

HitsWorld
http://www.hitsworld.com
If you're a fan of the weekly Top 40 or just enjoy tracking who's where on the music charts, this is the site for you. Not only are Casey's countdown and *Billboard*'s charts here, but there are also international charts, radio charts and playlists from more than 100 stations in North America, Internet charts influenced by visitors' picks and monthly reviews of chart-topping recordings.

Internet Movie Database
http://www.cm.cf.ac.uk/Movies
The Internet Movie Database includes thousands of movies, each with reviews, summaries, ratings and credits. Users can search by title, genre, year, cast and crew members.

Internet Public Library
http://www.ipl.org
This online library's "rooms" link to hundreds of information-packed sites, including Internet directories and encyclopedias. Separate areas for youth, teens and adults make finding online book and periodical resources easy. There's even a MOO, a role-playing game in which users choose to shush or be shushed as librarians or patrons.

Internet Underground Music Archive
http://www.iuma.com/IUMA–2.0/pages/home_page/homepage.html
Undoubtedly the most popular underground music archive on the 'Net, the IUMA represents more than 600 unsigned, independent bands and artists. IUMA also provides information on labels, publications and bands. Users can download sound clips from many of the bands.

Jazz Online
http://www.jazzonln.com
Jazz lovers should rush to bookmark this colorful, well-designed site featuring smart articles, live chats, insightful reviews and catalogs galore.

Movielink
http://www.movielink.com
No, this site by the creators of 777-Film doesn't offer a RealAudio version of the "Hello and welcome to MoviePhone" guy doing his shtick, but it does let moviegoers view trailers of new releases, learn showtimes and order tickets online at theaters in many cities.

Mr. Showbiz
http://web3.starwave.com/showbiz/
Everything you ever wanted to know about the biggest celebrities is now centralized on this funky site. Catch the latest gossip, chat with other surfers or see what albums made the latest *Billboard* charts.

OnVideo
http://www.cyberpod.com/cyberpod/onvideo.htm
Read about the newest releases, industry news, reviews and kids' picks before heading out to the video store for a weekend's worth of rentals.

Oxford University Libraries Automation Service FAQ Directory
http://www.lib.ox.ac.uk/internet /news/
Check out this directory of FAQs, "Frequently Asked Questions," searchable by category and newsgroup type, to avoid naive newbie queries when venturing onto unfamiliar Usenet groups.

Random Internet Camera
http://www.xmission.com/~bill/randcamera.html
For the voyeur in all of us. This site launches users to another site hooked up to a camera for some spontaneous spying.

Richard Wagner Archive
http://utu.fi/~hansalmi/wagner.html
This site devoted to "the most German of men" features the composer's letters, links to other opera sites, articles analyzing his musical influence and the complete list of his operas and other compositions.

shareware.com
http://www.shareware.com
This site is a mother lode of nearly 200,000 searchable and downloadable software files — shareware, demos, patches, upgrades and more — for both PCs and Macs. A subscription to the *Shareware Dispatch* keeps users abreast of what's new.

Sound Bytes: The WWW TV Themes Home Page
http://www.parkherre.com/tvbytes/
Can't remember the second verse to *The Jeffersons*? This site has snippets from TV shows dating back to the 1950s broken down into categories.

Tres Bizarre
http://ucunix.san.uc.edu/7.7Esolkode/tres_bizar/
A guy named Dave scours the 'Net for the freakiest sites around and posts his discoveries daily.

Ultimate Hip-Hop Directory
http://ubmail.ubalt.edu/~rmills/hiphop.html/
The guide to hip-hop and rap music includes links to artists' pages, awards and reviews, graffiti and breakdancing sites and magazine links.

The Ultimate TV List
www.tvnet.com
A must for those who can barely stand to leave the tube long enough to go online. This site provides TV schedules, industry press releases, a chat forum, reviews and even classifieds for users looking to buy a wide-screen set or sell the old black-and-white one.

World Wide Arts Resources
http://wwar.com
A searchable directory of all things artistic, from online museums and galleries to art history, performing arts and art education sites.

World Wide Internet Live Music Archive
http://underground.net/Wilma
This is the place to go for information — dates, reviews and venues — on live performances all over the world. Venues are listed by state, and tours are listed alphabetically.

20 Must-Have CD-ROMs

ANN HOOPER'S ULTIMATE SEX DISC

DK Multimedia; $39.95

British sex therapist Ann Hooper brings her best-selling how-to-do-it-better guide to a tasteful multimedia format. Live-action video and animation show the basics of positions, while personal questionnaires take advantage of the medium to customize the program. Features such as a "sex-opedia" reference to anatomy and technique and a collection of couples' case histories pick up where the seventh-grade gym teacher left off.

BEYOND THE WALL

Magnet Interactive; $49.98

This vivid, moving three-dimensional journey to the Vietnam Veterans Memorial in Washington D.C. brings a new understanding of the controversial war and the lives it affected. The interactive documentary explores the spectrum of emotions the conflict stirred through the soldiers' written and taped letters, newsreel footage, photographs and articles. It also follows the development of the Wall and includes a vast database on each person whose name appears on the majestic memorial. A thought-provoking and beautifully rendered package that delivers a powerful message about heroism and the aftermath of war.

CARMEN ADVANTAGE

Brøderbund; $79.95

This value-pack library includes two award-winning titles starring the shadowy globe-trotting villainess, *Where in the World Is Carmen Sandiego?* and *Where in the U.S.A. Is Carmen Sandiego?*, plus PC Globe's *Maps 'n' Facts* interactive atlas. The worldwide chase visits exotic sites as you gather evidence to unravel mysteries, identify crooks and discover their whereabouts. Digital sound, original score, *National Geographic* location photography and hilarious animation provide hours of educational entertainment. There are also two almanacs included to help decipher clues. A great buy.

COREL ALL-MOVIE GUIDE

Corel Corp.; $55

Don't know what to rent at the video store? Choose from nearly 90,000 in-depth reviews, searchable by category, on this jam-packed resource for the movie buff. Whether you're wondering who the gaffer was for *All About Eve* or just how much money *E.T.* raked in, this encyclopedic resource includes domestic grosses and comprehensive listings of movie credits, as well as a link to an on-line video store. For the true film aficionado whose tastes run from obscure gems to popular blockbusters.

DOOM II

GT Interactive; $40

In this lightning-fast, ultraviolent game, it's up to you, the superhero, to save the earth from flesh-eating mutants, monsters and demons of Hell. Like its predecessor, *Doom II* takes you through a labyrinth of corridors — a perfect opportunity to use your arsenal to blow away everything in your path. You can play this game solo or network with friends.

MAYO CLINIC FAMILY PHARMACIST

IVI Publishing; $35

This highly interactive home resource from the world-renowned Mayo Clinic provides exhaustive information on more than 7,600 prescription and non-prescription medications, first-aid techniques and early-detection procedures. A combination of text, illustration, animation and video answers questions clearly and thoroughly on everything from wrapping a sprain to determining a medicine's side effects. A Personal Profile feature allows users to record vital information.

MECHWARRIOR 2

Activision; $59.95

Welcome to the 31st century. After pledging your allegiance to one of two warring clans, you climb aboard a walking armored machine, choose your weapons (plasma blasters, lasers and rockets), receive your mission and prepare to fight. Not your run-of-the-mill blastfest, this combat game offers an unusually rich storyline, high-resolution animation, texture-mapped 3-D graphics and booming audio. Lucky gamers hooked up to a computer network can bombard up to eight players in this engrossing epic. Hard to believe this best-selling futuristic techno-wonder actually started as a simple board game.

MICROSOFT BOOKSHELF 1996–1997 EDITION

Microsoft; $55

The annual ultimate multimedia reference collection features a slick interface and updated material in all its books. Its nine multimedia tomes include the *Concise Encarta '96 World Atlas, National Five-Digit ZIP and Post Office Directory, The Concise Columbia Encyclopedia, The World Almanac and Book of Facts 1996, The American Heritage Dictionary, The Columbia Dictionary of Quotations, The Original Roget's Thesaurus, People's Chronology* and a new Internet directory with more than 5,000 Web addresses (though unfortunately not hyperlinked to the 'Net). Every entry can be accessed in a slew of ways, from searching for topics in several books simultaneously to leaping from hyperlink to hyperlink to find related material. While primarily text-based, the collection mixes in multimedia to capture historical moments on video or play soundbites from famous people.

MICROSOFT ENCARTA '96 ENCYCLOPEDIA

Microsoft; $49.99

Plenty of sound, color and activity accompany the interactive encyclopedia's 26,000 articles — more than an hour and a half of video, 8,000 photos and nearly constant voiceovers and aural effects. Starting with this volume, updates for the software are available for a fee from the Microsoft Network or Microsoft's Web site (http://www.microsoft.com).

MYST

Brøderbund; $54.95

Open the dusty book at your feet and begin to read. Suddenly you are on Myst, an island in another reality. Using clues hidden on the island, you solve mind-bending puzzles to unravel the age-old, family-tragedy mystery. Sure to be a classic, it will be tough to surpass *Myst's* pioneering intrigue.

NASCAR RACING

Papyrus Design Group, Inc.; $59.95

This challenging and realistic stock-car racing simulator offers computer-savvy Mario Andrettis the choice of nine tracks on which to tempt fate. True to NASCAR race specifications, the game's dashboard, pit board and key board come equipped with data on speed, laps remaining, tire temperature and pit status. Authentic sound effects and realistic racetrack video heighten the wheel-spinning action. But before you put your pedal to the metal, check out the manual to learn tips, track lingo, racing history and commentary from the heroes of the NASCAR circuit.

DIGITAL HOLLYWOOD AWARDS 1996

The second annual Digital Hollywood Awards were announced at the Digital Hollywood Conference, which was held February 20–22, 1996. The awards were created to honor individuals and companies pioneering the use of digital technologies in the entertainment industry. Internet users voted for the finalists via the Digital Hollywood Web site, while attendees of the conference selected the winners.

Best in Digital Hollywood
From film, TV, games, music, online, CD-ROM, literature and virtual realities
    Yahoo!

Best Digital Hollywood Movie
Feature-length enhanced, speculative or animated reality
    Toy Story

CD-ROM Music
From classical to rock 'n' roll
    The Individualist, Todd Rundgren

Best Performance
By an actor or virtual character
    Babe

Look of the Year
From film, TV, games, music, online and literature
    World Cup Soccer, Sony Signatures
    http://www.worldcupsoccer.com

Best in Digital Television
    The X-Files, Fox Television

Digital Kid Stuff — Television
    The Simpsons, Fox Television

SuperRealities: Animation and Special Effects
From film, TV, games and CD-ROM
    Jumanji, Columbia Pictures/TriStar

CD-ROM, Video Game and Computer Title of the Year
    You Don't Know Jack, Berkeley Systems and Jellyvision, Producers

CD-ROM Literature
    Charlton Heston's Voyage Through the Bible: New Testament, Jones Digital Century

Best Video and Computer Game
    The Indian in the Cupboard, Viacom New Media

CONTINUED ON NEXT PAGE ▶

Best Children's Title
CD-ROM, video game and computer
   The Indian in the Cupboard, Viacom New Media

CD-ROM Teen and Adult
   All This Time, Sting, Starwave

CD-ROM Reference
Education, news or general entertainment
   World of Whales, TeraMedia

Digital Magazine
Paper and CD-ROM
   Wired

Digital Darkness
   I Have No Mouth, and I Must Scream,
   Cyberdreams, Inc.

Internet Visionary Award
Honoring individual achievement
   Jerry Yang and David Filo, Yahoo!

Site of the Year
HotWired
http://www.hotwired.com

Webmaster of the Year
Best visual or graphic design on the 'Net
   Susan Mulcahy, publisher, Mr. Showbiz
   http://www.mrshowbiz.com

Computer and Internet 'Zines
   c/net: the computer network
   http://www.cnet.com

Cybercasting Special Events
   PC Magazine Awards for Technical Excellence

Entertainment Sites
Movies, music, TV and others
   Toy Story, Bonifer/Bogner Media, producer and
   webmaster
   http://www.toystory.com

Musicians, Personalities and Artists Sites
Honoring the individual
   Dr. Fiorella Terenzi on the Web
   http://www.fiorella.com

Literature on the Net
Poetry, fiction and criticism
   Sandscript
   http://scifi.com/pulp/htpulp/sandscript.htm/

News on the Net
   People Online
   http://pathfinder.com

NBA Live '96
Electronic Arts; $50
A hoop dream come true. This fast-paced, sophisticated court game lets you dunk, guard and run-and-gun like a pro. A special shot-accuracy feature controls your fellow players' performance based on 1995 statistics. But even if you haven't perfected your free throw, there's plenty of action on the sidelines — trade players, choose your starting lineup, call for a full-court press or substitute a guard. Particularly proud of your jump shot? Watch it again at different angles with the instant-replay feature.

Print Shop Deluxe CD Ensemble
Brøderbund; $49.95
Get the message out yourself and enjoy doing it. That's the idea behind this useful ensemble of five *Print Shop* programs for creating banners, calendars, cards, envelopes, letterhead and more. Intuitive click-and-drag commands make it easy to link up to a wide selection of layouts with more than 1,600 graphics and 73 scalable fonts.

Quicken CD-ROM Deluxe
Intuit; $60
The world's best-selling personal finance software combines the personal finance management tools introduced in earlier versions with added features. The new features are organized in a three-room suite: a conference room where business experts offer advice to help users make better financial decisions, a home office containing several organizational tools and a library that includes a mutual fund selector, a tax guidebook and a stock guide.

7th Guest
Virgin; $30
Crazed toy maker Henry Stauf has invited six guests to his mansion for a dark and mysterious visit. You, the seventh guest, explore the mansion solving puzzles and searching for clues to determine the fate of the other six guests.

Sim City 2000
Maxis; $29.95
Imagine a world where you can design and build your own city without making any structural and aesthetic compromises. Sim City 2000 allows you to create the city of your dreams — complete with an underground layer that includes subways and utilities. Mix and match different buildings in an unlimited number of graphic sets and then show off your work in color or black-and-white printouts.

STREET ATLAS USA

DeLorme; $80

Street Atlas USA provides a complete, up-to-date searchable road map of the entire United States from the largest interstates down to the tiniest back roads. The database provides access to more than one million lakes, ponds, rivers, railroads and monuments. Users can search for data by place name, ZIP code or telephone number.

TOY STORY ANIMATED STORYBOOK

Disney Interactive; $35

This sophisticated Disney title recasts Woody, Buzz and other characters from the animated hit film to keep tykes entertained for hours with point-and-click activities. The expertly animated scenes and sequences closely match those in the film to make kids feel they've become part of the toy adventure.

WING COMMANDER IV

Origin; $54

This epic flight strategy game grabbed headlines for its multimillion-dollar production budget and Hollywood star power — sci-fi heroes, including Mark Hamill and Malcolm McDowell. Information gleaned through conversations with them and other characters helps you build your strategy, whether it's escorting the troops, bombing the enemy or rescuing a hostage. Panning camera work, 16-bit movies with Dolby Surround Sound, a full-screen view for better visibility, digital music and detailed studio sets make this the ultimate flight-combat experience.

YOU DON'T KNOW JACK!

Berkeley Systems; $30

Imagine a manic-depressive Alex Trebek and you have the premise for this irreverent, rapid-fire interactive trivia game that tests your pop-culture knowledge with 800 questions of mind-numbing minutiae. Up to three people can participate in this battle of the wits, or you can play solitaire, but be warned — you'll be razzed "for playing with yourself." "Screw" another contestant by asking a question you're smugly convinced is a stumper, but if you come up short, don't expect sympathy — the obnoxious host sarcastically snarls, "Nice try," punctuated with a burp.

CyberRadio
National Public Radio
http://www.npr.org

Web Guides and Hot Lists
Yahoo!
http://www.yahoo.com

Children's Learning and Entertainment
Splash Kids Online Magazine
http://www.splash.com

Sports on the Net
ESPNet sportsZone
http://espnet.sportszone.com/

Fashion and Model Sites
fashionmall
http://www.fashionmall.com

Pop 'Zines and Other Web Phenomena
Culture Zone
http://www.culturezone.com

Pure Science on the Net
Earth View
http://www.fourmilab.ch/cgi-bin/uncgi/Earth/action?cpt=p

Best Reference
Education and general information
USA Today Weather
http://usatoday.com/weather/ufront.htm

Best Science Fiction Site
Babylon 5
http://www.babylon5.com

Best Art Site
Art galleries, exhibits and comics
Japan Online
http://www.japanonline.com

Environmental and Humanitarian Sites
The Names Project
http://www.aidsquilt.org

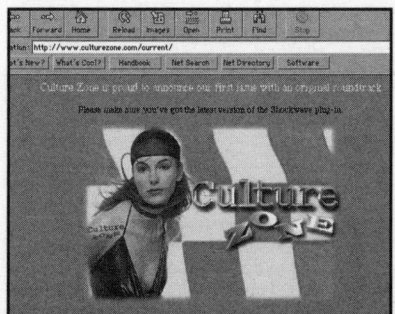

Educational CD-ROMs of 1995–1996

Overall it wasn't a blockbuster year for the CD-ROM industry, but among the new offerings, these educational CD-ROM releases caught our eye for combining learning with multimedia wizardry, imagination and just plain fun.

CHOP SUEY

Magnet Interactive; $34.98
Ages: 6 and up

More a whimsical multimedia story than an educational tool, this CD-ROM introduces Lily and June Bugg, two girls exploring their hometown of Cortland, Ohio. Eye-popping comic-book-style graphics, a dreamy plot and a sense of humor throughout make this far and away one of the year's most innovative products.

DISCOVERING MUSIC

Voyetra; $79.95
Ages: 7 and up

Young maestros can peruse this program's visual dictionary of instruments, glossary of musical terms, interactive timeline and scores of biographies, all with built-in audio and video clips as well as text and still images. That's the education part. Now for the fun — kids can "play" a veritable orchestra of instruments, compose their own songs and even print out sheet music.

ECHO LAKE

Delrina; $59.95
Ages: 6 and up

Great for kids and grown-ups, this program creates a cozy retreat — complete with wooden desk and lakeside view — that inspires self-expression. Its mix of creativity-stirring questions, clip-art images and sound effects make it easy to compose multimedia autobiographies and journals. Kids can share their masterpieces by either printing them out or copying them onto a floppy disc (though a floppy disc doesn't look nearly as impressive hanging on the refrigerator).

HOLLYWOOD

Theatrix Interactive; $39.95
Ages: 9 and up

A cast of animated characters guide budding Scorseses and Campions through the filmmaking process. By choosing among backgrounds, sound effects, facial expressions and other directives, kids begin piece together scripts. A super-cool voice-translation technology converts typed words into actual speech, and while most characters end up sounding like Robocop, there is a selection of voices, ranging from fast-talking to hoarse.

INVENTORLABS

Houghton Mifflin Interactive; $34
Ages: 10 and up

Travel through time to the laboratories of the world's greatest inventors Thomas Alva Edison, James Watt and Alexander Graham Bell. The labs and tools are historically accurate, giving users a true taste of 19th-century science. Kids with "Eureka!" fever can explore more than 40 photo-realistic 3-D inventions from every angle, re-creating the experiments and analyzing hundreds of possible outcomes. The interactive labs are a fun way to learn about the principles of electricity, optics, sound and light, illustrated through 100 historic films, photographs and original recordings, with real actors playing the geniuses.

MADELINE AND THE MAGNIFICENT PUPPET SHOW

Creative Wonders; $39.95
Ages: 5 and up

Ludwig Bemelmans's *jeune amie* comes to pixellated life in this CD-ROM adventure. The resourceful heroine is planning a puppet show to raise money for a less fortunate pal but needs the help of users to find the production's necessary props, which are hidden away in Paris's neighborhoods. Once they help Madeline and friends locate all the items, kids can further pitch in by painting backdrops, creating invitations and designing puppets. Users can even build their French and Spanish vocabulary in lessons from good-hearted Miss Clavel and their favorite Parisian schoolgirl.

MATH BLASTER JUNIOR

Davidson & Associates; $35
Ages: 4–7

This latest installation of the award-winning, best-selling *Math Blaster* series develops early math skills for younger children. Kids rocket into space on the Blaster ship to orbit a vivid 3-D galaxy where they can count stars and learn about quantities, equations and simple addition and subtraction from friendly inch worms. Catchy songs make learning easy, while print supplements continue the math lessons offline.

Significant New CD-ROM Magazines of 1995–1996

The past year saw several new CD-ROM magazines debut on newsstands, in bookstores, in record stores and in computer centers. While it's unlikely that these shiny, round publications will replace their glossy cousins anytime soon (considering the cost of a single issue), they're still a refreshing break from turning all those pages. Here's a sampling of the new consumer CD-ROM magazines that attracted small crowds around our computers.

DIGIZINE
Ahrens Interactive, Inc.; $9.95
Macintosh and PC

This hipper-than-thou "cultural adventure" follows in the funky footsteps of CD-ROM-magazine pioneer *Blender*. An assaulting mix of sound, video, graphic, games and text, *digiZINE* features more than 10 hours of content dedicated to movies, techonology reviews, audio samples and videos from rising alternative bands and counterculture topics such as 'zine reviews, tattoo artists and eight-track tape devotees. Psychedelic graphics, gritty background music and a cutting-edge WebRom™ feature, a technology that lets you download related information from the Internet, push this newcomer to the front of the pack.

IE: INTERACTIVE ENTERTAINMENT
Interactive Entertainment; $9.95
PC

Before you buy your next game, check out an issue of this interactive magazine for the latest demos, screenshots, previews and reviews. After you've made the purchase, rely on it to deliver bug fixes to cure the inevitable software glitch and to cull the best insider tips on improving your score. A good resource for the serious gamer.

LAUNCH
2Way Media, Inc.; $9.98
Macintosh and PC

This multimedia entertainment magazine chooses an urban backdrop as its interface that's just plain confusing if you don't keep the directions handy. Features on music, movies, games, interactive articles and animation are plentiful but not as slick as those in other magazines in this category.

LISTEN TO THE MUSIC
TransMedia Communications; $12.95
PC

Hundreds of song clips, interviews, reviews and videos from all music genres, including alternative, R&B, New Age, classical, folk and reggae, make this multimedia magazine a good buy for music lovers with eclectic tastes. A straightforward interface allows you to find the artists and articles that interest you without any trouble.

LIVINGHOME
Novo Media Group; $14.95
Macintosh and PC

An interactive resource for the Martha Stewart set, this smart multimedia publication uses virtual reality, design software, decorating tools, soothing graphics and full-motion video to explore the latest home-improvement tips. While this disc isn't full of information, it does offer creative ideas for making your pad more homey, from garden design to kitchen remodeling and decorating. For further exploring, there's a direct launch to the World Wide Web that links to the best home-improvement sites.

TROUBLE AND ATTITUDE
Marinex Multimedia Corporation; $9.95
Macintosh and PC

Troubling Attitude would be more like it. "The multimedia magazine for men" offers macho feature stories and regular columns on the usual categories of testosterone-fueled fare — "Wheels," "Threads," "Models" and "Gadgets" — set to a droning score of '80s guitar rock. But perhaps we're being too harsh — the interface is easy to navigate, and the editors do request that users send in their poetry. Then again, they also ask for home videos of subscribers "driving the porcelain bus." We don't even want to know.

A New Game in Town

■ BY JAMES K. WILLCOX

Nintendo 64

When Nintendo launched its much-awaited new game system, Nintendo 64, in September 1996, onscreen animated characters provided only some of the video-game action. The biggest battles were fought by the three companies — Nintendo, Sega and Sony Computer Entertainment America — vying for the loyalty and dollars of the millions of game fans who were expected to step up to the next generation of dedicated video-game consoles.

Nintendo certainly faced a challenge with the debut of its newest system. With 16-bit game sales steadily declining and new, 32-bit systems from Sony and Sega already established among consumers, Nintendo faced perhaps its biggest challenge since the mid-1980s, when it rejuvenated a dying video-game business that saw sales plummet from $3 billion in 1983 to just $100 million in 1985.

That same year Nintendo sent 100,000 8-bit Nintendo Entertainment Systems (NES) to the United States to gauge the market for video games. To everyone's surprise, the systems sold out immediately, and in 1986 Nintendo rolled out the NES in earnest. The rest is home entertainment history, with Nintendo so clearly dominating the business by the end of the 1980s that the name Nintendo became synonymous with video games.

VIDEO GAMES

But late in 1989, Nintendo's domination of the market began to wither, as a wave of new 16-bit game consoles with faster processors and better graphics arrived.

While NEC's TurboGrafx-16 system never seriously challenged Nintendo's hegemony, Sega's Genesis did, and by the end of 1990 the company's aggressive ad campaign had usurped the NES image as the cutting-edge system. Nintendo, not anxious to cannibalize sales of NES, held off introducing its own 16-bit Super NES console for nearly a year after Sega's Genesis launch. As a result, for the first time in its history Nintendo found itself playing catchup, as Sega and its cadre of licensees became the market-share leaders in 16-bit hardware and software sales. Nintendo regrouped and began a renewed marketing effort to reposition Super NES with consumers, which it accomplished in 1993 when industry sales exceeded $5 billion. Since then, the two companies have battled neck-and-neck, and together have sold approximately 40 million 16-bit game systems.

But for the past two years, video-game sales have been declining as 16-bit sales have waned, newer game systems have rolled out slowly and at dramatically higher prices and personal computers have competed for disposable entertainment income. Despite an unexpected resurgence during the 1995 Christmas buying season, industry sales in 1995 fell to approximately $3.8 billion, a decline of more than 20 percent from the previous year and the lowest total in 5 years.

Projections for 1996, however, are more optimistic, as the continued decline in 16-bit games is expected to be more than offset by sales of new, higher-priced systems offered by Sega, Sony and Nintendo. As a result, many analysts have upgraded their forecasts, with investment brokers Gerard Klauer Mattison now anticipating video-game sales to exceed $4 billion, a 17 percent increase from 1995.

The video-game business has traditionally been an industry of four- to five-year new product cycles, and last year one began anew as Sega introduced a 32-bit game console, called Saturn, which boasted even faster processors, much more detailed graphics, high-quality sound effects and more advanced games on CD-ROMs rather than cartridge ROMs. Sega began selling its Saturn in May 1996 on a limited basis, rolling out the system in full in September, when it was joined by Sony's first foray into the game market, a 32-bit console called PlayStation.

Nintendo announced it was working on its own next-generation game machine, called Ultra 64, which it was developing with Silicon Graphics, Inc. (SGI), whose high-end computer workstations have been used by Hollywood filmmakers to create special effects such as those in *Jurassic Park*. Instead of a 32-bit processor, Nintendo developed a 64-bit system it said would leapfrog the competition in both performance and price. After a number of delays, Nintendo finally introduced its new game system — now called Nintendo 64 — in Japan in June 1996 and began selling in the United States in September.

While software tends to be the differentiating feature between systems, it is nonetheless interesting to compare how Sega, Sony and Nintendo have engineered their respective game consoles. These newer systems employ multiple processors to achieve superb graphics unlike anything we've seen in the older, 16-bit machines.

For example, Sega's Saturn uses eight separate microprocessors, including a pair

Sega Saturn

BEST NEXT-GENERATION VIDEO GAMES

James K. Willcox shared his choices for the best 10 games to play on each gaming system. Many of the suggested titles will be available in 1996–1997.

NINTENDO 64

Super Mario 64
(Nintendo, for Nintendo 64; $69.95)
This is Nintendo's flagship title and one of the best games of all time. Engaging gameplay, eight different camera angles and mind-blowing 3-D graphics are sure to make this title both a critical and commercial success.

Pilotwings
(Paradigm Simulations/Nintendo, for Super Nintendo; $69.95)
This one-player flight sim features multiple perspectives, eight playable characters and a variety of death-defying missions and cool environments.

Turok: Dinosaur Hunter
(Acclaim Entertainment, for Nintendo 64; price not yet available)
In this comic-book-inspired game, you play as Turok, who must thwart the Campaigner's plans to use a time-altering device to take over the Lost Valley. The game features great polygonal characters and texture-mapped graphics, along with highly detailed backgrounds.

Mission Impossible
(Ocean of America; price not yet available)
Compelling espionage adventure pits players against smarter enemies that respond to all five senses, not just sight. The movie-based title also offers enough weapons, gadgets and intrigue to keep those fond of Bond happy.

Mortal Kombat Trilogy
(Williams; price not yet available)
Boasting one- or two-player head-to-head tournament fighting and all the characters from the three legendary *Mortal Kombat* games, *MK Trilogy* may be the fighting game to beat for Nintendo's new system.

Waverace 64
(Nintendo; $69.95)
A racing game with a unique twist, Waverace 64 challenges players to maneuver their jet skis through various race scenarios.

Wayne Gretsky 3D Hockey
(Williams; price not yet available)
With several realistic features, including fatigue and line changes, several play modes and smooth, fast action, *Gretsky 3-D Hockey* should be an important title in Nintendo's sports lineup.

CONTINUED ON NEXT PAGE ▶

■◣ CONTINUED FROM PREVIOUS PAGE

Star Wars Shadows of the Empire
(LucasArts; $79.95)
With appearances by popular Star Wars characters such as Darth Vader and Jabba The Hut, *Shadows of the Empire* — which takes place between the last two Star Wars movies — combines great graphics and fierce, multifaceted battle action.

Super Mario Kart 64
(Nintendo; $69.95)
Another Super NES-based update for Nintendo 64, *Super Mario Kart 64* includes textured backgrounds, polygonal characters and vehicles and four-player simultaneous play.

Doom 64
(Williams; price not yet available)
The standard-setting first-person shooter hits Nintendo's new hardware with more than 24 levels of action, improved graphics and heart-pounding audio. A slew of new monsters and weapons make this version a must for any *Doom* fan.

SONY PLAYSTATION

Crash Bandicoot
(Naughty Dog/Sony Computer Entertainment; $59.99)
This one-player platform title features eye-popping 3-D environments, cartoon characters and bonus rooms and levels. Players must guide Crash through a variety of colorful levels of adventure, avoiding enemies and natural pitfalls as he tries to save his girlfriend from the clutches of an evil doctor.

Final Doom
(Williams; price not yet available)
Despite the proliferation of *Doom* titles, this version — with more than 30 new levels and Death Match and Cooperative modes for multi-player gaming — adds enough new elements to keep the game exciting, even for the most jaded Doom fan.

Dark Forces
(LucasArts; price not yet available)
The popular Star Wars-inspired PC title hits PlayStation with great graphics, an intriguing storyline and enough action to keep everyone happy.

Magic Carpet
(Electronic Arts; price not yet available)
Part flight sim, part action-adventure game, Magic Carpet features a bounty of game levels, excellent morphing terrain and an engaging soundtrack as you try to restore balance to numerous 3-D worlds.

NBA Shootout
(Sony; $59.99)
Full teams featuring many of the game's superstars make this game more realistic but just as fun as *NBA Jam*. Players move smoothly — though control isn't always perfect — while characters and background graphics are sharp.

of custom SH2 32-bit RISC chips developed by Hitachi, which act as the system's main processors. In addition, Saturn uses two other 32-bit video digital processors (VDPs) that specifically handle graphics. One VDP generates the sprites — the game's main objects and characters — and effects such as scaling, rotation and texture-mapping to create a 3-D character or object. Saturn's first VDP also smoothes polygonal objects to reduce their geometric look, while the second creates background objects and effects such as scrolling. And unlike the Genesis, which only offered 64 colors, the Saturn can produce 16.8 million colors.

Saturn's other processors include a 32-bit RISC chip that controls the built-in double-speed CD-ROM drive; a system

Sony Playstation

control unit, which acts as the traffic cop in charge of synchronizing processing activity; a system manager and peripheral controller, which manages input from peripherals such as the game controllers; and a custom 32-voice Yamaha sound processor.

Sony's PlayStation also features multiple processors but relies more heavily on its main CPU — a custom 32-bit RISC processor developed by LSI Logic — which helps keep costs down and lets developers create games for the console more easily. The LSI chip is supported by five other processors: a geometry engine (GTE) and a graphics processing unit (GPU), responsible for creating the graphics; a data decompression engine (MDEC) for video playback; a CD-drive controller, which handles the information spooling off the CD-based games; and a sound processor.

The GTE and GPU work together to produce the PlayStation's graphics. The GPU renders the games' character sprites, effects such as rotation and scaling and the system's 16.8 million colors, while the GTE handles texture-mapping, object-shading and fog effects.

Nintendo 64, like the Sony PlayStation, is optimized for 3-D polygon-based games, which provide greater realism with their three-dimensional characters and objects. To perform the rapid, complex calculations it requires to make these objects move realistically, the companies constructed Nintendo 64 around two main processors: the CPU and a graphics processor.

Nintendo 64's main CPU is a customized version of an extremely fast R4000, 64-bit RISC chip, which is roughly three times as quick as Saturn or PlayStation. Nintendo 64's graphics are handled by a separate 64-bit processor, called the Reality Co-Processor, which consists of two components: a signal processor, which performs the geometric calculations required to render realistic, polygon-based images; and the display processor, which handles advanced features such as texture-mapping.

Nintendo also came up with a radical but highly effective wing-shaped game controller, comprised of a conventional directional joypad as well as an integrated analog "3-D Stick" that allows players to control movements in 360 degrees and manipulate the speed of a character's actions. The controller also contains a variety of conventional buttons, while a slot on the base of the controller accepts memory cartridges for saving games.

Unlike Sega and Sony, however, Nintendo does not use CD-based games, which it claims do not offer the speed required for great game play. Instead, it is using silicon ROM cartridges. Although the cartridges won't hold anywhere near the 650MB of data that CD-based games can, Nintendo says that by using compression it can store more than enough game data to be accessed much faster than with any CD-based system. Next year Nintendo plans to

Resident Evil
(Capcom; $59.99)
This best-selling PlayStation game is not for the squeamish, with its flesh-eating zombies, superb graphics and authentic horror-movie feel.

Destruction Derby 2
(Psygnosis; price not yet available)
Better tracks, improved graphics, flipping cars and a new Stunt mode allow this sequel to run laps around its predecessor. The best remedy yet for working out real-life road aggression.

Soul Storm
(Oddworld Inhabitants/GT Interactive; price not yet available)
With eye-catching graphics and an unusual twist on gaming — you avoid conflict rather than seek it — Soul Storm features an escaped slave named Abe as the main character who must solve numerous puzzles and overcome obstacles, often by learning songs or sentences.

Tomb Raider
(Eidos/U.S. Gold; price not yet available)
A female Indiana Jones-style archaeologist leads players on a virtual treasure hunt through ancient ruins in exotic locales. Excellent graphics bring the different locations to life, and a 3-D underwater level is particularly impressive.

Return Fire
(Time Warner Interactive; price not yet available)
A excellent war sim that deftly combines strategy with fast-paced martial action, Return Fire boasts more than 100 missions of increasing difficulty, an arsenal of weapons and a dramatic soundtrack that accompanies each vehicle into battle. Highly recommended for the armchair general.

SATURN

Nights
(Sega; $59.99)
Hailed as the next Sega Saturn blockbuster, this one-player game features two playable characters and planes of game play — a walk-around action mode and an intense air-bound mode — as well as stunning graphics.

Night Warriors: Darkstalker's Revenge
(Capcom; $54.99)
Superb animation tops the list of attributes for this excellent translation of the arcade fighting game. Impossibly athletic moves, a choice of 14 playable fighters and cool sound effects more than compensate for somewhat limited depth.

Die Hard Trilogy
(Fox Interactive; price not yet available)
A three-in-one action game that combines a search-and-rescue mission, an arcade-style shooter and a driving sim provides something for everyone, backed by strong graphics and gameplay.

CONTINUED ON NEXT PAGE

CONTINUED FROM PREVIOUS PAGE

Panzer Dragoon Zwei II
(Sega; $54.99)
This sequel ups the ante over the original with even better, highly detailed backgrounds and scenery, huge bosses and improved sound. Smooth control, engaging missions and intriguing enemies make this sequel the first-person shooter to beat on Saturn.

WWF Wrestlemania: The Arcade Game
(Acclaim Entertainment; $39.99)
Finally Saturn owners can punch, gouge and slam their way to the level of happiness PlayStation fans have enjoyed for a year now. Featuring the same fighters, action and moves as the PS game, *WrestleMania* for Saturn doesn't break new ground but does offer tons of two-player fun.

Magic Carpet
(Electronic Arts; $39.99)
Like the PlayStation version, *Magic Carpet* for Saturn features strong controls, great visuals and engaging game play as players take their trusty carpet on a first-person shooter spin through the countryside.

Virtua Cop 2
(Sega; $59.99)
Another Sega sequel that's better than the original, *Virtua Cop 2* offers more firepower, better backgrounds, smoother control and a new female partner. Most improved are the different scenarios, which spice up the action with car chases and a subway shootout.

Sonic X-Treme
(Sega; $49.99)
Sonic's first appearance on Saturn is sure to be popular with younger players, particularly with the added 3-D element, cool graphics and a cast of new and familiar characters.

NFL '97
(Sega; $59.99)
Vivid animation, statistics-tracking in all categories, multiple-play perspectives and all 30 NFL teams will make this a popular Saturn title even beyond the football season.

Virtua Fighter 3
(Sega; price not yet available)
Although so far we've only been able to view arcade-based demos, based on what we've seen this could be the most intense fighting game ever developed. Heart-stopping graphics, incredibly smooth control and engaging characters make this a must-have title for martial-arts fans. ■

offer a $150 accessory called DD64 that will play custom-designed magneto-optical "mini-disk" games. The disk can hold up to 150MB of data and are writeable so players will be able to store game data, player profiles and other customized information.

Most of the game developers, however, prefer working with CD-ROMs, which are much less expensive to manufacture. In addition, if it is to ultimately succeed, Nintendo will have to overcome several other obstacles in addition to its choice of software. Already the company has given in to competitive pressures and slashed its price from $249 to under $200. Sony and Sega both sell their systems for $199.

Nintendo 64 systems will be in short supply this year as the company ramps up manufacturing, while both Sony and Sega already have sold a significant number of systems. For example, Nintendo projects it will ship 500,000 units in the United States by Christmas 1996, selling one million systems by the end of March 1997. Sega is projecting sales of 1.6 million Saturn systems by the end of 1996, and Sony expects to have an installed base of 3 million PlayStation systems in North America by the end of March. And both companies have already sold approximately 2.5 million systems each in Japan. However, Nintendo sold 500,000 Nintendo 64 systems in Japan in June, the first month the console was available, and predicts it will sell 3.6 million systems there by the end of March.

So far, Sony has taken the early lead in the battle for next-generation supremacy. Despite its obstacles, few in the industry are willing to count Nintendo out given its past history of success.

Ultimately, of course, the real winners will be the millions of game players who will be the beneficiaries of the race between these companies to produce the most exciting, compelling game experience available. And chances are, four years from now, a new battle will just be beginning. ■

James K. Willcox is senior editor at TWICE, *a consumer-electronics magazine, and reports on interactive entertainment for several magazines and newspapers.*

Best-Selling Software of 1995

PC Data compiled these software titles as the top sellers of 1995.

CD-ROM TITLES

1. **Microsoft Windows '95 Upgrade** (Microsoft)
2. **Myst** (Brøderbund)
3. **Print Shop Deluxe CD Ensemble** (Brøderbund)
4. **Dark Forces** (LucasArts)
5. **Quicken Deluxe** (Intuit)
6. **Doom II** (GT Interactive)
7. **Microsoft Plus** (Microsoft)
8. **Microsoft Encarta** (Microsoft)
9. **Microsoft Flight Simulator** (Microsoft)
10. **Lion King Storybook** (Disney)

HOME EDUCATION TITLES FOR MS-DOS/WINDOWS

1. **Lion King Story Book** (Disney)
2. **Where in the World Is Carmen Sandiego?** (Brøderbund)
3. **Math Blaster: In Search of Spot** (Davidson)
4. **Oregon Trail II** (MECC)
5. **Aladdin Activity Center** (Disney)
6. **Reader Rabbit 1** (Softkey)
7. **Interactive Reading Journey** (Softkey)
8. **Winnie the Pooh** (Disney)
9. **Oregon Trail** (MECC)
10. **Where in the USA Is Carmen Sandiego?** (Brøderbund)

HOME EDUCATION TITLES FOR MACINTOSH

1. **Mavis Beacon Teaches Typing** (Mindscape)
2. **Kid Pix Studio** (Brøderbund)
3. **Aladdin Activity Center** (Disney)
4. **Lion King Story Book** (Disney)
5. **Mario Teaches Typing** (Interplay)
6. **Where in the World Is Carmen Sandiego?** (Brøderbund)
7. **Sim Town** (Maxis)

8. **Where in the USA Is Carmen Sandiego?** (Brøderbund)
9. **A.D.A.M. Inside Story** (A.D.A.M. Software)
10. **Oregon Trail** (MECC)

PC GAMES FOR MS-DOS, WINDOWS AND WINDOWS '95

1. **Myst** (Brøderbund)
2. **Doom II** (GT Interactive)
3. **Microsoft Flight Simulator** (Microsoft)
4. **Dark Forces** (LucasArts)
5. **NASCAR Racing** (Sierra On-Line)
6. **Ultimate Doom Thy Flesh** (GT Interactive)
7. **MechWarrior II** (Activision)
8. **D!Zone Collector's Edition** (Wizard Works)
9. **Phantasmagoria** (Sierra On-Line)
10. **Descent** (Interplay)
11. **Sim City 2000 Collection** (Maxis)
12. **Sim City 2000** (Maxis)
13. **Star Trek: TNG Final Unity** (Spectrum Holobyte)
14. **Best of Microsoft Entertainment Pack** (Microsoft)
15. **X-Wing Collector's CD** (LucasArts)
16. **7th Guest** (Virgin)
17. **Star Wars Rebel Assault II** (LucasArts)
18. **Wing Commander III** (Electronic Arts)
19. **Tie Fighter** (LucasArts)
20. **11th Hour** (Virgin)

MACINTOSH GAMES

1. **Myst** (Brøderbund)
2. **Dark Forces** (LucasArts)
3. **Doom II** (GT Interactive)
4. **Sim City 2000** (Maxis)
5. **Marathon** (Bungee)
6. **Star Wars Rebel Assault** (LucasArts)
7. **Links Pro** (Access)
8. **Top Ten Pack** (Electronic Arts)
9. **Wolfenstein 3D** (Interplay)
10. **Sim Tower** (Maxis)

All-Time Video and Laserdisc Charts

We compiled this list from various sources.

Top Video Rentals

1. **Star Wars**
   (Fox Video)

2. **On Golden Pond**
   (ITC)

3. **48 Hrs.**
   (Paramount Home Video)

4. **The Karate Kid**
   (Columbia Home Video)

5. **Romancing the Stone**
   (Fox Home Video)

6. **An Officer and a Gentleman**
   (Paramount Home Video)

7. **Flashdance**
   (Paramount Home Video)

8. **Back to the Future**
   (MCA Home Video)

9. **Beverly Hills Cop**
   (Paramount Home Video)

10. **First Blood**
    (Avid Home Entertainment)

11. **The Terminator**
    (Live Entertainment)

12. **Lethal Weapon**
    (Warner Home Video)

13. **Dirty Dancing**
    (Vestron)

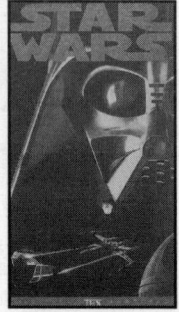

14. **Raiders of the Lost Ark**
    (Paramount Home Video)

15. **Police Academy**
    (Warner Home Video)

16. **Poltergeist**
    (MGM)

17. **Terms of Endearment**
    (Paramount Home Video)

18. **Ghost**
    (Paramount Home Video)

19. **Fort Apache, the Bronx**
    (Vestron Video)

20. **The Shawshank Redemption**
    (Columbia TriStar Home Video)

Top Video Sales

1. **The Lion King**
   (Disney Home Video)

2. **Jane Fonda's Workout**
   (Lorimar)

3. **Jane Fonda's New Workout**
   (Lorimar)

4. **Callanetics**
   (MCA/Universal Home Video)

5. **Jane Fonda's Low-Impact Aerobics**
   (Lorimar)

6. **Pinocchio**
   (Disney Home Video)

7. **Lady and the Tramp**
   (Disney Home Video)

8. **Raiders of the Lost Ark**
   (Paramount Home Video)

9. **The Sound of Music**
   (Fox Video)

10. **Beauty and the Beast**
    (Disney Home Video)

Top Laserdisc Sales

1. **Back to the Future**
   (MCA)

2. **Top Gun**
   (Paramount Home Video)

3. **Raiders of the Lost Ark**
   (Paramount Home Video)

4. **Dirty Dancing**
   (Vestron Video)

5. **The Karate Kid**
   (Columbia Home Video)

6. **Terminator 2: Judgment Day — Special Edition**
   (Carolco Video)

7. **RoboCop**
   (Orion Home Video)

8. **The Untouchables**
   (Paramount Home Video)

9. **Ghost**
   (Paramount Home Video)

10. **Speed**
    (Fox Video)

All-Time Software and CD-ROM Bestsellers

We compiled this list using PC Data's 1993-1995 bestseller charts and our own evaluation based on sales and product reviews.

CD-ROM TITLES

1. **Myst** (Brøderbund)
2. **Microsoft Windows '95 Upgrade** (Microsoft)
3. **Quicken CD-ROM Deluxe** (Intuit)
4. **Doom** (GT Interactive)
5. **Print Shop Deluxe CD Ensemble** (Brøderbund)
6. **Doom II** (GT Interactive)
7. **Microsoft Plus** (Microsoft)
8. **Microsoft Encarta** (Microsoft)
9. **Corel Printhouse** (Corel)
10. **Warcraft II: Tides of Darkness** (Davidson)

HOME EDUCATION TITLES FOR MS-DOS/WINDOWS

1. **Where in the World Is Carmen Sandiego?** (Brøderbund)
2. **Mavis Beacon Teaches Typing** (Software Toolworks)
3. **Math Blaster: In Search of Spot** (Davidson)
4. **Lion King Story Book** (Disney)
5. **Oregon Trail II** CD-ROM (Disney)

HOME EDUCATION TITLES FOR MACINTOSH

1. **Where in the World Is Carmen Sandiego?** CD-ROM (Brøderbund)
2. **Mavis Beacon Teaches Typing** (Software Toolworks)
3. **Kid Pix Studio** CD-ROM (Brøderbund)
4. **Lion King Story Book** CD-ROM (Disney)
5. **Pocahontas Animated Story Book** CD-ROM (Disney)

PC GAMES FOR MS-DOS/WINDOWS

1. **Myst** (Brøderbund)
2. **Doom** (GT Interactive)
3. **Doom II** (GT Interactive)
4. **Microsoft Flight Simulator** (Microsoft)
5. **Sim City 2000** (Maxis)
6. **Warcraft II** (Davidson)
7. **Sim City** (Maxis)
8. **7th Guest** (Virgin)
9. **Ultimate Doom Thy Flesh** (GT Interactive)
10. **Mechwarrior II** (Activision)

MACINTOSH GAMES

1. **Myst** (Brøderbund)
2. **Sim City 2000** (Maxis)
3. **FA-18 Hornet** (Graphic Simulations)
4. **Doom II** (GT Interactive)
5. **Links Pro** (Access)
6. **Star Wars Rebel Assault** (LucasArts)
7. **Top Ten Pack** (Electronic Arts)
8. **Links Pro** (Access)
9. **Sim City** (Maxis)
10. **Dark Forces** (LucasArts)

On-Line News Resources

On-line news resources have carved out a major presence on the Internet. Industry experts may squabble over exactly what's out there (most sources estimate about 1,000 newspapers have World Wide Web home pages) but agree growth will continue at the same swift pace. Following are major Web news sites, many of which are accessible free of charge and updated as news breaks:

NATIONAL NEWSPAPERS

Christian Science Monitor
http://www.csmonitor.com/

**Computer News Daily/
New York Times Syndicate**
http://nytsyn.com/cgi-bin/times/lead/go

The Earth Times
http://www.igc.apc.org/earthtimes

ElectionLine
http://www.electionline.com

Family World
http://family.com

InfiNet Webpaper
http://www.infi.net/webpaper/

NandO (News and Observer)
http://www.nando.net

New York Times
http://www.nytimes.com/

USA Today
http://www.usatoday.com

Wall Street Journal
http://update.wsj.com

**Your Health Daily/
New York Times Syndicate**
http://nytsyn.com/medic/

METRO NEWS SOURCES

Atlantic Journal Constitution
http://www.ajc.com

Chicago Tribune
http://www.chicago.tribune.com

Columbus Dispatch
http://www.cd.columbus.oh.us/

Dallas/Fort Worth Star-Telegram
http://www.startext.net

Detroit News
http://detnews.com

Hartford Courant
http://www.courant.com

Honolulu Star-Bulletin
http://starbulletin.com/

Houston Chronicle
http://www.chron.com

Indianapolis Star News
http://www.starnews.com

Kansas City Star
http://www.kcstar.com

Los Angeles Times
http://www.latimes.com

Minneapolis Pioneer
http://www.pioneerplanet.com

Minneapolis Star Tribune
http://www.startribune.com

New York Newsday
http://www.newsday.com

Norfolk Virginian Pilot
http://www.infi.net/pilot

Pittsburgh Tribune-Review
http://www.tribune.review.com

San Francisco Chronicle and Examiner
http://www.sfgate.com

San Jose Mercury News
http://www.sjmercury.com

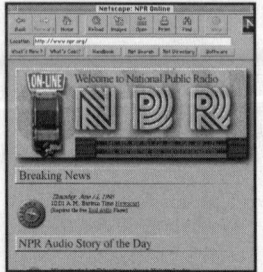

St. Louis Post-Dispatch
http://www.stlnet.com

Tampa/St. Petersburg Times
http://www.sptimes.com

Tampa/St. Petersburg Tribune
http://www.tamptrib.com

MAJOR NATIONAL NEWS NETWORKS

ABC Radio Network
http://www.realaudio.com

ABC-TV
http://www.abctv.com

BBC TV & Radio
http://www.bbcnc.org.uk

CBS Radio Networks
http://www.cbsradio.com

CBS-TV
http://www.cbs.com

Clarinet Online News Service
http://www/clarinet.com

CNN-TV
http://www.cnn.com

MSNBC
http://www.msnbc.com

National Public Radio
http://www.npr.org
http://gopher://gopher.npr.org

NBC-TV
http://www.nbc.com

PBS-TV
gopher.pbs.org

USIA European Wireless File
gopher://gopher.itu.ch

NEWSWIRES

Associated Press
cns.cscns.com

**Los Angeles Times/Washington Post
News Service**
http://www.newsservice.com

Reuters NewMedia
http://www.yahoo.com/headlines/current/news/summary.html

On-Line News Alternatives

The on-line self-publishing movement has given way to a broad spectrum of alternative news sources on the Internet, covering everything from progressive politics to small-town goings-on. Almost all are available free of charge.

The Anchorage Press (Anchorage, AK)
http://www.alaskana.com/press
On-line version of weekly has everything to get you through a cold Alaskan winter. Calendar, personals, movie reviews, even beer reviews.

Arkansas Times Online (Little Rock, AR)
http://www.aristotle.net/arktimes
On-line companion to local weekly featuring a statewide dining guide and a Whitewater archive.

The Austin Chronicle (Austin, TX)
http://www.auchron.com/current
On-line version of city newsweekly. News, features, arts and entertainment, excellent links to city and state organizations and even to Mexican and Canadian sites. "Best of Austin" annual listings. An all-around great resource.

The Baltimore Chronicle (Baltimore, MD)
http://www.charm.net/~marc/chronicle
National and local news and features taken from the monthly paper and from its nonprofit progressive insert, *The Sentinel,* with a little humor to lighten the tone. Hop from the Adventures of Kermit the Cyber Kitty to a debate on drug legalization.

Boulder Weekly Online (Boulder, CO)
http://www.earthnet.net/~altnews/home.html
On-line version of local newspaper self-described as "willing and able to do the hard stories." Investigative reporting, national and regional news, arts reviews and calendar. Straightforward, attractive interface.

Casco Bay Weekly (Portland, ME)
http://w3.maine.com/cbw/
On-line version of news, art and opinion weekly. Everything from sea kayaking to seasonal rentals, with a little gossip and a few weather links thrown into the mix.

The Casper Weekly Gazette (Casper, WY)
http://www.geocities.com/Bourbon Street/1094
Resolutely upbeat web companion to local weekly. "Good News" section lists happy local events, while "Thoughts for the Day" offers food for the soul. Links to "GeoCities," a virtual community site

that offers web space to those interested in becoming cyber-citizens.

Cincinnati CityBeat (Cincinnati, OH)
http://www.citybeat.com
Electronic version of weekly news and arts magazine. High-end virtual mall offers links to L.L. Bean, Speigel, The Nature Company and other catalog empires.

City Pages (St. Paul-Minneapolis, MN)
http://www.citypages.com
Twin Cities news and arts weekly, with a personals section and searchable events database. On-line conferencing covers everything from gas prices to sex.

City Paper Interactive (Philadelphia, PA)
http://www.cpcn.com
Web incarnation of city weekly. Comprehensive local news, features and listings.

City Paper Online (Baltimore, MD)
http://www.citypaper.com
Selections from city weekly. Cultural listings, television listings, restaurant directory, classifieds, personals, links to community information sites.

Colorado Daily (Boulder, CO)
http://bcn.boulder.co.us/media/colodaily/
On-line edition of local independent daily. News, opinion, sports, entertainment, earth/science section. Consult the "Best Of" section for a recommended local sushi bar or tattoo parlor.

Columbus Alive (Columbus, Ohio)
http://www.columbuspages.com
A wired guide to Columbus featuring news, weather, stocks, television listings, food, nightlife.

Community Crier (Tucson, AZ)
http://tucson.com/Crier
Homey on-line community resource run by a local web designer as a hobby. Includes regional news and listings and religion and family sections.

Creative Loafing Online (Atlanta, GA)
http://www.cln.com
Complete electronic version of news and entertainment weekly. Added attractions include the Southeast's largest web mall and live Internet chat sessions with Atlanta celebrities.

Crime Fighting Salem News Online (Salem, OR)
http://www.ncn.com/~snews
Selections from local monthly paper that is out to beat the bad guys. News and features cover gambling, street safety, delinquency and proposed solutions to crime.

Eugene Weekly (Eugene, OR)
http://www.efn.org/~ew
Text-based site with selections from weekly women-owned community paper. Headlines, arts and entertainment calendar, personals. Billed as an outspoken source of progressive views.

Flagpole (Athens, GA)
http://www.flagpole.com
On-line version of hip, ironic indie weekly emphasizing the local music scene. Includes local news, politics and arts listings.

Free Speech Newspaper (Phoenix, AZ)
http://com.primenet.com/callme
Monthly on-line scandal sheet dedicated to exposés of government, corporate and institutional conspiracies. On a lighter note, the site includes personals and a listing of Arizona casinos.

Hatch Courier (Hatch, NM)
http://www.zianet.com/files/users/wblase/courier
Home page of colorful populist newsweekly.

Icon (Iowa City, IA)
http://www.jeonet.com/icon
On-line version of self-described "smart news and entertainment" weekly. Emphasizes underdog stories, untold historical anecdotes and some colorful storytelling.

The Indianapolis Register (Indianapolis, IN)
http://www.inetdirect.net/indianapolis-register
Electronic version of monthly publication supplemented with everything you ever wanted to know about the nation's 14th largest city. Facts and figures, local events, arts and entertainment and sports.

In Pittsburgh Interactive (Pittsburgh, PA)
http://www.inpgh.com
On-line interactive edition of city newsweekly. Local news and culture, with an "Ipicks" section for choice weekly events. Find answers to life's problems in the "Hey, Rita" advice column.

The Isthmus Daily Page (Madison, WI)
http://www.thedailypage.com
Home page for even-toned progressive weekly. Investigative reports, regional news, reviews, sports and listings for kids to explore.

The Kokomo Herald (Kokomo, IN)
http://www.holli.com/herald
Selections from Howard County's oldest local weekly. Local news, classifieds and comprehensive Weather Watch links section.

Kokomo Perspective (Kokomo, IN)
http://www.airmax.net/perspective/default.htm
Electronic counterpart of weekly paper. Highlights include a religious insight section, stock quotes and a daily police blotter.

LA Weekly Worldwide (Los Angeles, CA)
http://www.villagevoice.com/laweekly
Selected news, reviews and features from print entertainment weekly. Catch up on gossip in the "Low Life" section. Comprehensive city information, "LA at Night" sections and access to "Village Voice New York at Night" listings.

The Lake Saint Louis Sentinel (St. Louis, MO)
http://www.videoalt.com/sentinel.html
On-line incarnation of local opposition weekly that was forced to shut down when controversy erupted over its publisher's amateur adult erotica business. Don't expect anything racy here — the hot spots are hospital and library news.

The Lebanon Daily Record NewsStand (Lebanon, MO)
http://www.llion.org/ldr/news.html
Text-only site with summaries of articles from daily newspaper.

Marlborough Electronic Messenger (Marlborough, CT)
http://gsl.com/messenger/messenger.html
Friendly, spirited community on-line newsweekly. Includes an environmental section and spotlight on local businesses and Marlborough Virtual Museum. Clear tone and attractive graphics make this a model local site.

The Messenger Online (Missoula, MT)
http://www.sisna.com/messenger/messenger.htm
Web page for regional classified weekly. Montana bargain hunters' paradise.

The Met Online (Dallas/Fort Worth, TX)
http://the met.computek.net
Web version of city news and entertainment weekly, with extra quirky features in the "Online" section. Extensive weather links.

Metro (Tampa, FL)
http://www.hpmetro.com
Electronic version of Tampa's biweekly lifestyle guide features colorful coverage of political races and cultural and sporting events.

MetroActive
http://boulevards.com/metroactive/
Home site for on-line versions of three Northern California alternative weeklies. All contain news and cultural features and listings. Navigate through each paper individually or use cross-referenced subject links. The three sites are:
Metro (San Jose, California)
http://www.boulevards.com/metroactive/metro/index.html
Metro Santa Cruz (Santa Cruz, CA)
http://www.boulevards.com/metroactive/cruz/index.html

Sonoma County Independent
http://www.boulevards.com/metroactive/sonoma/index.html

Milestone (Malden, MA)
http://www.milestones.com/civitas/ma/malden/malden.html
Community information source focusing on neighborhood and human interest stories. There's even a place for photos of local grandchildren.

Nashville Scene (Nashville, TN)
http://www.nashscene.com/
Electronic version of local arts and entertainment weekly with the latest in fun, useful features, such as searchable databases for movies, local events and dining.

New City Net (Chicago, IL)
http://www.suba.com/~newcity
On-line edition of culture and classifieds weekly. "Best of Chicago" listings from 1993 to the present offer choice insider tips on such topics as "Best Block to Ruin a Car On" and "Best Women's Hotel Bathroom."

Nuvo Online (Indianapolis, IN)
http://mercury.nuvo.net/nuvo/
On-line version of city news and entertainment weekly. Streamlined design and lively writing give this site a strong identity.

The Outrider (Washington, DC)
http://web.idirect.com/~outrider
On-line version of newspaper sold by homeless and needy people — the "outriders" who feel the first effects of social decay. Run by volunteer staff. News, features, arts and entertainment, food reviews by "Dumpster Dan the Gourmet Man." Links to resources that can help the disadvantaged get back on their feet.

Palo Alto Weekly (Palo Alto, California)
http://www.paweekly.com/paw/home.html
Text-based version of free local biweekly paper. Items of interest include listings of area classes and a history of Palo Alto's first 100 years.

Phoenix (Boston, MA)
http://www.phx.com
Comprehensive electronic offshoot of 30-year-old alternative weekly. Complete arts listings, gay and lesbian section including annual Gay Pride Guide, extensive guide to local bands, food listings, classifieds and personals.

Phoenix New Times.Com (Phoenix, AZ)
http://www.phoenix newtimes.com
"Newszine" companion to metropolitan weekly dedicated to good old-fashioned muckraking. Breaking news, features, arts and entertainment, classifieds, personals, a restaurant database and coverage of the local electronic community. Lively, colorful interface.

Point (Columbia, SC)
http://www.cris.com/~Scpoint
On-line version of proudly liberal news-
monthly emphasizing grassroots,
activist outlook. Features, commentary,
poetry, links to progressive organizations from the American Civil Liberties
Union to the Sierra Club.

Public News (Houston, TX)
http://www.neosoft.com/publicnews
Home page of weekly news magazine.
News, calendar, classifieds, personals,
local band register and extensive
restaurant database that even rates the
best local waitperson.

**The Round Top Register
(Round Top, TX)**
http://www.rtis.com/reg/roundtop
Funny, irreverent on-line newspaper
from the "biggest little town in Texas"
(population 81). Tongue-in-cheek news
and features, arts and entertainment.
Uncle Sack's Internet Depot is a treasure chest of links to everything from
weather forecasts to antiques.

**The San Francisco Bay Guardian
(San Francisco, CA)**
http://www.sfbayguardian.com
On-line version of established but funky
area newsweekly. National and local
news, area politics, arts and entertainment, personals. Bay Area listings
cover education, events, even nude
beaches.

The Village Voice Worldwide
http://www.villagevoice.com
On-line version of the 40-year-old alternative pioneer. Selections from print
weekly include news and features, arts
and entertainment reviews and listings,
classifieds, everything from sculpture to
body sculpting. Special "New York at
Night" section and access to sister site,
"L.A. at Night."

Savannah Today (Savannah, GA)
http://www.savga.com/news/today.htm
Well-organized on-line source of city
and local news, weather and events
information. Learn about the Waving
Girl Statue and other local lore.

Silicon Mesa News (Albuquerque, NM)
http://www.rt66.com/~kimzey
Experimental site created as forum for
news, interviews and background on
the high-tech transformation of the
New Mexico desert.

Syracuse New Times Net (Syracuse, NY)
http://www.rway.com/newtimes/
Web version of weekly news, arts and
entertainment magazine. Classifieds,
event listings and links to city and
regional resource sites.

**The Tallahassee News
(Tallahassee, FL)**
http://www.polaris.net/~mikems
Experimental on-line paper devoted to
the Capital Where Spring Begins. Local
news, links to school and state information and national news sources.

Tuscon Weekly (Tuscon, AZ)
http://desert.net/tw/twhome.htm
Well-designed, complete online version
of weekly news and events magazine
that aims to be anti-establishment
"journalistic fun." Local and regional
news, arts reviews and calendar.

Upwith Herald (Charleston, SC)
http://www.sc.net/organizations/upwith-
herald.html
Text-based electronic version of free
biweekly entertainment guide. Events
calendar, dining guide and newsbites.

The Virtual Times (Huntsville, AL)
http://www.hsv.com
Enthusiastic on-line community information resource. Publishes work by
local writers and artists, business
news, events listings. Look for dispatch-
es from Americans living in far-flung
places such as the Ukraine, Sweden
and Japan.

**Voices on the Internet
(State College, PA)**
http://www.epicom.com/voices
On-line version of regional news and
opinion monthly. Selected news, features, events, humor, from a self-
described liberal viewpoint. Easy-to-
navigate interface.

Washington Free Press (Seattle, WA)
http://www.speakeasy.org/wfp
On-line version of cooperatively run
bimonthly journal. Hard-hitting progressive news tries to "zap the complacent"
with articles on labor and environmental issues. Entertainment and humor are
also well represented.

**The Waterbury Observer
(Waterbury, CT)**
http//:www.sliceoflife.com/observer
Biweekly on-line newspaper takes an
independent, in-depth look at local
news, personalities and events in the
Brass City.

The Weekender Online (PA)
http://www.microserve.net/weekender/
Web version of northeastern
Pennsylvania events weekly. Light features, syndicated columns, links to
entertainment sites.

Zia Connection (Santa Fe, NM)
http://www.interart.net/zia.connection
Electronic sidekick to the daily Santa Fe
New Mexican. Weekly news features
regional topics. Cultural and shopping
information accessible through links to
Interart, a Southwest virtual mall.

1951
Bing Crosby finances the
first use of magnetic tape in
television, which employs
the Longitudinal Videotape
Recording Machine (LVR).

1960
The PDP-1, the first com-
mercial computer with a
keyboard and monitor is
introduced.

1962
Ivan Sutherland, a graduate student
at M.I.T., creates the science of
computer graphics.

Digital Equipment Corp. and MIT's
Lincoln Laboratory develop the first
personal computer, which sells for
$43,000.

CBS unveils the first video playing
units, the Electronic Video Recording
System.

1969
CompuServe, an on-line information
database, is introduced.

ARPAnet, the "mother of the
Internet," debuts as a government
experiment that links researchers
with remote computer centers.

1972
Nolan Bushnell produces Pong, the
black-and-white video game. Atari
releases the game in 1974, making it
the first electronic video game available in the United States.

Video, Games and New Media Magazines and Journals

Computer Entertainment News
CEN Publishing
P.O. Box 20508
Oakland, CA 94620
(510) 601-9275

Computer Gaming World
Ziff-Davis Publishing
950 Tower Lane
Foster City, CA 94404
(800) 827-4450
http://www.zdnet.com/gaming/

Cybersports
Sendai Publishing Group, Inc.
1920 Highland Ave., Suite 222
Lombard, IL 60148
(708) 916-7222
http://www.cybersports.com

Cyber Surfer
475 Park Ave. S.
New York, NY 10016
(212) 689-2830

EGM2
Sendai Publishing Group, Inc.
1920 Highland Ave., Suite 222
Lombard, IL 60148
(708) 916-7222

Electronic Entertainment
Infotainment World, Inc.
951 Mariner's Island Blvd., Suite 700
San Mateo, CA 94404
(415) 349-4300

Electronic Gaming Monthly
Sendai Publishing Group, Inc.
1920 Highland Ave., Suite 222
Lombard, IL 60148
(708) 916-7222
http://www.nuke.com/egm

Entertainment Weekly
1675 Broadway
New York, NY 10019
(212) 522-5600

Facets Video
1517 W. Fullerton Ave.
Chicago, IL 60614
(312) 281-9075

Family PC
Ziff-Davis Publishing
950 Tower Lane
Foster City, CA 94404
(800) 413-9749

Fusion
Sendai Publishing Group, Inc.
1920 Highland Ave., Suite 222
Lombard, IL 60148
(708) 268-2498

Game Players Sega-Nintendo
Imagine Publishing
1350 Old Bayshore Highway, Suite 210
Burlingame, CA 94010
(415) 696-1661

GamePro
Infotainment World, Inc.
951 Mariner's Island Blvd., Suite 700
San Mateo, CA 94404
(800) 879-0499

Inside the Internet
Cobb Group, Inc.
9420 Bunsen Pkwy., Suite 300
Louisville, KY 40232-9720
(502) 493-3200

Intelligent Gamer
Sendai Publishing Group, Inc.
1920 Highland Ave., Suite 222
Lombard, IL 60148
(708) 916-7222
http://igonline.escape.com

The Internet Underground
Sendai Publishing Group, Inc.
1920 Highland Ave., Suite 222
Lombard, IL 60148
(708) 916-7222
http://www.cdj.com.br/csv/news/iun-drgrd.htm

1975

Sony introduces the Beta-format VCR for consumer use.
IBM debuts the laser printer.

1976

JVC develops the Video Home System (VHS), which dominates the home market.

Steve Wozniak and Steve Jobs form Apple Computer Co.

1977

Bill Gates and Paul Allen form Microsoft Corp.

1979

Atari, Midway, Mattel, Cinematronics and Sega introduce the first video games such as Pac-Man and Space Invaders.

1980

The Sony Corporation introduces the camcorder.

1983

Radio Shack introduces the laptop computer with the TRS-80 Model 100.

1984

The first Macintosh computers are introduced with built-in graphical interface.

Philips and Sony introduce the compact disk, which can store up to 270,000 typewritten pages.

Internet World
Mecklermedia Corp.
20 Ketchum St.
Westport, CT 06880
(800) 573-3062
http://www.internetworld.com

Multimedia
Redgate Communications Corp.
660 Beachland Blvd.
Vero Beach, FL 32963
(407) 231-6904

Multimedia World
International Data Group
501 Second St., Suite 600
San Francisco, CA 94107
(800) 766-3294

The Net
Imagine Publishing
1350 Old Bayshore Highway, Suite 210
Burlingame, CA 94010
(415) 696-1688
http://www.thenet-usa.com/

Net Guide
CMP Publications
600 Community Drive
Manhasset, NY 11030
(516) 562-5000
http://www.techweb.cmp.com/tech-web/ng/current

NewMedia
Hypermedia Communications, Inc.
P.O. Box 1771
Riverton, NJ 08077-7371
(609) 786-4430
http://www.hyperstand.com

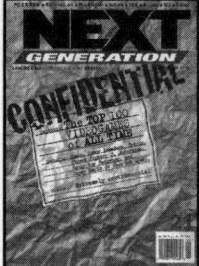

NEXT Generation
Imagine Publishing
1350 Old Bayshore Highway, Suite 210
Burlingame, CA 94010
(415) 696-1661
ngsubs@imagine-inc.com

PC Gamer
Imagine Publishing
1350 Old Bayshore Highway, Suite 210
Burlingame, CA 94010
(415) 696-1688
http://www.futurenet.co.uk/

PIX-Elation
P.O. Box 4139
Highland Park, NJ 08904
(908) 463-8787

PSX
Sendai Publishing Group, Inc.
1920 Highland Ave., Suite 222
Lombard, IL 60148
(708) 916-7222

Strategy Plus
Box 21
Hancock, VT 05748
(800) 283-3542

TWICE Magazine
245 West 17th St.
New York, NY 10011
(212) 337-6980

Video Event
Connell Communications, Inc.
86 Elm St.
Peterborough, NH 03458
(603) 924-7013

Video Magazine
Hachette Filipacchi Magazines, Inc.
1633 Broadway, 45th Floor
New York, NY 10019
(800) 601-8345

Videomaker
Box 4591
Chico, CA 95927-4591
(916) 891-8410

Video Watchdog
Box 5283
Cincinnati, OH 45205-0283
(513) 471-8989
Virtual City
Virtual Communications, Inc.
444 Madison Ave, Suite 803
New York, NY 10022
(212) 593-1537
http://www.virtcitnow.com/

Wired
520 Third St., 4th Fl.
San Francisco, CA 94107-1427
(800) 769-4733
info@wired.com

Yahoo! Internet Life
Ziff-Davis Publishing
One Park Ave.
New York, NY 10016
(800) 950-0484
http://www.zdnet.com/yil

1985
Nintendo arrives in the U.S. home video game market.

1989
VCRs are found in 62 percent of U.S. homes.

1991
Japan begins limited high definition television (HDTV) broadcasting. The technology delivers a television image equivalent in quality to film photography.
The World Wide Web is born.

1992
The reduction of hardware costs prompts the sudden growth of multimedia systems.

1993
3DO releases the first 32-bit video game console. Sales are poor, and consumers stick with existing 16-bit technology.

1994
The Internet hits the mainstream, complete with malls, banks, radio stations and Pizza Hut.

1995
Sony and Sega release 32-bit video-game consoles and Nintendo a 64-bit machine, signaling the obsolescence of 16-bit games.

Microsoft launches Windows '95.

Home Entertainment Glossary

access provider A company that sells Internet connections. Also called **service provider.**

bandwidth The size of the data pipeline through which information travels on a network. The higher the bandwidth, the faster information can flow.

binary file A computer file of a picture, audio clip or software program.

bps (bits per second) The rate at which data is transferred between two modems.

browser A program that allows World Wide Web users to download and display documents.

CCD (Charge Coupled Device) An electronic chip that replaced the vacuum tube in video cameras. CCDs are more durable, smaller and less expensive than tubes and are responsible for the miniaturization and price decrease of home-video equipment.

CD-i (Compact Disk-interactive) A multimedia technology that displays digital data from a compact disk when connected to a television or color computer monitor. CD-i brings crisp graphics and high-quality audio to games, interactive reference products and other educational materials.

digerati The hip, cerebral leaders of the digital movement.

Dolby Pro Logic A trademark for an encoding and decoding system that takes audio information on laserdisc or video and divides it into four channels, left, right, center and surround, to give an in-theater feel to home viewing.

DVD (Digital Video Disk) A new video disk format that will likely replace VCRs. DVDs offer detailed, lifelike picture quality and powerful surround sound and are the same size as an audio compact disk.

emoticon Text used to indicate emotions, humor or irony in electronic messages. It is best understood when viewed sideways. The most common symbols are : -) and : - (, which convey positive and negative emotions respectively. Also called **smiley.**

FAQ (Frequently Asked Questions) A file of questions and answers that addresses the most common queries on a particular subject in a newsgroup or mailing list.

FTP (File Transfer Protocol) A common method of downloading files between computers.

full-motion video An advanced gaming feature in which real video footage is incorporated into the graphics.

GIF (Graphic Image File) A common format used to transfer pictures on the Internet.

gopher A menu-based guide to directories on the Internet, usually organized by topic.

hit A means of measuring how many visitors have accessed a Web site.

HTML (Hypertext Markup Language) The programming language used to create Internet documents.

hypertext Highlighted words that link Internet documents to others with related subject matter.

jog/shuttle The VCR control that allows the user to quickly rewind or fast forward to a particular frame. It is useful for editing.

lurker Someone who regularly reads messages on a newsgroup or mailing list but never posts a message.

mailing list A group discussion or other communication that is automatically distributed through E-mail.

MUD (Multi-User Dungeon) A text-based Internet role-playing game in which participants assume characters to create a virtual fantasy world. MUDs have gained a notorious reputation for being highly addictive.

newbie A newcomer to the Internet, discussion group or on-line area.

newsgroup An on-line discussion group that is organized by subject.

post To send a message to a newsgroup.

QuickTime A multimedia technology developed by Apple to display video, sound, text and animation files.

role-playing game (rpg) An adventure game in which participants become characters, from monsters to medieval princesses, to create a digital world.

QuickTime A multimedia technology developed by Apple to display video, sound, text and animation files.

search engine An indexing application that helps users find specific information on the Internet or in a large text file.

service provider See **access provider.**

shareware Software distributed free of charge. Some manufacturers offer shareware free with the hope that users will eventually purchase an updated version, while others wait for a specified period of time before charging.

shooter A video or computer game in which the object is to blast away the enemy.

simulator A fantasy game that reproduces an experience, such as flying a MIG-17 or throwing a winning touchdown, through compelling graphics and interactive strategy.

smiley See **emoticon.**

spam 1. To post an inappropriate message, most often a blatant advertisement, to multiple newsgroups. 2. To send unsolicited junk mail to personal E-mail boxes.

S-VHS A high-resolution VHS video recording standard that provides more than 400 lines of resolution as opposed to 240 lines of resolution from a regular VHS VCR.

texture-mapping The technology used to create crisp, realistic graphics in video and computer games.

thread A series of related messages in a newsgroup.

3DO Multimedia software used for home-video games that delivers spectacular graphics, three-dimensional landscapes and bold color. The 3DO Company licenses the technology to game manufacturers such as Sony and Nintendo.

URL (Uniform Resource Locator) The addressing system for the World Wide Web.

Usenet (User's Network) A collection of networks and computers on the Internet that exchange messages, which are organized into newsgroups.

World Wide Web A vast Internet network of graphics and information resources connected by hypertext links. Often called the **Web.**

PERFORMING ARTS

Mit Paukenschläge

Here's to a New Era

■ BY ROSS WETZSTEON

**Ross Wetzsteon
is senior
editor of the
Village Voice
and recently
wrote a book
about the history
of Greenwich
Village.**

THE 1995-1996 THEATER SEASON WAS THE MOST SUCCESSFUL OF THE decade, both artistically and commercially, but the year will be remembered for a tragic loss. In late January, a then unknown 35-year-old composer-librettist named Jonathan Larson went to a New York emergency room suffering from acute chest and abdominal pains and was told he was merely reacting to a bad meal. Two days later he went to another hospital emergency room and was again perfunctorily released. The next night, alone in his Lower East Side apartment, he died of an aortic aneurysm. The opening of *Rent*, Larson's Off-Broadway musical, was only a week away, and he would never know that his work would not only receive ecstatic reviews and move uptown to a long run on Broadway, but that it would also win the

THEATER

three most prestigious awards in the American theater — the Tony for the best new musical on Broadway, the Pulitzer Prize for drama and an Obie for creative achievement Off-Broadway. And theatergoers enraptured by *Rent* would never know what glorious melodies and luminous lyrics would be left unsung.

Loosely based on Puccini's *La Boheme*, *Rent*'s characters transformed from painters and writers living in Parisian garrets to video artists and rock musicians struggling to make ends meet in the shabby tenements of New York's Alphabet City — and AIDS replaced tuberculosis as the deadly threat hanging over their lives. It was instantly acclaimed as the *Hair* of the '90s. Many observers predicted, in fact, that with its exultant blend of rock music and contemporary issues, Larson's work would revitalize the American musical so long mired in tourist-trade banality and technological gadgetry.

But *Rent* was only one of four breakthrough Off-Broadway musicals that shattered the mainstream mold. George Wolfe and Savion Glover's *Bring in 'da Noise, Bring in 'da Funk*,

Michael Daniel

Bring in 'da Noise, Bring in 'da Funk

Joan Marcus/Carol Rosegg

Rent

Carol Rosegg/Shirley Herz Assoc.

Bed and Sofa

which also moved to Broadway after premiering at the Joseph Papp Public Theater, joyously and sardonically traced three centuries of African-American history through the medium of tap dancing. Adam Guettel, Richard Rodgers's grandson, collaborated with avant-garde director Tina Landau on the Playwrights Horizon production of *Floyd Collins*, a lushly tuneful and darkly foreboding examination of the foolhardy optimism and commercial exploitation that so often underlie the American Dream. And *Bed and Sofa*, the latest of Polly Pen's chamber musicals at the Vineyard Theater, audaciously based on a Soviet silent film, depicted a bizarre ménage à trois with buoyant charm. Who would have guessed that the most artistic achievements of the downtown experimental theater season would bring renewed vigor to the most traditional of American theatrical forms?

I f Jonathan Larson's tragically premature death was the most significant event of the season, Julie Andrews's farcically immature announcement that she was declining her Tony nomination was the most talked about, sending the New York press into a tabloid frenzy. The Tony nominating committee, for once overlooking its annual function of serving as an advertising adjunct to the entertainment industry, shocked Broadway producers by declining to name *Victor/Victoria*, a big-budget, low-aspiration spectacle, among its best musical selections, prompting Andrews's petulant move. Many considered her a shoo-in anyway, but she turned out not even to win.

Ironically, those who were selected for the Great White Way's highest honor reflected Broadway's creative sterility, for with the single exception of Nathan Lane's performance in *A Funny Thing Happened on the Way to the Forum*, every one of the 21 Tonys went to a show that had developed either Off-Broadway or in a nonprofit theater — or, in the case of *The King and I*, in Australia. (And Lane's Tony, of course, was for a show developed on Broadway decades ago.) Terrence McNally won his second consecutive best play Tony for *Master Class*, his depiction of Maria Callas as a kind of genius-gorgon, but the uptown year was largely an umpteenth consecutive season of pre-packaged revivals of classic musicals or pre-sold adaptations of hit movies. Broadway was no longer "the fabulous invalid" so much as the comatose automaton.

Sam Shepard

Still, 1996 was the year Edward Albee returned to Broadway after a long absence, his *A Delicate Balance* moving from Houston's Alley Theater, and the year Sam Shepard had his first Broadway production *ever*, his 1979 Pulitzer Prize-winning *Buried Child* transferring from Chicago's Steppenwolf Theater. Even better, Shepard will be the 1996–1997 playwright at Off-Broadway's Signature Theater. The Signature's play-wrights of 1994 and 1995, Horton Foote and Edward Albee, won Pulitzer Prizes in drama, making it three years in a row the Pulitzer went to an Off-Broadway production. Continuing its unique format of devoting an entire season to one playwright, this year Signature featured the work of the exquisitely talented African-American playwright Adrienne Kennedy, including her Obie-winning best play *June and Jean in Concert*, a densely textured memory play about growing up black in 1940s Cleveland.

Broadway producers may have been dismayed by the end-of-season Tony hassles — in addition to Andrews's fit, David Merrick brought a lawsuit on behalf of Rodgers and Hammerstein's *State Fair* concerning the eligibility of several of its songs; the stagehands union threatened a last-minute strike; and the CBS telecast barely blipped on the Nielsen ratings — but they were quickly soothed by a glance at the box-office figures.

Adrienne Kennedy

According to statistics released by the League of American Theatres and Producers, 9.4 million people attended the theater in New York City alone in the 1995–1996 theater season, a 5 percent increase over last season and the largest audience in 15 years. This represented a 7.3 percent increase in revenues, for a total of $436 million. The number of new productions on Broadway increased from 29 to 38, and, aston-ishingly, there were two Shakespeares, a Moliére, a Strindberg and a Wilde. The average paid admission on Broadway was a whopping $45.97, but at least the price of tickets increased at a rate less than the New York area cost of living.

Nationwide, the power surge was almost as large — audience increased 4.6 percent to 18.2 million, the highest figure ever recorded, with ticket sales exceeding $1.24 billion, a 12.4 percent increase from last season. In total, American theater entertained — and in some cases actually enlightened — 27.6 million people, and no matter if they saw Shakespeare or Simon, Chekhov or Lloyd Webber, at least they strayed from the television and Internet long enough to witness live theater.

But, of course, in the commodity theater, high expenses go with high revenue, and the relative cost of doing business uptown and downtown is one of the major reasons Broadway producers have to rely on Off-Broadway theaters to take their risks for them. *Rent*, for instance, cost $200,000 to mount at the New York Theater Workshop on East 4th Street, but $2 million to produce at the Nederlander on West 41st Street — who would have been foolish enough to invest that kind of money in an unknown composer with a quirky idea? Freed from such burdensome financial constraints, no wonder Off Broadway is more adventurous, more creative — and considerably less predictable.

So if Broadway measures success at the box office, Off Broadway measures success on the stage — and, despite another year of drastic cuts in arts funding, a season of extraor-dinary artistic achievement was reflected in the granting of 33 Obies, the most in the his-tory of the 41-year-old awards. In addition to Adrienne Kennedy and the fabulous foursome of musicals, recipients included four young playwrights who hold great promise for the American stage. In *Wally's Ghost*, Ain Gordon examined the intermingling of memory and hope in the confusing present. Holocaust plays, of course, face a multitude of nearly insu-perable risks — trivializing tragedy and aestheticizing horror being the most obvious — but in *The Model Apartment*, Donald Margulies dealt obliquely but resonantly with the pain of a family of death-camp survivors. In *Venus*, Suzan-Lori Parks, in her early thirties and already one of the most narratively evocative and poetically expressive talents in theater, explored the life of Venus Hottentot, the African woman put on display as an exotic primitive in the salons and music halls of 19th-century Europe. And in *Quills*, a witty, gorgeously written, Grand Guignol study of the Marquis de Sade, Doug Wright asked a series of provocative questions: What barbarities will we inflict in the name of untrammeled personal freedom; what cruelties are we capable of in the name of civilized decorum; what balance can we find between our deepest psychic impulses and our need for social order?

Among the other outstanding Off-Broadway artists honored at the Obies were the legendary director Ingmar Bergman for his series of revelatory productions at the Brooklyn Academy of Music and the newcomer Scott Elliott, who, on the basis of his emotionally nuanced ensemble work in last year's *Ecstasy* and this year's *Curtains*, is clearly destined to become one of the American theater's preeminent directors. The sustained achievement award to Uta Hagen couldn't have been better named — sustained since her debut in 1937 with her achievements including a multitude of memorable performances (climaxing in this season's incisive portrayal of psychiatrist Melanie Klein in *Mrs. Klein*), acting classes that have trained many of our theater's finest talents and the most influential book on acting published in the past quarter-century.

America's Off Broadway — the nonprofit institutional theaters — has long outgrown its condescending designation as "regional" theater. August Wilson's *Seven Guitars*, which eventually wended its way to New York after development at Chicago's

Mrs. Klein

Goodman Theater, didn't need Broadway "validation" any more than did Albee's *Delicate Balance* or Shepard's *Buried Child*. Other highlights from around the country included Randy Newman's *Faust* at the La Jolla Playhouse, Robert Wilson's one-man *Hamlet* at

605

1995–1996 BROADWAY TOURING PRODUCTIONS

These productions mounted major national tours during the 1995–1996 theater season.

- Ain't Misbehavin'
- Beauty and the Beast (2)
- Big
- Carousel
- Damn Yankees
- Death of a Salesman
- Dial M for Murder
- Hello, Dolly!
- An Inspector Calls
- Jekyll & Hyde
- Master Class
- A Midsummer Night's Dream
- Moon Over Buffalo
- Music of the Night
- Seven Guitars
- Showboat
- Rodgers & Hammerstein's State Fair
- Three Tall Women
- Victor/Victoria
- West Side Story
- A Tuna Christmas (2)

Source: League of American Theatres and Producers

1995–1996 BROADWAY SEASON STATISTICS

	Attendance	Ticket Sales
Musical	7,210,636	$357,260,268
Straight Play	1,966,265	$67,686,354
Special Attraction	307,683	$11,054,112
TOTAL	9,484,584	$436,000,734

Average Paid Admission: $45.97

Source: League of American Theatres and Producers

Houston's Alley Theater, Susan Sontag's *Alice in Bed* and Claire Bloom in *Long Day's Journey Into Night* at Cambridge, Massachusetts's American Repertory Theater, and an end and a beginning — Garland Wright's farewell season at the Guthrie in Minneapolis and heralded young playwright and Susan Smith Blackburn-winner Naomi Wallace's debut production at the Humana Festival in Louisville.

And let's not "egregiously overlook" — in the Julie Andrews phrase so prominently featured on the Tony telecast — the Off-Broadway debuts of two movie stars turned playwrights, Steve Martin with his often hilarious and only occasionally pretentious *Picasso at the Lapin Agile* at the Promenade and Laurence Fishburne with his street-wise and stage-savvy *Riff-Raff* at Circle Rep. Even those disturbed by the Disneyfication of Broadway were heartened by the news that Walt's heirs have signed the gifted Off-Broadway puppeteer and designer Julie Taymor to bring her magic touch to the upcoming stage production of *The Lion King*. And don't forget the *Encores* series at New York's City Center — book-in-hand stagings of classic musicals that over the past couple of years have become the "in" ticket of the season, culminating this spring in an acclaimed *Chicago* and a *One Touch of Venus* featuring such a saucily elegant performance by Melissa Errico. It's obvious she'll soon become an over-the-title star. And an off-stage development bodes just as well for the American theater, especially for the Off-Broadway scene so often slighted by the "major" critics — the appointment of the brilliant young writer Ben Brantley as chief theater critic of the *New York Times*.

Among his other achievements, Jonathan Larson brought a younger generation to Broadway — now it's up to other artists and critics to keep them there. As *Rent*'s Wilson Jermaine Heredia put it in accepting his Tony for best featured actor in a musical — as an effervescent transvestite no less — "Here's to a new era in theater!" Let's hope these newcomers can handle the pressure. ■

1995 — 1996 Broadway Premieres

This year heralded a new heyday for Broadway, with an increased number of openings and breakthrough success for several productions that got their starts Off Broadway. The following alphabetical list presents Broadway shows that opened between September 1995 and August 1996.

THE APPLE DOESN'T FALL

By: Trish Vradenburg; **Director:** Leonard Nimoy; **Sets and Projections:** Kenneth Foy; **Costumes:** Gail Cooper-Hecht; **Lighting:** Kenn Billington; **Sound:** Tom Clark; **Music:** David Lawrence
Opened: 4/96 at the Lyceum Theater
Cast: Margaret Whitton, Florence Stanley, Lee Wallace, Janet Sarno, Richard Cox and Madeline Miller

When Selma Griswald (Stanley) is diagnosed with Alzheimer's disease, her husband of 42 years deserts her for another woman. Kate (Whitton), the couple's award-winning but unhappy television-writer daughter, is left to care for her mother, though the two struggle with an uneasy love-hate relationship. Relief comes when handsome, single Dr. Sam Gordon (Cox) produces a miracle drug that puts Selma into remission and inspires her to drag Kate along on a dude-ranch vacation spree. Wooden, sitcom-style language, painfully banal emotions and a depressing set overwhelm a competent cast to make this production a complete dud.

BIG

Book: John Weidman; **Music:** David Shire; **Lyrics:** Richard Maltby, Jr.; **Director:** Mike Ockrent; **Choreography:** Susan Stroman; **Sets:** Robin Wagner; **Costumes:** William Ivey Long; **Lighting:** Paul Gallo; **Sound:** Steve Canyon Kennedy
Opened: 4/96 at the Shubert Theater
Cast: Daniel Jenkins, Crista Moore, Jon Cypher, Barbara Walsh, Gene Weygandt, Brett Tabisel and Patrick Levis

Advance hype for this production centered on the huge marketing boost the show provided FAO Schwarz, purveyor of kiddie accessories and the scene of one dance number. The controversy is oddly appropriate to *Big*, a Broadway remake of the 1988 blockbuster movie in which child/man Tom Hanks brings wide-eyed innocence to the greedy, cynical world of — you guessed it — toy marketing. Twelve-year-old Josh Baskin (Levis) wishes so hard to be grown up that he suddenly finds himself in a 30-year-old body. As big Josh (Jenkins), he runs away to New York and goes to work for toy manufacturer MacMillan (Cypher). Still secretly a child himself, Big Josh can easily imagine things to play with, and he becomes a star toy inventor, meanwhile attracting the lustful attentions of Susan (Moore), the ambitious marketing director who

Joan Marcus/Carol Rosegg

Big

decides that Josh is her ticket to the top. Josh's innocence softens Susan's hardness into genuine affection, and she initiates him into manhood's mysteries. But Josh regretfully returns to childhood and is reunited with his lonely mother. Good performances by the leads, a wonderful corps of child dancers and a lively score make this *Big* fun and faithful to the spirit of the original.

BRING IN 'DA NOISE, BRING IN 'DA FUNK: A TAP/RAP DISCOURSE ON THE STAYING POWER OF THE BEAT

Book: Reg E. Gaines; **Music:** Daryl Waters, Zane Mark and Ann Duquesnay, conceived by George C. Wolfe and Savion Glover; **Director:** George C. Wolfe; **Choreography:** Savion Glover; **Sets:** Riccardo Hernandez; **Costumes:** Paul Tazewill; **Lighting:** Jules Fisher and Peggy Eisenhauer; **Sound:** Dan Moses Schreier; **Projections:** Batwin+Robin
Opened: 4/96 at the Ambassador Theater
Cast: Savion Glover, Baakari Wilder, Jimmy Tate, Vincent Bingham, Jeffrey Wright, Ann Duquesnay, Jared Crawford, Raymond King and Dule Hill

Originally an Off-Broadway production, this snappy tap-dance extravaganza re-creates black American history from the slave ships through plantation life and into the current era of supposed equal rights. Rhythm is the common thread running through the eras, and tap-dancing is showcased as a vital art form, not as throwaway light entertainment. The fine singing and forceful dancing, especially the brilliant tap work of 22-year-old Broadway veteran Savion Glover, pack a strong musical and emotional punch. Simple staging and innovative lighting effectively complement this powerful production.

BURIED CHILD

By: Sam Shepard; **Director:** Gary Sinise; **Sets:** Robert Brill; **Costumes:** Allison Reeds; **Lighting:** Kevin Rigdon; **Sound:** Rob Milburn
Opened: 4/96 at the Brooks Atkinson Theater
Cast: Leo Burmester, James Gammon, Terry Kinney, Jim Mohr, Kellie Overbey, Lois Smith and Jim True

Sam Shepard makes his Broadway debut with this Steppenwolf Theater Company revival of the 1979 Pulitzer Prize winner, the second play in his trilogy about the American family. When Vince (True) brings girlfriend Shelly (Overbey) home to the Illinois family farm, no one recognizes him. Eccentric grandfather Dodge (Gammon) argues with sleazy grandmother Halie (Smith), who is carrying on with Father Dewis (Mohr). Vince's hulking failure of a father, Tilden (Kinney), is blinded by his fixation on gathering vegetables. In their rundown farmhouse, the family immerses itself in common dark secrets and idiosyncrasies. While outsider Shelly refuses to be sucked into the dysfunctional environment, Vince is dragged down into the family past and forced to confront his ancestors. This effective production presents a classic fable of the American family's seamy underside. Unfortunately, even with the draw of Shepard and the production's artistic merits, it failed to emerge as one of the season's commercial successes.

BUS STOP

By: William Inge; **Director:** Josephine R. Abady; **Sets:** Hugh Landwehr; **Costumes:** Linda Fisher; **Lighting:** Dennis Parichy; **Sound:** Tom Gould
Opened: 2/96 at the Circle in the Square
Cast: Mary-Louise Parker, Ron Perlman, Billy Crudup, Michael Cullen, Patricia Dunnock, Larry Pine, Scott Sowers and Kelly Bishop

In this familiar study of love and romance in a small-town Kansas diner, eight characters are stranded overnight during a snowstorm: the pretty, self-styled working-class girl (Parker); the rodeo rider in love with her (Crudup); his shrewd friend (Pine); the alcoholic intellectual (Perlman); the Shakespeare-quoting teen waitress (Dunnock); the virile bus driver (Cullen); the local sheriff (Sowers); and the diner's proprietress (Bishop). As the night unfolds, secrets creep out and passions burn for an unsentimental commentary on love. Newcomer Crudup as the innocent cowboy Bo commands the theater-in-the-round as he willfully and naively pursues the hardened chanteuse, Cherie, played with skill by Parker. The rest of the cast turns in steady performances to lift this high-school drama-club favorite above the trademark

Joan Marcus

Fool Moon

conventionality that denied Inge a place among America's great playwrights.

COMPANY

Music and Lyrics: Stephen Sondheim; **Book:** George Furth; **Director:** Scott Ellis; **Musical Direction:** David Loud; **Musical Staging:** Rob Marshall; **Sets:** Tony Walton; **Costumes:** William Ivey Long; **Lighting:** Peter Kaczorowski; **Sound:** Tony Meola
Opened: 10/95 at the Roundabout Theatre Company
Cast: Boyd Gaines, Kate Burton, Robert Westenberg, Patricia Ben Peterson, Jonathan Dokuchitz, Diana Canova, John Hillner, Veanne Cox, Danny Burstein, Debra Monk, Timothy Landfield, La Chanze, Charlotte d'Amboise and Jane Krakowski

There were plenty of doubting Thomases who didn't have much confidence in the revival of the Tony-winning 1970 musical about a 38-year-old bachelor Robert (Gaines) and his married friends who want him to experience the bliss and travails of marriage. Any doubts were quickly put to rest. Through a series of flashbacks involving the successes and failures of his friends, Robert contemplates his own future. Judging from the number of Robert's one-night stands, one would think he was searching for the perfect mate, but deep down he is fearful of commitment. The women drive the production, giving strong, sometimes surprising performances. Cox wows the audience with "Getting Married Today."

DANNY GANS ON BROADWAY

Lighting: John Featherstone, Fred Irish and Norm Schwab; **Sound:** On Stage Audio and Tom Nicks; **General Management:** Leo K. Cohen; **Production Supervisor:** Chip Lightman
Opened: 11/95 at the Neil Simon Theatre
With: Danny Gans

This one-man act is an odd choice for a Broadway production — a Las Vegas venue would have been more appropriate. But Gans proves an amusing and convincing impressionist who entertains without offending. His repertoire includes uncanny impressions of Frank Sinatra, Bruce Springsteen, George Burns, Michael Jackson, Sammy Davis, Jr., Nat "King" and Natalie Cole, Elvis Presley, Tom Hanks and Al Pacino.

A DELICATE BALANCE

By: Edward Albee; **Director:** Gerald Guiterrez; **Sets:** John Lee Beatty; **Costumes:** Jane Greenwood; **Lighting:** Pat Collins; **Sound:** Aural Fixation
Opened: 4/96 at the Plymouth Theater at Lincoln Center
Cast: Rosemary Harris, George Grizzard, Elaine Stritch, John Carter, Elizabeth Wilson and Mary Beth Hurt
The Lincoln Center Theater once again gives an old play a new lease on life. Presenters of last season's acclaimed *The Heiress*, the company has brilliantly revived Albee's 1966 Pulitzer Prize winner, which originally starred Jessica Tandy and Hume Cronyn but enjoyed only a mediocre run. The current production emphasizes the blackly humorous side of middle-class suburban angst. Agnes (Harris) and Tobias (Grizzard) have long taken their marriage and material comforts for granted, sparring with each other and with Agnes's live-in alcoholic sister, Claire (Stritch). Anticipating the return of their daughter, Julia (Hurt), after the failure of her fourth marriage, they are surprised when Tobias's best friend, Harry (Carter), and his wife, Edna (Wilson), appear first, seeking refuge from the nameless fear that has suddenly overwhelmed them. When Julia returns and angrily demands her bedroom, the couples are forced to negotiate loyalties, and their uneasy complacency is shattered. Affluent suburbanite sets frame good performances from all, highlighted by Harris's perfectly tuned acting.

THE FATHER

By: August Strindberg, adapted by Richard Nelson; **Director:** Clifford Williams; **Sets:** John Lee Beatty; **Costumes:** Martin Pakledinaz; **Lighting:** Kenneth Posner; **Sound:** John Gromada
Opened: 1/96 at the Criterion Center
Cast: Frank Langella, Ivar Brogger, William Verderber, Garret Dillahunt, Gail Strickland, Tom Beckett, Irene Dailey and Angela Bettis
Langella elicits a career-making performance in the notoriously demanding role of the tortured husband and father in Strindberg's mesmerizing tale of domestic disintegration. Langella's Captain teeters on madness as his manipulating wife (Strickland) hints that their daughter (Bettis) was fathered by another man. As the marriage hurtles toward disaster, Langella's captivating command of the stage does not meet its match in the other performers. But with the well-conceived set and Nelson's deft adaptation, the production succeeds in finding a setting for its star's grandeur.

FOOL MOON

By: David Shiner and Bill Irwin; **Set:** Douglas Stein; **Costumes:** Bill Kellard; **Lighting:** Nancy Schertler; **Sound:** Tom Morse; **Music:** Red Clay Ramblers
Opened: 10/95 at the Ambassador Theater
Cast: David Shiner and Bill Irwin
A sweet, endearing night at the theater with two premier exponents of clowning tradition, Bill Irwin and David Shiner. Both alone and together, the baggy-pants duo spend much of the night playing with the audience, venturing out to steal seats, coats and cameras and, in the most involved audience participation segment (of which there are many), cast and direct a silent-film romance/tragedy that leads to outright hilarity rather than pathos. Irwin and Shiner are accompanied by the Red Clay Ramblers, an appropriately deadpan aggregation that lends musical support, sound effects and the occasional foil for a prank. The music also provides a backdrop for the clowns' serious soft-shoe and juggling expertise. These are performers who move seamlessly and athletically in a kind of mischievous ballet. By *Fool Moon*'s poignant close, you're not sure whether the tears on your cheeks are from laughter or from witnessing such pure, innocent beauty.

A FUNNY THING HAPPENED ON THE WAY TO THE FORUM

Book: Burt Shevelove and Larry Gelbart; **Music and Lyrics:** Stephen Sondheim; **Director:** Jerry Zaks; **Set and Costumes:** Tony Walton; **Lighting:** Paul Gallo; **Sound:** Tony Meola
Opened: 4/96 at the St. James Theater
Cast: Nathan Lane, Brad Aspel, Cory English, Ray Roderick, Jim Stanek, Jessica Boevers, Lewis J. Stadlen, Mary Testa, Mark Linn-Baker, Ernie Sabella, Pamela Everett, Cris Groenendaal and Leigh Zimmerman
Birdcage camp star Lane grabs audience attention in this much anticipated revival of Sondheim's indestructible 1962 musical farce. Lane plays Pseudolus, the Roman slave who so longs for freedom that he risks his life to procure the virgin Philia (Boevers) for his young master, Hero (Stanek). Philia lives with Marcus Lycus (Sabella), trader of courtesans, who has promised to sell

Joan Marcus

The Father

The 46th annual Outer Critics Circle Awards were presented on May 24, 1996, at New York's venerable Sardi's restaurant. The Outer Critics Circle includes theater writers who review New York theater productions for out-of-town publications.

Joan Marcus

Master Class

Outstanding Broadway Play
  Master Class

Outstanding Broadway Musical
  Victor/Victoria

Outstanding Revival — Play
  Inherit the Wind

Outstanding Revival — Musical
  The King and I

Outstanding Off-Broadway Play (tie)
  Molly Sweeney

  Picasso at the Lapin Agile

Outstanding Off-Broadway Musical
  Rent

Outstanding Performance by an Actor
  George C. Scott, *Inherit the Wind*

Outstanding Performance by an Actress
  Zoe Caldwell, *Master Class*

Outstanding Actor in a Musical
  Nathan Lane, *A Funny Thing Happened on the Way to the Forum*

Outstanding Actress in a Musical
  Julie Andrews, *Victor/Victoria*

Outstanding Solo Performance
  Patti LuPone, *Patti LuPone on Broadway*

her to the warrior Miles Gloriosus (Groenendaal). If Pseudolus can spirit the girl away, Hero will release him from slavery, but if he fails, Gloriosus will kill him. The involvement of cowardly slave Hysterium (Linn-Baker) and Hero's unattractive parents Senex (Stadlen) and Domina (Testa) adds further farcical twists to the life-and-death slapstick. The current production brings a tone of arch parody to what was originally a masterpiece of straightforward comic mayhem. Working hard to keep the laughs moving fast, the cast sweeps the audience away in manic hilarity.

GARDEN DISTRICT
(Two one-act plays, *Something Unspoken* and *Suddenly Last Summer*)
By: Tennessee Williams; **Director:** Theodore Mann and Harold Scott; **Sets and Costumes:** Zack Brown; **Lighting:** Marc B. Weiss; **Sound:** Bruce Cameron; **Fight Choreography:** B.H. Barry
Opened: 10/95 at the Circle in the Square
Cast: Elizabeth Ashley, Jordan Baker, Myra Carter, Pamela Payton-Wright, Peggy Cosgrave, Mitchell Lichtenstein, Leslie Lyles, Celia Weston and Victor Slezak

Something Unspoken
There are no men in this small play set in New Orleans's Garden District; they have all died after copiously providing for less-than-desirable women. Two of the women left behind, Cornelia (Carter) and Grace (Payton-Wright), her secretary, have lesbian feelings for each other, but they're not sure how to address their affection. Through persistence and persuasion, Cornelia finally prods Grace into admitting they have "something" to talk about.

Suddenly Last Summer
Also set in the Garden District, *Suddenly Last Summer* looks as if it should dazzle with its beautifully lit garden set. But the play, the main attraction in the double bill, falls short. The actors seem uncomfortable with the script and set, which impedes free movement onstage. Mrs. Venable (Ashley), a vicious and wealthy widower, is obsessed with her dead son, Sebastian, a dilettante and passionate homosexual. Mrs. Venable tries to purge the gory memories of her son's death from her niece Catherine (Baker) by having her lobotomized.

GETTING AWAY WITH MURDER
By: Steven Sondheim and George Furth; **Director:** Jack O'Brien; **Sets:** Douglas W. Schmidt; **Lighting:** Kenneth Posner; **Costumes:** Robert Wojewodski; **Sound:** Jeff Ladman; **Special Effects:** Gregory Meeh; **Fight Director:** Steve Rankin; **General Manager:** Jeff Lee
Opened: 2/96 at the Broadhurst Theater
Cast: John Rubinstein, Christine Ebersole, William Ragsdale, Michelle Hurd, Kandis Chappell, Josh Mostel, Terrence Mann, Frankie R. Faison, Jodi Long, Al Espinosa and Herb Foster

Seven patients of a distinguished psychiatrist gather for their weekly group-therapy session to discover their doctor bludgeoned to death. Suspecting each other of the crime, they bumble through their own investigation. While the ensemble cast delivers a sturdy performance, Sondheim and Furth disappoint with the mystery's shockingly dull, heavy-handed exposition. When the audience figures out the culprit long before the characters, the production bears the added burden of an anticlimactic ending. Atmospheric lighting and creepy special effects recover some of the requisite whodunit spookiness, but it's not enough to make up for the lackluster script.

HELLO, DOLLY!

Book: Michael Stewart, based on the play *The Matchmaker* by Thornton Wilder; **Music and Lyrics:** Jerry Herman; **Director:** Lee Roy Reams; **Associate Choreographer:** Bill Bateman; **Sets:** Oliver Smith; **Lighting:** Ken Billington; **Costumes:** Jonathan Bixby; **Sound:** Peter J. Fitzgerald; **Music Supervision:** Tim Stella; **Orchestrations:** Philip J. Lang; **Dance Arrangements:** Peter Howard; **Music Director and Conductor:** Jack Everly; **Production Stage Manager:** Thomas P. Carr
Opened: 10/95 at the Lunt-Fontanne Theatre
Cast: Carol Channing, Jay Garner, Michael DeVries, Florence Lacey, Cory English, Lori Ann Mahl, James Darrah, Monica M. Wemitt, Christine DeVito and Steve Pudenz
Channing's back on Broadway, proving she is the only worthy Dolly Gallagher Levi, the turn-of-the-century Yonkers matchmaker. Since 1964, when the show premiered, the husky-voiced star has played the role nearly 4,500 times, but she doesn't seem at all bored with the part. Quite the opposite. At 74, she dazzles with unrelenting energy as the widow enlisted to find a wife for the peevish, half-millionaire Horace Vandergelder (Garner), though she would like him for herself.

Joan Marcus

Hello, Dolly!

Outstanding Debut of an Actor
Lou Diamond Phillips, *The King and I*

Outstanding Debut of an Actress
Karen Kay Cody, *Master Class*

John Gassner Playwriting Award
Steve Martin, *Picasso at the Lapin Agile*

Outstanding Director of a Play
Lloyd Richards, *Seven Guitars*

Outstanding Director of a Musical
Jerry Zaks, *A Funny Thing Happened on the Way to the Forum*

Outstanding Choreography
Savion Glover, *Bring in 'da Noise, Bring in 'da Funk*

Outstanding Design
Brian Thomson, scenic design; Roger Kirk, costume design; Nigel Levings, lighting design, *The King and I*

Special Achievement Awards
Carol Channing, *Hello, Dolly!*

Betty Corwin, founder and director, Theatre on Film and Tape Archive of the New York Public Library

The cast of *Seven Guitars* for outstanding ensemble performance

1995 NEW YORK DRAMA CRITICS' CIRCLE AWARDS

The New York Drama Critics' Circle announced its 1995 winners on May 20, 1996. The 17-member group includes critics from all New York City's newspapers, magazines and wire services except the *New York Times.*

Best New Play
Seven Guitars

Best Foreign Play
Molly Sweeney

Best Musical
Rent

Special Citation
Encores! Great American Musicals in Concert, for its concert performances of overlooked musicals

The 1996 Los Angeles Drama Critics Awards were presented on March 18, 1996, at Studio City's Sportsmen's Lodge.

Productions
 Beauty and the Beast
 The Homecoming
 Wit

Lead Performances
 Zoe Caldwell, *Master Class*
 Megan Cole, *Wit*
 Julie Hagerty, *Raised in Captivity*
 Charles Hallahan, *Endgame*
 Gregory Itzin, *The Homecoming*
 Marcia Mitzman, *Chess*
 W. Morgan Sheppard, *The Homecoming*
 Sean Smith, *Chess*

Featured Performances
 Jane Carr, *She Stoops to Folly*
 Tsai Chin, *The Woman Warrior*
 Jane Kaczmarek, *Raised in Captivity*
 Douglas Sills, *She Stoops to Folly*

Writing
 Margaret Edson, *Wit*
 Brad Fraser, *Unidentified Human Remains and the True Nature of Love*
 Deborah Rogin, *The Woman Warrior* (adapted from the book by Maxine Hong Kingston)

Direction
 Martin Benson, *Wit*
 Andrew J. Robinson, *Endgame* and *The Homecoming*

Musical Direction
 Ron Abel, *Twist of Fate*

Choreography
 Rob Marshall, *Damn Yankees*

Original Music
 Ron Abel, *Twist of Fate*

Scenic Design
 Ralph Funicello, *She Stoops to Folly*
 Stan Meyer, *Beauty and the Beast*

Lighting Design
 Paulie Jenkins, *Wit*
 Natasha Katz, *Beauty and the Beast*

Costume Design
 Ann Hould-Ward, *Beauty and the Beast*
 Shigeru Yaji, *She Stoops to Folly*

Lifetime Achievement Award
 Carol Channing

HOLIDAY

By: Philip Barry; **Director:** David Warren; **Sets:** Derek McLane; **Costumes:** Martin Pakledinaz; **Lighting:** Donald Holder; **Sound and Score:** John Gromada; **Style and Movement:** Loyd Williamson
Opened: 12/95 at the Circle in the Square Theatre
Cast: Tony Goldwyn, Laura Linney, Kim Raver, Jim Oyster, Reese Madigan, Reg Rogers, Tom Lacy, Rod McLachlan, Becca Lish, Michael Countryman and Anne Lange

It's not easy to pull off a successful performance in the Circle, and director Warren and set designer McLane should be commended, possibly even recruited as permanent fixtures to the theater-in-the-round. This revival of the 1928 classic that *almost* starred Katharine Hepburn (she was an understudy) amuses when it could easily bore with its dated society mileu. Johnny Case (Goldwyn) believes in having fun and plans to retire when he has amassed $25,000 (remember, the original is almost 70 years old). It doesn't take him long to reach his goal with the help of the 1928 pre-crash stock market. His fiancée, Julia Seton (Raver), is appalled with his agenda; she expects a comfortable future with houses in the city and country. Her millionaire father, Edward (Lacy), is even more disgusted when he hears the news. Julia's sister, Linda (Linney), the independent thinker in the family, supports and encourages Johnny, and the two unite, making a much more suitable couple than the original pair.

AN IDEAL HUSBAND

By: Oscar Wilde; **Director:** Peter Hall; **Designer:** Carl Toms; **Lighting:** Joe Atkins, in association with Mike Baldassari
Opened: 4/96 at the Ethel Barrymore Theater
Cast: David Yelland, Penny Downie, Victoria Hasted, Michael Denison, Martin Shaw and Anna Carteret

After a 3-year London run, this polished revival of Wilde's 100-year-old drawing-room morality play arrives as a fitting end to a vibrant Broadway season. Scheming widow Mrs. Chevely (Carteret) is blackmailing irreproachably honest politician Sir Robert Chiltern (Yelland). Panicking that he will lose both his well-deserved reputation for integrity and his devoted but moralistic wife, Lady Chiltern (Downie), the politician turns to his friend Goring (Shaw), whose world-weary love for the couple leads him to mastermind a resolution. After many farcical plot twists, the Chilterns are reconciled and reach a new level of maturity and forgiveness. Elegant sets and understated lighting form a perfect backdrop for fluid performances by cast members, several of whom have been playing their parts for years.

INHERIT THE WIND

By: Jerome Lawrence and Robert E. Lee; **Director:** John Tillinger; **Sets:** James Noone; **Costumes:** Jess Goldstein; **Lighting:** Ken Billington; **Sound:** Aural Fixation

Opened: 4/96 at the Royale Theater
Cast: George C. Scott, Charles Durning, Kate Forbes, Garret Dillahunt, Tom Aldredge and Anthony Heald

Seventy years after science clashed with religion in the infamous Scopes "Monkey" Trial, creationism is enjoying a rebirth in the United States, and this 1955 play based on the trial remains oddly current. Clarence Darrow, the colorful defender of hopeless cases, was the inspiration for lawyer Henry Drummond (Scott), who is called in to represent a biology teacher accused of violating state law by teaching Darwin's theory of evolution. Since the defendant does not deny the charges, the trial becomes a moral confrontation between the incisive Drummond and gregarious prosecutor Matthew Harrison Brady (Durning), a character based on William Jennings Bryan. Denied permission to introduce scientific testimony, Drummond calls Brady to the stand as an expert Bible witness, and the two stage an intellectual wrestling match. Scott's commanding performance leads a good cast, including scores of extras who populate the evocative set.

JACK: A NIGHT ON THE TOWN WITH JOHN BARRYMORE

Conceived by: Nicol Williamson and Leslie Megahey; **Director:** Leslie Megahey; **Sets:** Bethia Jane Green; **Lighting:** Richard Winkler; **Sound:** Christopher Bond
Opened: 4/96 at the Belasco Theater
Cast: Nicol Williamson

This one-man show comes five years after Williamson's volatile Broadway stint as Barrymore's rambunctious ghost in *I Hate Hamlet*. Though Williamson bears no physical resemblance to Barrymore, he shares the star's legendary hell-raising reputation. After warming up the audience by recalling the notorious incident where he hit another actor during a stage fight, Williamson tempers feistiness with pathos, presenting Barrymore as a man beset by chronic insecurities that eventually drove him to drink. But by humanizing Barrymore, Williamson deprives the star of his devilish glamour, and the finished portrait, though enjoyable, lacks panache.

THE KING AND I

Music: Richard Rodgers; **Book and Lyrics:** Oscar Hammerstein II, based on the novel *Anna and the King of Siam* by Margaret Shaw; **Director:** Christopher Renshaw; **Musical Staging:** Lar Lubovitch; **Choreography:** Jerome Robbins; **Sets:** Brian Thomson; **Costumes:** Roger Kirk; **Lighting:** Nigel Levings; **Sound:** Tony Meola and Lewis Mead
Opened: 4/96 at the Neil Simon Theater
Cast: Donna Murphy, Lou Diamond Phillips, Jose Llana, Joohee Choi and Taewon Kim

A spirited but firm governess, a stern yet vulnerable king, a touch of exotic Oriental mystique and lively, lasting melodies combine to make *The King and I* an enduring favorite of Rodgers and Hammerstein audiences. This revival of the 1951 Yul Brynner/Gertrude Lawrence original adds a

The King and I

Joan Marcus

few touches borrowed from the 1956 film, which also starred Brynner. Not to be overshadowed, Phillips triumphs as a sexy, commanding King, the perfect foil for Murphy's determined, fabulously full-voiced Anna. Lovely performances by Choi as rebellious concubine Tuptim and Kim as her lover add to the show's musical wealth. Sumptuous sets and a faithful reproduction of Robbins's original choreography round out this rich, thoroughly enjoyable production.

LOVE THY NEIGHBOR

Conceived, Written and Directed by: Jackie Mason; **Designer:** Neil Peter Jampolis
Opened: 3/96 at the Booth Theater
With: Jackie Mason

In 90 minutes of tough, self-mocking standup humor, Mason covers all the bases, from his own Jewish childhood, to public figures such as O.J. and Bob Dole, to life in a cyberspace wasteland. There's something here to offend everyone, but comedy king Mason is a master at winning the audience back.

MASTER CLASS

By: Terrence McNally; **Director:** Leonard Foglia; **Sets:** Michael McGarty; **Costumes:** Jane Greenwood; **Lighting:** Brian MacDevitt; **Sound:** Jon Gottlieb; **Music Supervisor:** David Loud; **Production Stage Manager:** Dianne Trulock
Opened: 11/95 at the Golden Theatre
Cast: Zoe Caldwell, David Loud, Karen Kay Cody, Michael Friel, Audra McDonald and Jay Hunter Morrs

Opera diva Maria Callas (Caldwell) strolls onto the stage with the grandeur and airs one would expect from one of opera's most talented, glamorous and bitchy performers. Callas is conducting one of the master classes she taught between her retirement in 1965 and her death in 1977. Ready to devote her time and attention to her three students, Callas has no time for the second-rate and barely allows her first, Sophie (Cody), to get past the first syllable of her piece. She badgers Sharon

1996 DRAMA DESK AWARDS

The Drama Desk, a group of 150 theater critics and reporters, announced the 1996 award winners on May 20, 1996.

Outstanding Play
Master Class

Outstanding Musical
Rent

Outstanding Musical Revival
The King and I

Outstanding Play Revival
A Delicate Balance

Outstanding One-Person Show
Mary Louise Wilson, *Full Gallop*

Best Actor in a Play
Frank Langella, *The Father*

Best Actress in a Play
Zoe Caldwell, *Master Class*

Best Featured Actor in a Play
Martin Shaw, *An Ideal Husband*

Best Featured Actress in a Play
Elaine Stritch, *A Delicate Balance*

Best Actor in a Musical
Nathan Lane, *A Funny Thing Happened on the Way to the Forum*

Best Actress in a Musical
Julie Andrews, *Victor/Victoria*

Best Featured Actor in a Musical
Wilson Jermaine Heredia, *Rent*

Best Featured Actress in a Musical
Rachel York, *Victor/Victoria*

Best Director of a Play
Gerald Gutierrez, *A Delicate Balance*

Best Director of a Musical
Christopher Renshaw, *The King and I*

Set Design for a Play
Scott Bradley, *Seven Guitars*

Set Design for a Musical
Brian Thomson, *The King and I*

Choreography
Savion Glover, *Bring in 'da Noise, Bring in 'da Funk*

Lighting
Jules Fisher and Peggy Eisenhauer, *Bring in 'da Noise, Bring in 'da Funk*

Costumes
Roger Kirk, *The King and I*

Honorary Awards
George C. Scott
Repertorio Español
Signature Theatre Co.
Theaterworks/USA

(McDonald) to the point that the girl throws up but then coaches and encourages her when she recovers. In two scenes, Callas mentally leaves the session, becoming transfixed by the memory of her own performance at La Scala and by her chaotic relationship with Aristotle Onassis. A winner made mesmerizing by the star and her supporting cast.

A MIDSUMMER NIGHT'S DREAM

By: William Shakespeare; **Director:** Adrian Noble; **Designer:** Anthony Ward; **Lighting:** Chris Parry; **Music:** Ilona Sekacz; **Sound:** Paul Slocombe
Opened: 3/96 at the Lunt-Fontanne Theater
Cast: Alex Jennings, Lindsay Duncan, Barry Lynch, Alfred Burke, Monica Dolan, Daniel Evans, Kevin Robert Doyle, Emily Raymond, John Kane, Desmond Barrit and Mark Letheren

After an eight-year hiatus, the Royal Shakespeare Company returns to Broadway with the bard's madcap comedy of crossed destinies. Surrealist sets, lavish costumes and skillful lighting conjure up a forest world of fairies and carelessly cast spells, ruled by Titania (Duncan) and Oberon (Jennings). Irritated by Titania's disobedience, Oberon enlists the mischievous sprite Puck (Lynch) to drop a love potion on his sleeping wife's eyes, causing her to become infatuated with the first creature she sees upon waking. Human and fairy fates intermingle when the girl Hermia (Dolan) elopes to the forest with her lover, Lysander (Evans), to flee a death sentence for refusing to marry Demetrius (Doyle), the former beloved of her friend Helena (Raymond). Ordered by soft-hearted Oberon to set matters right between Demetrius and Helena, Puck unwittingly wreaks romantic havoc when he mistakenly applies the love potion to Lysander, causing him to fall in love with Helena. Meanwhile, Titania awakes to behold a clown disguised as an ass, and she is immediately smitten. Mortal and immortal hearts are at cross-purposes until Oberon and Puck remove their spells and romantic order is restored. Many members of this accomplished troupe have been playing their parts for two years, and they handle Shakespeare's language with magical fluency. While their fast-paced antics sometimes fail to invoke true starry-eyed romance, the production entrances the eye and the imagination.

MOON OVER BUFFALO

By: Ken Ludwig; **Director:** Tom Moore; **Sets:** Heidi Landesman; **Costumes:** Bob Mackie; **Lighting:** Ken Billington
Opened: 10/95 at the Martin Beck Theatre
Cast: Carol Burnett, Philip Bosco, Jane Connell, Randy Graff, Andy Taylor, Kate Miller, Dennis Ryan and James Valentine

Burnett returns to Broadway after a 30-year absence, proving she has not lost the goofy humor that catapulted her to stardom. In a play that was written for a male lead, Burnett unfortunately is underutilized as Charlotte Hay, a middle-aged actress, who, with her husband, George (Bosco), is touring in repertory with two productions. In one day, Charlotte learns the young ingénue of the troupe is carrying George's baby, which sends George off on a bender, and that Frank Capra, convinced that George is the actor to play the lead in *The Twilight of the Scarlet Pimpernel*, is due to watch their matinee. Further complicating an already sticky situation, half the actors think they are to perform *Private Lives* and the other half arrives costumed for *Cyrano de Bergerac*. Though *Moon Over Buffalo* was an overall disappointment, Burnett and Bosco did their best to provide some high moments.

THE NIGHT OF THE IGUANA

By: Tennessee Williams; **Director:** Robert Falls; **Sets:** Loy Arcenas; **Costumes:** Susan Hilferty; **Lighting:** James F. Ingalls; **Sound:** Richard Woodbury
Opened: 3/96 at the Criterion Center Stage Right
Cast: Cherry Jones, William Petersen, Marsha Mason, Lawrence McCauley, Paula Cale and Mary Beth Fisher
Fresh from her acclaimed performance in last season's *The Heiress*, Jones imbues this 1961 revival with both spiritual focus and star quality in her role as Nantucket spinster Hannah Jelkes. With her grandfather Nonno (McCauley), who calls himelf the "world's oldest practicing poet," Hannah barely scrapes by, living a gypsy life and relying on her sketch pad for income. The impoverished pair take refuge in a rundown Mexican hotel, where they encounter the Rev. T. Lawrence Shannon (Petersen), a former Episcopal minister now reduced to shepherding bus tours. Shannon is wracked by religious guilt, tormented by nameless ghosts and pursued by women who lust for him, including hotel owner Maxine (Mason). Struggling with his demons, he resists Hannah's generous attempts to save his soul. Lush sets and lighting, including a tropical thunderstorm, contribute to the overheated atmosphere of this semi-autobiographical classic.

PATTI LUPONE ON BROADWAY

Conceived and Directed by: Scott Wittman; **Musical Director:** Dick Gallagher; **Musical Arrangements:** John McDaniel; **Writer:** Jeffrey Richman; **Lighting:** John Hastings; **Sound:** Otts Munderloh; **Additional Arrangements:** Steven D. Bowen, Dick Gallagher, Glen Roven, Marc Shaiman and Jonathan Tunick;
Musical Coordinator: John Monaco
Opened: 10/95 at the Walter Kerr Theatre
With: Patti LuPone and the Mermen
LuPone is back on Broadway in a big way. In the first half of her two-act program, she borrows from Bette Midler's cabaret show, nervously playing the role of a tacky nightclub singer. She emotionally performs several Kurt Weill songs but adds little more to them than aggressiveness. In the second act, clearly the stronger of

Leslie Burke

Patti LuPone on Broadway

the two, LuPone recalls her earlier musical roles, including "Don't Cry for Me Argentina" from *Evita*, "Sleepy Man" from *The Robber Bridegroom*, "Meadowlark" from *The Baker's Wife* and "Bewitched, Bothered and Bewildered" from *Pal Joey*. LuPone introduces each theatrical song with an anecdote about her original performance.

PAUL ROBESON

By: Phillip Dean Hayes; **Director:** Harold Scott; **Lighting:** Shirley Prendergast; **Sound:** Tom Gould; **Original Choreography:** Dianne McIntyre; **Special Arrangements and Orchestrations:** Eva C. Brooks; **Musical Direction and Arrangements:** Ernie Scott
Opened: 12/95 at the Longacre Theatre
Cast: Avery Brooks and Ernie Scott
Though Hayes doesn't dig into the mind and affairs of Paul Robeson that deeply, the play succeeds in reverentially portraying a man who endured racial prejudice and parlayed his experiences into success as an athlete, singer, actor and spokesman for social issues. Brooks brilliantly captures the personality of Robeson whether performing the entertainer's favorites "Jacob's Ladder" and "Ol' Man River" or passionately denouncing racism before the House Committee on Un-American Activities. The play traces Robeson's rise from student-athlete at Rutgers University to international fame as an actor and captures his transformation into a political activist, which leads to blacklisting and near lynching.

Sacrilege

RACING DEMON

By: David Hare; **Director:** Richard Eyre; **Set and Costumes:** Bob Crowley; **Lighting:** Mark Henderson; **Projections:** Wendall K. Harrington; **Sound:** Scott Myers; **Music:** George Fenton
Opened: 11/95 at the Vivian Beaumont Theatre
Cast: Josef Sommer, George N. Martin, Michael Cumpsty, Paul Giamatti, Brian Murray, John C. Vennema, Kathryn Meisle, Patrice Johnson, Kathleen Chalfant, Denis O'Hare, John Curless and Richard Clarke

Hare examines the Church of England through the church's clergymen, who are struggling with their mission in London's inner city. The Rev. Lionel Espy (Sommer) is having doubts about his duty to dispense religious advice to parishioners — he's beginning to feel that his role should be simply to offer a sympathetic ear. In contrast, the born-again Christian Rev. Tony Ferris (Cumpsty) has taken to aggressive recruitment. Though Ferris's enthusiasm borders on fanaticism, his arrival to the parish draws even more attention to Espy's indifference. The two sides are well represented here, but it's too safe and suffers from a lack of debate or shock.

RENT

Book, Music and Lyrics: Jonathan Larson; **Director:** Michael Greif; **Choreographer:** Marlies Yearby; **Sets:** Paul Clay; **Costumes:** Angela Wendt; **Lighting:** Blake Burba; **Sound:** Kurt Fischer
Opened: 4/96 at the Nederlander Theater
Cast: Adam Pascal, Anthony Rapp, Daphne Rubin-Vega, Jesse L. Martin, Idina Menzel, Wilson Jermaine Heredia and Fredi Walker

The impoverished garret world of Puccini's *La Boheme* inspired Larson to create a musical based on his East Village neighborhood, with its artists, drug addicts, AIDS sufferers and street people. *Rent* premiered Off-Broadway immediately after the 35-year-old Larson's sudden death and was heralded as a landmark new musical. In its Broadway incarnation, *Rent* is still lively and passionate, though the 15 performers must work harder to fill the larger theater with the same emotional intensity. HIV-positive ex-junkie composer Roger (Pascal) loves S&M club dancer and addict Mimi (Rubin-Vega), who is also HIV-positive. Roger's roommate Mark films the tangled lives of their squatter roommates, who are thrown for a loop when their former classmate and landlord suddenly demands a year's back rent. Everyone fights for life, love and the chance to make it big without selling their souls. A dedicated, high-energy cast sing their hearts out to produce the most affecting musical of the season.

SACRILEGE

By: Diane Shaffer; **Director:** Don Scardino; **Set:** John Arnone; **Costumes:** Alvin Colt; **Lighting:** Howell Binkley; **Sound:** Aural Fixation
Opened: 11/95 at the Belasco Theatre
Cast: Ellen Burstyn, Brian Tarantina, Giancarlo Esposito, Jane Cecil, Damian Young, Herb Foster, Augusta Dabney, Reno Roop and Frank Raiter

Sister Grace (Burstyn) is making waves in the Roman Catholic Church. In fact, the pope has expressed his concern about an interview he read in which she demanded that women be allowed to become priests. The Pope is so disturbed by the renegade nun that he sends his adviser, Cardinal King (Foster), to deal with Sister Grace. Ironically, King was the parish priest who made Grace an altar girl, and their shared past makes him doubt his mission. As she is questioning her own faith, Grace befriends con artist Ramon (Esposito) and encourages him to become a priest. Straightforward to a fault, the play could easily pass for a television drama.

THE SCHOOL FOR SCANDAL

By: Richard Brinsley Sheridan; **Director:** Gerlad Freedman; **Sets:** Douglas W. Schmidt; **Costumes:** Theoni V. Aldredge; **Lighting:** Mary Jo Dondlinger; **Sound:** T. Richard Fitzgerald; **Music:** Robert Waldman
Opened: 11/95 at the Lyceum Theatre
Cast: Tony Randall, Mary Lou Rosato, Simon Jones, Philip Goodwin, Kate Forbes, Tom Hewitt and Ron Randell

Randall's National Actors Theatre has had its share of flops, mainly because the group often lacks the verve necessary to wow audiences. Unfortunately, *The School for Scandal* is no exception. Individually, the performances impress, but for some reason, they just don't meld well. Sir Peter Teazle (Randall) marries a young country girl (Forbes) and takes her to the city, where she falls under the influence of Lady Sneerwell (Rosato) and her clique, who infect Lady Teazle with questionable mores. Randall doesn't offer his character any originality; instead, he infuses his own personality into Sir Teazle, which actually works at times.

SEVEN GUITARS

By: August Wilson; **Director:** Lloyd Richards; **Sets:** Scott Bradley; **Costumes:** Constanza Romero; **Lighting:** Christopher Akerlind; **Sound:** Tom Clark
Opened: 3/96 at the Walter Kerr Theater
Cast: Michele Shay, Ruben Santiago-Hudson, Tommy Hollis, Viola Davis, Roger Robinson, Keith David and Rosalyn Coleman

The seventh and latest drama in Wilson's chronicle of African-American life begins just after the funeral of its central figure, blues musician Floyd "Schoolboy" Barton (David). When five of Floyd's closest companions get together behind their Pittsburgh tenement to swap unglamorized memories of their ill-fated friend, the year 1948 gives way to the past, and the departed blues player emerges to reenact his downfall. Returning from a Chicago studio, Floyd and his fellow musicians find that they have been cheated by the recording company out of royalties from their hit record. Hope reappears when the trio finds a manager, but he is soon arrested for fraud, and the downhill course of events leads inexorably to Floyd's untimely end. A suitably drab set is enlivened by vivid characters, who continue to pour energy into their lives, knowing that their dreams will be snatched away.

STATE FAIR

Music and Lyrics by: Richard Rodgers and Oscar Hammerstein II; **Book:** Tom Briggs and Louis Mattioli, based on the screenplay by Oscar Hammerstein and the novel by Phil Stong; **Directors:** James Hammerstein and Randy Skinner; **Choreography:** Randy Skinner; **Sets:** James Leonard Joy; **Costumes:** Michael Bottari and Ronald Case; **Lighting:** Natasha Katz; **Sound:** Brian Ronan
Opened: 3/96 at the Music Box Theater
Cast: John Davidson, Kathryn Crosby, Ben Wright, Andrea McArdle, Donna McKechnie and Scott Wise

Adapted for Broadway from the 1945 movie musical, *State Fair* tells the apple-pie American tale of a farm family going to the fair. While Melissa (Crosby) and Abel (Davidson) Frake parade their prize pigs, teenagers Margy (McArdle) and Wayne (Wright) discover some home truths. Wise steals the show with his brilliant dancing as Pat Gilbert, the ambitious reporter who captures Margy's heart, but powerful McKechnie doesn't get to really show her stuff as Emily Arden, the seductive singer who opens Wayne's eyes. Two songs lifted from *Oklahoma!* fail to relieve the overall flat tone of this production, which seems suited more to summer stock than to the bright lights. In a move that many theater-watchers deemed a publicity stunt, producers Natalie Lloyd and 84-year-old David Merrick took the Tony Award committee to court after it excluded 11 of the production's 15 songs from the Best Original Score category. A judge ruled that the songs could not be considered original to Broadway, as they were culled from two movie versions of the musical and other stage productions.

SWINGING ON A STAR: THE JOHNNY BURKE MUSICAL

Lyrics: Johnny Burke; **Music:** Johnny Burke, Joe Bushkin, Erroll Garner, Robert Haggart, Arthur Johnston, James Monaco, Harold Spina and Jimmy Van Heusen; **Writer and Director:** Michael Leeds; **Choreographer:** Kathleen Marshall; **Sets:** James Youmans; **Costumes:** Judy Dearing; **Lighting:** Richard Nelson; **Sound:** T. Richard Fitzgerald; **Musical Direction, Orchestrations and Vocal Arrangements:** Barry Levitt
Opened: 10/95 at the Music Box Theatre
Cast: Michael McGrath, Terry Burrell, Lewis Cleale, Alvaleta Guess, Denise Faye, Kathy Fitzgerald and Eugene Fleming

Burke is probably familiar only to the over-50 set, those who fondly remember "Misty," "Pennies From Heaven" and the *Road* movies starring Bob Hope, Bing Crosby and Dorothy Lamour, for which Burke wrote many of the lyrics. Leed's tribute to Burke, in the vein of *Smokey Joe's Cafe*, is surprisingly pleasant and enjoyable, though not a must-see. Each mini-revue, performed in chronological order, is set in a different location, from a Chicago speakeasy, to a radio show in New York City, to Paramount Studios for a tribute to the *Road* pictures.

TARTUFFE

By: Molière, adapted by Freyda Thomas; **Director:** David Saint; **Sets:** Allen Moyer; **Costumes:** Jess Goldstein; **Lighting:** Jeff Davis; **Sound:** John Kilgore; **Video:** Ben Rubin
Opened: 5/96 at the Circle in the Square
Cast: John Glover, Richard Bekins, Patricia Connolly, Haviland Morris, Alison Fraser, Kevin Dewey, Jane Krakowski, David Schramm and T. Scott Cunningham

The entire Circle in the Square theater was transformed into a television studio for this modern-day adaptation of Molière's 17th-century comic parable of moral hypocrisy. Tartuffe (Glover) is now a televangelist whose preaching has captivated studio owner Orgon (Schramm) so com-

Joan Marcus

Seven Guitars

Michael Daniel

The Tempest

lovers are united and Ariel the sprite is finally granted freedom for helping Prospero. Though more physically restrained than the outdoor version, this production attains a greater emotional richness.

VICTOR/VICTORIA

Director and Writer: Blake Edwards; **Music:** Henry Mancini; **Lyrics:** Leslie Bricusse; **Additional Music:** Frank Wildhorn; **Choreographer:** Rob Marshall; **Music Director:** Ian Fraser; **Sets:** Robin Wagner; **Costumes:** Willa Kim; **Lighting:** Jules Fisher and Peggy Eisenhauer; **Sound:** Peter Fitzgerald
Opened: 10/95 at the Marquis Theatre
Cast: Julie Andrews, Tony Roberts, Michael Nouri, Rachel York, Gregory Jbara, Richard B. Shull and Adam Heller

It has been the season for Broadway starlets to reprise earlier roles: Carol Channing appears again in rare form as Dolly Gallagher Levi in *Hello, Dolly!*, Patti Lupone performs favorites from shows past and 60-year-old Julie Andrews returns 13 years after the motion picture as the woman playing a man playing a woman in *Victor/Victoria*. Andrews shines in a production that certainly doesn't. Dressed in tuxedoed drag or sparkly spangles, she vibrantly gives 200 percent in every number. Roberts delivers as homosexual Toddy, Victor/Victoria's fellow nightclub performer, who transforms her into a wildly popular cabaret star who catches the eye of mobster King Marchan (Nouri). The problems arise with Edwards's script adaptation. Pace looms as the biggest problem, while the scenery and poor lighting often overshadow the actors. Still, Andrews's performance makes it a worthwhile night out. The star's real-life drama took center stage when she attempted to withdraw her Tony nomination for best actress in a musical after the awards committee chose not to nominate the production in any other category.

pletely that he's willing to donate his daughter Maryann (Krakowski) to the cause. Meanwhile, Tartuffe has his eye on Orgon's wife, Elmire (Morris), much to the disgust of Elmire's brother, Cleante (Bekins). Tartuffe's attempts to get his way while maintaining a righteous facade make for moments of hilarious physical comedy, but the original play's linguistic and social nuances are largely lost in translation.

THE TEMPEST

By: William Shakespeare; **Director:** George C. Wolfe; **Sets:** Riccardo Hernandez; **Costumes:** Toni-Leslie James; **Lighting:** Paul Gallo; **Sound:** Dan Moses Schreier; **Masks and Puppets:** Barbara Pollitt; **Music:** Carlos Valdez and Dan Moses Schreier; **Choreography:** Hope Clarke
Opened: 11/95 at the Broadhurst Theater
Cast: Avery Glymph, Adam Dannheisser, Miguel Perez, MacIntyre Dixon, Graham Winton, Nestor Serrano, Carrie Preston, Patrick Stewart, Aunjanue Ellis, Teagle F. Bougere, Paul Whitthorne, Neal Huff, Ross Lehman, Mario Cantone, Midori Nakamura, Hilary Chaplain and Sybyl Walker

New York Shakespeare Festival's spectacular *The Tempest* was originally performed at Central Park's outdoor theater, and this indoor production re-creates a similar, vibrant world. Prospero (Stewart), the reclusive former Duke of Milan, inhabits a mysterious island cave with his daughter, the beautiful Miranda (Preston), and various spirits, including mischievous Ariel (Ellis) and the grouchy monster Caliban (Bougere). After years of studying magical arts, Prospero has gained power over the elements and is able to founder the ship carrying his brother, Antonio (Serrano), and the King of Naples (Perez), who together betrayed him and robbed him of his heritage. Thanks to Ariel's help, everyone on the ship is safely washed ashore the enchanted isle, where the King's son Ferdinand (Whitthorne) is smitten with Miranda, and she in turn is entranced by the first young man she has ever seen. The survivors repent their evil deeds, the

Carol Rosegg/Joan Marcus

Victor/Victoria

1995 – 1996 Major Off-Broadway and Off-Off-Broadway Productions

Alice by Robert Wilson; based on *Alice's Adventures in Wonderland* and *Through the Looking Glass* by Lewis Carroll
Presented by the Brooklyn Academy of Music
Opened: 10/95 at the Brooklyn Academy of Music Opera House

The Amazing Metrano: An Accidental Comedy by Art Metrano and Cynthia Lee
Presented by Mitchell Maxwell and Victoria Maxwell in association with Workin' Man Theatricals Inc. and Fred H. Krones
Opened: 2/96 at the Union Square Theater

Ancient History by David Ives
Presented by Primary Stages
Opened 5/96

Antigone in New York by Janusz Glowacki
Presented by Vineyard Theater
Opened: 4/96

Arts and Leisure by Steve Tesich
Presented by Playwrights Horizons
Opened: 5/96

Bed and Sofa based on the film by Abram Room; music by Polly Pen; libretto by Laurence Klavan
Presented by Vineyard Theater
Opened: 2/96

Below the Belt by Richard Dresser
Presented by Julian Schlossberg, Meyer Ackerman and Anita Howe-Waxman
Opened: 3/96 at the John Houseman Theater

Black Girl by J. E. Franklin
Presented by the New Federal Theater
Opened: 11/95 at the Henry Street Settlement, Harry De Jur Playhouse

Blink of an Eye by Jeremy Dobrish
Presented by SoHo Think Tank
Opened: 9/95 the Ohio Theater

Blue Window by Craig Lucas
Presented by Manhattan Theater Club
Opened: 2/96 at City Center, Stage 1

Brine County Wedding by Christopher V. Alessi
Presented by WPA
Opened: 3/96

Michael Daniel

Bring in 'da Noise, Bring in 'da Funk

Bring in 'da Noise, Bring in 'da Funk: A Tap/Rap Discourse on the Staying Power of the Beat choreographed by Savion Glover; conceived by George C. Wolfe
Presented by Joseph Papp Public Theater/ New York Shakespeare Festival
Opened: 11/95 at the Joseph Papp Public Theater/Newman Theater

Cardenio attributed to William Shakespeare; adapted by Kermit Christman and Kevin Crawford, based on a text by Charles Hamilton
Presented by Kermit Christman, Jacqueline Anne Siegel and Kathleen Etherington, in association with the Palm Beach Shakespeare Festival and Musical Theater Works
Opened: 3/96 at the Linhart Theater

The Chang Fragments by Han Ong
Presented by the Joseph Papp Public Theater/ New York Shakespeare Festival
Opened: 5/96 at LuEsther Hall

Checkmates by Ron Milner
Presented by the Henry De Jur Playhouse
Opened: 4/96 at the Henry Street Settlement

Chinoiserie conceived by Ping Chong; text by Michael Matthews
Presented by the Brooklyn Academy of Music
Opened: 11/95 at the Majestic Theater

The 1996 Obie Awards, honoring distinguished achievement in Off-Broadway and Off-Off-Broadway productions, were presented on May 20, 1996, at New York's Manhattan Center.

Susan Johann

Sleep Deprivation Chamber

BEST PLAY
Adrienne Kennedy, *June and Jean in Concert* and *Sleep Deprivation Chamber*

PLAYWRITING
Ain Gordon, *Wally's Ghost*

Donald Margulies, *The Model Apartment*

Suzan-Lori Parks, *Venus*

Doug Wright, *Quills*

DIRECTION
Doug Hughes, *The Grey Zone*

PERFORMANCE
Julie Archer, *Epidog*

Gerry Bamman, *Nixon's Nixon*

Lisa Gay Hamilton, *Valley Song*

Terri Klausner, *Bed and Sofa*

Tom McGowan, *The Food Chain*

Mark Nelson, *Picasso at the Lapin Agile*

Barbara Pollitt, *Epidog*

Adina Porter, *Venus*

Marty Pottenger, *City Water Tunnel No. 3*

Virginia Rambal, *Troya de America* and *La Dama Duende*

A Christmas Carol by Charles Dickens
Presented by Madison Square Garden
Opened: 12/95 at the Paramount

Constant Stranger by John Kelly
Presented by the Joyce Theater Foundation
Opened: 10/95 at the Joyce Theater

City Water Tunnel No. 3 by Marty Pottenger
Presented by Dancing in the Streets and Dance Theater Workshop
Opened: 5/96 at the Dance Theater Workshop

Cowgirls conceived by Mary Murfitt; book by Betsy Howie; music and lyrics by Mary Murfitt
Presented by Denise Cooper, Susan Gallin, Rodger Hess and Suki Sandler
Opened: 4/96 at the Minetta Lane Theater

The Coyote Bleeds by Tony DiMurro
Presented by the Worth Street Theater
Opened: 11/95

Curtains by Stephen Bill
Presented by the New Group
Opened 4/96 at INTAR

La Dama Duende by Calderón de la Barca
Presented by Teatro Circulo and Thalia Spanish Theater
Opened: 1/96 at Thalia Spanish Theater

Dancing on Her Knees by Nilo Cruz
Presented by the Joseph Papp Public Theater/New York Shakespeare Festival
Opened: 2/96

Dangerous Corner by J. B. Priestley
Presented by the Atlantic Theater Company
Opened: 10/95

Dick Gregory Live!!
Presented by the Negro Ensemble Company
Opened: 12/95 at the Samuel Beckett Theater

Do Something With Yourself: The Life of Charlotte Brontë by Linda Manning
Presented by the Invisible Theater
Opened: 4/96

A Doll's House by Henrik Ibsen; translated by William Archer
Presented by the Pearl Theater Company
Opened: 9/95

Don Juan by Moliére
Presented by the Brooklyn Academy of Music
Opened: 4/96 at the Brooklyn Academy of Music Opera House

Don Juan Comes Back From the War by Odon von Horvath
Presented by Classic Stage Company and Cucaracha Theater
Opened: 4/96 at the Classic Stage Company

Du Barry Was a Lady book by Herbert Fields and B.G. DeSylva; music and lyrics by Cole Porter; adapted by David Ives and Walter Bobbie
Presented by City Center/Encores: Great American Musicals in Concert
Opened: 2/96 at City Center

The Duchess of Malfi by John Webster
Presented by the Brooklyn Academy of Music
Opened: 12/95 at the Majestic Theatre

Endgame by Samuel Beckett
Presented by the Classic Stage Company
Opened: 10/95

Entertaining Mr. Sloane by Joe Orton
Presented by Classic Stage Company
Opened: 2/96

Epidog by Lee Breuer
Presented by Mabou Mines
Opened: 1/96 at the HERE Theater

A Fair Country by Jon Robin Baitz
Presented by Lincoln Center Theater
Opened: 2/96 at the Mitzi E. Newhouse Theater

Floating Rhoda and the Glue Man by Eve Ensler
Presented by the HOME for Contemporary Theater and Art
Opened: 9/95 at the HERE Theater

Floyd Collins by Tina Landau; music and lyrics by Adam Guettel; additional lyrics by Tina Landau
Presented by Playwrights Horizons
Opened: 4/96

Forbidden Hollywood by Gerard Alessandrini
Presented by John Freedson, Harriet Yellin and Jon B. Platt
Opened: 3/96 at the Triad Theater

Frank Pig Says Hello by Pat McCabe
Presented by the Irish Repertory Theater
Opened: 1/96

Full Gallop by Mark Hampton and Mary Louise Wilson
Presented by the Manhattan Theater Club
Opened: 10/95 at City Center, Stage II

Funnyhouse of a Negro and **A Movie Star Has to Star in Black and White** by Adrienne Kennedy
Two one-act plays presented by the Signature Theater Company
Opened: 9/95 at the Joseph Papp Public Theater

Golden Boy by Clifford Odets
Presented by the Blue Light Theater Company
Opened: 11/95 at Primary Stages

The Green Bird by Carlo Gozzi; translated by Albert Bermel
Presented by The New Victory Theater
Opened: 3/96

Rocco Sisto, *Quills*

Steven Skybell, *Antigone in New York*

Derek Smith, *The Green Bird*

James Urbaniak, *The Universe*

Mary Louise Wilson, *Full Gallop*

DESIGN
Jeffrey S. Koger, sustained excellence of lighting design

Neil Patel, sustained excellence of set design

MUSIC
Bruce Coughlin and Adam Guettel, *Floyd Collins*

Polly Pen, *Bed and Sofa*

David Van Tieghem, sustained excellence of music

SPECIAL ACHIEVEMENT
Uta Hagen

SPECIAL CITATIONS
Ingmar Bergman, sustained excellence of direction

Kathleen Chalfant, sustained excellence of performance

Henry Stram, sustained excellence of performance

Scott Elliott and the cast of *Curtains*

Jonathan Larson, composer/writer; Michael Greif, director; and the cast of *Rent*

Savion Glover, *Bring in 'da Noise, Bring in 'da Funk*

Repertorio Español, *New Voices!* series

New Georges

Teatro Experimental Blue Amigos

Ingmar Bergman

Molly Sweeney

Greensboro: A Requiem by Emily Mann
Presented by the McCarter Theater
Opened: 2/96

The Grey Zone by Tim Blake Nelson
Presented by the MCC Theater
Opened: 1/96

The Hope Zone by Kevin Heelan
Presented by the Circle Repertory Theater
Opened: 1/96

Hubba City by Ishmael Reed
Presented by the American Theater of Actors
Opened: 1/96 at the Nuyorican Poets Cafe

I Do! I Do! book and lyrics by Tom Jones; music by
Harvey Schmidt
Presented by Arthur Cantor
Opened: 3/96 at the Lamb's Theater

In the Loneliness of the Cotton Fields by
Bernard-Marie Koltès
Presented by the Brooklyn Academy of Music
Opened: 2/96

The Island of Lost Shoes by Ray Dobbins
Presented by Performance Space 122 and
the National Performance Network
Opened: 9/95

June and Jean in Concert by Adrienne Kennedy
Presented by the Signature Theater Company
Opened: 11/95 at the Joseph Papp Public
Theater/Susan Stein Shiva Theater

King Lear by William Shakespeare
Presented by the Joseph Papp Public Theater
Opened: 1/96

The Lady From the Sea by Henrik Ibsen;
translated by Rolf Fjelde
Presented by the Jean Cocteau Repertory
Opened: 2/96 at the Bouwerie Lane Theater

A Line Around the Block by Marga Gomez
Presented by the Joseph Papp Public Theater/
New York Shakespeare Festival
Opened: 4/96 at the Anspacher Theater

Mata Hari by Jerome Coopersmith
Presented by the York Theater Company
Opened: 1/96 at the Theater at St. Peter's Church

Measure for Measure by William Shakespeare
Presented by Theater for a New Audience
Opened: 1/96 at the Playhouse at St. Clement's
Church

Mister Lincoln by Herbert Mitgang
Presented by Double W Productions
Opened: 9/95 at the Irish Arts Center

The Model Apartment by Donald Margulies
Presented by Primary Stages Company
Opened: 10/95

Molly Sweeney by Brian Friel
Presented by the Roundabout Theater Co., Gate
Theater Dublin and Emanuel Azenberg
Opened: 1/96 at the Roundabout's Laura Pels Theater

The Monogamist by Christopher Kyle
Presented by Playwrights Horizons
Opened: 11/95 at the Wilder Theater

Moonlight by Harold Pinter
Presented by the Roundabout Theater Company
Opened: 10/95 at the Criterion Center, Laura Pels
Theater

Moscow Stations adapted by Stephen Mulrine from
the novel *Moscow to Petushki* by Venedikt Yerofeyev
Presented by Julian Schlossberg, Brian Brooly, Alan
J. Schuster and Mitchell Maxwell
Opened: 10/95 at the Union Square Theater

Mrs. Klein by Nicholas Wright
Presented by David Richenthal, Lucille Lortel, Anita
Howe-Waxman and Jeffrey Ash
Opened: 10/95 at the Lucille Lortel Theatre

New England by Richard Nelson
Presented by Manhattan Theater Club
Opened: 11/95 at City Center, Stage I

Nixon's Nixon by Russell Lees
Presented by the Shubert Organization, Capital
Cities/ABC, Jujamcyn Theaters, Robert LuPone and
Bernard Telsey
Opened: 3/96 at the MCC Theater

Northeast Local by Tom Donaghy
Presented by Lincoln Center Theater
Opened: 10/95 at the Mitzi E. Newhouse Theater

Nude Nude Totally Nude by Andrea Martin
Presented by the Joseph Papp Public Theater/
New York Shakespeare Festival
Opened: 4/96 at the Papp Public Theater's
Anspacher Theater

Oblivion Postponed by Ron Nyswaner
Presented by Second Stage Theater
Opened: 12/95

Overtime by A. R. Gurney
Presented by Manhattan Theater Club
Opened: 3/96 at City Center, Stage II

Papa by John deGroot
Presented by Eric Krebs, Anne Strickland Squadron and Brian C. Smith
Opened 5/96 at the Douglas Fairbanks Theater

Picasso at the Lapin Agile by Steve Martin
Presented by Stephen Eich, Joan Stein, Leavitt/Fox Theatricals/Mages
Opened: 10/95 at the Promenade Theater

Por'Knockers by Lynn Nottage
Presented by the Vineyard Theater
Opened: 11/95

The Preservation Society by William S. Leavengood
Presented by Primary Stages Company
Opened: 1/96

The Principality of Sorrows by Keith Bunin
Presented by Pure Orange Productions
Opened: 12/95 at the Theater Row Theater

Quills by Doug Wright
Presented by New York Theater Workshop
Opened: 11/95

Rent by Jonathan Larson
Presented by New York Theater Workshop
Opened: 2/96

Riff Raff by Laurence Fishburne
Presented by Circle Repertory Theater
Opened: 11/95

Salome by Oscar Wilde
Presented by the Brooklyn Academy of Music
Opened: 10/95 at the Majestic Theater

Same Old Moon by Geraldine Aron
Presented by the Irish Repertory Theater
Opened: 9/95

Scenes From an Execution by Howard Barker
Presented by Blue Light Theater Company and Potomac Theater Project
Opened: 2/96 at the Atlantic Theater Company

Seascape by Edward Albee
Presented by Terese Hayden
Opened: 9/95 at Theater 22

The Shattering by Mark R. Shapiro
Presented by Shelmar Productions LLC
Opened: 4/96 at the Players Theater

Sin by Wendy MacLeod
Presented by Second Stage
Opened: 10/95

1996 LUCILLE LORTEL AWARDS FOR OUTSTANDING ACHIEVEMENT OFF-BROADWAY

The Lucille Lortel Awards, which include commercial and nonprofit productions, are the official awards of the League of Off-Broadway Theaters and Producers. Lortel rules exclude from consideration works that move to or are scheduled to move to Broadway. The 1996 Lortel Awards were presented on May 6, 1996, at the Lucille Lortel Theatre in New York's Greenwich Village.

Outstanding Play
  Molly Sweeney

Outstanding Musical
  Floyd Collins

Outstanding Revival
  Entertaining Mr. Sloan

Outstanding Director
  Scott Elliott, *The Monogamist*

Outstanding Actor in a Play
  Jim Dale, *Travels With My Aunt*

Outstanding Actress in a Play
  Uta Hagen, *Mrs. Klein*

Outstanding Actor in a Musical
  Jason Workman, *Bed and Sofa*

Outstanding Actress in a Musical
  Melissa Errico, *One Touch of Venus*

Outstanding Set Designer
  Tony Walton, *A Fair Country*

Outstanding Lighting Designer
  Michael Chybowski, *The Grey Zone*

Outstanding Costume Designer
  Jane Greenwood, *Sylvia*

Outstanding Body of Work
  Athol Fugard

Special Awards
  Cora Cahan

  Theatreworks U.S.A.

Outstanding Dedication to Off-Broadway
  Edith Oliver

The Size of the World by Charles Evered
Presented by the Circle Repertory Theater
Opened: 3/96

The Skriker by Caryl Churchill
Presented by the Joseph Papp Public Theater/
New York Shakespeare Festival
Opened: 5/96

Sleep Deprivation Chamber by Adrienne Kennedy
Presented by the Signature Theater Company
Opened: 2/96

The Slow Drag by Carson Kreitzer
Presented by American Place Theater
Opened: 4/96

Splendora by Peter Webb
Presented by the Bay Street Theater
Opened: 11/95 at the American Place Theater

Spoke Man by John Hockenberry
Presented by the American Place Theater
Opened: 2/96

Standing By by Norman Barasch
Presented by the York Theater Company
Opened: 9/95 at St. Peter's Church

Swinging on a Star music and lyrics by Johnny
Burke
Presented by Richard Seader, Mary Burke Kramer,
Paul B. Berkowsky and Angels of the Arts in
association with Sally Sears
Opened: 10/95 at the Music Box Theater

Swingtime Canteen by Linda Thorsen Bond, William
Repicci and Charles Busch
Presented by William Repicci and Michael
Minichello in association with Ken Jillson
Opened: 9/95 at the Blue Angel

Tovah: Out of Her Mind by Tovah Feldshuh
Presented by the Jewish Repertory Theater
Opened: 4/96 at Playhouse 91

True Crimes by Romulus Linney
Presented by the Theater for the New City
Opened: 12/95

The Universe by Richard Foreman
Presented by the Ontological Hysteric Theater
Opened: 1/96 at St. Mark's Church

Utopia by The Company
Presented by The Living Theater
Opened: 1/96 at the Vineyard Theater

Valley Song by Athol Fugard
Presented by Manhattan Theater Club
Opened: 12/95 at City Center, Stage II, reopened 5/96
at City Center, Stage I

Venus by Suzan-Lori Parks
Presented by the Joseph Papp Public Theater/
New York Shakespeare Festival
Opened: 4/96 at Martinson Hall

Victor, or Children Take Over by Roger Vitrac
Presented by Arden Party and Aaron Etra
Opened: 4/96 at the Ohio Theater

Virgins and Other Myths by Colin Martin
Presented by Primary Stages Company, in
association with Ted Snowdon
Opened: 2/96, reopened 4/96 at the Atlantic Theater

Waiting for Godot by Samuel Beckett
Presented by the Jean Cocteau Repertory
Opened: 10/95 at the Bouwerie Lane Theater

Wally's Ghost by Ain Gordon
Presented by the Soho Repertory Theater
Opened: 4/96

The Warm-up by Sammy Shore and Rudy DeLuca
Presented by the American Jewish Theater
Opened: 11/95 at the Susan Bloch Theater

WASP and Other Plays by Steve Martin
Presented by the New York Shakespeare Festival
Opened: 12/95 at the Joseph Papp Public Theater

When Ladies Battle by Eugène Scribe and Ernest
Legouvè; translated by Michael Feingold
Presented by the Pearl Theater Company
Opened: 12/95 at St. Mark's Place

Where the Truth Lies by Catherine Butterfield
Presented by the Weissberger Theater Group and
Jay Harris
Opened: 4/96 at the Irish Repertory Theater

A Whistle in the Dark by Thomas Murphy
Presented by the Irish Repertory Theater
Opened: 2/96

Wonderful Time by Jonathan Marc Sherman
Presented by the WPA Theater
Opened: 1/96

Working Title by Andrew Bergman
Presented by the American Jewish Theater
Opened: 3/96

The Yiddish Trojan Women by Carole Braverman
Presented by the American Jewish Theater
Opened: 1/96

Zombie Prom book and lyrics by John Dempsey,
based on a story by John Dempsey and Hugh M.
Murphy; music by Dana P. Rowe
Presented by Nat Weiss, in association with
Randall L. Wreghitt
Opened 4/96 at the Variety Arts Theater

1995 — 1996 Major Regional Theater Productions

ACTORS THEATRE OF LOUISVILLE
316 W. Main St.
Louisville, KY 40202-4218
(502) 584-1205

MAINSTAGE SERIES

Sleuth by Anthony Shaffer
9/20/95–10/21/95

The Romantic Comedy of Ferenc Molnar: The Play's the Thing and Olympia
10/25/95–11/18/95

Adventures of Huckleberry Finn by Mark Twain; adapted by Randal Myler
1/3/96–2/3/96

Blues in the Night conceived by Sheldon Epps
2/7/96–3/2/96

Humana Festival of New American Plays
3/7/96–4/6/96

All I Really Need to Know I Learned in Kindergarten by Ernest Zulia; adapted from the book by Robert Fulghum
4/4/96–5/26/96

The Comedy of Errors by William Shakespeare
5/8/96–6/2/96

OFF-BROADWAY SERIES

Flying Solo and Friends
9/5/95–9/24/95

A Perfect Ganesh by Terrence McNally
1/16/96–1/28/96

Humana Festival of New American Plays
2/27/96–3/31/96

SPECIAL PERFORMANCES

Dracula
10/3/95–11/5/95

A Christmas Carol by Charles Dickens; adapted by Jon Jory and Marcia Dixcy
11/22/95–12/30/95

The Gift of the Magi by O. Henry; adapted by Peter Ekstrom
12/6/95–12/23/95

Ken Friedman

**American Conservatory Theater,
The Cherry Orchard**

Rock 'n' Roles from the works of William Shakespeare; adapted by Jim Luigs
4/15/96–4/19/96

AMERICAN CONSERVATORY THEATER
30 Grant Ave., 6th Floor
San Francisco, CA 94108-5800
(415) 834-3218

Arcadia by Tom Stoppard
10/12/95–11/26/95

Seven Guitars by August Wilson
11/9/95–12/23/95

Gaslight by Patrick Hamilton
12/14/96–1/28/96

The Tempest by William Shakespeare
1/18/96–2/18/96

Dark Rapture by Eric Overmyer
2/29/96–3/31/96

The Cherry Orchard by Anton Chekhov
4/4/96–6/7/96

The Matchmaker by Thornton Wilder
4/18/96–6/9/96

AMERICAN REPERTORY THEATRE
64 Brattle St.
Cambridge, MA 02138
(617) 547-8300

The Tempest by William Shakespeare
11/29/96–12/31/96

Buried Child by Sam Shepard
1/10/96–2/4/96

Ubu Rock by Shelly Berc and Andrei Belgrader
3/13/96- 3/23/96

Tartuffe by Molière; adapted by Robert Auletta
2/14/96–3/10/96

The Naked Truth by Paul Rudnick
5/15/96–7/3/96

Long Day's Journey Into Night by Eugene O'Neill
5/28/96–7/14/96

DENVER CENTER THEATRE COMPANY
1245 Champa St.
Denver, CO 80204–2154
(303) 825-2117

Romeo and Juliet by William Shakespeare
9/28/95–11/11/95

You Never Can Tell by George Bernard Shaw
10/12/95–11/18/95

The Last Yankee by Arthur Miller
10/19/95–11/18/95

A Christmas Carol by Charles Dickens; adapted by
Dennis Powers and Laird Williamson
11/24/95–12/24/95

Beethoven 'n' Pierrot by Pavel M. Dobrusky and Per
Olav Sørensen
11/30/95–12/23/95

Two Trains Running by August Wilson
1/11/96–2/17/96

A Dybbuk or Between Two Worlds by S. Ansky
1/18/96–2/24/96

The Dresser by Ronald Harwood
1/25/96–3/23/96

Room Service by John Murray and Allen Boretz
3/14/96–4/20/96

Galileo by Bertoit Brecht
3/28/96–5/4/96

Appalachian Strings by Randal Myler and Dan
Wheetman
5/2/96–6/8/96

Prelude to Lime Creek by Joe Henry; adapted by
Anthony Zerbe
5/9/96–6/8/96

THE GUTHRIE THEATER
725 Vineland Place
Minneapolis, MN 55403
(612) 377-2224

Big White Fog by Theodore Ward
9/22/95–11/4/95

K: Impressions of Kafka's *The Trial* by Garland
Wright
9/26/95–11/5/95

King Lear by William Shakespeare
9/29/95–11/18/95

A Christmas Carol by Charles Dickens; adapted by
Barbara Field
12/1/95–12/24/95

Babes in Arms music by Richard Rodgers; lyrics by
Lorenz Hart
2/15/96–3/10/96

LONG WHARF THEATRE
222 Sargent Drive
New Haven, CT 06511
(203) 787-4284

NEWTON SCHENCK STAGE

As You Like It by William Shakespeare
10/10/95–11/19/95

Denial by Peter Sagal
11/28/95–12/31/95

The Amen Corner by James Baldwin
1/9/96–2/11/96

T. Charles Erickson

**American Repertory Theatre,
Long Day's Journey Into Night**

A Song at Twilight by Noel Coward
2/20/96–3/24/96

All in the Timing by David Ives
4/2/96–5/5/96

STAGE II

Robbers by Lyle Kessler
10/20/95–11/19/95

Getting Away by Carlo Goldoni; translated and adapted by Tom Simpson
12/5/95–12/17/95

Let's Do It by A.R. Gurney
3/19/96–4/21/96

THE MARK TAPER FORUM

Center Theatre Group
Music Center of Los Angeles County
135 N. Grand Ave.
Los Angeles, CA 90012
(213) 972-0700

Slavs! by Tony Kushner
10/15/95–11/19/95

The Family Business by Ain and David Gordon
11/26/95–12/24/95

Three Tall Women by Edward Albee
1/2/96–2/18/96

Blade to the Heat by Oliver Mayer
3/17/96–5/5/96

Psychopathia Sexualis by John Patrick Shanley
5/12/96–6/30/96

Changes of Heart by Pierre Carlet de Chamblain de Marivaux; adapted by Stephen Wadsworth
7/14/96–9/1/96

SEATTLE REPERTORY THEATRE

155 Mercer St.
Seattle, WA 98109
(206) 443-2222

Voir Dire by Joe Sutton
10/14/95–11/11/95

She Stoops to Conquer by Oliver Goldsmith
11/18/95–12/17/95

The Price by Arthur Miller
12/30/95–1/27/96

Waiting for Godot by Samuel Beckett
2/3/96–3/2/96

Psychopathia Sexualis by John Patrick Shanley
3/9/96–4/6/96

Blues in the Night by Sheldon Epps
4/13/96–5/19/96

Jay Thompson

The Mark Taper Forum,
A Blade to the Heat

STAGE 2

All in the Timing by David Ives
11/25/95–12/17/95

Buying Time by Michael Weller
1/27/96–2/18/96

The Cider House Rules (Part I) by Peter Parnell from John Irving's novel
3/2/96–3/31/96

SOUTH COAST REPERTORY

655 Town Center Drive
Costa Mesa, CA 92626
(714) 957-2602

MAINSTAGE

She Stoops to Folly by Tom Murphy
9/8/95–10/8/95

Raised in Captivity by Nicky Silver
10/20/95–11/19/95

A Christmas Carol by Charles Dickens; adapted by Jerry Patch
12/2/95–12/24/95

Ballad of Yachiyo by Philip Kan Gotanda
1/12/96–2/11/96

The Taming of the Shrew by William Shakespeare
3/1/96–3/31/96

New England by Richard Nelson
4/12/96–5/12/96

Arms and the Man by George Bernard Shaw
5/31/96–6/30/96

SECOND STAGE

The Things You Don't Know by David Hollander
9/22/95–10/22/95

The Interrogation of Nathan Hale by David Stanley Ford
11/3/95–12/3/95

Yale Repertory Theatre, *Uncle Vanya*

La Posada Magica by Octavio Solis
12/10/95–12/24/95

3 Viewings by Jeffrey Hunter
1/26/96–2/25/96

If We Are Women by Joanna McClelland Glass
3/15/96–4/14/96

A Mess of Plays by Christopher Durang
4/26/96–5/26/96

STEPPENWOLF THEATRE COMPANY
1650 N. Halstead St.
Chicago, IL 60614
(312) 335-1888

Buried Child by Sam Shepard
10/1/95–11/5/95

Everyman by Anonymous
12/3/95–1/14/96

The Libertine by Stephen Jeffreys
2/25/96–4/7/96

Supple in Combat by Alexandra Gersten
5/19/96–6/30/96

Molly Sweeney by Brian Friel
7/21/96–8/25/96

TRINITY REPERTORY COMPANY
201 Washington St.
Providence, RI 02903
(401) 521-1100

Once in a Lifetime by Moss Hart and George S. Kaufman
9/15/95–10/22/95

Long Day's Journey Into Night by Eugene O'Neill
10/6/95–11/19/95

A Christmas Carol by Charles Dickens; adapted by Adrian Hall and Richard Cumming
11/15/95–12/24/95

Voir Dire by Joe Sutton
1/4/96–2/18/96

Don Quixote by Miguel de Cervantes; adapted by Kyra Obolensky
2/2/96–3/3/96

Fires in the Mirror by Anna Deavere Smith
3/22/96–5/5/96

Angels in America by Tony Kushner
4/26/96–6/9/96

YALE REPERTORY THEATRE
222 York St.
New Haven, CT 06520
(203) 432-1515

Le Cirque Invisible
10/19/95–11/4/95

Pentecost by David Edgar
11/9/95–12/2/95

Mrs. Warren's Profession by George Bernard Shaw
1/11/96–2/3/96

The Beaux' Stratagem by George Farquhar
2/15/96–3/9/96

Venus by Suzan-Lori Parks
3/14/96–3/30/96

Landscape of the Body by John Guare
5/2/96–5/25/96

Star Turns

■ BY SUSAN REITER

Susan Reiter
is a contributing
editor to
Dance Magazine.

AS DANCE COMPANIES ADAPT TO THE PRIVATIONS OF THE 1990s, they often struggle to establish and maintain a clear, distinctive identity. Lacking a stellar dancer or celebrated choreographer to define its aesthetic and attract its audience, a company can find itself grasping for new repertory and dancers who possess that unique gift of individual presence combined with technical brilliance. Following the pinnacle of popularity and public awareness that dance achieved during the 1980 — when large, eager audiences greeted most dance events and touring engagements were plentiful — caution, fiscal responsibility and a concern for survival became primary concerns for companies that had previously enjoyed steady growth.

Fortunate is the troupe still led and defined by a major founding creative figure. The Merce Cunningham Dance Company and Paul Taylor Dance Company fall into this category and their vast, singular repertories continue to be replenished by these indefatigable veteran choreographers. Both companies have seen considerable turnover in personnel in recent years, losing some veteran performers who contributed significantly to the companies' profiles. But they have recruited intriguing new dancers who are quickly becoming vital members of the ensembles.

Both of these companies have also, unfortunately, been forced to curtail their presence on the New York City dance scene due to the enormous financial risk of presenting a local season. Taylor's troupe, which performed an annual four-week season throughout the 1980s, has cut back to a mere two weeks in the 1990s, and has eliminated nearly all live musical accompaniment. This year marked the first time the Cunningham company did not perform a two-week repertory season at City Center, its longtime New York base, and it is not scheduled to do so in 1997 either.

The Cunningham company did appear, however, in July and August 1996 as an important component of the new Lincoln Center Festival, a wide-ranging, three-week collection of music, theater, dance and opera events. Projected as an annual event, this festival makes an important addition to the city's performing arts scene. It offers a lively, diverse cultural smorgasbord during the less-busy summer weeks and emphasizes the vitality and creativity of Lincoln Center's constituent organizations. Thanks to the festival's fund-raising clout, ground-breaking, unusual works such as Cunningham's *Ocean* came to the city. Unlike the Kennedy Center in Washington D.C., which for years has been active as a presenter of dance, Lincoln Center has until now focused its presenting activities mostly on

Lois Greenfield

Merce Cunningham Dance Company,
Ocean

Costas/Courtesy of New York City Ballet

Peter Boal

Francia Russell and Kent Stowell
artistic directors, Pacific Northwest Ballet

Savion Glover
tap dancer

Peter Boal
principal dancer, New York City Ballet

1996 CAPEZIO DANCE AWARD

Rebecca Lester

Charles Reinhart

Charles Reinhart
president of the board and co-director
American Dance Festival

music events (with the occasional foray into dance or performance art as part of its Serious Fun! series). The festival, if it continues in the same vein, will serve as an annual occasion for major dance presentations (such as this summer's Lyons Opera Ballet, performing Maguy Marin's revisionist *Coppelia*), a cultural attraction New York has been lacking in recent years.

The current situation, again a sharp contrast to 10 or 15 years ago, is especially evident in the near-absence of foreign ballet troupes at the Metropolitan Opera House, which in a more golden era played host to four or five such visitors each summer. This summer, a 10-day run by the venerable Paris Opera Ballet was all the Met could muster. Important and welcome as it was to see this great company again after eight years, the limited repertory (nine performances of Rudolf Nureyev's overly elaborate, stodgy *La Bayadère* and three of Angelin Preljocaj's newsworthy but derivative *La Parc*) gave only the barest sketch of the company's extensive repertory.

Earlier in the season, one of the leading American ballet companies paid a significant visit to New York. With its three mixed programs at City Center in November 1995, the San Francisco Ballet demonstrated the intensity and the diversity (if not always the high quality) of its repertory. After 10 years under the intelligent, perceptive direction of Helgi Tomasson, this personable and committed company showcased its exceptional ballerinas (Elizabeth Loscavic, Tina LeBlanc and Jeanna Berman) and versatile male dancers (Anthony Randazzo, David Palmer and Yuri Possokhov). If its repertory was not always scintillating, a problem common to all ballet troupes these days, SFB at least has the advantage of a resident choreographer (Tomasson) who knows his dances well and who showcases them in a variety of styles, always within a framework of classical elegance.

New York's two major ballet troupes, American Ballet Theatre (ABT) and New York City Ballet (NYCB), continued to seek out new repertory and reveal exciting youthful talent within their ranks. ABT wisely continued its association with

Twyla Tharp, presenting a premiere by the legend choreographer for the second year in a row. Titled *The Elements*, it proved to be an exhilarating highlight of the season, a work that had her operating at peak inspiration (clearly urged on to bold innovations by the extraordinary baroque score by Jean-Fery Rebel) and finding new ways to challenge her dancers. Hopefully, this happy collaboration between Tharp and ABT will continue.

A less fortunate choice for enlarging ABT's repertory was the addition of Ben Stevenson's pallid 25-year-old staging of *Cinderella*. It is a well-known assumption that full-length narrative dances such as this are what bring the ticket-buyers to the box office; even if this held true in this case (and a less-than-packed house would indicate otherwise), it is hard to believe that anyone who saw this dramatically unfocused, often mean-spirited *Cinderella* would be likely to return soon for any additional ballet experience.

ABT's 20-year-old stars-in-the-making, Paloma Herrera and Angel Corella, continued to shine this season, drawing crowds and inspiring the kind of vociferous ovations not heard for a while. Both performed in many new roles this season, and while Corella remains primarily a technical wunderkind, Herrera revealed new depth and maturity.

Over at NYCB, equally young emerging talent — notably Maria Kowroski and Miranda Weese — took on new challenges, and the company went farther afield in commissioning new ballets. David Parsons's modern-dance sensibility did not mesh well with the dancers' classical strengths in *Touch*, but Kevin O'Day's *Bachonim* showed this intelligent, highly musical choreographer continuing to develop his craft and honing a blend of sleek modernism that still respects classical purity. Peter Martins's contribution to the season's repertory included a grim, turgid homage, *Reliquary*, which slavishly reproduced greatest moments from George Balanchine's works, and a brisk, intricate showpiece for four dancers, *Tchaikovsky Pas de Quatre*.

Dance Theatre of Harlem toured extensively but had no New York season, and the reborn Joffrey Ballet began to estab-

THE 11TH BESSIE AWARDS

The New York Dance and Performance Awards (Bessies), named in honor of renowned dance teacher Bessie Schönberg, honor the creative individuals and organizations that define modern dance. New York's Dance Theater Workshop presented the awards in September 1995 at New York City's 92nd Street Y.

Choreographers and Creators
Reza Abdoh (posthumous)
William Douglas
Janie Geiser
Neil Greenberg
Lisa Jones and Alva Rogers
Jennifer Miller
Mary Ellen Strom
Simone Forti

Performers
Jamie Bishton
Kristen Borg
Frédéric Gafner
Lawrence Goldhuber
Lisa Race
Renee Redding-Jones

Designers
Gretchen Bender
Elliot Caplan
David Fritz and Carol Mullins
Michael Stiller

Composers
Ysaye Barnwell
Raúl Jaurena
Guy Klucevsek
Philip Glass

Special Citations
Tina Ramirez, founder and director of Ballet Hispánico
Jeanette Ingbergman and Papo Colo, curators of *Let the Artists Live,* an experimental exhibition
Melvin Davis, director of the Thelma Hill Performing Arts Center (posthumous)

Riverside

lish itself in Chicago with national tours. The Feld Ballet showcased several premieres by Eliot Feld as well as an endearing, talented group of his school's students, for whom Feld choreographed the charming *Meshugana Dance*.

Mark Morris Dance Company presented its first major local repertory season in several years. The December 1995 engagement at the Brooklyn Academy of Music featured first-rate live musical accompaniment and a generous assortment of new Morris dances that once again made a sensitive, highly imaginative use of scores ranging from Mozart to Lou Harrison to Stephen Foster.

The Alvin Ailey American Dance Theatre continued to thrive under the inspired direction of Judith Jamison, who knows how to select and cultivate dancers and whose new *Riverside* was a lush, sensual adventure. This troupe provides a fine example of surmounting the loss of a visionary founder and carrying on his vision while moving in new directions.

Two significant companies reached the milestone 25th anniversary with their original visions and trademark styles mostly intact: Garth Fagan Dance, whose thrillingly distinctive and committed dancers tend to remain for many years and move like a select, highly evolved special breed, was in great form, especially in Fagan's typically disjointed but persuasive new work celebrating the occasion, *Mix 25*. Pilobolus Dance Theatre, the offbeat six-person collective that has evolved into an institution, performed some of its greatest hits as part of its anniversary season. Stimulated by new dancers but still directed by most of its original members, Pilobolus remains a unique success story. Its playful, sensual, gymnastically-oriented movement style sustains a high level of appeal year after year, as evidenced by the full houses that show up for its month-long seasons at New York's Joyce Theater. Like Fagan's dancers, Pilobolus cannot be confused with anyone else. That recognizable individuality helps sustain its popularity at a time when too much look-alike choreography and proficient but bland dancing has watered down the enthusiasm with which audiences view dance.

As the field refocuses and reinvents itself to confront the challenges of the current climate in the arts, it is the companies with strong individual profiles (and, ideally, dynamic choreographers who work closely with the dancers) that are most likely to sustain themselves and to thrive. Survival of the fittest, indeed. ■

Pilobolus

1995 – 1996 Major Dance Events

Robert Greskovic, a New York City critic for *Dance Magazine* and video editor for *Dance View*, selected the following major dance events as highlights of the 1995–1996 season.

THE ALVIN AILEY AMERICAN DANCE THEATER

Tribute to Masazumi Chaya
First program included *Memoria*
Choreography: Alvin Ailey; **Music:** Keith Jarrett; **Costumes:** A. Christina Giannini; **Lighting:** Chenault Spence
Second program included excerpts from:
Opus McShann — **Choreography:** Alvin Ailey; **Music:** Jay McShann and Walter Brown; **Sets and Costumes:** Randy Barcelo; **Lighting:** Timothy Hunter
Streams — **Choreography:** Alvin Ailey; **Music:** Miloslav Kabelac; **Lighting:** Chenault Spence
Hidden Rites — **Choreography:** Alvin Ailey; **Music:** Patrice Sciortino; **Costumes:** Bea Feitler; **Lighting:** Chenault Spence
The River — **Choreography:** Alvin Ailey; **Original Score:** Duke Ellington; **Costumes:** Christina Giannini; **Lighting:** Chenault Spence
Suite Otis — **Choreography and Costumes:** George Faison; **Music:** Otis Redding; **Lighting:** Chenault Spence
Third program included *Revelations*
Choreography: Alvin Ailey; **Decor and Costumes:** Ves Harper; **Lighting:** Nicola Cernovitch; Performed to traditional music
Opening: 12/95 at New York City's City Center
How fitting that this troupe of engaging, generous dancers honored artistic associate Masazumi Chaya in one of its gala performances of the season. "Chayasan," as the Japanese-born former Ailey dancer is affectionately known, is a good part of the reason the company performs so consistently well. Showcasing members of the Ailey school and its preprofessional repertory compa-

American Ballet Theatre,
Ballet Imperial

Martha Swope

ny, the gala's bill of fare included stirring excerpts from works Chayasan danced during his 15 years with the company. The touching evening ended with a rousing performance of Ailey's *Revelations*, which celebrated its 35th anniversary this year.

AMERICAN BALLET THEATRE

Triple Bill
First program included *The Leaves Are Fading*
Choreography: Antony Tudor; **Music:** Antonin Dvořák; **Costumes:** Patricia Zipprodt; **Lighting:** Jennifer Tipton
Second program included *Stepping Stones*
Choreography: Jiri Kylián; **Music:** John Cage and Anton Webern; **Costumes:** Joke Visser; **Scenery and Lighting:** Michael Simon
Third program included *Ballet Imperial*
Choreography: George Balanchine; **Music:** Peter Ilich Tchaikovsky; **Scenery and Costumes:** Rouben Ter-Arutunian; **Lighting:** Jennifer Tipton
Opening: 6/96 at New York City's American Ballet Theatre
Two classics of 20th-century ballet rooted the new, trendy work American Ballet Theatre introduced this season to its proudly eclectic repertory. Antony Tudor, once regarded as the company's "conscience," was responsible for the windswept lyricism breezing through *The Leaves Are Fading*, in a which an especially rapturous Julie Kent and an athletic Keith Roberts dominated a dance of young love. In a brilliant display of ballet's complex geometry, Balanchine's *Ballet Imperial* proved the perfect framework for the eager, young Paloma Herrera and the ardent José Manuel Carreño as her cavalier. In between, Jiri Kylián's *Stepping Stones* looked chic but slight.

Swan Lake
Choreography: Marius Petipa, Lev Ivanov and David Blair; **Music:** Peter Ilich Tchaikovsky; **Scenery:** Oliver Smith; **Costumes:** Freddy Wittop; **Lighting:** Thomas Skelton (after Jean Rosenthal)
Opening: 5/96 at New York City's American Ballet Theatre
When the exquisitely lithe, Russian-born Vladimir Malakhov dances opposite Julie Kent, American Ballet Theatre's most elegant Odette the Swan Queen, they might call him the Swan Prince instead of simply Prince Siegfried. While the exotic young Malakhov made a riveting but brief debut with the company last season, this year he staked a truly royal claim on an audience hungry for a

American Ballet Theatre,
All-Tharp Evening

new star. His performance of the melancholy and impassioned fairy-tale prince emerged as one of the season's most memorable.

AMERICAN BALLET THEATRE
All-Tharp Evening
First program included *The Elements*
Choreography: Twyla Tharp; **Music:** Jean-Féry Rebel; **Costumes:** Santo Loquasto; **Lighting:** Jennifer Tipton
Second program included *How Near Heaven*
Choreography: Twyla Tharp; **Music:** Benjamin Britten; **Costumes:** Gianni Versace; **Lighting:** Jennifer Tipton
Third program included *Americans We*
Choreography: Twyla Tharp; **Music:** Suite of Nineteenth-Century American Favorites arranged by Donald Hunsberger; **Costumes:** Santo Loquasto; **Lighting:** Jennifer Tipton
Opening: 5/96 at New York City's American Ballet Theatre
Tharp's triple whammy at American Ballet Theatre opened with a bang, as an unusually jolting light effect put her premiere, *The Elements*, square in the audience's face. Its nine subsequent segments made for dashing dance theater set to digitalized 18th-century music. Last year's *How Near Heaven*, sailed through the middle of the bill like some strangely populated ship, where handsome men and women pranced in either beachwear or sleepwear. *Americans We*, a remake of a trifle from last year, alternated fresh bursts of energy with sentimental vignettes of Americana to close an unforgettable evening of dance.

BALLET DE L'OPÉRA DE PARIS
La Bayadère
Choreography and Staging: Rudolf Nureyev (after Marius Petipa); **Original Music:** Ludwig Minkus; **Libretto:** Marius Petipa and Sergei Khudekov; **Decor:** Ezio Frigerio; **Costumes:** Franca Squarciapino;

Lighting: Vinicio Cheli
Opening: 6/96 at New York City's Metropolitan Opera
The world's oldest ballet troupe came to New York with the world's newest staging of a 19th-century landmark, *La Bayadère*, an extravagant production re-created by Nureyev. With the exception of one dancer, the first cast in New York City was the one Nureyev chose for his 1992 Paris premiere. A regal Isabelle Guérin, an elegant Laurent Hilaire and a strong Elizabeth Platel each resurrected their respective portrayals: Nikiya, the title-role temple dancer; Solor, the imperfect, warrior hero; and Gamzatti, the jealous princess. The exception was the irrepressible Patrick Dupond, who followed Nureyev as company director in Paris and here danced the cameo role of the "Golden Idol" with cheeky excess.

LES BALLETS AFRICAINS
Heritage
Choreography: Mohamed Kemoko Sano; **Costumes and Set Design:** Italo Zambo; **Lighting:** Tim Speechley
Opening: 4/96 at New York City's City Center
With its earthy settings of palm trees and thatched huts and dazzling explosions of instrumental, vocal and physical energy, the National Dance Company of Guinea created a thrilling hybrid display. The two-part program led the audience through a warm and colorful reverie on Guinean folk rituals. The individual branches all met in a mass celebration, presenting the 35-member troupe of acrobatic dancers and virtuoso musicians in a wildly alive spectacle. The nearly three-hour performance supported the World Music Institute (the evening's presenter) and culminated the organization's busy spring of music-and-dance events from faraway places.

LES BALLETS TROCKADERO DE MONTE CARLO
New York City Repertory Program
First program included *Le Lac de Cygnes*
Staging: Trutti Gasparinetti (after Ivanov); **Music:** Peter Ilich Tchaikovsky; **Costumes:** Mike Gonzales; **Lighting:** Kip Marsh; **Decor:** Clio Young
Second program included:
Grand Pas Classique — **Choreography:** after Victor Gsovsky; **Music:** Francois Auber; **Costumes:** Mike Gonzales; **Lighting:** Kip Marsh
Pas des Odalisques — **Staging:** Elena Kunikova (after Petipa); **Music:** Riccardo Drigo; **Costumes:** Mike Gonzales; **Lighting:** Kip Marsh
Go for Barocco — **Choreography:** Peter Anastos; **Music:** Johann Sebastian Bach; **Costumes:** Mike Gonzales; **Lighting:** Esquire Jauchem
Third program included *Gaîté Parisienne*
Choreography: Susan Trevino; **Music:** Jacques Offenbach; **Costumes and Decor:** Mike Gonzales; **Lighting:** Kip Marsh

Opening: 12/95 at the Sylvia and Danny Kaye Playhouse at Hunter College of The City University of New York

The Trocks, as these clever ballet spoofers have come to be called, returned to New York after a lengthy hiatus. Fears that the one-time ace satirists might have lost their lethally on-target touch proved unfounded — the troupe's mixed bill was sharper and funnier than ever before. Impeccable tutus, coiffeurs and choreographic elements such as *Swan Lake*, Act II, shine. Tatiana Youbetsyabootskaya in a drop-dead performance of *Grand Pas Classique* gained an immediate and impassioned following.

MERCE CUNNINGHAM DANCE COMPANY

Events

Choreography: Merce Cunningham; **Set Design:** Robert Rauschenberg; **Costumes:** Suzanne Gallo; **Lighting:** Kelly Atallah
Opening: 2/96 at New York City's Joyce Theater

First introduced in 1964, Cunningham's signature *Events* are one-time arrangements of excerpts recycled from past and present dances. Dressed in basic-black unitards, Cunningham's company opened its solitary New York City season in Manhattan's tiny Joyce Theater. The 90-minute affair showcased a 15-member troupe, including the 76-year-old silver-haired maestro himself. Cunningham devised an intriguing program of convoluted duets and densely configured groupings for a tantalizing sampler that left the audience hungry for full-scale performances.

Ocean

Concept: John Cage and Merce Cunningham; **Choreography:** Merce Cunningham; **Music:** Andrew Culver and David Tudor; **Decor:** Marsha Skinner
Opening: 7/96 at Damrosch Park as part of Lincoln Center Festival '96

Cunningham and Cage's *Ocean* finally washed up in New York after touring for the last couple of

Gadi Dagon

Merce Cunningham Dance Company,
Events

CONTINUED ON NEXT PAGE ▶

◀ CONTINUED FROM PREVIOUS PAGE

Summer Nights at the Ford
Ford Amphitheatre
Los Angeles, CA
(213) 466-1767

COLORADO

Aspen Music Festival
Aspen Festival Tent
Aspen, CO
(970) 925-3254
(970) 925-9042

Breckenridge Music Festival
Riverwalk Center
Breckenridge, CO
(970) 453-2120

Central City Opera Summer Series
Central City Opera House
Central City, CO
(303) 292-6700

Colorado Dance Festival
Boulder, CO
(303) 442-7666

Colorado Music Festival
Boulder, CO
(303) 449-1397

Colorado Opera Festival
Pikes Peak Center
Colorado Springs, CO
(719) 473-0073

CONNECTICUT

Connecticut Early Music Festival
Harkness Chapel
Connecticut College
New London, CT
(203) 444-2419

Norfolk Chamber Music Festival
Norfolk, CT
(203) 542-3000

Opera Theater of Connecticut Summer Production
Andrews Memorial Theatre
Clinton, CT
(203) 669-8999

DISTRICT OF COLUMBIA

DanceAfrica, D.C. Festival
Dance Place Theater
Washington D.C.
(202) 269-1600

CONTINUED ON PAGE 639 ▶

Margaretta K. Mitchell/Lori Belilove and Co.

Isadora Duncan Dance Ensemble,
America Dancing

years. Conceived a year before Cage died in 1992, the 90-minute nighttime, outdoor production was performed theater-in-the-round style, with the dancers center stage and the audience encircled by the work's 112 musicians. The event transpired as smoothly and serenely as lapping waves, and while Culver's Cagean score sounded more like an orchestral tune-up, Cunningham's dancers, costumed in rich, tropical-fish colors, conjured an exotic, flow of dreamy energy.

DANCE THEATRE OF HARLEM
World premiere of *Ground*
Choreography: Alonzo King; **Music:** Arvo Pärt, Henryk Gorecki and David LaMarche; **Costume Design:** Robert Rosenwasser; **Costumes:** Pamela Allen-Cummings; **Lighting:** Lisa Pinkham
Opening: 5/96 at The John F. Kennedy Center for the Performing Arts
King's *Ground*, created especially for the Dance Theatre of Harlem, drew from multiple musical sources, including compositions by modernists Pärt and Gorecki. The musical mood was shadowy and smoky; likewise, the tone of the dancing. Seven men and twelve women danced chicly, partially clad in what seemed to be second skins in shades of iridescent blue. Their eccentric moves alternated between the densely hyperactive and the dramatically enervated for an intriguing mix of movement and color.

ISADORA DUNCAN DANCE ENSEMBLE
America Dancing
Program included music from Schubert, Chopin, Strauss and Gluck
Choreography: Isadora Duncan; **Lighting:** Eric Fliss
Opening: 1/96 at the John F. Kennedy Center for the Performing Arts
A short speech by longtime Duncanite Julia Levien and 20 little dances by the Mother of

Modern Dance launched Kennedy Center's *America Dancing* with suitable simplicity and beauty. Seven young women, who have danced together since junior high school under artistic director Andrea Mandell-Seidel, tripped through potentially clichéd Duncan dancing on a poetically "light fantastic toe." Dressed in tissue-paper-thin silks of aurora-borealis hues, solo, duo and ensemble dancers technically did little more than hop, skip and jump, yet spiritually, they conjured marvelously colored theater by creating a distinctly different world with each brief number.

EIKO & KOMA

River

Choreography: Eiko and Koma; **Visual Elements:** Judd Weisberg; **Film:** James Byrne
Opening: 9/95 at Eddyside Park, Easton, PA
After nine summers of preparation in a creek in Lexington, New York, the husband and wife performing team of Eiko & Koma presented the premiere of *River*, one of the season's most highly original theatrical reveries. A deceptively lazy stretch of the Delaware River flowing through Easton, Pennsylvania, became the site for the debut of the one-hour event. In concert with sculptor Judd Weisberg and filmmaker James Byrne, the Japanese-born duo appear, disappear and reappear as luminous phantoms out of the river's hypnotic current. No two future performances will be alike, but each promises to be captivating.

DOUG ELKINS DANCE COMPANY

Altogether Different
First program included the world premiere of *The Sky Is Falling (so bury me standing)*
Choreography: Doug Elkins; **Music:** from the Montpellier Codex; **Set Design:** Ross Lewis
Second program included:
Scott, Queen Of Marys — **Choreography:** Doug Elkins; **Music:** Mio Morales; **Costumes:** Katrin Schnabl
Narcoleptic Lovers — **Words and Music:** Gavin Bryars, Lenny Bruce, Mio Morales, Mozart, Sinead O'Conner and Urban Species; **Costumes:** Katrin Schnabl
Opening: 1/96 at New York City's Joyce Theater
Dancer/choreographer Elkins appeared to be mellowing as a dancemaker, though he still retained his prankish good humor and audience rapport during curtain calls. *The Sky is Falling (so bury me standing)*, a premiere the Movement Man called a "first draft," offered a capella, reverie-inspired 13th-century motets that featured nine curvetting dancers. The limber performers tangled and tumbled gently and fluently for an inspired acrobatic journey.

GARTH FAGAN DANCE

First program included (all choreography by Garth Fagan):
Prelude — **Music:** Abdullah Ibrahim and Max Roach; **Lighting Design:** C.T. Oakes; **Costumes:** Zinda Williams
Oatka Trail — **Costumes:** Garth Fagan; **Music:** Antonin Dvořák; **Lighting Design:** C.T. Oakes.
River Song — **Music:** Don Pullen's African Brazilian Connection and The Chief Cliff Singers; **Lighting Design:** C.T. Oakes; **Costumes:** Linda King
Second program included the world premiere of *Mix 25*
Choreography: Garth Fagan; **Costumes:** Garth Fagan; **Lighting:** C.T. Oakes
Third program included (all choreography by Garth Fagan):
Spring Yaounde — **Music:** Wynton Marsalis; **Sets:** Martin Puryear; **Lighting:** C.T. Oakes
From Before — **Costumes:** Garth Fagan; **Music:** Ralph MacDonald; **Lighting:** C.T. Oakes
Opening: 4/96 at New York City's Joyce Theater
The centerpiece of Fagan's spring was a premiere called *Mix 25*. More a colorful patchwork sampler than a tightly woven tapestry, the five-part dance takes its inspiration from four different composers (jazz star Marsalis, a Fagan favorite and pal, is responsible for two parts). The final section, "Give Thanks" to Jamaican reggae, shows off the whole company in brightly colored swimsuits, gyrating like flying fish.

FELD BALLETS/NY

Kids Dance

Choreography: Eliot Feld and guest collaborators
While Eliot Feld's ballet companies have been consistently youthful, his spring season literally gave weekend matinees over to the kids. Called *Kids Dance*, these shows offered performing opportunities to students from the New Ballet School, a center founded in 1977 to introduce public schoolchildren to ballet. In addition to

Lois Greenfield

Feld Ballets/NY, *Meshugana Dance*

some new works, including a deftly dizzying *Meshugana Dance* to Klezmer music, Feld also sought collaboration from other choreographers, including Pilobolus veteran Alison Chase, who created *Kidsobolus* for the occasion. Among the performers shining in these programs was an eager and accomplished young dancer named Edgar Peterson, a kid ready, willing and able to move toward the big time.

HANDEL WITH CARE — SOLOS FROM A SUITCASE

U.S. Premiere
Choreography: Samuel Wuersten; **Music:** George Frederick Handel; **Costumes:** Emmy Schouten, Katherine Maurer and Edith Ordelmen; **Lighting:** Susanne Poulin
Opening: 1/96 at St. Mark's Church and administered by Danspace Project
Switzerland's Wuersten created a suite of solos showcasing four talented dancers — the United States's Brenda Daniels, The Netherlands's Anne Affourtit, South Africa's Tim Persent and Australia's Derek Porter. The foursome stretched, coiled, paced and leaped about to a mixture of excerpts lifted directly or very freely from Handel's *Messiah*. Each soloist proved worthy of spotlighting, but the gloriously gifted Porter emerged as a dance-world revelation and mesmerizing one-man theater.

MARIE-JEANNE/VIDEO TAPE SESSIONS

The George Balanchine Foundation
Opening: 6/96 at the New York City Ballet studios
In June, the Interpreters Archive of the George Balanchine Foundation conducted invaluable sessions aimed at documenting the memories of one of Balanchine's first American ballerinas. In the 1940s, Marie-Jeanne, who dropped her family name, Pelus, for the stage, played an instrumental role in the two now-classic Balanchine ballets *Concerto Barocco* and *Ballet Imperial* (both 1941) as well as in the currently titled "Russian Dance" in the ballet master's first American work, *Serenade* (1934). During a videotaped interview and demonstration sessions, the septuagenarian relayed tidbits of nostalgia as contemporary dancers, some still students, performed the choreography she inspired.

MARK MORRIS DANCE GROUP

Program A included (all choreography by Mark Morris):
Somebody's Coming To See Me Tonight — **Music:** Stephen Foster; **Lighting:** Michael Chybowski; **Costumes:** Susan Ruddie
A Spell — **Music:** John Wilson; **Lighting:** Michael Chybowski; **Costumes:** Susan Ruddie

The Office — **Music:** Antonin Dvorák; **Lighting:** Michael Chybowski; **Costumes:** June Omura.
Bedtime — **Music:** Franz Schubert; **Lighting:** James F. Ingalls; **Costumes:** Susan Ruddie
World Power — **Music:** Lou Harrison; **Lighting:** Michael Chybowski; **Costumes:** Susan Ruddie
Program B included (all choreography by Mark Morris and lighting by Michael Chybowski):
Lucky Charms — **Music:** Jacques Ibert
Rondo — **Music:** Wolfgang Amadeus Mozart
Jesu, Meine Freude — **Music:** Johann Sebastian Bach.
Grand Duo — **Music:** Lou Harrison; **Costumes:** Susan Ruddie
Opening: 12/95 at The Brooklyn Academy of Music
Mysteriously, all the ads for Morris's New York repertory season only announced the names of the composers whose music inspired these nine dances. With the exception of the grandly dark and vehement *Grand Duo* (1993), Morris was premiering the works to his large and loyal New York audiences. While such brief encounters with these complex creations did not serve up more than first impressions, the program — *Lucky Charms* (1994), a dazzling display of glitter and substance, *Bedtime* (1992), a simultaneously light and heavy look at lullabies, *The Office* (1994), a chilling contemporary folkdance, and *Rondo* (1994), a riveting Morris solo — received enthusiastic applause.

NEW YORK CITY BALLET

Tchaikovsky Suite No. 3
Choreography: George Balanchine; **Music:** Peter Ilich Tchaikovsky; **Scenery and Costumes:** Nicolas Benois; **Lighting:** Ronald Bates and Mark Stanley
Opening: 6/96 at New York City's City Ballet

Mark Morris Dance Group, *Somebody's Coming to See Me Tonight*

Dan Rest

Mark Morris Dance Company,
The Office

Just before he was due to leave New York City Ballet to join a European company, 23-year-old wunderkind Ethan Stiefel made his debut in the dazzling "Theme and Variations" movement of Balanchine's *Tchaikovsky Suite No. 3.* The young star, vibrant in white tights and gold-trimmed tunic, partnered with City Ballet's prodigious Miranda Weese for a wild and impetuous performance. Despite the demanding movements, Stiefel kept the ballet's precise framework in perfect focus. In light of the dazzling performance, it was hard to tell if the cocky American prince was having second thoughts about leaving ballets such as this or just saying a blazing good-bye.

Apollo
Choreography: George Balanchine; **Music:** Igor Stravinsky; **Lighting:** Ronald Bates and Mark Stanley
Opening: 5/96 at New York City's City Ballet
The biggest news at New York City Ballet in the spring wasn't new ballets — it was new and glorious talent in *Apollo*, a 68-year-old Balanchine gem. Though this cast performed the neoclassic only once, its two leading dancers honored the ballet's golden history with newfound radiance. Russian-trained Igor Zelensky created a glowing portrait of power and finesse in the title role, while burgeoning ballerina Maria Kowroski as the muse Terpsichore showed a playfulness, sweetness and expansive airiness that played off the stunning god of the sun.

NEW YORK INTERNATIONAL BALLET COMPETITION

Round I included *Les Sylphides*
Choreography: Michel Fokine; **Music:** Frédéric Chopin; **Costume Sketches:** Slava Toumine
Round II included *Raymonda*
Choreography: Marius Petipa; **Music:** Alexandre Glazounov

◀ CONTINUED FROM PAGE 636

Summer Opera Theatre Co.
Hartke Theatre
Catholic University
Washington D.C.
(202) 526-1669

GEORGIA

Atlanta Opera
Fox Theatre
Atlanta, GA
(404) 355-3311

ILLINOIS

Chicago Opera Theater Spring Fest
Merle Reskin Theater
Chicago, IL
(312) 292-7578

Grant Park Music Festival
Petrillo Band Shell
Grant Park
Chicago, IL
(312) 742-4763
(312) 742-7638

Ravinia Festival
Highland Park, IL
(312) 728-4642

IOWA

Des Moines Metro Opera Summer Festival
Blank Performing Arts Center
Indianola, IA
(515) 961-6221

Dorian Opera Theatre
Center for Faith and Life
Luther College
Decorah, IA
(319) 387-1124

35th Annual National Choreography Conference
Iowa City, IA
(713) 496-4670

MAINE

Bowdoin Summer Music Festival
Brunswick, ME
(207) 725-3895

CONTINUED ON NEXT PAGE ▶

◀ CONTINUED FROM PREVIOUS PAGE

MASSACHUSETTS

Amherst Early Music Festival
Amherst, MA
(413) 542-3236

Berkshire Opera Co.
Monument Mountain Regional High School Theater
Great Barrington, MA
(413) 528-4420

College Light Opera Co.
Highfield Theatre
Falmouth, MA
(508) 548-0668

Harvard Summer Dance Series
Cambridge, MA
(617) 495-5535

Jacob's Pillow Dance Festival
Ted Shawn Theater
Becket, MA
(413) 243-0745

Musicordia Festival
South Hadley, MA
(413) 538-2590

Tanglewood Festival
Lenox, MA
(617) 266-1492

MICHIGAN

Interlochen Arts Festival
Kresge Auditorium
Interlochen, MI
(616) 276-6230

Pine Mountain Music Festival
Calumet, Escanaba, Houghton,
Iron Mountain and Marquette, MI
(906) 487-2844

MINNESOTA

Minnesota Orchestra Viennese Sommerfest
Orchestra Hall
Minneapolis, MN
(612) 371-5656

MISSOURI

Summerfest St. Louis
St. Louis Symphony Community Music School
St. Louis, MO
(314) 534-1700

CONTINUED ON PAGE 642 ▶

Round III included *Who Cares?*
Choreography: George Balanchine; **Music:** George Gershwin
Round IV included *The Sleeping Beauty*
Choreography: Marius Petipa; **Music:** Peter Ilyich Tchaikovsky
Opening: 6/96 at New York City's Alice Tully Hall at Lincoln Center
There are no partisans like ballet partisans, especially at ballet competitions. The only regular U.S. version of such "contests" occurs triennially in New York City. This year's fifth anniversary event resulted in winners and, sometimes, losers who enjoyed great popularity with their audiences. The judges' gold medal went to favorite Barbora Kohoutkova of the Czech Republic, while Columbia's Carlos Molina, another audience darling, received a year's contract with American Ballet Theatre as the winner of the newly established Igor Youskevitch Award.

PLISETSKAYA GALA

Director: Guediminas Taranda; **Set Design:** Boris Krasnov; **Lighting:** Damir Ismagilov
Opening: 5/96 at New York City's City Center
Celebrating her 70th birthday year, legendary ballerina Maya Plisetskaya packed up her Cardin evening gown, tutu and toe-shoes and took her gala performance around the world. Billed as "direct from the Bolshoi Theater," the three-hour show of crowd-pleasing dancing by stellar performers from Eastern and Western Europe and the United States featured select items danced by the septuagenarian herself. In *The Dying Swan*, the still svelte star worked her evident, if fading strengths, to create images of a fragile fight for life. Climactically, Plisetskaya paraded like a runway model posing for a Richard Avedon shoot in a salute to her adoring audience.

Paul Taylor Dance Company,
Offenbach Overtures

PAUL TAYLOR DANCE COMPANY

World premiere of *Offenbach Overtures*
Choreography: Paul Taylor; **Music:** Jacques Offenbach; **Costumes:** Santo Loquasto; **Lighting:** Jennifer Tipton
Opening: 10/95 at New York City Center Theater
With dancers in bright scarlet and black costumes, Taylor's new *Offenbach Overtures* revisits an old world school of dancing with a sly, contemporary approach. Inspired by rousing oom-pah-pah music, the American modern-dance master poked a great deal of fun at yesteryear's Russian ballets with dapper dueling officers and can-canning mademoiselles. Setting the high-kicking high jinks to Offenbach's lively score, Taylor whipped up a brilliant production that soared with precision, humor and originality.

SAN FRANCISCO BALLET

First program included *Stravinsky Violin Concerto*
Choreography: George Balanchine; **Music:** Igor Stravinsky; **Lighting:** Lisa J. Pinkham (after Roland Bates)
Second program included:
Pacific — **Choreography:** Mark Morris; **Music:** Lou Harrison; **Costume:** Martin Pakledinaz; **Lighting:** James F. Ingalls
Tuning Game (world premiere) — **Choreography:** Helgi Tomasson; **Music:** John Corigliano; **Costumes:** Martin Pakledinaz; **Lighting:** Lisa J. Pinkham
Third program included *The Dance House*
Choreography: David Bintley; **Music:** Dmitry Shostakovich; **Scenery and Costumes:** Robert Heindel; **Lighting:** Lisa J. Pinkham
Opening: 11/95 at New York City's City Center
None of the premiering works San Francisco Ballet presented in New York, where artistic director Tomasson came of age aesthetically, packed much punch. But Tomasson's dancers more than did themselves and their art proud. Most impressive was former Bolshoi dancer Yuri Possokhov in Balanchine's *Stravinsky Violin Concerto*. Making his first local appearance with this company, the committed and scrupulously schooled Russian heated up the stage to an intense degree. In a showcase worthy of his formidable gifts, this riveting dancer, in a company where all of the male dancers exhibit impressive strength, emerged a prince among princes.

SCHOOL OF AMERICAN BALLET

32nd Annual Workshop Performances
First program included:
Concerto Barocco — **Choreography:** George Balanchine; **Music:** Johann Sebastian Bach
Valse Fantasie — **Choreography:** George Balanchine; **Music:** Mikhail Glinka
Second program included *Danses Bohémiennes*
Choreography: Christopher Wheeldon; **Music:** Claude Debussy; **Costumes:** Angela Kostritsky
Third program included *Rubies*
Choreography: George Balanchine; **Music:** Igor Stravinsky
Opening: 6/96 at the Juilliard Theater at Lincoln Center
This year's annual rite of artistic passage, showcasing the young talent of the School of American Ballet, turned even more youthful with the world premiere of *Danses Bohémiennes* by 23-year-old Wheeldon. Barely beyond his own student days (at Britain's Royal Ballet School), the up-and-coming dancer with New York City Ballet re-created a moonlit ballet class overflowing with beguiling talent. Wheeldon's five men and three women presented a dreamily playful scene inspired by the music of Debussy. What began in a simple classroom setting ended in a fanciful otherworld, where artfully schooled young people live, walk and ride on air.

Johan Elbers

San Francisco Ballet, *Pacific*

SALLY SILVERS & DANCERS

Pandora's Cake Stain
Choreography and Costumes: Sally Silvers; **Music Composition and Live Mixing:** Bruce Andrews; **Lighting:** Jennifer Tipton
Opening: 6/96 at New York City's Kitchen Center
Working from her interests in improvisation, experimentalist Silvers created an impressive world of odd movement to stock her latest mini-epic. Her two-act dance took as its oblique subject, Lulu, the femme fatale from Alban Berg's 1930s opera of the same name. The 11-dancer cast (including Silvers) performed an episodic array of funky yet dramatic moments that produced an unstoppable momentum. An appropriate subtitle for the whole loopy affair might well be *Little Lulu*, to indicate Silvers's whimsical comic-strip treatment of her grand opera subject.

◀ CONTINUED FROM PAGE 640

NEW HAMPSHIRE

Monadnock Music Festival
Pine Hill Waldorf Auditorium/Peterborough
Townhouse
Wilton, NH
(603) 924-7610

NEW JERSEY

New Jersey State Opera Summer Sounds
Garden State Arts Center
Holmdel, NJ
(908) 442-9200

Opera Festival of New Jersey
Kirby Arts Center
Lawrenceville, NJ
(609) 279-1795

NEW MEXICO

Santa Fe Chamber Music Festival
St. Francis Auditorium
Santa Fe, NM
(505) 983-2075

NEW YORK

Artpark/Artpark at the Church
Art Theater
Lewiston, NY
(716) 754-4375
(800) 659-7275

Bach Aria Festival & Institute
Stony Brook, NY
(516) 632-7239

Bridgehampton Chamber Music Fesival
Bridgehampton, NY
(212) 426-6952

Caramoor International Music Festival
Katonah, NY
(914) 232-1252
(800) 848-2742

Chautauqua Institution
Chautauqua, NY
(800) 836-2787

Dance Theater Workshop
Bessie Schönberg Theater
New York, NY
(212) 691-6500

STREB/RINGSIDE
POPAction
Choreography and Structural Design: Elizabeth
Streb; **Lighting:** Heather Carson; **Costumes:** Eileen
Thomas
Opening: 12/95 at the Joyce Theater
Taking over the popular Christmastime slot in
New York's Joyce Theater, Streb/Ringside offered
a two-part program showcasing a blend of raw
acrobatics, blunt gymnastics and daring stunts.
With athletic dancers costumed in primary col-
ors, Streb's eight "pop-action" (her term for her
unique branch of dance and choreography) num-
bers echoed the energy of cartoon violence. New
this year were two pieces choreographed for the
Museum of Contemporary Art in Los Angeles: the
first, an elaboration on flagpole stunts, the other,
post-modern trampolining.

DONNA UCHIZONO COMPANY
Ivy Grows
Choreography: Donna Uchizono; **Music:** Lawrence
D. "Butch" Morris and James Lo (for "quietly goes a
giant jane"); **Costumes:** Katherine Maurer; **Lighting:**
Stan Pressner
Opening: 11/95 at New York City's Dance Theater
Workshop
Uchizono divided her repertory concert in two
indelible halves. The four-part first half was
called "Polynesian Shorts;" the three-part second
half, "quietly goes a giant jane." In addition to her
ingenious, moving images, Uchizono's colorful
costume sense (illuminated by Pressner's brilliant lighting effects) provided her audience with
a visually stunning experience. Whether thinking
out loud about growing up as an Asian-American
woman while toying with scarlet "poi balls" or
articulating little more than finger joints alongside kindred spirit Nikki Castro (in a fantastic
indigo wig), Uchizono created stellar dance-the-
ater that glowed with color.

Miriam Lefkowitz

Streb/Ringside, *POPAction*

Donna Uchizono Company

THE WASHINGTON BALLET
Suzanne Farrell Stages Balanchine
First program included *Mozartiana*
Choreography: George Balanchine; **Music:** Peter Ilich Tchaikovsky; **Costumes:** Rouben Ter-Arutunian; **Lighting:** Tony Tucci
Second program included *Monumentum Pro Gesualdo* and *Movements for Piano and Orchestra*
Choreography: George Balanchine; **Music:** Igor Stravinsky; **Lighting:** Tony Tucci
Third program included:
Slaughter on Tenth Avenue — **Choreography:** George Balanchine; **Music:** Richard Rodgers; **Original Scenery:** Jo Mielziner; **Original Costumes:** Irene Sharaff; **Lighting:** Tony Tucci
Scotch Symphony — **Choreography:** George Balanchine; **Music:** Felix Mendelssohn; **Original Costumes:** Karinska; **Lighting:** Tony Tucci
Fourth program included *Tzigane*
Choreography: George Balanchine; **Music:** Maurice Ravel; **Costumes:** Karinska; **Lighting:** Tony Tucci
Fifth program included *Chaconne*
Choreography: George Balanchine; **Music:** Christoph Willibald von Gluck; **Costumes:** Karinska; **Lighting:** Tony Tucci
Opening: 10/95 at the John F. Kennedy Center for the Performing Arts
Former New York City Ballet ballerina Farrell took her act on the road, staging two programs including seven Balanchine ballets to open the 25th anniversary year of the Kennedy Center. Working with a core ensemble taken from Washington Ballet, Balanchine's best-known muse presented the ballets that defined her own legendary career. The leading dancers hailed from companies as close as New York City Ballet and as far as Germany's Bavarian State Ballet, but all came with the same lofty level of talent.

Glimmerglass Opera Festival
Alice Busch Opera Theater
Cooperstown, NY
(607) 547-2255

Huntington Summer Arts Festival
Huntington, NY
(516) 271-8442

Lake George Opera Festival
Queensbury High School Auditorium
Queensbury, NY
(518) 793-3859

Lincoln Center Out-of-Doors
New York, NY
(212) 875-5108

Lincoln Center Summer Festival
New York, NY
(212) 721-6500
(212) 875-5132

Maverick Concerts
Woodstock, NY
(914) 679-8217

Mohonk Music Week and Festival of the Arts
New Paltz, NY
(800) 772-6646

Mostly Mozart Festival
New York, NY
(212) 721-6500

New York Grand Opera
Rumsey Field
Central Park
New York, NY
(212) 245-8837

New York Philharmonic Parks Concerts
New York, NY
(212) 875-5709

Serious Fun! Festival
Lincoln Center
New York, NY
(212) 721-6500

NORTH CAROLINA

American Dance Festival
Durham, NC
(919) 684-6402

Brevard Music Festival
Brevard Music Center
Brevard, NC
(704) 884-2019

CONTINUED ON PAGE 651 ▶

Grand Entrances

■ BY DAVID PATRICK STEARNS

David Patrick
Stearns is the
theater and
classical music
critic for *USA
Today*.

OPERA HAS BEEN SIDESTEPPING ITSELF FOR YEARS, TRYING TO CONvince modern audiences that snazzy, updated productions and *Sunset Boulevard*-style flash will help the world get over the death of Maria Callas, the retirement of Joan Sutherland and the aging of Montserrat Caballe.

The big-show grandeur and contemporary themes can be stimulating and artistically significant, but only in the context of what opera was invented for: great singing. Almost by miracle, a whole school of first-class voices managed to arrive or artistically come of age in the 1995–1996 season, breaking through the distracting glare of opera's spectacle.

This was major news. For almost a generation, many opera fans have, paradoxically enough, drifted away from the opera house, lured back only by occasional performances by young superstars such as Cecilia Bartoli and Thomas Hampson. Audiences were often alienated by the superficial, jetsetting ways of modern singers. To borrow a phrase from opera sociologist Wayne Kostelbaum, they formed shut-in opera cults based mostly around great and old recordings. However, even these most hardened cynics have been softened and excited by Renee Fleming, who is no stranger to opera but has begun to sing with greater passion than before and a notable ecstatic quality. She had a remarkable year, establishing herself as a formidable singing actress in Gounod's *Faust* with Lyric Opera of Chicago, showing off her coloratura ability in Rossini's *Armida* with Opera Orchestra of New York and consolidating it all in a rendition of Charpentier's great aria, *Depius le Jour*,

OPERA

J. Henry Fair

Cecilia Bartoli

Courtesy of Lyric Opera of Chicago

Renee Fleming

**Angela Gheorghiu and Roberto Alagna at James Levine's
25th Anniversary Gala**

in the Metropolitan Opera gala celebrating James Levine's 25th anniversary as artistic director.

In many ways, the internationally televised Levine event proved to be a season-end showcase for young opera talent, offering the nation an introduction to French/Italian tenor Roberto Alagna (who was compared breathlessly to Luciano Pavarotti) and his new bride, Romanian soprano Angela Gheorghiu. The couple had a temporary setback with their performances of *La Boheme* at the Met — he was somewhat ill, and both of them were drowned out by a young, eager conductor. But their recordings inspired much favorable comment and their "Cherry Duet" from *L'Amico Fritz* at the Levine gala was captivating. Gheorghiu, in particular, proved to be a highly resourceful actress.

British soprano Jane Eaglen had already made isolated waves in the United States. There had been a successful *Norma* in Seattle and a hair-raising Wagner concert with the Boston Symphony Orchestra at Tanglewood. This year she broke out on a number of fronts. Besides being heard on the *Sense and Sensibility* soundtrack (reflecting her affinity for non-classical music), she sang the punishing role of Brunnhilde in Lyric Opera of Chicago's *Ring Cycle*. Eaglen also has an outstanding young Wagnerian leading man, Canadian tenor Ben Heppner, who consolidated his reputation in concert performances of *Die Meistersinger von Nurnberg* by the Chicago Symphony Orchestra under Sir Georg Solti and in a new production of *Andrea Chenier* with the Seattle Opera.

Welsh baritone Bryn Terfel, whose 1994–1995 season was cut short after a back injury, made good on last season's *Don Giovanni* cancellations at the Met by returning in the same opera (playing Leporello) and recording an album titled *Wagner Arias* with the Met orchestra. Perhaps his most complete artistic statement to date, though, was an album of infrequently heard British art songs titled *The Vagabond*, released in the fall. Other European singers with impressive followings elsewhere began to make career headway in the United States. Waltraud Meier, the German mezzo-soprano, was especially electrifying at the Met

Here is *The Entertainment Almanac*'s selection of recent, noteworthy opera recordings, ranging from old standbys to rediscovered masterpieces.

Cleopatra & Cesare
by Carl Heinrich Graun (c. 1703–1759)
Concerto Köln, conducted by René Jacobs;
Soloists: Janet Williams, Iris Vermillion, Lynne Dawson, Robert Gambill, Ralf Popken, Jeffrey Francis, Klaus Häger, Elisabeth Scholl and Maria-Cristina Kiehr
Harmonia Mundi (1996)
This opera by a contemporary of Handel features authentic period instruments and a smaller cast than is common today.

Cosi fan tutte
by Wolfgang Amadeus Mozart (1756-1791)
Chamber Orchestra of Europe, conducted by Sir George Solti; London Voices, chorus master: Terry Edwards; **Soloists:** Renée Fleming, Anne Sofie von Otter, Frank Lopardo, Olaf Bär, Adelina Scarabelli and Michele Pertusi
London (1996)
A sterling cast brings top-notch talent to this new version of Mozart's comic melodrama, performed this season by New York's Metropolitan Opera Company.

La Dafne by Marco da Gagliano (1582–1643)
Studio di musica antica Antonio il Verso; Ensemble Elyma conducted by Gabriel Garrido; **Soloists:** Maria Cristina Kiehr, Roberta Invernizzi, Adriana Fernandez, Jordi Ricart, Achim Schulz Anderson and Furio Zanasi
K 617 (1995)
This French recording of a first-generation Italian opera gives a taste of opera's very beginnings.

Le Domino Noir
by Daniel-François-Esprit Auber (1782–1871)
English Chamber Orchestra and London Voices, conducted by Richard Bonynge; **Soloists:** Sumi Jo, Isabelle Vernet, Bruce Ford, Patrick Power, Martine Olmeda, Jules Bastin, Doris Lamprecht, Jocelyne Taillon and Gilles Cachemaille
London (1995)
Fans of gorgeous singing will appreciate this recording, the perfect showcase for the pure, canary-like coloratura of star soprano Sumi Jo.

Golem and Arald by Nicolae Bretan (b. 1887)
Philharmonic Orchestra Moldova, conducted by Iasi Cristian Mandeal
Nimbus Records (1995)
These two recently unearthed one-act operas were composed by the Romanian master banned by the communist government in 1948.

gala, while French coloratura Natalie Dessay showed unusual theatrical savvy as the Queen of the Night in a new recording of Mozart's *The Magic Flute* by Les Arts Florissants, released in the spring of 1996.

Older singers were by no means eclipsed. Bartoli, Jessye Norman and Frederica von Stade all reminded the world of their formidable talents, while California-born Verdi soprano Aprile Millo emerged from years of bad vocal health with acclaimed Met performances of *Andrea Chenier* opposite Pavarotti. Long-retired Elisabeth Schwarzkopf generated the most controversy. Her 80th birthday celebrations were interrupted by a new biography by Alan Jefferson confirming her Nazi affiliations during World War II, rekindling volatile old questions about the line between career opportunism and collaboration.

Placido Domingo continued to amaze; at an age (55) when most tenors begin losing their powers, he seemed to gain. In addition, he prepared for his first season as artistic director of the Washington [D.C.] Opera, a company preparing to make a bid for international recognition. Thanks to a rich donor, the company bought a vacant department store with the intention of turning it into an opera house.

Elsewhere on the opera administration front, Paul Kellogg from the Glimmerglass Opera in Cooperstown, New York, also became general director of the New York City Opera after Christopher Keene died in the fall of 1995. He planned to have a fre-

Placido Domingo

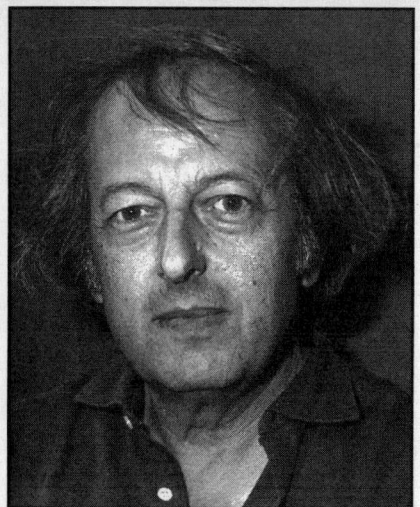

André Previn

quent exchange of productions between the two houses, which boded particularly well for the New York City Opera, since the Cooperstown organization is acclaimed for innovative productions of difficult-to-stage operas. Ardis Krainik, who heads Lyric Opera of Chicago, announced her intention to step down in a year because of health problems. Opera conductor Spiros Argiris, who held the top music post at Spoleto Festival USA in Charleston, South Carolina, died on the eve of the annual Memorial Day event. The San Francisco Opera announced that André Previn, who is best known as a conductor but is also a composer, would make an operatic adaptation of *A Streetcar Named Desire.*

And in typical consideration of the wave of young singers, the coveted roles of Blanche and Stanley were cast before they were even written. Marlon Brando's old role will be played by Rodney Gilfrey, one of the few singers known to look good with his shirt off. The lucky soprano is Sylvia McNair, who is as much at home singing Harold Arlen at a Boston Pops concert as she is singing Mozart at the rarefied Salzburg Festival. That's typical of the versatility of the new singers: In the future, you may see them where you least expect them. ∎

Iolanta by Peter Ilich Tchaikovsky (1840–1893)
Kirov Chorus and Orchestra, St. Petersburg, conducted by Valery Gergiev; chorus master: Valery Borisov; **Soloists:** Galina Gorchakova, Sergei Alexashkin, Dmitri Hvorostovsky, Gegam Grigorian, Nikolai Putilin, Nikolai Gassiev, Gennady Bezzubenkov, Larissa Diadkova, Tatiana Kravtsova and Olga Korzhenskaya
Phillips (1996)
Internationally renowned bass Dmitri Hvorostovsky is among the stars featured on this Russian recording of a beloved classic.

Lohengrin by Richard Wagner (1813–1883)
Bavarian Radio Symphony Orchestra and Chorus, conducted by Sir Colin Davis; **Soloists:** Jan Hendrik Rootering, Ben Heppner, Sharon Sweet, Sergei Leiferkus, Eva Marton and Bryn Terfel
RCA Victor (1995)
Outstanding singers on this newly recorded classic include Welsh bass-baritone Bryn Terfel, a current audience darling.

Peter Grimes by Benjamin Britten (1913–1976)
Opera London, London Symphony Chorus, chorus master: Stephen Westrop; City of London Sinfonia, conducted by Richard Hickox; **Soloists:** Philip Langridge, Ned Harrison, Janice Watson, Alan Opie, Ameral Gunson, Yvonne Barclay, Pamela Helen Stephen, John Graham Hall, John Connell, Anne Collins, John Fryatt, Roderick Williams and Matthew Best
Chandos (1996)
This new recording of Britten's best-known opera joins the long-established traditional version, which was recorded by the composer 40 years ago.

Roméo et Juliette by Charles Gounod (1919–1893)
Munich Radio Orchestra, conducted by Leonard Slatkin; Chorus of the Bavarian Radio, chorus master: Gustav Sjökvist; **Soloists:** Placido Domingo, Ruth Ann Swenson, Susan Graham, Sarah Walker, Paul Charles Clarke, Kurt Ollmann, Alain Vernhes, Alastair Miles and David Pittman-Jennings
RCA Victor (1996)
A new rendition of everyone's favorite romance, this recording received a boost when New York's Metropolitan Opera Company included the opera in its 1995–1996 season.

Salome by Richard Strauss (1864–1949)
Weiner Philharmoniker, conducted by Christoph von Dohnányi; **Soloists:** Catherina Malfitano, Bryn Terfel, Kenneth Riegel, Hanna Schwarz and Kim Begley
London (1995)
Bass-baritone giant Bryn Terfel's current popularity adds luster to this recent recording of the gory classic, also performed by the Metropolitan Opera Company this past season.

1995 – 1996 Opera Premieres and New Productions

David Patrick Stearns, theater and classical music critic for *USA Today*, selected these operas as highlights of the 1995–1996 season.

Marty Sohl

La Bohème

ANDREA CHENIER
Seattle Opera
Composer: Umberto Giordano; **Libretto:** Luigi Illica;
Conductor: Steven Mercurio; **Stage Director:**
Bernard Uzan; **Set Designers:** Michel Beaulac and
Bernard Uzan
Opening: 4/96 at Seattle Center Opera House
This was the season for *Andrea Chenier*. The
Metropolitan Opera also debuted a new production that saw a short-lived success by Luciano
Pavarotti (he canceled later performances) and
a comeback by Aprile Millo after a period of
vocal problems. However, many eyes turned to
the Seattle *Chenier* starring rising Canadian
tenor Ben Heppner and the popular American
soprano Diane Soviero, both singing their roles
onstage for the first time. As expected, their performances elicited critical acclaim, and so did
the production, which drew as much drama as
possible from its French Revolution setting.

BETROTHAL IN A DREAM
Washington Opera
Composer: Hans Krasa; **Libretto:** Rudolf Fuchs and
Rudolf Thomas; **Conductor:** Israel Yinon; **Stage
Director:** Karel Drgac; **Set and Costume Designer:**
Rainer Sinell
Opening: 1/96 at the Kennedy Center
With the 50th anniversary of World War II, orches-
tras and recording companies have been looking
back at the music that was banned or buried by
the Nazis, and inevitably, that spilled over into the
opera houses. Works by Bertolt Goldschmidt,
Viktor Ullmann and especially Erwin Schulhoff
were re-explored, though *Betrothal in a Dream,* by
Auschwitz victim Krasa, was the only World War
II-era opera to enjoy a full production by a major
U.S. opera house. The opera dates from 1933 and
tells the story of a woman attempting to marry an
ailing prince so she will have the money to help
the injured man she really loves. Some critics pronounced the work a bit youthful, though
London/Decca plans to record it. The cast included veteran British baritone John Shirley-Quirk.

BRAIN OPERA
Lincoln Center Festival '96
Composer: Todd Machover; **Libretto:** Todd Machover,
adapted from Marvin Minsky; **Stage Director and
Designer:** Maggie Orth; **Technology Design and
Direction:** Joe Paradiso; **Set and Instrument Design:**
Ray Knoshita; **Video and Visual Direction:** Sharon
Daniel
Opening: 7/96 at Juilliard School of Music
This technologically up-to-the-minute music theater piece attempted to incorporate audience
interaction, both from the Internet and from people playing on various theremin-style electronic
instruments. However, the visual elements were
similar to a run-of-the-mill planetarium show, the
musical ideas contributed by the audience often
weren't interesting and Machover's electronic
music score, though often inspired, was often too
dense to be appreciated on first hearing.

LA BOHÈME
San Francisco Opera
Composer: Giacomo Puccini; **Libretto:** Giuseppe
Giacosa and Luigi Illica; **Conductor:** Steven Mercurio
and others; **Stage Director:** Mark Lamos; **Set
Designer:** Michael Yeargan; **Costume Designer:**
Walter Mahoney
Opening: 6/96 at the Orpheum Theater
Attempting to make a virtue out of a problem,
the San Francisco Opera began its season in
exile from the War Memorial Opera House
(which closed for earthquake proofing and other
improvements) by staging the Puccini chestnut

in a smaller theater for a three-week, Broadway-style run with revolving casts for the near-daily performances. Critics praised the production for having a Great White Way energy with fun and energetic performances. Attendancewise, it was a record breaker, attracting more than 45,000 people, with each performance averaging 78.5 percent capacity and a box-office gross of $2 million. The previous record was 40,000 attending a 12-performance run of *Madame Butterfly* at the larger War Memorial Opera House in 1995. *La Boheme* casts included Patricia Racette, Mark Oswald and other up-and-coming singers.

THE EXCURSIONS OF MR. BROUCEK
Spoleto Festival USA, Charleston, S.C.
Composer: Leos Janácek; **Libretto:** Viktor Dyk and F.S. Prochazka; **Conductor:** Richard Bradshaw; **Stage Director:** Wolf Widder; **Set Design:** Jean Bauer; **Costume Design:** Eva Maria Weber
Opening: 6/96 at the Sottile Theater
Though Janácek has been enjoying a major vogue, this early opera has never had a professionally staged U.S. production. There's a reason for that: The story about a drunken Prague landlord who has hallucinations of going to the moon and then back in time appears to be full of topical references that are difficult to understand, much less to stage. The Spoleto production was fairly plain, but the musical preparation was superb, with a cast headed by Peter Kazaras.

LES ENFANTS TERRIBLES
Spoleto Festival USA, Charleston, S.C.
Composer: Philip Glass; **Libretto:** Jean Cocteau; **Director and Choreographer:** Susan Marshall; **Set Designer:** Douglas Stein; **Costume Designer:** Kasia Walicka-Malmone
Opening: 6/96 at the Sottile Theater
Glass has had considerable success turning Cocteau films into operas, and in this third installment of his Cocteau trilogy, he transformed Cocteau's story about a brother-and-sister pair who are two halves of the same personality into a dance opera, written in close collaboration with choreographer Marshall and the singers in the orchestra pit. Glass felt it was the strongest of his Cocteau pieces and planned to take it on a world tour. Philip Cutlip and Christin Arand played the two siblings.

FOUR SAINTS IN THREE ACTS
Houston Grand Opera
Composer: Virgil Thomson; **Libretto:** Gertrude Stein; **Conductor:** Dennis Russell Davies; **Stage Director and Set Designer:** Robert Wilson; **Costume Designer:** Francesco Clemente
Opening: 1/96 at the Wortham Center
This surreal 1933 Thomson/Stein meditation on the lives of Spanish saints has been discussed more often than performed, but director Wilson made up for that with a lavishly mounted, thoughtfully conceived production. It had all of the usual heavenly clichés, such as fluffy clouds and sheep, and some wacky touches, including giant giraffe heads lording over the singers. All imagery was served up with humor and affection. Singers included Ashley Putnam and Sanford Sylvan. The production later played in August at the Lincoln Center Festival '96.

THE MAKROPULOS CASE
Metropolitan Opera
Composer: Leos Janácek; **Libretto:** Leos Janácek (after a play by Karel Capek); **Conductor:** David Robertson; **Stage Director:** Elijah Moshinsky; **Set Designer:** Anthony War; **Costume Designer:** Dana Granata
Opening: 1/96 at the Metropolitan Opera
The cynical story of the 337-year-old mysterious opera diva Elena Makropulos, who has discovered an eternal youth formula, had a tragic debut at the Met. During the first moments of the opening night performance, tenor Richard Versalle dropped dead from heart failure. The second performance was snowed out. When finally performed, it was a success, thanks partly to Jessye Norman's glamorous, feline stage presence.

MATHIS DER MALER
New York City Opera
Composer and Librettist: Paul Hindemith; **Conductor:** Christopher Keene; **Set Designer:** John Conklin.
Opening: 9/95 at the Lincoln Center
Hindemith's 1935 opera about the painter Matthias Grunewald has long been famous thanks to a symphony the composer wrote based on music he also used in the opera. The opera itself, however, was banned by the Nazis because it was considered politically subversive, and since then, it has had a checkered history in theater. This

Winnie Klotz

The Makropulos Case

Mathis der Maler

Carol Rosegg

production was not considered a great success, though it was NYCO general director Christopher Keene's final conducting appearance; he died shortly after the run. The cast included Lauren Flanagan as Ursula and William Stone as Mathis.

DIE MEISTERSINGER VON NURNBERG
Chicago Symphony Orchestra
Composer and Librettist: Richard Wagner;
Conductor: Sir Georg Solti
Opening: 9/95 at Orchestra Hall
The Chicago Symphony's octogenarian conductor laureate Solti returned to his old stomping ground for a concert performance of Wagner's beloved comedy about singing guilds in medieval Nurnberg. Recorded live by London/Decca, the all-star cast included Jose van Dam, Rene Pape, Alan Opie, Ben Heppner and Karita Mattila.

ORFEO ED EURIDICE
Handel & Haydn Society, Boston
Composer: Willibald Christoph Gluck; **Libretto:**
Raniero de Calzabigi; **Director and Choreographer:**
Mark Morris; **Set Design:** Adrianne Lobel; **Costume Designer:** Martin Pakledinaz
Opening: 4/96 at the Wang Center
Choreographer Mark Morris has long been interested in opera, having created dances for John Adams's *Nixon in China* and *The Death of Klinghoffer*. However, this was his first time as an opera director, and audience interest was high enough that the Handel & Haydn Society gave it a national tour that stopped in Iowa City, Costa Mesa, Los Angeles, Berkeley and at the Brooklyn Academy of Music. Many critics praised Morris's contribution in this opera about the god of song who attempts to rescue the damsel he loves from the underworld, but Hogwood's conducting received lukewarm reviews. The title roles were sung by Michael Chance and Dana Hanchard.

ORLANDO
Les Arts Florissants
Composer: George Frederick Handel; **Libretto:**
Unknown; **Conductor:** William Christie; **Director:**
Robert Carsen; **Set and Costume Designer:** Anthony McDonald
Opening: 2/96 at the Brooklyn Academy of Music
Handel's 1733 opera about the legendary mad warrior was written when the composer was at the height of his operatic powers, but its revivals have been infrequent, partly because of the vocal difficulties it presents. Director Carsen's spare, Robert Wilson-style production was not universally credited with solving the piece's theatrical problems. However, Christie and his Paris-based early music group Les Arts Florissants were lavishly acclaimed for their musicality. Patricia Bardon sang the title role.

PAUL BUNYAN
Glimmerglass Opera, Cooperstown, N.Y.
Composer: Benjamin Britten; **Libretto:** W.H. Auden;
Conductor: Stewart Robertson; **Stage Director:** Mark Lamos; **Set Designer:** Paul Steinberg
Opening: 7/95 at Glimmerglass Opera
Britten's first opera, written in the United States during World War II, has always been an uneasy fusion of Broadway, folk opera and (thanks to librettist Auden) social satire. Adding to the theatrical limitations, its title character is never seen but is heard as a disembodied voice. However, director Lamos turned it into a witty cartoon of a piece (visual jokes about Bunyan's huge size abounded) without losing its message about respect for the elemental forces of the earth. The cast included Aaron Caves as Hel Helson, Jeffrey Lentz as John Inkslinger and Christine Arand as Tiny.

DER RING DES NIBELUNGEN
Lyric Opera of Chicago
Composer and Librettist: Richard Wagner;
Conductor: Zubin Mehta; **Stage Director:** August Everding; **Set Designer:** John Conklin
Opening: 1/96 at Civic Opera House
Four years in the making, the Chicago production of Wagner's four-part saga full of magic, deceit and many strange creatures from Nordic mythology climaxed in much the same spirit in which it began — with uncluttered, almost metallic sets and many sleights of hand, such as Rhinemaidens who swooped around the stage like bungee-jumpers and a Forest Bird that actually flew. Among performers, it was a major success for the oft-maligned former New York Philharmonic music director Mehta, and, among singers, was the first complete Brunnhilde by Jane Eaglen, the British soprano who promises to have a major Wagnerian career.

DER RING DES NIBELUNGEN
Seattle Opera

Composer and Librettist: Richard Wagner; **Conductor:** Hermann Michael; **Stage Director:** Francois Rochaix; **Scenery and Costume Designer:** Robert Israel

Opening: 8/95 at the Seattle Center Opera House

Since the mid-1980s, the Seattle Opera has tried to attract a public wanting an alternative to the *Ring* offered by the Metropolitan Opera. With each revival, it adds a number of features, and this time around, it was a new dragon for part three of the 16-hour saga, *Siegfried.* Taking into account ecology-minded Seattle citizens, the new dragon was intentionally repulsive, appearing as sort of a scrap heap on wheels, spewing all sorts of noxious gases. The singers weren't all of international fame, but had plenty of acclaim, including J. Patrick Raftery, Nadine Secunde, Marilyn Aschau and Joyce Castle.

LA RONDINE
Opera Theater of St. Louis

Composer: Giacomo Puccini; **Libretto:** Giuseppe Adami, Alfred W. Willner and Heinz Reichert; **Conductor:** Emmanuel Villaume; **Stage Director:** John Copley; **Set Designer:** John Conklin; **Costume Designer:** Jess Goldstein

Opening: 5/96 at the Loretto-Hilton Center for the Performing Arts

Puccini wanted to write something akin to a Franz Lehar opera with this libretto about a sophisticated Paris courtesan who hopes to find happiness with a young man from the country. However, this proved to be one of his most troubled creations, and whether or not this American premiere of his third revision makes any difference remains to be seen. Nonetheless, the production was acclaimed for its sumptuous, turn-of-the-century decor and excellent singing from Susan Patterson and Richard Drewes.

Tom Brazil

Orfeo ed Euridice

◀ CONTINUED FROM PAGE 643

OHIO

Cincinnati Opera Summer Festival
Music Hall
Cincinnati, OH
(513) 241-2742

Lyric Opera Cleveland Summer Festival
Kulas Hall, Cleveland Institute of Music
Cleveland, OH
(216) 231-2910

Ohio Ballet Summer Festival
Akron, OH
(330) 972-7900

Ohio Light Opera
Freedlander Theatre
Wooster, OH
(330) 263-2345

OKLAHOMA

Opera Festival of Oklahoma
Hardemann Auditorium
Oklahoma City, OK
(405) 297-3000

OREGON

Chamber Music Northwest
Portland, OR
(503) 294-6400

Oregon Bach Festival
Eugene, OR
(800) 457-1486

PENNSYLVANIA

American Music Theater Festival
Plays & Players Theater
Philadelphia, PA
(215) 893-1145

Mann Music Center Summer Festival
West Fairmount Park
Philadelphia, PA
(215) 878-7707

RHODE ISLAND

Newport Music Festival
Newport, RI
(401) 846-1133

CONTINUED ON NEXT PAGE ▶

◀ CONTINUED FROM PREVIOUS PAGE

SOUTH CAROLINA

Spoleto Festival U.S.A.
Dock Street Theatre
Charleston, SC
(803) 577-4500

TEXAS

International Summer Music Festival
Dallas, TX
(214) 692-0203

Round Top Festival
Round Top, TX
(409) 249-3129

UTAH

Moab Music Festival
Moab, UT
(801) 259-8431

Utah Festival Opera Co.
Ellen Eccles Theatre
Logan, UT
(800) 830-6088

VERMONT

Manchester Music Festival
P.O. Box 1165
Manchester Center, VT 05255-1165
(802) 362-1956
(800) 639-5868

Marlboro Music Festival
P.O. Box K
Marlboro, VT 05344
(215) 569-4690
(802) 254-2394

VIRGINIA

Ash Lawn — Highland Summer Festival
Boxwood Gardens
Charlottesville, VA
(804) 293-4500

WASHINGTON

Seattle Chamber Music Festival
Seattle, WA
(206) 328-1425

Seattle International Music Festival
Seattle, WA
(206) 233-0993

WYOMING

Grand Teton Music Festival
Teton Village
(307) 733-1128 ■

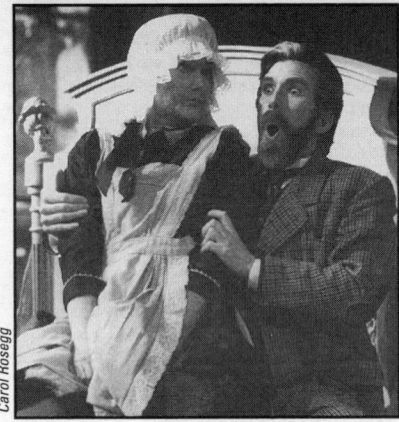

Carol Rosegg

Der Rosenkavalier

DER ROSENKAVALIER
New York City Opera
Composer: Richard Strauss; **Libretto:** Hugo von Hofmanthal; **Conductor:** Alex Sanders; **Stage Director:** Jonathan Miller; **Set Designer:** Peter Davison; **Costume Designer:** Sue Blane
Opening: 3/96 at New York State Theater
Richard Strauss's beloved 1911 opera is so firmly rooted in its 19th-century Viennese setting that it has resisted updating until now. Director Miller adapted it to reflect the time it was written, which turns the May-December romance between an aging princess and a teenage aristocrat into an act of female emancipation. In a particularly obvious Virginia Slims moment, the princess smoked a cigarette at the end of her famous Act I monologue. Cast included Elizabeth Holleque as the Marshallin, Emily Golden as Octavian and Nancy Allen Lundy as Sophie.

RUSALKA
San Francisco Opera
Composer: Antonin Dvorak; **Libretto:** Jaroslav Kvapil; **Conductor:** Charles Mackerras; **Stage Director:** Laurie Feldman; **Set Designer:** Gunther Schneider-Siemssen
Opening: 11/95 at the War Memorial Opera House
Dvorak's radiant score tells the story of a lovelorn water sprite who falls for with a prince and strikes a deal with a witch to make her human. The production is quickly becoming a fixture in U.S. opera houses, due in part to sympathetic interpretations by Renee Fleming, the sprite, and Felicity Palmer, the witch. This much-traveled, oft-cloned production is full of appropriately watery imagery and special effects that allow singers to appear as though they're rising from an onstage pond.

RUSLAN AND LYUDMILA
San Francisco Opera
Composer: Mikhail Glinka; **Libretto:** Mikhail Glinka, K. Bakhturin, A. Shakhovskoi and others; **Conductor:** Valery Gergiev; **Stage Director:** Lotfi Mansouri; **Set Designers:** Alexander Golovin and Konstantin Korovin; **Choreographer:** Alexander Shavrov (after Michel Fokine)
Opening: 9/95 at the War Memorial Opera House

Russian opera has been an increasing presence on the U.S. opera scene, thanks partly to the greater availability of Russian performers and charismatic leaders such as conductor Gergiev, who runs the Kirov Opera in St. Petersburg. He has been particularly savvy in mounting co-productions with more cash-rich Western opera companies. *Ruslan* is often considered the first truly Russian opera — it's based on a Pushkin poem about a bride abducted by an evil sorcerer — and has left critics wondering why it's so infrequently encountered in the West. The colorful San Francisco production was a copy of a production staged in 1904 in honor of Glinka's centennial. Singers included the great Russian veteran tenor Vladimir Atlantov.

SALOME
Metropolitan Opera
Composer: Richard Strauss; **Libretto:** Richard Strauss adapted from Oscar Wilde; **Conductor:** Donald Runnicles; **Stage Director:** Nikolaus Lehnhoff; **Set and Costume Designer:** Jurgen Rose
Opening: 3/96 at the Lincoln Center

This controversial production was resurrected for Catherine Malfitano, acclaimed in opera capitals around the world for her portrayal of the oversexed princess who demands the head of St. John the Baptist, and her New York performance was no exception. Some critics lauded her as the Salome of the decade. Cast members also included Bernd Weikl and Hanna Schwarz.

Rusalka

Salome

THE TIBETAN BOOK OF THE DEAD: A LIBERATION THROUGH HEARING
Music: Ricky Ian Gordon; **Libretto:** Jean-Claude van Itallie; **Conductor:** Charles Prince; **Stage Director:** Marcus Stern; **Set Designer:** Allison Koturbash; **Costume Designer:** Laura Patterson
Opening: 5/96 at the Wortham Center in Houston

Though the *Tibetan Book of Living and Dying* might seem an odd, morose idea for an opera, it turned out to be surprisingly stageworthy, dramatizing the progression of a soul from death to rebirth. However, the production was not considered a success, although the score by Gordon, a composer who blurs the line between opera and Broadway, was hailed as a breakthrough and future productions of the piece are planned. It was later presented in June at Philadelphia's American Music Theater Festival.

XERXES
Lyric Opera of Chicago
Composer: George Frederick Handel; **Libretto:** Niccolo Minato; **Conductor:** John Nelson; **Stage Director:** Nicholas Hytner; **Set Designer:** John Fielding
Opening: 10/95 at the Civic Opera House

Before Hytner became the much-in-demand director of Broadway's *Miss Saigon*, he worked extensively in opera; occasionally, he still does. This production of Handel's romantic comedy of mistaken identity was staged almost like a labyrinth through well-trimmed hedges and other trappings of English aristocracy, which was the opera's original audience. Cast included British Handel specialists such as Ann Murray, but also the promising American newcomer Elizabeth Futral.

The Tony Awards

The Antoinette Perry (Tony®) Awards, presented each June by the American Theatre Wing and the League of American Theatres and Producers, honor distinguished achievement in Broadway theater.

1947

ACTORS — PLAY
José Ferrer, *Cyrano de Bergerac*
Fredric March, *Years Ago*

ACTRESSES — PLAY
Ingrid Bergman, *Joan of Lorraine*
Helen Hayes, *Happy Birthday*

SUPPORTING OR FEATURED ACTRESS — PLAY
Patricia Neal, *Another Part of the Forest*

SUPPORTING OR FEATURED ACTOR — MUSICAL
David Wayne, *Finian's Rainbow*

DIRECTOR
Elia Kazan, *All My Sons*

COSTUME DESIGNER
Lucinda Ballard, *Happy Birthday, Another Part of the Forest, Street Scene, John Loves Mary* and *The Chocolate Soldier*

CHOREOGRAPHERS
Agnes De Mille, *Brigadoon*
Michael Kidd, *Finian's Rainbow*

SPECIAL AWARDS
Dora Chamberlain
Mr. and Mrs. Ira Katzenberg
Jules Leventhal
P.A. MacDonald
Burns Mantle
Arthur Miller
Vincent Sardi, Sr.
Kurt Weill

1948

PLAY
Mister Roberts

ACTORS — PLAY
Henry Fonda, *Mister Roberts*
Paul Kelly, *Command Decision*
Basil Rathbone, *The Heiress*

ACTRESSES — PLAY
Judith Anderson, *Medea*
Katharine Cornell, *Antony and Cleopatra*
Jessica Tandy, *A Streetcar Named Desire*

ACTOR — MUSICAL
Paul Hartman, *Angel in the Wings*

Henry Fonda

ACTRESS — MUSICAL
Grace Hartman, *Angel in the Wings*

AUTHORS
Thomas Heggen and Joshua Logan, *Mister Roberts*

PRODUCER
Leland Hayward, *Mister Roberts*

SCENIC DESIGNER
Horace Armistead, *The Medium*

COSTUME DESIGNER
Mary Percy Schenck, *The Heiress*

CHOREOGRAPHER
Jerome Robbins, *High Button Shoes*

STAGE TECHNICIANS
George Gebhardt
George Pierce

SPECIAL AWARDS
Vera Allen
Paul Beisman
Joe E. Brown
Robert Dowling
Experimental Theatre, Inc.
Rosamond Gilder
June Lockhart
Mary Martin
Robert Porterfield
James Whitmore

1949

PLAY
Death of a Salesman

MUSICAL
Kiss Me Kate

ACTOR — PLAY
Rex Harrison, *Anne of the Thousand Days*

ACTRESS — PLAY
Martita Hunt, *The Madwoman of Chaillot*

SUPPORTING OR FEATURED ACTOR — PLAY
Arthur Kennedy, *Death of a Salesman*

SUPPORTING OR FEATURED ACTRESS — PLAY
Shirley Booth, *Goodbye, My Fancy*

ACTOR — MUSICAL
Ray Bolger, *Where's Charley?*

ACTRESS — MUSICAL
Nanette Fabray, *Love Life*

AUTHOR — PLAY
Arthur Miller, *Death of a Salesman*

AUTHOR — MUSICAL
Bella and Samuel Spewack, *Kiss Me Kate*

DIRECTOR
Elia Kazan, *Death of a Salesman*

PRODUCERS — PLAY
Kermit Bloomgarden and Walter Fried, *Death of a Salesman*

PRODUCERS — MUSICAL
Saint-Subber and Lemuel Ayers, *Kiss Me Kate*

COMPOSER AND LYRICIST
Cole Porter, *Kiss Me Kate*

SCENIC DESIGNER
Jo Mielziner, *Sleepy Hollow, Summer and Smoke, Anne of the Thousand Days, Death of a Salesman* and *South Pacific*

COSTUME DESIGNER
Lemuel Ayers, *Kiss Me Kate*

CHOREOGRAPHER
Gower Champion, *Lend an Ear*

CONDUCTOR AND MUSICAL DIRECTOR
Max Meth, *As the Girls Go*

1950

PLAY
The Cocktail Party

MUSICAL
South Pacific

ACTOR — PLAY
Sidney Blackmer, *Come Back, Little Sheba*

ACTRESS — PLAY
Shirley Booth, *Come Back, Little Sheba*

ACTOR — MUSICAL
Ezio Pinza, *South Pacific*

ACTRESS — MUSICAL
Mary Martin, *South Pacific*

SUPPORTING OR FEATURED ACTOR — MUSICAL
Myron McCormick, *South Pacific*

SUPPORTING OR FEATURED ACTRESS — MUSICAL
Juanita Hall, *South Pacific*

AUTHOR — PLAY
T. S. Eliot, *The Cocktail Party*

AUTHORS — MUSICAL
Oscar Hammerstein II and Joshua Logan, *South Pacific*

DIRECTOR
Joshua Logan, *South Pacific*

PRODUCER — PLAY
Gilbert Miller, *The Cocktail Party*

PRODUCERS — MUSICAL
Richard Rodgers, Oscar Hammerstein II, Leland Hayward and Joshua Logan, *South Pacific*

COMPOSER
Richard Rodgers, *South Pacific*

SCENIC DESIGNER
Jo Mielziner, *The Innocents*

COSTUME DESIGNER
Aline Bernstein, *Regina*

CHOREOGRAPHER
Helen Tamiris, *Touch and Go*

CONDUCTOR AND MUSICAL DIRECTOR
Maurice Abravanel, *Regina*

STAGE TECHNICIAN
Joe Lynn, *Miss Liberty*

SPECIAL AWARDS
Maurice Evans

1951

PLAY
The Rose Tattoo

MUSICAL
Guys and Dolls,

ACTOR — PLAY
Claude Rains, *Darkness at Noon*

ACTRESS — PLAY
Uta Hagen, *The Country Girl*

SUPPORTING OR FEATURED ACTOR — PLAY
Eli Wallach, *The Rose Tattoo*

SUPPORTING OR FEATURED ACTRESS — PLAY
Maureen Stapleton, *The Rose Tattoo*

ACTOR — MUSICAL
Robert Alda, *Guys and Dolls*

ACTRESS — MUSICAL
Ethel Merman, *Call Me Madam*

SUPPORTING OR FEATURED ACTOR — MUSICAL
Russell Nype, *Call Me Madam*

SUPPORTING OR FEATURED ACTRESS — MUSICAL
Isabel Bigley, *Guys and Dolls*

AUTHOR — PLAY
Tennessee Williams, *The Rose Tattoo*

AUTHORS — MUSICAL
Jo Swerling and Abe Burrows, *Guys and Dolls*

DIRECTOR
George S. Kaufman, *Guys and Dolls*

PRODUCER — PLAY
Cheryl Crawford, *The Rose Tattoo*

PRODUCERS — MUSICAL
Cy Feuer and Ernest H. Martin, *Guys and Dolls*

COMPOSER AND LYRICIST
Frank Loesser, *Guys and Dolls*

SCENIC DESIGNER
Boris Aronson, *The Rose Tattoo, The Country Girl* and
  Season in the Sun

COSTUME DESIGNER
Miles White, *Bless You All*

CHOREOGRAPHER
Michael Kidd, *Guys and Dolls*

CONDUCTOR AND MUSICAL DIRECTOR
Lehman Engel, *The Consul*

STAGE TECHNICIAN
Richard Raven, *The Autumn Garden*

SPECIAL AWARD
Ruth Green

1952

PLAY
The Fourposter

MUSICAL
The King and I

ACTOR — PLAY
José Ferrer, *The Shrike*

ACTRESS — PLAY
Julie Harris, *I Am a Camera*

SUPPORTING OR FEATURED ACTOR — PLAY
John Cromwell, *Point of No Return*

SUPPORTING OR FEATURED ACTRESS — PLAY
Marian Winters, *I Am a Camera*

ACTOR — MUSICAL
Phil Silvers, *Top Banana*

ACTRESS — MUSICAL
Gertrude Lawrence, *The King and I*

SUPPORTING OR FEATURED ACTOR — MUSICAL
Yul Brynner, *The King and I*

SUPPORTING OR FEATURED ACTRESS — MUSICAL
Helen Gallagher, *Pal Joey*

DIRECTOR
José Ferrer, *The Shrike, The Fourposter* and *Stalag 17*

SCENIC DESIGNER
Jo Mielziner, *The King and I*

COSTUME DESIGNER
Irene Sharaff, *The King and I*

CHOREOGRAPHER
Robert Alton, *Pal Joey*

The King and I

CONDUCTOR AND MUSICAL DIRECTOR
Max Meth, *Pal Joey*

STAGE TECHNICIAN
Peter Feller, *Call Me Madam*

SPECIAL AWARDS
Edward Kook

Judy Garland

Charles Boyer

1953

PLAY
The Crucible

MUSICAL
Wonderful Town

ACTOR — PLAY
Tom Ewell, *The Seven Year Itch*

ACTRESS — PLAY
Shirley Booth, *Time of the Cuckoo*

SUPPORTING OR FEATURED ACTOR — PLAY
John Williams, *Dial M for Murder*

SUPPORTING OR FEATURED ACTRESS — PLAY
Beatrice Straight, *The Crucible*

ACTOR — MUSICAL
Thomas Mitchell, *Hazel Flagg*

ACTRESS — MUSICAL
Rosalind Russell, *Wonderful Town*

SUPPORTING OR FEATURED ACTOR — MUSICAL
Hiram Sherman, *Two's Company*

SUPPORTING OR FEATURED ACTRESS — MUSICAL
Sheila Bond, *Wish You Were Here*

AUTHOR — PLAY
Arthur Miller, *The Crucible*

AUTHORS — MUSICAL
Joseph Fields and Jerome Chodorov, *Wonderful Town*

DIRECTOR
Joshua Logan, *Picnic*

PRODUCER — PLAY
Kermit Bloomgarden, *The Crucible*

PRODUCER — MUSICAL
Robert Fryer, *Wonderful Town*

COMPOSER
Leonard Bernstein, *Wonderful Town*

SCENIC DESIGNER
Raoul Pène Du Bois, *Wonderful Town*

COSTUME DESIGNER
Miles White, *Hazel Flagg*

CHOREOGRAPHER
Donald Saddler, *Wonderful Town*

CONDUCTOR AND MUSICAL DIRECTOR
Lehman Engel, *Wonderful Town* and
    Gilbert and Sullivan season

STAGE TECHNICIAN
Abe Kurnit, *Wish You Were Here*

SPECIAL AWARDS
Beatrice Lillie

Danny Kaye

Equity Community Theatre

1954

PLAY
The Teahouse of the August Moon

MUSICAL
Kismet

ACTOR — PLAY
David Wayne, *The Teahouse of the August Moon*

ACTRESS — PLAY
Audrey Hepburn, *Ondine*

SUPPORTING OR FEATURED ACTOR — PLAY
John Kerr, *Tea and Sympathy*

SUPPORTING OR FEATURED ACTRESS — PLAY
Jo Van Fleet, *The Trip to Bountiful*

ACTOR — MUSICAL
Alfred Drake, *Kismet*

ACTRESS — MUSICAL
Dolores Gray, *Carnival in Flanders*

SUPPORTING OR FEATURED ACTOR — MUSICAL
Harry Belafonte, *John Murray Anderson's Almanac*

SUPPORTING OR FEATURED ACTRESS — MUSICAL
Gwen Verdon, *Can-Can*

AUTHOR — PLAY
John Patrick, *The Teahouse of the August Moon*

AUTHORS — MUSICAL
Charles Lederer and Luther Davis, *Kismet*

DIRECTOR
Alfred Lunt, *Ondine*

PRODUCERS — PLAY
Maurice Evans and George Schaefer, *The Teahouse of
    the August Moon*

PRODUCER — MUSICAL
Charles Lederer, *Kismet*

COMPOSER
Alexander Borodin, *Kismet*

SCENIC DESIGNER
Peter Larkin, *Ondine* and *The Teahouse of the August Moon*

COSTUME DESIGNER
Richard Whorf, *Ondine*

CHOREOGRAPHER
Michael Kidd, *Can-Can*

MUSICAL CONDUCTOR
Louis Adrian, *Kismet*

STAGE TECHNICIAN
John Davis, *Picnic*

1955

PLAY
The Desperate Hours

MUSICAL
The Pajama Game

ACTOR — PLAY
Alfred Lunt, *Quadrille*

ACTRESS — PLAY
Nancy Kelly, *The Bad Seed*

SUPPORTING OR FEATURED ACTOR — PLAY
Francis L. Sullivan, *Witness for the Prosecution*

SUPPORTING OR FEATURED ACTRESS — PLAY
Patricia Jessel, *Witness for the Prosecution*

ACTOR — MUSICAL
Walter Slezak, *Fanny*

ACTRESS — MUSICAL
Mary Martin, *Peter Pan*

SUPPORTING OR FEATURED ACTOR — MUSICAL
Cyril Ritchard, *Peter Pan*

SUPPORTING OR FEATURED ACTRESS — MUSICAL
Carol Haney, *The Pajama Game*

AUTHOR — PLAY
Joseph Hayes, *The Desperate Hours*

AUTHORS — MUSICAL
George Abbott and Richard Bissell, *The Pajama Game*

DIRECTOR
Robert Montgomery, *The Desperate Hours*

PRODUCERS — PLAY
Howard Erskine and Joseph Hayes, *The Desperate Hours*

PRODUCERS — MUSICAL
Frederick Brisson, Robert Griffith and Harold S. Prince,
    The Pajama Game

COMPOSER AND LYRICIST
Richard Adler and Jerry Ross, *The Pajama Game*

SCENIC DESIGNER
Oliver Messel, *House of Flowers*

COSTUME DESIGNER
Cecil Beaton, *Quadrille*

CHOREOGRAPHER
Bob Fosse, *The Pajama Game*

CONDUCTOR AND MUSICAL DIRECTOR
Thomas Schippers, *The Saint of Bleecker Street*

STAGE TECHNICIAN
Richard Rodda, *Peter Pan*

SPECIAL AWARD
Proscenium Productions

1956

PLAY
The Diary of Anne Frank

MUSICAL
Damn Yankees

ACTOR — PLAY
Paul Muni, *Inherit the Wind*

ACTRESS — PLAY
Julie Harris, *The Lark*

SUPPORTING OR FEATURED ACTOR — PLAY
Ed Begley, *Inherit the Wind*

SUPPORTING OR FEATURED ACTRESS — PLAY
Una Merkel, *The Ponder Heart*

ACTOR — MUSICAL
Ray Walston, *Damn Yankees*

ACTRESS — MUSICAL
Gwen Verdon, *Damn Yankees*

SUPPORTING OR FEATURED ACTOR — MUSICAL
Russ Brown, *Damn Yankees*

SUPPORTING OR FEATURED ACTRESS — MUSICAL
Lotte Lenya, *The Threepenny Opera*

AUTHORS — PLAY
Frances Goodrich and Albert Hackett, *The Diary of Anne Frank*

AUTHORS — MUSICAL
George Abbott and Douglass Wallop, *Damn Yankees*

DIRECTOR
Tyrone Guthrie, *The Matchmaker*

PRODUCER — PLAY
Kermit Bloomgarden, *The Diary of Anne Frank*

PRODUCERS — MUSICAL
Frederick Brisson, Robert Griffith and Harold S. Prince in association with Albert B. Taylor, *Damn Yankees*

COMPOSER AND LYRICIST
Richard Adler and Jerry Ross, *Damn Yankees*

SCENIC DESIGNER
Peter Larkin, *Inherit the Wind* and *No Time for Sergeants*

COSTUME DESIGNER
Alvin Colt, *Pipe Dream*

CHOREOGRAPHER
Bob Fosse, *Damn Yankees*

CONDUCTOR AND MUSICAL DIRECTOR
Hal Hastings, *Damn Yankees*

STAGE TECHNICIAN
Harry Green, *Middle of the Night* and *Damn Yankees*

SPECIAL AWARDS
The Threepenny Opera
The Theatre Collection of the New York Public Library

1957

PLAY
Long Day's Journey Into Night

MUSICAL
My Fair Lady

ACTOR — PLAY
Fredric March, *Long Day's Journey Into Night*

ACTRESS — PLAY
Margaret Leighton, *Separate Tables*

SUPPORTING OR FEATURED ACTOR — PLAY
Frank Conroy, *The Potting Shed*

SUPPORTING OR FEATURED ACTRESS — PLAY
Peggy Cass, *Auntie Mame*

ACTOR — MUSICAL
Rex Harrison, *My Fair Lady*

ACTRESS — MUSICAL
Judy Holliday, *Bells Are Ringing*

SUPPORTING OR FEATURED ACTOR — MUSICAL
Sydney Chaplin, *Bells Are Ringing*

SUPPORTING OR FEATURED ACTRESS — MUSICAL
Edith Adams, *Li'l Abner*

AUTHOR — PLAY
Eugene O'Neill, *Long Day's Journey Into Night*

AUTHOR — MUSICAL
Alan Jay Lerner, *My Fair Lady*

DIRECTOR
Moss Hart, *My Fair Lady*

PRODUCERS — PLAY
Leigh Connell, Theodore Mann and José Quintero, *Long Day's Journey Into Night*

PRODUCER — MUSICAL
Herman Levin, *My Fair Lady*

COMPOSER
Frederick Loewe, *My Fair Lady*

SCENIC DESIGNER
Oliver Smith, *My Fair Lady*

COSTUME DESIGNER
Cecil Beaton, *My Fair Lady*

CHOREOGRAPHER
Michael Kidd, *Li'l Abner*

CONDUCTOR AND MUSICAL DIRECTOR
Franz Allers, *My Fair Lady*

STAGE TECHNICIAN
Howard McDonald, *Major Barbara*

SPECIAL AWARDS
American Shakespeare Festival
Jean-Louis Barrault — French Repertory
Robert Russell Bennett
William Hammerstein
Paul Shyre

Jerome Robbins

COMPOSER AND LYRICIST
Meredith Willson, *The Music Man*

SCENIC DESIGNER
Oliver Smith, *West Side Story*

COSTUME DESIGNER
Motley, *The First Gentleman*

CHOREOGRAPHER
Jerome Robbins, *West Side Story*

CONDUCTOR AND MUSICAL DIRECTOR
Herbert Greene, *The Music Man*

STAGE TECHNICIAN
Harry Romar, *Time Remembered*

SPECIAL AWARDS
New York Shakespeare Festival

Mrs. Martin Beck

1958

PLAY
Sunrise at Campobello

MUSICAL
The Music Man

ACTOR — PLAY
Ralph Bellamy, *Sunrise at Campobello*

ACTRESS — PLAY
Helen Hayes, *Time Remembered*

SUPPORTING OR FEATURED ACTOR — PLAY
Henry Jones, *Sunrise at Campobello*

SUPPORTING OR FEATURED ACTRESS — PLAY
Anne Bancroft, *Two for the Seesaw*

ACTOR — MUSICAL
Robert Preston, *The Music Man*

ACTRESSES — MUSICAL
Thelma Ritter, *New Girl in Town*
Gwen Verdon, *New Girl in Town*

SUPPORTING OR FEATURED ACTOR — MUSICAL
David Burns, *The Music Man*

SUPPORTING OR FEATURED ACTRESS — MUSICAL
Barbara Cook, *The Music Man*

AUTHOR — PLAY
Dore Schary, *Sunrise at Campobello*

AUTHORS — MUSICAL
Meredith Willson and Franklin Lacey, *The Music Man*

DIRECTOR — PLAY
Vincent J. Donehue, *Sunrise at Campobello*

PRODUCERS — PLAY
Lawrence Langner, Theresa Helburn, Armina Marshall and
    Dore Schary, *Sunrise at Campobello*

PRODUCERS — MUSICAL
Kermit Bloomgarden, Herbert Greene and Frank Productions,
    The Music Man

1959

PLAY
J. B.

MUSICAL
Redhead

ACTOR — PLAY
Jason Robards, Jr., *The Disenchanted*

ACTRESS — PLAY
Gertrude Berg, *A Majority of One*

SUPPORTING OR FEATURED ACTOR — PLAY
Charlie Ruggles, *The Pleasure of His Company*

SUPPORTING OR FEATURED ACTRESS — PLAY
Julie Newmar, *The Marriage-Go-Round*

ACTOR — MUSICAL
Richard Kiley, *Redhead*

ACTRESS — MUSICAL
Gwen Verdon, *Redhead*

SUPPORTING OR FEATURED ACTORS — MUSICAL
Russell Nype, *Goldilocks*
Cast of *La Plume de Ma Tante*

**SUPPORTING OR FEATURED ACTRESSES —
MUSICAL**
Pat Stanley, *Goldilocks*
Cast of *La Plume de Ma Tante*

AUTHOR — PLAY
Archibald MacLeish, *J. B.*

AUTHORS — MUSICAL
Herbert and Dorothy Fields, Sidney Sheldon and David Shaw,
    Redhead

DIRECTOR
Elia Kazan, *J. B.*

PRODUCER — PLAY
Alfred de Liagre, Jr., *J. B.*

PRODUCERS — MUSICAL
Robert Fryer and Lawrence Carr, *Redhead*

COMPOSER
Albert Hague, *Redhead*

SCENIC DESIGNER
Donald Oenslager, *A Majority of One*

COSTUME DESIGNER
Rouben Ter-Arutunian, *Redhead*

CHOREOGRAPHER
Bob Fosse, *Redhead*

CONDUCTOR AND MUSICAL DIRECTOR
Salvatore Dell'Isola, *Flower Drum Song*

STAGE TECHNICIAN
Sam Knapp, *The Music Man*

SPECIAL AWARDS
John Gielgud

Howard Lindsay and Russel Crouse

1960

PLAY
A Raisin in the Sun

MUSICALS
Fiorello!

The Sound of Music

ACTOR — PLAY
Melvyn Douglas, *The Best Man*

ACTRESS — PLAY
Anne Bancroft, *The Miracle Worker*

SUPPORTING OR FEATURED ACTOR — PLAY
Roddy McDowall, *The Fighting Cock*

SUPPORTING OR FEATURED ACTRESS — PLAY
Anne Revere, *Toys in the Attic*

ACTOR — MUSICAL
Jackie Gleason, *Take Me Along*

ACTRESS — MUSICAL
Mary Martin, *The Sound of Music*

SUPPORTING OR FEATURED ACTOR — MUSICAL
Tom Bosley, *Fiorello!*

SUPPORTING OR FEATURED ACTRESS — MUSICAL
Patricia Neway, *The Sound of Music*

AUTHOR — PLAY
William Gibson, *The Miracle Worker*

AUTHORS — MUSICAL
Jerome Weidman and George Abbott, *Fiorello!*

Howard Lindsay and Russel Crouse, *The Sound of Music*

DIRECTOR — PLAY
Arthur Penn, *The Miracle Worker*

DIRECTOR — MUSICAL
George Abbott, *Fiorello!*

PRODUCER — PLAY
Fred Coe, *The Miracle Worker*

PRODUCERS — MUSICAL
Robert Griffith and Harold S. Prince, *Fiorello!*

Leland Hayward and Richard Halliday, *The Sound of Music*

COMPOSERS
Jerry Bock, *Fiorello!*

Richard Rodgers, *The Sound of Music*

SCENIC DESIGNER — DRAMATIC
Howard Bay, *Toys in the Attic*

SCENIC DESIGNER — MUSICAL
Oliver Smith, *The Sound of Music*

COSTUME DESIGNER
Cecil Beaton, *Saratoga*

CHOREOGRAPHER
Michael Kidd, *Destry Rides Again*

CONDUCTOR AND MUSICAL DIRECTOR
Frederick Dvonch, *The Sound of Music*

STAGE TECHNICIAN
John Walters, *The Miracle Worker*

SPECIAL AWARDS
John D. Rockefeller III

James Thurber and Burgess Meredith, *A Thurber Carnival*

1961

PLAY
Becket, Jean Anouilh

MUSICAL
Bye, Bye Birdie

ACTOR — PLAY
Zero Mostel, *Rhinoceros*

ACTRESS — PLAY
Joan Plowright, *A Taste of Honey*

SUPPORTING OR FEATURED ACTOR — PLAY
Martin Gabel, *Big Fish, Little Fish*

SUPPORTING OR FEATURED ACTRESS — PLAY
Colleen Dewhurst, *All the Way Home*

ACTOR — MUSICAL
Richard Burton, *Camelot*

ACTRESS — MUSICAL
Elizabeth Seal, *Irma la Douce*

SUPPORTING OR FEATURED ACTOR — MUSICAL
Dick Van Dyke, *Bye, Bye Birdie*

SUPPORTING OR FEATURED ACTRESS — MUSICAL
Tammy Grimes, *The Unsinkable Molly Brown*

AUTHOR — PLAY
Jean Anouilh, *Becket*

AUTHOR — MUSICAL
Michael Stewart, *Bye, Bye Birdie*

DIRECTOR — PLAY
Sir John Gielgud, *Big Fish, Little Fish*

DIRECTOR — MUSICAL
Gower Champion, *Bye, Bye Birdie*

PRODUCER — PLAY
David Merrick, *Becket*

PRODUCER — MUSICAL
Edward Padula, *Bye, Bye Birdie*

SCENIC DESIGNER — PLAY
Oliver Smith, *Becket*

Richard Burton, *Camelot*

SCENIC DESIGNER — MUSICAL
Oliver Smith, *Camelot*

COSTUME DESIGNER — PLAY
Motley, *Becket*

COSTUME DESIGNERS — MUSICAL
Adrian and Tony Duquette, *Camelot*

CHOREOGRAPHER
Gower Champion, *Bye, Bye Birdie*

CONDUCTOR AND MUSICAL DIRECTOR
Franz Allers, *Camelot*

STAGE TECHNICIAN
Teddy Van Bemmel, *Becket*

SPECIAL AWARDS
David Merrick

The Theatre Guild

1962

PLAY
A Man for All Seasons

MUSICAL
How to Succeed in Business Without Really Trying

ACTOR — PLAY
Paul Scofield, *A Man for All Seasons*

ACTRESS — PLAY
Margaret Leighton, *Night of the Iguana*

SUPPORTING OR FEATURED ACTOR — PLAY
Walter Matthau, *A Shot in the Dark*

SUPPORTING OR FEATURED ACTRESS — PLAY
Elizabeth Ashley, *Take Her, She's Mine*

ACTOR — MUSICAL
Robert Morse, *How to Succeed in Business Without Really Trying*

ACTRESSES — MUSICAL
Anna Maria Alberghetti, *Carnival*

Diahann Carroll, *No Strings*

SUPPORTING OR FEATURED ACTOR — MUSICAL
Charles Nelson Reilly, *How to Succeed in Business Without Really Trying*

SUPPORTING OR FEATURED ACTRESS — MUSICAL
Phyllis Newman, *Subways Are for Sleeping*

AUTHOR — PLAY
Robert Bolt, *A Man for All Seasons*

AUTHORS — MUSICAL
Abe Burrows, Jack Weinstock and Willie Gilbert, *How to Succeed in Business Without Really Trying*

DIRECTOR — PLAY
Noel Willman, *A Man for All Seasons*

DIRECTOR — MUSICAL
Abe Burrows, *How to Succeed in Business Without Really Trying*

PRODUCERS — PLAY
Robert Whitehead and Roger L. Stevens, *A Man for All Seasons*

PRODUCERS — MUSICAL
Cy Feuer and Ernest Martin, *How to Succeed in Business Without Really Trying*

COMPOSER
Richard Rodgers, *No Strings*

SCENIC DESIGNER
Will Steven Armstrong, *Carnival*

COSTUME DESIGNER
Lucinda Ballard, *The Gay Life*

CHOREOGRAPHERS
Agnes De Mille, *Kwamina*

Joe Layton, *No Strings*

CONDUCTOR AND MUSICAL DIRECTOR
Elliot Lawrence, *How to Succeed in Business Without Really Trying*

STAGE TECHNICIAN
Michael Burns, *A Man for All Seasons*

SPECIAL AWARDS
Brooks Atkinson

Franco Zeffirelli

Richard Rodgers

Richard Rodgers, *No Strings*

1963

PLAY
Who's Afraid of Virginia Woolf?

MUSICAL
A Funny Thing Happened on the Way to the Forum

ACTOR — PLAY
Arthur Hill, *Who's Afraid of Virginia Woolf?*

ACTRESS — PLAY
Uta Hagen, *Who's Afraid of Virginia Woolf?*

SUPPORTING OR FEATURED ACTOR — PLAY
Alan Arkin, *Enter Laughing*

SUPPORTING OR FEATURED ACTRESS — PLAY
Sandy Dennis, *A Thousand Clowns*

ACTOR — MUSICAL
Zero Mostel, *A Funny Thing Happened on the Way to the Forum*

ACTRESS — MUSICAL
Vivien Leigh, *Tovarich*

SUPPORTING OR FEATURED ACTOR — MUSICAL
David Burns, *A Funny Thing Happened on the Way to the Forum*

SUPPORTING OR FEATURED ACTRESS — MUSICAL
Anna Quayle, *Stop the World — I Want to Get Off*

AUTHORS — MUSICAL
Burt Shevelove and Larry Gelbart, *A Funny Thing Happened on the Way to the Forum*

DIRECTOR — PLAY
Alan Schneider, *Who's Afraid of Virginia Woolf?*

DIRECTOR — MUSICAL
George Abbott, *A Funny Thing Happened on the Way to the Forum*

PRODUCERS — PLAY
Richard Barr and Clinton Wilder, Theatre 1963, *Who's Afraid of Virginia Woolf?*

PRODUCER — MUSICAL
Harold S. Prince, *A Funny Thing Happened on the Way to the Forum*

COMPOSER AND LYRICIST
Lionel Bart, *Oliver!*

SCENIC DESIGNER
Sean Kenny, *Oliver!*

COSTUME DESIGNER
Anthony Powell, *The School for Scandal*

CHOREOGRAPHER
Bob Fosse, *Little Me*

CONDUCTOR AND MUSICAL DIRECTOR
Donald Pippin, *Oliver!*

STAGE TECHNICIAN
Solly Pernick, *Mr. President*

SPECIAL AWARDS
W. McNeil Lowry
Irving Berlin
Alan Bennett
Peter Cook
Jonathan Miller
Dudley Moore

1964

PLAY
Luther

MUSICAL
Hello, Dolly!

ACTOR — PLAY
Alec Guinness, *Dylan*

ACTRESS — PLAY
Sandy Dennis, *Any Wednesday*

SUPPORTING OR FEATURED ACTOR — PLAY
Hume Cronyn, *Hamlet*

SUPPORTING OR FEATURED ACTRESS — PLAY
Barbara Loden, *After the Fall*

ACTOR — MUSICAL
Bert Lahr, *Foxy*

ACTRESS — MUSICAL
Carol Channing, *Hello, Dolly!*

SUPPORTING OR FEATURED ACTOR — MUSICAL
Jack Cassidy, *She Loves Me*

SUPPORTING OR FEATURED ACTRESS — MUSICAL
Tessie O'Shea, *The Girl Who Came to Supper*

AUTHOR — PLAY
John Osborne, *Luther*

AUTHOR — MUSICAL
Michael Stewart, *Hello, Dolly!*

DIRECTOR — PLAY
Mike Nichols, *Barefoot in the Park*

DIRECTOR — MUSICAL
Gower Champion, *Hello, Dolly!*

PRODUCER — PLAY
Herman Shumlin, *The Deputy*

PRODUCER — MUSICAL
David Merrick, *Hello, Dolly!*

COMPOSER AND LYRICIST
Jerry Herman, *Hello, Dolly!*

SCENIC DESIGNER
Oliver Smith, *Hello, Dolly!*

COSTUME DESIGNER
Freddy Wittop, *Hello, Dolly!*

CHOREOGRAPHER
Gower Champion, *Hello, Dolly!*

CONDUCTOR AND MUSICAL DIRECTOR
Shepard Coleman, *Hello, Dolly!*

SPECIAL AWARD
Eva Le Gallienne

Alec Guinness, *Dylan*

1965

PLAY
The Subject Was Roses

MUSICAL
Fiddler on the Roof

ACTOR — PLAY
Walter Matthau, *The Odd Couple*

ACTRESS — PLAY
Irene Worth, *Tiny Alice*

SUPPORTING OR FEATURED ACTOR — PLAY
Jack Albertson, *The Subject Was Roses*

SUPPORTING OR FEATURED ACTRESS — PLAY
Alice Ghostley, *The Sign in Sidney Brustein's Window*

ACTOR — MUSICAL
Zero Mostel, *Fiddler on the Roof*

ACTRESS — MUSICAL
Liza Minnelli, *Flora, the Red Menace*

SUPPORTING OR FEATURED ACTOR — MUSICAL
Victor Spinetti, *Oh, What a Lovely War*

SUPPORTING OR FEATURED ACTRESS — MUSICAL
Maria Karnilova, *Fiddler on the Roof*

AUTHOR — PLAY
Neil Simon, *The Odd Couple*

AUTHOR — MUSICAL
Joseph Stein, *Fiddler on the Roof*

DIRECTOR — PLAY
Mike Nichols, *Luv* and *The Odd Couple*

DIRECTOR — MUSICAL
Jerome Robbins, *Fiddler on the Roof*

PRODUCER — PLAY
Claire Nichtern, *Luv*

PRODUCER — MUSICAL
Harold S. Prince, *Fiddler on the Roof*

COMPOSER AND LYRICIST
Jerry Bock and Sheldon Harnick, *Fiddler on the Roof*

SCENIC DESIGNER
Oliver Smith, *Baker Street*

COSTUME DESIGNER
Patricia Zipprodt, *Fiddler on the Roof*

CHOREOGRAPHER
Jerome Robbins, *Fiddler on the Roof*

SPECIAL AWARDS
Gilbert Miller
Oliver Smith

1966

PLAY
Marat/Sade

MUSICAL
Man of La Mancha

ACTOR — PLAY
Hal Holbrook, *Mark Twain Tonight!*

ACTRESS — PLAY
Rosemary Harris, *The Lion in Winter*

SUPPORTING OR FEATURED ACTOR — PLAY
Patrick Magee, *Marat/Sade*

SUPPORTING OR FEATURED ACTRESS — PLAY
Zoe Caldwell, *Slapstick Tragedy*

ACTOR — MUSICAL
Richard Kiley, *Man of La Mancha*

ACTRESS — MUSICAL
Angela Lansbury, *Mame*

SUPPORTING OR FEATURED ACTOR — MUSICAL
Frankie Michaels, *Mame*

SUPPORTING OR FEATURED ACTRESS — MUSICAL
Beatrice Arthur, *Mame*

DIRECTOR — PLAY
Peter Brook, *Marat/Sade*

DIRECTOR — MUSICAL
Albert Marre, *Man of La Mancha*

COMPOSER AND LYRICIST
Mitch Leigh and Joe Darion, *Man of La Mancha*

SCENIC DESIGNER
Howard Bay, *Man of La Mancha*

COSTUME DESIGNER
Gunilla Palmstierna-Weiss, *Marat/Sade*

CHOREOGRAPHER
Bob Fosse, *Sweet Charity*

SPECIAL AWARD
Helen Menken (posthumous)

1967

PLAY
The Homecoming

MUSICAL
Cabaret

ACTOR — PLAY
Paul Rogers, *The Homecoming*

ACTRESS — PLAY
Beryl Reid, *The Killing of Sister George*

SUPPORTING OR FEATURED ACTOR — PLAY
Ian Holm, *The Homecoming*

SUPPORTING OR FEATURED ACTRESS — PLAY
Marian Seldes, *A Delicate Balance*

ACTOR — MUSICAL
Robert Preston, *I Do! I Do!*

ACTRESS — MUSICAL
Barbara Harris, *The Apple Tree*

SUPPORTING OR FEATURED ACTOR — MUSICAL
Joel Grey, *Cabaret*

SUPPORTING OR FEATURED ACTRESS — MUSICAL
Peg Murray, *Cabaret*

DIRECTOR — PLAY
Peter Hall, *The Homecoming*

DIRECTOR — MUSICAL
Harold S. Prince, *Cabaret*

COMPOSER AND LYRICIST
John Kander and Fred Ebb, *Cabaret*

SCENIC DESIGNER
Boris Aronson, *Cabaret*

COSTUME DESIGNER
Patricia Zipprodt, *Cabaret*

CHOREOGRAPHER
Ron Field, *Cabaret*

1968

PLAY
Rosencrantz and Guildenstern Are Dead

MUSICAL
Hallelujah, Baby!

ACTOR — PLAY
Martin Balsam, *You Know I Can't Hear You When the Water's Running*

ACTRESS — PLAY
Zoe Caldwell, *The Prime of Miss Jean Brodie*

SUPPORTING OR FEATURED ACTOR — PLAY
James Patterson, *The Birthday Party*

SUPPORTING OR FEATURED ACTRESS — PLAY
Zena Walker, *Joe Egg*

ACTOR — MUSICAL
Robert Goulet, *The Happy Time*

ACTRESSES — MUSICAL
Patricia Routledge, *Darling of the Day*
Leslie Uggams, *Hallelujah, Baby!*

SUPPORTING OR FEATURED ACTOR — MUSICAL
Hiram Sherman, *How Now, Dow Jones*

SUPPORTING OR FEATURED ACTRESS — MUSICAL
Lillian Hayman, *Hallelujah, Baby!*

DIRECTOR — PLAY
Mike Nichols, *Plaza Suite*

DIRECTOR — MUSICAL
Gower Champion, *The Happy Time*

PRODUCER — PLAY
David Merrick Arts Foundation, *Rosencrantz and Guildenstern Are Dead*

PRODUCERS — MUSICAL
Albert Selden, Hal James, Jane C. Nusbaum and Harry Rigby, *Hallelujah, Baby!*

COMPOSER AND LYRICIST
Jule Styne, Betty Comden and Adolph Green, *Hallelujah, Baby!*

SCENIC DESIGNER
Desmond Heeley, *Rosencrantz and Guildenstern Are Dead*

COSTUME DESIGNER
Desmond Heeley, *Rosencrantz and Guildenstern Are Dead*

CHOREOGRAPHER
Gower Champion, *The Happy Time*

SPECIAL AWARDS
Audrey Hepburn
Carol Channing
Pearl Bailey

David Merrick
Maurice Chevalier
APA-Phoenix Theatre
Marlene Dietrich

1969

PLAY
The Great White Hope

MUSICAL
1776

ACTOR — PLAY
James Earl Jones, *The Great White Hope*

ACTRESS — PLAY
Julie Harris, *Forty Carats*

SUPPORTING OR FEATURED ACTOR — PLAY
Al Pacino, *Does a Tiger Wear a Necktie?*

SUPPORTING OR FEATURED ACTRESS — PLAY
Jane Alexander, *The Great White Hope*

ACTOR — MUSICAL
Jerry Orbach, *Promises, Promises*

ACTRESS — MUSICAL
Angela Lansbury, *Dear World*

SUPPORTING OR FEATURED ACTOR — MUSICAL
Ronald Holgate, *1776*

SUPPORTING OR FEATURED ACTRESS — MUSICAL
Marian Mercer, *Promises, Promises*

DIRECTOR — PLAY
Peter Dews, *Hadrian VII*

DIRECTOR — MUSICAL
Peter Hunt, *1776*

SCENIC DESIGNER
Boris Aronson, *Zorba*

COSTUME DESIGNER
Louden Sainthill, *Canterbury Tales*

CHOREOGRAPHER
Joe Layton, *George M!*

SPECIAL AWARDS
The National Theatre Company of Great Britain
The Negro Ensemble Company
Rex Harrison
Leonard Bernstein
Carol Burnett

1970

PLAY
Borstal Boy

MUSICAL
Applause

ACTOR — PLAY
Fritz Weaver, *Child's Play*

ACTRESS — PLAY
Tammy Grimes, *Private Lives* (Revival)

SUPPORTING OR FEATURED ACTOR — PLAY
Ken Howard, *Child's Play*

SUPPORTING OR FEATURED ACTRESS — PLAY
Blythe Danner, *Butterflies Are Free*

ACTOR — MUSICAL
Cleavon Little, *Purlie*

ACTRESS — MUSICAL
Lauren Bacall, *Applause*

SUPPORTING OR FEATURED ACTOR — MUSICAL
René Auberjonois, *Coco*

SUPPORTING OR FEATURED ACTRESS — MUSICAL
Melba Moore, *Purlie*

DIRECTOR — PLAY
Joseph Hardy, *Child's Play*

DIRECTOR — MUSICAL
Ron Field, *Applause*

SCENIC DESIGNER
Jo Mielziner, *Child's Play*

COSTUME DESIGNER
Cecil Beaton, *Coco*

CHOREOGRAPHER
Ron Field, *Applause*

LIGHTING DESIGNER
Jo Mielziner, *Child's Play*

SPECIAL AWARDS
Noel Coward

Alfred Lunt and Lynn Fontanne

New York Shakespeare Festival

Barbra Streisand

1971

PLAY
Sleuth

MUSICAL
Company

ACTOR — PLAY
Brian Bedford, *The School for Wives*

ACTRESS — PLAY
Maureen Stapleton, *Gingerbread Lady*

SUPPORTING OR FEATURED ACTOR — PLAY
Paul Sand, *Story Theatre*

SUPPORTING OR FEATURED ACTRESS — PLAY
Rae Allen, *And Miss Reardon Drinks a Little*

ACTOR — MUSICAL
Hal Linden, *The Rothschilds*

ACTRESS — MUSICAL
Helen Gallagher, *No, No, Nanette*

SUPPORTING OR FEATURED ACTOR — MUSICAL
Keene Curtis, *The Rothschilds*

SUPPORTING OR FEATURED ACTRESS — MUSICAL
Patsy Kelly, *No, No, Nanette*

DIRECTOR — DRAMATIC
Peter Brook, *A Midsummer Night's Dream*

Lauren Bacall

DIRECTOR — MUSICAL
Harold S. Prince, *Company*

PRODUCERS — PLAY
Helen Bonfils, Morton Gottlieb and Michael White, *Sleuth*

PRODUCER — MUSICAL
Harold Prince, *Company*

BOOK — MUSICAL
George Furth, *Company*

LYRICS — MUSICAL
Stephen Sondheim, *Company*

SCORE — MUSICAL
Stephen Sondheim, *Company*

SCENIC DESIGNER
Boris Aronson, *Company*

COSTUME DESIGNER
Raoul Pène Du Bois, *No, No, Nanette*

CHOREOGRAPHER
Donald Saddler, *No, No, Nanette*

LIGHTING DESIGNER
H. R. Poindexter, *Story Theatre*

SPECIAL AWARDS
Elliot Norton

Ingram Ash

Playbill

Roger L. Stevens

1972

PLAY
Sticks and Bones

MUSICAL
Two Gentlemen of Verona

ACTOR — PLAY
Cliff Gorman, *Lenny*

ACTRESS — PLAY
Sada Thompson, *Twigs*

SUPPORTING OR FEATURED ACTOR — PLAY
Vincent Gardenia, *The Prisoner of Second Avenue*

SUPPORTING OR FEATURED ACTRESS — PLAY
Elizabeth Wilson, *Sticks and Bones*

ACTOR — MUSICAL
Phil Silvers, *A Funny Thing Happened on the Way to the Forum*

ACTRESS — MUSICAL
Alexis Smith, *Follies*

SUPPORTING OR FEATURED ACTOR — MUSICAL
Larry Blyden, *A Funny Thing Happened on the Way to the Forum*

SUPPORTING OR FEATURED ACTRESS — MUSICAL
Linda Hopkins, *Inner City*

DIRECTOR — PLAY
Mike Nichols, *The Prisoner of Second Avenue*

DIRECTORS — MUSICAL
Harold S. Prince and Michael Bennett, *Follies*

BOOK — MUSICAL
Two Gentlemen of Verona, John Guare and Mel Shapiro

SCORE — MUSICAL
Follies, Stephen Sondheim, music and lyrics

SCENIC DESIGNER
Boris Aronson, *Follies*

COSTUME DESIGNER
Florence Klotz, *Follies*

CHOREOGRAPHER
Michael Bennett, *Follies*

LIGHTING DESIGNER
Tharon Musser, *Follies*

SPECIAL AWARDS
The Theatre Guild — American Theatre Society

Richard Rodgers

Fiddler on the Roof

Ethel Merman

1973

PLAY
That Championship Season

MUSICAL
A Little Night Music

ACTOR — PLAY
Alan Bates, *Butley*

ACTRESS — PLAY
Julie Harris, *The Last of Mrs. Lincoln*

SUPPORTING OR FEATURED ACTOR — PLAY
John Lithgow, *The Changing Room*

SUPPORTING OR FEATURED ACTRESS — PLAY
Leora Dana, *The Last of Mrs. Lincoln*

ACTOR — MUSICAL
Ben Vereen, *Pippin*

ACTRESS — MUSICAL
Glynis Johns, *A Little Night Music*

SUPPORTING OR FEATURED ACTOR — MUSICAL
George S. Irving, *Irene*

SUPPORTING OR FEATURED ACTRESS — MUSICAL
Patricia Elliot, *A Little Night Music*

Phil Silvers, *A Funny Thing Happened on the Way to the Forum*

DIRECTOR — PLAY
A. J. Antoon, *That Championship Season*

DIRECTOR — MUSICAL
Bob Fosse, *Pippin*

BOOK — MUSICAL
A Little Night Music, Hugh Wheeler

SCORE — MUSICAL
A Little Night Music, Stephen Sondheim, music and lyrics

SCENIC DESIGNER
Tony Walton, *Pippin*

COSTUME DESIGNER
Florence Klotz, *A Little Night Music*

CHOREOGRAPHER
Bob Fosse, *Pippin*

LIGHTING DESIGNER
Jules Fisher, *Pippin*

SPECIAL AWARDS
John Lindsay

Actors' Fund of America

Shubert Organization

1974

PLAY
The River Niger

MUSICAL
Raisin

ACTOR — PLAY
Michael Moriarty, *Find Your Way Home*

ACTRESS — PLAY
Colleen Dewhurst, *A Moon for the Misbegotten*

SUPPORTING OR FEATURED ACTOR — PLAY
Ed Flanders, *A Moon for the Misbegotten*

SUPPORTING OR FEATURED ACTRESS — PLAY
Frances Sternhagen, *The Good Doctor*

ACTOR — MUSICAL
Christopher Plummer, *Cyrano*

ACTRESS — MUSICAL
Virginia Capers, *Raisin*

SUPPORTING OR FEATURED ACTOR — MUSICAL
Tommy Tune, *Seesaw*

SUPPORTING OR FEATURED ACTRESS — MUSICAL
Janie Sell, *Over Here!*

DIRECTOR — PLAY
José Quintero, *A Moon for the Misbegotten*

DIRECTOR — MUSICAL
Harold Prince, *Candide*

BOOK — MUSICAL
Candide, Hugh Wheeler

SCORE
Gigi, Frederick Loewe, music; Alan Jay Lerner, lyrics

SCENIC DESIGNERS
Franne and Eugene Lee, *Candide*

COSTUME DESIGNER
Franne Lee, *Candide*

CHOREOGRAPHER
Michael Bennett, *Seasaw*

LIGHTING DESIGNER
Jules Fisher, *Ulysses in Nighttown*

SPECIAL AWARDS
Liza Minnelli

Bette Midler

Peter Cook and Dudley Moore, *Good Evening*

A Moon for the Misbegotten

Candide

Actors' Equity Association

Theatre Development Fund

John F. Wharton

Harold Friedlander

1975

PLAY
Equus

MUSICAL
The Wiz

ACTORS — PLAY
John Kani and Winston Ntshona, *Sizwe Banzi Is Dead* and
The Island

ACTRESS — PLAY
Ellen Burstyn, *Same Time, Next Year*

SUPPORTING OR FEATURED ACTOR — PLAY
Frank Langella, *Seascape*

SUPPORTING OR FEATURED ACTRESS — PLAY
Rita Moreno, *The Ritz*

ACTOR — MUSICAL
John Cullum, *Shenandoah*

ACTRESS — MUSICAL
Angela Lansbury, *Gypsy*

SUPPORTING OR FEATURED ACTOR — MUSICAL
Ted Ross, *The Wiz*

SUPPORTING OR FEATURED ACTRESS — MUSICAL
Dee Dee Bridgewater, *The Wiz*

DIRECTOR — PLAY
John Dexter, *Equus*

DIRECTOR — MUSICAL
Geoffrey Holder, *The Wiz*

BOOK — MUSICAL
Shenandoah, James Lee Barrett, Peter Udell and Philip Rose

SCORE
The Wiz, Charlie Smalls, music and lyrics

SCENIC DESIGNER
Carl Toms, *Sherlock Holmes*

COSTUME DESIGNER
Geoffrey Holder, *The Wiz*

CHOREOGRAPHER
George Faison, *The Wiz*

LIGHTING DESIGNER
Neil Peter Jampolis, *Sherlock Holmes*

SPECIAL AWARDS
Neil Simon

Al Hirschfeld

1976

PLAY
Travesties

MUSICAL
A Chorus Line

ACTOR — PLAY
John Wood, *Travesties*

ACTRESS — PLAY
Irene Worth, *Sweet Bird of Youth*

FEATURED ACTOR — PLAY
Edward Herrmann, *Mrs. Warren's Profession*

FEATURED ACTRESS — PLAY
Shirley Knight, *Kennedy's Children*

ACTOR — MUSICAL
George Rose, *My Fair Lady*

ACTRESS — MUSICAL
Donna McKechnie, *A Chorus Line*

FEATURED ACTOR — MUSICAL
Sammy Williams, *A Chorus Line*

FEATURED ACTRESS — MUSICAL
Carole Bishop, *A Chorus Line*

DIRECTOR — PLAY
Ellis Rabb, *The Royal Family*

DIRECTOR — MUSICAL
Michael Bennett, *A Chorus Line*

BOOK — MUSICAL
A Chorus Line, James Kirkwood and Nicholas Dante

SCORE
A Chorus Line, Marvin Hamlisch, music; Edward Kleban, lyrics

SCENIC DESIGNER
Boris Aronson, *Pacific Overtures*

COSTUME DESIGNER
Florence Klotz, *Pacific Overtures*

CHOREOGRAPHERS
Michael Bennet and Bob Avian, *A Chorus Line*

LIGHTING DESIGNER
Tharon Musser, *A Chorus Line*

SPECIAL AWARDS
Mathilde Pincus, *Circle in the Square*

Thomas H. Fitzgerald, *The Arena Stage*

Richard Burton, *Equus*

1977

PLAY
The Shadow Box

MUSICAL
Annie

ACTOR — PLAY
Al Pacino, *The Basic Training of Pavlo Hummel*

ACTRESS — PLAY
Julie Harris, *The Belle of Amherst*

FEATURED ACTOR — PLAY
Jonathan Pryce, *Comedians*

FEATURED ACTRESS — PLAY
Trazana Beverley, *For Colored Girls Who Have Considered
    Suicide When the Rainbow is Enuf*

ACTOR — MUSICAL
Barry Bostwick, *The Robber Bridegroom*

ACTRESS — MUSICAL
Dorothy Loudon, *Annie*

FEATURED ACTOR — MUSICAL
Lenny Baker, *I Love My Wife*

FEATURED ACTRESS — MUSICAL
Delores Hall, *Your Arm's Too Short to Box With God*

DIRECTOR — PLAY
Gordon Davidson, *The Shadow Box*

DIRECTOR — MUSICAL
Gene Saks, *I Love My Wife*

BOOK — MUSICAL
Annie, Thomas Meehan

SCORE
Annie, Charles Strouse, music; Martin Charnin, lyrics

SCENIC DESIGNER
David Mitchell, *Annie*

COSTUME DESIGNERS
Theoni V. Aldredge, *Annie*

Santo Loquasto, *The Cherry Orchard*

CHOREOGRAPHER
Peter Gennaro, *Annie*

LIGHTING DESIGNER
Jennifer Tipton, *The Cherry Orchard*

MOST INNOVATIVE PRODUCTION OF A REVIVAL
Porgy and Bess, Sherwin M. Goldman and Houston Grand
    Opera, producers

SPECIAL AWARDS
Lily Tomlin

Barry Manilow

Diana Ross

National Theatre for the Deaf

Mark Taper Forum

Equity Library Theatre

1978

PLAY
Da

MUSICAL
Ain't Misbehavin'

ACTOR — PLAY
Barnard Hughes, *Da*

ACTRESS — PLAY
Jessica Tandy, *The Gin Game*

FEATURED ACTOR — PLAY
Lester Rawlins, *Da*

FEATURED ACTRESS — PLAY
Ann Wedgeworth, *Chapter Two*

ACTOR — MUSICAL
John Cullum, *On the Twentieth Century*

ACTRESS — MUSICAL
Liza Minnelli, *The Act*

FEATURED ACTOR — MUSICAL
Kevin Kline, *On the Twentieth Century*

FEATURED ACTRESS — MUSICAL
Nell Carter, *Ain't Misbehavin'*

DIRECTOR — PLAY
Melvin Bernhardt, *Da*

DIRECTOR — MUSICAL
Richard Maltby, Jr., *Ain't Misbehavin'*

BOOK — MUSICAL
On the Twentieth Century, Betty Comden and Adolph Green

SCORE
On the Twentieth Century, Cy Coleman, music; Betty Comden
    and Adolph Green, lyrics

Liza Minnelli

SCENIC DESIGNER
Robin Wagner, *On the Twentieth Century*

COSTUME DESIGNER
Edward Gorey, *Dracula*

CHOREOGRAPHER
Bob Fosse, *Dancin'*

LIGHTING DESIGNER
Jules Fisher, *Dancin'*

MOST INNOVATIVE PRODUCTION OF A REVIVAL
Dracula, Jujamcyn Theatre, Elizabeth I. McCann, John Wulp,
   Victor Lurie, Nelle Nugent and Max Weitzenhoffer, producers

SPECIAL AWARD
The Long Wharf Theatre

1979

PLAY
The Elephant Man

MUSICAL
Sweeney Todd

ACTOR — PLAY
Tom Conti, *Whose Life Is It Anyway?*

ACTRESSES — PLAY
Constance Cummings, *Wings*
Carole Shelley, *The Elephant Man*

FEATURED ACTOR — PLAY
Michael Gough, *Bedroom Farce*

FEATURED ACTRESS — PLAY
Joan Hickson, *Bedroom Farce*

ACTOR — MUSICAL
Len Cariou, *Sweeney Todd*

ACTRESS — MUSICAL
Angela Lansbury, *Sweeney Todd*

FEATURED ACTOR — MUSICAL
Henderson Forsythe, *The Best Little Whorehouse in Texas*

FEATURED ACTRESS — MUSICAL
Carlin Glynn, *The Best Little Whorehouse in Texas*

DIRECTOR — PLAY
Jack Hofsiss, *The Elephant Man*

DIRECTOR — MUSICAL
Harold Prince, *Sweeney Todd*

BOOK — MUSICAL
Sweeney Todd, Hugh Wheeler

SCORE
Sweeney Todd, Stephen Sondheim, music and lyrics

SCENIC DESIGNER
Eugene Lee, *Sweeney Todd*

COSTUME DESIGNER
Franne Lee, *Sweeney Todd*

CHOREOGRAPHERS
Michael Bennett and Bob Avian, *Ballroom*

LIGHTING DESIGNER
Roger Morgan, *The Crucifer of Blood*

SPECIAL AWARDS
Henry Fonda
Walter F. Diehl
Eugene O'Neill Memorial Theatre Center
American Conservatory Theater

1980

PLAY
Children of a Lesser God

MUSICAL
Evita

REPRODUCTION — PLAY OR MUSICAL
Morning's at Seven

ACTOR — PLAY
John Rubinstein, *Children of a Lesser God*

ACTRESS — PLAY
Phyllis Frelich, *Children of a Lesser God*

FEATURED ACTOR — PLAY
David Rounds, *Morning's at Seven*

FEATURED ACTRESS — PLAY
Dinah Manoff, *I Ought to Be in Pictures*

ACTOR — MUSICAL
Jim Dale, *Barnum*

ACTRESS — MUSICAL
Patti LuPone, *Evita*

FEATURED ACTOR — MUSICAL
Mandy Patinkin, *Evita*

FEATURED ACTRESS — MUSICAL
Priscilla Lopez, *A Day in Hollywood* and *A Night in the Ukraine*

DIRECTOR — PLAY
Vivian Matalon, *Morning's at Seven*

DIRECTOR — MUSICAL
Harold Prince, *Evita*

BOOK — MUSICAL
Evita, Tim Rice

SCORE
Evita, Andrew Lloyd Webber, music; Tim Rice, lyrics

SCENIC DESIGNERS
John Lee Beatty, *Talley's Folly*
David Mitchell, *Barnum*

COSTUME DESIGNER
Theoni V. Aldredge, *Barnum*

CHOREOGRAPHERS
Tommy Tune and Thommie Walsh, *A Day in Hollywood* and
   A Night in the Ukraine

LIGHTING DESIGNER
David Hersey, *Evita*

SPECIAL AWARDS
Mary Tyler Moore
Actors Theatre of Louisville
Goodspeed Opera House

Kevin Kline, *The Pirates of Penzance*

1981

PLAY
Amadeus

MUSICAL
42nd Street

REPRODUCTION — PLAY OR MUSICAL
The Pirates of Penzance

ACTOR — PLAY
Ian McKellen, *Amadeus*

ACTRESS — PLAY
Jane Lapotaire, *Piaf*

FEATURED ACTOR — PLAY
Brian Backer, *The Floating Light Bulb*

FEATURED ACTRESS — PLAY
Swoosie Kurtz, *Fifth of July*

ACTOR — MUSICAL
Kevin Kline, *The Pirates of Penzance*

ACTRESS — MUSICAL
Lauren Bacall, *Woman of the Year*

FEATURED ACTOR — MUSICAL
Hinton Battle, *Sophisticated Ladies*

FEATURED ACTRESS — MUSICAL
Marilyn Cooper, *Woman of the Year*

DIRECTOR — PLAY
Peter Hall, *Amadeus*

DIRECTOR — MUSICAL
Wilford Leach, *The Pirates of Penzance*

BOOK — MUSICAL
Woman of the Year, Peter Stone

SCORE
Woman of the Year, John Kander, music; Fred Ebb, lyrics

SCENIC DESIGNER
John Bury, *Amadeus*

COSTUME DESIGNER
Willa Kim, *Sophisticated Ladies*

CHOREOGRAPHER
Gower Champion, *42nd Street*

LIGHTING DESIGNER
John Bury, *Amadeus*

SPECIAL AWARDS
Lena Horne

Trinity Square Repertory Company

1982

PLAY
The Life and Adventures of Nicholas Nickleby

MUSICAL
Nine

REPRODUCTION — PLAY OR MUSICAL
Othello

ACTOR — PLAY
Roger Rees, *The Life and Adventures of Nicholas Nickleby*

ACTRESS — PLAY
Zoe Caldwell, *Medea*

FEATURED ACTOR — PLAY
Zakes Mokae, *'Master Harold' . . . and the Boys*

FEATURED ACTRESS — PLAY
Amanda Plummer, *Agnes of God*

ACTOR — MUSICAL
Ben Harney, *Dreamgirls*

ACTRESS — MUSICAL
Jennifer Holliday, *Dreamgirls*

FEATURED ACTOR — MUSICAL
Cleavant Derricks, *Dreamgirls*

FEATURED ACTRESS — MUSICAL
Liliane Montevecchi, *Nine*

DIRECTORS — PLAY
Trevor Nunn and John Caird, *The Life and Adventures of
    Nicholas Nickleby*

DIRECTOR — MUSICAL
Tommy Tune, *Nine*

BOOK — MUSICAL
Dreamgirls, Tom Eyen

SCORE
Nine, Maury Yeston, music and lyrics

SCENIC DESIGNERS
John Napier and Dermot Hayes, *The Life and Adventures of
    Nicholas Nickleby*

COSTUME DESIGNER
William Ivey Long, *Nine*

CHOREOGRAPHERS
Michael Bennett and Michael Peters, *Dreamgirls*

LIGHTING DESIGNER
Tharon Musser, *Dreamgirls*

SPECIAL AWARDS
The Guthrie Theatre

The Actors Fund of America

1983

PLAY
Torch Song Trilogy

MUSICAL
Cats

REPRODUCTION — PLAY OR MUSICAL
On Your Toes

ACTOR — PLAY
Harvey Fierstein, *Torch Song Trilogy*

ACTRESS — PLAY
Jessica Tandy, *Foxfire*

FEATURED ACTOR — PLAY
Matthew Broderick, *Brighton Beach Memoirs*

FEATURED ACTRESS — PLAY
Judith Ivey, *Steaming*

ACTOR — MUSICAL
Tommy Tune, *My One and Only*

ACTRESS — MUSICAL
Natalia Makarova, *On Your Toes*

FEATURED ACTOR — MUSICAL
Charles "Honi" Coles, *My One and Only*

FEATURED ACTRESS — MUSICAL
Betty Buckley, *Cats*

DIRECTOR — PLAY
Gene Saks, *Brighton Beach Memoirs*

DIRECTOR — MUSICAL
Trevor Nunn, *Cats*

BOOK — MUSICAL
Cats, T. S. Eliot

SCORE
Cats, Andrew Lloyd Webber, music; T. S. Eliot, lyrics

SCENIC DESIGNER
Ming Cho Lee, *K2*

COSTUME DESIGNER
John Napier, *Cats*

CHOREOGRAPHERS
Tommy Tune and Thommie Walsh, *My One and Only*

LIGHTING DESIGNER
David Hersey, *Cats*

SPECIAL AWARDS
The Theatre Collection, Museum of the City of New York

Shakespearean Festival Association

1984

PLAY
The Real Thing

MUSICAL
La Cage aux Folles

REPRODUCTION — PLAY OR MUSICAL
Death of a Salesman

ACTOR — PLAY
Jeremy Irons, *The Real Thing*

ACTRESS — PLAY
Glenn Close, *The Real Thing*

FEATURED ACTOR — PLAY
Joe Mantegna, *Glengarry Glen Ross*

FEATURED ACTRESS — PLAY
Christine Baranski, *The Real Thing*

ACTOR — MUSICAL
George Hearn, *La Cage aux Folles*

ACTRESS — MUSICAL
Chita Rivera, *The Rink*

FEATURED ACTOR — MUSICAL
Hinton Battle, *The Tap Dance Kid*

FEATURED ACTRESS — MUSICAL
Martine Allard, *The Tap Dance Kid*

DIRECTOR — PLAY
Mike Nichols, *The Real Thing*

DIRECTOR — MUSICAL
Arthur Laurents, *La Cage aux Folles*

BOOK — MUSICAL
La Cage aux Folles, Harvey Fierstein

SCORE — MUSICAL
La Cage aux Folles, Jerry Herman, music and lyrics

SCENIC DESIGNER
Tony Straiges, *Sunday in the Park With George*

COSTUME DESIGNER
Theoni V. Aldredge, *La Cage aux Folles*

CHOREOGRAPHER
Danny Daniels, *The Tap Dance Kid*

LIGHTING DESIGNER
Richard Nelson, *Sunday in the Park With George*

SPECIAL AWARDS
San Diego Old Globe Theatre

La Tragedie de Carmen

Al Hirschfeld (Brooks Atkinson Award)

Peter Feller

1985

PLAY
Biloxi Blues

MUSICAL
Big River

REPRODUCTION — PLAY OR MUSICAL
Joe Egg

ACTOR — PLAY
Derek Jacobi, *Much Ado About Nothing*

ACTRESS — PLAY
Stockard Channing, *Joe Egg*

FEATURED ACTOR — PLAY
Barry Miller, *Biloxi Blues*

FEATURED ACTRESS — PLAY
Judith Ivey, *Hurlyburly*

FEATURED ACTOR — MUSICAL
Ron Richardson, *Big River*

FEATURED ACTRESS — MUSICAL
Leilani Jones, *Grind*

DIRECTOR — PLAY
Gene Saks, *Biloxi Blues*

DIRECTOR — MUSICAL
Des McAnuff, *Big River*

BOOK — MUSICAL
Big River, William Hauptman

SCORE
Big River, Roger Miller

SCENIC DESIGNER
Heidi Landesman, *Big River*

COSTUME DESIGNER
Florence Klotz, *Grind*

LIGHTING DESIGNER
Richard Riddell, *Big River*

SPECIAL AWARDS
Yul Brynner
Edwin Lester
New York State Council on the Arts
Steppenwolf Theatre

1986

PLAY
I'm Not Rappaport

MUSICAL
The Mystery of Edwin Drood

REPRODUCTION — PLAY OR MUSICAL
Sweet Charity

ACTOR — PLAY
Judd Hirsch, *I'm Not Rappaport*

ACTRESS — PLAY
Lily Tomlin, *The Search for Signs of Intelligent Life in the Universe*

FEATURED ACTOR — PLAY
John Mahoney, *The House of Blue Leaves*

FEATURED ACTRESS — PLAY
Swoosie Kurtz, *The House of Blue Leaves*

ACTOR — MUSICAL
George Rose, *The Mystery of Edwin Drood*

ACTRESS — MUSICAL
Bernadette Peters, *Song & Dance*

FEATURED ACTOR — MUSICAL
Michael Rupert, *Sweet Charity*

FEATURED ACTRESS — MUSICAL
Bebe Neuwirth, *Sweet Charity*

DIRECTOR — PLAY
Jerry Zaks, *The House of Blue Leaves*

DIRECTOR — MUSICAL
Wilford Leach, *The Mystery of Edwin Drood*

BOOK — MUSICAL
The Mystery of Edwin Drood, Rupert Holmes

SCORE
The Mystery of Edwin Drood, Rupert Holmes

SCENIC DESIGNER
Tony Walton, *The House of Blue Leaves*

COSTUME DESIGNER
Patricia Zipprodt, *Sweet Charity*

CHOREOGRAPHER
Bob Fosse, *Big Deal*

LIGHTING DESIGNER
Pat Collins, *I'm Not Rappaport*

SPECIAL AWARD
American Repertory Theatre

1987

PLAY
Fences

MUSICAL
Les Misérables

REVIVAL
All My Sons

ACTOR — PLAY
James Earl Jones, *Fences*

ACTRESS — PLAY
Linda Lavin, *Broadway Bound*

FEATURED ACTOR — PLAY
John Randolph, *Broadway Bound*

FEATURED ACTRESS — PLAY
Mary Alice, *Fences*

ACTOR — MUSICAL
Robert Lindsay, *Me and My Girl*

ACTRESS — MUSICAL
Maryann Plunkett, *Me and My Girl*

FEATURED ACTOR — MUSICAL
Michael Maguire, *Les Misérables*

FEATURED ACTRESS — MUSICAL
Frances Ruffelle, *Les Misérables*

James Earl Jones

DIRECTOR — PLAY
Lloyd Richards, *Fences*

DIRECTORS — MUSICAL
Trevor Nunn and John Caird, *Les Misérables*

BOOK — MUSICAL
Les Misérables, Alain Boublil and Claude-Michel Schönberg

SCORE
Les Misérables, Claude-Michel Schönberg, music; Herbert Kretzmer and Alain Boublil, lyrics

SCENIC DESIGNER
John Napier, *Les Misérables*

COSTUME DESIGNER
John Napier, *Starlight Express*

CHOREOGRAPHER
Gillian Gregory, *Me and My Girl*

LIGHTING DESIGNER
David Hersey, *Les Misérables*

SPECIAL AWARDS
George Abbott
Jackie Mason
San Francisco Mime Troupe

1988

PLAY
M. Butterfly

MUSICAL
The Phantom of the Opera

REVIVAL
Anything Goes

ACTOR — PLAY
Ron Silver, *Speed-the-Plow*

ACTRESS — PLAY
Joan Allen, *Burn This*

FEATURED ACTOR — PLAY
B. D. Wong, *M. Butterfly*

FEATURED ACTRESS — PLAY
L. Scott Caldwell, *Joe Turner's Come and Gone*

ACTOR — MUSICAL
Michael Crawford, *The Phantom of the Opera*

ACTRESS — MUSICAL
Joanna Gleason, *Into the Woods*

FEATURED ACTOR — MUSICAL
Bill McCutcheon, *Anything Goes*

FEATURED ACTRESS — MUSICAL
Judy Kaye, *The Phantom of the Opera*

DIRECTOR — PLAY
John Dexter, *M. Butterfly*

DIRECTOR — MUSICAL
Harold Prince, *The Phantom of the Opera*

BOOK — MUSICAL
Into the Woods, James Lapine

SCORE — MUSICAL
Into the Woods, Stephen Sondheim, music and lyrics

SCENIC DESIGNER
Maria Björnson, *The Phantom of the Opera*

COSTUME DESIGNER
Maria Björnson, *The Phantom of the Opera*

CHOREOGRAPHER
Michael Smuin, *Anything Goes*

LIGHTING DESIGNER
Andrew Bridge, *The Phantom of the Opera*

SPECIAL AWARDS
Brooklyn Academy of Music
South Coast Repertory of Costa Mesa, CA

1989

PLAY
The Heidi Chronicles

MUSICAL
Jerome Robbins' Broadway

REVIVAL
Our Town

ACTOR — PLAY
Philip Bosco, *Lend Me a Tenor*

ACTRESS — PLAY
Pauline Collins, *Shirley Valentine*

FEATURED ACTOR — PLAY
Boyd Gaines, *The Heidi Chronicles*

FEATURED ACTRESS — PLAY
Christine Baranski, *Rumors*

ACTOR — MUSICAL
Jason Alexander, *Jerome Robbins' Broadway*

ACTRESS — MUSICAL
Ruth Brown, *Black and Blue*

FEATURED ACTOR — MUSICAL
Scott Wise, *Jerome Robbins' Broadway*

FEATURED ACTRESS — MUSICAL
Debbie Shapiro, *Jerome Robbins' Broadway*

DIRECTOR — PLAY
Jerry Zaks, *Lend Me a Tenor*

DIRECTOR — MUSICAL
Jerome Robbins, *Jerome Robbins' Broadway*

SCENIC DESIGNER
Santo Loquasto, *Cafe Crown*

COSTUME DESIGNERS
Claudio Segovia and Hector Orezzoli, *Black and Blue*

CHOREOGRAPHERS
Cholly Atkins, Henry LeTang, Frankie Manning and Fayard Nicholas, *Black and Blue*

LIGHTING DESIGNER
Jennifer Tipton, *Jerome Robbins' Broadway*

SPECIAL AWARD
Hartford Stage Company

1990

PLAY
The Grapes of Wrath

MUSICAL
City of Angels

REVIVAL
Gypsy

ACTOR — PLAY
Robert Morse, *Tru*

ACTRESS — PLAY
Maggie Smith, *Lettice and Lovage*

FEATURED ACTOR — PLAY
Charles Durning, *Cat on a Hot Tin Roof*

FEATURED ACTRESS — PLAY
Margaret Tyzack, *Lettice and Lovage*

ACTOR — MUSICAL
James Naughton, *City of Angels*

ACTRESS — MUSICAL
Tyne Daly, *Gypsy*

FEATURED ACTOR — MUSICAL
Michael Jeter, *Grand Hotel, the Musical*

FEATURED ACTRESS — MUSICAL
Randy Graff, *City of Angels*

DIRECTOR — PLAY
Frank Galati, *The Grapes of Wrath*

DIRECTOR — MUSICAL
Tommy Tune, *Grand Hotel, the Musical*

BOOK — MUSICAL
City of Angels, Larry Gelbart

SCORE
City of Angels, Cy Coleman, music; David Zippel, lyrics

SCENIC DESIGNER
Robin Wagner, *City of Angels*

COSTUME DESIGNER
Santo Loquasto, *Grand Hotel, the Musical*

CHOREOGRAPHER
Tommy Tune, *Grand Hotel, the Musical*

LIGHTING DESIGNER
Jules Fisher, *Grand Hotel, the Musical*

SPECIAL TONY AWARD
Seattle Repertory Theatre

TONY HONOR
Alfred Drake for excellence in the theater

1991

PLAY
Lost in Yonkers

MUSICAL
The Will Rogers Follies

REVIVAL
Fiddler on the Roof

Mercedes Ruehl

ACTOR — PLAY
Nigel Hawthorne, *Shadowlands*

ACTRESS — PLAY
Mercedes Ruehl, *Lost in Yonkers*

FEATURED ACTOR — PLAY
Kevin Spacey, *Lost in Yonkers*

FEATURED ACTRESS — PLAY
Irene Worth, *Lost in Yonkers*

ACTOR — MUSICAL
Jonathan Pryce, *Miss Saigon*

ACTRESS — MUSICAL
Lea Salonga, *Miss Saigon*

FEATURED ACTOR — MUSICAL
Hinton Battle, *Miss Saigon*

FEATURED ACTRESS — MUSICAL
Daisy Eagan, *The Secret Garden*

DIRECTOR — PLAY
Jerry Zaks, *Six Degrees of Separation*

DIRECTOR — MUSICAL
Tommy Tune, *The Will Rogers Follies*

BOOK — MUSICAL
The Secret Garden, Marsha Norman

SCORE — MUSICAL
The Will Rogers Follies, Cy Coleman, music; Betty Comden and Adolph Green, lyrics

SCENIC DESIGNER
Heidi Landesman, *The Secret Garden*

COSTUME DESIGNER
Willa Kim, *The Will Rogers Follies*

CHOREOGRAPHER
Tommy Tune, *The Will Rogers Follies*

LIGHTING DESIGNER
Jules Fisher, *The Will Rogers Follies*

SPECIAL TONY AWARD
Yale Repertory Theatre

TONY HONOR
Father George Moore

1992

PLAY
Dancing at Lughnasa

MUSICAL
Crazy for You

REVIVAL
Guys and Dolls

ACTOR — PLAY
Judd Hirsch, *Conversations With My Father*

ACTRESS — PLAY
Glenn Close, *Death and the Maiden*

FEATURED ACTOR — PLAY
Larry Fishburne, *Two Trains Running*

FEATURED ACTRESS — PLAY
Brid Brennan, *Dancing at Lughnasa*

ACTOR — MUSICAL
Gregory Hines, *Jelly's Last Jam*

ACTRESS — MUSICAL
Faith Prince, *Guys and Dolls*

FEATURED ACTOR — MUSICAL
Scott Waara, *The Most Happy Fella*

FEATURED ACTRESS — MUSICAL
Tonya Pinkins, *Jelly's Last Jam*

DIRECTOR — PLAY
Patrick Mason, *Dancing at Lughnasa*

DIRECTOR — MUSICAL
Jerry Zaks, *Guys and Dolls*

BOOK — MUSICAL
Falsettos, William Finn and James Lapine

SCORE
Falsettos, William Finn, music and lyrics

SCENIC DESIGNER
Tony Walton, *Guys and Dolls*

COSTUME DESIGNER
William Ivey Long, *Crazy for You*

CHOREOGRAPHER
Susan Stroman, *Crazy for You*

LIGHTING DESIGNER
Jules Fisher, *Jelly's Last Jam*

SPECIAL TONY AWARD
The Goodman Theatre of Chicago

TONY HONOR
The Fantasticks

1993

PLAY
Angels in America: Millennium Approaches

MUSICAL
Kiss of the Spider Woman — The Musical

REVIVAL
Anna Christie

ACTOR — PLAY
Ron Leibman, *Angels in America: Millennium Approaches*

ACTRESS — PLAY
Madeline Kahn, *The Sisters Rosensweig*

FEATURED ACTOR — PLAY
Stephen Spinella, *Angels in America: Millennium Approaches*

FEATURED ACTRESS — PLAY
Debra Monk, *Redwood Curtain*

ACTOR — MUSICAL
Brent Carver, *Kiss of the Spider Woman — The Musical*

ACTRESS — MUSICAL
Chita Rivera, *Kiss of the Spider Woman — The Musical*

FEATURED ACTOR — MUSICAL
Anthony Crivello, *Kiss of the Spider Woman — The Musical*

FEATURED ACTRESS — MUSICAL
Andrea Martin, *My Favorite Year*

DIRECTOR — PLAY
George C. Wolfe, *Angels in America: Millennium Approaches*

DIRECTOR — MUSICAL
Des McAnuff, *The Who's Tommy*

BOOK — MUSICAL
Kiss of the Spider Woman — The Musical, Terrence McNally

SCORES — MUSICAL
Kiss of the Spider Woman — The Musical, John Kander, music; Fred Ebb, lyrics

The Who's Tommy, Pete Townshend, music and lyrics

SCENIC DESIGNER
John Arnone, *The Who's Tommy*

COSTUME DESIGNER
Florence Klotz, *Kiss of the Spider Woman — The Musical*

CHOREOGRAPHER
Wayne Cilento, *The Who's Tommy*

LIGHTING DESIGNER
Chris Parry, *The Who's Tommy*

SPECIAL TONY AWARDS
Oklahoma! — 50th Anniversary

La Jolla Playhouse

TONY HONORS
IATSE

Broadway Cares/Equity Fights AIDS

1994

PLAY
Angels in America: Perestroika

MUSICAL
Passion

REVIVAL — PLAY
An Inspector Calls

REVIVAL — MUSICAL
Carousel

ACTOR — PLAY
Stephen Spinella, *Angels in America: Perestroika*

ACTRESS — PLAY
Diana Rigg, *Medea*

Ken Howard

Matthew Broderick, *How to Succeed in Business Without Really Trying*

FEATURED ACTOR — PLAY
Jeffrey Wright, *Angels in America: Perestroika*

FEATURED ACTRESS — PLAY
Jane Adams, *An Inspector Calls*

ACTOR — MUSICAL
Boyd Gaines, *She Loves Me*

ACTRESS — MUSICAL
Donna Murphy, *Passion*

FEATURED ACTOR — MUSICAL
Jarrod Emick, *Damn Yankees*

FEATURED ACTRESS — MUSICAL
Audra Ann McDonald, *Carousel*

DIRECTOR — PLAY
Stephen Daldry, *An Inspector Calls*

DIRECTOR — MUSICAL
Nicholas Hytner, *Carousel*

BOOK — MUSICAL
Passion, James Lapine

ORIGINAL MUSICAL SCORE
Passion, Stephen Sondheim, music and lyrics

SCENIC DESIGNER
Bob Crowley, *Carousel*

COSTUME DESIGNER
Ann Hould-Ward, *Beauty and the Beast*

CHOREOGRAPHER
Sir Kenneth MacMillan, *Carousel*

LIGHTING DESIGNER
Rick Fisher, *An Inspector Calls*

SPECIAL TONY AWARDS
Jessica Tandy and Hume Cronyn, lifetime achievement
McCarter Theatre

1995

PLAY
Love! Valour! Compassion!

MUSICAL
Sunset Boulevard

REVIVAL — PLAY
The Heiress

REVIVAL — MUSICAL
Show Boat

ACTOR — PLAY
Ralph Fiennes, *Hamlet*

ACTRESS — PLAY
Cherry Jones, *The Heiress*

ACTOR — MUSICAL
Matthew Broderick, *How to Succeed in Business
    Without Really Trying*

ACTRESS — MUSICAL
Glenn Close, *Sunset Boulevard*

FEATURED ACTOR — PLAY
John Glover, *Love! Valour! Compassion!*

FEATURED ACTRESS — PLAY
Frances Sternhagen, *The Heiress*

FEATURED ACTOR — MUSICAL
George Hearn, *Sunset Boulevard*

FEATURED ACTRESS — MUSICAL
Gretha Boston, *Show Boat*

DIRECTOR — PLAY
Gerald Gutierrez, *The Heiress*

DIRECTOR — MUSICAL
Harold Prince, *Show Boat*

BOOK — MUSICAL
Sunset Boulevard, Christopher Hampton and
    Don Black

SCORE — MUSICAL
Sunset Boulevard, Andrew Lloyd Webber, music; Christopher
    Hampton and Don Black, lyrics

SCENIC DESIGNER
John Napier, *Sunset Boulevard*

COSTUME DESIGNER
Florence Klotz, *Show Boat*

CHOREOGRAPHER
Susan Stroman, *Show Boat*

LIGHTING DESIGNER
Andrew Bridge, *Sunset Boulevard*

SPECIAL TONY AWARDS
Carol Channing, lifetime achievement

Harvey Sabinson, executive director of the League of
American Theatres and Producers, lifetime achievement

Goodspeed Opera House

National Endowment for the Arts

All-Time Top Tony Winners and Nominees

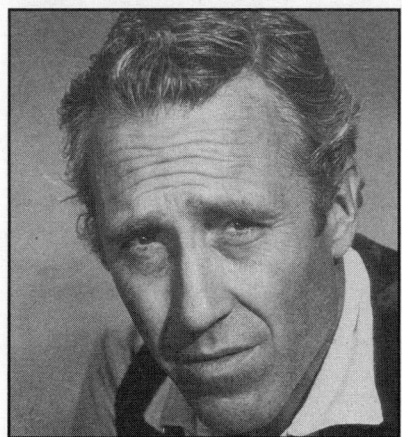

Jason Robards, Jr.

ACTOR — PLAY

	Nominations	Wins
Jason Robards, Jr.	7	1
Brian Bedford	4	1
Hume Cronyn	4	0
Donald Pleasance	4	0

ACTRESS — PLAY

	Nominations	Wins
Julie Harris	8	5
Colleen Dewhurst	6	1
Rosemary Harris	6	1
Jane Alexander	5	0
Margaret Leighton	4	2
Maureen Stapleton	4	1
Jessica Tandy	4	3
Irene Worth	4	2

ACTOR — MUSICAL

	Nominations	Wins
Raul Julia	4	0
Len Cariou	3	1
John Cullum	3	2
Alfred Drake	3	1
Joel Grey	3	0
Gregory Hines	3	1
Richard Kiley	3	2
Robert Morse	3	1
Robert Preston	3	2
George Rose	3	2
Phil Silvers	3	2

ACTRESS — MUSICAL

	Nominations	Wins
Chita Rivera	6	2
Gwen Verdon	5	3
Carol Channing	4	1
Mary Martin	4	3
Bernadette Peters	4	1

FEATURED ACTOR — PLAY

	Nominations	Wins
Joseph Maher	3	0
Philip Bosco	2	0
Michael Gough	2	1
George Grizzard	2	0
Zeljko Ivanek	2	0
Walter Matthau	2	1
Edward Petherbridge	2	0

FEATURED ACTRESS — PLAY

	Nominations	Wins
Francis Sternhagen	4	2
Swoosie Kurtz	3	2
Rae Allen	2	1
Christine Baranski	2	2
Leora Dana	2	1
Alice Ghostley	2	1
Eileen Heckart	2	0
Mary Beth Hurt	2	0
Judith Ivey	2	2
Zohra Lampert	2	0
Debra Monk	2	1
Rosemary Murphy	2	0

Jessica Tandy

Marian Seldes	2	1
Carole Shelley	2	0
Maureen Stapleton	2	1
Margaret Tyzack	2	1
Zoe Wannamaker	2	0

FEATURED ACTOR — MUSICAL

	Nominations	Wins
René Auberjonois	3	1
Hinton Battle	3	3
Bruce Adler	2	0
Tom Aldredge	2	0
Jack Cassidy	2	1
Harry Groener	2	0
George S. Irving	2	1
Russell Nype	2	2
Gilbert Price	2	0
Charles Nelson Reilly	2	1
Edward Winter	2	0

FEATURED ACTRESS — MUSICAL

	Nominations	Wins
Helen Gallagher	2	1
Patsy Kelly	2	1
Priscilla Lopez	2	1
Marie Julienne	2	0
Millicent Martin	2	0

DIRECTOR — PLAY

	Nominations	Wins
Mike Nichols	8	5
Peter Hall	7	2
Marshall W. Mason	5	0
Alan Schneider	5	1
Joseph Anthony	4	0
Elia Kazan	4	2
José Quintero	4	1
Lloyd Richards	4	1
Gene Saks	4	1

Tim Boxer, Pictorial Parade

Neil Simon

Stephen Sondheim

DIRECTOR — MUSICAL

	Nominations	Wins
Harold Prince	15	8
Gower Champion	8	3
Michael Bennett	6	2
Bob Fosse	6	1
Tommy Tune	6	3
Trevor Nunn	5	2

AUTHOR — PLAY

	Nominations	Wins
Neil Simon	10	2
Edward Albee	5	1
August Wilson	5	1
Athol Fugard	4	0
Arthur Miller	4	2
John Osborne	4	1
David Rabe	4	1
Peter Shaffer	4	2

BOOK — MUSICAL

	Nominations	Wins
Michael Stewart	7	2
James Lapine	4	3
Hugh Wheeler	4	3
Betty Comden	3	1
Adolph Green	3	1
George Abbott	3	3

BEST SCORE (MUSIC AND/OR LYRICS) — MUSICAL

	Nominations	Wins
Stephen Sondheim	9	6
Andrew Lloyd Webber	9	3
Cy Coleman	6	3
Fred Ebb	5	2
John Kander	5	2
Tim Rice	4	1
Richard Maltby, Jr.	4	0
Charles Strouse	4	1
Stephen Schwartz	4	0

Source: The American Theatre Wing

The Obie Awards

The Obie Awards, administered by New York's *Village Voice,* recognize distin-guished achievement in Off-Broadway and Off-Off-Broadway productions. The Obies honor people and productions in informally structured award categories.

1955–1956

BEST NEW PLAY
Lionel Abel, *Absalom*

BEST ALL-AROUND PRODUCTION
Uncle Vanya

BEST MUSICAL
The Threepenny Opera

BEST DIRECTOR
José Quintero, *The Iceman Cometh*

BEST ACTOR (TIE)
Jason Robards, Jr., *The Iceman Cometh*
George Voskevec, *Uncle Vanya*

BEST ACTRESS
Julie Bovasso, *The Maids*

BEST SUPPORTING ACTOR
Gerald Hiken, *The Cherry Orchard* and *Uncle Vanya*

BEST SUPPORTING ACTRESS
Peggy McCay, *Uncle Vanya*

DISTINGUISHED PERFORMANCES (ACTORS)
Alan Ansara, *The Private Life of the Master Race*
Roberts Blossom, *A Village Wooing*
Addison Powell, *The Iceman Cometh*

DISTINGUISHED PERFORMANCES (ACTRESSES)
Shirlee Emmons, *The Mother of Us All*
Frances Sternhagen, *The Admirable Basheville*
Nancy Wickwire, *The Cherry Orchard*

FOR HIGH TECHNICAL ACCOMPLISHMENT IN SETS, LIGHTING AND COSTUMES
Klaus Holm and Alvin Cold (Phoenix Theatre)

1956–1957

BEST NEW PLAY
Louis A. Lippa, *A House Remembered*

BEST ALL-AROUND PRODUCTION
Exiles

BEST DIRECTOR
Gene Frankel, *Volpone*

BEST ACTOR
William Smithers, *The Sea Gull*

BEST ACTRESS
Colleen Dewhurst, *The Taming of the Shrew, The Eagle Has Two Heads* and *Camille*

Arthur Miller

DISTINGUISHED PERFORMANCES (ACTORS)
Thayer David, *Saint Joan* and *Oscar Wilde*
Michael Kane, *Exiles*
Arthur Malet, *Volpone, The Misanthrope* and *The Apollo of Bellac*

DISTINGUISHED PERFORMANCES (ACTRESSES)
Marguerite Lenery, *House of Breath*
Betty Miller, *Exiles*
Jutta Wolf, *Exiles*

1957–1958

BEST PLAY (ADAPTATION)
Boris Tumarin and Jack Sydow, *The Brothers Karamazov*

BEST REVIVAL
Arthur Miller, *The Crucible*

BEST ONE-ACT PLAY
Neil McKenzie, *Guests of the Nation*

BEST COMEDY
George Panetta, *Comic Strip*

BEST FOREIGN PLAY
Samuel Beckett, *Endgame*

BEST DIRECTOR
Stuart Vaughan, New York Shakespeare Festival

BEST ACTOR
George C. Scott, *Richard III, As You Like It* and
    Children of Darkness

BEST ACTRESS
Anne Meacham, *Garden District*

DISTINGUISHED PERFORMANCES (ACTORS)
Jack Cannon, New York Shakespeare Festival and
    Children of Darkness

Leonardo Cimino, *The Brothers Karamazov*

Robert Geiringer, New York Shakespeare Festival and
    Guests of the Nation

Michael Higgins, *The Crucible*

DISTINGUISHED PERFORMANCES (ACTRESSES)
Tammy Grimes, *Clerambard*

Grania O'Malley, *Guests of the Nation*

Nydia Westman, *Endgame*

1958–1959

BEST NEW PLAY
Brendan Behan, *The Quare Fellow*

BEST ALL-AROUND PRODUCTION
Ivanov

BEST MUSICAL
A Party With Betty Comden and Adolph Green

BEST REVUE
Steven Vinaver, *Diversions*

BEST DIRECTOR (AMERICAN PLAY)
Jack Ragotzy, Arthur Laurents cycle

BEST DIRECTOR (FOREIGN PLAY)
William Ball, *Ivanov*

BEST ACTOR
Alfred Ryder, *I Rise in Flame, Cried the Phoenix*

BEST ACTRESS
Kathleen Maguire, *The Time of the Cuckoo*

DISTINGUISHED PERFORMANCES (ACTORS)
Zero Mostel, *Ulysses in Nighttown*

Lester Rawlins, *The Quare Fellow*

Harold Scott, *Deathwatch*

DISTINGUISHED PERFORMANCES (ACTRESSES)
Rosina Fernhoff, *Fashion* and *The Geranium Hat*

Anne Fielding, *Ivanov*

Nancy Wickwire, *A Clearing in the Woods*

BEST MUSIC
David Amram

BEST OPEN-STAGE SET
David Hays, *The Quare Fellow*

BEST PROSCENIUM SET
Will Stevens Armstrong, *Ivanov*

BEST LIGHTING
Nikola Cernovich

Brendan Behan

1959–1960

BEST NEW PLAY
Jack Gelber, *The Connection*

BEST ALL-AROUND PRODUCTION
The Connection

BEST FOREIGN PLAY
Jean Genet, *The Balcony*

DISTINGUISHED PLAYS
Edward Albee, *The Zoo Story*

Samuel Beckett, *Krapp's Last Tape*

Jack Richardson, *The Prodigal*

BEST DIRECTOR
Gene Frankel, *Machinal*

BEST ACTOR
Warren Finnerty, *The Connection*

BEST ACTRESS
Eileen Brennan, *Little Mary Sunshine*

DISTINGUISHED PERFORMANCES (ACTORS)
William Daniels, *The Zoo Story*

Donald Davis, *Krapp's Last Tape*

Vincent Gardenia, *Machinal*

John Heffernan, *Henry IV, Part 2*

Jock Livingston, *The Balcony*

DISTINGUISHED PERFORMANCES (ACTRESSES)
Patricia Falkenhain, *Peer Gynt* and *Henry IV*

Elisa Loti, *Come Share My House*

Nancy Marchand, *The Balcony*

SETS
David Hays, *The Balcony*

1960–1961

BEST NEW PLAY
Jean Genet, *The Blacks*

BEST OVERALL PRODUCTION
Hedda Gabler

BEST OFF-OFF-BROADWAY PRODUCTION
The Premise

BEST DIRECTOR
Gerald A. Freedman, *The Taming of the Shrew*

BEST ACTOR
Khigh Dhiegh, *In the Jungle of Cities*

BEST ACTRESS
Anne Meacham, *Hedda Gabler*

DISTINGUISHED PERFORMANCES (ACTORS)
Godfrey M. Cambridge, *The Blacks*

James Coco, *The Moon in the Yellow River*

Lester Rawlins, *Hedda Gabler*

DISTINGUISHED PERFORMANCES (ACTRESSES)
Joan Hackett, *Call Me by My Rightful Name*

Gerry Jedd, *She Stoops to Conquer*

Surya Kumari, *The King of the Darn Chamber*

BEST MUSIC
Teiji Ito, *In the Jungle of Cities, Three Modern Japanese Plays* and *Ubu*

1961–1962

BEST AMERICAN PLAY
Frank D. Gilroy, *Who'll Save the Plowboy?*

BEST MUSICAL
Fly Blackbird, C. Jackson, James Hatch and Jerome Eskow

BEST FOREIGN PLAY
Samuel Beckett, *Happy Days* (Walter Kerr abstaining)

BEST ACTORS
James Earl Jones, *Clandestine on the Morning Line, The Apple* and *Moon on a Rainbow Shawl*

BEST ACTRESS
Barbara Harris, *Oh, Dad, Poor Dad, Mamma's Hung You in the Closet and I'm Feelin' So Sad*

DISTINGUISHED PERFORMANCES (ACTORS)
Clayton Corzatte, APA Repertory

Geoff Garland, *The Hostage*

Gerald O'Loughlin, *Who ll Save the Plowboy?*

Paul Roebling, *This Side of Paradise*

DISTINGUISHED PERFORMANCES (ACTRESSES)
Sudie Bond, *Theatre of the Absurd*

Vinnette Carroll, *Moon on a Rainbow Shawl*

Rosemary Harris, APA Repertory

Ruth White, *Happy Days*

BEST SET
Norris Houghton, *Who'll Save the Plowboy?*

1962–1963

BEST PRODUCTION (PLAY)
Luigi Pirandello, *Six Characters in Search of an Author*

BEST PRODUCTION (MUSICAL)
The Boys From Syracuse

BEST DIRECTOR
Alan Schneider, *The Pinter Plays*

BEST ACTOR
George C. Scott, *Desire Under the Elms*

BEST ACTRESS
Colleen Dewhurst, *Desire Under the Elms*

DISTINGUISHED PERFORMANCES
Jacqueline Brookes, *Six Characters in Search of an Author*

Joseph Chaikin, *A Man's a Man*

Olympia Dukakis, *A Man's a Man*

Anne Jackson, *The Typists* and *The Tiger*

Michael O'Sullivan, *Six Characters in Search of an Author*

James Patterson, *The Collection: The Pinter Plays*

Madeleine Sherwood, *Hey You, Light Man!*

Eli Wallach, *The Typists* and *The Tiger*

1963–1964

BEST PLAY
Samuel Beckett, *Play*

BEST AMERICAN PLAY
Le Roi Jones, *Dutchman*

BEST PRODUCTION (PLAY)
The Brig

BEST PRODUCTION (MUSICAL)
What Happened

DISTINGUISHED PLAYS
Rosalyn Drexler, *Home Movies*

Adrienne Kennedy, *Funnyhouse of a Negro*

BEST DIRECTION
Judith Malina, *The Brig*

DISTINGUISHED DIRECTION
Lawrence Kornfeld, *What Happened*

BEST PERFORMANCE
Gloria Foster, *In White America*

DISTINGUISHED PERFORMANCES
Philip Bruns, *Mr. Simian*

Joyce Ebert, *The Trojan Women*

Lee Grant, *The Maids*

David Hurst, *A Month in the Country*

Taylor Mead, *The General Returns From One Place to Another*

Estelle Parsons, *Next Time I'll Sing to You* and *In the Summer House*

Diana Sands, *The Living Premise*

Marian Seldes, *The Ginger Man*

Jack Warden, *Epiphany*

Ronald Weyland, *The Lesson*

BEST MUSIC
Al Carmines, *Home Movies* and *What Happened*

BEST DESIGN
Julian Beck, *The Brig*

1964–1965

BEST AMERICAN PLAY
Robert Lowell, *The Old Glory*

BEST MUSICAL PRODUCTION
The Cradle Will Rock

DISTINGUISHED PLAYS
Maria Irene Fornes, *Promenade* and *The Successful Life of Three*

BEST DIRECTION
Ulu Grosbard, *A View From the Bridge*

BEST PERFORMANCES
Roscoe Lee Browne, Frank Langella and Lester Rawlins, *The Old Glory*

DISTINGUISHED PERFORMANCES
Brian Bedford, *The Knock*

Roberts Blossom, *Do Not Pass Go*

Joseph Chaikin, *Victims of Duty* and *The Exception and the Rule*

Margaret De Priest, *The Place for Chance*

Dean Dittmann, *The Cradle Will Rock*

Robert Duvall, *A View From the Bridge*

Rosemary Harris, APA Repertory

James Earl Jones, *Beal*

Frances Sternhagen, *The Room* and *A Slight Ache*

Sada Thompson, *Tartuffe*

BEST COSTUMES
Willa Kim, *The Old Glory*

1965–1966

BEST AMERICAN PLAY
Ronald Ribman, *The Journey of the Fifth Horse*

DISTINGUISHED PLAYS
Emanuel Peluso, *Good Day*

Sam Shepard, *Chicago, Icarus's Mother* and *Red Cross*

DISTINGUISHED DIRECTION
Remy Charlip, *A Beautiful Day*

Jacques Levy, *You're Only as Old as Your Arteries, Red Cross* and *The Next Thing*

BEST ACTOR
Dustin Hoffman, *The Exhaustion of Our Son's Love*

BEST ACTRESS
Jane White, *Coriolanus* and *Love's Labour's Lost*

DISTINGUISHED PERFORMANCES
Clarice Blackburn, *The Exhaustion of Our Son's Love*

Mari-Claire Charba, *Birdbath*

Gloria Foster, *Medea*

Sharon Gans, *Soon Jack November*

Frank Langella, *Good Day* and *The White Devil*

Michael Lipton, *The Trigon*

Kevin O'Connor, *Chicago*

Jess Osuna, *Bugs* and *Veronica*

Florence Tarlow, *Istanbul, Red Cross* and *A Beautiful Day*

Douglas Turner, *Days of Absence*

SET DESIGN
Lindsey Decker, *Red Cross*

Ed Wittstein, *Serjeant Musgrace's Dance*

1966–1967

DISTINGUISHED PLAYS
Henry Livings, *Eh?*

Rochelle Owens, *Futz*

Sam Shepard, *La Turista*

BEST DIRECTOR
Tom O'Horgan, *Futz*

BEST ACTOR
Seth Allen, *Futz*

DISTINGUISHED PERFORMANCES
Tom Aldredge, *Measure for Measure* and *Stock Up on Pepper Cause Turkey's Going to War*

Robert Bonnard, *The Chairs*

Alvin Epstein, *Dynamite Tonite*

Neil Flanagan, *The Madness of Lady Bright*

Bette Henritze, *Measure for Measure,* the Wilder plays, *The Distinguished Person* and *The Rimers of Eldrich*

Stacy Keach, *MacBird!*

Terry Kiser, *Fortune and Men's Eyes*

Eddie McCarthy, *Kitchenette*

Robert Salvio, *Hemp*

Rip Torn, *The Deer Park*

BEST LIGHTING
John Dodd, *The White W, The Madness of Lady Bright* and Charles Dickens' *"Christmas Carol"*

1967–1968

DISTINGUISHED PLAYS
John Guare, *Muzzeha*

Israel Horovitz, *The Indian Wants the Bronz*

Sam Shepard, *Forensic and the Navigator* and *Melodrama Play*

BEST MUSICAL
Gertrude Stein and Al Carmines, *In Circles*

BEST FOREIGN PLAY
Vaclav Havel, *The Memorandum*

BEST DIRECTOR
Michael A. Schultz, *Song of the Lusitanian Bogey*

DISTINGUISHED DIRECTION
John Hancock, *A Midsummer Night's Dream*

Rip Torn, *The Beard*

BEST ACTOR
Al Pacino, *The Indian Wants the Bronz*

BEST ACTRESS
Billie Dixon, *The Beard*

DISTINGUISHED PERFORMANCES
John Cazale, *Line* and *The Indian Wants the Bronx*

James Coco, *Fragments*

Jean David, *Istanbul*

Cliff Gorman, *The Boys in the Band*

Mari Gorman, *The Memorandum* and *Walking to Waldheim*

Moses Gunn, The Negro Ensemble Company repertory

Peggy Pope, *Maaamama*

Roy R. Scheider, *Stephen D.*

BEST DESIGN
Robert LaVigne, *A Midsummer Night's Dream* and *Endecott and the Red Circus*

1968–1969

There were no category classifications this year.

Julian Beck, *Antigone*

Julie Bovasso, *Gloria and Esperansa*

Jules Feiffer, *Little Murders*

Nathan George and Ron O'Neal, *No Place to Be Somebody*

Israel Horovitz, *The Honest-to-God Schnozzola*

The Living Theatre, *Frankenstein*

Judith Molina, *Antigone*

OM Theatre, *Riot*

Open Theatre, *The Serpent*

Performance group, *Dionysus in '69*

Arlene Rothlein, *The Poor Little Match Girl*

Ronald Tavel, *The Boy on the Straight Back Chair*

Theatre Genesis, sustained excellence

Jeff Weiss, *The International Wrestling Match*

1969–1970

BEST AMERICAN PLAY
Megan Terry, *Approaching Simone*

Paul Zindel, *The Effect of Gamma Rays on Man-in-the-Moon Marigolds*

BEST MUSICAL
Gretchen Cryer and Nancy Ford, *The Last Sweet Days of Isaac*

Robert Livingston, Gary William Friedman and Will Holt, *The Me Nobody Knows*

BEST FOREIGN PLAY
Joe Orton, *What the Butler Saw*

DISTINGUISHED PLAYS
Vaclav Havel, *The Increased Difficulty of Concentration*

Murray Mednick, *The Deer Kill*

DISTINGUISHED DIRECTION
Alan Arkin, *The White House Murder Case*

Melvin Bernhardt, *The Effect of Gamma Rays on Man-in-the-Moon Marigolds*

Maxine Klein, *Approaching Simone*

Gilbert Moses, *Slave Ship*

BEST PERFORMANCE
Sada Thompson, *The Effect of Gamma Rays on Man-in-the-Moon Marigolds*

Alan Arkin

DISTINGUISHED PERFORMANCES
Beeson Carroll, *The Unseen Hand*

Vincent Gardenia, *Passing Through Exotic Places*

Harold Gould, *The Increased Difficulty of Concentration*

Anthony Holland, *The White House Murder Case*

Lee Kissman, *The Unseen Hand*

Ron Leibman, *Transfers*

Roberta Maxwell, *Whistle in the Dark*

Rue McClanahan, *Who's Happy Now?*

Pamela Payton-Wright, *The Effect of Gamma Rays on Man-in-the-Moon Marigolds*

Austin Pendleton, *The Last Sweet Days of Isaac*

Fredericka Weber, *The Last Sweet Days of Isaac*

1970–1971

BEST AMERICAN PLAY
John Guare, *House of Blue Leaves*

BEST FOREIGN PLAY
Athol Fugard, *Boesman and Lena*

Derek Walcott, *Dream on Monkey Mountain*

Heathcote Williams, *AC/DC*

DISTINGUISHED PLAYS
Ed Bullins, *The Fabulous Miss Maria* and *In New England Winter*

David Rabe, *Basic Training of Pavlo Hummel*

DISTINGUISHED PRODUCTION
The Trial of the Catonsville 9

DISTINGUISHED DIRECTION
John Berry, *Boesman and Lena*

Jeff Bleckner, *Basic Training of Pavlo Hummel*

Gordon Davidson, *The Trial of the Catonsville 9*

John Hirsch, *AC/DC*

Larry Kornfeld, *Dracular Sabbat*

BEST PERFORMANCE BY AN ACTOR
Jack MacGowran, *Beckett*

BEST PERFORMANCE BY AN ACTRESS
Ruby Dee, *Boesman and Lena*

DISTINGUISHED PERFORMANCES
Susan Batson, *AC/DC*

Margaret Braidwood, *Saved*

Hector Elizondo, *Steambath*

Donald Ewer, *Saved*

Sonny Jim, *The Fabulous Miss Marie*

Stacy Keach, *Long Day's Journey Into Night*

Kirk Kirksey, consistent excellence of performance

Harris Laskawy, *Uncle Vanya*

Joan MacIntosh, *Commune*

William Schallert, *The Trial of the Catonsville 9*

James Woods, *Saved*

SET DESIGN
John Scheffler, *AC/DC*

1971–1972

BEST THEATER PIECE
The Open Theatre, *The Mutation Show*

DISTINGUISHED DIRECTION
Wilford Leach and John Braswell, *The Only Jealousy of Emer*

Mel Shapiro, *Two Gentlemen of Verona*

Michael Smith, *Country Music*

Tom Sydorick, *20th Century Tar*

DISTINGUISHED PERFORMANCES
Salome Bey, *Love Me, Love My Children*

Maurice Blanc, *The Celebrations: Joos/Guns/Movies/
    The Abyss*

Alex Bradford, *Don't Bother Me, I Can't Cope*

Marilyn Chris, *Kaddish*

Ron Faber, *And They Put Handcuffs on Flowers*

Jeanne Hepple, *The Reliquary of Mr. and Mrs. Potterfield*

Danny Sewell, *The Homecoming*

Marilyn Sokol, *The Beggar's Opera*

Kathleen Widdoes, *The Beggar's Opera*

Elizabeth Wilson, *Sticks and Bones*

Ed Zang, *The Reliquary of Mr. and Mrs. Potterfield*

MUSIC AND LYRICS
Micki Grant, *Don't Bother Me, I Can't Cope*

COMPOSER
Liz Swados, *Medea*

VISUAL EFFECTS
Video Free America, *Kaddish*

1972–1973

BEST AMERICAN PLAY
Joseph A. Walker, *The River Niger*

Lanford Wilson, *The Hot L Baltimore*

BEST FOREIGN PLAY
Samuel Beckett, *Not I*

Peter Handke, *Kaspar*

Ruby Dee

DISTINGUISHED PLAYS
J.E. Gaines, *What if It Had Turned up Heads?*

Sam Shepard, *The Tooth of Crime*

Ronald Tavel, *Big Foot*

DISTINGUISHED DIRECTION
Jack Gelber, *The Kid*

William E. Lathan, *What if It Had Turned up Heads?*

Marshall W. Mason, *The Hot L Baltimore*

DISTINGUISHED PERFORMANCES
Hume Cronyn, *Krapp's Last Tape*

Mari Gorman, *The Hot L Baltimore*

James Hilbrandt, *A Boy Named Dog*

Stacy Keach, *Hamlet*

Christopher Lloyd, *Kaspar*

Charles Ludlam, *Corn* and *Camille*

Lola Pashalinski, *Corn*

Alice Playten, *Lemmings*

Roxie Roker, *The River Niger*

Jessica Tandy, *Not I*

Douglas Turner Ward, *The River Niger*

Sam Waterston, *Much Ado About Nothing*

1973–1974

BEST AMERICAN PLAY
Miguel Pinero, *Short Eyes*

BEST FOREIGN PLAY
David Storey, *The Contractor*

DISTINGUISHED PLAYS
Paul Carter Harrison, *The Great MacDaddy*

Terrence McNally, *Bad Habits*

Mark Medoff, *When You Comin' Back, Red Ryder?*

DISTINGUISHED DIRECTION
Marvin Felix Camillo, *Short Eyes*

Robert Drivas, *Bad Habits*

David Light, *Hard to Be a Jew*

John Pasquin, *Moonchildren*

Harold Prince, *Candide*

DISTINGUISHED PERFORMANCES
Barbara Barrie, *The Killdeer*

Joseph Buloff, *Hard to Be a Jew*

Kevin Conway, *When You Comin' Back, Red Ryder*

Conchata Ferrell, *The Sea Horse*

Loretta Greene, *The Sirens*

Barbara Montgomery, *My Sister, My Sister*

Zipora Spaizman, *Stepemyu*

Elizabeth Sturges, *When You Comin' Back, Red Ryder*

MUSIC
Bill Elliott, *C.O.R.F.A.X.*

COSTUMES
Theoni Aldredge (The Public Theatre)

SET DESIGN
Holmes Easley (The Roundabout Theatre)

Christopher Thomas, *The Lady From the Sea*

1974–1975

BEST NEW AMERICAN PLAY
Leslie Lee, *The First Breeze of Summer*

PLAYWRITING
Ed Bullins, *The Taking of Miss Janie*

Wallace Shawn, *Our Late Night*

Sam Shepard, *Action*

Lanford Wilson, *The Mound Builders*

DIRECTION
Lawrence Kornfeld, *Listen to Me*

Marshall W. Mason, *Battle of Angels* and *The Mound Builders*

Gilbert Moses, *The Talking of Miss Janie*

PERFORMANCES
Tanya Berezin, *The Mound Builders*

Cara Duff-MacCormick, *Craig's Wife*

Tovah Feldshuh, *Yentl the Yeshiva Boy*

Moses Gunn, *The First Breeze of Summer*

Dick Latessa, *Philemon*

Kevin McCarthy, *Harry Outside*

Stephen D. Newman, *Polly*

Reyno, *The First Breeze of Summer*

Priscilla Smith, *Trilogy*

Ian Trigger, *The True History of Squire Jonathan*

Christopher Walken, *Kid Champion*

DESIGN
John Lee Beatty, distinguished set design, *Down by the River . . ., Battle of Angels* and *The Mound Builders*

Robert U. Taylor, distinguished set design, *Polly*

SPECIAL 20-YEAR OBIES
Judith Malina and Julian Beck

Ted Mann and the Circle in the Square

Joseph Papp

Ellen Stewart

The Fantasticks

1975–1976

BEST NEW AMERICAN PLAYS
David Mamet, *American Buffalo* and *Sexual Perversity in Chicago*

BEST THEATER PIECE
Richard Foreman, *Rhoda in Potatoland*

DIRECTION
JoAnne Akalaitis, *Cassandra*

Marshall Mason, *Knock Kryla* and *Serenading Louie*

PERFORMANCES
Joyce Aaron, *Academics*

Roberts Blossom, *Ice Age*

Robert Christian, *Blood*

Crystal Field, *Day Old Bread*

June Gable, *Comedy of Errors*

Mike Kellin, *American Buffalo*

Tony Lo Bianco, *Yanks 3 Detroit 0 Top of the Seventh*

Priscilla Lopez, *A Chorus Line*

Kate Manheim, *Rhoda in Potatoland*

T. Miratti, *The Shortchanged Review*

Pamela Payton-Wright, *Jesus and the Bandit Queen*

Priscilla Smith, *Good Woman of Setzuan*

David Warrilow, *The Warrilow* and *The Last Ones*

Sammy Williams, *A Chorus Line*

1976–1977

BEST NEW AMERICAN PLAY
Sam Shepard, *Curse of the Starving Class*

DISTINGUISHED PRODUCTIONS
Eve Merriam, playwright; Tommy Tune, director; Kate Carmel, costume designer; entire cast, *The Club*

Ntozake Shange, poet; Oz Scott, director; entire cast, *For Colored Girls Who Have Considered Suicide When the Rainbow Is Enuf*

Mabou Mines, *Dressed Like an Egg*

PLAYWRITING
David Berry, *G.R. Point*

Maria Irene Fornes, *Fefu and Her Friends*

William Hauptmann, *Domino Courts*

Albert Innaurato, *German* and *The Transfiguration of Benno Blimpie*

David Rudkin, *Ashes*

DIRECTION
Melvin Bernhardt, *Children*

Gordon Davidson, *Savages*

PERFORMANCES
Danny Aiello, *German*

Martin Balsam, *Cold Storage*

Lucinda Childs, *Einstein on the Beach*

James Coco, *The Transfiguration of Benno Blimpie*

Anne DeSalvo, *German*

John Heard, *G.R. Point*

Jo Henderson, *Ladyhouse Blues*

William Hurt, *My Life*

Joseph Maher, *Savages*

Roberta Maxwell, *Ashes*

Brian Murray, *Ashes*

Lola Pashalinski, *Der Ring Gott Farblonjet*

Martin Seldes, *Isadora Duncan Sleeps With the Russian Navy*

Margaret Wright, *A Manoir*

1977–1978

BEST NEW AMERICAN PLAY
Lee Breuer, *Shaggy Dog Animation*

DIRECTION
Robert Allan Ackerman, *Prayer for My Daughter*

Thomas Bullard, *Statements After an Arrest Under the Immorality Act*

Elizabeth Swados, *Runaways*

PERFORMANCES
Richard Bauer, *Landscape of the Body* and *The Dybbuk*

Nell Carter, *Ain't Misbehavin'*

Alma Cuervo, *Uncommon Women*

Swoosie Kurtz, *Uncommon Women*

Kaiulani Lee, *Safe House*

Bruce Myers, *The Dybbuk*

Lee S. Wilkof, *The Present Tense*

DESIGN
Garland Wright and John Arnone, *K*

Robert Yudice, *Museum*

LIFETIME ACHIEVEMENT
Peter Schumann's Bread & Puppet Theatre

1978–1979

BEST NEW AMERICAN PLAY
Michael McClure, *Josephine*

PLAYWRITING
Rosalyn Drexler, *The Writer's Opera*

Susan Miller, *Nasty Rumors* and *Final Remarks*

Richard Nelson, *Vienna Notes*

Bernard Pomerance, *The Elephant Man*

Sam Shepard, *Buried Child*

DIRECTION
Maria Irene Fornes, *Eyes on the Harem*

Jack Holssiss, *The Elephant Man*

PERFORMANCES
Mary Alice, *Nongogo* and *Julius Caesar*

Philip Anglim, *The Elephant Man*

Joseph Buloff, *The Price*

Constance Cummings, *Wings*

Fred Gwynne, *Grand Magic*

Judd Hirsch, *Talley's Folly*

Marcell Rosenblatt, *Vienna Notes*

Elizabeth Wilson, *Taken in Marriage*

DESIGN
Theatre X, set design and lighting design, *A Fierce Longing*

Jennifer Tipton, Public Theatre, set design and lighting design

SUSTAINED ACHIEVEMENT
Al Carmines

1979–1980

PLAYWRITING
Lee Breuer, *A Prelude to Death in Venice*

Christopher Durang, *Sister Mary Ignatius Explains It All for You*

Romulus Linney, *Tennessee*

Roland Muldoon, *Full Confessions of a Socialist*

Jeff Weiss, *That's How the Rent Gets Paid* (Part Three)

DIRECTION
A. J. Antoon, *The Art of Dining*

Edward Cornell, *Johnny on a Spot*

Elizabeth LeCompte, *Point Judith*

PERFORMANCES
Michael Burrell, *Hess*

Michael Cristofer, *Chinchilla*

Lindsay Crouse, *Reunion*

Elizabeth Franz, *Sister Mary Ignatius Explains It All for You*

Morgan Freeman, *Mother Courage* and *Coriolanus*

John Heard, *Othello* and *Split*

Michael Higgins, *Reunion*

Madeleine Le Houx, *La Justice*

Jon Polito, performances with Dodger Theatre Company and the BAM Theater Company

Bill Raymond, *A Prelude to Death in Venice*

Dianne Wiest, *The Art of Dining*

Hattie Winston, *Mother Courage* and *The Michigan*

DESIGN
Laura Crow, costume design, *Mary Stuart*

Beverly Emmons, distinguished lighting design

Sally Jacobs, *Conference of the Birds*

Ruth Maleczech and Julie Archer, *Vanishing Pictures*

SUSTAINED ACHIEVEMENT
Sam Shepard

1980–1981

BEST NEW AMERICAN PLAY
David Henry Hwang, *FOB*

BEST PRODUCTION
Emily Mann, *Still Life*

PLAYWRITING
Charles Fuller, *Zooman and the Sign*

Amlin Gray, *How I Got That Story*

Len Jenkin, *Limbo Tales*

DIRECTION
Melvin Bernhardt, *Crimes of the Heart*

Wilford Leach, *The Pirates of Penzance*

Toby Robertson, *Pericles*

Meryl Streep

PERFORMANCES
Giancarlo Esposito, *Zooman and the Sign*
Bob Gunton, *How I Got That Story*
Mary Beth Hurt, *Crimes of the Heart*
Kevin Kline, *The Pirates of Penzance*
John Lone, *FOB* and *The Dance and the Railroad*
Mary McDonnell, *Still Life*
Timothy Near, *Still Life*
William Sadler, *Limbo Tales*
Michele Shay, *Meetings*
John Spencer, *Still Life*
Meryl Streep, *Alice in Concert*
Christopher Walken, *The Sea Gulf*

DESIGN
Bloolips, costume design, *Lust in Space*
Manuel Lutgenhorst and Douglas Ball, *Request Concert*
June Maeda, sustained excellence in set design
Donnie Perichy, sustained excellence in lighting design

SUSTAINED ACHIEVEMENT
Negro Ensemble Company

1981–1982

BEST NEW AMERICAN PLAYS
Metamorphosis in Miniature
Mr. Dead and Mrs. Free

BEST THEATER PIECE
Tadeusz Kantor, *Wielopole, Wielopole*

PLAYWRITING
Robert Auletta, *Stops* and *Virgins*
Caryl Churchill, *Cloud 9*

DIRECTION
Tommy Tune, *Cloud 9*

PERFORMANCES
Kevin Bacon, *Forty Deuce* and *Poor Little Lambs*
James Barbosa, *Soon Jack November*
Ray Dooley, *Peer Gynt*
Christine Estabrook, *Pastorale*
Michael Gross, *No End of Blame*
E. Katherine Karr, *Cloud 9*
Kenneth McMillan, *Weekends Like Other People*
Kevin O'Connor, *Chucky's Hunch, Birdbath* and *Crossing the Crab Nebula*
Carole Shelley, *Twelve Dreams*
Josef Sommer, *Lydie Breeze*
Irene Worth, *The Chalk Garden*

DISTINGUISHED ENSEMBLE PERFORMANCES
Lisa Banes, Brenda Currin, Elizabeth McGovern and Beverly May, *My Sister in This House*
Adolph Caesar, Larry Riley and Denzel Washington, *A Soldier's Play*

DESIGN
Jim Clayburgh, sustained excellence in set design
Arden Fingerhut, sustained excellence in lighting design

SUSTAINED ACHIEVEMENT
Maria Irene Fornes

1982–1983

BEST NEW AMERICAN PLAY
Tina Howe, Harry Kondoleon and David Mamet shared the $1,000 prize.

PLAYWRITING
Caryl Churchill, *Top Girls*
Tina Howe, distinguished playwriting
Harry Kondoleon, most promising young playwright
David Mamet, *Edmond*

DIRECTION
Gregory Mosher, *Edmond*
Gary Sinise, *True West*

PERFORMANCES
Ernest Abuba, *Yellow Fever*
Christine Baranski, *A Midsummer Night's Dream*
Glenn Close, *The Singular Life of Albert Nobbs*
Jeff Daniels, *Johnny Got His Gun*
Ruth Maleczech, *Haff*
John Malkovich, *True West*
Donald Moffat, *Painting Churches*
Harry Wise, *The Tooth of Crime*

ENSEMBLE PERFORMANCES
Kenneth Frankel, director; cast, *Quartermaine's Terms*
Max Sufford-Clark, director; Royal Court cast, *Top Girls*
The New York Shakespeare Festival cast, *Top Girls*

DESIGN
Heidi Landesman, *A Midsummer Night's Dream* and *Painting Churches*

SUSTAINED ACHIEVEMENT
Lanford Wilson, Marshall Mason and the Circle Repertory Company

1983–1984

BEST NEW AMERICAN PLAY
Sam Shepard, *Fool for Love*

BEST MUSICAL
Lee Bruer and Bob Telson, *Gospel at Colonus*

PLAYWRITING
Samuel Beckett, *Ohio Impromptu, What Where, Catastrophe* and *Pocket*
Maria Irene Fornes, *The Danube, Sarita* and *Mud*
Vaclav Havel, *A Private View*
Len Jenkin, *Five of Us*
Franz Xaver Kroetz, *Through the Leaves* and *Mensch Meier*
Ted Tally, *Terra Nova*

DIRECTION
JoAnne Akalaitis, *Through the Leaves*
Maria Irene Fornes, *The Danube, Sarita* and *Mud*
Lawrence Sacharow, *Five of Us*
Sam Shepard, *Fool for Love*

PERFORMANCES
F. Murray Abraham, *Uncle Vanya*
Kathy Baker, *Fool for Love*
Sheila Dabney, *Sarita*
Morgan Freeman, *Gospel at Colonus*
George Guidall, *Cinders*
Ed Harris, *Fool for Love*
Frederick Haumann, *Through the Leaves*
Richard Jordan, *A Private View*
Ruth Maleczech, *Through the Leaves*
Stephen McHattie, *Mensch Meier*
Will Patton, *Fool for Love*
Pamela Reed, sustained excellence of performance
Dianne Wiest, *Serenading Louie* and *Other Places*

DESIGN
Adrianne Lobel, set design, *The Vampires* and *All Night Long*
Anne Militello, sustained excellence of lighting design
Bill Stabile, set design, *Spookhouse, Damnee Hanon* and *Sacree Sandre*
Douglas Stein, set design, *Through the Leaves*

SUSTAINED ACHIEVEMENT
Music-Theatre Group/Lenox Arts Center

1984–1985

NEW AMERICAN PLAY
Maria Irene Fornes, *The Conduct of Life*

PLAYWRITING
Rosalyn Drexler, *Transients Welcome*
Christopher Durang, *The Marriage of Bette and Boo*
William M. Hoffman, *As Is*

DIRECTION
John Malkovich, *Balm in Gilead*
Barbara Vann, *Bound to Rise*
Jerry Zaks, *The Foreigner* and *The Marriage of Bette and Boo*

Eric Bogosian

PERFORMANCES
Dennis Boutsikaris, *The Nest of the Woodgrouse*
Frances Foster, sustained excellence in performance
Jonathan Hadary, *As Is*
Anthony Heald, *Henry V, The Foreigner* and *Digby*
Laurie Metcalf, *Balm in Gilead*
John Turturro, *Danny and the Deep Blue Sea*
Ron Vawter, sustained excellence in performance

ENSEMBLE PERFORMANCES
Charles Ludlam and Everett Quinton, *The Mystery of Irma Vep*
Entire cast, *The Marriage of Bette and Boo*

MUSIC
Peter Gordon, *Otello*
Max Roach, *Shepardsets*

DESIGN
Judy Dearing, costume design
Victor En Yu Tan, lighting design
Loren Sherman, set design

SUSTAINED ACHIEVEMENT
Meredith Monk

1985–1986

DISTINGUISHED PLAYWRITING
Wallace Shawn, *Aunt Dan and Lemon*

PLAYWRITING
Eric Bogosian, *Drinking in America*
Martha Clarke, *Vienna: Lusthaus*
John Jesurun, *Deep Sleep*
Tadeusz Kantor, *Let the Artist Die*
Lee Nagrin, *Bird/Bear*

DIRECTION
Richard Foreman, *Largo Desolato*

BEST PERFORMANCE
Swoosie Kurtz, *The House of Blue Leaves*

PERFORMANCES
Norma Aleandro, *About Love and Other Stories About Love*
Dylan Baker, *Not About Heroes*
Tom Cayler, *A Matter of Life and Death*
Jill Eikenberry, *Lemon Sky* and *Life Under Water*
Farley Granger, *Talley & Son*
Kathryn Posson, *Aunt Dan and Lemon*
Josef Sommer, *Largo Desolato*
Helen Stenborg, *Talley & Son*
Elisabeth Welch, *Time to Start Living*
Elizabeth Wilson, *Anteroom*

SUSTAINED EXCELLENCE IN PERFORMANCE
Edward Herrmann
Kevin Kline

DESIGN
Paul Gallo, lighting design
Edward T. Gianfrancesco, set design
Rita Ryack, costume design

SUSTAINED ACHIEVEMENT
Mabou Mines

1986–1987

BEST NEW AMERICAN PLAYS
Richard Foreman, *The Cure* and *Film Is Evil, Radio Is Good*

DIRECTION
Garland Wright, *On the Verge*

PERFORMANCES
Robin Bartlett, *The Early Girl*
Rob Besserer, *The Hunger Artist*
Morgan Freeman, *Driving Miss Daisy*
Laura Hicks, *On the Verge*
Anthony Holland, *The Hunger Artist*
Dana Ivey, *Driving Miss Daisy*
John Kelly, *Pass the Blutwurst* and *Bitte (The Egon Schiele Story)*
Gcina Mhlophe, *Born in the RSA*
Bill Raymond, *Cold Harbor*
Clarice Taylor, *Moms*

SUSTAINED EXCELLENCE OF PERFORMANCE
Blackeyed-Susan
Philip Bosco
Andrew Jackson

DESIGN
Paul Gallo, lighting design, *The Hunger Artist*
James F. Ingalls, sustained excellence of lighting design
Robert Israel, set and costume design, *The Hunger Artist*

SUSTAINED ACHIEVEMENT
Charles Ludlam and the Ridiculous Theatrical Company

1987–1988

BEST NEW AMERICAN PLAY
Caryl Churchill, *Serious Money*
Maria Irene Fornes, *Abingdon Square*

DIRECTION
Anne Bogart, *No Plays No Poetry . . .*
Peter Brook, *The Mahabharata*
Julie Taymor, *Juan Darien*

PERFORMANCES
Kathy Bates, *Frankie & Johnny in the Clair de Lune*
Larry Bazzell, *The Signal Season of Dummy Hoy*
Yvonne Bryceland, *The Road to Mecca*
Victor Garber, *Wenceslas Square*
Amy Irving, *The Road to Mecca*
Erland Josephson, *The Cherry Orchard*
Gordana Rashovich, *A Shayna Maidel*
John Seitz, *Abingdon Square*
Peggy Shaw, *Dress Suits to Hire*
Tina Shepard, *The Three Lives of Lucie Cabrol*
Lauren Tom, *American Notes*

DESIGN
Eva Buchmuller, sustained excellence of stage design
Huck Snyder, sustained excellence of scenic design

SUSTAINED ACHIEVEMENT
Richard Foreman

1988–1989

PLAYWRIGHTING
Intar Hispanic Playwrights-in-Residence Laboratory
The Frank Silva Writers Workshop

DIRECTION
Ingmar Bergman, *Hamlet*
Rene Buch, sustained excellence of direction
Peter Stein, *Falstaff*

PERFORMANCES
Mark Blum, *Gus and Al*
Niall Buggy, *Aristocrats*
William Converse-Roberts, *Love's Labor's Lost*
Fyvush Finkel, *Cafe Crown*
Gloria Foster, *The Forbidden City*
Paul Hecht, *Enrico IV*
Nancy Marchand, *The Cocktail Hour*
Tim McDonnell, *Diary of a Madman*
Kathy Najimy and Mo Gaffney, *The Kathy and Mo Show*
Will Patton, *What Did He See?*
Lonny Price, *The Immigrant*
Everett Quinton, *A Tale of Two Cities*
Rocco Sisto, *The Winter's Tale*

DESIGN
Gabriel Berry, sustained excellence of costume design
Donald Eastman, sustained excellence of set design

SUSTAINED ACHIEVEMENT
Irene Worth

1989–1990

BEST NEW AMERICAN PLAYS
Craig Lucas, *Prelude to a Kiss*
Suzan-Lori Parks, *Imperceptible Mutabilities in the Third Kingdom*
Mac Wellman, *Bad Penny*, *Crowbar* and *Terminal Hip*

DIRECTION
Liz Diamond, *Imperceptible Mutabilities in the Third Kingdom*
Norman Rene, *Prelude to a Kiss*
Jim Simpson, *Bad Penny*
George C. Wolfe, *Spunk*

PERFORMANCES
Alec Baldwin, *Prelude to a Kiss*
Elzbieta Czyzewska, *Crowbar*
Karen Evans-Kandel, *Lear*
Marcia Jean Kurtz, *The Loman Family Picnic* and
    When She Danced
Ruth Maleczech, *Lear*
Greg Mehrten, *Lear*
Stephen Mellor, *Terminal Hip*
Isabell Monk, *Lear*
Jean Stapleton, *Mountain Language* and *The Birthday Party*
Pamela Tyson, *Imperceptible Mutabilities in the Third Kingdom*
Courtney B. Vance, *My Children! My Africa!*
Danitra Vance, *Spunk*
Lillias White, *Romance in Hard Times*
Mary Shultz, sustained excellence in performance

DESIGN
Daniel Moses Schreler, sustained excellence of sound design
George Tsypin, sustained excellence of set design

SUSTAINED ACHIEVEMENT
Money awarded to ACT-UP for the fight against AIDS

1990–1991

BEST NEW AMERICAN PLAY
Wallace Shawn, *The Fever*

PLAYWRITING
John Guare, *Six Degrees of Separation*
Mac Wellma, *Sincerity Forever*

DIRECTION
Michael Grief, *Machinal*
Lisa Peterson, *Light Shining in Buckinghamshire*

PERFORMANCES
Eileen Atkins, *A Room of One's Own*
Stockard Channing, *Six Degrees of Separation*
Joan Copeland, *The American Plan*
Angela Goethals, *The Good Times Are Killing Me*
Tony Goldwyn, *The Sum of Us*
Jan Leslie Harding, *Sincerity Forever*
John Leguizamo, *Mambo Mouth*
Michael Lombard, *What's Wrong With This Picture?*

Jodie Markell, *Machinal*
Anne Pitoniak, *Pygmalion*
Ron Rifkin, *The Substance of Fire*
Kathleen Widdoes, *Tower of Evil*
Betty Bourne, Precious Pearl, Peggy Shaw and Lois Weaver,
    ensemble performance, *Belle Reprieve*

DESIGN
Frances Aronson, sustained excellence of lighting design
Mark Board, sustained excellence of set design
William Ivey Long, sustained excellence of costume design
John Gromada, sound design, *Machinal*

SUSTAINED ACHIEVEMENT
The Wooster Group

1991–1992

BEST NEW AMERICAN PLAYS (TIE)
Donald Margulies, *Sight Unseen*
Robbie McCauley, *Sally's Rape*
Paula Vogel, *The Baltimore Waltz*

PLAYWRITING
Neal Bell, sustained excellence
Romulus Linney, sustained excellence

DIRECTION
Anne Bogart, *The Baltimore Waltz*
Mark Wing-Davy, *Mad Forest*

PERFORMANCES
Dennis Boutsikaris, *Sight Unseen*
Larry Bryggman, sustained excellence of performance
Randy Danson, sustained excellence of performance
Laura Esterman, *Marvin's Room*
Ofelia Gonzales, sustained excellence of performance
Deborah Hedwall, *Sight Unseen*
Cherry Jones, *The Baltimore Waltz*

Stockard Channing

Nathan Lane, sustained excellence of performance

James McDaniel, *Before It Hits Home*

S. Epatha Merkerson, *I'm Not Stupid*

Roger Rees, *The End of the Day*

Lynne Thigpen, *Boesman and Lena*

DESIGN

John Arnone, sustained excellence of set design

Marina Dragnici, sets and costumes, *Mad Forest*

SUSTAINED ACHIEVEMENT

Athol Fugard

1992–1993

PLAYWRITING

Harry Kondoleon, *The Houseguests*

Larry Kramer, *The Destiny of Me*

José Rivera, *Marisol*

Paul Rudnick, *Jeffrey*

DIRECTION

Christopher Ashley, *Jeffrey*

Michael Maggio, *Wings*

Frederick Zollo, *Aven' U Boys*

PERFORMANCES

Jane Alexander, *The Sisters Rosensweig*

Miriam Colon, sustained excellence of performance

Frances Conroy, *The Last Yankee*

David Drake, *The Night Larry Kramer Kissed Me*

Giancarlo Esposito, *Distant Fires*

Geoffrey C. Ewing, *Ali*

Hallie Foote, *The Roads to Home*

Edward Hibbert, *Jeffrey*

Bill Irwin, *Texts for Nothing*

John Cameron Mitchell, *The Destiny of Me*

Ellen Parker, sustained achievement of performance

Linda Stephens, *Wings*

DESIGN

Loy Arcenas, sustained excellence of set design

Howard Thies, sustained excellence of lighting design

SUSTAINED ACHIEVEMENT

JoAnne Akalaitis

1993–1994

BEST PLAY

Anna Deavere Smith, *Twilight: Los Angeles, 1992*

PLAYWRITING

Eric Bogosian, *Pounding Nails in the Floor With My Forehead*

Howard Korder, *The Lights*

DIRECTION

Andre Ernotte, *Christina Aberta's Father*

David Warren, *Pterodactyls*

PERFORMANCES

Carolee Carmello, *Hello Again*

Myra Carter, *Three Tall Women*

Gail Grate, *The America Play*

Danny Hoch, *Some People*

Judith Ivey, *The Moonshot Tape*

Peter Francis James, *The Maids*

Jefferson Mays, *Orestes*

Christopher McCann, *The Lights*

Tom Nelis, *The Medium*

Alice Playten, *The First Lady Suite*

Michael Potts, *The America Play*

Robert Stanton, *All in the Timing*

DESIGN

Kyle Chepulis, sustained excellence of set design

Brian MacDevitt, sustained excellence of lighting design

SUSTAINED ACHIEVEMENT

Edward Albee

1995

BEST PLAY

David Mamet, *Cryptogram*

PLAYWRITING

David Hancock, *The Convention of Cartography*

Tony Kushner, *Slavs!*

Terrence McNally, *Love! Valour! Compassion!*

Susan Miller, *My Left Breast*

DIRECTION

Robert Falls, *SubUrbia*

Don Scardino, *A Cheever Evening*

Susan Shulman, *Merrily We Roll Along*

PERFORMANCES

Joanna Adler, *The Boys in the Basement*

Eileen Atkins and Vanessa Redgrave, *Vita and Virginia*

Paul Calderon, *Blade to the Heart*

Malcolm Gets, *Merrily We Roll Along* and *Two Gentlemen of Verona*

Felicity Huffman, *Cryptogram*

Linda Lavin, *Death Defying Acts*

Ron Leibman, *The Merchant of Venice*

Camryn Manheim, *Missing Persons*

Joe Mantello, director; entire cast, *Love! Valour! Compassion!*

Kristine Nielsen, *Dog Opera*

Mary Beth Peil, *The Naked Truth, Missing Persons* and *A Cheever Evening*

Barbara Eda Young, *Slavs!*

DESIGN

Wendall K. Harrington, sustained excellence of projection

Jennifer von Mayrhauser, sustained excellence of costume design

SUSTAINED ACHIEVEMENT

Ming Cho Lee

New York Drama Critics' Circle Awards

The New York Drama Critics' Circle Awards are presented each May by a 17-member group that includes critics from all New York City's newspapers, magazines and wire services except the *New York Times*.

1935–1936
Winterset, Maxwell Anderson

1936–1937
High Tor, Maxwell Anderson

1937–1938
Of Mice and Men, John Steinbeck
Citation for Best Foreign Play
Shadow and Substance, Paul
    Vincent Carroll

1938–1939
No award
Citation for Best Foreign Play
The White Steed, Paul Vincent Carroll

1939–1940
The Time of Your Life, William Saroyan

1940–1941
Watch on the Rhine, Lillian Hellman
Citation for Best Foreign Play
The Corn Is Green, Emlyn Williams

1941–1942
No award
Citation for Best Foreign Play
Blithe Spirit, Noel Coward

1942–1943
The Patriots, Sidney Kingsley

1943–1944
No award
Citation for Best Foreign Play
Jacobowsky and the Colonel, Franz
    Werfel and S. N. Behrman

1944–1945
The Glass Menagerie, Tennessee
    Williams

1945–1946
No award
Citation for Best Musical
Carousel, Richard Rodgers and
    Oscar Hammerstein II

1946–1947
All My Sons, Arthur Miller
Citation for Best Foreign Play
No Exit, Jean-Paul Sartre
Citation for Best Musical
Brigadoon, Alan Jay Lerner and
    Frederick Loewe

Richard Rodgers and Oscar Hammerstein II

1947–1948
A Streetcar Named Desire, Tennessee
    Williams
Citation for Best Foreign Play
The Winslow Boy, Terence Rattigan

1948–1949
Death of a Salesman, Arthur Miller
Citation for Best Foreign Play
The Madwoman of Chaillot, Jean
    Giraudoux and Maurice Valency
Citation for Best Musical
South Pacific, Richard Rodgers, Oscar
    Hammerstein II and Joshua Logan

1949–1950
The Member of the Wedding, Carson
    McCullers
Citation for Best Foreign Play
The Cocktail Party, T. S. Eliot
Citation for Best Musical
The Consul, Gian Carlo Menotti

1950–1951
Darkness at Noon, Sidney Kingsley
Citation for Best Foreign Play
The Lady's Not for Burning,
    Christopher Fry
Citation for Best Musical
Guys and Dolls, Abe Burrows, Jo
    Swerling and Frank Loesser

1951–1952
I Am a Camera, John Van Druten
Citation for Best Foreign Play
Venus Observed, Christopher Fry
Citation for Best Musical
Pal Joey, Richard Rodgers, Lorenz Hart
    and John O'Hara
**Distinguished and Original Contribution
to Theater**
Don Juan in Hell, George Bernard Shaw

1952–1953
Picnic, William Inge
Citation for Best Foreign Play
The Love of Four Colonels,
    Peter Ustinov
Citation for Best Musical
Wonderful Town, Joseph Fields, Jerome
    Chodorov, Betty Comden, Adolph
    Green and Leonard Bernstein

1953–1954
The Teahouse of the August Moon,
    John Patrick
Citation for Best Foreign Play
Ondine, Jean Giraudoux
Citation for Best Musical
The Golden Apple, John Latouche and
    Jerome Moross

1954–1955
Cat on a Hot Tin Roof, Tennessee
    Williams
Citation for Best Foreign Play
Witness for the Prosecution,
    Agatha Christie

Citation for Best Musical
The Saint of Bleecker Street,
  Gian Carlo Menotti

1955–1956
The Diary of Anne Frank, Frances
  Goodrich and Albert Hackett

Citation for Best Foreign Play
Tiger at the Gates, Jean Giraudoux and
  Christopher Fry

Citation for Best Musical
My Fair Lady, Frederick Loewe and
  Alan Jay Lerner

1956–1957
Long Day's Journey Into Night,
  Eugene O'Neill

Citation for Best Foreign Play
Waltz of the Toreadors, Jean Anouilh

Citation for Best Musical
The Most Happy Fella, Frank Loesser

1957–1958
Look Homeward, Angel, Ketti Frings

Citation for Best Foreign Play
Look Back in Anger, John Osborne

Citation for Best Musical
The Music Man, Meredith Willson

1958–1959
A Raisin in the Sun, Lorraine Hansberry

Citation for Best Foreign Play
The Visit, Friedrich Duerrenmatt-
  Maurice Valency

Citation for Best Musical
La Plume de ma Tante, Robert Dhery
  and Gerard Calvi

1959–1960
Toys in the Attic, Lillian Hellman

Citation for Best Foreign Play
Five Finger Exercise, Peter Shaffer

Citation for Best Musical
Fiorello!, Jerome Weidman, George
  Abbott, Jerry Bock and Sheldon
  Harnick

1960–1961
All the Way Home, Tad Mosel

Citation for Best Foreign Play
A Taste of Honey, Shelagh Delaney

Citation for Best Musical
Carnival, Michael Stewart

1961–1962
The Night of the Iguana, Tennessee
  Williams

Citation for Best Foreign Play
A Man for All Seasons, Robert Bolt

Citation for Best Musical
*How to Succeed in Business Without
  Really Trying,* Abe Burrows, Jack
  Weinstock, Willie Gilbert and Frank
  Loesser

1962–1963
Who's Afraid of Virginia Woolf?, Edward
  Albee

Special Citation
Beyond the Fringe, Alan Bennett, Peter
  Cook, Jonathan Miller and Dudley
  Moore

1963–1964
Luther, John Osborne

Citation for Best Musical
Hello, Dolly, Michael Stewart and
  Jerry Herman

Special Citation
The Trojan Women, Euripides

1964–1965
The Subject Was Roses, Frank D. Gilroy

Citation for Best Musical
Fiddler on the Roof, Joseph Stein, Jerry
  Bock and Sheldon Harnick

1965–1966
*The Persecution and Assassination of
  Marat as Performed by the
  Inmates of the Asylum of
  Charenton Under the Direction of
  the Marquis de Sade,* Peter Weiss
The Man of La Mancha, Dale
  Wasserman, Mitch Leigh and
  Joe Darion

1966–1967
The Homecoming, Harold Pinter

Citation for Best Musical
Cabaret, Joe Masteroff, John Kander
  and Fred Ebb

1967–1968
*Rosencrantz and Guildenstern Are
  Dead,* Tom Stoppard

Citation for Best Musical
Your Own Thing, Donald Driver, Hal
  Hester and Danny Apolinar

1968–1969
The Great White Hope, Howard
  Sackler

Citation for Best Musical
1776, Sherman Edwards and
  Peter Stone

1969–1970
Borstal Boy, Frank McMahon

Citation for Best American Play
*The Effect of Gamma Rays on Man-in-
  the-Moon Marigolds,* Paul Zindel

Citation for Best Musical
Company, George Furth and
  Stephen Sondheim

1970–1971
Home, David Storey

Citation for Best American Play
The House of Blue Leaves, John Guare

Citation for Best Musical
Follies, James Goldman and
  Stephen Sondheim

1971–1972
That Championship Season,
  Jason Miller

Citation for Best Foreign Play
The Screens, Jean Genet

Citation for Best Musical
Two Gentlemen of Verona, adapted by
  John Guare and Mel Shapiro

1972–1973
The Changing Room, David Storey

Citation for Best American Play
The Hot l Baltimore, Lanford Wilson

Citation for Best Musical
A Little Night Music, Hugh Wheeler and
  Stephen Sondheim

1973–1974
The Contractors, David Storey

Citation for Best American Play
Short Eyes, Miguel Pinero

Citation for Best Musical
Candide, Leonard Bernstein, Hugh
  Wheeler and Richard Wilbur

1974–1975
Equus, Peter Shaffer

Citation for Best American Play
The Taking of Miss Janie, Ed Bullins

Citation for Best Musical
A Chorus Line, James Kirkwood and
  Nicholas Dante

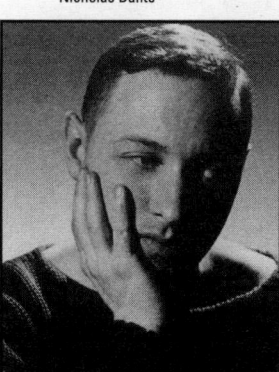

Tennessee Williams

1975–1976
Travesties, Tom Stoppard

Citation for Best American Play
Streamers, David Rabe

Citation for Best Musical
Pacific Overtures, Stephen Sondheim,
John Weidman and Hugh Wheeler

1976–1977
Otherwise Engaged, Simon Gray

Citation for Best American Play
American Buffalo, David Mamet

Citation for Best Musical
Annie, Thomas Meehan, Charles
Strouse and Martin Charnin

1977–1978
Da, Hugh Leonard

Citation for Best Musical
Ain't Misbehavin', conceived by
Richard Maltby, Jr.

1978–1979
The Elephant Man, Bernard Pomerance

Citation for Best Musical
Sweeney Todd, Hugh Wheeler and
Stephen Sondheim

1979–1980
Talley's Folly, Lanford Wilson

Evita, Andrew Lloyd Webber and
Tim Rice

Citation for Best Foreign Play
Betrayal, Harold Pinter

1980–1981
A Lesson From Aloes, Athol Fugard

Citation for Best American Play
Crimes of the Heart, Beth Henley

1981–1982
*The Life and Adventures of Nicholas
Nickleby,* adapted by David Edgar

Citation for Best American Play
A Soldier's Play, Charles Fuller

1982–1983
Brighton Beach Memoirs, Neil Simon

Citation for Best Foreign Play
Plenty, David Hare

Citation for Best Musical
Little Shop of Horrors, Alan Menken and
Howard Ashman

1983–1984
The Real Thing, Tom Stoppard

Citation for Best American Play
Glengarry Glen Ross, David Mamet

Citation for Best Musical
Sunday in the Park With George,
Stephen Sondheim and
James Lapine

1984–1985
Ma Rainey's Black Bottom,
August Wilson

1985–1986
Lie of the Mind, Sam Shepard

Citation for Best Foreign Play
Benefactors, Michael Frayn

Special Citation
*The Search for Signs of Intelligent Life
in the Universe,* Lily Tomlin and
Jane Wagner

1986–1987
Fences, August Wilson

Citation for Best Foreign Play
Les Liaisons Dangereuses,
Christopher Hampton

Citation for Best Musical
Les Misérables, Claude-Michel
Schönberg and Alain Boublil

1987–1988
Joe Turner's Come and Gone,
August Wilson

Citation for Best Foreign Play
The Road to Mecca, Athol Fugard

Citation for Best Musical
Into the Woods, Stephen Sondheim and
James Lapine

1988–1989
The Heidi Chronicles, Wendy
Wasserstein

Citation for Best Foreign Play
Aristocrats, Brian Friel

Special Citation
Largely New York, Bill Irwin

1989–1990
The Piano Lesson, August Wilson

Citation for Best Foreign Play
Privates on Parade, Peter Nichols

Citation for Best Musical
City of Angels, Larry Gelbart, Cy
Coleman and David Zippel

1990–1991
Six Degrees of Separation, John Guare

Citation for Best Foreign Play
Our Country's Good, Timberlake
Wertenbaker

Citation for Best Musical
The Will Rogers Follies, Cy Coleman,
Peter Stone, Betty Comden and
Adolph Green

Special Citation
Eileen Atkins, *A Room of One's Own*

Tom Stoppard

1991–1992
Dancing at Lughnasa, Brian Friel

Citation for Best American Play
Two Trains Running, August Wilson

1992–1993
*Angels in America: Millennium
Approaches,* Tony Kushner

Citation for Best Foreign Play
Someone Who'll Watch Over Me,
Frank McGuinness

Citation for Best Musical
Kiss of the Spider Woman, John Kander,
Fred Ebb and Terrence McNally

1993–1994
Three Tall Women, Edward Albee

Twilight: Los Angeles, 1992, Anna
Deavere Smith, writer/actress,
received an award "for unique
contribution to theatrical form."

1994–1995
Arcadia, Tom Stoppard

Citation for Best American Play
Love! Valour! Compassion!,
Terrence McNally

Citation for Best Musical
No award given

Outstanding Achievement Award
Signature Theatre Company, which
dedicated its season to the
works by Horton Foote

Broadway's Longest-Running Shows

SHOW	DATES	PERFORMANCES
A Chorus Line	10/75–4/90	6,137
Oh, Calcutta!	9/76–8/89	5,962
Cats	10/82–present	5,692
Les Misérables	3/87–present	3,782
Phantom of the Opera	1/88–present	3,504
42nd Street	8/80–1/89	3,485
Grease	2/72–4/80	3,388
Fiddler on the Roof	9/64–7/72	3,242
Life With Father	11/39–7/47	3,224
Tobacco Road	12/33–5/41	3,182
Hello, Dolly!	1/64–12/70	2,844
My Fair Lady	3/56–9/62	2,717
Annie	4/77–1/83	2,377
Man of La Mancha	11/65–6/71	2,329
Abie's Irish Rose	5/22–10/27	2,327
Oklahoma!	3/43–5/48	2,212
Miss Saigon	4/91–present	2,150
Pippin	10/72–6/77	1,944
South Pacific	4/49–1/54	1,925
Magic Show	5/74–12/78	1,920
Gemini	5/77–9/81	1,819
Deathtrap	2/78–6/82	1,793
Harvey	11/44–1/49	1,775
Dancin'	3/78–6/82	1,774
La Cage Aux Folles	6/83–11/87	1,761
Hair	4/68–7/72	1,742
The Wiz	1/75–1/79	1,672
Crazy for You	2/92–present	1,648
Born Yesterday	2/46–12/49	1,642
Ain't Misbehavin'	5/78–2/82	1,604
Best Little Whorehouse in Texas	6/78–3/82	1,584
Mary, Mary	3/61–12/64	1,572
Evita	9/79–6/83	1,567
Voice of the Turtle	12/43–1/48	1,557
Barefoot in the Park	10/63–6/64	1,532
Dreamgirls	12/81–7/85	1,521
Mame	5/66–1/70	1,503
Same Time, Next Year	3/76–9/78	1,453
Arsenic and Old Lace	1/41–6/44	1,444
The Sound of Music	11/59–6/63	1,443
Me and My Girl	X/86–X/89	1,420
How to Succeed in Business Without Really Trying	10/61–3/65	1,417
Hellzapoppin'	9/38–12/41	1,404
The Music Man	12/57–4/61	1,375
Funny Girl	3/64–7/67	1,348
Mummenschantz	3/77–4/80	1,326
Oh, Calcutta!	6/69–8/72	1,314
Brighton Beach Memoirs	3/83–5/86	1,299
Angel Street	12/41–12/44	1,295

Oh, Calcutta!

SHOW	DATES	PERFORMANCES
Lightnin'	8/18–8/21	1,291
Promises, Promises	12/68–1/72	1,281
The King and I	4/51–4/54	1,246
Cactus Flower	12/65–11/68	1,234
Sleuth	11/70–10/73	1,222
Torch Song Trilogy	6/82–5/85	1,222
1776	3/69–2/72	1,217
Equus	10/74–10/77	1,209
Sugar Babies	10/79–8/82	1,208
Guys and Dolls	11/50–6/53	1,200
Cabaret	11/66–9/69	1,166
Amadeus	12/80–9/83	1,161
Mister Roberts	2/48–1/51	1,157
Annie Get Your Gun	5/46–2/49	1,147
Guys and Dolls	4/92–1/95	1,143
The Seven Year Itch	11/52–8/55	1,141
Butterflies Are Free	10/69–7/72	1,128
Pins and Needles	11/37–6/40	1,108
Plaza Suite	2/68–10/70	1,097
They're Playing Our Song	2/79–9/81	1,082
Kiss Me, Kate	12/48–7/51	1,071
Don't Bother Me, I Can't Cope	4/72–11/74	1,065
Pajama Game	5/54–11/56	1,063
Shenandoah	1/75–8/77	1,050
Teahouse of the August Moon	10/53–4/56	1,027
Damn Yankees	5/55–10/57	1,019
Grand Hotel	11/89–4/92	1,018
Never Too Late	11/62–4/65	1,007
Beatlemania	6/77–10/79	1,006

Source: League of American Theatres and Producers

Broadway Season Statistics

New York Convention & Visitors Bureau

SEASON	GROSS (IN MILLIONS)	ATTENDANCE (IN MILLIONS)	NEW PRODUCTIONS	TOURING GROSS (IN MILLIONS)
1957–1958	$ 38	7.2	56	$ 23
1958–1959	40	7.7	56	23
1959–1960	46	7.9	58	27
1960–1961	44	7.7	48	34
1961–1962	44	6.8	53	39
1962–1963	44	7.4	54	32
1963–1964	40	6.8	63	34
1964–1965	50	8.2	67	36
1965–1966	54	9.6	68	32
1966–1967	55	9.3	69	44
1967–1968	59	9.5	74	45
1968–1969	58	8.6	67	43
1969–1970	53	7.1	62	48
1970–1971	55	7.4	49	50
1971–1972	52	6.5	55	50
1972–1973	45	5.4	55	56
1973–1974	46	5.7	43	46
1974–1975	57	6.6	54	51
1975–1976	71	7.3	55	53
1976–1977	93	8.8	54	83
1977–1978	114	9.8	42	106
1978–1979	134	9.6	50	141
1979–1980	146	9.6	61	181
1980–1981	197	11.0	60	219
1981–1982	223	10.1	48	250
1982–1983	209	8.4	50	184
1983–1984	227	7.9	36	202
1984–1985	213	7.4	33	226
1985–1986	191	6.6	33	236
1986–1987	209	7.05	41	224
1987–1988	253	8.14	32	223
1988–1989	262	7.97	30	256
1989–1990	283	8.03	35	367
1990–1991	267	7.32	28	450
1991–1992	292	7.37	37	503
1992–1993	328	7.86	33	621
1993–1994	356	8.10	37	688
1994–1995	406	9.04	29	810

Source: League of American Theatres and Producers

Broadway Theaters

Thirty-four theaters grace the Great White Way, the Broadway theater district, which lies bordered by 41st to 53rd streets and Sixth to Ninth avenues.

Ambassador Theatre
215 W. 49th St.
New York, NY 10019
(212) 239-6200

Brooks Atkinson Theatre
256 W. 47th St.
New York, NY 10036
(212) 307-4100

Ethel Barrymore Theatre
243 W. 47th St.
New York, NY 10036
(212) 239-6200

Martin Beck Theatre
302 W. 45th St.
New York, NY 10036
(212) 239-6200

Belasco Theatre
111 W. 44th St.
New York, NY 10036
(212) 239-6200

Booth Theatre
222 W. 45th St.
New York, NY 10036
(212) 239-6200

Broadhurst Theatre
235 W. 44th St.
New York, NY 10036
(212) 239-6200

Broadway Theatre
1681 Broadway
New York, NY 10019
(212) 239-6200

Circle in the Square
1633 Broadway
New York, NY 10019
(212) 239-6200

Cort Theatre
138 W. 48th St.
New York, NY 10036
(212) 239-6200

Gershwin Theatre
222 W. 51st St.
New York, NY 10019
(212) 307-4100

John Golden Theatre
252 W. 45th St.
New York, NY 10036
(212) 239-6200

Helen Hayes Theatre
240 W. 44th St.
New York, NY 10036
(212) 307-4100

Imperial Theatre
249 W. 45th St.
New York, NY 10036
(212) 239-6200

Walter Kerr Theatre
219 W. 48th St.
New York, NY 10036
(212) 239-6200

Longacre Theatre
220 W. 48th St.
New York, NY 10036
(212) 239-6200

Lunt-Fontanne Theatre
205 W. 46th St.
New York, NY 10036
(212) 307-4100

Lyceum Theatre
149 W. 45th St.
New York, NY 10036
(212) 239-6200

Majestic Theatre
245 W. 44th St.
New York, NY 10036
(212) 239-6200

Marquis Theatre
1535 Broadway
New York, NY 10036
(212) 307-4100

Minskoff Theatre
200 W. 45th St.
New York, NY 10036
(212) 307-4100

Music Box Theatre
239 W. 45th St.
New York, NY 10036
(212) 239-6200

Nederlander Theatre
208 W. 41st St.
New York, NY 10036
(212) 307-4100

Eugene O'Neill Theatre
230 W. 49th St.
New York, NY 10036
(212) 239-6200

Palace Theatre
1564 Broadway
New York, NY 10036
(212) 307-4100

Plymouth Theatre
236 W. 45th St.
New York, NY 10036
(212) 239-6200

New York Convention & Visitors Bureau

Richard Rodgers Theatre
226 W. 46th St.
New York, NY 10036
(212) 307-4100

Roundabout Theatre
1530 Broadway
New York, NY 10036
(212) 869-8400

Royale Theatre
242 W. 45th St.
New York, NY 10036
(212) 239-6200

St. James Theatre
246 W. 44th St.
New York, NY 10036
(212) 239-6200

Neil Simon Theatre
250 W. 52nd St.
New York, NY 10019
(212) 307-4100

Shubert Theatre
225 W. 44th St.
New York, NY 10036
(212) 239-6200

Virginia Theatre
245 W. 52nd St.
New York, NY 10036
(212) 239-6200

Winter Garden Theatre
1634 Broadway
New York, NY 10019
(212) 239-6200

Capezio Dance Awards

The Capezio Dance Awards, presented annually by the Capezio/Ballet Makers Dance Foundation, Inc., honor the performer, choreographer, critic, teacher, producer or administrator who has made a significant contribution to the art.

Eric H. Antoniou/Courtesy of Boston Ballet

Bruce Marks

1952
Zachary Solov

1953
Lincoln Kirstein

1954
Doris Humphrey

1955
Louis Horst

1956
Genevieve Oswald

1957
Ted Shawn

1958
Alexandra Danilova

1959
Sol Hurok

1960
Martha Graham

1961
Ruth St. Denis

1962
Barbara Karinska

1963
Donald McKayle

1964
José Limón

1965
Maria Tallchief

1966
Agnes de Mille

1967
Paul Taylor

1968
Lucia Chase

1969
John Martin

1970
William Kolodney

1971
Arthur Mitchell

1972
La Meri

Reginald and Gladys Laubin

1973
Isadora Bennett

1974
Robert Joffrey

1975
Robert Irving

1976
Jerome Robbins

1977
Merce Cunningham

1978
Hanya Holm

1979
Alvin Ailey

1980
Walter Terry

1981
Dorothy Alexander

1982
Alwin Nikolais

1983
Harvey Lichtenstein

1984
William Christensen

Harold Christensen

Lew Christensen

1985
Doris Hering

1986
Antony Tudor

1987
Fred Astaire

Bob Fosse

Rudolf Nureyev

Jac Venza

1988
Charles "Honi" Coles

1989
Edward Villella

1990
Jacques d'Amboise

1991
John Curry

Katherine Dunham

Darci Kistler

Igor Youskevitch

1992
Frederic Franklin

1993
Dance/USA

1994
Urban Bush Women

1995
Bruce Marks

PERFORMING ARTS TIMELINE

534 B.C.

Thespis wins the first public contest for tragic poets in Greece, and the term thespian derives from his name. He also introduces masks, which become a staple of Greek and Roman theater.

525–385 B.C.

The Athenian or Classical period introduces a dramatic era of tragic poets that includes Aeschylus

(*Agamemnon,* 458 B.C.), Sophocles (*Antigone,* 441 B.C.; *Oedipus Rex,* 430 B.C.) and Euripides (*Medea,* 431 B.C.).

Euripides, considered the first choreographer, incorporates dance into his plays.

350–250 B.C.

The Hellenistic or Colonial period marks an era when comedy is preferred over tragedy.

Old Comedy, buffoonery and farce that often attacks individuals and

portrays the foibles of a social class, evolves into New Comedy, a more polished and refined humor that centers on the shortcomings of the middle class.

Comic drama moves from politics and philosophy to everyday life.

27 B.C. – A.D. 476

The Romans invent pantomime.

c. 500–800

Theater is all but extinct in both the western and eastern Roman Empires

Major U. S. Dance Companies

Alvin Ailey American Dance Theatre
211 W. 61st St., 3rd Floor
New York, NY 10023
(212) 767-0940

American Ballet Theatre
890 Broadway
New York, NY 10003
(212) 477-3030

Ballet Hispanica of New York
167 W. 89th St.
New York, NY 10024
(212) 362-6710

Ballet West
50 W. 200th S.
Salt Lake City, UT 84101
(801) 524-8300

Boston Ballet
19 Clarendon St.
Boston, MA 02116
(617) 695-6950

Trisha Brown Co.
211 W. 61st, 4th Floor
New York, NY 10023
(212) 582-0040

Lucinda Childs Dance Co.
541 Broadway
New York, NY 10012
(212) 431-7599

Cunningham Dance Foundation
55 Bethune St.
New York, NY 10014
(212) 255-8240

Dance Theatre of Harlem
466 W. 152nd St.
New York, NY 10031
(212) 690-2800

Garth Fagan Dance
50 Chesnut St.
Rochester, NY 14604
(716) 454-3260

Carol Rosegg

American Ballet Theatre

Feld Ballets/NY
890 Broadway, 8th Floor
New York, NY 10003
(212) 777-7710

Martha Graham Dance Co.
360 E. 63rd St.
New York, NY 10021
(212) 832-9166

Erick Hawkins Dance Co.
375 W. Broadway, 5th Floor
New York, NY 10012
(212) 226-5363

Houston Ballet
1921 W. Bell
P.O. Box 130487
Houston, TX 77219-0487
(713) 523-6300

Hubbard Street Dance Chicago
218 S. Wabash Ave., 3rd Floor
Chicago, IL 60604
(312) 663-0853

Joffrey Ballet
434 Avenue of the Americas
New York, NY 10011
(212) 254-8520

Bill T. Jones Dance Co.
853 Broadway, Suite 1706
New York, NY 10003
(212) 477-1850

Paula Josa-Jones
185 Green St.
Cambridge, MA 02139
(617) 864-3191

Liz Lerman Dance Exchange
1664 Columbia Road N.W., Suite 21
Washington D.C. 20009
(202) 232-0833

Lewitsky Dance Co.
1055 Wilshire Blvd., Suite 1140
Los Angeles, CA 90017
(213) 580-6338

José Limón Dance Foundation
611 Broadway, 9th Floor
New York, NY 10012
(212) 777-3353

Nikolais Louis Dance Theatre
611 Broadway, Suite 221
New York, NY 10012
(212) 420-0700

Lar Lubovitch Dance Co.
15 W. 18th St., 7th Floor
New York, NY 10011-4604
(212) 242-0633

Miami City Ballet
905 Lincoln Road
Miami Beach, FL 33139
(305) 532-4880

---

during the Dark Ages because Christians oppose the entertainment.

c. 900

The church introduces dramatic performances to Easter services, acting out the story of the Resurrection. Ironically, the institution that discouraged theater is responsible for its rebirth.

1495

Everyman, the best surviving example of a morality play, is written. The morality play touches on large con-temporary issues with moral overtones and describes the lives of everyday people facing temptation.

1489

Ballet is performed for the first time.

1550

Commedia dell'arte flourishes in Italy and Western Europe. Literally "professional comedy," the theater form features improvisation from a standard script and stock characters.

1570

Count Giovanni Bardi debuts the Elizabethan masque, an aristocratic form of entertainment that features music, dance and elaborate costuming.

1576

The Theatre, the first commercial theater, opens in London. It is also the first Elizabethan playhouse.

Momix Dance Co.
P.O. Box 1035
Washington, CT 06793
(203) 868-7454

Elisa Monte Dance Co.
1170 Broadway, Suite 912
New York, NY 10001
(212) 251-0789

Mark Morris Dance Co.
225 Lafayette St., Suite 504
New York, NY 10012
(212) 219-3660

Jennifer Muller
131 W. 24th St., 4th Floor
New York, NY 10011
(212) 691-3803

New York City Ballet
20 Lincoln Center
New York, NY 10023
(212) 870-5656

Ohio Ballet
354 E. Market St.
Akron, OH 44325
(216) 972-7900

David Turner

Lar Lubovitch Dance Company

Pacific Northwest Ballet
301 Mercer St.
Seattle, WA 98109
(206) 441-9411

The Parsons Dance Co.
130 W. 56th St.
New York, NY 10019
(212) 247-3203

Pennsylvania Ballet
1101 S. Broad St.
Philadelphia, PA 19147
(215) 551-7000

Philadanco
9 N. Preston St.
Philadelphia, PA 19104
(215) 387-8200

Pilobolus Dance Theatre
P.O. Box 388
Washington Depot, CT 06794
(203) 868-0538

Pittsburgh Ballet Theater
2900 Liberty Ave.
Pittsburgh, PA 15201-1500
(412) 281-0360

San Francisco Ballet
455 Franklin St.
San Francisco, CA 94102
(415) 861-5600

Paul Taylor Dance Co.
552 Broadway
New York, NY 10012-3947
(212) 431-5562

Twyla Tharp Dance Co.
336 Central Park W.
New York, NY 10025
(212) 932-3000

Washington Ballet
3515 Wisconson Ave., N.W.
Washington D.C. 20016
(202) 362-3606

White Oak Dance Project
1830 Rittenhouse Square
Philadelphia, PA 19103
(215) 731-0722

Lois Greenfield

Feld Ballets/NY

1594

The Chamberlain's Men, the leading Elizabethan and Jacobean theatrical company of the day, is formed. William Shakespeare is the chief playwright and Richard Burbage its most famous actor. After 1603 the group is known as the King's Men. The Admiral's Men, the group that performs the works of Christopher Marlowe, is also formed and rivals the Chamberlain's Men.

1597

Jacopo Peri's musical fable, *Dafne,* often considered the first opera, is performed at the palace of Jacopo Corsi. Opera becomes the preferred entertainment of the aristocracy.

1598–1608

William Shakespeare writes *Much Ado About Nothing, As You Like It, All's Well That Ends Well, Julius Caesar, Hamlet, Othello, King Lear, Macbeth* and *Anthony and Cleopatra.*

1607

Claude Monteverdi's *Orfeo,* regarded as the first masterpiece in opera history, is performed and revolutionizes music by establishing a tonal system and giving the recitative a more flexible accompaniment.

1619

Teatro Farnese in Parma, Italy, uses the proscenium arch for the first time.

CONTINUED ON PAGE 702 ▶

Favorite Opera Stories

Opera plots form the backdrop to the rich music and staging that make the opera experience. To help you follow the action, we've outlined the stories from the most frequently performed operas.

AÏDA

Music: Giuseppe Verdi; **Libretto:** Antonio Ghislanzoni
Premiere: Cairo, December 24, 1871

Verdi's grandest and most classically perfect opera unfolds in the royal palace in ancient Egypt, where the beautiful Ethiopian princess Aïda is a captive slave of Egyptian Princess Amneris. When Ethiopian forces attack in an attempt to rescue Aïda, Radames, captain of the Egyptian guard and Aïda's sworn beloved, leads a triumphant defense, capturing King Amonasro, Aïda's father. As a reward for his victory, the Egyptian king bestows on Radames the hand of his daughter, Princess Amneris, who is infatuated with the captain and jealous of Aïda. Torn between patriotism and passion, a despairing Aïda obeys her father's urgings to betray Radames, but Amneris discovers the plot and vengefully orders Radames to renounce Aïda or be buried alive. Silent and unrepentant, Radames is led to the dungeon, where he reunites tragically with Aïda, who has stolen away to join him in death.

IL BARBIERE DI SIVIGLIA (THE BARBER OF SEVILLE)

Music: Gioacchino Rossini; **Libretto:** Cesare Sterbini, based on the play by Pierre Beaumarchais
Premiere: Rome, February 20, 1816

Though its premiere was an infamous flop, *The Barber of Seville* has become a standard of comic opera repertory. Irrepressible Figaro, town barber and jack-of-all-trades, learns that dashing Count Almaviva loves the young, rich and beautiful Rosina, the ward and intended wife of strict Dr. Bartolo. Rosina is equally smitten with the count, whom she has never met, and tosses him a love note from her balcony. Figaro gleefully masterminds an elopement, employing a series of disguises and ruses that bring the lovers together in the nick of time.

LA BOHÈME

Music: Giacomo Puccini; **Libretto:** Giuseppe Giacosa and Luigi Illica, based on *Scènes de la vie de Bohème* by Henri Murger
Premiere: Turin, February 1, 1896

Puccini's most expressive opera draws from a collection of true-life sketches describing life among the original bohemians, the poor artists of Paris's Latin Quarter. Hungry but cheerful, the poet Rodolfo shares a garret with the painter Marcello and two others. One moonlit Christmas Eve, the

Giuseppe Verdi

frail seamstress Mimi comes to Rodolfo's door for help, and the two fall passionately in love, while Marcello carries on a turbulent affair with flirtatious Musetta. But Rodolfo is impossibly jealous of Mimi, and the two regretfully part, until Musetta reveals that Mimi is dying of consumption. Rodolfo flies to Mimi's side, and the lovers are united, only to be separated forever by Mimi's death.

BORIS GODUNOV

Music: Modest Mussorgsky; **Libretto:** from the play by Alexander Pushkin and Nikolai Karamzin's *History of the Russian State*
Premiere: St. Petersburg, January 27, 1874

The most majestic of all Russian operas, *Boris Godunov* was considered revolutionary for its music and lyrics as well as its somber portrayal of a turbulent period in Russian history. In legend (not in fact), Boris becomes Tsar of Russia after murdering Dmitri, the rightful heir, and though he rules humanely, the land falls into chaos and poverty. The young monk Grigory convinces the neighboring Polish king that he is actually the murdered Dmitri and marries Marina, a Polish noblewoman who disguises her lust for power as passionate love. Grigory/Dmitri and the Poles invade Russia, taking power after Boris, terrified and guilt-stricken by Dmitri's apparent resurrection, dies. As a stark background, the war-torn Russian populace bitterly voices its utter misery.

CARMEN

Music: Georges Bizet; **Libretto:** Henri Meilhac and Ludovic Halévy, based on the novel by Prosper Mérimée
Premiere: Paris, March 3, 1875

Though *Carmen* is now a universal favorite, the opera's first performances failed miserably, and a disheartened Bizet died three months later. Soon after his death overwhelming audience acclaim greeted work, set in a vividly romanticized Spanish world, where the gypsy cigarette girl Carmen taunts corporal Don Josè with her flamboyant charms. Even the gentle peasant girl Micaela, who loves Don Josè, cannot break Carmen's spell, and the corporal gives up everything to follow the fickle gypsy into the mountains. She quickly tires of Don Josè and runs off with the handsome matador Escamillo, fatalistically embracing the warning of death she has seen in the cards. As Escamillo triumphs in the bullring, Carmen is confronted by Don Josè in a nearby alley, and this time, her defiance cannot save her.

CAVALLERIA RUSTICANA (RUSTIC CHIVALRY)

Music: Pietro Mascagni; **Libretto:** G. Menasci and G. Targioni-Tozzetti, based on a story of G. Verga
Premiere: Rome, May 17, 1890

A phenomenally successful drama of betrayal and retribution, *Cavalleria Rusticana* made the 26-year-old Mascagni an overnight sensation. As the story begins, Sicilian villagers make their way to church on a balmy Easter morning. Santuzza appears, distraught that her lover Turiddu has betrayed her with Lola, his first love, who is now married to the teamster Alfio. She pours out her desperation to Mamma Lucia, Turiddu's mother, and vainly attempts to persuade Turiddu to return. But he shuns her to follow Lola, and Santuzza blurts out to Alfio the tale of his wife's deception. At this moment, destiny prevails, as Sicilian honor requires Alfio to redeem his honor with the stiletto, and the guilty Turiddu must submit to his fate.

LA CENERENTOLA (CINDERELLA)

Music: Gioacchino Rossini; **Libretto:** Jacopo Ferretti
Premiere: Rome, January 25, 1817

Widely popular in the 19th century but neglected later, this comic retelling of the classic rags-to-riches fairytale has recently returned to favor. Cenerentola is the poor stepsister Cinderella, who is at the mercy of Don Magnifico and his two unpleasant daughters, Clorinda and Thisbe. When Prince Ramiro, disguised as the valet Dandini, calls on his way to the ball, he and Cinderella fall instantly in love. Costumed as a mysterious lady, Cinderella slips out to the ball, where the prince finds her and again declares his love. But Cinderella disappears, leaving the prince with one of her bracelets, telling him he must find her. Later, when the prince visits Don Magnifico, he recognizes a matching bracelet on Cinderella's arm, and the truth is revealed.

LES CONTES D'HOFFMANN (TALES OF HOFFMANN)

Music: Jacques Offenbach; **Libretto:** Michel Carré and Jules Barbier
Premiere: Paris, February 10, 1881

Loosely based on the life of the German writer E.T.A. Hoffmann, *Tales of Hoffmann* portrays a mysterious world where human and supernatural forces meet. In a tavern, the poet Hoffmann tells of his three ill-fated romances. In the first tale, he pursues the doll Olympia until she dances him into a mechanical frenzy, and he wearily realizes that she is not human. Next, he falls passionately in love with the sickly but gifted Antonia, who is compelled by her mother's portrait to sing away her last ounce of strength. Finally, Hoffmann is drawn against his will to Giulietta, who steals his reflection for the sorcerer Dapertuto. Blind with passion, Hoffmann murders Giulietta's lover Schlemil, only to see her entice yet another man. As the last tale ends, Hoffmann, lost in a bitter haze of drink and memory, fails to notice Stella, the woman who truly loves him, as she tosses him a flower.

CONT. FROM PAGE 700

1637

Venice becomes the home of the first public opera house, the San Cassiano Theater.

1642–1660

Following the civil war of 1642, the Puritans close or burn down all English theaters and forbid acting.

1643

Molière incorporates an acting troupe called Illustre Theatre.

Although initially unsuccessful with his troupe, Moliére goes on to be one of history's most famous and enduring playwrights. His work includes *Tartuffe* (1664), *Misanthrope* (1666) and *Bourgeois Gentleman* (1670).

1660

Women start appearing in French and English plays. Elizabeth Barry and Anne Bracegirdle are among the pioneers.

1661

Louis XIV officially recognizes dance instruction by establishing the Académie Royale de Danse.

1665

William Darby's *Ye Bare and Ye Cubb*, reportedly the first English-language play presented in the colonies, is performed in Accomac County, Virginia.

COSI FAN TUTTE ("THEY ALL DO IT")

Music: Wolfgang Amadeus Mozart;
Libretto: Lorenzo da Ponte
Premiere: Vienna, January 26, 1790

Mozart's final comic opera, *Cosi fan tutte*, a laughing look at the twists and turns of romantic love, was originally attacked for portraying faithless women. Some early performances were even accompanied by apologies for the frivolous plot. The story begins in a Neapolitan café, where two young men, Ferrando and Guglielmo, argue with the older and more skeptical Don Alfonso that their fiancées, the sisters Fiordiligi and Dorabella, would never betray them. Aided by Despina, the sisters' maid, the men hatch a plot to test the women's loyalty. They disguise themselves as soldiers and woo each other's lovers, managing through various tricks to win over the initially reluctant women. As deeper feelings surface, however, the suitors become uneasy with their antics, and once the deception is unmasked, the four reunite, though who pairs up with whom remains a mystery.

DON GIOVANNI

Music: Wolfgang Amadeus Mozart;
Libretto: Lorenzo da Ponte
Premiere: Prague, October 29, 1787

One of the most praised operas, *Don Giovanni* combines high drama with comedy to illustrate the escapades and eventual fiery end of the mythical womanizer. As the story opens, Don Giovanni steals away from Donna Anna's house, but she pursues him. The commotion alarms her father, the Commendatore, who duels with and is killed by Don Giovanni. He sets off again with his servant, Leporello, and meets the grieving Donna Elvira, who loves him although he has betrayed her. Making a quick exit, he next encounters a lively bunch of peasants, among them the pretty Zerlina and her clumsy fiancé, Masetto. Wily Don Giovanni spirits Zerlina away, but her enraged scream alerts the suspicious Masetto, and the Don is unmasked as a seducer and murderer. He escapes, only to be confronted later by a statue of

Wolfgang Amadeus Mozart

the murdered Commendatore, who extends an icy grip to drag an unrepentant Don Giovanni to the depths of hell.

DON PASQUALE

Music: Gaetano Donizetti; **Libretto:** Donizetti and Giovanni Ruffini
Premiere: Paris, January 3, 1843

Donizetti's exuberant farce chronicles the ill-fated attempts of elderly bachelor Don Pasquale to snare a wife while he tries to stop his nephew, Ernesto, from doing the same. Ernesto loves the lively widow Norina, and the couple are persuaded to assist Don Pasquale's friend Malatesta in a plot to ruin the old man's fantasies of marriage. Norina, posing as Don Pasquale's innocent bride-to-be, becomes a shrew after their marriage is finalized, terrorizing her husband and even boxing his ears. As a last straw, Don Pasquale finds a carefully planted love note from Ernesto to Norina that leads him and Malatesta to "discover" the lovers in the garden. The wise Malatesta reconciles everyone, and all ends well.

---

c. 1670

Pierre Beauchamps codifies the five foot positions in ballet.

1681

Pierre Beauchamps and Jean Baptiste write *Le Triomphe de l'Ammour,* which features LaFontaine, the first woman to dance professionally in a ballet.

1685

Alessandro Scarlatti founds the Neapolitan School of Opera, which

establishes the da capo, or three-part aria.

1689

The young women at Josias Priest's finishing school in Chelsea, England, perform Henry Purcell's *Dido and Aeneas,* the first English operatic masterpiece.

1730

Romeo and Juliet, the first play by Shakespeare to be presented in America, is performed in New York.

1733

La Serva Padrona by Giovanni Pergolesi is performed in Naples, heralding the popularity of opera buffa or comic opera.

1734

French ballerina Marie Camargo stirs controversy when she raises dancing skirts above the ankle for greater freedom of movement.

EUGENE ONEGIN

Music: Peter Ilyich Tchaikovsky; **Libretto:** Tchaikovsky and K. S. Shilovsky, based on the poem by Pushkin
Premiere: Moscow, March 29, 1879

Tchaikovsky himself is said to have been enamored of the character Tatiana, virtuous heroine of his classic *Eugene Onegin*. As the story opens on a Russian estate, sisters Tatiana and Olga await Olga's fiancé, Lenski, and his friend Onegin. Only 17 years old, Tatiana falls in love for the first time with the older Onegin and pens him a passionate declaration of her feelings, which he kindly but coolly rejects. Bored Onegin offends Lenski's honor by flirting with Olga, and the two comrades duel until Lenski is killed. A repentant Onegin disappears from society, but on returning years later, he sees the elegant, mature and married Tatiana and is overwhelmed by love. He declares his passion, but it is too late. Tatiana, though torn by her continuing love for Onegin, devotedly remains true to her husband.

FAUST

Music: Charles Gounod; **Libretto:** Michel Carré and Jules Barbier
Premiere: Paris, March 19, 1859

Rich drama and ornate occultism made *Faust* an immediate popular success. The elderly philosopher Faust, lamenting his lost powers and wasted life, lifts a glass of poison to his lips, but stops short when he hears youthful voices and bitterly calls on Satan for help. The devil Mephistopheles materializes, offering Faust the gift of youth if he will sacrifice his soul, and they seal the pact. With Mephistopheles smirking in the background, a now young Faust seduces and betrays Marguerite, killing her brother, Valentine, when he defends his sister. Marguerite, too, is damned and murders her illegitimate child, for which she is condemned to death. But ultimately, Marguerite's goodness wins out, and the angels who escort her to heaven also rescue a repentant Faust from the devil's clutches.

Peter Ilich Tchaikovsky

DIE FLEDERMAUS (THE BAT)

Music: Johann Strauss; **Libretto:** Henri Meilhac and Ludovic Halévy
Premiere: Vienna, April 5, 1874

Strauss's ever-popular operetta is a madcap comedy of light-hearted deceit, filled with lively dance music. Bourgeois citizen Eisenstein must go to prison because of an oversight by his lawyer. Hearing this news, Alfred, former lover of Eisenstein's wife, Rosalinda, decides to use her husband's absence to renew his suit. Then Eisenstein's friend Falke arrives, dressed as a bat, and invites the unwitting husband to postpone his imprisonment for a few hours and attend a masquerade. The pair depart and Alfred arrives, only to be mistaken for Eisenstein and carted off to jail. At the ball, Eisenstein is dazzled by a mysterious Hungarian countess, who is none other than his wife in disguise. Afterwards, he turns himself in at the jail, only to find Alfred and Rosalinda already there. As the three confront each other, the rest of the cast magically appears, tension dissolves and all unite in singing the praises of champagne.

1735

Ballet arrives in America. Englishman Henry Holt stages the first production for the amusement of the Charleston, South Carolina, elite.

John Hippisley's *Flora,* the first opera performed in America, is also presented in Charleston, South Carolina.

1751

The first professional theater company in the colonies, the Virginia Company of Comedians, opens a temporary wooden playhouse in Williamsburg, Virginia.

1762

Christoph Willibald von Gluck's *Orfeo ed Euridice* premieres at the Hofburgtheater in Vienna, marking revolutionary changes and reform in opera seria.

1766

The first permanent American theater building, Southwark Theater, is erected in Philadelphia.

1778

Milan's Teatro alla Scala, Italy's leading opera house and one of the world's most renowned, is built.

1786

Mozart collaborates with Lorenzo da Ponte on *The Marriage of Figaro,* which premieres in Vienna. He completes *Don Giovanni* the following year, and it premieres in Prague.

DER FLIEGENDE HOLLANDER (THE FLYING DUTCHMAN)

Music: Richard Wagner; **Libretto:** Wagner, based on Heine
Premiere: Dresden, January 2, 1843

Wagner based the spooky plot of *Der Fliegende Hollander* on the legend of a Dutch sea captain who vows to sail around the Cape of Good Hope, even if it takes forever. Condemned by the devil to be endlessly at sea, he may land once every seven years and search for the faithful woman whose true love will be his only salvation. During a furious storm, Norwegian sea captain Daland has taken shelter with his ship when the deathly masts of the Flying Dutchman's vessel loom nearby. Daland agrees that the Dutchman will follow him home to meet his daughter, Senta, who has become entranced by a portrait bearing an eerie resemblance to the Flying Dutchman. At first sight, Senta knows the Dutchman to be the man of her dreams and tears herself away from friends and family to throw herself into the sea as he departs, thus freeing her beloved from the devil's curse and uniting with him for eternity.

HÄNSEL AND GRETEL

Music: Engelbert Humperdinck; **Libretto:** Adelheid Wette
Premiere: Weimar, December 23, 1893

The classic fairy tale tells of a poor broommaker who lives in a forest hut with his wife, Gertrude, and their children, Hänsel and Gretel. One day, irritated by her children's playfulness, Gertrude accidentally spills the family's only pitcher of milk and is forced to send Hänsel and Gretel into the woods to gather berries for dinner. When the broommaker returns home, he tells her with horror of an evil witch in the woods, who likes to bake children and eat them. By this time, Hänsel and Gretel have eaten all their berries, and as it grows dark, they fall asleep in the woods, protected by guardian angels. When they awake, they are captured by the evil witch, who binds them with a magic spell and prepares to cook them. But clever Gretel undoes the spell, and the two children trick the witch into the oven, where she is baked into a giant cake.

LADY MACBETH OF MTSENSK (KATERINA ISMAILOVA)

Music: Dmitri Shostakovich; **Libretto:** Shostakovich and Alexander Preis, based on the story by N. Leskov
Premiere: Leningrad, January 22, 1934

Stalinists denounced *Lady Macbeth of Mtsensk* after a few performances for being too modern, and the opera almost disappeared from the stage. Katerina Ismailova, the heroine, is bored and unhappy with her husband, Zinovy, and intensely dislikes her father-in-law Boris, who in turn suspects her of wanting to have an affair. Zinovy hires the flirtatious Sergei, who immediately begins seducing Katerina, but Boris catches the pair and orders Sergei to be flogged. Katerina vengefully poisons Boris and continues her passionate affair with Sergei until Zinovy surprises the lovers together. To keep their secret, the pair murder Zinovy, bury his body in the cellar and prepare to wed. But at the lovers' wedding feast, the body is discovered. Katerina and Sergei are arrested and sentenced to a convict gang, where Sergei woos saucy Sonyetka. Overwhelmed with jealousy and misery, Katerina leaps from a bridge into the river, taking Sonyetka with her.

Dmitri Shostakovich

1816

Gaslighting is used for the first time in American theater at Philadelphia's Chestnut Street Theatre.

Thomas Drummond invents the limelight, which is used in the same manner as the spotlight is used today.

1828

Minstrel dancing debuts with Thomas Dartmouth "Daddy" Rice appearing as Jim Crow in a song-and-dance act.

1830–1850

The Romantic period in ballet sees ballerinas making technical and artistic strides in the art form. Until this period, men dominated the stage.

1841

Composer Adolphe Adam, poets Heinrich Heinke and Théophile Gautier and choreographers Jean Coralli and Jules Perrot collaborate on *Giselle*, which is a prototype of the Romantic period and is still found in many modern repertories.

1843

The Theatre Regulation Act of 1843 bans drinking in legitimate theaters. Many tavern owners take advantage of the situation and renovate their establishments to accommodate live performances.

1859

The French Opera House, the first great opera house in America, is built in New Orleans.

LUCIA DI LAMMERMOOR

Music: Gaetano Donizetti; **Libretto:** Salvatore
Cammarano, based on the novel by
Sir Walter Scott
Premiere: Naples, September 26, 1835

Donizetti's tragic romance relates the fortunes of
Lucy, sister of Lord Henry of Lammermoor, who
arranges a marriage for Lucy to salvage his own
financial and political fortunes. When Henry discovers that Lucy loves Edgar, son of a rival family, he deceives her into believing that Edgar is
unfaithful, and she agrees to marry the man her
brother has chosen. Returning from abroad, an
innocent Edgar curses Lucy's apparent infidelity,
and Henry challenges him to a duel. But Lucy,
mad with grief, slays her husband and kills herself, leaving Edgar to die by his own hand in the
graveyard of his ancestors.

MADAMA BUTTERFLY

Music: Giacomo Puccini; **Libretto:** Giuseppe
Giacosa and Luigi Illica
Premiere: Milan, February 17, 1904

One of the world's most popular operas, *Madama
Butterfly* passionately explores the consequences

Giacomo Puccini

of obsessive devotion. Pinkerton, a U.S. Navy officer in Japan, contracts what he considers a temporary marriage to Cio-Cio-San, called Butterfly,
who renounces religion and family in her adoration for him. When Pinkerton leaves for America,
Butterfly blissfully ignores warnings of his unfaith-
fulness and awaits his return, even turning down a
marriage proposal from Yamadori, a rich Japanese
businessman. With all avenues of escape closed to
her, she is shattered when Pinkerton returns with
an American wife. Butterfly ends her unbearable
misery with her father's sword, thus preserving
her honor.

DIE ZAUBERFLÖTE (THE MAGIC FLUTE)

Music: Wolfgang Amadeus Mozart; **Libretto:**
Emanuel Schikaneder
Premiere: Vienna, September 30, 1791

First performed only two months before Mozart's
death, *The Magic Flute* is the story of true lovers
who must survive magical ordeals before they can
be together. Prince Tamino stumbles into the land
of the Queen of Night, where he is attacked by a
giant serpent. He is rescued by three ladies, who
show him a picture of the beautiful Pamina, and
Tamino instantly falls in love. Protected by a gold-
en flute, he sets off with the bird-catcher
Papageno to rescue Pamina from the clutches of
the sorcerer Sarastro. But the sorcerer is actually
a wise priest, who tells Pamina that though she
and Tamino are destined for each other, they must
first prove their love. When the gods instruct
Tamino to take a vow of silence, Pamina fears that
all is lost and contemplates suicide, but she is
comforted by kind spirits and finds new strength
to aid Tamino through the trials of fire and water.
Triumphing over all adversity, the lovers unite, as
the forces of light banish the darkness, and the
magic flute carries the final melody.

1865

Former circus clown Tony Pastor
opens the first variety theater in
New York.

1868

Lydia Thompson and her British
Blondes bring burlesque to the
United States.

1871

Giuseppe Verdi's *Aïda* premieres in
Cairo, Egypt.

The first collaboration of W.S. Gilbert

and Sir Arthur Sullivan, *Thespis*, is
performed at London's Gaiety
Theatre.

1876

The first complete production of
Wagner's *Ring*, a titanic cycle of four
musical dramas, opens the first
Bayreuth Festival.

1879

Henrik Ibsen's *A Doll's House*, a revolutionary play that centers on the
repression of women, deeply offends
conservatives and thrills a newly

awakened European conscience
when it premieres at the
Copenhagen's Royal Theatre.

1881

The first modern cabaret, Le Chat
Noir (The Black Cat), opens in Paris.

London's Savoy Theatre opens and is
the first to be lit by electricity.

Vaudeville debuts at Tony Pastor's
New 14th Street Theater in New
York.

LE NOZZE DI FIGARO
(THE MARRIAGE OF FIGARO)
Music: Wolfgang Amadeus Mozart; **Libretto:** Lorenzo da Ponte, based on the poem by Pierre Beaumarchais
Premiere: Vienna, May 1, 1786

The Marriage of Figaro recounts the further comic adventures of Figaro, first introduced in Mozart's previous opera, *The Barber of Seville*. Figaro's master, Count Almaviva, is now married to his love Rosina but has tired of her and pursues the affections of her comely maid Susanna, who is engaged to Figaro. The count hatches a plot to convince Figaro that Susanna is deceiving him and that he should instead marry the noblewoman Marcellina, but Figaro in turn schemes to reunite the count and countess. After many ruses and disguises have backfired, Figaro discovers that Marcellina is his long-lost mother. Figaro and Susanna regain their trust in each other and the count must stoop to begging Rosina's pardon.

THE MERRY WIDOW
Music: Franz Lehár; **Libretto:** Victor Léon and Leon Stein, based on the comedy by Henri Meilhac
Premiere: Vienna, December 28, 1905

Joyful music, dance and light romance have made *The Merry Widow* a universal favorite since the operetta's first performance. In gay Paris, a birthday party for the ruler of the imaginary land of Marsovia is in full swing. Wealthy Sonia is surrounded by suitors, to the despair of Marsovian diplomat Baron Popoff, who fears she will bankrupt their country if she marries a foreigner. He cleverly convinces Prince Danilo, the minister of finance, to woo Sonia, though the prince has been rejected once. While Sonia lavishes special attention on the prince, he feigns indifference until she announces her engagement to a Frenchman. In agony, he at last reveals his true love to Sonia and discovers with joy that her engagement is a fiction and that she shares his most passionate feelings.

THE MIKADO
Music: Arthur Sullivan; **Libretto:** William S. Gilbert
Premiere: London, March 14, 1885

Parodying contemporary British taste for all things Japanese, the original production of *The Mikado* played in London for two full years. In the town of Titipu, where flirting is a capital crime, the nervous nobles have appointed former prisoner Ko-Ko as Lord High Executioner. Condemned for flirting, Ko-Ko cannot execute anyone unless he beheads himself first. Offended by Ko-Ko's lowly origins, the town officials resign, and Pooh-Bah takes charge of all functions as Lord High Everything Else. Into this setting wanders an unknown minstrel, Nanki-Poo, disguised son of the mighty Mikado, who has displeased his father by refusing to marry elderly Katisha. Nanki-Poo seeks Yum-Yum, the beautiful, self-absorbed ward of Ko-Ko, who is to marry her protector shortly.

Learning of the upcoming marriage, Nanki-Poo is preparing to hang himself in despair when an edict arrives from the Mikado warning that Titipu is overdue for an execution. Ko-Ko devises a clever plan to marry Yum-Yum to Nanki-Poo for one month, after which the groom will be executed, fulfilling the Mikado's order and leaving the bride free to marry Ko-Ko. Hilarious complications ensue, and when the Mikado discovers that his son has apparently been beheaded, Ko-Ko must marry Katisha to escape execution. Yum-Yum and Nanki-Poo, alive and secretly wedded, emerge from hiding and Ko-Ko uses his zany, illogical reasoning to appease the Mikado.

NABUCCO
Music: Giuseppe Verdi; **Libretto:** Temistocle Solera
Premiere: Milan, March 9, 1842

Verdi's first truly successful opera opens in ancient Jerusalem, as King Nabucco of Babylon, whose daughter Fenena is a hostage to the Jews, invades and sacks the Jewish Temple. Installed by Nabucco as Regent of Jerusalem and inspired by her love for the Jew Ismaele, Fenena converts to Judaism and frees the Jewish prisoners. The slave Abigaille, who claims to be Fenena's sister, also loves Ismaele and masterminds a vengeful plot to

---

1883

The Metropolitan Opera House opens in New York with Gounod's *Faust*.

1890

Modern dance emerges when choreographers and dancers begin to rebel against traditional ballet.

1901

Founder of the Moscow Art Theatre, Konstantin Stanislavski formulates the revolutionary Stanislavski

Method of acting, which requires actors to see and hear on stage as they do in real life, enabling them to react to theatrical situations in the same way they would in real life. He is credited with launching the age of the great director in modern theater.

1902

Claude Debussy introduces impressionism in *Pelléas and Mélisande* at the Opéra Comique in Paris.

1904

Anton Chekhov introduces modern realism at the premiere of *The Cherry Orchard* at the Moscow Art Theatre.

1905

Isadora Duncan establishes the first school of modern dance in Berlin.

1909

Serge Diaghilev opens the Ballets Russes de Serge Diaghilev, which begins the era of modern ballet and

imprison Nabucco and steal the crown of Jerusalem for herself. In his cell, Nabucco dreams that Fenena is about to be executed, but he escapes in time to free her and also converts to Judaism, as a repentant Abigaille poisons herself.

OTELLO

Music: Giuseppe Verdi; **Libretto:** Arrigo Boito, based on Shakespeare's *Othello*
Premiere: Milan, February 5, 1887

Although Verdi planned to retire from composing, he was tempted by Boito's libretto to write the score for *Otello*, which has remained popular since its first glorious success. As the tragedy opens, the triumphant Venetian general Othello returns to port, braving a furious storm, and is joyfully reunited with his wife, Desdemona. But the jealous ensign Iago schemes with Roderigo, who also loves Desdemona, to undermine Othello's victory. Iago orchestrates the downfall of Cassio, Othello's trusted lieutenant, and then suggests to Cassio that he turn to Desdemona for support. When Desdemona pleads Cassio's case, Othello becomes suspicious, and Iago's further ruses convince the general that his wife is unfaithful. Desdemona's denials are in vain, and as Othello's admirers unknowingly pay tribute to their hero, he smothers his wife in bed. Moments later, discovering that Iago is the true villain, he drives his sword through his own breast in despair.

I PAGLIACCI (THE CLOWNS)

Music and Libretto: Ruggiero Leoncavallo
Premiere: Milan, May 21, 1892

Leoncavallo's sentimental play-within-a-play unfolds in an Italian village, where a group of traveling actors are to perform. The intensely jealous Canio, head of the troupe, discovers that his actress-wife Nedda has decided to run off with a lover. Vowing revenge, he declares that the guilty man will somehow reveal himself at that evening's performance. During the play, when Nedda as Columbine addresses Harlequin, her stage lover, Canio breaks through his disguise as Pagliaccio and bullies his wife to reveal her lover's real name. Terrified, Nedda flees the stage,

but Canio pursues her and stabs her to death. With her dying breath, Nedda whispers the name of Silvio, and Canio slays him on the spot. The audience is paralyzed with fear by the drama that has suddenly and tragically come to life.

PELLÉAS ET MÉLISANDE

Music: Claude Debussy; **Libretto:** based on the play by Maeterlinck
Premiere: Paris, April 30, 1902

For *Pelléas et Mélisande*, Debussy composed a score as subtle and haunting as the story of the mysterious creature Mélisande, coaxed from her dark forest home to secretly wed Golaud, grandson of King Arkël of Allemonde. The King forgives Golaud, but Mélisande, wandering in the garden with her brother-in-law Pelléas, drops her wedding ring in a pool, magically causing her husband to be injured in a fall from his horse. From his bed, Golaud sends Mélisande after the enchanted ring, and when Pelléas accompanies her, the two fall innocently into childlike love. Jealous Golaud warns Mélisande away from Pelléas, but she agrees to a last meeting, and the couple abandon themselves to their premonitions of doom. Suddenly Golaud bursts on to the scene, slays Pelléas and chases Mélisande, wounding her slightly. After giving birth to a girl, Mélisande quietly dies, resisting repentant Golaud's pleadings and denying any guilt to the end.

DER RING DES NIBELUNGEN (THE RING OF NIBELUNG)

Das Rheingold (The Rhinegold)
Die Walküre (The Valkyrie)
Siegfried
Götterdämmerung (The Twilight of the Gods)
Music and Libretto: Richard Wagner
Premiere: Bayreuth, August 1876

Wagner's four-part *Ring* cycle follows the fortunes of gods, giants, gnomes and humans as they battle greed and betrayal to reach a final redemption. In the first drama, *Das Rhinegold*, the Nibelung dwarf Alberich renounces love to gain possession of the mysterious Rhine gold, from which he fashions the ring that grants him mighty powers.

---

his 20-year reign as ballet's leading figure. Moving away from full-length works characteristic of Romantic ballet, he creates new, shorter ballets. Mikhail Fokine is Diaghilev's choreographer and is considered the most influential choreographer of the 20th century.

1911

Der Rosenkavalier, Richard Strauss's masterpiece, premieres in Dresden.

1913

Darktown Follies opens in Harlem and helps to make Harlem a black cultural center.

1915

Ruth St. Denis and her husband, Ted Shawn, establish the Denishawn dance school in Los Angeles, where Martha Graham and Doris Humphrey study.

1920

Eugene O'Neill's first full-length play, *Beyond the Horizon*, is produced on Broadway and wins a Pulitzer Prize, marking the beginning of modern American drama.

Rising popular interest in African-American literature sparks the beginning of the Harlem Renaissance.

1923

Harlem's Cotton Club opens and presents all-black performances to

Meanwhile Wotan, king of the gods, regrets his promise to trade Freia, goddess of youth and beauty, for the giants' help in building Valhalla, home of the gods. Wotan dupes Alberich and steals the magic Ring, giving it to the giants in place of Freia. But Alberich has cursed the ring and all who touch it, and Wotan has brought this curse upon the gods.

As *Die Walküre* opens, Siegmund staggers into the hut where Sieglinde fearfully awaits the return of Hunding, whom she was forced to marry. The two fall in love, unaware that both are Wotan's human children. Wotan commands his favorite daughter, Brünnhilde of the fierce Valkyries, to defend Siegmund against Hunding, but his wife, the goddess Fricka, reminds him that Siegmund has violated Sieglinde's marriage vows and must die. Heartbroken and still under the Ring's curse, Wotan orders Brünnhilde to help Hunding defeat Siegmund in battle. Brünnhilde admires the strength of Siegmund's passion and defies her father, but at the last moment Wotan furiously intervenes, causing Siegmund's death. To punish his Valkyrie daughter, Wotan puts her to sleep on Brünnhilde Rock, inside a ring of fire that only a true hero would dare to defy. Brünnhilde tells her father that Sieglinde has hidden in the forest to give birth to Siegfried, who will help the gods defeat their enemies.

Siegfried relates how Sieglinde's baby is rescued from his dead mother's side and raised by Mime, a Nibelung dwarf who plots that Siegfried will grow up to slay the giant Fafner and reclaim the magic ring. Siegfried fearlessly welds the halves of his father Siegmund's splintered sword and slays Fafner. but kills Mime for his treachery, while Alberich's evil laugh is heard in the background. Meanwhile, the exhausted god Wotan gives up his kingship, abandoning the world to the rule of human love. A bird guides brave Siegfried to Brünnhilde Rock, where he battles through the ring of flames to reach the sleeping maiden. Inspired by his passion, Brünnhilde renounces her magical Valkyrie powers, and the lovers are joyfully united by the cursed ring.

But the gods' final reckoning awaits them in the fourth drama, *Götterdämmerung*. Hagen, son of the

Richard Wagner

evil Alberich, devises a devilish plot to kill Siegfried and steal the Ring from Brünnhilde's finger. He convinces his half-sister Gutrune to feed Siegfried a potion that erases the hero's memory of Brünnhilde and makes him lust after Gutrune. The besotted Siegfried agrees to kidnap his former love as a bride for Gutrune's brother Gunther, and as Brünnhilde vainly defends herself, Siegfried seizes the ring from her. Unaware of the treachery afoot, Brünnhilde denounces Siegfried's betrayal, but he can remember nothing and denies all guilt. After the double wedding, the Rhine maidens, who are rightful owners of the Ring, beg Siegfried to return it to them, but he refuses, not realizing that he is under its curse. In his lust for the Ring, Hagen drives his spear into Siegfried's back. But when Hagen reaches to steal the Ring from Siegfried's corpse, the dead man's hand raises itself to shake him off, and Brünnhilde appears on her magic charger. Seizing the ring, she lights a funeral pyre and rides into the flames, immolating the corrupt reign of the gods forever. Brünnhilde's sacrifice returns the cursed ring to the Rhine maidens and purifies the world for the new rule of human love.

---

white-only audiences. Entertainers include Lena Horne, the Nicholas Brothers and Cab Calloway.

1926

Martha Graham, the American pioneer of the modern-dance revolt, gives her first New York performance, which features 18 barefoot, evocatively-costumed dancers.

1927

The Broadway musical links with opera in Jerome Kern's revolutionary *Show Boat*.

1930

Jean Rosenthal, one of the greatest lighting designers in theater history, pioneers the concept of stage lighting.

1935

George Gershwin combines black folk idiom and Broadway musical techniques in *Porgy and Bess*.

1943

Rodgers & Hammerstein's *Oklahoma!* opens and changes American musical theater by com-

bining entertainment and serious subjects. Agnes de Mille choreographs the musical, capturing the essence of American folk dance.

1946

George Balanchine and Lincoln Kirstein establish the New York City Ballet. It makes its home at Lincoln Center in 1964.

RIGOLETTO

Music: Giuseppe Verdi; **Libretto:** Francesco Maria Piave based on Victor Hugo's *Le Roi s'amuse*
Premiere: Venice, March 11, 1851

Vivid characters and lively music have made *Rigoletto* a long-time favorite of both performers and audiences, second only to *Aïda* among Verdi's works. Rigoletto is the bitter, hunchbacked court jester whose treasured daughter, Gilda, has caught the eye of the womanizing Duke of Mantua. Approaching Gilda, the duke declares his love, and the girl discovers a passion for him. Court nobles, seeking revenge for the jester's many insults, dupe Rigoletto into helping them kidnap Gilda, who is delivered to the Duke and seduced by him. Determined to show his daughter the Duke's true nature, Rigoletto takes her to the house of the assassin Sparafucile, whose sister Maddalena offers the duke her gypsy favors. Rigoletto has hired Sparafucile to kill the duke, but Maddalena convinces her assassin brother to murder a random victim instead. Knowing she will be murdered, Gilda appears in disguise, is stabbed, stuffed in a sack and delivered to Rigoletto in place of the duke's body. At the last minute, the horrified hunchback opens the sack and discovers his daughter, who whispers her last words of love for the duke and dies.

DER ROSENKAVALIER (THE KNIGHT OF THE ROSE)

Music: Richard Strauss; **Libretto:** Hugo von Hofmannsthal
Premiere: Dresden, January 26, 1911

Strauss's first successful comic opera begins in the bedroom of the Marschallin of Werdenberg, where the 32-year-old princess has spent a passionate night with 17-year-old Octavian. The marschallin's pleasure is mixed, for she knows that Octavian will soon seek a younger lover. She appoints Octavian to take a silver betrothal rose to a young girl, Sophie, on behalf of her country relative, Baron von Lerchenau, and the two teenagers fall in love. Sophie's angry father orders her to a convent, but Octavian, determined to win her hand, concocts a scheme to discredit the baron. Comic confusion reigns until the marschallin appears and reestablishes order, forgiving Octavian and nobly pushing him into Sophie's arms.

SALOME

Music: Richard Strauss; **Libretto:** translation by Hedwig Lachmann of Oscar Wilde's stage poem
Premiere: Dresden, December 9, 1905

Salome shocked early audiences with its gory portrayal of lust and obsession, and was withdrawn from The Metropolitan Opera stage after one production. Sultry Salome is the virgin daughter of wicked Herodias, who murdered her husband to marry Herod, Tetrarch of Judea. Smitten with desire for his stepdaughter, Herod begs her to dance, and Salome agrees when Herod promises to grant her one wish. After performing the enticing dance of the seven veils, Salome demands in return the life of Jokanaan, or John the Baptist, for whom she has developed a single-minded, unrequited lust. Though he protests fearfully, Herod orders Jokanaan executed, and the bloody head is offered to Salome on a silver plate. When Salome steals a frenzied, ghoulish kiss from the dead man's lips, a horrified Herod orders his guards to kill her.

TOSCA

Music: Giacomo Puccini; **Libretto:** Giuseppe Giacosa and Luigi Illica
Premiére: Rome, January 14, 1900

Flamboyant *Tosca* opens in a church, where the artist Cavaradossi paints a Mary Magdalen portrait while dreaming of his lover, Tosca, a famously passionate yet devout singer. Suddenly the escaped political prisoner Angelotti staggers in, on the run from the savage police chief Scarpia. When Tosca arrives and overhears the two men talking, she is devoured with suspicion that Cavaradossi has another lover, but the painter soothes her and hides Angelotti. The angry Scarpia bursts in, hot on the escapee's heels and burning with lust for Tosca. Sizing up the situation, he schemes to make the jealous singer betray her lover's secret. Cavaradossi is arrested and brutally tortured, blackmailing Tosca into revealing Angelotti's whereabouts. As the artist is dragged to the scaffold, Scarpia demands Tosca's favors as payment

1952
Jose Quintero's revival of Tennessee Williams's *Summer and Smoke* premieres at Broadway's Circle in the Square Theatre and is the first major Off-Broadway success.

1962
The first dance concert is held at New York's Judson Memorial Church, marking the beginning of the Judson Movement and postmodern dance. Judson dancers also introduce the use of a performance space instead of a stage. Judsonites include Meredith Monk, Trisha Brown and Lucinda Childs.

1966
The old Metropolitan Opera House is abandoned as the company moves to Lincoln Center. The new Metropolitan Opera opens with Samuel Barber's *Antony and Cleopatra*.

1980
Mark Morris establishes the Mark Morris Dance Group in New York and is widely received as the most promising modern-dance choreographer of his generation.

1983
Harvey Fierstein's *Torch Song Trilogy* wins the New York Drama Critics' Circle Award and Tony Award for best play, marking the acceptance of gay theater.

1995
The Metropolitan Opera installs screens on audience seats that display captions, to attract a wider audience.

TOP 20 MOST FREQUENTLY PERFORMED OPERAS

1. *La Bohème*	6. *Barber of Seville*	11. *Aïda*	16. *Die Fledermaus*
2. *La Traviata*	7. *Tosca*	12. *Cosi fan Tutte*	17. *La Cenerentola*
3. *Madama Butterfly*	8. *Carmen*	13. *Turandot*	18. *Il Trovatore*
4. *Marriage of Figaro*	9. *Magic Flute*	14. *Lucia di Lammermoor*	19. *Der Rosenkavalier*
5. *Rigoletto*	10. *Don Giovanni*	15. *Faust*	20. *Salome*

Source: Opera America

for her lover's life, but the agonized Tosca meets his embrace with a fatal knife thrust. Joyfully, she goes to free Cavaradossi, but Scarpia's final cruel ruse leads her instead to witness her lover's execution. As the police pursue her, Tosca throws herself from a parapet to her death.

LA TRAVIATA
(THE FALLEN WOMAN)
Music: Giuseppe Verdi; **Libretto:** Francesco Maria Piave, based on Alexandre Dumas's *La Dame aux Camélias*
Premiere: Venice, March 6, 1853

La Traviata created an outrage with its sympathetic portrayal of Violetta, the ailing courtesan who is redeemed by love. When she learns of Alfredo's adoration for her, sickly Violetta hesitantly abandons a life of revelry to live with her lover, and the two are blissfully happy. But Alfredo's father warns Violetta that her scandalous past threatens his son's future and asks her to abandon her lover. A tormented Violetta agrees to return to her old ways, leaving Alfredo furious at her apparent betrayal. Overcome with grief, Violetta falls mortally ill, and Alfredo's father, taking pity on her, informs his son of her sacrifice. Alfredo rushes to Violetta's side, arriving in time for a rapturous deathbed duet.

IL TROVATORE
(THE TROUBADOUR)
Music: Giuseppe Verdi; **Libretto:** Salvatore Cammarano, based on the play by Antonio Garcia Gutiérrez
Premiere: Rome, January 19, 1853

The complicated melodrama of *Il Trovatore* revolves around the gypsy Azucena, whose mother was burned at the stake for bewitching the elder count di Luna's baby son. To revenge her mother's death, Azucena hysterically kidnaps the count's baby, then mistakenly casts her own infant son into the flames. Horror-struck, she escapes with the count's stolen baby and raises him as her own son, Manrico. As the opera opens, the younger count, Manrico's unknowing brother, jealously awaits the arrival of the mysterious troubadour who has captured the heart of the Duchess Leonora. The troubadour Manrico appears, and the two men fight a duel, unaware that they are brothers. When Leonora hears a rumor that Manrico has been slain by the count's forces, she vows to become a nun, but her lover, still very much alive, hastens to her side. The count's forces besiege the couple's hideaway, and old Azucena, wandering into the enemy camp, is sentenced to death. Trying to save his mother, Manrico is also captured and thrown into prison. Leonora desperately promises to marry the count if he will free Manrico, but when he agrees, she poisons herself, dying in her lover's arms. A furious count forces Azucena to watch her supposed son Manrico's execution, but the malicious gypsy has the last word, screaming that the count has killed his own brother.

TURANDOT
Music: Giacomo Puccini **Libretto:** Giuseppe Adami and Renato Simoni, based on Carlo Gozzi's fable
Premiere: Milan, April 25, 1926

Puccini's last opera was left unfinished at his death, and what he had intended to be a final, transcendent love duet was completed by a younger colleague, Franco Alfano. In Peking's Imperial Palace, the fatally beautiful Princess Turandot receives unlucky suitors from far and wide, who must answer three riddles to win her hand — or die. Calaf, son of the exiled King Timur of Tartary, is struck with Turandot's beauty, and ignoring protests from his father and Liù, the servant girl who loves him, he matches wits with the princess. Although he guesses the three riddles, Calaf offers his life to Turandot if she can discover his secret name. Searching the city in vain, the princess finally tortures faithful Liù, driving her to suicide. Faced with Liù's sacrifice and Calaf's stern devotion, Turandot crumbles, and weeping in Calaf's arms, she declares that his secret name is Love.

Major U.S. Opera Companies

Courtesy of The Metropolitan Opera Co.

The Metropolitan Opera Company performs Mozart's *The Magic Flute*

Arizona Opera
3501 N. Mountain Ave.
P.O. Box 42828
Tucson, AZ 85733
(602) 293-4336

Baltimore Opera Co.
1202 Maryland Ave.
Baltimore, MD 21201
(410) 625-1600

Central City Opera
621 17th St., Suite 1601
Denver, CO 80293
(303) 292-6500

Cincinnati Opera Associates
1241 Elm St.
Cincinnati, OH 45210
(513) 621-1919

Cleveland Opera
1422 Euclid Ave., Suite 1052
Cleveland, OH 44115-2001
(216) 575-0900

The Dallas Opera
3102 Oaklawn Ave., Suite 450
Dallas, TX 75219
(214) 443-1043

Florentine Opera Company
735 N. Water St., Suite 1315
Milwaukee, WI 53202-4106
(414) 291-5700

Florida Grand Opera Associates
1200 Coral Way
Miami, FL 33145
(305) 854-1643

Houston Grand Opera Association
510 Preston
Houston, TX 77002-1594
(713) 546-0200

Kentucky Opera
101 S. Eighth St. at Main
Louisville, KY 40202
(502) 584-4500

Los Angeles Music Center Opera
135 N. Grand Ave.
Los Angeles, CA 90012
(213) 972-7211

Lyric Opera of Chicago
20 N. Wacker Drive
Chicago, IL 60606
(312) 332-2244

Lyric Opera of Kansas City
1029 Central St.
Kansas City, MO 64105
(816) 471-4933

Metropolitan Opera Association
Lincoln Center
New York, NY 10023
(212) 799-3100

Michigan Opera Theatre
Lothrop Landing
104 Lothrop
Detroit, MI 48202
(313) 874-7850

The Minnesota Opera
620 N. First St.
Minneapolis, MN 55401
(612) 333-2700

New York City Opera
20 Lincoln Center
New York, NY 10023
(212) 870-5500

The Ohio Light Opera
The College of Wooster
Wooster, OH 44691
(216) 263-2090

Opera Colorado
695 S. Colorado Blvd., Suite 20
Denver, CO 80222
(303) 778-1500

Opera Company of Philadelphia
530 Walnut St., Suite 1450
Philadelphia, PA 19106
(215) 928-2100

Opera Pacific
9 Executive Circle, Suite 190
Irvine, CA 92714
(714) 474-4488

Opera Theatre of St. Louis
P.O. Box 191910
St. Louis, MO 63119
(314) 961-0171

Pittsburgh Opera, Inc.
711 Penn Ave., 8th Floor
Pittsburgh, PA 15222
(412) 281-0912

Portland Opera Association
1515 S.W. Morrison
Portland, OR 97205
(503) 241-1401

San Diego Opera
P.O. Box 988
San Diego, CA 92112
(619) 232-7636

San Francisco Opera
301 Van Ness Ave.
San Francisco, CA 94102
(415) 861-4008

Seattle Opera Association
1020 John St.
P.O. Box 9248
Seattle, WA 98109-0248
(206) 389-7600

Virginia Opera
160 Virginia Beach Blvd.
Norfolk, VA 23510
(804) 627-9545

Utah Opera Company
50 W. 200th S.
Salt Lake City, UT 84101
(801) 323-6868

The Washington Opera
Kennedy Center
Washington D.C. 20566-0012
(202) 416-7890

OPERA COMPANIES

Performing Arts Magazines and Journals

THEATER

American Theatre
355 Lexington Ave.
New York, NY 10017
(212) 697-5230

Backstage
1515 Broadway
New York, NY 10036-8986
(212) 764-7300

BCA News
Business Committee for the Arts, Inc.
1775 Broadway, Suite 510
New York, NY 10019-1942
(212) 664-0600

Ford Foundation Report
Office of Communications
320 E. 43rd St.
New York, NY 10017
(212) 573-5000

Lighting Dimensions
32 W. 18th St.
New York, NY 10011
(212) 229-2965

TCI
32 W. 18th St.
New York, NY 10011-4612
(212) 229-2965

Theater Week
28 W. 25th St., 4th Floor
New York, NY 10010
(212) 627-2120

Theatre Design and Technology
10 W. 19th St., Suite 5A
New York, NY 10011
(212) 924-9088

Variety
245 W. 17th St., 5th floor
New York, NY 10011
(212) 645-0067

DANCE

Dance Chronicle
Marcel Dekker, Inc.
270 Madison Ave.
New York, NY 10016
(212) 696-9000

Dance/USA Journal
1156 15th St. N.W., Suite 820
Washington D.C. 20005-1704
(202) 833-1717

OPERA

Opera Fanatic Bel Canto Society
11 Riverside Drive
New York, NY 10023-2504
(212) 877-1595

Opera News
Metropolitan Opera Guild
70 Lincoln Center Plaza
New York, NY 10023-6593
(212) 769-7080

Dance Ink
145 Central Park W.
New York, NY 10023
(212) 228-0540

Dance Magazine
33 W. 60th St., 10th Floor
New York, NY 10023
(212) 245-9050

Dance Research Journal
Congress on Research in Dance
SUNY — Brockport
Department of Dance
350 New Campus Drive
Brockport, NY 14420-2939
(716) 395-2590

Performing Arts Glossary

act A unit of theatrical action composed of several scenes.

apron The area of a stage extending beyond the proscenium.

aria An accompanied solo vocal performance, usually found in opera or oratorio.

backing The flat used to block the view of the area beyond the doors and windows in a theater.

barn door The four-doored device that fits around a lighting instrument, shaping the light beam and keeping it in place.

bel canto Operatic singing in the Italian manner, characterized by legato, rich tone, evenness and agility in passagework. It is usually found in works from the 17th and 18th centuries.

blackout 1. The sudden extinguishment of theater stage lights to indicate the passage of time or the end of an act or a scene. **2.** A short vaudeville skit that ends with lights out.

blocking The director's plan for the actors' movements.

boards A theater stage.

book 1. A libretto. **2.** The script of a play.

border 1. The material hung above the stage that prevents audiences from seeing into the fly space. **2.** The lighting hung above the stage.

box set The standard form of an interior set that shows three walls of a room.

buffo A male singer of comic-opera roles.

climax The apex of the action and conflict in a drama.

corps de ballet The dancers in a ballet company who perform as a group.

curtain raiser A short performance offered before the main presentation.

cyclorama The curved drop that, when illuminated, simulates the sky or creates an abstract background. Also called **cyc.**

dark The term used to describe a theater that is closed or not giving performances.

denouement The resolution of action and conflict occurring after the climax.

dimmer The electronic device that controls the brightness of a lighting instrument.

downstage The area of the stage closest to the audience.

drop A large piece of fabric painted and used as scenery.

entr'acte 1. The interval between two acts of a theatrical performance. **2.** A music or dance performance provided between two acts of a theatrical performance.

flat A flat piece of painted scenery, generally made from wood or fabric.

fly The area over the stage that contains lighting instruments, scenery and equipment to raise and lower scenery.

follow spot A bright spotlight used to track an actor's movements on the stage.

footlights The strip of lights near the apron on the stage floor.

fourth wall The imaginary wall that exists between the stage and the audience.

gelatin The colored plastic sheets placed in front of lighting instruments. Also called **gel.**

green room The room backstage where actors and crew wait for their call or cue.

grip A stagehand who helps move scenery.

house manager The theater employee who deals with issues related to the audience or theater.

impresario The sponsor or producer of an entertainment, especially the director of an opera company.

libretto The text of an opera, oratorio or other musical drama.

light opera See **operetta.**

loge 1. A box in a theater. **2.** The front rows of the mezzanine.

mezzanine The lowest balcony in a theater or the first few rows of that balcony.

off book The term that refers to the point in the rehearsal process when the actors have memorized their lines so they no longer need to carry scripts.

opéra bouffe A comic, often farcical opera.

operetta A short, light opera often with spoken dialogue. Also called **light opera.**

oratorio An unstaged composition for voices and orchestra that tells a sacred story. It is performed without scenery, costumes or action.

orchestra The entire main level of a modern theater.

pit The section directly in front of and below the stage, where the musicians sit. Also called **orchestra pit.**

places The call given by the stage manager before the curtain rises.

practical A prop or piece of scenery that is used or handled by the actors.

prompt To give an actor his or her lines during a rehearsal or performance.

proscenium The area of a theater located between the curtain and the orchestra.

rake To elevate the stage at an angle.

recitative The speechlike singing style found in opera or oratorio.

repertoire The body of plays that a company is prepared to perform. Also called **repertory.**

set The scenery that delineates the performing space of a play.

supertitle A written translation of the dialogue or lyrics of a foreign-language opera or choral performance that is shown on a screen above the performers. Also called **surtitle.**

thrust stage A stage that extends into the audience and often has seats facing it on three sides.

trap A door in the stage that allows actors to enter and exit.

upstage 1. The rear of the stage. **2.** To speak while upstage, forcing other actors to turn their backs to the audience.

wings The flats at the sides of the stage and parallel to the front of the stage that hide the backstage area.

(PUBLISH-ING)

The Fiction Lottery

■ BY DAVID STREITFELD

David Streitfeld covers books and publishing for the *Washington Post*. He wrote the story that unmasked Joe Klein as the anonymous author of *Primary Colors*.

EVERY ONCE IN A WHILE, SOME BITTER SOUL ON THE FRINGES OF THE literary world goes to the trouble of retyping a few prize-winning short stories by well-known writers. He then submits the stories under a pseudonym to prestigious magazines, which inevitably bounce them without even a "promising, keep trying" note attached. This result confirms the cynical view that who you are is more important than the quality of what you write, and that the talented but unknown newcomer has essentially no chance of making it into the club.

Key West writer William J. Schlicht, Jr. recently undertook this always-interesting experiment. The stories he chose, by Jane Smiley, Ethan Canin, Ann Beattie, Tobias Wolff and Alice Adams, had all appeared in "best of the year" anthologies, which should mean that their virtues were immediately apparent. But when Schlicht sent "his" stories to 20 different literary publications, only once was one of them accepted. (In a handful of cases, the editors recognized the story under submission as the work of its real author.)

BOOKS

"Selection of short fiction based on literary merit is a matter of subjective judgment to such a degree that acceptance is not significantly different than the selection of lottery winners," Schlicht concluded.

To an extent, this was probably always true. Never, however, has the intrinsic quality of a work of fiction mattered less than today. The degree to which the author is connected, the amount the publisher has invested in him and, most of all, the book's "hype quality" are at least as important and probably more.

Of course, serious young writers often recoil from the mere mention of the word "hype." They want to be loved for their work, they say, not because a publisher has whipped up a froth of interest. This stance backfired when the literary quarterly *Granta* went to considerable pains to come up with a list of the 20 best young fiction writers in the country.

Many of the writers talented enough to be under consideration actively disdained the competition; there was talk of a boycott. One of the anointed, Jonathan Franzen, asserted that "good fiction is one of the last remaining pockets of resistance to a culture of hype-able commodities," and that he hoped it would stay that way.

Franzen got his wish. When the list was published, the media basically ignored it, and so did everyone else. This might have kept the writers pure, but it kept them poor as well and didn't do much for the cause of literature in our time, either.

So what's a hapless scribbler to do? The best suggestion is to recast your autobiographical novel as conventional autobiography, which will give it the immediacy and the force of truth. (Don't worry if it's still heavily fictionalized: No one will notice.) There were dozens of autobiographies by new writers in 1996, all bent on recapturing the respect and long-running success attained by Mary Karr's *The Liars' Club* (growing up poor and troubled in a grim Texas town). None did, although Caroline Knapp's *Drinking: A Love Story* and Mark Matousek's *Sex Death Enlightenment* came close.

Yet you can't make a career out of talking about your wretched life, which is why this new crop of memoirists will eventually have to turn to fiction if they want to keep writing. But it's increasingly hard to make a career out of fiction, too.

Let's say, for instance, you have actually succeeded in your lifelong dream: A publisher has accepted your novel about life and love at the end of the '90s. For it to succeed in the marketplace, it will need some extra support. A movie deal, or at least an option, comes in handy here, but it's easiest to get one of these if your book is already making a splash. Catch-22.

A magazine feature will sell your book at least as much as a favorable review, but features are much harder to come by. Are you good-looking? If not — this is particularly true if you are a woman — the fashion magazines will not be interested; a photo of your ugly mug might upset readers. All the other periodicals ask one question: If you don't have an interesting and, preferably, tragic background — addiction (overcome, naturally), abuse, world-class angst — why should anyone want to read about you? But, of course, if you had one of these backgrounds, you would have written an autobiography, not fiction.

Still, sometimes this process works out nicely. David Foster Wallace wrote what was clearly the year's best novel in *Infinite Jest,* an 1,079-page mind-blower about addiction and salvation, even if much of the attention was sparked by the author's grungy good looks and hints of past dissipation.

The novel sold 40,000 copies and will do even better if it picks up a couple of awards. A prize gives the media a reason to write about an author and

a publisher a reason to schedule readings. In recent years, those who have taken the big trophies and then hustled themselves — E. Annie Proulx with *The Shipping News,* Jane Smiley with *A Thousand Acres,* David Guterson with *Snow Falling on Cedars* — found themselves with literally millions of readers and veritable fortunes.

Getting prizes is so crucial, in fact, that it's surprising more cases don't crop up like the one in France. The most important prize there is the Goncourt, which lifts a book from a few thousand copies to as many as half a million. Traditionally, the Goncourt winner is someone who hasn't received any of the other major prizes. That explains why, in 1995, the publisher Grasset was accused of maneuvering to let a competitor's novel get another major prize — so the way would be clear for a Grasset author to nab the Goncourt.

Joe Klein

The ruse was discovered and the plot blown, but the events served as a long-distance warning for American literary folk. "Two years, tops, before something like that is uncovered here," commented one publisher.

The only thing better than winning a prize is causing a sensation. You can't bribe your way into this; you can only get lucky. No one was more blessed in 1996 than the anonymous author of *Primary Colors,* eventually revealed to be political journalist Joe Klein. It was all so improbable — living through the 1992 Clinton campaign once should have been enough. Who would want to read a thinly fictionalized version of it?

About a million people, it turned out, plus droves more in paperback, and undoubtedly a whole bunch more if the $65-million, Mike Nichols-directed movie is any good. At the high point of the madness, Random House couldn't print copies fast enough, and at least one desperate soul in Los Angeles reportedly offered booksellers $50 for a copy.

This furious activity was generated by a small group of White House operatives and political reporters, many of whom speculated endlessly in the press about how the real author must be someone they knew. It's so true to life, they said, it must be based on inside information. The possibility that some outsider could merely have a very vivid imagination apparently wasn't a possibility.

Even in death, whom you knew is beginning to count for more than what you did. Two novelists who died in the first weeks of 1996 provide a useful contrast. Harold Brodkey was wired into the literary world: He lived in Manhattan, was a lively interview (often claiming that he was so good that other novelists either plagiarized from him or based characters on him) and wrote for *The New Yorker.*

But he was mostly famous for being famous; a great deal of hype surrounded his 32-years-in-the-making first novel, *The Runaway Soul.* Yet when it was finally published in 1991, reviewers tended to hate it ("heartsinkingly charmless" was a typical description), and the public stayed away.

None of this mattered; the literary world takes care of its own. Brodkey got the literary equivalent of a 21-gun salute: lengthy obituary and appreciation in the *New York Times,* lengthy appreciation in the *Washington Post,* photo and autobiographical snippets in *The New Yorker,* etc.

By contrast, Walter M. Miller, Jr. shunned not only the literary world but also everyone else, too. He wrote one novel, *A Canticle for Leibowitz,* which appeared in 1959. A dark and disturbing look at religious life after a nuclear holocaust, it's been perennially in print, selling more than two million copies. Miller was a troubled man and took his own life. Six months after his death, no newspaper outside of his native Florida had bothered to report the fact. That wouldn't surprise W.J. Schlicht, Jr., but it's still rather sad.

All these are dire omens; it's easy to wonder if there's any point to novels any more. David Foster Wallace, as it happened, provided the most eloquent defense of the art when he noted that "fiction's one of the few experiences where loneliness can be both confronted and relieved. Drugs, movies where stuff blows up, loud parties — all these chase away loneliness by making me forget my name's Dave, and I live in a one-by-one box of bone no other party can penetrate or know. Fiction, poetry, music, really deep, serious sex, and, in various ways, religion — these are the places (for me) where loneliness is countenanced, stared down, transfigured, treated."

Luckily, Wallace is not the only one who feels this way. Despite all the gloomy predictions about the death of reading, he probably has more company than you might think. ■

1995's Longest-Running Bestsellers

The following books appeared on *Publishers Weekly*'s year-end, cumulative bestseller list in the January 1, 1996, issue. Number of weeks on the bestseller list refers to the amount of time the book spent on the charts in 1995. Here are *The Entertainment Almanac*'s capsule reviews of 1995's bestsellers.

HARDCOVER
FICTION

THE CELESTINE PROPHECY
Author: James Redfield
Publisher: Warner Books($17.95)
Release: 3/94
Number of weeks on bestseller list: 51
In matters of the spirit, many Americans look south, most notably with Carlos Castañeda's hallucinogenic-enhanced Don Juan series. For '90s soul seekers, *The Celestine Prophecy* offers the path to discovering a "completely spiritual culture on Earth." Disillusioned and burned out, the unnamed narrator journeys to Machu Picchu, where he finds the Manuscript, an ancient document possessing the nine key insights into human life.

THE BRIDGES OF MADISON COUNTY
Author: Robert James Waller
Publisher: Warner Books ($16.95)
Release: 4/92
Number of weeks on bestseller list: 40
Clint Eastwood directed the 1995 film starring Eastwood and Meryl Streep. Worldly, self-absorbed photographer Robert Kincaid falls madly in love with middle-aged farm wife Francesca Johnson while passing through Madison County, Iowa, on a photo shoot. The pair, taking advantage of Francesca's empty house, spend four passionate days together.

POLITICALLY CORRECT BEDTIME STORIES
Author: James Finn Garner
Publisher: Macmillan ($8.95)
Release: 4/94
Number of weeks on bestseller list: 24
Garner puts a humorous spin on classic stories including *Little Red Riding Hood, The Three Little Pigs, Snow White* and *Cinderella*. He rewrites the tales in politically and environmentally correct prose, eliminating the discriminatory and insensitive language often found in classic tales.

THE RAINMAKER
Author: John Grisham
Publisher: Doubleday ($25.95)
Release: 5/95
Number of weeks on bestseller list: 23
Grisham's sixth legal thriller pits a scrupulous young lawyer against a giant corporation and its powerful legal team. After unsuccessfully knocking on hundreds of doors, recent law-school grad Rudy Baylor joins Bruiser Stone's "firm," which is as questionable as the owner's name. In his first case, Baylor represents a leukemia victim who dies because his insurance company refused to pay for a bone-marrow transplant. Grisham adds extra spice (and too many subplots) with a love story, a will and underworld types.

BEACH MUSIC
Author: Pat Conroy
Publisher: Doubleday/Talese ($27.50)
Release: 6/95
Number of weeks on bestseller list: 23
Haunted by his wife's suicide, Jack McCall moves to Rome with his daughter. McCall's escape is shortlived as his sister-in-law begs him to return home and two old friends seek his help in tracking down another friend who has been missing for years. Back in his native South Carolina, McCall must come to terms with his troubled past and tackle personal conflicts.

LADDER OF YEARS
Author: Anne Tyler
Publisher: Knopf ($24)
Release: 5/95
Number of weeks on bestseller list: 17
While feminist pioneers such as Gloria Steinem were breaking new ground for women, Delia Grinstead was rearing children as the perfect surburban housewife. After 20 years of marriage, Grinstead begins to question her life and the choices she made along the way. She abandons her family while on vacation and tries to start a new life but then takes a job as a nanny and housekeeper. Grinstead finds herself at a crossroads, unable to decide if she should continue on with her new life or return to her family.

Moo

Author: Jane Smiley
Publisher: Knopf ($24)
Release: 4/95
Number of weeks on bestseller list: 16

Smiley attacks the country's education system, the excesses of the 1980s, politics and bureaucracy in this satire set in a fictional Iowa university, Moo U. The characters — professors, students and administrators — are self-serving at best and promote their personal agendas at the expense of education.

Coming Home

Author: Rosamunde Pilcher
Publisher: St. Martin's Press ($25.95)
Release: 9/95
Number of weeks on bestseller list: 16

Judith Dunbar, enrolled in a British boarding school when her parents are sent abroad, "adopts" a schoolmate's family. With the imminent approach of World War II, she must make sense of her new life and find a real home for herself. Pilcher incorporates many of her own wartime experiences in *Coming Home*.

Border Music

Author: Robert James Waller
Publisher: Warner Books ($17.95)
Release: 2/95
Number of weeks on bestseller list: 15

Waller has created another passionate novel about a lovey-dovey, middle-aged couple. Linda Lobo, a topless dancer in Minnesota's Rainbow bar, and Jack Carmine, a Vietnam vet, sneak out the back door of the bar and set out on an all-day drive that ends with the pair naked in a motel room. The characters in *Border Music* are more fully drawn than others in Waller's books.

NONFICTION

Men Are From Mars, Women Are From Venus

Author: John Gray
Publisher: HarperCollins ($23)
Release: 6/92
Number of weeks on bestseller list: 51

In what has been labeled the relationship book of the '90s, Gray suggests that in order to improve relationships between men and women, people should focus on the differences between the sexes, not analyze why the differences exist.

Midnight in the Garden of Good and Evil

Author: John Berendt
Publisher: Random House ($24)
Release: 1/94
Number of weeks on bestseller list: 45

Berendt, *Esquire* columnist and former editor of *New York* magazine, spent eight years in Savannah, Georgia, compiling anecdotes and meeting the city's inhabitants. The personalities he encountered could easily pass for the main characters in a best-selling novel: a black drag queen, an inventor with enough poison to contaminate Savannah's water supply and a voodoo priestess. Looming over Savannah is the trial of antiques dealer Jim Williams, who is charged with murdering his young companion.

Sisters

Authors: Carol Saline and Sharon Wohlmuth
Publisher: Running Press ($27.50)
Release: 10/94
Number of weeks on bestseller list: 45

Journalist Saline and photojournalist Wohlmuth explore relationships between female siblings using essays and black-and-white photos to highlight 36 famous and not-so-famous sets of sisters. The Turlington sisters talk about their supermodel sister Christy; Coretta Scott King and her sister Edythe correspond about Martin Luther King, Jr.; and Janice Coffey discusses her sister Elizabeth, who used to be her brother.

The Seven Spiritual Laws of Success

Author: Deepak Chopra
Publisher: New World Library ($14)
Release: 1/95
Number of weeks on bestseller list: 43

Multi-best-selling author Chopra breaks his self-help program into seven principles that promise success at every turn. He teaches readers how to achieve harmony with their true nature and natural law, a process which results in fulfilled relationships, a sense of well being, increased energy and material abundance.

THE HOT ZONE
Author: Richard Preston
Publisher: Random House ($23)
Release: 9/94
Number of weeks on bestseller list: 29

This is probably not the book for the queasy or the chronic worrier. Journalist Preston describes in excruciating detail the symptoms and terrible death caused by the Ebola virus. He visited a cave (donning a space suit) in Kenya where scientists think the virus originated and then traveled to Reston, Virginia, where, in 1989, a group of lab monkeys contracted a form of the virus. Perhaps more distressing than his gory descriptions is Preston's warning that we are not safe from other deadly viruses that could be easily transmitted to the United States through animals and humans.

MARS AND VENUS IN THE BEDROOM
Author: John Gray
Publisher: HarperCollins ($24)
Release: 4/95
Number of weeks on bestseller list: 26

Gray is back at it again, this time dispensing bedroom advice. In his sex manual, Gray suggests ways for couples to achieve optimal pleasure and satisfaction, maintain the spark in a relationship and talk openly about sexual needs and desires without offending the other. Curiously absent in "the sex guide for the 1990s" is coverage of AIDS and other sexually transmitted diseases.

HOW TO ARGUE AND WIN EVERY TIME
Author: Gerry Spence
Publisher: St. Martin's Press ($22.95)
Release: 3/95
Number of weeks on bestseller list: 26

Successful trial lawyer Spence provides readers the tools necessary to achieve positive results in everyday arguments, whether they be with a spouse, co-worker, child or teacher. Claiming argument is both an art and a technique, Spence recommends that people argue out of the "heart zone," use fear as an ally, let their emotions run free and know when to argue.

THE DEATH OF COMMON SENSE
Author: Philip K. Howard
Publisher: Random House ($18)
Release: 1/95
Number of weeks on bestseller list: 25

New York attorney Howard believes there are too many rules and regulations in the United States that complicate even the simplest project and offend

common sense. He uses anecdotes to prove his point and to attack nearly every form of regulation, including fire-safety codes, environmental laws, OSHA rules and bureaucratic guidelines. Though he does have a point, Howard seems to be longing for the good ole days when there were fewer regulations but many more accidents.

A GOOD WALK SPOILED
Author: John Feinstein
Publisher: Little, Brown ($23.95)
Release: 6/95
Number of weeks on bestseller list: 21

This account may be a little long, but it's certainly thorough. Feinstein followed a group of professional golfers on the tour, beginning with 1993's Ryder Cup and wrapping up with 1994's PGA Championship, aiming to "really get inside the heads of the players." He succeeds in familiarizing readers with Curtis Strange, Tom Watson, Nick Faldo and Greg Norman (to name a few). Lots of biographical information on the players and background on the tournaments.

IN THE KITCHEN WITH ROSIE
Author: Rosie Daley
Publisher: Knopf ($14.95)
Release: 4/94
Number of weeks on bestseller list: 23

Oprah Winfrey's personal chef, Daley, helped the talk-show maven finally overcome the diet roller coaster by serving up delicious, low-fat, low-calorie meals. Winfrey's favorites include the Unfried Fried Chicken, Unfried  French Fries and low-fat cheesecake. Mmm mmm.

THE BEARDSTOWN LADIES' COMMONSENSE INVESTMENT GUIDE
Author: Leslie Whitaker
Publisher: Hyperion ($19.95)
Release: 1/95
Number of weeks on bestseller list: 17

Serious investors may be hesitant to take investment advice from a group of 16 women, averaging 55 years old, from Beardstown, Illinois, but given their record, even Peter Lynch may think twice. The Beardstown Ladies investment club has enjoyed a 23.4 percent average annual return since 1980 on 20 stocks. In 1991, they scored a 59.5 percent gain. The book includes actual minutes from their meetings, case histories of their stocks, recommended research resources and anecdotes. An entertaining and informative investment guide.

The 45th annual National Book Awards were presented November 15, 1995, at New York City's Plaza Hotel.

Fiction
> *Sabbath's Theater,*
> Philip Roth
> (Houghton Mifflin)

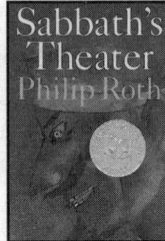

Nonfiction
> *The Haunted Land:*
> *Facing Europe's Ghosts*
> *After Communism,*
> Tina Rosenberg
> (Random House)

Poetry
> *Passing Through: The Later Poems, New and*
> *Selected,* Stanley Kunitz (Norton)

1995 NATIONAL BOOK CRITICS CIRCLE AWARDS

The 1995 National Book Critics Circle Awards were presented March 21, 1996, at New York University.

Fiction
> *Mrs. Ted Bliss,* Stanley
> Elkin (Hyperion)

General Nonfiction
> *A Civil Action,*
> Jonathan Harr
> (Random House)

Biography or
Autobiography
> *Savage Art: A*
> *Biography of Jim*
> *Thompson,*
> Robert Polito (Knopf)

Poetry
> *Time & Money,* William Matthews
> (Houghton Mifflin)

Criticism
> *The Forbidden Best Sellers of Pre-Revolutionary*
> *France,* Robert Darnton (Norton)

MY POINT ... AND I DO HAVE ONE

Author: Ellen DeGeneres
Publisher: Bantam ($19.95)
Release: 8/95
Number of weeks on bestseller list: 16

If she has a point, DeGeneres does not include it in her book. Her stand-up routines are funny and her television show is sharp, but her talent doesn't carry over to the written word. *My Point* lacks both her subtle humor and witty self-deprecating stories. DeGeneres can't be put entirely at fault — it seems every other stand-up comic/sitcom star is going the book route with his or her take on quirky, inconsequential subjects.

NEW PASSAGES: MAPPING YOUR LIFE ACROSS TIME

Author: Gail Sheehy
Publisher: Random House ($25)
Release: 6/95
Number of weeks on bestseller list: 15

Twenty years ago Sheehy couldn't imagine life after 50. Hell, she'd have one foot in the grave by then. In the sequel to 1976's 10-million seller, *Passages,* Sheehy changes her tune significantly, asserting that middle age can be the most productive and healthy period in life. She arrived at this conclusion after interviewing more than 500 people between the ages of 20 and 70, including Joni Mitchell and Gloria Steinem, and found plenty of personal and professional vitality in the middle-aged set. Perfect timing for those baby boomers turning 50.

COUPLEHOOD

Author: Paul Reiser
Publisher: Bantam ($19.95)
Release: 10/94
Number of weeks on bestseller list: 15

Reiser, the star of NBC's *Mad About You,* offers his take on being part of a couple, lightheartedly highlighting the good and bad associated with relationships.

PAPERBACK
MASS MARKET

THE ALIENIST

Author: Caleb Carr
Publisher: Random House ($6.99)
Release: 7/95
Number of weeks on bestseller list: 26

Set in turn-of-the-century New York, Carr's historical thriller reveals the corruption in the city's police department that led to the appointment of Theodore Roosevelt as police commissioner. Dr. Lazlo Kreizler, the "alienist," enlists the help of two reformist detectives, a *New York Times* reporter, Roosevelt and his secretary to capture a deranged serial killer who preys on young male prostitutes.

The Chamber

Author: John Grisham
Publisher: Doubleday ($7.50)
Release: 4/95
Number of weeks on bestseller list: 25

Straying from Grisham's characteristic legal-suspense genre, *The Chamber* explores family relationships and a man's troubled past rather than focusing on an explosive courtroom battle. After years of appeal, Sam Cayhall, convicted of bombing the office of a civil-rights lawyer and killing the lawyer's two sons, awaits "the chamber" in a Mississippi state penitentiary. Cayhall's grandson, recently admitted to the bar, stages a last-ditch effort to save Cayhall.

Embraced by the Light

Author: Betty J. Eadie
Publisher: Gold Leaf Press ($5.99)
Release: 10/94
Number of weeks on bestseller list: 24

Of all the near-death experience books on the market, Eadie's account of heaven and its dwellers stands out for its originality. Eadie, 31 at the time, "died" on a hospital bed just prior to surgery. Instead of a celestial paradise, she found a heaven resembling a not-so-perfect Earth.

The Day After Tomorrow

Author: Allan Folsom
Publisher: Warner Vision ($6.99)
Release: 4/94
Number of weeks on bestseller list: 21

Much publicity surrounded the deal made for *The Day After Tomorrow,* Folsom's first novel, which earned him an unprecedented $5.3 million in book and movie rights. His advance, the largest ever for a first novel, was $750,000. The story: Paul Osborn, sitting in a Paris cafe, spots the man who killed his father 20 years earlier. The man gets away, but Osborn begins an obsessive quest to find him, ask him why he committed the murder and then kill him. The high-tech thriller zooms between Paris, New York, London, Los Angeles and Switzerland.

The Hot Zone

Author: Richard Preston
Publisher: Doubleday/Anchor ($6.99)
Release: 8/95
Number of weeks on bestseller list: 20
See page 721

Circle of Friends

Author: Maeve Binchy
Publisher: Dell ($6.50)
Release: 11/91
Number of weeks on bestseller list: 19

Pat O'Connor directed the 1995 film starring Minnie Driver, Chris O'Donnell and Geraldine O'Rawe.
Eve, raised in an orphanage, and Benny, who comes from a middle-class background, continue their childhood friendship as they attend the same university in Dublin. The girls come of age while studying in the city, and the plump, homely Benny wins the heart of the school's heartthrob, Jack.

Congo

Author: Michael Crichton
Publisher: Ballantine ($6.99)
Release: 1/93
Number of weeks on the bestseller list: 18

Frank Marshall directed the 1995 film starring Dylan Walsh, Laura Linney, Ernie Hudson, Joe Don Baker, Tim Curry and Taylor Nichols.
Amy, a gorilla with a 620-word sign language vocabulary, has an understanding of the Congo that is coveted by explorers in pursuit of treasures in King Solomon's mines. A professor who has been studying Amy takes her back to the jungle, and the fortune hunters join the pair, hoping to capitalize on Amy's knowledge of the Congo.

Tom Clancy's Op-Center

Author: Tom Clancy
Publisher: Berkley ($6.99)
Release: 2/95
Number of weeks on bestseller list: 17

Based on the NBC miniseries starring Harry Hamlin, Lindsay Frost, Kim Cattrall, Wilford Brimley and Rod Steiger
The day that Paul Hood steps in as director of the National Crisis Management Center, a government agency that keeps an eye on international hot spots, rebel KGB guards steal three nuclear warheads from the Ukraine. Hood's problems at home are just as menacing, and the President he serves would rather be in bed with a reporter/spy than at work in the Oval Office.

The Body Farm

Author: Patricia Cornwell
Publisher: Berkley ($6.99)
Release: 9/95
Number of weeks on bestseller list: 16

Not the best from Cornwell but certainly the most predictable. The FBI pulls medical examiner/sleuth Dr. Kay Scarpetta and her sidekick, Capt. Pete Marino, from their familiar Richmond digs to work on a North Carolina murder case. The victim is a young girl, and all evidence points to an escaped serial killer whom Marino and Scarpetta have tangled with before. Scarpetti is not convinced and takes the investigation in another direction.

Nothing Lasts Forever

Author: Sidney Sheldon
Publisher: Warner Books ($6.99)
Release: 9/95
Number of weeks on bestseller list: 16

It's not surprising the schlockmeister set his latest bestseller in a hospital and made the main characters beautiful residents. The theme is all the rage on television, so how could he go wrong? Set in San Francisco's Embarcadero County Hospital, three women doctors confront drama in their personal lives as well as on the job. Dr. Paige Taylor tackles murder charges for euthanizing a patient, Dr. Kat Hunter faces the emotional scars left from childhood sexual abuse and Dr. Honey Taft must rely on more than her brains to be a successful doctor.

Debt of Honor

Author: Tom Clancy
Publisher: Putnam ($7.50)
Release: 8/95
Number of weeks on bestseller list: 15

Since the Cold War is no longer topical, Clancy has decided to focus on other forms of international intrigue, but judging by *Debt of Honor*, he has not yet found his niche. Jack Ryan returns as Clancy's protagonist, but he disappears in the whirlwind of subplots that include hostile U.S.-Japanese relations, rape charges against the vice president, the capture of two C.I.A. operatives by a Mideast drug terrorist, a stock-market crash and a crusade against defective automobile gas tanks.

Trade

Seven Habits of Highly Effective People

Author: Stephen R. Covey
Publisher: Simon & Schuster/Fireside ($12)
Release: 8/90
Number of weeks on bestseller list: 51

Though indulging in the free-to-be-synergy language of self-help, *7 Habits of Highly Effective People* effectively addresses the ills of life and work. In his runaway bestseller, management consultant Covey brings a sensible, soulful approach to professional and personal empowerment.

Chicken Soup for the Soul

Editors: Jack Canfield and Mark Hansen
Publisher: Health Communications ($12.95)
Release: 5/93
Number of weeks on bestseller list: 22

Taking the advice of their audiences, motivational speakers Canfield and Hansen compiled and published their inspirational stories. Also included are stories from Art Buchwald, Gloria Steinem and Bennett Cerf.

Ten Stupid Things Women Do to Mess Up Their Lives

Author: Laura Schlessinger
Publisher: HarperPerennial ($10)
Release: 1/95
Number of weeks on bestseller list: 45

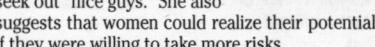

Schlessinger uses examples from her psychotherapy practice and her nationally syndicated radio show to help women take control of their lives. She recommends that women in unhappy relationships dump the "jerks" and seek out "nice guys." She also suggests that women could realize their potential if they were willing to take more risks.

What to Expect When You're Expecting

Authors: A. Eisenberg, H. Murkoff and S. Hathway
Publisher: Workman ($10.95)
Release: 5/91
Number of weeks on bestseller list: 44

The bible for pregnant women, *What to Expect When You're Expecting* outlines the month-by-month physical and emotional changes a mother experiences and the attendant growth and development of her baby.

Reviving Ophelia

Author: Mary Pipher
Publisher: Ballantine ($12.50)
Release: 3/95
Number of weeks on bestseller list: 36

Pipher, a clinical psychologist who has worked with adolescent girls for more than 20 years, lets young women tell their own personal and painful stories of living in a "girl-poisoned culture" — one that stifles girls' creativity and intelligence and dictates that females should be thin and beautiful. Pipher, urging parents to address these issues, provides strategies to confront growing sexism and violence against women.

A Second Helping of Chicken Soup

Editors: Jack Canfield and Mark Hansen
Publisher: Health Communications ($12.95)
Release: 4/95
Number of weeks on bestseller list: 35

Back by popular demand, Canfield and Hansen have collected more inspirational and uplifting stories that provide readers with anecdotes of love, perserverance and the joys of everyday life.

CARE OF THE SOUL

Author: Thomas Moore
Publisher: HarperPerennial ($13)
Release: 2/94
Number of weeks on bestseller list: 34

Care of the Soul explores human spiritual needs and offers sound, reassuring advice on using everyday life as a guide to personal depth. Moore, a Jung-inspired therapist, lived in a Catholic seminary for 12 years before he began his writing career.

THE STONE DIARIES

Author: Carol Shields
Publisher: Penguin ($10)
Release: 4/95
Number of weeks on bestseller list: 34

Canadian novelist Shields won a Pulitzer Prize and National Book Award for *The Stone Diaries*, the fictional autobiography of Daisy Stone Goodwill. Goodwill, an octogenarian, looks back on her life, reminiscing matter-of-factly about her sorrows, joys and regrets as a wife and mother.

THE SHIPPING NEWS

Author: E. Annie Proulx
Publisher: Simon & Schuster/Touchstone ($12)
Release: 5/94
Number of weeks on bestseller list: 33

Deserted by his wife and left with two small daughters, hapless journalist Quoyle returns to his family's original Newfoundland home. As eccentric as the locals, he enters village life and discovers disturbing secrets about his ancestors.

THE CELESTINE PROPHECY: EXPERIENTIAL GUIDE

Authors: James Redfield and Carol Adrienne
Publisher: Warner Books ($8.99)
Release: 9/95
Number of weeks on bestseller list: 25

Meant to be a companion to *The Celestine Prophecy,* the *Experiential Guide* helps readers expand and intensify the nine insights detailed in the original book and use them to improve their own lives and the lives of loved ones.

THE ARTIST'S WAY

Authors: Judith Cameron with Mark Bryan
Publisher: Jeremy Tarcher ($13.95)
Release: 7/92
Number of weeks on bestseller list: 36

For aspiring and established artists, *The Artist's Way* includes a comprehensive 12-week program to enhance and improve creativity. The book helps creative types overcome and eliminate such stumbling blocks as fear, jealousy, guilt and self-sabotage, replacing them with confidence and productivity.

O.J.'S LEGAL PAD

Authors: Henry Beard and John Boswell
Publisher: Villard ($8.95)
Release: 5/95
Number of weeks on bestseller list: 22

Co-authors Beard, co-founder of the *National Lampoon,* and Boswell claim this yellow legal pad is the real thing — the notebook O.J. scribbled on during his trial. The collection of doodles, defense strategies, alibis and legal theories mercilessly parodies 1995's daytime-television star.

WHAT TO EXPECT THE TODDLER YEARS

Authors: A. Eisenberg, H. Murkoff and S. Hathaway
Publisher: Workman ($15.95)
Release: 12/94
Number of weeks on bestseller list: 19

Why not keep going after the enormous success of *What to Expect When You're Expecting* and *What to Expect the First Year?* The toddler book provides everything parents have come to expect and rely on in the *What to Expect* books: physical and mental changes of young ones, health tips, dos and don'ts and advice and answers to common questions.

DRIVEN TO DISTRACTION

Authors: Edward Hallowell and John J. Ratey
Publisher: S&S/Touchstone ($12)
Release: 3/95
Number of weeks on bestseller list: 17

Most people associate Attention Deficit Disorder (ADD) with children, but Hallowell and Ratey illustrate that the condition afflicts adults as well. Through success stories of other sufferers, they offer hope to adults with the disorder and ways to battle it. State-by-state listings of support groups, medications, symptoms and treatment tips are also included.

A MAP OF THE WORLD

Author: Jane Hamilton
Publisher: Doubleday/Anchor ($12)
Release: 6/95
Number of weeks on bestseller list: 16

It's rare that a family can exist without problems, but the Goodwins seemed to be one of those few families. The family's bliss is shattered when one of the children Mrs. Goodwin is babysitting falls into a pond and is rescued only to be left brain dead. She is then accused of child molestation. Goodwin and her husband nearly self-destruct as their lives fall apart. Though it sounds like a trashy novel, Hamilton's prose makes it a haunting, compelling read.

Publishers Weekly's Best Books of 1995

Publishers Weekly editors annually select what they think are the best books of the year based on "literary excellence, originality, timeliness and the promise of an enduring contribution to our culture." These are titles that usually don't make the bestseller lists — but should. (You won't find any books with "O.J." in the title here.)

FICTION

ALL SOUL'S RISING
by Madison Smartt Bell (Pantheon)

Set during the struggle for Haiti's independence in the late 1700s, this intensely imagined epic novel of racial hatred and bloody upheaval illuminates the enmities among the astonishingly complex ethnic populations of the Caribbean island. Bell evokes a society caught in the crucible of violence with superb characterizations, ranging from the arrogant grand blanc plantation owners to the black slaves — including Toussaint L'Ouverture, the leader of the black revolt. Both graphic and subtle, it is a haunting, magisterial work, produced by a writer in complete control of his craft.

THE FIRST MAN
by Albert Camus (Knopf)

Even in its unfinished state, the work in progress left by Camus at his death has a compelling authenticity and emotional impact. The protagonist, a thinly disguised Camus, recalls his youth in an illiterate, poor, but warmly cushioning family in Algeria, his search to know his dead father and the flowering of his intellect.

WONDER BOYS
by Michael Chabon (Villard)

Bright promise gone awry is the theme of this exuberantly comic novel, whose convoluted plot sparkles with inventiveness and wit. The narrator is a writer at an inspirational dead end; his long-awaited second novel is bloated, seriously flawed and truly unpublishable. A series of encounters — professional, amatory, domestic, collegial — sweep him from one darkly hilarious situation to the next, while the reader basks in Chabon's deft, satiric prose.

SIGNALS OF DISTRESS
by Jim Crace (Farrar, Straus & Giroux)

In the 1830s, when an American steamer founders off the English coast, the inhabitants of a hard-scrabble fishing village are caught up in tragicomic events that cast light on the social fabric and intellectual issues of the day. With irony and a firm knowledge of human nature, Crace spins a beguiling tale whose richly comic scenes do not obscure the dark reality of these peoples' lives.

THE POINT
by Charles D'Ambrosio (Little, Brown)

This debut collection of engrossing short stories establishes D'Ambrosio as a writer to watch. With fluid and compelling prose, he limns some pivotal moments in the lives of people trying to escape private emotional hells; some succeed.

INTERSTATE
by Stephen Dixon (Holt)

Edgy, insistent, run-on dialogue is one feature of a story told eight times, with subtle variations and a basic question: What would you do if the unthinkable occurred? A minivan pulls up alongside a car bearing a father and his two daughters; a bullet is fired; one of the girls dies. The narrative brilliantly explores the permutations of memory, trauma and guilt.

PHOSPHOR IN DREAMLAND
by Rikki Ducornet (Dalkey Archive)

In this wondrous, fantastical novel, Ducornet portrays a 17th-century poet and (very) early photographer as he grapples with issues of permanence and impermanence. By adding a madly loquacious priest, a giant extinct bird and Swiftian wit, Ducornet has created a book that is both touching and slyly funny. Paperback original.

MRS. TED BLISS
by Stanley Elkin (Hyperion)

Hilarity and pathos mingle in Elkin's resonant tale of an elderly Miami widow who undergoes surprising changes as she begins to examine her circumscribed life. A master of playful and eloquent prose, which he employs here with deadpan accuracy, the late Elkin has made of a woman and her times a work of lasting literary merit.

INDEPENDENCE DAY
by Richard Ford (Knopf)

Frank Bascombe, met first in *The Sportswriter,* continues to search for self-knowledge and meaning in a skillful narrative set over the holiday weekend. Now a real-estate agent, Frank attempts to sell a house, to restore a relationship with his ex-wife and retain one with his lover and to establish communication with his troubled teenage son. With a rich grounding of atmospheric details, Ford achieves an acutely observed, virtually seamless chronicle of contemporary archive.

THE CHESS GARDEN
by Brooks Hansen (Farrar, Straus & Giroux)

As difficult to characterize as it is enchanting to read, Hansen's strikingly imaginative novel consists mainly of letters from a doctor who has volunteered to serve in a British concentration camp during the 19th-century Boer War. Dr. Unterhoeven writes, however, about an imaginary kingdom, the Antipodes, whose inhabitants are chess pieces come to life. These fabulist explorations become part of the daily existence of the doctor's family and community back in Dayton, Ohio.

THE WEIGHT OF LOVE
by John Herman (Doubleday/Talese)

An affluent, happily married New York man is suddenly smitten with erotic longings for many women, and the resulting events are surprising even as they unfold with tragic implacability. Herman writes authoritatively about lives in a sophisticated social strata, and his bittersweet story is a page-turner.

THE UNCONSOLED
by Kazuo Ishiguro (Knopf)

Deliberately disorienting, unpredictable and surreal, Ishiguro's almost claustrophobic rendering of a man caught in a nightmarish situation relates to anxieties and psychological crises of modern society. His narrator, a famous musician, utterly lacks self-knowledge and can't sustain emotional relationships. This ambitious work demands close reading.

ANNOTATIONS
by John Keene (New Directions)

Fragmented and highly experimental, Keene's slim first novel (96 pages) is also beautiful and affecting. In spare but richly imagistic language, he evokes not only the physical reality of the St. Louis of his youth, but also the complex emotions of growing up. Paperback original.

A RIVER TOWN
by Thomas Keneally (Doubleday/Talese)

Tim Shea, proprietor of a general store in a little river town in New South Wales at the turn of the century, is the kind of ordinary, decent, principled character that Keneally draws so well. Threatened with financial ruin because of his outspoken comments about social justice, Tim is also in danger of losing his life to the bubonic plague. Keneally shapes his narrative with understated skill, fashioning a powerful story with strong moral undertones.

WAITING FOR THE DARK, WAITING FOR THE LIGHT
by Ivan Klima (Grove/Atlantic)

Klima's bleak but powerful novel portrays the enduring effects of a totalitarian regime on a man's soul. A Czech filmmaker who could not achieve his potential under the Communist yoke finds that freedom has come too late for professional or personal fulfillment.

BLUE SPRUCE
by David Long (Scribner)

The characters in these 12 short stories, who live in a range of perfectly evoked settings that include rural Montana, Washington D.C. and New England, have no hopes except for the possibility of love, but they carry their burdens with strength born of having no alternatives.

RESURRECTION MAN
by Eoin McNamee (Picador)

Belfast in the 1980s is the setting for this wrenching first novel, whose rich prose and analytic intelligence are employed in the service of a riveting narrative. Four men involved in sectarian violence are emblematic of the breakdown of language and communication in a hellish atmosphere of unrelenting hatred.

BATTLEFIELDS AND PLAYGROUNDS
by Janos Nyiri, translated by William Brandon and Janos Nyiri (Farrar, Straus & Giroux)

In one of the most powerful novels about the Holocaust, Nyiri reflects the suffering of Hungarian Jews through the eyes of a bright, spirited, irreverent, courageous young boy. The novel is lively and often funny as we follow Janos Sondor's schoolboy adventures and obsession with sports; as violence and brutality escalate, so does his maturation in the crucible of war.

THE TRUEST PLEASURE
by Robert Morgan (Algonquin)

Restrained yet eloquent, this is the story of a marriage and of a time and place. A hardworking Appalachian farm wife who attends Pentecostal revival meetings and is moved to speak in tongues earns the disdain of her husband, who scorns such practices. This wise and affecting novel offers insight into family life and marriage while poetically evoking the landscape and culture of the North Carolina mountains.

HORSES INTO THE NIGHT
by Baltasar Porcel, translated by John L. Getman (University of Arkansas)

Catalan author Porcel's novel is the story of one family's brutal founding and its centuries-long demise. Although gothic, almost ghoulish, this 1976 Spanish Literary Critics Award winner is also wildly imaginative and lyrically written, with a translation to match. Paperback original.

CHOICES
by Mary Lee Settle (Doubleday/Talese)

The saga of a woman who makes difficult political and moral choices during some of the defining events of the 20th century, Settle's sweeping novel celebrates the grand tradition of social activism. A debutante with a conscience, the protagonist survives the carnage of Spain's Civil War and London during the Blitz and returns to the United States to take part in the civil rights movement.

MEN IN BLACK
by Scott Spencer (Knopf)

A struggling writer finally has a bestseller, but it's a hack book on UFOs that he's written under a pseudonym. As money pours in, his wife finds out about an extramarital affair and his son goes missing. In other hands, this could be a trite story, but Spencer's wry take on moral values, midlife crisis and family relationships shows a mature and thoughtful writer at work.

MORALITY PLAY
by Barry Unsworth (Doubleday/Talese)

Medieval England is the setting for Unsworth's taut drama about a group of traveling players who unwittingly uncover the circumstances surrounding a murder and are plunged into a situation that puts their own lives at risk. Unsworth examines the tenuous influence of piety on human conduct.

THE RIDERS
by Tim Winton (Scribner)

Once in the grip of Winton's tumultuous, haunting story about a man obsessively seeking his missing wife, readers will suspend all disbelief. Winton is a mesmerizing raconteur, and he infuses the narrative with throbbing energy and lyrically charged prose as the Australian protagonist and his bewitching 7-year-old daughter careen across Europe in quest of spiritual peace.

OBJECTS IN THE MIRROR ARE CLOSER THAN THEY APPEAR
by Katherine Weber (Crown)

Witty, poignant and insightful, this accomplished first novel is seen through the eyes of a woman photographer who visits a friend in Geneva and witnesses a destructive liaison.

MYSTERIES

BURNING ANGEL
by James Lee Burke (Hyperion)

Characters from both sides of the law — and places in between — dance through a complex tale set in steamy Louisiana and starring Cajun deputy Dave Robicheaux.

THE SHAMAN LAUGHS
by James Doss (St. Martin's Press)

In southwestern Colorado, a Ute reservation policeman and a local police chief pair up to solve mutilation murders with links to sacred Indian rituals.

77TH STREET REQUIEM
by Wendy Hornsby (Dutton)

While producing a film about the unsolved murder of an L.A. cop in 1974, Maggie MacGowen discovers a surrealistic past with revelations and repercussions that threaten the present.

A WILD AND LONELY PLACE
by Marcia Muller (Mysterious)

Ranging from San Francisco to the Caribbean, a mellow, authoritative Sharon McCone tangles with diplomats from the Mideast and the threats of a serial bomber.

BROWN
by James Polster (Longstreet)

An East Coast sportswriter ends up working as a California PI in a case driven by outrageous circumstances and singular characters.

Under the Beetle's Cellar

by Mary Willis Walker (Doubleday)

1994's Edgar winner for Best Mystery returns with a knockout story of game Texas journalist Molly Cates and a religious fanatic who kidnaps — and buries — a bus full of schoolkids.

SCIENCE FICTION

Legacy

by Greg Bear (Tor)

Bear extrapolates a scientifically complex future from the basic stuff of human nature. Fascinating descriptions of the planet Lamarckia establish it as a world that assimilates and learns from other organisms, making it the perfect test tube for examining the personal and political dramas that engulf the characters.

Sailing Bright Eternity

by Gregory Benford (Bantam)

In the concluding volume of his Galactic Center series, Benford skillfully elucidates fascinating ideas about the stuff of hard SF: quantum effects and particle physics.

Four Ways to Forgiveness

by Ursula K. Le Guin (HarperPrism)

Four interrelated novellas deal with the Hainish culture on the twin planets of Werel and Yeowe and examine the relationship between love, freedom and forgiveness.

Pasquale's Angel

by Paul J. McAuley (Morrow/AvoNova)

Renaissance Florence provides the historical backdrop for this ambitious novel of alternative history in which Leonardo da Vinci, Raphael and Savonarola play pivotal roles.

Door Number Three

by Patrick O'Leary (Tor)

Tantalizing jokes and asides fill this zany, imaginative debut novel in which a therapist encounters a woman who claims to be an alien abducted to Earth; soon he himself begins to blip back and forth in time.

The Diamond Age

by Neal Stephenson (Bantam/Spectra)

Simultaneously SF, fantasy and a political thriller, this intriguing novel set in a far-future Shanghai, when nations have been superseded by enclaves of common cultures, presents its sometimes difficult technical concepts in accessible ways.

1996 PEN/Faulkner Award for Fiction

The PEN/Faulkner Award for Fiction, established in 1980, annually honors an American fiction writer with a $15,000 prize. Located at Washington D.C.'s Folger Shakespeare Library, the award is funded by grants, contributions, special events and benefit readings.

Richard Ford, *Independence Day* (Knopf)

1996 PEN Literary Award Winners

The 1996 PEN Literary Awards were presented in New York City on May 20, 1996. The Hemingway Award was presented April 21, 1996, in Boston.

Ernest Hemingway Foundation/PEN Award for First Fiction
Chang-rae Lee, *Native Speaker* (Riverhead)

PEN/Book-of-the-Month Club Translation Prize
Stanislaw Baranczak and Clare Cavanagh, translators, *View With a Grain of Sand* (Harcourt Brace) by Wislawa Szymborska

PEN Award for Poetry in Translation
Guy Davenport, editor and translator, *7 Greeks* (New Directions)

PEN/Voelcker Award for Poetry
Franz Wright

PEN/Martha Albrand Award for First Nonfiction
Mary Karr, *The Liars' Club* (Viking)

PEN/Spielvogel-Diamonstein Award for the Art of the Essay
Thomas Nagel, *Other Minds—Critical Essays 1969–1994* (Oxford)

Gregory Kolovakos Awards recognizing lifetime dedication to bringing works of Hispanic literatures to English-language readers
Suzanne Jill Levine

Jean Franco

Emerging Writer Award/Renato Poggioli Translation Award
Louise Rozier, *Little Jesus of Sicily* by Fortunato Pasqualino (in progress)

POETRY

THE MASTER LETTERS
by Lucie Brock-Broido (Knopf)

Posthumously discovered letters by Emily Dickinson propel a young, highly accomplished poet into startlingly new realms of syntax, style and vision.

PLAINWATER
by Anne Carson (Knopf)

Classicism, intellect and a vibrant immediacy mark the freewheeling, superbly crafted writings of a Canadian poet.

ENEMIES OF LEISURE
by John Gery (Story Line)

Traditional meters and forms and such images of middle-American life as cowboys and chores are provocatively refashioned in this first collection.

POEMS FOR THE MILLENNIUM, VOL. 1
Edited by Jerome Rothenberg and Pierre Joris (University of California)

This massive, brilliantly orchestrated collection demonstrates the movements and ambitions energizing this century's first 40 years of poetry.

A HUMMOCK IN THE MALOOKAS
by Matthew Rohrer (Norton)

Everything — from motes of dust to desire — is animate and startling in this surrealistic, hip and firmly controlled first collection.

NONFICTION

THE BRONTËS
by Juliet Barker (St. Martin's Press/Dunne)

Here are the Brontës — siblings Charlotte, Emily, Anne and Branwell and their father, the Rev. Patrick — as if met for the first time. This exhaustively researched revisionary depiction by a Brontë scholar and former curator of the Brontë Parsonage Museum will likely stand as definitive for some time.

ZOLA: A LIFE
by Frederick Brown (Farrar, Straus & Giroux)

This shrewd biography, with discussions of all the novels set against the seamy politics of the Second Empire, makes one appreciate Zola's (1840–1902) greatness and originality anew. Brown teaches French literature at the State University of New York.

THE DEATH OF SATAN: HOW AMERICANS HAVE LOST THE SENSE OF EVIL
by Andrew Delbanco
(Farrar, Straus & Giroux)

Columbia University literary scholar Delbanco weighs in with a plea for revival not of old-time religion but of the sense of personal responsibility fostered by traditional religious notions of evil. This is serious cultural history, as witty and elegant as it is impassioned.

THE FUTURE EATERS
by Tim Flannery (Braziller)

Australian research scientist Flannery makes a compelling and accessible argument for the interdependence of man and environment. He describes the impact of time, glaciers, dung beetles, fire and agriculture in a narrative that will interest even those who didn't think they cared about the environment or Australasia. Paperback original.

FIVE EQUATIONS THAT CHANGED THE WORLD: THE POWER AND POETRY OF MATHEMATICS
by Michael Guillen (Hyperion)

In a seamless blend of dramatic biography and mathematical documentary that links the personal with the scientific, Harvard mathematician and physicist Guillen profiles five pioneers whose mathematical equations had far-reaching consequences: Isaac Newton, Albert Einstein, Daniel Bernoulli, Rudolf Clausius and Michael Faraday.

BLACK CONFEDERATES AND AFRO-YANKEES IN CIVIL WAR VIRGINIA
by Ervin L. Jordan Jr. (University Press of Virginia)

Although focusing on Virginia, this well-researched study details an astonishingly broad range of African-American participation in the Civil War, describing not just those who fought for the Union but also those slaves and freedmen who served the Confederacy. Paperback original.

VIRGINIA WOOLF

by James King (Norton)

In an uncanny literary biography of enormous riches, King maintains that Woolf's writing was her attempt to stave off her obsession with death, her self-loathing and the frequent depressions that led to her suicide in 1941.

JAMES THURBER: HIS LIFE AND TIMES

by Harrison Kinney (Holt)

Exhaustive and sprightly, at 1,200 pages this is probably the fullest, most revealing portrait to date of humorist and *The New Yorker* staffer, James Thurber (1894–1961). Liberally sprinkled with Thurber's own words and cartoons, this encyclopedic biography helps us understand how Thurber transmuted personal frustration into engaging doodles and sophisticated satire of human folly and pretense.

EDWARD HOPPER: AN INTIMATE BIOGRAPHY

by Gail Levin (Knopf)

Levin, professor of art at City University of New York, throws Hopper's life and art into sharp new perspective, focusing on the laconic, introverted painter's stormy 43-year marriage to outspoken, gregarious Josephine Nevison, herself an artist, as revealed by her diaries.

WILLIAM MORRIS: A LIFE FOR OUR TIME

by Fiona MacCarthy (Knopf)

Morris (1834–1896) was an astringent critic of Victorian England who nearly became its poet laureate; a manufacturer of lush housewares who rejected his father as a "capitalist villain"; a man at once worldly and naïve, stymied by his wife's affair with artist Dante Gabriel Rossetti.

EDMUND WILSON: A BIOGRAPHY

by Jeffrey Meyers (Houghton Mifflin/Davison)

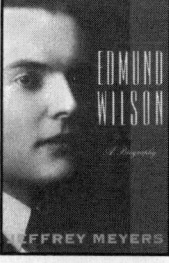

A remarkable feat of biographical sleuthing, this refreshingly down-to-earth life of Wilson (1895–1972), written by a biographer of Hemingway and Fitzgerald, peers beneath the crusty persona to portray a tormented, restless, sexually hyperactive man, a difficult, heavy-drinking husband to four wives, a domineering, lecturing father to his three children.

1996 CALDECOTT MEDAL

The Caldecott Medal is awarded annually by the American Library Association for the most distinguished American picture book for children.

Caldecott Medal for Best Picture Book
Officer Buckle and Gloria, illustrated and written by Peggy Rathmann (Putnam)

Caldecott Honor Books
Alphabet City, illustrated by Stephen T. Johnson (Viking)

Zin! Zin! Zin! a Violin, illustrated by Marjorie Priceman, written by Lloyd Moss (Simon & Schuster Books for Young Readers)

The Faithful Friend, illustrated by Brian Pinkney, written by Robert D. San Souci (Simon & Schuster Books for Young Readers)

Tops & Bottoms, adapted and illustrated by Janet Stevens (Harcourt Brace)

1996 JOHN NEWBERY MEDAL

The Newbery Medal is awarded annually by the American Library Association for the most distinguished contribution to American literature for children.

Newbery Medal for Best Book
The Midwife's Apprentice, Karen Cushman (Clarion)

Newbury Honor Books
What Jamie Saw, Carolyn Coman (Front Street)

The Watsons Go to Birmingham — 1963, Christopher Paul Curtis (Delacorte)

Yolonda's Genius, Carol Fenner (Margaret K. McElderry Books/Simon & Schuster)

The Great Fire, Jim Murphy (Scholastic)

Byzantium: The Decline and Fall
by John Julius Norwich (Knopf)

Completing his popular trilogy begun with *Byzantium: The Early Centuries* and continued in *Byzantium: The Apogee*, British historian Norwich vividly chronicles the last four tumultuous centuries of the Byzantine Empire.

A Concise History of the Russian Revolution
by Richard Pipes (Knopf)

By synthesizing and condensing his *The Russian Revolution* (1990) and *Russia Under the Bolshevik Regime* (1994) into a superb narrative, Harvard historian Pipes has produced the single most readable, useful and illuminating chronicle of the revolution and its aftermath.

Walt Whitman's America: A Cultural Biography
by David S. Reynolds (Knopf)

In a study that roots Whitman (1819–1892) firmly in his times, Reynolds balances the familiar image of the visionary optimist against the disillusioned social critic.

Dark Sun: The Making of the Hydrogen Bomb
by Richard Rhodes (Simon & Schuster)

As compelling as Rhodes's 1986 Pulitzer Prize-winning *The Making of the Atomic Bomb,* this monumental chronicle of the rivalry between the U.S. and the U.S.S.R. to invent, build, test and stockpile hydrogen bombs reveals how perilously close the world came to nuclear Armageddon.

Emerson: The Mind on Fire
by Robert D. Richardson (University of California)

Richardson, biographer of Thoreau, balances the often chilling puritanism of Ralph Waldo Emerson's writing with a portrait of the man as hungry for friendship and maintaining close relationships with Carlyle, Thoreau, Bronson Alcott and Margaret Fuller, arguing that the thinker's icy doctrine of individualism reflected his loneliness.

Emblems of Mind: The Inner Life of Music and Mathematics
by Edward Rothstein (Times Books)

In an elegantly written inquiry, *New York Times* critic-at-large Rothstein explores the links between music and mathematics. His uncanny insight will startle and reward literate generalists, including those with no technical knowledge of either music or math.

Christ on the Rue Jacob
by Severo Sarduy, translated by Suzanne Jill Levine and Carol Maier (Mercury House)

This last book by the Cuban-born Sarduy, who died of AIDS in 1993, maps his life in brief, imagistic essays. This is often melancholic, as Sarduy describes friends who have died, but it is first and foremost a beautiful meditation on a life lived fully. Paperback original.

Landscape and Memory
by Simon Schama (Knopf)

In a rich, labyrinthine survey, Schama explores the role of landscape in myth, art and culture. Arguing that the boundaries between the wild and the cultivated are more flexible than is commonly assumed, this rewarding synthesis maps an uncharted geography of the imagination.

Robert E. Lee: A Biography
by Emory M. Thomas (Norton)

Unlike previous biographers, distinguished Civil War historian Thomas presents Lee as neither an icon nor a flawed figure, but rather as a man who made the best of his lot, whose comic vision of life ultimately shaped him into an individual who was both more and less than his legend.

From the Beast to the Blonde: On Fairy Tales and Their Tellers
by Marina Warner (Farrar, Straus & Giroux)

In a richly illustrated feminist study, cultural historian Warner argues that instead of seeking psychoanalytic meanings in fairy tales, we must first understand them in their social and emotional contexts. Reluctant brides, silent daughters, crones, witches, fates, muses, sirens, Saint Anne, Angela Carter's fiction and Walt Disney's movies all provide grist for her delightfully subversive inquiry.

Alfred Stieglitz: A Biography
by Richard Whalen (Little, Brown)

Whalen's critical portrait presents Stieglitz (1864–1946) as an obsessive perfectionist, a man whose colossal self-righteousness and need for control distorted his dealings with loved ones and fellow artists, including his second wife, Georgia O'Keeffe.

Bestsellers of 1996

The Entertainment Almanac's bestseller list for the first half of 1996 includes books that appeared regularly or for long stretches on the *Publisher's Weekly*, *New York Times* and *Wall Street Journal* lists. Some of the titles listed below, in estimated order of sales, were released over the summer and got off to a great start. We included them because we anticipate they will continue to do well for the remainder of the year.

HARDCOVER

FICTION

THE RUNAWAY JURY

Author: John Grisham
Publisher: Doubleday ($26.95)
Release: 5/96
Veering from his trademark predictability, Grisham mixes it up with clever twists and turns and a page-turning ending. The result? His best, most complicated plot yet. Celeste Wood is suing cigarette manufacturer Pynex, blaming the company for her husband's death from lung cancer. Freelance jury investigator Rankin Fitch has every juror pegged except for one, Nicholas Easter, who has the defense worried. He's a smart guy who has gained the respect of and influence over the other jurors. Trying to figure out Easter's motives is half the fun — the other half is picking the cast for the upcoming film.

HOW STELLA GOT HER GROOVE BACK

Author: Terry McMillan
Publisher: Viking ($23.95)
Release: 5/96

Stella Payne, a 43-year-old divorced mother, lives a pretty good life. She's a $200,000-a-year investment analyst who drives a BMW, lives in an expensive house outside San Francisco and has a personal trainer who has whipped her into phenomenal shape. She misses the thrill of a relationship, though she doesn't necessarily want to open up to a man. When her 11-year-old son goes on vacation with his father, she steals away to a Jamaican resort and meets a 20-year-old local and sparks fly. It may not be McMillan's best, but you'll root for the couple 100 percent.

PRIMARY COLORS

Author: Anonymous (Joe Klein)
Publisher: Random House ($24)
Release: 1/96
Would *Primary Colors* have done so well if the author's identity weren't such a well-kept secret? Probably not. The guessing game was part of the appeal. George Stephanopoulos, James Carville and Joe Klein were short-listed, but each denied penning the fictional exposé. Klein came clean in July 1996 after the *Washington Post* ran a story that outted him as Anonymous. The story is based on President Clinton's 1992 primary campaign (all names have been changed), and for the most part the anecdotes have captured every detail, right down to the meals served on the campaign trail. A little preachy at times but deserves credit for making a potentially dull topic captivating.

THE HORSE WHISPERER

Author: Nicholas Evans
Publisher: Delacorte ($23.95)
Release: 9/95

A long-winded Robert James Waller and somehow even less bearable. Annie, a New York career woman with an impressive résumé, will do anything to lift her daughter's spirits after the teenage Grace and her horse were hit by an 18-wheeler. Grace lost a leg in the accident and her horse, Pilgrim, was injured almost beyond repair. Annie contacts Montana "horse whisperer" Tom, who can cure a horse by whispering in its ear. They travel to Montana, Tom cures Pilgrim and Grace walks and rides again. And, by the way, Annie falls in love with Tom and questions her marriage and hectic city life.

THE TENTH INSIGHT

Author: James Redfield
Publisher: Warner Books ($19.95)
Release: 4/96

Redfield's *The Celestine Prophecy* has taken up permanent residence on the bestseller lists, and it looks as if *The Tenth Insight* will do the same, no matter how disappointing it is even to the most loyal New Agers. The unnamed narrator returns, now navigating the Appalachians, which are strewn with "openings" that lead to another dimension where your soul plots your future. There are also the requisite villains bent on destroying the environment.

THE CELESTINE PROPHECY

Author: James Redfield
Publisher: Warner Books ($17.95)
Release: 3/94
See page 719

ABSOLUTE POWER

Author: David Baldacci
Publisher: Warner Books ($22.95)
Release: 2/96

Another made-for-motion-picture book that is full of intrigue — and holes. Camping out in a Virginia mansion, an aging burglar watches as inebriated President Alan Richmond has animated sex with his mistress, the super-model wife of a rich and powerful octogenarian. He then witnesses Secret Service agents killing the woman. Richmond and his chief of staff, Gloria Russle, maneuver and scramble to keep the President and his image clean. Clint Eastwood will play the burglar and direct the film.

INTENSITY

Author: Dean Koontz
Publisher: Knopf ($25)
Release: 1/96

Not one likely to garner critical praise, Koontz wowed and terrified the most discriminating reviewers with *Intensity*, which takes place over 24 hours and features only two main characters. Chyna Shepherd is a psychology graduate student and the prey of serial killer Edgler Vess. Shepherd, staying in a guest house, spends a day and night trying to stay a step ahead of Vess and thus stay alive. Vess, a meticulous killer, likes to keep his victims close by, so he photographs their dead bodies and eats the pictures.

FIVE DAYS IN PARIS

Author: Danielle Steele
Publisher: Delacorte ($15.95)
Release: 12/95

Predictable and cliché-ridden, but what else to expect from the queen of romance? Peter Haskell, president of an international pharmaceutical company, is in Paris awaiting test results that, if positive, will change the course of chemotherapy (and put millions in his pocket). He meets Olivia Thatcher, the unhappy wife of a senator who has his eye on the White House, and the two spend five passionate days together in Paris. The pair realize they are made for each other and that their marriages are empty and loveless. Oh, what to do, when Thatcher's husband offers her $1 million a year to stand by his side?

MOONLIGHT BECOMES YOU

Author: Mary Higgins Clark
Publisher: Simon & Schuster ($24)
Release: 4/96

Newport is the setting for Clark's 13th novel, and the story remains pretty much true to formula: murder among high society. New York photographer Maggie and her father's former wife, Nuala Moore, reunite at a family reunion. Shortly after the event, Moore is murdered during a seemingly random break-in. Suspicious, Maggie investigates, finds a string of similarly mysterious deaths and becomes the next victim on the killer's list.

NONFICTION

MEN ARE FROM MARS, WOMEN ARE FROM VENUS

Author: John Gray
Publisher: HarperCollins ($23)
Release: 6/92
See page 720

IN CONTEMPT

Authors: Christopher A. Darden with Jess Walter
Publisher: Regan Books ($26)
Release: 3/96

Hands down the best (only positive) thing to come out of the O.J. Simpson trial. *In Contempt* tells Darden's personal story of growing up poor but determined in Richmond, California, with a heroin-addicted brother. Darden does offer his opinion of the trial's leading figures: Judge Ito was "drunk with media attention" and F. Lee Bailey is a "foul-mouthed, arrogant SOB." But he reserves his most scathing remarks for Johnnie Cochran, who suggested that Darden's involvement in the trial was a move by the district attorney's office to include a token African American on the prosecution team.

THE SEVEN SPIRITUAL LAWS OF SUCCESS
Author: Deepak Chopra
Publisher: New World Library ($12.95)
Release: 1/95
See page 720

BAD AS I WANNA BE
Author: Dennis Rodman with Tim Keown
Publisher: Delacorte ($22.95)
Release: 6/96

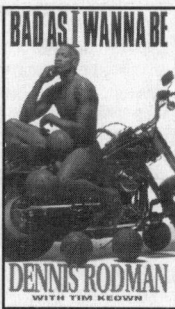

This one will sell based on the sole fact that people want to know what makes the tattooed, hair-dyed rebel tick. In his memoir, the Chicago Bulls star rebounder reveals "secrets" about fame, money, sex, Madonna, drugs and the NBA.

SIMPLE ABUNDANCE: A DAY BOOK OF COMFORT AND JOY
Author: Sarah Ban Breathnach
Publisher: Warner Books ($18.95)
Release: 11/95
For women only, this inspirational guide provides an exercise or meditation for each day of the year that will help women clear their minds and make their chaotic lives more manageable.

RUSH LIMBAUGH IS A BIG FAT IDIOT AND OTHER OBSERVATIONS
Author: Al Franken
Publisher: Delacorte ($21.95)
Release: 2/96
What goes around comes around. For years, Limbaugh has been skewering Democrats, and now Franken, a *Saturday Night Live* writer and performer, has a go at the big man. Using half-truths and out-of-context quotes, tactics borrowed from Limbaugh, Franken's humorous collection of essays attacks not only Limbaugh, but also many of his Republican cronies, including Newt Gingrich, Jerry Falwell and Phil Gramm. Franken also provides a retrospective on Limbaugh's life, which portrays him as a leech who lived off unemployment and didn't register to vote until he was 35.

IT TAKES A VILLAGE AND OTHER LESSONS CHILDREN TEACH US
Author: Hillary Rodham Clinton
Publisher: Simon & Schuster ($20)
Release: 1/96

A big campaign-year pitch for her husband and his support of family values. The first lady draws on personal experiences as a mother, public servant and child advocate to suggest ways to improve the life of children worldwide.

EMOTIONAL INTELLIGENCE
Author: Daniel Goleman
Publisher: Bantam ($23.95)
Release: 10/95
Goleman, a science writer for the *New York Times,* argues that one's emotions play a much larger part in the decision-making process and in determining success than ever before believed. He introduces the reader to "emotional intelligence," which is a set of skills one uses to control impulses in self-motivation and relationships. He suggests ways to use one's emotional intelligence constructively.

UNDAUNTED COURAGE: MERIWETHER LEWIS, THOMAS JEFFERSON AND THE OPENING OF THE AMERICAN WEST
Author: Stephen E. Ambrose
Publisher: Simon & Schuster ($27.50)
Release: 2/96
Using many of William Clark's journals, Ambrose chronicles the triumphs and travails of the explorers' journey to open the American frontier, focusing on Meriwether Lewis's role in the quest. President Thomas Jefferson selected his secretary to make the journey, which was dogged by problems, including an alcoholic boat builder and other alcohol-related hindrances involving both Lewis and Clark.

MIDNIGHT IN THE GARDEN OF GOOD AND EVIL
Author: John Berendt
Publisher: Random House ($24)
Release: 1/94
See page 720

PAPERBACK

MASS MARKET

THE RAINMAKER
Author: John Grisham
Publisher: Dell ($7.99)
Release: 2/96
See page 719

THE GREEN MILE (#1 TWO DEAD GIRLS)
Author: Stephen King
Publisher: Signet ($2.99)
Release: 3/96
A clever marketing tool — write a serialized novel with the first installment being the author's best work in years. King has pretty much insured him-

self and his publisher that at least the next few episodes will also make the bestseller list (and they did). Paul Edgecombe, a death-row superintendent, has never been rattled by any of his charges, but John Coffey is different. Convicted of raping and murdering two 9-year-old sisters, Coffey's gentle demeanor bothers Edgecombe. Also introduced are inmate Eduard Delacroix, who has a friendship with a brown mouse, and malicious prison guard Percy Wetmore.

LET ME CALL YOU SWEETHEART
Author: Mary Higgins Clark
Publisher: Pocket ($7.50)
Release: 5/96
Investigator Kerry McGrath's latest investigation is more troubling than any other case she has handled. Visiting a plastic surgeon with her daughter, McGrath discovers that the doctor is changing his patients' faces to resemble a woman who was murdered two years ago. As she delves deeper in the investigation, McGrath finds people so obsessed with beauty they're willing to kill for it.

APOCALYPSE WATCH
Author: Robert Ludlum
Publisher: Bantam ($7.50)
Release: 5/96

American agent Harry Latham spent three years undercover with an underground neo-Nazi movement amassing a list of the group's followers, which includes government officials of the United States and its allies. Suddenly Harry disappears, and his brother, Drew, frantically searches for him. When Harry surfaces, ready to go public with the list, Drew questions the list and Harry's reliability.

WAITING TO EXHALE
Author: Terry McMillan
Publisher: Pocket Books ($6.99)
Release: 12/95
Forest Whitaker directed the 1995 film starring Whitney Houston, Angela Bassett, Loretta Devine, Lela Rochon and Gregory Hines.
Four Arizona women are not lucky in love. In fact, the men they are with pretty much suck, and the women know that. Each is successful in her career but in a state of flux when it comes to love. Savannah can't decide if she should continue an affair with a married man; Bernadine has been dumped by her husband for his white bookkeeper; Robin keeps picking the wrong man; and Gloria is recently separated from her bisexual husband but does have hopes for her developing relationship with Marvin.

THE GLASS LAKE
Author: Maeve Binchy
Publisher: Dell ($7.50)
Release: 4/96
When Kit McMahon was 12 years old, her mother supposedly drowned in Ireland's Lough Glass. But Kit found a suicide note her mother wrote to her father. Fearing her mother won't get a proper burial, Kit burns the letter and keeps the secret to herself. Years later, Kit finds her mother living in London with a new name and a successful career. Mother and daughter suffer more than they ever could have imagined from the discovery. A real tear-jerker.

SOPHIE'S WORLD
Author: Jostein Gaarder
Publisher: Berkley ($6.99)
Release: 3/96
Sophie, a 15-year-old Norwegian girl, receives a letter in the mail that asks two questions: Who are you? Where does the world come from? She answers the letter and begins a correspondence course in philosophy with the author, an anonymous philosopher. She also starts receiving another batch of strange letters, which are for another girl, Hilde. Sophie's lessons in critical thinking have her doubting her existence. An enjoyable browse in philosophy.

ROSE MADDER
Author: Stephen King
Publisher: Signet ($7.50)
Release: 6/96
After years of physical and sexual abuse, Rosie Daniels finally summons the courage to leave her savage husband, Norman. When Norman discovers she has fled, his already frail sanity is shattered, and he embarks on a murderous journey in pursuit of Rosie. King's 29th novel is ripe with feminist themes, from the sense of sorority Rosie feels at a women's shelter to the mystical and revengeful powers she finds in a bewitching painting.

THE COVE
Author: Catherine Coulter
Publisher: Jove ($6.99)
Release: 3/96
Escaping a sanitarium, where she was falsely placed, Sally Brainerd flees to her aunt's house in the Cove. FBI Special Agent James Quinlan follows her to the small town, seeking information about her father's murder. Brainerd, alone and scared, falls in love with Quinlan. The pair links two other murders to Brainerd's father's death and tries to uncover the secret beneath the connection.

EYES OF A CHILD

Author: Richard North Patterson
Publisher: Ballantine
($6.99)
Release: 1/96

In the sequel to Patterson's *Degree of Guilt*, hotshot lawyer Christopher Paget returns, this time as the defendant rather than the defender. He's accused of killing his lover's sleazy ex-husband, Ricardo Arias. Things don't bode well for Paget. He had ample motive: Arias claimed Paget's son, Carlo, sexually assaulted his 5-year-old daughter and he was blackmailing Paget, who had his eyes on the U.S. Senate. To make matters worse, Paget's weak alibi is hole-ridden. The accused hires the only lawyer who could win this impossible case, Caroline Masters, the judge who heard Paget's last high-profile case.

TRADE

SNOW FALLING ON CEDARS

Author: David Guterson
Publisher: Vintage ($12)
Release: 10/95

Meditative and lyrical, Guterson's first novel appealed to both literary snobs and the average Joe looking for a good mystery. And hordes of both bought the book, with sales of more than 350,000. Not bad for a rookie. In 1954, on Washington's San Piedro Island, Kabuo Miyamoto is on trial for killing fellow fisherman and childhood friend Carl Heine, Jr. There had been some bad blood between Miyamoto and Heine stemming from an agreement gone sour between the fathers of both men. Flashbacks woven throughout the trial reveal a pre-war San Piedro torn apart when its Japanese-American citizens were sent to internment camps. The trial forces Miyamoto's wife, Hatsue, to come to terms with the failure of her first relationship, which was with a white boy.

CHICKEN SOUP FOR THE SOUL

Editors: Jack Canfield and Mark Hansen
Publisher: Health Communications ($12.95)
Release: 5/93
See page 724

A 3RD SERVING OF CHICKEN SOUP FOR THE SOUL

Editors: Jack Canfield and Mark Hansen
Publisher: Health Communications ($12.95)
Release: 4/96

It may be the third serving, but it's the fourth book in the *Chicken Soup* series. This course features 101 new inspirational stories by luminaries such as Michael Jordan, Erma Bombeck, Maya Angelou and Jimmy Carter.

INDEPENDENCE DAY

Author: Richard Ford
Publisher: Vintage ($13)
Release: 5/96

Frank Bascombe, last seen in Ford's 1986 *The Sportswriter*, returns from the road, where he covered baseball games for a national magazine. He's settled down as a New Jersey real-estate agent, though he remains embittered and depressed. Over a July 4th weekend, Bascombe fights with his ex-wife, nearly ends another relationship, almost sells a house, tries to bond with his troubled son and mourns the death of a stranger. Ford won the Pulitzer Prize for *Independence Day*.

THERE'S TREASURE EVERYWHERE: A CALVIN AND HOBBES COLLECTION

Author: Bill Watterson
Publisher: Andrews & McMeel ($14.95)
Release: 3/96

Though Watterson called it quits December 31, 1995, you can continue to enjoy the adventures of the beloved 6-year-old Calvin and his loyal sidekick, Hobbes, with Watterson's largest collection of comic strips. The duo venture to the regions of Spaceman Spiff and Stupendous Man, race at warp speed down a hill and ponder the irony of life.

SEVEN HABITS OF HIGHLY EFFECTIVE PEOPLE

Author: Stephen R. Covey
Publisher: Simon & Schuster/Fireside ($12)
Release: 8/90
See page 724

1995 NOBEL PRIZE FOR LITERATURE

Seamus Heaney, Ireland

1996 PULITZER PRIZES IN LETTERS

The 1996 Pulitzer Prizes were awarded on April 9, 1996, by Columbia University.

Fiction
Independence Day, Richard Ford (Knopf)

General Nonfiction
The Haunted Land: Facing Europe's Ghosts After Communism, Tina Rosenberg (Random House)

History
William Cooper's Town: Power and Persuasion on the Frontier of the Early American Republic, Alan Taylor (Knopf)

Biography or Autobiography
God: A Biography, Jack Miles (Knopf)

Poetry
The Dream of the Unified Field, Jorie Graham (Ecco Press)

Drama
Rent, Jonathan Larson

1995 BOOKER PRIZE

Britain's most prestigious literary award, the Booker Prize, was presented on November 7, 1995, at London's Guildhall.

The Ghost Road,
Pat Barker (Dutton)

REVIVING OPHELIA
Author: Mary Pipher
Publisher: Ballantine ($12.50)
Release: 3/95
See page 724

DEAD MAN WALKING
Author: Sister Helen Prejean
Publisher: Vintage ($12)
Release: 6/94
Tim Robbins directed the 1995 film starring Susan Sarandon and Sean Penn. Sister Helen Prejean was admittedly naive when she agreed to write to death-row inmate Elmo Pat Sonnier, who was convicted of murdering a young couple. She didn't expect him to write back, but he did. Letters

became visits, and the visits led to a spiritual relationship. Sister Prejean tried to have Sonnier's sentence commuted, citing a grossly inadequate defense. Though she failed, she helped Sonnier come to terms with his crimes and his fate.

DR. ATKINS' NEW DIET REVOLUTION
Author: Dr. Robert C. Atkins
Publisher: M. Evans ($12.95)
Release: 12/94
Atkins' diet program teaches people how to change their metabolism, which he cites as a culprit in weight gain and obesity. He helps readers adjust their rate of metabolism, enabling the body to burn fat more efficiently. His diet claims to allow people to eat as much as they like without packing on the pounds.

TEN STUPID THINGS WOMEN DO TO MESS UP THEIR LIVES
Author: Laura Schlessinger
Publisher: HarperPerennial ($10)
Release: 1/95
See page 724

Do It Yourself

■ BY R.SETH FRIEDMAN

Hordes of people are quickly becoming published writers, and they aren't seeing their bylines in *The New Yorker* or on the cover of a best-selling novel. Far from it. They are the self-published who are using their computers and Xerox machines to spread the word cheaply on everything from politics to body piercing.

Rather than trying to break into more established, mainstream magazines, these self-publishers go it alone, writing about their hobbies and obsessions on their own terms. They range from high-school students confessing the triumphs and travails of angst-ridden adolescence to parents chronicling the demands of child rearing. However, twentysomethings dominate the 'zine movement, seizing on self-publishing as a forum for their opinions and passions.

The idea of publishing a personal magazine isn't a new one; Ben Franklin was doing it in the 18th century. But 'zines as we know them today evolved from underground publications that first emerged in the 1940s.

In the first fanzines, people primarily wrote about their favorite science-fiction stories. Eventually, personal anecdotes began to overwhelm the commentary. In the 1950s, poetry chapbooks became popular with the rise of the beats. These pamphlets featured collections of poetry that the major publishing houses ignored. Then, in the 1970s, punk rock took teens by storm. The mainstream publications overlooked the radical new music, leaving fans to create their own style of music journalism. These influential fanzines continue to dictate the character of the modern-day 'zine.

Over the years, the lines between science-fiction fanzines, music fanzines and poetry chapbooks began to blur. The term 'zine was coined (by shortening fanzine) to describe this new trend in homespun publishing, which didn't fit any one journalistic category.

It didn't take long for the trend to flourish. There are 'zines for virtually every topic imaginable. It's almost impossible to determine the exact number of 'zines currently published worldwide, but *Factsheet 5,* a publication that covers the 'zine world, estimates the number to be around 50,000 and counting. Sure, many fold after the first few issues, but the effort and the interest remain.

Many 'zines explore culture and politics, with coverage of civilizations far and wide. A recent hot trend has been the exploration of the American West. For years, Hollywood has overexposed and sanitized the West. 'Zine publishers look beyond the cowboy-and-Indian stories, focusing on other attractions, including the West's endless highways and quirky roadside attractions.

In a flurry of publishing activity, there are four new 'zines devoted to exploring various aspects of Americana. My favorite is the Minneapolis-based *State Fair.* The second issue has yet to hit the stands, but the first celebrates true Americana with a personal touch and sense of irony and includes stories about 4-H animal judging, carnival rides and the abominable food that's offered all over the countryside.

Having trouble finding a selection of quality 'zines? Below are some of our favorites with addresses.

ANSWER Me!
Price: $5 per issue
Jim and Debbie Goad
Goad to Hell Enterprises
P.O. Box 31009
Portland, OR 97231
E-mail: Goad2Hell@aol.com

Asian Trash Cinema
Price: $6 per issue or $20 for 4 issues
Craig Ledbetter
P.O. Box 5367
Kingwood, TX 77325
E-mail: 74563.1756@compuserve.com

At-Home Dad
Promoting the Home-Based Father
Price: $1 plus a self-addressed stamped envelope per issue or $12 for 4 issues
Peter Baylies
61 Brightwood Ave.
North Andover, MA 01845
E-mail: athomedad@aol.com

Basement Children 'Zine Distribution
Price: $1 per catalog
Shayna
Basement Children
2502 N. Rockwell
Basement Apartment
Chicago, IL 60647

Beer Frame
The Journal of Inconspicuous Consumption
Price: $2 per issue
Paul Lukas
160 St. Johns Place
Brooklyn, NY 11217
E-mail: krazykat@pipeline.com

The Curious West
For People Who Love the Unusual and Mysterious West
Price: $2.95 per issue or $15 for 6 issues
Judy Miller
634 Main St., Suite 5
Grand Junction, CO 81501
E-mail: desertpubl@aol.com

The spirit of the West encompasses many different elements: sprawling cities, mountain adventures, a sense of freedom and the occasional oddball settler. *Edging West* has a handle on this diversity, offering a sensibility that can't be found east of the Rockies. Published out of the small town of Logan, Utah, *Edging West* profiles real Americans and their contribution to the American patchwork.

Created in the heart of the country, *Devil's Elbow* dwells on the peculiarities that can be found in the Midwest. For one issue, the publishers of the 'zine ventured from their home in Chicago and followed the highways to Missouri, highlighting their adventures. *The Curious West* has a more outdoorsy, back-to-nature feel, but still includes its share of Western oddities, including a visit to Marie Odgen's "Home of Truth" in Utah. Odgen claims God appears before her, telling her about the end of the world.

The granddad of all Western exploration 'zines is undoubtedly *Out West*, which has been around for ages. Twice a year, the publisher and his family leave their home in Nevada City, California, searching out the weirdness that awaits them along our nation's highways. On their last outing they discovered a historical monument to "ladies of the evening," a 32-foot log that's been converted into a one-room travel trailer, a junkyard/museum and a ranch that grows nothing but maggots.

Another group of 'zine publishers are looking East, too, and we're not talking about New England. They explore the enigmatic cultures of China and Japan. Bored with McDonald's, basketball and Coke, many publishers find cultures that combine a thousand-year-old history with a modern character intriguing.

Giant Robot and Asian Trash Cinema are the two most popular 'zines devoted to Asian culture. Giant Robot has a huge following and covers all the latest trends in the East and everything else Asian from Manga to Hello Kitty and Godzilla to Ultraman.

For purely cinematic explorations, nothing beats Asian Trash Cinema. Mainstream America (well, cutting-edge mainstream America) has only recently discovered the  talents of John Woo and Jackie Chan, but the publishers of this 'zine are longtime fans, publishing this leading Asian B-movie chronicle for five years. Editors Craig Ledbetter and Tom Weisser give side-by-side reviews of the latest guilty pleasures from Asia. The synopsis for each film is so complete that you could safely rent one of these from your neighborhood Chinese video store and not worry about subtitles. Their publishing schedule has been a bit erratic, but if you drop 'em a line you should be able to pick up a back issue or two.

With the upcoming presidential election, political commentary has also seen a surge in popularity in the past year. Think the op-ed pages express frustration about the political landscape? That's nothing compared to what's turning up in the political 'zines. Seeing little outlet for their often marginalized viewpoints, publishers lash out with vitriolic screeds not often seen (allowed?) in the daily papers.

'Zine publishers are similarly passionate about television. The White Dot, out of Chicago, advocates throwing out the television — the publisher did just that. Now, instead of watching Friends, he actually goes out with them.

S.E.T. Free is the long-running newsletter of the Society for the Elimination of Television, an organization devoted to exposing the evils of watching TV. Their

Devil's Elbow
A Magazine for People Who Don't Care Where They're Going
Price: $2 per issue or $7 for 4 issues
Lori Robbins
2850 N. Sheridan Road
Chicago, IL 60657
Web address:
http://members.aol.com/develbow/private/dehtml.html
E-mail: develbow@aol.com

Edging West
And Teetering on the Millennium
Price: $2.50 per issue or $10 for 6 issues
Edging West
5 W. Center St.
Logan, UT 84321
E-mail: edgingwest@aol.com

Factsheet 5
Price: $6 per issue or $20 for 6 issues
Factsheet Five
P.O. Box 170099
San Francisco, CA 94117

Giant Robot
A Magazine for You
Price: $5 per issue
Eric Nakamura
P.O. Box 2053,
Los Angeles, CA 90064
E-mail: grobot@netvoyage.net

HipMama
The Parenting 'Zine
Price: $3.95 per issue or $15 for 4 issues
Ariel Gore
HipMama
4165 Emerald St.
Oakland, CA 94609

Hip-Hop Housewife
For Homemakers With Attitude
Price: $1 per issue or $19.95 for 12 issues
Fran Pelzman Liscio
TLR Publishing Corp.
19 Bellegrove Drive
Upper Montclair, NJ 07043

CONTINUED ON NEXT PAGE ▶

◀ CONTINUED FROM PREVIOUS PAGE

Machination

Plots, Plans and Schemes of the Seattle Cacophony Society
Price: 2 stamps per issue or $10 for 12 issues
Seattle Cacophony Society
923 27th Ave.
Seattle, WA 98122
Web address:
http://www.halcyon.com/anitar/cacoph.html
E-mail: scacophn@seanews.akita.com

Meaningless Madness

The Official Organ of the Portland Cacophony Society
Price: $10 for 12 issues
P.O. Box 25093
Portland, OR 97225
Web address:
http://www.iccom.com/cacohome.html
E-mail: arogers@graphicmedia.com

Nicks and Scratches

One More Drop in the 'Zine Pool
Price: $1 per issue
Erik Lindquist
1671 Bayview Drive
Fort Wayne, IN 46815
E-mail: linded01@holmes.ipfw.indiana.edu

Out West

The Newspaper That Roams
Price: $3.50 per issue or $11.95 for 4 issues
Out West
408 Broad St., Suite 11
Nevada City, CA 95959
E-mail: outwestcw@aol.com

Pills-a-Go-Go

Journal of Pills
Price: $2 per issue or $12 for 6 issues
Pills-a-Go-Go
1202 E. Pike St., #849
Seattle, WA 98122-3934

Radio Free Ybor City

Price: $1 per issue or $7 for 7 issues
Kelly Kombat
2203 Fifth Ave.
Tampa, FL 33604

Radio Resistor's Bulletin

Price: $1 per issue or $5 for 5 issues
Radio Resistor's Bulletin
P.O. Box 3038
Bellingham, WA 98227-3038
E-mail: haulgren@well.com

occasional newsletter features news clips and other bits for people disgusted with the power of TV.

Of course, not everyone hates TV, and Dean Williams is one of those folks who enjoys watching. In his 'zine, *TV Grind,* he writes about his passion for TV but with a cynical and critical attitude. He once compared the castaways of *Gilligan's Island* to the Seven Deadly Sins and believes that *Three's Company* is essentially Shakespearean in nature.

Clearly, 'zines publish an alternative view and serve to challenge mainstream institutions. Some 'zine publishers consider the bicycle the first choice in transportation, citing the economic and environmental advantages over the automobile. The biking 'zines (and there are zillions of them) cover everything from the localized struggle for safe urban biking to the preservation of bike trails. *Biker Pride* certainly captures the attitude and energy of many biking 'zines.

They may be many, but most biking 'zines are hard to find. The best place to find hard-core bike 'zines is at hard-core bike events such as San Francisco's Critical Mass. Once a month, hundreds of riders meet downtown for a long, meandering ride though the streets of San Francisco. These long, slow group bike rides snarl traffic and are meant to increase bike visibility. The concept has spread to Minneapolis and across the Atlantic to London.

Also flourishing are 'zines about parenthood. *Hip Mama, Hip-Hop Housewife* and *At-Home Dad* all share the ups and downs of parenting. *Hip Mama,* with its slick covers and upbeat writing, is the most successful of the

bunch, but *Hip-Hop Housewife* and *At-Home Dad* are two newcomers certain to carve out their own niche.

The fact that several 'zine publishers have inked book deals highlights the 'zines' success. We're not talking small potatoes. St. Martin's Press recently published '*Zine*, based on Pagan Kennedy's 'zine, *Pagan's Head,* and Paul Lucas, who publishes the well-known *Beer Frame,* has signed with Crown.

But it's not a perfect world, and there is some bad news to report on the 'zine front. *ANSWER Me!* was recently the center of attention at a Bellingham, Washington

obscenity trial. Some people were offended by two rape victims' frank discussion about their ordeals and alerted the local district attorney, who immediately tried to suppress the 'zine. The struggle escalated into a prolonged court battle. The American Civil Liberties Union stepped in, and the sellers of the publication were cleared of obscenity charges.

Distribution problems continue to dog some publishers. It used to be a simple and painless process: Publishers sent their 'zines to their distributors, who in turn sent smaller batches out to bookstores. Rising paper prices and overall financial woes have led to chaos and uncertainty with the smaller magazine-distribution business.

Thankfully, there are several groups that bypass the corporate structure and manage to distribute 'zines effectively. Most notable are Basement Children 'Zine Distribution and Subway Sissy 'Zine Distribution. These do-it-yourself collectives drop off 'zines at local stores, sell them at punk rock concerts or offer them through mail order. While these groups can't get 'zines into all bookstores across the country, they are providing an option for 'zine publishers who want to bypass the corporate structure of national bookstore chains.

'Zine publishers have also turned to conventions for distribution. There have been several events in the past year, but so far the hoped-for droves of buyers haven't materialized. But the conventions have

Rough Draft
The Official Organ of the San Francisco Cacophony Society
Price: $12 for 12 issues
The Cacophony Society
P.O. Box 424969
San Francisco, CA 94142-4969
Web address: http://www.zpub.com/caco

S.E.T. Free
The Newsletter Against Television
Price: A self-addressed stamped envelope per issue
Society for the Elimination of Television
P.O. Box 10491
Oakland, CA 94610-0491

State Fair
Price: $1 cash plus 2 stamps per issue
BSBN Publishing
Dept. SF
P.O. Box 7205-F5
Minneapolis, MN 55407
E-mail: bsbn@pro-algonquin.mn.org

Subway Sissy 'Zine Distribution
Price: 1 stamp per catalog
Witknee Alien
17337 Tramonto, #306
Pacific Palisades, CA 90272

TV Grind
Price: $3 per issue or $12 for 4 issues
Dean Williams
P.O. Box 14043
Chicago, IL 60614-0043
Web address: http://www.suba.com/~tvgrind
E-mail: TVGRIND@suba.com

The White Dot
Tune It Out. Turn It Off.
Price: $2 per issue or $8 for 4 issues
Jean Lotus
P.O. Box 577257
Chicago, IL 60657

The National Magazine Awards, sponsored by the American Society of Magazine Editors and administered by the Columbia University Graduate School of Journalism, were presented April 23, 1996, at New York's Waldorf-Astoria Hotel.

General Excellence
Business Week (circulation more than 1,000,000)
Outside (circulation 400,000 to 1,000,000)
Civilization (circulation 100,000 to 400,000)
The Sciences (circulation less than 100,000)

Personal Service
SmartMoney

Special Interests and Photography
Saveur

Reporting
The New Yorker

Essays and Criticism
The New Yorker

Feature Writing
GQ

Public Interest
Texas Monthly

Design
Wired

Fiction
Harper's

Single-Topic Issue
Bon Appétit

How I spent six years of my life in the underground and finally... found myself... I think.

pagan kennedy

given 'zine publishers an opportunity to meet each other and discuss the business. The big kahuna is the annual Underground Press Conference in Chicago and there are other events in Seattle, San Jose, Los Angeles and Hawaii.

Of course, there are other outlets that carry 'zines. Tower Records and Tower Books have been longtime supporters and often offer a good crop. A visit to a Borders Books may also turn up a few of the more widely distributed music and culture 'zines.

Many thought 'zine publishing was a passing fad, but it's alive and well and looks as if it's here to stay. The Internet ain't the only new medium in town. ∎

R. Seth Friedman is the editor of Factsheet 5.

Top 100 Consumer Magazines by Paid Circulation for the Last Half of 1995

Rank	Magazine	Circulation
1.	**NRTA/AARP Bulletin**	21,100,610
2.	**Modern Maturity**	21,064,030
3.	**Reader's Digest**	15,103,830
4.	**TV Guide**	13,175,549
5.	**National Geographic Magazine**	8,988,444
6.	**Better Homes & Gardens**	7,603,207
7.	**Good Housekeeping**	5,372,786
8.	**Ladies' Home Journal**	5,045,644
9.	**Family Circle**	5,007,542
10.	**Woman's Day**	4,707,330
11.	**McCall's**	4,520,186
12.	**Car & Travel Magazine**	4,150,352
13.	**Time**	4,083,105
14.	**People Weekly**	3,321,198
15.	**Playboy**	3,283,272
16.	**Prevention**	3,252,115

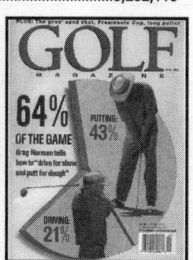

Rank	Magazine	Circulation
17.	**Redbook**	3,173,313
18.	**Sports Illustrated**	3,157,303
19.	**Newsweek**	3,155,155
20.	**American Legion Magazine**	2,852,332
21.	**Avenues**	2,777,749
22.	**National Enquirer**	2,613,647
23.	**Cosmopolitan**	2,569,186
24.	**Southern Living**	2,471,170
25.	**Star**	2,406,150
26.	**Motorland**	2,334,938
27.	**U.S. News & World Report**	2,220,327
28.	**Home & Away**	2,204,014
29.	**Seventeen**	2,172,923

Rank	Magazine	Circulation
30.	**YM**	2,165,079
31.	**Smithsonian**	2,151,172
32.	**Glamour**	2,141,752
33.	**V.F.W. Magazine**	2,013,258
34.	**Field & Stream**	2,001,875
35.	**Ebony**	1,927,675
36.	**Money**	1,922,737
37.	**Parents**	1,848,008
38.	**Country Living**	1,838,808
39.	**Popular Science**	1,805,525
40.	**American Rifleman**	1,666,398
41.	**Popular Mechanics**	1,586,137
42.	**Life**	1,556,189
43.	**Golf Digest**	1,501,525
44.	**Sunset, The Magazine of Western Living**	1,451,846
45.	**Martha Stewart Living**	1,449,744
46.	**Soap Opera Digest**	1,372,316
47.	**Woman's World**	1,363,240
48.	**Teen**	1,360,411
49.	**Outdoor Life**	1,358,647
50.	**Discover**	1,320,701
51.	**Men's Health**	1,314,802
52.	**American Hunter**	1,303,067
53.	**Golf Magazine**	1,283,925
54.	**Mademoiselle**	1,280,169
55.	**Elks Magazine**	1,269,677
56.	**New Woman**	1,262,003
57.	**Consumers Digest**	1,254,879
58.	**First for Women**	1,237,449
59.	**Boys' Life**	1,229,052
60.	**Cooking Light**	1,213,158
61.	**Self**	1,211,024
62.	**Us**	1,201,327
63.	**Entertainment Weekly**	1,195,926
64.	**Rolling Stone**	1,180,217
65.	**Vanity Fair**	1,173,077
66.	**Vogue**	1,146,037

Rank	Magazine	Circulation
67.	*Bon Appetit*	1,128,932
68.	*Car & Driver*	1,108,975
69.	*PC Magazine*	1,107,187
70.	*Penthouse*	1,100,679
71.	*Family Handyman*	1,046,398
72.	*Scouting*	1,038,009
73.	*Scholastic Parent & Child*	1,037,622
74.	*Country Home*	1,030,694

Rank	Magazine	Circulation
75.	*Endless Vacation*	1,024,287
76.	*Sesame Street Magazine*	1,021,807
77.	*Kiplinger's Personal Finance*	1,020,931
78.	*PC World*	1,016,889

Rank	Magazine	Circulation
79.	*Home Mechanix*	1,012,411
80.	*Home*	1,005,916
81.	*Weight Watchers Magazine*	1,001,148
82.	*Essence*	1,000,184
83.	*Travel & Leisure*	988,055
84.	*Globe*	981,889
85.	*House Beautiful*	980,423
86.	*Parenting Magazine*	979,849
87.	*Motor Trend*	968,719
88.	*Jet*	965,870
89.	*PC/Computing*	964,507
90.	*Victoria*	963,277
91.	*Country America*	961,106
92.	*Health*	947,728
93.	*Elle*	922,048
94.	*Gourmet*	896,352
95.	*Business Week* (North America)	882,583
96.	*Shape*	865,257
97.	*Nation's Business*	863,156
98.	*Condé Nast Traveler*	850,007
99.	*The New Yorker*	847,201
100.	*Midwest Living*	838,969

Source: Publishers Information Bureau

1995's Top 100 Magazines by Revenue

Rank	Magazine	Total Revenue
1.	*People Weekly*	$437,663,406
2.	*Sports Illustrated*	435,709,953
3.	*TV Guide*	406,944,634
4.	*Time*	404,462,265
5.	*Newsweek*	331,853,174
6.	*PC Magazine*	331,072,030
7.	*Better Homes & Gardens*	274,444,527
8.	*Business Week*	267,632,090
9.	*Good Housekeeping*	238,675,415
10.	*U.S. News & World Report*	222,420,487
11.	*Forbes*	205,703,659
12.	*Woman's Day*	197,514,800
13.	*Reader's Digest*	186,587,930
14.	*Fortune*	179,524,270
15.	*Family Circle*	163,970,813

Rank	Magazine	Total Revenue
16.	*Cosmopolitan*	$159,714,706
17.	*Ladies' Home Journal*	158,469,433
18.	*Vogue*	116,438,723
19.	*Redbook*	112,512,757
20.	*Money*	105,340,506
21.	*McCall's*	104,082,241
22.	*Glamour*	103,692,870
23.	*PC Computing*	101,262,125
24.	*Southern Living*	100,440,312
25.	*Rolling Stone*	97,779,589
26.	*Golf Digest*	94,267,686
27.	*Entertainment Weekly*	88,940,568
28.	*Country Living*	86,141,398
29.	*Car & Driver*	84,944,706
30.	*The New Yorker*	79,172,620

RANK	MAGAZINE	TOTAL REVENUE
31.	*Parents*	$74,455,297
32.	*Inc.*	72,445,617
33.	*Bride's*	71,337,578
34.	*Vanity Fair*	70,853,972
35.	*Elle*	70,720,548
36.	*Harper's Bazaar*	65,562,916
37.	*Golf*	65,323,272
38.	*Modern Maturity*	63,292,485
39.	*Modern Bride*	59,484,311
40.	*Road & Track*	57,341,755
41.	*House Beautiful*	55,369,852
42.	*Travel & Leisure*	53,835,235
43.	*Self*	53,375,628
44.	*National Geographic*	52,295,215
45.	*Seventeen*	51,592,892
46.	*Sunset*	51,386,471
47.	*Gentlemen's Quarterly*	50,340,075
48.	*Parenting*	49,024,287
49.	*New York Magazine*	48,297,661
50.	*Playboy*	47,234,898
51.	*Condé Nast Traveler*	47,143,566
52.	*Mademoiselle*	46,467,852
53.	*Ebony*	46,196,010
54.	*Motor Trend*	45,295,040
55.	*Architectural Digest*	44,488,171
56.	*W.*	44,362,323
57.	*Allure*	43,661,420
58.	*Gourmet*	43,469,923
59.	*Prevention*	43,191,135
60.	*Popular Photography*	41,817,457
61.	*Popular Mechanics*	41,535,732
62.	*Home.*	41,460,952
63.	*Smithsonian*	40,772,832
64.	*Sky Magazine*	40,517,084
65.	*Economist*	40,024,459

RANK	MAGAZINE	TOTAL REVENUE
66.	*Hemispheres*	$39,632,023
67.	*Field & Stream*	39,430,962
68.	*Essence*	37,446,137
69.	*Automobile Magazine*	36,736,689
70.	*Popular Science*	36,105,148
71.	*Life*	35,222,375
72.	*Outside Magazine*	34,233,059
73.	*Penthouse*	33,531,191
74.	*Martha Stewart Living*	33,273,468
75.	*Entrepreneur*	33,023,738

RANK	MAGAZINE	TOTAL REVENUE
76.	*Country Home*	32,993,598
77.	*Esquire*	32,684,286
78.	*New Woman*	32,565,282
79.	*Men's Health*	32,547,582
80.	*American Way*	32,522,175
81.	*Financial World*	31,965,123
82.	*Muscle & Fitness*	31,705,372
83.	*American Baby*	31,343,786
84.	*Bon Appetit*	31,060,139
85.	*Stereo Review*	31,028,776
86.	*Tennis*	29,763,572
87.	*Boating*	29,708,990
88.	*SmartMoney*	29,177,416
89.	*Kiplinger's Personal Finance*	28,761,247
90.	*Town & Country*	28,758,868
91.	*Working Mother*	28,275,108
92.	*Family Fun*	27,886,674
93.	*Details*	27,628,135
94.	*Us*	27,326,174
95.	*Child*	26,342,304
96.	*Computer Life*	25,511,103
97.	*Ski.*	25,230,431
98.	*Bridal Guide*	24,209,395
99.	*Cooking Light*	23,864,856
100.	*Premiere.*	23,843,803

Source: Publishers Information Bureau

National Book Awards

The National Book Awards, administered by the National Book Foundation, are considered one of the most prestigious literary honors, rivaled only by the Pulitzer Prizes.

William Faulkner

1950

FICTION
The Man With the Golden Arm, Nelson Algren

NONFICTION
Ralph Waldo Emerson, Ralph L. Rusk

POETRY
Paterson: Book III and Selected Poems, William Carlos
    Williams

1951

FICTION
The Collected Stories of William Faulkner, William Faulkner

NONFICTION
Herman Melville, Newton Arvin

POETRY
The Auroras of Autumn, Wallace Stevens

1952

FICTION
From Here to Eternity, James Jones

NONFICTION
The Sea Around Us, Rachel Carson

POETRY
Collected Poems, Marianne Moore

1953

FICTION
Invisible Man, Ralph Ellison

NONFICTION
The Course of an Empire, Bernard A. De Voto

POETRY
Collected Poems, 1917–1952, Archibald MacLeish

1954

FICTION
The Adventures of Augie March, Saul Bellow

NONFICTION
A Stillness at Appomattox, Bruce Catton

POETRY
Collected Poems, Conrad Aiken

1955

FICTION
A Fable, William Faulkner

NONFICTION
The Measure of Man, Joseph Wood Krutch

POETRY
The Collected Poems of Wallace Stevens, Wallace Stevens

SPECIAL CITATION
Poems, 1923–1954, e. e. cummings

1956

FICTION
Ten North Frederick, John O'Hara

NONFICTION
An American in Italy, Herbert Kubly

POETRY
The Shield of Achilles, W. H. Auden

1957

FICTION
The Field of Vision, Wright Morris

NONFICTION
Russia Leaves the War, George F. Kennan

POETRY
Things of This World, Richard Wilbur

1958

FICTION
The Wapshot Chronicle, John Cheever

NONFICTION
The Lion and the Throne, Catherine Drinker Bowen

POETRY
Promises: Poems, 1954–1956, Robert Penn Warren

1959

FICTION
The Magic Barrel, Bernard Malamud

NONFICTION
Mistress to an Age: A Life of Madame de Stael,
J. Christopher Herold

POETRY
Words for the Wind, Theodore Roethke

1960

FICTION
Goodbye, Columbus, Philip Roth

NONFICTION
James Joyce, Richard Ellmann

POETRY
Life Studies, Robert Lowell

1961

FICTION
The Waters of Kronos, Conrad Richter

NONFICTION
The Rise and Fall of the Third Reich, William L. Shirer

POETRY
The Woman at the Washington Zoo, Randall Jarrell

1962

FICTION
The Moviegoer, Walker Percy

NONFICTION
*The City in History: Its Origins, Its Transformations and Its
Prospects,* Lewis Mumford

POETRY
Poems, Alan Dugan

1963

FICTION
Morte D'Urban, J. F. Powers

NONFICTION
Henry James, Vol. II: The Conquest of London and *Henry
James, Vol. III: The Middle Years,* Leon Edel

POETRY
Traveling Through the Dark, William Stafford

1964

ARTS AND LETTERS
John Keats: The Making of a Poet, Aileen Ward

FICTION
The Centaur, John Updike

HISTORY AND BIOGRAPHY
The Rise of the West: A History of the Human Community,
William H. McNeill

POETRY
Selected Poems, John Crowe Ransom

SCIENCE, PHILOSOPHY AND RELIGION
Man-Made America, Christopher Tunnard and
Boris Pushkarev

1965

ARTS AND LETTERS
Oysters of Locmariaquer, Eleanor Clark

FICTION
Herzog, Saul Bellow

HISTORY AND BIOGRAPHY
The Life of Lenin, Louis Fischer

POETRY
The Far Field, Theodore Roethke

SCIENCE, PHILOSOPHY AND RELIGION
*God and Golem, Inc.: A Comment on Certain Points Where
Cybernetics Impinges on Religion,* Norbert Wiener

1966

ARTS AND LETTERS
Paris Journal, 1944–65, Janet Flanner

FICTION
The Collected Stories of Katherine Anne Porter,
Katherine Anne Porter

HISTORY AND BIOGRAPHY
A Thousand Days, Arthur M. Schlesinger, Jr.

POETRY
Buckdancer's Choice: Poems, James Dickey

SCIENCE, PHILOSOPHY AND RELIGION
No award

1967

ARTS AND LETTERS
Mr. Clemens and Mark Twain: A Biography, Justin Kaplan

FICTION
The Fixer, Bernard Malamud

HISTORY AND BIOGRAPHY
*The Enlightenment, Vol. I: An Interpretation: The Rise of
Modern Paganism,* Peter Gay

POETRY
Nights and Days, James Merrill

SCIENCE, PHILOSOPHY AND RELIGION
La Vida, Oscar Lewis

TRANSLATION
Julio Cortazar's Hopscotch, Gregory Rabassa
Casanova's History of My Life, Willard Trask

Katherine Anne Porter

Lillian Hellman

1968

ARTS AND LETTERS
Selected Essays, William Troy

FICTION
The Eighth Day, Thornton Wilder

HISTORY AND BIOGRAPHY
Memoirs: 1925–1950, George F. Kennan

POETRY
The Light Around the Body, Robert Bly

SCIENCE, PHILOSOPHY AND RELIGION
Death at an Early Age, Jonathan Kozol

TRANSLATION
Soren Kierkegaard's Journals and Papers, Howard and
 Edna Hong

1969

ARTS AND LETTERS
*The Armies of the Night: History as a Novel, the Novel as
 History,* Norman Mailer

CHILDREN'S LITERATURE
Journey From Peppermint Street, Meindert DeJong

FICTION
Steps, Jerzy Kosinski

HISTORY AND BIOGRAPHY
*White Over Black: American Attitudes Toward the Negro,
 1550–1812,* Winthrop D. Jordan

POETRY
His Toy, His Dream, His Rest, John Berryman

THE SCIENCES
Death in Life: Survivors of Hiroshima, Robert J. Lifton

TRANSLATION
Calvino's Cosmicomics, William Weaver

1970

ARTS AND LETTERS
An Unfinished Woman: A Memoir, Lillian Hellman

CHILDREN'S BOOKS
A Day of Pleasure: Stories of a Boy Growing Up in Warsaw,
 Isaac Bashevis Singer

FICTION
Them, Joyce Carol Oates

HISTORY AND BIOGRAPHY
Huey Long, T. Harry Williams

PHILOSOPHY AND RELIGION
Gandhi's Truth: On the Origins of Militant Nonviolence,
 Erik H. Erikson

POETRY
The Complete Poems, Elizabeth Bishop

TRANSLATION
Celine's Castle to Castle, Ralph Manheim

1971

ARTS AND LETTERS
Cocteau: A Biography, Francis Steegmuller

CHILDREN'S BOOKS
The Marvelous Misadventures of Sebastian, Lloyd Alexander

FICTION
Mr. Sammler's Planet, Saul Bellow

HISTORY AND BIOGRAPHY
Roosevelt: The Soldier of Freedom, James MacGregor Burns

POETRY
To See, To Take, Mona Van Duyn

THE SCIENCES
Science in the British Colonies of America,
 Raymond Phineas Sterns

TRANSLATION
Brecht's Saint Joan of the Stockyards, Frank Jones

Yasunari Kawabata's The Sound of the Mountain,
 Edward G. Seidensticker

1972

ARTS AND LETTERS
The Classical Style: Haydn, Mozart, Beethoven, Charles Rosen

BIOGRAPHY
*Eleanor and Franklin: The Story of Their Relationship, Based on
 Eleanor Roosevelt's Private Papers,* Joseph P. Lash

CHILDREN'S BOOKS
*The Slightly Irregular Fire Engine or the Hithering Thithering
 Djinn,* Donald Barthelme

CONTEMPORARY AFFAIRS
The Last Whole Earth Catalog, Stewart Brand, editor

FICTION
The Complete Stories of Flannery O'Connor, Flannery O'Connor

HISTORY
*Ordeal of the Union, vols. VII and VIII: The Organized War,
 1863–1864* and *The Organized War to Victory,*
 Allan Nevins

PHILOSOPHY AND RELIGION
Righteous Empire: The Protestant Experience in America,
 Martin E. Marty

POETRY
Selected Poems, Howard Moss

The Collected Poems of Frank O'Hara, Frank O'Hara

THE SCIENCES
The Blue Whale, George L. Small

TRANSLATION
Jacques Monod's Chance and Necessity, Austryn Wainhouse

1973

ARTS AND LETTERS
Diderot, Arthur M. Wilson

BIOGRAPHY
George Washington, Vol. IV: Anguish and Farewell, 1793–1799,
James Thomas Flexner

CHILDREN'S BOOKS
The Farthest Shore, Ursula K. LeGuin

CONTEMPORARY AFFAIRS
*Fire in the Lake: The Vietnamese and the Americans in
Vietnam,* Frances FitzGerald

FICTION
Chimera, John Barth
Augustus, John Williams

HISTORY
The Children of Pride, Robert Manson Myers
Judenrat, Isaiah Trunk

PHILOSOPHY AND RELIGION
A Religious History of the American People, S. E. Ahlstrom

POETRY
Collected Poems, 1951–1971, A. R. Ammons

THE SCIENCES
The Serengeti Lion: A Study of Predator-Prey Relations,
George B. Schaller

TRANSLATION
The Aeneid of Virgil, Allen Mandelbaum

1974

ARTS AND LETTERS
Deeper Into the Movies, Pauline Kael

BIOGRAPHY
Macaulay: The Shaping of the Historian, John Clive
Malcolm Lowry: A Biography, Douglas Day

CHILDREN'S BOOKS
The Court of the Stone Children, Eleanor Cameron

CONTEMPORARY AFFAIRS
The Briar Patch, Murray Kempton

FICTION
Gravity's Rainbow, Thomas Pynchon
A Crown of Feathers and Other Stories, Isaac Bashevis Singer

HISTORY
Macaulay: The Shaping of the Historian, John Clive

PHILOSOPHY AND RELIGION
Edmund Husserl: Philosopher of Infinite Tasks,
Maurice Natanson

POETRY
The Fall of America: Poems of These States, Allen Ginsberg
Diving Into the Wreck: Poems 1971–1972, Adrienne Rich

THE SCIENCES
Life: The Unfinished Experiment, S. E. Luria

TRANSLATION
The Confessions of Lady Nijo, Karen Brazell
Octavio Paz' Alternating Current, Helen R. Lane
Paul Valery's Monsieur Teste, Jackson Mathews

1975

ARTS AND LETTERS
Marcel Proust, Roger Shattuck
The Lives of a Cell: Notes of a Biology Watcher, Lewis Thomas

BIOGRAPHY
The Life of Emily Dickinson, Richard B. Sewall

CHILDREN'S BOOKS
M. C. Higgins the Great, Virginia Hamilton

CONTEMPORARY AFFAIRS
All God's Dangers: The Life of Nate Shaw,
Theodore Rosengarten

FICTION
Dog Soldiers, Robert Stone
The Hair of Harold Roux, Thomas Williams

HISTORY
The Ordeal of Thomas Hutchinson, Bernard Bailyn

PHILOSOPHY AND RELIGION
Anarchy, State and Utopia, Robert Nozick

POETRY
Presentation Piece, Marilyn Hacker

THE SCIENCES
Interpretation of Schizophrenia, Silvano Arieti
The Lives of a Cell: Notes of a Biology Watcher, Lewis Thomas

TRANSLATION
*Miguel D. Unamuno's The Agony of Christianity and Essays on
Faith,* Anthony Kerrigan

1976

ARTS AND LETTERS
The Great War and Modern Memory, Paul Fussell

CHILDREN'S LITERATURE
Bert Breen's Barn, Walter D. Edmonds

CONTEMPORARY AFFAIRS
Passage to Ararat, Michael J. Arlen

Allen Ginsberg

FICTION
Jr, William Gaddis

HISTORY AND BIOGRAPHY
The Problem of Slavery in the Age of Revolution, 1770–1823, David Brion Davis

POETRY
Self-Portrait in a Convex Mirror, John Ashbery

1977
BIOGRAPHY AND AUTOBIOGRAPHY
Norman Thomas: The Last Idealist, W. A. Swanberg

CHILDREN'S LITERATURE
The Master Puppeteer, Katherine Paterson

CONTEMPORARY THOUGHT
The Uses of Enchantment: The Meaning and Importance of Fairy Tales, Bruno Bettelheim

FICTION
The Spectator Bird, Wallace Stegner

HISTORY
World of Our Fathers, Irving Howe

JUDGES' STATEMENT: Because Alex Haley's *Roots* does not accommodate itself to the category of History but transcends that and other categories, members of the History panel were unable to name it as one of the nominees in History. They are at one, however, that its distinguished literary quality justifies according it a special citation of merit.

POETRY
Collected Poems, 1930–1976, Richard Eberhart

TRANSLATION
Master Tung's Western Chamber Romance, Li-Li Ch'en

1978
BIOGRAPHY AND AUTOBIOGRAPHY
Samuel Johnson, W. Jackson Bate

CHILDREN'S LITERATURE
The View From the Oak, Judith Kohl and Herbert Kohl

CONTEMPORARY THOUGHT
Winners and Losers, Gloria Emerson

Alex Haley

FICTION
Blood Ties, Mary Lee Settle

HISTORY
The Path Between the Seas: The Creation of the Panama Canal 1870–1914, David McCullough

POETRY
The Collected Poems of Howard Nemerov, Howard Nemerov

TRANSLATION
Uwe George's In the Deserts of This Earth, Richard Winston and Clara Winston

1979
BIOGRAPHY AND AUTOBIOGRAPHY
Robert Kennedy and His Times, Arthur M. Schlesinger, Jr.

CHILDREN'S LITERATURE
The Great Gilly Hopkins, Katherine Paterson

CONTEMPORARY THOUGHT
The Snow Leopard, Peter Matthiessen

FICTION
Going After Cacciato, Tim O'Brien

HISTORY
Intellectual Life in the Colonial South, 1585–1763, Richard Beale Davis

POETRY
Mirabell: Book of Numbers, James Merrill

TRANSLATION
Cesar Vallejo's The Complete Posthumous Poetry, Clayton Eshleman and José Rubia Barcia

1980
AUTOBIOGRAPHY
HARDCOVER
Lauren Bacall by Myself, Lauren Bacall

PAPERBACK
And I Worked at the Writer's Trade: Chapters of Literary History 1918–1978, Malcolm Cowley

BIOGRAPHY
HARDCOVER
The Rise of Theodore Roosevelt, Edmund Morris

PAPERBACK
Max Perkins: Editor of Genius, A. Scott Berg

CHILDREN'S BOOKS
HARDCOVER
A Gathering of Days: A New England Girl's Journal, Joan W. Blos

PAPERBACK
A Swiftly Tilting Planet, Madeleine L'Engle

CURRENT INTEREST
HARDCOVER
Julia Child and More Company, Julia Child

PAPERBACK
The Culture of Narcissism, Christopher Lasch

FICTION
HARDCOVER
Sophie's Choice, William Styron

PAPERBACK
The World According to Garp, John Irving

FIRST NOVEL
Birdy, William Wharton

GENERAL NONFICTION
HARDCOVER
The Right Stuff, Tom Wolfe
PAPERBACK
The Snow Leopard, Peter Matthiessen

GENERAL REFERENCE BOOKS
HARDCOVER
Congressional Quarterly's Guide to the U.S. Supreme Court,
    Elder Witt, editor
PAPERBACK
The Complete Directory of Prime Time Network TV Shows:
    1946–Present, Tim Brooks and Earle Marsh

HISTORY
HARDCOVER
The White House Years, Henry A. Kissinger
PAPERBACK
A Distant Mirror: The Calamitous 14th Century,
    Barbara W. Tuchman

MYSTERY
HARDCOVER
The Green Ripper, John D. MacDonald
PAPERBACK
Stained Glass, William F. Buckley, Jr.

POETRY
Ashes, Philip Levine

RELIGION/INSPIRATION
HARDCOVER
The Gnostic Gospels, Elaine Pagels
PAPERBACK
A Severe Mercy, Sheldon Vanauken

SCIENCE
HARDCOVER
Gödel, Escher, Bach: An Eternal Golden Braid,
    Douglas Hofstadter
PAPERBACK
The Dancing Wu Li Masters: An Overview of the New Physics,
    Gary Zukav

SCIENCE FICTION
HARDCOVER
Jem, Frederik Pohl
PAPERBACK
The Book of the Dun Cow, Walter Wangerin, Jr.

TRANSLATION
Cesare Pavese's Hard Labor, William Arrowsmith
Osip E. Mandelstam's Complete Critical Prose and Letters,
    Jane Garry Harris and Constance Link

WESTERN
Bendigo Shafter, Louis L'Amour

1981
AUTOBIOGRAPHY/BIOGRAPHY
HARDCOVER
Walt Whitman, Justin Kaplan
PAPERBACK
Samuel Beckett, Deirdre Bair

CHILDREN'S BOOKS, FICTION
HARDCOVER
The Night Swimmers, Betsy Byars
PAPERBACK
Ramona and Her Mother, Beverly Cleary

Tom Wolfe

CHILDREN'S BOOKS, NONFICTION
HARDCOVER
Oh, Boy! Babies, Alison Cragin Herzig and Jane Lawrence Mali

FICTION
HARDCOVER
Plains Song, Wright Morris
PAPERBACK
The Stories of John Cheever, John Cheever

FIRST NOVEL
Sister Wolf, Ann Arensberg

GENERAL NONFICTION
HARDCOVER
China Men, Maxine Hong Kingston
PAPERBACK
The Last Cowboy, Jane Kramer

HISTORY
HARDCOVER
Christianity, Social Tolerance and Homosexuality,
    John Boswell
PAPERBACK
Been in the Storm So Long: The Aftermath of Slavery,
    Leon F. Litwak

POETRY
The Need to Hold Still, Lisel Mueller

SCIENCE
HARDCOVER
The Panda's Thumb: More Reflections in Natural History,
    Stephen Jay Gould
PAPERBACK
The Medusa and the Snail, Lewis Thomas

TRANSLATION
The Letters of Gustave Flaubert, Francis Steegmuller
Arno Schmidt's Evening Edged in Gold, John E. Woods

1982
AUTOBIOGRAPHY/BIOGRAPHY
HARDCOVER
Mornings on Horseback, David McCullough
PAPERBACK
Walter Lippmann and the American Century, Ronald Steel

John Updike

CHILDREN'S BOOKS, FICTION
HARDCOVER
Westmark, Lloyd Alexander

PAPERBACK
Words by Heart, Ouida Sebestyen

CHILDREN'S BOOKS, NONFICTION
HARDCOVER
A Penguin Year, Susan Bonners

CHILDREN'S BOOKS, PICTURE BOOKS
HARDCOVER
Outside Over There, Maurice Sendak

PAPERBACK
Noah's Ark, Peter Spier

FICTION
HARDCOVER
Rabbit Is Rich, John Updike

PAPERBACK
So Long, See You Tomorrow, William Maxwell

FIRST NOVEL
Dale Loves Sophie to Death, Robb Forman Dew

GENERAL NONFICTION
HARDCOVER
The Soul of a New Machine, Tracy Kidder

PAPERBACK
Naming Names, Victor S. Navasky

HISTORY
HARDCOVER
People of the Sacred Mountain: A History of the Northern Cheyenne Chiefs and Warrior Societies, 1830–1879, Father Peter John Powell

PAPERBACK
The Generation of 1914, Robert Wohl

POETRY
Life Supports: New and Collected Poems, William Bronk

SCIENCE
HARDCOVER
Lucy: The Beginnings of Humankind, Donald C. Johanson and Maitland A. Edey

PAPERBACK
Taking the Quantum Leap: The New Physics for Nonscientists, Fred Alan Wolf

TRANSLATION
Higuchi Ichiyo's In the Shade of Spring Leaves, Robert Lyons Danly

The Ten Thousand Leaves: A Translation of the Man'Yoshu, Japan's Premier Anthology of Classical Poetry, Ian Hideo Levy

1983
AUTOBIOGRAPHY/BIOGRAPHY
HARDCOVER
Isak Dinesen: The Life of a Storyteller, Judith Thurman

PAPERBACK
Nathaniel Hawthorne in His Time, James R. Mellow

CHILDREN'S FICTION
HARDCOVER
Homesick: My Own Story, Jean Fritz

PAPERBACK
A Place Apart, Paula Fox

Marked by Fire, Joyce Carol Thomas

CHILDREN'S BOOKS, NONFICTION
Chimney Sweeps, James Cross Giblin

CHILDREN'S PICTURE BOOKS
HARDCOVER
Miss Rumphius, Barbara Cooney

Doctor De Soto, William Steig

PAPERBACK
A House Is a House for Me, Mary Ann Hoberman; Betty Fraser, illustrator

FICTION
HARDCOVER
The Color Purple, Alice Walker

PAPERBACK
Collected Stories of Eudora Welty, Eudora Welty

FIRST NOVEL
The Women of Brewster Place, Gloria Naylor

GENERAL NONFICTION
China: Alive in the Bitter Sea, Fox Butterfield

PAPERBACK
National Defense, James Fallows

Alice Walker

HISTORY
HARDCOVER
Voices of Protest: Huey Long, Father Coughlin and the Great Depression, Alan Brinkley

PAPERBACK
Utopian Thought in the Western World, Frank E. Manuel and Fritzie P. Manuel

ORIGINAL PAPERBACK
The Red Magician, Lisa Goldstein

POETRY
Selected Poems, Galway Kinnell

Country Music: Selected Early Poems, Charles Wright

SCIENCE
HARDCOVER
"Subtle Is the Lord . . .": The Science and Life of Albert Einstein, Abraham Pais

PAPERBACK
The Mathematical Experience, Philip J. Davis and Reuben Hersh

TRANSLATION
Charles Baudelaire's Les Fleurs du Mal, Richard Howard

1984
FICTION
Victory Over Japan: A Book of Stories, Ellen Gilchrist

FIRST WORK OF FICTION
Stones for Ibarra, Harriet Doerr

NONFICTION
Andrew Jackson and the Course of American Democracy, 1833–1845, Robert V. Remini

1985
FICTION
White Noise, Don DeLillo

FIRST WORK OF FICTION
Easy in the Islands, Bob Shacochis

NONFICTION
Common Ground: A Turbulent Decade in the Lives of Three American Families, J. Anthony Lukas

1986
FICTION
World's Fair, E. L. Doctorow

NONFICTION
Arctic Dreams, Barry Lopez

1987
FICTION
Paco's Story, Larry Heinemann

NONFICTION
The Making of the Atom Bomb, Richard Rhodes

1988
FICTION
Paris Trout, Pete Dexter

NONFICTION
A Bright Shining Lie: John Paul Vann and America in Vietnam, Neil Sheehan

1989
FICTION
Spartina, John Casey

John Gilbert Fox/Courtesy of Scribner

E. Annie Proulx

NONFICTION
From Beirut to Jerusalem, Thomas L. Friedman

1990
FICTION
Middle Passage, Charles Johnson

NONFICTION
The House of Morgan: An American Banking Dynasty and the Rise of Modern Finance, Ron Chernow

1991
FICTION
Mating, Norman Rush

NONFICTION
Freedom, Orlando Patterson

POETRY
What Work Is, Philip Levine

1992
FICTION
All the Pretty Horses, Cormac McCarthy

NONFICTION
Becoming a Man: Half a Life Story, Paul Monette

POETRY
New and Selected Poems, Mary Oliver

1993
FICTION
The Shipping News, E. Annie Proulx

NONFICTION
United States: Essays 1952–1992, Gore Vidal

POETRY
Garbage, A. R. Ammons

1994
FICTION
A Frolic of His Own, William Gaddis

NONFICTION
How We Die: Reflections on Life's Final Chapter, Sherwin B. Nuland

POETRY
Worshipful Company of Fletchers, James Tate

Pulitzer Prizes in Letters

The Pulitzer Prizes, established and endowed by Joseph Pulitzer (1847–1911), honor excellence in American literature, journalism, drama and music. The prizes, administered by Columbia University, bestow on winners both literary prestige and a cash prize.

Fiction

1918
His Family, Ernest Poole

1919
The Magnificent Ambersons, Booth Tarkington

1920
No award

1921
The Age of Innocence, Edith Wharton

1922
Alice Adams, Booth Tarkington

1923
One of Ours, Willa Cather

1924
The Able McLaughlins, Margaret Wilson

1925
So Big, Edna Ferber

1926
Arrowsmith, Sinclair Lewis

1927
Early Autumn, Louis Bromfield

1928
The Bridge of San Luis Rey, Thornton Wilder

1929
Scarlet Sister Mary, Julia Peterkin

1930
Laughing Boy, Oliver La Farge

1931
Years of Grace, Margaret Ayer Barnes

1932
The Good Earth, Pearl S. Buck

1933
The Store, T. S. Stribling

1934
Lamb in His Bosom, Caroline Miller

1935
Now in November, Josephine Winslow Johnson

1936
Honey in the Horn, Harold L. Davis

1937
Gone With the Wind, Margaret Mitchell

1938
The Late George Apley, John Phillips Marquand

1939
The Yearling, Marjorie Kinnan Rawlings

1940
The Grapes of Wrath, John Steinbeck

1941
No award

1942
In This Our Life, Ellen Glasgow

1943
Dragon's Teeth, Upton Sinclair

1944
Journey in the Dark, Martin Flavin

1945
A Bell for Adano, John Hersey

1946
No award

1947
All the King's Men, Robert Penn Warren

1948
Tales of the South Pacific, James A. Michener

1949
Guard of Honor, James Gould Cozzens

1950
The Way West, A. B. Guthrie, Jr.

1951
The Town, Conrad Richter

Edith Wharton

1952
The Caine Mutiny, Herman Wouk

1953
The Old Man and the Sea, Ernest Hemingway

1954
No award

1955
A Fable, William Faulkner

1956
Andersonville, MacKinlay Kantor

1957
No award

1958
A Death in the Family, James Agee

1959
The Travels of Jaimie McPheeters, Robert Lewis Taylor

1960
Advise and Consent, Allen Drury

1961
To Kill a Mockingbird, Harper Lee

1962
The Edge of Sadness, Edwin O'Connor

1963
The Reivers, William Faulkner

1964
No award

1965
The Keepers of the House, Shirley Ann Grau

Ernest Hemingway

1966
Collected Stories of Katherine Anne Porter, Katherine Anne Porter

1967
The Fixer, Bernard Malamud

1968
The Confessions of Nat Turner, William Styron

1969
House Made of Dawn, N. Scott Momaday

1970
Collected Stories, Jean Stafford

1971
No award

1972
Angle of Repose, Wallace Stegner

1973
The Optimist's Daughter, Eudora Welty

1974
No award

1975
The Killer Angels, Michael Shaara

1976
Humboldt's Gift, Saul Bellow

1977
No award

1978
Elbow Room, James Alan McPherson

1979
The Stories of John Cheever, John Cheever

1980
The Executioner's Song, Norman Mailer

1981
A Confederacy of Dunces, John Kennedy Toole

1982
Rabbit Is Rich, John Updike

1983
The Color Purple, Alice Walker

1984
Ironweed, William Kennedy

1985
Foreign Affairs, Alison Lurie

1986
Lonesome Dove, Larry McMurtry

1987
A Summons to Memphis, Peter Taylor

1988
Beloved, Toni Morrison

1989
Breathing Lessons, Anne Tyler

1990
The Mambo Kings Play Songs of Love, Oscar Hijuelos

1991
Rabbit at Rest, John Updike

1992
A Thousand Acres, Jane Smiley

1993
A Good Scent From a Strange Mountain, Robert Olen Butler

Toni Morrison

1994
The Shipping News, E. Annie Proulx

1995
The Stone Diaries, Carol Shields

General Nonfiction

1962
The Making of the President, 1960, Theodore H. White

1963
The Guns of August, Barbara W. Tuchman

1964
Anti-Intellectualism in American Life, Richard Hofstadter

1965
O Strange New World, Howard Mumford Jones

1966
Wandering Through Winter, Edwin Way Teale

1967
The Problem of Slavery in Western Culture, David Brion Davis

1968
Rousseau and Revolution, Will and Ariel Durant

1969
So Human an Animal, Rene Jules Dubos and *The Armies of the Night,* Norman Mailer

1970
Gandhi's Truth, Erik H. Erikson

1971
The Rising Sun, John Toland

1972
Stilwell and the American Experience in China, 1911–1945, Barbara W. Tuchman

1973
Fire in the Lake: The Vietnamese and the Americans in Vietnam, Frances FitzGerald

Children of Crisis (vols.1 and 2), Robert M. Coles

1974
The Denial of Death, Ernest Becker

1975
Pilgrim at Tinker Creek, Annie Dillard

1976
Why Survive? Being Old in America, Robert N. Butler

1977
Beautiful Swimmers: Watermen, Crabs and the Chesapeake Bay, William W. Warner

1978
The Dragons of Eden, Carl Sagan

1979
On Human Nature, Edward O. Wilson

1980
Gödel, Escher, Bach: An Eternal Golden Braid, Douglas R. Hofstadter

1981
Fin-de-Siecle Vienna: Politics and Culture, Carl E. Schorske

1982
The Soul of a New Machine, Tracy Kidder

1983
Is There No Place on Earth for Me?, Susan Sheehan

1984
Social Transformation of American Medicine, Paul Starr

1985
The Good War: An Oral History of World War II, Studs Terkel

1986
Move Your Shadow: South Africa, Black and White, Joseph Lelyveld

Common Ground: A Turbulent Decade in the Lives of Three American Families, J. Anthony Lukas

1987
Arab and Jew: Wounded Spirits in a Promised Land, David K. Shipler

1988
The Making of the Atomic Bomb, Richard Rhodes

1989
A Bright Shining Lie, Neil Sheehan

1990
And Their Children After Them, Dale Maharidge and Michael Williamson

1991
The Ants, Bert Holldobler and Edward O. Wilson

1992
The Prize: The Epic Quest for Oil, Money and Power, Daniel Yergin

1993
Lincoln at Gettysburg: The Words That Remade America, Garry Wills

1994
Lenin's Tomb: The Last Days of the Soviet Empire, David Remnick

1995
The Beak of the Finch: A Story of Evolution in Our Time, Jonathan Weiner

Poetry

1918
Love Songs, Sara Teasdale

1919
Old Road to Paradise, Margaret Widdemer and *Corn Huskers,* Carl Sandburg

1922
Collected Poems, Edwin Arlington Robinson

1923
The Ballad of the Harp-Weaver; A Few Figs From Thistles; eight sonnets in American Poetry, 1922, A Miscellany, Edna St. Vincent Millay

1924
New Hampshire: A Poem With Notes and Grace Notes, Robert Frost

1925
The Man Who Died Twice, Edwin Arlington Robinson

1926
What's O'Clock, Amy Lowell

1927
Fiddler's Farewell, Leonora Speyer

1928
Tristram, Edwin Arlington Robinson

1929
John Brown's Body, Stephen Vincent Benét

1930
Selected Poems, Conrad Aiken

1931
Collected Poems, Robert Frost

1932
The Flowering Stone, George Dillon

1933
Conquistador, Archibald MacLeish

1934
Collected Verse, Robert Hillyer

1935
Bright Ambush, Audrey Wurdemann

1936
Strange Holiness, Robert P. T. Coffin

1937
A Further Range, Robert Frost

1938
Cold Morning Sky, Marya Zaturenska

1939
Selected Poems, John Gould Fletcher

1940
Collected Poems, Mark Van Doren

1941
Sunderland Capture, Leonard Bacon

1942
The Dust Which Is God, William Rose Benét

1943
A Witness Tree, Robert Frost

1944
Western Star, Stephen Vincent Benét

1945
V-Letter and Other Poems, Karl Shapiro

1946
No award

1947
Lord Weary's Castle, Robert Lowell

1948
The Age of Anxiety, W. H. Auden

1949
Terror and Decorum, Peter Viereck

1950
Annie Allen, Gwendolyn Brooks

1951
Complete Poems, Carl Sandburg

1952
Collected Poems, Marianne Moore

1953
Collected Poems, 1917–1952, Archibald MacLeish

1954
The Waking, Theodore Roethke

1955
Collected Poems, Wallace Stevens

1956
Poems — North & South, Elizabeth Bishop

1957
Things of This World, Richard Wilbur

1958
Promises: Poems, 1954–1956, Robert Penn Warren

1959
Selected Poems, 1928–1958, Stanley Kunitz

Robert Frost

1960
Heart's Needle, William Snodgrass

1961
Times Three: Selected Verse From Three Decades, Phyllis McGinley

1962
Poems, Alan Dugan

1963
Pictures From Breughel, William Carlos Williams

1964
At the End of the Open Road, Louis Simpson

1965
77 Dream Songs, John Berryman

1966
Selected Poems, Richard Eberhart

1967
Live or Die, Anne Sexton

1968
The Hard Hours, Anthony Hecht

1969
Of Being Numerous, George Oppen

1970
Untitled Subjects, Richard Howard

1971
The Carrier of Ladders, William S. Merwin

1972
Collected Poems, James Wright

1973
Up Country, Maxine Winokur Kumin

1974
The Dolphin, Robert Lowell

1975
Turtle Island, Gary Snyder

1976
Self-Portrait in a Convex Mirror, John Ashbery

1977
Divine Comedies, James Merrill

1978
Collected Poems, Howard Nemerov

1979
Now and Then: Poems, 1976–1978, Robert Penn Warren

Robert Lowell

1980
Selected Poems, Donald Rodney Justice

1981
The Morning of the Poem, James Schuyler

1982
The Collected Poems, Sylvia Plath

1983
Selected Poems, Galway Kinnell

1984
American Primitive, Mary Oliver

1985
Yin, Carolyn Kizer

1986
The Flying Change, Henry Taylor

1987
Thomas and Beulah, Rita Dove

1988
Partial Accounts: New and Selected Poems, William Meredith

1989
New and Collected Poems, Richard Wilbur

1990
The World Doesn't End, Charles Simic

1991
Near Changes, Mona Van Duyn

1992
Selected Poems, James Tate

1993
The Wild Iris, Louise Gluck

1994
Neon Vernacular, Yusef Komunyakaa

1995
Simple Truth, Philip Levine

Biography or Autobiography

1917
Julia Ward Howe, Laura E. Richards and Maude Howe Elliott, assisted by Florence Howe Hall

1918
Benjamin Franklin, Self-Revealed, William Cabell Bruce

1919
The Education of Henry Adams, Henry Adams

1920
The Life of John Marshall, Albert J. Beveridge

1921
The Americanization of Edward Bok, Edward Bok

1922
A Daughter of the Middle Border, Hamlin Garland

1923
The Life and Letters of Walter H. Page, Burton J. Hendrick

1924
From Immigrant to Inventor, Michael Idvorsky Pupin

1925
Barrett Wendell and His Letters, M. A. DeWolfe Howe

1926
The Life of Sir William Osler, Harvey Cushing

1927
Whitman, Emory Holloway

1928
The American Orchestra and Theodore Thomas, Charles Edward Russell

1929
The Training of an American: The Earlier Life and Letters of Walter H. Page, Burton J. Hendrick

1930
The Raven, Marquis James

1931
Theodore Roosevelt, Henry F. Pringle

1932
Charles W. Eliot, Henry James

1933
Grover Cleveland, Allan Nevins

1934
John Hay, Tyler Dennett

1935
R. E. Lee, Douglas S. Freeman

1936
The Thought and Character of William James, Ralph Barton Perry

1937
Hamilton Fish, Allan Nevins

1938
Pedlar's Progress, Odell Shepard
Andrew Jackson, Marquis James

1939
Benjamin Franklin, Carl Van Doren

1940
Woodrow Wilson. Life and Letters, vols. *VII* and *VIII,* Ray Stannard Baker

1941
Jonathan Edwards, Ola E. Winslow

1942
Crusader in Crinoline, Forrest Wilson

1943
Admiral of the Ocean Sea, Samuel Eliot Morison

John F. Kennedy

1944
The American Leonardo: The Life of Samuel F. B. Morse, Carleton Mabee

1945
George Bancroft: Brahmin Rebel, Russel Blaine Nye

1946
Son of the Wilderness, Linnie Marsh Wolfe

1947
The Autobiography of William Allen White

1948
Forgotten First Citizen: John Bigelow, Margaret Clapp

1949
Roosevelt and Hopkins, Robert E. Sherwood

1950
John Quincy Adams and the Foundations of American Foreign Policy, Samuel Flagg Bemis

1951
John C. Calhoun: American Portrait, Margaret Louise Coit

1952
Charles Evans Hughes, Merlo J. Pusey

1953
Edmund Pendleton, 1721–1803, David J. Mays

1954
The Spirit of St. Louis, Charles A. Lindbergh

1955
The Taft Story, William S. White

1956
Benjamin Henry Latrobe, Talbot F. Hamlin

1957
Profiles in Courage, John F. Kennedy

Russell Baker

1958
George Washington, Douglas Southall Freeman (Vols. 1–6) and John Alexander Carroll and Mary Wells Ashworth (Vol. 7)
1959
Woodrow Wilson, American Prophet, Arthur Walworth
1960
John Paul Jones, Samuel Eliot Morison
1961
Charles Sumner and the Coming of the Civil War, David Donald
1962
No award
1963
Henry James: Vol. II, The Conquest of London, 1870–1881; Vol. III, The Middle Years, 1881–1895, Leon Edel
1964
John Keats, Walter Jackson Bate
1965
Henry Adams (3 Vols.), Ernest Samuels
1966
A Thousand Days, Arthur M. Schlesinger, Jr.
1967
Mr. Clemens and Mark Twain, Justin Kaplan
1968
Memoirs, 1925–1950, George F. Kennan
1969
The Man From New York, B. L. Reid
1970
Huey Long, T. Harry Williams
1971
Robert Frost: The Years of Triumph, 1915–1938, Lawrence Thompson
1972
Eleanor and Franklin: The Story of Their Relationship, Based on Eleanor Roosevelt's Private Papers, Joseph P. Lash
1973
Luce and His Empire, W. A. Swanberg

1974
O'Neill, Son and Artist, Louis Sheaffer
1975
The Power Broker: Robert Moses and the Fall of New York, Robert A. Caro
1976
Edith Wharton: A Biography, Richard W. B. Lewis
1977
A Prince of Our Disorder, John E. Mack
1978
Samuel Johnson, Walter Jackson Bate
1979
Days of Sorrow and Pain: Leo Baeck and the Berlin Jews, Leonard Baker
1980
The Rise of Theodore Roosevelt, Edmund Morris
1981
Peter the Great, Robert K. Massie
1982
Grant: A Biography, William S. McFeely
1983
Growing Up, Russell Baker
1984
Booker T. Washington, Louis R. Harlan
1985
The Life and Times of Cotton Mather, Kenneth Silverman
1986
Louise Bogan: A Portrait, Elizabeth Frank
1987
Bearing the Cross: Martin Luther King, Jr. and the Southern Christian Leadership Conference, David J. Garrow
1988
Look Homeward: A Life of Thomas Wolfe, David Herbert Donald
1989
Oscar Wilde, Richard Ellmann
1990
Machiavelli in Hell, Sebastian de Grazia
1991
Jackson Pollock: An American Saga, Steven Naifeh and Gregory White Smith
1992
Fortunate Son: The Healing of a Vietnam Vet, Lewis B. Puller, Jr.
1993
Truman, David McCullough
1994
W.E.B. DuBois: Biography of a Race, 1868–1919, David Levering Lewis
1995
Harriet Beecher Stowe: A Life, Joan D. Hedrick

History of the United States

1917
With Americans of Past and Present Days, J. J. Jusserand, ambassador of France to United States
1918
A History of the Civil War, 1861–1865, James Ford Rhodes
1919
No award
1920
The War With Mexico, Justin H. Smith
1921
The Victory at Sea, William Sowden Sims in collaboration with Burton J. Hendrick
1922
The Founding of New England, James Truslow Adams
1923
The Supreme Court in United States History, Charles Warren
1924
The American Revolution — A Constitutional Interpretation, Charles Howard McIlwain
1925
A History of the American Frontier, Frederic L. Paxson
1926
The History of the United States, Edward Channing
1927
Pinckney's Treaty, Samuel Flagg Bemis
1928
Main Currents in American Thought, Vernon Louis Parrington
1929
The Organization and Administration of the Union Army, 1861–1865, Fred Albert Shannon
1930
The War of Independence, Claude H. Van Tyne
1931
The Coming of the War: 1914, Bernadotte E. Schmitt
1932
My Experiences in the World War, John J. Pershing
1933
The Significance of Sections in American History, Frederick J. Turner
1934
The People's Choice, Herbert Agar
1935
The Colonial Period of American History, Charles McLean Andrews

1936
The Constitutional History of the United States, Andrew C. McLaughlin

1937
The Flowering of New England, Van Wyck Brooks

1938
The Road to Reunion, 1865–1900, Paul Herman Buck

1939
A History of American Magazines, Frank Luther Mott

1940
Abraham Lincoln: The War Years, Carl Sandburg

1941
The Atlantic Migration, 1607–1860, Marcus Lee Hansen

1942
Reveille in Washington, Margaret Leech

1943
Paul Revere and the World He Lived In, Esther Forbes

1944
The Growth of American Thought, Merle Curti

1945
Unfinished Business, Stephen Bonsal

1946
The Age of Jackson, Arthur M. Schlesinger, Jr.

1947
Scientists Against Time, James Phinney Baxter, 3rd

1948
Across the Wide Missouri, Bernard DeVoto

1949
The Disruption of American Democracy, Roy Franklin Nichols

1950
Art and Life in America, Oliver W. Larkin

1951
The Old Northwest, Pioneer Period 1815–1840, R. Carlyle Buley

1952
The Uprooted, Oscar Handlin

1953
The Era of Good Feelings, George Dangerfield

1954
A Stillness at Appomattox, Bruce Catton

1955
Great River: The Rio Grande in North American History, Paul Horgan

1956
The Age of Reform, Richard Hofstadter

1957
Russia Leaves the War: Soviet-American Relations, 1917–1920, George F. Kennan

1958
Banks and Politics in America: From the Revolution to the Civil War, Bray Hammond

Carl Sandburg

1959
The Republican Era: 1869–1901, Leonard D. White, assisted by Jean Schneider

1960
In the Days of McKinley, Margaret Leech

1961
Between War and Peace: The Potsdam Conference, Herbert Feis

1962
The Triumphant Empire, Thunder-Clouds Gather in the West, Lawrence H. Gipson

1963
Washington, Village and Capital, 1800–1878, Constance McLaughlin Green

1964
Puritan Village: The Formation of a New England Town, Sumner Chilton Powell

1965
The Greenback Era, Irwin Unger

1966
Life of the Mind in America, Perry Miller

1967
Exploration and Empire: The Explorer and Scientist in the Winning of the American West, William H. Goetzmann

1968
The Ideological Origins of the American Revolution, Bernard Bailyn

1969
Origins of the Fifth Amendment, Leonard W. Levy

1970
Present at the Creation: My Years in the State Department, Dean Acheson

1971
Roosevelt: The Soldier of Freedom, James McGregor Burns

1972
Neither Black Nor White, Slavery and Race Relations in Brazil and the United States, Carl N. Degler

1973
People of Paradox: An Inquiry Concerning the Origin of American Civilization, Michael Kammen

1974
The Americans: The Democratic Experience, Vol. 3, Daniel J. Boorstin

1975
Jefferson and His Time, Dumas Malone

1976
Lamy of Santa Fe, Paul Horgan

1977
The Impending Crisis: 1841–1861, David M. Potter (posthumous)

1978
The Invisible Hand: The Managerial Revolution in American Business, Alfred D. Chandler, Jr.

1979
The Dred Scott Case: Its Significance in Law and Politics, Don E. Fehrenbacher

1980
Been in the Storm So Long, Leon F. Litwack

1981
American Education: The National Experience; 1783–1876, Lawrence A. Cremin

1982
Mary Chestnut's Civil War, C. Vann Woodward, editor

1983
The Transformation of Virginia, 1740–1790, Rhys L. Isaac

George Kennan

Richard Goodwin/Courtesy of Simon & Schuster

Doris Kearns Goodwin

1984
No award

1985
The Prophets of Regulation, Thomas K. McCraw

1986
. . . the Heavens and the Earth: A Political History of the Space Age, Walter A. McDougall

1987
Voyagers to the West: A Passage in the Peopling of America on the Eve of the Revolution, Bernard Bailyn

1988
The Launching of Modern American Science 1846–1876, Robert V. Bruce

1989
Parting the Waters, Taylor Branch

Battle Cry of Freedom, James M. McPherson

1990
In Our Image: America's Empire in the Philippines, Stanley Karnow

1991
A Midwife's Tale: The Life of Martha Ballard, Based on Her Diary 1785–1812, Laurel Thatcher Ulrich

1992
The Fate of Liberty: Abraham Lincoln and Civil Liberties, Mark E. Neely, Jr.

1993
The Radicalism of the American Revolution, Gordon S. Wood

1994
The Disruption of American Democracy, Roy Franklin Nichols

1995
No Ordinary Time: Franklin and Eleanor Roosevelt: The Home Front in World War II, Doris Kearns Goodwin

Drama

1918
Why Marry?, Jesse Lynch Williams

1919
No award

1920
Beyond the Horizon, Eugene O'Neill

1921
Miss Lulu Bett, Zona Gale

1922
Anna Christie, Eugene O'Neill

1923
Icebound, Owen Davis

1924
Hell-Bent fer Heaven, Hatcher Hughes

1925
They Knew What They Wanted, Sidney Howard

1926
Craig's Wife, George Kelly

1927
In Abraham's Bosom, Paul Green

1928
Strange Interlude, Eugene O'Neill

1929
Street Scene, Elmer L. Rice

1930
The Green Pastures, Marc Connelly

1931
Alison's House, Susan Glaspell

1932
Of Thee I Sing, George S. Kaufman, Morrie Ryskind and Ira Gershwin

1933
Both Your Houses, Maxwell Anderson

1934
Men in White, Sidney Kingsley

1935
The Old Maid, Zoe Akins

1936
Idiot's Delight, Robert E. Sherwood

1937
You Can't Take It With You, Moss Hart and George S. Kaufman

1938
Our Town, Thornton Wilder

1939
Abe Lincoln in Illinois, Robert E. Sherwood

1940
The Time of Your Life, William Saroyan

1941
There Shall Be No Night, Robert E. Sherwood

1942
No award

1943
The Skin of Our Teeth, Thornton Wilder

1944
No award

1945
Harvey, Mary Chase

1946
State of the Union, Russel Crouse and Howard Lindsay

Eugene O'Neill

➤

PUBLISHING TIMELINE

808
The world's oldest known printed book, *The Diamond Sutra,* a seven-page scroll printed with wood blocks on paper, is produced in China.

11th century
The Chinese and Koreans continue to experiment with movable type, using clay, wood, bronze and iron. The complexity of Chinese and Korean symbols creates a major stumbling block in the process.

1440
German Johann Gutenberg invents movable type by developing foundry-cast metal characters and a wooden printing press.

1455
Gutenberg prints his first book, a Latin Bible.

1475
Englishman William Caxton produces the first book printed in English, *The Recuyell of the Historyes of Troye.*

1559
Pope Paul IV issues the Index of Forbidden Books, which lists books the Roman Catholic Church considers dangerous to faith and morals.

1639
Stephen Day prints *Freeman's Oath* and *An Almanack* in Cambridge, Massachusetts, the first books published in the American colonies.

1947
No award

1948
A Streetcar Named Desire, Tennessee Williams

1949
Death of a Salesman, Arthur Miller

1950
South Pacific, Richard Rodgers, Oscar Hammerstein II and Joshua Logan

1951
No award

1952
The Shrike, Joseph Kramm

1953
Picnic, William Inge

1954
The Teahouse of the August Moon, John Patrick

1955
Cat on a Hot Tin Roof, Tennessee Williams

1956
The Diary of Anne Frank, Frances Goodrich and Albert Hackett

1957
Long Day's Journey Into Night, Eugene O'Neill

1958
Look Homeward, Angel, Ketti Frings

1959
J.B., Archibald MacLeish

1960
Fiorello!, George Abbott, Jerome Weidman, Jerry Bock and Sheldon Harnick

1961
All the Way Home, Tad Mosel

1962
How to Succeed in Business Without Really Trying, Frank Loesser and Abe Burrows

1963
No award

1964
No award

1965
The Subject Was Roses, Frank D. Gilroy

1966
No award

1967
A Delicate Balance, Edward Albee

1968
No award

1969
The Great White Hope, Howard Sackler

1970
No Place to Be Somebody, Charles Gordone

1971
The Effect of Gamma Rays on Man-in-the-Moon Marigolds, Paul Zindel

1972
No award

1973
That Championship Season, Jason Miller

1974
No award

1975
Seascape, Edward Albee

1976
A Chorus Line, conceived by Michael Bennett

1977
The Shadow Box, Michael Cristofer

1978
The Gin Game, Donald L. Coburn

1979
Buried Child, Sam Shepard

1980
Talley's Folly, Lanford Wilson

1981
Crimes of the Heart, Beth Henley

1982
A Soldier's Play, Charles Fuller

1983
Night, Mother, Marsha Norman

1984
Glengarry Glen Ross, David Mamet

Wendy Wasserstein

1985
Sunday in the Park With George, Stephen Sondheim and James Lapine

1986
No award

1987
Fences, August Wilson

1988
Driving Miss Daisy, Alfred Uhry

1989
The Heidi Chronicles, Wendy Wasserstein

1990
The Piano Lesson, August Wilson

1991
Lost in Yonkers, Neil Simon

1992
The Kentucky Cycle, Robert Schenkkan

1993
Angels in America: Millennium Approaches, Tony Kushner

1994
Three Tall Women, Edward Albee

1995
The Young Man From Atlanta, Horton Foote

1663

Erbauliche Monaths-Unterredungen (Edifying Monthly Discussions), considered the world's first magazine, is published in Germany.

1690

America's first newspaper, *Publick Occurrences Both Forreign and Domestick,* is printed in Boston, Massachusetts, and subsequently suspended for operating without a royal license.

1731

The Gentleman's Magazine, considered the first modern magazine, is published in England. The periodical is intended for entertainment and includes essays, stories, poems and political commentary.

1741

Benjamin Franklin plans to publish America's first magazine, *General Magazine* but is beaten to the punch when *American Magazine* comes out three days before Franklin's.

1764

Pierre Fournier of France develops the point system to measure type sizes. His system is further refined by Francois Didot, establishing consistency in type measure throughout the world.

1771

Encyclopaedia Brittanica, the first English-language encyclopedia, is published in Edinburgh, Scotland.

Nobel Prize for Literature

The Nobel Prize for Literature, one of the six international awards administered by the Nobel Foundation, honors outstanding achievement in letters. The estate of Alfred Bernhard Nobel (1833–1896), the Swedish inventor of dynamite, funds the awards.

W. B. Yeats

1901
René F. A. Sully Prudhomme, France

1902
Theodor Mommsen, Germany

1903
Björnstjerne Björnson, Norway

1904
Frédéric Mistral, France and
José Echegaray, Spain

1905
Henryk Sienkiewicz, Poland

1906
Giosuè Carducci, Italy

1907
Rudyard Kipling, England

1908
Rudolf Eucken, Germany

1909
Selma Lagerlöf, Sweden

1910
Paul von Heyse, Germany

1911
Maurice Maeterlinck, Belgium

1912
Gerhart Hauptmann, Germany

1913
Rabindranath Tagore, India

1914
No award

1915
Romain Rolland, France

1916
Verner von Heidenstam, Sweden

1917
Karl Gjellerup, Denmark and Henrik
Pontoppidan, Denmark

1918
No award

1919
Carl Spitteler, Switzerland

1920
Knut Hamsun, Norway

1921
Anatole France, France

1922
Jacinto Benavente, Spain

1923
William B. Yeats, Ireland

1924
Wladyslaw Reymont, Poland

1925
George Bernard Shaw, Ireland

1926
Grazia Deledda, Italy

1927
Henri Bergson, France

1928
Sigrid Undset, Norway

1929
Thomas Mann, Germany

1930
Sinclair Lewis, United States

1931
Erik A. Karlfeldt, Sweden

1932
John Galsworthy, England

1933
Ivan G. Bunin, Russia

1934
Luigi Pirandello, Italy

1935
No award

1936
Eugene O'Neill, United States

Saul Bellow

1793
The Pennsylvania Evening Post becomes America's first daily newspaper.

1796
German Alois Senefelder develops lithography, a method of image transfer that produces high-quality printed images.

c. 1800
The Third Earl of Stanhope manufactures an all-metal printing press.

1810
In London, Friedrich Koenigh uses steam power to operate a printing press. His system involves rolling a cylinder over paper that lies on top of inked type — moving away from the flat-hand press.

1822
American-born William Church invents the first mechanical typesetting device.

1828
Noah Webster, often referred to as the "father of his country's language," publishes the *American Dictionary of the English Language* in an attempt to encourage American independence in both written and spoken English.

1829
Encyclopaedia Americana, America's first encyclopedia, is published in Philadelphia.

1937
Roger Martin du Gard, France

1938
Pearl S. Buck, United States

1939
Frans Eemil Sillanpää, Finland

1940
No award

1941
No award

1942
No award

1943
No award

1944
Johannes V. Jensen, Denmark

1945
Gabriela Mistral, Chile

1946
Hermann Hesse, Switzerland

1947
André Gide, France

1948
Thomas Stearns Eliot, England

1949
William Faulkner, United States

1950
Bertrand Russell, England

1951
Pär Lagerkvist, Sweden

1952
François Mauriac, France

1953
Sir Winston Churchill, England

1954
Ernest Hemingway, United States

1955
Halldór Kiljan Laxness, Iceland

1956
Juan Ramón Jiménez, Spain

1957
Albert Camus, France

1958
Boris Pasternak, U.S.S.R. (declined)

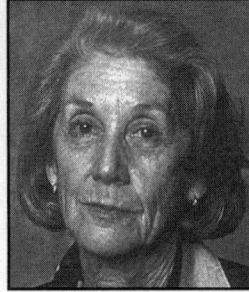

Nadine Gordimer

1959
Salvatore Quasimodo, Italy

1960
St-John Perse (Alexis St.-Léger Léger), France

1961
Ivo Andric, Yugoslavia

1962
John Steinbeck, United States

1963
Giorgios Seferis (Seferiades), Greece

1964
Jean-Paul Sartre, France (declined)

1965
Mikhail Sholokhov, U.S.S.R.

1966
Shmuel Yosef Agnon, Israel and Nelly Sachs, Sweden

1967
Miguel Angel Asturias, Guatemala

1968
Yasunari Kawabata, Japan

1969
Samuel Beckett, Ireland

1970
Aleksandr Solzhenitsyn, U.S.S.R.

1971
Pablo Neruda, Chile

1972
Heinrich Böll, Germany

1973
Patrick White, Australia

1974
Eyvind Johnson, Sweden and Harry Martinson, Sweden

1975
Eugenio Montale, Italy

1976
Saul Bellow, United States

1977
Vicente Aleixandre, Spain

1978
Isaac Bashevis Singer, United States

1979
Odysseus Elytis, Greece

1980
Czeslaw Milosz, United States

1981
Elias Canetti, Bulgaria

1982
Gabriel García Márquez, Colombia

1983
William Golding, England

1984
Jaroslav Seifert, Czechoslovakia

1985
Claude Simon, France

1986
Wole Soyinka, Nigeria

1987
Joseph Brodsky, United States

1988
Naguib Mahfouz, Egypt

1989
Camilo José Cela, Spain

1990
Octavio Paz, Mexico

1991
Nadine Gordimer, South Africa

1992
Derek Walcott, Trinidad

1993
Toni Morrison, United States

1994
Kenzaburo Oe, Japan

1842

Illustrated London News uses woodcuts and engravings for the first time, prompting the growth of illustrated journals throughout the second half of the century.

c. 1845

Paperbacks are introduced to the United States as newspaper supplements and soon appear as small-sized reprints of existing books.

1846

Richard Hoe patents the first rotary press, which allows publishers to increase circulation exponentially.

1851

Selling for a penny a copy, the *New York Times* debuts.

1861

The *Chicago Times* publicizes its motto: "It is a newspaper's duty to print the news and raise hell."

1891

The Copyright Act of 1891 prohibits the reprinting of English titles in paperback form, making paperbacks virtually nonexistent.

William Morris establishes the Kelmscott Press to improve the quality of books produced in England. His books are known for their high quality illustrations and typography.

Major U.S. Trade Publishing Houses

Abbeville Press
488 Madison Ave.
New York, NY 10022
(212) 888-1969
Includes: Artabras, Canopy Books and Cross River

Harry N. Abrams Inc.
Subsidiary of the Times Mirror Company
100 Fifth Ave.
New York, NY 10011
(212) 206-7715
Includes: Abradale

Addison-Wesley-Longman Publishing Co., Inc.
Subsidiary of Pearsons PLC
1 Jacob Way
Reading, MA 01867
(617) 944-3700

Bantam Doubleday Dell Publishing Group Inc.
Affiliate of Bertelsmann AG
1540 Broadway
New York, NY 10036
(212) 354-6500
Bantam includes: Bantam Classics, Bantam Doubleday Dell Books for Young Readers, Golden Apple, New Age Books, New Fiction, New Sciences, Peacock Press, Perigord Press, Spectra and Sweet Dreams

Doubleday includes: Anchor Books, Broadway Books, Currency, Dolphin Books, Double D Western, Foundation Books, Galilee Books, Image Books, Loveswept, Made Simple Books, Main Street/Back List, Nan A. Talese Books, Perfect Crime and Spy Books

Dell includes: Delacorte Press, Dell Books, Dell Hardcovers, Delta Books, Dial Press, DTP Trade Paperbacks, Island Books and Laurel Books

Chronicle Books
275 Fifth St.
San Francisco, CA 94103
(415) 777-7240

DK Publishing
95 Madison Ave., 10th Floor
New York, NY 10016
(212) 213-4800

Farrar, Straus & Giroux Inc.
Subsidiary of the Holtzbrinck Group
19 Union Square W.
New York, NY 10003
(212) 741-6900
Includes: Noonday Press, North Point Press and Sunburst Books

Grove-Atlantic
841 Broadway, 4th Floor
New York, NY 10003
(212) 614-7850
Includes: Grove Press and Atlantic Monthly Press

Harcourt Brace and Co.
Division of Harcourt General
15 E. 26th St.
New York, NY 10010
(212) 592-1000
Includes: Brown Deer Press, Gulliver Books, Gulliver Green, Harvest Books, Red Wagon Books, Kurt and Helen Wolff Books and Jane Yolen Books

HarperCollins Publishers
Subsidiary of News Corp.
10 E. 53rd St.
New York, NY 10022
(212) 207-7000
Includes: Basic Books, Collins San Francisco, Harper Business, HarperCollins Children's Books, HarperCollins Trade, Harper Perennial, Harper Reference and Harper San Francisco

Henry Holt and Co., Inc.
Subsidiary of the Holtzbrinck Group
115 W. 18th St.
New York, NY 10011
(212) 886-9200
Includes: Books for Young Readers, Henry Holt Books, Henry Holt Reference, Metropolitan Books, Owl Books and 21st Century Books

Houghton Mifflin Co.
222 Berkeley St.
Boston, MA 02116
(617) 351-5000
Includes: Clarion Books

Hyperion
Division of Disney Book Publishing Inc.
114 Fifth Ave.
New York, NY 10011
(212) 633-4400
Includes: Hyperion Paperbacks for Children and Miramax Books

Little, Brown and Co.
Subsidiary of Time Warner Inc.
1271 Ave. of the Americas
New York, NY 10020
(212) 522-8700
Includes: Bullfinch Press and Back Bay Books

William Morrow & Company Inc.
Subsidiary of the Hearst Group
1350 Ave. of the Americas
New York, NY 10019
(212) 261-6500
Includes: Avon, Green Willow Books, Hearst Books, Mulberry, Beachtree Books, Lothrop, Lee and Shepard, William Morrow Books, Morrow Junior Books, Quill Books and Tamborine Books

---

1895

In its first issue, American magazine *The Bookman* includes a list of "Books in Demand," which predates the bestseller list, later developed by Frank Mott in his book, *Golden Multitudes.*

1902

McClure's Magazine prints "Tweed Days in St. Louis" by C.H. Wetmore and Lincoln Steffens. The article introduces the muckraking era.

1912

Photoplay debuts as the first magazine for movie fans.

1917

The first Pulitzer Prizes are awarded for editorial writing, reporting, history of the United States and biography or autobiography. Fiction, drama and poetry debut in 1918.

The first op-ed page appears in the *New York Times.*

1926

The Book-of-the-Month Club is founded and begins to sell books at reduced prices by mail and on a subscription basis.

1933

Anti-pornography laws are cited as the reason that James Joyce's *Ulysses* is prohibited from being imported to the United States.

W. W. Norton & Company Inc.
500 Fifth Ave.
New York, NY 10110
(212) 354-5500

Penguin U.S.A.
375 Hudson St.
New York, NY 10014
(212) 366-2000
Includes: Dutton, Penguin, Penguin
Classics, Plume, Puffin, Signet, Signet
Classics, Viking and Viking Studio

The Putnam Berkley Group Inc.
Subsidiary of MCA, Inc.
200 Madison Ave.
New York, NY 10016
(212) 951-8400
Includes: Ace, Berkley Prime Crime,
Coward-McCann, Diamond, Grosset &
Dunlap, Grosset Books, HP Books, Jove,
Perigee Books, Philomel, Platt & Munk,
Price Stern Sloan, G.P. Putnam's Sons,
Riverhead Books, Sandcastle,
Serendipity, Jeremy P. Tarcher, Wee
Sing and Wonder Books

Random House Inc.
Subsidiary of Advance Publications
201 E. 50th St.
New York, NY 10022
(212) 751-2600
Includes: Ballantine, Crown, Fawcett,
Fodor's, Harmony, Ivy, Alfred A. Knopf,
Modern Library, Pantheon, Clarkson
Potter Publishers, Random House Adult
Books, Schocken, Times Books, Villard
and Vintage

Simon & Schuster
Division of Viacom Inc.
1230 Ave. of the Americas
New York, NY 10020
(212) 698-7000
Includes: Baseball America, H&R Block,
Collier Books, Lisa Drew Books,
Fireside, Hudson River Editions,
Macmillan Publishing USA, MTV Books,
Pocket Books, Prentice Hall, Rawson
Associates, Scribner, Charles Scribner's
Sons, Thorndike Press, Touchstone and
Twayne Publishers

St. Martin's Press Inc.
Subsidiary of Macmillan Publishers Ltd.
(England)
175 Fifth Ave.
New York, NY 10010
(212) 674-5151
Includes: Bedford Books, Forge, Orb,
Picador, Tor Books and A. Wyatt Books

Warner Books
Division of Time Warner Inc.
1271 Ave. of the Americas
New York, NY 10020
(212) 522-7200

Workman Publishing Co.
708 Broadway
New York, NY 10003
(212) 254-5900
Includes: Algonquin Books and Artisan
Books

1936

Allen Lane's Penguin Press, an
English publishing house, reintro-
duces the paperback book.

1967

Rolling Stone and *New York
Magazine* debut, spawning the popularity of special-interest and regional
magazines.

c. 1980

About 70 percent of the books sold in
the United States are paperbacks.

1985

With the availability of relatively
inexpensive laser printers and computers, tools for desktop publishing
begin to be commonly used.

1986

*The Academic American
Encyclopedia* is available on CD-
ROM, the first reference work pub-
lished in this medium.

1994

For the first time in history, chain
bookstores outsell independent
stores, signaling what many fear to
be the death of smaller booksellers
at the hands of superstores.

Book and Magazine Publications

American Book Review
Unit for Contemporary Literature
Campus Box 4241
Illinois St. University
Normal, IL 61790-4241
(309) 438-3026

American Bookseller
American Booksellers Association
828 S. Broadway
Tarrytown, NY 10591
(914) 591-2665

Book World
The Washington Post Co.
1150 15th St., N.W.
Washington D.C. 20071
(202) 334-6000

Boston Book Review
30 Brattle St., 4th Floor
Cambridge, MA 02138
(617) 497-0344

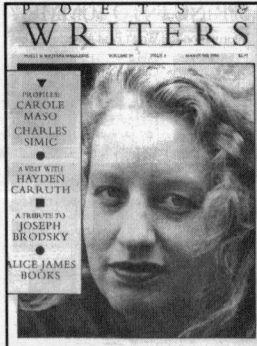

Editor and Publisher
11 W. 19th St.
New York, NY 10011
(212) 675-4380

Entertainment Weekly
1675 Broadway
New York, NY 10019
(212) 522-5600

Firsts: Collecting Modern First Editions
Lucerne Group
575 N. Lucerne Blvd.
Los Angeles, CA 91104-4805
(213) 469-9189

Horn Book Magazine
11 Beacon St., Suite 1000
Boston, MA 02108
(617) 227-1555

New York Review of Books
251 W. 56th St., Suite 1321
New York, NY 10107
(212) 556-3598

New York Times Book Review
229 W. 43rd St.
New York, NY 10036
(212) 556-1234

Poets and Writers
72 Spring St.
New York, New York 10012
(212) 226-3586

Publishers Weekly
Cahners Publishing Co.
249 W. 17th St.
New York, NY 10011
(212) 645-0067

Small Press
The Jacobs Group
121 E. Front Street, Suite 401
Trevor City, MI 49684
(616) 933-0445

Women's Review of Books
Wellesley College
Center for Research on Women
Wellesley, MA 02181
(617) 283-2555

The Writer
120 Boylston St.
Boston, MA 02116
(617) 423-3157

Writer's Digest
P.O. Box 2124
Harlon, IA 51593
(800) 333-0133

PEOPLE

Biography®

You'll find this selection of notables from the world of entertainment in *The Entertainment Almanac* or on the *Biography*® series on A&E Network.

George Abbott
6/25/1887–1/31/1995; Forestville, New York. Pulitzer Prize- and Tony Award-winning playwright, actor, director and producer, known as "Mr. Broadway," whose career paralleled and influenced the development of modern theater. His career began in 1912 and extended into the late 1980s. He was involved with more than 120 productions, including *Three Men on a Horse* (1935), *Damn Yankees* (1955) and *Fiorello* (1959).

Aerosmith Grammy Award-winning hard-rock band known for its blues-influenced style, flamboyant stage presence and an amazing 1984 comeback. After a long battle with drugs and bad blood within the band, the group broke up in the 1970s. Current band members include singer **Steven Tyler (Steven Tallarico, b. 3/26/48; New York City),** guitarist **Joe Perry (b. 9/10/50; Lawrence, Massachusetts),** guitarist **Brad Whitford (b. 2/23/52; Winchester, Massachusetts),** bassist **Tom Hamilton (b. 12/31/51; Colorado Springs, Colorado)** and drummer **Joey Kramer (b. 6/21/50; New York City).** The band's recordings include *Toys in the Attic* (1975), *Permanent Vacation* (1987) and *Get a Grip* (1993).

Alvin Ailey, Jr. 1/5/31–12/1/89; Rogers, Texas. Modern dancer and choreographer known for his theatrical, energetic dances that combine modern, jazz and African dance elements. He studied dance with Martha Graham and Charles Weidman before forming his Alvin Ailey American Dance Theater in 1958. His dances include *Blue Swan* (1958), *Night Creature* (1975) and *Precipice* (1983).

George Abbott

Edward Albee b. 3/12/28; Washington D.C. Tony Award and Pulitzer Prize-winning dramatist associated with the theater of the absurd and known for his biting dialogue and satire. His plays include *The Zoo Story* (1958), *Who's Afraid of Virginia Woolf* (1962) and *A Delicate Balance* (1967).

Alan Alda b. 1/28/36; New York City. Emmy Award-winning television, film and stage actor best known for his portrayal of Hawkeye Pierce on *M*A*S*H* (1972–83). He has also appeared in several films, including *Same Time Next Year* (1978), *The Four Seasons* (1981) and *Crimes and Misdemeanors* (1989). He is the son of actor Robert Alda.

Gracie Allen 7/20/06–8/27/64; San Francisco. Actress who was the scatterbrained half of Hollywood's beloved husband-and-wife comedy team. Her husband, **George Burns (see obituary on page 797),** was her straight man. The pair performed in vaudeville, on radio, in movies and on television. Their television show, *The Burns and Allen Show*, ran from 1950 to 1958.

Steve Allen b. 12/26/21; New York City. Grammy Award-winning comedian, actor, author and

musician best known for his intelligent, informal comic style. He was the first host (1954–56) and creator of *The Tonight Show*. His *Steve Allen Show* (1956–64) was a major influence on a generation of comedians and launched the careers of Tom Posten, Louis Nye and others. His films include *The Story* (1955).

Tim Allen b. 6/1/53; Denver, Colorado. Television and film actor who started his career as a standup comic before landing the lead role on television's *Home Improvement* (1991–present). His films include *The Santa Clause* (1994) and *Toy Story* (1995).

Woody Allen (Allen Stewart Konigsberg) b. 12/1/35; Brooklyn, New York. Academy Award-winning film director, writer, actor and playwright whose films range from comic fantasies (*Bananas*, 1971; *Sleeper*, 1973) to urban, contemplative comedies (*Manhattan*, 1979; *Hannah and Her Sisters*, 1986). Allen won Best Director honors for *Annie Hall* (1977), which was also named Best Picture.

Robert Altman b. 2/20/25; Kansas City, Missouri. Film director whose sprawling, stylized films deglamorize and shatter myths surrounding history, Hollywood and politics. His films include *McCabe and Mrs. Miller* (1971), *Nashville* (1975) and *The Player* (1992).

Julie Andrews (Julia Elizabeth Wells) b. 10/1/35; Walton-on-Thames, England. Academy Award-winning film and stage actress known for her fresh-faced, innocent appeal first on stage in *My Fair Lady* (1956) and then in films, including *Mary Poppins* (1964) and *The Sound of*

Music (1965). She created a controversy in 1996 when she tried to withdraw her name from the Tony Award ballot. She is married to film and stage director **Blake Edwards (b. 7/26/22; Tulsa, Oklahoma)**.

Maya Angelou b. 4/4/28; St. Louis, Missouri. Grammy Award-winning poet, writer, composer and actress who has appeared in several Off-Broadway productions, including Jean Genet's *The Blacks* (1960). She wrote *I Know Why the Caged Bird Sings* (1970), a humorous autobiography about growing up in segregated Arkansas. She read her poem "On the Pulse of Morning" at President Clinton's 1993 inauguration.

Louis "Satchmo" Armstrong 7/4/1900–7/9/71; New Orleans. Jazz musician known for his virtuosic skills on the cornet and trumpet. Armstrong popularized the scat style of singing and remains one of jazz's most important and influential musicians. He was a member of King Oliver's band in the 1920s, and he formed several bands of his own, namely the Hot Fives and Sevens.

Fred Astaire (Frederick Austerlitz) 5/10/1899–6/22/1987; Omaha, Nebraska. Dancer and actor who appeared with dancing partner Ginger ROGERS in several romantic comedies that elevated dance to cinematic artistry. Though Astaire started his career as a stage performer, he is best remembered for his screen roles including *Top Hat* (1935) and *Swing Time* (1936).

Sir Richard Attenborough b. 8/29/23; Cambridge, England. Academy Award-winning director and actor best known for his

Robert Altman

sweeping biopics, including *Gandhi* (1982) and *Cry Freedom* (1987).

Gene Autry b. 9/29/07; Tioga, Texas. Singer and actor best known as the "Singing Cowboy." Autry was a popular radio figure in the early 1930s, performing at the Grand Ole Opry. He emerged as a movie star in 1935, when he signed with Republic Pictures and made his big-screen debut with *The Phantom Empire.* He is credited with creating the musical Western. In 1938, Roy ROGERS also joined Republic and the two actors became the country's most loved cowboy team. Autry's other films include *Tumbling Tumbleweeds* (1935), *The Singing Cowboy* (1937) and *Rhythm of the Saddle* (1938). He parlayed his stardom into a fortune and is the former owner of baseball's California Angels.

Kathy Baker b. 6/8/50; Midland, Texas. Emmy Award-winning actress best known for her role as the compassionate mother, doctor and citizen, Jill Brock, on *Picket Fences* (1991–96).

Russell Baker b. 1925; Loudoun County, Virginia. Pulitzer Prize-winning columnist for the *New York Times*. In 1993, he replaced Alistair Cook as host of PBS's *Masterpiece Theatre*. Collections of Baker's columns include *An American in Washington* (1961) and *Poor Russell's Almanac* (1971); his two memoirs are *Growing Up* (1982) and *The Good Times* (1989).

George Balanchine (Georgi Melitonovich Balanchivadze) 1/22/04–4/30/83; St. Petersburg, Russia. Creative and experimental choreographer and dancer considered the most influential figure in 20th-century dance. Balanchine's career began in Russia, where he was a student at the Imperial Ballet School. He danced with and choreographed Diaghilev's Ballets Russes before coming to the United States, where he became ballet director of the Metropolitan Opera (1934–37), co-founder with Lincoln Kirstein of the School of American Ballet (1934) and princi-

pal choreographer of the New York City Ballet. He created more than 200 dances for the NYCB, including *Serenade* and *Don Quixote*.

Lucille Ball 8/6/11–4/26/89; Jamestown, New York. Emmy Award-winning television and film actress best remembered for her starring role in television's *I Love Lucy* (1951–57). A talented comedienne and slapstick genius, Ball was television's most popular actress. Her films include *Stage Door* (1937) and *Mame* (1974).

Anne Bancroft b. 9/17/31; New York City. Academy- and Tony Award-winning film and stage actress best known for her portrayal of Annie Sullivan, Helen Keller's teacher, in the stage (1960) and film (1962) versions of *The Miracle Worker.* Her other films include *The Graduate* (1967) and *The Turning Point* (1977). She is married to actor and director **Mel Brooks (b. 6/28/26; Brooklyn, New York)**, whose films include *The Producers* (1968), *Blazing Saddles* (1974) and *History of the World — Part 1* (1981).

Brigitte Bardot b. 9/28/34; Paris, France. Actress who often portrayed sexy, sensual women in films such as *And God Created Woman* (1956) and *The Truth* (1961). She abandoned her film career to become an animal-rights advocate.

John Barrymore (John Blythe) 2/15/1882–5/29/1942; Philadelphia. Film and stage actor known for his acting skills and tempestuous personal life. In 1922 and 1923, he gave 101 performances as Hamlet. His films include *A Bill of Divorcement* (1932) and *Twentieth Century* (1934). John's father, **Maurice (1847–1905; Agra, India)**, immigrated to the United States in 1875 and appeared in Augustin Daly's play *Under the Gaslight.* Maurice's wife, **Georgianna Drew (1856–1893; Philadelphia)**, also from a family of actors, appeared with her husband in the play *Diplomacy* (1886). John's brother, **Lionel (4/28/1878–11/15/1954;**

Philadelphia), an Academy Award-winning actor, appeared in the films *Free Soul* (1931) and *Dinner at Eight* (1933). John's sister, **Ethel (8/15/1879–6/18/1959; Philadelphia)**, best known as a stage actress, appeared in *The Corn Is Green* (1940–1942) and has a Broadway theater named in her honor. She won an Academy Award for *None but the Lonely Heart* (1944). John's son, **John Drew (John Blythe Barrymore; b. 6/4/32; Beverly Hills, California)**, appeared in several films, including *While the City Sleeps* (1956), as has his granddaughter, **Drew Barrymore (b. 2/22/75; Los Angeles)**, who appeared in *E.T. the Extra-Terrestrial* (1982) and *Boys on the Side* (1995).

Mikhail Baryshnikov b. 1/27/48; Riga, Latvia. Dancer and choreographer widely considered the best male classical dancer of the 20th century. Baryshnikov defected to the United States in 1974 and danced with the American Ballet Theatre (1974–78) and the New York City Ballet (1978–79). He has performed in *Swan Lake, Medea* and *Push Comes to Shove*, which Twyla THARP created for him. He is also involved in modern dance and leads his own modern-dance company, The White Oak Dance Project. He appeared in the film *White Nights* (1985).

Count Basie 8/24/04–4/26/84; Red Bank, New Jersey. Grammy Award-winning jazz pianist, composer and bandleader known for his powerful, rhythmic sound and his dominant-right-hand piano style. He played in New York and Kansas City bands in the 1920s and 1930s before forming his own band in 1935, which he performed with for 40 years.

Kathy Bates b. 6/28/48; Memphis, Tennessee. Academy Award-winning film, stage and television character actress whose films include *Come Back to the Five and Dime, Jimmy Dean, Jimmy Dean* (1982), *Misery* (1990) and *Fried Green Tomatoes* (1991). Her Broadway appearances include '*Night, Mother* (1983).

The Beatles British rock group that inspired the psychedelic movement of the 1960s and shaped the course of rock and roll. No band has yet equalled The Beatles's popularity and influence. Members included singer **John LENNON**, singer and pianist **Paul McCARTNEY**, drummer **Ringo Starr (Richard Starkey; b. 7/7/40; Liverpool, England)** and guitarist **George Harrison (b. 2/25/43; Liverpool, England)**. Lennon and McCartney played together in the late 1950s in The Quarrymen. With Harrison they formed The Silver Beatles in 1959, added Starr in 1962 and dropped the Silver. The 1964 song "I Want to Hold Your Hand" sparked "Beatlemania" in the United States and the band became an international success. The group's albums include *A Hard Day's Night* (1964), *Revolver* (1966) and *Sgt. Pepper's Lonely Hearts Club Band* (1967), and their films include *A Hard Day's Night* (1964) and *Help!* (1965). The group disbanded in 1970, claiming they had reached their potential as a band.

Warren Beatty b. 3/30/37; Richmond, Virginia. Academy Award-winning director, actor, producer and writer known for his appealing physical features and his ambitious directorial efforts. He directed the films *Reds* (1981) and *Dick Tracy* (1990) and appeared in *McCabe and Mrs. Miller* (1971), *Bonnie and Clyde* (1967) and *Bugsy* (1991). His sister is actress Shirley MacLAINE. He is married to actress **Annette Bening (b. 5/5/58; Topeka, Kansas)**

John Belushi 1/24/49–3/5/82; Chicago. Emmy Award-winning television and film comedian and writer best remembered for his offbeat, outrageous wit. He was one of the original cast members of *Saturday Night Live* (1975–79), appearing in skits featuring the Samurai warrior, the Blues Brothers and the bees. His films include *Animal House* (1978) and *The Blues Brothers* (1980). He died of a heroin overdose.

Ingmar Bergman

Tony Bennett (Anthony Dominick Benedetto) b. 8/13/26; Queens, New York. Grammy Award-winning singer of classic jazz-inflected music who was popular in the late 1950s and 1960s and enjoyed an enormous comeback in the 1990s, appealing to both baby boomers and the MTV generation. His recordings include *Basie Swings, Bennett Sings* (1959), "I Left My Heart in San Francisco" (1962) and *MTV Unplugged* (1994).

Jack Benny (Benjamin Kubelsky) 2/14/1894–12/26/1974; Chicago. Emmy Award-winning radio and television comedian remembered for his self-ridicule, his awful violin playing and his stinginess. He starred in the *Jack Benny Show* (1950–65) and was a regular guest on *Shower of Stars* (1955–58).

Robert Benton b. 9/29/32; Waxahachie, Texas. Academy Award-winning director and screenwriter known for his sentimental films, which include *Kramer vs. Kramer* (1979), *Places in the Heart* (1984) and *Nobody's Fool* (1994). He wrote the screenplay of *Bonnie and Clyde* (1967).

Candice Bergen b. 5/8/46; Beverly Hills, California. Emmy Award-winning television and film actress who enjoyed a successful film career but found wider praise and recognition starring as broadcast journalist Murphy Brown in the show of the same name (1988–present). Her films include *The Group* (1966) and *Carnal Knowledge* (1971). She also worked as a model and a photojournalist, and her photos have appeared in *Life* and *Playboy*. She was married to **Louis Malle (see obituary on page 802)**. Her father was ventriloquist **Edgar Bergen (2/16/03–9/30/78; Chicago)**, who appeared on several variety shows with his puppet, Charlie McCarthy.

Ingmar Bergman b. 7/14/18; Uppsala, Sweden. Academy and Tony Award-winning Swedish screen and stage writer, director and producer known for his films that explore the philosophical and spiritual. His films include *The Seventh Seal* (1957), *Persona* (1966) and *Fanny & Alexander* (1983).

Ingrid Bergman 8/29/15–8/29/82; Stockholm, Sweden. Academy Award-winning Swedish film and stage actress who often portrayed strong, sophisticated women. Her films include *Intermezzo* (1939), *Casablanca* (1942) and *Gaslight* (1944).

Milton Berle (Milton Berlinger) b. 7/12/08; Harlem, New York. Emmy Award-winning television, film and stage comic actor known as "Mr. Television." He starred in television's *The Texaco Star Theater* (1948–53) and appeared in the film *It's a Mad Mad Mad Mad World* (1963). Berle's widespread appeal helped spark the popularity of television.

Chuck Berry b. 10/18/26; Wentzville, Missouri. Singer, songwriter and guitarist who was a pioneer in the development of rock music. His recordings, known for their witty lyrics and blues-influenced guitar, include "Maybellene" (1955), "Roll Over, Beethoven" (1956) and "Johnny B. Goode" (1958). He appeared in the films *Rock, Rock, Rock* (1956) and *Go, Johnny, Go* (1959).

Shirley Temple Black b. 4/23/28; Santa Monica, California. Actress famous for her childhood roles. Her curly hair, dimples and charm captivated America in the films *Little Miss Marker* (1934), *Heidi* (1937) and *The Little Princess* (1939). Later in life, Black became active in the Republican party, serving under presidents Nixon, Ford and Bush.

Humphrey Bogart 12/25/1899–1/14/1957; New York City. Academy Award-winning film and stage actor known for his roles as a tough, cynical guy with a big heart. His films include *Casablanca* (1942), *The Maltese Falcon* (1941) and *The African Queen* (1951). He was married to the Tony Award-winning actress **Lauren Bacall (Betty Joan Perske; b. 9/16/24; New York City)**, who appeared with him in *The Big Sleep* (1946).

Pierre Boulez b. 3/26/25; Montbrison, France. Grammy Award-winning conductor and composer considered a leader of the avant-garde. His works include *Le Marteau sans maître* (1954) and *Pli selon pli* (1960). He was music director and conductor of the New York Philharmonic-Symphony Orchestra (1971–77) and is currently director of the Insitut de Recherche et de Coordination Acoustique/Music in Paris (1976–present).

Marlon Brando b. 4/3/24; Omaha, Nebraska. Academy Award-winning actor whose inward-looking style and rough but sexy appeal established him as one of Hollywood's most respected actors. Brando, a practitioner of Method acting, appeared in *A Streetcar Named Desire* (1951), *On the Waterfront* (1954) and *The Godfather* (1972). He won the Best Actor Oscar for *The Godfather* but refused the award in protest of Hollywood's treatment of Native Americans.

Garth Brooks (Troyal Garth Brooks) b. 2/2/62; Tulsa, Oklahoma. Wildly popular Grammy Award-winning country singer who has attracted scores of rock and pop fans as well as country and western followers. His recordings include *No Fences* (1990), *Ropin' the Wind* (1991), which sold a record-shattering 11 million copies and was the first album to debut at number 1 on both *Billboard*'s pop and country charts, and *In Pieces* (1993).

James Brown b. 5/3/33; Augusta, Georgia. Energetic, intense singer best known for his gospel-tinged, rhythm and blues

songs that influenced the direction of funk, soul and disco. Still a constantly touring showman, the Godfather of Soul's recordings progress from the early, soul-stirring shout of "Please, Please, Please" (1956) to the proto-funk of "Papa's Got a Brand New Boy" (1965) to the black power anthem "Say It Loud — I'm Black and I'm Proud" (1968).

Yul Brynner 7/11/15–10/10/85; Sakhalin, Russia. Academy- and Tony Award-winning film and stage actor best known for his portrayal of the King of Siam in *The King and I*. He appeared in the Broadway play (1951) and the film (1956). His other film credits include *Anastasia* (1956) and *The Magnificent Seven* (1960).

Carol Burnett b. 4/26/34; San Antonio, Texas. Emmy Award-winning television, film and stage comedienne. She starred in the *Carol Burnett Show* (1967–78) and appeared in the films *The Four Seasons* (1981) and *Annie* (1982). In 1981, she became the first person to win a libel suit against the tabloid *National Enquirer*.

Richard Burton (Richard Jenkins) 11/10/25–8/5/84; Pontrhydfen, Wales. Tony Award-winning film and stage actor who gained fame working with the Old Vic, London's premier theater company. Burton starred in Broadway's *Camelot* (1960) and *Hamlet* (1964). He appeared in several films with his then-wife, Elizabeth TAYLOR, including *Cleopatra* (1962) and *Who's Afraid of Virginia Woolf* (1966).

Marlon Brando

Sid Caesar b. 9/8/22; Yonkers, New York. American comedian and actor who, with his comedy partner, **Imogene Coca (b. 11/18/08; Philadelphia),** starred in television's *Your Show of Shows* (1950–54). He also starred in *Caesar's Hour* (1954–57) and appeared in the film *It's a Mad Mad Mad Mad World* (1963).

Nicolas Cage (Nicolas Coppola) b. 1/7/64; Long Beach, California. Academy Award-winning actor whose credits range from serious dramas to wacky comedies to action-adventure films. His films include *Raising Arizona* (1987), *Moonstruck* (1987), *Leaving Las Vegas* (1995) and *The Rock* (1996).

James Cagney 7/17/1899–3/30/1986; New York City. Academy Award-winning actor best known for his brash gangster role in *Public Enemy* (1931). But Cagney first performed as a song-and-dance man, appearing in comedies and musicals. His other films include *Yankee Doodle Dandy* (1942), *Love Me or Leave Me* (1955) and *Ragtime* (1981).

Michael Caine (Maurice Micklewhite) b. 3/14/33; London. Academy Award-winning British actor whose versatility and unlimited acting range has lead to constant work. His films include *Alfie* (1966), *Sleuth* (1972) and *Hannah and Her Sisters* (1986).

Zoe Caldwell b. 9/14/33; Australia. Tony Award-winning stage actress known for her roles in both classical and modern productions. Her Broadway plays include *The Prime of Miss Jean Brodie* (1968), *Medea* (1982) and *Master Class* (1995).

Glen Campbell b. 4/22/36; Billstown, Arkansas. Grammy Award-winning country-pop singer and guitarist who worked as a session musician for Frank Sinatra, Johnny Cash and Phil Spector before he made it big solo with "Gentle on My Mind" (1967). His other recordings include "Wichita Lineman" (1968) and "Rhinestone Cowboy" (1975).

Jim Carrey

He hosted television's *The Glen Campbell Show* (1969–72).

John Candy 12/31/50–3/4/94; Toronto, Canada. Portly film and television actor best known for his comedic roles opposite Dan Aykroyd. In 1974, he formed a Canadian spinoff of Chicago's popular Second City Comedy Troupe. His films include *The Blues Brothers* (1980), *Stripes* (1981) and *Planes, Trains and Automobiles* (1987). He died of a heart attack while filming *Wagons East* in Mexico.

Frank Capra 5/18/1897–9/3/1991; Palermo, Sicily. Academy Award-winning director known for his films that depict the triumph of the little guy. His films include *It Happened One Night* (1934), *Mr. Deeds Goes to Town* (1936) and *It's a Wonderful Life* (1946).

Mariah Carey b. 3/27/70; Long Island, New York. Grammy Award-winning singer and songwriter known for her seven-octave range and her popular gospel-influenced, dance-pop songs. Her recordings include *Mariah Carey* (1990), *Emotions* (1991) and the eight-million selling *Music Box* (1993). She is married to Columbia Records head Tommy Mottola.

Jim Carrey b. 1/17/62; Ontario, Canada. Film and television actor known for his inane, physical comedy. In 1995, he became Hollywood's highest paid actor, earning $20 million for *The Cable Guy* (1996). His other films include *Ace Ventura, Pet Detective* (1994) and *The Mask* (1995). His television credits include *The Duck Factory* (1984) and *In Living Color* (1990–94).

Johnny Carson b. 10/23/25; Corning, Iowa. Emmy Award-winning television entertainer famous for his 30-year stint as host of *The Tonight Show* (1962–92), television's most popular late-night show. Carson began his show-business career as a magician.

Betty Carter (Lillie Mae Jones) b. 5/16/30; Flint, Michigan. Grammy Award-winning jazz and blues singer whose career started at the age of 16. Though she did not enjoy fame until she reached her 40s, she is now considered one of the best bebop singers. She has performed with Muddy Waters, Miles Davis and Thelonious Monk. Her recordings include *The Audience With Betty Carter* (1981) and *Whatever Happened to Love* (1982).

Johnny Cash b. 2/26/32; Kingsland, Arkansas. Grammy Award-winning country and western singer known as "the man in black." From his earliest rockabilly sessions at Memphis's Sun Studios, Cash has had an enduring influence on rock. His recordings include *Johnny Cash at Folsom Prison* (1967) and *American Recordings* (1994).

Raymond Chandler 7/23/1888–5/26/1959; Chicago. Author of detective novels that depict the seedy, dark side of Los Angeles. His novels, which include *The Big Sleep* (1939) and *Farewell, My Lovely* (1940), feature the tough private detective Philip Marlowe.

Lon Chaney (Alonso Chaney) 4/1/1883–8/26/1930; Colorado Springs, Colorado. Actor known as "the man of a thousand faces." Chaney specialized in using make-up to transform himself into grotesque, often distorted, figures. His films include *The Hunchback of Notre Dame* (1923) and *The Phantom of the Opera* (1925). His son, **Lon Chaney, Jr. (Creighton Chaney; 2/10/06–7/12/73; Oklahoma City, Oklahoma),** also appeared in horror films and is remembered as "the Wolfman."

Tracy Chapman b. 3/20/64; Cleveland, Ohio. Grammy Award-winning folk-rock singer and songwriter known for her rich alto voice and her socially conscious lyrics. Her recordings include *Tracy Chapman* (1988) and *Crossroads* (1989).

Ray Charles (Ray Charles Robinson) b. 3/23/30; Albany, Georgia. Grammy Award-winning singer, pianist and composer known for his popular, soul-inflected pop and country music and his lavish stage productions. His recordings include "I Got a Woman" (1955), "What I'd Say" (1959) and "Georgia on My Mind" (1960).

Cher (Cherilyn Sarkisian La Piere) b. 5/20/46; El Centro, California. Academy Award-winning pop star turned actress turned infomercial queen whose films include *Moonstruck* (1987) and *The Witches of Eastwick* (1987). Cher and her first husband, Sonny Bono, sang as a duo and had a hit television series, *The Sonny and Cher Comedy Hour* (1971–74). Her recordings include *Heart of Stone* (1989).

Deepak Chopra b. 1947; India. Best-selling author who abandoned his profession as an endocrinologist and adopted the alternative healing method called Maharishi Ayur-Veda, which involves herbal remedies, meditation, massage and yoga. His books include *Ageless Body, Timeless Mind* (1993) and *The Seven Spiritual Laws of Success* (1995).

Dame Agatha Christie 9/15/1890–1/12/1976; England. British mystery writer and playwright with more than 80 novels

Dame Agatha Christie

to her credit. Most of her books featured either Hercule Poirot, a Belgian detective, or Miss Marple, an elderly spinster with a knack for solving murders. Christie's books include *The Murder of Roger Ackroyd* (1926), *Murder on the Orient Express* (1934) and *Death on the Nile* (1937). She also wrote the plays *Mousetrap* (1952) and *Witness for the Prosecution* (1954).

Eric Clapton (Eric Clapp) b. 3/30/45; Ripley, England. Grammy Award-winning blues-rock singer, guitarist and composer whose virtuosic guitar skills caused some critics to proclaim "Clapton is God." He played in the Yardbirds (1963–65), John Mayall's Bluesbreakers (1965–66), Cream (1966–68), Blind Faith (1969) and Derek and the Dominos (1970–71). He began his solo career in 1974, and his solo recordings include "Layla" (1970), "Cocaine" (1977), "Lay Down Sally" (1977) and *Unplugged* (1992).

John Cleese b. 10/27/39; Weston-Super-Mare, England. Film and television comic actor whose deadpan humor makes life's mundane annoyances hilarious. He played country hotel manager Basil Fawlty in England's brilliant television series *Fawlty Towers* (1975–79) and appeared in the Monty Python films, including *Monty Python and the Holy Grail* (1975) and *Monty Python's The Meaning of Life* (1983). His other films include *Time Bandits* (1981) and *A Fish Called Wanda* (1988).

Van Cliburn (Harvey Lavan Cliburn, Jr.) b. 7/12/34; Shreveport, Louisiana. Pianist known for his outstanding technique and his interpretation of works by Romantic composers. In 1958, he became the first American to win the International Tchaikovsky Prize.

Montgomery Clift 10/17/20–7/23/66; Omaha, Nebraska. Fine-featured, high-strung movie actor who often played sensitive loners. His films include *Red River* (1946), *A Place in the Sun* (1951), *From Here to Eternity* (1953) and *Judgment at

Nuremberg* (1961). Disfigured in a 1957 car accident, Clift took to drink, ruining his health and career.

George Clooney b. 5/6/61; Lexington, Kentucky. Film and television actor who briefly appeared in several television shows including *E/R* (1984) and *The Facts of Life* (1985–86), before landing a role on NBC's hit *ER* (1994–present). His films include *From Dusk Till Dawn* (1995).

Glenn Close b. 3/19/47; Greenwich, Connecticut. Tony Award-winning stage and film actress who surprised many when she displayed a strong soprano in Broadway's *Sunset Boulevard* (1994–95). Her films include *The Big Chill* (1983) and *Fatal Attraction* (1987).

Nat "King" Cole (Nathaniel Adams Coles) 3/17/19–2/15/65; Montgomery, Alabama. Grammy Award-winning singer and composer known for his velvety voice and romantic ballads. He was the first African American to host a network television series, *The Nat "King" Cole Show* (1956–57). His recordings include "Unforgettable" and "Mona Lisa." In 1991, his daughter, **Natalie (b. 02/06/50; Los Angeles),** released *Unforgettable,* an album of duets she sang with earlier recordings of her father.

John Coltrane 9/23/26–7/17/67; Hamlet, North Carolina. Jazz tenor and soprano saxophonist and composer who was a leader of the New Wave jazz movement. Coltrane began his career playing in big bands and gained wide respect and fame for his stylistic innovations while playing with Miles Davis in the 1950s. His modal approach and spiritual depth influenced the free jazz explorations of the 1960s and 1970s.

Sean Connery (Thomas Connery) b. 8/25/30; Edinburgh, Scotland. Academy Award-winning, genially handsome film actor whose name became synonymous with James Bond, the imperturbable superspy hero of *Dr. No* (1962), *Goldfinger* (1964), *Diamonds Are Forever* (1971) and others. Connery broke the Bond mold to establish himself as an all-around Hollywood star, aging remarkably well in *Indiana Jones and the Last Crusade* (1989), *The Hunt for Red October* (1990) and *The Rock* (1996).

Bill Cosby b. 7/12/37; Philadelphia. Emmy and Grammy Award-winning television and film actor and comedian who was the first African American to star in a television series, *I Spy* (1965–68). He also starred in *The Cosby Show* (1984–92), the multi-Emmy Award-winning family sitcom. He returned to television in 1996's *Cosby*.

Kevin Costner b. 1/18/55; Los Angeles. Academy Award-winning actor and director who often plays stoic but vulnerable heroes. His films include *Bull Durham* (1988), *JFK* (1991), *Dances With Wolves* (1990), which he also directed, and *Waterworld* (1995), which he also produced and is the most expensive movie to date.

Joan Crawford (Lucille Fay Le Sueur) 3/23/08–5/10/77; San Antonio, Texas. Academy Award-winning actress whose portrayal of independent women is associated with Hollywood's most glamorous era. Her films include *Mildred Pierce* (1945), *Johnny Guitar* (1955) and *The Best of Everything* (1959).

Walter Cronkite b. 11/4/16; St. Joseph, Missouri. News broadcaster often called "the most trusted journalist" in the United States, Cronkite anchored *The CBS Evening News* (1962–81). His career with CBS began in 1950, and in 1952, he covered the first televised presidential convention.

Bing Crosby (Harry Lillis Crosby) 5/2/04–10/14/77; Tacoma, Washington. Academy Award-winning singer and actor. The crooner starred in dozens of films including *Going My Way* (1944) and released more than 1,000 recordings, including the 30-million seller "White Christmas."

Walter Cronkite

George Cukor 7/7/1899–1/24/1983; New York City. Academy Award-winning film and stage director known for his high quality, classy films, which include *The Philadelphia Story* (1940), *Gaslight* (1944) and *My Fair Lady* (1964). Cukor is credited with discovering Katharine HEPBURN, and the two worked together in several films between 1932 and 1979.

Merce Cunningham b. 4/16/19; Centralia, Washington. Dancer and choreographer whose avant-garde dances focus on pure movement and chance. He has often collaborated with American artists, including Andy Warhol, Robert Rauschenberg, Frank Stella and the composer John Cage. Cunningham danced with Martha GRAHAM (1940–55) and formed his own company in 1950. His dances include *Suite by Chance* (1952) and *Locale* (1980).

Jane Curtin b. 9/6/47; Cambridge, Massachusetts. Emmy Award-winning television comedienne and actress who was a regular on *Saturday Night Live* during its heyday (1975–80). She also starred in *Kate and Allie* (1984–89) and currently appears in *3rd Rock From the Sun* (1996–present).

Jamie Lee Curtis b. 11/22/58; Los Angeles. Film and television actress who rose from the dubious distinction of being the "Queen of Crud" to star in several successful comedies. Her films include *Trading Places* (1983), *A Fish Called Wanda* (1988) and *True Lies* (1994). She

is the daughter of actors Tony Curtis and Janet Leigh.

Ted Danson b. 12/29/49; San Diego, California. Emmy Award-winning television and film actor best known for his role as the womanizing bartender on *Cheers* (1982–93). He recently returned to television starring opposite his wife, **Mary Steenburgen (b. 02/08/53; Newport, Arkansas),** in *Ink* (1996). His films include *Three Men and a Baby* (1987), its sequel, *Three Men and a Little Lady* (1990) and *Made in America* (1993).

Bette Davis (Ruth Elizabeth Davis) 5/5/08–10/6/89; Lowell, Massachusetts. Academy Award-winning film and television actress known for her distinctive appearance and voice and her roles as troubled women. She earned a reputation for toughness as a result of battling studio boss Jack Warner. Her films include *Dangerous* (1935), *Jezebel* (1938) and *Whatever Happened to Baby Jane?* (1962).

Sammy Davis, Jr. 12/18/25–1990; New York City. Popular singer and stage and film actor who started touring with his family's troupe, the Will Mastin Trio, at age three. He was a member of Frank SINATRA's "Rat Pack." He nearly died in a 1954 car accident that resulted in the loss of his left eye. His films include *Johnny Cool* (1963) and *Robin and the Seven Hoods* (1964). His stage credits include *Mr. Wonderful* (1956).

James Dean 2/2/31–9/30/55. Film actor who achieved cult-figure status after making only three films, *Rebel Without a Cause* (1955), *East of Eden* (1955) and *Giant* (1956). A car accident ended a troubled life and promising career.

Ruby Dee (Ruby Ann Wallace) b. 10/27/24; Cleveland, Ohio. Emmy Award-winning stage, film and television actress whose Broadway and Off-Broadway performances include *A Raisin in the Sun* (1959), *Purlie Victorious* (1961) and *Boesman and Lena*

(1970). Her films include *Do the Right Thing* (1989).

Robert De Niro b. 8/17/43; New York City. Academy Award-winning actor known for his demanding, tough-guy roles in Martin SCORSESE films. His films include *The Godfather Part II* (1974), *Raging Bull* (1980) and *GoodFellas* (1990).

Danny De Vito b. 11/17/44; Neptune, New Jersey. Film and television actor, director and producer who appeared in television's *Taxi* (1978–83) before moving to film. His films include *The War of the Roses* (1989), which he also directed, *Twins* (1988) and *Hoffa* (1992), which he also directed. He is married to actress Rhea PERLMAN.

Placido Domingo b. 1/21/41; Madrid, Spain. Grammy Award-winning operatic tenor known for his warm voice and his roles in Italian operas. He has appeared in the operas *Carmen, Pagliacci* and *Madame Butterfly*. In 1994, he participated in the most successful vocal showcase ever, *The Three Tenors* with Luciano PAVAROTTI and José Carreras.

The Doors Rock group remembered for its dark, poetic lyrics, psychedelic guitars and the drug-induced antics of singer **Jim Morrison (12/08/43–7/3/71; Melbourne, Florida).** Other band members include keyboardist **Ray Manzarek (b. 2/12/35; Chicago),** guitarist **Robby Krieger (b. 1/8/46; Los Angeles)** and drummer **John Densmore (b. 12/1/44; Los Angeles).** The Doors' recordings include *The Doors* (1967), *Strange Days* (1967) and *L.A. Woman* (1971).

Michael Douglas b. 9/25/44; New Brunswick, New Jersey. Academy Award-winning actor, director and producer whose films include *Romancing the Stone* (1984), *Wall Street* (1987), *Fatal Attraction* (1987) and *Basic Instinct* (1992). He produced *One Flew Over the Cuckoo's Nest* (1975). His father is actor and producer **Kirk Douglas (Issur Danielovitch Demsky) (b. 12/9/16; Amsterdam, New York).**

David Duchovny b. 3/7/60; New York City. Actor who plays FBI agent Fox Mulder, a monotone believer in U.F.O.s and extraterrestrials, on *The X-Files* (1993–present). Duchovny also played Denise, a transvestite detective, on television's *Twin Peaks* (1990–91).

Faye Dunaway (Dorothy Faye) b. 1/14/41; Bascom, Florida. Academy Award-winning film and stage actress whose role in *Bonnie and Clyde* (1967) brought her critical acclaim and wide recognition. Her other films include *Chinatown* (1974), *Network* (1976) and *Barfly* (1987).

Federico Fellini

Bob Dylan (Robert Allen Zimmerman) b. 5/24/41; Duluth, Minnesota. Grammy Award-winning singer, songwriter and guitarist known for his angry folk-rock protest songs and his harsh delivery. Dylan is one of the seminal figures of modern music and a creator of rock and roll. His recordings include "The Times They Are a-Changin'" (1964), "Like a Rolling Stone" (1965), "Knockin' on Heaven's Door" (1973) and *Blood on the Tracks* (1975). He appeared in the films *Don't Look Back* (1967) and *Hearts of Fire* (1987).

Clint Eastwood 5/31/30; San Francisco. Academy Award-winning director and actor known for portrayal of anti-heroes, especially in Westerns. His films include *The Good the Bad and the Ugly* (1966), *Dirty Harry* (1971) and *Unforgiven* (1992). Eastwood served as mayor of Carmel, California (1986–88).

Duke Ellington (Edward Kennedy Ellington) 4/29/1899–5/24/1974; Washington D.C. Grammy Award-winning jazz pianist, composer and orchestra leader considered the most prolific composer and best-known figure in jazz history. Ellington's orchestra featured jazz's biggest names and achieved an almost perfect unity of style, making tremendous progress in the jazz idiom. His works include "Mood Indigo" (1930), "Black, Brown and Beige" (1943) and "Night Creatures" (1955).

Melissa Etheridge b. 5/29/61; Leavenworth, Kansas. Grammy Award-winning rock singer and guitarist known for her raspy voice, raw love songs and intense guitar playing. Her recordings include *Melissa Etheridge* (1988) and *Yes I Am* (1993).

Federico Fellini 1/20/20–10/31/93; Rimini, Italy. Academy Award-winning filmmaker, writer and actor internationally renowned for his artistic, humanistic film fantasies. His films include *La Strada* (1954), *La Dolce Vita* (1960) and *8 1/2* (1963). His wife, **Giuletta Masina (2/22/20–3/23/94; Giorgio di Piavo, Italy),** appeared in many of his films, including *Juliet of the Spirits* (1965), *La Strada* and *Nights of Cabiria* (1956).

W. C. Fields (William Claude Dukenfield) 1/29/1879–12/25/1946; Philadelphia. Comic stage, film and radio actor best known for his raspy voice, bulbous nose and portrayals of drunk, down-and-out scoundrels. His films include *It's a Gift* (1934), *The Man on the Flying Trapeze* (1935) and *David Copperfield* (1935).

F(rancis) Scott Fitzgerald 9/24/1896–12/21/1940; Saint Paul, Minnesota. Novelist and short-story writer credited with chronicling the Jazz Age and considered one of the greatest writers of the 20th century. His novels, which include *The Great Gatsby* (1925), *Tender Is the Night* (1934) and *The Last Tycoon* (1941), often center on morally weak characters prone to heavy drinking and talking — a mirror of Fitzgerald's own lifestyle.

Errol Flynn 6/20/09–10/14/59; Hobart, Tasmania. Film actor known for his roles as a swashbuckling romantic. His films include *Captain Blood* (1935) and *The Sea Hawk* (1940).

Henry Fonda 5/16/05–8/12/82; Grand Island, Nebraska. Academy and Tony Award-winning film and stage actor who, as a young man, portrayed honest, hardworking men, and as an adult, often played heroic characters. He appeared in nearly 90 films, which include *The Grapes of Wrath* (1940), *Young Mr. Lincoln* (1939) and *On Golden Pond* (1981). His daughter, Academy-Award winning actress Jane Fonda (b. 12/21/37; New York City), began her career playing sexy roles and later opted for films that were more in line with her liberal, often radical, agenda. Her films include *Barefoot in the Park* (1967), *Klute* (1971) and *The China Syndrome* (1979). In the 1980s, she became a fitness guru with a series of videotapes. She is married to media mogul **Ted Turner (b. 11/19/38; Cincinnati, Ohio)**. Henry's son, **Peter (b. 2/23/40; New York City)**, appeared in and produced the successful independent film *Easy Rider* (1967).

John Ford (Sean Aloysius O'Feeny) 2/1/1895–8/31/1973; Cape Elizabeth, Maine. Academy Award-winning director known for his visually striking, well-acted movies, notably Westerns, that capture restless spirits trying to find a meaningful place in the world. His films include *Stagecoach* (1939), *How Green Was My Valley* (1941) and *The Battle of Midway* (1942).

Milos Forman b. 2/18/32; Káslov, Czechoslovakia. Academy Award-winning film director known for his observant, often challenging, films, which include *One Flew Over the Cuckoo's Nest* (1974), *Hair* (1979) and *Amadeus* (1984).

Jodie Foster

Jodie Foster (Alicia Christian Foster) b. 11/19/62; Los Angeles. Academy Award-winning actress, director and producer whose career in show business began when she appeared at the age of three in a Coppertone ad. Her films as an actress include *Taxi Driver* (1976), *The Accused* (1988) and *Silence of the Lambs* (1991). She directed *Little Man Tate* (1991) and *Home for the Holidays* (1995).

Michael J. Fox b. 6/9/61; Edmonton, Canada. Emmy Award-winning television and film actor who played the conservative teenager of hippie parents on *Family Ties* (1982–89). His films include the three *Back to the Future* movies (1985, '89, '90) and *The American President* (1995). He returned to television in 1996's *Spin City*.

Aretha Franklin b. 3/25/42; Memphis, Tennessee. Grammy Award-winning soul singer known for her influence on pop music. Her music combines gospel, jazz, pop and rythm and blues. Her recordings include "Respect" (1967), "Chain of Fools" (1968) and "Freeway of Love" (1985).

Athol Fugard b. 6/11/32; Middleburg, Cape Province, South Africa. South Africa's premier playwright whose works, many which have been banned in his country, deal with contemporary South Africa and the psychological and physical barriers confronted in trying to overcome apartheid. His works include *Blood Knot* (1960), *Boesman and Lena* (1970) and *A Lesson From Aloes* (1978).

Annette Funicello b. 10/22/42; Utica, New York. Television and film actress who gained early fame as a perky Mouseketeer on television's *The Mickey Mouse Club* (1955–57). Funicello went on to star with teen idol Frankie Avalon in a series of lighthearted beach movies including *Beach Party* (1963).

Clark Gable 2/1/01–11/16/60; Cadiz, Ohio. Academy Award-winning film actor, known in Hollywood as "the king," who is remembered for his seductive looks and charming swagger. His films include *It Happened One Night* (1934), *Gone With the Wind* (1939) and *Mogambo* (1953).

Ava Gardner (Lucy Johnson) 12/24/22–1/25/90; Grabton, North Carolina. Glamorous actress known for her roles as a romantic leading lady. Her films include *The Killers* (1946), *The Snows of Kilimanjaro* (1952) and *Night of the Iguana* (1964). She was married to Mickey ROONEY, Artie Shaw and Frank SINATRA.

Judy Garland (Frances Gumm) 6/10/22–6/22/69; Grand Rapid, Minnesota. Academy and Grammy Award-winning actress and singer remembered for her role as Dorothy in *The Wizard of Oz* (1939). Her other films include *Meet Me in St. Louis* (1944) and *A Star is Born* (1954). She also had a successful singing career, with her influence seen in daughter Liza MINNELLI's performances. She was married to director Vincente Minnelli.

Bill Gates (William Henry Gates III) b. 10/28/55; Seattle. Businessman and entrepreneur who founded Microsoft in 1974 with Paul Allen. They created MS-DOS, the operating system for IBM's first personal computer, OS/2 and Windows, making Microsoft the world's largest software manufacturer. Gates is one of the world's richest men, with a current net worth estimated at $18 billion.

Marvin Gaye 4/2/39–4/1/84; Washington D.C. Grammy Award-winning singer, songwriter and instrumentalist who was one of Motown's most successful recording artists and is remembered for his sensual delivery and collaborations with Tammi Terrell. His recordings include "Ain't No Mountain High Enough" (1967), "I Heard It Through the Grapevine" (1968) and "Sexual Healing" (1982).

George Gershwin 9/26/1889–7/11/1937; Brooklyn, New York. Grammy Award- and Pulitzer Prize-winning composer known for his popular songs and orchestral compositions. His works, which often combined jazz and folk rhythms, include "Swanee" (1919), *Rhapsody in Blue* (1924) and *Porgy and Bess* (1935). His brother, **Ira (16/6/1896–8/17/1983; Brooklyn, New York),** often wrote the lyrics to George's songs.

Mel Gibson b. 1/3/56; Peekskill, New York. Academy Award-winning actor, director and producer who first appeared in Australian cult films, including *Mad Max* (1979) and *The Road Warrior* (1981), before making his mark in Hollywood. His other films include *The Year of Living Dangerously* (1983) and *Hamlet* (1990). He directed the films *The Man Without a Face* (1993) and *Braveheart* (1995), in which he also starred.

Allen Ginsberg b. 6/3/26; Newark, New Jersey. Prominent poet whose confessional, rhythmic writings made him a leading figure in the 1950s Beat generation. His works include *Howl and Other Poems* (1956) and *The Fall of America* (1974).

Betty Grable

Whoopi Goldberg (Caryn Johnson) b. 11/13/49; New York City. Academy Award-winning, outspoken African-American comedienne turned film and television actress. Her films include *The Color Purple* (1985), *Ghost* (1990) and *Sister Act* (1992).

Nadine Gordimer b. 11/20/23; South Africa. Nobel Prize-winning author whose novels and stories explore the domestic realities of life under apartheid. Her works include *The Lying Days* (1953), *A Guest of Honor* (1970), *Burger's Daughter* (1979) and *None to Accompany Me* (1994).

Betty Grable 12/18/16–7/2/73; St. Louis, Missouri. Vivacious leading lady of Fox movie musicals, who began as a chorus girl and became famous for her legs, which helped make her the top pinup girl of World War II. Her films include *The Gay Divorcee* (1934), *Tin Pan Alley* (1940) and *Pin-Up Girl* (1944).

Martha Graham 5/11/1894–4/1/1991; Allegheny, Pennsylvania. Pioneering dancer and choreographer who is credited with establishing the principals of modern dance. She danced with the Denishawn troupe (1919–23) and formed her own studio in New York City in 1927. Her angular and highly demanding dances include *Primitive Mysteries* (1931), *Appalachian Spring* (1944) and *Rite of Spring* (1984). She was married to choreographer Erick Hawkins from 1948 to 1954.

Kelsey Grammer b. 2/20/55; St. Thomas, Virgin Islands. Emmy Award-winning actor who played the highbrow, intellectual psychiatrist Dr. Frasier Crane on *Cheers* (1984–93) and now plays the same character on his own show, *Frasier* (1993–present).

Cary Grant (Archibald Alexander Leach) b. 1/18/04–11/29/86; Bristol, England. Comfortable with comedy, suspense and costume drama, Grant defined debonair and suave both on- and off-screen. His films include *His Girl Friday* (1940), *The Philadelphia Story* (1940) and *Notorious* (1946).

The Grateful Dead Groundbreaking band that was an innovator in psychedelic and country rock. The group is best known for its cult-like following, trance-inducing songs and drug use. Most recent band members include singer and guitarist **Jerry Garcia (8/1/42–8/9/95; San Francisco),** singer and guitarist **Bob Weir (b. 10/16/47; San Francisco),** bass player **Phil Lesh (b. 3/15/40; Berkeley, California)** and drummer **Bill Kreutzmann (b. 6/7/46; Palo Alto, California).** When Garcia died in 1995, the remaining members disbanded to pursue other projects. The band's recordings include *The Grateful Dead* (1967), *American Beauty* (1970) and *In the Dark* (1987).

John Grisham b. 2/8/55; Jonesboro, Arkansas. Author and attorney whose fast-paced, suspenseful courtroom dramas have sold millions and topped international bestseller lists. All of Grisham's blockbuster hits, including *The Firm* (1993), *The Pelican Brief* (1993) and *The Client* (1993), have been made into motion pictures.

John Guare b. 2/5/38; New York City. Playwright known for his comic, satirical works, which have found critical success Off Broadway. His plays include *The House of Blue Leaves* (1971) and *Six Degrees of Separation* (1990). He wrote the screenplay to the film *Atlantic City* (1981).

Bryant Gumbel b. 9/29/48; New Orleans. Television journalist who has hosted NBC's *Today Show* since 1982. Before joining *Today*, Gumbel hosted NBC's *NFL '81*.

Woody Guthrie (Woodrow Wilson Guthrie) 7/14/12–10/4/67; Okemah, Oklahoma. Folk singer, composer and songwriter known for his political songs (numbering more than 1,000) about social injustice and poverty. His recordings include "This Land Is Your Land" (1967) and the collections *The Greatest Songs of Woody Guthrie* (1988) and *Songs to Grow on for Mother and Child* (1993). His son, **Arlo Guthrie (b. 7/10/47; New York City),** is also a folk singer and composer. His recordings include "Alice's Restaurant" (1967). He played himself in the 1969 film of the same name.

Gene Hackman b. 1/30/31; San Bernardino, California. Academy Award-winning film actor known for his gritty performances in dramatic roles. His films include *The French Connection* (1971), *Mississippi Burning* (1988) and *Unforgiven* (1992).

Alex Haley 8/11/21–2/10/92; Ithaca, New York. Pulitzer Prize-winning author best known for *Roots* (1976), his ancestral saga encompassing the entire African-American experience.

Tom Hanks 7/9/56; Concord, California. Academy Award-winning comic and dramatic actor who won consecutive Oscars for *Philadelphia* (1993) and *Forrest Gump* (1994). He also starred in the offbeat comedies *Splash* (1984) and *Big* (1988) and the romance *Sleepless in Seattle* (1993).

Jean Harlow (Harlean Carpenter) 3/3/11–6/7/37; Kansas City, Missouri. Film actress and archetypal pinup, known for her roles as a wise-cracking sexpot. Her films include *Hell's Angels* (1930), *Dinner at Eight* (1933) and *Libeled Lady* (1936). She died at the age of 26 from a kidney infection.

Julie Harris b. 12/2/25; Grosse Pointe Park, Michigan. Tony Award-winning stage, film and television actress who is one of Broadway's most respected actresses. Her stage roles include *The Lark* (1956), *The Belle of Amherst* (1977) and *The Glass Menagerie* (1994).

Sir Rex Harrison 3/5/08–6/1/90; Huyton, England. Academy and Tony Award-winning film and stage actor known for his suave, nonchalant style. He appeared in the stage (1956–58) and film (1964) versions of *My Fair Lady*. His other Broadway performances include *Anne of a Thousand Days*

(1948–49), and his other films include *Cleopatra* (1962).

Howard Hawks 5/30/1896–12/26/1977; Goshen, Indiana. American film director whose work spanned nearly all movie genres — musicals, gangster movies, comedies, action adventures, war films, detective movies and westerns. His films include *The Dawn Patrol* (1930), *Scarface* (1932) and *Bringing Up Baby* (1938).

Helen Hayes 10/10/1900–3/17/93; Washington D.C. Academy and Tony-Award winning film and stage actress who began acting when she was 9 years old and became a leading figure on Broadway and the big screen. Her plays include *Victoria Regina* (1935) and *Caesar and Cleopatra* (1932). Her films include *A Farewell to Arms* (1932) and *Airport* (1970).

Rita Hayworth (Margarita Carmen Cansino) 10/17/18–5/14/87; Brooklyn, New York. Fiery movie actress who began her career as a dancer and made her major film debut in *Only Angels Have Wings* (1939). Hayworth's beauty and talent made her a top Hollywood star and popular World War II pinup. Her other films include *Gilda* (1946), *The Lady From Shanghai* (1948) and *Pal Joey* (1957).

Lillian Hellman 6/20/07–6/30/84; New Orleans. Playwright and essayist known for her intelligent, melodramatic works that passionately defend social justice. Her plays include *The Children's Hour* (1934), *The Little Foxes* (1939) and *Toys in the Attic* (1960).

Ernest Hemingway 7/21/1899–7/2/1961; Oak Park, Illinois. Nobel Prize-winning novelist and short-story writer considered spokesman of the "lost generation." His works, which include *The Sun Also Rises* (1926), *A Farewell to Arms* (1929) and *For Whom the Bell Tolls* (1940), often told of people who courageously face the perils of living adventurous lives.

Audrey Hepburn

Audrey Hepburn 5/4/29–1/20/93; Brussels, Belgium. Poised, naturally chic movie and stage actress whose sense of style and graceful demeanor made her a star in films such as *Gigi* (1951), *Roman Holiday* (1953), *Breakfast at Tiffany's* (1961), *My Fair Lady* (1964) and the thriller *Wait Until Dark* (1967). From 1988, Hepburn worked for the U.N. Children's Fund, and she received a posthumous Academy Award for her humanitarian efforts.

Katharine Hepburn b. 5/12/07; Hartford, Connecticut. Academy Award-winning film, stage and television actress whose career spans nearly 70 years. Spencer TRACY was Hepburn's leading man and romantic partner in mid-career, and they appeared in nine films together including *State of the Union* (1948) and *Adam's Rib* (1949). Hepburn's other films include *Morning Glory* (1933), *The Philadelphia Story* (1940) and *On Golden Pond* (1982).

Charlton Heston (Charlton Carter) b. 10/4/24; Evanston, Illinois. Academy Award-winning screen actor known for his roles in epic films, including *The Ten Commandments* (1956), *Ben-Hur* (1959) and *El Cid* (1961).

Sir Alfred Hitchcock 8/13/1899–4/29/1980; London, England. British director famous for his dark, voyeuristic suspense films. He is best known for *Strangers on a Train* (1951), *Rear Window* (1954), *North by Northwest* (1959) and *Psycho* (1960). Though revered by cinephiles and other directors, Hitchcock never won an Academy Award.

Dustin Hoffman b. 8/8/37; Los Angeles. Academy Award-winning film and stage actor known for his acting range and the eccentric characters he has portrayed. His films include *The Graduate* (1967), *Kramer vs. Kramer* (1979) and *Rain Man* (1988).

William Holden (William Beedle, Jr.) 4/17/18–11/16/81; O'Fallon, Illinois. Academy Award-winning film actor whose early virile appeal deepened into rich characterizations. His films include *Sunset Blvd.* (1950), *Stalag 17* (1953), *The Wild Bunch* (1969) and *Network* (1976).

Billie Holiday (Eleanora Fagan) 4/7/15–7/17/59; Baltimore, Maryland. Jazz singer known for her emotion-laden vocal performances. She performed with Benny Goodman, Duke ELLINGTON, Count BASIE and Teddy Wilson before embarking on a successful solo career in 1940. Her recordings include "Strange Fruit" (1939) and "God Bless the Child" (1941). Holiday's drug addiction destroyed her career and was responsible for her early death.

Buddy Holly (Charles Harden Holly) 9/7/36–2/2/59; Lubbock, Texas. Singer and guitarist who was one of the first rock and roll musicians. With his band, The Crickets, Holly recorded "That'll Be the Day" (1957) and "Peggy Sue" (1957). Holly was a major influence on The Beatles and Bob Dylan. He died in a plane crash.

Bob Hope (Leslie Towne Hope) b. 5/29/03; Eltham, England. American film, radio and television comedian known for his topical jokes, quick delivery and long career in show business. He appeared in several "Road" films with comedy partner Bing Crosby and Dorothy Lamour. His films include *Road to Utopia* (1940) and *The Paleface* (1947). Since 1940, Hope has tirelessly entertained U.S. troops stationed overseas.

Sir Anthony Hopkins b. 12/31/37; Port Talbot, Wales. Academy Award-winning British film and stage actor whose performance

in *The Silence of the Lambs* (1991) made him one of the most respected film actors of the 1990s. His other films include *Howards End* (1992), *Shadowlands* (1993) and *Nixon* (1995). His stage credits include London's *Macbeth* (1972), *King Lear* (1986) and Broadway's *Equus* (1974).

Dennis Hopper b. 5/17/36; Dodge City, Kansas. Film actor, director and producer known for his swaggering screen persona and colorful personal life. Hopper made his film debut in *Rebel Without a Cause* (1955), directed the hit road movie *Easy Rider* (1969) and played crazed misfits in *Apocalypse Now* (1979) and *Blue Velvet* (1986). He is also an accomplished photographer.

Whitney Houston b. 8/9/63; East Orange, New Jersey. Grammy Award-winning pop singer and actress known for her remarkable vocal range and powerful, gospel-inspired ballads. Her recordings include *Whitney Houston* (1985), *Whitney* (1987) and *I'm Your Baby Tonight* (1990). Her films include *The Bodyguard* (1992) and *Waiting to Exhale* (1995). She is (sometimes) married to R&B bad-boy Bobby Brown.

Ron Howard b. 3/1/54; Duncan, Oklahoma. Actor, producer and director who was television's "all-American boy" and is one of film's most respected directors and producers. He portrayed Opie Taylor on *The Andy Griffith Show* (1960–68) and the letter-sweater-wearing teenager Richie Cunningham on *Happy Days* (1974–80). He directed films

including *Cocoon* (1985) and *Apollo 13* (1995).

Rock Hudson (Roy Harold Scherer) 11/17/25–10/2/85; Winnetak, Illinois. Film and television actor best remembered as a romantic leading man and for his stunning good looks. His films include *A Farewell to Arms* (1957) and *Pillow Talk* (1959). He starred in the television series *McMillan and Wife* (1971–77). His death from AIDS helped increase public awareness of the disease.

Helen Hunt b. 6/15/63; Los Angeles. Emmy Award-winning television and film actress best known for her role as Jamie Buchman on *Mad About You* (1992–present). She began acting at the age of seven when she appeared on *The Mary Tyler Moore Show* as Murray Slaughter's daughter. Her other television credits include *Swiss Family Robinson* (1975–76) and *It Takes Two* (1982–83). Her films include *Project X* (1987), *Kiss of Death* (1995) and *Twister* (1996).

John Huston 8/5/06–8/28/87; Nevada, Missouri. Film director, writer and actor who directed *The Maltese Falcon* (1941) and *The African Queen* (1951) and appeared in *Chinatown* (1974). His daughter **Anjelica Huston (b. 7/8/51; Los Angeles)**, an actress and director, won an Academy Award for her role in *Prizzi's Honor* (1985). His father, **Walter Huston (4/6/1884–4/7/1950; Toronto, Canada)**, was a film and stage actor who appeared in the stage (1934) and film (1936) versions of *Dodsworth* and the film *Treasure of the Sierra Madre* (1948), which John directed.

Jeremy Irons b. 9/19/48; Isle of Wight, England. Academy and Tony Award-winning film, stage and televsion actor known for his intensity and patrician cool. His films include *The French Lieutenant's Woman* (1981) and *Reversal of Fortune* (1990). His stage appearances include *Godspell* (1971) and *The Real Thing* (1984).

Helen Hunt

Janet Jackson b. 5/16/66; Gary, Indiana. Grammy Award-winning pop-funk singer whose soft, sexy singing often takes a backseat to her athletic, energetic dancing and artistic videos. Her recordings include *Control* (1986), *Janet Jackson's Rhythm Nation 1814* (1989) and *janet* (1993). In 1996, she became the country's highest paid female recording artist. Her brother is Michael JACKSON.

Michael Jackson b. 8/29/58; Gary, Indiana. Grammy Award-winning pop singer and dancer known for his controversial behavior on- and offstage, his phenomenal commercial success and his big-budget, flashy videos. He began his career in the 1960s performing with his siblings in the Jackson Five. In 1978, Jackson re-emerged with his solo album *Off the Wall* and a new persona and appearance. His other recordings include *Thriller* (1982), *Dangerous* (1992) and *HIStory: Past, Present and Future* (1995). He was married to Lisa Marie Presley (1995–96). His sister is Janet JACKSON.

Waylon Jennings b. 6/15/37; Littlefield, Texas. Grammy Award-winning country music singer who, with Willie NELSON, invented progressive or "outlaw" country music. His recordings include "MacArthur Park" (1969), *Ol' Waylon* (1977) and "Mamas Don't Let Your Babies Grow Up to Be Cowboys" (1978). In 1985, he formed the Highwaymen with Nelson, Johnny CASH and Kris Kristofferson.

Steve Jobs b. 1955; San Francisco. Businessman and entrepreneur, who designed, built and introduced the Apple computer, a user-friendly alternative to IBM's personal computer with Steve Wozniak in 1976. Jobs and Wozniak saw Apple grow into a billion dollar company. Jobs lost a 1985 power struggle, left Apple and formed NeXT Computer.

Al Jolson (Asa Yoelson) 5/26/1888–10/23/1950; Lithuania. Entertainer who performed in theater, films, circuses, minstrel shows and vaudeville. He was known for his sentimental performances, and appeared in the first talkie, *The Jazz Singer* (1927).

James Earl Jones b. 1/17/31; Arkabutla, Mississippi. Tony and Grammy Award-winning film and stage actor known for his authoritative voice. His stage appearances include *The Great White Hope* (1968) and *Fences* (1985), and his movie roles include *The Star Wars* films, in which he was the voice of Darth Vader, and *Field of Dreams* (1989).

Quincy Jones b. 3/14/33; Chicago. Grammy Award-winning pop-soul composer, arranger, instrumentalist and producer known for his behind-the-scenes influence in the music industry. He started his music career as a trumpeter with Lionel Hampton and Dizzy Gillespie and briefly formed his own band, Free and Easy Musicians. He abandoned performing for the boardroom when he joined Mercury Records. He has scored more than 50 films, including *The Wiz* (1978) and *The Color Purple* (1985). He also produced Michael JACKSON's *Off the Wall* (1978) and co-produced Jackson's *Thriller* (1982). He leads his own recording label, Quest, and is involved in movie, television and multimedia production. Jones was the co-producer of the 1995 Academy Awards broadcast.

Janis Joplin 1/19/43–10/4/70; Port Arthur, Texas. Rock singer who is remembered for her passionate, wailing voice. She sang with the blues-rock group Big Brother and the Holding Company and her solo recordings include "Piece of My Heart" (1968) and "Me and Bobby McGee" (1971). She died of a heroin overdose.

Elia Kazan b. 9/7/09; Istanbul, Turkey. Academy and Tony Award-winning film and stage director, producer, writer and actor who earned renown direct-

k.d. lang

ing plays by Arthur MILLER and Tennessee WILLIAMS. His credits include the stage (1947) and film (1951) versions of *A Streetcar Named Desire* and the film *On the Waterfront* (1954). In 1952, he testified before the House Committee on Un-American activities admitting membership in the Communist Party, naming other Hollywood members.

Buster Keaton 10/4/1895–2/1/1966; Piqua, Kansas. American film actor and director widely considered the greatest comic actor in film history. Keaton used his acrobatic skills in his many roles as a deadpan hero who overcame potentially disastrous situations. His films include *The General* (1926), *The Navigator* (1924) and *Sherlock Jr.* (1924).

Diane Keaton (Diane Hall) b. 1/5/46; Santa Ana, California. Academy Award-winning actress and director known for her comic roles in Woody ALLEN films in which she often played neurotic, urban characters. Her films include *Annie Hall* (1977), *Manhattan* (1979) and *Baby Boom* (1987).

Grace Kelly 11/12/29–9/14/82; Philadelphia. Academy Award-winning film actress whose cool beauty launched her career in such films as *The Country Girl* (1954), *Dial M for Murder* (1954) and *Rear Window* (1954). In 1956 she married Prince Rainier III of Monaco and ended her acting career.

Jack Kerouac (Jean Louis Kerouac) 3/12/22–10/21/69; Lowell, Massachusetts. Novelist and leader of the Beat generation. His books include *On the Road* (1957), considered the lasting testament of the Beat movement, and *The Subterraneans* (1958).

Carole King b. 2/9/42; Brooklyn, New York. Grammy Award-winning pop songwriter and singer best known for her 1971 recording *Tapestry*. With her former husband, Gerry Goffin, she wrote more than 100 songs, including "Will You Still Love Me Tomorrow?" (1960).

Larry King (Larry Zeiger) b. 11/19/33; Brooklyn, New York. Prime-time talk-show host whose show, *Larry King Live* (1985–present), often attracts the biggest names in poltics and show business.

Ben Kingsley (Krishna Banji) b. 12/31/43; Yorkshire, England. Academy Award-winning polished stage and movie actor whose films include *Gandhi* (1982), *Betrayal* (1983) and *Turtle Diary* (1985).

Kevin Kline b. 10/24/47; St. Louis, Missouri. Academy and Tony Award-winning film and stage actor known for his comedic and musical roles. His films include *The Big Chill* (1983), *A Fish Called Wanda* (1988) and *Dave* (1993). His Broadway performances include *Pirates of Penzance* (1980) and *On the Twentieth Century* (1978).

Spike Lee

Alison Krauss b. 7/23/71; Champaign, Illinois. Grammy Award-winning bluegrass singer and fiddler whose music combines both traditional and contemporary styles, making her the premier musician of the genre. With her backup band, Union Station, she released *Two Highways* (1989) and *Every Time You Say Goodbye* (1992). Her solo recordings include *I've Got That Old Feeling* (1990) and *Now That I've Found You: A Collection* (1995).

Akira Kurosawa b. 3/23/10; Toyko, Japan. Academy Award-winning Japanese film director, writer and producer responsible for bringing Japanese film to the West. His films include *Rashomon* (1950), *The Seven Samurai* (1954), which saw several Western imitations, and the Shakespeare adaptations *Ran (King Lear)* (1986) and *Throne of Blood (Macbeth)* (1957).

Tony Kushner b. 1956; Lake Charles, Louisiana. Tony Award- and Pulitzer Prize-winning playwright known for his plays that politicize the AIDS crisis. His works include the two-part critical and commercial success *Angels in America: Millennium Approaches* (1993) and *Perestroika* (1993).

Ricki Lake b. 9/21/68; New York City. Talk-show host and actress who appeared in John Waters's cult films *Hairspray* (1988) and *Cry-Baby* (1990) before gaining fame as the formerly rotund princess of daytime talk.

Burt Lancaster 11/2/13–10/20/94; New York City. Academy Award-winning actor and director who parlayed an imposing presence into an impressive range of Hollywood roles. His credits include *Elmer Gantry* (1960) and *Bird Man of Alcatraz* (1962).

k.d. lang (Kathryn Dawn Lang) b. 11/2/61; Alberta, Canada. Grammy Award-winning country-rock singer and songwriter known for her velvety, emotive voice and her socially conscious views. Her recordings include *A Truly Western Experience* (1984) and *Ingénue* (1992).

Angela Lansbury b. 10/16/26; London, England. Tony Award-winning stage, film and television actress best known for her role as crime solver Jessica Fletcher on television's *Murder, She Wrote* (1984–96). She has also had great success in plays and films. Her plays include *Mame* (1966) and *Gypsy* (1975). Her films include *The Manchurian Candidate* (1962) and *The Pirates of Penzance* (1983).

John Larroquette b. 11/25/47; New Orleans. Emmy Award-winning actor who portrayed womanizing Asst. D.A. Dan Fielding on *Night Court* (1984–92). He now plays John Hemingway, a reformed alcholic who manages a bus station and dabbles in writing on the *John Larroquette Show* (1993–present). His other television credits include *Baa Baa Black Sheep* (1976–78).

Sir David Lean 3/25/08–4/16/91; Croydon, England. Academy Award-winning director, editor, producer and writer known for his craftmanship behind the camera. His films include *The Bridge on the River Kwai* (1957), *Lawrence of Arabia* (1962) and *Passage to India* (1984).

Bruce Lee (Lee Yuen Kam) 11/27/40–7/19/73; San Francisco. American star of Hong Kong martial-arts films who was a martial-arts instructor to celebrities before beginning his own acting career. His films include *Return of the Dragon* (1973) and *Enter the Dragon* (1973). His mysterious premature death was mirrored years later by the accidental death of his son, Brandon Lee.

Spike Lee (Shelton Jackson Lee) b. 3/20/57; Atlanta, Georgia. Film writer, director, producer and actor known for his controversial films that tackle race relations and African-American issues. His films include *Do the Right Thing* (1989), *Jungle Fever* (1991) and *Malcolm X* (1992).

Jack Lemmon b. 2/8/25; Boston. Academy Award-winning film and stage actor best known as a comic actor but also successful in dramatic roles. His films include *Mister Roberts* (1955), *The Odd Couple* (1968) and *Glengarry Glen Ross* (1992).

John Lennon 10/9/40–12/8/80; Liverpool; England. British singer, guitarist and harmonica player for THE BEATLES. After The Beatles broke up in 1970, Lennon launched a successful solo career, releasing *Imagine* (1971). In 1980, he and his wife, **Yoko Ono** (b. 2/18/33; Tokyo, Japan), released *Double Fantasy*. Lennon was murdered outside his New York apartment building by Mark Chapman.

Jay Leno b. 4/28/50; New Rochelle, New York. Emmy Award-winning television comedian who has hosted the *The Tonight Show* since Johnny CARSON retired in 1992. Leno started his career as a standup comic and got his break in the early 1980s when he appeared several times on *Late Night With David Letterman*.

David Letterman b. 4/12/47; Indianapolis, Indiana. Emmy Award-winning nighttime talk-show host known for his dry, sardonic humor. He hosted NBC's *Late Night With David Letterman* (1982–93) and moved to CBS in 1993. His show was renamed *The Late Show*.

Jerry Lee Lewis b. 9/2/35; Ferriday, Louisiana. Rock musician, often presented as the dark, wild side of Elvis PRESLEY, known for his flamboyant, slamming piano playing and controversial personal life. His recordings include "Great Balls of Fire" (1957), "Whole Lotta Shakin' Going On" (1957) and "Breathless" (1958). The 1989 film *Great Balls of Fire!*, starring Dennis Quaid, chronicled Lewis's life.

Jerry Lewis (Joseph Levitch) b. 3/16/26; Newark, New Jersey. Comedian, actor, writer and director whose rubber-faced, often juvenile, characters earned him a place in entertainment history as one of the great physical comics of all time. In the late 1940s, Lewis teamed with **Dean Martin** (see obituary page 802) and they became one of the

country's best-known musical comedy duos. They appeared together on television, the night-club stage and in 17 films together before going separate ways in 1956. Lewis's credits include the films *Geisha Boy* (1958), *Bellboy* (1960), *The Nutty Professor* (1963) and *The King of Comedy* (1983). More recently, he has become as renowned for hosting the muscular dystrophy telethons.

Liberace (Wladziu Valentine Liberace) 5/16/19–2/4/87; West Allis, Wisconsin. Flamboyant pianist known for his talent, showmanship and outrageous costumes. His repertoire included boogie woogie, cocktail jazz and movie music. In the 1960s and 1970s, he was the highest paid entertainer in the United States, earning an estimated $5 million a year.

John Lithgow b. 10/19/45; Rochester, New York. Tony Award-winning stage, television and film actor known for his dry humor. His films include *The World According to Garp* (1982). He returned to television in 1996, starring in the hit *3rd Rock From the Sun*.

Christopher Lloyd b. 10/22/38; Stamford, Connecticut. Emmy Award-winning television and film actor known for his roles as eccentric, spaced-out characters. He played former flower child "Reverend Jim" Ignatowski on *Taxi* (1979–83) and the befuddled scientist in the three *Back to the Future* films (1985, 1989 and 1990).

Sir Andrew Lloyd Webber b. 3/22/48; London, England. Tony Award-winning composer known for his larger-than-life works of the 1970s and 1980s that made London the city of new musicals. His works include *Jesus Christ Superstar* (1970), *Evita* (1978), *Phantom of the Opera* (1986) and *Sunset Boulevard* (1993). He often collaborates with lyricist Tim Rice.

Courtney Love b. 7/9/64; San Francisco. Pop-punk singer and songwriter known for her strong,

David Mamet

emotional vocals, volatile behavior on- and offstage and for being the widow of Kurt Cobain of the band NIRVANA. She is the singer in the band Hole, whose recordings include *Pretty on the Inside* (1991) and the critically acclaimed *Live Through This* (1994).

Bela Lugosi (Bela Blasko) 10/20/1882–8/16/1956; Lugos, Hungary. Film and stage actor best known for his role in *Dracula* (1931). His convincing performance as the count and his trouble with English left him typecast as a horror actor, and his talents were never fully explored. His other films include *White Zombie* (1932) and *Son of Frankenstein* (1939).

Sidney Lumet b. 6/25/24; Philadelphia. Academy Award-winning film and television director known for his rough, often low-budget films. His credits include *Long Day's Journey Into Night* (1962), *Dog Day Afternoon* (1975) and *Network* (1976). He authored *Making Movies,* an incisive account of the movie-production process.

Loretta Lynn b. 4/14/42; Butchers Hollow, Kentucky. Country and western singer known for her plaintive singing style and her rags-to-riches life story portrayed in the 1980 film *Coal Miner's Daughter*. Her recordings include "Honky Tonk Girl" (1960) and *Honky Tonk Heroes* (1978). She made several records with Conway Twitty.

Madonna (Madonna Louise Veronica Ciccone) b. 8/16/58; Bay City, Michigan. Singer, songwriter and actress whose eroticism, determination and provocative concert performances have brought her huge commercial success and made her a pop icon. Her albums include *Madonna* (1983), *Like a Virgin* (1984) and *Bedtime Stories* (1995). Her films include *Desperately Seeking Susan* (1986) and *Evita* (1996).

David Mamet b. 11/30/47; Chicago. Pulitzer Prize-winning playwright, screenwriter and film director known for his biting, elliptical dialogue and works about the shattering of the American dream. His plays include *American Buffalo* (1975), *Glengarry Glen Ross* (1984) (he also wrote the screenplay for the 1992 film) and *Speed-the-Plow* (1988). He directed the films *House of Games* (1987), *Things Change* (1988) and *Oleanna* (1994).

Joseph L. Mankiewicz 2/11/09–2/5/93; Wilkes-Barre, Pennsylvania. Academy Award-winning film director, screenwriter and producer who directed *Dragonwyck* (1946), *The Ghost and Mrs. Muir* (1947) and *All About Eve* (1950) and wrote and directed *The Barefoot Contessa* (1954), *The Quiet American* (1958) and *Suddenly, Last Summer* (1959).

Jayne Mansfield 4/19/33–6/29/67; Bryn Mawr, Pennsylvania. Film and stage actress known for her roles as a dizzy sexpot. Her films include *The Girl Can't Help It* (1956), *Will Success Spoil Rock Hunter?* (1957) and *The Wayward Bus* (1957).

Fredric March (Frederick McIntyre Bickel) 8/31/1897–4/14/1975; Racine, Wisconsin. Academy and Tony Award-winning actor who played a range of characters but shone in emotional roles. His films include *Dr. Jekyll and Mr. Hyde* (1932) and *The Best Years of Our Lives* (1946). His Broadway plays include *Long Day's Journey Into Night* (1956).

Bob Marley 2/6/45–5/11/81; St. Ann, Jamaica. Grammy Award-winning reggae singer, songwriter and guitarist whose music sparked an international interest in reggae music. In 1964, he formed The Wailers with Peter Tosh and Bunny Livingston. Their recordings include "Stir It Up" (1972), "No Women No Cry" (1975) and *Uprising* (1981).

Wynton Marsalis b. 10/18/61; New Orleans. Grammy Award-winning jazz trumpeter known for his brilliant technique and championing traditional jazz forms. His recordings include *Soul Gestures in Southern Blue* (1991) and *Hot House Flowers* (1984).

Steve Martin b. 8/14/45; Waco, Texas. Emmy and Grammy Award-winning actor, comedian and playwright known for his broad physical comedy and nice-guy screen appeal. The self-titled "wild and crazy guy's" films include *The Jerk* (1979), *Roxanne* (1987) and *Father of the Bride* (1992). His plays include *Picasso at the Lapin Agile* (1993).

Marx Brothers New York City–born team of film, vaudeville and Broadway comedians known for surreal humor and groundbreaking movie comedy. **Chico (Leonard; 3/22/1887–10/11/1961)** specialized in distorted logic and Italian-dialect routines; **Harpo (Adolph; 11/23/1888–9/28/1964)** played the harp and chased girls; and bushy-browed **Groucho (Julius; 10/2/1890–8/19/1977)** lead the group with his wild wisecracks and puns. Two other brothers **Gummo (Milton; 1893–4/21/1977)** and **Zeppo (Herbert; 2/25/01–11/30/1979)** performed only occasionally with the group. Groucho had a second career on television as the host of *You Bet Your Life* (1950–1961).

Ethel Merman

(James) Paul McCartney b. 6/18/42; Liverpool, England. Grammy Award-winning British singer, composer and pianist for THE BEATLES. His songwriting credits for The Beatles include "Yesterday," "Eleanor Rigby" and "Hey Jude." After The Beatles broke up in 1970, McCartney launched a successful solo career and formed the band Wings (1971–81) with his wife, **Linda (Eastman) McCartney (b. 9/24/42; Scarsdale, New York)**.

Shirley MacLaine b. 4/24/34; Richmond, Virginia. Academy Award-winning actress whose screen talents range from dancing the can-can to playing the part of an aging eccentric. Her films include *The Apartment* (1960), *Terms of Endearment* (1983) and *Guarding Tess* (1994). Her brother is actor, director and producer Warren BEATTY.

Reba McEntire b. 3/25/55; McAlester, Oklahoma. Grammy Award-winning country and western singer who is considered the most popular and successful female performer in the industry. Her recordings include "I Don't Want to Be a One-Night Stand" (1976), "Can't Even Get the Blues" (1982) and *What Am I Gonna Do About You* (1986). McEntire is also a shrewd businesswoman; she and her husband, Narvel Blackstock, run Starstruck Enterprises, a management company that oversees her career and runs a thoroughbred farm.

Steve McQueen 3/24/30–1980; Slater, Missouri. Television and film actor known for his roles as a cool loner. He appeared in the television series *Wanted — Dead or Alive* (1958–61). His film credits include *The Magnificent Seven* (1960), *Bullitt* (1968) and *Papillon* (1973). He was married to actress Ali McGraw.

Ethel Merman (Ethel Zimmerman) 1/16/09–2/15/84; Astoria, New York. Tony Award-winning musical comedy entertainer known for her booming voice and extroverted style. Her Broadway performances include *Girl Crazy* (1930),

Annie Get Your Gun (1946) and *Call Me Madam* (1950).

Bette Midler b. 12/1/45; Honolulu, Hawaii. Grammy and Emmy Award-winning singer and stage and film actress known for her vibrant personality on- and off-stage. Her recordings include *The Divine Miss M* (1972) and *Broken Blossom* (1977). Her films include *The Rose* (1979), *Ruthless People* (1986) and *Beaches* (1988). She also appeared in Broadway's *Fiddler on the Roof* (1966–69).

Arthur Miller b. 10/17/15; New York City. Pulitzer Prize- and Tony Award-winning playwright whose works deal with familial turmoil and moral and political issues. His plays include *Death of a Salesman* (1949), *The Crucible* (1953) and *A View From the Bridge* (1955). He was married to actress and icon Marilyn MONROE.

Liza Minnelli b. 3/12/46; Hollywood, California. Academy and Tony Award-winning actress known for her powerful voice and stage presence and for being the daughter of director Vincente Minnelli and Judy GARLAND. Her films include *Cabaret* (1972) and *Arthur* (1981). Her plays include *The Act* (1977) and *The Rink* (1984).

Joni Mitchell (Roberta Joan Anderson) b. 11/7/43; Alberta, Canada. Grammy Award-winning folk singer and guitarist known for her cutting, powerful lyrics and her vocal range. Her recordings include *Clouds* (1969), *Blue* (1971) and *Dog Eat Dog* (1985).

Robert Mitchum b. 8/6/17; Bridgeport, Connecticut. Film and television actor best known for his authoritative, tough-guy roles. His films include *The Night of the Hunter* (1955), *The Last Tycoon* (1976) and *The Big Sleep* (1978).

Thelonious Monk 10/10/18–2/17/82; Rocky Mount, North Carolina. Jazz pianist, composer and arranger known for his influence on avant-garde jazz and for making the first bebop records with fellow musi-cians Charlie PARKER and Dizzy GILLESPIE. He composed "Round Midnight," "Straight No Chaser" and "Epistrophy."

Marilyn Monroe (Norma Jeane Mortenson or Baker) 6/1/26–8/5/62; Los Angeles. Actress who was, and remains, one of the most famous celebrities of the 20th century. Her mixture of vulnerability and sex appeal has haunted Hollywood since her early death. She was married to baseball legend Joe DiMaggio and playwright Arthur MILLER. Her films include *Gentlemen Prefer Blondes* (1953) and *Some Like It Hot* (1959). She died of an overdose of sleeping pills, which many believe was suicide.

Demi Moore (Demetria Guynes) b. 11/11/62; Roswell, New Mexico. Film and television actress who played Jackie Templeton on *General Hospital* (1981–83) before she became a film star. Her films include *St. Elmo's Fire* (1985), *Ghost* (1990) and *Striptease* (1996). She is married to actor Bruce WILLIS.

Dudley Moore b. 4/19/35; London, England. Composer, cabaret comedian and film and stage actor who was at his best when performing with **Peter Cook (11/17/37–1/9/95; Torquay, England)** in the comedy revue Beyond the Fringe. His films include *10* (1979), *Arthur* (1981) and *Micki and Maude* (1984).

Mary Tyler Moore b. 12/29/37; Brooklyn, New York. Emmy Award-winning television, film and stage actress best known for her television roles as witty, intelligent women. Her television credits include *The Dick Van Dyke Show* (1961–66) and *The Mary Tyler Moore Show* (1970–77). Her films include *Ordinary People* (1980) and *Flirting With Disaster* (1996).

Roger Moore b. 10/14/27; London, England. Urbane British television and film actor who starred in the television series *The Saint* before becoming Sean Connery's successor as James Bond beginning with *Live and Let Die* (1973).

Alanis Morissette b. 6/1/74; Ottawa, Canada. Grammy Award-winning pop singer who burst onto the American music scene in 1995 with her 11-million-selling *Jagged Little Pill* after a career as Canada's top teen-pop star.

Mark Morris b. 8/29/56; Seattle, Washington. Modern dancer and choreographer known for his unique, stylish dances, which appeal to dance aficionados and mainstream audiences alike. Morris's dances include *Dido and Aeneas* (1989) and *The Office* (1995). He formed the Mark Morris Dance Group in 1980, which was the resident dance company of Brussels's Theatre Royal de la Monnaie (1988–91).

Toni Morrison (Chloe Anthony Wofford) b. 2/18/31; Lorain, Ohio. Pulitzer and Nobel Prize-winning novelist whose emotional, intense books portray African-American life. Her novels include *Song of Solomon* (1977), *Beloved* (1987) and *Jazz* (1992).

Van Morrison (George Ivan Morrison) b. 8/31/45; Belfast, Northern Ireland. Singer and songwriter known for his singular style that combines jazz, folk, rhythm and blues and rock. Morrison was a member of the Irish group Them (1963–66) before he became a solo star. His solo recordings include *Astral Weeks* (1968), *Moondance* (1970) and *St. Dominic's Preview* (1972).

Edward R. Murrow 4/24/08–4/23/65; Pole Creek, North Carolina. Emmy Award-winning radio and news broadcaster remembered for his work as CBS's war correspondent and his attack on Sen. Joseph McCarthy's investigation into American Communists, which ultimately led to the senator's demise.

Willie Nelson b. 3/30/33; Abbott, Texas. Grammy Award-winning country-music singer and songwriter known for his spare style and for inventing with Waylon JENNINGS progressive or "outlaw" country music. His recordings include *Yesterday's Wine* (1969), "Always on My Mind"

(1982) and *Across the Borderline* (1993). Nelson organizes Farm Aid concerts to raise money for American farmers.

Paul Newman b. 1/26/25; Shaker Heights, Ohio. Academy Award-winning actor and director known for his piercing blue eyes and the immediacy of his acting. His films include *Cool Hand Luke* (1967), *The Sting* (1973) and *The Color of Money* (1986). He is married to Academy Award-winning actress Joanne WOODWARD.

Mike Nichols (Michael Igor Peschkowsky) b. 11/6/31; Berlin, Germany. Academy and Tony Award-winning film and stage director and actor known for his ability to elicit virtuoso performances from the actors he directs. He started his career doing a standup routine with Elaine May before moving to directing plays and films. His stage credits include *The Odd Couple* (1965) and *Plaza Suite* (1968). His films include *The Graduate* (1967), *Carnal Knowledge* (1971) and *The Birdcage* (1996). He is married to broadcast reporter Diane Sawyer.

Jack Nicholson b. 4/22/37; Neptune, New Jersey. Academy Award-winning actor, director and producer known for portraying cynical, dissolute characters. His films include *Easy Rider* (1969), *One Flew Over the Cuckoo's Nest* (1975) and *The Witches of Eastwick* (1987).

Nirvana Seattle-based grunge band that brought 1970s punk sound and sensibility into the mainstream during the early 1990s. The band's lyrics spoke to a generation of frustrated, disillusioned twentysomethings. Most recent band members included singer and guitarist **Kurt Cobain (2/20/67–5/5/94; Hoquiam, Washington),** bassist **Krist Novoselic (b. 5/10/65; Compton, California)** and drummer **Dave Grohl (b. 1/14/69; Warren, Ohio).** Nirvana's recordings include *Bleach* (1989), *Nevermind* (1991) and *In Utero* (1993). Cobain's 1994 suicide caused much mourning and reflection on the influence of pop stars on youth.

Carroll O'Connor b. 8/2/22; New York City. Emmy Award-winning television and stage actor best known for his portrayal of the bigot Archie Bunker on *All in the Family* (1971–79), one of television's most successful shows. He also appeared in *Archie Bunker's Place* (1979–83) and *In the Heat of the Night* (1988–92).

Sir Laurence Olivier 5/22/07–7/11/89; Dorking, England. Academy and Emmy Award-winning film and stage actor best known for his roles in Shakespearean works. His films include *Henry V* (1945) and *Hamlet* (1948). He headed London's National Theatre Company (1962–73). England's premier theater awards are named in his honor.

Eugene O'Neill 10/16/1888–11/27/1953; New York City. Nobel and Pulitzer Prize-winning playwright whose plays portray tormented families and people torn between wealth and noble ideals. His plays include *Beyond the Horizon* (1920), *Anna Christie* (1921), *Strange Interlude* (1928) and the semiautobiographical *Long Day's Journey Into Night* (1956).

Al Pacino b. 4/25/40; New York City. Academy and Tony Award-winning film and stage actor known for his intensity portraying sensitive men caught in brutal circumstances. His films include *The Godfather* (1972; Part II, 1974), *Dog Day Afternoon* (1975) and *Scent of a Woman* (1992). He won a Tony Award for *Does a Tiger Wear a Necktie?* (1969).

Jack Nicholson

Charlie "Bird" Parker 8/29/20–3/12/55; Kansas City, Kansas. Grammy Award-winning jazz alto saxophonist credited with releasing the first bebop records with fellow musicians Dizzy GILLESPIE and Thelonious MONK. Parker is remembered for his brilliant improvisations and his influence on other jazz musicians.

Luciano Pavarotti b. 10/12/35; Modena, Italy. Perhaps the definitive tenor of his generation and certainly the most popular. He has performed works by Bellini, Donizetti, Puccini and Verdi. In 1994 he released *The Three Tenors* with Placido DOMINGO and José Carreras.

Gregory Peck b. 4/5/16; La Jolla, California. Academy Award-winning film actor known for his strong, dignified roles. His films include *Gentleman's Agreement* (1947), *To Kill a Mockingbird* (1962) and *The Boys From Brazil* (1978).

Sam Peckinpah 2/21/25–12/28/84; Fresno, California. Director known for his violent films that depicted men pushed to their limits. His movies include *The Wild Bunch* (1969) and *Straw Dogs* (1971).

Itzhak Perlman b. 8/31/45; Tel Aviv, Israel. Concert violinist who fought childhood polio and went on to be one of the most respected musicians of the 20th century. He is known for his brilliant technique and success with 19th- and 20th-century works.

Rhea Perlman b. 3/31/48; Brooklyn, New York. Emmy Award-winning television and film actress best known for her role as the pugnacious waitress Carla Tortelli on *Cheers* (1982–93). Her films include *Canadian Bacon* (1995) and *Sunset Park* (1996). She returned to television in 1996's *Pearl*. She is married to actor, director and producer Danny DE VITO.

Mary Pickford (Gladys Mary Smith) 4/8/1893–5/29/1979; Toronto, Canada. Academy Award-winning actress and businesswoman who enjoyed enormous success in silent films but faded when talkies arrived. With her second husband, Douglas Fairbanks, and Charlie Chaplin, she established United Artists in 1919. Her films include *Rebecca of Sunnybrook Farm* (1917) and *Coquette* (1929).

Edgar Allan Poe 1/19/1809–10/7/1849; Boston. Poet, short-story writer and critic considered the father of the modern detective story and one of the most brilliant writers in American literature. His works, written with a passionate intensity, were marked by dreamlike, macabre prose and include "The Fall of the House of Usher" (1839), "The Murders in the Rue Morgue" (1841) and *The Raven and Other Poems* (1845).

Sidney Poitier b. 2/24/24; Miami, Florida. Academy Award-winning actor who was the first African-American Hollywood actor to play a leading man. His films, many of which address race, include *The Defiant Ones* (1958), *Lilies of the Field* (1963) and *Guess Who's Coming to Dinner* (1967).

Katherine Anne Porter 5/15/1890–9/18/1980; Indian Creek, Texas. Pulitzer Prize-winning short-story writer and novelist whose elegant prose earned her wide renown. Porter's work includes the collections *Pale Horse, Pale Rider* (1939), *The Leaning Tower* (1944) and *The Collected Short Stories of Katherine Ann Porter* (1965), as well as the best-selling novel *Ship of Fools* (1962).

Elvis Presley 1/8/35–8/16/77; Tupelo, Mississippi. Singer and actor whose first recordings fused black rural blues with gospel and country, igniting the rock explosion and making Presley an enduring pop icon. His hits include "Heartbreak Hotel"(1956), "Hound Dog" (1956) and "Jailhouse Rock" (1957). His films include *Love Me Tender* (1956) and *Viva Las Vegas* (1964). His home, Graceland, remains a much-visited tourist attraction.

Gilda Radner

Vincent Price 5/27/11–10/25/93; St. Louis, Missouri. Film and stage actor who had a respectable screen career, including his most famous role in *Laura* (1944) before becoming king of horror. Price began acting on the London stage, where he appeared in *Victoria Regina* and *Heartbreak House*. His films include *House of Wax* (1953), *The Ten Commandments* (1956) and *The House of Usher* (1960).

Harold Prince b. 1/30/28; New York City. Tony Award-winning theatrical producer and director known for his successful Broadway musicals. His productions include *Pajama Game* (1954), *West Side Story* (1957) and *Phantom of the Opera* (1988).

Richard Pryor b. 12/1/40; Peoria, Illinois. Grammy Award-winning film actor and comedian known for his rude, crude and hilarious characterizations of the dark side of the African-American experience. Pryor's success also brought problems, and he currently suffers from multiple sclerosis. His films include *Lady Sings the Blues* (1972), *Blazing Saddles* (1973) and *Stir Crazy* (1980).

Joseph Pulitzer 4/10/1847–10/29/1911; Mako, Hungary. Newspaperman who emigrated to the United States in 1864 and began a successful career as editor and publisher of the St. Louis *Post-Dispatch*. He bought the New York *Post* in 1883. He bequeathed funds to establish Columbia University's School of Journalism and endow the Pulitzer Prizes, which honor

excellence in journalism, letters and music.

Gilda Radner 6/28/46–5/20/89; Detroit. Emmy Award-winning television, film and stage comedienne who is best remembered for her appearances on *Saturday Night Live* (1975–80). Her regular characters on the show included Ba Ba Wawa, Roseanne Rosanna-Dana and Emily Litella. She died of ovarian cancer after authoring a book on her battle with the disease. She was married to actor and comedian **Gene Wilder (b. 6/11/35; Milwaukee, Wisconsin).**

Bonnie Raitt b. 11/8/49; Burbank, California. Grammy Award-winning blues-rock singer and guitarist known for her powerful voice and late-career comeback. Her recordings include *Bonnie Raitt* (1971), *Glow* (1979), *Nick of Time* (1989) and *Luck of the Draw* (1991).

Ronald Reagan b. 2/6/11; Tampico, Illinois. The 40th President of the United States, sportscaster and actor who appeared in 53 films before turning to politics. After graduating Eureka College in 1932, Reagan became a radio sportscaster, landing a job with NBC. In 1937, he signed with Warners, acted in B films for about 10 years and eventually became a solid supporting actor in features. His films include *Knute Rockne, All American* (1940), *King's Row* (1942) and *Bedtime for Bonzo* (1951). Reagan also served as governor of California (1966–74), hosted television's *G.E. Theater* (1954–61) and served as president of the Screen Actors' Guild (1947–52). He was married to actress Jane Wyman and is currently married to former actress Nancy (Davis) Reagan.

Robert Redford b. 8/18/37; Santa Monica, California. Academy Award-winning film actor, producer and director considered one of Hollywood's most popular and sought-after leading men. His films include *Butch Cassidy and the Sundance Kid* (1969), *All the President's Men* (1976) and

The Natural (1984). Redford runs the Sundance Institute, an organization that promotes and supports independent filmmakers and sponsors the annual Sundance Film Festival.

Vanessa Redgrave b. 1/30/37; London, England. Academy and Emmy Award-winning film, stage and television actress known for her onscreen dignity and radical politics. Her films include *Julia* (1977) and *Howard's End* (1992). She was married to director Tony RICHARDSON, and they had two daughters, actresses **Natasha Richardson (b. 5/11/63; London, England)** and **Joely Richardson (b. 1/9/65; London, England).** Redgrave's father, **Sir Michael Redgrave (3/20/08–3/21/85; Bristol, England),** was knighted for his contribution to the British stage. His stage performances include *Uncle Vanya, As You Like It* and *Hamlet.* His films include *Dead of Night* (1945) and *The Browning Version* (1951). Vanessa's sister, **Lynn Redgrave (b. 3/8/43; London, England),** has appeared in several films, including *Georgy Girl* (1966), television shows and plays.

Christopher Reeve b. 9/25/52; New York City. Classically handsome film, stage and television actor who became a movie icon as the title character of *Superman* (1978). Reeve avoided standard male hunk roles and instead acted in several Merchant-Ivory features, including *The Bostonians* (1984) and *The Remains of the Day* (1993). He is also an acclaimed stage actor who has appeared in Broadway plays and at the prestigious Williamstown Theatre Festival. In 1995, a fall from a horse left Reeve paralyzed and wheelchair-bound, but still showing great courage, aplomb and ambition.

Carl Reiner b. 3/20/22; Bronx, New York. Emmy Award-winning actor, writer and director considered one of television's most creative minds. His credits include *Caesar's Hour* (1954–57) and *The Dick Van Dyke Show* (1961–66), which he wrote, produced and played the role of

Alan Brady in. He directed the films *Oh God!* (1977) and *The Jerk* (1979).

Rob Reiner b. 3/6/47; New York City. Emmy Award-winning television and film actor, writer, director and producer who portrayed Mike Stivic, Archie Bunker's politically correct meathead son-in-law, on *All in the Family* (1971–78). Reiner has found even more success in the movies, having directed *This Is Spinal Tap* (1984), *When Harry Met Sally* (1989) and *A Few Good Men* (1992). He appeared in *Sleepless in Seattle* (1993).

Paul Reiser b. 3/30/57; New York City. Television and film actor known for his comic roles, especially as documentary filmmaker Paul Buchman on *Mad About You* (1992–present). His films include *Beverly Hills Cop* (1984), *Aliens* (1986) and *Bye, Bye Love* (1995).

Debbie Reynolds (Mary Frances Reynolds) b. 4/1/32; El Paso, Texas. Singer, dancer and actress known for her tireless energy and pertness. Her films include *Singin' in the Rain* (1952), *The Affairs of Dobie Gillis* (1953) and *Goodbye Charlie* (1964). She also starred in the sitcom *The Debbie Reynolds Show* (1969–70).

Anne Rice (Howard Allen O'Brien) b. 10/4/41; New Orleans. Author of vampire novels and, under the name A. N. Roquelaure, a series of pornographic books. Rice's works include *The Vampire Chronicles: Interview With the Vampire* (1976), *Vampire Lestat* (1985), *Tale of the Body Thief* (1993) and *Memnoch the Devil* (1995).

Michael Richards b. 7/21/48; Culver City, California. Emmy Award-winning television and film actor best known for his role as the outrageous, master-of-the-big-entrance Cosmo Kramer on *Seinfeld* (1990–present). He also appeared on *Fridays* (1980–82). His film credits include *UHF* (1989) and *Unstrung Heroes* (1995).

Tony Richardson 6/5/28–11/15/91; Shipley, England. Academy Award-winning film and stage

director influential in shaping modern British film and theater. His films include *The Entertainer* (1960), *Tom Jones* (1963) and *Blue Sky* (1991). He was married to actress Vanessa REDGRAVE, and they had two daughters, actresses Natasha and Joely Richardson.

Jerome Robbins b. 10/11/18; New York City. Academy and Tony Award-winning choreographer and dancer. He was associate artistic director of the New York City Ballet (1949–59). He choreographed the musicals *The King and I* (1951), *West Side Story* (1957) and *Fiddler on the Roof* (1964) and co-directed the film *West Side Story* (1961).

Julia Roberts b. 10/18/67; Smyrna, Georgia. Film actress known for her southern charm and her failed relationships. Her films include *Steel Magnolias* (1989), *Pretty Woman* (1990) and *Mary Reilly* (1996). She was married to musician Lyle Lovett.

William "Smokey" Robinson b. 2/19/40; Detroit. Grammy Award-winning singer and songwriter known for his falsetto voice and as a premier songwriter with more than 4,000 songs to his credit. He formed the band the Miracles in 1955, and the band recorded the hits "Shop Around" (1960), "I Second That Emotion" (1967) and "Tracks of My Tears" (1967). He also served as president of Motown Records.

Ginger Rogers (Virginia McMath) 7/16/11–4/25/95; Independence, Missouri. Academy Award-winning film and stage actress and dancer who appeared in several romantic comedies with her dancing partner Fred ASTAIRE. She also gave several successful dramatic performances. Her films include *Swing Time* (1939) and *Kitty Foyle* (1940).

Roy Rogers (Leonard Slye) b. 11/5/12; Cincinnati, Ohio. Actor and singer who starred in more than 80 Westerns, earning the moniker "King of the Cowboys." He signed with Republic Pictures in 1938, and with Gene AUTRY, became the country's most famous cowboy team. His films include *Under Western Stars* (1938), *King of the Cowboys* (1943) and *The Yellow Rose of Texas* (1944). He is married to actress Dale Evans.

Will Rogers 11/4/1879–8/15/1935; Oologah, Indian Territory (now Claremore, Oklahoma). Actor and humorist known as a homespun, straight-talking cowboy philosopher. His films include *Guile of Woman* (1921), *The Headless Horseman* (1922) and *A Connecticut Yankee* (1931).

The Rolling Stones British rock band considered one of the most influential of all time. The Stones appeared on the music scene at about the same time as THE BEATLES and balanced the mop tops' clean-cut appeal with a reverence for black blues and an appetite for excess. The Stones continue to record and tour. Current band members include singer **Mick Jagger (b. 7/26/43; Dartford, England),** guitarist **Keith Richards (b. 12/18/43; Dartford, England),** bassist **Bill Wyman (b. 10/24/41; London, England),** drummer **Charlie Watts (b. 6/2/41; Islington, England)** and guitarist **Ron Wood (b. 6/1/47; Hillingdon, England).** Guitarist **Brian Jones (2/28/42–7/3/69; Cheltenham, England)** drowned in a pool. The band's recordings include *Let It Bleed* (1969), *Sticky Fingers* (1971), *Exile on Main Street* (1972) and *Steel Wheels* (1989). Jagger, Richard and Watts have also had variably successful solo careers.

Mickey Rooney b. 9/23/20; Brooklyn, New York. Academy Award-winning film, television and stage actor who gained fame as a child actor and continued acting throughout his adult life. His films include *Boys Town* (1938), *Huckleberry Finn* (1939) and *National Velvet* (1944).

Roseanne (Roseanne Barr) b. 11/3/53; Salt Lake City, Utah. Emmy Award-winning outspoken actress best known for her role as white-trash queen Roseanne Conner on *Roseanne* and for her controversial behavior offscreen.

Martin Scorsese

She caused a stir in 1990 when, while screeching the national anthem at a San Diego baseball game, she grabbed her crotch and spat. She was married to actor **Tom Arnold (b. 3/6/59; Ottawa, Iowa),** who appeared on *Roseanne* and briefly had his own show, *Tom* (1994). His film credits include *True Lies* (1994) and *Nine Months* (1995).

Susan Sarandon (Susan Abigail Tomalin) b. 10/4/46; New York City. Academy Award-winning, self-possessed film actress who is known for her intelligent, sensual presence. Her films include *Atlantic City* (1980), *Bull Durham* (1988), *Thelma and Louise* (1991) and *Dead Man Walking* (1995). She and her significant other, director and actor **Tim Robbins (b. 10/16/58; West Covina, California),** are known for their outspoken support of progressive causes.

John Schlesinger b. 2/26/26; London, England. Academy Award-winning film and television director whose *Midnight Cowboy* (1970) is the only X-rated film to win a best-picture Oscar. His other films include *Sunday, Bloody Sunday* (1967) and *The Day of the Locust* (1975).

Charles Schulz b. 11/26/22; Minneapolis, Minnesota. Cartoonist who created "Peanuts," the most commercially successful syndicated comic strip of all time.

Arnold Schwarzenegger b. 7/30/47; Graz, Austria. Hulk-like actor best known for his roles in sci-fi action/thrillers. Schwarzenegger immigrated to the United

States in 1968 after winning several European body-building championships. He also won the Mr. Universe title five times. He first came to Hollywood's attention in the documentary *Pumping Iron* (1977) and has appeared in *Conan the Barbarian* (1982), *The Terminator* (1984), its sequel, *Terminator 2: Judgment Day* and *Eraser* (1996). He is an owner of the Planet Hollywood restaurant chain and is married to Kennedy family member and newscaster Maria Shriver.

Martin Scorsese b. 11/17/42; Flushing, New York. Director considered one of the most influential of the late 20th century. His films, which draw on his experiences growing up as the son of Italian immigrants and his encyclopedic knowledge of film history, include *Taxi Driver* (1976), *Raging Bull* (1980) and *GoodFellas* (1990).

George C. Scott b. 10/18/27; Wise, Virginia. Academy Award-winning film and stage actor known for his powerful presence. His films include *Dr. Strangelove* (1964) and *Patton* (1970). He appeared in the New York Shakespeare Festival's *Richard III* and *The Merchant of Venice* and Broadway's *Uncle Vanya* (1973).

Jerry Seinfeld b. 4/29/55; Brooklyn, New York. Comedian and actor who was a successful standup comic before landing his own television series, the Emmy Award-winning *Seinfeld* (1990–present).

Selena (Quintanilla Perez) 4/16/71–3/31/95; Lake Jackson, Texas. Grammy Award-winning *tejano* singer who was gunned down in 1995 by deranged fan Yolanda Saldivar. Her recordings include *Live* (1993) and *Dreaming of You* (1995).

Tom Selleck b. 1/29/45; Detroit, Michigan. Emmy Award-winning telelvision and film actor best known for his role as the suave, mustachioed private investigator Thomas Magnum on *Magnum, P.I.* (1980–88). His films include *Three Men and a Baby* (1987) and its sequel, *Three Men and a*

Little Lady (1990). He returned to television in 1996, appearing in several episodes of *Friends*.

Peter Sellers 9/5/25–7/24/80; Southsea, England. Inimitable, eccentric film actor who starred in the British comic radio series *The Goon Show* before making his mark as the bemused Inspector Clouseau in the much-loved *Pink Panther* movies, which premiered in 1964. Sellers played multiple characers in *The Mouse That Roared* (1959) and *Dr. Strangelove* (1964).

David O. Selznick 5/10/22–6/22/65; Pittsburgh, Pennsylvania. Hollywood producer and magnate who was the driving force behind *Gone With the Wind* (1939). After working for Paramount, RKO and MGM, he formed Selznick International Pictures in 1936. The studio's credits include *Rebecca* (1940) and *Spellbound* (1945). He was married to actress Jennifer Jones.

Maurice Sendak b. 6/10/29; Brooklyn, New York. Children's book writer and illustrator and playwright known for his wildly fantastic drawings and tales that convey childhood experiences. His books include *Where the Wild Things Are* (1963), *In the Night Kitchen* (1970) and *Outside Over There* (1981).

George Bernard Shaw 7/26/1856–11/2/1950; Dublin, Ireland. Nobel Prize-winning playwright, essayist and critic known for his witty, intelligent dramas of ideas. He was a founder of the Fabian Society (1883), a group of writers committed to promoting socialism. His plays include *Candida* (1896) and *Pygmalion* (1913).

Sam Shepard (Samuel Shepard Rogers) b. 11/5/43; Fort Sheridan, Illinois. Pulitzer Prize-winning playwright and actor known for his dramas that combine myth and reality, past and present. His plays include *Buried Child* (1978) and *A Life of the Mind* (1985).

Cybill Shepherd b. 2/18/50; Memphis, Tennessee. Television and film actress who appeared in several films and then made the move to television. Her films include *The Last Picture Show* (1971) and *Taxi Driver* (1976). Her television credits include *The Yellow Rose* (1983–84), *Moonlighting* (1985–89) and *Cybill* (1995–present).

Dinah Shore 3/1/17–2/24/94. Emmy Award-winning radio, television and film entertainer who achieved fame as a singer and became better known as the hostess of several television shows. Her programs include *The Dinah Shore Show* (1951–57) and *The Dinah Shore Chevy Show* (1956–63). Her recordings include "Yes, My Darling Daughter" (1941).

Beverly Sills (Belle Silverman) b. 5/25/29; Brooklyn, New York. Animated coloratura widely regarded as America's greatest soprano. She has appeared as the heroine in more than 50 operas, including Handel's *Julius Caesar,* Offenbach's *Tales of Hoffman* and Donizetti's *Anna Bolena.* She served as director of the New York City Opera (1979–89) and since 1994 has been chairwoman of the Lincoln Center for the Performing Arts.

Phil Silvers 5/11/12–11/1/85; Brooklyn, New York. Emmy and Tony Award-winning television and stage actor remembered for creating Sgt. Ernie Bilko, the fast-talking but endearing con man in *The Phil Silvers Show* (1955–59). His Broadway credits include *High Button Shoes* (1947) and *Top Banana* (1951).

Neil Simon b. 7/4/27; Bronx, New York. Pulitzer Prize- and Tony Award-winning playwright known for his popular plays about middle-class America that often touch on sex, marriage and middle age. His plays include *Barefoot in the Park* (1963), *The Odd Couple* (1965), *Brighton Beach Memoirs* (1983) and *Lost in Yonkers* (1991). Many of Simon's plays have been made into films.

Paul Simon b. 10/13/41; Newark, New Jersey. Grammy Award-winning singer, guitarist and songwriter best known for being half of the folk-rock duo Simon and Garfunkel and for his intelligent, polished recordings. When the pair disbanded in 1970, Simon embarked on a successful solo career and released *Paul Simon* (1972) and *Graceland* (1986).

Frank Sinatra b. 12/12/15; Hoboken, New Jersey. Academy and Grammy Award-winning singer and actor who matured from the bobby-soxers' heart-throb to one of the most influential song stylists of his day. Similarly, Sinatra surprised critics who expected little from a band singer with credible screen performances in *From Here to Eternity* (1953), *The Manchurian Candidate* (1962) and *The Man With the Golden Arm* (1955). Sinatra continued to pack auditoriums with tours that sometimes included his "Rat Pack" pals from the 1950s. His recordings include "Young at Heart" (1954) and "Strangers in the Night" (1966).

Jimmy Smits b. 7/9/58; New York City. Emmy Award-winning television and film actor who played Hispanic lawyer Victor Sifuentes on *L.A. Law* (1985–91) and replaced David Caruso on *NYPD Blue* (1995). His films include *My Family: Mi Familia* (1995).

Stephen Sondheim b. 3/22/30; New York City. Pulitzer Prize-, Tony and Academy Award-winning lyricist and composer known for his successful, sophisticated Broadway musicals. He wrote the lyrics for *West Side Story* (1957), and lyrics and music for *Company* (1970), *Sweeney Todd* (1979), *Sunday in the Park With George* (1984) and *Passion* (1995). He has continued to expand the emotional and musical boundaries of the Broadway stage.

Steven Spielberg b. 12/18/47; Cincinnati, Ohio. Academy Award-winning director whose films, which range from action-adventure to science fiction to historical drama, have come to be equated with box-office smash. His credits include *Jaws* (1975), *E.T. the Extra-Terrestrial* (1982), *Jurassic Park* (1993) and *Schindler's List* (1993). In 1995 he formed an entertainment mega-studio, DreamWorks SKG, with Hollywood heavyweights Jeffrey Katzenberg and David Geffen. He is married to actress Kate Capshaw.

Bruce Springsteen b. 9/23/49; Freehold, New Jersey. Grammy Award-winning singer and song-writer whose songs reflect sympathy for the working class and tell of the American experience. His recordings include *Born to Run* (1975), *Nebraska* (1980) and *Born in the U.S.A.* (1984).

Sylvester Stallone b. 7/6/46; New York City. Actor known for his roles in action-adventure films that are big on muscle and carnage. His films include the five *Rocky* films (1976; II, 1979; III, 1981; IV, 1985; V, 1990), the three Rambo movies (*First Blood*, 1982; *Rambo: First Blood Part II*, 1985; *Rambo III* , 1988) and *Cliffhanger* (1993).

Howard Stern b. 1/2/54; New York City. Shock jock and author who takes pleasure and pride in offending as many as possible with racist and sexist jokes. He has cost his employer, Infinity Broadcasting, more than $2 million in fines for indecency. His books include his autobiography *Private Parts* (1993) and *Miss America* (1996).

George Stevens 12/18/04–3/8/75; Oakland, California. Leading film director of the 1930s and 1940s known for movie standards such as *Swing Time* (1936), *Gunga Din* (1939) and *Woman of the Year* (1942). After his World War II service, Stevens returned to Tinseltown and made *I Remember Mama* (1948) and *A Place in the Sun* (1951), but his later work became grandiose and overblown.

James (Jimmy) Stewart b. 5/20/08; Indiana, Pennsylvania. Academy Award-winning actor known for his slow drawl and sincere, all-American charm. His films include *It's a Wonderful*

Quentin Tarantino

Life (1946), *Mr. Smith Goes to Washington* (1939) and *The Philadelphia Story* (1940).

Michael Stipe b. 1/4/60; Decatur, Georgia. Lead singer of the Grammy Award-winning band R.E.M., one of the first bands to earn the alternative label. R.E.M.'s recordings include *Murmur* (1983), *Document* (1987) and *Monster* (1994). Stipe was involved in his band's award-winning videos and he is expanding his interest to fea-ture-film production.

Oliver Stone b. 9/15/46; New York City. Academy Award-winning director and writer known for his controversial historical films. His films include *Born on the Fourth of July* (1989), *Platoon* (1986), *JFK* (1991) and *Nixon* (1995).

Tom Stoppard b. 7/3/37; Gottwaldov, Czechoslovakia. Tony Award-winning playwright known for his dazzling wordplay and clever constructions. His plays include *Rosencrantz and Guildenstern Are Dead* (1966), *Travesties* (1974) and *The Real Thing* (1982).

Meryl Streep (Mary Louise Streep) b. 6/22/49; Summit, New Jersey. Academy Award-winning film, stage and television actress known for her versatility and ability to create an interior life for her characters with telling details of manner, action or accent. Her films include *Kramer vs. Kramer* (1979), *Out of Africa* (1985) and *The Bridges of Madison County* (1995).

Barbra Streisand b. 1942; New York City. Academy Award-winning film and stage actress, singer, known for her strong soprano voice, and film producer and director. She appeared in the film (1968) and stage (1964) versions of *Funny Girl* and the films *The Way We Were* (1973) and *Yentl* (1983). Her recordings include *The Barbra Streisand Album* (1963), *A Star Is Born* (1976) and *The Concert* (1994).

Ed Sullivan 9/25/02–10/13/74; New York City. Television per-sonality known for his monotone voice, wooden mannerisms and ability to recognize America's tastes and fads. He hosted *The Ed Sullivan Show* (1948–71), and his guests included The Beatles, Walt Disney, Dean Martin and Elvis Presley.

Donna Summer (Donna Gaines) b. 12/31/48; Boston. Grammy Award-winning singer who was disco's diva, surviving the period, emerged as a 1980s pop star. Her recordings include *Bad Girls* (1979), *She Works Hard for the Money* (1983) and "This Time I Know It's for Real" (1989).

Donald Sutherland b. 7/17/34; St. John, New Brunswick, Canada. Film actor who struggled for years as a supporting actor before establishing himself as a lead in *M*A*S*H* (1970). His other films include *Klute* (1971) and *A Dry White Season* (1989). His son, Kiefer, is a well-known film actor.

Quentin Tarantino b. 3/27/63; Knoxville, Tennessee. Academy Award-winning writer, director and actor known for his violent, witty films. Tarantino, a high-school dropout, learned the art of film by watching thousands of movies and videos. His films include *Reservoir Dogs* (1992) and *Pulp Fiction* (1994).

Elizabeth Taylor b. 2/27/32; London, England. Academy Award-winning film and televi-sion actress known for both her beauty and her seven marriages. Her films include *National Velvet* (1944), *Butterfield 8* (1960) and

Who's Afraid of Virginia Woolf? (1966). Her former husbands include Eddie Fisher, Richard Burton (twice) and most recently construction worker Larry Fortensky.

Twyla Tharp b. 7/1/41; Portland, Indiana. Dancer and choreographer whose innovative, energetic style combines jazz, tap, ballet and modern dance. She has danced with the Paul Taylor Dance Company, choreographed for the American Ballet Theatre and formed her own troupes.

Marlo Thomas b. 11/21/38; Detroit. Emmy Award-winning actress who is best known for her role as one of television's first independent women, Ann Marie, on *That Girl* (1966–71). She is married to talk-show host **Phil Donahue (b. 12/21/35; Cleveland, Ohio)**, who has hosted *Donahue* since 1967. He announced in 1996 that he planned to retire at the end of the television season. Her father was Emmy Award-winning **Danny Thomas (1/6/14–2/6/91; Deerfield, Michigan)**, a popular entertainer of the 1950s, '60s and '70s who starred in *The Danny Thomas Show* (originally called *Make Room for Daddy*) (1953–64) and *The Danny Thomas Hour* (1967–68).

Emma Thompson b. 4/15/59; London, England. Academy Award-winning film and television actress and screenwriter known for her intelligence and lively wit. Her films include *Henry V* (1989), *Howards End* (1992), *Remains of the Day* (1993) and *Sense and Sensibility* (1995), for which she also wrote the screenplay. She was married to actor and director **Kenneth Branagh (b. 12/10/60; Belfast, Northern Ireland)**.

The Three Stooges Best known as a threesome, the Stooges started as a twosome, with **Moe Howard (1897–1975; Brooklyn, New York)** and his brother **Samuel "Shemp" (1900–55; Brooklyn, New York)**. The pair performed their shtick in vaudeville for five years before **Larry**

Fine (1911–74; Philadelphia) made the two Stooges three. As the magic of vaudeville began to wane, the Stooges took their head-knocking act to the big screen, making 200 short films between 1934 and 1958. Shemp Howard left the group in the early 1930s and **Jerome "Curly" Howard (1906–52; Brooklyn, New York)** signed on. When Curly suffered a stroke in 1946, Shemp returned. **Joe Besser** replaced Shemp when he died in 1955 and **Joe De Rita** replaced Besser in 1959. The Stooges made feature films, including *Have Rocket Will Travel* (1959) and *Snow White and the Three Stooges* (1961), but their current renown and status as pop icons depends on the incessant television exposure in the 1950s and '60s of their short films.

Leo Tolstoy 9/9/1828–11/20/1910; Yasnaya Polyana, Russia. Novelist and philosopher considered one of the greatest writers of all time. His pacifist beliefs were often reflected in his later works. His masterpieces include *War and Peace* (1862–69), *Anna Karenina* (1873–76) and *The Confession* (1879).

Spencer Tracy 4/5/1900–6/10/67; Milwaukee, Wisconsin. Academy Award-winning actor who often played opposite his lover, Katharine Hepburn. His films include *Boys Town* (1938), *Woman of the Year* (1942) and *Guess Who's Coming to Dinner* (1968).

Daniel J. Travanti b. 3/7/40; Kenosha, Wisconsin. Emmy Award-winning actor best known for his role as Capt. Frank Furillo in *Hill Street Blues* (1981–87).

John Travolta b. 2/18/54; Englewood, New Jersey. Film and television actor first known for his role on television's *Welcome Back Kotter* (1975–79) and as disco king Tony Manero in the 1977 film *Saturday Night Fever*. His career languished from the mid-1980s to the mid-1990s, but his appearance in 1994's *Pulp Fiction* reestablished Travolta as

a box-office draw and made him the king of cool. His other films include *Grease* (1978) and *Get Shorty* (1995).

Tommy Tune b. 2/28/39; Wichita Falls, Texas. Tony Award-winning dancer and choreographer known for his innovative dances and his work in musical films. His Broadway musicals include *Irma La Douce* (1965), *My One and Only* (1983) and *The Will Rogers Follies* (1991). His films include *Hello, Dolly!* (1969) and *The Boyfriend* (1972).

Tina Turner (Annie Mae Bullock) b. 11/26/39; Nutbush Borough, Tennessee. Grammy Award-winning rhythm and blues singer known for her powerful vocals and her athletic dancing. Her career began in 1956 with her husband's band, Ike Turner and the Kings of Rhythm, but fell apart when she left the band and the abusive Ike. She reemerged in 1984 with *Private Dancer*. Her other recordings include *Simply the Best* (1991), "Proud Mary" (1972) and "River Deep, Mountain High."

Mark Twain (Samuel Langhorne Clemens) 11/30/1835–4/21/1910; Florida, Missouri. Writer and social observer considered master of humor and sarcasm and one of the most influential modern American writers. His *The Adventures of Huckleberry Finn* (1884) is often called the first modern American novel. His other books include *The Adventures of Tom Sawyer* (1876), *The Prince and the Pauper* (1882) and *A Connecticut Yankee in King Arthur's Court* (1889).

Liv Ullman b. 12/16/38; Tokyo, Japan. Norwegian film and stage actress known for her work with Ingmar Bergman. Her films include *Persona* (1966), *Cries and Whispers* (1972) and *Autumn Sonata* (1978).

U2 Grammy Award-winning Irish rock group known for its political songs, anthemic guitars and big, high-tech concerts. Formed in 1977, band members are vocalist **Bono (Paul Hewson; b. 5/10/60; Dublin, Ireland)**, guitarist **The**

Edge (David Evans; b. 8/8/61; Barking, England), bassist **Adam Clayton (b. 3/13/60; Oxford, England)** and drummer **Larry Mullen, Jr. (b. 10/31/61; Dublin, Ireland).** U2's recordings include *Boy* (1980), *Joshua Tree* (1987) and *Zooropa* (1993).

Dick Van Dyke b. 12/13/25; West Plains, Missouri. Emmy Award-winning television, film and stage actor best known for his portrayal of Rob Petrie, the lanky, bumbling comedy writer on *The Dick Van Dyke Show* (1961–66). His films include *Bye Bye Birdie* (1963), *Mary Poppins* (1964) and *Chitty Chitty Bang Bang* (1968). His other television credits include *Diagnosis Murder* (1992–present).

Kurt Vonnegut, Jr. b. 11/11/22; Indianapolis, Indiana. Science-fiction writer known for his dark humor and social satire. His novels include *Cat's Cradle* (1963), *Slaughterhouse Five* (1969) and *Breakfast of Champions* (1973).

Alice Walker b. 2/9/44; Eatonton, Georgia. Pulitzer Prize-winning author whose novels and stories portray the hardships endured by Southern blacks. Her work includes *Meridian* (1976), *In Love and Trouble* (1973) and *The Color Purple* (1982), which was filmed in 1985.

Denzel Washington b. 12/28/54; Mount Vernon, New York. Academy Award-winning film and television actor whose films include *Cry Freedom* (1987), *Glory* (1989) and *Malcolm X* (1992). His career began on television's *St. Elsewhere* (1982–88).

Wendy Wasserstein b. 10/18/50; Brooklyn, New York. Tony Award- and Pulitzer Prize-winning dramatist known for her plays about educated women facing challenges in post-liberation America. Her plays include *Uncommon Women and Others* (1977), *Isn't It Romantic* (1983) and *The Heidi Chronicles* (1988).

Muddy Waters (McKinley Morganfield) 4/4/15–4/30/83; Rolling Fork, Mississippi. Blues singer and guitarist who plugged in Delta blues and is considered one of rock's most influential musicians. Though he never enjoyed huge commercial success, Waters inspired the likes of Bob DYLAN, Elvis PRESLEY and Mick Jagger. His recordings include "Rollin' Stone" (1948), "I Just Wanna Make Love to You" (1954) and "Got My Mojo Working" (1954).

John Wayne (Marion Michael Morrison) 5/26/07–6/11/79; Winterset, Iowa. Academy Award-winning film actor whose tough screen persona was the archetypal hero of the western. Wayne was at his best in the "cavalry trilogy" of westerns directed by John Ford. His films include *Stagecoach* (1939), *She Wore a Yellow Ribbon* (1949) and *True Grit* (1969).

Orson Welles 5/6/15–10/10/85; Kenosha, Wisconsin. Academy Award-winning film and stage director, actor, writer and producer who redefined film language with his groundbreaking, critically acclaimed *Citizen Kane* (1941), considered by many to be the greatest film ever made. His 1938 radio adaptation of H.G. WELLS's *War of the Worlds* caused a nationwide panic when listeners thought aliens had landed in New Jersey. Welles spent much of his life in a restless pursuit of projects that would fit the measure of his genius and his ego.

H(erbert) G(eorge) Wells 9/21/1866–8/13/1946; Bromley, Kent, England. Pioneering writer whose novels *The Time Machine* (1985), *The Invisible Man* (1897) and *War of the Worlds* (1898) were among the first science-fiction books. Wells wrote popular comic novels, essays examining the problems of modern life, a one-volume history of the world and an autobiography.

Dianne Wiest

Mae West 8/17/1892–11/22/1980; Brooklyn, New York. Stage and film actress who was the queen of double entendre and exaggerated, humorous sexiness. Her films include *She Done Him Wrong* (1933) and *Go West , Young Man* (1936). Her plays include *Sex* (1926) and *Diamond Lil* (1928).

Edith Wharton 1/24/1862–8/11/1937; New York City. Pulitzer Prize-winning novelist whose work gives an intelligent, ironic picture of post-Civil War society life. Wharton's books include *The House of Mirth* (1905), *The Custom of the Country* (1913), *The Age of Innocence* (1920), filmed by Martin SCORSESE in 1993, and *Ethan Frome* (1911) also filmed in 1993.

Dianne Wiest b. 3/28/48; Kansas City, Missouri. Academy Award-winning film and stage actress known for her quirky, appealing screen personality. Her films include *Hannah and Her sisters* (1986), *Parenthood* (1989) and *Bullets Over Broadway* (1994).

Billy Wilder b. 6/22/06; Vienna, Austria. Academy Award-winning director, writer and producer known for dark film noir and social comedy with a biting edge. His films include *Double Indemnity* (1944), *The Lost Weekend* (1945) and *The Apartment* (1960).

Tennessee Williams (Thomas Lanier Williams) 3/26/11–2/25/83; Columbus, Mississippi. Pulitzer Prize- and Tony Award-winning dramatist and author of film scripts, short stories, novels and poems. He is known for his emotional dialogue, tense plotting and passionate, often shocking, themes that explore sexual tension and characters victimized by a brutal society. His plays include *The Glass Menagerie* (1945), *A Streetcar Named Desire* (1947) and *Cat on a Hot Tin Roof* (1955).

Bruce Willis b. 3/1/55; Penns Grove, New Jersey. Emmy Award-winning film and television actor who gained fame as David Addison on *Moonlighting* (1985–89). His films include the *Die Hard* series (1988, 1990 and 1995) and *Pulp Fiction* (1994). He is married to actress Demi MOORE.

Lanford Wilson b. 4/13/37; Lebanon, Missouri. Prolific playwright whose works center on dynamic characters, often plagued by psychological problems. In 1969, he co-founded the Circle Repertory Company. His plays include *So Long at the Fair* (1963), *The Mound Builders* (1975) and *Redwood Curtain* (1993).

August Wilson b. 1945; Pittsburgh. Tony Award- and Pulitzer Prize-winning playwright, poet and writer whose work focuses on the struggle of African Americans. His plays include *Ma Rainey's Black Bottom* (1984), *Fences* (1987) and *The Piano Lesson* (1990).

Oprah Winfrey b. 1/29/54; Kosciusko, Mississippi. Emmy Award-winning television talk-show host, actress and producer. Her *Oprah Winfrey Show* (debut 1986) is the highest-rated talk show in syndication history. She owns a production company, Harpo, and is one of the highest-paid celebrities in the world. She appeared in the film *The Color Purple* (1985) and the television movie *The Women of Brewster Place* (1989).

Stevie Wonder (Stevland Morris) b. 5/13/50; Saginaw, Michigan. Grammy Award-winning singer, composer, producer, arranger and instrumentalist known for his unlimited ability to produce a kind of spiritually informed, upbeat rhythm and blues that crossed over to millions of fans. Born blind, Wonder signed with Motown Records at age 10 and has been recording since. His recordings include *Innervisions* (1973), *Songs in the Key of Life* (1976) and *Square Circle* (1985).

Alfre Woodard b. 11/2/53; Tulsa, Oklahoma. Emmy Award-winning television and film actress who played Dr. Roxanne Tucker on *St. Elsewhere* (1985–87) before moving to film. Her films include *Cross Creek* (1983), *Passion Fish* (1992) and *How to Make an American Quilt* (1995).

Joanne Woodward b. 2/27/30; Thomasville, Georgia. Academy Award-winning actress whose films include *The Three Faces of Eve* (1957) and *The Glass Menagerie* (1987), which was directed by her husband, Paul NEWMAN.

Steve Wozniak b. 8/11/51; San Jose, California. Electronics engineer who designed, built and introduced the Apple computer, a user-friendly alternative to IBM's personal computer with Steve JOBS in 1976. Jobs and Wozniak formed Apple and saw it grow into a billion dollar company. Wozniak left the company in 1985 and went on to pursue interests in home video.

William Wyler 7/1/02–7/27/81; Alsace, France. Academy Award-winning director credited with adding a new level of maturity to American films during the 1940s and 1950s. His films include *Dodsworth* (1936), *The Best Years of Our Lives* (1946) and *The Heiress* (1949).

Tammy Wynette (Wynette Pugh) b. 5/5/42; Red Bay, Alabama. Country and western singer who gained national recognition with

the release of "D-I-V-O-R-C-E" (1968) and "Stand By Your Man" (1968). She also appeared on radio's Grand Ole Opry. She was married to country singer George Jones with whom she sang several duets.

William Butler Yeats 6/13/1865–1/28/1939; Dublin, Ireland. Nobel Prize-winning Anglo-Irish poet whose work interweaves mysticism, Irish history, love and self-analysis. Yeat's books include *The Rose* (1893), *The Wind Among the Reeds* (1899), *Responsibilities* (1914) and *The Tower* (1928). He also wrote essays and plays, was active in the Irish National Theatre and served as an Irish senator.

Loretta Young (Gretchen Young) b. 1/6/13; Salt Lake City, Utah. Academy and Emmy Award-winning film and television actress who tirelessly made almost 100 films in the 1930s and 1940s. She also hosted television's *Loretta Young Show* (1950–60). Her films include *A Man's Castle* (1933) and *The Farmer's Daughter* (1947).

Robert Young b. 2/22/07; Chicago. Emmy Award-winning television and film actor known for his gentle, patriarchal television roles on the shows *Father Knows Best* (1954–60) and *Marcus Welby, M.D.* (1969–76). *Father Knows Best* was originally a radio show, and CBS transferred it to television in 1954. Though the show was well-received, it fared poorly in the ratings, and CBS canceled it. A write-in campaign convinced NBC to pick up the show, the first successful campaign of its kind.

Frank Zappa 12/21/40–12/4/93; Baltimore, Maryland. Grammy Award-winning rock musician remembered for his complex, virtuosic musical satires. He formed The Mothers of Invention in 1964, and the band specialized in experimental music, surreal comedy and high-tech light shows. Zappa's recordings include *Freak Out !* (1966), *Hot Rats* (1969) and *Jazz From Hell* (1988).

Gone but Not Forgotten

Salvatore Aiello *dance troupe leader* — led North Carolina Dance Theater; danced with the Joffrey Ballet, the Harkness Ballet and the Royal Winnipeg Ballet (194?–1995)

Max Allentuck *theater manager* — worked with theater greats Kermit Bloomgarden, Emanuel Azenberg and James and Joseph Nederlander (1911–1995)

John Alton *cinematographer* — Working with many of America's greatest directors during Hollywood's golden era, Alton was an innovator in lighting techniques that helped establish the film noir movement. (1901–1996)

Sir Kingsley Amis *British novelist* — The prolific author is best known for his first novel, *Lucky Jim,* a 1954 satire about academic life. The book placed him among Britain's Angry Young Men, a group of educated men who denounced Britain's class system. The once-radical became a conservative later in life. He was knighted in 1990. His other books include *That Uncertain Feeling* and *The Old Devils,* for which he won the Booker Prize. (1922–1995)

Maxene Andrews *an Andrews sister* — The Andrews Sisters became stars in 1937 with their enthusiastic harmonies and close association with popular swing bands. The trio became *the* radio voice during World War II and an inspiration to servicemen. Their hits include "Boogie-Woogie Bugle Boy," "Beer Barrel Polka," "Don't Sit Under the Apple Tree" and "Rum and Coca-Cola." Sister LaVerne died in 1967 and Patty is still living. (1916–1995)

Rene Anselmo *television- and satellite-network founder* — started SIN, the Spanish broadcast network in the United States and founded PanAmSat, which challenged the government monopoly on satellite transmission of video images (192?–1995)

Word Baker *director* — directed the world's longest-running musical, *The Fantasticks* (1923–1995)

Martin Balsam *actor* — Balsam won both an Oscar and a Tony Award for his versatile work as a character actor. He made his onscreen debut in 1954 in *On the Waterfront.* His other films include *Twelve Angry Men, Psycho, All the President's Men,* and the 1962 and 1991 versions of *Cape Fear.* Balsam's Broadway credits include Willie Loman in *Death of a Salesman* and *You Know I Can't Hear You When the Water's Running.* (1919–1996)

Saul Bass *animator, graphic designer, filmmaker* — Bass turned feature-film credits into an art form by incorporating sophisticated graphics and animation into the opening title sequences of such films as *The Man With the Golden Arm, Psycho, West Side Story* and *Big.* He won a 1968 documentary short subject Oscar for *Why Man Creates.* (1920–1996)

Sandy Becker *radio announcer, children's TV host* — network-radio announcer and quiz-show voice who became host of early children's variety shows for which he invented characters and skits (192?–1996)

John Beradino *soap-opera star* — played Dr. Steve Hardy on *General Hospital* for 33 years, acted in the *Our Gang* comedies as a child and played for the 1948 World Series-winning Cleveland Indians (1917–1996)

Ruth Berghaus *director, choreographer* — One of postwar Europe's most influential figures in theater, Berghaus directed

George Burns

many of Paul Dessau's (her late husband) operas and was known for her original productions of Mozart, Wagner, Strauss and works by Berg. (1927–1996)

Pandro Berman *film producer* — A producer for RKO in its heyday, Berman put his stamp on a collection of classic films, including *Swing Time, Gunga Din, The Hunchback of Notre Dame* and *Butterfield 8.* (1905–1996)

Whit Bissell *actor* — supporting actor who appeared in more than 350 TV roles and 85 films, including *The Great Missouri Raid* and *Birdman of Alcatraz* (1909–1996)

Lady Caroline Blackwood *writer* — author of several wry, witty novels, including *The Last of the Duchess* and *The Stepdaughter* (1931–1996)

Vivian Blaine *stage actress* — created the role of Miss Adelaide in the original 1950 production of *Guys and Dolls* (1921–1995)

Ralph Blane *songwriter* — scored the 1944 musical *Meet Me in St. Louis* (1914–1995)

Raphael Blau *writer* — screenwriter whose credits include *Bedtime for Bonzo* (191?–1996)

Erma Bombeck *columnist, author* — After having three children, Bombeck turned her homemaking experience into humorous columns that became widely syndicated as "At Wit's End." Her books include *The Grass Is Always Greener Over the Septic Tank*. (1927–1996)

Roger Bowen *actor* — played Col. Henry Blake in Robert Altman's 1970 film *M*A*S*H* (193?–1996)

Jeremy Brett *actor* — played Freddy Eynsford-Hill in *My Fair Lady* (1956) and later became television's favorite Sherlock Holmes, playing the famous sleuth in 41 episodes of *Mystery* (1935–1995)

Harold Brodkey *novelist* — Brodkey was best known for *The Runaway Soul*, his 1991 novel which was 32 years in the making. He was a writer for *The New Yorker* and is also remembered for using 31 pages to describe a single sex act in his short story "Innocence." (1930–1996)

Joseph Brodsky *poet* — Russian-born Brodsky won the 1987 Nobel Prize for Literature and was named Poet Laureate of the United States in 1991. His work, though not political, was condemned by Russian authorities. He was arrested in 1964 on charges of "parasitism" and expelled from Russia in 1972. His works include *A Part of Speech*, *Less Than One* and *To Urania*. (1940–1996)

Albert (Pud) Brown *jazz musician* — Dixieland jazz clarinetist and saxophonist who composed "Johnson Rag" (1917–1996)

Mary Bruce *tap-dance teacher* — dance students included Ruby Dee, Martina Arroyo and Marlon Brando (1900–1995)

John Brunner *science-fiction novelist* — British writer who penned *Stand on Zanzibar*, *The Shockwave Rider* and *A Maze of Stars* (193?–1995)

Herman Buchman *makeup artist* — former director of makeup for the New York City Opera; film credits include *12 Angry Men*, *The Miracle Worker* and *Long Day's Journey Into Night* (192?–1996)

George Burns *actor, comedian* — Legendary, cigar-smoking personality who, with his wife Gracie Allen, formed a highly successful radio/TV comedy act. He won an Oscar in 1975 for his role in *The Sunshine Boys* and starred in the film *Oh God*. (1896–1996)

Margaret G. Cahill *first Miss America* — became the first Miss America at age 16 in 1921 (1905–1995)

William Caunitz *author* — Once a New York City policeman, Caunitz turned to writing spy and cop thrillers, including the best-selling *One Police Plaza*. (193?–1996)

Rosalind Cash *stage and screen actress* — appeared in Broadway and Off-Broadway productions, films and television movies and was an original member of the Negro Ensemble Company (1938–1995)

John Chancellor *television anchorman* — Joining NBC in 1950, Chancellor eventually became the anchor of *NBC Nightly News*, a position he held for 12 years before becoming senior analyst and political commentator for the network. (1927–1996)

Chas Chandler *rock bassist and manager* — Chandler co-founded and was drummer of '60s rock band the Animals. He is credited with discovering Jimi Hendrix and producing the legend's first two albums, *Are You Experienced* and *Axis: Bold as Love*. (193?–1996)

Don Cherry *jazz musician* — Trumpeter Cherry worked with the Ornette Coleman Quartet, John Coltrane, Lou Reed and many other musicians. He formed the acoustic quartet New and Old Dreams and was a pioneer in exploring world music. (1936–1995)

Giraud Chester *game show executive* — developed *The Price Is Right*, *Family Feud* and *What's My Line* (1922–1995)

Eleanor Clark *writer* — Although not distinctly guides for the

tourist and traveler, Clark's works describe cities so lucidly, so eloquently and with such detail that many cannot help but follow her prose page by page when touring a foreign place. (1913–1996)

Richard Coe *theater critic* — Coe was the *Washington Post* theater critic for more than 40 years, reviewing many Broadway-bound shows. The Directors' Guild of America named him Critic of the Year in 1963; he was also honored as Washingtonian of the Year in 1980. (1916–1995)

Claudette Colbert *stage and screen actress* — Academy Award-winning actress who often portrayed headstrong, sophisticated women. Her films include *It Happened One Night* (1934) and *The Palm Beach Story* (1939). (1905–1996)

Ray Combs *game show host, stand-up comic* — hosted *The New Family Feud* game show from 1988 to 1994 (1956–1996)

Richard Condon *political novelist* — A longtime Hollywood publicist, Condon wrote his first novel at age 42, and his second book, *The Manchurian Candidate*, became both a bestseller and a classic film. He wrote *Prizzi's Honor* (1982), which was also made into a film. (1915–1996)

Willis Conover *disc jockey* — Largely responsible for bringing jazz to Eastern European airwaves, Conover became the *Voice of America* disc jockey in 1954. (1920–1996)

Claudette Colbert

Pam Conrad *author* — her children's books include *I Don't Live Here!, What I Did for Roman* and *Taking the Ferry Home* (194?–1996)

Morty Corb *jazz bassist* — performed with Louis Armstrong, Ella Fitzgerald, Pearl Bailey and Nat King Cole (1917–1996)

John Craven *actor* — played George in the original Broadway production of *Our Town;* also appeared in movies and on television (1916–1995)

Leo J. Damore *writer* — wrote *Senatorial Privilege: The Chappaquiddick Cover-Up,* which drew on his experience as a reporter on Cape Cod (192?–1995)

Frank Daniel *filmmaker* — The Czech-born filmmaker made the Academy-Award winning *The Shop on Main Street* (1965). He emigrated in 1968 to the United States, becoming a friend, teacher and mentor to the likes of David Lynch, Paul Schrader and Terrence Mallick. (1926–1996)

Minna Lederman Daniel *music editor* — Lederman edited *Modern Music* magazine from 1924 until the magazine folded in 1946. She continued to write on music and dance and contributed to *The Nation, Saturday Review* and other magazines. (1896–1995)

Alexander D'Arcy *actor* — debuted in Rex Ingram's *Garden of Allah* (1928) and went on to enjoy a 60-year film career (1908–1996)

Saul David *movie producer* — Before becoming a producer of such films as *Von Ryan's Express* and the James Bond spoofs *Our Man Flint* and *In Like Flint,* David was an editor at Bantam Books in the mid-1950s. (1921–1996)

Robertson Davies *Canadian author* — Davies published more than 30 works, including 3 trilogies, fiction, essays and criticism. His 1972 novel, *The Manticore,* won Canada's Governor General Award for fiction. He also edited and published Ontario's *Peterborogh Examiner* from 1942 to 1962. (1913–1995)

Judy Dearing *costume designer, dancer* — designed costumes for Broadway and Off-Broadway productions, the New York Shakespeare Festival and the Alvin Ailey Dance Theater; won 1985 Obie for *A Soldier's Play* (1940–1995)

Annie Elizabeth (Bessie) Delany *dentist, writer* — Delany became New York's second black woman dentist in 1923 and continued her Harlem practice for almost 30 years. With her sister Sadie, she co-authored *Having Our Say: The Delany Sisters' First 100 Years* (1993), a bestseller that became a Broadway hit. (1891–1995)

William Delligan *screenwriter, novelist* — wrote for *All My Children* and penned 15 novels, including *The Maze* and *Time Nor Tide* (194?–1996)

Charles Denner *actor* — Denner worked with many of France's most famous movie directors including François Truffaut, Louis Malle, Claude Chabrol, Claude Lelouch, Yves Allégret and Claude Berri. He also starred in Costa-Gavras's *Z.* Denner is best remembered for his role in Truffaut's *The Man Who Loved Women.* (1926–1995)

Pasquale De Santis *cinematographer* — won a 1968 Academy Award for his camera work in *Romeo and Juliet;* also worked with many of Italy's neorealist directors (1927–1996)

Guy Doleman *actor* — radio, theater, television and film actor whose credits include *The Deadly Bees, The Avengers* and *Murder, She Wrote* (1924–1996)

Virginia Donaldson *ballet press agent* — longtime New York City Ballet press agent and ballet supporter whose career was inspired by her early friendship with choreographer Léonide Massine (192?–1996)

Zeno Dostal *filmmaker, screenwriter, novelist* — Dostal was one of the leading filmmakers in the Czech Republic, best known for his last film, *The Golet in the Valley (Golet v Udoli).* (1934 – 1996)

Scott Douglas *ballet dancer, choreographer* — performed in ballets by Jerome Robbins, Agnes de Mille, Antony Tudor and George Balanchine (192?–1996)

Ulysses Dove *choreographer* — Dove created modern dances that have been performed by the Alvin Ailey American Dance Theater and the New York City Ballet. (1947–1996)

Jacob Druckman *composer, teacher* — Pulitzer Prize-winning composer and contemporary music teacher (1928–1996)

Marguerite Duras *writer* — Duras had a small but loyal literary following until she was 70, when the publication of *The Lover* gave her a world-wide audience. Her 1960 screenplay for Alain Resnais's *Hiroshima, Mon Amour* is considered a classic. (1914–1996)

Paul Eddington *actor* — starred in the British sitcoms *Yes, Minister* and *Yes, Prime Minister* (1927–1995)

Bernard Edwards *disco musician, pop producer* — co-founded the hot disco group Chic (1952–1996)

Vince Edwards *actor* — played the inspired but pensive Dr. Ben Casey on the hit TV show *Ben Casey* (1926–1996)

Eddie Egan *former policeman, actor* — Egan's career as a New York City cop was the basis for the 1971 film *The French Connection.* He also appeared in several television series, including *Joe Forrester* and *Mike Hammer.* (c. 1930–1995)

Lonne Elder 3d *playwright* — appeared in the first Broadway version of *A Raisin in the Sun* and wrote for the stage, television and film (1926–1996)

Michael Ende *children's book author* — Ende penned *Momo,* which was the source of the

1979 film *The NeverEnding Story.*
(c. 1930–1995)

Evan Esar *author* — Esar wrote books of humor, including the *Dictionary of Humorous Quotations.* (1899–1995)

Fred Fehl *dance and theatrical photographer* — Fehl revolutionized theatrical and dance photography, abandoning staged photo sessions for what he termed "performance photography," using rapid-fire shots to capture the living moment. His photographs from the *New York Times, Dance Magazine, Life* and *Theater Arts* were published in several books, including *On Broadway* and *Stars of the American Ballet.* (190?–1995)

Edward Fenton *children's book author* — books include *Nine Lives: Or, The Celebrated Cat of Beacon Hill, Duffy's Rocks* and *The Phantom of Walkaway Hill,* for which he won an Edgar award (191?–1995)

Leonor Fini *artist, set designer* — designed sets for George Balanchine's *The Crystal Palace* and for Milan's La Scala opera house (1908–1996)

Donald Fink *television engineer* — published the standard work *Principles of TV Engineering* (1940) (191?–1996)

Jack Finney *science-fiction writer* — Finney, who specialized in time-travel novels and thrillers, was best known for his 1955 book, *The Body Snatchers,* which was reissued as *Invasion of the Body Snatchers* and made into films in 1956, 1978 and 1994. (1911–1995)

Ella Fitzgerald *jazz singer* — One of the premiere jazz singers, "the first lady of song" blessed thousands of listeners around the world with her unmistakable voice. Considered by many to be the greatest jazz vocalist of all time, she is credited with influencing a generation of singers, including Frank Sinatra, Tony Bennett and Mel Tormé. In a career that spanned six decades, Fitzgerald recorded more than 250 albums with jazz's elite players. (1911–1996)

Susan Fleetwood *actress* — gained fame working in London's Royal Shakespeare Company; played Lady Russell in the 1995 film *Persuasion* (1944–1995)

Chet Forte *television director* — famous for directing *Monday Night Football* and developing state-of-the-art sportscasting techniques (1935–1996)

Joseph M. Fox *editor* — As a prominent senior editor at Random House, Fox edited some of the publisher's most respected authors, including Truman Capote, John Irving, Philip Roth, Ralph Ellison, Anthony Lewis and Martin Cruz Smith. (1926–1995)

Michael Fox *actor* — Performing in theater, television and film, Fox was best known for his eight-year stint as Saul Feinberg on *The Bold and the Beautiful.* (1920–1996)

Richard Edward Frank *actor* — television, theater and film actor; appeared in Broadway's *Kiss of the Spider Woman* (195?–1995)

Francisco M. Garcia *bandleader* — Led the 1960s' pop quartet Cannibal and the Headhunters, known for the hit "Land of 1,000 Dances" and as the opening act for The Beatles 1965 U.S. tour. (194?–1996)

Arthur Getz *magazine illustrator* — more than 200 of his illustrations graced the cover of *The New Yorker* (191?–1996)

Paul Gillette *screenwriter, novelist* — wrote *Play Misty for Me* (194?–1996)

Peter Glenville *theater director* — A highly acclaimed director in London's West End and on

Ella Fitzgerald

Broadway who worked with some of the stage's greatest actors and playwrights, Glenville garnered fame on both sides of the Atlantic, staging Terence Rattigan's *The Browning Version* and *Romeo and Juliet.* (1913–1996)

Linda Goodman *astrologer* — Goodman's books on astrology moved the topic from the occult to the mainstream. *Sun Signs,* her first book, appeared on the *New York Times* bestseller list shortly after it was published in 1968, becoming the first astrology book to make the list. Her other books include *Love Signs* and *Star Signs.* (1925–1995)

Morton Gould *composer* — In his prolific career, Gould made many attempts to bridge different aspects of popular culture through his music. He wrote for Broadway, movies, ballet and television, encompassing jazz, pop, folk and marches in his style. He won the 1995 Pulitzer Prize in music for his *String Music.* (1913–1996)

Peter Grant *rock manager* — managed Led Zeppelin and Bad Company (1935–1995)

Edward Greenberg *musical director* — directed *The King and I, The Merry Widow* and *Kismet* for Lincoln Center (1924–1995)

Florence Greenberg *record company executive* — Greenberg discovered the Shirelles, who were classmates of her daughters. In 1959, she founded the label Scepter and recorded the Shirelle's first hit, "Will You Still Love Me Tomorrow?" (1913–1995)

John L. Greene *television writer* — Greene created *My Favorite Martian,* the popular 1960s series. He also wroter for *Ozzie and Harriet, The Real McCoys, Bewitched, I Dream of Jeannie, Andy Griffith* and *Green Acres.* (1912–1995)

Don Grolnick *songwriter, pianist* — best known for backing up popular musicians such as Paul Simon, Bonnie Raitt and James Taylor; his solo recordings include *Weaver of Dreams* and *Nighttown* (1947–1996)

Edith Haggard *literary agent* — In her 30-year career, Haggard represented Adela Rogers St. Johns, Sinclair Lewis, Daphne Du Maurier and Richard Llewellyn. (190?–1995)

Robert Hamner *television writer and producer* — wrote episodes for *Cannon, Planet of the Apes* and *McGyver* and created the series *S.W.A.T.* (192?–1996)

Robin Hardy *writer* — author of 20 novels and founder of the Publishing Triangle, an association of gays and lesbians involved in publishing (195?–1995)

Oliver Harrington *cartoonist* — In the 1930s, Harrington, a pioneering black cartoonist, created the comic character Bootsie, who became a celebrity in Harlem. (191?–1995)

David Healey *actor* — Healey starred in London's 1982 production of *Guys and Dolls* and won an Olivier Award, the British equivalent of a Tony Award, for the performance. (1931–1995)

Brigitte Helm *actress* — Before Marlene Dietrich arrived on the scene, Helm was the most renowned actress of German film's first golden era. Though she played many roles, she will always be remembered as the working girl who was transformed into the malevolent robot in Fritz Lang's *Metropolis.* (1906–1996)

Tom Helmore *actor, writer* — appeared in the films *Lucy Gallant, Designing Women* and *The Tender Trap* and wrote the novel *Affair at Quala* (1904–1995)

Margaux Hemingway *model, actress* — Hemingway was a successful model in the 1980s and had a brief film career, making her glamorous screen debut in *Lipstick.* She was the granddaughter of Ernest Hemingway. (1955–1996)

Roy Herbert *magazine editor* — As editor of *Reader's Digest*, Herbert ended the magazine's

Margaux Hemingway

longtime support of the Vietnam war. (193?–1996)

Barton Heyman *actor* — Best remembered for uttering the three-word title line in *Dead Man Walking,* Heyman also acted in countless plays, including several New York Shakespeare Festival productions, and various films. (193?–1996)

Martha Hill *dance instructor* — A passionate proponent of modern dance, Hill founded the American Dance Festival and dance departments at Connecticut College, Bennington College and the Juilliard School. (1901–1995)

Shannon Hoon *singer* — Hoon was the lead singer of the rock group Blind Melon. The band achieved moderate success with its 1992 self-titled debut album and was best known for the song "No Rain," whose video featured a young dancing girl dressed in a bee costume. Hoon died of a drug overdose while on tour promoting the band's second album, *Soup.* (1967–1995)

Richard Hornung *costume designer* — Hornung's film credits include *Raising Arizona, Miller's Crossing, Natural Born Killers* and *Barton Fink,* for which he received an Oscar nomination. (1951–1996)

Ross Hunter *film producer* — Hunter's melodramas included *Pillow Talk, Magnificent Obsession* and *Imitation of Life.* (1916–1996)

Harry Hurwitz *filmmaker, artist* — director of low-budget comedies and thrillers, including the

cult classic *The Projectionist* (193?–1995)

Dorothy Hyson *actress* — Said to have inspired the 1935 Rodgers and Hart hit song "The Most Beautiful Girl in the World," Hyson turned many heads in her time. She made her mark on stage, appearing in *Pink String and Sealing Wax.* (1915–1996)

Dorothy Jeakins *costume designer* — Jeakins won Oscars for her designs in the films *Joan of Arc, Samson and Delilah* and *Night of the Iguana.* She also designed costumes for *The Sound of Music, The Way We Were, The Greatest Show on Earth* and *The Music Man.* (1914–1995)

Timothy Jenkins *opera singer* — tenor at the Metropolitan Opera (195?–1995)

Ben Johnson *Western actor* — appeared in the films *She Wore a Yellow Ribbon* and *Rio Grande;* won an Oscar for his aging pool shark in *The Last Picture Show* (1918–1996)

Robert Johnson *magazine editor* — executive editor of *Jet* magazine for three decades; wrote a biography of Bill Cosby (191?–1996)

Johnny Johnston *big-band singer* — recorded "That Old Black Magic," "I Don't Want to Walk Without You," and "Dearly Beloved" for Capitol Records (191?–1996)

Isabel Kambert *opera singer* — Kambert was well known in German and Paris opera houses until she was banned from performing after refusing to join the Nazi party. She emigrated to New York and, after finding few suitable opera roles, opened a successful business designing cashmere sweaters. (1892–1996)

Danny Kamekona *actor* — television tough guy in *Hawaii Five-O, Magnum P.I.* and *Jake and the Fat Man* (193?–1996)

George Keane *television and stage actor* — appeared in Broadway's *Hamlet* and *Brigadoon* (191?–1995)

Helen Keane *jazz manager and producer* — Pioneering jazz businesswoman who represented pianist Bill Evans, guitarist Kenny Burrell, trumpeter Art Farmer and others. She sought to promote women singers such as Sylvia Sims and Morgana King. (192?–1996)

Christopher Keene *conductor, arts administrator* — associated with the New York City Opera for more than 25 years; conducted Italy's Spoleto Festival and Elliot Feld's American Ballet Company (1946–1995)

Gene Kelly *dancer, actor, singer choreographer, director* — Kelly was an innovator in musical films, bringing the exuberance and athleticism of his dance to the genre. He is perhaps best remembered for 1952's *Singin' in the Rain*, in which he sang the title song while dancing through the streets in a downpour. He earned an Oscar nomination for *Anchors Aweigh* (1945), in which he appeared with Jerry the Mouse, the first time animation and live action were used together in a film. His other screen credits include *An American in Paris* (1951), *Brigadoon* (1954) and *Cover Girl* (1944). He also appeared in several Broadway productions, including *Pal Joey* and *Best Foot Forward*. (1912–1996)

Krzysztof Kieslowski *filmmaker* — Kieslowski was one of the world's most acclaimed filmmakers. His most recent work, his "Three Colors" trilogy, brought him unrivaled international acclaim. *Blue* (1993), *White* (1994) and *Red* (1994) focused on

Gene Kelly

the colors of the French flag and their emotional counterparts: liberty, equality and fraternity. With *Red*, Kieslowski received an Oscar nomination for Best Director. Although he had publicly announced that *Red* would be his final work, sources close to the director say he was planning projects at the time of his death. (1941–1996)

George Kirby *comedian* — Las Vegas headliner who performed impressions of John Wayne, Jerry Lewis, Pearl Bailey, Ella Fitzgerald and Sarah Vaughan (1924–1995)

Lincoln Kirstein *arts patron, co-founder of the New York City Ballet* — Kirstein's influence on ballet is immeasurable. Born into a wealthy Boston family, he used his resources to bring George Balanchine to the United States in 1933, and together they founded the New York City Ballet, considered the best classical-dance troupe of the 20th century. They also established the School of American Ballet. Kirstein was a firm proponent of traditional dance and looked down upon modern dance. He was awarded the President Medal of Freedom in 1984 and the National Medal of Arts in 1985. (1907–1996)

Patric Knowles *British actor* — began his career in London theater and later moved to Hollywood, appearing in films *The Charge of the Light Brigade* and *The Adventures of Robin Hood* (1911–1995)

Jennings Lang *film executive* — best known for producing *Airport* and its sequels (1915–1996)

Larry LaPrise *singer* — wrote the children's standard "The Hokey Pokey," a dance song originally intended to amuse adult resort skiers (191?–1996)

William Larsen *character actor* — veteran of Broadway, Off-Broadway and regional theater; best known for his portrayal of the sheriff in *The Best Little Whorehouse in Texas* (1928–1996)

Jonathan Larson *composer, playwright* — Larson struggled for

years as a writer and composer, waiting tables to support himself while waiting for his big break. His break came, though he never lived to enjoy the fame or the success of *Rent*, his rock opera that wowed critics and fans alike. *Rent* opened Off-Broadway, moved to Broadway and won four 1996 Tony Awards, including Best Musical, and the Pulitzer Prize for Drama. (1961–1996)

Evelyn Laye *comic actress* — British musical-comedy star who enjoyed an 80-year career on Broadway and London stages and in films. Her credits include the Broadway production of *Bitter Sweet* and the films *The Night Is Young* and *Second Star to the Right*. (1900–1996)

Timothy Leary *counterculture guru* — Leary was forced from academia and his post as a Harvard psychology professor after he turned on to hallucinogenic drugs. He would become one of the 1960's most well-known, controversial advocates of the alternative lifestyle, famous for his line which encouraged people to "tune in, turn on and drop out." (1920–1996)

Lou Levy, Jr *music publisher* — published The Beatles's "I Want to Hold Your Hand," provided Frank Sinatra with material and nurtured Bob Dylan, Sammy Cahn and Henry Mancini (1910–1995)

Stanley Lewis *bookseller, publisher* — operated the Parnassus literary bookshop on Manhattan's Upper West Side for more than a decade and published the journal *Parnassus: Poetry in Review* (193?–1995)

Viveca Lindfors *actress* — The Swedish actress starred in the films *Stargate*, *Adventures of Don Juan*, *Four in a Jeep* and *Last Summer in the Hamptons* and in Broadway's *Anastasia*. (1920–1995)

Paul Lipson *stage actor* — Lipson played Tevye in *Fiddler on the Roof* more than 2,000 times. His other Broadway credits include *Remains to Be Seen*, *Carnival in Flanders*, *The Vamp* and *Bells Are Ringing*. (1914–1996)

Leon Lisher *bass-baritone* — performed with the New York City Opera (1913–1995)

Shelley List *television producer, novelist* — produced television's *Cagney and Lacey* and wrote the novels *Did You Love Daddy When I Was Born* and *Nobody Makes Me Cry* (193?–1996)

Arthur Loew, Jr. *film producer* — Loew came from a legendary film family: his maternal grandfather was Adolph Zukor, who founded Paramount Pictures, and his paternal grandfather, Marcus Loew, founded MGM and Loew's Theaters. Loew's credits include *The Rack* and *The Affairs of Dobie Gillis.* (192?–1995)

Pilar Lorengar *soprano* — Lorengar, a Spanish soprano, was famous for her renditions of Mozart heroines. Though she recorded with numerous orchestras and companies, Lorengar stayed with the Berlin Deutsche Opera for most of her career. (1928–1996)

Rita Lynn *actress* — television credits include *Perry Mason, The Streets of San Francisco* and *Maverick* (192?–1996)

Robie Macauley *writer, editor* — former executive editor of Houghton Mifflin Company and senior editor of *Playboy;* his works include *The Disguises of Love, A Secret History of Time* and *The End of Pity* (191?–1995)

Guy Madison *actor* — star of the 1950's television series *The Adventures of Wild Bill Hickok;* films include *Honeymoon, The Command* and *Bullwhip* (1922–1996)

Louis Malle *director* — Malle, first associated with the French New Wave, quickly moved to expand his horizons. After early successes such as The Luvett (1958) and Zazie dans le Metro (1960), Malle's restless curiosity took him to India, Mexico, Brazil and finally to the United States and his first Hollywood film, *Pretty Baby.* He is perhaps most well known in this country as the director of *My Dinner With Andre* and *Atlantic City.* (1932–1995)

William Marchant *playwright* — wrote *The Desk Set,* which was both a 1955 Broadway play starring Shirley Booth and a 1957 film starring Katharine Hepburn and Spencer Tracy (1923–1995)

Dean Martin *actor, singer* — The crooner and actor appeared in 55 films, had 40 singles on the *Billboard* charts between 1950 and 1969 and had two successful television series. He appeared in a number of films opposite Jerry Lewis. Their first outing together was 1949's *My Friend Irma.* Martin also appeared in *Some Came Running, The Silencers* and *Robin and the Seven Hoods,* which also starred fellow Rat Packers Sammy Davis, Jr. and Frank Sinatra. His television shows were *The Dean Martin Show* and *The Dean Martin Comedy World.* (1917–1995)

Pamela Mason *author, actress, talk-show host* — Mason wrote several books, including *Marriage Is the First Step Toward Divorce.* She appeared in Broadway productions and hosted two syndicated talk shows; she was married to actor James Mason. (1918–1996)

Tom McDermott *actor* — appeared in numerous Broadway, film and television roles, including the first stage adaptation of *Billy Budd* and the 1950s TV series *Captain Video* (191?–1996)

Brownie McGhee *blues guitarist and singer* — introduced Piedmont blues to an international audience (1915–1996)

Arona McHugh *author* — best-selling novels include *A Banner With a Strange Device* and *The*

Dean Martin

Calling of the Mercenaries (192?–1996)

Daniel McLain *country musician* — known as Country Dick Montana, McLain started the country-rock band the Beat Farmers (1955–1995)

Barbara McLean *film editor* — McLean overcame 1930s Hollywood sexism to become Darryl F. Zanuck's most trusted editor and eventually head of Twentieth Century-Fox's editing division. (1909–1996)

David McLean *film and television actor* — McLean starred in the short-lived 1960 series, *Tate,* which gave him the identity of American cowboy. He appeared in several television ads as the Marlboro Man. He died of lung cancer. (192?–1995)

Butterfly McQueen *actress* — McQueen was best known for her role as Prissy, the maid in *Gone With the Wind.* (1911–1995)

Robert A. Mead *television producer* — producer of NBC's *Weekend Nightly News* (193?–1996)

Audrey Meadows *actress, singer* — Meadows's portrayal of the smart-mouthed housewife Alice Kramden on television's *The Honeymooners* earned her a place among TV's comedy elite. She began her career as a coloratura soprano, debuting at age 16 at Carnegie Hall. A number of stage and television roles followed, including the lead role

Louis Malle

opposite Phil Silvers in the Broadway production of *Top Banana.* While Jackie Gleason initially dismissed Meadows as too pretty for the part of Alice, her persistence won her the role. Meadows's tart — often ad-libbed — retorts made Gleason's Ralph to shake his fist and fume, "One of these days, Alice. Pow! Right in the kisser!" (1926–1996)

John Megna *actor, brother of actress Connie Stevens* — appeared in Broadway productions, movies and television shows (1952–1995)

Jonathan Melvoin *rock musician* — Melvoin, touring keyboardist and percussionist for the hit alternative rock band Smashing Pumpkins, died of a drug overdose. (196?–1996)

Grace Miceli *costumer* — provided costumes for several theater, ballet, opera, film and television productions; worked closely with the American Ballet Theatre and the New York City Ballet (191?–1995)

J. D. Miller *music producer* — wrote "It Wasn't God Who Made Honky-Tonk Angels" (1922–1996)

Jessica Mitford *author* — British author famous for her 1963 best-selling book, *The American Way of Death,* a relentless critique of the funeral industry (1917–1996)

Patsy Montana *country-music singer* — cowgirl yodeler who wrote and performed "I Want to Be a Cowboy's Sweetheart" (1935), the first song by a woman country singer and songwriter to sell a million copies (1914–1996)

Richard Morris *film, television and stage writer* — head writer and director of *The Loretta Young Show;* other credits include Broadway's *The Unsinkable Molly Brown* (1924–1996)

Gerry Mulligan *baritone saxophonist* — Mulligan, with Miles Davis, was one of the founders of cool jazz. Though closely associated with the West Coast jazz scene he helped create with Chet Baker and Lee Konitz, Mulligan

may be best known for his membership in the prime Dave Brubeck ensemble. (1927–1996)

Jim Nash *record label head* — founder of Wax Trax!, an industrial-music label and chain of music stores (1948–1995)

Helen Nearing *writer* — Nearing and her husband, Scott Nearing, left New York City in 1932 to live the simple, self-sufficient life the couple promoted in their books, including *Living the Good Life* (1954), which became a back-to-the-land bible in the 1970s. (190?–1995)

Wade Nichols *publisher* — published *Good Housekeeping* magazine (191?–1996)

Gerry Mulligan

Liam O'Brien *screenwriter* — After working as a poet, cartoonist, labor organizer and signal corpsman, O'Brien was nominated for a 1951 Academy Award for his first Hollywood screenplay, *Here Comes the Groom.* O'Brien's first play, *The Remarkable Mr. Pennypacker,* was a 1954 Broadway hit, and he later became a successful TV writer. (1913–1996)

David J. O'Connell *television producer* — won an Emmy for *Marcus Welby, M.D.* (191?–1996)

Lynn O'Donnell *documentary producer* — produced *Crumb,* the disturbing portrait of cartoonist R. Crumb (195?–1996)

David Opatoshu *actor* — began his acting career in theater and is best known for his portrayal of a Jewish resistance fighter in the film *Exodus* (191?–1996)

George Osterman *playwright, actor* — known for his work with the Ridiculous Theater Company (195?–1995)

John Panozzo *rock drummer* — cofounder and drummer of the '70's rock group Styx (194?–1996)

Edith Pargeter *British author* — Under the pen name Ellis Peters, Pargeter wrote a series of mystery novels about 12th-century monk Brother Cadfael. (1913–1995)

Robert Parrish *film editor and director* — Parrish won a 1947 Academy Award for his editing work in *Body and Soul.* His other editing credits include *All the King's Men* and *Battle of Midway.* He directed *Cry Danger* and *The Purple Rain* and acted in *City Lights, The Informer* and *All Quiet on the Western Front.* He began his editing career as an apprentice to John Ford. (1916–1995)

John Patrick *writer* — Patrick won the 1954 Pulitzer Prize in Drama for *Teahouse of the August Moon.* His other plays include *Curious Savage* and *The Hasty Heart;* his screenplays include *Three Coins in the Fountain, Love Is a Many Splendored Thing* and *High Society.* (1905–1995)

Luana Patten *actress* — early Disney child star who debuted in *Song of the South* (1938–1996)

Robert Patterson *opera baritone* — sang with the Metropolitan opera in the 1960s (1930–1995)

Minnie Pearl *country singer, comedian* — With her trademark straw flowered hat (with a $1.98 pricetag dangling by a thread) and greeting, "How-dee!," Pearl made a name for herself on the stage of the Grand Ole Opry. (1912–1996)

Jeffrey Lee Pierce *rock musician* — singer and guitarist who founded pioneer Los Angeles punk band Gun Club (1958–1996)

Orville Prescott *book critic* — Longtime book critic for the *New York Times* who challenged the superstar status of accepted literary heroes such as William Faulkner, John Steinbeck, Saul

Bellow and John Updike. (190?–1996)

Eugenia Price *romance novelist* — Price's popular antebellum romantic books sold more than 40 million copies. (191?–1996)

Philip Rapp *comedy writer* — Rapp created the wildly popular Bickersons, the squabbling couple played by Don Ameche and Frances Langford on the 1940s radio program of the same name. (191?–1996)

Samuel D. Ratcliffe *television scriptwriter* — won a 1991 Emmy for his work on the daytime drama *Santa Barbara* (1945–1995)

Phil Regan *entertainer* — Regan worked his way from New York City policeman to Hollywood performer, earning the nickname "the singing cop." His honeyed tenor voice won him high-visibility gigs performing for the 1944 Democratic Convention and 1949 Presidential inauguration. He appeared in more than two dozen films, performed with George Burns and Gracie Allen and hosted radio's *The Phil Regan Armed Forces Show.* (1906–1995)

James Reston *journalist* — Arguably the most celebrated and respected print journalist of the 20th century, Reston held positions as foreign correspondent, columnist and executive editor of the *New York Times.* Based in Washington D.C., for most of his career, Reston was the quintessential Washington insider. He won two Pulitzer Prizes, in 1945 for coverage of the 1944 Dumbarton Oaks Conference and in 1957 for a series of articles that analyzed the effects of Dwight Eisenhower's illness on the presidency. (1909–1995)

Adam Roarke *actor, acting coach* — familiar face in biker films, including *Play It as It Lays* and *Dirty Mary, Crazy Larry;* opened the Film Actors Lab in 1982 (193?–1996)

Darren Robinson *rapper* — The 450-pound musician was a member of the comical rap group, The Fat Boys. (1967–1995)

Roxie Roker

Roxie Roker *actress* — Roker played Helen Willis on *The Jeffersons.* On the show, she was married to Franklin Cover; the pair was television's first interracial couple. Her son is recording artist Lenny Kravitz. (1929–1995)

Jack Rose *screenwriter* — Rose penned several scripts for Bob Hope, including *The Road to Rio, My Favorite Brunette* and *The Seven Little Foys.* His other credits include *Papa's Delicate Condition* and *A Touch of Class,* for which he earned an Oscar nomination. (1911–1995)

Ralph Rosenblum *film editor, author* — edited six Woody Allen movies including *Annie Hall, Take the Money and Run* and *Sleeper* (1925–1995)

M.L. Rosenthal *poet, critic* — wrote the acclaimed *The Modern Poetic Sequence: The Genius of Modern Poetry* (191?–1996)

Jimmy Rowles *jazz composer and accompanist* — Thought to be one of jazz's most accomplished sidemen, Rowles performed with virtually every important singer, including Billie Holiday, Ella Fitzgerald and Carmen McRae. He also proved himself adequate as an improvier, playing with the likes of Lester Young, Stan Getz and Zoot Sims. (1918–1996)

Vermont Royster *editor* — Royster helped make the *Wall Street Journal* the most respected business daily. He won two Pulitzer Prizes. (1914–1996)

Richard Ryder *actor* — credits include *One Life to Live* and the plays *See Saw, Via Galactica* and *Sweet Charity* (194?–1995)

Victor Samrock *theatrical manager* — credits include *Abe Lincoln in Illinois, Knickerbocker Holiday, Key Largo* and *Truckline Cafe* (190?–1995)

John Scali *ABC reporter* — Scali, a colorful ABC war correspondent, secretly played a pivotal role in resolving the Cuban missile crisis, acting as courier, negotiator and spokesman for the Kennedy Administration. (1918–1995)

Martin M. Schaeffer *theater and cabaret critic* — *Variety's* nightclub critic and an Off-Broadway critic for the *Hollywood Reporter* (194?–1996)

Jeffrey Schaire *magazine editor* — former editor of *Art Magazine* (195?–1995)

Charles Scribner, Jr. *publishing executive* — Scribner was the president and chairman of Charles Scribner's Sons publishing company and edited Ernest Hemingway. (1921–1995)

Robert J. Shaw *TV writer* — Shaw wrote serials, soaps and dramas, including *Peyton Place* and *General Hospital.* His biggest coup was the 1980 "Who Shot J.R.?" episode of *Dallas,* which broke all viewing records. (191?–1996)

Robert Shelton *music critic, author* — As a music critic for the *New York Times,* Shelton brought attention to Bob Dylan, Judy Collins and Janis Joplin. His books include a biography of Dylan, a book about Woody Guthrie and *The Face of Folk Music.* (1926–1995)

Jerry Siegel *Superman co-creator* — Siegel conceived the idea of Superman in 1934 shortly after he graduated high school. His partner, Joe Shuster, illustrated the comic strip. The pair sold the rights to DC Comics in 1938 for $130. In 1978, after making millions on the product, DC Comics agreed to pay Siegel and

Shuster $20,000 (later $30,000) annually for their creation. (1915–1996)

Don Simpson *movie producer* — Simpson was one of Hollywood's most influential producers. With his former partner, Jerry Bruckheimer, he produced *Flashdance, Beverly Hills Cop, Top Gun, Crimson Tide* and *Dangerous Minds.* (1943–1995)

Eleanor Aller Slatkin *cellist* — Slatkin, a respected musician, came from a musical family. Her father, Gregory Aller, was a cellist as was his father. She was married to Felix Slatkin, conductor, violinist and concertmaster, and her two sons, conductor Leonard Slatkin and Frederick Zlotkin are also well-known in the music world. (1917–1995)

Nicolas Slonimsky *musicologist, conductor, composer, pianist* — Slonimsky wrote several music reference books, including *Music Since 1900, A Lexicon of Musical Invective* and numerous editions of *Baker's Biographical Dictionary of Musicians.* His dictionary entries were known for their animated and witty definitions. He founded and conducted the Chamber Orchestra of Boston. (1894–1995)

Terry Southern *screenwriter, novelist* — Southern's work, which included 1964's *Dr. Strangelove or: How I Learned to Stop Worrying and Love the Bomb* and 1969's *Easy Rider* (both nominated for Best Screenplay Oscars), symbolized the fear and humor of the 1960s. His other screenwriting credits include *The Loved One, The Cincinnati Kid* and *Barbarella.* His novels include *Candy.* (1924–1995)

Alison Steele *disc jockey* — Steele became one of the country's first female disc jockeys in 1966 at New York's WNEW-FM and built a loyal following among late-night radio listeners who knew her as "the Nightbird." She is a member of the Rock-and-Roll Hall of Fame. (193?–1995)

Sir Robert Stephens *British actor* — Stephens was a well-known actor with Britain's National

Theatre Company in the 1960s, starring in Peter Shaffer's *Royal Hunt of the Sun,* Franco Zeffirelli's *Much Ado About Nothing* and Noel Coward's *Hay Fever.* After a 20-plus-year hiatus, Stephens returned to the stage in the 1990s with the Royal Shakespeare Company. (1931–1995)

McLean Stevenson *actor* — Played Lt. Col. Henry Blake in the hit comedy series *M*A*S*H.* He was also a frequent guest host of *The Tonight Show.* (1929–1996)

Geoffrey Stokes *writer* — A former columnist for *The Village Voice* and the *Boston Globe* and the author of several books, Stokes wrote on subjects ranging from sports to music to cooking. (1940–1995)

Al Stump *sportswriter* — Stump wrote two chronicles of Ty Cobb's life, the first as a collaborator with Cobb on *My Life in Baseball,* which Stump later referred to as a "coverup." He later penned *Cobb: A Biography,* which was made into the 1994 movie starring Tommy Lee Jones, which portrayed the Georgia Peach as an abusive racist as well as a baseball legend. (191?–1995)

Linda Sutter *comic-strip writer* — wrote the story line for the comic strip *Brenda Starr* (1941–1995)

Grady Sutton *actor* — character actor who appeared in more than 180 movies; best known for his role as the comic foil to W. C. Fields in *The Bank Dick* (1908–1995)

Lyle Talbot *character actor* — appeared in more than 150 movies, including *20,000 Years in Sing Sing;* played Joe Randolf, the neighbor of the title characters on *The Adventures of Ozzie and Harriet* (1902–1996)

Bert Terborgh *dancer* — Terborgh was a principal dancer with the Martha Graham Dance Company. (194?–1996)

Bob Thiele *jazz producer label head* — As the head of Impulse Records in the 1960s, Thiele produced jazz greats including

Coleman Hawkins, Count Basie, Earl Hines, Duke Ellington, Charles Mingus and Charlie Haden's Liberation Music Orchestra. His finest moments may be producing John Coltrane's *A Love Supreme* and *Crescent.* (192?–1996)

Ross Thomas *author* — Critics compare the hard-boiled fiction of Thomas to Raymond Chandler and Dashiell Hammett. His novels include *The Cold War Swap, Briarpatch,* which won an Edgar Award, *Cast a Yellow Shadow* and *Out on the Rim.* (1926–1995)

Richard Tobin *journalist* — former reporter for the *New York Herald Tribune* and editor for *The Saturday Review* (c. 1910–1995)

Tamara Toumanova *ballerina* — Toumanova, "the black pearl of the Russian ballet," became an internationally acclaimed ballerina at the age of 13. The daughter of a Russian czarist colonel, she is remembered as a dramatic, classical ballerina who starred in Balanchine's *Le Palais de Cristal* and Serge Lifar's *Phèdre.* (1919–1996)

Jo Van Fleet *actress* — Known for playing matriarchal figures, Van Fleet played Paul Newman's mother in *Cool Hand Luke* and James Dean's mother in Elia Kazan's *East of Eden,* for which she won an Academy Award. (1919–1996)

Joseph Vasquez *filmmaker* — Vasquez's 1991 low-budget film, *Hangin' With the Homeboys,* won the screenwriting award at the 1991 Sundance Film Festival. (1962–1995)

Nina Verchinina *ballerina* — Verchinina studied with choreographer Bronislava Nijinska and danced with Ballets Russes for choreographer Léonide Massine. (1910–1995)

Frederic Waldman *conductor* — Waldman taught at the Juilliard School, was music director of the Juilliard Opera Theater until 1985 and founded the ensemble Musica Aeterna in 1957. At Juilliard, Waldman conducted the American premieres of several forgotten works, including Strauss's *Capriccio,* Kodaly's *Hary Janos* and Britten's arrangement of *The Beggar's Opera.* (1903–1995)

Randy Walker *rap artist* — Under the name Stretch, Walker rapped with Live Squad. (1968–1995)

Ira Wallach *screenwriter* — credits include *Hot Millions, Don't Make Waves, Hopalong-Freud* and *Hopalong-Freud Rides Again* (191?–1995)

Ruth Warshawsky *actress* — A veteran of stage, screen and television, Warshawsky played the leads in national theater touring productions and appeared in *Hill Street Blues, Lou Grant, Barney Miller* and *Quincy.* (191?–1996)

Johnny "Guitar" Watson *rhythm and blues guitarist* — influenced musicians such as Jimi Hendrix and Frank Zappa (1935–1996)

Mary-Scott Welch *writer, editor* — popularized career networking for women in *Networking: The Great New Way for Women to Get Ahead;* wrote and edited for *Redbook, Vogue, Ladies Home Journal* and other magazines (192?–1995)

Pete Welding *producer and label head* — founded Testament Records and produced for Prestige, Bluesville, Elektra and Arhoolie (1935–1995)

Jack Weston *character actor* — movie, television and Broadway veteran whose movie credits include *Wait Until Dark* (1926–1996)

Slappy (Melvin) White *comedian* — one of the first black comedians to perform for white audiences in the 1950s; often performed with Nipsey Russell, Dean Martin and Redd Foxx (1921–1995)

Mary Wickes *actress* — Her name may not be recognizable, but her face certainly was. Wickes appeared in more than 50 movies, 25 Broadway plays and musicals and 60 television shows, most often playing an acerbic housekeeper, a wicked stepmother or a spinster. She appeared in the two *Sister Act* movies, *Postcards From the Edge, Little Women* and *White Christmas.* (1916–1995)

Frank Wigglesworth *composer, teacher* — Part of the New York music scene since the 1950s, Wigglesworth's music ranged from the lyrical to the atonal. (1918–1996)

Barney Wilen *jazz saxophonist* — The French saxophonist played a large role in legitimizing European jazz and jazz musicians. Wilen's breakthrough came in 1957 when he performed as a sideman for Miles Davis on the now classic soundtrack to Louis Malle's *Ascenseur pour l'Echafaud* (*Elevator to the Gallows*). In addition to Davis, Wilen played with many legendary jazzers, including J.J. Johnson, Thelonious Monk and Dizzie Gillespie. (1937–1996)

Garth Williams *book illustrator* — Trained as a painter and sculptor, Williams became a children's book illustrator after *The New Yorker* rejected his cartoons as too wild. Beginning with E. B. White's *Stuart Little,* he illustrated many well-loved children's classics, including White's *Charlotte's Web,* Laura Ingalls Wilder's *Little House on the Prairie* books and George Selden's *The Cricket in Times Square.* (191?–1996)

Rober Russell (Chubby) Wise *fiddler* — Wise was an influential bluegrass fiddler. He wrote the showpiece "Orange Blossom Special" and was a member of Bill Monroe's Blue Grass Boys. (1915–1996)

Peter Wisher *dance pioneer* — As a coach at Gallaudet University, Wisher was so taken by the flow of sign language that he created a dance form, marked by exaggerated hand, arm and body movement, for the deaf based on signing. The Gallaudet Dance Company toured nationally and internationally. (191?–1995)

William Woodman *theater director* — former artistic director of Chicago's Goodman Theater; also worked with the Denver Center for the Performing Arts, the American Shakespeare Festival in Stratford, Connecticut, and the Juilliard School (1932–1995)

Howard Wyeth *drummer, pianist* — toured with Bob Dylan's Rolling Thunder Revue and drummed on albums by Dylan and other artists (194?–1996)

José Yglesias *novelist* — Yglesias wrote fiction and non-fiction books about Latin Americans affected by revolutions. His books include *The Goodbye Land, In the Fist of Revolution, Tristan and the Hispanics* and *Double Double.* (c. 1920–1995)

Marguerite Young *author* — Young's enormous novel, *Miss MacIntosh, My Darling* gained a cult following. She traveled in literary circles with the likes of Truman Capote, Dylan Thomas and Carson McCullers. (1908–1995)

Joseph C. Youngerman *Directors Guild of America official* — As executive secretary of the DGA, Youngerman built the organization from an unorganized group of 900 directors to a 10,000-member powerful industry union. He was also an assistant director on almost 100 films, including *Beau Geste, Sullivan's Travels* and *For Whom the Bell Tolls.* (190?–1995)

Lee Zhito *former publisher of* Billboard — Zhito started his career with *Billboard* as a reporter in 1945 and rose to editor in chief and publisher. (1918–1995)

Everyone has an opinion when it comes to movies, music, TV and the other subjects included in this book. We want to hear yours. Did we miss anything? Anything you would like to see more of? Less of? Please write us with your comments.

THE ENTERTAINMENT ALMANAC
INSO CORP.
31 ST. JAMES AVE.
BOSTON, MA 02116-4101

EMMY
AWARDS

HOME
ENTERTAIN-
MENT

PERFORMING
ARTS

TONY
AWARDS

PUBLISHING

BOOK
AWARDS

PEOPLE